Sensation & Perception

FIFTH EDITION

Sensation & Perception

FIFTH EDITION

Jeremy M. Wolfe
Brigham & Women's Hospital
Harvard University Medical School

Keith R. Kluender
Purdue University

Dennis M. Levi
University of California, Berkeley

Linda M. Bartoshuk
University of Florida

Rachel S. Herz
Brown University

Roberta L. Klatzky
Carnegie Mellon University

Daniel M. Merfeld
The Ohio State University

 SINAUER ASSOCIATES

NEW YORK   OXFORD
OXFORD UNIVERSITY PRESS

About the cover

Mark Guglielmo, *El Pintor Lincoln Camué* | *The Painter Lincoln Camué*, Santiago de Cuba, 2015, photo-mosaic, 50 × 94 inches.

Sensation & Perception, Fifth Edition

Oxford University Press is a department of the University of Oxford. It furthers the University's objective of excellence in research, scholarship, and education by publishing worldwide. Oxford is a registered trade mark of Oxford University Press in the UK and certain other countries.

Published in the United States of America by Oxford University Press
198 Madison Avenue, New York, NY 10016, United States of America

© 2018 Oxford University Press
Sinauer Associates is an imprint of Oxford University Press.

For titles covered by Section 112 of the US Higher Education Opportunity Act, please visit www.oup.com/us/he for the latest information about pricing and alternate formats.

Address editorial correspondence to:
Sinauer Associates
23 Plumtree Road
Sunderland, MA 01375 U.S.A.
publish@sinauer.com

Address orders, sales, license, permissions, and translation inquiries to:
Oxford University Press U.S.A.
2001 Evans Road
Cary, NC 27513 U.S.A.
Orders: 1-800-445-9714

Library of Congress Cataloging-in-Publication Data

Names: Wolfe, Jeremy M., author. | Kluender, Keith R., author. | Levi, Dennis M,. author.
Title: Sensation & perception / Jeremy M. Wolfe, Brigham & Women's Hospital/Harvard University Medical School, Keith R. Kluender, Purdue University, Dennis M. Levi, University of California, Berkeley, Linda M. Bartoshuk, University of Florida, Rachel S. Herz, Brown University, Roberta Klatzky, Carnegie Mellon University, Daniel M. Merfeld, Ohio State University.
Other titles: Sensation and perception
Description: Fifth Edition. | New York, NY : Sinauer Associates is an imprint of Oxford University Press, 2017. | Revised edition of Sensation & perception, [2015] | Includes bibliographical references and index.
Identifiers: LCCN 2017042012 | ISBN 9781605356419 (hardback)
Subjects: LCSH: Senses and sensation. | Perception. | BISAC: PSYCHOLOGY / General.
Classification: LCC QP431 .S445 2017 | DDC 612.8084/6--dc23
LC record available at https://lccn.loc.gov/2017042012

9 8 7 6 5 4 3 2 1
Printed in the United States of America

Companion Website Activities and Essays

Throughout the textbook, you will see references to Companion Website resources in **blue text**. These refer to specific activities and essays that are relevant to the topic being discussed. Below is the full list of activities and essays, by chapter.

CHAPTER	ACTIVITY	ACTIVITY	ESSAY
1	1.1 Psychophysics 1.2 Fourier Analysis	1.3 Sensory Areas in the Brain 1.4 Neurons	1.1 Senses of Reality Through the Ages
2	2.1 Visual System Overview 2.2 From Sun to Eye 2.3 Eye Structure 2.4 Simulated Scotoma	2.5 Retinal Structure 2.6 Phototransduction 2.7 Acuity versus Sensitivity 2.8 Ganglion Receptive Fields	2.1 How Many Quanta Does It Take? 2.2 Clinical Case: The Man Who Couldn't Read 2.3 Seeing Illusory Stripes and Spots
3	3.1 Visual Angle 3.2 Foveal Acuity 3.3 Gabor Patches	3.4 Striate Receptive Fields 3.5 Hypercolumns	3.1 Hyperacuity 3.2 The Whole Brain Atlas 3.3 Seeing Images on the Cortex
4	4.1 Object Substitution Masking 4.2 Gestalt Grouping Principles 4.3 Object Ambiguity 4.4 Infant Object Perception	4.5 Pandemonium 4.6 Viewpoint Effects 4.7 The Face Inversion Effect	4.1 The Role of Knowledge in Figure–Ground Assignment 4.2 Dynamic Occlusion 4.3 Bayesian Analysis 4.4 Face Blindness
5	5.1 The Principle of Univariance 5.2 Trichromacy 5.3 Color Mixing	5.4 Afterimages 5.5 Color Constancy 5.6 Illusions of Lighting	5.1 More About Opponent Processing in Color Vision 5.2 The Philosophical Problem of "Inverted Qualia" 5.3 Experiencing Color Blindness 5.4 Color Constancy in the Lab
6	6.1 Monocular Depth Cues 6.2 Binocular Disparity	6.3 Stereoscopes and Stereograms 6.4 Stereoscopic Correspondence	6.1 Making the Implicit Explicit 6.2 Stereo Images on the Web 6.3 Stereo Movies, TV, and Video Games 6.4 The Moon Illusion
7	7.1 Attentional Cueing 7.2 Visual Search 7.3 The RSVP Paradigm	7.4 The Attentional Blink and Repetition Blindness 7.5 Change Blindness 7.6 The Attentional Bottleneck	7.1 Balint Syndrome 7.2 Boundary Extension 7.3 Attentional Capture
8	8.1 Motion Aftereffects 8.2 Motion Detection Circuit 8.3 Types of Motion	8.4 Motion Correspondence 8.5 Eye Movements	8.1 Perceiving Motion in Static Images 8.2 Beyond Second-Order Motion
9	9.1 What We Hear 9.2 Structure of the Auditory System	9.3 Equal-Loudness Curves	
10	10.1 Auditory Localization Cues 10.2 The Missing-Fundamental Effect 10.3 Timbre	10.4 Auditory Stream Segregation 10.5 Continuity and Restoration Effects	10.1 Reverberations and the Precedence Effect
11	11.1 Notes, Chords, and Octaves 11.2 Categorical Perception	11.3 The McGurk Effect 11.4 Word Breaks	11.1 Studying Brain Areas for Language Processing
12	12.1 A Guided Tour of the Vestibular System 12.2 Sinusoidal Motion	12.3 Observing Torsional Eye Movement	12.1 Gravity versus Linear Acceleration 12.2 Canal–Otolith Integration 12.3 Space Motion Sickness
13	13.1 The Need for Touch 13.2 Somatosensory Receptors 13.3 The Sensory Homunculus	13.4 The Rubber Hand Illusion 13.5 Two-Point Touch Thresholds 13.6 Haptic Object Recognition	13.1 Living without Kinesthesis 13.2 Body Image 13.3 Phantom Limbs 13.4 Lego Blocks Front and Back
14	14.1 Olfactory Anatomy 14.2 Odor Adaptation and Habituation	14.3 Sensory Memory Cues	14.1 Smell-O-Vision 14.2 Olfactory Lateralization 14.3 Verbal–Olfactory Interactions
15	15.1 Taste without Smell	15.2 Gustatory Anatomy	15.1 Water Tastes

Brief Contents

About the Authors

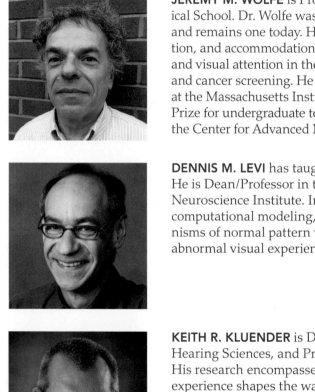

JEREMY M. WOLFE is Professor of Ophthalmology and Radiology at Harvard Medical School. Dr. Wolfe was trained as a vision researcher/experimental psychologist and remains one today. His early work includes papers on binocular vision, adaptation, and accommodation. The bulk of his recent work has dealt with visual search and visual attention in the lab and in real-world settings such as airport security and cancer screening. He taught Introductory Psychology for over twenty-five years at the Massachusetts Institute of Technology, where he won the Baker Memorial Prize for undergraduate teaching in 1989. He directs the Visual Attention Lab and the Center for Advanced Medical Imaging of Brigham and Women's Hospital.

DENNIS M. LEVI has taught at the University of California, Berkeley since 2001. He is Dean/Professor in the School of Optometry and Professor at the Helen Wills Neuroscience Institute. In the lab, Dr. Levi and colleagues use psychophysics, computational modeling, and brain imaging (fMRI) to study the neural mechanisms of normal pattern vision in humans, and to learn how they are degraded by abnormal visual experience (amblyopia).

KEITH R. KLUENDER is Department Head, Professor of Speech, Language, and Hearing Sciences, and Professor of Psychological Sciences at Purdue University. His research encompasses: how people hear complex sounds such as speech; how experience shapes the way we hear; how what we hear guides our actions and communication; clinical problems of hearing impairment or language delay; and practical concerns about computer speech recognition and hearing aid design. Dr. Kluender is deeply committed to teaching, and has taught a wide array of courses—philosophical, psychological, and physiological.

LINDA M. BARTOSHUK is Bushnell Professor, Department of Food Science and Human Nutrition at the University of Florida. Her research on taste has opened up broad new avenues for further study, establishing the impact of both genetic and pathological variation in taste on food preferences, diet, and health. She discovered that taste normally inhibits other oral sensations such that damage to taste leads to unexpected consequences like weight gain and intensified oral pain. Most recently, working with colleagues in Horticulture, her group found that a considerable amount of the sweetness in fruit is actually produced by interactions between taste and olfaction in the brain. This may lead to a new way to reduce sugar in foods and beverages.

RACHEL S. HERZ is an Adjunct Assistant Professor in the Department of Psychiatry and Human Behavior at Brown University's Warren Alpert Medical School and Part-time Faculty in the Psychology Department at Boston College. Her research focuses on a number of facets of olfactory cognition and perception and on emotion, memory, and motivated behavior. Using an experimental approach grounded in evolutionary theory and incorporating both cognitive–behavioral and neuropsychological techniques, Dr. Herz aims to understand how biological mechanisms and cognitive processes interact to influence perception, cognition, and behavior.

ROBERTA L. KLATZKY is the Charles J. Queenan, Jr. Professor of Psychology at Carnegie Mellon University, where she also holds faculty appointments in the Center for the Neural Basis of Cognition and the Human–Computer Interaction Institute. She has done extensive research on haptic and visual object recognition, space perception and spatial thinking, and motor performance. Her work has application to haptic interfaces, navigation aids for the blind, image-guided surgery, teleoperation, and virtual environments.

DANIEL M. MERFELD is a Professor at The Ohio State University and also serves as the Senior Vestibular Scientist at the Naval Medical Research Unit in Dayton (NAMRUD). Much of his research career has been spent studying how the brain combines information from multiple sources, with a specific focus on how the brain processes ambiguous sensory information from the vestibular system in the presence of noise. Translational work includes research developing new methods to help diagnose patients experiencing vestibular symptoms and research developing vestibular implants for patients who have severe problems with their vestibular organs.

Contents

7 Attention and Scene Perception   218

8 Visual Motion Perception   256

 **Touch 420**

Touch Physiology 422
Touch Receptors 422
From Skin to Brain 430
Pain 436
  Scientists at Work: Tickling Rats 438

Tactile Sensitivity and Acuity 441
*How Sensitive Are We to Mechanical
  Pressure? 441*
How Finely Can We Resolve Spatial Details? 442
*How Finely Can We Resolve Temporal
  Details? 444*
Do People Differ in Tactile Sensitivity? 444

Haptic Perception 446
Perception for Action 446
Action for Perception 447
*The What System of Touch: Perceiving Objects
  and Their Properties 448*
*The Where System of Touch: Locating
  Objects 454*
Tactile Spatial Attention 455
Social Touch 456
*Interactions between Touch and Other
  Modalities 457*
  Sensation & Perception in Everyday Life:
  Haptic Simulation for Surgical Training 459

Summary 460

 **Olfaction 462**

Olfactory Physiology 464
Odors and Odorants 464
The Human Olfactory Apparatus 465
  Sensation & Perception in Everyday Life:
  Anosmia 469

Neurophysiology of Olfaction 470
The Genetic Basis of Olfactory Receptors 473
The Feel of Scent 476

From Chemicals to Smells 477
Theories of Olfactory Perception 477
The Importance of Patterns 480
Is Odor Perception Synthetic or Analytical? 481
The Power of Sniffing 483
Odor Imagery 484

**Olfactory Psychophysics, Identification,
and Adaptation 484**
Detection, Discrimination, and Recognition 484
*Psychophysical Methods for Detection and
  Discrimination 486*

Identification 486
Individual Differences 488
  Scientists at Work: A New Test to Diagnose
  Parkinson's Disease 490
Adaptation 491
Cognitive Habituation 493

Olfactory Hedonics 494
Familiarity and Intensity 495
Nature or Nurture? 495
An Evolutionary Argument 497
Caveats 498

**Associative Learning and Emotion:
Neuroanatomical and Evolutionary
Considerations 499**
*The Vomeronasal Organ, Human Pheromones,
  and Chemosignals 500*
  Sensation & Perception in Everyday Life:
  Odor-Evoked Memory and the Truth behind
  Aromatherapy 503

Summary 505

15 Taste   508

Preface

If you are lucky, you will have a career doing something that you really enjoy. We, the authors of this book, are lucky. We are fascinated by the human senses and we are fortunate enough to be employed to investigate how different aspects of different senses work. We want to know the answers to fundamental questions about the senses: How does our brain create a three-dimensional perception of the world from two-dimensional images, formed on the back of each eye? Why do some substances taste "sweet"? We also want to know the answers to perceptual questions that arise from important problems in the world, so we work on problems like oral pain or disorders of balance that have medical applications, or issues such as airport security that have broader societal implications.

We wrote this undergraduate textbook in the hope that we might spread some of our enthusiasm to you, our reader. In service of that goal, each of the 15 chapters of this book aims to tell a coherent and interesting story that will give the reader enough background and exposure to current research to understand why these topics are interesting and how they might be further investigated. For every topic in the book, we are acutely aware that there is vastly more information than we can squeeze into a chapter. Moreover, we are not naive or immodest enough to believe that you will devour a chapter on "The Perception of Color" or "Perceiving and Recognizing Objects" in the way that you might devour a good novel. However, we do hope that you will find each chapter to be more than a compilation of facts. We hope to be like Cleopatra in Shakespeare's play "Anthony and Cleopatra": while other texts may "cloy the appetites they feed," we hope our work "makes hungry where most it satisfies" (Act 2, Scene 2). It is our hope that this book teaches enough to inspire the reader to want to know more.

In service of these goals, we have produced a textbook that is reasonably comprehensive while still being digestible. It is possible that you, the student, may not think so at 3:00 a.m. the day before the final exam, but that was the goal. We want to present a coherent introduction to the important topics in our field. As noted, we can't cover *everything*. If you, the instructor, or you, the interested student, think we missed something that should be in here, please feel encouraged to drop us an email. Each time we revise the book, we add some new topics and we take some material out.

Some of that extra material can be found on the text's companion website, oup.com/us/wolfe5e. There you will find a number of brief essays on topics that we broken-heartedly removed from earlier versions of our chapters. Given the chance, each of us can talk your ear off on the topics in this book, but we have sincerely tried to avoid doing this. In addition to the essays, the website features a host of great demonstrations made possible by Evan Palmer of San Jose State University, the guardian of our website.

In trying to convey our enthusiasm for this material, we wanted to create a beautiful book. If we have succeeded, it is in no small part due to our publisher, Sinauer Associates. The people at Sinauer produce beautiful books and we have enjoyed working with their talented editors to produce a book that strives to be both aesthetically and intellectually appealing.

We were pleased by the reception of the earlier editions of our textbook and pleased that this reception warranted a Fifth Edition. Between editions, each of us keeps an eye out for new findings that seem worthy of note in the textbook. When it comes to writing, we always discover that we have more new material that we can squeeze in but, in each chapter, you will find some of what we have learned since the Fourth Edition. One new feature in the Fifth Edition is called *Scientists at Work*. In these highlighted sections, you will find a more extended discussion of one piece of research. The goal of this feature is to show you how to think like a scientist, and what the thought process is in designing experiments that yield scientific results. Another feature of the textbook are *Sensation & Perception in Everyday Life* boxes. Here we discuss the application of basic scientific knowledge to practical problems in the real world. For example, as you will see in Chapter 5, aspects of the color picker in your graphics program can be directly traced to our understanding of how your eye and brain derive the experience of color from different mixtures of wavelengths of light. We trust that you will recognize or even invent other applications of the information presented here. That, as they say, is an exercise for the reader. Speaking of readers, it is always a question whether or not anyone actually reads the preface. If you did and you are reading this, please send a note to jwolfe@bwh.harvard.edu. It is fun to hear from folks in the field. If you are reading this for a course, tell us who is teaching. Odds are that one of us knows your instructor. Please also feel encouraged to send us notes and comments about the actual text. There are quite a few changes in the current edition that were driven by intelligent reader comments about the previous editions. Thanks.

ACKNOWLEDGMENTS

Our editor, Sydney Carroll has kept this project going over several editions and always manages to gracefully cajole us into doing our work more-or-less on time. Lou Doucette did a fantastic job copyediting. She caught our errors, improved our words, and made our text fit for public use. Mark Siddall came up with an endless set of clever ideas for better images and photos (check out Figure 7.33). Danna Lockwood coordinated and oversaw the entire production process, as well as developed figures, helped clarify prose, and corrected any leftover inconsistencies or unclear writing. We also wish to thank the entire production department at Sinauer, especially Christopher Small and Ann Chiara, who created an elegant book design and cover. Mike Demaray, Craig Durant, and colleagues at Dragonfly Media Group created the beautiful art program of this text.

The following reviewers read and critiqued drafts and/or previous versions of the text, and we are grateful for their expert assistance:

Nicole D. Anderson, MacEwan University

Jeffrey Andre, James Madison University

Martin Arguin, University of Montreal

Simona Buetti, University of Illinois at Urbana-Champaign

Cheryl A. Camenzuli, Molloy College

Leslie Cameron, Carthage College

Linda C. Carson, University of Waterloo

Kathleen Cullen, McGill University

Thomas A. Daniel, Westfield State University

Nicolas Davidenko, University of California, Santa Cruz

Christopher DiMattina, Florida Gulf Coast University

Joshua Dobias, Rutgers, The State University of New Jersey

Colin Ellard, University of Waterloo

Stephen Emrich, Brock University

Rhea Eskew, Northeastern University

Danielle Gagne, Alfred University

Carmela Gottesman, University of South Carolina, Salkehatchie

Michael E. Hildebrand, Carleton University

Eric Jackson, University of New Mexico

Aaron Johnson, Concordia University

Ingrid S. Johnsrude, Western University

Jane Karwoski, University of Nevada, Las Vegas

Brock Kirwan, Brigham Young University

Roger Kreuz, University of Memphis

Leslie D. Kwakye, Oberlin College

Michael Landy, New York University

Michael Lantz, Concordia University at Loyola

Glenn Legault, Laurentian University

Max Levine, Siena College

Olga Lipatova, Christopher Newport University

Zili Liu, University of California, Los Angeles

Alejandro Lleras, University of Illinois at Urbana-Champaign

Justin A. MacDonald, New Mexico State University

Kristen L. Macuga, Oregon State University

Janice C. McMurray, University of Nevada, Las Vegas

John Monahan, Central Michigan University

Richard Murray, York University

Gina O'Neal-Moffitt, Florida State University

Michael Owren, Emory University

Jennifer Peszka, Hendrix College

Robert Remez, Barnard College, Columbia University

Adrián Rodríguez-Contreras, The City College of New York

Lisa Sanders, University of Massachusetts, Amherst

Eriko Self, California State University, Fullerton

Kevin Seybold, Grove City College

Steve Shevell, University of Illinois at Chicago

Rachel Shoup, California State University, East Bay

T.C. Sim, Sam Houston State University

Joel Snyder, University of Nevada, Las Vegas

Miriam Spering, University of British Columbia

Kenneth Steele, Appalachian State University

Julia Strand, Carleton College

William Stine, University of New Hampshire

Greg Stone, Arizona State University

Duje Tadin, University of Rochester

Jeroen van Boxtel, University of California, Los Angeles

Rachel Walker, Charleston Southern University

Dirk B. Walther, University of Toronto

Scott N.J. Watamaniuk, Wright State University

Laurie Wilcox, York University

Finally, many, many colleagues sent us reprints and answered questions about points both specific and general. We gratefully acknowledge their help even if we cannot list all of their names (and even if we may *still* have failed to get things *exactly* right). We are also indebted to the users of the text, students, and faculty who pointed out errors, typos, and other shortcomings in the first four editions. We hope we caught them all and we hope that the readers of this edition will continue to offer us assistance. As noted earlier in the preface, if you find a flaw or if you have any other comment—even a positive one—please feel encouraged to let us know. You can use jwolfe@bwh.harvard.edu as a point of contact for all of us.

Media and Supplements

FOR THE STUDENT

Companion Website (oup.com/us/wolfe5e)

The *Sensation & Perception*, Fifth Edition companion website provides students with a variety of interactive resources and study and review materials to help them master the important concepts covered in the textbook. The site is available to students free of charge and includes the following resources:

- *Introductions* give students an engaging entry point into the important concepts presented in each chapter.

- *Web Activities* lead students through important processes, phenomena, and structures. These interactive exercises give students the opportunity to explore a variety of topics in an interactive, exploratory format, including perception experiments, illusions that illustrate key concepts, models of cognitive processes, and interactive diagrams of important structures.

- *Web Essays* expand on selected topics from the textbook and provide additional coverage and examples.

- *Flashcards* help students master the hundreds of new terms introduced in the textbook.

- An online *Glossary* provides definitions for all textbook bolded terms.

Dashboard (www.oup.com/us/dashboard)

Dashboard delivers a wealth of automatically-graded quizzes and study resources for *Sensation & Perception*, along with an interactive eBook, all in an intuitive, web-based learning environment. See below for details.

FOR THE INSTRUCTOR

Ancillary Resource Center (oup-arc.com/access/wolfe-5e)

- *Textbook Figures and Tables*: All of the figures and tables from the textbook, formatted for optimal legibility when projected. Complex images are provided in both a whole and split version.

- *PowerPoint Presentations*: For each chapter of the textbook, two PowerPoint presentations are provided:

  - *Figures & Tables*: All of the figures and tables from the chapter, with titles on each slide, and complete captions in the Notes field.

  - *Lecture*: A complete lecture presentation that consists of a detailed lecture outline with selected figures and tables.

- *Instructor's Manual*: A variety of resources to aid in course development, lecture planning, and assessment. The Instructor's Manual includes the following resources for each textbook chapter: Chapter Overview, Chapter Outline, Chapter Summary, Learning Objectives, and References for Lecture Development.

- *Test Bank*: A complete set of multiple-choice, short answer, and essay questions for each chapter of the textbook. Questions cover the full range of material covered in each chapter, including both factual and conceptual questions, and all are keyed to specific textbook sections, learning objectives, and Bloom's taxonomy. Available in Microsoft Word, Diploma, and LMS formats.

Dashboard (www.oup.com/us/dashboard)

Dashboard by Oxford University Press delivers a wealth of study resources and automatically-graded quizzes for *Sensation & Perception* in an intuitive, web-based learning environment. A built-in color-coded gradebook allows instructors to track student progress. Dashboard includes:

- *Interactive eBook*: A complete eBook is integrated into Dashboard and includes in-text links to Activities and Essays.

- *All Student Companion Website Resources*: Activities, Overviews, Web Essay, Flashcards, and Glossary.

- *Activity Quizzes*: Each activity is accompanied by a brief assignable quiz, giving instructors the option to use the activities as assignments.

- *Study Questions*: A set of questions designed to give students the opportunity to test their understanding of each chapter's material.

- *Chapter Summaries*: Review activities that combine a detailed overview of each chapter's content with a fill-in-the-blanks exercise to check comprehension.

To learn more about any of these resources, or to get access, please contact your local OUP representative.

VALUE OPTIONS

eBook

(ISBN 978-1-60535-715-7)

Sensation & Perception, Fifth Edition is available as an eBook, in several different formats, including RedShelf, VitalSource, and Chegg. All major mobile devices are supported.

Looseleaf Textbook

(ISBN 978-1-60535-727-0)

Sensation & Perception is also available in a three-hole punched, looseleaf format. Students can take just the sections they need to class and can easily integrate instructor material with the text.

Sensation & Perception
FIFTH EDITION

Introduction

■ Questions to Contemplate ■

Think about the following questions as you read this chapter. By the chapter's end, you should be able to answer and discuss them.

- How can scientists study something as personal as your internal sensations and perceptions?

- Are there laws that relate the physics of the world to your subjective experience?

- What is happening when you think that you might have heard something or felt something but you're not sure? If a stimulus is detectable, why isn't it detectable all the time?

- Are there rules that relate the activity of your brain to your subjective experience?

- How do sensation and perception change over the life span?

Welcome to Our World

You've taken the plunge to read at least part of a textbook on "sensation and perception." You may be majoring in psychology or studying an allied field, such as neuroscience or biology, or you may be simply curious. No matter what interests you most, your understanding will be informed by sensation and perception.

"Why?" you ask. Most everything you know or think that you know about the world around you depends on how you sense and how you perceive. These foundational experiences began even before you were born. Your senses help you to keep upright, stay warm or cool, avoid pain and poisonous things, and be safe from danger. Your experiences of the rich tapestry of life through movement, touch, smell, taste, hearing, and vision inform most everything that you believe to be true.

Aaron Jasinski, *Clarity II*, 2015

It is small wonder that the questions posed in this textbook have been front and center for big thinkers since the first written words, and probably sooner. Today, a small army of researchers continue to pursue answers. This first chapter provides an introduction to the sorts of questions that captivate the authors of this book and the sorts of methods that researchers have developed to answer those questions. These are only examples, as the list of possible others is endless. The rest of the book will introduce you to a panorama of questions that have occupied and continue to occupy the attention of anyone who really wants to know how we know what we think we know.

Sensation and Perception

What does your smartphone feel as you run your finger down its touch screen (**Figure 1.1**)? What does it hear as you whisper into its receiver? We assume that

Figure 1.1 Would it make sense to ask what a cell phone feels when you stroke its screen?

sensation The ability to detect a stimulus and, perhaps, to turn that detection into a private experience.

perception The act of giving meaning to a detected sensation.

Figure 1.2 Étienne Bonnot de Condillac imagined how a statue could develop a mental life.

these are silly questions, though it would not be silly to ask about the lightest touch that the screen could sense or the faintest vibration in the air that the microphone could sense. What does your cat feel as you run your finger down its back? That seems a more reasonable question, though you have no access to the private experience of the cat. You don't even have access to the private sensations of a person whose back you might stroke. Your own sensory experience is directly accessible only to you.

This book is titled *Sensation & Perception*. The ability to detect the pressure of a finger and, perhaps, to turn that detection into a private experience is an example of **sensation**. **Perception** can be thought of as the act of giving meaning and/or purpose to those detected sensations. How do you *understand* the finger that runs down your back? Is it a gesture of affection? Is it an officer at an airport security checkpoint looking for contraband? This book will trace the path from stimuli in the world, through your sense organs, to the understanding of the world that you perceive.

Everything we feel, think, and do depends on sensations and perceptions. For this reason, philosophers have thought, talked, and written about the topic in profound and systematic ways for over two millennia. (See **Web Essay 1.1: Senses of Reality Through the Ages**.) The idea that mental life depends on sensation and perception has deep roots. The eighteenth-century French philosopher Étienne Bonnot de Condillac (1715–1780) (**Figure 1.2**) famously asked his readers to imagine the mental life of a statue with no senses, and he concluded that the statue would have no mental life. Then Condillac imagined opening the statue's nose and giving it a whiff of the scent of a rose. Then, he thought, the entire mental life of the statue would consist of that smell. If more senses and more experience were provided to the statue, Condillac imagined, a real mental life would develop. If our mental life depends on information from our senses, then it follows that the place for the study of the senses is within the science of human behavior and human mental life—that is, within psychology. Of course, psychologists do not have the topic entirely to themselves. Researchers studying topics in sensation and perception can be found in biology, computer science, medicine, neuroscience, and many other fields. Indeed, the authors of this book come from academic departments of ophthalmology, radiology, optometry, speech, language and hearing sciences, and community dentistry in addition to psychology. Critically, however, we approach the study of sensation and perception as a scientific pursuit. As such, it needs scientific methods. That's why the next sections of this chapter are devoted to an array of methods used in the study of the senses.

METHOD 1: THRESHOLDS What is the faintest sound you can hear? How would you know? What is the loudest sound you can hear? This last question is not as stupid as it may sound, though it could be rephrased like this: What is the loudest sound you can hear safely or without pain? If you listened to sounds above that limit, perhaps by blasting your music too enthusiastically, you would change the answer to the first question. You would damage your auditory system. Then, you would be unable to hear the faintest sound that you used to be able to hear. Your threshold would have changed (for the worse). How would you measure that? As we'll learn in this chapter, a variety of methods are available for measuring just how sensitive your senses are.

METHOD 2: SCALING—MEASURING PRIVATE EXPERIENCE When you say that you "hear" or "taste" something, are those experiences—what the philosophers call **qualia** (singular *quale*)—the same as the experiences of the person you're talking to? We can't really answer the question of whether your qualitative experience of "red" is like my qualitative experience of "green" or, for that matter, "middle C." We still have no direct way to experience someone else's experiences. However, we can demonstrate that different people do, in some cases, inhabit different sensory worlds. Our discussion in this chapter will show how scaling methods can be used to perform this act of mind reading.

qualia In reference to philosophy, private conscious experiences of sensation or perception.

FURTHER DISCUSSION of qualia can be found in Chapter 5 on page 158.

METHOD 3: SIGNAL DETECTION THEORY—MEASURING DIFFICULT DECISIONS   A radiologist looks at a mammogram, the X-ray test used to screen for breast cancer. There's something on the X-ray that might be a sign of cancer, but it is not perfectly clear. What should the radiologist do? Suppose she decides to call it benign, not cancerous, and suppose she is wrong. Her patient might die. Suppose she decides to treat it as a sign of malignancy. Her patient will need more tests, perhaps involving surgery. The patient and her family will be terribly worried. If the radiologist is wrong and the spot on the mammogram is, in fact, benign, the consequences may be less dire than those of missing a cancer, but there will be consequences. This is a perceptual decision, made by an expert, that has real consequences. Our discussion of signal detection theory will show how decisions of this sort can be studied scientifically.

METHOD 4: SENSORY NEUROSCIENCE   Grilled peppers appear on your table as an appetizer. They have an appealing, smoky smell. When you bite into one, it has a complex flavor that includes some of that smokiness. Fairly quickly you also experience a burning sensation. There is no actual change in the temperature in your mouth, and your tongue is no warmer than it was, but the "burn" is unmistakable. How does the pepper fool your nervous system into thinking that your tongue is on fire? This chapter's exploration of sensory neuroscience will introduce the ways in which sensory receptors and nerves undergird your perceptual experience.

METHOD 5: NEUROIMAGING—AN IMAGE OF THE MIND   Suppose you arrange to view completely different images with different eyes. We might present a picture of a house to one eye and of a face to the other (Tong et al., 1998). The result would be an interesting effect known as binocular rivalry (see Chapter 6). The two images would compete to dominate your perception: sometimes you would see a house, and sometimes you would see a face. You would not see the two together. One reason binocular rivalry is interesting is that it represents a dissociation of the stimuli, presented to the eyes, and your private perceptual experience. Even if we cannot share the experience, modern brain-imaging techniques enable us to see traces of that experience as it takes place in the brain. Methods of neuroimaging will be our final methodological topic in this chapter.

DEVELOPMENT   Development, the study of the changes over the life span, is not really a "method," but it is an approach to the study of sensation and perception that should be introduced in this opening chapter, so we will do so in the last section.

Figure 1.3 Gustav Fechner invented psychophysics and is thought by some to be the true founder of experimental psychology. Fechner is best known for his pioneering work relating changes in the physical world to changes in our psychological experiences.

dualism The idea that the mind has an existence separate from the material world of the body.

materialism The idea that the only thing that exists is matter, and that all things, including the mind and consciousness, are the results of interaction between bits of matter.

panpsychism The idea that the mind exists as a property of all matter—that is, that all matter has consciousness.

psychophysics The science of defining quantitative relationships between physical and psychological (subjective) events.

two-point touch threshold The minimum distance at which two stimuli (e.g., two simultaneous touches) are just perceptible as separate.

Thresholds and the Dawn of Psychophysics

Early on, study of the senses was a mix of experimental science and philosophy. Fascinating work can be found in ancient Greek philosophy, in medieval Islamic science, and in the writings of sages in China or India. We will start much later with the very interesting and versatile nineteenth-century German scientist-philosopher Gustav Fechner (1801–1887) (**Figure 1.3**). Fechner is sometimes considered to be the true founder of experimental psychology (Boring, 1950), even if that title is usually given to Wilhelm Wundt (1832–1920), who began his work sometime later.

Before making his first contributions to psychology, Fechner had an eventful personal history. Young Fechner earned his degree in medicine, but his interests turned from biological science to physics and mathematics. By 1833, he was a full professor of physics in Leipzig, Germany. Though this might seem an unlikely way to get to psychology, events proved otherwise. He became absorbed with the relationship between mind and matter. This pursuit placed him in the middle of a classic philosophical debate between adherents of **dualism** and **materialism**. Dualists hold that the mind has an existence separate from the material world of the body. Materialists hold that the mind is not separate. A modern materialist position, probably the majority view in scientific psychology, is that the mind is what the brain does. Fechner proposed to effectively split the difference by imagining that the mind, or consciousness, is present in all of nature. This **panpsychism**—the idea that the mind exists as a property of all matter—extended not only to animals, but to inanimate things as well. Fechner described his philosophy of panpsychism in a provocative book entitled *Nanna, or Concerning the Mental Life of Plants*. This title alone gives a pretty good idea of what Fechner had in mind.

Fechner was a very hardworking young scientist. He worked himself to exhaustion. In addition to being overworked, he suffered severe eye damage from gazing too much at the sun while performing vision experiments (a not uncommon problem for curious vision researchers in the days before reliable, bright, artificial light sources). The visually incapacitated Fechner had some form of mental breakdown that left him sometimes unable to speak or eat. Not only did he need to resign from his position at the university, he also withdrew from almost all his friends and colleagues. For 3 years he spent almost all of his time alone with his thoughts.

He apparently solved his eating problem with a diet of "fruit, strongly spiced ham and wine" (Fancher, 1990, p. 133). His vision was also recovering. Then on October 22, 1850 (a date still celebrated as "Fechner Day" by some), while lying in bed, Fechner had a specific insight into the relationship between mental life and the physical world. From his experience as a physicist, Fechner thought it should be possible to describe the relation between mind and body using mathematics. His goal was to formally describe the relationship between sensation (mind) and the energy (matter) that gave rise to that sensation. He called both his methods and his theory **psychophysics** (*psycho* for "mind," and *physics* for "matter").

In his effort, Fechner was inspired by the findings of one of his German colleagues, Ernst Weber (1795–1878) (**Figure 1.4**), an anatomist and physiologist who was interested in touch. Weber tested the accuracy of our sense of touch by using a device much like the compass one might use to draw circles. He used this device to measure the smallest distance between two points that was required for a person to feel touch on two points instead of one. Later, Fechner would call the distance between the points the **two-point touch threshold**. We will discuss two-point touch thresholds, and touch in general, in Chapter 13.

For Fechner, Weber's most important findings involved judgments of lifted weights. Weber would ask people to lift one standard weight (a weight that stayed the same over a series of experimental trials) and one comparison weight that differed from the standard. Weber increased the comparison weight in incremental amounts over the series of trials. He found that the ability of a person to detect the difference between the standard and comparison weights depended greatly on the weight of the standard. When the standard was relatively light, people were much better at detecting a small difference when they lifted a comparison weight. When the standard was heavier, people needed a bigger difference before they could detect a change. He called the difference required for detecting a change in weight the **just noticeable difference**, or **JND**. Another term for JND, the smallest change in a stimulus that can be detected, is the **difference threshold**.

Weber noticed that JNDs changed in a systematic way. The smallest change in weight that could be detected was always close to 1/40 of the standard weight. Thus, a 1-gram change could be detected when the standard weighed 40 grams, but a 10-gram change was required when the standard weighed 400 grams. Weber went on to test JNDs for a few other kinds of stimuli, such as the lengths of two lines, for which the detectable change ratio was 1:100. For virtually every measure—whether brightness, pitch, or time—a constant ratio between the change and the standard could describe the threshold of detectable change quite well. This ratio rule holds true except when intensities, size, and so on are very small or very large, nearing the minimum and maximum of our senses. In recognition of Weber's discovery, Fechner called these ratios **Weber fractions**. He also gave Weber's observation a mathematical formula. Fechner named the general rule—that the size of the detectable difference (ΔI) is a constant proportion (K) of the level of the stimulus (I)—**Weber's law**.

In Weber's observations, Fechner found what he was looking for: a way to describe the relationship between mind and matter. Fechner assumed that the smallest detectable change in a stimulus (ΔI) could be considered a unit of the mind because this is the smallest bit of change that is perceived. He then mathematically extended Weber's law to create what became known as **Fechner's law** (Figure 1.5):

$$S = k \log R$$

where S is the psychological sensation, which is equal to the logarithm of the physical stimulus level ($\log R$) multiplied by a constant, k. This equation describes

Figure 1.4 Ernst Weber discovered that the smallest detectable change in a stimulus, such as the weight of an object, is a constant proportion of the stimulus level. This relationship later became known as Weber's law.

just noticeable difference (JND) or **difference threshold** The smallest detectable difference between two stimuli, or the minimum change in a stimulus that enables it to be correctly judged as different from a reference stimulus.

Weber fraction The constant of proportionality in Weber's law.

Weber's law The principle describing the relationship between stimulus and resulting sensation that says the just noticeable difference (JND) is a constant fraction of the comparison stimulus.

Fechner's law A principle describing the relationship between stimulus and resulting sensation that says the magnitude of subjective sensation increases proportionally to the logarithm of the stimulus intensity.

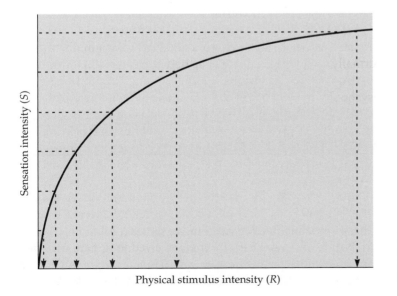

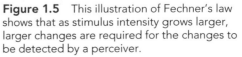

Figure 1.5 This illustration of Fechner's law shows that as stimulus intensity grows larger, larger changes are required for the changes to be detected by a perceiver.

absolute threshold The minimum amount of stimulation necessary for a person to detect a stimulus 50% of the time.

method of constant stimuli A psychophysical method in which many stimuli, ranging from rarely to almost always perceivable (or rarely to almost always perceivably different from a reference stimulus), are presented one at a time. Participants respond to each presentation: "yes/no," "same/different," and so on.

the fact that our psychological experience of the intensity of light, sound, smell, taste, or touch increases less quickly than the actual physical stimulus increases. With this equation, Fechner provided a mathematical expression that formally demonstrated a relationship between psyche and physics (psychophysics).

Consider the similarity between Fechner's law and Albert Einstein's famous equation:

$$E = mc^2$$

Like mind and body, energy (*E*) and mass (*m*) had, before Einstein, been thought of as distinct things. (The letter *c* corresponds to the speed of light, almost a billion feet per second.) Just as Einstein showed how to equate energy and mass, Fechner provided us with at least one way to equate mind and matter. As you learn about the senses when reading this book, you will find that we typically make a distinction between units of physical entities (light, sound) and measures of people's perception. For example (as we'll learn in Chapter 9), we measure the physical intensity of a sound (sound pressure level) in decibels, but we refer to our sensation as "loudness." Similarly, frequency is a measure of a physical phenomenon, while pitch describes a psychophysical response to that physical phenomenon. Frequency and pitch are not the same thing, but they are closely correlated. Over a wide range, as frequency increases, so does pitch, though it is unclear whether there is a perception of pitch for high frequencies.

Fechner invented new ways to measure what people see, hear, and feel. All of his methods are still in use today. In explaining these methods here, we will use absolute threshold as an example because it is, perhaps, the most straightforward, but we would use the same methods to determine difference thresholds such as Δ*I*. An **absolute threshold** is the minimum intensity of a stimulus that can be detected (**Table 1.1**). This returns us to the question we raised earlier: What is the faintest sound you can hear? Of course, we could ask the same question about the faintest light, the lightest touch, and so forth. (See **Web Activity 1.1: Psychophysics**.)

■ Table 1.1

Absolute thresholds in the real world

Sense	Threshold
Vision	Stars at night, or a candle flame 30 miles away on a dark, clear night
Hearing	A ticking watch 20 feet away, with no other noises
Vestibular	A tilt of less than half a minute on a clock face
Taste	A teaspoon of sugar in 2 gallons of water
Smell	A drop of perfume in three rooms
Touch	The wing of a fly falling on your cheek from a height of 3 inches

Source: From Galanter, 1962.

Psychophysical Methods

How can we measure an absolute threshold in a valid and reliable manner? One method is known as the **method of constant stimuli**. This method requires creating many stimuli with different intensities in order to find the tiniest intensity that can be detected (**Figure 1.6**). If you've had a hearing

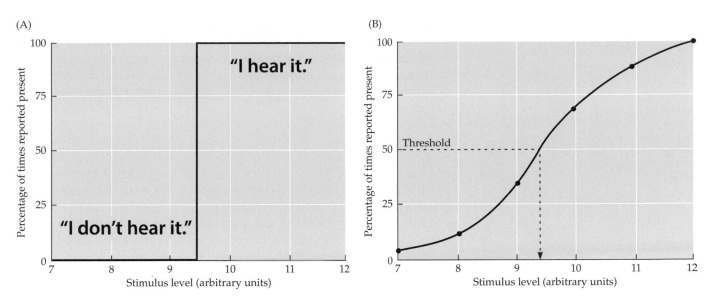

Figure 1.6 The method of constant stimuli. (A) We might expect the threshold to be a sharp change in detection from never reported to always reported, as depicted here, but this is not so. (B) In reality, experiments measuring absolute threshold produce shallower functions relating stimulus to response. A somewhat arbitrary point on the curve, often 50% detection, is designated as the threshold.

test, you had to report when you could and could not hear a tone that the audiologist played to you over headphones, usually in a very quiet room. In this test, intensities of all of the tones were relatively low, not too far above or below the intensity where your threshold was expected to be. The tones, varying in intensity, were presented randomly, and tones were presented multiple times at each intensity.

The "multiple times" piece is important. Subtle perceptual judgments (e.g., threshold judgments) are variable. The stimulus varies for physical reasons. The observer varies. Attention waivers and sensory systems fluctuate for all sorts of reasons. As a consequence, one measure is almost never enough. You need to repeat the measure over and over and then average responses or otherwise describe the pattern of results. Some experiments require thousands of repetitions (thousands of "trials") to establish a sufficiently reliable data point.

Returning to our auditory example, as the listener, you would report whether you heard a tone or not. You would always report hearing a tone that was relatively far above threshold, and almost never report hearing a tone that was well below threshold. In between, however, you would be more likely to hear some tone intensities than not to hear them, and you would hear other, lower intensities on only a few presentations. In general, the intensity at which a stimulus would be detected 50% of the time would be chosen as your threshold.

That 50% definition of absolute threshold is rather interesting. Weren't we looking for a way to measure the weakest detectable stimulus? Using the hearing example, shouldn't that be a value below which we just can't hear anything (see Figure 1.6A)? It turns out that no such hard boundary exists. Because of variability in the nervous system, stimuli near threshold will be detected sometimes and missed at other times. As a result, the function relating the probability of detection with the stimulus level will be more gradual (see Figure 1.6B), and we must settle for a somewhat arbitrary definition of an absolute threshold. (We will return to this issue when we talk about signal detection theory.)

Trial series

Intensity (arbitrary units)	↓1	↑2	↓3	↑4	↓5	↑6	↓7	↑8
20	Y						Y	
19	Y		Y		Y		Y	
18	Y		Y		Y		Y	
17	Y		Y		Y		Y	
16	Y		Y		Y		Y	Y
15	Y	Y	Y	Y	Y	Y	Y	Y
14	Y	N	Y	N	Y	N	Y	Y
13	N	N	Y	N	Y	N	N	Y
12		N	N	N	N	N		N
11		N		N		N		N
10		N		N		N		N
	13.5	14.5	12.5	14.5	12.5	14.5	13.5	12.5

Crossover values (average = 13.5)

Figure 1.7 The method of limits. Here the listener attends to multiple series of trials. For each series, the intensity of the stimulus is gradually increased or decreased until the listener detects (Y) or fails to detect (N), respectively, the stimulus. For each series, an estimate of the threshold (red dashed line) is taken to be the average of the stimulus level just before and after the change in perception.

method of limits A psychophysical method in which the particular dimension of a stimulus, or the difference between two stimuli, is varied incrementally until the participant responds differently.

method of adjustment A method of limits in which the participant controls the change in the stimulus.

magnitude estimation A psychophysical method in which the participant assigns values according to perceived magnitudes of the stimuli.

The method of constant stimuli is simple to use, but it is an inefficient way to conduct an experiment, because much of the listener's time is spent with stimuli that are clearly well above or below threshold. A more efficient approach is the **method of limits (Figure 1.7)**. With this method, the experimenter begins with the same set of stimuli—in this case, tones that vary in intensity. Instead of random presentations, tones are presented in order of increasing or decreasing intensity. When tones are presented in ascending order, from faintest to loudest, listeners are asked to report when they first hear the tone. With descending order, the task is to report when the tone is no longer audible. Data from an experiment such as this show that there is some "overshoot" in judgments. It usually takes more intensity to report hearing the tone when intensity is increasing, and it takes more decreases in intensity before a listener reports that the tone cannot be heard. We take the average of these crossover points—when listeners shift from reporting hearing the tone to not hearing the tone, and vice versa—to be the threshold.

The third and final of these classic measures of thresholds is the **method of adjustment**. This method is just like the method of limits, except the person being tested is the one who steadily increases or decreases the intensity of the stimulus. The method of adjustment may be the easiest method to understand, because it is much like day-to-day activities such as adjusting the volume dial on a stereo or the dimmer switch for a light. Even though it's the easiest to understand, the method of adjustment is not usually used to measure thresholds. The method would be perfect if threshold data were like those plotted in Figure 1.6A. But, a graph of real data looks more like Figure 1.6B. The same person will adjust a dial to different places on different trials, and measurements get even messier when we try to combine the data from multiple people.

Scaling Methods

Moving beyond absolute thresholds and difference thresholds, suppose we wanted to know how strong your experiences are. For example, we might show you a light and ask how much additional light you would need to make another light look twice as bright. Though that might seem like an odd question, it turns out to be answerable. We could give you a knob to adjust so that you could set the second light to appear twice as bright as the first, and you could do it.

In fact, we don't need to give the observers a light to adjust. A surprisingly straightforward way to address the question of the strength or size of a sensation is to simply ask observers to rate the experience. For example, we could give observers a series of sugar solutions and ask them to assign numbers to each sample. We would just tell our observers that sweeter solutions should get bigger numbers, and if solution A seems twice as sweet as solution B, the number assigned to A should be twice the number assigned to B. This method is called **magnitude estimation**. This approach actually works well, even when observers are free to choose their own range of numbers. More typically, we might begin the experiment by presenting one solution at an intermediate level and telling the taster to label this level as a specific value—10, for instance. All of the responses should then be scaled sensibly above or below this standard of 10. If you do this for sugar solutions, you will get data that look like the blue "sweetness" line in **Figure 1.8**.

Harvard psychologist S. S. Stevens (1962, 1975) invented magnitude estimation. He, his students, and successors measured functions like the one in Figure 1.8 for many different sensations. Even though observers were asked

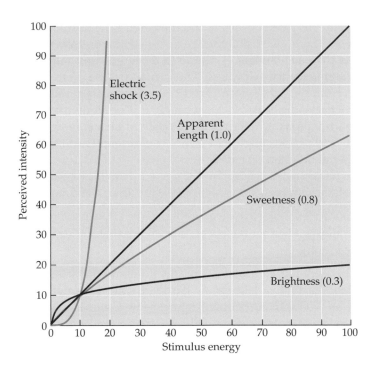

Figure 1.8 Magnitude estimation. The lines on this graph represent data from magnitude estimation experiments using electric shocks of different currents, lines of different lengths, solutions of different sweetness levels, and lights of different brightness levels. The exponents for the "power functions" that describe these lines are 3.5, 1.0, 0.8, and 0.3, respectively. For exponents greater than 1, such as for electric shock, Fechner's law does not hold, and Stevens's power law must be used instead.

to assign numbers to private experience, the results were orderly and lawful. However, they were not the same for every type of sensation. That relationship between stimulus intensity and sensation is described by what is now known as **Stevens's power law**:

$$S = aI^b$$

which states that the sensation (S) is related to the stimulus intensity (I) by an exponent (b). (The letter a is a constant that corrects for the units you are using. For example, if you measured your stimulus in meters then switched to measuring it in centimeters, you would need to multiply by 0.01 [divide by 100] to keep your sensation numbers the same.) So, for example, experienced sensation might rise with intensity squared ($I \times I$). That would be an exponent of 2.0. If the exponent is less than 1, this means that the sensation grows less rapidly than the stimulus. This is what Fechner's law and Weber's law would predict.

Suppose you have some lit candles and you light 10 more. If you started with 1 candle, the change from 1 to 11 candles must be quite dramatic. If you add 10 to 100, the change will be modest. Adding 10 to 10,000 won't even be noticeable. In fact, the exponent for brightness is about 0.3. The exponent for sweetness is about 0.8 (Bartoshuk, 1979). Properties like length have exponents near 1, so, reasonably enough, a 12-inch-long stick looks twice as long as a 6-inch-long stick (S. S. Stevens and Galanter, 1957). Note that this relationship is true over only a moderate range of sizes. An inch added to the size of a spider changes your sensory experience much more than an inch added to the height of a giraffe. Some stimuli have exponents greater than 1. In the painful case of electric shock, the pain grows with $I^{3.5}$ (Stevens, Carton, and Shickman, 1958), so a 4-fold increase in the electrical current is experienced as a 128-fold increase in pain!

Weber's and Fechner's laws have rather broad implications beyond questions of apparent brightness or loudness. Suppose you are a plant that is fertilized by bees that visit your flowers because you have sweet nectar. How much sugar do you need to put into that nectar? After all, that sugar is going to "cost" you

Stevens's power law   A principle describing the relationship between stimulus and resulting sensation that says the magnitude of subjective sensation is proportional to the stimulus magnitude raised to an exponent.

cross-modality matching The ability to match the intensities of sensations that come from different sensory modalities. This ability allows insight into sensory differences. For example, a listener might adjust the brightness of a light until it matches the loudness of a tone.

supertaster An individual who experiences the most intense taste sensations. Some stimuli are dramatically more intense for supertasters than for medium tasters or nontasters. Supertasters also tend to experience more intense oral burn and oral touch sensations.

signal detection theory A psychophysical theory that quantifies the response of an observer to the presentation of a signal in the presence of noise. Measures obtained from a series of presentations are sensitivity (d') and criterion of the observer.

something. If your nectar has 2 units of sugar and the neighbor flower only has 1, you probably have a competitive advantage over the neighbor. However, if you have 12 units and the neighbor has 11, that difference of 1 unit might fall below the bee's Weber fraction for sweetness. Thus, there will be more evolutionary pressure to go from 1 to 2 than from 11 to 12. Flowers will respond to the psychophysical experience of the bees (Nachev et al., 2011). Similarly, a peacock with 51 feathers in his tail probably does not have much of an advantage over a 50-feather peacock. The peahen might not notice the difference, putting an evolutionary brake on tail inflation (Ferris, 2017).

At this point in our discussion of psychophysics, it is worth taking a moment to compare the three laws that have been presented: Weber's, Fechner's, and Stevens's.

1. *Weber's law* involves a clear objective measurement. We know how much we varied the stimulus, and either the observers can tell that the stimulus changed or they cannot.

2. *Fechner's law* begins with the same sort of objective measurements as Weber's, but the law is actually a calculation based on some assumptions about how sensation works. In particular, Fechner's law assumes that all JNDs are perceptually equivalent. In fact, this assumption turns out to be incorrect and leads to some places where the "law" is violated, such as in the electric shock example just given.

3. *Stevens's power law* describes rating data quite well, but notice that rating data are qualitatively different from the data that supported Weber's law. We can record the observer's ratings and we can check whether those ratings are reasonable and consistent, but there is no way to know whether they are objectively right or wrong.

A useful variant of the scaling method can show us that different individuals can live in different sensory worlds, even if they are exposed to the same stimuli. The method is **cross-modality matching** (J. C. Stevens, 1959). In cross-modality matching, an observer adjusts a stimulus of one sort to match the perceived magnitude of a stimulus of a completely different sort. For example, we might ask a listener to adjust the brightness of a light until it matches the loudness of a particular tone. Again, though the task might sound odd, people can do this, and for the most part, everyone with "normal" vision and hearing will produce the same pattern of matches of a sound to a light. We still can't examine someone else's private experience, but at least the relationship of visual experience and auditory experience appears to be similar across individuals.

Not so when it comes to the sense of taste. There is a molecule called propylthiouracil (PROP) that some people experience as very bitter, while others experience it as almost tasteless. Still others fall in between. This relationship can be examined formally with cross-modality matching (Marks et al., 1988). If observers are asked to match the bitterness of PROP to other sensations completely unrelated to taste, we do not find the sort of agreement that is found when observers match sounds and lights (**Figure 1.9**). Some people—we'll call them nontasters—match the taste of PROP to very weak sensations like the sound of a watch or a whisper. A group of **supertasters** assert that the bitterness of PROP is similar in intensity to the brightness of the sun or the most intense pain ever experienced. Medium tasters match PROP to weaker stimuli, such as the smell of frying bacon or the pain of a mild headache (Bartoshuk, Fast, and Snyder, 2005). As we will see in Chapter 15, there is a genetic basis for this variation, and it has wide implications for our food preferences and, consequently, for health. For the present discussion, this

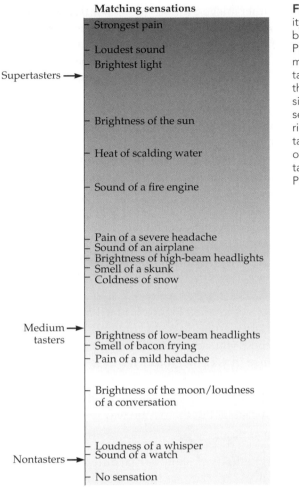

Matching sensations

Supertasters →

- Strongest pain

- Loudest sound
- Brightest light

- Brightness of the sun

- Heat of scalding water

- Sound of a fire engine

- Pain of a severe headache
- Sound of an airplane
- Brightness of high-beam headlights
- Smell of a skunk
- Coldness of snow

Medium tasters →

- Brightness of low-beam headlights
- Smell of bacon frying
- Pain of a mild headache

- Brightness of the moon/loudness of a conversation

- Loudness of a whisper
- Sound of a watch

Nontasters →

- No sensation

Figure 1.9 Cross-modality matching. The levels of bitterness of concentrated PROP perceived by nontasters, medium tasters, and supertasters of PROP are shown on the left. The perceived intensities of a variety of everyday sensations are shown on the right. The arrow from each taster type indicates the level of sensation to which those tasters matched the taste of PROP. (Data from Fast, 2004.)

example shows that we can use scaling methods to quantify what appear to be real differences in individuals' taste experiences.

Signal Detection Theory

Let's return to thresholds—particularly to the fact that they are not absolute. An important way to think about this fact and to deal with it experimentally is known as **signal detection theory** (D. M. Green and Swets, 1966). Signal detection theory begins with the fact that the stimulus you're trying to detect (the "signal") is always being detected in the presence of "noise." If you sit in the quietest place you can find and you wear your best noise-canceling headphones, you will find that you can still hear *something*. Similarly, if you close your eyes in a dark room, you still see something—a mottled pattern of gray with occasional brighter flashes. This is internal noise, the static in your nervous system. When you're trying to detect a faint sound or flash of light, you must be able to detect it in the presence of that internal noise. Down near threshold, it will be hard to tell a real stimulus from a surge of internal noise.

There is external noise, too. Consider again that radiologist reading a mammogram looking for signs of breast cancer. In **Figure 1.10**, it is the marked fuzzy white region that is the danger sign. As you can see, however, the mammogram contains lots of other similar regions. We can think of the cancer as the signal. By the time it is presented to the radiologist in an X-ray, there is a signal plus noise.

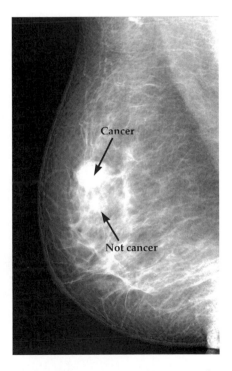

Cancer

Not cancer

Figure 1.10 Mammograms, X-rays of the breast, are used to screen women for breast cancer. Reading such images is a difficult perceptual task, even for a trained radiologist.

Elsewhere in the image, and in other images, are stimuli that are nothing other than noise. The radiologist is a visual expert, trained to find these particular signals, but sometimes the signal will be lost in the noise and missed, and sometimes some noise will look enough like cancer to generate a false alarm (Nodine et al., 2002). Thus, the radiologist will be faced with uncertainty, introduced both as external and internal noise.

Of course, sometimes neither internal nor external noise is much of a problem. When you see this dot, •, you are seeing it in the presence of internal noise, but the magnitude of that noise is so much smaller than the signal generated by the dot that it has no real impact. Similarly, the dot may not be exactly the same as other dots, but that variation, the external noise, is also too small to have an impact. If asked about the presence of a dot here, •, and its absence here, , you will be correct in your answer essentially every time. Signal detection theory exists to help us understand what's going on when we make decisions under conditions of uncertainty.

Because we are not expert mammographers, let's introduce a different example to illustrate the workings of signal detection theory. You're in the shower. The water is making a noise that we will imaginatively call "noise." Sometimes the noise sounds louder to you; sometimes it seems softer. We could plot the distribution of your perception of noise as shown in **Figure 1.11A**. On the x-axis, we have the magnitude of your sensation from "less" to "more." Imagine that we asked you, over and over again, about your sensation. Or imagine we took many repeated measures of the response in your nervous system to the sound. For

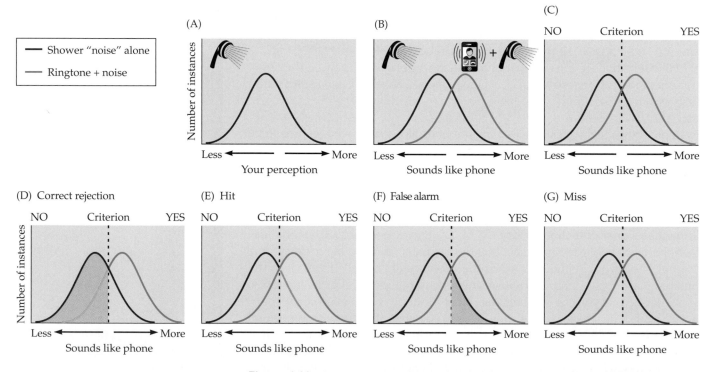

Figure 1.11 Detecting a stimulus using signal detection theory (SDT). (A) SDT assumes that all perceptual decisions must be made against a background of noise (the red curve) generated in the world or in the nervous system. (B) Your job is to distinguish nervous system responses due to noise alone (red) or to signal plus noise (blue). (C) The best you can do is establish a criterion (dotted line) and declare that you detect something if the response is above that criterion. SDT includes four classes of responses: (D) correct rejections (you say "no" and there is, indeed, no signal); (E) hits (you say "yes" and there is a signal); (F) false-alarm errors (you say "yes" to no signal); and (G) miss errors (you say "no" to a real signal).

some instances, the response would be "less." For some, it would be "more." On average, it would lie somewhere in between. If we tabulated all of the responses, we would get a bell-shaped (or "normal") distribution of answers, with the peak of that distribution showing the average answer that you gave.

Now a ringtone plays. That will be our "signal." Your perceptual task is to detect the signal in the presence of the noise. What you hear is a combination of the ringtone and the shower. That is, the signal is added to the noise, so we can imagine that now we have two distributions of responses in your nervous system: a noise-alone distribution and a signal-plus-noise distribution (**Figure 1.11B**).

For the sake of simplicity, let's suppose that "more" response means that it sounds more like the phone is ringing. So now your job is to decide whether it's time to jump out of the shower and answer what might be the phone. The problem is that you have no way of knowing at any given moment whether you're hearing noise alone or signal plus noise. The best you can do is to decide on a **criterion** level of response (**Figure 1.11C**). If the response in your nervous system exceeds that criterion, you will jump out of the shower and run naked and dripping to find the phone. If the level is below the criterion, you will decide that it is not a ringtone and stay in the shower. Note that this "decision" is made automatically; it's not that you sit down to make a conscious (soggy) choice. Thus a criterion, in signal detection theory, is a value that is somehow determined by the observer. A response, inside the observer, above criterion will be taken as evidence that a signal is present. A response below that level will be treated as noise.

There are four possible outcomes in this situation: You might say "no" when there is no ringtone; that's a correct rejection (**Figure 1.11D**). You might say "yes" when there is a ringtone; that's known as a hit (**Figure 1.11E**). Then there are the errors. If you jump out of the shower when there's no ringtone, that's a false alarm (**Figure 1.11F**). If you miss the call, that's a miss (**Figure 1.11G**).

How sensitive are you to the ringtone? In the graphs of Figure 1.11, the sensitivity is shown as the separation between the noise-alone and signal-plus-noise distributions. If the distributions are on top of each other (**Figure 1.12A**), you can't tell noise alone from signal plus noise. A false alarm is just as likely as a hit. By knowing the relationship of hits to false alarms, you can calculate a **sensitivity** measure known as d' (*d*-prime), which would be about zero in Figure 1.12A. In **Figure 1.12C** we see the case of a large d'. Here you could detect essentially all the ringtones and never a false alarm. The situation we've been discussing is in between (**Figure 1.12B**).

criterion In reference to signal detection theory, an internal threshold that is set by the observer. If the internal response is above criterion, the observer gives one response (e.g., "yes, I hear that"). Below criterion, the observer gives another response (e.g., "no, I hear nothing").

sensitivity In reference to signal detection theory, a value that defines the ease with which an observer can tell the difference between the presence and absence of a stimulus or the difference between Stimulus 1 and Stimulus 2.

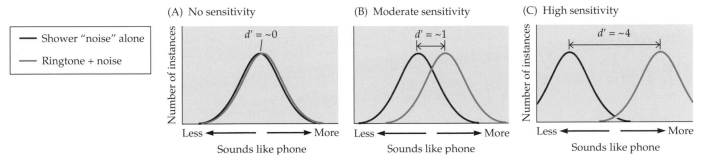

Figure 1.12 Your sensitivity to a stimulus is illustrated by the separation between the distributions of your response to noise alone (red curve) and to signal plus noise (blue). This separation is captured by the measure d' (*d*-prime). (A) If the distributions completely overlap, d' is almost 0 and you have no ability to detect the signal. (B) If d' is intermediate, you have some sensitivity but your performance will be imperfect. (C) If d' is big, then distinguishing signal from noise is easy.

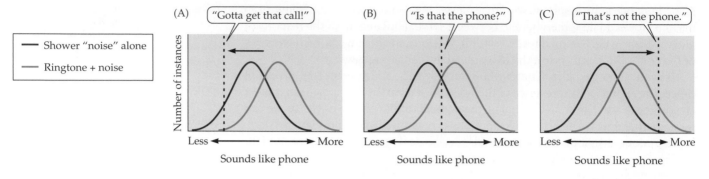

Figure 1.13   For a fixed d', all you can do is change the pattern of your errors by shifting the response criterion. If you don't want to miss any signals, you move your criterion to the left (A), but then you have more false alarms. If you don't like false alarms, you move the response criterion to the right (C), but then you make more miss errors. In all these cases (A–C), your sensitivity, d', remains the same.

receiver operating characteristic (ROC) curve   In reference to studies of signal detection, the graphical plot of the hit rate as a function of the false-alarm rate. If these are the same, points fall on the diagonal, indicating that the observer cannot tell the difference between the presence and absence of the signal. As the observer's sensitivity increases, the curve bows upward toward the upper left corner. That point represents a perfect ability to distinguish signal from noise (100% hits, 0% false alarms).

Now suppose you're waiting for an important call. Even though you really don't want to miss the call, you can't magically make yourself more sensitive. All you can do is move the criterion level of response, as shown in **Figure 1.13**. If you shift your criterion to the left, you won't miss many calls, but you will have lots of false alarms (Figure 1.13A). That's annoying. You're running around naked, dripping on the floor, and traumatizing the cat for no good reason. If you shift your criterion to the right, you won't have those annoying false alarms, but you will miss most of the calls (Figure 1.13C). For a fixed value of d', changing the criterion changes the hits and false alarms in predictable ways. If you plot false alarms on the x-axis of a graph against hits on the y-axis for different criterion values, you get a curve known as a **receiver operating characteristic (ROC) curve** (**Figure 1.14**).

Suppose you were guessing (the Figure 1.12A situation); then you might guess "yes" on 40% of the occasions when the phone rang, but you would also guess "yes" on 40% of the occasions when the phone did not ring. If you moved your criterion and guessed "yes" on 80% of phone-present occasions, you would also guess "yes" on 80% of phone-absent occasions. Your data would fall on that "chance performance" diagonal in Figure 1.14. If you were perfect (the Figure 1.12C situation), you would have 100% hits and 0% false alarms and your data point would lie at the upper left corner in Figure 1.14. Situations in between (Figure 1.12B) produce curves between guessing and perfection (the green, purple, and blue curves in Figure 1.14). If your data lie below the chance line, you did the experiment wrong!

Let's return to our radiologist. She will have an ROC curve whose closeness to perfection reflects her expertise. On that

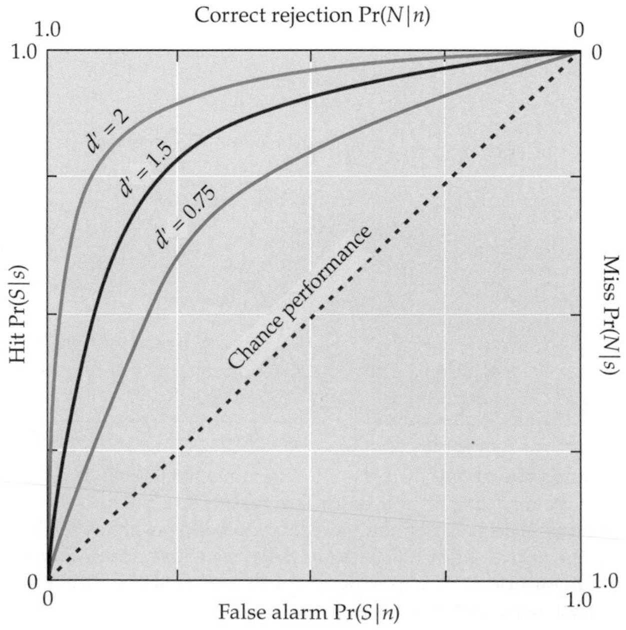

Figure 1.14   Theoretical receiver operating characteristic (ROC) curves for different values of d'. Note that $d' = 0$ when performance is at the chance level. When d' increases, the probability of hits and correct rejections increases, and the probability of misses and false alarms decreases. $Pr(N|n)$ = probability of the response "no signal present" when no signal is present (correct rejection); $Pr(N|s)$ = probability of the response "no signal present" when signal is present (miss); $Pr(S|n)$ = probability of the response "signal present" when no signal is present (false alarm); $Pr(S|s)$ = probability of the response "signal present" when signal is present (hit).

ROC, her criterion can slide up and to the right, in which case she will make more hits but also more false alarms, or down and to the left, in which case she will have fewer false alarms but more misses. Where she places her criterion (consciously or unconsciously) will depend on many factors. Does the patient have factors that make her more or less likely to have cancer? What is the perceived "cost" of a missed cancer? What is the perceived cost of a false alarm? You can see that what started out as a query about the lack of absolute thresholds can become, quite literally, a matter of life and death.

Signal detection theory can become a rather complicated topic in detail (e.g., what happens if those noise and signal + noise curves are not exactly the same shape?). To learn about how to calculate *d'* and about ROC curves, you can take advantage of many useful websites and several texts (e.g., Macmillan and Creelman, 2005). (See Burgess, 2010, if you're interested in the application to radiology.)

Fourier Analysis

While we're on the topic of signals, there's just one more tool in the researcher's arsenal that will prove helpful to you as you learn about sensation and perception. French mathematician Joseph Fourier (1768–1830) (**Figure 1.15**) developed analyses that help modern perception scientists to better describe how complex sounds such as music and speech, complex head motions, and complex images can be decomposed into a set of simpler components. To understand Fourier's analytical technique, let's begin with sounds, because they're relatively easy to describe.

One of the simplest kinds of sounds is a **sine wave** (in hearing, a *pure tone*). Air pressure in a sine wave changes continuously (sinusoidally) at one frequency (**Figure 1.16**). The time taken for one complete cycle of a sine wave, or for a **wavelength** to pass a point, is the **period** of the sine wave. The height of the wave is its amplitude. The **phase** of the wave is its position relative to a fixed marker. Phase is measured in degrees, with 360 degrees of phase across one period, like the 360 degrees around a circle. Thus, in Figure 1.16 the red and blue sine waves differ by 90 degrees in phase.

Sine waves are not common, everyday sounds, because few vibrations in the world are so pure. If you've taken a hearing test or used tuning forks, you may have heard sine waves. Flutes can produce musical notes that are close to pure tones, but other musical instruments, human voices, birds, cars, and almost all other sound sources in the world produce complex sounds.

If pure tones are so uncommon, you may wonder why we're bothering to discuss them. It turns out that all sounds, no matter how complex, can be described as a combination of

Figure 1.15 Joseph Fourier showed how very complex signals could be understood more easily as a combination of simple sine wave components.

sine wave A simple, smoothly changing oscillation that repeats across space. Higher-frequency sine waves have more oscillations, and lower frequencies have fewer oscillations, over a given distance. 1. In reference to hearing, a waveform for which variation as a function of time is a sine function. Also called *pure tone*. 2. In reference to vision, a pattern for which variation in a property like brightness or color as a function of space is a sine function.

wavelength The distance required for one full cycle of oscillation for a sine wave.

period In reference to hearing, the time required for a full wavelength of an acoustic sine wave to pass by a point in space.

phase A fraction of the cycle of the sine wave described in degrees (0° to 360°) or radians (0π to 2π). In reference to hearing, phase can be used to describe fractions of a period that relate to time.

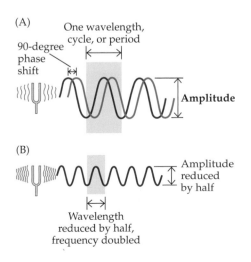

Figure 1.16 Sine waves. (A) A vibrating tuning fork produces sinusoidal variations in air pressure—variations that are the stimulus for hearing. We can plot those variations as sine waves. The period is the time taken for one complete cycle or the passage of one wavelength. The amplitude is the height of the wave. The position of the wave relative to a fixed marker is its phase—measured in degrees out of a total of 360 degrees, like the 360 degrees around a circle. The red and blue sine waves shown here are separated by 90 degrees of phase. (B) This tuning fork produces a sine wave that has half the amplitude and half the wavelength of the waves in (A). In hearing, the frequency of a sine wave is the number of cycles per second (see Chapter 9). In vision, you might have sinusoidal variation of light over space; then the frequency would be in cycles per degree of visual angle (see Chapter 3).

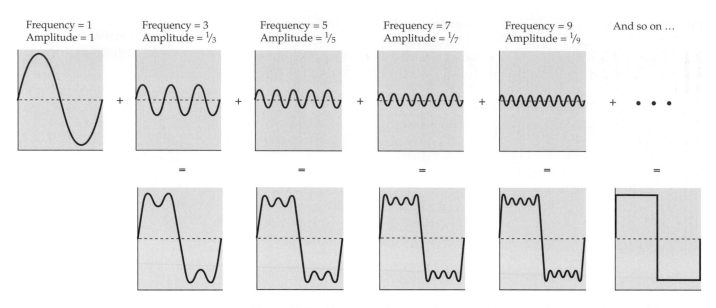

Frequency = 1
Amplitude = 1

Frequency = 3
Amplitude = ⅓

Frequency = 5
Amplitude = ⅕

Frequency = 7
Amplitude = ⅐

Frequency = 9
Amplitude = ⅑

And so on ...

Figure 1.17 Every complex sound wave can be analyzed as a combination of sine waves, each with its own frequency, amplitude, and phase. Here, multiple, specific sine waves (top) are added together to form more complex waveforms (bottom). When infinitely more sine waves with even higher frequencies are added, a square wave (bottom right) can be constructed.

Fourier analysis A mathematical procedure by which any signal can be separated into component sine waves at different frequencies. Combining these sine waves will reproduce the original signal.

spatial frequency The number of cycles of a grating (e.g., changes in light and dark) per unit of visual angle (usually specified in cycles per degree).

cycles per degree The number of pairs of light and dark bars (cycles of grating) per degree of visual angle.

sine waves (**Figure 1.17**). Fourier proved that even the cacophony of a room full of people talking or the swelling sound of a full orchestra can be broken down into combinations of sine waves at many different frequencies with different amplitudes and phases. Any complex sound can be broken down into individual sine wave components through this process, which is called **Fourier analysis**. (See **Web Activity 1.2: Fourier Analysis**.)

Fourier analysis is a powerful mathematical tool that is used in many research fields. As we will see in Chapter 12, Fourier analysis is used extensively by vestibular and spatial orientation researchers. Vision researchers use Fourier analysis to explore the visual system in ways quite similar to those employed by hearing researchers. While sounds are described as changes in pressure across time, images can be described as changes in light and dark across space. Images can be broken down into components that capture how often changes from light to dark occur over a particular region in space, called **spatial frequencies**. Spatial frequencies are defined as the number of these light/dark changes across 1 degree of a person's visual field. There are 360 degrees around the head. One degree is about the size of a thumbnail at arm's length. Thus, in vision the units of spatial frequency are **cycles per degree** of visual angle (**Figure 1.18**). Just as a complex sound can be broken down into a set of sine wave pure tones, a visual stimulus can be broken down into component spatial frequencies. We will have more to say about this in Chapter 3.

Fourier analysis is more than a mathematical curiosity. To a first approximation, your auditory and visual systems appear to break down real-world sounds and images into sine wave components. When we study how individual neurons respond to sounds and images, we find many neurons that have strong preferences for some frequency components over others, and this is especially true for early stages of auditory and visual processing. Understanding how simpler sounds and images are encoded provides essential insights into how we hear and see real events and objects in our world.

(A) High-frequency
square wave

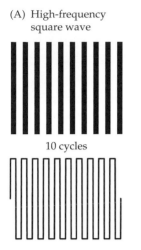

10 cycles

(B) Low-frequency
square wave

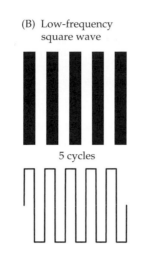

5 cycles

(C) High-contrast
sinusoidal spatial grid

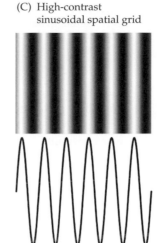

(D) Low-contrast
sinusoidal spatial grid

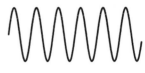

(E) Normal

(F) High frequencies filtered out

(G) Low frequencies filtered out

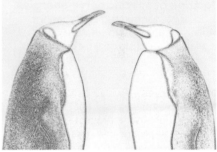

Figure 1.18 The spacing between dark and light stripes in (A) has a spatial frequency that is twice the spatial frequency of (B). When spatial frequency is represented as sinusoids (C, D), there are greater amplitude differences for high contrast (C) than for low contrast (D). A photograph of penguins (E) illustrates how images appear when high spatial frequencies are filtered out (taken away) (F) and when low spatial frequencies are filtered out (G). (From Breedlove and Watson, 2013.)

Sensory Neuroscience and the Biology of Perception

Many students taking this course will have had some introduction to neuroscience. Our discussion of neuroscience that is relevant to the study of sensation and perception should serve as a reminder of what you have learned elsewhere. If this is your first encounter with neuroscience, you may want to consult a neuroscience text to give yourself a more detailed background than we will provide here.

During the nineteenth century, when Weber and Fechner were initiating the experimental study of perception, physiologists were hard at work learning how the senses and the brain operate. Much of this work involved research on animals. It's worth spending a moment on a key assumption here: studies of animal senses tell us something about human senses. That may seem obvious, but the assumption requires the belief that there is some continuity between the way animals work and the way humans work.

The most powerful argument for a continuity between humans and animals came from Darwin's theory of evolution. During the 1800s, Charles Darwin (1809–1882) proposed his revolutionary theory in *The Origin of Species* (1859). Although many of

Figure 1.19   Johannes Müller formulated the doctrine of specific nerve energies, which says that we are aware only of the activity in our nerves, and we cannot be aware of the world itself. For this reason, what is most important is *which* nerves are stimulated, not *how* they are stimulated.

doctrine of specific nerve energies
A doctrine, formulated by Johannes Müller, stating that the nature of a sensation depends on which sensory fibers are stimulated, rather than how they are stimulated.

cranial nerves   Twelve pairs of nerves (one for each side of the body) that originate in the brain stem and reach sense organs and muscles through openings in the skull.

olfactory (I) nerves   The first pair of cranial nerves. The axons of the olfactory sensory neurons bundle together after passing through the cribriform plate to form the olfactory nerve, which conducts impulses from the olfactory epithelia in the nose to the olfactory bulb.

optic (II) nerves   The second pair of cranial nerves, which arise from the retina and carry visual information to the thalamus and other parts of the brain.

vestibulocochlear (VIII) nerves
The eighth pair of cranial nerves, which connect the inner ear with the brain, transmitting impulses concerned with hearing and spatial orientation. The vestibulocochlear nerve is composed of the cochlear nerve branch and the vestibular nerve branch.

oculomotor (III) nerves   The third pair of cranial nerves, which innervate all the extrinsic muscles of the eye except the lateral rectus and the superior oblique muscles, and which innervate the elevator muscle of the upper eyelid, the ciliary muscle, and the sphincter muscle of the pupil.

the ideas found in that book had been brewing for some time, controversy expanded with vigor following Darwin's provocative statements in *The Descent of Man* (1871), where he argued that humans and apes evolved from a common ancestor. If there was continuity in the structure of the bones, heart, and kidneys of cows, dogs, monkeys, and humans, then why wouldn't there be continuity in the structure and function of their sensory and nervous systems? An inescapable implication of the theory of evolution is that we can learn much about human sensation and perception by studying the structure and function of our nonhuman relatives.

At the same time that Darwin was at work in England, the German physiologist Johannes Müller (1801–1858) (**Figure 1.19**) was writing his very influential *Handbook of Physiology* during the early 1830s. In this book, in addition to covering most of what was then known about physiology, Müller formulated the **doctrine of specific nerve energies**. The central idea of this doctrine is that we cannot be directly aware of the world itself, and we are only aware of the activity in our nerves. Further, what is most important is *which* nerves are stimulated, and not *how* they are stimulated. For example, we experience vision because the optic nerve leading from the eye to the brain is stimulated, but it does not matter whether light, or something else, stimulates the nerve. To prove to yourself that this is true, close your eyes and press very gently on the outside corner of one eye through the lid. (This works better in a darkened room.) You will see a spot of light toward the inside of your visual field by your nose. Despite the lack of stimulation by light, your brain interprets the input from your optic nerve as informing you about something visual.

The **cranial nerves** leading into and out of the skull illustrate the doctrine of specific nerve energies (**Figure 1.20**). The pair of optic nerves is one of 12 pairs of cranial nerves that pass through small openings in the bone at the base of the skull. The cranial nerves are dedicated mainly to sensory and motor systems. Cranial nerves are labeled both by names and by Roman numerals that roughly correspond to the order of their locations, beginning from the front of the skull. Three of the cranial nerves—**olfactory (I)**, **optic (II)**, and **vestibulocochlear (VIII)**—are exclusively dedicated to sensory information. The vestibulocochlear nerve serves two sensory modalities: the vestibular sensations that support our sense of equilibrium (see Chapter 12) and hearing (discussed in Chapter 9). Three more cranial nerves—**oculomotor (III)**, **trochlear (IV)**, and **abducens (VI)**—are dedicated to muscles that move the eyes. The other six cranial nerves either are exclusively motor (spinal accessory [XI] and hypoglossal [XII]) or convey both sensory and motor signals (trigeminal [V], facial [VII], glossopharyngeal [IX], and vagus [X]). With respect to our study of perception, in later chapters we will return to the first six cranial nerves described here, because each one plays an important role in our ability to use our senses to learn about the world around us.

The doctrine of specific nerve energies extends beyond the cranial nerves, as illustrated especially well by our senses of hot and cold on the skin. Two special types of nerve cells are warmth fibers and cold fibers, which respond to increases and decreases in temperature on the skin (see Chapter 13). Capsaicin, a chemical that naturally occurs in chili peppers, causes warmth fibers to fire, creating a sense of increasing heat even though the temperature has not changed. On the other hand, menthol, which imparts a minty flavor in cough drops, stimulates cold fibers (Bautista et al., 2007), so skin feels cooler without getting physically colder. In sufficiently high amounts, both capsaicin and menthol stimulate pain receptors in the skin. Paradoxically, this is why ointments often contain capsaicin or menthol, where their effect is to mask real physical pain.

Just as different nerves are dedicated to individual sensory and motor tasks, areas of the brain stem and cerebral cortex are similarly dedicated to particular

trochlear (IV) nerves The fourth pair of cranial nerves, which innervate the superior oblique muscles of the eyeballs.

abducens (VI) nerves The sixth pair of cranial nerves, which innervate the lateral rectus muscle of the eyeballs.

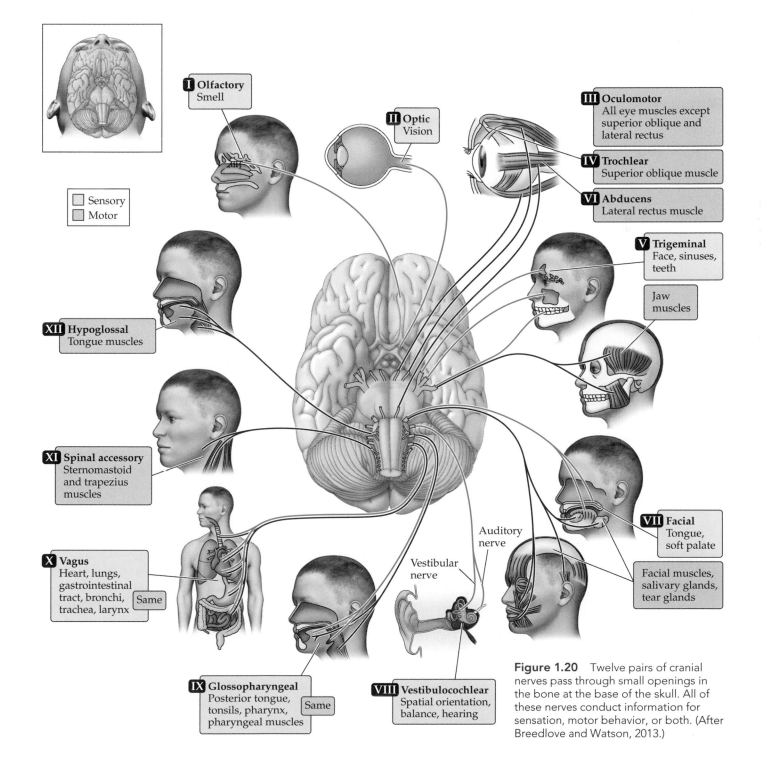

Sensory
Motor

I Olfactory Smell

II Optic Vision

III Oculomotor All eye muscles except superior oblique and lateral rectus

IV Trochlear Superior oblique muscle

VI Abducens Lateral rectus muscle

V Trigeminal Face, sinuses, teeth

Jaw muscles

XII Hypoglossal Tongue muscles

XI Spinal accessory Sternomastoid and trapezius muscles

VII Facial Tongue, soft palate

Facial muscles, salivary glands, tear glands

Auditory nerve

Vestibular nerve

X Vagus Heart, lungs, gastrointestinal tract, bronchi, trachea, larynx   Same

IX Glossopharyngeal Posterior tongue, tonsils, pharynx, pharyngeal muscles   Same

VIII Vestibulocochlear Spatial orientation, balance, hearing

Figure 1.20 Twelve pairs of cranial nerves pass through small openings in the bone at the base of the skull. All of these nerves conduct information for sensation, motor behavior, or both. (After Breedlove and Watson, 2013.)

Figure 1.21 Cortex of the human brain. The darkened areas show where information from four of our sensory modalities first reaches the cortex. Also shown is the motor cortex, which is engaged in balance, touch, and some auditory processing.

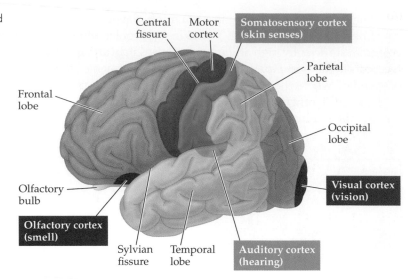

polysensory   Referring to blending multiple sensory systems.

vitalism   The idea that there is a force in life that is distinct from physical entities.

Figure 1.22 Hermann von Helmholtz was one of the greatest scientists of all time. He made many important discoveries in physiology and perception.

tasks. Areas of the cortex dedicated to perception actually are much larger than the darkened areas in **Figure 1.21**. The areas depicted here are primary sensory areas; more complex processing is accomplished across cortical regions that spread well beyond these primary areas. For example, visual perception uses cortex that extends both anteriorly (forward) into parietal cortex and ventrally (lower) into regions of the temporal lobe (see Figures 4.2 and 4.4). In addition, as processing extends beyond primary areas, cortex often becomes **polysensory**, meaning that information from more than one sense is being combined in some manner. (See **Web Activity 1.3: Sensory Areas in the Brain**.)

Hermann Ludwig Ferdinand von Helmholtz (1821–1894) (**Figure 1.22**), one of the greatest scientists of the nineteenth century, was greatly influenced by Müller at the Free University of Berlin. Although initially inspired by Müller, Helmholtz truly disliked one of Müller's beliefs: **vitalism**, the idea that there is a force in life that is distinct from physical entities. By contrast, Helmholtz thought that all behavior should be explained by only physical forces. Vitalism violated the physical law of conservation of energy, and Helmholtz wanted the brain and behavior to obey purely physical laws. He chose a very smart place to begin his attack on vitalism. Müller had claimed that the nerve impulse could never be measured experimentally. So, Helmholtz set out to show that the activity of neurons obeys normal rules of physics and chemistry by being the first to effectively measure how fast neurons transmit their signals. (See **Web Activity 1.4: Neurons**.)

In an early effort, Helmholtz estimated that the speed of signal transmission in the nerves in frog legs was about 90 feet per second, comfortably within the range of ordinary physical events. Later he concluded that sensory nerves in people transmitted signals at speeds of between 165 and 330 feet per second. In all cases, this transmission was slower than many people believed at the time. Helmholtz emphasized this point when he noted that a "whale probably feels a wound near its tail in about one second, and requires another second to send back orders to the tail to defend itself" (Koenigsberger, 1906/1965, p. 72). As you may already have guessed, not all neurons are equal when it comes to speed; some are faster than others. It's still interesting to realize that when you stub your toe, a measurable amount of time elapses before you feel the consequences.

(A)

(B)

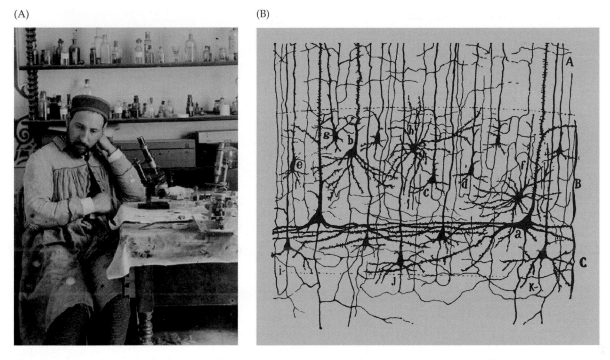

Figure 1.23 Neurons in the brain. (A) Santiago Ramón y Cajal (perhaps not on his happiest day in the lab). (B) Ramón y Cajal created these drawings of brain neurons while peering into a microscope for many hours. Because of his painstaking care and accuracy, his early drawings are still cited today.

Neuronal Connections

During the second half of the nineteenth century, when Helmholtz was making stunning discoveries concerning vision and hearing, other scientists were learning a great deal about how neurons and brains work. After nearly dying of malaria in Cuba, the Spaniard Santiago Ramón y Cajal (1852–1934) **(Figure 1.23A)** returned to his homeland to develop some of the most painstaking and breathtaking insights into the organization of neurons in the brain. Spending many hours peering into a microscope, he made spectacularly detailed drawings of neurons and their connections that remain useful 100 years after they were created. **Figure 1.23B** shows an example.

Ramón y Cajal's drawings suggested that neurons do not actually touch one another. Instead, he depicted neurons as separate cells with tiny gaps between them. Sir Charles Scott Sherrington (1857–1952) **(Figure 1.24)** named the tiny gap between the axon of one neuron and the dendrite of the next a **synapse** **(Figure 1.25)**, from the Greek word meaning "to fasten together." Sherrington made very careful measurements demonstrating that the speed of neural transmission decreases at synapses, and this work helped us understand that something special happens at this junction where neurons meet to communicate.

Initially, people thought that some sort of electrical wave traveled across the synapse from one neuron to the next. Otto Loewi (1873–1961) **(Figure 1.26)**, however, was convinced that this could not be true. One reason is that some neurons increase the response of the next neuron (they are *excitatory*) but other neurons decrease the response of the next neuron (they are *inhibitory*). Loewi proposed that something chemical, instead of electrical, might be at work at the synapse. This insight launched many studies about molecules that travel from the axon across the synapse to bind to receptor molecules on the dendrite of the

synapse The junction between neurons that permits information transfer.

Figure 1.24 Sir Charles Scott Sherrington was an English neurophysiologist who earned a Nobel Prize for his pioneering discoveries concerning neural activities.

Figure 1.25   A synapse. An axon terminal in the presynaptic cell communicates with a dendrite of the postsynaptic cell. Neurotransmitter molecules are released by synaptic vesicles in the axon and fit into receptors on the dendrite on the other side of the synapse, thus communicating from the axon of the first neuron to the dendrite of the second neuron.

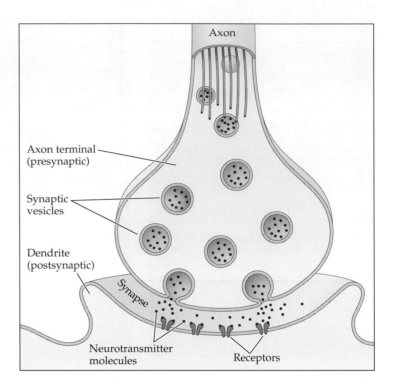

neurotransmitter   A chemical substance used in neuronal communication at synapses.

next neuron. The molecules, released by the axon, are called **neurotransmitters**. There are many different kinds of neurotransmitters in the brain, and individual neurons are selective with respect to which neurotransmitters excite them or inhibit them from firing. Drugs that are psychoactive, such as amphetamines, work by increasing or decreasing the effectiveness of different neurotransmitters. Today, scientists use chemicals that influence the effects of neurotransmitters in efforts to understand pathways in the brain, including those used in perception.

Neural Firing: The Action Potential

After Loewi's discovery of neurotransmitters, scientists learned what it really means to have a neuron "fire." Investigators made the greatest early advances by taking advantage of the fact that some squids have giant neurons as thick as 1 millimeter. At the laboratory of the Marine Biological Association in Plymouth, England, Sir Alan Hodgkin (1914–1998) and Sir Andrew Huxley (1917–2012) (**Figure 1.27**) seized their opportunity when trawlers operating beyond Plymouth Sound brought catches of fresh squid to port. Hodgkin and Huxley conducted experiments in which they isolated a single neuron from the squid and tested how the nerve impulse traveled along the axon. With such large axons, they could pierce the axon with an electrode to measure voltage, and they could even inject different chemicals inside. They learned that neural firing is actually electrochemical (**Figure 1.28**). Voltage increases along the axon are caused by changes in the membrane of the neuron that permit positively charged sodium ions (Na^+) to rush very quickly into the axon from outside. Then, the membrane very quickly changes again in a way that pushes positively charged potassium ions (K^+) out of the axon, restoring the neuron to its initial resting voltage. All of this—sodium in and potassium out—occurs in about a thousandth of a second every time a neuron fires.

Because even the biggest axons in mammals are much, much smaller than the giant squid axon, it is difficult to insert an electrode inside a neuron. Usually we measure electrical changes from just outside mammalian neurons

Figure 1.26   Otto Loewi was a German pharmacologist who received a Nobel Prize for demonstrating that neurons communicate with one another by releasing chemicals called neurotransmitters.

(A) Hodgkin

(B) Huxley

(C) Hodgkin and Huxley's squid

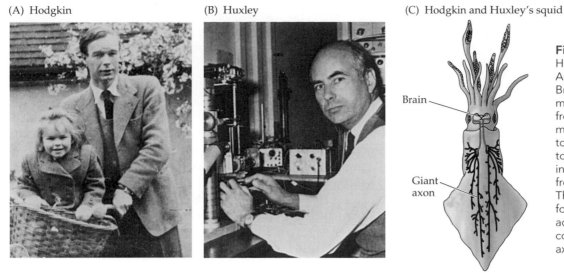

Brain

Giant axon

Figure 1.27 Sir Alan Hodgkin (A) and Sir Andrew Huxley (B) were British physiologists who made the first recordings from inside a neuron. They moved from Cambridge to Plymouth, England, to record voltages from inside the giant axons of fresh Atlantic squid (C). They earned a Nobel Prize for discovering how the action potential works to conduct signals along the axons of neurons.

(Figure 1.29). By measuring different aspects of neurons firing, we can learn about how individual neurons encode and transmit information from sense organs through higher levels of the brain.

One way to investigate what a neuron encodes is to try to identify the stimulus that makes it fire the most vigorously. For example, a neuron in the primary visual cortex (see Chapter 3) might respond best to lines that are vertical, less to lines tilted to the left or right, and not at all to horizontal lines. When you get to the auditory system in Chapter 9, you will see that the timing and the rate of firing are important.

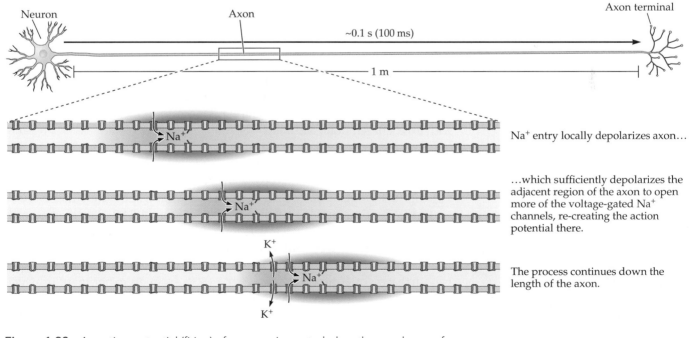

Neuron

Axon

Axon terminal

~0.1 s (100 ms)

1 m

Na^+

Na^+ entry locally depolarizes axon…

Na^+

…which sufficiently depolarizes the adjacent region of the axon to open more of the voltage-gated Na^+ channels, re-creating the action potential there.

K^+

Na^+

K^+

The process continues down the length of the axon.

Figure 1.28 An action potential (firing) of a neuron is created when the membrane of the neuron permits sodium ions (Na^+) to rush into the cell, thus increasing the voltage. Very quickly afterward, potassium (K^+) flows out of the cell, bringing the voltage back to resting voltage. This process occurs along the length of the axon until the action potential reaches the axon terminal.

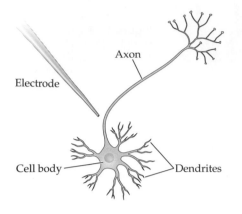

Figure 1.29 Neuroscientists record the activity of single neurons with electrodes close to the axons. Modern techniques permit the insertion of multiple electrodes to measure activity in multiple neurons so that we can better understand how neurons work in concert when encoding sensory information.

Sometimes we learn a lot by simply finding the threshold for getting a neuron to fire at all. For example, you will learn that different neurons in the auditory nerve, on the way from the ear to the brain, are most sensitive to particular frequencies of sounds. In **Figure 1.30**, you can see curves obtained by measuring responses of six different neurons to sounds of different frequencies and intensities. These are called tuning curves because they show how patterns of neural firing are selectively "tuned" to different frequencies that vary from 0 to 50 kilohertz (kHz = 1000 hertz, or 1000 cycles per second; plotted on the x-axis). The minimum sound intensity that is required for a neuron to respond is shown in decibels (dB) on the y-axis. Thus, the best frequency for the neuron whose responses are plotted in red in Figure 1.30 is about 1.3 kHz. To get that cell to respond to another frequency, the sound will need to be louder. The yellow plot is for a cell that responds to a completely different, markedly higher range of frequencies.

Neuroimaging

Modern perception researchers use other tools to understand how thousands or millions of neurons work together within the human brain. In many cases, we look at the results of these methods by making pictures of the brain that reveal its structure and functions. These methods can be collectively referred to as **neuroimaging** methods. Of course, neuroanatomists have long described the structure of the human brain, and neuropsychological studies of individuals with brain damage have taught us much about the functions of different parts of the brain. However, a great advance in recent decades has been the invention of neuroimaging methods that allow us to look at the structure and function of the human brain in healthy, very much living human observers.

For example, **electroencephalography** (**EEG**) measures electrical activity through dozens of electrodes placed on the scalp (**Figure 1.31A**). EEG does not allow researchers to learn what individual neurons are doing or to pinpoint the exact area of neural activity. However, EEG can be used to roughly localize whole populations of neurons (**Figure 1.31D**) and to measure their activities with excellent temporal accuracy.

Like a single behavioral measurement, a single EEG signal recorded for a single event is usually not terribly informative. If you want to know the brain's response to a prick of the skin or a flash of light, you record the responses to many, many repetitions of that stimulus (**Figure 1.31B**). You then average all the responses aligned to the moment that the stimulus was present. The resulting averaged waveform is known as an **event-related potential** (**ERP**) (**Figure 1.31C**). For example, **Figure 1.32** shows the ERPs from an experiment in which observers saw very brief flashes of light lasting for 0.1 to 5 milliseconds (ms); a millisecond is a thousandth of a second. A flash of each duration was shown to the observer 400 times. The EEGs for the 300 ms after each flash were averaged together to produce the waveforms—the ERPs—shown in the figure. For the millions of neurons contributing to the particular signal, nothing happens for the first 50 ms or so. Then there is a small

neuroimaging A set of methods that generate images of the structure and/or function of the brain. In many cases, these methods allow us to examine the brain in living, behaving humans.

electroencephalography (EEG) A technique that, using many electrodes on the scalp, measures electrical activity from populations of many neurons in the brain.

event-related potential (ERP) A measure of electrical activity from a subpopulation of neurons in response to particular stimuli that requires averaging many EEG recordings.

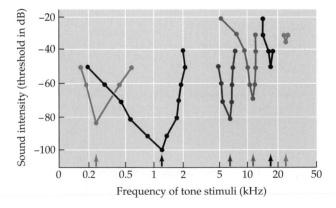

Figure 1.30 Tuning curves of auditory neurons. See the text for details. (After Kiang, 1965.)

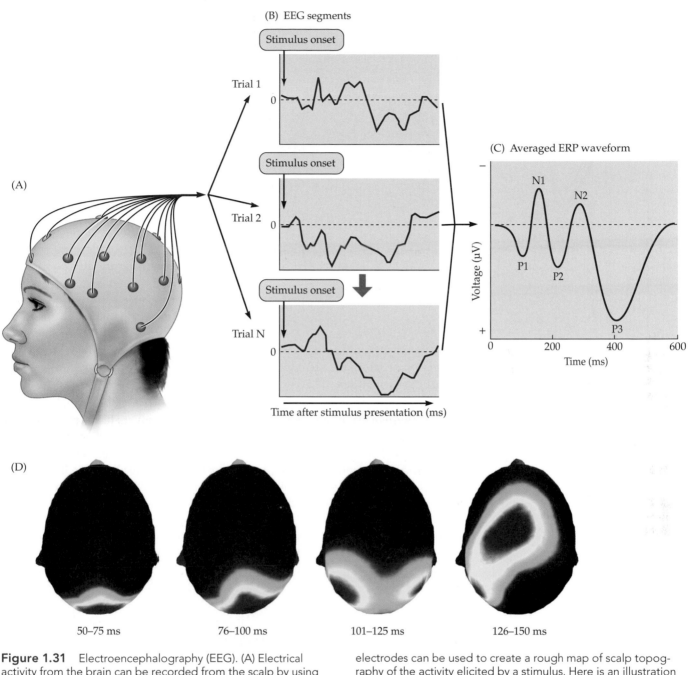

(B) EEG segments

Stimulus onset

Trial 1

Stimulus onset

Trial 2

Stimulus onset

Trial N

Time after stimulus presentation (ms)

(A)

(C) Averaged ERP waveform

N1

N2

P1

P2

P3

Voltage (μV)

Time (ms)

(D)

50–75 ms   76–100 ms   101–125 ms   126–150 ms

Figure 1.31 Electroencephalography (EEG). (A) Electrical activity from the brain can be recorded from the scalp by using an array of electrodes. (B) The activity from one electrode is quite variable, even if the same stimulus (perhaps a flash of light) is presented multiple times. (C) However, if many such signals are averaged, a regular pattern of electrically positive (P) and negative (N) waves can be seen. Electrical activity (voltage) is measured in microvolts (μV). (D) Different signals from different electrodes can be used to create a rough map of scalp topography of the activity elicited by a stimulus. Here is an illustration of the typical changes one might see from 50 to 150 ms after the onset of a visual stimulus. Notice that the signal is initially focused over early visual cortex (50–100 ms), then shifts to more anterior areas of visual cortex (101–125 ms) and then begins to activate frontal cortex (126–150 ms). (A–C after Breedlove, Watson, and Rosenzweig, 2010; D courtesy of Steven Luck.)

negative deflection of the signal, followed by a larger positive deflection. You can see how this sort of recording could tell us about the average timing of nervous system responses to stimuli in the world.

A related method known as **magnetoencephalography (MEG)** (Figure 1.33) maintains much of the timing of populations of neurons while providing a better

magnetoencephalography (MEG) A technique, similar to electroencephalography, that measures changes in magnetic activity across populations of many neurons in the brain.

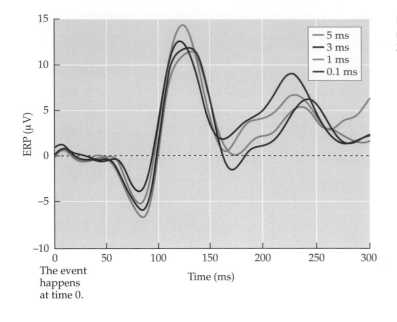

The event happens at time 0.

Time (ms)

Figure 1.32 Event-related potentials (ERPs) produced in response to very brief flashes of light. (After Yesilyurt et al., 2009.)

idea of where in the brain neurons are most active. MEG takes advantage of the fact that neurons make very small changes in their local magnetic fields in addition to small electrical changes. With MEG, researchers use extremely sensitive devices to measure these tiny magnetic field changes. Why use EEG if you can have MEG's better spatial resolution? EEG recording is relatively simple and relatively cheap. MEG devices use superconducting quantum interference devices (SQUIDs, but different from the squids in Figure 1.27). These are much more expensive and complex.

As noted above, one of the most exciting and important changes in neuroscience in the last generation has been the advent of methods that enable us to see the brain while it is still in its owner's living head. We have had X-rays for over 100 years, but an image like the X-ray in **Figure 1.34** gives only a ghostly impression of soft tissues like those making up the brain. Compare that image to the images in **Figure 1.35**. Figure 1.35A shows a **computed tomography**, or **CT**, image. To create CT images, standard X-rays are used in a different manner. A beam of X-rays is passed through the target—the head in this case. The device emitting that beam spins around the head, sending the beam on many paths through the same "slice" of the head. This process is repeated for many slices, until the whole head has been scanned. Each time the beam passes through the head, some amount of the emitted energy is absorbed by the intervening tissue. Dense tissue absorbs more energy than lighter tissue. The detector on the other side of the head measures the amount of energy that has been lost on the way through the head. If you have this information from many, many passes through the head from many different positions, you can put the pieces of information together to create a three-dimensional picture of the head.

computed tomography (CT) An imaging technology that uses X-rays to create images of slices through volumes of material (e.g., the human body).

(A) An MEG machine

(B) Reconstruction of brain responses to a visual stimulus

Figure 1.33 Magneto-encephalography (MEG). (A) What looks like a huge helmet contains superconducting magnets. (B) The output of MEG recording can be used to visualize activity in the brain. In this case, the individual saw pictures of objects. "Hotter" colors indicate more activity. The hot spot at the back of the brain is the primary visual cortex. The floating squares represent the array of MEG detectors. (B courtesy of Daniel Baldauf.)

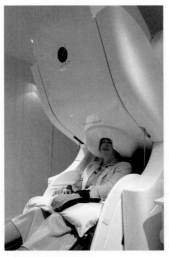

Figure 1.34 A standard X-ray does not provide much of a look at the structure of the brain.

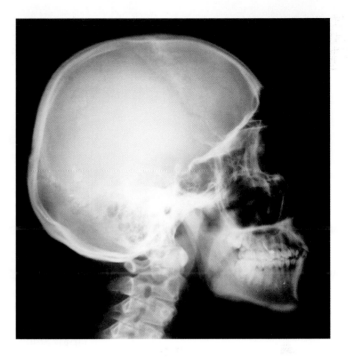

Figure 1.35B shows an image produced by **magnetic resonance imaging**, or **MRI**. MRI uses a very different method to make its often spectacular images. The brain and its owner are placed in a very powerful magnetic field that influences the way the atoms spin. The physics is complicated and beyond the scope of our text, but by pulsing the magnetic field, it is possible to measure a signal that can indicate the presence of specific elements in the tissue. If you ask about hydrogen in the brain, you are (mostly) asking about water, and your computer can use that signal to reconstruct the structure of the water-rich tissue inside your head.

For the study of the senses and, indeed, for the study of many topics in psychology, the most remarkable use of MRI technology is known as **functional magnetic resonance imaging**, or **fMRI**. With fMRI, we can see the activity of the living brain. Here the critical factor is that active brain tissue is hungry brain tissue. It needs oxygen. Oxygen and other supplies are delivered by the blood, so an active brain demands more blood. The result is that there is a **blood oxygen level–dependent (BOLD) signal** that can be measured by the MRI device. Instead of indicating the presence of water, the magnetic pulses and recording are used to pick up evidence of the demand for more oxygenated blood. There are some drawbacks. It takes a few seconds for the BOLD signal to rise after a bit of brain becomes more active, so the temporal resolution of the method is quite slow compared with EEG/ERP methods, for example. The machines are noisy, making auditory experiments difficult. Moreover, acquiring and running these machines is expensive. Still, none of these drawbacks have prevented the method from revolutionizing the study of the brain.

Figure 1.36 shows some of the results from a very basic fMRI experiment. The observer was watching a screen. A visual stimulus was on for 30 seconds and off for 30 seconds in alternation. Regions of the brain that are made more active

magnetic resonance imaging (MRI) An imaging technology that uses the responses of atoms to strong magnetic fields to form images of structures like the brain. The method can be adapted to measure activity in the brain, as well.

functional magnetic resonance imaging (fMRI) A variant of magnetic resonance imaging that makes it possible to measure localized patterns of activity in the brain. Activated neurons provoke increased blood flow, which can be quantified by measuring changes in the response of oxygenated and deoxygenated blood to strong magnetic fields.

blood oxygen level–dependent (BOLD) signal The ratio of oxygenated to deoxygenated hemoglobin that permits the localization of brain neurons that are most involved in a task.

(A) CT

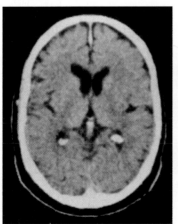

(B) MRI

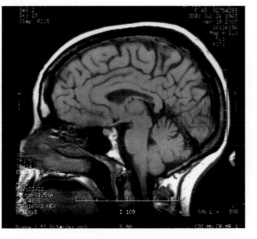

Figure 1.35 CT and MRI. (A) This CT image is one horizontal slice through the head, from the eyes at the top of the image to the back of the head. The dark areas are the fluid-filled ventricles in the brain, the bright white is bone, and the gray is the brain itself. (B) This structural MRI image shows a vertical slice through the middle of the head. You can see the folded cortex of the brain, the spinal cord descending down the neck, and much more.

Figure 1.36 Functional MRI. The warm colors show places where the BOLD signal was elevated by the presence of a visual stimulus. Blues show decreases in BOLD activity. The big region of signal elevation corresponds to the primary visual areas of the brain (see Chapter 3). (Courtesy of Steve Smith, University of Oxford FMRIB Centre.)

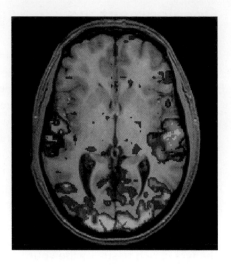

by the presentation of a visual stimulus demand more supplies in response to the presence of the stimulus, so there is a difference between the BOLD responses to stimulus-on and stimulus-off conditions (with that lag of several seconds). Subtracting the stimulus-off fMRI signal from the stimulus-on signal reveals the difference in BOLD responses. Typically, these are shown as colors superimposed on a structural MRI of the brain.

Positron emission tomography (**PET**) is an imaging technique in which a small amount of a safe, biologically active, radioactive material (a tracer) is introduced into the participant's bloodstream, and a specialized camera detects gamma rays emitted from brain regions where the tracer is being used most (Phelps, 2000) (**Figure 1.37**). The logic is similar to that of fMRI: the idea is to detect activity in neurons by looking for increased metabolic activity. The most common tracer used in perception experiments is oxygen-15, an unstable form of oxygen that has a half-life of only a little more than 2 minutes. Neurons that are most active in the brain should have the greatest requirement for this oxygen. Although PET is a somewhat inconvenient method because you have to inject a tracer, it has the advantage of being silent, which is helpful in studies of brain activity related to hearing.

Modern labs often use multiple methods in the same experiment or series of experiments. You might use behavioral methods to determine the nature of a particular perceptual capability, but such methods might take hours and hundreds or thousands of trials. If your observers can't spend that much time in the scanner, you might have them perform a shorter, stripped-down version of the study while being imaged. You might do yet another version of the task, specialized for the demands of EEG recording. By means of these "converging operations," you could build up quite a detailed picture of what a person perceives and how her brain gives rise to those perceptions.

positron emission tomography (PET) An imaging technology that enables us to define locations in the brain where neurons are especially active by measuring the metabolism of brain cells using safe radioactive isotopes.

| Looking | Listening | Thinking | Remembering | Working |

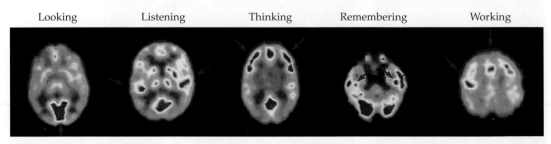

Figure 1.37 Positron emission tomography (PET) is a form of neuroimaging that uses positron-emitting radioisotopes to create images of biological processes in the living brain. Here we see different patterns of glucose usage in the brain while an individual is performing different tasks. (From Phelps, 2000.)

Development over the Life Span

Before we end this chapter, it is worth reminding ourselves that no sensory system has fixed properties over the course of the life span. "Development" is not a method, like PET or scaling, but it is an approach to thinking about sensation and perception. Development will be mentioned in many of the chapters of this book. Broadly, it is worth keeping three big questions in mind:

1. *What comes with the system?* What aspects of sensation and perception does a baby have at birth? Clearly, infants have senses. Typically developing children are not blind or deaf at birth, but what do they make of that sensory input? The great American philosopher and psychologist William James famously speculated, "The baby, assailed by eyes, ears, nose, skin, and entrails at once, feels it all as one great blooming, buzzing confusion" (James, 1890, vVol 1, p. 488). However, James may have underestimated the infant's ability to make meaning out of that chaos. Babies may be sensitive to faces even before they are born. (How would you know this? See Chapter 4, page 132, to find out.) They are exposed to smells and tastes in the womb, and they emerge into the world with clear taste preferences. As we will see in Chapter 15 (page 530), a newborn infant likes sweet and dislikes bitter. Similarly, the newborn's suckling reflex relies on a sense of touch that is already conveying information (see Chapter 13).

2. *What has to be learned?* That baby who has built-in, hardwired preferences for sweet and against bitter does not have hardwired responses to smell. The fetus has developed a fully functional sense of smell by the end of the first trimester of pregnancy. Therefore, volatile compounds that a mother consumes during pregnancy, such as those in cigarette smoke, alcohol, and pungent foods like garlic, can be perceived by the fetus because these compounds enter the amniotic fluid. Once born, the infant may have preferences for some smells that were experienced in the womb, because odor familiarity is highly correlated with odor liking. The more familiar we are with an odor, the more accepting we are of it—and becoming familiar with an odor begins before birth. Interestingly, this implies that a mother who consumes a healthy, varied diet during pregnancy may have an infant who is willing to accept a wider range of food. These are learned preferences. You might think that the smell of a dirty diaper would be aversive to baby and parent alike, but in fact, that nearly universal olfactory response is not reliable in children until around the time they are toilet trained.

   Of course, most of the details of your perceptual world must be learned. No one comes into the world understanding the meaning of emojis (**Figure 1.38**). Babies might have a head start, though, if there is some innate understanding of facial expressions—a topic that remains controversial (Farroni et al., 2007).

3. *What changes with age?* Development doesn't stop when we become adults. Changes occur across the life span. Mostly, the news is not good, at least not at a basic sensory level. Your senses become less acute as you age. For instance, **Figure 1.39** shows sensitivity to sounds of different frequencies declining with

Figure 1.38 Would a newborn understand anything about the meaning of emojis (even if we made sure that the emoji was big and bold enough to be seen by the infant)?

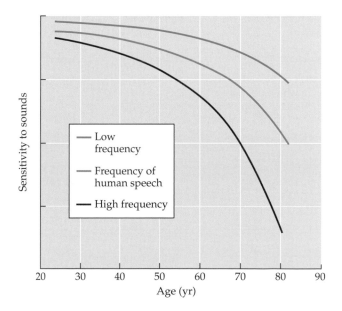

Figure 1.39 Sensitivity to sounds declines with age, more markedly for high-frequency sounds. (After Sommers et al., 2011.)

age (Sommers et al., 2011). This decline is more marked for high-frequency sounds. Similarly, the sensory detector cells that support your sense of smell do not regenerate as effectively as you age, so by age 85 approximately half of that population is functionally unable to detect odors. There is no evidence that your perceptual world—the meaning you make out of the sensory signals you detect—declines markedly with age. Perhaps life's experiences make it richer. And even on the sensory side, Shakespeare's Jacques in *As You Like It* was too pessimistic when he imagined old age as "sans [meaning 'without'] teeth, sans eyes, sans taste, sans everything." You start with an innate repertoire of sensory responses, you learn a lot, and you will carry most of that into what we hope will be a successful and contented old age. With that sweeping summary of the span of your life, you should be ready to embark on a more comprehensive examination of sensation and perception. We hope you enjoy the journey.

Go to the
Sensation & Perception
Companion Website at
oup.com/us/wolfe5e
for chapter overviews, activities, essays, flashcards, and other study aids.
Go to **DASHBOARD** for additional resources and assessments.

Summary

1. Sensation and perception are central to, and often precede, almost all aspects of human behavior and thought. There are many practical applications of our increased understanding of sensation and perception.

2. Gustav Fechner invented several clever methods for measuring the relationship between physical changes in the world and consequent psychological changes in observers. These methods remain in use today. Using Fechner's methods, researchers can measure the smallest levels of stimulus that can be detected (absolute threshold) and the smallest differences that can be detected (difference thresholds, or just noticeable differences).

3. A more recent development for understanding performance—signal detection theory—permits us to simulate changes in the perceiver (e.g., internal noise and biases) in order to understand perceptual performance better.

4. Studying simple stimuli (such as pure tones) is useful because complex stimuli can be decomposed into simple components. In vision and audition, Fourier analysis is a mathematical tool that helps researchers break down complex images and sounds in ways that permit better understanding of how they are sensed and perceived.

5. We learn a great deal about perception by understanding the biological structures and processes involved. One early observation—the doctrine of specific nerve energies—expresses the fact that people are aware only of the activity of their nervous systems. For this reason, what matters is which nerves are stimulated, not how they are stimulated. The central nervous system reflects specializations for the senses, from cranial nerves to areas of the cerebral cortex involved in perception.

6. The essential activities of all neurons, including those involved in sensory processes, are chemical and electrochemical. Neurons communicate with each other through neurotransmitters, molecules that cross the synapse from the axon of one neuron to the dendrite of the next. Nerve impulses are electrochemical; voltages change along the axon as electrically charged sodium and potassium ions pass in and out of the membranes of nerve cells.

7. Recordings of individual neurons enable us to measure the lowest level of stimulus required for a neuron to fire (absolute threshold). Both the rate and the timing pattern of neural firing provide additional information about how the brain encodes stimuli in the world.

8. Neuroimaging methods have revolutionized the study of sensation and perception by allowing us to study the brain in healthy, living human observers. Useful methods include electroencephalography (EEG), magnetoencephalography (MEG), positron emission tomography (PET), and functional magnetic resonance imaging (fMRI). Each comes with its own combination of temporal and spatial properties, making one method suitable for researching some questions and other methods more suitable for other questions.

9. Developmental studies concern themselves with the changes that occur over the lifetime of the organism: What are the sensory and perceptual capabilities of a newborn? What is learned after birth? What changes from childhood, to adulthood, to old age?

2

The First Steps in Vision: From Light to Neural Signals

■ Questions to Contemplate ■

Think about the following questions as you read this chapter. By the chapter's end, you should be able to answer and discuss them.

- How are images of the world formed on the retina?

- How is energy from light converted into the electrical neural signals that lead to "seeing"?

- When the eye doctor says you have 20/20 vision, what does she mean?

- How is it that you are able to see over a huge range of brightness levels?

I magine looking into the night sky at your favorite star. The light coming from that star reaches your eye after traveling as far as 2000 light-years (almost 6 trillion miles). Remarkably, in a dark winter sky far from city lights, the neighboring galaxy, Andromeda, is visible at over 2 *million* light-years away! This chapter describes the first steps in seeing. To understand how we see, we must first consider a little physics and optics, and then we'll look at how the eye is built to capture light, and how specialized cells in the retina act to change physical light energy into electrical neural energy.

In Chapters 3–8 we'll see how light information gleaned by the eyes travels back through the head to the brain, and how the brain transforms this information into a meaningful interpretation of the outside world. For a preview of the entire visual process, work through **Web Activity 2.1: Visual System Overview**.

A Little Light Physics

Light is a form of electromagnetic radiation—energy produced by vibrations of electrically charged material. There are two ways to conceptualize light: as a

Alicia Hunsicker, *Soul Window*, 2009

wave or as a stream of **photons**, tiny particles that each consist of one quantum of energy. This dual nature of light can be confusing to physics and psychology students alike. In this discussion we'll try to avoid confusion as much as possible by treating light as being made up of waves when it moves around the world, and being made up of photons when it is absorbed.

Although the full spectrum of electromagnetic radiation is very wide, light makes up only a tiny portion of this spectrum. **Figure 2.1A** illustrates the electromagnetic spectrum, from gamma rays (which have very short wavelengths) to radio and television waves (which have very long wavelengths). Visible light waves have wavelengths between 400 and 700 nanometers (nm; 1 nm = 10^{-9} meter), as illustrated on the bottom of the figure. Note that as the wavelength varies in the visible spectrum, the **hue** we observe changes, from violet at about 400 nm through the whole spectrum of the rainbow up to red at about 650 nm. (As we'll discuss in Chapter 5, however, the light waves themselves are not

wave An oscillation that travels through a medium by transferring energy from one particle or point to another without causing any permanent displacement of the medium.

photon A quantum of visible light or other form of electromagnetic radiation demonstrating both particle and wave properties.

hue The perceptual attribute of colors that enables them to be classed as similar to red, green or blue, or something in between.

Figure 2.1 The electromagnetic energy spectrum. (A) The spectrum of electromagnetic energy (specified in nanometers), with the visible spectrum (400–700 nm) expanded. Note that 1 nm = 10^{-9} m. (B) Rayleigh scatter. Light scatter causes the sky to look blue when the sun is high, and to look red when the sun is low.

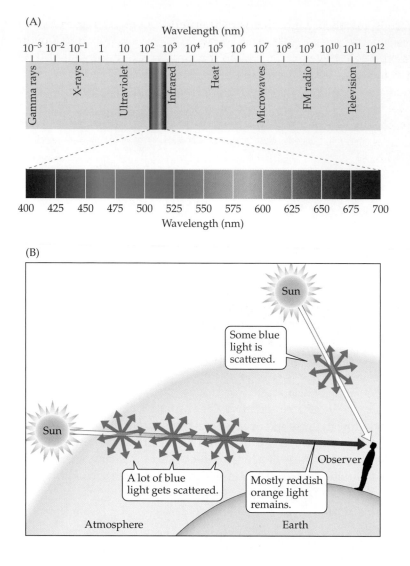

colored; it is only after our visual system interprets an incoming wave that we perceive the light as a specific color.)

Let's consider what happens to light on its way from a star to an eye. (See **Web Activity 2.2: From Sun to Eye**.) In empty space the electromagnetic radiation from a star travels in a straight line at the speed of light (about 186,000 miles per second). Once it reaches the atmosphere, some of the starlight's photons are **absorbed** by encounters with dust, vaporized water, and so on; and some of the light is **scattered** (sometimes called diffracted) by these particles. Scattering of sunlight by small particles (Rayleigh scattering, named after Lord Rayleigh) gives the sky its color: blue when the sun is high, because short-wavelength (blue) light is scattered more strongly than other wavelengths; red at sunset, when the sun is near the horizon, because the sunlight must pass through more atmosphere near the Earth's surface, scattering more of the short-wavelength (blue) light (**Figure 2.1B**), allowing the longer wavelength (red and yellow) light to reach your eyes. Most of the photons, however, make it through the atmosphere and eventually hit the surface of an object.

If the ray of starlight were to strike a light-colored surface, most of the light would be **reflected**. Indeed, the fact that most of the light bounces off the surface accounts for that surface's "light" appearance. However, most of the light striking

absorb To take up something—such as light, noise, or energy—and not transmit it at all.

scatter To disperse something—such as light—in an irregular fashion.

reflect To redirect something that strikes a surface—especially light, sound, or heat—usually back toward its point of origin.

a dark surface is absorbed. Light that is neither reflected nor absorbed by the surface is **transmitted** through the surface. If we are gazing at our star through a window as the light travels from air into the glass, some of the rays will be bent, or **refracted**, as light is transmitted.

Refraction also occurs when light passes from air into water or into the eyeball. In fact, the part of an eye exam in which the eye doctor checks the patient's prescription is often called a refraction because the doctor determines how much the light must be bent by eyeglasses for it to be properly focused on the retina. In the next section we'll see how the optic system of our eyes performs this same kind of focusing.

Eyes That Capture Light

In order to see stars or anything else, we need some type of physiological mechanism for sensing light. Even single-celled organisms such as amoebas respond to light, changing their direction of motion to avoid bright light when it is detected. But eyes go well beyond mere light detection. An eye can form an **image** of the outside world, enabling animals that possess eyes to use light to recognize objects, not just to determine whether light is present and what direction it's coming from.

Before explaining how eyes form images, let's take a tour through the human eye to become familiar with its important parts. **Figure 2.2** shows a front-to-back slice through a human eye, with the most important structures labeled. (See **Web Activity 2.3: Eye Structure.**)

The first tissue that light from the star will encounter is the **cornea**. The cornea provides a window to the world because it is **transparent** (that is, most light photons are transmitted through it, rather than being reflected or absorbed). It is transparent because it is made of a highly ordered arrangement of fibers and because it contains no blood vessels or blood, which would absorb light. The cornea

transmit To convey something (e.g., light) from one place or thing to another.

refract 1. To alter the course of a wave of energy that passes into something from another medium, as water does to light entering it from the air. 2. To measure the degree of refraction in a lens or eye.

image A picture or likeness.

cornea The transparent "window" into the eyeball.

transparent Referring to the characteristic of a material that allows light to pass through it with no interruption such that objects on the other side can be clearly seen.

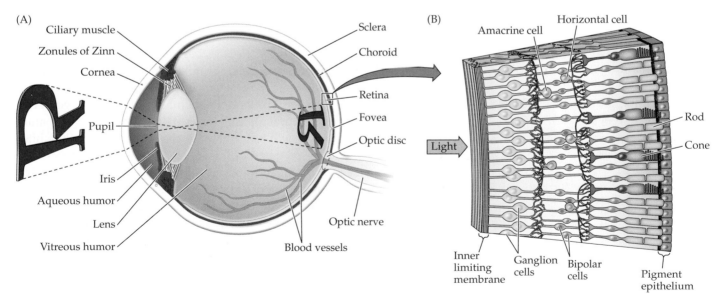

Figure 2.2 The human right eye in cross section (viewed from above). Note that the *R* on the retina is reversed right to left, and it is upside down. The "hole" in the retina where the optic nerve leaves the eyeball is the optic disc (where the absence of photoreceptors results in a blind spot). (B) This enlargement of a cross section through the retina shows the main cell types. These will be discussed in detail later in the chapter. (After Breedlove and Watson, 2013.)

does, however, have a rich supply of transparent sensory nerve endings, which are there to force the eyes to close and produce tears if the cornea is scratched, to preserve its transparency. If you have ever scratched your cornea or worn contact lenses too long, you know exactly how painful this can be! Fortunately, the external layers of the cornea regenerate very quickly, so even when a cornea is scratched, it usually heals within 24 hours.

If you wear contact lenses, you will know that they sit on a thin film of tears in front of the cornea. The tear film is important because it provides the eyes with a smooth, clear surface, helps to protect and lubricate the eyes, and washes away dust and particles. Tears also help to reduce the risk of eye infections. Besides, without tears, crying just wouldn't be the same.

You might be wondering how the cells of the cornea get their oxygen and nutrients if it has no blood supply. The **aqueous humor**, a fluid derived from blood, fills the space immediately behind the cornea and supplies oxygen and nutrients to, and removes waste from, both the cornea and the **lens**. Like the cornea, the lens has no blood supply, so it can be completely transparent. As we'll see later, the shape of the lens is controlled by the ciliary muscle.

To get to the lens, the light from our star must pass through the **pupil**, which is simply a hole in a muscular structure called the **iris**. The iris gives the eye its distinctive color and controls the size of the pupil, and thus the amount of light that reaches the retina, via the pupillary light reflex. When the level of light increases or decreases, the iris automatically expands or contracts to allow more or less light into the eye, respectively. Interestingly, like the aperture of a camera, the pupil of the iris plays an important role in the image quality. Under low illumination, when the pupil is large, the depth of focus (the range of distances over which the image is sharply focused) is reduced, resulting in poor image quality.

After passing through the lens, our starlight will enter the vitreous chamber (the space between the lens and the retina), where it will be refracted for the fourth and final time by the **vitreous humor**. This is the longest part of the journey through the eyeball; this chamber comprises 80% of the internal volume of the eye. The vitreous is gel-like and viscous (a bit like egg white), and it is generally transparent. While staring up at the bright blue sky on a lazy sunny day, however, you may have noticed "floaters," small bits of debris (biodebris) that drift around in the vitreous. Floaters are quite common, and they are usually not a cause for concern.

Finally, after traveling through the vitreous chamber, the light emitted by our favorite star will (hopefully) be brought into focus at the **retina**. To be a bit more precise, only some of the light will actually reach the retina. Much of the light energy will have been lost in space or the atmosphere, because of absorption and scattering, as described already. In addition, a good deal of light will have become lost in the eyeball, so only about half of the starlight that arrives at the cornea will actually reach the retina. The role of the retina is to detect light and "tell the brain about aspects of light that are related to objects in the world" (Oyster, 1999). In other words, the retina is where seeing really begins, because it is here that light energy is turned into electrical neural signals—a process known as transduction.

Focusing Light onto the Retina

To focus a distant star onto the retina, the refractive power of the four optical components of the eye—cornea, aqueous humor, lens, and vitreous humor—must be perfectly matched to the length of the eyeball. Because the cornea is highly curved and has a higher refractive index than air (1.376 versus 1), it forms the most powerful refractive surface in the eye. The aqueous and vitreous humors

aqueous humor The watery fluid in the anterior chamber of the eye.

lens The structure inside the eye that enables the changing of focus.

pupil The dark, circular opening at the center of the iris in the eye, where light enters the eye.

iris The colored part of the eye, consisting of a muscular diaphragm surrounding the pupil and regulating the light entering the eye by expanding and contracting the pupil.

vitreous humor The transparent fluid that fills the vitreous chamber in the posterior part of the eye.

retina A light-sensitive membrane in the back of the eye that contains photoreceptors and other cell types, that transduce light into electrochemical signals and transmits them to the brain through the optic nerve.

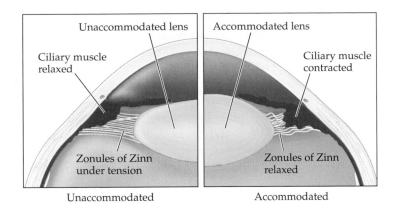

Figure 2.3 Accommodation enables the power of the lens to vary. The left side of this cross section shows the relaxed (unaccomodated) lens. The right side shows the bulging accommodated lens, due to decreased tension of the zonules when the ciliary muscle contracts.

also help refract light. However, the refractive power of each of these three structures is fixed, so they cannot be used to bring close objects into focus. This job is performed by the lens, which can alter the refractive power by changing its shape—a process called **accommodation**.

Accommodation (change in focus) is accomplished through contraction of the ciliary muscle. The lens is attached to the ciliary muscle through tiny fibers (suspensory ligaments known as the zonules of Zinn) (**Figure 2.3**). When the ciliary muscle is relaxed, the zonules are stretched and the lens is relatively flat. In this state, the eye will be focused on very distant objects (like our star). But to focus on something closer—say, a wristwatch or smartphone—the ciliary muscle must contract. This contraction reduces the tension on the zonules and enables the lens to bulge. The fatter the lens is, the more power it has, and the closer you can focus.

Accommodation enables the power of the lens to vary. Lens power $(P) = 1/f$, where f is the **focal distance** in meters. So, if your unaccommodated eyes were perfectly corrected for distant vision, 15 **diopters** (**D**) of accommodation would enable you to read your watch at a distance of about 0.067 meter (1/15) or 6.7 centimeters (cm; to convert meters to centimeters, simply multiply by 100). If you can read your watch at 6.7 cm (while wearing your distance correction), you are either very lucky or very young. Our ability to accommodate declines with age, starting from about 8 years old, and we lose about 1 diopter of accommodation every 5 years up to age 30 (and even more after age 30). By the time most people are between 40 and 50 years old, they find that their arms are too short because they can no longer easily accommodate the 2.5 diopters or so needed to see clearly at 40 cm (1/0.4 = 2.5). This condition is called **presbyopia** (meaning "old sight"), and it is, like death and taxes, inevitable! **Figure 2.4** illustrates the precipitous drop in accommodation with age.

Why do we all have presbyopia to look forward to? The main reason is that the lens becomes harder, and the capsule that encircles the lens, enabling it to change shape, loses its elasticity. Lucky for us, Benjamin Franklin (1706–1790) invented bifocals—lenses that have one power at the top (permitting us to see distant objects) and a different power at the bottom (allowing us to focus on objects at a comfortable reading distance).

Like the other optical components of the eye, the lens is normally transparent. It is transparent because the crystallins (a class of proteins that make up the lens) are packed together very densely and therefore are very regular. Anything that interferes with the regularity of the crystallins will result in loss of transparency (that is, result in areas that are opaque, or opacities). Opacities of the lens are known

accommodation The process by which the eye changes its focus (in which the lens gets fatter as gaze is directed toward nearer objects).

focal distance The distance between the lens (or mirror) and the viewed object, in meters.

diopter (D) A unit of measurement of the optical power of a lens. It is equal to the reciprocal of the focal length, in meters. A 2-diopter lens will bring parallel rays of light into focus at ½ meter (50 cm).

presbyopia Literally "old sight." The age-related loss of accommodation, which makes it difficult to focus on near objects.

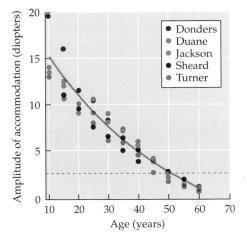

Figure 2.4 The precipitous drop in amplitude of accommodation with age. The dashed line indicates the amplitude of accommodation required to focus at a distance of 40 cm. Each colored symbol represents data from a different classical study.

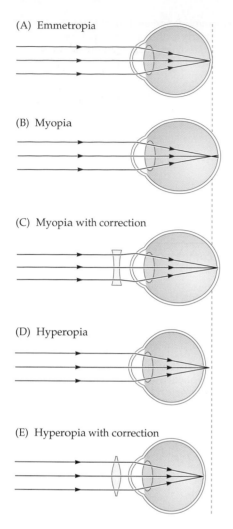

(A) Emmetropia

(B) Myopia

(C) Myopia with correction

(D) Hyperopia

(E) Hyperopia with correction

Figure 2.5 Optics of the human eye. See the text for details. (After Oyster, 1999.)

as **cataracts**. Cataracts can occur at different ages and take many different forms. Congenital cataracts (present at birth) are relatively rare, but if they are dense (and therefore interfere with retinal image quality), they can have devastating effects on normal visual development if not treated promptly. Most cataracts are discovered after age 50, and the prevalence of cataracts increases with age, so by 70 almost everyone has some loss of transparency. Cataracts can interfere with vision because they absorb and scatter more light than the normal lens does. Fortunately, treatment of cataracts (in which the opacified lens is extracted and replaced with a plastic or silicone implant) has become quite routine—often just a 30-minute procedure in the eye doctor's office. There is much ongoing effort to develop new types of lens implants that can change focus—hopefully these will be perfected before you need cataract surgery!

When the refractive power of the four optical components of the eye (cornea, aqueous humor, lens, and vitreous humor) are perfectly matched to the length of the eyeball, this perfect match is known as **emmetropia** (**Figure 2.5A**). A person who is emmetropic does not need corrective lenses to see distant objects. On average, the adult human eye is 24 millimeters (mm) long, about the diameter of a quarter. However, eyeballs can be quite a bit longer or shorter and still be emmetropic because eyes generally grow to match the power of the optical components we're born with. (Most newborns are hyperopic because the optical components of their eyes are relatively well developed at birth compared with the length of their eyeballs.)

Refractive errors occur when the eyeball is too long or too short relative to the power of the four optical components. If the eyeball is too long for the optics (**Figure 2.5B**), the image of our star will be focused *in front* of the retina, and the star will thus be seen as a blur rather than a spot of light. This condition is called **myopia** (or nearsightedness). Individuals with myopia cannot see distant objects clearly; luckily, myopia can be corrected with negative (minus) lenses, which diverge the rays of starlight before they enter the eye (**Figure 2.5C**). If the eyeball is too short for the optics (**Figure 2.5D**), the image of our star will be focused *behind* the retina—a condition called **hyperopia** (or farsightedness). If the hyperopia is not too severe, a young hyperope can compensate and see clearly by accommodating, thereby increasing the power of the eye. If accommodation fails to correct the hyperopia, the star's image will again be blurred. Hyperopia can be corrected with positive (plus) lenses, which converge the rays of starlight before they enter the eye (**Figure 2.5E**).

As noted above, the most powerful refracting surface in the eye is the cornea, which contributes about two-thirds of the eye's focusing power. In an emmetrope, the cornea is spherical, like a basketball or soccer ball (**Figure 2.6A**). However, if the cornea is not spherical, but rather shaped like a football (i.e., the curvature is different in the horizontal and vertical meridians; **Figure 2.6B**), the result is **astigmatism**. With astigmatism, vertical lines may be focused slightly in front of the retina,

Figure 2.6 Two balls with different shapes. (A) Basketballs and soccer balls are spherical. (B) Rugby and American football balls are elliptical. If the cornea is shaped like a rugby ball, with different curvatures in the horizontal and vertical meridians, it will result in astigmatism.

(A)

(B)

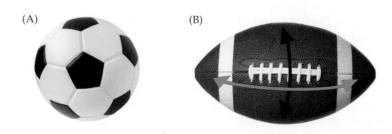

while horizontal lines may be focused slightly behind it (or vice versa). If you have a reasonable degree of uncorrected astigmatism, one or more of the lines in **Figure 2.7** may appear to be out of focus while other lines appear sharp. Lenses that have two focal points (that is, lenses that provide different amounts of focusing power in the horizontal and vertical planes) can correct astigmatism. The development of refractive surgery such as LASIK (laser-assisted in situ keratomileusis) as an alternative to glasses or contact lenses is based on the cornea's refractive power.

The Retina

The preceding discussion covered how the human visual system delivers a focused image of our favorite star onto the retina, which is spread across the back of the eyeball. The optics involved (see Figure 2.2) include a mechanism for regulating the amount of light (the iris) and a lens for adjusting focal length (see Figure 2.3) so that both near and distant objects can be focused on the retina. However, unlike a camera, the purpose of the human visual system is to interpret this image. This is the difference between taking a picture and seeing a picture. And the process of seeing begins with the retina, where the light energy from our star is **transduced** into neural energy that can be interpreted by the brain.

What the Doctor Saw

Eye doctors use an instrument called an ophthalmoscope to look at the back surface of their patients' eyes, which is called the **fundus** (plural *fundi*). (You probably remember all too well having that bright light shining into your eye while the doctor examined your fundus.) **Figure 2.8** shows a normal fundus. The white circle is known as the optic disc. This is the point where the arteries and veins that feed the retina enter the eye, and where the axons of ganglion cells (which we will get to shortly) leave the eye via the optic nerve. This portion of the retina contains no **photoreceptors**, and consequently it is blind. For that reason, it is referred to as the blind spot or physiological blind spot. You can experience your own blind spot, corresponding to the optic disc, by closing your left eye, fixating on the *F* in **Figure 2.9A** with your right eye, and adjusting the distance

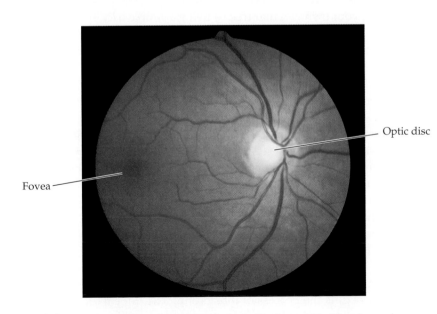

Optic disc

Fovea

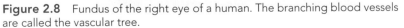

Figure 2.8 Fundus of the right eye of a human. The branching blood vessels are called the vascular tree.

Figure 2.7 Fan chart for astigmatism. Take off your glasses (if you wear glasses) and view this "fan." If you have a significant degree of astigmatism, one or more of the lines will appear to have lower contrast.

cataract An opacity of the crystalline lens.

emmetropia The condition in which there is no refractive error, because the refractive power of the eye is perfectly matched to the length of the eyeball.

refractive error A very common disorder in which the image of the world is not clearly focused on the retina. The most common refractive errors are myopia, hyperopia, astigmatism, and presbyopia.

myopia Nearsightedness, a common condition in which light entering the eye is focused in front of the retina and distant objects cannot be seen sharply.

hyperopia Farsightedness, a common condition in which light entering the eye is focused behind the retina and accommodation is required in order to see near objects clearly.

astigmatism A visual defect caused by the unequal curving of one or more of the refractive surfaces of the eye, usually the cornea.

transduce To convert from one form of energy to another (e.g., from light to neural electrical energy, or from mechanical movement to neural electrical energy). Neurons use electrical signals in their communication.

fundus The back layer of the retina: what the eye doctor sees through an ophthalmoscope.

photoreceptor A light-sensitive receptor in the retina.

Figure 2.9 To experience your blind spot, close your left eye, fixating on the *F* in (A) with your right eye. Hold the book about 15 cm away from your eye to begin, and adjust the distance of the book from your eyes until the red circle disappears. This is your blind spot. Ordinarily you are not aware of it, because the visual system "fills in" the blind spot with information from the surrounding area. If you fixate on the *F* in (B) with your right eye and again adjust the distance, when the gap in the line falls in your blind spot, it will fill in and you will see a continuous red line.

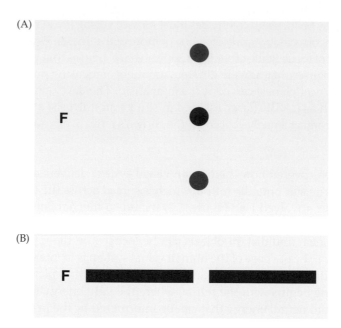

of the book from your eyes until the red circle disappears. You don't normally notice this large blind spot in your visual field, because we have two eyes and objects whose images fall into the blind spot of one eye can be seen by the other eye (see Chapter 6). However, even with the other eye closed, the visual system "fills it in" with information from the surrounding area (**Figure 2.9B**).

Another prominent feature of the fundus is the fovea (the center of the brownish spot in Figure 2.8), which is located near the center of the **macula**. The fundus is the only place in the body where one can see the arteries and veins directly, so it provides doctors with an important window on the well-being of the body's vascular system. The vascular "tree" (i.e., the branching blood vessels) spreads out across the retina in a characteristic way but stops short of the fovea.

You can see your own vascular tree by using a simple trick that requires only a penlight. In a dark room, close your eyes and place the penlight against the outside corner of one eye. Holding the penlight against the eye, gently move the light around (up and down, and back and forth). Within a few seconds you should see the shadows cast by your blood vessels looking like the branches of a tree. We don't normally see them, because the blood vessels move with our eyes, so their shadows are stabilized retinal images and, as with the blind spot, the visual system fills in behind them. The motion of the penlight makes the shadows move, enabling us to see them.

Even when viewed through an ophthalmoscope with a lot of magnification, the fundus does not provide a detailed view of the retina. The retina is the neural structure of the eye where transduction takes place. To get a good look at the structure of the retina, we need a photomicrograph (**Figure 2.10**), which reveals that the retina is a layered sheet of clear neurons, about half the thickness of a credit card (Rodieck, 1998), with another layer of darker cells, the pigment epithelium, lying behind the final layer.

As we'll see in the next section, together these neurons constitute a mini-computer that begins the process of interpreting the information contained in visual images. The transduction of light energy into neural energy begins in the backmost layer of the retina, which is made up of photoreceptors (see Figure 2.10).

macula The pigmented region with a diameter of about 5.5 mm near the center of the retina. It is sometimes referred to as the macula lutea (from the Latin) because of its yellow appearance.

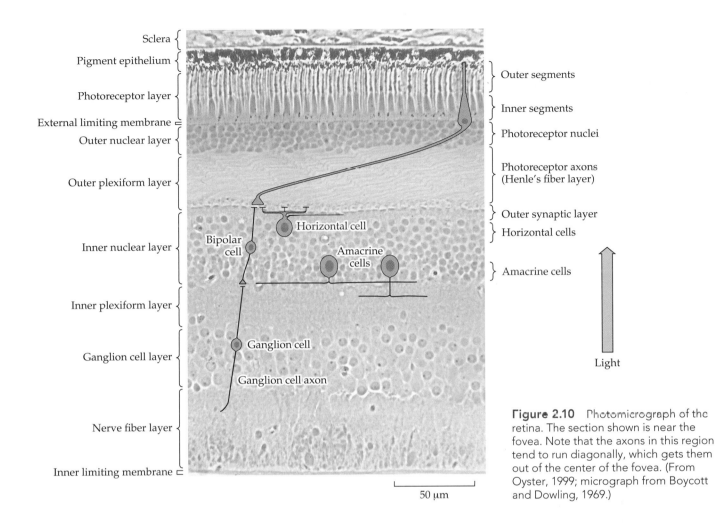

Sclera

Pigment epithelium

Photoreceptor layer

External limiting membrane

Outer nuclear layer

Outer plexiform layer

Inner nuclear layer

Inner plexiform layer

Ganglion cell layer

Nerve fiber layer

Inner limiting membrane

Horizontal cell

Bipolar cell

Amacrine cells

Ganglion cell

Ganglion cell axon

Outer segments

Inner segments

Photoreceptor nuclei

Photoreceptor axons (Henle's fiber layer)

Outer synaptic layer

Horizontal cells

Amacrine cells

Light

50 μm

Figure 2.10 Photomicrograph of the retina. The section shown is near the fovea. Note that the axons in this region tend to run diagonally, which gets them out of the center of the fovea. (From Oyster, 1999; micrograph from Boycott and Dowling, 1969.)

When photoreceptors sense light, they can stimulate neurons in the intermediate layers, including bipolar cells, horizontal cells, and amacrine cells. These neurons then connect with the frontmost layer of the retina, made up of ganglion cells, whose axons pass through the optic nerve to the brain.

Before we describe the function of these layers, we should address an obvious question regarding the structure of the retina: Why are the photoreceptors at the back—that is, in the last layer? This arrangement requires light to pass through the ganglion, horizontal, and amacrine cells before making contact with the photoreceptors. However, these neurons are mostly transparent, whereas cells in the pigment epithelium, which provide vital nutrients and recycling (or housekeeping) functions to the photoreceptors, are opaque. Once we see that the photoreceptors must be next to both the pigment epithelium, for nutrition and recycling, and the other neurons, in order to pass along their signals, the layering order makes much more sense.

Retinal Geography and Function

Each retina contains roughly 100 million photoreceptors. These are the neurons that capture light and initiate the act of seeing by producing chemical signals. The human retina contains at least two types of photoreceptors: **rods** and **cones**. These two types not only have different shapes (which is how they earned their names; **Figure 2.11**), but they have different distributions across the retina and serve different functions.

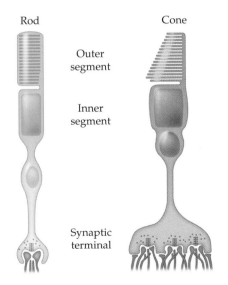

Rod

Cone

Outer segment

Inner segment

Synaptic terminal

Figure 2.11 Rod and cone. (From Rodieck, 1998.)

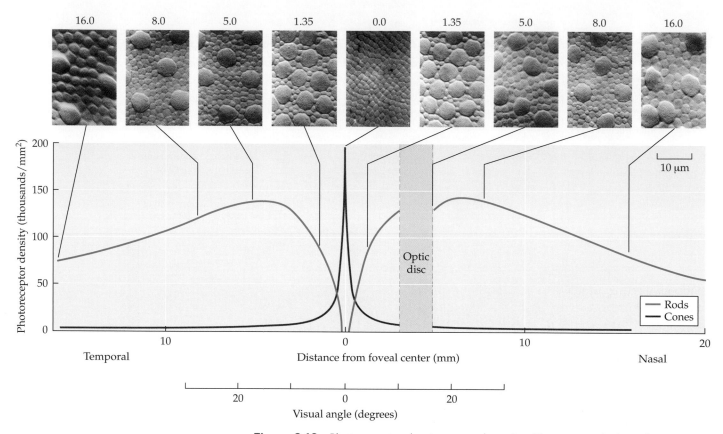

Figure 2.12 Photoreceptor density across the retina. The top panels show slices through the photoreceptor inner segments at different eccentricities (distances from the fovea). The graph shows the density of rods and cones plotted as a function of distance from the fovea. Note that in the peripheral slices, the cones are always the larger cells. (After Oyster, 1999; micrographs from Curcio et al., 1990.)

rod A photoreceptor specialized for night vision.

cone A photoreceptor specialized for daylight vision, fine visual acuity, and color.

fovea A small pit located near the center of the macula and containing the highest concentration of cones and no rods. It is the portion of the retina that produces the highest visual acuity and serves as the point of fixation.

eccentricity The distance between the retinal image and the fovea.

duplex In reference to the retina, consisting of two parts: the rods and cones, which operate under different conditions.

visual angle The angle that an object subtends at the eye.

Humans have many more rods (about 90 million in each eye) than cones (about 4–5 million in each eye), and the two types of cells have very different geographic distributions on the retina (**Figure 2.12**). Rods are completely absent from the center of the fovea, and their density increases to a peak at about 20 degrees and then declines again. The cones are most concentrated in the center of the **fovea**, and their density drops off dramatically with retinal **eccentricity** (distance from the fovea). The fovea is the "pit" in the inner retina that is specialized for seeing fine detail. Because human retinas have both rods and cones, they are considered to be **duplex** retinas. Some animals, such as rats and owls, have mostly rod retinas; others (e.g., certain lizards) have mostly cone retinas.

As the photographs of photoreceptors at different eccentricities in Figure 2.12 illustrate, cones are also smaller and more tightly packed in the foveal center (0.0 in Figure 2.12). This rod-free area (about 300 square micrometers [μm] on the retina) is directly behind the center of the pupil and subtends an angle at the eye (the **visual angle**) of about 1 degree. How big is 1 degree? Here's a rule of thumb, illustrated in **Figure 2.13**: your thumb, when viewed at arm's length, subtends an angle of about 2 degrees on the retina, assuming your thumb is about 2 cm across and your outstretched arm extends about 57 cm from your eye). So if we look directly at an object whose image is smaller than 1 degree, the image will land on a region of the retina that has only cones. **Table 2.1** illustrates some of the fundamental differences in the properties of the fovea compared with the

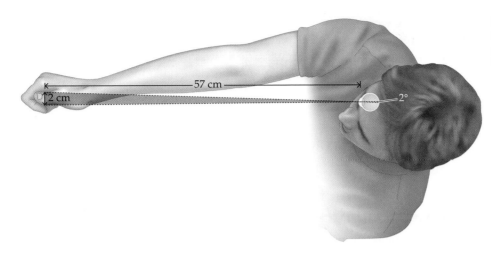

Figure 2.13 The "rule of thumb": when viewed at arm's length, your thumb subtends an angle of about 2 degrees on the retina.

peripheral retina. Most important for us, the fovea has high acuity and we use it to identify objects, to read, and to inspect fine detail. On the other hand, we use the periphery when detecting and localizing stimuli that we aren't looking at directly (e.g., seeing a moving truck out of the "corner of the eye").

The cones become larger and more sparse away from the foveal center, and the small cells that appear outside the fovea (e.g., at 1.35 mm in Figure 2.12) are rods, which are about the same size as the foveal cones. In all of the micrographs except for the one at 0.0, the large cells are always the cones.

Rods and cones operate best under different lighting conditions: Rods function relatively well under conditions of dim (scotopic) illumination (which is why animals such as opossums with all-rod retinas are nocturnal), but cones require brighter (photopic) illumination (e.g., sunlight or room lights) to operate efficiently. Having an area at the center of the fovea with no rods means that under dim illumination the central 1 degree or so around the fovea is effectively blind! Indeed, practiced stargazers know that it is often easier to spot a dim star by looking out of the corner of one's eye than by looking directly at it. We will revisit photopic and scotopic vision again in Chapter 5.

Rods and cones differ functionally in another important way. Because all rods have the same type of photopigment, they cannot signal differences in color. Each cone, on the other hand, has one of three different photopigments that differ in the wavelengths at which they absorb light most efficiently. Therefore, cones can signal information about wavelength, and thus they provide the basis for our color vision.

■ Table 2.1 ■

Properties of the fovea and periphery in human vision

Property	Fovea	Periphery
Photoreceptor type	Mostly cones	Mostly rods
Bipolar cell type	Midget	Diffuse
Convergence	Low	High
Receptive-field size	Small	Large
Acuity (detail)	High	Low
Light sensitivity	Low	High

You may wonder why we have both rods and cones, and why 95% of our photoreceptors are rods, given that for city dwellers in this day and age, our vision is almost entirely mediated by cones. The answer is that roughly 400–500 million years ago, a particular fishy ancestor of ours developed rods (they already had cones), and this provided an advantage in survival at very low light levels at the bottom of the ocean. That advantage has survived till now (Lamb, *Eye*, 2015).

> **FURTHER DISCUSSION** of cones and color detection can be found in Chapter 5 on pages 138–139.

Dark and Light Adaptation

When you emerge from a dark room into bright light (e.g., coming out of a movie theater), your pupil constricts to reduce the amount of light arriving at your retina. This automatic reflex is nothing to sneeze at, but there's a good chance that you will! Sneezing in response to being exposed to a bright light—the "photic sneeze reflex"—is not yet understood, even though it has intrigued some of history's greatest minds. Aristotle (384–322 BCE) thought the heat of the sun on the nose might be responsible. However, Francis Bacon (1561–1626) showed that Aristotle was wrong. Bacon stepped into the sun with his eyes closed and did not sneeze; the heat was still there, but the sneeze was not. Bacon guessed that the sun's light makes the eyes water, and that moisture ("braine humour," in his words) then seeps into and irritates the nose. We now know that the sneeze takes place too soon after light exposure to be the result of the comparatively slow formation of tears. Current thinking suggests that the photic sneeze reflex is a result of crossed wires in the brain.

When you enter a dark room from bright sunlight, the number of photons of light entering your eye might be reduced by a factor of several billion (more than 12 log units) (**Figure 2.14**). Initially you will have trouble seeing anything, but after about 30 minutes in the dark, you will be able to detect even just a few photons. The purple curve in **Figure 2.15** illustrates the change in the threshold light intensity needed to detect a peripheral spot (see Chapter 1 for a discussion

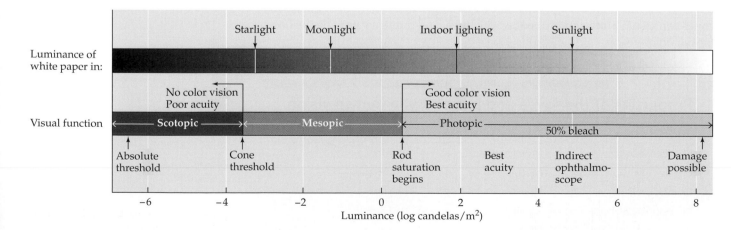

Figure 2.14 The visual system operates over a huge range of luminance levels, from just a few photons to very bright sunshine. (After Purves et al., 2013.)

of thresholds). Initially the threshold is very high, indicating low sensitivity. But over 20 minutes or so the threshold is greatly reduced (meaning sensitivity is increased). And when you emerge from the dark and return to the sunlight, you will be able to see almost instantly. How does the visual system alter its sensitivity over such a large operating range?

There are four primary ways in which the visual system adjusts to changes in illumination: pupil size, photopigment regeneration, the duplex retina, and neural circuitry.

Pupil Size

When a flashlight is shone in someone's eye in a dimly lit room, the pupil quickly constricts. The diameter of the pupil can vary by about a factor of 4, from about 2 mm in bright illumination to about 8 mm in the dark (**Figure 2.16**). Because the amount of light entering the eye is proportional to the area of the pupil, the 4-fold increase in diameter accounts for a 16-fold improvement in sensitivity. In other words, 16 times as many quanta can enter the eye when the pupil is completely dilated, compared with when it is constricted. Although this adaptive ability certainly helps, pupil dilation has a time course of a few seconds, while dark adaptation takes many minutes. Thus pupil size accounts for only a small part of the visual system's overall ability to adapt to light and dark conditions.

Photopigment Regeneration

A second mechanism for achieving a large sensitivity range is provided by the way photopigments are used up and replaced in receptor cells. In dim lighting conditions, plenty of photopigment is available, and rods and cones absorb and respond to as many photons as they can. As already noted, rods provide better sensitivity in such situations than do cones. Indeed, the rod system is capable of detecting a single quantum of light! (See **Web Essay 2.1: How Many Quanta Does It Take?**) After a photopigment molecule is bleached (used to detect a photon), the molecule must be regenerated before it can be used again to absorb another photon.

As the overall light level increases, the number of photons starts to overwhelm the system: photopigment molecules cannot be regenerated fast enough to detect all the photons hitting the photoreceptors. This slow regeneration is a good thing for increasing our sensitivity range. If photons are scarce, we use them all to see; if we have an overabundance, we simply throw some of them away and use the leftovers.

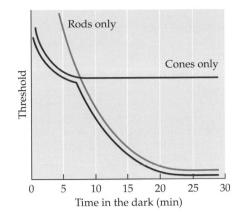

Figure 2.15   Dark adaptation curve. The purple curve shows the threshold light intensity required to detect a peripheral spot following several minutes of adaptation to a bright light. The red curve illustrates the rapid adaptation of the cones. The blue curve shows the slower recovery of the rods to much lower threshold intensities (that is, greater sensitivity). The purple curve represents the more sensitive of the two at any given time.

(A) Darkness

(B) Bright illumination

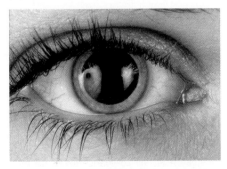

8-mm pupil

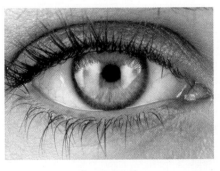

2-mm pupil

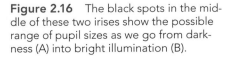

Figure 2.16   The black spots in the middle of these two irises show the possible range of pupil sizes as we go from darkness (A) into bright illumination (B).

receptive field   The region on the retina in which visual stimuli influence a neuron's firing rate.

age-related macular degeneration (AMD)   A disease associated with aging that affects the macula. AMD gradually destroys sharp central vision, making it difficult to read, drive, and recognize faces. There are two forms of AMD: wet and dry.

retinitis pigmentosa (RP)   A progressive degeneration of the retina that affects night vision and peripheral vision. RP commonly runs in families and can be caused by defects in a number of different genes that have recently been identified.

The Duplex Retina

The light compensation mechanism is enhanced by humans' duplex retinas. Rods provide exquisite sensitivity at low light levels, but they become overwhelmed when the background light becomes moderately bright, leading to a loss in information quality. Cones are much less sensitive than rods (they function poorly under very dim light), but their operating range is much larger, stretching from about ten photons per second (just enough light to see color) to hundreds of thousands of photons per second (e.g., a snowcapped mountain in bright sunlight). So we use rods to see when the light is low, and the cones take over when there is too much light for the rods to function well. After adapting to a bright light, cones recover sensitivity quickly (red curve in Figure 2.15) and then saturate. They are not very sensitive to very dim light. Rods recover more slowly (blue curve in Figure 2.15), but after 20 minutes or so they are very sensitive to dim light.

Neural Circuitry

Although pupil size, photopigment regeneration rates, and the rod/cone dichotomy all play a role in dark and light adaptation, the most important reason we are not bothered by variations in overall light levels has to do with the neural circuitry of the retina. As we will see below, ganglion cells are most sensitive to *differences* in the intensity of the light in the center and in the surround of their receptive fields, and they are less affected by the average intensity of the light. The **receptive field** is the region on the retina (and the corresponding region in visual space) in which visual stimuli influence the neuron's firing rate. But the cells will still fire at an above-spontaneous rate when light falls on the entire receptive field, as long as the photoreceptors feeding the ganglion cells are not completely saturated. Thus, the ganglion cells will encode the pattern of relatively light and relatively dark areas in the retinal image. And the pattern of illumination, not the overall light level, is the primary concern of the rest of the visual system.

To sum up, the answer to the question of how the visual system deals with such large variations in overall light levels has two parts. First, we reduce the scale of the problem by regulating the amount of light entering the eyeball, by using different types of photoreceptors in different situations, and by effectively throwing away photons we don't need. Second, by responding to the contrast between adjacent retinal regions, the ganglion cells do their best to ignore whatever variation in overall light level is left over.

■ Sensation & Perception in Everyday Life ■

When Good Retina Goes Bad

Millions of people around the world suffer from blinding diseases in which the rods and/or cones degenerate. These include **age-related macular degeneration (AMD)** and **retinitis pigmentosa (RP)**. (See **Web Essay 2.2: Clinical Case: The Man Who Couldn't Read** and **Web Activity 2.4: Simulated Scotoma**.) At present, there are no effective cures to prevent the progressive degeneration of the photoreceptors that occur in these diseases. For people with AMD this may lead to an inability to read or recognize faces. For people with long-standing RP, this leads inevitably to irreversible blindness.

Fortunately, there are several exciting technological developments that provide hope for these people. These are all based on the notion that while the photoreceptors are dead or dying, postreceptoral neurons and their connections are largely intact. One approach is to substitute an electronic prosthesis (an artificial device to

■ **Sensation & Perception in Everyday Life** *(continued)* ▬▬▬▬

replace or augment a missing or impaired part of the body) into the retina. Typically the prosthesis uses a camera to convert light into energy; an array of electrodes implanted in the retina generates an electrical stimulation pattern based on the light pattern on the camera and delivers this stimulation pattern to the intact postreceptoral neurons (**Figure 2.17**). Unfortunately, while these retinal prostheses can restore some sight, there are technical challenges to implanting them, and they suffer low spatial resolution (Weiland, Cho, and Humayun, 2011), allowing only perception of spots of light and very high-contrast edges.

Another approach that has had some early success in animal models is to use gene therapy to express light-activated channels in surviving photoreceptors using adeno-associated viral (AAV) vectors. This approach has been successfully used in several clinical trials in patients.

A third strategy is to chemically modify endogenous channels in retinal ganglion cells to make them light-sensitive. This approach essentially adds a synthetic small molecule "photoswitch" to confer light sensitivity onto retinal ganglion cells, and it has been shown to reinstate light sensitivity in blind mice (Tochitsky et al., 2014).

Each of these approaches provides promise for new treatments for people with blinding retinal disorders.

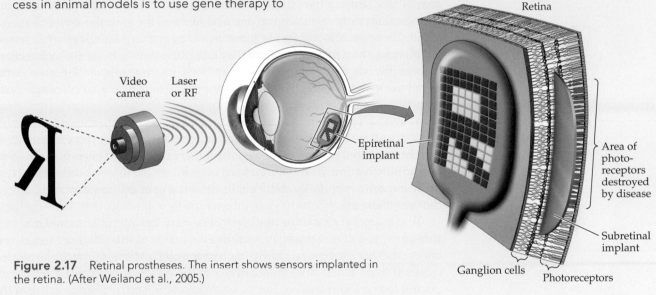

Figure 2.17 Retinal prostheses. The insert shows sensors implanted in the retina. (After Weiland et al., 2005.)

Retinal Information Processing

The retina contains five major classes of neurons: photoreceptors, horizontal cells, bipolar cells, amacrine cells, and ganglion cells mentioned earlier in this chapter (see Figure 2.10). Let's take a closer look at the functions of each of these cell types. (See **Web Activity 2.5: Retinal Structure**.)

Light Transduction by Rod and Cone Photoreceptors

When photoreceptors capture light, they produce chemical changes that start a cascade of neural events ending in a visual sensation. Photoreceptors send their signals by way of the synaptic terminals, specialized structures for contacting other retinal neurons. Figure 2.11 shows examples of rod and cone synaptic terminals. The synaptic terminals contain connections from the neurons that photoreceptors "talk to": the horizontal and bipolar cells.

Both types of photoreceptors consist of an **outer segment** (which is adjacent to the pigment epithelium), an **inner segment**, and a **synaptic terminal**.

outer segment The part of a photoreceptor that contains photopigment molecules.

inner segment The part of a photoreceptor that lies between the outer segment and the cell nucleus.

synaptic terminal The location where axons terminate at the synapse for transmission of information by the release of a chemical transmitter.

Molecules called visual pigments are made in the inner segment (which is like a little factory, filled with mitochondria) and stored in the outer segment, where they are incorporated into the membrane. Each visual pigment molecule consists of a protein (an opsin), the structure of which determines which wavelengths of light the pigment molecule absorbs, and a **chromophore**, which captures light photons. The chromophore is the part of the pigment molecule that determines its color by selectively absorbing specific wavelengths of light. The chromophore, known as Retinal, is derived from vitamin A, which is in turn manufactured from beta-carotene, which is why your mother told you to eat your carrots! The opsin and chromophore are connected. Each photoreceptor has only one of the four types of visual pigments found in the human retina. The pigment **rhodopsin** is found in the rods, concentrated mainly in the stack of membranous discs in the outer segment. Each cone has one of the other three pigments, each of which responds to long, medium, or short wavelengths only. Figure 5.1 shows the absorption spectra of the four photoreceptor types.

Evidence suggests that there may be another type of photoreceptor—one that "lives" among the ganglion cells and that is involved in adjusting our biological rhythms to match the day and night of the external world (Baringa, 2002). These photoreceptors are sensitive to the ambient light level and contain the photopigment **melanopsin**, and they send their signals to the suprachiasmatic nucleus, the home of the brain's circadian clock, which regulates 24-hour patterns of behavior and physiology. The melanopsin signals may also influence pupil responses (Spitschan et al., 2014).

When a photon from our favorite star makes its way into the outer segment of a rod and is absorbed by a molecule of rhodopsin, it transfers its energy to the chromophore portion of the visual pigment molecule. This process, known as **photoactivation** (also referred to as bleaching), initiates a biochemical cascade of events eventually resulting in the closing of cell membrane channels that normally allow ions to flow into the rod's outer segment. Closing these channels alters the balance of electrical current between the inside and outside of the rod's outer segment, making the inside of the cell more negatively charged. This process is known as **hyperpolarization**. Hyperpolarization closes voltage-gated calcium channels at the synaptic terminal, thereby reducing the concentration of free calcium inside the cells. The lowering of the calcium concentration, in turn, reduces the concentration of neurotransmitter (glutamate) molecules released in the synapse, and this change signals to the bipolar cell that the rod has captured a photon. The entire sequence of events takes only a matter of milliseconds. While we have focused this discussion on rhodopsin, cone visual pigment molecules act in a qualitatively similar fashion. A full discussion of the biochemical cascade is beyond the scope of this book, but you can learn more about phototransduction at **Web Activity 2.6: Phototransduction**.

The amount of glutamate present in the photoreceptor–bipolar cell synapse at any one time is inversely proportional to the number of photons being absorbed by the photoreceptor. Thus, unlike most other types of neurons, photoreceptors do not respond in an all-or-nothing fashion. They pass their information on to bipolar cells via **graded potentials**, which vary in size, instead of all-or-none action potentials or spikes, which are found throughout the nervous system (see Chapter 1).

The three cone photopigments are not distributed equally among the cones (**Figure 2.18**). Short wavelength–sensitive cones (S-cones) constitute only about

chromophore The light-catching part of the visual pigments of the retina.

rhodopsin The visual pigment found in rods.

melanopsin A photopigment that is sensitive to ambient light.

photoactivation Activation by light.

hyperpolarization A change in membrane potential such that the inner membrane surface becomes more negative than the outer membrane surface.

graded potential An electrical potential that can vary continuously in amplitude.

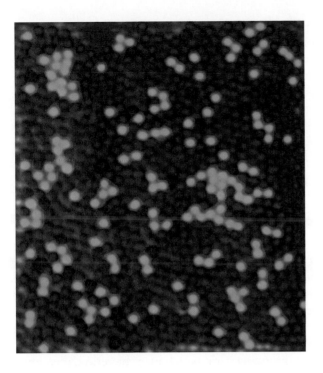

Figure 2.18 Blue, green, and red represent the S-, M-, and L-cones, respectively, of a living human being in a patch of retina at 1 degree from the fovea. This pseudocolor image was made by the use of adaptive optics, to measure and bypass the aberrations of the eye, and of selective bleaching, to isolate the different photopigments. (From Roorda and Williams, 1999; courtesy of Austin Roorda.)

5–10% of the total cone population, and they are essentially missing from the center of the fovea. Thus, the foveal center is dichromatic (it has only two color-sensitive cone types). We also know that there are more long wavelength–sensitive cones (L-cones) than medium wavelength–sensitive cones (M-cones); it has been estimated that there are, on average, about twice as many L-cones as M-cones, although the ratio of L- to M-cones varies enormously among individuals. **Table 2.2** illustrates some of the fundamental differences in the properties of the photopic (high-illumination) and scotopic (low-illumination) visual systems.

■ Table 2.2 ■
Properties of human photopic and scotopic vision

Property	Photopic system	Scotopic system
Photoreceptor	4–5 million cones	90 million rods
Location in retina	Throughout retina, with highest concentration close to fovea	Outside of fovea
Spatial acuity (detail)	High	Low
Light sensitivity	Low	High
Response speed	Fast	Slow
Saturation	No saturation	Saturate at ~ twilight levels
Dark adaptation	Recovery in ~ 5 min	Recovery in ~ 40 min
Light adaptation	Fast (Weber's law)	Slow (square root law)
Color vision	Trichromatic	None

Lateral Inhibition through Horizontal and Amacrine Cells

As the name implies, **horizontal cells** run perpendicular to the photoreceptors, making contacts between nearby photoreceptors. These lateral connections play an important functional role in the form of **lateral inhibition**, which enables the signals that reach retinal ganglion cells to be based on differences in activation between nearby photoreceptors. Lateral inhibition plays an important role in visual perception, as well as in several visual illusions (e.g., Mach bands and the Hermann grid—see **Web Essay 2.3: Seeing Illusory Stripes and Spots**). We will have more to say about lateral inhibition in the "Center-Surround Receptive Fields" section on the next page.

Amacrine cells are also part of the lateral pathway. Like horizontal cells, amacrine cells run perpendicular to the photoreceptors in the inner layers of the retina, where they receive inputs from bipolar cells and other amacrine cells and send signals to bipolar, amacrine, and retinal ganglion cells. Amacrine cells come in many flavors, by some estimates as many as 40 (Rodieck, 1998). Although amacrine cells have been implicated in both contrast enhancement and temporal sensitivity (the detection of changes in light patterns over time), their precise function remains unclear.

Convergence and Divergence of Information via Bipolar Cells

If horizontal and amacrine cells form a lateral pathway in the retina, then photoreceptors, bipolar cells, and ganglion cells can be considered to form a vertical pathway (see Figure 2.10). Bipolar cells are the intermediaries. There are various types of bipolar cells, and their wiring determines the information that is passed from the photoreceptors to the ganglion cells. For example, in peripheral vision a **bipolar cell** receives input from as many as 50 photoreceptors, pools this information, and passes it on to a ganglion cell. This convergence of information from many photoreceptors to a **diffuse bipolar cell** (a single bipolar cell) is a characteristic of the rod pathway, and the same sort of convergence also occurs in the cone pathway in the peripheral retina.

Pooling of information from many photoreceptors is a very important mechanism for increasing visual **sensitivity**. Indeed, the fact that most rods communicate with ganglion cells through diffuse bipolar cells largely accounts for the ability of the rod system to function well in dim lighting conditions. A diffuse bipolar cell may respond at the same rate in response to a single point of bright light or several spots of dim light, since multiple photoreceptors synapse on each diffuse bipolar cell, and a ganglion cell listening to the diffuse bipolar cell will be unable to tell which pattern of light is present. The high degree of neural convergence in peripheral vision has important consequences for **visual acuity**, which falls off rapidly with eccentricity (see Table 2.1).

FURTHER DISCUSSION of visual acuity can be found in Chapter 3 on pages 62–65.

In contrast, in the fovea, **midget bipolar cells** receive input from single cones and pass this information on to single ganglion cells. The fact that one-to-one pathways between cones and ganglion cells exist only in the fovea accounts for why images are seen most clearly when they fall on this part of the retina. The high degree of convergence in the retinal periphery ensures high sensitivity to light but poor acuity. The low degree of convergence in the fovea ensures high acuity but poor sensitivity to light (see Table 2.2). You can explore this trade-off of sensitivity and acuity in **Web Activity 2.7: Acuity versus Sensitivity**.

horizontal cell   A specialized retinal cell that contacts both photoreceptor and bipolar cells.

lateral inhibition   Antagonistic neural interaction between adjacent regions of the retina.

amacrine cell   A retinal cell found in the inner nuclear layer that makes synaptic contacts with bipolar cells, ganglion cells, and other amacrine cells.

bipolar cell   A retinal cell that synapses with either rods or cones (not both) and with horizontal cells and then passes the signals on to ganglion cells.

diffuse bipolar cell   A bipolar retinal cell whose processes are spread out to receive input from multiple cones.

sensitivity   1. The ability to perceive via the sense organs. 2. Extreme responsiveness to radiation, especially to light of a specific wavelength. 3. The ability to respond to transmitted signals.

visual acuity   A measure of the finest detail that can be resolved by the eyes.

midget bipolar cell   A small bipolar cell in the central retina that receives input from a single cone.

Each foveal cone actually contacts two bipolar cells (representing a divergence of information): one depolarizes in response to an increase in light captured by the cone and is called an **ON bipolar cell**; the other hyperpolarizes and is called an **OFF bipolar cell**. ON and OFF bipolar cells respond differently to the same photoreceptor input because they express different types of postsynaptic glutamate receptors that ultimately lead to changes in membrane potential in opposite directions.

The existence of both ON and OFF bipolar cells provides information about whether the retinal illumination increased or decreased, and as we will see, the ON/OFF distinction built into the anatomical structure of the retina is present at many levels of the visual pathway.

Communicating to the Brain via Ganglion Cells

By the time signals arrive at the **ganglion cells**, the final layer of the retina, there has already been a lot of information processing. Some information has been pooled through convergence; some has been enhanced or inhibited by lateral pathways.

By now you are probably getting the idea that each cell type comes in many varieties, and ganglion cells are no exception. The human retina contains about 1,250,000 ganglion cells, about 1% of the number of photoreceptors. Midget bipolar cells send their signals to small ganglion cells, which are widely referred to as **P ganglion cells** because they feed the parvocellular ("small cell") layer of the lateral geniculate nucleus (LGN) (discussed in Chapter 3). P ganglion cells constitute about 70% of the ganglion cells in the human retina. Diffuse bipolar cells project to ganglion cells that are known as **M ganglion cells (Figure 2.19)** because they feed the magnocellular ("large cell") layer of the LGN. The dendrites of the M ganglion cells spread out much more than those of the P ganglion cells, giving them an umbrellalike appearance. About 8–10% of ganglion cells in the human retina are of the M variety. The dendrites of both P and M ganglion cells increase in size with retinal eccentricity, but at all eccentricities the P ganglion cells have much smaller dendritic trees than do the M ganglion cells.

The astute reader may have noticed that M and P ganglion cells together constitute about 80% of all ganglion cells. Other ganglion cell types, known as **koniocellular cells**, project to koniocellular layers in the LGN. Some of these, with input from S-cones, may be part of a "primordial" blue-yellow pathway, while yet other ganglion cells that project to the koniocellular layers are thought to correspond to "nonblue" koniocellular cells.

CENTER-SURROUND RECEPTIVE FIELDS   Much of what we know about how retinal ganglion cells work comes from painstaking physiological studies in which tiny electrodes are used to study the electrical changes in individual ganglion cells. Ganglion cells fire action potentials spontaneously, at about one spike per

ON bipolar cell   A bipolar cell that depolarizes in response to an increase in light captured by the cones.

OFF bipolar cell   A bipolar cell that hyperpolarizes in response to an increase in light captured by the cones.

ganglion cell   A retinal cell that receives visual information from photoreceptors via two intermediate neuron types (bipolar cells and amacrine cells) and transmits information to the brain and midbrain.

P ganglion cell   A small ganglion cell that receives excitatory input from single midget bipolar cells in the central retina and feeds the parvocellular layer of the lateral geniculate nucleus.

M ganglion cell   A ganglion cell resembling a little umbrella that receives excitatory input from diffuse bipolar cells and feeds the magnocellular layer of the lateral geniculate nucleus.

koniocellular cell   A neuron located between the magnocellular and parvocellular layers of the lateral geniculate nucleus. This layer is known as the koniocellular layer.

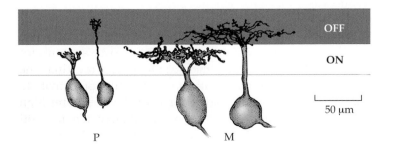

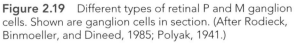

Figure 2.19   Different types of retinal P and M ganglion cells. Shown are ganglion cells in section. (After Rodieck, Binmoeller, and Dineed, 1985; Polyak, 1941.)

second, even in the absence of visual stimulation. However, each ganglion cell has a small window on the world known as its receptive field. As noted earlier, the receptive field is the region on the retina (and the corresponding region in visual space) in which visual stimuli influence the neuron's firing rate. This influence can be either excitatory, increasing the ganglion's firing rate, or inhibitory, decreasing the ganglion's firing rate.

FURTHER DISCUSSION of receptive fields can be found in Chapter 3 on pages 78–82.

Work on horseshoe crabs and frogs provided some of our earliest information on the receptive fields of retinal neurons (Hartline, 1940). But it was Stephen Kuffler who first mapped out the receptive fields of individual retinal ganglion cells in the cat, using small spots of light (Kuffler, 1953). **Figure 2.20** illustrates Kuffler's main findings, which also apply to the retina in primates, and provides some important insights into how the retina processes visual information. Kuffler's experiments are simulated in **Web Activity 2.8: Ganglion Receptive Fields**.

Let's consider Figure 2.20B. Kuffler's visual stimulus was a small spot of light on a projector screen, which moved about on the retina, turning on and off while he recorded impulses from a single retinal ganglion cell (RGC). When the spot was placed on a specific small region of the retina, the ganglion cell *increased* its firing rate when the light was turned on (this response is indicated by a plus sign in the figure). This area of the retina is called the "center" of the ganglion cell's receptive field. When the spot was moved to an adjacent area of the retina, the ganglion cell *decreased* its firing rate when the light was turned on (indicated by a minus sign). It is interesting that turning the light *off* in this area surrounding the receptive-field center led to a brief surge in the cell's firing rate, after which the cell settled down to its spontaneous rate.

The cell just described is known as an **ON-center cell**. It increases its firing rate when a light is turned on in the center of its receptive field, and it decreases its firing rate when the light is turned on in the surround. However, nearly as many ganglion cells do exactly the opposite: their firing rates decrease when a light is turned on in a spot in the center of the receptive field, and increase when a light is turned on in a spot in the surround. These are known as **OFF-center cells** (Figure 2.20C). Most retinal ganglion cells have one of these two types of concentric center-surround organization.

An important finding of Kuffler's was that the spatial layout of the ganglion cell's receptive field is essentially concentric; that is, a small circular area in the center responds to an increase in illumination, and a surrounding ring responds to a decrease in illumination, and size matters! The ganglion cell fires fastest when the size of the spot of light matches the size of the excitatory center. (The size of the receptive-field center reflects the convergence discussed above, that is, the number of photoreceptors and bipolar cells that feed into the RGC center.) The ganglion cell reduces its firing rate when the spot of light begins to encroach on its inhibitory surround (Figure 2.20D). This antagonistic interaction between the center and surround is known as lateral inhibition and is mediated in part by horizontal cells.

The center-surround organization has two important functional consequences. First, as noted above, each ganglion cell will respond best to spots of a particular size (and will respond less to spots that are either bigger or smaller). In this way, retinal ganglion cells act as a **filter** by responding best to stimuli that are just the right size and less to stimuli that are larger or smaller. Second, ganglion cells

ON-center cell A cell that increases firing in response to an increase in light intensity in its receptive-field center.

OFF-center cell A cell that increases firing in response to a decrease in light intensity in its receptive-field center.

filter An acoustic, electrical, electronic, or optical device, instrument, computer program, or neuron that allows the passage of some frequencies or digital elements and blocks the passage of others.

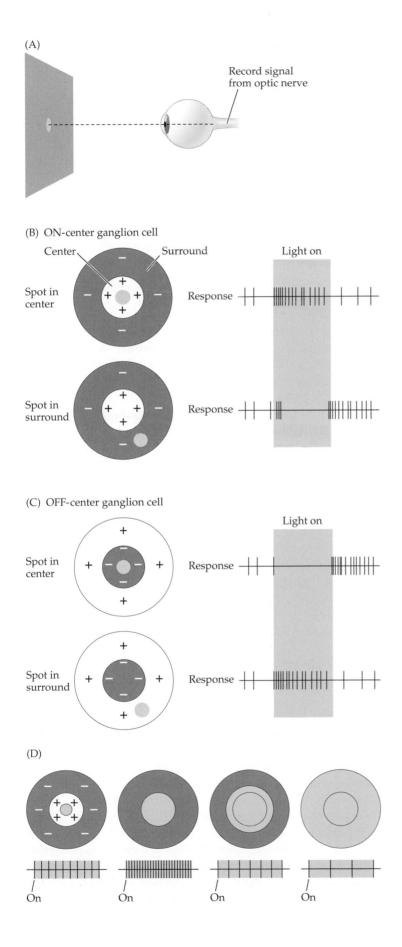

(A)

Record signal from optic nerve

(B) ON-center ganglion cell

Center — Surround

Spot in center

Response

Light on

Spot in surround

Response

(C) OFF-center ganglion cell

Light on

Spot in center

Response

Spot in surround

Response

(D)

On   On   On   On

Figure 2.20 Retinal ganglion cell receptive fields. (A) Mapping retinal receptive fields. (B) ON-center field. In each image on the left, the small white circle illustrates the region on the retina where the retinal ganglion cell increased its firing rate when the spot (small yellow circle) was turned on. The large gray circle illustrates the region on the retina where the retinal ganglion cell decreased its firing rate when the spot was turned on and increased its rate when the spot was turned off. The plots on the right illustrate the spikes fired by the associated retinal ganglion cell. (C) OFF-center field. In each image on the left, the large white circle illustrates the region on the retina where the retinal ganglion cell increased its firing rate when the spot was turned on. The small gray circle illustrates the region on the retina where the retinal ganglion cell decreased its firing rate when the spot was turned on and increased its rate when the spot was turned off. The plots on the right illustrate the spikes fired by the associated retinal ganglion cell. (D) The effect of varying the spot size. Note that firing is fastest when the spot just fills the receptive-field center. Increasing the spot size further results in reduced firing due to lateral inhibition from the surround. (C, D after Hubel and Wiesel, 1961.)

Figure 2.21 Diagram showing a classic neuronal explanation for the optical illusion of stripes where none actually appear (known as Mach bands). See the text for details on center-surround organization and antagonism.

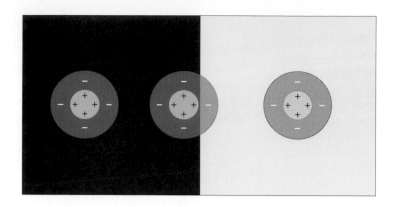

are most sensitive to *differences* in the intensity of the light in the center and in the surround, and they are less affected by the average intensity of the light. This is a useful quality because the average intensity of the light falling on the retina varies a lot, depending on whether you are indoors or outdoors, whether it is daytime or nighttime, how far away you and the objects you're looking at are from the source of illumination, and so on. But the **contrast**—the difference in luminance or brightness between adjacent bits of the scene—will be roughly the same regardless of lighting conditions.

The center-surround antagonism, or lateral inhibition, also has other important perceptual consequences, resulting in the illusions of stripes and spots (**Figure 2.21**). (See **Web Essay 2.3: Seeing Illusory Stripes and Spots.**)

Phenomenologically, we have the impression that our eyes work like video cameras, capturing faithful snapshots of the world around us. Note, though, that the rest of the visual system sees only what the retinal ganglion cells show it, and the ganglion cells are not content simply to pass along the raw images encoded by the photoreceptors. Instead, the ganglion cells, together with the bipolar, amacrine, and horizontal cells, act as an image filter, transforming the raw image into a new representation. This new representation highlights certain important information, such as contrast, and largely discounts other types of less useful information, such as ambient light intensity. In fact, the whole visual system can be considered a long series of filters, with each stage in the system responsible for extracting a particular aspect of the visual world and passing this aspect on to the next stage.

P AND M GANGLION CELLS REVISITED   As already mentioned, retinal ganglion cells come in several types; for human visual perception the most important of these are the P and M cells. The receptive fields of these two types of ganglion cells differ in some important ways. First, at all eccentricities P cells have smaller receptive fields than M cells have. This isn't too surprising, because the size of the receptive field is determined by the size of its dendritic field and the type of bipolar cells it is connected to (see Figure 2.19); since M cells listen to more photoreceptors (via mainly diffuse bipolar, horizontal, and amacrine cells) than P cells do, M cells respond to a larger portion of the visual field.

An additional consequence of the differing sizes of M and P receptive fields is that M cells are much more sensitive—better able to detect visual stimuli—than are P cells under low-light conditions (e.g., at night). However, the smaller receptive fields of P cells enable them to provide finer resolution (greater acuity) than M cells can, if there is enough light for the P cells to operate. See **Web Activity 2.7: Acuity versus Sensitivity** for more on this trade-off.

contrast   The difference in luminance between an object and the background or between lighter and darker parts of the same object.

P and M ganglion cells also differ in their temporal responses. P cells tend to respond with changes in sustained firing while light shines on their excitatory regions. M cells tend to respond more transiently: an M cell will respond with a brief burst of impulses when the spot is turned on, and then it will quickly return to its spontaneous rate, even if the spot remains lit. Thus, M and P ganglion cells signal different information to the brain. P cells provide information mainly about the contrast in the retinal image, and M cells signal information about how the image changes over time.

Finally, P and M cells differ in what they say to the brain about the color of the light they detect (see Chapter 5).

■ Scientists at Work

Is One Photon Enough to See?

■ **Question** The seminal experiments of Hecht, Schlaer, and Pirenne (1942) and others suggest that under ideal conditions, humans are able to detect as few as five to seven photons. However, the long-standing question is, Can the human visual system detect a single photon?

■ **Hypothesis** Evolution has optimized the visual system and post-processing performed by the retina and brain to detect a single photon.

■ **Test** All previous studies were hampered by light sources that were intrinsically and irreducibly variable in the number of photons emitted. In this ingenious work, the researchers built a special single-photon quantum light source that produced correlated pairs of photons. With this, the researchers could detect one of the photons and send the other to the subject's eye, enabling them to identify trials in which it was clear that only one photon was sent to the subject's eye (Tinsley et al. 2016).

■ **Results** Human observers can detect a single-photon incident on the cornea with a probability well above chance.

■ **Conclusion** Evolution has optimized the visual system and post-processing performed by the retina and brain to detect a single photon.

■ **Future work** The single-photon quantum light source may provide a new method for directly measuring and understanding the visual system's internal noise.

Summary

1. This chapter provided some insight into the complex journey that is required for us to see stars and other spots of light. The path of the light was traced from a distant star through the eyeball and to its absorption by photoreceptors and its transduction into neural signals. In subsequent chapters we'll learn how those signals are transmitted to the brain and translated into the experience of perception.

2. Light, on its way to becoming a sensation (a visual sensation, that is), can be absorbed, scattered, reflected, transmitted, or refracted. It can become a sensation only when it's absorbed by a photoreceptor in the retina.

3. Vision begins in the retina, when light is absorbed by rods or cones. The retina is like a minicomputer that transduces light energy into neural energy.

Go to the
Sensation & Perception
Companion Website at
oup.com/us/wolfe5e
for chapter overviews, activities, essays, flashcards, and other study aids.
Go to **DASHBOARD** for additional resources and assessments.

4. The high degree of convergence in the retinal periphery ensures high sensitivity to light but poor acuity.

5. The low degree of convergence in the fovea ensures high acuity but poor sensitivity to light.

6. The one-to-one pathways between cones and ganglions exist only in the fovea and account for why images are seen most clearly when they fall on this part of the retina.

7. The visual system deals with large variations in overall light intensity by (a) regulating the amount of light entering the eyeball, (b) using different types of photoreceptors in different situations, and (c) effectively throwing away photons we don't need.

8. The retina sends information to the brain via ganglion cells, neurons whose axons make up the optic nerves. Retinal ganglion cells have center-surround receptive fields and are concerned with changes in contrast (the difference in intensity between adjacent bits of the scene).

9. Age-related macular degeneration (AMD) is a disease associated with aging that affects the macula. The leading cause of visual loss among the elderly in the United States, AMD gradually destroys sharp central vision, making it difficult to read, drive, and recognize faces.

10. Retinitis pigmentosa (RP) is a family of hereditary diseases characterized by the progressive death of photoreceptors and degeneration of the pigment epithelium. In the most common form of the disease, patients first notice vision problems in their peripheral vision and under low-light conditions—situations in which rods play the dominant role in collecting light.

11. Several exciting developments are aimed at restoring sight in individuals with blinding retinal diseases.

3 Spatial Vision: From Spots to Stripes

■ Questions to Contemplate

Think about the following questions as you read this chapter. By the chapter's end, you should be able to answer and discuss them.

- How do the images of the world formed on the retina reach the brain and enable us to see the world?

- How do we see things "right side up" when the image on our retina is upside down?

- What can a baby see?

In Chapter 2 we learned that the macroscopic structures of the human eye function essentially as a biological camera: The iris regulates the amount of light entering the eyeball. The cornea, lens, and aqueous and vitreous humors focus the light rays so that a clear image is formed on the retina. The rod and cone photoreceptors capture this image in a way that is roughly analogous to the way the film in a camera captures photographic images.

It is here, however, that the analogy between visual system and camera ends. Cameras take pictures. Visual systems see. How do we get from an image of the world in front of us to an interpretation of that world—what is out there, where it is, and what we can do to it? The process starts in the eyeball itself, where the postreceptoral layers of the retina translate the raw light array captured by the photoreceptors into the patterns of spots surrounded by darkness, or vice versa, detected by the ganglion cells (see Figure 2.20). As we discussed in Chapter 2, this retinal translation helps us perceive the pattern of light and dark areas in the visual field, regardless of the overall light level (e.g., it enables us to see almost as well at dusk as we can at noon).

In this chapter we follow the path of image processing from the eyeball to the brain (**Figure 3.1**). Ganglion cells in the retina respond preferentially to spots

Mishael Coggeshall-Burr, *V'lisu II*, 2014

of light. As we will see, neurons in the cerebral cortex prefer lines, edges, and stripes. Furthermore, this portion of visual cortex is organized into thousands of tiny computers, each responsible for determining the orientation, width, color, and other characteristics of the stripes in one small portion of the visual field. In Chapter 4 we will continue this story by examining how other parts of the brain assemble the outputs from these minicomputers to produce a coherent representation of the objects whose reflected light started the photoreceptors firing in the first place.

Visual Acuity: Oh Say, Can You See?

> The King said, "I haven't sent the two Messengers, either. They're both gone to the town. Just look along the road, and tell me if you can see either of them."
>
> "I see nobody on the road," said Alice.
>
> "I only wish I had such eyes," the King remarked in a fretful tone. "To be able to see Nobody! And at that distance, too!"
>
> — Lewis Carroll, *Through the Looking Glass*

Since we'll be talking in this chapter about how the visual system codes images in terms of oriented stripes, let's start by determining just how well we see stripes when they are very close together and/or when the **contrast**—the difference

(A)

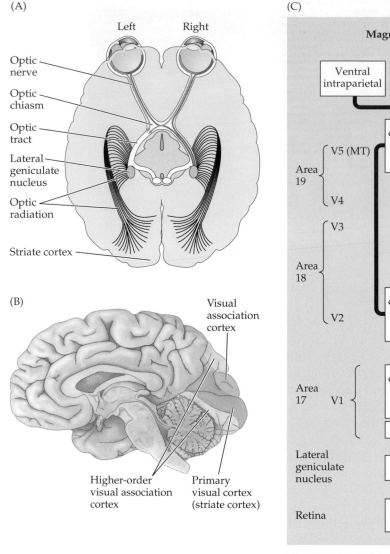

(B)

(C)

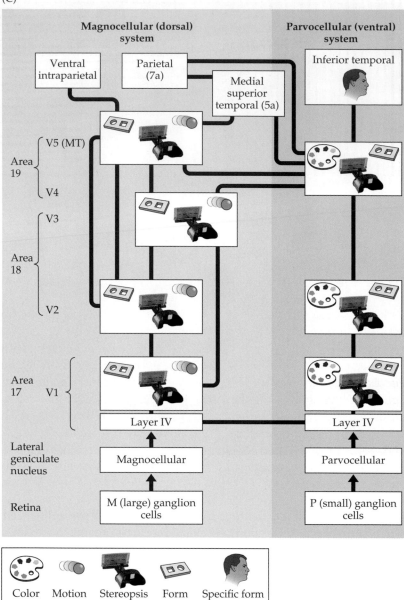

Figure 3.1 Cortical visual pathways. (A) The basic organization of the primary visual pathway from eyeball to striate cortex, in transverse section. (B) A lateral view of the brain, illustrating primary visual cortex, visual association cortex, and higher-order visual association cortex. (C) The flow of information for motion, form, and color analysis from retinal ganglion cells to higher-order visual association cortex. (A after Purves et al., 2012; B after Breedlove and Watson 2013; C after Rosenzweig, Breedlove, and Leiman, 2002.)

contrast The difference in luminance between an object and the background, or between lighter and darker parts of the same object.

in illumination between the stripes and the background—is very low. In addition to setting the boundary conditions for how well we should expect the visual system to be able to perform, we will use this section to introduce some important jargon that we'll need in the rest of the chapter.

Get a tape measure, prop your textbook up, and, while looking at the X in the middle of **Figure 3.2**, back up until you cannot tell the orientation of the black and white stripes. Measure how far your eye is from the page. Now walk

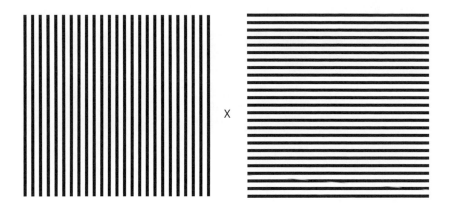

Figure 3.2 A visual acuity test. See the text for details.

forward a bit until you're sure you can see which grating includes vertical stripes and which horizontal stripes, and again measure your distance from the page. Congratulations! You just completed a fast (but not terribly accurate) measurement of your own visual resolution **acuity**.

Eye doctors specify acuity in terms like *20/20* (more about this in a moment), but vision scientists prefer to talk about the smallest visual angle of a cycle of the grating that we can perceive (**Figure 3.3**). A **cycle** is simply one repetition of a black and a white stripe (both of the gratings in Figure 3.2 have 25 total cycles). **Visual angle**, which we mentioned briefly in Chapter 2, is the angle that would be formed by lines going from the top and bottom (or left and right, depending on the orientation of the stripes) of a cycle on the page, passing through the center of the lens, and ending on the retina. You can learn more about this concept in **Web Activity 3.1: Visual Angle**.

More precisely, to calculate the visual angle of your resolution acuity, divide the size of the cycle in Figure 3.2 (which is 2 millimeters, or 1/16 inch) by the viewing distance at which you could just barely make out the orientation of the gratings (average your first and second measurements to get a rough estimate of this distance), and then take the arctangent of this ratio. Under ideal conditions, humans with very good vision can resolve gratings like those in Figure 3.2 when one cycle subtends an angle of approximately 1 minute of arc (1 arc minute, or 0.017 degree). As a rough rule of thumb (see Figure 2.13), 1 centimeter (cm) ≈ 1 degree (60 arc minutes) at a viewing distance of 57 cm. If the size of the just resolvable cycle were 1 cm, you would need to back up to about 3.42 meters (57 × 60 = 3420 cm) in order to be at the acuity limit.

acuity The smallest spatial detail that can be resolved at 100% contrast.

cycle For a grating, a pair consisting of one dark bar and one bright bar.

visual angle The angle subtended by an object at the retina.

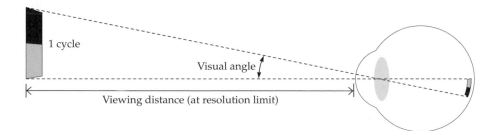

Figure 3.3 Visual angle. Shown here is the angle size of one cycle of a grating at the retina.

Figure 3.4   A sine wave grating (A) and a square wave grating (B). (C) The stripes of the sine wave grating are wider than the photoreceptors (pink circles in the top panel), and the grating can be reconstructed vertically. (D) The stripes of the sine wave grating are narrower than the photoreceptors, so both black and white bars will fall inside a single receptor (top panel), resulting in a uniform gray field (bottom panel).

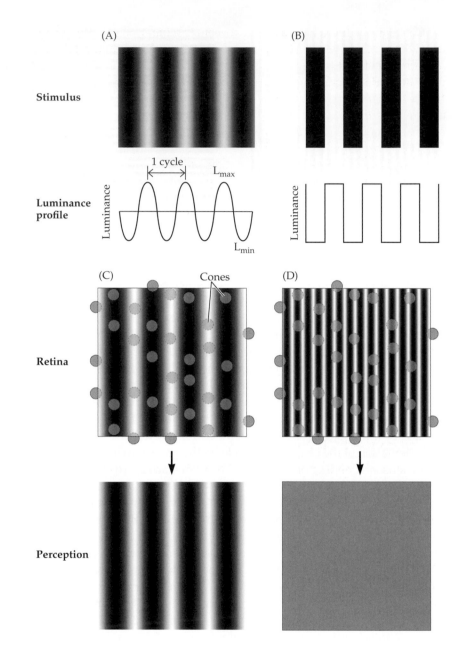

sine wave grating   A grating with a sinusoidal luminance profile as shown in Figure 3.4A.

This resolution acuity represents one of the fundamental limits of spatial vision: it is the finest high-contrast detail that can be resolved. The limit is determined primarily by the spacing of photoreceptors in the retina. To see why, imagine that we're projecting the **sine wave gratings** shown in **Figure 3.4A** onto the retina. The light intensity in such gratings varies smoothly and continuously across each cycle (unlike the gratings in Figures 3.2 and 3.4B, and **3.4B**, in which intensity changes abruptly from black to white and back to black). However, the visual system "samples" the grating discretely, through the array of receptors at the back of the retina (in this respect the eye is more like a digital camera than like a traditional camera that uses film). If the receptors are spaced such that the whitest and blackest parts of the grating fall on separate cones (**Figure 3.4C**), we should be able to make out the grating. But if the entire cycle falls on a single cone (**Figure 3.4D**), we will see nothing but a gray field.

Cones in the fovea have a center-to-center separation of about 0.5 minute of arc (0.008 degree), which fits nicely with the observed acuity limit of 1 minute of arc (remember that we need two cones per cycle to be able to perceive the grating accurately). Rods and cones in the periphery are packed together less tightly (recall that in the periphery, rods are physically more tightly packed [denser] than cones, as shown in Figure 2.10), and here many receptors converge on each ganglion cell. As a result, visual acuity is much poorer in the periphery than in the fovea. For a demonstration of the difference between foveal and peripheral vision, see **Web Activity 3.2: Foveal Acuity**. (See also **Web Essay 3.1: Hyperacuity**.)

Visual acuity in peripheral vision is not uniform—it falls off more rapidly along the vertical midline of the visual field than along the horizontal midline. This is known as horizontal and vertical asymmetry. Thus, if you fix your eyes on one point, you have (slightly but measurably) better acuity 5 degrees left or right than you do 5 degrees up or down. We also have better acuity a fixed distance below the midline of the visual field than above. This is known as vertical meridian asymmetry (Abrams, Nizam, and Carrasco, 2012).

There is also another surprising difference between central vision and peripheral vision—central vision is considerably slower than peripheral vision. Recent work (Sinha et al., 2017) suggests that peripheral cones respond about twice as quickly to light as do foveal cones (30 versus 60 milliseconds). Foveal cones have longer axons than peripheral cones, in order to allow dense packing in the central fovea, and the longer axons transmit slow signals better than fast ones (Masland, 2017). The slow response may allow foveal cones to increase their reliability by integrating their inputs over a longer time.

A Visit to the Eye Doctor

Eye doctors don't describe acuity in terms of visual angles and cycles. The last time you visited your eye doctor, she may have asked you to read letters, decreasing the size of the letters until you made several errors. Then she may have told you that your visual acuity was 20/20 if your vision was good, or 20/40 if you needed glasses, or possibly 20/10 if you could read the smallest letters on the eye chart. This method for designating visual acuity was invented in 1862 by a Dutch eye doctor, Herman Snellen (1834–1908). Snellen constructed a set of block letters for which the letter as a whole was five times as large as the strokes that formed the letter (**Figure 3.5**). Note that the resulting patterns are reminiscent of the gratings in Figure 3.2. He then defined visual acuity as follows:

$$\frac{\text{(distance at which a person can just identify the letters)}}{\text{(distance at which a person with "normal" vision can just identify the letters)}}$$

In later adaptations of the Snellen test, the viewer was positioned at a constant distance of 20 feet, and the size of the letters, rather than the position of the viewer, was altered. So normal vision came to be defined as 20/20. To relate this measure back to visual angle, a 20/20 letter is designed to subtend an angle of 5 arc minutes (0.083 degree) at the eye, and each stroke of a 20/20 letter subtends an angle of 1 arc minute (the familiar 0.017 degree). Thus, if you can read a 20/20 letter, you can discern detail that subtends 1 minute of arc. If you have to be at 20 feet to read a letter that someone with normal vision can read at 40 feet, you have 20/40 vision (worse than normal). Although 20/20 is often considered the gold standard, most healthy young adults have an acuity level closer to 20/15. Note that while the acuity for stripes and letters is quite similar for individuals, the two types of stimuli provide different cues and are subject to different constraints. Indeed, in

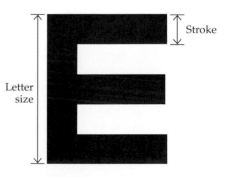

Figure 3.5 A Snellen *E*. The letter size is five times the stroke size.

■ Table 3.1 ▬▬▬▬▬▬▬

Summary of the different forms of acuity and their limits

Type of acuity	Measured	Acuity (degree)
Minimum visible	Detection of a feature	0.00014
Minimum resolvable	Resolution of two features	0.017
Minimum recognizable	Identification of a feature	0.017
Minimum discriminable	Discrimination of a change in a feature	0.00024

some patients with **amblyopia**, acuity with Snellen letters may be much more affected than acuity with gratings.

More Types of Visual Acuity

So far we've discussed two forms of visual acuity: the finest stripes that can be resolved (sometimes referred to as the minimum resolvable acuity) and the smallest letter that can be recognized (the minimum recognizable acuity). How should we define the keenness of sight? *Visual acuity* is used to specify a spatial limit. Over the centuries there have emerged various ideas about how to define, measure, and specify visual acuity. **Table 3.1** lists four of the most common definitions and we discuss them next.

MINIMUM VISIBLE ACUITY   Minimum visible acuity refers to the smallest object that one can detect. As early as the seventeenth century, Benito Daça de Valdés (1591–1634) measured the distance at which a row of mustard seeds could no longer be counted, and early astronomers like Robert Hooke (1635–1703) were interested in the size of stars that could be detected and their relation to retinal anatomy. Under ideal conditions, humans can detect a long, dark wire (like a cable of the Golden Gate Bridge) against a very bright background (like the sky on a bright sunny day) when they subtend an angle of just 0.5 arc second (about 0.00014 degree). It is widely accepted that the minimum visible acuity is so small for two reasons: first, the optics of the eye (described later in this chapter) spread the image of the thin line, making it much wider on the retina; second, the fuzzy retinal image of the line casts a shadow that reduces the light on a row of cones to a level that is just detectably less than the light on the row of cones on either side. In other words, although we specify the minimum visible acuity in terms of the angular size of the target at the retina, it is actually limited by our ability to discriminate the intensity of the target relative to its background. Although the minimum visible acuity represents one limit to spatial vision, it is in fact a limit in the ability to discern small changes in contrast, rather than a spatial limit per se, and *minimum visible acuity* is not used clinically.

MINIMUM RESOLVABLE ACUITY   Minimum resolvable acuity refers to the smallest angular separation between neighboring objects that one can resolve. Ancient Egyptians assessed visual acuity by the ability of an observer to resolve double stars. However, today the minimum resolvable acuity is much more like-ly to be assessed by determining the finest black and white stripes that can be

amblyopia   A developmental disorder characterized by reduced spatial vision in an otherwise healthy eye, even with proper correction for refractive error. Also known as *lazy eye*.

resolved. Under ideal conditions (e.g., high contrast and luminance), humans with very good vision can resolve black and white stripes when one cycle subtends an angle of approximately 1 minute of arc (0.017 degree). This minimum resolvable acuity represents one of the fundamental limits of spatial vision: it is the finest high-contrast detail that can be resolved. In foveal vision the limit is determined primarily by the spacing of photoreceptors in the retina.

MINIMUM RECOGNIZABLE ACUITY   Minimum recognizable acuity refers to the angular size of the smallest feature that one can recognize or identify. Although this method has been used since the seventeenth century, the approach still used by eye doctors today was introduced more than a century ago by Herman Snellen and his colleagues, as discussed above.

MINIMUM DISCRIMINABLE ACUITY   Minimum discriminable acuity refers to the angular size of the smallest *change* in a feature (e.g., a change in size, position, or orientation) that one can discriminate. Perhaps the most studied example of minimum discriminable acuity is our ability to discern a difference in the relative positions of two features. Our visual system is very good at telling where things are relative to each other. Consider two abutting horizontal lines, one slightly higher than the other. The smallest misalignment that we can reliably discern is known as Vernier acuity—named after the Frenchman Pierre Vernier (1580–1637), whose scale, developed in the seventeenth century, was widely used to aid ships' navigators. The success of the Vernier scale was based on the fact that humans are very adept at judging whether nearby lines are lined up or not. Thus, Vernier alignment is still widely used in precision machines, and even in the dial switches in modern ovens. Under ideal conditions, Vernier acuity may be just 3 arc seconds (about 0.0008 degree)! This performance is even more remarkable when you consider that it is about ten times smaller than even the smallest foveal cones. Note that the optics of the eye spread the image of a thin line over a number of retinal cones, and that the eyes are in constant motion, and this performance appears even more remarkable.

Vernier acuity is not the most remarkable form of hyperacuity. *Guinness World Records 2005* describes the "highest hyperacuity" as follows: "In April 1984, Dr. Dennis M. Levi" (yes—that's one of the authors of this book) "… repeatedly identified the relative position of a thin, bright green line within 0.8 seconds of arc (0.00024 degree). This is equivalent to a displacement of some 0.25 inches (6 mm) at a distance of 1 mile (1.6 km)."

Acuity for Low-Contrast Stripes

Up to now we've been discussing the tiniest high-contrast details that we can resolve. We learned that high-contrast sine wave gratings can be distinguished from a uniform gray field, as long as adjacent pairs of light or dark stripes are separated by at least 1 arc minute of visual angle. But what happens if the contrast of the stripes is reduced—that is, if the light stripes are made darker and the dark stripes lighter?

This was the question asked by Otto Schade in 1956, when he was working for the RCA Corporation. Schade showed people sine wave gratings with different spatial frequencies and had them adjust the contrast of the gratings until they could just be detected. **Spatial frequency** refers to the number of times a pattern, such as a sine wave grating, repeats in a given unit of space. For example, if you view your book from about 120 cm (about 47 inches) away, the visual angle between

spatial frequency   The number of grating cycles (i.e., dark and bright bars) in a given unit of space.

(A)

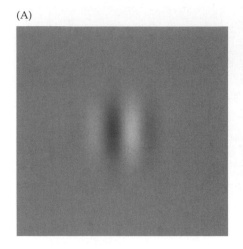

(B)

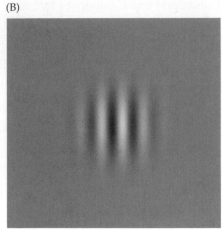

(C)

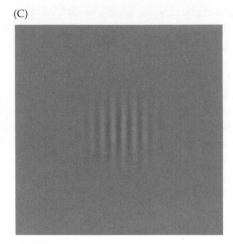

Figure 3.6 Sine wave gratings illustrating low (A), medium (B), and high (C) spatial frequencies.

cycles per degree The number of grating cycles per degree of visual angle.

contrast sensitivity function (CSF) A function describing how the sensitivity to contrast (defined as the reciprocal of the contrast threshold) depends on the spatial frequency (size) of the stimulus.

contrast threshold The smallest amount of contrast required to detect a pattern.

each pair of white stripes in **Figure 3.6A** shows a grating with a relatively low spatial frequency—about 2 **cycles per degree**. **Figure 3.6B** is about 0.25 degree, so the spatial frequency of this grating is 1/0.25 = 4 cycles per degree, and **Figure 3.6C** illustrates a relatively higher spatial frequency (about 8 cycles per degree). **Web Activity 3.3: Gabor Patches** provides additional illustrations of sine wave gratings at different spatial frequencies.

Intuitively, you might think that the wider the stripes (that is, the lower the spatial frequency), the easier it would be to distinguish the light stripes from the dark stripes. But this is not what Schade found. He, and later Fergus Campbell and Dan Green (1965), demonstrated that the human **contrast sensitivity function** (**CSF**) is shaped like an upside-down *U*, as shown in **Figure 3.7**. The y-axis on the right is the observer's contrast threshold. We obtain the units for the left side of the y-axis by taking the reciprocal of the **contrast threshold**. For example, for a 1-cycle/degree grating to be just distinguishable from uniform gray, the stripes must have a contrast of about 1.0% (that is, if the mean luminance is 1000 photons, then a tiny patch of a light stripe reflects 1010 photons and a patch of a dark stripe should reflect 990 photons). The contrast, C, of a grating is generally specified according to the definition described by the first American to win the Nobel Prize, the physicist, Albert Michelson. (He won the Nobel Prize in 1907 for his work on the measurement of the speed of light.) According to the Michelson definition, $C = (L_{max} - L_{min})/(L_{max} + L_{min})$, where L_{max} and L_{min} are the maximum and minimum luminance, respectively. In our example, C = (1010 − 990)/(1010 + 990) = 0.01 or 1% (0.01 × 100). The reciprocal of this threshold is 1/0.01 = 100, so this is the point plotted on the red CSF line in Figure 3.7 for this spatial frequency.

Note that a contrast of 100% corresponds to a contrast sensitivity value of 1. The CSF reaches this value on the

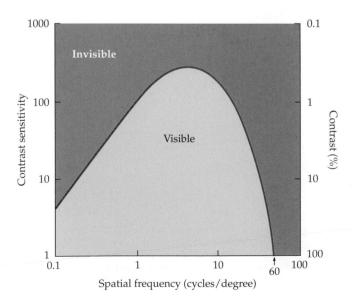

Figure 3.7 The contrast sensitivity function (red line): the window of visibility. Any objects whose spatial frequencies and contrasts fall within the yellow region will be visible. Those outside the yellow region are outside the window of visibility. The red line delimits the "threshold" between seeing and not seeing.

far right side of the curve in Figure 3.7, at about 60 cycles/degree. Sixty cycles/degree corresponds to a cycle width of 1 minute of arc, the resolution limit we measured previously for high-contrast stripes, which, recall, is determined primarily by cone spacing. The falloff in the CSF on the other side of the curve cannot be explained by cone spacing or by limitations in the optics of the eye. Instead, this part of the function must be due to neural factors, which we will discuss later in the chapter.

You can visualize your own CSF by using **Figure 3.8**. Here we see a sinusoidal grating whose contrast increases continuously from the top of the figure to the bottom, and whose spatial frequency increases continuously from the left side of the graph to the right. If you view the figure from a distance of about 2 meters, you will notice the inverted *U* shape where the grating fades from visibility to invisibility. If you bring the book closer to your eye, you should be able to see the stripes on the right side of the figure going farther up, whereas the tops of the stripes on the left side will become less distinct.

There are many factors that influence the exact form of the CSF. These include the adaptation level of the eye (**Figure 3.9A**), the temporal modulation of the targets (**Figure 3.9B**), and the age (**Figure 3.9C**) and refractive state of the individual.

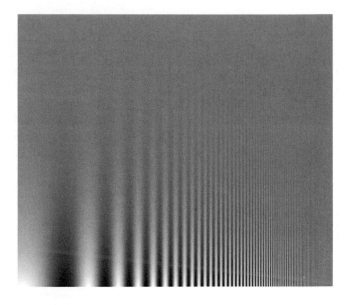

Figure 3.8 A grating modulated by contrast (vertically) and by spatial frequency (horizontally). (Courtesy of Izumi Ohzawa with credit to John Robson and Fergus W. Campbell.)

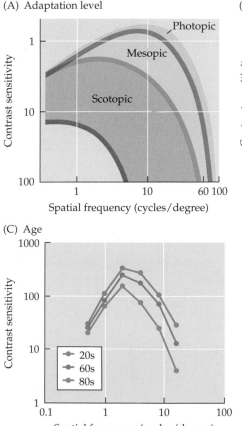

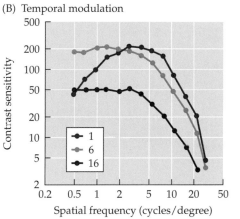

Figure 3.9 The shape and height of the contrast sensitivity function (CSF) is influenced by a wide variety of factors such as adaptation level (A), temporal modulation (B) where each curve represents the CSF at a different temporal frequency (1, 6, and 16 Hz), and age (C) where each curve represents the CSF at a different age (20s, 60s, and 80s).

Why Sine Wave Gratings?

One answer to this question is that, although "pure" sine wave gratings may be rare in the real world, patterns of stripes with more or less fuzzy boundaries are quite common: think of trees in a forest, books on a bookshelf, and a map of Manhattan (the latter includes a pattern of horizontal stripes superimposed on a pattern of vertical stripes). Furthermore, the edge of any object produces a single stripe, often blurred by a shadow, in the retinal image.

On a larger scale, the visual system appears to break down real-world images into a vast number of components, each of which is, essentially, a sine wave grating with a particular spatial frequency. This method of processing is analogous to the way in which the auditory system deals with sound and is called Fourier analysis. **Figure 3.10** illustrates how a square wave can be constructed by adding a series of sine waves with the appropriate amplitudes and phases (Fourier synthesis; also see Chapters 1 and 12). We'll return to this idea later in the chapter. For now, rest assured that scientists don't use sine wave gratings just because they're convenient to manipulate in experiments (although they do make very nice stimuli).

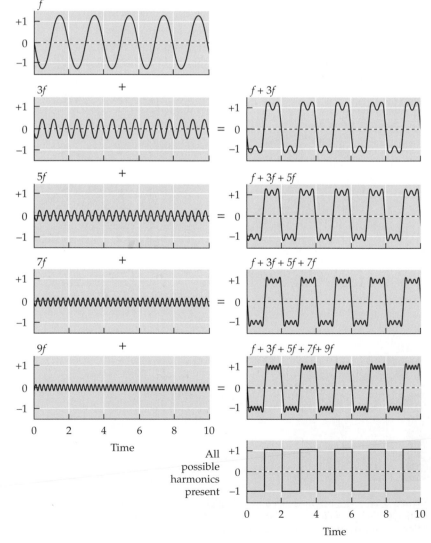

Figure 3.10 Fourier analysis. The left column shows sine waves of different spatial frequencies and amplitudes. From top to bottom: first row, the "fundamental" spatial frequency (*f*) with amplitude = *a*; second row, 3*f*, *a* = 1/3; third row, 5*f*, *a* = 1/5; fourth row, 7*f*, *a* = 1/7; fifth row, 9*f*, *a* =1/9.

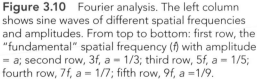

Retinal Ganglion Cells and Stripes

In Chapter 2 we learned that retinal ganglion cells respond vigorously to spots of light. As it turns out, each ganglion cell also responds well to certain types of stripes or gratings. **Figure 3.11** shows how an ON-center retinal ganglion cell responds to gratings of different spatial frequencies. When the spatial frequency of the grating is too low (Figure 3.11A), the ganglion cell responds weakly because part of the fat, bright bar of the grating lands in the inhibitory surround, damping the cell's response. Similarly, when the spatial frequency is too high (Figure 3.11C), the ganglion cell responds weakly because both dark and bright stripes fall within the receptive-field center, washing out the response. But when the spatial frequency is just right (Figure 3.11B), with a bright bar filling the center and with dark bars filling the surround, the cell responds vigorously. Thus, these retinal ganglion cells are "tuned" to spatial frequency: each cell acts like a **filter**, responding best to a specific spatial frequency that matches its receptive-field size, and responding less to both higher and lower spatial frequencies.

Christina Enroth-Cugell and John Robson (1984) were the first to record the responses of retinal ganglion cells to sine wave gratings. In addition to showing that these cells respond vigorously to gratings of just the right size, these investigators discovered that responses depend on the **phase** of the grating—its position within the receptive field. **Figure 3.12** illustrates how an ON-center retinal ganglion cell might respond to a grating of just the right spatial frequency (a bar width about the size of the receptive-field center) in four different phases.

When the grating has a light bar filling the receptive-field center and dark bars filling the surround (Figure 3.12A), this ON-center ganglion cell responds vigorously, increasing its firing rate. If the grating phase is shifted by 90 degrees (Figure 3.12B), half the receptive-field center will be filled by a light bar and half by a dark bar, and similarly for the surround. In other words, there will be no net difference between the light intensity in the receptive field's center and its surround. In this case the cell's response rate will not change from its resting rate when the grating is turned on—just what we would predict if the ganglion cell were averaging the amount of light

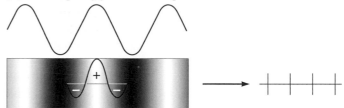

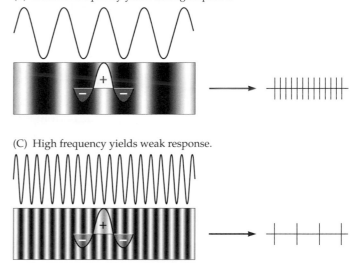

Figure 3.11 The response (right) of an ON-center retinal ganglion cell to gratings of different spatial frequencies (left): (A) low, (B) medium, and (C) high.

filter An acoustic, electrical, electronic, or optical device, instrument, computer program, or neuron that allows the passage of some range of parameters (e.g., orientations, frequencies) and blocks the passage of others.

phase The relative position of a grating.

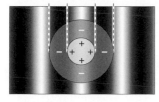

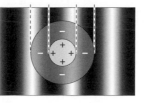

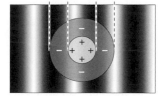

Figure 3.12 The response of a ganglion cell to a grating depends on the phase of the grating. This figure illustrates the response of an ON-center retinal ganglion cell to four different phases of an optimally sized grating.

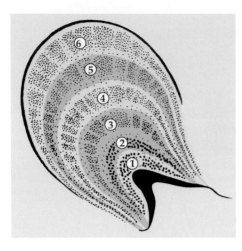

Figure 3.13 The primate lateral geniculate nucleus. (From Breedlove and Watson, 2013.)

lateral geniculate nucleus (LGN)
A structure in the thalamus, part of the midbrain, that receives input from the retinal ganglion cells and has input and output connections to the visual cortex.

magnocellular layer Either of the bottom two neuron-containing layers of the lateral geniculate nucleus, the cells of which are physically larger than those in the top four layers.

parvocellular layer Any of the top four neuron-containing layers of the lateral geniculate nucleus, the cells of which are physically smaller than those in the bottom two layers.

koniocellular cell A neuron located between the magnocellular and parvocellular layers of the lateral geniculate nucleus. This layer is known as the koniocellular layer.

contralateral Referring to the opposite side of the body (or brain).

ipsilateral Referring to the same side of the body (or brain).

falling on its center and its surround. A second 90-degree shift puts the dark bar in the center and the light bars in the surround, producing a negative response (Figure 3.12C); and a third phase shift returns us to the situation after the first shift, with the overall intensities in the center and surround equivalent and the cell therefore blind to the grating (Figure 3.12D). (Note that other ganglion cells located to the left or right of our target cell might respond to the 90-degree and 270-degree phases but not to the 0-degree and 180-degree phases, which is why the visual system as a whole is able to see all four phases equally well.)

The Lateral Geniculate Nucleus

The axons of retinal ganglion cells synapse in the two **lateral geniculate nuclei (LGNs)**, one in each cerebral hemisphere. These act as relay stations on the way from the retina to the cortex (see Figure 3.1). **Figure 3.13** shows that the LGN of primates is a six-layered structure, a bit like a stack of pancakes that has been bent in the middle (*geniculate* means "bent"). The neurons in the bottom two layers are physically larger than those in the top four layers; for this reason, the bottom two are called **magnocellular layers**, and the top four are called **parvocellular layers** (*magno-* and *parvo-* are Latin for "large" and "small," respectively). The two types of layers also differ in another, more important, way: the magnocellular layers receive input from M ganglion cells in the retina, and the parvocellular layers receive input from P ganglion cells. The layers differ in more than the size of the cells. Studies in which magnocellular and parvocellular layers are chemically lesioned indicate that the magnocellular pathway responds to large, fast-moving objects, and the parvocellular pathway is responsible for processing details of stationary targets. This distinction is interesting because it shows that the visual system splits input from the image into different types of information.

Even more splitting takes place *between* the layers. There we find the layers consisting of **koniocellular cells** (*konio-* is Greek for "dust"; these little cells were ignored for many years). The koniocellular layers are in the spaces between the magno and parvo layers, which are clearly labeled in Figure 3.13 (Casagrande et al., 2007; Nassi and Callaway, 2009; Szmajda, Grünert, and Martin, 2008). Each koniocellular layer seems to be involved in a different aspect of processing. For example, one layer is specialized for relaying signals from the S-cones and may be part of a "primordial" blue-yellow pathway (Hendry and Reid, 2000).

The organization of the retinal inputs to the LGNs, diagrammed in **Figure 3.14**, provides some important insights into how our visual world is mapped to the brain. First, the left LGN receives projections from the left side of the retina in both eyes, and the right LGN receives projections from the right side of both retinas. Second, each layer of the LGN receives input from one or the other eye. From bottom to top, layers 1, 4, and 6 of the right LGN receive input from the left (**contralateral**) eye, while layers 2, 3, and 5 get their input from the right (**ipsilateral**) eye.

FURTHER DISCUSSION of koniocellular cells can be found in Chapter 2 on page 53.

Each LGN layer contains a highly organized map of a complete half of the visual field. Figure 3.14 shows schematically how objects in the right visual field (objects to the right of where our gaze is fixated) are mapped onto the different

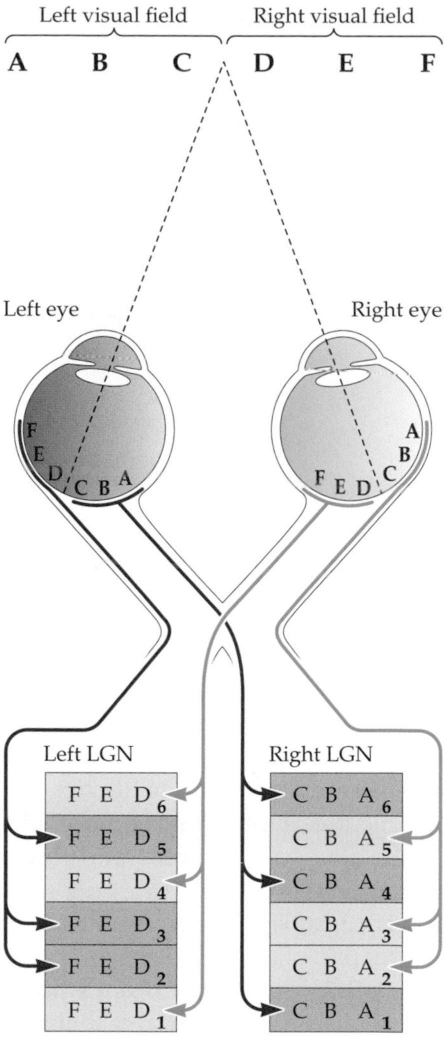

Left visual field   Right visual field

A   B   C   D   E   F

Left eye   Right eye

Left LGN   Right LGN

F E D 6   C B A 6
F E D 5   C B A 5
F E D 4   C B A 4
F E D 3   C B A 3
F E D 2   C B A 2
F E D 1   C B A 1

Figure 3.14   Input (in this case the letters *ABCDEF*) from the right visual field is mapped in an orderly fashion onto the different layers of the left LGN, and input from the left visual field is mapped to the right LGN. Information from the two eyes is segregated into separate layers. Layers 1 and 2 are the magnocellular layers; layers 3–6 are the parvocellular layers.

layers of the left LGN (the right side of the world falls on the left side of the retina, whose ganglion cells project to the left LGN). This ordered mapping of the world onto the visual nervous system, known as **topographical mapping**, provides us with a neural basis for knowing where things are in space (we will return to this point a little later).

LGN neurons have concentric receptive fields that are very similar to those of retinal ganglion cells: they respond well to spots and gratings. Given that the LGN cells respond to the same patterns as the ganglion cells that provide their input, you might wonder why the visual system bothers with the LGN. Why don't the ganglion cell axons simply travel directly back to the cerebral cortex? One important reason is that the LGN is not merely a stop on the line from retina to cortex. There are many connections between other parts of the brain and the LGN (Babadi et al., 2010; Dubin and Cleland, 1977). Moreover, there are more feedback connections from the visual cortex to the LGN than feed-forward connections from the LGN to the cortex.

It seems that the LGN is a location where various parts of the brain can modulate input from the eyes. For example, the LGN is part of a larger brain structure called the thalamus (the medial geniculate nucleus, part of the auditory pathway, is another portion of the thalamus; see Chapter 9). When you go to sleep, the entire thalamus is inhibited by circuitry elsewhere in the brain that works to keep you asleep. Thus, even if your eyelids were open while you were sleeping at night, you would not see anything in your dimly lit room. Input would travel from your retinas to your LGNs, but the neural signals would stop there before reaching the cortex, so they would never be registered. The thalamic inhibition is not complete, which is why loud noises (e.g., the alarm clock) or bright lights will be perceived, causing you to wake up.

topographical mapping   The orderly mapping of the world in the lateral geniculate nucleus and the visual cortex.

The Striate Cortex

If you place one hand at the back of your head, about an inch or two above the top of your neck, you should be able to feel a small bump known as the inion. The receiving area for LGN inputs in the cerebral cortex lies below the inion.

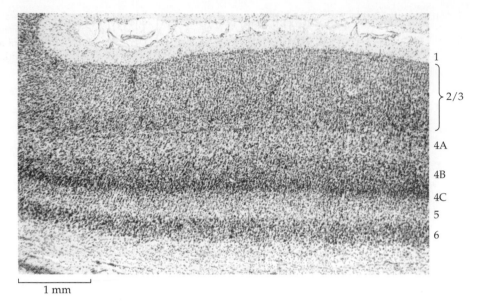

1 mm

Figure 3.15 Striate cortex. Note that like the LGN, striate cortex consists of six distinct layers. (From Hubel, 1988.)

This area has several names: **primary visual cortex (V1)**, **area 17**, or **striate cortex** (*striate* means "striped," for the striped pattern V1 develops following a certain type of staining procedure). By now you're probably getting the idea that layers are an important property of neural structures in the visual pathway. The striate cortex consists of six major layers, some of which have sublayers (**Figure 3.15**). Fibers from the LGN project mainly (but not exclusively) to layer 4, with magnocellular axons coming in to the upper part of layer 4C (known as 4Cα) and parvocellular axons projecting to the lower part of layer 4C (known as 4Cβ) (Yabuta and Callaway, 1998). (See **Web Essay 3.2: The Whole Brain Atlas**.)

Like the LGN, the striate cortex has a systematic topographical mapping of the visual field. But the striate cortex is not simply a bigger version of the LGN. A major and complex transformation of visual information takes place in the striate cortex. For starters, striate cortex contains on the order of 200 million cells—more than 100 times as many as the LGN has! This massive expansion of the number of neurons in V1 may be important for representing our complex natural visual world (Olshausen and Field, 1996; Olshausen SPIE, 2013).

Figure 3.16 illustrates two important features of the visual cortex: topography and magnification. First, the fact that the image of the woman's right eyebrow (*her* right; it appears on the left in Figure 3.16) is mapped onto regions corresponding to the numbers 3 and 4 in the striate cortex tells the visual system that the eyebrow must be in positions 3 and 4 of the visual field. This is topographical mapping. Second, information is dramatically scaled from different parts of the visual field. In Figure 3.16, the fovea is represented by number 5 on the retina. Objects imaged on or near the fovea are processed by neurons in a large part of the striate cortex, but objects imaged in the far right or left periphery are allocated only a tiny portion of the striate cortex. This distortion of the visual-field map on the cortex is known as **cortical magnification** because the cortical representation of the fovea is greatly magnified compared with the cortical representation of peripheral vision. (See **Web Essay 3.3: Seeing Images on the Cortex**.)

To gain a sense of the extent of this cortical magnification factor, hold your two arms out in front of you, put up your index fingers, hold them about 10 cm

primary visual cortex (V1), area 17, or striate cortex The area of the cerebral cortex of the brain that receives direct inputs from the lateral geniculate nucleus, as well as feedback from other brain areas.

cortical magnification The amount of cortical area (usually specified in millimeters) devoted to a specific region (e.g., 1 degree) in the visual field.

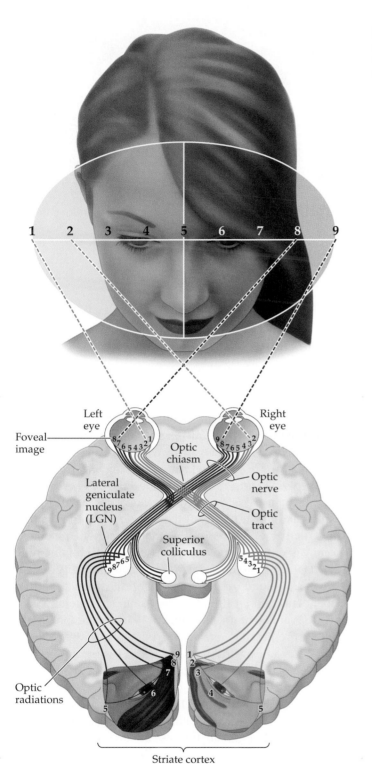

Figure 3.16 The mapping of objects in space onto the visual cortex. This figure illustrates both the topographical mapping and the dramatic magnification of the foveal representation in the cortex. (After Frisby, 1980.)

(4 inches) apart, close your left eye, and fixate your right finger. In this position, your right fingernail, which is taking up about 1 degree of visual angle on the fovea, is being processed by neurons in about 20 millimeters (mm) of striate cortex. Your left fingernail, which is covering the same amount of visual angle but is falling 10 degrees to the left of the fovea, is being processed by only 1.5 mm of cortex.

(A)

(B)

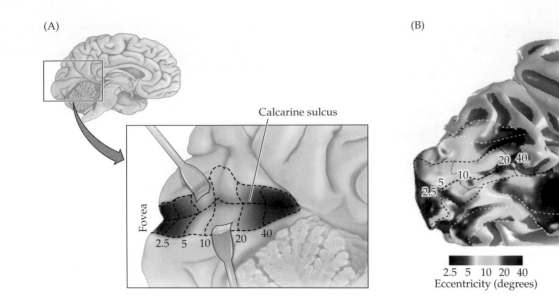

Calcarine sulcus

Fovea

2.5 5 10   20   40

20 40

10

5

2.5

2.5 5 10 20 40
Eccentricity (degrees)

1 cm

Figure 3.17 Mapping the visual field onto the cortex, as deduced from studying lesions (A) and from functional MRI (B). Different parts of the visual field are mapped onto the cortex according to the color code provided. The red area is just the central few degrees, whereas the blue areas cover substantially more of the peripheral field, from 20 to 40 degrees. (A after Horton and Hoyt, 1991; B from Wandell and Winawer, 2011.)

The Topography of the Human Cortex

Much of what we know about cortical topography and magnification comes from anatomical and physiological studies in animals. The earliest studies in humans were based on correlating visual-field defects with cortical lesions. That is, someone with damage to this part of visual cortex would be blind in that part of the visual field. **Figure 3.17A** illustrates how eccentricity (distance from the fovea) maps onto visual cortex, as deduced from studying lesions. However, in the last 20 years or so there have been major advances in our knowledge of human visual cortex—in large part through developments in brain-imaging techniques. If you've ever injured your knee or back, you may be familiar with magnetic resonance imaging (MRI). MRI is very useful for anatomical imaging of soft tissues, including the brain.

MRI lets us see the structure of the brain. *Functional* magnetic resonance imaging (fMRI) is a noninvasive technique for measuring and localizing brain activity. As discussed in Chapter 1, fMRI does not measure neural activity directly. Rather, it measures changes in blood oxygen level that reflect neural activity. Blood oxygen level–dependent (BOLD) signals reflect a range of metabolically demanding neural signals (Wandell and Winawer, 2011). If you compare blood flow when visual stimuli are presented in one portion of the visual field to blood flow when the field is blank, you can find portions of the brain that respond specifically to that stimulation of that portion of the field. In this way it is possible to map the topography of V1 in the living human brain (**Figure 3.17B**). Different parts of the visual field are mapped onto Figure 3.17 with a color code. Notice that the red area is just the central few degrees. The blue areas cover vast parts of the more peripheral field, from 20 to 40 degrees. Because of cortical magnification of the central field, these red and blue regions are similar in size. In Chapter 4, we will see that fMRI can be used to localize other visual functions in striate cortex and beyond, in "extrastriate" cortex, the cortex surrounding striate cortex. Recent advances in fMRI make it possible to reconstruct the visual images viewed by humans (Miyawaki et al., 2008; Nishimoto et al., 2011) (**Figure 3.18**). In the future, we may be able to use fMRI to tell what you are thinking. Stay tuned!

FURTHER DISCUSSION of the use of fMRI to reconstruct visual images can be found in Chapter 4 on page 126.

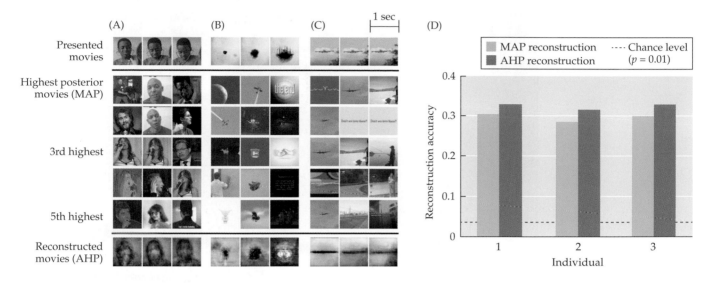

Figure 3.18 Using fMRI to reconstruct images from the brain elicited by natural movies. (A) Top row: three frames from a movie. Row 2: the maximum a posteriori (MAP) reconstruction. Rows 3–6: frames from the clips with the highest posterior probability. Row 7: the averaged high posterior (AHP) reconstruction. (B, C) Additional examples. (D) Reconstruction accuracy for the three individuals. (From Nishimoto et al., 2011.)

Some Perceptual Consequences of Cortical Magnification

One important consequence of cortical magnification is that visual acuity declines in an orderly fashion with eccentricity (Levi, Klein, and Aitsebaomo, 1985)—a phenomenon demonstrated by Hermann Rudolf Aubert well over a century ago (Aubert, 1886). **Web Activity 3.2: Foveal Acuity** allows you to demonstrate this phenomenon yourself, as does **Figure 3.19**, in which the letters are scaled in size such that each one covers an approximately equal cortical area.

Why is the foveal representation in the cortex so highly magnified? The visual system must make a trade-off. High resolution requires a great number of resources: a dense array of photoreceptors, one-to-one lines from photoreceptors to retinal ganglion cells, and a large chunk of striate cortex (not to mention the real estate in other areas of cortex necessary to do something with the visual information coming out of V1). To see the entire visual field with such high resolution, we might need eyes and brains too large to fit in our heads! Thus, we have evolved a visual system that provides high resolution in the center and lower resolution in the periphery. If you need to process the details of an object in the corner of your eye, you can simply turn your eye or head so that the object falls on the fovea instead (see Chapter 8 for a discussion of eye movements).

Figure 3.19 A letter chart in which the letter size increases with eccentricity in proportion to the inverse cortical magnification factor. If you fixate your gaze on the far left side of the figure, all seven letters should be equally easy to see because those on the right, which are in the periphery, are so much larger.

Figure 3.20 Visual crowding. (A) Visual crowding occurs in natural scenes. When fixating the bull's-eye near the construction zone, note that it is difficult or impossible to recognize that there is a child on the left-hand side of the road, simply because of the presence of the nearby signs. However, it is relatively easy to recognize the child on the right-hand side. (B) While fixating each cross, it is easy to identify the shape (left cross), line orientation (middle cross), or letter (right cross) above it, but it is difficult or impossible to identify the same shape, line orientation, or letter when it is in the middle of a group below the cross. However, it is easy to do when looking at the patterns directly. Crowding in peripheral vision impairs the ability to recognize objects, but it does not make them disappear. (From Whitney and Levi, 2011.)

Interestingly, although visual acuity falls off rapidly in the visual periphery, it is not the major obstacle to reading or object recognition. The real problem in the periphery is known as **visual crowding**. Visual crowding refers to the deleterious effect of clutter on peripheral object recognition (Levi, 2008; Whitney and Levi, 2011). Objects that can be easily identified in isolation seem indistinct and jumbled when surrounded by other objects (**Figure 3.20**).

Crowding is an essential bottleneck, setting limits on object perception, eye and hand movements, visual search, reading, and perhaps other functions in peripheral vision. Crowding impairs not only the discrimination of object features and contours but the ability to recognize and respond appropriately to objects in clutter. Interestingly, crowded objects don't simply disappear. Rather, crowded objects appear "jumbled" (the target and neighboring objects are combined into a single texture or object). Thus, crowding may be a process that simplifies the appearance of the peripheral array by promoting consistent appearance among adjacent objects, at the expense of an ability to pick out individual objects. Luckily, we are able to make eye movements in order to foveate and scrutinize individual objects in clutter.

Receptive Fields in Striate Cortex

In 1958, David Hubel and Torsten Wiesel began work as postdoctoral students in Stephen Kuffler's laboratory. Their goal was to extend Kuffler's groundbreaking work on retinal ganglion cells and to apply it to the cortex. So they began trying to map the receptive fields of neurons in striate cortex of cats, using spots of light, much as Kuffler (1953) had done earlier (see Chapter 2). Recall that the receptive field of a neuron is the region in space in which the presence of a

visual crowding The deleterious effect of clutter on peripheral object recognition.

stimulus alters the neuron's firing rate (see Chapter 2). To Hubel and Wiesel's dismay, they found that a cat's cortical cells hardly responded at all to the same spots that made its ganglion cells fire like crazy. To project their stimuli onto the retina, Hubel and Wiesel inserted a glass slide with a black spot into a slot in a special ophthalmoscope (that's the instrument the doctor uses when she shines a bright light into your eye in order to see your retina). One day, they had been recording from a neuron without much luck, when suddenly the cell emitted a strong burst of firing as they inserted the glass slide into the slot. Eventually they realized that the response had nothing to do with the spot itself; instead, the cell had been responding to the shadow cast by the edge of the glass slide as it swept across the ophthalmoscope's light path. And the rest, as they say, is history. Hubel related this story when he and Wiesel received the 1981 Nobel Prize in Physiology or Medicine for uncovering many of the remarkable properties of the visual cortex (**Figure 3.21A**).

Hubel and Wiesel's most fundamental discovery was that the receptive fields of striate cortex neurons are not circular, as they are in the retina and LGN. Rather, they are elongated. As a result, they respond much more vigorously to bars, lines, edges, and gratings than to round spots of light.

Orientation Selectivity

Further investigation by Hubel and Wiesel (1962) uncovered a number of other important properties of the receptive fields of neurons in striate cortex. First, an individual neuron will not respond equivalently to just any old stripe in its receptive field. It responds best when the line or edge is at just the right orientation, and hardly at all when the line is tilted more than 30 degrees away from the optimal orientation (a change equivalent to movement of the minute hand of a clock from 12 to 1). Scientists call this selective responsiveness **orientation tuning**: the cell is tuned to detect lines in a specific orientation.

A typical orientation tuning function looks like the plot in **Figure 3.21B**. The neuron featured here fires vigorously when the line is oriented vertically, but the response tapers off rapidly as the line is tilted one way or another, diminishing to close to the cell's resting rate when the line is tilted about 30 degrees in either direction. Other cells in striate cortex are selective for horizontal lines and lines at 45 degrees, 20 degrees, 62 degrees, and so on, so the population of neurons as a whole detects all possible orientations. However, more cells are responsive to horizontal and vertical orientations than to obliques (De Valois, Yund, and Hepler, 1982; B. Li, Peterson, and Freeman, 2003). This physiological finding meshes well with the psychophysical finding that humans have somewhat lower visual acuity and contrast sensitivity for oblique targets than for horizontal and vertical targets.

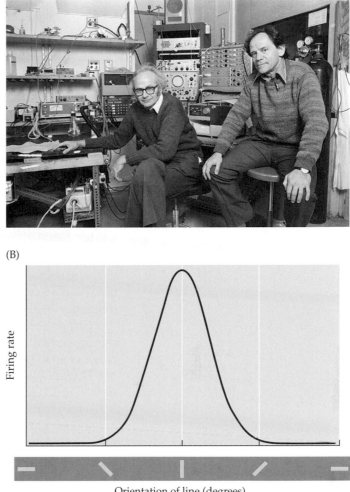

(A)

(B)

Firing rate

Orientation of line (degrees)

Figure 3.21 Hubel and Wiesel, shown here in their lab (A), received the Nobel Prize for their discoveries that furthered understanding of information processing in the visual system. (B) Orientation tuning function of a cortical cell. The neuron fires vigorously when the line is oriented vertically, but it fires hardly at all when the line orientation is changed by 30 degrees. While this example is for a cell tuned to vertical lines, other cells are tuned to different orientations.

orientation tuning The tendency of neurons in striate cortex to respond optimally to certain orientations and less to others.

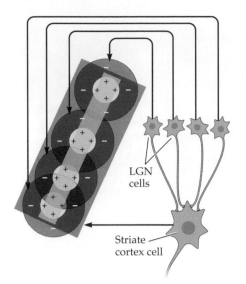

LGN cells

Striate cortex cell

Figure 3.22 Hubel and Wiesel's model of how striate cortex cells get their orientation tuning: they hypothesized that LGN cells were lined up in a row, feeding into the elongated arrangement of the striate cortex receptive fields (left).

How are the circular receptive fields in the LGN transformed into the elongated receptive fields in striate cortex? Hubel and Wiesel suggested a very simple scheme to explain this transformation (**Figure 3.22**). Simply put, their idea was that the concentric LGN cells that feed into a cortical cell are all in a row. Later studies (e.g., J. S. Anderson et al., 2000) have shown that the arrangement of LGN inputs is indeed crucial for establishing the orientation selectivity of striate cortex cells. However, other evidence suggests that neural interactions (e.g., lateral inhibition; see Chapter 2) within the cortex also play an important role in the dynamics of orientation tuning (Pugh et al., 2000).

Other Receptive-Field Properties

Cortical cells respond not just to bars, lines, and edges. Like retinal ganglion cells, they also respond well to gratings (which are, after all, collections of lines). And like ganglion cells, they respond best to gratings that have just the right spatial frequency to fill the receptive-field center. That is, each striate cortex cell is tuned to a particular spatial frequency, which corresponds to a particular line width. Indeed, cortical cells are much more narrowly tuned (they respond to a smaller range of spatial frequencies) than retinal ganglion cells (De Valois, Albrecht, and Thorell, 1982). These narrow tuning functions mean that each striate cortex neuron functions as a filter for the portion of the image that excites the cell. We will return to the idea of striate cortex as a collection of filters later in the chapter.

Another important discovery made by Hubel and Wiesel was that many cortical cells respond especially well to *moving* lines, bars, edges, and gratings. Moreover, many neurons respond strongly when a line moves in one direction—say, from left to right—but not at all when the same line moves, say, from right to left.

As noted earlier, information from the two eyes is kept separate in the LGN: each LGN cell responds to one eye or the other, but never to both eyes. This arrangement changes dramatically in striate cortex, where a majority of cells can be influenced by input from both the left eye and the right eye. In other words, if a striate cortex neuron responds best to a 5-cycle/degree grating oriented at 45 degrees, it will respond to such a stimulus whether that stimulus is presented in the right eye or the left eye. However, striate cortex neurons often have a preference, responding somewhat more strongly when a stimulus is presented in one eye than when it is presented in the other. Hubel and Wiesel called this property of striate receptive fields **ocular dominance**.

Given that we see a single, unified world, intuitively it makes sense that information from the two eyes should be brought together at some point. Until Hubel and Wiesel's discovery, however, there were heated arguments about whether the information converged at all and, if so, whether it was in a specialized "fusion center" in the brain—a notion that dates back to Descartes (1664) (see Howard and Rogers, 2001). We'll describe some of these issues in Chapter 6, when we discuss binocular vision.

Simple and Complex Cells

Like precortical neurons, cortical neurons come in a wide variety of types. Hubel and Wiesel characterized some neurons as **simple cells**. Simple cells are cortical neurons whose receptive fields have clearly defined excitatory and inhibitory regions.

ocular dominance The property of the receptive fields of striate cortex neurons by which they demonstrate a preference, responding somewhat more rapidly when a stimulus is presented in one eye than when it is presented in the other.

simple cell A cortical neuron whose receptive field has clearly defined excitatory and inhibitory regions.

Figure 3.23 shows two varieties of simple-cell receptive fields and their preferred stimuli. An edge detector (Figure 3.23A) is most highly excited when there is light on one side of its receptive field and darkness on the other side. A stripe detector (Figure 3.23B) responds best to a line of light that has a particular width, surrounded on both sides by darkness. If a grating with the appropriate spatial frequency drifts across the receptive field of this cell, the cell's response will be modulated as dark and bright bars drift across the receptive-field center, in exactly the same way the response of the retinal ganglion cell shown in Figure 3.12 is modulated.

Other neurons show responses that cannot be simply predicted from their responses to stationary bars of light. Hubel and Wiesel called these **complex cells**. Complex cells are cortical neurons whose receptive fields do not have clearly defined excitatory and inhibitory regions. Like simple cells, each complex cell is tuned to a particular orientation and spatial frequency and shows an ocular preference. However, whereas a simple cell might respond only if a stripe is presented in the center of its receptive field, a complex cell will respond regardless of where the stripe is presented, as long as it is somewhere within the cell's receptive field (**Figure 3.24**). Another way of stating this difference is to say that simple cells are "phase-sensitive," and complex cells are "phase-insensitive." When tested with a drifting grating, the complex cell gives a robust response, with little or none of the modulation shown by simple cells (as well as retinal ganglion and LGN cells).

As with all other neurons in the visual system, with the exception of retinal photoreceptors, the receptive fields of complex cells represent a pooling of the responses of several subunits. The subunits give the complex cell its spatial frequency and orientation tuning, but the complex pooling operation makes the complex cell insensitive to the precise position of the stimulus within its receptive field. Hubel and Wiesel hypothesized a hierarchy in which LGN cells fed into simple cells, which in turn provided excitatory inputs to complex cells. However, substantial evidence now suggests that complex cells represent a separate parallel pathway (that is, that both simple and complex cells get direct input from LGN neurons).

Further Complications

Hubel and Wiesel described another property of some cells in striate cortex that they called **end stopping**. When they tested an end-stopped cell with bars of increasing lengths, the response rate first increased as the bar filled up the cell's receptive field, and then decreased markedly as the bar was lengthened further

(A) Edge detector

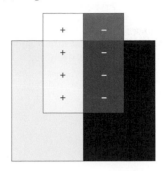

(B) Stripe detector

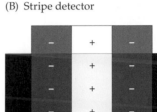

Figure 3.23 Two flavors of simple cells: (A) an edge detector and (B) a stripe detector.

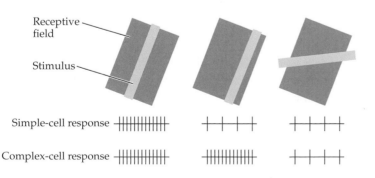

Figure 3.24 A simple cell and a complex cell might both be tuned to the same orientation and stripe width (spatial frequency), but the complex cell will respond to that stripe presented anywhere within its receptive field, whereas the simple cell might respond to the stripe in only one position.

complex cell A cortical neuron whose receptive field does not have clearly defined excitatory and inhibitory regions.

end stopping The process by which a cell in the cortex increases its firing rate as the length of a bar increases until the bar fills up its receptive field, and then it decreases its firing rate as the bar is lengthened further.

Figure 3.25 When the stimulus (bar) does not reach the outside edge of the receptive field or it extends beyond the receptive field of an end-stopped cortical neuron, the neuron fires less than when the stimulus is just the right length.

(**Figure 3.25**). Hubel and Wiesel called these cells "hypercomplex" cells, although they now appear to be subclasses of the simple and complex cells already discussed here (that is, there are simple end-stopped cells and complex end-stopped cells). End stopping is thought to play an important role in our ability to detect luminance boundaries and discontinuities.

Research has revealed additional idiosyncrasies in the receptive fields of striate cortex neurons. For example, the size of a particular cell's receptive field appears to vary with target contrast; for instance, the cell might respond to a smaller portion of the visual field when the grating stimulus has a high contrast than it will when the difference between light and dark bars is more subtle (Sceniak et al., 1999). And neurons can be influenced by stimuli that fall outside the classic receptive field, via short- or long-range lateral connections and/or via feedback from neurons in other layers (Zipser, Lamme, and Schiller, 1996).

As is the case for most of the visual system, what we don't know about the workings of striate cortex neurons almost certainly dwarfs what we do know. But to review what we do know, spend some time with **Web Activity 3.4: Striate Receptive Fields**, where you can try your hand at determining the receptive field of an unknown virtual neuron.

Columns and Hypercolumns

As we've discussed, each of the approximately 200 million neurons in striate cortex responds to a distinctive set of stimulus properties: stripes, edges, and/or gratings that are oriented at a particular angle, with a particular width or spatial frequency, possibly moving in a particular direction. Some neurons are simple cells and some are complex cells, and each one is end-stopped or not. Most neurons also respond preferentially to stimuli presented in one eye or another. And each neuron responds only when its preferred stimulus is presented in one particular part of the visual field.

Hubel and Wiesel noticed very early on that these various receptive-field properties are not scattered haphazardly around striate cortex. Once they had figured out what the cells were looking for (stripes rather than spots), they discovered that if they pushed the recording electrode down through the layers of the cortex in a direction perpendicular to the cortical surface, all the cells they encountered showed similar orientation preferences. If they shifted the electrode position over a tiny distance and made another perpendicular penetration, all the cells then responded best to a slightly different orientation, perhaps 10 or 15 degrees from the original orientation. On the basis of these observations, Hubel and Wiesel concluded that neurons with similar orientation preferences are arranged in **columns** that extend vertically through the cortex.

When Hubel and Wiesel made tangential penetrations into striate cortex (inserting an electrode in a direction parallel to the cortical surface, rather than

column A vertical arrangement of neurons. Neurons within a single column tend to have similar receptive fields and similar orientation preferences.

(A) Orientation columns

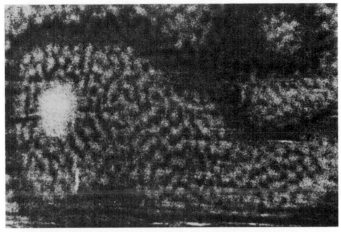

(B) Ocular dominance columns

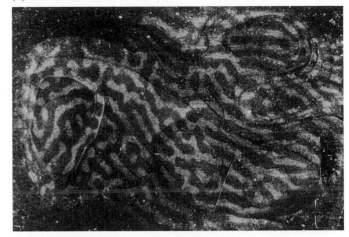

(C) Orientation maps

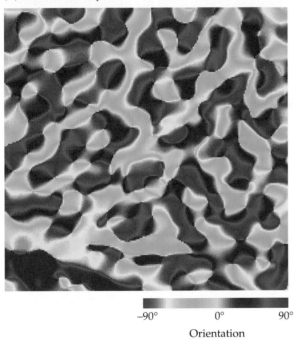

−90°   0°   90°
Orientation

Figure 3.26 Orientation (A) and ocular dominance (B) columns of the striate cortex, revealed by staining. (C) Optical imaging of the orientation maps in monkey cortex. (A, B from Hubel, Wiesel, and Stryker, 1978; C from Nauhaus et al., 2008.)

perpendicular), they found a systematic and progressive change in preferred orientation and encountered essentially all the orientations in a distance of about 0.5 mm. This finding has been confirmed via alternative physiological techniques. **Figure 3.26A** shows a small portion of a monkey's striate cortex prepared so that neurons responding to vertically oriented lines are stained black, while other neurons remain white. The distance between the vertical orientation columns revealed by this technique is, sure enough, just about 0.5 mm (LeVay, Hubel, and Wiesel, 1975).

Orientation is not the only property arranged in columns in the visual cortex. Neurons that share the same eye preference (exhibiting ocular dominance) also have a columnar arrangement (**Figure 3.26B**). Furthermore, single-cell recording experiments, as well as staining experiments, indicate that eye preference switches (you guessed it) every 0.5 mm or so.

hypercolumn A 1-millimeter block of striate cortex containing two sets of columns, each covering every possible orientation (0–180 degrees), with one set preferring input from the left eye and one set preferring input from the right eye.

Roughly 30 years ago, it became possible to make detailed maps of the orientation tuning of cells in the cortex, using optical imaging. **Figure 3.26C** shows an optical imaging study in which light reflected from the surface of the exposed brain reflects the activity of underlying neurons. In this figure, each color shows a set of neurons, activated by one orientation. You can see the complex, yet orderly organization of orientation tuning in the cortex (Blasdel and Salama, 1986). More recent work (Paik and Ringach, 2011) suggests that this beautiful arrangement arises during early development as a consequence of statistical wiring mechanisms combined with evenly spaced mosaics of ON- and OFF-center retinal ganglion cells.

Through their studies, Hubel and Wiesel arrived at the model of striate cortical architecture illustrated in **Figure 3.27**. They proposed that a 1-mm block of striate cortex contains "all the machinery necessary to look after everything the visual cortex is responsible for, in a certain small part of the visual world" (Hubel, 1982). Each of these sections of cortex is called a **hypercolumn**. It contains at least two sets of columns, each covering every possible orientation (0–180 degrees), with one set preferring input from the left eye and one set preferring input from the right eye.

Hypercolumns are roughly 1 mm across throughout the striate cortex, but because of the cortical magnification factor discussed earlier, not all hypercolumns see the world at the same level of detail. A hypercolumn in the part of the cortex that represents the fovea may "see" a portion of the visual field that is 0.05 degrees of visual angle across; a hypercolumn responding to input 10 degrees to the right of the fovea should cover about 14 times as large an area (0.7 degrees across).

Orientation and ocular dominance are probably not the only stimulus dimensions that have a systematic columnar arrangement in the visual cortex. For

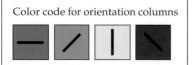

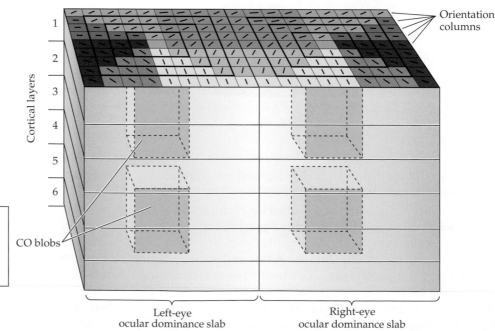

Figure 3.27 This model of a hypercolumn shows two ocular dominance columns (one for each eye) and many orientation columns, and it illustrates the locations of the cytochrome oxidase (CO) blobs. (From Breedlove and Watson, 2007.)

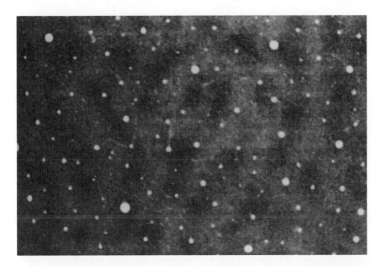

Figure 3.28 Cytochrome oxidase (CO) blobs. (From Hubel, 1988.)

example, another staining technique, which takes advantage of an enzyme called **cytochrome oxidase** (**CO**), has revealed a regular array of "CO blobs" (shown in section in **Figure 3.28**), spaced that magical distance of about 0.5 mm apart (see Figure 3.27). The functional role of these blobs remains unclear, but CO blob columns have been implicated in processing color, with the interblob regions (note the elegant scientific jargon that has developed around this field of study) processing motion and spatial structure (Livingstone and Hubel, 1988). This view is probably too simplistic, but the blob array does suggest some kind of additional organizational layer on top of the orientation and ocular dominance arrays.

> **FURTHER DISCUSSION** of CO blobs, which are also implicated in processing color, can be found in Chapter 5 on pages 154–155.

In sum, the current state of understanding is that striate cortex is concerned with analyzing the orientation, size, shape, speed, and direction of motion of objects in the world and that it does so using modular groups of neurons—hypercolumns—each of which receives input from and processes a small piece of the visual world. (You can explore these organizational principles interactively in **Web Activity 3.5: Hypercolumns**.) We can think of this arrangement as a big bank of filters. Combining information from multiple hypercolumns is presumably the job of other portions of cortex farther downstream in the visual system. We will consider some of these portions in Chapter 4, when we discuss the representation and recognition of whole objects.

Selective Adaptation: The Psychologist's Electrode

Most of the physiological research reported up to this point in the chapter was done using cats, monkeys, or other animals as subjects. Does the human visual system also include neurons selective for orientation, line width, direction of motion, and so on? The difficult thing about answering this question is that we can't normally poke electrodes into a human's brain (which is why Hubel, Wiesel, and their peers had to use cats and monkeys in the first place), so indirect methods of learning about brain function had to be devised. One such method is called **adaptation**, a technique that gives psychologists a noninvasive

cytochrome oxidase (CO)
An enzyme used to reveal the regular array of "CO blobs," which are spaced about 0.5 millimeter apart in the primary visual cortex.

adaptation A reduction in response caused by prior or continuing stimulation.

Figure 3.29 The psychologist's electrode. This schematic diagram shows how selective adaptation may alter the distribution of neural responses and therefore perception. See the text for details.

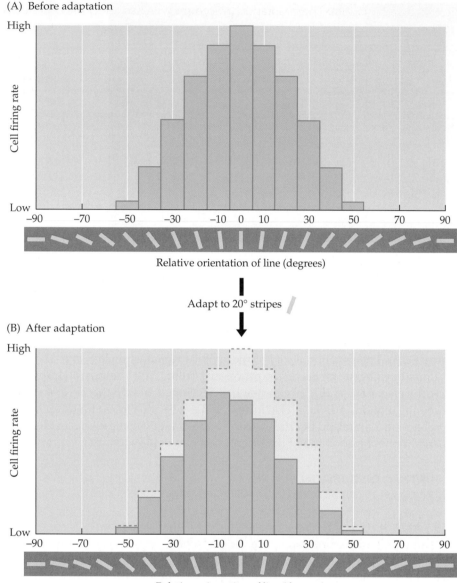

(A) Before adaptation

Cell firing rate

Relative orientation of line (degrees)

Adapt to 20° stripes

(B) After adaptation

Cell firing rate

Relative orientation of line (degrees)

"electrode" they can use to probe the human brain. Although often attributed to John Frisby (1980), the term "the psychologist's electrode" was actually coined by Sir Colin Blakemore in the 1970s.

Selective adaptation can provide insights into the properties of cortical neurons, as illustrated in **Figure 3.29**. The green bars in Figure 3.29A illustrate the normal firing rates of cells tuned to various orientations (0, 10, –10, 20,–20 degrees, and so on) relative to a vertical grating. By definition, gratings oriented at 0 degrees (vertical) elicit the strongest response from the 0-degree selective cells, followed closely by the 10-degree and –10-degree selective cells, followed by the 20-degree and –20-degree selective cells, and so on (see Figure 3.29A). Now suppose we expose the visual system that contains these cells to a 20-degree grating for an extended period of time. This adapting stimulus will cause the 20-degree selective cells to be most active, and the extended activity will fatigue these cells (that is, their maximum firing rate will be reduced for a short period following adaptation). The adaptation procedure will also affect the other cells to some extent: the 10-degree and 30-degree cells will be the next most fatigued, followed by the 0-degree and 40-degree cells, and so on.

Figure 3.29B shows what should happen when we present the vertical grating again after adaptation to the 20-degree grating, assuming that our orientation perception is really due to populations of orientation-selective cells like those that Hubel and Wiesel found in the cat cortex. As the darker green bars show, because the 0-degree cells have been fatigued more than the –10-degree cells, the –10-degree cells are now firing fastest. (The lighter-shaded bars indicate the amount of firing before adaptation, so the difference between the lighter and darker bars corresponds to the degree of fatigue for each type of cell.) As a result, we should perceive the vertical test stimulus as being oriented 10 degrees to the left. Thus adaptation results in both a decrease in firing rate and a change in the tuning curve.

You can test the validity of this technique yourself using the stimuli in **Figure 3.30**. Start by carefully fixating the black line between the two sets of tilted stripes in Figure 3.30A for a few seconds. This exercise will result in adaptation to left-tilted stripes in the upper visual field, and to right-tilted stripes in the lower field. Now, look quickly at the fixation point (black dot) between the two sets of vertical stripes in Figure 3.30B. Move back and forth a few times—looking at the adapting stimuli (Figure 3.30A) for a few seconds and quickly looking at the test stimuli (Figure 3.30B). You should notice that Figure 3.30A looks like a chevron pointing right and that Figure 3.30B has come to look like it points a little to the left. That is the **tilt aftereffect**, just as predicted by the model of the human visual system based on the cat research and diagrammed in Figure 3.29. The tilt aftereffect strongly supports the idea that the human visual system contains individual neurons selective for different orientations.

tilt aftereffect The perceptual illusion of tilt, produced by adaptation to a pattern of a given orientation.

(A)   (B)

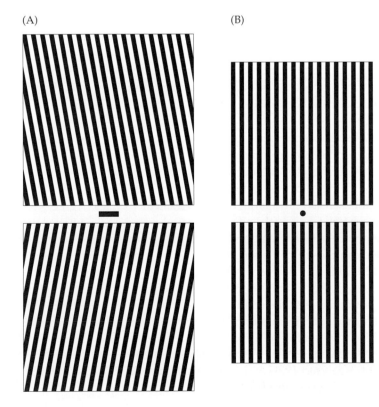

Figure 3.30 Stimuli for demonstrating selective adaptation. See the text for details. (After Frisby and Stone, 2010.)

(A)

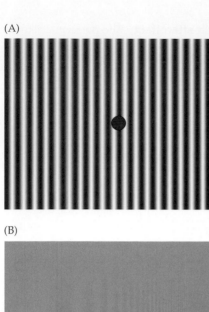

(B)

(C)

(D)

Figure 3.31 A demonstration of adaptation that is specific to spatial frequency. (A) The adapting grating. (B) A grating modulated in contrast (vertically) and spatial frequency (horizontally). This pattern lets you visualize your own contrast sensitivity function (CSF) (see also Figure 3.8). Before adaptation, your CSF should have the appearance of an inverted *U*. After adaptation to (A), your CSF should look something like the red curve in (C). The red curve illustrates the effect of adaptation. The notch indicates reduced contrast sensitivity for spatial frequencies that are close to the adapting spatial frequency. Adapting to the horizontal grating in (D) results in little or no reduction in sensitivity. (B, C courtesy of Izumi Ohzawa with credit to John Robson and Fergus W. Campbell.)

Selective adaptation also provides evidence that the human visual system contains neurons selective for spatial frequency. You can check this with the gratings shown in **Figure 3.31**. First, look at Figure 3.31B and make a mental note of your CSF (the inverted *U*–shaped area where the gratings fade into the gray background; see Figure 3.8). Next, adapt for about 10–20 seconds to the grating in Figure 3.31A, and then quickly shift your gaze back to Figure 3.31B and make a mental note of your CSF now. After you repeat this procedure a few times, the outline of your CSF in Figure 3.31B should look something like the red curve in Figure 3.31C. It should have a notch (indicating reduced contrast sensitivity for spatial frequencies that are close to the adapting spatial frequency in Figure 3.31A). This demonstration shows that adaptation to the high-contrast top panel is selective—resulting in a loss of sensitivity for spatial frequencies close to the adapting frequency but no loss for spatial frequencies that are much higher or lower than the adapting frequency. Note that adaptation to the bottom panel (Figure 3.31D) does not result in a similar notch, since spatial-frequency adaptation is orientation-selective. Thus, there is little or no effect on sensitivity to vertical gratings following adaptation to a horizontal grating.

As noted earlier, selective adaptation causes the neurons most sensitive to the adapting stimulus to become fatigued. In this demonstration, neurons sensitive to the spatial frequency of the adapting stimulus have their contrast sensitivity reduced. That is, higher contrast is needed after adaptation in order for a test grating to stimulate these neurons. Neurons responsive to much higher or much lower spatial frequencies are not fatigued by the adaptation procedure, so contrast sensitivity for these spatial frequencies is not affected.

Figure 3.32A shows more precisely how selective adaptation to a 7-cycle/degree grating produces a selective loss of contrast sensitivity at spatial frequencies of about 7 cycles/degree, with little or no loss at, for example, 1 cycle/degree or 15 cycles/degree. After adaptation, the CSF has a "notch," as if the detectors sensitive to spatial frequencies near 7 cycles/degree were selectively desensitized (luckily the effects of spatial-frequency adaptation are reversible!). From these measurements of contrast sensitivity before and after adaptation, we can construct the spatial-frequency tuning function shown in **Figure 3.32B**. This function represents the change in contrast threshold (contrast threshold after adaptation, divided by contrast threshold before adaptation) plotted against the spatial frequency of the test grating. This curve represents the spatial-frequency tuning function for a "channel" that is most sensitive to a grating of 7 cycles/degree. The shape and selectivity of this channel are very similar to the spatial-frequency tuning functions for striate cortex neurons of cats and monkeys. **Figure 3.32C** illustrates that the CSF (gray curve) represents the "upper envelope" of the sensitivities of

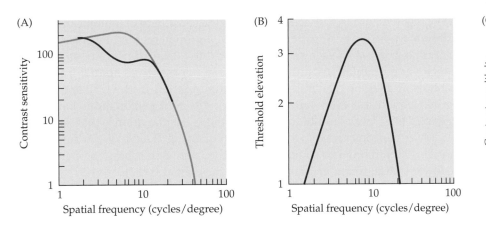
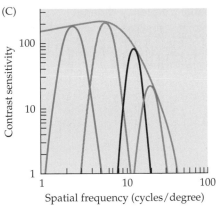

Figure 3.32   Spatial-frequency adaptation. (A) Selective adaptation to a 7-cycle/ degree grating produces a selective loss of contrast sensitivity at spatial frequencies of about 7 cycles/degree, leaving a notch (indicated by the red line) in the contrast sensitivity function (CSF, gray line). (B) Threshold elevation (the change in contrast threshold) following adaptation. (C) Physiologically measured spatial-frequency tuning functions for striate cortex neurons in monkeys (colored curves represent different neurons). The gray curve, the CSF, represents the "upper envelope" of the sensitivities of the underlying channels. (A, B after C. Blakemore and Campbell, 1969.)

many spatial-frequency channels, each tuned to a different spatial frequency. The key idea here is that you can see the pattern when at least one mechanism (channel) detects it.

The Site of Selective Adaptation Effects

The adaptation experiments replicated here provide strong evidence that orientation and spatial frequency are coded by neurons somewhere in the human visual system. In cats and monkeys, we know that these neurons are located in striate cortex, not in the retina or LGN. Can we localize the orientation-selective and spatial frequency–selective neurons in humans?

As it turns out, we can do just that with a clever variation on the adaptation experiments. Repeat the orientation (Figure 3.30) and spatial-frequency (Figure 3.31) adaptation demonstrations, but this time view the adapting stimuli with your left eye only (keep your right eye closed during the adaptation period), and then view the test stimuli with your right eye (close your left eye and open your right eye as you shift your gaze to the test stimuli). You should find that the tilt aftereffect and the decreased contrast sensitivity transfer from one eye to the other, although the effect may be somewhat less pronounced than when you did the demonstrations with both eyes open. This transfer of adaptation from the adapted to the nonadapted eye is known as interocular transfer (Blakemore and Campbell, 1969).

Now recall that information from the two eyes is kept completely separate in the retinas and in the two LGNs; no single neuron receives input from both eyes until the striate cortex. The transfer of adaptation effects from one eye to the other thus implies that selective adaptation occurs in cortical neurons, just as we would predict from animal physiology studies.

Spatial Frequency–Tuned Pattern Analyzers in Human Vision

Selective adaptation to spatial frequency, as well as other evidence, provides strong support for the notion, first suggested by Fergus Campbell and John Robson

spatial-frequency channel A pattern analyzer, implemented by an ensemble of cortical neurons, in which each set of neurons is tuned to a limited range of spatial frequencies.

(1968), that the human CSF actually reflects the sensitivity of multiple individual pattern analyzers. These pattern analyzers are implemented by ensembles of cortical neurons, with each set of cells tuned to a limited range of spatial frequencies and orientations, and they are often referred to as **spatial-frequency channels**. Remember the initially unexplained falloff in the CSF at very low spatial frequencies? Although a number of different explanations have been suggested (e.g., lateral inhibition), the most likely explanation is that we simply have fewer neurons tuned to low spatial frequencies (De Valois, Albrecht, and Thorell, 1982) in order to compensate for the over-representation of energy in the lower spatial frequencies in natural scenes (Field, 1987).

The multiple-spatial-frequency model of vision implies that spatial frequencies that stimulate different pattern analyzers will be detected independently, even if the different frequencies are combined in the same image. Consider the compound grating pattern in **Figure 3.33**, made by adding a sine wave with frequency f to a sine wave with frequency $3f$. Graham and Nachmias (1971) found that the contrast sensitivity for this compound pattern was almost the same as the contrast sensitivity for detecting the individual components of the pattern separately. If the two component sine waves had stimulated a common pattern analyzer, then their effects on the analyzer should have been added, so contrast sensitivity should have been greatly improved. This may sound a bit like the Fourier analysis idea discussed early in this chapter. However, it's now pretty clear that the visual system doesn't carry out an actual Fourier analysis, analyzing the world into very narrow bands of spatial frequencies. Rather, it filters the image into spatially localized receptive fields that have a limited range of spatial frequencies. (Something like a Fourier analysis may be important in quickly appreciating the gist of a scene; see Chapter 7.)

Why would the visual system use spatial-frequency filters to analyze images? One important reason may be that different spatial frequencies emphasize different types of information. **Figure 3.34B** and **C** show only high-frequency or low-frequency components, respectively, of the face in **Figure 3.34A**. These images show that low frequencies (Figure 3.34C) emphasize the broad outlines of the face, and high frequencies (Figure 3.34B) carry information about fine details. If we want to know how many people are in a scene, it is most efficient to consult our low-frequency channels. But if we want to know about the fine details—for example, whether the people are frowning or smiling—we must rely on our high-frequency channels.

Note that high spatial frequencies can mask low spatial frequencies. You can experience this for yourself in **Figure 3.35**, where the high spatial frequencies introduced by the small blocks mask the low spatial

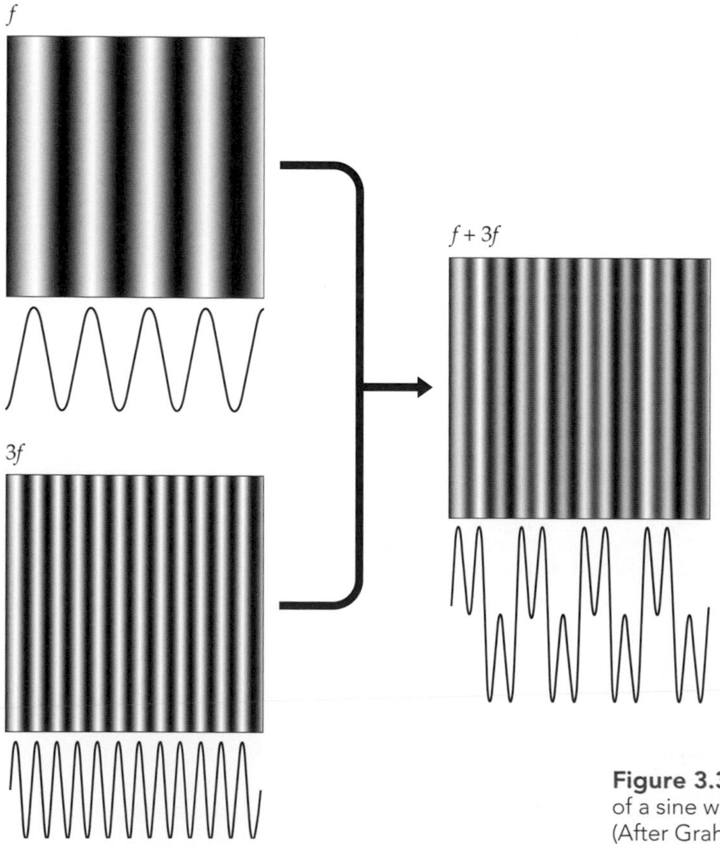

Figure 3.33 A compound grating pattern (right), made by the addition of a sine wave of frequency f (top left) to one of frequency $3f$ (bottom left). (After Graham and Nachmias, 1971.)

(A) (B) (C)

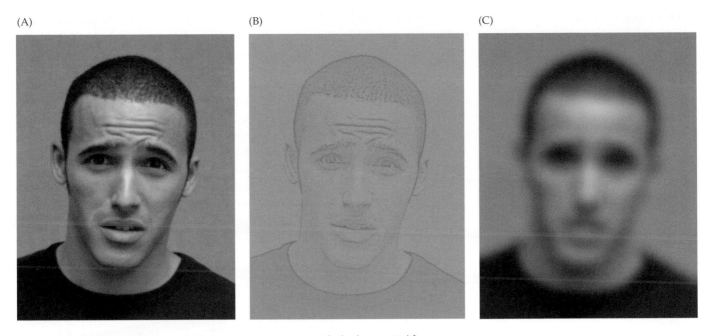

Figure 3.34 A complete image (A) and reconstructions: with the low spatial frequencies removed, leaving only the high-frequency components of that image (B), and with the high spatial frequencies removed, leaving only the low-frequency components of that image (C). For another example, see Figure 1.18.

frequencies that convey an underlying portrait of a famous American. Squinting your eyes will blur the blocks, minimizing the effect of the mask to a point where the face you've seen countless times on the 5-dollar bill will probably show through.

Figure 3.35 Who is hidden behind the high-spatial-frequency mask in this image? (From Harmon and Julesz, 1973.)

The Development of Vision

William James (1890) described the infant's world as "a blooming, buzzing confusion." However, studies over the past several decades have shown that the visual system is much more developed at birth than we used to think. One of the difficulties in assessing vision in infants is that we can't simply ask them what they see. Rather, we have to think of tricky ways to coax that information from them. The most widely used method for studying infant vision is based on an observation that Robert Fantz made in the early 1960s. What Fantz noticed is that if infants are shown two scenes, they invariably stare at the more complex scene (the scene with the most contours). So, if an infant is shown two patches, one containing stripes and the other uniform gray, the infant will prefer to look at the stripes. Of course, an infant who couldn't see the stripes would be equally likely to stare at the gray patch as at the striped patch. Thus, preferential looking is one important method used by infant researchers (grown psychologists studying infant vision, not babies in lab coats) to learn what infants can see and respond to behaviorally (**Figure 3.36A**).

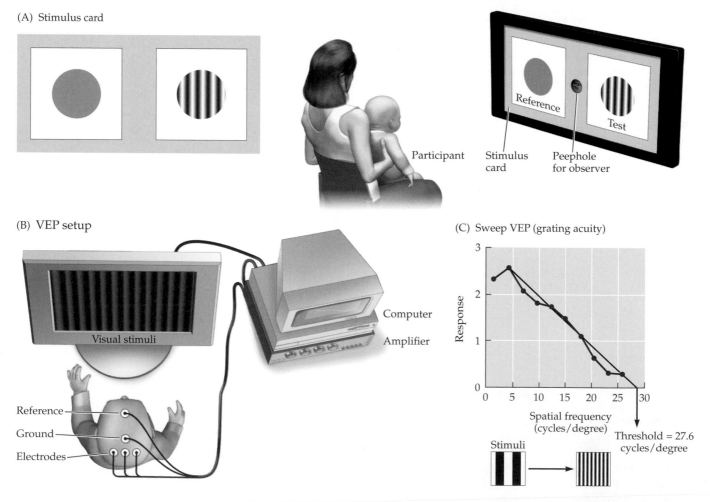

Figure 3.36 Assessing vision in infants. (A) Forced-choice preferential-looking stimuli (left) and the experimental setup (right). (B) Visually evoked electrical potential (VEP) setup. (C) Results of a sweep VEP experiment in which the spatial frequency of the stimulus is swept (continuously varied from low to high spatial frequency), illustrating the extrapolated acuity (threshold—in this case, 27.6 cycles/degree). This particular experiment was done at 80% contrast. (C after Norcia, Tyler, and Hamer, 1990.)

The success of preferential looking depends on the willingness of babies to stare at stimuli near threshold level. An alternative approach, used with considerable success in more recent years, is to measure visually evoked electrical potentials (VEPs)—that is, electrical signals from the brain that are evoked by visual stimuli—by attaching electrodes to the scalp and measuring the changes in electrical activity that are elicited by the changing visual stimulus (**Figure 3.36B, C**). Using this technique, we can measure an entire contrast sensitivity function in as little as 10 seconds in a nonverbal infant.

These techniques have provided a great deal of insight into the development of visual mechanisms and sensitivities. One insight is that different visual functions may emerge at different times and may develop at different rates. Thus, for example, the rod system appears to be functional in early infancy (Powers et al., 1981; Werner, 1982; Teller and Bornstein 1986; Fulton, 1988; Brown, 1990). While rods and rhodopsin are functional early, postreceptoral mechanisms may mature later, since dark-adapted spatial summation areas of infants are considerably enlarged compared with those of adults (Hamer and Schneck, 1984). Many investigations of cone-mediated vision have focused on the development of mechanisms of color vision, visual acuity, and contrast sensitivity. It is now reasonably well established that by 2–3 months after birth, infants must have three functioning cone types. The question of when each of the three cone types functions normally is less clear. Infants less than 1 month old fail to make chromatic discriminations; however, what remains unclear is whether these failures reflect immature cones or postreceptoral mechanisms (Teller and Movshon, 1986; Teller and Bornstein, 1986) or lack of attention. Uniform field flicker sensitivity appears to be adult-like by 3 months of age (Regal, 1981), while acuity and contrast sensitivity for high spatial frequencies develops slowly and may not reach adult levels until several years of age (see below).

critical period A phase in the life span during which abnormal early experience can alter normal neuronal development.

■ Sensation & Perception in Everyday Life

The Girl Who Almost Couldn't See Stripes

Normal visual development requires normal visual experience. Abnormal early visual experience can have serious and often permanent consequences for seeing patterns, as illustrated by the story of a girl named Jane. Jane was born with a dense cataract (an opacity of the lens) in her left eye, which prevented clear patterns from forming on her left retina. In addition to causing form deprivation in the left eye, the cataract prevented Jane's two eyes from seeing the same images at the same time.

Studies in cats and monkeys dating back to Hubel and Wiesel in the early 1960s have shown that monocular form deprivation can cause massive changes in cortical physiology that result in a devastating and permanent loss of spatial vision (Wiesel, 1982). Hubel and Wiesel, and many other workers subsequently, demonstrated that there is

a **critical period** of early visual development when normal binocular visual stimulation is required for normal cortical development. In cats and monkeys this critical period covers the first 3–4 months of life; in humans it is extended to something on the order of the first 3–8 years. During the critical period, cortical neurons are still being wired up to their inputs from the two eyes. This is a period of neural plasticity, when abnormal visual experience can alter the normal neural wiring process. If one eye is not receiving normal stimulation, the neurons that should be destined to respond to that eye do not become properly connected. In fact, some evidence suggests that these neurons are actually co-opted by inputs from the other, normally functioning eye.

If cataracts are left untreated during the critical period, the misplaced cortical connections can

(Continued)

■ Sensation & Perception in Everyday Life *(continued)* ■

never be repaired. The result is often amblyopia (reduced visual acuity in one eye because of abnormal early visual experience—commonly known as lazy eye) and an inability to perceive stereopsis (a lack of binocular depth perception; see Chapter 6). Correcting the condition later in life will thus have little effect, because the information from the now-functioning eye can never be properly conveyed to or processed by the cortex.

Luckily for Jane, her pediatrician found the cataract early, and the cataractous lens was surgically replaced by an artificial lens when she was 3 months old. The visual acuity in Jane's left eye just after the replacement lens was inserted was 20/1200, about four times worse than the normal value for a 3-month-old. But when tested again 1 month later, acuity in her left eye had already begun to catch up with the acuity in her right eye. In fact, a study of 28 infants (Maurer et al., 1999) found significant acuity improvements only an hour after corrective measures had been taken.

Not all individuals with congenital cataracts are as lucky as Jane. For example, in much of the third world, because of poverty, children born with congenital cataracts (often in both eyes) go untreated and grow up essentially blind. According to the World Health Organization, India is home to the largest population of blind children in the world. Recently, Pawan Sinha and his collaborators initiated an undertaking (Project Prakash) to perform corrective cataract surgeries for free and to track how these "blind" children learn to see. These studies are providing important new insights into brain plasticity.

Congenital cataracts are not the only cause of amblyopia. Early in life, two other disorders— **strabismus** (in which one eye is turned so that it is receiving a view of the world from an abnormal angle) and **anisometropia** (in which the two eyes have very different refractive errors; e.g., one eye is farsighted and the other not)—may also cause amblyopia. These forms of amblyopia are typically less severe, and often they have a later onset than congenital cataracts. The standard clinical treatment for amblyopia, for over 250 years, has been to patch the good eye and "force" the amblyopic eye to work. This treatment is ordinarily performed only in young children (typically younger than 8 years). However, several recent studies suggest that there may be hope for recovery of vision in older children, and even in adults through "perceptual learning"—repeated practice of a demanding visual task (Levi and Li, 2009) or playing action video games (Li et al., 2011).

---

strabismus A misalignment of the two eyes such that a single object in space is imaged on the fovea of one eye and on a nonfoveal area of the other (turned) eye.

anisometropia A condition in which the two eyes have different refractive errors (e.g., one eye is farsighted and the other not).

Development of the Contrast Sensitivity Function

The emerging picture suggests that sensitivity to low spatial frequencies develops much more rapidly than sensitivity to high spatial frequencies. Thus, at low spatial frequencies, contrast sensitivity may reach nearly adult levels as early as about 9 weeks of age, whereas sensitivity at higher spatial frequencies continues to develop dramatically (**Figure 3.37**). There remains a substantial difference in the contrast sensitivity of adults and 33-week-olds at high spatial frequencies (Norcia, Tyler, and Hamer, 1990).

What limits the development of acuity and contrast sensitivity? The primary postnatal changes in the retina concern differentiation of the macular region (Boothe, Dobson, and Teller, 1985). After birth, foveal receptor density and cone outer segment length both increase, as foveal cones become thinner and more elongated. There is a dramatic migration of ganglion cells and inner nuclear layers from the foveal region as the foveal pit develops during the first 4 months of life, and not until about 4 years of age is the fovea fully adultlike (Yuodelis and Hendrickson, 1986).

From birth to beyond 4 years of age, cone density increases in the central region, because of both the migration of receptors and decreases in their dimensions. Both of these factors result in finer cone sampling (by decreasing the distance between neighboring cones). Alterations in cone spacing and the light-gathering

Figure 3.37 The development of contrast sensitivity. Note that the shape of the CSF is "lowpass" (that is, there is no drop in sensitivity at low spatial frequencies) because the gratings were temporally modulated. (After Norcia, Tyler, and Hamer, 1990.)

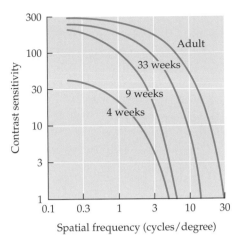

properties of the cones during early development probably contribute a great deal toward the improvements in acuity and contrast sensitivity during the first months of life. The massive migration of retinal cells, and the alterations in the size of retina and eyeball (along with changes in interpupillary distance), may necessitate the plasticity of cortical connections early in life. Interestingly, the peripheral retina appears to develop much more rapidly than the fovea (Yuodelis and Hendrickson, 1986).

■ Scientists at Work

Does the Duck's Left Eye Know What the Right Eye Saw?

■ **Question** The question that two zoologists from Oxford University (Martinho and Kacelnik, 2016) asked was, If a duckling imprinted on its mother with one eye, would it recognize her with the other eye?

■ **Hypothesis** The corpus callosum is the bundle of fibers that enables the left and right brain hemispheres to communicate with each other in humans. However, birds don't have a corpus callosum (although that's not why we refer to bird brains!). Therefore, in ducklings, information obtained through the left eye might not be recognized when viewed through the right eye.

■ **Test** One eye of each of 64 ducklings was covered with a blindfold, and then they were presented with a fake red or blue adult duck. The ducklings imprinted on the colored duck, which became "Mom," and the ducklings followed it around.

■ **Results** When the blindfold was switched to the previously open eye, the ducklings no longer recognized their "mom." Instead, they were equally likely to follow red or blue fake ducks.

■ **Conclusion** Each side of the brain seems to have a separate record of memory.

■ **Future work** Given that ducks do not have a corpus callosum, it will be important to understand how they integrate the separate information streams from the two eyes in order to make decisions.

Go to the
Sensation & Perception
Companion Website at
oup.com/us/wolfe5e
for chapter overviews, activities, essays, flashcards, and other study aids.
Go to **DASHBOARD** for additional resources and assessments.

Summary

1. In this chapter we followed the path of image processing from the eyeball to the brain. Neurons in the cerebral cortex translate the array of activity signaled by retinal ganglion cells into the beginnings of forms and patterns. The primary visual cortex is organized into thousands of tiny computers, each responsible for determining the orientation, width, color, and

other characteristics of the stripes in one small portion of the visual field. In Chapter 4 we will continue this story by seeing how other parts of the brain combine the outputs from these minicomputers to produce a coherent representation.

2. Perhaps the most important feature of image processing is the remarkable transformation of information from the circular receptive fields of retinal ganglion cells to the elongated receptive fields of the cortex.

3. Cortical neurons are highly selective along a number of dimensions, including stimulus orientation, size, direction of motion, and eye of origin.

4. Neurons with similar preferences are often arranged in columns in primary visual cortex.

5. Selective adaptation provides a powerful, noninvasive tool for learning about stimulus specificity in human vision.

6. The human visual cortex contains pattern analyzers that are specific to spatial frequency and orientation.

4 Perceiving and Recognizing Objects

■ Questions to Contemplate ■

Think about the following questions as you read this chapter. By the chapter's end, you should be able to answer and discuss them.

- Can the identity and location of an object be processed separately by the brain?

- How do we know what object (if any) an edge belongs to?

- How do we know if an object continues behind another, occluding object?

- When do two bits of a visual image belong together in the same group or object?

- How do we recognize objects?

- How do we recognize the same object from different points of view?

We have been traveling up the visual system from the eyes into the brain. By the end of Chapter 3, we had reached primary visual cortex (V1, striate cortex), where we encountered cells that were optimally stimulated by bars and gratings of different orientations. Of course, when you look at the world, you do not see an array of bars and gratings; you see coherent objects and extended surfaces. Moreover, you recognize specific objects even if they are odd objects, as in **Figure 4.1**. This chapter continues our journey through the visual system and considers how that visual system manages the task of perceiving and recognizing objects.

Mark Guglielmo, *Albero della Vita*, 2013

From Simple Lines and Edges to Properties of Objects

To begin, let's extend the visual pathways beyond V1 and beyond what was shown in Figure 3.1. Recall that cells in V1 are interested in the basic features of the visual image, responding to edges or lines of specific orientation, motion, size, and so forth. These neurons have relatively small and precise receptive

Figure 4.1 We see a world full of identifiable objects even if we have never seen them in this particular arrangement before.

fields. That is, a cell will respond to its preferred stimulus only if that stimulus is presented in a very specific location relative to the point where the observer (monkey, cat, human) is fixating its (or his or her) gaze. Beyond V1 is the **extrastriate cortex**, a set of visual areas so called because they lie just outside the primary visual (or striate) cortex. In the monkey, these areas are named V2, V3, and so on, though they are not a simple chain of processing areas and the naming convention breaks down pretty rapidly. **Figure 4.2** shows the main visual areas of the macaque monkey brain, and **Figure 4.3** shows one "wiring" diagram of these and a few other visual areas. The human visual system is not identical to that of a macaque. However, the basic plan, mapped out in **Figure 4.4**, is similar. Basic, local properties are pulled out of the image by early stages of visual cortex, but sophisticated tasks like object recognition require a great deal of subsequent processing and a large number of apparently distinct visual-processing areas.

We can sketch a broad structure of the visual areas beyond V1. In the extrastriate regions just beyond V1 (such as V2), receptive fields begin to show an interest in properties that will be important for object perception. As we saw in Chapter 3, cells in the primary visual cortex have preferences for lines and edges of specific orientations in specific locations in the visual field. Imagine a cell, tuned to edges tilted to the left of vertical with the darker side on the right. Such a cell would be activated if its receptive field lined up with the red ovals in any of the panels of **Figure 4.5**.

The hypothetical V1 cell would not care that the edge in Figure 4.5B is the edge of a black square while the edge in Figure 4.5C is the edge of a gray square.

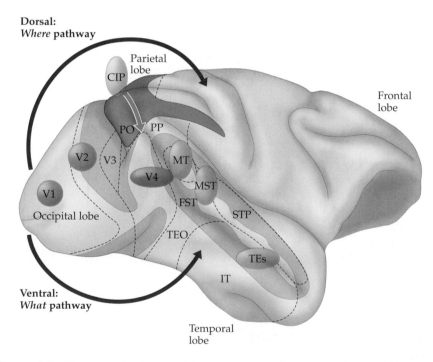

Figure 4.2 The main visual areas of the macaque monkey cortex. Humans have comparable visual areas (see Figure 3.1). The drawing of the brain has been distorted to show areas that lie deep in the folds (sulci) of the cortex. Each abbreviation refers to a different visual area, not all of which will be discussed here. Visual cortical processing can be divided into two broad streams. One, heading for the parietal lobe, can be thought of as being interested in where things are. The other, heading down into the temporal lobe, is concerned with what things are. (After Parker, 2007.)

extrastriate cortex The region of cortex bordering the primary visual cortex and containing multiple areas involved in visual processing.

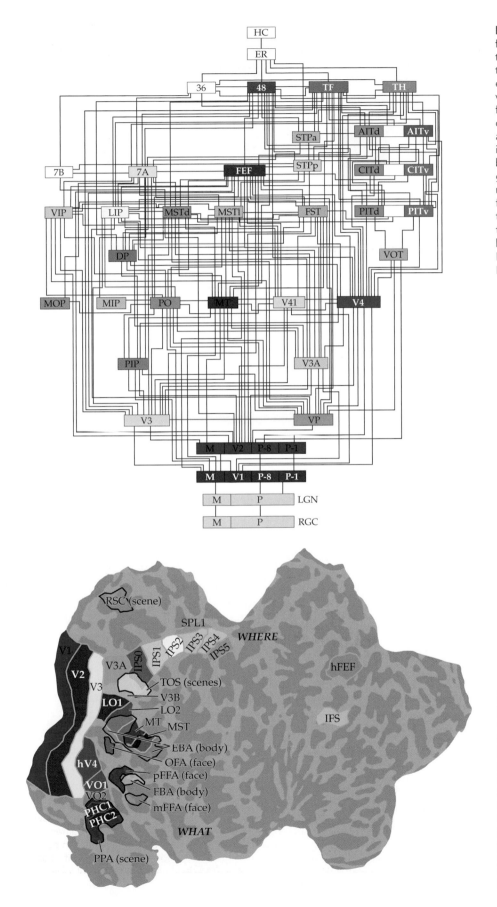

Figure 4.3 A partial "wiring" diagram for the main visual areas of the brain of the macaque monkey. (We don't have these data for humans). As in Figure 4.2, each abbreviation refers to a different visual area. The main message of this figure is that the visual pathways are very complex and that there are many visual areas. For a bit of orientation, visual information from the eyes enters at the bottom of the diagram, via the retinal ganglion cells (RGC). Feed-forward information generally flows "upward" in this figure. However, visual processing is a two-way street. From the LGN onward, there are both feed-forward and feed-back connections between areas (see Figure 3.1). (After Felleman and Van Essen, 1991.)

Figure 4.4 The main visual areas of the human cortex (compare with Figure 4.2 and Figure 3.1). Here the convoluted, wrinkled surface of the brain has been flattened. Each abbreviation refers to a different visual area. If you are curious, a little surfing on the internet will yield the definitions of all the acronyms and several other maps that will give you an idea of the complexities of figuring out the map of human visual processing. Here you should notice the *what* and *where* pathways and the areas specialized for faces, bodies, and scenes. (Courtesy of Sabine Kastner and Mike Arcaro.)

Figure 4.5 All the edges inside the receptive field, marked by the red oval, are the same. However, in the larger scene, (B) shows the edge of a black square while (C) shows the edge of a gray square.

You, the perceiver, do care about this. You care about what Zhou, Friedman, and von der Heydt (2000) called "border ownership." When an object, like the black square in Figure 4.5B is sitting on a background, the edges defining the border between object and background "belong" to the object. When Zhou et al. recorded from area V2, they found many cells that cared about border ownership. Suppose that a cell was activated by a dark edge on the right side of its receptive field (as in Figure 4.5A). In V2, a border ownership cell would respond more strongly to Figure 4.5B, the edge of a black square, than to Figure 4.5C, the locally identical edge of a gray square.

■ Scientists at Work

Rüdiger von der Heydt, Border Ownership, and Transparency

■ **Hypothesis** Figure 4.5B, C shows a pretty simple situation: an isolated square on a background. How sophisticated are these V2 cells? Rüdiger von der Heydt and his students hypothesized that cells in V2 would understand about transparency (Qiu and von der Heydt, 2007).

■ **Test** The stimuli in **Figure 4.6** illustrate the stimuli used to test the question. In Stimulus 1, the dark border is clearly "owned" by the square. In Stimulus 2, the same edge is the product of overlapping transparent rectangles and appears to be owned by the white vertical bar. In Stimulus 3, a very small change gives ownership of the same white-dark edge back to a dark square. Monkeys were trained to pay attention to a subtle change in a small target at the point of fixation. Meantime, Von der Heydt and colleagues recorded from a V2 cell whose receptive field was located someplace else in the visual field. The monkey was rewarded for noticing that change at the point of fixation, but the researchers' real interest was in the V2 cell's responses to edges like those shown in Figure 4.6.

■ **Results** The graph in Figure 4.6 compares the responses of a cell that prefers dark edges to the right to responses of cells the like bright edges to the left.

This cell responds well to the edge of a dark object on the right (Stimulus 1). The cell's response to Stimulus 2 is suppressed relative to other cells that prefer edges owned by an item to the left. Finally, in Stimulus 3 just a few pixels are removed from Stimulus 2, breaking up the white bar but leaving the edge and all the other pixels the same. Now, the response returns.

■ **Conclusion** Cells in area V2 of the macaque monkey cortex "understand" transparency. This is one more step to understanding edges in the real world. As we will discuss later, carving a continuous image into distinct objects is a difficult task, but these V2 cells are up to their part of the challenge. If a cell responded best to an edge that was dark on the left, it would respond well to oval 1 in **Figure 4.7** but not to oval 2. In oval 1, the dark left edge is part of the penguin. In oval 2 it isn't (Williford and von der Heydt, 2016).

■ **Future work** At this time, we don't really know how the visual system creates cells that are sensitive to border ownership, but von der Heydt's work makes it clear that, fairly early in the visual-processing pathway, the responses of single cells are driven by the structure of the objects and the scene far beyond the simple receptive field of the cell.

■ **Scientists at Work** *(continued)*

Stimulus 1

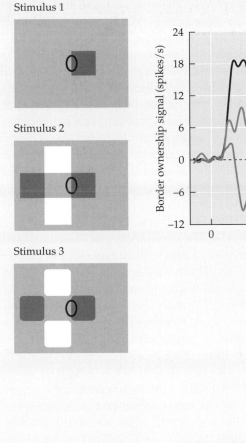

Stimulus 2

Stimulus 3

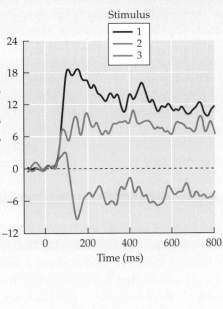

Figure 4.6 Border ownership cells can "understand" transparency. The graph compares the activity of cells that prefer edges owned by an object to the right to the responses of cells that prefer edges owned by an object to the left. In Stimulus 1, the edge belongs to a square on the right, so the to-the-right kind of cell is more active and the difference (purple line) is positive. In Stimulus 2, the edge looks like the edge of a white bar on the left, so the second kind of cell is more active and the difference is negative (yellow line). In Stimulus 3, a few pixels are removed and the edge is again owned by the item on the right (green line). (After Qiu and von der Heydt, 2007.)

Figure 4.7 The dark edge in oval 1 belongs to the penguin. The dark edge in oval 2 doesn't.

What and *Where* Pathways

From the extrastriate regions of the occipital lobe of the brain, visual information moves out along two main pathways (see Figure 4.2). One pathway heads up into the parietal lobe. Visual areas in this pathway seem to be important for processing information relating to the location of objects in space and the actions required to interact with them (moving the hands, the eyes, and so on). This pathway is sometimes known as the *where* pathway. As we will see in Chapter 7, this pathway plays an important role in the deployment of attention. The other pathway heads down into the temporal lobe and is known as the *what* pathway. This pathway appears to be the locus for the explicit acts of object recognition that are of particular importance in this chapter (Ungerleider and Mishkin, 1982). As we move down into the temporal lobe, receptive fields get much bigger. As the pathway's name implies, *what* is in view seems more important than where it is. However, though it is a useful organizing principle, one should not become too addicted to this *what* and *where* distinction. For instance, some basic object

lesion In reference to neurophysiology, 1. (n) A region of damaged brain. 2. (v) To destroy a section of the brain.

agnosia A failure to recognize objects in spite of the ability to see them. Agnosia is typically due to brain damage.

inferotemporal (IT) cortex Part of the cerebral cortex in the lower portion of the temporal lobe, important in object recognition.

homologous regions Brain regions that appear to have the same function in different species.

information is simultaneously represented in both pathways (Konen and Kastner, 2008), and some *where* information is encoded in the temporal lobe *what* pathway.

Early evidence for a relationship between the temporal lobe and object recognition came from studies in which large sections of the temporal lobe were **lesioned** (surgically excised) in monkeys. When Klüver and Bucy (1938, 1939) did this, they found that their monkeys behaved as though they could see but did not know what they were seeing. This deficit, also seen in some human stroke victims, is known as **agnosia**, though Klüver and Bucy called it "psychic blindness." Later work pointed to one part of the temporal lobe, the **inferotemporal (IT) cortex**, as particularly important in the visual problems of these monkeys. In the 1970s, Charlie Gross and his colleagues began to record the activity of single cells in this area. What they found was quite striking. We have seen that neurons in striate cortex are activated by simple stimuli and respond only if their preferred stimuli are presented in very restricted portions of the visual field. In contrast, cells in the IT cortex were discovered to have receptive fields that could spread over half or more of the monkey's field of view. Even more striking were the sorts of stimuli that activated IT cells. The usual spots and lines didn't work well at all, but the silhouette of a monkey hand worked fantastically for some cells. Monkey faces excited other cells. There was even a cell with a distinct preference for a toilet brush shape (Gross, Rocha-Miranda, and Bender, 1972).

Findings like this led Horace Barlow (1972) and others to suggest a hierarchical model of visual perception in which the small receptive fields and simple features of visual cortex are combined with ever-greater complexity as one moves from striate cortex to IT cortex, eventually culminating in small networks of cells that might fire when you see your grandmother or your *Sensation & Perception* textbook. Indeed, the term *grandmother cell,* coined by Jerry Lettvin, has entered the jargon of the field to stand for any cell that seems to be selectively responsive to one specific object (Barlow, 1995). We discuss grandmother cells again later in this chapter.

We do not know what brain activity actually corresponds to your recognition of your grandmother. It is probably a bit extreme to imagine that this is the work of a few neurons in the IT cortex. Grandmother recognition is more likely to involve quite a large network of cells with individual cells participating in recognition of more than one stimulus. Nevertheless, it does seem clear that cells in that part of the brain are critically involved in object recognition. The IT cortex maintains close connections with parts of the brain involved in memory formation (notably the hippocampus). This is important because those IT cells need to *learn* their receptive-field properties. The receptive-field properties of primary visual cortex could be written into the genetic code in some manner, but neurons that respond to grandmothers clearly cannot be hardwired, since everyone's grandmother is different. Nikos Logothetis and his coworkers demonstrated that cells in IT cortex have precisely this type of plasticity (Logothetis, Pauls, and Poggio, 1995). After training monkeys to recognize novel objects, these researchers found IT neurons that responded with high firing rates to those objects, but only when the objects were seen from viewpoints similar to those from which they had been learned.

Human cortex has areas that appear to be the equivalent of monkey IT cortex and hippocampus (the anatomy of human and macaque monkey brains is not identical, so we talk about **homologous regions**). One of the more amazing demonstrations of this fact comes from a 2005 study by Quiroga et al. They made recordings from single cells in the temporal lobe (hippocampus and its neighbors) of human observers. Normally, we do not put electrodes into the human brain, but these observers were patients being prepared for brain surgery to treat epilepsy. Implanting electrodes was part of the treatment plan, and

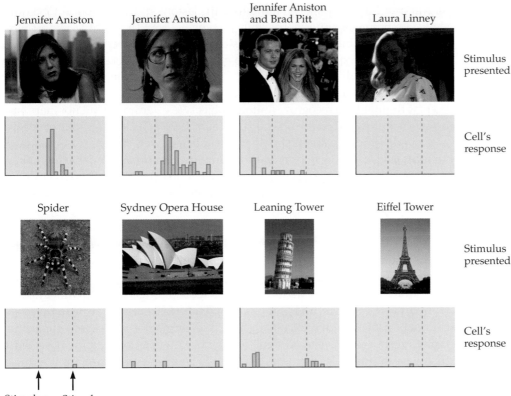

Figure 4.8   Results of recording the activity of one cell in the temporal lobe (hippo-campus and its neighbors) of a human patient. This cell responded to pictures of the actress Jennifer Aniston. The cell did not respond to pictures of anything else, including those of other actresses. (After Quiroga et al., 2005.)

recording visual responses from these cells involved no extra risk to the patient or interference with treatment. In the experiment, the observer just looked at a collection of images while the activity of a cell was monitored. As **Figure 4.8** shows, some of these cells turned out to have very specific tastes. The cell shown in the figure responded only to the actress Jennifer Aniston and to nothing else presented to the observer. Other cells had preferences for other people, like former president Bill Clinton. One cell responded to the Sydney Opera House; another, to the Eiffel Tower and the Leaning Tower of Pisa but not to other landmarks (Quiroga et al., 2005).

While we do not have a lot of systematic data on the responses of single cells in the human visual system, we have a growing volume of functional imaging data that documents areas in the human brain that appear be specialized for different sorts of stimuli. Conveniently, as shown in Figure 4.4, many of these have been given names that make that proposed specialization clear. Thus, cells in the fusiform face area (FFA) are interested in faces (Kanwisher, McDermott, and Chun, 1997), while an area like the parahippocampal place area (PPA) has cells that respond to spaces in the world like rooms with furniture in them (Epstein and Kanwisher, 1998). The visual system has many different problems to solve—like the problem of face processing—and it appears to have modules that are specialized for working on different problems (Kanwisher, 2017). Other evidence comes from brain lesions caused by strokes or other accidents. Like

feed-forward process A process that carries out a computation (e.g., object recognition) one neural step after another, without need for feedback from a later stage to an earlier stage.

reverse-hierarchy theory A theory that fast, feed-forward processes can give you crude information about objects and scenes based on activity in high-level parts of the visual cortex. You become aware of details when activity flows back down the hierarchy of visual areas to lower-level areas where the detailed information is preserved.

Klüver and Bucy's monkeys, humans with lesions in the temporal lobe often show symptoms of agnosia, the ability to see without the ability to know what is being seen. Sometimes these agnosias can be quite specific. Prosopagnosia, an inability to recognize faces, is one example that has received a lot of study and that will be discussed at the end of this chapter (Damasio, Damasio, and Van Hoesen, 1982). There are other interesting subdivisions of agnosia as well, such as the ability to recognize animate objects (e.g., animals) but not inanimate objects (e.g., tools) (Newcombe and de Haan, 1994). The implications of specific agnosias in specific patients should not be taken too far. While areas specialized for faces or places seem to be readily documented in humans and you might have areas specialized for some other categories of objects, like tools (Hutchison et al., 2014), you probably do not have a separate area for each and *every* category of object that you can recognize (Kanwisher and Dilks, 2013).

Some processing that leads to the categorization of objects and scenes can be very fast. Electrical activity from the brain can be recorded from electrodes placed on the scalp. If we flash a picture to an observer and ask whether it contains an animal, we can record a signal in the observer that reliably differentiates animal from nonanimal scenes within 150 milliseconds (ms) from the onset of the stimulus (Thorpe, Fize, and Marlot, 1996). That's fast enough to mean that there cannot be a lot of feedback from higher visual or memory processes, suggesting that it must be possible to do some rough object recognition on the basis of the first wave of activity as it moves, cell by cell, synapse by synapse, from retina to striate cortex to extrastriate cortex and beyond. That **feed-forward process** must be able to generate an "animal" signal from a wide range of animals in different positions, sizes, and so on (Serre, Oliva, and Poggio, 2007). At the same time, it is important to remember that all those many areas in Figure 4.3 have feedback connections as well as those that feed forward. More complex acts of recognition ("That is my cat, Totoro. He is looking plump.") will rely on this feedback. Hochstein and Ahissar (2002) proposed a **reverse-hierarchy theory**. It argues that the feed-forward processes give you a general, categorical impression of the world but that you don't become aware of the details until "re-entrant" feedback (Di Lollo, 2012) goes back down the visual pathway. This "re-entrant processing" will become important in Chapter 7 when we discuss what it means to "pay attention" to one part of the visual input. (For an interesting effect related to re-entrant processing, see **Web Activity 4.1: Object Substitution Masking**.)

To summarize, two pathways emerge from visual cortex. The *where* pathway will be taken up in later chapters. The *what* pathway moves through a succession of stages (backward as well as forward), building a representation of your grandmother or the Eiffel Tower out of the very specific, very localized spots, lines, and bars that interest the cells in the retina, lateral geniculate nucleus (LGN), and primary visual cortex. That's a start, but don't be lulled into thinking we fully understand the process of object recognition simply because we have some notion of the neural pathways involved. It is a really difficult problem, and in the rest of the chapter we will illustrate why this problem is hard and how the visual system attempts to solve different parts of it.

The Problems of Perceiving and Recognizing Objects

Figure 4.9A is clearly a picture of a house. The image may contain some other things as well, but the chief object of interest is the house. It is pretty clear that **Figure 4.9D** also shows a house, perhaps with a similar shape and chimney,

Figure 4.9 The problem of object recognition. The image of the house in (A) and the oil painting by Monet in (D) look completely different, but they both clearly show red houses. The image in (B) is also very different from the image in (A), but they both clearly show the same house. While (C) shows a red house, it is clear that it is fairly similar to but different from the house in (A) and (B).

though in this case the house is part of a scene painted by the French artist Claude Monet in the late nineteenth century. **Figures 4.9B** and **C** are two more pictures of houses. It is quite clear that Figure 4.9B shows the same house as Figure 4.9A, while Figure 4.9C does not. These seemingly simple acts of object identification require a lot from the *what* pathway, and they constitute the main topic of the rest of this chapter. Like many seemingly simple acts, object perception is actually a collection of complex and remarkable accomplishments.

Consider **Figure 4.10A**. It shows yet another house. How do we recognize it as a house? First we need to gather some basic visual features. The preceding chapters showed us how single cells in the early visual system respond to stimuli such as simple lines. In **Figure 4.10B** each circle is a cartoon of the receptive field of a simple cortical cell. Those cells in striate cortex will respond well to the high-contrast lines in the outline of the house. That limited receptive field is like a window that allows the cell to "see" only a small part of the world. None of these simple cells see a house. They just collect local features like horizontal, vertical, and oblique lines.

At the very least, the local features will need to be assembled into a house. This process could be imagined as the natural extension of a process we have already discussed. One way to "construct" the lines detected by simple cells is to imagine combining a row of dots detected by retinal ganglion cells. Dots could be grouped together into lines. A pair of lines, each collected by a different cell, could be combined by another cell that would sense a corner. This process could go on and on until we had a house. On closer examination, however, it is

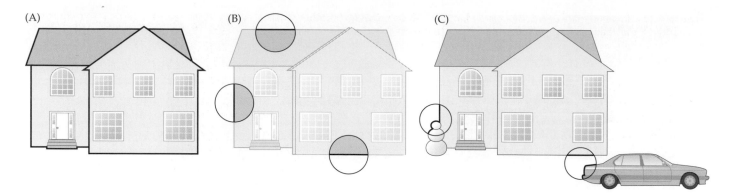

Figure 4.10 The problem continued. (A) Another house. (B) Cells in primary visual cortex respond well to the local features (circled) of the house. But how do we go from recognizing a collection of local features to perceiving a house? (C) In this slightly more complicated scene, how do we know which bits belong together?

clear that this process would not be easy. Consider, for example, **Figure 4.10C**. Again, simple cells would have no problem detecting the lines and edges in this scene, but how do we know which edges go with which objects? How do we avoid considering the snowman part of the house? The house and snowman make corners, as do the house and its door and steps. The car and house are separate. None of their lines touch. But this is also true of the outline of the house and its windows.

Clearly we must have processes that successfully combine features into objects. That is one of the tasks that defines **mid-level** (or **middle**) **vision** (as opposed to low-level vision, which was the topic of Chapters 2 and 3). The next part of this chapter looks at some of the processes of mid-level vision. The following part takes the feature combinations given to us by mid-level vision and asks how we come to know what the object is. The act of recognition must involve matching what we perceive now to a memory of something we perceived in the past. How can we do that? For example, how do we know that all of the images in Figures 4.9 and 4.10 show houses? Without having seen these exact objects before, how do we go about placing them in the "house" category? Furthermore, how do we know that Figures 4.9A and B portray the same house, given that the images delivered to our retinas from the two are radically different? In the final section of this chapter we'll discuss the high-level visual processes that enable us to recognize familiar objects, novel views of familiar objects, and new instances of familiar object categories.

Mid-level Vision

The goal of mid-level vision is to organize the elements of a visual scene into groups that we can then recognize as objects. Let's begin with the simplest case of an object isolated on a simple background. Finding the edges of this object will be a good starting place on the road to recognizing the object.

Finding Edges

In Chapter 3 we discussed at length how neurons in striate cortex can detect bits of lines, but how do we decide which bits belong to which objects? We already established that we can't just group all the edges that touch each other into an object. Because objects abut and overlap other objects, simple connectedness

mid-level (or middle) vision
A loosely defined stage of visual processing that comes after basic features have been extracted from the image (low-level, or early, vision) and before object recognition and scene understanding (high-level vision).

Figure 4.11 In some places this object is darker than the background. In other places it is lighter. If the changes are continuous, it follows that there must be places where the edge of this shape simply disappears, even if you see the edges as continuous.

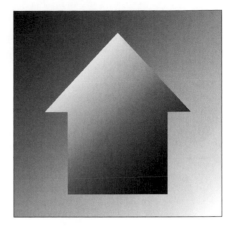

will not work. Worse yet, before we can concern ourselves with grouping edges, we need to worry about the quality of the raw edge information. In **Figure 4.11**, part of the house of Figure 4.10 is reduced to a simple, arrow-shaped outline. It is easy to see that arrow. Notice, however, that in some places the object is lighter than the background, while in other places it is darker. This means that if we trace the edge of the object with a finger, we *must* pass through locations where there is no difference between the luminance of the object and the luminance of the background. In other words, at these points the shape has no edge at all.

Interestingly, this occasional lack of an edge doesn't seem to bother our visual system at all. In fact, it may be hard to see the gap. Asking simple computer graphics software to find the edges in Figure 4.11 would yield something like **Figure 4.12A**. The visual system knows that the gaps are accidents of the lighting and fills in the contour. **Figure 4.12B, C** shows another example. In Figure 4.12C, notice that the edge-finding software finds all sorts of edges. The human visual system, however, is doing something quite different. In the early stages of processing, it is figuring out which edges mark the boundaries of objects and which represent surface features (like the texture of the feathers). All these different bits of information are then combined to make the system's best guess about the presence of a contour.

The inferential nature of contour perception can be appreciated in the more extreme demonstration shown in **Figure 4.13**. This is an example of a Kanizsa figure—named after Gaetano Kanizsa (1913–1993), an Italian psychologist who spent many years investigating such stimuli. Here it is still easy to see the

(A)

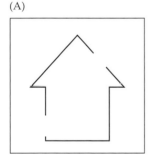

(B)

(C)

Figure 4.12 (A) The "find edges" function in a popular graphics program finds gaps in the borders of the image in Figure 4.11—gaps that we do not see. When a computer algorithm looks for the edges in this photo of a bird (B), it finds what is shown in (C). (B courtesy of Farahnaz Wick.)

Figure 4.13 This "house" outline is constructed from illusory contours. Even though the contour is clearly visible, there is no physical difference between the white background and the white house.

arrow outline, even though the vast majority of the shape's lines are missing. Check it yourself. There really is no border between the white figure and the white background. These edges, called **illusory contours**, are perceived because they are the best guess about what is happening in the world at that location. It really does seem likely that a contour is present, even if there is no physical evidence at that location.

illusory contour A contour that is perceived even though nothing changes from one side of it to the other in an image.

OCCLUSION Why is that illusory contour a good guess about the world? We can imagine the visual system asking why the vertical line at the bottom of Figure 4.13 suddenly stops. One reasonable guess might be that it stops because something else gets in the way, hiding it from our view. The visual system seems to come up with the hypothesis that there is another contour *occluding* the vertical line. That contour could be of any orientation, but if we average all the possible orientations, we might guess that the occluding edge is oriented perpendicular to the occluded line. That is shown in **Figure 4.14B**.

Once we support the guess about the occlusion of the vertical line with similar guesses about the notches in the circles in **Figure 4.14A**, we have pretty good

Figure 4.14 The making of illusory contours. The gray arrows in (B) and (D) represent the visual system's best guess about what is going on in (A) and (C). The illusory disk in (C) arises when the visual system combines a whole collection of guesses about the line terminations, as shown in (D). (E, F) These images show very sophisticated use of subjective contours by American graphic artist C. Coles Phillips (1880–1927).

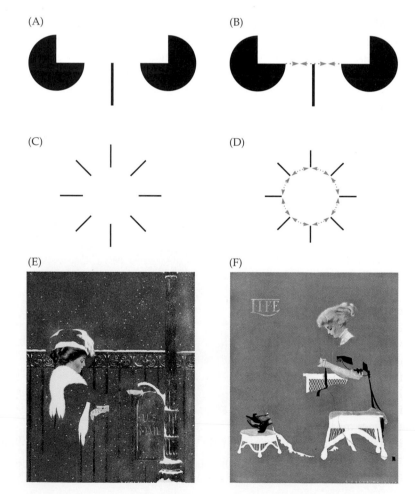

reason to infer an illusory horizontal contour. In fact, that contour looks like the bottom of a solid surface extending upward. **Figure 4.14C** shows another example of the same inference of occlusion. If each black line generated weak illusory contours at right angles to its end point, then this figure would contain a set of inferred line segments (**Figure 4.14D**) that could imply the illusory circle that we see in Figure 4.14C. By the way, illusory contours like this make excellent doodles when you would rather be doing informal perception experiments than paying attention. See what happens if you tilt the lines so that they do not all radiate from a single point. If you happen to be a very fine artist, you could doodle subjective contours like those in these old magazine covers by C. Coles Phillips (1880–1927) (**Figures 4.14E,** and **F**). Notice how his subjective contours are really subjective three-dimensional volumes with rounded arms and legs under a seemingly visible dress (Tse, 1999).

RULES OF EVIDENCE   This tendency of the visual system to make inferential leaps like those that form the illusory contours of Figures 4.13 and 4.14 was problematic for one of the earliest groups of perceptual psychologists, the **structuralists**. Structuralists such as Wilhelm Wundt (1832–1920) and Edward Bradford Titchener (1867–1927) argued that perceptions are the sum of atoms of sensation—bits of color, orientation, and so forth. In the structuralist view, perception is built up of local sensations the way a crystal might be built up of an array of atoms. An illusory contour challenges this view because an extended edge is seen bridging a gap where no local atom of "edgeness" can be found.

Over time, it became clear that there are many examples where the structuralist argument seems to fail. Inspired by these examples, a second group of psychologists, led by Max Wertheimer (1880–1943), Wolfgang Köhler (1887–1967), and Kurt Koffka (1886–1941), formed the **Gestalt** school (Wagemans et al., 2012). Gestalt theory held that the perceptual whole is more than the sum of its sensory parts. Perhaps the most enduring contribution of this school was to begin the description of a set of organizing principles, sometimes known as **Gestalt grouping rules**, that describe the visual system's interpretation of the raw retinal image. In the following sections, we will describe some of those rules. More than the specific rules, it is important to remember the overarching goal. The visual system is trying to make sense of the vast and often ambiguous and noisy inputs from the early stage of visual processing. These rules are useful parts of that effort because they reflect regularities in the world. They allow the visual system to say, "If the input looks like that, I can infer that this is the state of the visual world."

With that in mind, consider **Figure 4.15A**, where we have a collection of short line segments. One set of these seems to form a contour—an irregular, dented loop. The "rule," shown in **Figure 4.15B**, is that we tend to see similarly oriented lines as part of the same contour (Field, Hayes, and Hess, 1992). Polat and Sagi (1993) measured how pieces of a contour support each other. The effect will be hard to see in print, but the fainter lines in the middle of the triplets of lines in **Figure 4.15C** will be easier to see when they are collinear with the flanking lines. Those flankers provide evidence for lines of the same orientation in between. If a set of lines forms a closed shape like the roughly circular contour in Figure 4.15A, then the short segments support each other even more strongly (Kovacs and Julesz, 1993). Geisler and Perry (2009) documented the regularity in the world that supports the rule shown in Figure 4.15B. They labeled many, many contours in natural scenes. Then they examined pairs of contour pieces and asked, "What is the chance that *this* piece *here* at *this* orientation is part of

structuralism   In reference to perception, a school of thought that believed that complex objects or perceptions could be understood by analysis of the components.

Gestalt   In German, literally "form." In reference to perception, a school of thought stressing that the perceptual whole can be greater than the apparent sum of the parts.

Gestalt grouping rules   A set of rules describing which elements in an image will appear to group together. The original list was assembled by members of the Gestalt school of thought.

Figure 4.15 Contour completion. (A) The roughly circular contour seen in the center of this diagram results from the visual system's application of the rule shown in (B). (C) Polat and Sagi (1993) found that it was easier to see a faint set of bars if they were flanked by bars of the same orientation. (D) Geisler and Perry (2009) actually measured the relationships between nearby line segments in natural scenes. The figure shows the probability that a horizontal line segment would co-occur with other line segments in the image at different distances and orientations. The most likely pairs are colinear or nearly so. (C after Polat and Sagi, 1993; D after Geisler and Perry, 2009.)

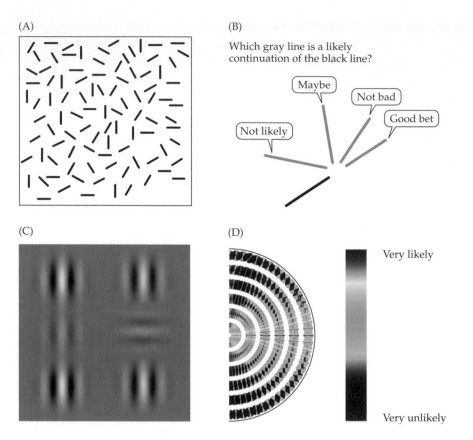

(A)

(B) Which gray line is a likely continuation of the black line?

(C)

(D)

the same contour as *that* piece *there* at *that* orientation?" These likelihoods are color-coded in **Figure 4.15D**, and they show that in the real world, if two contour elements are close to colinear, they are likely to come from the same contour. Sharp turns are much rarer.

The Gestaltists called this the principle of **good continuation**, and they illustrated it with examples like the one shown in **Figure 4.16A**. We tend to see this figure as a pair of intersecting lines, so it is most likely that you would see dot 1 as connected to dot 4. A connection to dot 2 is possible, while a connection to dot 3 would require a less probable sharp turn. In **Figure 4.16B**, the connection of dot 1 to dot 2 is strengthened by the Gestalt principle of **closure**. The visual system has a bias toward closed contours. In **Figure 4.17** good continuation is strong enough to create an apparently transparent child.

good continuation A Gestalt grouping rule stating that two elements will tend to group together if they seem to lie on the same contour.

closure In reference to perception, the Gestalt principle that holds that a closed contour is preferred to an open contour.

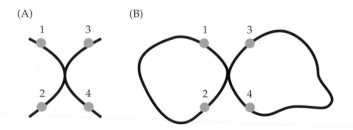

(A)

(B)

Figure 4.16 Does dot 1 connect most strongly with dot 2, 3, or 4. In (A), good continuation biases perception in favor of dot 4. In (B), closure biases perception in favor of dot 2.

Texture Segmentation and Grouping

Connecting short line segments will get us only so far in dividing the raw image into objects. If you look at **Figure 4.18**, you will immediately see a border dividing the left from the right side even though an edge-detecting cell or algorithm would not find an edge. In this case, the border is found by the visual system's sophisticated mechanisms for **texture segmentation** (Beck, 1982; Bergen and Adelson, 1988; Malik and Perona, 1990). One way that the visual system decides that two regions are different is by looking at the statistics of all the features in one region and determining that those statistics differ from the statistics in the neighboring region (Alvarez, 2011; Chong and Treisman, 2003). However, not every statistic works for this purpose. Thus, the difference between left and right in Figure 4.18 is based on something like "number of line terminations" (Gurnsey and Browse, 1987). The distinction between the plusses in the top left and the very different shape in the lower left is much less obvious (Wolfe and DiMase, 2003). Figuring out the properties of a group of items is not a matter of scrutinizing each one. In **Figure 4.19**, for example, it is immediately obvious that the average of the blue lines on the left is near vertical. However, you will have to search to determine whether any individual blue line is perfectly vertical. The green lines in the middle have the same average orientation, but you can tell that there is more variability, and it is easy to notice that

Figure 4.17 When good continuation goes bad. Laura Williams cleverly exploits good continuation by lining up the edge of the field with the reflected edge in the mirror. This allows the good continuation cue to trump the occlusion cue (see the "Dealing with Occlusion" section later in this chapter) to produce this striking image.

Figure 4.18 Regions defined by texture.

texture segmentation Carving an image into regions of common texture properties.

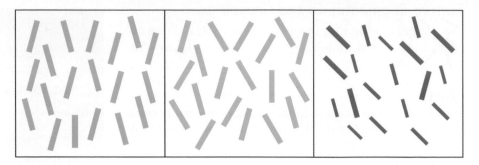

Figure 4.19   It is easy to see the approximate average orientation and size of the lines in the three regions of this figure. It will take more work to determine whether any one line is vertical.

similarity   A Gestalt grouping rule stating that the tendency of two features to group together will increase as the similarity between them increases.

proximity   A Gestalt grouping rule stating that the tendency of two features to group together will increase as the distance between them decreases.

parallelism   A rule for figure-ground assignment stating that parallel contours are likely to belong to the same figure.

symmetry   A rule for figure-ground assignment stating that symmetrical regions are more likely to be seen as figure.

the purple items on the right differ in average size and average orientation from the other items.

Texture segmentation is closely related to the Gestalt grouping principles that we've been discussing. **Figure 4.20A** illustrates two of the strongest principles: similarity and proximity. **Similarity** means that image chunks that are similar to each other will be more likely to group together. Similar in what ways? Grouping of elements can be based on similarity in a limited number of features such as color, size, orientation, and as illustrated here, aspects of form. Notice that these are similar to (maybe the same as) the features that can be used for texture segmentation and the averaging shown in Figure 4.19. Combinations ("conjunctions") of features do not support grouping or segmentation (Treisman, 1986b). Thus, the texture segmentation between the left and right sides of **Figure 4.20B** is not clear, even though the left side contains orange diamonds and green squares and the right side contains green diamonds and orange squares.

The principle of **proximity** holds that items near each other are more likely to group together than are items more widely separated. Proximity grouping gives Figure 4.20A its horizontally striped appearance. The original descriptions of these Gestalt principles did not involve extensive experimentation. Illustrative demonstrations, like those of Figure 4.20, seemed to make the point. Since that early Gestalt work, careful experiments have confirmed and quantified what the early demonstrations illustrated. For example, Kubovy and his colleagues (Kubovy and Cohen, 2001) quite precisely measured the strength of the proximity effect.

Figure 4.21 illustrates two somewhat weaker grouping principles: **parallelism** and **symmetry**. Most people see the *parallel* pair of contours (lines 2 and 3) as a group and the *symmetrical* pair (lines 7 and 8) as another group, and **Figure 4.22** shows the grouping effects of enclosing or connecting items (S. E. Palmer, 1992).

(A)   (B)

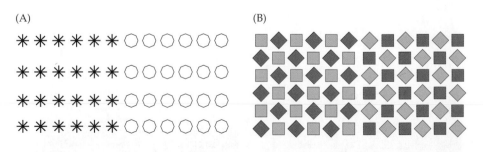

Figure 4.20   Similarity and proximity. (A) Grouping by similarity and by proximity is useful. (B) Grouping by a conjunction of color and form does not work.

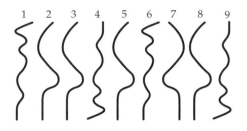

Figure 4.21 Parallelism and symmetry. Which pairs of lines go together?

We can't list all the rules (even if we knew them all, which we probably don't). More important, for our purposes, is to remember that the visual system's goal is to decide which bits of the input belong with which other bits of the input. (See **Web Activity 4.2: Gestalt Grouping Principles** for examples of grouping by common fate and synchrony—two principles not covered here [S.-H. Lee and Blake, 1999].)

CAMOUFLAGE   The same principles that are normally used to help us find objects in the world can be exploited to hide them. The art of camouflage is, to a great extent, the art of getting your features to group with the features of the environment so as to persuade an observer that your features do not form a perceptual group of their own. **Figure 4.23** shows two examples from the animal kingdom. The exercise for you is to determine which principles of grouping are

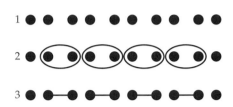

Figure 4.22 Proximity grouping (line 1) can be overruled by grouping by common region (line 2) or grouping by connectedness (line 3). (After S. E. Palmer, 1992.)

(A)

(B)

(C)

(D)

Figure 4.23 Panel (B) shows the hidden animal in (A). We leave (C) as an exercise for the reader. (D) Sometimes camouflage is meant to confuse the viewer, rather than to hide the object.

ambiguous figure A visual stimulus that gives rise to two or more interpretations of its identity or structure.

Necker cube An outline that is perceptually bi-stable. Unlike the situation with most stimuli, two interpretations continually battle for perceptual dominance.

accidental viewpoint A viewing position that produces some regularity in the visual image that is not present in the world (e.g., the sides of two independent objects lining up perfectly).

at work hiding the camouflaged animals in Figures 4.23A and C. Camouflage does not need to be entirely about hiding things. In World War I, navies painted some of their ships with very dramatic patterns. The "dazzle camouflage" in Figure 4.23D was designed to make a clearly visible object hard to understand.

AMBIGUITY AND PERCEPTUAL "COMMITTEES" How do we put all these grouping rules together into a single percept of the world? If you go back and scrutinize Figure 4.16B, you can see that it is ambiguous and you can feel the two Gestalt principles striving for dominance. As the Gestalt psychologists knew, and as we will see, a host of rules, principles, and good guesses contribute to our organized perception of the world. These seem to operate according to a sort of committee model. Everyone gets together and voices opinions about how the stimulus ought to be understood. In Figure 4.16B, it is the good continuation and closure committee members who are arguing, with closure probably winning the debate about whether dot 1 is connected to dot 2 or 4 in this case. The supremacy of closure over good continuation is not absolute. When the opinions of different "committee members" collide, the results can be somewhat ambiguous. In normal, everyday vision, though, a consensus view almost always quickly emerges and we settle on a single interpretation of the visual scene. This committee metaphor is very useful and will recur throughout this chapter.

COMMITTEE RULES: HONOR PHYSICS AND AVOID ACCIDENTS Though we usually come to a single coherent interpretation of the current contents of the sensory world, the decisions made by perceptual committees need not be final. An **ambiguous figure** is a figure that generates two or more plausible interpretations. For example, **Figure 4.24A** shows the famous **Necker cube**. Mid-level-vision committees of the visual system are willing to entertain either of the two solids shown in **Figures 4.24B** and **C** as interpretations of the wire frame pictured in Figure 4.24A. However, the system is unwilling to readily consider any of the infinite number of other possible interpretations of the wire image—for example, the flat one in **Figure 4.24D**. Another classic ambiguous figure, now pressed into the service of commerce, is seen in **Figure 4.25**.

Necker cubes and duck-rabbits are really the exceptions that prove the rule. *Every* image is, in theory, ambiguous, but the perceptual committees almost always agree on a single interpretation. Consider, for example, **Figure 4.26A**. This pattern might represent the retinal image projected by the scene depicted in **Figure 4.26B**: four surfaces with different shapes, arranged in different orientations, and at different distances. However, for Figure 4.26B to produce Figure 4.26A, you would have to be viewing the scene from exactly one, very precise location—what object recognition researchers call an **accidental viewpoint**.

(A)   (B)   (C)   (D)

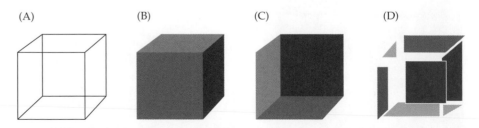

Figure 4.24 The wire-frame Necker cube (A) can look like either of the solids shown in (B) or (C). It is much less likely to be seen as a collection of flat regions on the page (D), even though that's really what it is!

Any slight shift in viewpoint—say, moving just slightly to the left—would destroy the illusion of the four equidistant square regions. (**Web Activity 4.3: Object Ambiguity** illustrates this situation with an animation that makes the relationship between Figures 4.26A and B clearer.)

The perceptual committees know about accidental viewpoints. More specifically, they know enough not to bet on them. The chances that Figure 4.26A is the two-dimensional representation of the three-dimensional scene in Figure 4.26B are so slim that the visual system refuses even to consider this possibility. **Figure 4.27** shows us that sometimes the visual system can be fooled (in whole or in part) by an accidental viewpoint. At some level, you know that this young woman is not holding the Leaning Tower of Pisa, but it looks quite convincing. If the camera moved just a little, the illusion would vanish.

The visual system also makes some assumptions based on an implicit understanding of some aspects of the physics of the world. For example, returning to the Kanizsa figure (see Figure 4.13), we infer the arrow-shaped object, in part, because of our *implicit* understanding that solid objects block light. This understanding of opacity causes us to infer that the lines disappear because something is blocking our view of them. Calling this understanding "implicit" means that we need not be able to verbalize the rule in order to use it. Monkeys seem to see the subjective contours without benefit of instruction in physics (von der Heydt, Peterhans, and Baumgartner, 1984), and we may assume that similar abilities extend far into the animal kingdom. We and our visual systems "know" this and other physical principles in the same way that a ball "knows" about gravity.

These principles and assumptions may seem so obvious as to be meaningless. But remember that an image has no meaning whatsoever until mid-level and high-level visual processes dig into it. One committee uses the knowledge that opaque objects occlude other objects behind them to generate plausible interpretations of image elements like the notched circles and dead-end edges in Figures 4.13 and 4.14. Another committee considers all the possibilities and devalues any that involve accidental viewpoints, reducing what is initially a theoretically unsolvable problem (finding the one correct interpretation out of the infinite number of possible ones) to a potentially solvable one. And so we proceed further and further into the visual system, until a single, generally correct interpretation emerges.

Figure 4.25 A classic ambiguous figure gets a new role.

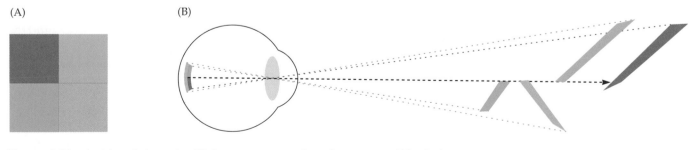

Figure 4.26 Accidental viewpoint. (A) Suppose you see these four squares. What is the state of the world that produced this view? (B) Maybe the eye just happens to be in the right position to see four arbitrary shapes at arbitrary depths line up to form the pattern. That would be quite a coincidence. That would be what is called an accidental viewpoint.

Figure 4.27 In this case, the view from an accidental viewpoint is accepted.

Figure and Ground

figure-ground assignment The process of determining that some regions of an image belong to a foreground object (figure) and other regions are part of the background (ground).

Armed with this understanding of the ground rules of committee deliberation, we can continue with the effort to go from simple features to recognizable objects. The edge- and region-finding mechanisms discussed earlier would divide **Figure 4.28** into yellow and red regions without much difficulty. But how should those regions be understood? It is extremely likely that we would interpret the illustration as two red figures on a yellow background. That is, we would infer that the yellow would continue behind the red objects if we could lift them up to check. That need not be the case, however. We could be looking at yellow and red puzzle pieces, cut to fit each other perfectly. Or we could be looking at two yellow objects, a smaller one on the left and a larger one with a squiggly hole on the right, both sitting on top of a red background.

The ability to distinguish figures (objects in the foreground) from ground (surfaces or objects lying behind the figures) is a critical step on the path from image to object recognition. Like the finding of edges and regions, it is a process governed by a collection of principles acting together, as if in another of these perceptual committees, to decide how the visual world should be understood. As before, the governing goal is to determine the most likely reality behind the image on the retina.

Like the grouping principles, the topic of **figure-ground assignment** became important in visual perception because of the work of the Gestalt psychologists. **Figure 4.29** shows the classic vase/face figure introduced in the 1920s by the Danish psychologist Edgar Rubin (1886–1951). It must be the best-known illustration from the Gestalt school, and it is analogous to the Necker cube in that it illustrates one of those rare cases in which a perceptual committee has a difficult time reaching consensus. All visual stimuli may be inherently ambiguous, but the processes that determine figure and ground almost always manage to come to a single conclusion, as they do in Figure 4.28. We are surprised when the

Figure 4.28 What is figure and what is ground and why?

process fails and delivers two or more interpretations. The surprise we register when the Rubin vase "flips" to a pair of faces (or vice versa) reminds us of the perceptual stability that we usually take for granted.

What principles are at work in the assignment of regions to figure or ground? We can list some of them:

- *Surroundedness.* If one region is entirely surrounded by another, it is likely that the surrounded region is the figure. This **surroundedness** is a factor in labeling the red region on the right in Figure 4.28 as figure.

- *Size.* The smaller region is likely to be figure. The cow is smaller than the field in which she stands, so she is the figure.

- *Symmetry.* A symmetrical region is more likely to be seen as figure. How likely is it that the two yellow regions in Figure 4.28 just happen to have the symmetrical contours facing each other over what would be the red gap on the left?

- *Parallelism.* Regions with parallel contours are more likely to be seen as figure (does blue or purple "win" as figure in **Figure 4.30**?). Again, how likely is it that two contours would be parallel with one another if they did not belong to the same object?

- *Relative motion.* How surface details move relative to an edge can also determine which portion of a display is the foreground figure and which is the background (Yonas, Craton, and Thompson, 1987). (See **Web Activity 4.2: Gestalt Grouping Principles**.)

A COMPLICATED BUSINESS   Although the assignment of figure and ground is governed by rules, it is not a simple process. Consider, for example, **Figure 4.31**. The surroundedness, size, symmetry, and parallelism rules combine to firmly establish the purple squares as figures on the green background. But what about the circle in the middle of each square? Each one is smaller than the

Figure 4.29 The Rubin vase/face figure. Do you see a vase or two faces in profile? Notice that the boundary marked by the green line changes its allegiance when the figure flips interpretation. The boundary is "owned" by the figure.

surroundedness A rule for figure-ground assignment stating that if one region is entirely surrounded by another, it is likely that the surrounded region is the figure.

Figure 4.30 Why do the pale blue stripes appear to be the figure when the blue and purple regions are about equal in size? Parallel contours are often taken to belong to the figure.

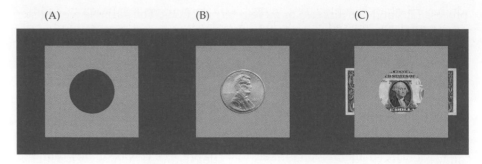

(A) (B) (C)

Figure 4.31 Which circles are figures and which are holes?

relatability The degree to which two line segments appear to be part of the same contour.

heuristic A mental shortcut.

purple square and completely surrounded by it. Moreover, each circle is perfectly symmetrical. Yet, of the three, only the center circle (Figure 4.31B) is perceived as being a separate object (figure); the circles on the left and right are seen as holes in the purple squares.

You can (and should) speculate about the factors that determine whether a circle is seen as a hole or a spot (C. Yin, Kellman, and Shipley, 1997). In Figure 4.31C, the answer has something to do with the fact that we interpret those three isolated patches of a dollar as one object, occluded by the purple square. Given that theory, the circle must be a hole. One lesson from this figure is that the journey from image features to perceptual objects is not a simple one-way street. Figure-ground processes divide up the image into regions that can be recognized as specific objects. At the same time, object recognition influences figure-ground assignment (Peterson and Skow, 2008). (See **Web Essay 4.1: The Role of Knowledge in Figure-Ground Assignment**.) In some sense, object recognition is happening both before and after figure-ground assignment.

Dealing with Occlusion

Objects are rarely kind enough to present themselves to us in splendid isolation on blank backgrounds. In the real world, objects are often partially hidden by other objects. Indeed, three-dimensional objects hide parts of themselves (you don't see the back of a ball, for example). We've already discussed how edge-finding processes can fabricate illusory contours on the basis of the physics of occlusion. Now, let us think about the work required to connect the visible pieces of occluded objects by inferring the presence of hidden pieces of the object when necessary.

The Gestalt principle of good continuation comes into play here (see Figure 4.17). How do we understand the continuation of a contour when it disappears from view, behind an occluder? Philip Kellman and Thomas Shipley (1991) speak about the **relatability** of two contour segments. Relatability is illustrated in **Figure 4.32**. Do the two black line segments in each part look like they belong to the same curve, occluded by the black square? For Figure 4.32A, the answer is "yes." For Figure 4.32B, the answer is "no." Kellman and his colleagues argue that the critical difference is that the lines in Figure 4.32A can be related by a simple curve like an elbow or a bend in the road. The lines in Figure 4.32B require a more complex *S* curve to make a smooth connection between them. The visual system is unwilling to propose such an elaborate relationship, so it concludes that the lines are not related at all (that is, they are not parts of the same object). Like the figure-ground rules, this **heuristic** (mental shortcut) is not infallible (after all, some objects really

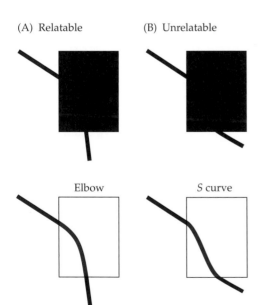

(A) Relatable (B) Unrelatable

Elbow *S* curve

Figure 4.32 Two edges are relatable if they can be connected with a smooth convex or smooth concave curve (A), but not if the connection requires an *S* curve (B). (After Kellman, 1998.)

do have *S*-shaped contours). The occlusion committee is apparently willing to accept a few missed completions in order to reduce the vast number of possible completions we would have to consider if we tried to connect every pair of occluded edges. (For more on dealing with occlusion, see **Web Essay 4.2: Dynamic Occlusion** and **Web Activity 4.4: Infant Object Perception**.)

Additional heuristics emerge when we move from two dimensions to three, as **Figure 4.33** shows. Here we see a pair of box-shaped objects, one partially occluding the other. The overlap of the boxes produces a variety of different line junctions, all of which can be classified as *Y*, *T*, or arrow junctions. *T* junctions almost always occur when one surface occludes another; *Y* and arrow junctions almost always correspond to corners and thus don't signal occlusions. These rules fail to hold true only when we're viewing the scene from an accidental viewpoint. Hence, the various junction types are known as **nonaccidental features** (Lowe, 1985), and they provide another potential tool for use by the perceptual committees charged with dividing the scene into objects and deciding whether one object is occluding another.

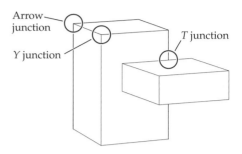

Figure 4.33 Different sorts of line junctions have different meanings. *T* junctions indicate occlusion of one region by another. *Y* and arrow junctions indicate corners.

Parts and Wholes

Objects in the world tend to have parts. Indeed, it is not obvious how to define a visual object. Look at yourself in the mirror. In some sense, you are an object; so is your nose, each eye, your shirt, and so forth, but your lips, eyes, and so on, can be thought of as objects in their own right. In the lab, stimuli like those in **Figure 4.34** have been used to investigate the relationship of visual objects to their component parts. Look for *H*s in Figure 4.34. Did you find the big (global) *H* more quickly than the little (local) *H*s? Using stimuli like these, David Navon (1977) found that the global letters interfered with naming of the local letters more than the local letters interfered with recognition of the global letters. This **global superiority effect** is consistent with an implicit assumption we've been making throughout our discussion of mid-level vision: that the first goal is to carve the retinal image into large-scale objects.

In the Navon letters, the division into parts and wholes, local and global, is easy. It is not so easy to ask how to "carve" a human form into parts like legs and arms. One heuristic is illustrated in **Figure 4.35**. Don Hoffman and Whitman Richards (1984) noted that when one blob is pushed into another, a pair of concavities is created in the silhouette of the resulting two-part object (Figure 4.35A). A process that embodied this bit of physics would conclude that valleys, rather than bumps, should be used to mark part boundaries. Thus, we are inclined to parse the object into two parts as shown in Figure 4.35B, not into three parts as in Figure 4.35C.

Summarizing Mid-level Vision

Before moving on, it is worth briefly reviewing how we got here. Early-vision processes gave us the local features in the visual world. Mid-level–vision processes began the work of understanding what those local features might be telling us

nonaccidental feature A feature of an object that is not dependent on the exact (or accidental) viewing position of the observer.

global superiority effect The finding in various experiments that the properties of the whole object take precedence over the properties of parts of the object.

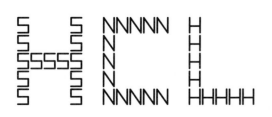

Figure 4.34 Global letters composed of local letters. David Navon argued that perceptual processes work from the global to the local.

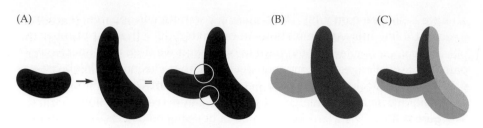

Figure 4.35 Finding parts from object boundaries. (A) When one blob is pushed into another, a pair of concavities is created. We know this (implicitly, of course), and we work backward from this fact to carve this figure into the two parts shown in (B) rather than according to a different scheme, such as the one shown in (C).

Bayesian approach   A way of formalizing the idea that our perception is a combination of the current stimulus and our knowledge about the conditions of the world—what is and is not likely to occur. The Bayesian approach is stated mathematically as Bayes' theorem: $P(A|O) = P(A) \times P(O|A)/P(O)$, which enables us to calculate the probability (P) that the world is in a particular state (A) given a particular observation (O).

about the state of the world. The work of the mid-level–vision processes discussed so far in this chapter might be summarized in five principles:

1. *Bring together that which should be brought together.* We have the Gestalt grouping principles (similarity, proximity, parallelism, symmetry, and so forth), and we have the processes that complete contours and objects even when they are partially hidden behind occluders (e.g., the relatability heuristic).

2. *Split asunder that which should be split asunder.* Complementing the grouping principles are the edge-finding processes that divide regions from each other. Figure-ground mechanisms separate objects from the background. Texture segmentation processes divide one region from the next on the basis of image statistics.

3. *Use what you know.* Two-dimensional edge configurations are taken to indicate three-dimensional corners or occlusion borders, and objects are divided into parts on the basis of an implicit knowledge of the physics of image formation.

4. *Avoid accidents.* Avoid interpretations that require the assumptions of highly specific, accidental combinations of features or accidental viewpoints.

5. *Seek consensus and avoid ambiguity.* Every image is ambiguous. There are always multiple, even infinite, physical situations that could generate a given image. Using the first four principles, the "committees" of mid-level vision must eliminate all but one of the possibilities, thereby resolving the ambiguity and delivering a single solution to the perceptual problem at hand.

From Metaphor to Formal Model

We have been talking about perceptual committees in mid-level vision. While we hope that is a useful way to think about what's going on, it is just a metaphor. There are formal, mathematical ways to model the way in which knowledge about regularities in the world can constrain the interpretation of ambiguous sensory input. One of the most fruitful approaches is known as the **Bayesian approach** (Yuille and Kersten, 2006). Thomas Bayes (1702–1761), an eighteenth-century Presbyterian minister, was the first to describe the relevant mathematics.

Look at **Figure 4.36**. Our visual system looks at the stimulus and makes an observation. As noted earlier, there is an infinite set of hypotheses that could be based on the observation. How does our visual system decide that one of these is the best hypothesis? The Bayesian approach asks us to think about two factors. First, before you look at anything, how likely is what you are proposing? This is known as the prior probability. The prior probability of a unicorn is much lower

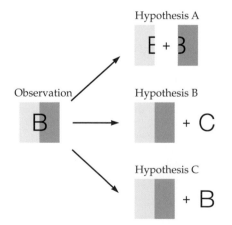
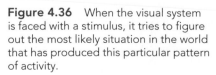

Figure 4.36 When the visual system is faced with a stimulus, it tries to figure out the most likely situation in the world that has produced this particular pattern of activity.

than the prior probability of a cow. Thus, if you make an observation that seems consistent with either unicorn or cow, you should be more inclined to accept the cow hypothesis. Second, how consistent is each hypothesis with observation? Suppose you had the hypothesis that you were looking at a red square in Figure 4.36. The prior probability of a red square is no lower than the prior probability of a green square, but observation does not support the red square hypothesis.

So, in Figure 4.36, let's consider three hypotheses: Hypothesis A proposes that we're looking at two green rectangles. The light one has a narrow letter *E* on it, and the dark one has a narrow numeral 3. These just happen to precisely line up in order to produce a *B* like the one we observed. That is consistent with the observation, but its prior probability is low because the *E* and 3 would need to line up very precisely—an accidental viewpoint. Hypothesis B suggests that this is a green square with a *C* on it. That is not particularly unlikely, but it is not consistent with the sensory data. Hypothesis C proposes that this is a green square with a *B* on it. That does not require anything very unlikely in the world, and it is consistent with the observation.

What is really powerful about the Bayesian approach is that these sorts of ideas can be reduced to formal, mathematical equations. That math is beyond the scope of this text, but a brief introduction can be found in **Web Essay 4.3: Bayesian Analysis**.

> **FURTHER DISCUSSION** of the Bayesian approach can be found in Chapter 6 on pages 204–206.

■ Sensation & Perception in Everyday Life

Material Perception: The Everyday Problem of Knowing What It Is Made Of

We have assembled a collection of mid-level–vision tools that will be very useful when it comes to recognizing objects, but before we move on to object recognition, let's take a moment to think about what things are made of. You are very good at what we can call "material perception." If you look at **Figure 4.37**, you will be able to say something about each of these surfaces. For instance, Figure 4.37B is shiny while Figure 4.37C is not. From very simple examples like this, we can derive some important principles of material perception. First, material perception is not about recognizing the object and knowing what such objects are made of. You could have a rubber ball, a metal ball, or a ball made of rock or ice. They would all be simple spheres, but you would know from their surface properties that each was made of something different. Moreover, some surfaces aren't parts of objects at

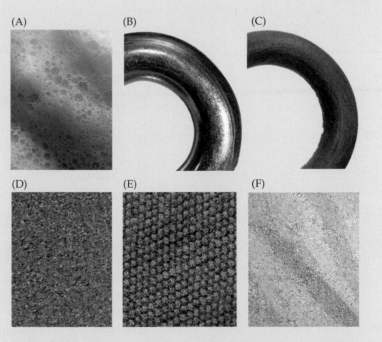

Figure 4.37 You are remarkably good at figuring out what things are made of.

(Continued)

■ Sensation & Perception in Everyday Life *(continued)* ■■■■■■

all; at least, not in the usual sense of "object." In Figure 4.37F, you can identify sand. Sand, like snow or water, isn't an object like a rock or a desk. It is "stuff" (Adelson, 2001), but you can still identify it from its surface properties.

Figure 4.37 illustrates a second important aspect of material perception. You can use the visual properties of a material to perform two related but not identical tasks. You can *categorize* the material; so, Figure 4.37E is cloth. And you can *estimate* how the thing would behave. Would that cloth be rough and itchy against your skin? What would it feel like to try to pick up the stuff in Figure 4.37A (Fleming, 2014)?

How do you perform these acts of material perception? There are reliable visual cues that are generated by the ways that light interacts with physical materials. Think about a shiny ball or a surface like the one in Figure 4.37B. There are "highlights," bright spots, on a shiny surface. These have specific properties. For instance, they tend to be less richly colored than the rest of the shiny surface. Indeed, if you take away the highlights, a shiny ball will no longer look very shiny. Computer graphics have gotten very good at simulating the physics of different surfaces. The problem is that it is easier to go from the physics to the creation of a visual stimulus than it is to go from the visual stimulus back to the physics. Think about plastic. You have a pretty good idea of when you are looking at something made of plastic, but just think of all the varieties of surfaces that fall into that category, from clear plastic bags to shopping bags to children's toys to plastic deck chairs. The latest animated movie may do a great job rendering shopping bags and deck chairs, but you won't find a simple rule that will let you categorize all those things as plastic. How are you doing this very tricky task? One possibility is that you are learning that specific features correspond to a substance like plastic in this specific case. Then you are creating a "generative" model (Fleming, 2014) where you estimate what that substance would look like under a range of different conditions (dimmer light, light source over to one side, and so on). From this, you build up an internal definition of plastic that allows you to categorize plastic the next time you see it, even under quite different conditions. This is a bit like your definition of object categories—a topic we will return to later. What, after all, is the definition of "chair"? It might be a thing with four legs that you can sit on. Unless it has three legs or no legs, or it is a table that you could sit on but shouldn't or it is a horse. However you do these tasks, you do them remarkably fast. Given an exposure of 40 ms (1/25 of a second), you can identify many types of material and even tell whether they are real or fake (Sharan, Rosenholtz, and Adelson, 2009).

Object Recognition

Now, armed with tools that should be useful for object recognition, let us return to Quiroga's discovery of cells that respond to highly specific objects (Quiroga et al., 2005). Traveling the *what* pathway from V1 into the temporal lobe, we can see a progressive change in the responses of cells in different visual areas. In V1, cells respond best to lines and edges in very specific areas of the visual field. In V2, we get early steps from local features to objects. As noted before, these cells have a sensitivity to "border ownership." They are also sensitive to illusory contours (Peterhans et al., 1986; von der Heydt, Peterhans, and Baumgartner, 1984). By area V4, cells appear to be interested in much more complex attributes, like those shown in **Figure 4.38**. No one has ever definitively determined the perfect set of stimuli for V4 cells. Figure 4.38A shows some geometric ideas from Gallant, Braun, and Van Essen (1993); Figure 4.38B shows a small subset of a collection of bumpy blobs from the work of Kourtzi and Connor (2011). The images in Figure 4.38 illustrate a fact about objects: while you can vary orientation or color or other basic features in a systematic way, it is much harder to imagine how you vary object shape. What are the dimensions of shape? We really do not know. In Figure 4.38B the darkness of the circles indicates how well a specific

(A)

(B)

Figure 4.38 Response of V4 cells to different shapes. (A) Gallant, Braun, and Van Essen tried this set of stimuli. Warm colors indicate more response from one particular cell. (B) Connor and his colleagues presented these shapes to V4 neurons. Darker circles indicate more response. (A from Gallant, Braun, and Van Essen, 1993; B from Pasupathy and Connor, 2002.)

cell responded to each of these items. As you can see, this cell seems to have a taste for stimuli with a feature pointing to the right. The connection to object perception is illustrated in **Figure 4.39**. This V4 cell might respond to a stimulus like the one in Figure 4.39A, but it will not respond well to a stimulus like the one in Figure 4.39B, because that black object doesn't really have a feature pointing right. Its point is an accident of occlusion. The border ownership rules, established in V2, now become part of the process of understanding object shape (Bushnell et al., 2011).

Things get more complex as we move farther into the temporal lobe. **Figure 4.40** illustrates the hopeful hypothesis that a vast family of shapes like those in Figure 4.38 might be a basis for object perception just as letters and syllables can be the basis for words (Ungerleider and Bell, 2011). We may not know exactly what optimally activates individual cells as we progress down the *what* pathway into the temporal lobe. However, as mentioned before, *functional imaging studies* can show us that different regions of the cortex are activated better by some categories of stimuli than by others. One way to show this is a so-called **subtraction method**. If you show a human observer a series of pictures of spaces like rooms and fields and city streets, lots of pieces of the brain will be activated by these places. Now show the observer other pictures with similar properties that do not happen to be places—maybe scrambled versions of the places, maybe objects or abstract designs. Again, large areas of brain will be active. However, if you subtract the two patterns of activation, there will be at least one region,

(A)   (B)
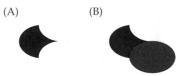

Figure 4.39 A cell in V4 that responded well to sharp features pointing to the right would respond well to (A) but not to (B) because that sharp point is the "accidental" product of occlusion.

subtraction method In functional magnetic imaging, comparison of brain activity measured in two conditions: one with and one without the involvement of the mental process of interest. The difference between the images for the two conditions may show regions of brain specifically activated by that mental process.

Figure 4.40 Neurons might be sensitive to shapes that can be put together into a recognizable object even if no cell's preferred shape looks like anything that we have seen.

Figure 4.41 Object-decoding methods in functional magnetic resonance imaging (fMRI). First, researchers train a computer system by showing a large set of images to an observer in a scanner. Then, they attempt to decode the brain activity produced by a new image. By finding the best match to the previously recorded brain activity, researchers can often guess the identity of the new image and can map the parts of the brain that contain that information.

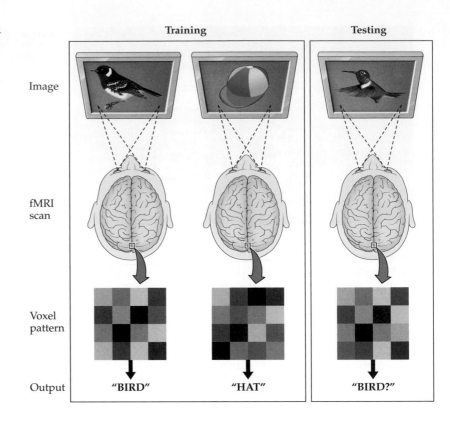

parahippocampal place area (PPA) A region of extrastriate visual cortex in humans that is specifically and reliably activated more by images of places than by other stimuli.

fusiform face area (FFA) A region of extrastriate visual cortex in humans that is specifically and reliably activated by human faces.

extrastriate body area (EBA) A region of extrastriate visual cortex in humans that is specifically and reliably activated by images of the body other than the face.

decoding The process of determining the nature of a stimulus from the pattern of responses measured in the brain or, potentially, in an artificial system like a computer network. The stimulus could be a sensory stimulus or it could be an internal state (e.g., the contents of a dream).

now known as the **parahippocampal place area** (**PPA**), mentioned earlier, that is specifically and reliably activated more by places than by other stimuli (Epstein and Kanwisher, 1998). Other well-established specialized areas include the **fusiform face area** (**FFA**), also mentioned earlier, and the **extrastriate body area** (**EBA**) (see Figure 4.4).

More modern functional imaging studies can make use of **decoding** methods as shown in **Figure 4.41**. First, you present an observer in a magnetic resonance imaging scanner with a range of different images, for example, a vast series of objects, each in many different sizes, positions, and so forth. You catalogue the responses of the brain to each image. Next, you present a new image of one of these objects, and you use the patterns of activity to try to guess the identity of the object. Perhaps there is some part of the brain that generates patterns that allow you to correctly determine that this stimulus was a cat and that stimulus was a shoe. This does not prove that this specific piece of brain was the locus of recognition, but it does show that information about object identity is present in that region (Kay et al., 2008). Eventually, decoding could take us to some rather interesting places. If you knew the patterns of activity associated with a wide set of objects presented while someone was awake, could you decode that person's dreams if you let her sleep in the scanner? We are not there yet, but a start has been made (Horikawa et al., 2013).

Can we build it? Chapters 2, 3, and 4 have described a story in which more and more complex attributes of the visual input are processed as we move from the eyes to the LGN to early visual cortex and beyond. Recent advances in computer science have shown that models, built on an approximation of this architecture, can do a good job in classifying objects in scenes. Oliver Selfridge (1959) suggested a version of such a model more than 50 years go. His "Pandemonium model" was an account of letter recognition, a relatively simple subset of the object recognition

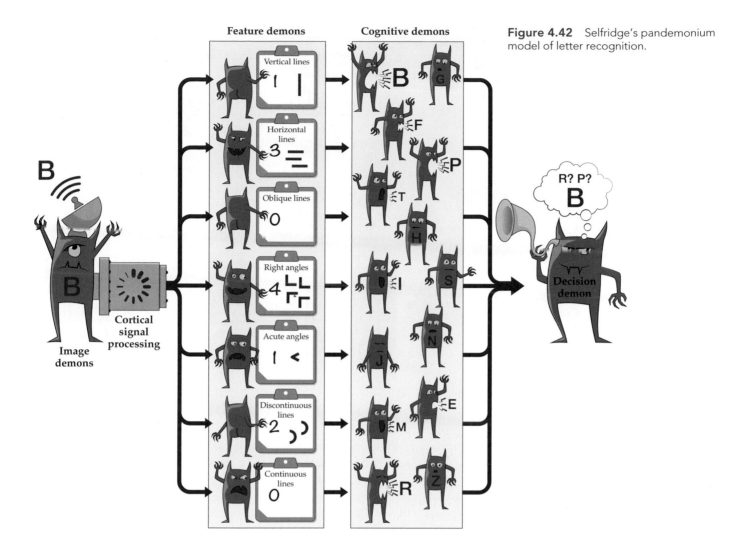

Feature demons

Vertical lines

Horizontal lines

Oblique lines

Right angles

Acute angles

Discontinuous lines

Continuous lines

Cognitive demons

Image demons

Cortical signal processing

R? P? B

Decision demon

Figure 4.42 Selfridge's pandemonium model of letter recognition.

problem (**Figure 4.42**). Selfridge used "demons" as metaphor for processes that we would discuss in neural terms today. Indeed, the word *pandemonium*, which we define as "noise and chaos," was originally coined by the poet John Milton (1608–1674) as the name of the home of all demons in *Paradise Lost*. Selfridge had an initial early-vision signal-processing stage. Next, features were extracted: oriented lines, curves, and so on. In his third step, a set of "cognitive demons" each looked for the features of one letter while the decision demon pooled information across all the third-layer demons and chose the loudest demon as the answer. (See **Web Activity 4.5: Pandemonium** for more on Selfridge's model.)

That is not a bad start but, of course, the real network will be more complicated than Selfridge's fairly simple network of demons. Even for a constrained task like letter recognition, the network needs to accept all the letter *A*s in **Figure 4.43** as *A*s. It needs to recognize *A*s in many locations, many sizes, and many orientations. And an *A* is a simple case. The object recognition network needs to be able to categorize each object in **Figure 4.44** as a cow. No simple cow **template** will do that. The basic idea of a template is rather like a lock and key. As we will see in Chapters 14 and 15, the lock-and-key metaphor is quite apt in smell and taste, where the "key" to be recognized is a molecule like a specific odorant and where that molecular key presents itself in more or less the same shape every time. For instance, look at the "shape-pattern" theory of olfaction

template The internal representation of a stimulus that is used to recognize the stimulus in the world. Unlike its use in, for example, making a key, a mental template is not expected to actually look like the stimulus that it matches.

A *A* A A

a *a* A a

Figure 4.43 The problem with templates is that we need a lot of them.

Figure 4.44   What would a cow template look like?

in Chapter 14. Objects, however, are not like molecules. The same category of object can present itself in an infinity of ways.

One way out of this problem is to notice that all the *A*s—at least all the capital *A*s in Figure 4.43—share a basic structure. Instead of matching each point in the image to a point in a template, perhaps we perform a more conceptual match. Just about any capital *A* can be described by the relationship of its three lines: the two flanking lines meet, and the third line spans the angle created by those two lines. Now the image of the *A* is being matched to a **structural description** of an *A*, a specification of an object in terms of its parts and the relationships between the parts.

Biederman (1987) in his **recognition-by-components model** proposed something like this for objects more generally. He suggested that a set of **geons** ("geometric ions") could be the basic building blocks of the perception of objects in the world. **Figure 4.45** shows a few geons in isolation and a few simple objects composed of two geons. The idea is that the visual system should be able to recognize an object on the basis of the relationship of its geons, regardless of how the geon is oriented in space (as long as it's not an accidental view). There are problems with structural description models. Real object recognition is not as viewpoint-independent as the model would propose. Moreover, no one has ever come up with a set of geon-like primitives that would work over all objects. Would the geon description of a book differ from the description of a box containing that book? This objection merely points out that a structural description would have to be just a part of the answer to the problem of object recognition. Other parts of the answer would include information about materials and surface markings. Those factors, for instance, would tend to differentiate a box and a book. In addition, it is important to remember that object identities are learned and that learning may be influenced

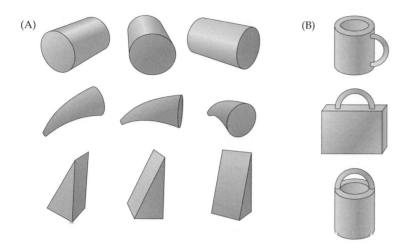

Figure 4.45 Building objects from geons. (A) Three of the 36 or so geons in Biederman's recognition-by-components model of object recognition. (B) Three of the many objects that could be made from just two geons.

by the viewpoint(s) at which the object is seen (Gauthier et al., 1998). (**Web Activity 4.6: Viewpoint Effects** lets you test yourself in a short experiment showing some of these effects.)

As hinted at the start of this section, the real breakthrough in the area of object recognition has come from computer science. The advent of faster computers with more and more memory has allowed researchers to build **deep neural network** (**DNN**) models with many more layers than Selfridge's and with a set of rules that let the model learn to categorize objects (Kriegeskorte, 2015). In broad outline, the ideas behind DNNs should sound familiar. A set of features is extracted from the image (**Figure 4.46A, B**). In the first layer of a DNN, this is quite like what *simple cells* in visual cortex are doing (see page 80). Then that information is pooled in a manner that is something like what *complex cells* are doing (**Figure 4.46C**). You can think of these operations as creating a new image that the next layer of the DNN will take as its input for feature extraction and pooling (**Figure 4.46D, E**). These processes of feature extraction and pooling are repeated for a number of layers (**Figure 4.46F**). Then, at the top of this stack of layers you have what amounts to a set of "grandmother cells," one for each category of object that you are trying to identify. If the set of object categories included "grandmother," then one of these cells really would be a grandmother cell. It would be looking at the pattern of activity across the top layer of the

deep neural network (DNN)
A type of "machine learning" in artificial intelligence in which a computer is programmed to learn something (here object recognition). First the network is "trained" using input for which the answer is known ("that is a cow"). Subsequently, the network can provide answers from input that it has never seen before.

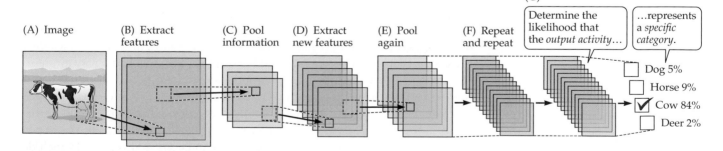

Figure 4.46 A deep neural network recognizing a cow. The network has previously been trained using a wide range of animals. Now, faced with an image it has never seen before, it can declare that "cow" is the most likely category.

network to determine how likely it was that the pattern indicated the presence of "grandmother" (**Figure 4.46G**). A different cell would look for "cat" or "egg beater" or whatever categories you cared to ask about.

All of the myriad connections between bits of this big network are governed by weights that say, "This is a strong connection, while that is a weak connection." It is not possible to set all these weights by hand. Instead, the network learns its weights. Initially, the weights are random and the network produces random results. Show it a grandmother and, perhaps, it says that the most likely answer is "cat." If you show the network a set of images whose identities you know, you can calculate the size of the error that the network is making. Now you can change all the weights a bit and repeat. If the error gets smaller, that is good. If it gets larger, you made the wrong changes. Repeat this process many times (with some good rules for how to change weights), and you find a set of weights that minimizes the network's error. Now you have a "trained" network. If you feed a properly trained network some new images that it has never seen before, it will categorize most of those images successfully.

Notice that this has a quite natural feel to it. Once upon a time, you were a little child with a good network but not much training. You might not have known much about animals. Over time you were shown examples of cats, dogs, kangaroos, and wombats. We can imagine that the weights in your network were adjusted appropriately and then, faced with a specific cat that you had never seen before, you were likely to correctly categorize it. Learning the weights is how the specific features in a network are created. Interestingly, these object recognition networks learn features that seem to make some physiological sense. The first layer tends to grow features that look like oriented line and edge detectors with various color combinations. Intermediate layers become more complex, responding to textures and shapes like those in Figure 4.38, while the features in the final layers can look quite specific, reminiscent of cells in inferotemporal cortex that might respond to something face-like, for example.

This description of DNNs glosses over a great deal of sophisticated computer science. Moreover, it would be a mistake to think that DNNs have *solved* vision. Nevertheless, they are going to have increasing impact on our world, from self-driving cars to medical diagnosis where, for example, a DNN can diagnose skin cancer from images as well as expert dermatologists can (Esteva et al., 2017).

Multiple Recognition Committees?

If this chapter has had one theme, it is that no step on the road from image to recognition is taken by a single process acting alone. From the grouping of similar pieces of the image to the segregation of figure and ground, every step has been based on consensus—a committee decision. It seems likely that the act of recognition is similar. Indeed, recognition may not be a single act. We can recognize an object in multiple ways, perhaps simultaneously. As an example, **Figure 4.47** shows two birds. In the terminology of Pierre Jolicoeur and his colleagues (Jolicoeur, Gluck, and Kosslyn, 1984), "bird" is the **entry-level category** for these objects—the first word that comes to mind when we're asked to name them. But these objects are also quite clearly different. At a subordinate level—a more specific level beneath the entry level—Figure 4.47A shows a fox sparrow and Figure 4.47B shows a cardinal. At a superordinate level—a broader level above the entry level—these two objects, as well as the one in Figure 4.47C, are all animals.

We can imagine that each of these acts of recognition ("fox sparrow," "bird," "animal") might rely on different stored representations and different analyses of the visual stimulus. This is one reason to think that DNNs have not "solved"

entry-level category For an object, the label that comes to mind most quickly when we identify it (e.g., "bird"). At the subordinate level, the object might be more specifically named (e.g., "eagle"); at the superordinate level, it might be more generally named (e.g., "animal").

Figure 4.47 Two quite different birds (A, B), a yet more different animal (C), and a third "bird" (D).

vision yet. A good DNN might identify a fox sparrow, but you and what might be your vast collection of DNNs can answer many questions about that bird as a visual stimulus. In spite of amazing progress, it will be a while before artificial vision systems approach the visual world with the flexibility of the human system.

Faces: An Illustrative Special Case

Faces are an interesting special case of object recognition. Take, for example, the images in **Figure 4.48A**. You should have little difficulty recognizing these as faces, but you will probably have some difficulty quickly identifying which one has been modified. If you turn the faces right side up, however, one of the pictures will look quite strikingly wrong (Thompson, 1980). Effects like these (see **Web Activity 4.7: The Face Inversion Effect**) are taken as evidence for **holistic processing** of faces. That is, you don't recognize your friend's face by recognizing her specific eye and nose and mouth and then combining those features into a face. Instead, you seem to process the complex face as a single thing and your face-analyzing processes seem to be very concerned with the precise configuration of eyes, nose, and mouth. However, it is not clear how that configuration is specified. For example, if you look at **Figure 4.48B**, you will see that recognition seems to survive stretching the face even though that changes the relative distances between different features (Burton, 2013).

Work on the neural basis of face perception underlines the complexity of the face as an "object." Earlier, we mentioned the fusiform face area (FFA) as a patch

holistic processing Processing based on analysis of the entire object or scene and not on adding together a set of smaller parts or features.

(A)

Figure 4.48 Faces. (A) Which of these two photos has been altered? As you can see for yourself, both of these images of one of the authors look quite normal upside down, but one of them looks quite strikingly "wrong" when turned right side up. (B) The "wholistic" interpretation of this face does not seem to be greatly disturbed by stretching the image. (After Thompson, 1980.)

(B)

of brain that is very interested in faces. It is not alone. Different parts of the visual pathway appear to be interested in different aspects of face processing. Bruce and Young (1986) argued that faces conveyed seven distinct types of information. For example, the identity of the face is separable from the emotion expressed by the face, which is separable from the analysis of lip movements that support speech perception (see Chapter 11). More recent advances in neural imaging have started to identify specific brain regions that are important for different aspects of face processing. Haxby, Hoffman, and Gobbini (2000) propose a two-pathway story in which a pathway through FFA deals with invariant aspects of the face (Who is this?) while a different pathway deals with more dynamic aspects of face processing (What is she saying? Is she happy?). Like *what* and *where* pathways (see Figure 4.2), these pathways are not completely separate. They interact and support each other (Duchaine and Yovel, 2015).

Neuropsychology provides further evidence that face processing can be separated into different functions. Damage to specific areas in the temporal lobe of the brain can produce **prosopagnosia**, a disorder in which someone cannot identify faces. (See **Web Essay 4.4: Face Blindness**.) He may be able to recognize an object as a face, and he may know that the face looks angry. However, he will not know who the person is. If the person speaks, then auditory information, processed elsewhere, might provide identity information. Interestingly, it is possible to be born with a specific impairment in the ability to recognize faces. The existence of this **congenital prosopagnosia** is a good indication that there is a specific neural module for face recognition (Behrmann and Avidan, 2005). You may think you're suffering from this disorder when you fail to match a name to a face. However, that is a much more common failure of memory. You can recognize the face; you just can't remember the name that goes with it. Someone with prosopagnosia would not know that this particular face was familiar while another one was not. If you can be born without this face-recognizing ability, it seems likely that you are born with some ability. One study even suggests that some face-processing ability is present *before* birth. Reid et al. (2017) projected very schematic faces onto the abdomens of pregnant women. The abdominal wall is not much of a screen, so these were just triangles of dots mimicking two eyes and a nose or mouth. Nevertheless, Reid et al. reported that there were more fetal head turns toward the "upright face." Once the baby is born, it is much easier to show that very young infants have a preference for faces (Mondloch et al., 1999).

prosopagnosia An inability to recognize faces.

congenital prosopagnosia A form of face blindness apparently present from birth, as opposed to acquired prosopagnosia, which would typically be the result of an injury to the nervous system.

Summary

1. A series of extrastriate visual areas continue the work of visual processing. Emerging from V1 (primary visual cortex) are two broad streams of processing: one going into the temporal lobe and the other into the parietal lobe. The temporal pathway seems specifically concerned with *what* a stimulus might be. This chapter follows that pathway. (The parietal *where* pathway will be considered in later chapters.)

2. After early visual processes extract basic features from the visual input, it is the job of mid-level vision to organize these features into the regions, surfaces, and objects that can, in turn, serve as input to object recognition and scene-understanding processes.

3. Perceptual "committees" serve as an important metaphor in this chapter. The idea is that many semi-independent processes are working on the input at the same time. Different processes may come to different conclusions about the presence of an edge or the relationship between two elements in the input. Under most circumstances, we see the single conclusion that the committees settle upon. Bayesian models are one way to formalize this process of finding the most likely explanation for input. Deep neural networks may be a way to build members/parts of the committee.

4. Multiple processes seek to carve the input into regions and to define the edges of those regions, and many rules are involved in this parsing of the image. For example, image elements are likely to group together if they are similar in color or shape, if they are near each other, or if they are connected. Many of these grouping principles were first articulated by members of the Gestalt school.

5. Other, related processes seek to determine whether a region is part of a foreground figure (like this black *O*) or part of the background (like the white area around the *O*). These rules of grouping and figure-ground assignment are driven by an implicit understanding of the physics of the world. Thus, events that are very unlikely to happen by chance (e.g., two contours parallel to each other) are taken to have meaning. (Those parallel contours are likely to be part of the same figure.)

6. The processes that divide visual input into objects and background have to deal with many complexities. Among these are the fact that parts of objects may be hidden behind other objects (occlusion) and the fact that objects themselves have structure. Is your nose an object or a part of a larger whole? What about glasses or hair or a wig?

7. In addition to perceiving the shapes of objects and their parts, we are also very adept at categorizing the material that an object seems to be made of—glass, stone, cloth, and so on. We use material perception to estimate physical properties. What would it feel like? Can it be grasped like a bottle or would it slip through our fingers like sand?

8. It is common to talk about the role of "templates" in object recognition. The idea is that an object in the world is recognized when its image fits a particular representation in the brain in the way that a key fits a lock. It has always been hard to see how naïve template models could work, because of the astronomical number of templates required: we might need one "lock" for every object in every orientation in every position in the visual field.

Go to the
Sensation & Perception
Companion Website at
oup.com/us/wolfe5e
for chapter overviews, activities, essays, flashcards, and other study aids.
Go to **DASHBOARD** for additional resources and assessments.

9. Deep neural networks (DNNs) are modern efforts to create computer algorithms that can categorize objects very well. Unlike a literal, lock-and-key template, a DNN tries to match an image with a complex pattern of activity in a network that arises when the network encounters an object in a specific category. This allows the network to categorize an infinite set of images as "cat," "coffee cup," and so on.

10. Faces are an interesting special case of object processing. Viewpoint is very important. Upright faces are much easier to recognize than inverted faces. Moreover, some regions of the brain seem to be specifically interested in faces. Different regions may be important for different aspects of face processing (Who is it? versus How is he feeling?).

5 The Perception of Color

Questions to Contemplate

Think about the following questions as you read this chapter. By the chapter's end, you should be able to answer and discuss them.

- What is color for?

- Does everyone see the same colors?

- Suppose you have an orange on your plate for lunch. It looks orange. If you send a photo of that orange, the photo will look orange, too. The physical bases of those two orange experiences are very different. How does that work?

- Why couldn't people agree about the color of a dress that was all over the internet in 2015?

In 2015, a fairly ordinary picture of a dress swept the internet. The picture that caused all the fuss is shown in Figure 5.26, later in this chapter, where we will discuss the dress in more detail. For now, you can flip ahead and ask yourself, What colors do I see in the stripes? Some people assert that the stripes appear to be black and blue. Others (including the author of this chapter) insist on white and gold. If you saw this dress on someone out on the street, almost everyone would agree that the dress looks black and blue. We will come back to why people might report the "wrong" color later. For the start of this chapter on color perception, the dress can make the crucial point that color is not a physical property of things in the world; rather, it is a creation of the mind. A rose looks red, not because it is red in some physical sense, but because we look at that rose with our particular visual system. The central goal of this chapter is to explain what that means.

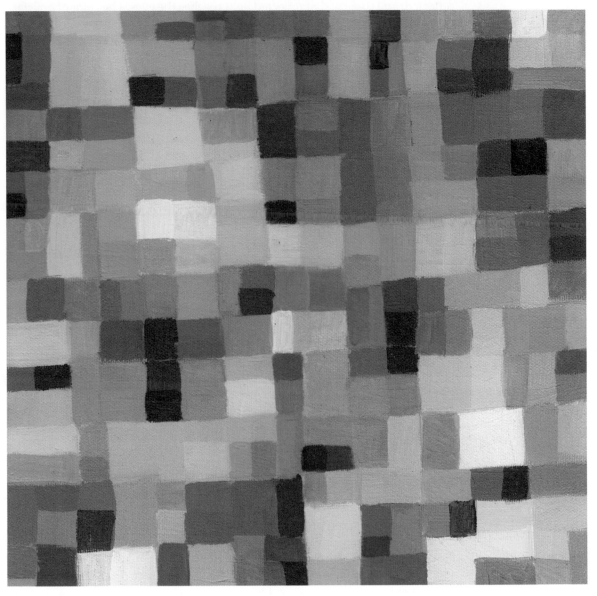

Tali Yalonetzki, Untitled painting, 2017

Basic Principles of Color Perception

Although color itself is not a physical property of things in the world, it is related to a physical property. As discussed in Chapter 2, humans see a narrow range of the electromagnetic spectrum between the wavelengths of about 400 and 700 nanometers (nm). The apparent color of a piece of the visible world is correlated with the wavelengths of the light rays reaching the eye from that piece of the world.

Most of the light that we see is reflected light. Typical light sources, like the sun or a lightbulb, emit a broad spectrum of wavelengths that hit surfaces in the world around us. Some wavelengths are absorbed by the surfaces they hit. The more light a surface absorbs, the darker it appears. Other wavelengths are reflected, and some of that reflected light reaches the eyes. The color of a surface depends on the mix of wavelengths that reach the eye from the surface (and, as we will see later, from the other surfaces and lights that are present in the scene). In the case of red roses, more of the longer-wavelength light (>600 nm) is reflected into the eyes of the observer. Even though (almost) all humans would declare this collection of wavelengths to appear red, it would be a big mistake to think of specific wavelengths of light as being specific colors. As Steven Shevell (2003) puts it, "There is no red in a 700 nm light, just as there is no pain in the hooves of a kicking horse." Like pain, color is the result of the interaction of a physical stimulus with a particular nervous system.

Three Steps to Color Perception

Several problems must be solved in order to go from physical wavelengths to the perception of color. We will organize our discussion around three steps (Stockman and Brainard, 2010):

1. *Detection.* Wavelengths must be detected.

2. *Discrimination.* We must be able to tell the difference between one wavelength (or mixture of wavelengths) and another.

3. *Appearance.* We want to assign perceived colors to lights and surfaces in the world. Moreover, we want those perceived colors to go with the object (that rose looks red) and not to change dramatically as the viewing conditions change (that rose should remain red in sun and shadow, for example).

We can say at the outset that color researchers have pretty convincing accounts of how color detection and discrimination work. Color appearance is a trickier problem.

Step 1: Color Detection

Detection was largely covered in Chapter 2. To briefly review, we have three types of cone photoreceptors. These cones differ in the photopigment they carry, and as a result, they differ in their sensitivity to light of different wavelengths. **Figure 5.1** shows those sensitivities as a function of wavelength. Each cone type is named for the location of the peak of its sensitivity on the spectrum: The cones that have a peak at about 420 nm are known as short-wavelength cones,

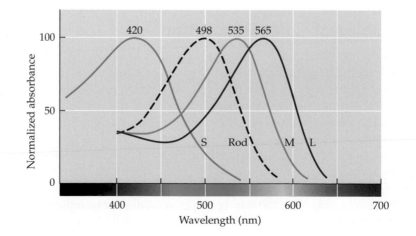

Figure 5.1   The retina contains four types of photoreceptors. These differ in their sensitivity to the wavelengths of light. Three cone types are maximally sensitive at short (S), medium (M), and long (L) wavelengths. The single type of rod photoreceptor has its peak sensitivity between those of the S- and M-cones.

or **S-cones**. The medium-wavelength cones, or **M-cones**, peak at about 535 nm. Long-wavelength cones, or **L-cones**, peak at about 565 nm. As you can see from Figure 5.1, cones are not exclusively sensitive to different parts of the spectrum. That is, even though the L-cone is maximally sensitive at about 565 nm, the M-cone can detect that wavelength as well. Their **spectral sensitivities** overlap. As mentioned in Chapter 2, S-cones are relatively rare, and they are less sensitive than M- and L-cones. The combination of sensitivities of the three types of cones gives us our overall ability to detect wavelengths from about 400 nm to about 700 nm (see Figure 5.1). Remember also that cones work at **photopic** (daylight) light levels. We have one type of rod photoreceptor; it works in **scotopic** (dimmer) light and has a somewhat different sensitivity profile, peaking at about 500 nm.

Step 2: Color Discrimination

We can detect wavelengths between 400 and 700 nm, but how do we distinguish, for example, between lights of 450, 550, and 625 nm? To see how discrimination differs from detection, let's examine the response of a single photoreceptor to a single wavelength of light. **Figure 5.2** shows how one kind of human photoreceptor responds to light of a specific wavelength while the intensity of the light is held constant. Because of the properties of the photopigment in the photoreceptor cell, 400-nm light produces only a small response in each cell of this type, 500-nm light produces a greater response, and 550-nm light even more. However, 600-nm light produces less than the maximal response, and 650-nm light produces a minimal response. Light of 625 nm produces a response of moderate strength.

The Principle of Univariance

So far, so good. We know that different wavelengths of light give rise to different experiences of color, and the varying responses of this photoreceptor to different wavelengths could provide a basis for color vision. But there is a problem, as illustrated in **Figure 5.3**. Suppose we change the wavelength from 625 nm to 450 nm. Figure 5.3 shows that an equal amount of 450-nm light will produce the same response from this photoreceptor that 625-nm light does. If we were looking at the output of the photoreceptor, we would have no way of distinguishing between the two lights. But when we look with a normal human color vision system, the 625-nm light looks orange and the 450-nm light looks bluish.

S-cone   A cone that is preferentially sensitive to short wavelengths; colloquially (but not entirely accurately) known as a "blue cone."

M-cone   A cone that is preferentially sensitive to middle wavelengths; colloquially (but not entirely accurately) known as a "green cone."

L-cone   A cone that is preferentially sensitive to long wavelengths; colloquially (but not entirely accurately) known as a "red cone."

spectral sensitivity   The sensitivity of a cell or a device to different wavelengths on the electromagnetic spectrum

photopic   Referring to light intensities that are bright enough to stimulate the cone receptors and bright enough to "saturate" the rod receptors (that is, drive them to their maximum responses).

scotopic   Referring to light intensities that are bright enough to stimulate the rod receptors but too dim to stimulate the cone receptors.

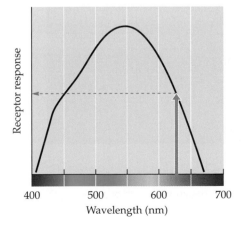

Figure 5.2 A single photoreceptor shows different responses to lights of different wavelengths but the same intensity. A 625-nm light of this intensity, indicated by the arrow, produces a response midway between the maximum and minimum responses.

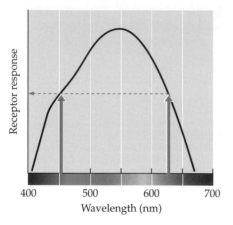

Figure 5.3 Lights of 450 and 625 nm both elicit the same response from the photoreceptor whose responses are shown here and in Figure 5.3. This situation illustrates the principle of univariance.

Actually, the problem is much worse. Remember that Figures 5.2 and 5.3 represent the photoreceptor's response rate when all wavelengths are presented at the same intensity. Under these conditions, the graphs indicate that light at either 450 or 625 nm produces a response lower than the peak response obtained at about 535 nm. If we had a 535-nm light, we could reduce its intensity until it produced exactly the same level of response from our photoreceptor as the 450- or 625-nm light did at the higher intensity. Indeed, we could take a "white light" or any mix of wavelengths and, by properly adjusting the intensity, get exactly the same response out of the photoreceptor.

Thus, when it comes to seeing color, the output of a single photoreceptor is completely ambiguous. An infinite set of different wavelength-intensity combinations can elicit exactly the same response, so the output of a single photoreceptor cannot by itself tell us anything about the wavelengths stimulating it. This constraint is known as the **principle of univariance** (Rushton, 1972). (See **Web Activity 5.1: The Principle of Univariance**.)

Obviously, the human visual system has solved the problem, but not under all circumstances. Univariance explains the lack of color in dimly lit scenes. Remember that there is only one type of rod photoreceptor. All rods contain the same type of photopigment molecule: rhodopsin. Thus, they all have the same sensitivity to wavelength. As a consequence, although it is possible to tell light from dark under scotopic conditions, the problem of univariance makes it impossible to discriminate colors. Our nighttime color blindness is one hint that color is psychophysical and not physical. The world seen under a bright moon (**Figure 5.4**) has not been physically drained of color. The same mix of wavelengths that produces color perception during the day remains present on that moonlit night, but we fail to see colors under dim illuminants like moonlight, because dim light stimulates only the rods, and the output of that single variety of photoreceptor does not permit color vision.

principle of univariance The fact that an infinite set of different wavelength-intensity combinations can elicit exactly the same response from a single type of photoreceptor. One photoreceptor type cannot make color discriminations based on wavelength.

Figure 5.4 The moonlit world appears drained of color because we have only one type of rod photoreceptor transducing light under these scotopic conditions. With just one type of photoreceptor, we cannot make discriminations based on wavelength, so we cannot see color.

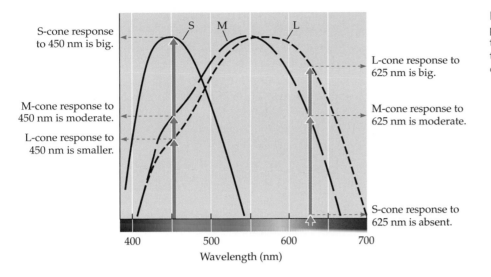

S-cone response to 450 nm is big.

M-cone response to 450 nm is moderate.

L-cone response to 450 nm is smaller.

L-cone response to 625 nm is big.

M-cone response to 625 nm is moderate.

S-cone response to 625 nm is absent.

Wavelength (nm)

Figure 5.5 The two wavelengths that produce the same response from one type of cone (M) produce different patterns of responses across the three types of cones (S, M, and L).

The Trichromatic Solution

We can detect differences between wavelengths or mixtures of wavelengths precisely because we have more than one kind of cone photoreceptor. **Figure 5.5** shows how, with our three cone types, we can tell the difference between lights of different wavelengths. Look at the three cones' responses to the two wavelengths—450 and 625 nm—that produced the same response from the single cone in Figure 5.3. The two wavelengths of light still produce the same response from that type of cone, now revealed to be the M-cone. However, these two wavelengths produce different outputs from the L-cones and S-cones. In fact, as you will see if you try **Web Activity 5.2: Trichromacy**, any wavelength from about 420 to 660 nm produces a unique set of three responses from the three cone types. This combined signal, a triplet of numbers for each "pixel" in the visual field, can be used as the basis for color vision. (We can see from about 400 to 700 nm, but the very long and very short wavelengths each stimulate only one type of cone.)

In our discussion of the univariance problem, we noted that we can make any wavelength produce the same response as any other from a single cone type by adjusting the intensity of the light. That is not a problem in the three-cone world of human color vision. A specific light produces a specific set of three responses from the three cone types. Suppose that the light produces twice as much M response as S response and twice as much S response as L response. If we increase the intensity of the light, the response sizes will change but the relationships will not. There will still be twice as much M response as S response and twice as much S response as L response, and those relationships will define our response to the light and, eventually, the color that we see. (Think what might happen if the lights were really bright.) The idea that ability to discriminate one light from another is defined in our visual system by the relationships among three numbers is the heart of **trichromacy**, or more elaborately, the **trichromatic theory of color vision**.

Metamers

The examples presented thus far involve the responses of the visual system to single wavelengths. However, you may have noticed that we have referred to "wavelengths or mixtures of wavelengths." That's because we are not typically

trichromacy or **trichromatic theory of color vision** The theory that the color of any light is defined in our visual system by the relationships of three numbers—the outputs of three receptor types now known to be the three cones. Also called the *Young-Helmholtz theory*.

Figure 5.6 Objects in the real world reflect light across the spectrum in different amounts. This graph plots the reflectances of raw and cooked hamburger meat. Which one looks redder? Which one reflects more of the long wavelengths?

exposed to single wavelengths. Almost every light and every surface that we see is emitting or reflecting a wide range of wavelengths. A laser pointer would emit a very narrow range of wavelengths, but a more normal situation is shown in **Figure 5.6**. It shows the relative amounts of light reflected from raw and cooked hamburger. How can we discriminate the raw from the cooked? When we're studying color vision, this real-world concern gets reduced to a different question: How do our cones respond to combinations of wavelengths of light?

To answer this question, consider what happens if we mix just two wavelengths. For the sake of this example, we will oversimplify by ignoring the S-cones and redrawing the M- and L-cones to make the numbers simpler. Imagine that we shine a wavelength that looks red and a wavelength that looks green onto a white piece of paper so that a mixture of both is reflected back to the eyes (**Figure 5.7A**). Suppose that the light that looks green produces 80 units of activity in the M-cones and 40 in the L-cones (remember, we are ignoring the S-cones for now). In addition, suppose that the light that looks red produces 40 units of activity in the M-cones and 80 in the L-cones. If we assume that we can add the cone responses together, then summing the "red" and "green"

Figure 5.7 In (A), the long-wavelength light that looks red and the shorter-wavelength light that looks green mix together to produce the same response from the cones as does the medium-wavelength light that looks yellow in (B). If two sets of lights produce the same responses, they are metamers and must look identical, so the red plus the green will look yellow.

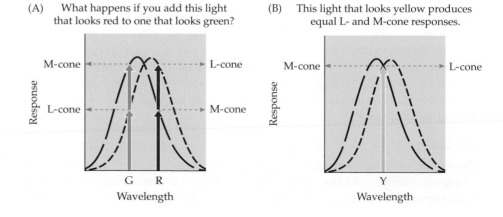

lights produces a response of 120 units in each cone. The absolute value is not important, because it could change if the intensity of the light changed. What is important is that these two lights, mixed together, produce a mixture that excites the L- and M-cones equally.

The key point is that the rest of the nervous system knows *only* what the cones tell it. If the mixture of lights that look red and green produces the same cone output as the single wavelength of light that looks yellow (**Figure 5.7B**), then the mixture and the single wavelength *must look identical*. Mixtures of different wavelengths that look identical are called **metamers**. The single wavelength that produces equal M- and L-cone activity will look yellow, and the correct mixture of longer- and shorter-wavelength lights will also look yellow.

Two quick warnings:

1. Mixing wavelengths does not change the physical wavelengths. If we mix 500- and 600-nm lights, the physical stimulus contains wavelengths of 500 and 600 nm. It does not contain the average (550 nm). It does not contain the sum (1100 nm) (which we would not be able to see anyway). Color mixture is a mental event, not a change in the physics of light.

2. For a mixture of a red and green to look perfectly yellow, we would have to have just the right red and just the right green. Other mixes might look a bit reddish or a bit greenish.

This example generalizes to *any* mixture of lights. All the light reaching the retina from one patch in the visual field will be converted into three numbers by the three cone types. If those numbers are sufficiently different from the numbers in another patch, you will be able to discriminate those patches. If not, those patches will be metamers: they will look identical, even if the wavelengths are physically different.

The History of Trichromatic Theory

From what you've read so far in this book, you would be forgiven for supposing that clever anatomists and physiologists identified the three cone types and built the trichromatic theory of color vision from there. Indeed, there have been beautiful experiments of this sort: For instance, Schnapf, Kraft, and Baylor (1987) managed to record the activity of single photoreceptors. Nathans, Thomas, and Hogness (1986) found the genes that code for the different photopigments. David Williams and his students even developed a method for photographing and identifying different cone types in the living human eye (see Figure 2.18).

Such research has cemented our understanding of the physical basis of trichromacy, but the basic theory was established by psychophysical experimentation. The theorizing started with Isaac Newton's great discovery that a prism would break up sunlight into the spectrum of hues, and a second prism would put the spectrum back together into light that looked white. In 1666, Newton understood that "the rays to speak properly are not coloured" (from *Opticks*, published originally in 1704). Newton knew that color is a mental event.

The three-dimensional nature of the experience of color was worked out in the nineteenth century by Thomas Young (1773–1829) and subsequently by Hermann von Helmholtz (1821–1894). In their honor, trichromatic theory is often called the "Young-Helmholtz theory." James Clerk Maxwell (1831–1879) developed a color-matching technique that was central to Helmholtz's work on this topic. (Somehow Maxwell missed having his name attached, or we would have the Young-Maxwell-Helmholtz theory.) Maxwell's technique is illustrated

metamers Different mixtures of wavelengths that look identical. More generally, any pair of stimuli that are perceived as identical in spite of physical differences.

Figure 5.8 In a modern version of Maxwell's color-matching experiment, a color is presented on the left. On the right, the observer adjusts a mixture of the three lights to match the color on the left.

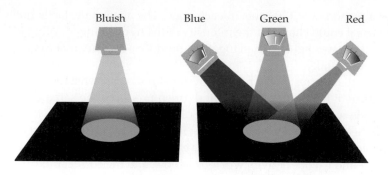

in **Figure 5.8**. The observer in a modern version of Maxwell's experiments would try to use different amounts of "primary" colored lights (e.g., the lights looking red, green, and blue on the right side of the figure) to exactly match another reference color (e.g., the light looking cyan, or bluish, on the left side).

The central observation from these experiments was that only three mixing lights are needed to match any reference light. Two primaries are not enough, and four are more than are needed. Long before physiology could prove it, these results led Young and Helmholtz to deduce that three different color mechanisms must limit the human experience of color.

A Brief Digression into Lights, Filters, and Finger Paints

The ubiquity of video screens in the twenty-first century may make color mixing and metamers reasonably intuitive. If you've never done so, find a magnifying glass and take a very close look at a yellow patch on your computer screen. You'll find that the patch is actually composed of thousands of intermixed red and green dots. The "red + green = yellow" formula is an example of **additive color mixture** because we are taking one wavelength or set of wavelengths and *adding* it to another.

For most of us, color mixture begins in kindergarten or earlier, with paints. In that world, red plus green doesn't make yellow; that mixture typically looks brown. A finger paint, or any other pigment, looks a particular color because it absorbs some wavelengths, subtracting them from the broadband ("white") light falling on a surface covered with the pigment. When a toddler smears together red and green, almost all wavelengths are absorbed by one pigment or the other, so we perceive the **subtractive color mixture** as a dark color like brown.

Actually, finger paint mixtures are rather complicated, with some pigment particles sitting next to each other and effectively adding their reflected light to the result. Other particles occlude each other, and still others are engaged in other complex interactions. Colored filters, like those you might put over stage lights, are a cleaner example of subtractive color mixture. **Figure 5.9** shows how a subtractive mixture of yellow and blue filters would subtract wavelengths, leaving only wavelengths in a middle range, which appear green. An additive mixture of lights that look blue and yellow will look white (if you have exactly the right blue and yellow) (**Figure 5.10**) because that combination produces a mix of wavelengths that stimulate the three cone types roughly equally. (See **Web Activity 5.3: Color Mixing**.)

Additive color mixture with paints is possible. Georges Seurat (1859–1891) and other Postimpressionist artists of the late nineteenth century experimented with Pointillism, a style of painting that involved creating many hues by placing

additive color mixture A mixture of lights. If light A and light B are both reflected from a surface to the eye, in the perception of color the effects of those two lights add together.

subtractive color mixture A mixture of pigments. If pigments A and B mix, some of the light shining on the surface will be subtracted by A, and some by B. Only the remainder will contribute to the perception of color.

1. Take "white" light that contains a broad mixture of wavelengths.

2. Pass it through a filter that absorbs shorter wavelengths. The result will look yellowish.

3. Pass that through a bluish filter that absorbs all but a middle range of wavelengths.

4. The wavelengths that make it through both filters will be a mix that looks greenish.

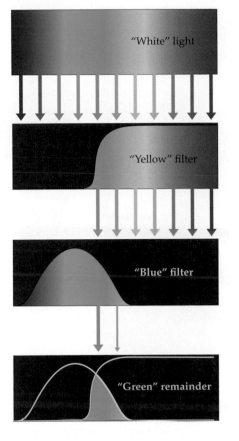

Figure 5.9 In this example of subtractive color mixture, "white"—broadband—light is passed through two filters. The first one absorbs shorter wavelengths, transmitting a mix of wavelengths that looks yellow. The second absorbs longer wavelengths and the shortest wavelengths, transmitting a mix that looks blue. The wavelengths that can pass through both filters without being subtracted are a middle range of wavelengths that appear green.

small spots of just a few colors in different textures (**Figure 5.11**). Viewing the painting up close, as illustrated in the figure, we can see each individual dot of color. Like the red, green, and blue phosphor dots on a computer monitor, the dots in the painting combine additively to produce a wide range of colors. Thus, from a distance the water's surface is appropriately silvery gray even if, up close, it is composed of spots of blue and yellow that would not be seen on the surface of a (clean) harbor.

From Retina to Brain: Repackaging the Information

The cones in the retina are the neural substrate for detection of lights. What is the neural basis for discriminating between lights with different wavelength composition? To tell the difference between different lights, the nervous system will look at differences in the activities of the three cone types. This work begins in the retina. We could send separate L, M, and S signals to the brain, but that approach would be less useful than one might think. For example, the L- and M-cones have very similar sensitivities (see Figure 5.1), so most of the time they are in close agreement: L says, "Lots of light coming from location X." "Yes, lots of light coming from location X," M agrees.

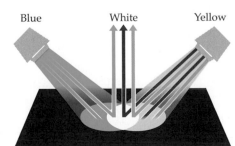

Figure 5.10 If we shine a light that looks blue and a light that looks yellow on the same patch of paper, the wavelengths will add, producing an additive color mixture. Remember that the light that looks yellow is equivalent to a mix of a long wavelength and a medium wavelength, so blue plus yellow results in a mix of short, medium, and long wavelengths. The mixture looks white (or gray, if it is not the brightest patch in view).

Figure 5.11 Pointillism is usually illustrated with a picture by Seurat. For variety, here is a painting by Paul Signac (1863–1935) using additive color mixture in the manner of a modern computer monitor. Thus, from a distance the domes look grayish, even if, up close, they are composed of spots of blue, green, and white.

Computing differences between cone responses turns out to be a much more useful way to transmit information to the brain. The nervous system computes two differences: $(L - M)$ and $([L + M] - S)$. Why these two? Comparisons across species suggest that the comparison between S-cones and an LM-cone happened first, perhaps 500 million years ago (Mollon, 1989). Then, about 40 million years ago, the LM-cone split into very similar L- and M- cones, and the difference between those cone types turned out to be useful. We don't know exactly why the L-M comparison became important in color vision, but there are theories. For example, blushing and turning pale are useful signals to observe, and our specific photopigments may have evolved to help us see those signals (Changizi, Zhang, and Shimojo, 2006) by making it possible to discriminate different amounts of blood in skin. That is not the only possibility. The $(L - M)$ difference may also be very useful if you want to tell the difference between fruit and leaves, different shades of green in the foliage, or the ripeness of a berry (Regan et al., 2001).

In addition to $(L - M)$, we could create $(L - S)$ and $(M - S)$ signals. However, because L and M are so similar, a single comparison between S and $(L + M)$ can capture almost the same information that would be found in $(L - S)$ and $(M - S)$ signals. Finally, combining L and M signals is a pretty good measure of the intensity of the light (S-cones make a rather small contribution to our perception of brightness). Thus, on theoretical grounds, it might be wise to convert the three cone signals into three new signals—$(L - M)$, $([L + M] - S)$, and $(L + M)$ (Buchsbaum and Gottschalk, 1983; Zaidi, 1997)—and the visual system does something reasonably close to this.

Cone-Opponent Cells in the Retina and LGN

The earliest work on the combination of cone signals was done with fish (Svaetichin and Macnichol, 1959). By the 1960s, Russell De Valois and others had begun to show that these sorts of signals actually exist in the **lateral geniculate** nucleus (**LGN**) of macaque monkeys (De Valois, Abramov, and Jacobs, 1966). As described in Chapter 3, many ganglion cells in the retina and the LGN of the thalamus are maximally stimulated by spots of light. These cells have receptive fields with a characteristic center-surround organization. For example, some cells are excited when a light turns on in the central part of their receptive fields and inhibited when a light turns on in the surround (see Figure 2.20).

A similar antagonistic relationship characterizes color. Some of these retinal and LGN ganglion cells are excited by the L-cone onset in their center and inhibited by M-cone onsets in their surround. These (L − M) cells are one type of **cone-opponent cell**, so named because different sources of chromatic information are pitted against each other. There are also (M − L), ([M + L] − S), and (S − [M + L]) cells—just the sorts of cells we would like to have to support the repackaging of cone signals, as described in the previous section. The cells that were excited by light onset could be thought of as (L + M) cells. Thus, we have the three signals that we wanted on theoretical grounds. The actual physiology is quite complicated. As mentioned in Chapters 2 and 3, for example, the S-cone signals go through the **koniocellular** layers in the LGN, while the M- and L-cone opponent signals are mostly found in the **parvocellular** layers (Xiao, 2014).

Suppose you could stimulate a single cone. What color would you see? Any spot of light you could put up on a screen would cover many photoreceptors. However, recall from Figure 2.12 that Roorda and Williams (1999) figured out how to use some very sophisticated optics to allow them to see and classify individual cones in the retina of a human observer. Now Roorda and his colleagues (Sabesan et al., 2016) have managed to focus tiny spots of light onto individual cones and ask those observers what they see (**Figure 5.12**). Often, as you might think, L-cones produce red responses and M-cones produce green regardless of the wavelength of stimulus (remember "univariance"). However, interestingly, much of the time, the spots look white. Amazingly, when the same cone is tested in sessions many days apart, the pattern of responses can stay quite stable. Why do we have all these "white" cones? Cones could be contributing to many circuits. For example, an L-cone could be part of an (L − M) circuit that responds to color and an (L + M) circuit that responds to brightness. Maybe the (L + M) brightness response is just stronger, so the spot looks white even though that cone might also contribute to the apparent color of a more normal patch of light. Alternatively, it could be that the response looks white because some cones just don't contribute to color sensation. This might help explain why spatial resolution (acuity, contrast sensitivity, see Chapters 2 and 3) is quite bad if you use **equiluminant** stimuli—stimuli that vary in color but not in luminance (Mullen, 1985). It may be that many cones just don't contribute to perception of such stimuli.

A Different Ganglion Cell Helps to Keep Track of Day and Night

If you have ever flown a significant distance east or west, you have probably experienced jet lag. The time on your cell phone clock changed by a few hours one way or the other, but your internal clock didn't get the message and remained on your home time. Over a couple of days, you adjusted to the new time. The primary force adjusting your internal **circadian** clock is sunlight (LeGates, Fernandez, and Hattar, 2014). Interestingly, mice bred to have no functioning photoreceptors continued to entrain their circadian clocks to light. Some apparently blind humans also seem to have that ability (Czeisler et al., 1995; Klerman et al., 2002). How could this be? There has been speculation about photoreceptors in the skin, but in recent years, we have learned that there is a previously unknown

lateral geniculate nucleus (LGN) A structure in the thalamus, part of the midbrain, that receives input from the retinal ganglion cells and has input and output connections to the visual cortex.

cone-opponent cell A cell type—found in the retina, lateral geniculate nucleus, and visual cortex—that, in effect, subtracts one type of cone input from another.

koniocellular Referring to cells in the koniocellular layer of the lateral geniculate nucleus of the thalamus. *Konio* from the Greek for "dust" referring to the appearance of the cells.

parvocellular Referring to cells in the parvocellular layers of the lateral geniculate nucleus of the thalamus. *Parvo* from the Greek for "small" referring to the size of the cells.

equiluminant Referring to stimuli that vary in color but not in luminance.

circadian Referring to the biological cycle that recurs approximately every 24 hours, even in the absence of cues to time of day (via light, clocks, etc.).

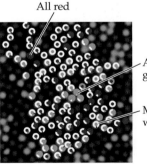

All red

Almost all green

Mostly white

Figure 5.12 A piece of the retina with the L-, M- and S-cones colored red, green, and blue. On top of many cones are white rings of varying degrees of completion. These show the responses of that cone to tiny spots of light. A full white ring, for example, means the observer always said the spot looked white. (From Sabesan et al., 2016.)

melanopsin A photopigment, found in a class of photoreceptive retinal ganglion cells.

mesopic Referring to the middle range of light intensities.

color space The three-dimensional space, established because color perception is based on the outputs of three cone types, that describes the set of all colors.

photosensitive cell in the retina. It is a ganglion cell. It receives input from the rods and the cones, but it also contains its own photopigment, **melanopsin** (see Chapter 2), so it can detect light even when normal photoreceptors are absent. You don't consciously see the outputs of this cell. Its outputs go to centers in the brain that control functions such as your circadian clock (Hughes et al., 2016). It is as if two (or more) visual systems were occupying your body, sharing the same eyes. Indeed, under the right circumstances, a few seconds of blue light can have an impact on cognitive function, even in individuals who have no conscious light perception, via this melanopsin-based system (Vandewalle et al., 2013).

Step 3: Color Appearance

Returning to the visual system that is giving rise to our conscious perception of the visual world, we have seen that the three cones detect a range of wavelengths. Rods make a small, important contribution to color vision, but only in fairly dim light (Stabell and Stabell, 2002). Interestingly, the three cone types and the rods are all active in a middle range of light intensities (call the **mesopic** range) but the visual system never developed "tetrachromacy," color perception based on four photoreceptor types (Webster, 2017) (but we will return to this topic later in this chapter, in the section on genetic differences). The retina and LGN contain cells that have repackaged the three cone signals into cone-opponent difference signals that constrain our ability to see differences between regions. Now is the time to think about what colors will be perceived.

Three Numbers, Many Colors

To begin, it is useful to have a system for talking about all the colors we can see. Because we have exactly three different types of cone photoreceptors, the light reaching any part of the retina will be translated into three responses, one for each local population of cones. After that translation, the rest of the nervous system cannot glean anything more about the physical wavelengths of the light. If the light rays reflecting off two isolated surfaces produce the same set of cone responses, the two surfaces must and will appear to be exactly the same color. They will be metamers, even if their physical characteristics are quite different. Thus, it is possible to produce bloodred color on the page without mimicking the physical properties of blood.

Working with just three numbers might not sound very promising, but it has been estimated that, with this system, we can discriminate the surfaces of more than 2 million different colors (Linhares, Pinto, and Nascimento, 2008; Pointer and Attridge, 1998). A lot of these colors are lightness variations of what we would colloquially consider the same color: bloodred in dim light, bloodred in brighter light, and so on. But even if we ignore lightness, we can still distinguish about 26,000 colors (Foster, 2011). Unless you're in paint sales, you don't know this many distinctive color *names*, but you could tell two different colors apart even if they were both named "pea green" or "sky blue."

We need some way to talk about all those colors in an orderly way. We can describe each of the colors in the spectrum with a single number—for example, the light's wavelength. Going beyond the spectrum, we have a three-dimensional **color space** analogous to a three-dimensional physical space. Of course, it doesn't make much sense to talk about height, length, and width in color space, but the space that contains the set of all perceptible colors has three dimensions based on the three numbers that come from the outputs of the three cone types.

■ Sensation & Perception in Everyday Life ■

Picking Colors

Representing the three-dimensional color space becomes a practical problem when you are using your computer. Many applications let you pick the colors of fonts, objects, and so on, and the app developers needed to devise an interface that would make that practical. One solution has been simply to present a fixed set of options (e.g., the crayon-box color-picking tool in many applications). However, if the developers want to provide access to all the possible colors, then they can present one or more color pickers that represent a three-dimensional color space. For example, look at **Figure 5.13**. It shows two different ways of using three "sliders" to define colors (here, borrowed from PowerPoint). In Figure 5.13A are three sliders for red, green, and blue. These RGB sliders are useful because com-

puter monitors have red, green, and blue elements in each pixel, and using RGB values is a good way to specify the signal to send to each of those elements. Thus, the green shown in the figure is what you get from 62 units (out of 255) delivered by the red elements, 180 from the green, and 60 from the blue. These RGB sliders define a three-dimensional space that can be represented by the cube shown in Figure 5.13C. Notice that white is in the upper corner closest to you on the cube. Black is hidden on the back corner, farthest from you.

In Figure 5.13B, we see the same shade of green defined by a different set of three numbers. This time, the variables are hue (H), saturation (S), and brightness (B). Part of the resulting HSB color space is shown in Figure 5.13D. These variables are very different concepts from red, green, and blue, but notice that again the system is three-dimensional. Look at the circular, top surface of the HSB space. Hue is the chromatic aspect of a light. It changes as you move around the circumference of the circle. Each point on the spectrum defines a different hue. As you can see from the HSB sliders, the whole family of colors with a hue of 120 (out of 360 degrees around the circle) will look like some version of green. The saturation dimension corresponds to the amount of hue present in a light. In the HSB space (Figure 5.13D), it is shown as the distance from the center of the circle. At the center, where saturation is 0, the resulting color would appear somewhere on the achromatic axis from black to white. Here, 67 (out of 100) describes a fairly saturated green. The final term, brightness, describes that black-to-white achromatic axis. The black bottom of the HSB

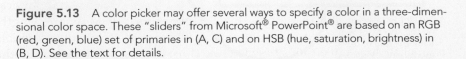

Figure 5.13 A color picker may offer several ways to specify a color in a three-dimensional color space. These "sliders" from Microsoft® PowerPoint® are based on an RGB (red, green, blue) set of primaries in (A, C) and on HSB (hue, saturation, brightness) in (B, D). See the text for details.

(Continued)

■ Sensation & Perception in Everyday Life *(continued)* ■

cone has a brightness of 0 (out of 100). The space tapers to a point because when brightness is 0, hue and saturation no longer have meaning. The full three-dimensional space, in this case, includes a cone, rising from a black point to a multicolored surface at a brightness of 100 and then climbing to a white peak (not shown in the figure). Brightness is the perceptual consequence of the physical intensity of a light. For instance, the physically intense light of the sun looks brighter than the less intense moon.

Thus, when you use your color picker to find just the right color, you are illustrating the fundamental nature of trichromacy. There is one interesting

exception. Along with RGB and HSB color pickers, many applications will also give you CMYK. This is a four-dimensional system, with sliders for cyan (C), magenta (M), yellow (Y), and black (K because "B" might be thought to stand for blue). You might notice that these are the colors of the ink cartridges in your color printer. Color printing is a subtractive process, and CMYK is designed for printing. The black slider is a convenience because using black ink is a better way to get to the black point in your color space than mixing cyan, magenta, and yellow inks. We will leave it as an exercise for the reader to figure out why CMYK uses C, M, and Y rather than R, G, and B inks.

The Limits of the Rainbow

The spectrum that you can see in the "hue" slider in Figure 5.13B is like the rainbow/wavelength spectrum that you can see at the bottom of **Figure 5.14A**, but it is not identical. There are hues that you can see that do not exist on the wavelength spectrum. Figure 5.14 illustrates how this comes to be. For example, suppose we combined a pure 420-nm light with a pure 680-nm light. This combination would strongly stimulate the L- and S-cones and produce minimal stimulation in the M-cones. No single wavelength of light could do that, but such a mixture is visible and must look like *something*. In fact, such mixtures will produce purplish magentas that seem to us to lie naturally between red and blue

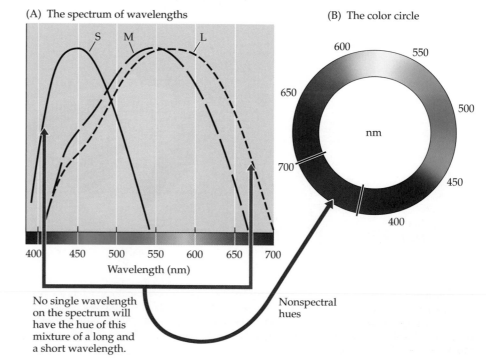

Figure 5.14 If you combine lights that look red and blue, the result will look purple, but there is no purple on the spectrum (A). Purples are nonspectral colors that join the ends of the spectrum into a color circle (B).

No single wavelength on the spectrum will have the hue of this mixture of a long and a short wavelength.

Nonspectral hues

on a color circle (**Figure 5.14B**). When we wrap the wavelength spectrum into a color circle, we join the red and blue ends with a set of colors that are called nonspectral hues—hues that can arise only from mixtures of wavelengths. While we are on the topic, it is worth noting that there are other commonly perceived colors that are not included in the spectrum's "all the colors of the rainbow." Brown is one such color. There are no brown lights. Brown is seen when a mixture of wavelengths that would look yellow, greenish yellow, or orange is seen in the company of other, brighter patches of color. You cannot see an isolated brown light in the dark (Buck, 2015).

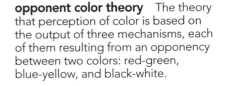

opponent color theory The theory that perception of color is based on the output of three mechanisms, each of them resulting from an opponency between two colors: red-green, blue-yellow, and black-white.

Opponent Colors

In the nineteenth century, Ewald Hering (1834–1918) described a curious feature of color vision: some combinations of colors seem to be perceptually "illegal." We can have a bluish green, a reddish yellow (which we would call "orange"), or a bluish red (which we would call "purple"), but reddish green and bluish yellow don't exist. Red and green are, in some fashion, opposed to each other, as are blue and yellow (Hering, 1878). Young and Helmholtz described a trichromatic theory with three basic colors (red, green, and blue); Hering's **opponent color theory** had four basic colors in two opponent pairs: red versus green, and blue versus yellow. A black-versus-white component formed a third opponent pair.

Figure 5.15 illustrates this idea. The center ring shows the hue dimension of HSB space, wrapped into the color circle as in Figure 5.14B. The outer ring offers a cartoon of four color mechanisms in two pairs. The inner patch on the center left looks yellow, in opponent color theory, because it stimulates the yellow pole of the yellow-blue opponency and does not stimulate either red or green.

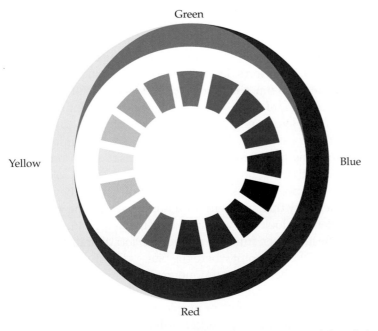

Figure 5.15 Hering's idea of opponent colors. Hering noted that all the colors on the "color circle" (the center ring) could be represented by two pairs of opposing colors: blue versus yellow, and red versus green (shown in the outer ring). Thus, a color could be a reddish yellow or a bluish green, but not a reddish green or a bluish yellow. (After Stockman and Brainard, 2010.)

Figure 5.16 A hue cancellation experiment starts with a color—here, bluish green (A) and a greener hue (B)—and attempts to determine how much of the opponent color of one of the starting color's components must be added to eliminate any hint of that component from the starting color. In this example, the observer adds red to cancel green (B, E), leaving only the blue component of the bluish green (C, E).

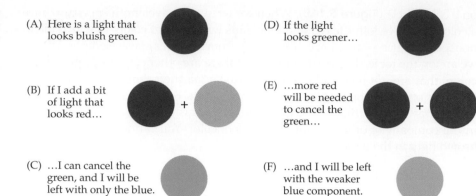

(A) Here is a light that looks bluish green.

(B) If I add a bit of light that looks red…

(C) …I can cancel the green, and I will be left with only the blue.

(D) If the light looks greener…

(E) …more red will be needed to cancel the green…

(F) …and I will be left with the weaker blue component.

Move a bit counterclockwise, and the orange patches add increasing red to the decreasing yellow.

Leo Hurvich and Dorothea Jameson (1957) revived Hering's ideas and developed one way to quantify this opponency. The method, called hue cancellation, is shown in **Figure 5.16**. In this example we start with a light that appears to be a bluish green (Figure 5.16A). We can cancel the perceptual greenness by adding its opponent color, red (Figure 5.16B). We measure the amount of a light that looks red that is needed to just remove all traces of green. The result will appear neither red nor green. It will be a shade of blue (Figure 5.16C). Since it is a mix of lights that look bluish green and red, it will be a rather desaturated-looking blue. If we do this for a greener color, as in Figure 5.16D, it will take more added light that looks red to cancel the green, and the result will be an even fainter blue remnant (Figure 5.16E, F). If we started with pure green, once it was cancelled, the result would be an achromatic patch because there would be no blue to be left over. We could cancel the perception of blue in our bluish-green patches by adding light that looked yellow. In this case, the remnant would appear green.

If we did hue cancellation experiments for lights across the spectrum, we would get results that look like those in **Figure 5.17**—not exactly like these, because these are Dorothea Jameson's data and everyone has slightly different results. If we start at about 400 nm, the lights look reddish blue (or violet) and we need to add some green and some yellow to cancel them. But look what happens at about 470 nm. Here is a light that has no red or green to cancel; it looks perfectly blue. This location on the spectrum is known as unique blue. Continuing to scan along the spectrum in the figure reveals the locations of two other **unique hues**—hues that can be described with only a single color term. Only four hues can be described in this way. As you might guess, they are red, green, yellow, and blue. Only three of them have unique loci on the spectrum. All the very long wavelengths look red (with, maybe, a touch of residual yellow). The two crossings of the red-green function provide the loci of unique blue and unique yellow (Figure 5.17A). The point where the blue-yellow function crosses from positive to negative is the locus of unique green, the green that has no blue or yellow in it (and, of course, no red) (Figure 5.17B). There are excellent exemplars of other colors, such as orange or purple, but they are not unique in the same way; orange, no matter how pure, can still be described as a reddish yellow. We can think of gray as a unique hue, too (or antihue). It is what you get if you cancel both red-green and blue-yellow (Webster, 2017).

This opponent-process, color-appearance story sounds rather similar to the (L − M) and ([L + M] − S) story. However, (L − M) is not the same as red versus

unique hue Any of four colors that can be described with only a single color term: red, yellow, green, blue. Other colors (e.g., purple or orange) can also be described as compounds (reddish blue, reddish yellow).

(A)

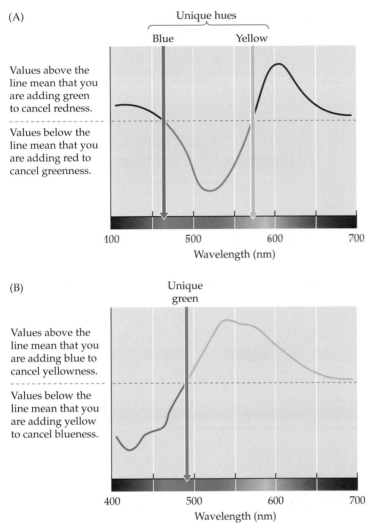

Values above the line mean that you are adding green to cancel redness.

Values below the line mean that you are adding red to cancel greenness.

(B)

Values above the line mean that you are adding blue to cancel yellowness.

Values below the line mean that you are adding yellow to cancel blueness.

Figure 5.17 Results from a hue cancellation experiment. The locations where the hue cancellations cross the neutral midpoint are the locations of the unique blue and yellow (A) and green (B) hues—for example, the green hue with no hint of blue or yellow in it. "Unique red" is not defined by just one spectral locus. (After Hurvich and Jameson, 1957.)

green, and ([L + M] − S) is not the same as yellow versus blue. If this were the case, an ([L + M] − S) cell should be a yellow-blue cell: a cell that would be maximally excited by unique yellow and maximally inhibited by unique blue. However, that ([L + M] − S) cell would actually be stimulated most strongly by a yellowish-greenish hue and least by a purplish hue.

The (L − M) cells aren't in quite the right place either. The L-cone end of the axis is near perceptual red, but the M-cone end is a bluish green (Eskew, 2008). Krauskopf, Williams, and Heeley (1982) call these endpoints the "cardinal directions" in color space, but they are not perceptual red, green, yellow, and blue. We need at least three steps to get to color appearance. These are shown in **Figure 5.18**. First, three cones detect light in different ranges of wavelengths. Then, opponent processes measure the differences in activity between cone types. Finally, some further transformations are needed to create the color opponency described by Hering (Stockman and Brainard, 2010). (See **Web Essay 5.1: More about Opponent Processing in Color Vision.**)

Color in the Visual Cortex

We know that transformations that produce perceived color take place in the visual cortex; it is not clear how the physiology gives rise to perception

Figure 5.18 Three steps to color perception. (A) Detection: light is differentially absorbed by three photopigments in the cones. (B) Discrimination: differences are taken between cone types, creating cone-opponent mechanisms, important for wavelength discriminations. (C) Appearance: further recombination of the signals creates color-opponent processes that support the color-opponent nature of color appearance. (After Stockman and Brainard, 2010.)

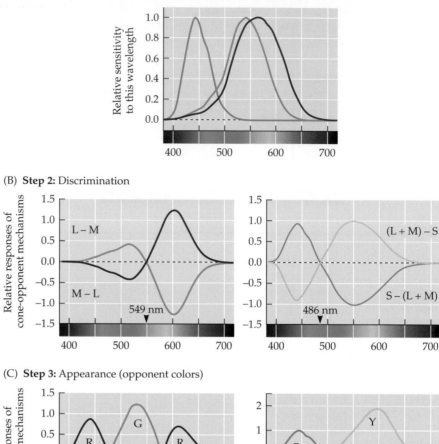

(A) **Step 1:** Detection (cones)

(B) **Step 2:** Discrimination

(C) **Step 3:** Appearance (opponent colors)

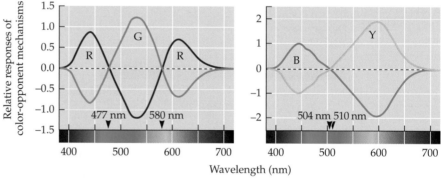

Wavelength (nm)

(Webster, 2017). Many cells in cortex are interested in color but do not seem to linearly add and subtract inputs from different cone types. There is some evidence that they add and subtract in a *nonlinear* manner. For instance, a cell might be responding to something more like $(L^2 - M^2 + S^2)$, though exactly how this would produce the colors we see remains a topic for future work (Horwitz and Hass, 2012; Wandell and Chichilnisky, 2012). For now, we may have to agree with Conway (2014, p. 201): "There is still no good neural explanation for Hering's psychologically important colors … or … the unique hues often associated with them."

Is there a specific area or are there areas in the brains of monkeys and humans specialized for color vision? In the 1980s, evidence favored a separate pathway for color. There were "blobs" in V1 where cells did not seem interested in orientation but seemed very interested in color. The blobs sent output to "thin stripe" regions in V2 (Livingstone and Hubel, 1988) and from there to V4, an area that Semir Zeki argued was specialized for color, with cells that responded not to wavelength but to perceived color (Zeki, 1983a, 1983b). More recently, functional imaging in monkeys has been used to uncover color hot spots in visual cortex. These have been named "globs" (really!) (Conway, Moeller, and Tsao, 2007), and cells in these regions also seem more interested in color than do cells outside. However, although these anatomical pathways are there (Federer et al., 2009), it has become less clear that we can separate color processing from other perceptual processes in cortical anatomy (Shapley and Hawken, 2011). Indeed, you may remember from Chapter 4 that V4 is a popular candidate for a "shape" area. This doesn't mean that it is uninterested in color, but merely that it is probably not *only* interested in color (Roe et al., 2012).

> **FURTHER DISCUSSION** of the elegantly named "blobs" can be found in Chapter 3 on page 85.

Modern imaging studies show some areas of the human visual cortex that seem particularly interested in color (Grill-Spector and Malach, 2004), but we can't record from single cells in humans under most circumstances. Perhaps the best evidence for specialized brain areas for color in humans comes from certain cases of **achromatopsia**, a loss of color vision after brain damage (Zeki, 1990). People with achromatopsia may be able to find the boundaries between regions of different colors, but they cannot report what those colors might be. In these individuals, vision is largely intact, while the experience of color seems specifically impaired.

Individual Differences in Color Perception

Thus far, with a little caution, we have been talking about color as if we all see colors the same way, but do we? This is one of those questions that everyone asks at one point or another, often as a child. Like many "childish" questions, this has been the topic of much decidedly unchildlike philosophical work. (See **Web Essay 5.2: The Philosophical Problem of "Inverted Qualia."**)

Language and Color

Putting aside the finer points of philosophy, suppose you are in a clothing store and you find a shirt that you like but you want a different color. You might go to the clerk and ask, "Do you have this in blue?" You simply assume that you and that clerk agree about the meaning of *blue*. You can discriminate on the order of millions of different colors, but you don't have a separate word for each of these. There is a vast range of color words, but in looking for that shirt, you would not typically ask for "azuline" or "cerulean" (both, varieties of blue). You would use a word like *blue* that almost every speaker of your language would use quickly and consistently in naming colors. These colors names are the **basic color terms** of the language. What makes a color term basic? Berlin and Kay (1969) asserted that it must be common (like *red* and not like *beige*), not an object or substance name (excluding *bronze* and *olive*), and not a compound word (no *blue green* or *light purple*). This classification is a little subjective (is *beige* that uncommon?), but Berlin and Kay argued that, in English, these rules yield a list of 11 terms: *red, green, blue, yellow, black, white, gray, orange, purple, brown,* and *pink.*

Interestingly, the numbers of "basic" color terms differ dramatically across cultures, down to as few as 2 or 3. At one time it was thought that the differing numbers of basic color terms in different languages meant that color categorization was arbitrary. This notion was called **cultural relativism**, meaning that

achromatopsia An inability to perceive colors that is caused by damage to the central nervous system.

basic color terms Color words that are single words (like "blue," not "sky blue"), are used with high frequency, and have meanings that are agreed upon by speakers of a language.

cultural relativism In sensation and perception, the idea that basic perceptual experiences (e.g., color perception) may be determined in part by the cultural environment.

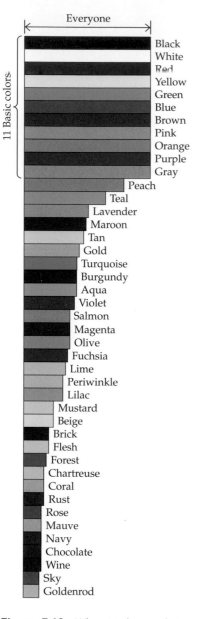

Figure 5.19 When Lindsey and Brown (2014) asked Americans to name color patches, everyone used the 11 "basic" color names. The other color terms were used by fewer and fewer people, going toward the bottom of the graph. A few of these other terms, like *peach* and *teal*, may be considered basic color names over time.

each group was free to create its own linguistic map of color space. Berlin and Kay's important discovery was that the various maps used in different cultures are actually rather similar (Lindsey and Brown, 2006). After surveying many languages, they found that the 11 basic color terms in English are about as many as any group possesses. Of course, the words themselves differ. Red becomes *rouge* in French or *adom* in Hebrew. Moreover, languages do not select randomly among the possible color terms. If a language has only two basic color terms, speakers of the language divide colors into "light" and "dark." If a language has three color terms (one chromatic term beyond *light* and *dark*), what do you think the third usually is? If you guessed *red*, you are correct. Typically, the fourth color term would be *yellow*, then *green* and *blue*. This ordering is not absolute, but you won't find a language with, for example, just *purple*, *green*, and *gray* as its basic color terms.

How do new basic color terms emerge? Berlin and Kay argued that a big color term is partitioned into two smaller terms. Levinson (2000) suggested that new basic terms tend to emerge at the boundary between two existing color terms, in the area where neither existing term works well. In fact, both processes may be at work. Lindsey and Brown (2014) looked at the use of color words in American English by asking 51 Americans to name the color of each of 330 color patches (like paint chips). These observers were told to use a single word. That word had to be a word that could be used for anything of that color (you can't have a "blond" car, can you?). Lindsey and Brown were looking for the sort of word you might use in everyday speech to name the color of a car or a shirt. Those 51 Americans used 122 terms for 330 colors. *Everyone* used the basic 11, but there was evidence that American English might be moving beyond the 11 basics. A color term *teal* may become basic. It emerges in the no man's land of colors that are neither blue nor green. A term like *purple* may eventually be partitioned, with a term like *lavender* or *lilac* taking over some of the purple real estate in color space (**Figure 5.19**).

If our set of basic color terms increased, would that change the way we *see* color? If a language has only two or three basic color terms, do its speakers *see* colors differently than we do with our 11 basic terms? Eleanor Rosch (Heider, 1972) studied this question among the Dani of New Guinea, a tribe whose language has only two basic color terms: *mola* for light-warm colors and *mili* for dark-cool colors. Now, it is hard enough to ask your neighbor to define the experience of "blue" and then to ask if that is the same as your experience of "blue." It is much more difficult to ask these questions across a great cultural divide. But there are tricks, as the experiment illustrated in **Figure 5.20** demonstrates. Suppose you are shown a bluish color chip and asked to remember it. Then you are shown two test chips and asked to pick the color you saw before. Obviously, the less similar the two test colors are, the easier this task is. But more important, you will do better if the wrong choice is on the other side of a color categorical boundary. Color boundaries are sharper than you might think. If you show people a collection of colors and ask, "Which are blue and which are green?" people do the task without much difficulty. If you have to remember a color, as in the task shown in Figure 5.20, you are likely to give it a label like "green" or "blue." If the next color has the same label, you are more likely to be confused than if it has a different label.

Rosch found that the Dani's performance on such tasks reflected the same color boundaries, even when their language did not recognize the distinction between the two colors (a Dani might use the term *mili* for all the colors in Figure 5.20 but would still do better with the task in Figure 5.20B). This finding leads

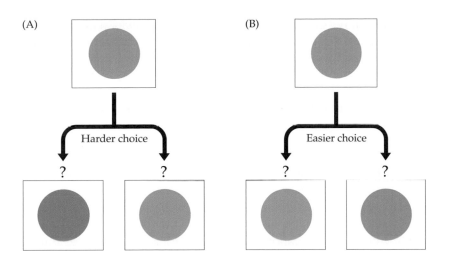

Figure 5.20 It is easier to remember which of two colors you have seen if the choices are categorically different. For example, suppose you had to remember the "blue" patch shown at the top of each part of the figure. Picking between two "blues," as in (A), would be rather hard. The task would be easier if one of the choices were "blue" and the other "green," as in (B), even if the distances in color space were the same in the two cases.

to the conclusion that color perception is not especially influenced by culture and language; blue and green are *seen* as categorically different, even if one's language does not employ color terms to express this difference.

In the late 1990s, Debi Roberson went up the Sepik River in New Guinea to study the Berinmo, whose language, like the Dani's, has a limited set of basic color terms. Unlike previously studied groups, the Berinmo have terms that form novel boundaries in color space. For example, their *nol/wor* distinction lies in the middle of colors we categorize as green, and may roughly distinguish live from dead or dying foliage. Moreover, when the Berinmo did the color memory task, they performed better across their *nol-wor* boundary than across the blue-green boundary. English speakers showed the opposite result (Davidoff, Davies, and Roberson, 1999).

You might think that this was just about the role of language in memory. If you call a spot "blue" or "green," the word acts as a cue when you see two spots and only one of them is green. However, color boundaries have an influence, even if the task doesn't have a memory component. As you can see in **Figure 5.21**, Witzel and Gegenfurtner (2016) measured how long it took to say which one of four patches was of a different color. They used four different pairs of

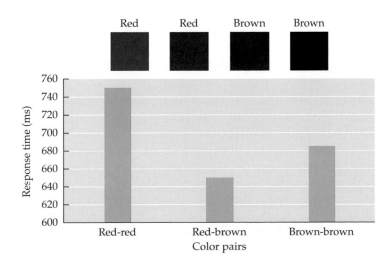

Figure 5.21 Observers see four color patches and simply locate the one patch that is different from the other three. Responses are faster and more accurate when the two colors cross a color boundary—in this case, between red and brown. (After Witzel and Gegenfurtner, 2016.)

qualia In philosophy, a private conscious experience of sensation or perception.

tetrachromatic Referring to the rare situation (in humans, at least) where the color of any light is defined by the relationships of four numbers—the outputs of those four receptor types.

colors selected from red and brown patches. Each patch was separated from the next patch by two just noticeable differences. (If you don't remember "just noticeable differences," revisit Chapter 1 page 7). They found that people were faster to identify the different one and more accurate when the patches were separated by the border between red and brown than when both patches were within the "red" or "brown" category. So the color names matter, even when you compare two colors side by side.

Genetic Differences in Color Vision

The individual differences described in the previous two sections are either small or, in the case of inverted **qualia** (singular *quale*), hypothetical. Under most circumstances, if you declare two lights to be metamerically matched, those around you will generally agree, even if we can't make definitive statements about their qualia. There will be some variation between individuals. For example, unique green can vary between observers from at least 495 to 530 nm (Nerger, Volbrecht, and Ayde, 1995). Some of these differences will be due to factors like age, which turns the lens of the eye yellow (Werner, Peterzell, and Scheetz, 1990). To a first approximation, however, your performance on standard measures of color vision will be the same as others'.

However, there is a significant exception to this universality of color matching. Some 8% of the male population and 0.5% of the female population have a form of color vision deficiency commonly known as "color blindness," in which there is a malfunction in one or more of the genes coding the three cone photopigments. It's a "guy thing" because the genes that code for the M- and L-cone photopigments are on the X chromosome (Nathans, 1986). Males have only one copy of the X chromosome, so if one is defective, the male in question will have a problem. Females have two copies and can have normal color vision even if one copy is abnormal. In fact, some women can end up with four different cone pigments, and in very rare cases, that produces **tetrachromatic** color vision—color vision based on four numbers per patch of light (Jordan et al., 2010). Such individuals may actually see colors that trichromats cannot see. The S-cone photopigment is coded elsewhere, so everyone has two copies, and therefore S-cone color deficiencies are rare (Alpern, Kitahara, and Krantz, 1983). (See **Web Essay 5.3: Experiencing Color Blindness**.)

There are a number of different types of color blindness. One determining factor is the type of cone affected. A second factor is the type of defect; either the photopigment for that cone type is anomalous (different from the norm) or the cone type is missing altogether. Although we call people who are missing one cone type "color-blind," it is a mistake to think that this means they cannot see colors at all. As you will recall, if you have all three cones with their standard photopigments, you need three primary colors to make a metameric match with an arbitrary patch of color. If you have two cone types rather than three, the normally three-dimensional color space becomes a two-dimensional space. The world will still be seen in color, but you will have a "flatter" color experience, different from that of people with normal color vision.

Because M- and L-cone defects are the most common, most color-blind individuals have difficulty discriminating lights in the middle-to-long-wavelength range. For example, consider the wavelengths 560 and 610 nm. Neither of these lights activates S-cones very much, and the L-cones fire at about the same rate for both. But most of us can distinguish the lights on the basis of the M-cone outputs they elicit, which will be higher for the 560-nm light than for the 610-nm light (you can confirm these assertions by consulting Figure 5.5). English-speaking trichromats would label the colors of these two lights as "green" and "reddish orange," respectively.

Now consider a **deuteranope**, someone who has no M-cones. His photoreceptor output to these two lights will be identical. Following our maxim that the rest of the visual system knows only what the photoreceptors tell it, 560- and 610-nm lights must and will be classified as the same color by our deuteranopic individual.

A **protanope**—someone who has no L-cones—will have a different set of color matches based on the outputs of his two cone types (M and S). And a **tritanope**—with no S-cones—will be different again. Genetic factors can also make people **color-anomalous**. Color-anomalous individuals typically have three cone photopigments, but two of them are so similar that these individuals experience the world in much the same way as individuals with only two cone types.

We actually have some notion of exactly what the world looks like to color-deficient individuals, because there are a few, very rare cases of individuals who are color-blind in only one eye. They can compare what they see with the color-blind eye to what they see with the normal eye, enabling us to reconstruct the appearance of the color-blind world (MacLeod and Lennie, 1976).

True color blindness does occur but it is very unusual. It is possible to be a **cone monochromat**, with only one type of cone in the retina. Cone monochromats (who also have rods) live in a one-dimensional color space, seeing the world only in shades of gray. Even more visually impaired are **rod monochromats**, who are missing cones altogether. Because the rods work well only in dim light and are generally absent in the fovea, these individuals not only fail to discriminate colors, but also have very poor acuity and serious difficulties seeing under normal daylight conditions.

We already mentioned one other very interesting class of color blindness, coming not from photoreceptor problems but from damage to the visual cortex. Lesions of specific parts of the visual cortex beyond primary visual cortex can cause achromatopsia. An achromatopsic individual sees the world as drained of color, even while showing evidence that wavelength information is processed at earlier stages in the visual pathway. Brain lesions can also produce various forms of color agnosia or anomia (Oxbury, Oxbury, and Humphrey, 1969). In **agnosia**, the patient can *see* something but fails to know what it is. **Anomia** is an inability to name—in this case, an inability to name colors. A patient with anomia might be able to pick the banana that "looks right" but unable to report that the banana is or should be yellow.

From the Color of Lights to a World of Color

Now for a bit of depressing news. The material presented so far in this chapter about color is quite complex, but the sad fact is that it has only addressed the relatively *simple* problems related to the detection, discrimination, and appearance of isolated lights. We pointed to the limits of this approach to color when we noted that there are no "brown" lights. A surface looks brown when there are other, typically brighter surfaces in the neighborhood. A nonspectral color like brown just scratches the surface of the puzzles that must be solved if we want to understand color in the world. Think about this. **Figure 5.22** shows a black-and-white zebra on grass. Let us assume that you are looking at this in print (the story would be different on a screen). The black, white, and green are products of reflection from paper, covered with specific inks. Let us suppose you are reading this deep in the bowels of the library, by the light of a yellowish

deuteranope An individual who suffers from color blindness that is due to the absence of M-cones.

protanope An individual who suffers from color blindness that is due to the absence of L-cones.

tritanope An individual who suffers from color blindness that is due to the absence of S-cones.

color-anomalous A better term for the commonly used term *color-blind*. Most "color-blind" individuals can still make discriminations based on wavelength. Those discriminations are different from the norm—that is, *anomalous*.

cone monochromat An individual with only one cone type. Cone monochromats are truly color-blind.

rod monochromat An individual with no cones of any type. In addition to being truly color-blind, rod monochromats are badly visually impaired in bright light.

agnosia A failure to recognize objects in spite of the ability to see them. Agnosia is typically due to brain damage.

anomia An inability to name objects in spite of the ability to see and recognize them (as shown by usage). Anomia is typically due to brain damage.

Figure 5.22 This zebra looks like a black-and-white beast in a green field whether you are looking at this book under a dim yellow bulb inside, under the bright sky outside, or for that matter, on your computer screen. How does that work?

incandescent lightbulb. Now, you take the book outside and continue to read in sunlight. The number of photons coming from the page to your eye is now thousands of times greater than it was inside. Outside, a patch of "black" stripe is now sending much more energy to your photoreceptors than did a patch of "white" stripe inside. Moreover, the mix of wavelengths reflected from the grass will be very different if the light source is the sun rather than a dim bulb. Nevertheless, the grass looks green and the zebra looks black-and-white in both locations. How (and why) do you do that?

Let's start by just putting colors next to each other. We live in a world where regions of one color abut regions of another, and this proximity changes the appearance of colors, as **Figure 5.23** shows. In **color contrast** effects, the color of one region induces the opponent color in a neighboring region. Thus, in Figure 5.23A the yellow surround weakens the yellow of a central square and strengthens the blue. In **color assimilation** effects, two colors bleed into each other, each taking on some of the chromatic quality of the other. So, in Figure 5.23B the blue in the first column looks reddish or purplish in the top image and greenish on the bottom.

Not only can other colors in the scene alter the color of a target region, but scenes can contain colors that cannot be experienced in isolation. Though it may be hard to believe unless you try it, you cannot sit in complete darkness and see a gray light, all by itself. That light will look white if seen as an isolated or **unrelated color**. To be seen as gray, it must be seen in relationship to other patches of color. Thus it is a **related color**. Brown is another related color. We can distinguish a few thousand unrelated colors. Allowing for context effects is what boosts the number of distinguishable colors to the millions (Shevell, 2003).

Adaptation and Afterimages

Color contrast effects show how the spatial relations between colors can influence color appearance. Temporal relations matter, too. What you saw before has an influence on the color you see now. You already know this from the discussion

color contrast A color perception effect in which the color of one region induces the opponent color in a neighboring region.

color assimilation A color perception effect in which two colors bleed into each other, each taking on some of the chromatic quality of the other.

unrelated color A color that can be experienced in isolation.

related color A color, such as brown or gray, that is seen only in relation to other colors. For example, a "gray" patch in complete darkness appears white.

(A) Color contrast

Figure 5.23 Color contrast and color assimilation. (A) In color contrast, the central square takes on chromatic attributes that are opposite those of the surround, so the green central square looks greener on the red background than on the green background. (B) In color assimilation, colors blend together locally. So, in the second column the yellow squares look a bit reddish in the upper square and a bit greenish in the lower square. (From Stockman and Brainard, 2010.)

(B) Color assimilation

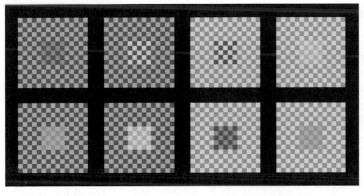

of light adaptation in Chapter 2. Adapting to a bright light makes a moderate light look darker. Adapting to darkness would make that same moderate light appear brighter.

> **FURTHER DISCUSSION** of the time course of dark adaptation can be found in Chapter 2 on pages 47–49.

Now let's extend that principle to color. Adaptation can be color-specific, as we see in the phenomenon of **negative afterimages**. If you look at one color for a few seconds, a subsequently viewed achromatic region will appear to take on a color opposite to the original color. We can call the first colored stimulus the **adapting stimulus**. The illusory color that is seen afterward is the negative afterimage. (See **Web Activity 5.4: Afterimages**.)

The principle is illustrated in **Figure 5.24**. Figure 5.24A consists of a circle of gray spots. Now, stare at the black dot at the center of Figure 5.24B and consider what happens as you expose one bit of your retina and visual system to the red dot at the top of Figure 5.24B. The L-cones will be more stimulated than the M- or S-cones. L+/M− opponent processes will be stimulated. You will see "red." When you move your eyes back to fixate on the black dot at the center of Figure 5.24A, the red is withdrawn from that area of the visual field. The L-cones will be more adapted than M- or S-cones, as will the later processes in the retina and brain that were more stimulated by the red spot. Adapted processes behave as though they are somewhat tired. They respond less vigorously than unadapted processes. The result is a bit like what would happen if you held a pendulum up

negative afterimage An afterimage whose polarity is the opposite of the original stimulus. Light stimuli produce dark negative afterimages. Colors are complementary; for example, red produces green, and yellow produces blue.

adapting stimulus A stimulus whose removal produces a change in visual perception or sensitivity.

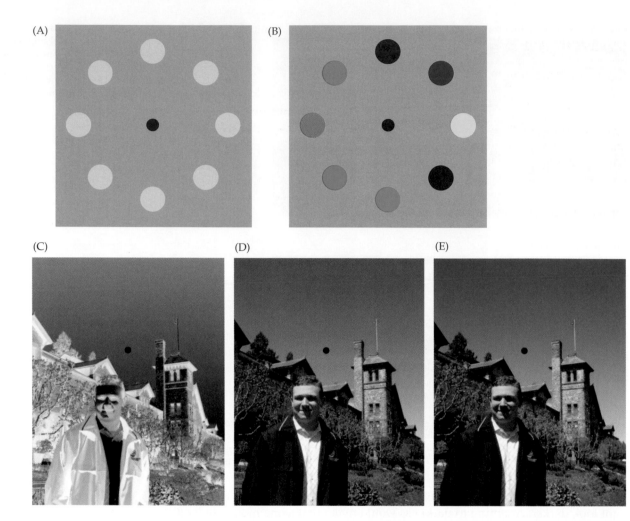

(A)   (B)

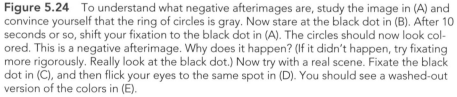

(C)   (D)   (E)

Figure 5.24 To understand what negative afterimages are, study the image in (A) and convince yourself that the ring of circles is gray. Now stare at the black dot in (B). After 10 seconds or so, shift your fixation to the black dot in (A). The circles should now look colored. This is a negative afterimage. Why does it happen? (If it didn't happen, try fixating more rigorously. Really look at the black dot.) Now try with a real scene. Fixate the black dot in (C), and then flick your eyes to the same spot in (D). You should see a washed-out version of the colors in (E).

neutral point The point at which an opponent color mechanism is generating no signal. If red-green and blue-yellow mechanisms are at their neutral points, a stimulus will appear achromatic. (The black-white process has no neutral point.)

and released it. The red-green opponent color mechanism swings back toward the **neutral point**, overshoots this point, and slides over to the green side. As a consequence, the gray spot appears greenish until the opponent mechanism settles back to the neutral point.

If you look at the green dot at the bottom of Figure 5.24B and then look back at the gray image (Figure 5.24A), you will see the result of pushing the red-green mechanism in the other direction. Other colors will produce other results, which you should now be able to predict. In Figures 5.24C–E, you can try this with a real scene. If you stare at the black dot in Figure 5.24C and then quickly move your eyes to the same dot in Figure 5.24D, you will see a pale, tinted version of the real photograph (Figure 5.24E), though this effect will be more dramatic if you look at the version in **Web Activity 5.4: Afterimages**. Notice that we are not attributing negative afterimages to *just* the cones or *just* one set of cone- or color-opponent processes. Adaptation occurs at multiple sites in the nervous system, though the primary generators are in the retina (Zaidi et al., 2012).

Color Constancy

Let us return to the zebra. The fact that the picture looks black, white, and green whether viewed inside or outside is an illustration of **color constancy**, the tendency for the colors of objects to appear relatively unchanged in spite of substantial changes in the lighting conditions. All the color figures in this book will seem to have more or less the same colors wherever you read the book (though there is an entire research area hidden in what we might mean by "more or less"; Foster, 2011).

Figure 5.25 illustrates why color constancy is yet another difficult problem for the visual system to solve. The heart of the problem is that the **illuminant**,

color constancy The tendency of a surface to appear the same color under a fairly wide range of illuminants.

illuminant The light that illuminates a surface.

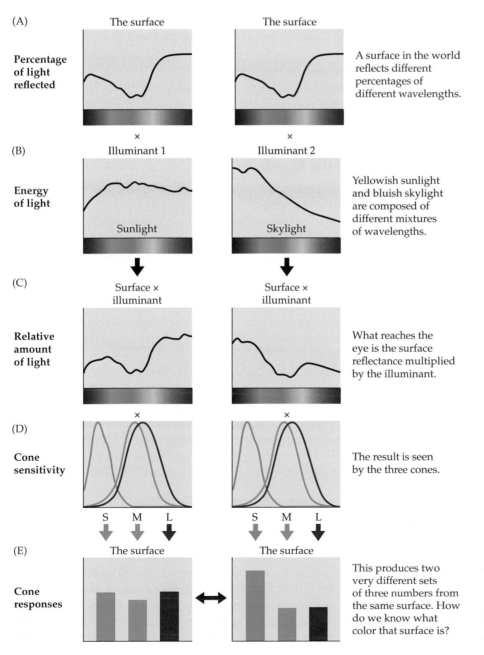

(A) **Percentage of light reflected**

The surface The surface

A surface in the world reflects different percentages of different wavelengths.

(B) **Energy of light**

Illuminant 1 Illuminant 2

Sunlight Skylight

Yellowish sunlight and bluish skylight are composed of different mixtures of wavelengths.

(C) **Relative amount of light**

Surface × illuminant Surface × illuminant

What reaches the eye is the surface reflectance multiplied by the illuminant.

(D) **Cone sensitivity**

S M L S M L

The result is seen by the three cones.

(E) **Cone responses**

The surface The surface

This produces two very different sets of three numbers from the same surface. How do we know what color that surface is?

Figure 5.25 The same surface (A) illuminated by two different lights (B) will generate two different patterns of activity in the S-, M-, and L-cones (C–E). However, the surface will appear to be the same color under both illuminants. This phenomenon is known as color constancy. (After Smithson, 2005.)

spectral reflectance function   The percentage of a particular wavelength that is reflected from a surface.

spectral power distribution   The physical energy in a light as a function of wavelength.

the light that illuminates a surface, is not constant. Lighting changes as we go from indoors to outdoors or as the sun moves from the horizon to high in the sky. Figure 5.25A shows the **spectral reflectance function** for a surface—the percentage of each wavelength that is reflected from a particular surface. With its preponderance of long and short wavelengths and that dip in the middle wavelengths, this surface probably looks purplish. Let's call it "lilac." Figure 5.25B shows the **spectral power distribution**—the relative amount of light at different visible wavelengths—of two different types of "daylight": sunlight and skylight. Sunlight is a yellowish light, richer in middle and long wavelengths; skylight is more bluish, with more short-wavelength energy. Figure 5.25C shows that the light reflected to our eyes is the product of the surface and the illumination. For example, a surface might reflect 90% of 650-nm light, but no 650-nm light would reach the eye unless there was some in the original illumination. Figure 5.25D, E show that those two different products of surface and illumination are converted into two different sets of three numbers by the L-, M- and S-cones. (See **Web Essay 5.4: Color Constancy in the Lab** and **Web Activity 5.5: Color Constancy**.)

Here's the problem. Even though the three numbers from the three cones are different in the two conditions, that lilac-colored surface will look lilac under both illuminants. White paper will look white. A banana will look yellow. This color constancy is beneficial because we want to know the color of the object. Under normal circumstances, we don't care about the spectral composition of the lights.

The Problem with the Illuminant

Let's think about color constancy as a math problem. In simple terms, we have an illuminant (call it I) and a surface (S). As shown in Figure 5.25C, what we can sense is a result—the product of $I \times S$—but what we want to know is S. It is as if we were given a number (say, 48), told that it is the product of two other numbers, and asked to guess what those two numbers might be. The answer could be 12 and 4. Or it could be 16 and 3. Or 6 and 8. Given just the number 48, we cannot solve the problem. Nevertheless, given the result of $I \times S$, the visual system does a pretty good job of figuring out S.

We sometimes talk about "discounting" the illuminant as if our whole goal were to throw away the I term and just see the surface color. However, this is not quite right. For instance, you can get different answers if you point to two patches under two different illuminants and ask if these two were "cut from the same cloth" or if they are the "same color" (Arend and Reeves, 1986). If you just discarded the illuminant information, these answers would be the same—but they are not. Similarly, you can tell the difference between a scene lit by the morning sun and a scene illuminated by the sun at high noon. Thus, not only can you recover the color of the surface, but you also know something about the illuminant. How do you do this?

Physical Constraints Make Constancy Possible

As noted in the previous section, it is impossible to know which two integers are multiplied to produce 48. However, if you are told that the first number is between 9 and 14, you're saved. The first number must be 12, and the second, then, must be 4. In an analogous way, color constancy must be based on some information or assumptions that constrain the possible answers. There are many possible assumptions that could help. Suppose we assumed that, in a complex scene, the brightest region was white (Land and McCann, 1971) or that the average color across the whole scene was gray (Buchsbaum, 1980). We could scale the other colors relative to these white or gray anchors. However, this can't be entirely right. Think what would happen if you were in a dark room with two spots of light on the wall: a red one and a blue one. Under a simple version of a bright-is-white theory, the brighter spot should look white and the other spot should change color. That can't be right (and theorists knew this, so the actual theories are more subtle, but they still do not work perfectly).

There are other possible constraining pieces of information. Assumptions can be made about the illuminant. For instance, natural light sources (and most artificial ones, such as standard lightbulbs) are generally "broadband." That is, they contain many wavelengths, even if some wavelengths are not as intense as others. Furthermore, their spectral composition curves (see Figure 5.25) are usually smooth; spikes at particular wavelengths are uncommon, though this generalization is violated by some artificial light sources. Highly unnatural (e.g., monochromatic) light sources make the world look highly unnatural—a fact exploited in nightclubs the world over. Indeed, with a monochromatic source, color vision is impossible, though not much broadband light is needed to get color back.

Assumptions can be made about surfaces. Real surfaces also tend to be broadband in their **reflectances** (recall the hamburger distributions of Figure 5.6). It would be very unlikely, for example, to find a surface that reflected 100% of 535-nm light, 0% of 538-nm light, and 100% again of 540-nm light. Even surfaces that look like single wavelengths of light typically reflect a wide range of wavelengths. That is, the red bars in Figure 5.25 may be metameric with something like a 600-nm light, but that region is sending many other wavelengths to your eye. There are other limits on the reflectance of real surfaces. The whitest surface rarely reflects more than 95% of any wavelength, and the blackest rarely reflects less than 5%. The brightest thing in the visual field is likely to be white. A "specular reflection" (like the shiny spot on a billiard ball) has a wavelength composition very similar to that of the illuminant. Any of these facts might help.

This brings us back to the dress introduced at the start of the chapter. Why does that dress look white and gold or black and blue? We are not really sure, but it seems that people are making different assumptions about the light source in the original photograph (**Figure 5.26A**). Some people assume that the illuminant is white (**Figure 5.26B**). They would see the dress as black and blue (the actual colors). Others may be assuming a more complicated situation with one diffuse blue light and a more direct, more yellow light (**Figure 5.26C**). This could persuade those observers to see the black as a sort of golden brown and the blue as a bluish white. Then, when asked about the cloth, they might report (as would the author of this bit of the text) that the dress looks

reflectance The percentage of light hitting a surface that is reflected and not absorbed into the surface. Typically reflectance is given as a function of wavelength.

(A)

(B)    (C)

Figure 5.26 What color is this dress? (A) The color of this dress may not look the same to different people because each observer is making different assumptions about the nature of the light shining on the dress. (B) Maybe the light is just broadband white light. Then the dress appears to be blue and black. (C) Maybe there are a couple of light sources: one bluish and the other more yellow. Then the dress could appear to be white and gold. (B, C after Macknik and Martinez-Conde, 2015.)

like a white-and-gold dress under a bluish light. If you asked such an observer to match the *color* of the lighter stripes, the patch that matched the color might be quite blue. Remember, "Are these cut from the same cloth?" and "Are these the same color?" are different questions (Arend and Reeves, 1986).

The real mystery about the dress is that it looks dramatically different to different people. Normally, this does not happen. You might disagree with your friend about whether a shirt is bluish green or greenish blue, but if both of you are normal trichromats, it would be very unusual for you to think the shirt was dark blue while your friend insisted on white. To be sure, there are ambiguous stimuli (remember the Necker cube of Figure 4.24). In those cases, even if the two interpretations are very different, one person can see them both. Usually, perception will alternate between the possibilities. It is unusual for one person to see one possibility and to be unable to see the other (sounds like politics, not perception). As this is being written, the dress remains a hot topic (Brainard and Hurlbert, 2015; Gegenfurtner, Bloj, and Toscani, 2015; Lafer-Sousa, Hermann, and Conway, 2015; Wallisch, 2017), but we don't have a clear explanation for the dramatic differences between perceptions. Nevertheless, we think it must be telling us something significant about the mechanisms of color perception in complex scenes.

Assumptions about illumination are not the only route to color constancy. Other assumptions can be made about the structure of the world. Sharp borders in an image are almost always the result of boundaries between surfaces, not boundaries between light sources. Thus, if you see something that looks pink next to something that looks golden, it is very unlikely to be the result of cleverly placed pink and golden light sources (unless you're in a theater, perhaps). Shadow borders can be an exception to this rule (Adelson, 1993; Cavanagh and Leclerc, 1989). A shadow can produce a sharp edge that is unrelated to any change in the underlying surface. However, the change across a shadow border is typically a change in brightness and not a change in the chromatic properties of the regions. In **Figure 5.27A**, you can easily imagine that you're looking at three rectangles with a circular patch of shadow, lying across their middles. Not so in **Figure 5.27B**; though the top and bottom in Figure 5.27B are brighter than the middle, the darker region does not look like a shadow, because for that darkening to be the result of a shadow, the shadow would have to be coincidentally aligned with a set of hue changes. Our implicit knowledge of these sorts of constraints helps us sort out the visual world.

Cues like this, perhaps in clever combination, can be used to solve the otherwise unsolvable problem of color constancy (Smithson, 2005). All of these assumptions about the state of the world might sound a lot like the "prior probabilities" that are important in Bayesian theories of the sort introduced in Chapter 4. Bayesian ideas have been put to work to explain color constancy (Brainard, 2009; Brainard and Freeman, 1997). The hard part, whether you're working in an explicitly Bayesian framework or not, is to get the prior probabilities exactly right (Foster, 2011). What are the precise assumptions that give us our level of color constancy? We are still not sure.

> **FURTHER DISCUSSION** of Bayesian theories in the context of vision can be found in Chapter 4 on page 122 and in **Web Essay 4.3: Bayesian Analysis**.

Nonetheless, we can broadly describe how the visual system might use these assumptions to achieve color constancy. Suppose, for example, that you're

(A) Luminance change without hue change looks like a shadow.

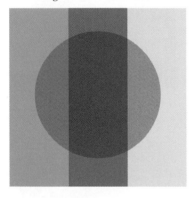

(B) Luminance change *with* hue change looks less like a shadow.

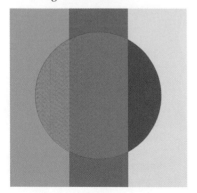

Figure 5.27 The visual system "knows" that brightness changes across a shadow boundary but hue does not. As a result, the difference in (A) looks more like a shadow than the one in (B).

Figure 5.28 The strawberries in a complex scene will look red even if there is not much long-wavelength light in the illuminant.

standing in a kitchen illuminated by a light source composed primarily of short and middle wavelengths (**Figure 5.28**). None of the surfaces in your visual field will reflect much long-wavelength light, because there isn't much of this light to be reflected. But given the assumption that the illumination is evenly distributed around the room, you will still perceive the strawberries as red, because they reflect *more* long-wavelength light than any other surface does. (See **Web Activity 5.6: Illusions of Lighting**.)

What Is Color Vision Good For?

Having introduced some of the basics and some of the complications of color vision, we will wrap up this chapter by asking about the usefulness of color vision. The ability to use wavelength information has evolved several times in several ways during the course of time. Evolutionary theory tells us that, for this to be true, color vision must provide an advantage that makes it worth the trouble. Color is not an absolute requirement. If we could not make wavelength discriminations, we could still identify a lion (**Figure 5.29A**), and we could still find our way through the forest (**Figure 5.29B**). Although color vision might make the lion stand out a bit better from the background, we would be much more impaired if we lacked "orientation vision" or "motion vision." Across the animal kingdom, however, there seem to be at least two realms of behavior where color vision is especially useful: eating and sex. More generally, color vision seems to be particularly helpful in visual search tasks (see Chapter 7).

Having color vision does seem to make it easier to find candidate foods and to discriminate good food from bad food. Comparing the two versions of **Figure 5.30**, it is clear that finding berries is easier with color vision (Bompas,

(A) (B)

Figure 5.29 Do humans need color vision? (A) A black-and-white lion is still a lion, and (B) you could still find a path in the woods without color vision.

Kendall, and Sumner, 2013). Notice also that it makes it easier to decide which of these berries is ripe. You may recall that we mentioned this possibility when discussing the L- and M-cones, earlier in the chapter. Most diurnal animals have two photopigments: roughly an S-cone and an LM-cone. Some primates have evolved separate L and M photopigments and the neural circuitry to exploit the rather small differences between the responses of those cone types. There has been considerable debate regarding whether this really conveys an advantage in telling ripe from unripe fruit or distinguishing subtle differences among green leaves (Troscianko et al., 2003). Some have argued that shape and texture information, along with dichromatic color vision, are good enough for these purposes. How can we find out? In some monkey species (e.g., capuchins) is a mix of dichromats and trichromats (as in the human species). Do the trichromats have an advantage in hunting for food? Rather than test this in capuchins, Melin et al. (2013) carefully simulated six varieties of capuchin color vision in human observers and had those observers search for capuchin food in photographs of those fruits as they would appear in the Costa Rican forests where the monkeys live. The result was a clear advantage for trichromatic vision.

Figure 5.30 Finding a raspberry is easier if you have color vision, as is deciding if that berry is ripe.

(A)

(B)

Figure 5.31   Color vision in different species. (A) These black-eyed Susans are shown as they are seen with human photoreceptors and color vision. (B) A honeybee can see UV light. In UV, the flower's "black eye" (or maybe the pupil of that eye) is much larger—a better target for the bee. (Courtesy of Tom Eisner.)

The food-color vision connection is not limited to primates. The colors of wildflowers did not develop to please the aesthetic sense of humans. As a general rule, they are advertisements to bees and other insects, offering to trade food for sex (well, at least for pollination of the flower). In fact, many flowers have dramatic patterns that we cannot see, because they are variations in the reflection of short-wavelength (ultraviolet) light, which is outside our range. Bees can see these short wavelengths, and it is the bees that flowers have evolved to attract (**Figure 5.31**). While we're on the subject of the relationship of plants and animals, it is worth a detour to point out that plants exploit several sensory systems in an effort to attract the attention of the right animal. The smell of a flower is intended as a signal to pollinators, and even the shape of specialized leaves can create an auditory beacon to attract echolocating bats (Simon et al., 2011).

In addition to searching for and assessing food, animals spend significant time and effort searching for and assessing potential mates. Here, too, color plays a central role. Colorful displays—from the dramatic patterns on tropical fish (**Figure 5.32A**) to the tail of a peacock (**Figure 5.32B**) to the face of the mandrill (**Figure 5.32C**)—are all sexual signals. What makes the male peacock that has the most colorful tail the most desirable mate for a female peacock? We can't ask her, of course, but a colorful tail might somehow indicate that this peacock's genes are better than his competitors'. A female peacock that sees the world in black and white won't be able to perceive this information and will therefore be at an evolutionary disadvantage. In another example that we mentioned earlier, the development of separate L- and M-cones may have made primate color vision particularly well suited to detecting the amount of blood in a blushing or blanched cheek (Changizi, Zhang, and Shimojo, 2006).

Color vision is accomplished in different ways in different species. We are trichromats, with three different types of cone photoreceptors. Dogs appear to be dichromats, with two types of cone photoreceptors (Neitz, Geist, and Jacobs, 1989). Chickens, surprisingly enough, turn out to be tetrachromats, with four (Okano, Fukada, and Yoshizawa, 1995). There is not much gain in information if the number of cone types is increased beyond 3 or 4 (Maloney, 1986), which probably explains why octachromats or dodecachromats—individuals with 8

(A) (B) (C)

Figure 5.32 The colors of animals—from (A) tropical fish to (B) peacocks to (C) mandrills—are often advertisements to potential mates.

or 12 types of cones—are very rare. Rare, but not nonexistent. If you have some time, look into the case of the mantis shrimp, a wonderfully eccentric beast with at least 12 types of photoreceptors (Marshall and Arikawa, 2014).

Our S-, M-, and L-cones are different because they contain different photopigments (**Figure 5.33A**). It is also possible to use a single photopigment to create more than one functional type of cone. The trick is to put a different filter

(A) Different photopigments can tune photoreceptors to different wavelengths.

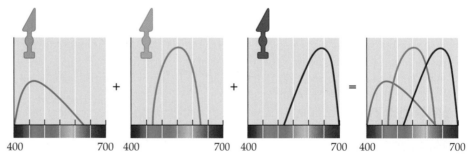

Figure 5.33 Two ways to make photoreceptors with different spectral sensitivities. (A) Our S-, M-, and L-cones are different because they contain different photopigments. (B) Some animals have only one type of photopigment. These animals can have color vision because colored oil droplets sitting on top of photoreceptors create groups of photoreceptors with different sensitivities to wavelength.

(B) Colored oil droplets can also tune photoreceptors to different wavelengths.

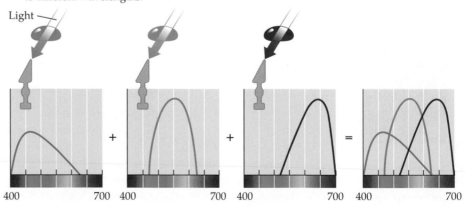

in front of each type of cone so that some wavelengths are subtracted before light reaches the photoreceptor (**Figure 5.33B**). A cone with a reddish oil droplet in front of it will respond more vigorously to long-wavelength light than will a cone covered by a greenish droplet. Chicks and other birds have these droplets, as do a variety of reptiles (Govardovskii, 1983).

Even fireflies get into this act in a limited way. Fireflies signal each other with bioluminescence: they make their own light. Different species have different lights, and each species' visual system appears to be tuned to its particular wavelength signature. A combination of a photopigment and a colored filter makes signals of conspecifics (members of the same species) appear brighter than the flashes of other fireflies in the vicinity (Cronin et al., 2000). With this sort of visual system, the firefly will never appreciate the palette of colors in a sunset. But it will be able to locate an appropriate mate, and that, after all, was the pressure shaping the development of this limited sensitivity to wavelength.

■ Scientists at Work

Filtering Colors

■ **Question** How well can you direct your attention to one color?

■ **Hypothesis** A "feature-based attention" mechanism should allow an observer to select all the items of one color and treat them as a group, effectively ignoring the other items.

■ **Test** The researchers showed their observers images like those in the first column of **Figure 5.34** (Sun et al., 2016). (The colors were much more carefully chosen than we can print here.) Observers were asked to mark the centroid of the three dots of a particular color. If you imagine the triangle formed by the three dots, the centroid is that triangle's center of mass. People can do this easily enough with three dots (as in the three dots in the upper right panel of the figure). If filtering by color worked, the dots of different colors would have no effect on ability to judge the centroid of one target color.

■ **Results** When the different dots varied in hue (see page 35), this task was quite easy. The researchers could calculate the impact of each color dot on the centroid, and in the hue condition, observers could create an attentional filter that effectively removed every dot except those of the correct hue (here green). If the dots varied along a saturation axis as they do in the second row, observers couldn't easily select just the dots of one saturation. (The actual experiment was a bit different from what is shown.)

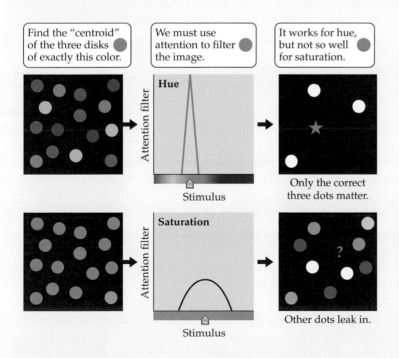

Figure 5.34 The setup of the Sun et al. attention filter experiment. Column 1 shows sample stimuli. Observers would be asked to pay attention to just three dots in each image, defined by their color. Column 2 shows the "attention filter" that can be inferred from the data. Column 3 shows the hypothetical strength of the dots in the mind of the observer when the filter has been applied. When the dots differ in hue (top row), the filter leaves only the target dots. When the dots vary in saturation (bottom row) nontarget dots get past the filter and influence behavior.

(Continued)

■ Scientists at Work *(continued)* ■

■ **Conclusion** We can use our attention to select a group of items on the basis of hue. Other dimensions of color cannot be filtered as effectively. The authors speculate that "hue is a more reliable cue to material identity than either lightness or saturation" (p. E6717), so it might not be as useful to filter along those dimensions.

■ **Future work** Are there other features of the visual world for which it might be useful to have this kind of filtering ability? Suppose you were a product designer; might this result influence the way that you designed the bottles for a line of shampoo?

Go to the
Sensation & Perception
Companion Website at
oup.com/us/wolfe5e
for chapter overviews, activities, essays, flashcards, and other study aids.
Go to **DASHBOARD** for additional resources and assessments.

Summary

1. Probably the most important fact to know about color vision is that lights and surfaces look colored because a particular distribution of wavelengths of light is being analyzed by a particular visual system. Color is a mental phenomenon, not a physical phenomenon. Many animal species have some form of color vision. It seems to be important for identifying possible mates, possible rivals, and good things to eat. Color vision has evolved several times in several different ways in the animal kingdom.

2. Rod photoreceptors are sensitive to low (scotopic) light levels. There is only one type of rod photoreceptor; it yields one "number" for each location in the visual field. Rods can support only a one-dimensional representation of color, from dark to light. Thus, scotopic vision is achromatic vision.

3. Humans have three types of cone photoreceptors, each having a different sensitivity to the wavelengths of light. Cones operate at brighter light levels than rods, producing three numbers at each location; the pattern of activity over the different cone types defines the color.

4. If two regions of an image produce the same response in the three cone types, they will look identical; that is, they will be metamers. And they will look identical even if the physical wavelengths coming from the two regions are different.

5. In additive color mixture, two or more lights are mixed. Adding a light that looks blue to a light that looks yellow will produce a light that looks white (if we pick the right blue and yellow). In subtractive color mixture, the filters, paints, or other pigments that absorb some wavelengths and reflect others are mixed. Mixing a typical blue paint and a typical yellow paint will subtract most long and short wavelengths from the light reflected by the mixture, and the result will look green.

6. Color blindness is typically caused by the congenital absence or abnormality of one cone type—usually the L- or M-cones, usually in males. Most color-blind individuals are not blind to differences in wavelength. Rather, their color perception is based on the outputs of two cone types instead of the normal three.

7. A single type of cone cannot be used, by itself, to discriminate between wavelengths of light. To enable discrimination, information from the three cones is combined to form three cone-opponent processes. In the first,

cones sensitive to long wavelengths (L-cones) are pitted against medium-wavelength (M) cones to create an (L – M) process that is *roughly* sensitive to the redness or greenness of a region. In the second cone-opponent process, L- and M-cones are pitted against short-wavelength (S) cones to create an ([L + M] – S) process *roughly* sensitive to the blueness or yellowness of a region. The third process is sensitive to the overall brightness of a region.

8. Color appearance is arranged around opponent colors: red versus green, and blue versus yellow. This color opponency involves further reprocessing of the cone signals from cone-opponent processes into color-opponent processes.

9. The visual system tries to disentangle the properties of surfaces in the world (e.g., the "red" color of a strawberry) from the properties of the illuminants (e.g., the "golden" light of evening), even though surface and illuminant information are combined in the input to the eyes. Mechanisms of color constancy use implicit knowledge about the world to correct for the influence of different illuminants and to keep that strawberry looking red under a wide range of conditions.

10. The colors of the dress discussed at the start of the chapter look different to different people. We understand a great deal about the factors that lead to the perceived colors in that image. We do not really understand why some people see one set of colors while others see different colors.

6 Space Perception and Binocular Vision

Questions to Contemplate

Think about the following questions as you read this chapter. By the chapter's end, you should be able to answer and discuss them.

- Given the curved, two-dimensional images on the retina of each eye, how does the brain reconstruct our rich three-dimensional world?

- What tricks do artists use to give the rich sense of depth in drawings and paintings?

- Why do we have two eyes?

- How does the brain combine different cues to depth?

- How does three-dimensional vision develop?

Imagine that you're moving quietly through a meadow, trying to get close enough to a bear cub to get a good picture. Suddenly you discover that Mother Bear is not happy about your photo session. She charges, and you run—back across the field, through a thicket of trees. A quick leap across a stream brings you to a slope that leads down to the road where your partner is waiting in a Jeep. You dive into the passenger side and roar off down the track to safety. As the bear lumbers off and your heartbeat returns to normal, your thoughts naturally turn to the acts of visual space perception that you just performed: You picked a path through the three-dimensional world that brought you to safety. You behaved as though you knew where the trees were. You acted as though you understood how far it was across the stream. All in all, you demonstrated a sophisticated grasp of the layout of the physical world around you.

Humans share this sophistication with a large part of the animal kingdom. Faced with the same bear, a rabbit or deer would have shown a similar grasp of the relevant issues in space perception (without the Jeep). The ability to perceive

Ellen Augarten, #7 from the *Boardwalk Doubles Series*, 2016

and interact with the structure of space is one of the fundamental goals of the visual system. It is also quite a formidable accomplishment, and in this chapter we'll explore how we do it.

As a starting place, let's assume that the external world exists. This is a philosophical position known as **realism**. It is not the only possibility. The **positivists** note that all you really have to go on is the evidence of your senses, so the world could be nothing more than an elaborate hallucination. For less philosophical elaborations of this viewpoint, we could consult the writings of Philip K. Dick and other science fiction authors. In this book, we'll just assume that there is a real world out there to perceive.

The problem that the visual system needs to solve is how to construct a three-dimensional world based on the inverted images on the retina of each eye. Parallel lines in the world do not necessarily remain parallel in the retinal image, as **Figure 6.1** illustrates. The angles of triangles don't always add up to 180 degrees. The retinal area occupied by an object gets smaller as the object moves farther away from the eyeball. What all this means is that if we want to appreciate the three-dimensional world, we have to reconstruct it from the distorted retinal input.

To be more precise, as a general rule our visual experience is a reconstruction of the world based on two distorted inputs: the two distinct retinal images.

realism A philosophical position arguing that there is a real world to sense.

positivism A philosophical position arguing that all we really have to go on is the evidence of the senses, so the world might be nothing more than an elaborate hallucination.

Figure 6.1 The Euclidean geometry of the three-dimensional world turns into something quite different on the curved, two-dimensional retina. In the Euclidean world, the angles of a triangle add up to 180 degrees. In the non-Euclidean world of the retinal image, this need not be so.

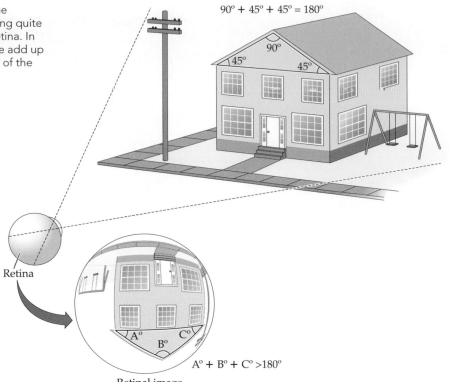

$90° + 45° + 45° = 180°$

$90°$

$45°$ $45°$

Retina

$A°$ $B°$ $C°$

$A° + B° + C° > 180°$

Retinal image

Close your left eye, stretch your left arm out in front of you, and hold up your left index finger. Then hold up your right index finger about 6 inches in front of your face so that it appears to be positioned just to the left of the left index finger, as illustrated in **Figure 6.2**. Now, quickly open your left eye and close your right eye. If you positioned your fingers properly, your right finger will jump to the other side of your left finger. Although this demonstration is designed to exaggerate the different views of your two eyes, the point is a general one: the two retinal images always differ. They differ because your two eyeballs (and their two retinas) are in slightly different places in your head. Just as you and the person standing next to you see somewhat different views of the world, so do your two eyes. Much of this chapter will be devoted to explaining how the visual system goes to quite elaborate lengths both to exploit and to reconcile these differences.

Why have two eyes at all? Perhaps most fundamentally, having two eyes confers the same evolutionary advantage as having two lungs or two kidneys: you can lose one eye and still be able to see. A second advantage to doubling the number of eyes is that they enable you to see more of the world. This is especially true for animals like rabbits

(A)

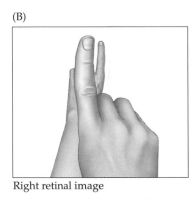

(B)

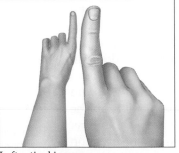

Right retinal image

Left retinal image

Figure 6.2 The two retinal images of a three-dimensional world are not the same. See the text for details.

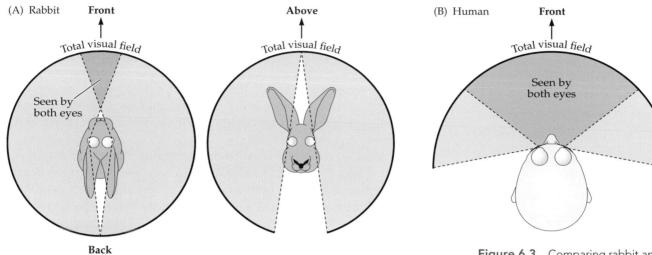

(A) Rabbit **Front**

Total visual field

Seen by both eyes

Back

Above

Total visual field

(B) Human **Front**

Total visual field

Seen by both eyes

Figure 6.3 Comparing rabbit and human visual fields. (A) A rabbit's lateral eyes can see all around its head. It can even see above its head, making its visual field something like a planetarium dome (with ears). (B) The human visual field is more like a windshield covering a large region in front of the eyes. Light purple indicates the entire visual field; dark purple, the part of the visual field seen by both eyes.

who have *lateral* eyes on the sides of their heads. A rabbit can actually see for 360 degrees around its head (**Figure 6.3A**). This explains why it is so hard to sneak up on a rabbit. Moreover, the rabbit can also see straight up above its head (Hughes, 1977).

Humans, with *frontal* eyes, still see more of the world with two eyes than with one. Our visual field is limited to about 190 degrees from left to right, 110 degrees of which is covered by both eyes (**Figure 6.3B**). The field is more restricted vertically: about 140 degrees, 60 degrees up to a limit defined by your eyebrows and 80 degrees down to your cheeks, as is shown in **Web Essay 2.2: Clinical Case: The Man Who Couldn't Read**. The exact size of your visual field will be limited by the specific anatomy of your cheeks and eyebrows. Overlapping, frontal, **binocular** visual fields give predator animals such as humans a better chance to spot small, fast-moving objects in front of them that might provide dinner. Prey animals, like rabbits, are often those with very wide visual fields allowing them to monitor the whole scene for predators.

With frontal eyes and overlapping visual fields, you also get the advantage of two detectors looking at the same thing. For example, if two independent people each had a 50% chance of missing a target, the chance that both of them would miss it would be 50% × 50% = 25%. So the chance that at least one of the two would find that target is 100% − 25%, or 75%. This is known as **probability summation**. Something similar happens if the two eyes both look for the same hard-to-see target. In vision, this would be called **binocular summation** (Blake, Sloane, and Fox, 1981). Binocular summation may have provided the evolutionary pressure that first moved eyes toward the front of some birds' and mammals' faces. Under most circumstances, we do not get complete probability summation. The increase from a 50% chance to a 75% chance assumes two completely independent observers, but our two eyes are not independent, because they are embedded in one person. Nevertheless, we will do better at many tasks with two eyes than with just one (R. K. Jones and Lee, 1981).

Once the eyes moved to the front, though, evolution found an additional use for overlapping visual fields. Try this: Take the top off a pen and hold the top in one hand and the pen in the other. Hold both about a foot in front of your face, with your elbows bent. Now, close one eye and try to quickly put the cap on the pen. Repeat the same task with both eyes open. For most (but not all) people,

binocular Referring to two eyes.

probability summation The increased detection probability based on the statistical advantage of having two (or more) detectors rather than one.

binocular summation The combination (or "summation") of signals from both eyes in ways that make performance on many tasks better than with either eye alone.

binocular disparity The differences between the two retinal images of the same scene. Disparity is the basis for stereopsis, a vivid perception of the three-dimensionality of the world that is not available with monocular vision.

monocular Referring to one eye.

stereopsis The ability to use binocular disparity as a cue to depth.

monocular depth cue A depth cue that is available even when the world is viewed with one eye alone.

binocular depth cue A depth cue that relies on information from both eyes. Stereopsis is the primary example in humans, but convergence and the ability of two eyes to see more of an object than one eye sees are also binocular depth cues.

this task is easier with two eyes than with one. This is a quick demonstration of the usefulness of **binocular disparity**—the differences between the two retinal images of the same world. Disparity is the basis for a vivid perception of the three-dimensionality of the world that is not available with purely **monocular** (one-eyed) vision. The technical term for this binocular perception of depth is **stereopsis**. The geometric and physiological bases for stereopsis are the topic of a large portion of this chapter (see also I. P. Howard and Rogers, 2001). Stereopsis is special in that it can provide very-high-resolution depth information, in the absence of other cues (McKee, 1983).

When you decide you need a break from reading this chapter, take that break with one eye closed. You should be able to notice the loss of stereopsis (and of part of your visual field), but a period of one-eyed visual experience will also make it clear that stereopsis is not a necessary condition for depth perception or space perception. Rabbits do very well with very little binocular vision, and painters and movie directors manage to convey realistic impressions of depth on flat canvases and movie screens. On the other hand, stereopsis does add a richness to perception of the three-dimensional world, as vividly described by Oliver Sacks (2006) in his article about "Stereo Sue," a neuroscientist who regained stereopsis at the age of 48. We will talk about her later.

In this chapter, first we describe the set of **monocular depth cues** to three-dimensional space. After that, we turn to the more complicated topic of binocular stereopsis, a **binocular depth cue**. Finally, we consider how the various cues are combined to produce a unified perception of space.

Monocular Cues to Three-Dimensional Space

M. C. Escher (1898–1972) titled the drawing in **Figure 6.4** *Relativity*. Escher was a master of the rules that govern our perception of space. Each bit of stairway, each landing, every person—all are drawn using cues that enable us to infer three dimensions from two. But when we try to follow those stairs, we find that Escher's drawing cleverly fails to add up to a coherent representation of a place that could exist. Even when no one is trying to fool us, it is geometrically impossible for the visual system to create a perfectly faithful reconstruction of the true layout of space, given the distorted, two-dimensional input we receive through each eye. The best we can do is to use depth cues to *infer* aspects of the three-dimensional world from our two-dimensional retinal images. On the basis of the retinal images and an implicit understanding of physics and geometry, we collect cues that provide hints about the likely structure of the space in front of us and the disposition of objects in that space.

Unless we're stuck in an extremely impoverished perceptual environment (say, the Sahara

Figure 6.4 M. C. Escher, *Relativity*, 1953. Escher deploys monocular cues to depth in a way that is essentially correct at each location but that adds up to an impossible world.

during a sandstorm), every view of the world provides multiple depth cues. Usually the cues reinforce each other, combining to produce a convincing and reliable representation of the three-dimensional world. Occasionally, however, the cues are contradictory. Escher could fool us by deliberately manipulating depth cues and other routine visual inferences. He arranged sensible local cues into a globally implausible story. What cues does the visual system use to infer depth relations, and how do we use those cues to create a representation of the three-dimensional world? (See **Web Activity 6.1: Monocular Depth Cues**.)

Pictorial Depth Cues

Artists have long used clever tricks to depict depth in their paintings. These are known as **pictorial depth cues**. These cues are the natural consequence of the projection of the three-dimensional world onto the two-dimensional surface of the retina. A realistic picture or photograph is the result of projecting the three-dimensional world onto the two-dimensional surface of film or canvas. When that image is viewed from the correct position, the retinal image (in one eye, at least) formed by the two-dimensional picture will be the same as the retinal image that would have been formed by the three-dimensional world, and hence, we see depth in the picture. In theory, this means that a picture should look correct from only one, precise viewing position. In fact, pictures look reasonable over quite a range of views. Were this not so, there would be only one good seat in the movie theater. As we will now discuss, these pictorial cues include occlusion, size and position cues, and perspective cues.

Occlusion

Some of the cues to the layout of the three-dimensional world were introduced earlier in this book, because hints to the layout of space can also be hints about the structure of objects in that space. **Occlusion** is an example (see the section titled "Finding Edges" in Chapter 4). In Chapter 4, occlusion was a cue to the presence of an otherwise invisible edge. As a depth cue, occlusion gives information about the relative position of objects. Thus, in **Figure 6.5** we are happy to infer a circle in front of a square in front of a triangle. Occlusion is present in almost every visual scene (we challenge you to find a situation in normal life where nothing blocks your view of anything else), and many researchers argue that it is the most reliable of all the depth cues. It is misleading only in the case of "accidental viewpoints" (remember those, from Chapter 4?). That is, the retinal image shown in Figure 6.5 could be produced by a circle and two oddly shaped puzzle pieces, as shown in **Figure 6.6A**. That scenario would require careful placement of the objects and the viewer. It is much more likely that Figure 6.5 would arise from a more generic view of a circle occluding a square occluding a triangle (**Figure 6.6B**).

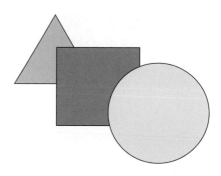

Figure 6.5 Occlusion makes it easy to infer relative position in depth.

pictorial depth cue A cue to distance or depth used by artists to depict three-dimensional depth in two-dimensional pictures.

occlusion A cue to relative depth order in which, for example, one object obstructs the view of part of another object.

(A) (B)

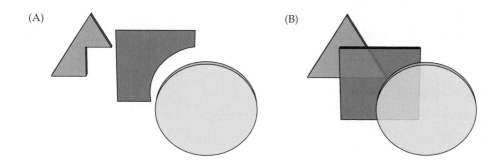

Figure 6.6 Figure 6.5 could be an "accidental" view of the pieces shown here in (A). It is much more likely, however, that it is a generic view of circle, square, and triangle, as shown in (B).

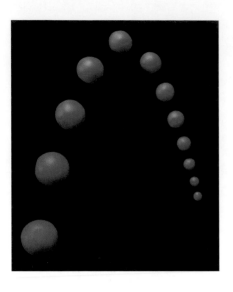

Figure 6.7 This is a photograph of a collection of Plasticine balls that are resting on the same surface at the same distance from the camera. Nevertheless, the small ones appear to be farther away. Some portion of the visual system assumes that all of these items are the same. If one ball projects a smaller image on the retina and if we assume that the balls really are the same size, then the smaller one must be farther away. This is the cue of relative size.

We do not know from the occlusion cue alone whether the red square in Figure 6.5 is in front of a small green triangle, a larger but more distant triangle (maybe a green tree), or an even larger but even more distant green mountain. Occlusion is a **nonmetrical depth cue**; it just gives us the relative orderings of occluders and occludees. A **metrical depth cue** is one that does provide information about distance in the third dimension.

Size and Position Cues

The image on the retina formed by an object out in the world gets smaller as the object gets farther away. (See **Web Activity 3.1: Visual Angle** for a review.) Moreover, your visual system knew this fact of **projective geometry** implicitly before you ever picked up this book and learned it explicitly. Projective geometry describes how the world is *projected* onto a surface. For example, a shadow is a projection of an object onto a surface. An implicit (nonconscious) understanding of the rules of projective geometry can be said to undergird many of the depth cues described here. In this case, the visual system knows that, all else being equal, smaller things are farther away. Hence, the Plasticine balls in **Figure 6.7** may appear to lie in different depth planes. We can call this depth cue **relative size**.

The impression of three-dimensionality in **Figure 6.8** is more powerful than that in Figure 6.7 because we've added another cue. The critical difference is in the organization of the objects in the two figures. In Figure 6.8, the rabbits form an orderly **texture gradient**, with larger objects in one area and smaller objects in

nonmetrical depth cue A depth cue that provides information about the depth order (relative depth) but not depth magnitude (e.g., his nose is in front of his face).

metrical depth cue A depth cue that provides quantitative information about distance in the third dimension.

projective geometry For purposes of studying perception of the three-dimensional world, the geometry that describes the transformations that occur when the three-dimensional world is *projected* onto a two-dimensional surface. For example, parallel lines do not converge in the real world, but they do in the two-dimensional projection of that world.

relative size A comparison of size between items without knowing the absolute size of either one.

texture gradient A depth cue based on the geometric fact that items of the same size form smaller images when they are farther away. An array of items that change in size smoothly across the image will appear to form a surface tilted in depth.

Figure 6.8 This rabbit texture gradient shows that the size cue is more effective when size changes systematically.

Figure 6.9 Organized differently, the same rabbits as those shown in Figure 6.8 do not produce the same sense of depth in this illustration. A size cue is most effective when it is consistent with objects arranged on the ground, not on a wall.

another. Because smaller is interpreted as farther away, this arrangement creates the perception of a ground plane receding into the distance.

In **Figure 6.9**, the rabbits are again arrayed in an orderly texture, but here we get less of a sense of depth. The difference between Figures 6.8 and 6.9 is that Figure 6.8 includes another depth cue that is not present in Figure 6.9: **relative height**. Imagine that you're actually standing in a field of rabbits. Consider the rabbit at your feet (**Figure 6.10**). It will project its image in your lower visual field. The smaller image of a more distant rabbit will be projected higher in your

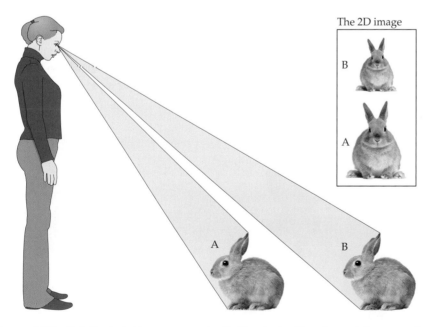

The 2D image

Figure 6.10 Relative height as a cue to depth. If we're looking down at the ground plane, the image of a closer rabbit will lie above the image of a farther rabbit in the retinal image. Because the image is inverted, the closer rabbit lies lower in the visual field than the farther rabbit.

relative height As a depth cue, the observation that objects at different distances from the viewer on the ground plane will form images at different heights in the retinal image. Objects farther away will be seen as higher in the image.

Figure 6.11 The rabbit image at the top far left is the same size as the one at the bottom far right. If they don't seem the same size, then you have been fooled by the depth cues.

visual field. Here, then, is another geometric regularity produced by projective geometry that the visual system can exploit: for objects on the ground plane, objects that are more distant will be higher in the visual field. Indeed, Ooi, Wu, and He (2001) have shown that humans use the angle between the horizon and an object to judge that object's distance.

Texture fields that provide an impression of three-dimensionality are really combinations of relative size and relative height cues. Remember the metaphor of perceptual "committees" in Chapter 4? Different modules in the visual system perform different tasks. The brain then combines the outputs to come up with a committee-like decision about the state of the world. In the case of a texture field, multiple cues interact to produce a final perception. **Figure 6.11** shows how this interaction can give rise to a size illusion. The rabbit at the upper left of the figure is actually the same physical size on the page as the rabbit at the lower right, but the one at the bottom looks smaller to most of us than the one at the top. Why? We infer, on the basis of relative height, that the rabbit at the bottom must be closer. If it is closer and it forms an image of the same size as the little rabbit at the top, it follows that the little rabbit at the bottom must be really little.

If we know what size something *ought* to be, that knowledge can be a depth cue in its own right. We infer that the woman in **Figure 6.12A** is holding her hand out at the end of an outstretched arm. Why do we make this guess? One alternative is that she's holding her hand near her shoulder, as in **Figure 6.12B**. But if that were the case in Figure 6.12A, the hand would need to be a *very* big hand. Here, our knowledge of the normal relationship of hand size to head size makes all the difference. This is the depth cue of **familiar size**.

familiar size A depth cue based on knowledge of the typical sizes of objects, such as humans or pennies.

(A)   (B)

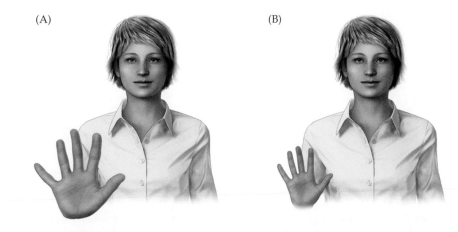

Figure 6.12 The cue of familiar size. The hand in (A) looks closer than the one in (B) because we know how big hands should be relative to heads.

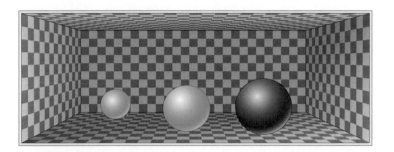

Figure 6.13 The metrical cues of relative size and height can give the visual system more information than a nonmetrical cue like occlusion can. Not only does the red sphere in this image appear to be closest and the green sphere farthest away, but also the blue sphere is seen to be closer in depth to the red sphere than to the green sphere.

Recall that occlusion is a nonmetrical cue, providing only depth *order*. The relative size and relative height cues, especially taken together, provide some metrical information. This is illustrated in **Figure 6.13**, where the three balls appear to lie at measurable distances from each other. The blue ball seems closer to the red ball than to the green ball in depth, for example. Relative size and height do not tell us the *exact* distance to an object or between objects. These are **relative metrical depth cues**. Familiar size, however, could be an **absolute metrical depth cue**. If your visual system knew the actual size of an object and the visual angle of the object's projection on the retina, it could (at least in theory) calculate the exact distance from object to eye. In practice, however, even if you know that your friend is 5 feet 10 inches tall, the visual system does not seem to know that fact with a precision that would let you know he's standing exactly 12 feet away.

Aerial Perspective

In addition to its implicit knowledge of geometry and its learned knowledge of familiar size, the visual system "knows" about properties of the atmosphere. The triangles in **Figure 6.14A** give only a faint sense of depth, if any. They are just an array of identical shapes. Adding some grayscale information, however, as in **Figure 6.14B**, provides the impression of something like a mountain range receding in the distance. More specifically, the fainter mountains (triangles) may appear to be farther away than the darker ones. The depth cue at work here relies on an implicit understanding that light is scattered by the atmosphere and that more light is scattered when we look through more atmosphere. Thus, objects farther away are subject to more scatter and appear fainter and less distinct.

relative metrical depth cue A depth cue that could specify, for example, that object A is twice as far away as object B without providing information about the absolute distance to either A or B.

absolute metrical depth cue A depth cue that provides quantifiable information about distance in the third dimension (e.g., his nose sticks out 4 centimeters in front of his face).

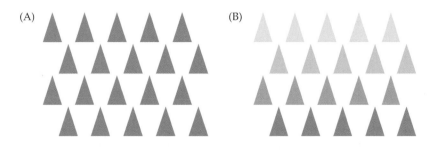

(A)   (B)

Figure 6.14 The triangles seem to recede into depth more in (B) than in (A).

Figure 6.15 A real-world example of aerial perspective. Scattering of light by the atmosphere makes more-distant features appear hazy and blue.

haze or **aerial perspective** A depth cue based on the implicit understanding that light is scattered by the atmosphere. More light is scattered when we look through more atmosphere. Thus, more distant objects are subject to more scatter and appear fainter, bluer, and less distinct.

linear perspective A depth cue based on the fact that lines that are parallel in the three-dimensional world will appear to converge in a two-dimensional image.

This cue is known as **haze**, or **aerial perspective**. **Figure 6.15** shows a real-world example. Short wavelengths (blue) are scattered more than medium and long wavelengths (see Figure 2.1B). This is why the sky looks blue and why objects farther away look not only hazy, but bluish. Relative to the rows of triangles in Figure 6.14, Figure 6.15 provides a stronger sense of depth. By now, it should be clear that this effect results from the contribution of other depth cues such as occlusion and the known size of boats.

Linear Perspective

It would not be difficult to imagine the six lines shown in **Figure 6.16** to be a sketch of the view out the windshield of a car moving down a road in a flat landscape. The depth cue in this case—**linear perspective**—is based on the rules that determine how lines in three-dimensional space are projected onto a two-dimensional image. The core piece of projective geometry in this case is that lines that are parallel in the three-dimensional world will appear to converge in the two-dimensional image, except when the parallel lines lie in a plane that is parallel to the plane of the two-dimensional image. Artists of the Italian Renaissance are said to have "discovered" linear perspective. That is not quite right. Your dog or cat knows about linear perspective. What Renaissance artists discovered was how to make the rules explicit, write them down, and turn linear perspective into a method for generating realistic depth in otherwise flat paintings. Filippo di Ser Brunellesco (1377–1446) is typically given credit for bringing linear perspective into European art. Leon Battista Alberti (1404–1474) wrote the first book on the topic in 1435 (Alberti, 1970). **Figure 6.17** shows an example of what could be done. This *Architectural View* is by Francesco di Giorgio Martini, a painter from the Italian city of Siena. Painted around

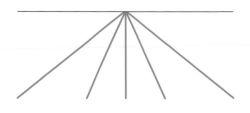

Figure 6.16 Linear perspective. If we titled this image "Driving across Kansas," you would understand, because the converging lines give the impression of parallel lines receding toward the horizon.

Figure 6.17 *Architectural View* by Francesco di Giorgio Martini (1477), a very clear example of linear perspective. Parallel lines in the image plane, such as the pillars at the front center, remain parallel in the image. Parallel lines that would recede in depth in the three-dimensional world converge to a vanishing point in the two-dimensional image.

1477, it is not the greatest work of Renaissance art, but it demonstrates his use of the basic rules of perspective. Parallel lines in the image plane, like the two front center pillars, would be parallel in the world. Look at all those other lines converging toward a **vanishing point**. Clearly, these are intended to show the parallel lines on the ground or on the sides of buildings running in depth. Of course, you can see occlusion, size, and texture cues at work, too.

In the real world, there isn't just one vanishing point, somewhere out in the harbor of Figure 6.17. The vanishing point will move as you move your eyes and head. This can be captured in a painting by having more than one vanishing point, as can be seen in **Figure 6.18** in a painting by Canaletto (1697–1768).

vanishing point The apparent point at which parallel lines receding in depth converge.

Seeing Depth in Pictures

To correctly interpret the shapes of three-dimensional objects from two-dimensional pictures, people take the orientation of the flat surface of the image into account. This allows them to understand that the picture is, in fact, a picture and not the real thing;

Figure 6.18 An example of "two-point perspective" *in Bucentaur's Return to the Pier by the Palazzo Ducale* by Canaletto (1697–1768). The pink and yellow lines are added to make the vanishing points clear.

(A)

(B)

Figure 6.19 Picture in a picture. (A) One of the authors, Dennis Levi, is seen standing next to a photograph of himself. In this panel the "picture in the picture" appears reasonable. (B) The framed picture, isolated without the context. Does the picture appear distorted? (Courtesy of Dhanraj Vishwanath and Martin S. Banks.)

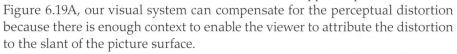

anamorphosis or **anamorphic projection**   Use of the rules of linear perspective to create a two-dimensional image so distorted that it looks correct only when viewed from a special angle or with a mirror that counters the distortion.

at the same time, they can calculate an accurate impression of the thing that is portrayed (Vishwanath, Girshik, and Banks, 2005). To illustrate this point, Marty Banks snapped the photo of one of this book's authors standing alongside a picture of himself that is shown in **Figure 6.19A**; here the "picture in the picture" appears reasonable. In **Figure 6.19B**, the same picture is shown stripped of its context. Now it appears quite distorted. In Figure 6.19A, our visual system can compensate for the perceptual distortion because there is enough context to enable the viewer to attribute the distortion to the slant of the picture surface.

The technique known as **anamorphosis**, or **anamorphic projection**, illustrates that the ability to cope with distortion is limited. In anamorphic projection, the rules of linear perspective are pushed to an extreme. Now the projection of three dimensions into two dimensions creates a two-dimensional image that is recognizable only from an unusual vantage point (or sometimes with a curved mirror). The results are known as anamorphic art. As an example, there is an odd diagonal smear in the lower center of Hans Holbein's sixteenth-century painting *The Ambassadors* (**Figure 6.20A**). If you could put your eye in exactly the right position to view the image, the smear would prove to be the skull shown in **Figure 6.20B**. Despite its successful recovery of the shapes in Figure 6.19A, the visual system cannot use knowledge about surface orientation to compensate

(A)

Figure 6.20   In 1533, Hans Holbein painted the double portrait in (A) with an odd object (B) at the feet of the two men.

(B)

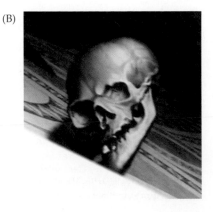

Figure 6.21 Modern-day anamorphic art. (A) In this photograph, artist Leon Keer creates what appears to be a large three-dimensional version of the classic video game, Pacman. But, as shown in (B), this is just a clever bit of anamorphic art. It is just a flat image that looks three-dimensional when viewed from the correct position.

(A)

(B)

© Leon Keer

for the distortion in Figure 6.20. In our own day, the sidewalk chalk artist Leon Keer creates amazing anamorphic images that look spectacularly real from the right vantage point and spectacularly distorted from elsewhere (**Figure 6.21**). More on the role of pictorial depth cues in art can be found in **Web Essay 6.1: Making the Implicit Explicit**.

Triangulation Cues to Three-Dimensional Space

Beyond the pictorial depth cues, a number of additional sources of information are available to our visual system when we view real-world scenes—cues that cannot be reproduced in a static two-dimensional picture. We refer to these as triangulation cues due to viewing the image from different vantage points. These cues can be either monocular (motion parallax and focus) or binocular (convergence and stereopsis).

Motion Cues

The first triangulation cue we will discuss is **motion parallax**. Motion parallax allows you to see the world from multiple viewpoints at different times by

motion parallax An important depth cue that is based on head movement. The geometric information obtained from an eye in two different positions at two different times is similar to the information from two eyes in different positions in the head at the same time.

(A)

Train

You

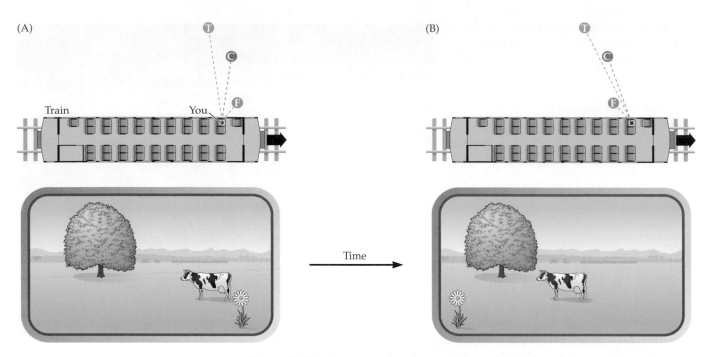

Time

(B)

Figure 6.22 Motion parallax. As you look out the window of a moving train, objects closer to you (like the flower in this illustration) shift position more quickly than do objects farther away (the tree) from one moment (A) to the next (B). This regularity can be exploited as a depth cue.

moving your head. To appreciate its power (and to understand why photographs of the forest often don't come out well), the best thing to do is to go outside and lie under a tree. Gaze up into the branches and leaves with one eye covered and your head stationary. You will notice that leaves and branches form a relatively flat texture. You can see all the details, but you may have trouble deciding whether one little branch lies in front of or behind another. If you open the other eye, stereopsis (introduced earlier and discussed in detail later in the chapter) will allow the branches and leaves to fill out a three-dimensional volume that was lacking before. Close the eye, and the volume collapses again. Now, move your head from side to side, and motion parallax will restore some of this sense of depth.

How does motion provide a cue for depth? Suppose you're sitting on a train, looking out the window at the countryside. At one instant you see the scene sketched in **Figure 6.22A**. A moment later, the scene has changed to the one in **Figure 6.22B**. Notice that as your train moved from left to right in the figure, all the objects shifted from right to left. But note that some things shifted more than others. The flower (labeled F in the figure) moved almost all the way across your retinal image, the cow (C) moved a much shorter distance, and the tree (T) hardly changed position at all. The term *parallax* refers to the geometric relationship revealed here: when you change your viewpoint while rolling down the tracks, objects closer to you shift position more than objects farther away. Of course, you don't need to be on a train to experience motion parallax; just moving your head will do. The geometric information obtained from an eye in two different positions at two different times (motion parallax) is similar to the information from two eyes in different positions in the head at the same time (binocular stereopsis) (Durgin et al., 1995; Rogers and Collett, 1989).

Motion parallax provides relative metrical information about how far away objects are; as the experiment with the tree branches demonstrates, it can provide a compelling sense of depth in some situations in which other cues are not very effective. The downside of motion parallax is that it works only if the head moves (just moving the eyes back and forth won't do, as you can easily prove to yourself). Now you know why a cat might bob its head back and forth as it plans a spectacular leap from the sofa to the table.

Other motion signals produce information about depth. For example, objects get bigger and smaller as they get closer and farther away, so an object that is simply getting bigger on a screen can appear to be looming toward you. If everything is looming at once in a large field, this **optic flow** may make you feel like you are moving toward the screen rather than like the objects on the screen are moving toward you. These topics are discussed in more detail in Chapter 8.

Accommodation and Convergence

Like a camera, the eyes need to be focused to see objects at different distances clearly. As we learned in Chapter 2, the human eye focuses via a process called **accommodation**, in which the lens gets fatter as we direct our gaze toward nearer objects (see Figure 2.3). We also need to point our eyes differently to focus on objects at different distances. As the schematic eyeballs in **Figure 6.23** move from the red dot to the blue dot, they rotate inward—a process called **convergence** (Figure 6.23A); refocusing on the red dot would require rotation outward, which is known as **divergence** (Figure 6.23B).

Focus cues can in principle enable us to see depth because we see the image from various points across the pupil, and if we could monitor our state of accommodation and/or the extent to which our eyes were converged, we could use this information as a cue to the depth of the object we were trying to bring into focus: the more we have to converge and the more the lens has to bulge in order to focus

optic flow The pattern of apparent motion of objects in a visual scene produced by the relative motion between the observer and the scene.

accommodation The process by which the eye changes its focus (in which the lens gets fatter as gaze is directed toward nearer objects).

convergence The ability of the two eyes to turn inward, often used in order to place the two images of a feature in the world on corresponding locations in the two retinal images (typically on the fovea of each eye). Convergence reduces the disparity of that feature to zero (or nearly zero).

divergence The ability of the two eyes to turn outward, often used in order to place the two images of a feature in the world on corresponding locations in the two retinal images (typically on the fovea of each eye). Divergence reduces the disparity of that feature to zero (or nearly zero).

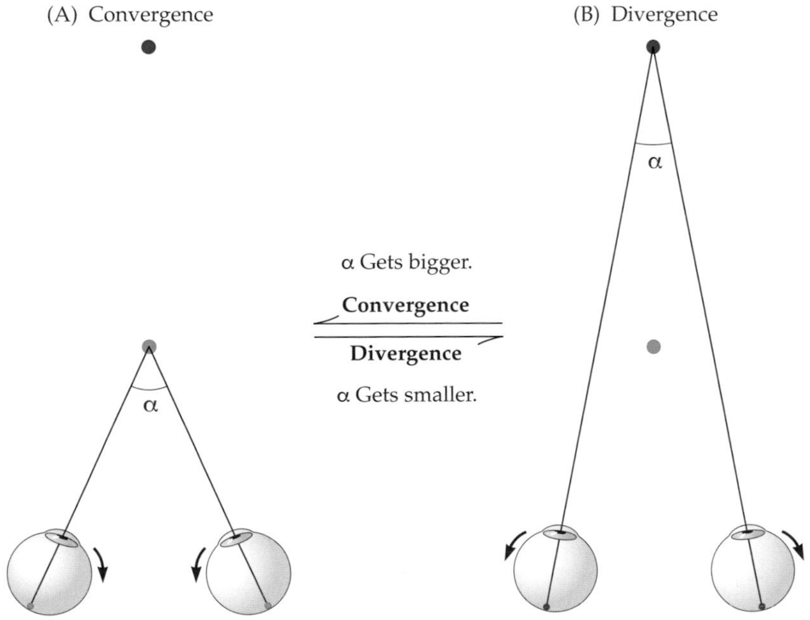

Figure 6.23 Vergence. (A) As we shift focus from a far to a near point, our eyes converge. (B) As we go from near to far, the eyes diverge. The size of the angle (labeled α) is a cue to depth.

on the object, the closer it is. In fact, we do use this information. For example, Hoffman and Banks (2010) showed that depth discrimination improves when the focus is correct. However, when we focus on objects more than about 2–3 meters away, the lens is as thin as it can get and the eyes are diverged about as much as possible, so neither cue provides much useful information. But careful studies have shown that the visual system takes advantage of both cues for objects closer than this limit. Convergence is used more than accommodation (Fisher and Ciuffreda, 1988; Owens, 1987). Moreover, in principle these cues can tell us the *exact* distance to an object. However, humans are not particularly precise about measuring the exact angles shown in Figure 6.23. Chameleons, on the other hand, do use the absolute metrical depth information from convergence to catch prey insects with their sticky tongues. Harkness (1977) showed this by fitting a chameleon with glasses that distorted the angle of convergence. The result was that the poor chameleon flicked out its tongue to the wrong distance and missed its intended dinner.

Binocular Vision and Stereopsis

As defined earlier, the term *binocular disparity* refers to differences between the images falling on our two retinas, and *stereopsis* refers to the impression of three-dimensionality—of objects "popping out in depth"—that most humans get when they view real-world objects with both eyes. Like the accounts of other depth cues, the story of the route from binocular disparity to stereopsis is a story of the visual system exploiting the regularities of projective geometry to recover the three-dimensional world from its projections—this time, onto a pair of two-dimensional surfaces. We will illustrate the translation from disparity to stereopsis using the situation shown in **Figure 6.24A**, in which the viewer (let's call him Bob) is facing a scene that includes four colored crayons at different depths. Suppose that Bob is focusing his gaze on the red crayon, as shown in **Figure 6.24B**. The two lines in this figure trace the paths of the light rays that reflect off the red crayon and onto Bob's two retinas. (Similar experiences with crayon scenes are also demonstrated in **Web Activity 6.2: Binocular Disparity**.)

(A) (B)

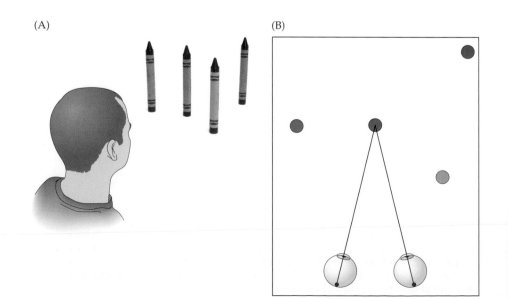

Figure 6.24 This simple visual scene illustrates how geometric regularities are exploited by the visual system to achieve stereopsis from binocular disparity. (A) The viewer, Bob, is assumed to be fixing his gaze on the red crayon. (B) This top view traces the rays of light bouncing off the red crayon onto Bob's retinas.

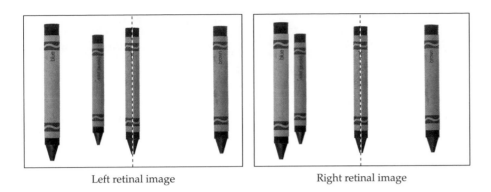

Left retinal image   Right retinal image

Figure 6.25 The overlapping portions of the images falling on Bob's left and right retinas. Because the retinal image is reversed, the blue and purple crayons on the right side of the scene in Figure 6.24 project to the left side of each retina, whereas the brown crayon on the left side of the scene projects to the right side of each retina. The size differences between the retinal images of the crayons in the two retinas are exaggerated in this figure compared with the differences we would observe if we saw this scene in the real world.

Because the visual system is designed so that the object of our gaze *always* falls on the fovea, the rays from the red crayon fall on the fovea in each of Bob's eyes. **Figure 6.25** shows the retinal image for the crayons in each eye. The red crayon is in the center of both images. We've added a dashed vertical line in front of this crayon in each image, to emphasize the fact that this is the location of the fovea.

Now consider the retinal images of the blue crayon. As you saw in Chapter 2, the optics of the eye reverse left-right and up-down (see Figure 2.2A). Thus, the blue crayon on the right side of the scene in Figure 6.24 falls on the left side in each of the two retinal images shown in Figure 6.25. In our imaginary scene, the blue crayon is placed so that the monocular retinal images of that crayon are formed at the same distance from the fovea in both eyes. We say that this crayon's images fall on **corresponding retinal points**. The same can be said of the images of the red crayon, which fall on the two foveas.

In fact, any object lying on the **Vieth-Müller circle**—the imaginary circle that runs through the two eyeballs and the object on which Bob is fixated—should project to corresponding retinal points. This imaginary circle is drawn in gray in **Figure 6.26**. Objects that fall on corresponding retinal points are said to have zero binocular disparity. If the two eyes are looking at one spot (such as the red crayon), then there will be a surface of zero disparity running through that spot. That surface is known as the **horopter**. Any object placed on that imaginary surface in the world will form images on corresponding retinal points. As it happens, the horopter and the Vieth-Müller circle are not quite the same. If you are *extremely* fond of rather complicated geometry, you may want to pursue this topic in one of the following sources: I. P. Howard and Rogers, 1995 or 2001; or Tyler, 1991. Otherwise, the important point is that there is a surface of zero disparity whose position in the world depends on the current state of convergence of the eyes.

Objects that lie on the horopter are seen as single objects when viewed with both eyes. Objects significantly closer to or farther away from the surface of zero disparity form images on decidedly noncorresponding points in the two eyes, and we see two of each of those objects. This double vision is known as **diplopia**. Objects that are close to the horopter but not quite on it can still be seen

corresponding retinal points Two monocular images of an object in the world are said to fall on corresponding points if those points are the same distance from the fovea in both eyes. The two foveas are also corresponding points.

Vieth-Müller circle The location of objects whose images fall on geometrically corresponding points in the two retinas. If life were simple, this circle would be the horopter, but life is not simple.

horopter The location of objects whose images lie on corresponding points. The surface of zero disparity.

diplopia Double vision. If visible in both eyes, stimuli falling outside of Panum's fusional area will appear diplopic.

Figure 6.26 Bob is still gazing at the red crayon. This view from above traces the light rays reflecting from the red and blue crayons onto Bob's retinas. The blue crayon projects to *corresponding retinal points*—positions that are equidistant from and on the same side of the fovea. The same would be true of any object falling on the gray curve shown in the figure. (The horopter and Vieth-Müller circle are not exactly the same, but they would be very similar in this case.)

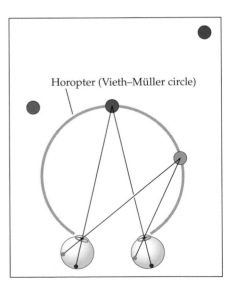

Horopter (Vieth–Müller circle)

(A)

(B)

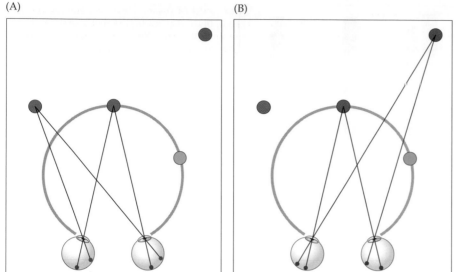

Figure 6.27 Light rays projecting from the brown (A) and purple (B) crayons onto Bob's retinas as he continues to gaze at the red crayon.

Panum's fusional area The region of space, in front of and behind the horopter, within which binocular single vision is possible.

as single objects. This region of space in front of and behind the horopter, within which binocular single vision is possible, is known as **Panum's fusional area** (Panum, 1940). You can check this ability quite simply, by holding a red crayon (or pen) directly in front of you with your left hand, at a distance of about 20 centimeters (cm), and keeping both eyes on it. Now hold a blue crayon (or pen) about 5 cm to either side of the red one with your right hand, and slowly move it nearer to your eyes and then farther away, while maintaining careful fixation on the red one. You should initially see the blue crayon/pen as single, when it is about the same distance from you as the red one, because it is within Panum's fusional area. However, when it falls outside Panum's area, it will appear double. Panum's area provides a little room for small errors in eye alignment, while still maintaining single vision.

Armed with this terminology, let's return to Bob and his crayons. Consider the retinal images of the brown crayon, lying just off the horopter. As Figure 6.24 and the view from above in **Figure 6.27A** show, rays of light bouncing off this crayon do *not* fall on corresponding retinal points: the crayon's image is farther away from the fovea on the left retina than on the right retina. Relative to the horopter, this crayon forms retinal images with a nonzero binocular disparity. The purple crayon is even farther off the horopter (**Figure 6.27B**); it forms retinal images that are even more disparate (**Figure 6.28**).

The geometric regularity that the visual system uses to extract metrical depth information from binocular disparity should now be growing clear. The larger the disparity, the greater the distance in depth of the object from the horopter.

The direction in depth is given by the *sign* (that is, "crossed" or "uncrossed") of the disparity, as illustrated in **Figure 6.29**. Suppose that Bob is looking at a red crayon with his eyes converged so that the red crayon falls on the fovea in each eye. A closer, blue crayon will form images on noncorresponding, disparate points. On the left retina, blue will lie to the left of red. Because the image is reversed, this means that, viewed from the left

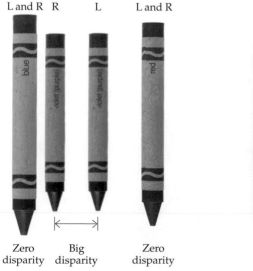

Zero disparity   Big disparity   Zero disparity

Small disparity

Figure 6.28 Superposition of Bob's left (L) and right (R) retinal images of the crayons in Figure 6.25, showing the relative disparity for each crayon. Size differences are ignored here. The red and blue crayons sit on the horopter and have zero disparity. They form retinal images in corresponding locations. The brown crayon forms images with a small binocular disparity. The purple crayon, farther from the horopter, has larger binocular disparity.

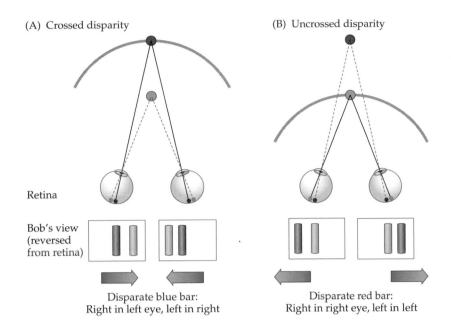

(A) Crossed disparity

(B) Uncrossed disparity

Retina

Bob's view
(reversed
from retina)

Disparate blue bar:
Right in left eye, left in right

Disparate red bar:
Right in right eye, left in left

Figure 6.29 *Crossed and uncrossed disparity.* (A) Here Bob is foveating the red crayon. In the Bob's-eye views, the closer, blue object is seen to the right in the left eye and to the left in the right eye. In this scenario the disparity is crossed. (B) Here Bob has shifted his gaze and his horopter to the blue crayon. In the Bob's-eye views, the farther, red object is seen to the left in the left eye and to the right in the right eye. In this scenario the disparity is uncrossed

eye, blue is to the right of red. Viewed from the right eye, blue is to the left. Right in left, and left in right. This is known as **crossed disparity** (Figure 6.29A), and crossed disparity always means "in front of the horopter." In Figure 6.29B, Bob is looking at the blue crayon, and the red is seen to the left with the left eye and to the right with the right. That's **uncrossed disparity**, and uncrossed disparity always means "behind the horopter." Note that if we change our fixation, the horopter is now at a different location in space. Stereopsis is a relative depth cue that provides very-high-resolution depth information for objects that are close to the horopter.

Figure 6.30 illustrates the relationship between binocular disparity and perceived relative depth. In the middle of the graph, just to either side of the

crossed disparity The sign of disparity created by objects in front of the plane of fixation (the horopter). The term *crossed* is used because images of objects located in front of the horopter appear to be displaced to the left in the right eye and to the right in the left eye.

uncrossed disparity The sign of disparity created by objects behind the plane of fixation (the horopter). The term *uncrossed* is used because images of objects located behind the horopter will appear to be displaced to the right in the right eye and to the left in the left eye.

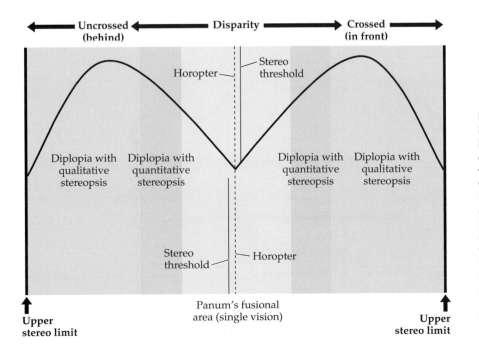

Uncrossed
(behind)

Disparity

Crossed
(in front)

Horopter

Stereo
threshold

Diplopia with
qualitative
stereopsis

Diplopia with
quantitative
stereopsis

Diplopia with
quantitative
stereopsis

Diplopia with
qualitative
stereopsis

Stereo
threshold

Horopter

Panum's fusional
area (single vision)

Upper
stereo limit

Upper
stereo limit

Figure 6.30 In this figure, disparity increases from zero at the horopter (dashed line in the middle of the figure). Going in either the crossed or uncrossed direction, we first find the smallest disparity that would support stereopsis (stereo threshold). Next, there is a range of single vision with quantitative stereo (green), a range of diplopia or "double vision" with quantitative stereopsis (blue), and diplopia with qualitative (just near or far) stereopsis (orange). Finally, there is an upper stereo limit, the disparity beyond which stereoscopic processing does not occur. The black curve gives a feeling for the relative size of the depth impression for that disparity. (After Ogle, 1952; Wilcox and Allison, 2009.)

stereoscope A device for simultaneously presenting one image to one eye and another image to the other eye. Stereoscopes can be used to present dichoptic stimuli for stereopsis and binocular rivalry.

horopter, are the lower limits of stereopsis—the smallest crossed and uncrossed disparities that can be detected (i.e., the stereo thresholds). Farther from the center in either direction, disparity increases. The limit of Panum's fusional area (the green zone in Figure 6.30) marks the end of the zone of single vision. Beyond that the images are diplopic. Items will look doubled but, interestingly, they are still seen in relative depth. When the disparity is not too large (the blue zones in Figure 6.30), the depth information from stereopsis is quantitative. Here stereopsis still provides an accurate estimate of the relative depth. As disparity increases beyond this range into the purple zones, it still provides usable depth order information, but it is now qualitative rather than quantitative. An item will appear to be in front or behind, but that is about all that stereopsis can provide in this range. Finally, once disparities are larger than the upper disparity limit, there is no longer any useful depth information.

Stereoscopes and Stereograms

Interestingly, although scientists had studied the geometry of binocular vision for millennia (the geometer Euclid was at it in the third century BCE), not until the nineteenth century was binocular disparity properly recognized as a depth cue. In the 1830s, Sir Charles Wheatstone invented a device called the **stereoscope** (**Figure 6.31**) that presented one image to one eye and a different image to the other eye. The stereoscope confirmed that the visual system treats binocular disparity as a depth cue, regardless of whether the disparity is produced by actual or simulated images of a scene.

For the average citizen at the time, the stereoscope was not science; it was home entertainment. The Wheatstone stereoscope held two different images in two different places. In the 1850s, however, David Brewster and Oliver Wendell Holmes invented viewers (**Figure 6.32A**) that held a card with a double image like that shown in **Figure 6.32B**. The double images were captured by cameras with two lenses separated by about 2.5 inches (≈ 63 cm), the distance between the average human's eyes. This arrangement allows stereo cameras to take a pair of pictures that mimic the images produced by the projective geometry of human binocular vision. Photographers traveled the world with these stereo cameras, capturing far-off scenes in a way that enabled a London schoolchild to

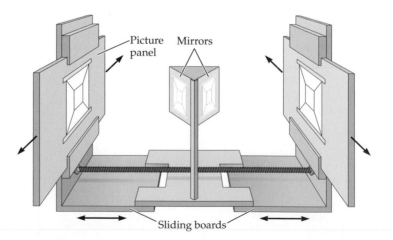

Figure 6.31 Wheatstone's stereoscope. The viewer would bring her nose up to the vertical rod at the center of the apparatus so that each eye was looking at the image reflected in one of the two mirrors. (After Wheatstone, 1838.)

(A) (B)

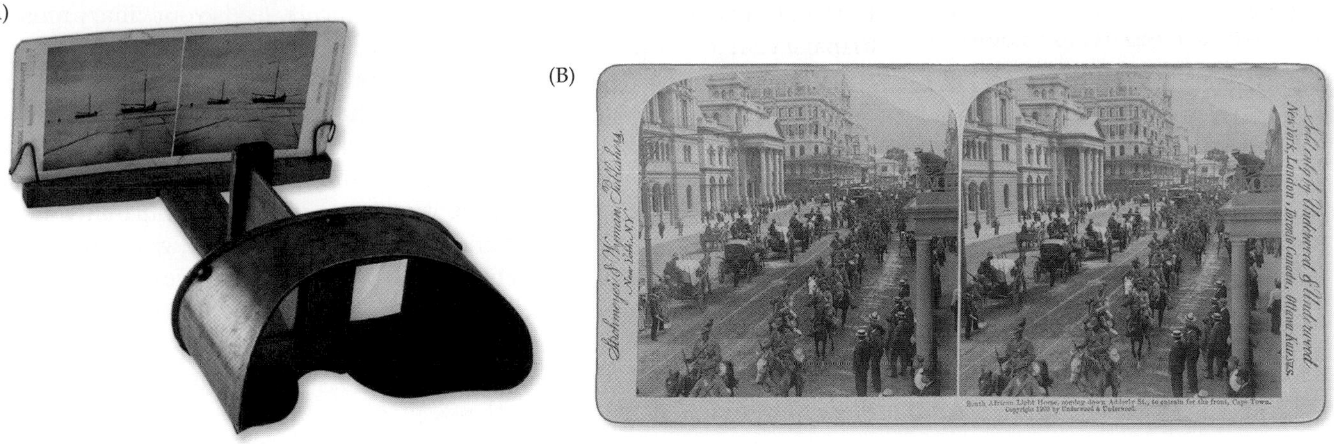

Figure 6.32 Stereopsis for the masses. (A) This Holmes stereoscope—among others—brought stereo photos into many mid-nineteenth-century homes. (B) A stereo photo of South African Light Horse, a scouting regiment of the British Army, on Adderly Street in Cape Town, South Africa, in 1900. If you can free-fuse (explained later in this section), you will be able to see this scene jump out in depth.

see, for example, a vivid three-dimensional image of the British Army in Cape Town, South Africa. (For a guide to more of these historical images, as well as many other stereograms, see **Web Essay 6.2: Stereo Images on the Web**.)

A stereoscope is very helpful, but you don't actually need one to experience stereopsis. You can teach yourself a technique known as **free fusion**, which John Frisby (1980) called "the poor man's stereoscope." **Figure 6.33** contains two almost identical pictures. If you cross your eyes hard, you should see four sets of squares. This is the phenomenon of double vision (diplopia), described in the previous section. Two of those sets of squares are seen with the left eye, and two with the right. The trick is to relax just a bit until you see just three sets of squares. The far-left set is seen only in the left eye; the far-right set, only in the right; but the middle set is the fusion of two sets, one seen by the left eye and another seen by the right eye. This fusion of the separate images seen by the two eyes makes stereopsis possible.

Achieving the perception of three, instead of four or two, sets of squares in Figure 6.33 is the first step toward free fusion. The second step is to bring the middle set into focus. Convergence and accommodation, discussed earlier, normally

free fusion The technique of converging (crossing) or diverging the eyes in order to view a stereogram without a stereoscope.

Figure 6.33 Try to converge (cross) or diverge (uncross) your eyes so that you see exactly three big blue squares here, rather than the two on the page. If you succeed, you will probably be able to see that the three little white squares lie at different depths in the middle set of big squares.

stereoblindness An inability to make use of binocular disparity as a depth cue. This term is typically used to describe individuals with vision in both eyes. Someone who has lost one (or both) eyes is not typically described as "stereoblind."

work in lockstep, so crossing your eyes automatically leads your ciliary muscles to make your lenses more spherical (unless you are presbyopic—see Chapter 2). Similar problems (in the opposite direction) will occur if you diverge your eyes. To see the middle set of squares clearly, you have to decouple accommodation and convergence. This is hard to do, but if you can manage it, then the image will come into focus and the three white squares will appear to lie at different depths in the middle set of squares. When you view them normally, notice that the white squares in the left and right panels look misaligned in opposite directions. Those are the monocular views. When you free-fuse, the opposite misalignments become the binocular disparity, and your visual system converts that disparity into a perception of depth.

The depth that you see depends on whether you converged or diverged your eyes. We described crossing, or converging, the eyes. It is also possible to free-fuse the images in Figure 6.33 by *diverging* your eyes. Divergence requires focusing on a point beyond the plane of the page so that the image of the left-hand set of squares falls on the left fovea and the image of the right-hand set falls on the right fovea. Because the images falling on the two retinas in the divergence method are reversed compared with the convergence situation, the disparities are reversed and the perceived depth will be reversed. That is, if you converge, the top square will be the farthest back. If you diverge, it will appear closest to you. Either converging or diverging will produce a clear stereoscopic effect, so give it a try.

Before we go on, we should note that approximately 3–5% of the population lacks stereoscopic depth perception—a condition known as **stereoblindness**. Stereoblind individuals might be able to achieve the perception of three sets of squares in Figure 6.33, but the little white squares will not pop out in depth. Stereoblindness is usually a secondary effect of childhood visual disorders such as strabismus, in which the two eyes are misaligned. (See the Sensation & Perception in Everyday Life box "Recovering Stereo Vision" below.) If you had such a visual disorder during childhood and/or you've been diagnosed with stereoblindness, we apologize, but you just won't perceive depth in the stereograms presented here and on the website. That said, many people who try and fail to see depth in stereograms have "normal" vision (wearing glasses doesn't count as "abnormal" in this case). Those people just need practice, so don't give up. **Web Activity 6.3: Stereoscopes and Stereograms** provides more stereograms for practice, and **Web Essay 6.2: Stereo Images on the Web** leads to another website with more tips for free-fusing.

FURTHER DISCUSSION of strabismus can be found in Chapter 3 on page 94.

■ Sensation & Perception in Everyday Life ■

Recovering Stereo Vision

As noted earlier, about 3–5% of the population are stereoblind, usually as a result of early childhood visual disorders. Can stereo vision be recovered later in life? Meet Stereo Sue and Binocular Bruce.

Susan Barry, a professor of neurobiology, had strabismus as an infant and had been stereoblind essentially all her life. Her book *Fixing My Gaze* (2009) provides a fascinating, informative, and beautifully written

■ Sensation & Perception in Everyday Life *(continued)* ■

account of her acquisition of stereopsis following vision therapy. It describes her transformative journey from the many visual, social, and psychological challenges of a turned eye (a squint or strabismus) early in life, to the sudden enrichment of her perceptions of the world following successful unconventional visual therapy begun at 48 years of age. (An earlier article about her visual recovery was published in *The New Yorker* under the title of "Stereo Sue" by Oliver Sacks.)

Barry vividly recounts how acquiring stereoscopic vision led to a dramatic improvement of her perception of depth, or the appreciation of the "space between objects." A particularly valuable insight is her argument for the inability of people with normal vision to appreciate the visual experience of being stereoblind. Naively one might think that this experience could be duplicated simply by closing one eye so all information about depth was conveyed by monocular cues. Not so, however, Barry argues: the monocular experience of a typically reared person who closes one eye has been informed by a lifetime of experience with stereoscopic vision and so is far different from that of a person who is stereoblind. As a result, Barry's new stereoscopic vision brought much more to her life than just depth perception: objects became clearer, motion perception became more veridical, and her movement around the world became more confident. Even more poignant is her vivid description of the enhanced sense of touch she had developed over the years and its key role in informing her newly acquired sense of stereo vision.

Barry did not simply "recover" stereopsis, but rather had to relearn to see with stereo vision. As blind or deaf individuals often describe, individuals deprived of a sense are not just "missing" a sense.

Rather, they have developed an entirely different way of sensing the world. Upon sensory restitution, a fascinating but rather disturbing experience unfolds as the brain has to adapt to a new way of functioning.

Even more dramatic is the experience of Binocular Bruce (the late Bruce Bridgeman), a very perceptive vision scientist who had been stereo-deficient all his life. Remarkably, he recovered stereopsis after watching the 3D movie *Hugo* (Bridgeman, 2014). Whether this sort of immersive experience, with very large disparities along with many other depth cues, will be a generally effective treatment for abnormal stereopsis remains to be tested. However, these case studies, along with lab studies of perceptual learning that have resulted in the recovery of stereopsis (Ding and Levi, 2011; Vedamurthy et al., 2015), call into question the notion that has been the received wisdom, that recovery of stereopsis can only occur during early childhood. The idea, dating back to the early twentieth century, has been that there is a "critical period" of development when the visual system is still plastic and capable of change. After that, it was thought, our basic visual capabilities are fixed. This led a number of practitioners to tell Susan Barry and her mother that "nothing could be done" about her vision (one suggested that she might need a psychiatrist). Since binocular neurons are present in the visual cortex of primates within the first week of life (see the "Development of Binocular Vision and Stereopsis" section below), Barry surmises that some of the innate wiring of her binocular connections remained intact and that vision therapy taught her to move her eyes into position for stereo vision, "finally giving these neurons the information they were wired to receive" (Barry, 2009).

Random Dot Stereograms

For 100 years or so after the invention of the stereoscope, it was generally supposed that stereopsis occurred relatively late in the processing of visual information. The idea was that the first step in free-fusing images such as those in **Figure 6.34** would be to analyze the input as a face. We would then use the slight disparities between the left-eye and right-eye images of the nose, eyes, chin, and other objects and parts to enrich the sense that the nose sticks out in front of the face, that the eyes are slightly sunken, and so on.

Bela Julesz, a Hungarian radar engineer who spent most of his career at Bell Labs in New Jersey, thought the conventional wisdom might be backward. He theorized that stereopsis might be used to *discover* objects and surfaces in

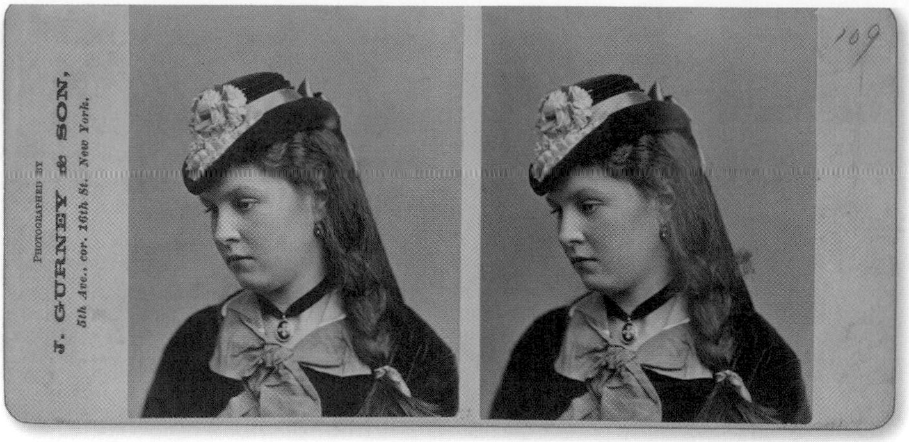

Figure 6.34 A stereo photograph of a woman's face.

random dot stereogram (RDS)
A stereogram made of a large number (often in the thousands) of randomly placed dots. Random dot stereograms contain no monocular cues to depth. Stimuli visible stereoscopically in random dot stereograms are Cyclopean stimuli.

Cyclopean Referring to stimuli that are defined by binocular disparity alone. Named after the one-eyed Cyclops of Homer's *Odyssey*.

the world. Why would this be useful? Julesz thought that stereopsis might help reveal camouflaged objects. A mouse might be the same color as its background, but out in the open it would be in front of the background. A cat that could use stereopsis to break the mouse's camouflage would be a more successful hunter. (Cats do have stereopsis, by the way [Blake, 1988; R. Fox and Blake, 1971].) To prove his point, Julesz (1964, 1971) made use of **random dot stereograms** (**RDSs**). An example is shown in **Figure 6.35**. If you can free-fuse these images, you will see a pair of squares, one sticking out like a bump, the other looking like a hole in the texture (which one is the bump and which one is the hole depends, again, on whether you converge or diverge your eyes).

The important point about RDSs is that we cannot see the squares in either of the component images. We cannot see the squares using any monocular depth cues. These are shapes that are defined by binocular disparity alone. Julesz called such stimuli **Cyclopean**, after the one-eyed Cyclops of Homer's *Odyssey*. Wheatstone showed with his stereoscope that binocular disparity is a necessary condition for stereopsis. Julesz demonstrated with RDSs that disparity is *sufficient* for stereopsis. To understand how RDSs are made, see **Web Activity 6.3: Stereoscopes and Stereograms**. And to learn something about 3D movies and games see **Web Essay 6.3: Stereo Movies, TV, and Video Games**.

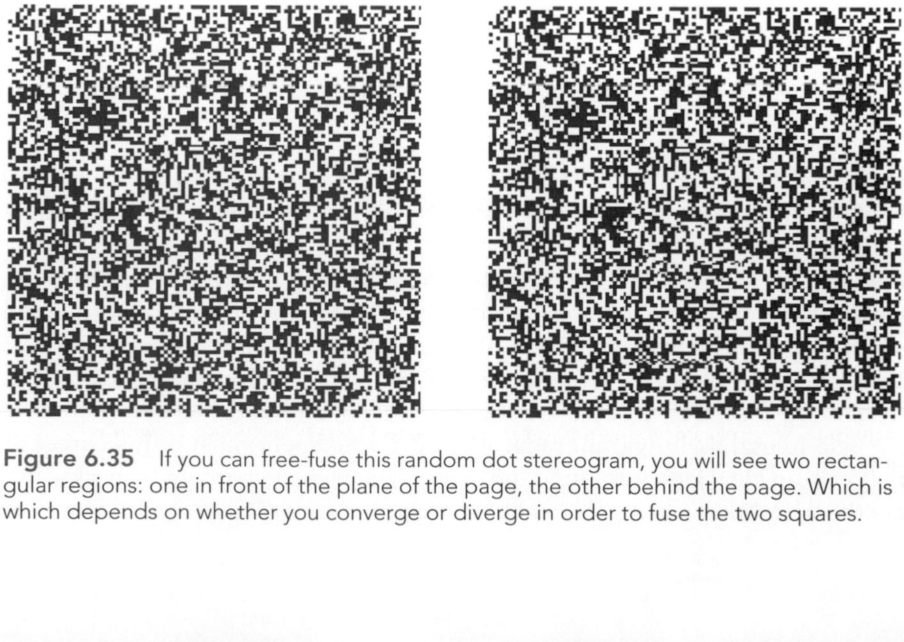

Figure 6.35 If you can free-fuse this random dot stereogram, you will see two rectangular regions: one in front of the plane of the page, the other behind the page. Which is which depends on whether you converge or diverge in order to fuse the two squares.

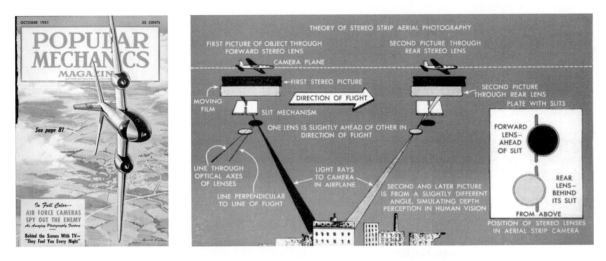

Figure 6.36 It is possible to make effective stereoscopic images of terrain by taking two aerial pictures from two, quite widely separated viewpoints. (From Goddard, 1951; Hearst Communications Inc.., reprinted with permission.)

Using Stereopsis

Stereopsis has been put to work in a number of fields. The military has known for a long time that you can get more information out of aerial surveillance if your view of the ground is stereoscopic. However, if you've ever looked out the window from thousands of meters in the air, you may have noticed the ground looks rather flat. This is due to yet more geometry. Stereopsis can provide useful information about metric depth only for distances up to 40 meters (Palmisano et al., 2010). With eyes a few centimeters apart, you don't get adequate disparity from more distant targets. What you need are eyes separated by hundreds of meters. This can be done if you have a plane and a special camera. **Figure 6.36** reprints a figure from a 1951 issue of *Popular Mechanics* in which Colonel George W. Goddard showed the public how images taken from two vantage points produced stereo images during the Korean War.

We can also use stereopsis to have a better look inside the body. **Figure 6.37** shows a stereo view of a mammogram, an X-ray of the breast of the sort used to detect breast cancer. In order to create another free-fusion demonstration, we've

Figure 6.37 This stereo mammogram was created by taking X-rays of a woman's breast from two viewpoints. If you can free-fuse, you will see the structures in the image separate in depth, making it easier to decide whether the filament is part of the breast tissue or is a different structure. (Courtesy of David Getty.)

correspondence problem In reference to binocular vision, the problem of figuring out which bit of the image in the left eye should be matched with which bit in the right eye. The problem is particularly vexing when the images consist of thousands of similar features, like dots in random dot stereograms.

printed the one image of the breast twice, to the left and the to right of a second image of the same breast, placed in the middle of this figure. The two images are taken from slightly different viewpoints, creating a binocular disparity if one view is presented to one eye and the other view to the other eye. Thus, if you free-fuse the images so that you see four breast images, one of the two center images will have the correct disparities (depending on whether you diverge or converge your eyes to free-fuse). The correct one will show the white wire—a marker for the surgeon—on top of the breast. You can see that the breast tissue is characterized by a network of intersecting structures. This is like our earlier example of looking at the little branches of a tree while lying on your back with just one eye open. It can be very hard to tell which line-like structures actually intersect and which ones lie at different depths. This turns out to be important when reading a mammogram. A starburst structure might be a sign of cancer, but not if it is an accidental viewpoint (see Chapter 4) of structures at different depths in the breast that just happen to form a suspicious pattern in a two-dimensional projection. Stereopsis can disambiguate this situation. If you can free-fuse these images, you will see the texture in three dimensions, and you will be able to determine how different structures relate to each other in depth. Stereoscopic displays are beginning to be used in radiology (Held and Hui, 2011), and they can reduce the error rate in these important tasks (Getty, D'Orsi, and Pickett, 2008).

Is stereopsis useful in everyday life? In people with normal binocular vision, visually guided hand movements are significantly impaired when viewing is restricted to one eye (Fielder and Mosely, 1996), likely owing to the fact that binocular depth thresholds are about a factor of 10 better than monocular thresholds (McKee and Taylor, 2010). These results are mirrored in patients with amblyopia ("lazy eye") for whom many observed visuomotor deficits are due to impaired stereopsis, and in particular impaired visual feedback control of movements, rather than visual acuity loss (Grant and Moseley, 2011). Loss of stereopsis may also result in unstable gait, especially reduced accuracy when a change of terrain (e.g., steps) occurs, and difficulties for children in playing some sports.

> **FURTHER DISCUSSION** of stereo sensation can be found in Chapter 10 (sound localization; pages 316–321) and Chapter 14 (binaral rivalry in olfaction; page 481).

Stereoscopic Correspondence

If you successfully free-fused the random dot patterns in Figure 6.35, you solved a truly daunting problem. Even if you didn't, if you have normal binocular vision, you are solving the **correspondence problem** all the time. The correspondence problem is the problem of figuring out which bit of the image in the left eye should be matched with which bit in the right eye. **Figures 6.38** and **6.39** use an extremely simple situation to illustrate why correspondence is so tricky. There are, of course, just three dots in Figure 6.38. Figure 6.39A traces the paths of the rays of light from the printed circles on the page to the images on the viewer's retinas. The retinal images of the circles are labeled to make it clear which image on the left retina corresponds to which image on the right retina, but your visual system has no such labels. All it knows about is the retinal images, as shown in Figure 6.39B. Figure 6.39C shows another possible geometric interpretation of the situation: if the left retinal image of circle 2 is matched to the right retinal image of circle 1, and the left retinal image of circle 3 is matched to the right retinal image of circle 2, you will perceive *four* circles, with the inner pair of

Figure 6.38 Is this a simple picture or a complicated computational problem?

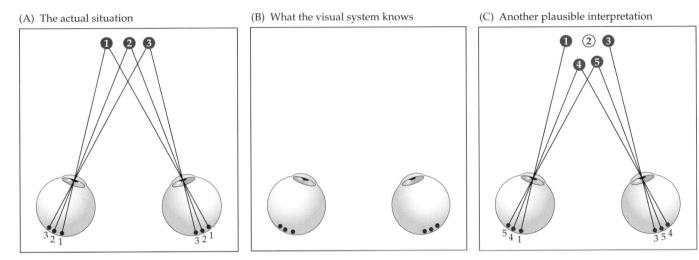

(A) The actual situation

(B) What the visual system knows

(C) Another plausible interpretation

Figure 6.39 Interpreting the visual information from the three circles in Figure 6.38 (A, B). It would require careful placement, but four dots in the world could produce three dots in each eye as in (C).

circles perceived as floating in front of the outer pair. In fact, you may be able to experience this for yourself if you can cross your eyes correctly.

With only three elements in the visual scene, it isn't hard to imagine how the visual system might achieve the proper correspondence: first match the two circles whose images fall on the foveas; then match the two images to the left of the foveas with each other; then match the two images to the right of the foveas. Before the introduction of random dot stereograms, a similar logic seemed reasonable for more complex scenes, too. Go back to the face in Figure 6.34. Our visual systems could solve the correspondence problem by first finding the parts of the two faces and then matching nose to nose, mouth to mouth, and so forth. The RDS in Figure 6.35, however, contains thousands of identical black and white dots falling on each retina. How can we be sure that the dot in the center of the fovea of one eye corresponds to the dot in the center of the other eye? Even if we knew that, could we really match each dot in the right eye with just one dot in the left eye? If there were a little dirt on the page, would the whole process collapse? How in the world does our visual system succeed in making the proper matches?

Matching thousands of left-eye dots to thousands of right-eye dots in Figure 6.35 would require a lot of work for any computational system. However, the problem is simpler if we look at a blurred version of the stereogram. Blurring leaves only the low-spatial-frequency information. **Figure 6.40** shows the low spatial frequencies of the stereogram from

Figure 6.40 A low-spatial-frequency filtered version of the stereogram in Figure 6.35.

uniqueness constraint In reference to stereopsis, the observation that a feature in the world is represented exactly once in each retinal image. This constraint simplifies the correspondence problem.

continuity constraint In reference to stereopsis, the observation that, except at the edges of objects, neighboring points in the world lie at similar distances from the viewer. This is one of several constraints that have been proposed as helpful in solving the correspondence problem.

Figure 6.35. Now, rather than thousands of dots, we have just a few large blobs. Now you could imagine a process that, for example, matched the black blob in the upper left corner of the left image with the very similar blob in the right image. Crude matches of this sort could act as anchors, allowing the visual system to fill in the finer (high-spatial-frequency) matches from there.

In addition to starting with low-spatial-frequency information, David Marr and Tomaso Poggio (1979) suggested two more heuristics for solving the correspondence problem. They called these the uniqueness and continuity constraints. The **uniqueness constraint** acknowledges that a feature in the world is represented exactly once in each retinal image. Working in the opposite direction, the visual system knows that each monocular image feature (e.g., a nose or a dot) should be paired with exactly one feature in the other monocular image. Notice that Figure 6.39C would not violate uniqueness. Each dot in the world would be represented exactly once in each retinal image. The odd thing is that two dots in the real world could be represented by the same dot in the retinal image. The **continuity constraint** holds that, except at the edges of objects, neighboring points in the world lie at similar distances from the viewer. Accordingly, disparity should change smoothly at most places in the image. (These constraints are difficult to illustrate on a static page, but **Web Activity 6.4: Stereoscopic Correspondence** provides dynamic explanations.) With those constraints, the correspondence problem is not entirely solved, but it is made much more tractable. There are not so many possible solutions. However, recent work suggests that identifying correct matches may not be the optimal strategy (Goncalves and Welchman, 2017). Rather, they suggest that the brain uses "what not detectors" that sense dissimilar features in the two eyes. These suppress unlikely interpretations of the scene and facilitate stereopsis by providing evidence against interpretations that are incompatible with the true structure of the scene.

The Physiological Basis of Stereopsis and Depth Perception

Now that we know something about the theoretical basis of stereopsis, we can ask how it is implemented by the human brain. The most fundamental requirement is that input from the two eyes must converge onto the same cell. As noted in Chapter 3, this convergence does not happen until the primary visual cortex, where most neurons can be influenced by input from both the left and right eyes—that is, they are binocular (Hubel and Wiesel, 1962). A binocular neuron has two receptive fields, one in each eye. In binocular primary visual cortex neurons, the receptive fields in the two eyes are generally very similar, sharing nearly identical orientation and spatial-frequency tuning, as well as the same preferred speed and direction of motion (Hubel and Wiesel, 1973). Thus, these cells are well suited to the task of matching images in the two eyes.

Many binocular neurons respond best when the retinal images are on corresponding points in the two retinas, thereby providing a neural basis for the horopter. However, many other binocular neurons respond best when similar images occupy slightly *different* positions on the retinas of the two eyes (Barlow, Blakemore, and Pettigrew, 1967; Pettigrew, Nikara, and Bishop, 1968). In other words, these neurons are tuned to a particular binocular disparity, as diagrammed in **Figure 6.41**.

Recall the distinction, from earlier in this chapter, between metrical and nonmetrical depth cues. Stereopsis can be used both metrically and nonmetrically. Nonmetrical stereopsis might just tell you that a feature lies in front of or behind the plane of fixation. Gian Poggio and his colleagues (Poggio and Talbot, 1981) found disparity-tuned neurons of this sort in V2 (which stands for "visual

(A)　　　　　　　(B)　　　　　　　(C)

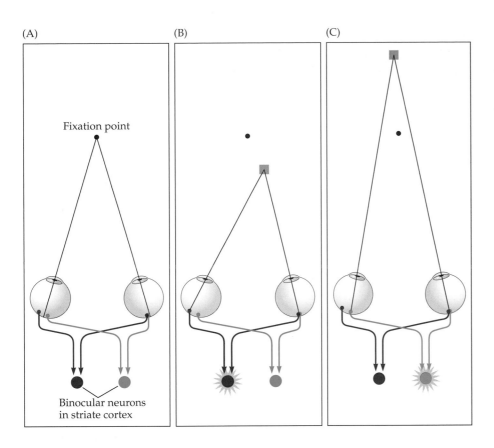

Fixation point

Binocular neurons
in striate cortex

Figure 6.41 In these simplified diagrams of receptive fields for two binocular-disparity–tuned neurons in primary visual cortex, the red neuron "sees" stimuli falling on the red receptive fields, and the blue neuron responds to stimuli falling on the blue receptive fields (these receptive fields overlap on the right retina). (A) The overall picture, showing the fixation point in relation to the two retinas. (B) The red neuron responds best to a stimulus closer to and slightly to the right of the fixation point. (C) The blue neuron responds best if its preferred stimulus is behind and slightly to the left of fixation.

area 2") and some higher cortical areas. Some neurons responded positively to disparities near zero—that is, to images falling on corresponding retinal points. Other neurons were broadly tuned to a range of crossed (near) or uncrossed (far) disparities. On the other hand, stereopsis can also be used in a very precise, metrical manner. Indeed, stereopsis is a "hyperacuity" like Vernier acuity (see **Web Essay 3.1: Hyperacuity**), with thresholds smaller than the size of a cone. Both of these forms of stereopsis have their uses, and functional magnetic resonance imaging (fMRI) data suggest that the dorsal *where* pathway is most interested in metrical stereopsis, while the ventral *what* pathway makes do with more categorical, near-versus-far information (Preston et al., 2008) (see Chapter 4).

The neural bases of other depth cues have also been investigated. For example, when we discussed motion parallax earlier, we suggested moving your head back and forth while looking into the branches of a tree in order to create a more vivid impression of the depth relationships among the branches and twigs. To exploit that cue properly, you need to know how your head is moving (see Chapter 12) and how items in the visual field are moving (see Chapter 8). Nadler, Angelaki, and DeAngelis (2008) looked for the neural substrate of parallax in the middle temporal area (area MT) of the brain of macaque monkeys. As we will see in Chapter 8, this area is very important in the perception of motion. Nadler et al. set up an apparatus where the monkey was moved from side to side while items on the screen also moved. If the monkey was integrating signals about its head movement with the motion signals, then the objects on the screen should have been seen in depth. Otherwise, they would have been seen as just moving in the plane of the screen. It turns out that cells in area MT can signal the sign of depth (near or far) based on this motion parallax signal alone.

Bayesian approach A way of formalizing the idea that our perception is a combination of the current stimulus and our knowledge about the conditions of the world—what is and is not likely to occur. The Bayesian approach is stated mathematically as Bayes' theorem—$P(A|O) = P(A) \times P(O|A)/P(O)$. This theorem enables us to calculate the probability (P) that the world is in a particular state (A) given a particular observation (O).

Other visual areas also contribute to the complex business of inferring the three-dimensional world from two-dimensional retinal images. Anzai and DeAngelis (2010) suggest that early visual areas, particularly V2, are involved in computing depth order (who's in front?), based on the contour completion and border ownership process we discussed in Chapter 4 (see Figures 4.5–4.7). Intermediate visual areas such as V4 (meaning "visual area 4") encode depth intervals, based on relative disparities, and higher cortical areas such as inferotemporal cortex are involved in the representation of complex three-dimensional shapes.

> **FURTHER DISCUSSION** of phase as it relates to vision can be found in Chapter 3 on pages 71–72. Sensitivity to phase is also important for temporal coding of sound frequency (see Chapter 9, page 294).

Combining Depth Cues

If the chapters of this book were novels, this chapter could be said to have the same plot as the discussion of object recognition in Chapter 4, but with different characters. In Chapter 4 we talked about a set of cues that enable us to group local features together into possible objects and then to recognize those objects. We described the process as a sort of committee effort in which different sources of information all contribute their opinions and where we see the committee decision without necessarily knowing how that decision was reached. In this chapter we've covered multiple sources of depth information and they, too, need to be combined. Any or all of these cues might be available to the visual system when we're viewing any visual scene. None of the cues are foolproof, and none work in every possible situation. For example, relative height produces inconsistent or misleading information if we can't see the point at which an object touches the ground. All we really have is a collection of guesses about possible depth relations between different objects in our visual field.

By carefully combining and weighting these guesses, the visual system generally arrives at a coherent, and more or less accurate, representation of three-dimensional space. Helmholtz, writing in the nineteenth century (and translated into English in the twentieth), called this automatic cue combination process "unconscious inference" (Helmholtz, 1924). In recent years, a number of vision researchers have been attempting to put this sort of argument on the more rigorous mathematical footing of the **Bayesian approach** that we mentioned in Chapter 4, and that is the subject of a more detailed essay on the website, **Web Essay 4.3: Bayesian Analysis**.

The Bayesian Approach Revisited

Recall that the basic insight of Reverend Thomas Bayes was that prior knowledge could influence estimates of the probability of a current observation. Let's apply this idea to a concrete, depth perception example. Suppose our visual system is confronted with the retinal image shown in **Figure 6.42**. There are infinite possible ways to produce this retinal image. Actually, this is a bit of a problem for the use of Bayes' theorem. We don't *really* know the prior probabilities (M. Jones and Love, 2011). Still, we can acknowledge that limitation, and we can still make good use of the basic insight that some hypotheses are more likely than others and that these prior probabilities can shape our interpretation of the world. Three hypotheses about our pennies are shown in **Figure 6.43**. Maybe the two pennies are the same

Figure 6.42 Retinal image of a simple visual scene.

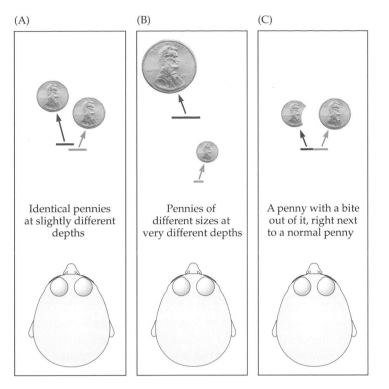

Figure 6.43 Three of the infinite number of scenes that could generate the retinal image in Figure 6.42. Is (A), (B), or (C) the most probable?

(A) Identical pennies at slightly different depths

(B) Pennies of different sizes at very different depths

(C) A penny with a bite out of it, right next to a normal penny

size, but the one on the left is slightly farther away than the one on the right (Figure 6.43A). Maybe the penny on the right is much smaller, but also much closer, than the penny on the left (Figure 6.43B). Maybe the two pennies are equidistant, but the penny on the left is smaller and has had a bite taken out of it (Figure 6.43C). If you don't see how the set of possibilities could be infinite, remember that size and distance can vary continuously over a large range. In Figure 6.43B, the big penny could be on the moon (but it would have to be a *really* big penny).

How does the visual system decide what we're actually seeing? Which interpretation seems most likely? That is the core of the Bayesian approach (except that it's all automatic; our conscious selves do not get to make the decision). In our experience, all pennies are the same size. This cue of familiar size is one source of prior knowledge in this case. This makes the *prior probability* of the hypotheses shown in Figure 6.43A higher than the prior probabilities of the other two hypotheses. Furthermore, for the scene in Figure 6.43C to produce the retinal image in Figure 6.42, we would have to be seeing the scene from one of those unusual and unlikely "accidental viewpoints." It is much more likely that the points of contact between the images of the two pennies reflect occlusion. If we were to plug all these probabilities into the math of Bayes' equation, we would find that, given the image in Figure 6.42, the most likely answer is the scene depicted in Figure 6.43A.

In thinking about combining depth cues, our choice of the metaphor of a committee is not arbitrary. We could have talked about an election, but that would have implied something like "one cue, one vote." On a committee, you might have one member who is stronger than the others and wins all the arguments. You might give more weight to the committee member who comes prepared with the best information. The committee might defer to one member on one topic and another member on a different topic. Something like this last option is described by Held, Cooper, and Banks (2012). Binocular-disparity information

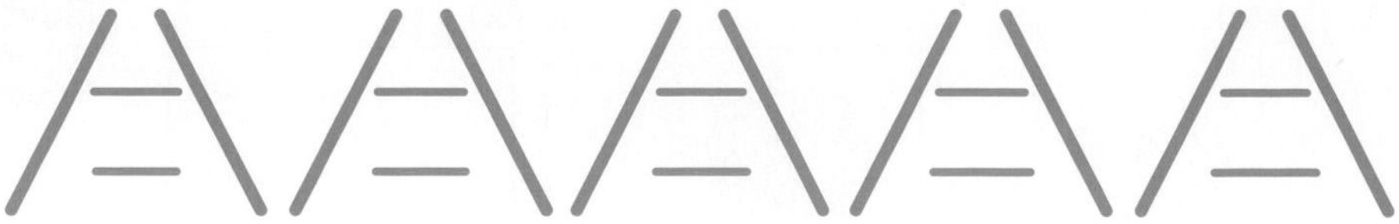

Figure 6.44   In which image are the two horizontal lines the same length?

can be very precise, but that is only true near the plane of fixation (remember Panum's fusional area?). Blur can be quite a good cue, too, but it is actually better away from the plane of fixation. When Held et al. made stimuli that had disparity cues, blur cues, or both, they found that disparity drove responses where disparity was more reliable and that blur drove responses in parts of the three-dimensional world where blur was more reliable. This is different from just letting every cue have its say, and it makes us realize that the visual system must be estimating how reliable each depth cue might be.

Illusions and the Construction of Space

If our visual perception of the world is our best guess about the causes of visual input, then interesting things should happen when a guess is wrong. In some sense, as with the pennies we just discussed, a guess is wrong whenever we look at a two-dimensional picture and see it as three-dimensional. As noted, however, we are not really fooled into thinking that the picture is three-dimensional. It would be more accurate to say that we make a plausible guess about the three-dimensional world that is being represented in the two-dimensional picture.

What about a situation like that shown in **Figure 6.44**? One of the five pairs of horizontal lines (and only one) shows two lines of the same length. Can you pick the correct pair (without a ruler)? In fact, it is the second from the left. Odds are, you picked the third or fourth pair, even though the bottom line in both of those images is physically longer than the top line. This is known as the Ponzo illusion, named after Mario Ponzo, who described the effect in 1913. What causes this illusion? For many years, a popular family of theories has held that the illusion is a guess gone wrong—a situation in which we overinterpret the depth cues in a two-dimensional image. The basic idea is illustrated in **Figure 6.45**. Maybe the two tilted lines that induce the illusion in each image of Figure 6.44 are being interpreted by the visual system as linear-perspective cues like the train tracks in Figure 6.45. If

Figure 6.45   The two lizards crossing these train tracks are the same size in the image. You can verify this by measuring them. However, the more distant lizard would need to be much larger in the real three-dimensional world to produce this image in the two-dimensional figure.

(A)

(B)

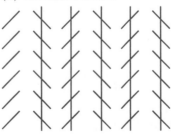

Figure 6.46 All of the red lines in this illustration (A) are the same length, as you can see in (B). Line E looks bigger than B, which looks bigger than A (similar to the railroad tracks in 6.45). But Line D does not look bigger than C, revealing a limit to the perceived-distance account of the Ponzo illusion.

so, then objects that were the same size in the two-dimensional image would represent objects of different sizes in the three-dimensional world and the far lizard would be a more disturbing animal than the closer one.

Such accounts are very compelling and exist for a wide range of visual illusions (Gillam, 1980). (See **Web Essay 6.4: The Moon Illusion**.) They are consistent with the idea that the job of the visual system is to use available cues to make an intelligent guess about the world (Gregory, 1966, 1970). Just because an answer is plausible, however, doesn't mean it's entirely correct. In **Figure 6.46**, line B looks longer than line A within the scene in Figure 6.46A, though we can see that they are the same length in Figure 6.46B. That makes sense if we're interpreting these lines as lines lying at different distances on the wall of the colonnade. As in the Ponzo illusion, if line B is farther away than A, then the same image size implies a larger size in the real world. But what about lines C and D? Surely D would be interpreted as farther away than C, but it does not look convincingly larger.

Prinzmetal, Shimamura, and Mikolinski (2001) use a demonstration like this as part of their argument that the Ponzo illusion is not really a by-product of depth cues. They argued that it reflects a more general aspect of the visual system's response to tilted lines and is related to illusions like the Zollner and Hering illusions illustrated in **Figure 6.47** (which we will *not* try to explain; see Prinzmetal and Beck, 2001). The point

(A) The Zollner illusion   (B) The Hering illusion

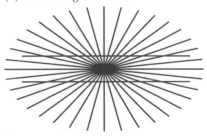

Figure 6.47 Despite their appearance, the vertical lines are parallel in (A), as are the horizontal lines in (B).

binocular rivalry The competition between the two eyes for control of visual perception, which is evident when completely different stimuli are presented to the two eyes.

is debatable. After all, line E looks very big down there at the apparent end of the colonnade in Figure 6.46A. Who is right? It could be that both arguments hold a piece of the truth. Perhaps the visual system's response to tilted lines is related to the role of those lines in creating an impression of depth. Going back to Figure 6.45, that would mean that the Ponzo illusion was not based on some version of the railroad track story but that the processes that give rise to a three-dimensional interpretation of Figure 6.45 also give rise to illusions like those in Figures 6.44, 6.46, and 6.47.

Binocular Rivalry and Suppression

The preceding sections demonstrated that objects in the world often project images on our two retinas that do not overlap (that is, the images fall on noncorresponding retinal points) and that the visual system is physiologically prepared to deal with these discrepancies via disparity-tuned neurons in striate cortex and beyond. But what happens when completely different stimuli are presented to the two eyes? You can answer this question for yourself by fixating on a small object across the room, such as a clock, and moving your hand up so that your fingers occlude the object in the right eye (making sure the left eye still has an unobstructed view). It would be a mistake for the visual system to fuse the images of your fingers and the clock into a single perception of something that does not exist in the world. Accordingly, the visual system chooses instead to *suppress* one image and perceive the other. In the present situation, you probably see the clock as though you were looking through a hole in your hand. (For an even more compelling perception of a hole in your hand, click on "Another Demonstration" in **Web Activity 6.2: Binocular Disparity**.)

How does the visual system "decide" what to see? The more interesting of the two stimuli is likely to be dominant. *Interesting* in this case has several meanings. The most important factor is which stimulus is more salient to the early stages of cortical visual processing. High contrast is more salient than low contrast, bright is better than dim, moving objects are more interesting than stationary ones, and so forth (Fahle, 1982). The meaning of the stimulus also has an effect (Yu and Blake, 1992), as does what you're attending to (Ooi and He, 1999).

The competition between the two eyes for control of visual perception, known as **binocular rivalry**, is never completely won by either eye (Alais and Blake, 2005; Wheatstone, 1852) or either stimulus (Blake and Logothetis, 2002). If you stare at the combination of the clock and hand long enough, your fingers will eventually conquer the visual territory, only to surrender it back to the clock a moment later. The battle is easier to see if the two combatants are more closely matched. If you free-fuse the two panels of **Figure 6.48**, your visual system will not actually combine the perpendicular stripes in the two center squares. Instead, you will see a battle between the

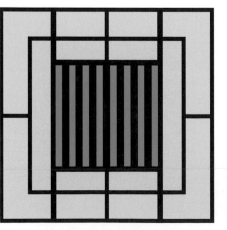

Figure 6.48 Binocular rivalry. If you free-fuse these two images, you will be able to watch the blue verticals and orange horizontals engage in the perceptual battle known as binocular rivalry.

Figure 6.49 If blue vertical bars are shown to one eye while orange horizontal bars are shown to the other, the two stimuli will battle for dominance.

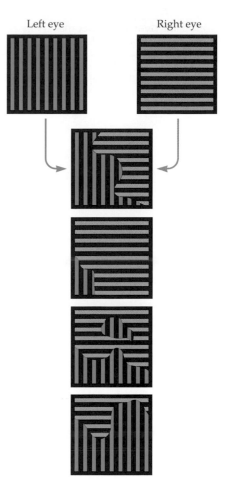

Left eye   Right eye

vertically and horizontally striped patches, with regions of dominance growing and shrinking over time, as illustrated in **Figure 6.49**.

Binocular rivalry might seem an odd situation that would arise only in a vision lab or a perception course, but a moment's reflection should convince you that the stimuli for rivalry are actually very common. If you cover one eye and then the other while looking at the three-dimensional world, you should notice that there are various features visible to only one eye (for example, near the edges of nearby objects). If something is visible in only one eye, something else is present in the corresponding location in the other eye. When the stimuli presented to corresponding points in the two eyes are unrelated, rivalry occurs. The classic demonstrations of rivalry pit a stimulus in one eye against a stimulus in the other eye. More recently, it has become clear that rivalry is part of a larger effort by the visual system to come up with the most likely version of the world, given the current retinal images (sounds Bayesian again, doesn't it?) (Clifford, 2009). If you can free-fuse **Figure 6.50A**, you will see the chimp and the text battle each other. That is just standard binocular rivalry. Interestingly, you will see a similar chimp/text rivalry if you free-fuse **Figure 6.50B**. In that case the chimp is being put together from bits in the two eyes. Your brain is not trying to pick a winner in a battle between the eyes. It is trying to figure out the world, and if that interesting chimp is seen with one eye in one spot and the other eye in another spot, the brain can put those different bits together into a coherent perception (Blake and Wilson, 2011). This effort to come up with a coherent view of the world requires attention (the topic of the next chapter). Without attention, rivalry ceases. This is hard to see, because if you want to check whether rivalry is occurring at a location, you need to pay attention to that location. With attention,

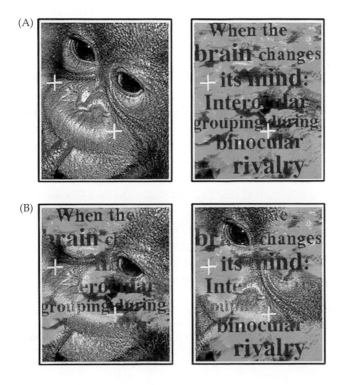

(A)

(B)

Figure 6.50 Binocular rivalry is not just a fight between the two eyes. If you can free-fuse these pairs of images, you will see a typical example of rivalry. (A) Different images in each eye struggle for dominance. The chimp and the text struggle for dominance in panel (B) too, but this is pattern rivalry: the two eyes are actually cooperating to put together coherent views of the chimp or the text. (From Kovacs et al., 1996; © 1996 National Academy of Sciences, U.S.A.)

a relatively fast interocular competition process and a slower cooperation between the eyes produce a single, usually quite stable view of the world (Li et al., 2017).

Rivalry is a very useful tool for probing one of the more vexing problems in the neuroscience of perception: what parts of the visual system give rise to the conscious experience of seeing something? For these purposes, the great feature of rivalry is that it dissociates the stimulus on the retina from the stimulus that you see. Now, imagine that you record from single cells somewhere in the monkey visual system (Logothetis and Schall, 1989) or you use fMRI to look at the working human brain. If you train the monkeys or ask humans to monitor their perception ("Do you see vertical or horizontal?"), you can ask whether the neural signal in a specific part of the visual pathway follows the physical stimulus or the perceived stimulus. It is a complex and evolving story, but one that clearly shows that conscious visual awareness is not something that happens in one discrete step in a chain of visual processing (Tong, Meng, and Blake, 2006).

Development of Binocular Vision and Stereopsis

What is binocular vision like in infants? Babies are born with two eyes, but are they born with stereopsis? If not, how does binocular function develop? In a wonderful conversation about visual development, Davida Teller and Tony Movshon (1986) recalled a lecture by a disillusioned developmental psychologist, John McKee, who argued that the field could be summed up by three laws:

1. As children get older, they get better at things.

2. Whatever it is, girls do it before boys.

3. Everything develops along with everything else.

To these "laws," Teller added a summary statement: "Things start out badly, then they get better; then, after a long time, they get worse again" (Teller and Movshon, 1986).

As it turns out, research over the last 30 years or so has shown that visual development provides support for the first and second laws but not for a strict form of the third. The development of binocular vision and stereopsis provides one of the strongest violations of that third law.

Most visual functions indeed start off badly (but not as badly as we used to think) and then improve steadily until they reach adult levels; however, the development of stereopsis is surprising, in that infants are essentially blind to disparity until about 3–4 months of age. At that point, stereopsis appears quite suddenly—almost out of the blue. Of course, measuring stereopsis (or anything else) in infants is no easy task, but developmental psychologists have been very inventive in designing methods for assessing development.

It is now quite well established that infants 6 months or older are sensitive to depth based on pictorial cues, and more recent studies show that infants as young as 4 months are sensitive to relative height (Tsuruhara et al., 2014). But how about stereoscopic depth, based on binocular disparity? Despite differences in techniques and procedures, most investigators agree about the onset of stereoscopic depth. **Figure 6.51** summarizes the results

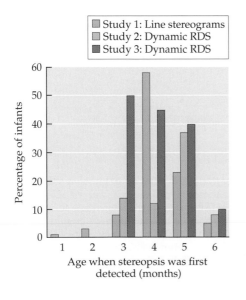

Figure 6.51 The onset of stereopsis. This figure shows the percentage of infants demonstrating stereopsis for the first time as a function of their age. In three separate studies (the three different colors), almost all infants showed stereopsis for the first time between 3 and 5 months. (After Birch, 1993.)

of several studies, showing the age at which stereopsis can first be detected. These studies (and others like them) looked for evidence indicating that infants could reliably detect a large binocular disparity (typically on the order of 30–60 arc minutes). The agreement among the studies is remarkable. Infants are essentially stereoblind before 3 months, with most infants showing a sudden onset of stereopsis between 3 and 5 months.

Stereopsis is not an all-or-none phenomenon. Just as an individual's acuity is a measure of his ability to resolve spatial detail, **stereoacuity** is a measure of the smallest binocular disparity that can generate a sensation of depth. Once an infant develops stereopsis, stereoacuity increases rapidly to near adult levels (**Figure 6.52**). Birch and Petrig (1996) found that stereoacuity rose from essentially nothing before 4 months to near adult levels by 6 months! This time course is very different from the time course in the development of simple acuity. Though coarsely present at birth, basic acuity takes years to reach adult levels. The same difference between basic acuity and stereoacuity is seen in monkeys (O'Dell and Boothe, 1997), but the overall rate of development is faster in monkeys. Interestingly, not only stereoacuity but several other visual functions develop at a rate approximately four times faster than in humans, as if one monkey week were the equivalent of one human month. In keeping with this rule of one human month being equal to one monkey week, stereopsis can be detected in monkeys within the first 3–5 weeks of life, compared with the 3-to-5-month window of onset observed in humans.

How, then, do we explain the sudden emergence of stereopsis in humans at about 4 months? Although a newborn infant makes convergence eye movements to track a target as it approaches her nose, accurate and consistent convergence probably does not occur until 3–4 months of age (Sreenivasan, et al., 2016). But we can't conclude that inaccurate convergence prevents stereopsis from developing earlier than 4 months, because convergence need not be very accurate in order to

stereoacuity A measure of the smallest binocular disparity that can generate a sensation of depth.

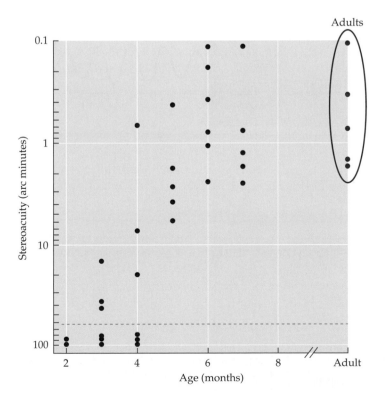

Figure 6.52 The development of stereoacuity. Stereoacuity develops to adult levels within the first 6–7 months of life. Data points below the dashed line indicate unmeasurable stereoacuity. (After Birch and Petrig, 1996.)

dichoptic Referring to the presentation of two different stimuli, one to each eye. Different from *binocular* presentation, which could involve both eyes looking at a single stimulus.

detect large disparities. Moreover, several studies used repeating gratings, which would be fused at some disparity even if convergence were inaccurate. Before 4 months, babies don't respond to these stereoscopic stimuli either.

An alternative view is that the failure of stereopsis to develop prior to 4 months might mean that some part of the visual system is immature. Disparity-sensitive neurons in the primary visual cortex (V1) are one plausible candidate for that immature part, but recent anatomical and physiological data suggest that we need to look beyond V1 for an explanation of why infants do not exhibit stereopsis.

Yuzo Chino and his colleagues made the most detailed quantitative study of the binocular responses of V1 neurons of infant monkeys (Chino et al., 1997). They presented a pair of drifting sine wave gratings **dichoptically** (one to each eye). The sine waves were identical in spatial frequency, orientation, contrast, and velocity, and these values were chosen to maximize the cell's response. A phase difference between the two monocular gratings will also create binocular disparity. Some cells in the visual cortex are sensitive to this phase shift (Ohzawa and Freeman, 1986a, 1986b). When Chino et al. varied the relative spatial phase of the two drifting sine waves (**Figure 6.53A**), the response of a binocular neuron waxed and waned (**Figure 6.53B**). The dashed lines in Figure 6.53B show the levels of

(A)

Left eye

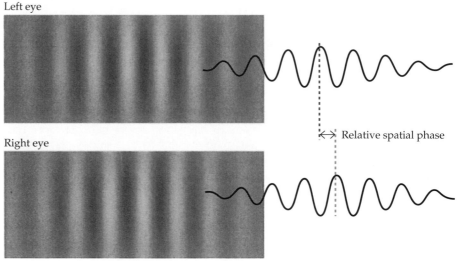

Right eye

(B)

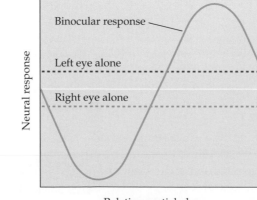

Figure 6.53 Interocular phase difference gratings are used to study disparity tuning. (A) The sinusoidal grating drifts differently in one eye than in the other, producing a sinusoidal change in spatial phase disparity. (B) The response of a binocular neuron. Notice that the binocular response varies with phase, and the monocular responses do not. (After Chino et al., 1997.)

response for the two eyes, stimulated alone. Notice that for some interocular phase differences, the binocular response was considerably higher than the response through either eye alone. At other interocular phase differences, the binocular response was lower than the response through either eye alone. This sinusoidal binocular phase tuning is the hallmark of this type of binocular neuron in the visual cortex. Using this sensitive method, Chino et al. (1997) found that within the first week of life—well before the onset of stereopsis—infant monkeys had practically the same proportion of phase disparity–sensitive neurons that adults have in primary visual cortex.

In addition, the ocular dominance properties of these infant monkeys were essentially identical to those of adults. Other investigators have also found that ocular dominance columns in the input layers of V1 are essentially adult-like at birth (Horton and Hocking, 1996).

> **FURTHER DISCUSSION** of ocular dominance can be found in Chapter 3 on page 80.

What do these studies tell us about the development of stereopsis? The results suggest that the neural apparatus in V1 of newborns is capable of combining signals from the two eyes and that it is sensitive to interocular disparities. So why are newborns blind to disparity? One possibility is that the extraction of relative disparity, which is needed for stereoacuity, takes place beyond V1, possibly in V2. At this time we do not know much about how V2 neurons in newborns respond to disparity, but emerging evidence suggests that other receptive-field properties mature later in V2 than in V1 (Zhang et al., 2005; Zheng et al., 2007).

Another possibility is that the problem is in V1. Although V1 cells of newborn monkeys are adult-like in their response to interocular phase disparity, these neurons remain immature in several important ways. They do not have adult sensitivity to monocular spatial frequency or direction of motion. Moreover, they are much less responsive overall than are adult neurons (that is, their peak firing rates are considerably lower). In addition, these neurons display more interocular suppression than adult neurons do. Thus, it is also possible that because of the immaturity in V1 neurons, the signals they send to the next stage of processing are too weak or confused to support stereopsis.

Abnormal Visual Experience Can Disrupt Binocular Vision

The presence of all this binocular hardware, even if it is immature, strongly suggests that extensive binocular visual experience is not necessary for binocular connections to form in V1. These connections are present at birth or very shortly thereafter, so we don't need to "learn" or develop binocular vision. However, the normal development of adult binocular vision and stereopsis does require visual experience. In Chapter 3 we learned about Hubel and Wiesel's work on the **critical period**, the period during early visual development when normal binocular visual stimulation is required for normal cortical development. During this period the visual cortex is highly susceptible to any disorder that alters normal binocular visual experience. In cats and monkeys this critical period is approximately the first 3–4 months of life.

We cannot study a child's visual cortex the way we might study a monkey's or a cat's. How, then, can we estimate the critical period in humans? Some humans are born with two eyes that do not point at the same spot in the world. This not uncommon disorder is known as **strabismus**, as we learned in Chapter 3. The incidence is about 3%. In **esotropia**, one eye is pointed too far toward

critical period   A period of time during development when the organism is particularly susceptible to developmental change. There are critical periods in the development of binocular vision, human language, and so on.

strabismus   A misalignment of the two eyes such that a single object in space is imaged on the fovea of one eye and on a nonfoveal area of the other (turned) eye.

esotropia   Strabismus in which one eye deviates inward.

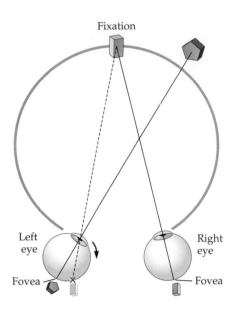

Fixation

Left eye

Right eye

Fovea

Fovea

Figure 6.54 Left esotropia. The person wants to fixate on the yellow brick, but the left eye is turned too far toward the nose; as a result, the left fovea is pointing at a different location (here the purple pentagon), while the image of the yellow brick falls to the right of the left fovea.

exotropia Strabismus in which one eye deviates outward.

tilt aftereffect The perceptual illusion of tilt, produced by adaptation to a pattern of a given orientation.

suppression In reference to vision, the inhibition of an unwanted image. Suppression occurs frequently in people with strabismus.

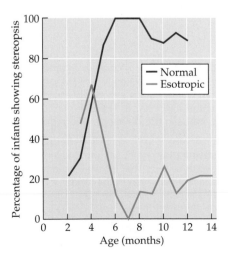

Figure 6.55 Development of stereopsis in normal infants (red line) and in esotropes (blue). Beyond 4 months, very few esotropic infants demonstrated stereopsis. (After Stager and Birch, 1986.)

the nose ("cross-eyed"). In **exotropia**, the deviating eye is pointed too far to the side. There are various ways to treat strabismus. For example, it is possible to surgically correct the position of the eyes. For the present discussion, however, the important point is that it is possible to test adults who had misaligned eyes at different times and for different durations during childhood.

Recall from Chapter 3 that exposure to lines tilted to one side of vertical will make vertical lines appear tilted to the other side. This is known as the **tilt aftereffect**. One characteristic of the tilt aftereffect is that it shows interocular transfer (transfer of the effect from one eye to the other). If we show the adapting lines to one eye, we can measure an aftereffect through the other eye. This result is generally taken to show that the cells responsible for the effect are binocular: they receive input from both eyes (for some details, see Wolfe and Held, 1981). Individuals who exhibited strabismus during the first 18 months of life do not show normal interocular transfer (Banks, Aslin, and Letson, 1975; Hohmann and Creutzfeldt, 1975). This result provides an indirect estimate of the period during which binocular connections in humans are susceptible to abnormal input.

Let's explore in a bit more detail why strabismus disrupts binocular vision. We will use left esotropia as an example. In left esotropia (**Figure 6.54**), the left eye is turned in. As a consequence, although the object of fixation (the yellow brick, in this case) lands on the fovea of the right eye, in the left eye it lands on a region in the "nasal" retina. (The nasal retina is the half of the retina closer to the nose.) This means that the images of the yellow brick are in noncorresponding points in the two eyes. What will the person see? If an adult becomes esotropic (perhaps because of an injury), she will experience diplopia (double vision), seeing two bricks instead of one. However, people who exhibit strabismus early in life often experience no such problem. Why? Notice that *something* is present at the fovea of the left eye. In Figure 6.54, this something is a purple pentagon. Thus, in strabismus, normally corresponding points in the two eyes receive conflicting information (this situation is known—not unreasonably—as "confusion"). To eliminate diplopia and confusion, the brain **suppresses** one of the two images. It is simply not consciously perceived. In esotropia, the most common pattern is suppression of the input from the eye that is turned in. So, in the example in Figure 6.54, the person would most likely suppress visual input from the left eye.

Binocular rivalry is a form of suppression, so some suppression is an important part of normal visual experience. Unfortunately, early-onset strabismus can have other, more serious effects on the developing visual nervous system, and on visual performance. For example, strabismus greatly reduces the number of binocular neurons in the visual cortex (Wiesel, 1982). Cells that would normally be driven by both eyes are dominated by only one. You would be correct if you suspected that this situation would disrupt stereopsis. Birch and her colleagues (e.g., Stager and Birch, 1986) followed the development of stereopsis in normal and esotropic infants. **Figure 6.55** illustrates the percentage of infants who showed a measurable ability to perceive stereoscopic depth. The red line shows that by about 6 months of age, almost all normal infants demonstrate stereopsis. In contrast, the esotropes (all of whom were diagnosed with esotropia by 6 months of age) initially demonstrated a normal pattern of stereopsis development. After 4 months, however, very few esotropic infants demonstrated stereopsis, although recent work suggests that "coarse" stereopsis (i.e., sensitivity to very large disparities) may be spared in some children with strabismus and amblyopia (Giaschi et al., 2013).

This result has an interesting parallel in cortical physiology. Chino and his colleagues made otherwise normal monkeys strabismic (Kumagami et al., 2000). They found that a brief period of experimental strabismus shortly after the age of onset of stereopsis produced a greater loss of disparity sensitivity and more binocular suppression in V1 neurons than did an earlier episode of strabismus. These physiological and perceptual deficits appear to be permanent and have important implications for the surgical treatment of infantile esotropia. Almost all surgeons agree that treatment should be early, but there has been a lot of debate about just how early. These results suggest that the treatment should take place before the age at which stereopsis normally develops, in order to minimize the damage done by esotropia.

■ Scientists at Work

Stereopsis in a Hunting Insect

■ **Question** How can you tell if a praying mantis has stereopsis?

■ **Hypothesis** Judging distance (depth) accurately is critically important both for predators hunting for food and for prey trying not to be dinner. Praying mantises love to catch bugs and eat them for dinner, leading to the hypothesis that the praying mantis should have stereoscopic depth perception.

■ **Test** The researchers made very, very small anaglyphic glasses—with one lens blue and the other green—and stuck them to the foreheads of a few mantises, using beeswax and a type of resin (Nityananda et al., 2016) (**Figure 6.56**). For each trial, they then placed a mantis in hunting position, but instead of being in the real world of bugs in the bushes, the mantis was in front of a computer screen showing three-dimensional movies of simulated bugs. Binocular disparity was used to move the bugs to different virtual distances from the mantis. If the mantis had stereoscopic depth perception, it should attempt to strike its prey when it perceived that the bug was at exactly the right distance. That would be about 2 cm away, the grabbing distance of the mantis's extended front claws.

■ **Results** When the researchers played two-dimensional movies of simulated bugs, the mantises didn't react. However, when they played three-dimensional movies, they struck in attempts to nab their dinners when virtual bugs were at the apparently correct

distance. Of course, there were no real bugs to grasp. We can only speculate about how the mantises felt about being tricked in this way.

■ **Conclusions** Whether or not the mantises were frustrated by the experience, this experiment provides clear and dramatic proof that the praying mantis has stereoscopic vision and will respond to depth defined by disparity.

■ **Future work** Mantises and humans are far apart on the evolutionary tree. Further research of this sort with other species will help us to understand the forces that shape the number of eyes an organism has and how those eyes work together.

Figure 6.56 A praying mantis wearing anaglyphic glasses. When presented with stereoscopic "bugs," the mantis strikes at a distance consistent with the information in the binocular-disparity signal. (From Nityananda et al., 2016.)

Summary

1. Reconstructing a three-dimensional world from two non-Euclidean, curved, two-dimensional retinal images is one basic problem faced by the brain.

2. A number of monocular cues provide information about three-dimensional space. These include occlusion, various size and position cues, aerial perspective, linear perspective, motion cues, accommodation, and convergence.

3. Having two eyes is an advantage for a number of reasons, some of which have to do with depth perception. It is important to remember, however, that it is possible to reconstruct the three-dimensional world from a single two-dimensional image. Two eyes have other advantages over just one: expanding the visual field, permitting binocular summation, and providing redundancy if one eye is damaged.

4. Having two laterally separated eyes connected to a single brain also provides us with important information about depth through the geometry of the small differences between the images in each eye. These differences, known as binocular disparities, give rise to stereoscopic depth perception.

5. Random dot stereograms show that we don't need to know what we're seeing before we see it in stereoscopic depth. Binocular disparity alone can support shape perception.

6. Stereopsis has been exploited to add, literally, depth to entertainment—from nineteenth-century photos to twenty-first-century movies. It has also served to enhance the perception of information in military and medical settings.

7. The difficulty of matching an image element in one eye with the correct element in the other eye is known as the correspondence problem. The brain uses several strategies to solve the problem. For example, it reduces the initial complexity of the problem by matching large "blobs" in the low-spatial-frequency information before trying to match every high-frequency detail.

8. Single neurons in the primary visual cortex and beyond have receptive fields that cover a region in three-dimensional space, not just the two-dimensional image plane. Some neurons seem to be concerned with a crude in-front/behind judgment. Other neurons are concerned with more precise, metrical depth perception.

9. When the stimuli on corresponding loci in the two eyes are different, we experience a continual perceptual competition between the two eyes, known as binocular rivalry. Rivalry is part of the effort to make the best guess about the current state of the world based on the current state of the input.

10. All of the various monocular and binocular depth cues are combined (unconsciously) according to what prior knowledge tells us about the probability of the current event. Making the wrong guess about the cause of visual input can lead to illusions. Bayes' theorem is the basis of one type of formal understanding of the rules of combination.

11. Stereopsis emerges suddenly at about 4 months of age in humans, and it can be disrupted through abnormal visual experience during a critical period early in life.

7 Attention and Scene Perception

■ Questions to Contemplate ■

Think about the following questions as you read this chapter. By the chapter's end, you should be able to answer and discuss them.

- Why can't we process everything at once?

- Is attention really like a spotlight? What would that mean?

- How do we find what we are looking for?

- What changes in the brain when we "pay attention"?

- If we can attend to only one (or a very few) objects at once, why does the world seem to be filled with many, many clearly perceived objects?

- How much do we actually notice and/or remember of what we see?

If you're reading this, you are probably a student. If you're a student, you are probably taking more than one course and are therefore very busy. Here's an idea: why not read two books at the same time? Chapter 2 will have told you that the limit on peripheral acuity is one reason that this won't work. The acuity problem could be overcome if the size of the print were increased, as in **Figure 7.1**. Nevertheless, even with suitably large letters, it will be clear to you that you cannot look at the column of Xs in the figure and read the two sentences. We just cannot read two messages at the same time. Note that you *can* read the words on one side or the other of the Xs while looking at the Xs. You just can't read both sides simultaneously. This is a specific example of a more general problem—that the retinal array contains far more information than we can process. **Figure 7.2** shows another example. We cannot possibly recognize all the objects in this picture at once. That's why "Where's Waldo?"

Rick Pas, *nothing, stuck in traffic*, 2014

and "I Spy" games are a challenge. This is not just a visual problem. All of the senses receive more input than we can handle (see Chapter 10 for a discussion of attention in hearing). One more introductory example: why not drive down the street and text your friend at the same time? It is obvious that this can be a problem if the act of texting takes your eyes off the road, but you should be beginning to suspect that there is more to the problem than that. Doing two things at the same time can be a problem—in the case of texting and driving, a dangerous problem.

Why can't we process everything at once? Quite literally, we don't have the brains for it. Remember from Chapter 4 that recognizing a single object like an elephant requires a sizable chunk of the brain and its processing power, especially when that elephant could be seen in many different orientations, under different lighting conditions, at different retinal sizes, and so on. Moreover, in order to understand Figure 7.2, we also need to process the relationships between objects—like the fact that the elephant is dousing the yellow car with its trunk. If we do the math for even a fairly small subset of all possible visual stimuli, it turns out that processing everything, everywhere, all at once requires a brain that will not fit in the human head (Tsotsos, 1990).

These   x   Is
letters   x   it
are   x   time
big   x   for
and   x   a
easy   x   quick
to   x   snack
read.   x   yet?

Figure 7.1   Even though the letters are big enough to resolve while looking at the Xs, we simply cannot read the left-hand and right-hand sentences at the same time.

If it is not possible to process everything all at once, what *should* be processed? This matter can't be left to chance. If you are crossing a road, you need to determine that no car will hit you; devoting your visual capacity to the vital tweet that just appeared on your phone can be dangerous. (Many YouTube videos will demonstrate this. Just stop walking before you watch!) To deal with this problem, we "pay attention" to some stimuli and not to others. As we will see in this chapter, **attention** is not a single *thing*, and it does not have a single locus in the nervous system (Chun, Golomb, and Turk-Browne, 2011). Rather, *attention* is the name we give to a family of mechanisms that restrict or bias processing in various ways.

Here are some of the distinctions we can make when considering varieties of attention:

- Attention can be internal or external. *External attention* refers to attention to stimuli in the world (our primary concern here), but we should not forget *internal attention*, our ability to attend to one line of thought as opposed to another or to select one response over another.

Figure 7.2   Search for the unicorn in this piece of a "Where's Waldo?" picture. You can search for Waldo, too, but he is a bit small in this reproduction. (From *Where's Waldo?* © Martin Handford 2005.)

- Attention can be overt or covert. *Overt attention* usually refers to directing a sense organ at a stimulus—fixating the eyes on a single word, for example. If you point your eyes at this page while directing attention to a person of interest off to the left, you are engaging in *covert attention*.

- Reading this text while continuing to be aware of music playing in the room is an example of *divided attention*.

- Watching the pot to note the moment the water begins to boil is a *vigilance* task requiring *sustained attention*.

- The ability to pick one (or a few) out of many stimuli is a job for **selective attention**. That form of attention receives the most attention in this chapter.

These different forms of attention are not mutually exclusive. Staring straight ahead while attending only to an interesting person off to one side, to the exclusion of all else, might be described as an act of external, sustained, covert, selective attention.

Although we will focus on visual attention, it is important to remember that attentional mechanisms operate in all of the senses. For example, because of the different amounts of attention we give to each event, getting a shot in the doctor's office may hurt a lot, while an equivalent injury on the playing field may not seem to hurt much at all. We can also use attentional mechanisms to give priority to one sense over others. Right now, you are probably selecting visual stimuli over auditory, even if you have music on in the background. And you didn't even notice the pressure of your posterior on the seat until we mentioned it (sorry for disrupting your attention).

In this chapter, first we discuss evidence that we attend to only one (or perhaps a few) objects at any single moment. We consider attentional selection in space (I am attending to this object and not that object) and selection in time (I was attending to that object, but now I've selected this object). Next we examine the changes that occur in the brain when we attend to one object rather than another, and we will see what happens when the neural substrate of attention is damaged. Having convinced you, we hope, that we can recognize only one object at a time, we will turn to scenes. If we're attending to one object, what does it mean to say that we see a whole scene?

Selection in Space

To begin, let's consider what it means to attend to a stimulus. A good place to start is with a cueing experiment of the sort pioneered by Michael Posner (1980). Start with the situation shown in **Figure 7.3A**. The participant in the experiment fixates on a central point (*). After a variable delay, a test probe (X) appears in one of the two boxes. All the participant needs to do is hit a response key as fast as possible when the probe appears. The measure of interest is the average **reaction time** (**RT**)—the amount of time that elapses between the point when the probe appears and the point when the participant hits the response key.

Suppose now that the situation is slightly changed: during the waiting period, the participant is given a **cue**, a stimulus that provides a hint about where the target might appear. In **Figure 7.3B**, the cue is a change in the outline color of one of the two boxes (a "peripheral cue"). Because the test probe appears in the cued location, this peripheral cue is said to be a "valid cue." With a valid cue,

attention   Any of the very large set of selective processes in the brain. To deal with the impossibility of handling all inputs at once, the nervous system has evolved mechanisms that are able to bias processing to a subset of things, places, ideas, or moments in time.

selective attention   The form of attention involved when processing is restricted to a subset of the possible stimuli.

reaction time (RT)   A measure of the time from the onset of a stimulus to a response.

cue   A stimulus that might indicate where (or what) a subsequent stimulus will be. Cues can be valid (giving correct information), invalid (incorrect), or neutral (uninformative).

(A)

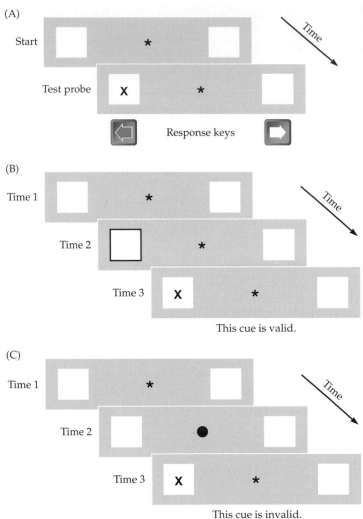

Start

Test probe

X   *

Response keys

(B)

Time 1

Time 2

Time 3   X   *

This cue is valid.

(C)

Time 1

Time 2

Time 3   X   *

This cue is invalid.

Figure 7.3 The Posner cueing paradigm. (A) This simple probe detection experiment has two possible probe locations. Here all you have to do is hit one key if the probe appears on the left and another if it appears on the right. (B) A valid peripheral cue indicates where the target will be. This time the cue is valid; we are telling the truth. (C) An invalid cue points to the wrong side. (This is also a different kind of cue—a symbolic cue—where color indicates the location. Symbolic cues direct attention more slowly.)

Posner found, the RT decreases. Compared with the no-cue control situation, the participant generally responds faster to the probe because she is "paying attention" to the correct location. In **Figure 7.3C**, we have a different kind of cue. The red dot is a "symbolic cue," but it can also direct attention. Here the rule is this: If the cue is green, the probe is likely to be on the left; if the cue is red, the probe is likely to be on the right. In Figure 7.3C, however, the cue is misleading, or "invalid," because the cued location is on the right but the probe appears on the left. RTs are slower here than in the control condition, because the participant has been fooled into attending to the wrong location.

The peripheral cue (the outlined box) is an example of an **exogenous cue**. Exogenous cues seem to summon attention automatically by virtue of their physical salience. The symbolic cue (red dot) is an example of an **endogenous cue**. Endogenous cues can be considered something like instructions that can be voluntarily obeyed. The endogenous cue says "go right," so you go right, while the exogenous cue could drag you to the right, whether you wanted to go there or not. *Endo* and *exo* refer to "inside" and "outside," respectively, as in our *endo*skeleton and the *exo*skeleton on the outside of an insect (Posner, 1980).

Peripheral/exogenous and symbolic/endogenous cues can be valid or invalid. As in Figure 7.3C, an invalid cue might tell you to go right, when the target actually appears on the left. In a typical experiment, the cue might be valid on 80% of the trials and invalid on the remaining 20%. Since the observer doesn't know if the cue is valid, it would be in the observer's interest to deploy attention on the assumption that the cue is valid. This means that the experimenter can compare RTs from trials that had valid cues, where attention was cued left and the stimulus appeared on the left, and trials that had invalid cues, where the cue moved attention to the left but the stimulus appeared on the right.

How long does it take for a cue to redirect our attention? It depends on the nature of the cue. At the beginning of a trial in a Posner cueing experiment, the participant is attending to the fixation point (Time 1 in Figure 7.3B, C). The cue appears at Time 2, and the probe appears at Time 3. We can measure the timing of the attentional shift by varying the interval between Time 2 and Time 3. This is called the **stimulus onset asynchrony**, a psychophysical variable that typically goes by its acronym, **SOA**. If the SOA is 0 milliseconds (ms), the cue and probe appear simultaneously. There is no time for the cue to be used to direct attention,

exogenous cue In directing attention, a cue that is located out (*exo*) at the desired final location of attention.

endogenous cue In directing attention, a cue that is located in (*endo*) or near the current location of attention.

stimulus onset asynchrony (SOA) The time between the onset of one stimulus and the onset of another.

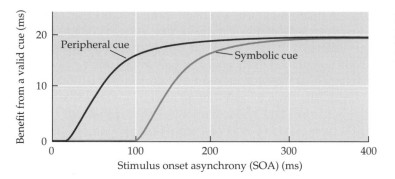

Figure 7.4 The effect of a cue develops over time. A peripheral cue (like that in Figure 7.3B) becomes fully effective 100–150 ms after it appears. A symbolic cue (see Figure 7.3C) takes longer to get started and to rise to full effect.

and there is no difference between the effects of valid or invalid cues. As the SOA increases to about 150 ms, the magnitude of the cueing effect from a valid peripheral cue increases, as shown by the red line in **Figure 7.4**. After that, the effect of the cue levels off or declines a bit.

Symbolic/endogenous cues, such as the colored dot, take longer to work, presumably because we need to do some work to interpret them (the SOA is shown by the blue line in Figure 7.4). Interestingly, some rather symbolic cues behave like fast peripheral cues. For example, we are very quick to deploy our attention to arrow cues and even faster to respond to a pair of eyes looking in one direction or another (**Figure 7.5**), as if we were built to get information from the gaze of others (Kuhn and Kingstone, 2009). You can try the cueing experiment in some of its important variations in **Web Activity 7.1: Attentional Cueing**.

Interestingly, if you move your attention or your eyes to a location and then look away from that location, it is harder to look back at it again for a little while. This is known as **inhibition of return** (Klein, 2000). Inhibition of return helps to keep you from getting stuck continually revisiting one spot. For instance, suppose you were looking for Waldo in Figure 7.2 and your attention was attracted to the Santa in the lower right. If your attention kept going back to Santa, that would be rather useless. Inhibition of return helps your search to move forward (Klein and MacInness, 1999).

inhibition of return The relative difficulty in getting attention (or the eyes) to move back to a recently attended (or fixated) location.

The "Spotlight" of Attention

In a cueing experiment, attention starts at the fixation point and somehow ends up at the cued location. But does it actually *move* from one point to the next? Attention could be deployed from spot to spot in a number of ways. It might move in a manner analogous to the movements of our eyes. When we shift our gaze, our point of fixation sweeps across the intervening space (although, as we will see in Chapter 8, "saccadic suppression" keeps us from noticing, and being disturbed by, this movement). Attention might sweep across space in a similar manner, like a spotlight beam (Posner, 1980).

The spotlight metaphor makes good sense and has become, perhaps, the most common way for cognitive psychologists to talk about attention. But there are other possibilities. For example, attention might expand from fixation, growing to fill the

Figure 7.5 Which way does your attention shift when you look at this photo?

visual search A search for a target in a display containing distracting elements.

target The goal of a visual search.

distractor In visual search, any stimulus other than the target.

set size The number of items in a visual display.

whole region from the fixation spot to the cued location, and then it might shrink to include just the cued location. This would be a version of a zoom lens model of attention (Eriksen and Yeh, 1985). Or, when attention is withdrawn from the fixation spot, it might not move at all. It might simply melt away at that location and then reappear at the cued location (Sperling and Weichselgartner, 1995). It is hard to say for sure which metaphor is "correct," because we have no direct way to measure the location and extent of attention. However, the best evidence suggests that attention is not *moving* from point to point in the brain in the way a physical spotlight would move across the world (Cave and Bichot, 1999). Moreover, there is no guarantee that there is just one "spotlight." It might be split (look ahead to Figure 7.16) (McMains and Somers, 2004), though most of the time, visual selective attention is probably directed to one thing in one location. One last point to make about the spotlight is that you can see *something* in the locations where the spotlight is not shining. The Nobel Prize winner Francis Crick put it nicely: "In this metaphor, the searchlight is not supposed to light up part of a completely dark landscape but, like a searchlight at dusk, it intensifies part of a scene that is already visible to some extent" (Crick, 1984). It seems that there are two pathways to your visual awareness: a selective pathway that constitutes the spotlight and a nonselective pathway that fills in the rest of your visual experience (Wolfe et al., 2011).

Visual Search

Cueing experiments provide important insight into the deployment of attention. But the situation is rather artificial, in that all of the experiments involve telling the observer exactly when and where to attend. **Visual search** experiments provide a closer approximation of some of the actions of attention in the real world. In a typical visual search experiment, the observer looks for a **target** item among **distractor** items. Visual searches are ubiquitous in the real world: we look for faces in a crowd, mugs in a cupboard, books on a shelf, and so forth. Some searches are so easy that we hardly think of them as searches (e.g., finding the cold-water tap on a sink). Others, like looking for the unicorn in the "Where's Waldo?" puzzle of Figure 7.2, are more demanding. Some are, literally, matters of life and death, as when radiologists look for tumors in X-rays or airport security officers look for threats in luggage.

The quest to understand what makes some search tasks easy and others hard has proven to be one of the most productive and interesting lines of cognitive psychology research in the past half century. **Figure 7.6** shows examples of the simplified visual search tasks often used in the lab. In Figure 7.6A, B, the target is a red vertical bar. In Figure 7.6C, the target is the letter *T* (in any of four possible rotations). Two factors are being varied in this figure: First, moving across the figure, the tasks increase in difficulty from left to right. Second, the **set size** (the number of items) increases as we move down each column. As a general (and unsurprising) rule, it is harder to find a target as the set size increases.

To measure the efficiency of a visual search, often we ask how much time is added (on average) for each item added to the display. To find out, the experimenter measures the RT required for the observer to say "yes" if the target is present or "no" if there is no target in the display, and observers perform the same type of search over and over. The functions relating RT to set size are graphed at the bottom of Figure 7.6. The efficiency of the search is described by the slope of the function relating RT to set size (higher slopes mean lower efficiency). *Efficiency* describes the ease with which we can work our way through a display. It is a

Figure 7.6 Laboratory visual search tasks. Each part of the figure shows a different search task, with difficulty increasing from (A) to (C). Each row shows a different number of items (the set size), with difficulty increasing as set size increases. Here we show only examples with the target present. In a typical experiment, a target might be absent in half of the trials. The graphs at the bottom depict typical patterns of results for each type of task. The purple line in each graph represents average reaction times for different set sizes on target-absent trials; the green line shows results for target-present trials.

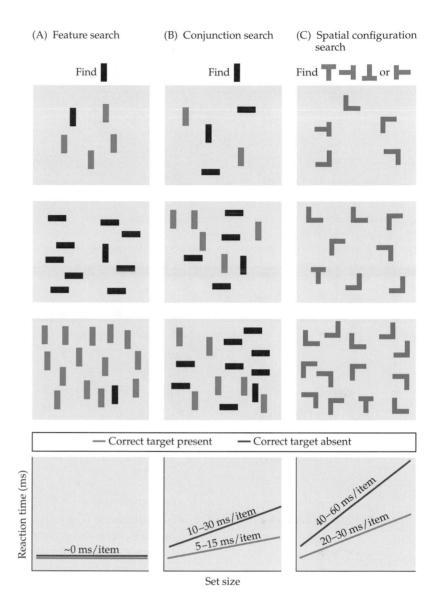

way to compare search tasks. If we can direct attention to the target as soon as the display appears, regardless of the set size, then we have an efficient search, like the feature searches in Figure 7.6A. Here the slope is near zero because adding more blue distractors or more horizontal distractors does not make it any harder to find a red or a vertical target. If we must examine each item in turn until we find the target, then we have an inefficient search. Figure 7.6C shows an inefficient search where each *L* needs to be examined until the observer stumbles upon a *T*. Notice that saying "yes, the target is present" is typically faster and more efficient than saying "no, it is not," because even in the hardest task, a lucky observer might stumble on the presence of the target with her first deployment of attention, but it is not possible to stumble on the *absence* of the target in the same way.

Although all the displays in Figure 7.6 include a target, in a typical experiment the target is present in 50% of the trials and absent in the other 50%. You can try a number of different visual search tasks in **Web Activity 7.2: Visual Search**. It's much easier to get a feel for the difficulty of these tasks when you do them yourself.

Feature Searches Are Efficient

The task in Figure 7.6A is called a simple **feature search**. Here the target is defined by the presence of a single feature. Each example contains an item with a unique color or orientation. If the unique item is sufficiently **salient** (if it stands out visually from its neighbors), it really doesn't matter how many distractors there are. The target seems to "pop out" of the display. Apparently we can process the color or orientation of all the items at once (often called a **parallel search**). When we measure the RT, it does not change with the set size. The results will approximate the flat lines plotted at the bottom of Figure 7.6A; more technically, the slope of the function relating RT to set size is about 0 ms per item.

Between one dozen and two dozen basic attributes seem able to support parallel visual search (Wolfe and Horowitz, 2017). These include obvious

feature search Search for a target defined by a single attribute, such as a salient color or orientation.

salience The vividness of a stimulus relative to its neighbors.

parallel search Search in which multiple stimuli are processed at the same time.

(A)

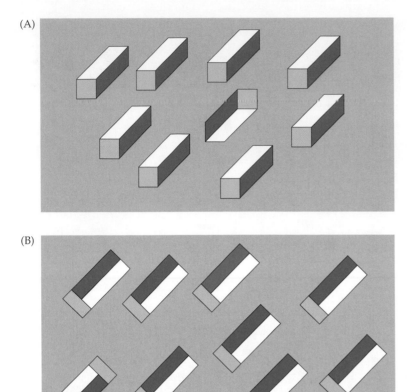

(B)

Figure 7.7 Three-dimensional orientation is a basic feature used in the guidance of search. (A) The oddly oriented bar in this image is easy to find, even though all the bars have the same orientation in the two-dimensional image plane. (B) To show that the ease of the task in (A) had to do with the three-dimensional effects and not just with the relative positions of different regions, the experiment was repeated with apparently two-dimensional items composed of similar parts in similar positions. This made it harder to find the odd item. (After Enns and Rensink, 1990.)

stimulus properties such as color, size, orientation, and motion (A. Treisman, 1986a, 1986b) and some less obvious attributes, like lighting direction (Enns and Rensink, 1990).

In **Figure 7.7A**, look for the bar that is oriented differently in depth. This task is quite easy, even though all the items have the same orientation in the two-dimensional plane of the page. Notice that the target object in Figure 7.7A is just a 180-degree rotation of the distractor objects, and this rotation changes its depth orientation. In **Figure 7.7B**, the target is also a 180-degree rotation of the distractors, but you will probably find it harder to locate the target that has light green at the top rather than the bottom. That's interesting because the objects in Figures 7.7A and B are all composed of elongated white and dark green regions with a smaller light green region at one end. The overall shapes and orientations of all objects are about the same. The critical change in Figure 7.7B is that the objects no longer look like three-dimensional bricks and no longer differ in their apparent orientation in depth. Without that distinguishing feature, the light-green-on-top target is harder to find.

Many Searches Are Inefficient

When the target and distractors in a visual search task contain the same basic features, as in Figure 7.6C, search is inefficient. Here, we are looking for *T*s among *L*s where both targets and distractors are composed of a vertical and a horizontal bar. It is not hard to distinguish a *T* from an *L*, but we need to attend to each item until we stumble on the target. Even if, as in Figure 7.1, the letters are big enough that we don't have to move our eyes to distinguish *T* from *L*, each additional distractor adds about 20–30 ms to a successful search for a target, and about twice that amount of time (40–60 ms) to a search that ends without finding a target. We call this an inefficient search.

Why do we get the particular pattern of results seen in Figure 7.6C? One straightforward proposal is that these tasks involve a **serial self-terminating search**, in which items are examined one after another (serially) either until the target is found or until all items have been checked. Consider the case in which a target is present. Sometimes the observer will get lucky and find the target on the first deployment of attention. Sometimes she will be unlucky and have to search all the items before stumbling on the target. On average, she will have to search through about half the items on each trial before the search can be

serial self-terminating search
A search from item to item, ending when a target is found.

terminated. When no target is present, our observer will always need to search through all the items. There are other models of this behavior that would not propose an exhaustive examination of each item (J. Palmer, 1995). The important point is that some searches are inefficient, meaning that each additional item in the display imposes a significant cost on the searcher.

The inefficient search for a *T* among *L*s is nothing like the hardest search we could devise, of course. For starters, if we need to spend a lot of time with each item, search will be much slower, as it is in the search for a particular Chinese character in **Figure 7.8** (unless, of course, you happen to read Chinese). Other search tasks, like spotting missile sites in satellite images, could take days even if, once you found one, the missile site was readily identifiable. The *T*-among-*L*s search is interesting because it is a simpler case where a target can "hide in plain sight." The items are easy to see and very familiar, but search is still inefficient.

In Real-World Searches, Basic Features Guide Visual Search

In the real world, it would be very rare to have a true feature search for the only red item among homogeneous distractors. How often do you have to find the strawberry among the limes? It is probably even rarer to have to search through a scene containing objects that all share the same basic features—perhaps the proverbial needle in the haystack. Usually, basic features can be used to narrow down the search, even if they cannot eliminate all distractions. This is known as **guided search** (Wolfe, 1994; Wolfe, Cave, and Franzel, 1989). If you're looking for a tomato in **Figure 7.9**, you will be able to find it quite quickly, even though it is not the only red thing or the only round thing or, indeed, the only

Find: Among:

优   福   恕   花
"Grace"   "Happiness" "Forgiveness" "Flower"

Figure 7.8 Search can be much more laborious if you're not familiar with what you're searching for. Here, the search for the Chinese character for "grace" will be much easier if you can read Chinese.

guided search Search in which attention can be restricted to a subset of possible items on the basis of information about the target item's basic features (e.g., its color).

Figure 7.9 A real-world conjunction search. Find the big, round, red tomatoes among things that might be big or round or red but do not have all three basic features.

Figure 7.10 Search for arbitrary objects is not very efficient. Find the faucet, the violin, or the window.

possessor of any unique feature. Tomatoes are distinguished from most of the distractors by a *conjunction* of several features. If you can guide your attention to red and round and large, you will have eliminated most of the competition. In the lab, we use **conjunction searches** like those in Figure 7.6B. In a conjunction search, no single feature defines the target. Instead, the target is defined by the conjunction—the co-occurrence—of two or more features. In this case we're looking for the red, vertical items. In terms of efficiency, conjunction searches tend to lie between the very efficient feature searches and the inefficient serial searches.

In Real-World Searches, Properties of Scenes Guide Visual Search

If guidance by the basic features of the target object were the whole solution to finding objects in the real world, then search for a faucet in **Figure 7.10** should be efficient. The searcher would think of the basic features of faucets—shiny, silver, rounded—and then the search for a faucet would be a matter of guiding attention to a complex conjunction of features. However, search for arbitrary objects is not efficient (Vickery, King, and Jiang, 2005). Certainly, feature guidance can help—for example, look for the *green* paintbrush in Figure 7.10—but the ease with which we search in the real world must involve more than feature guidance.

It is quite easy to find the faucet in the kitchen scene in **Figure 7.11**, even though it is less visible than the faucet in Figure 7.10. You are helped by various forms of **scene-based guidance** (Castelhano and Heaven, 2010). Even though you've never seen this kitchen before, you know about kitchens. They have sinks in typical places.

Figure 7.11 Scene-based guidance would help you find the faucet in this scene.

You know that sinks have faucets in typical places and, behold, there is the faucet. If you were searching for bowls, you would be guided by the knowledge that bowls must rest on surfaces; they do not float. Moreover, you know about the average size of bowls. This knowledge would allow you to figure out that only a few objects in this scene are plausibly bowl-sized in the space defined by this picture. In that case, that guidance would speed your conclusion that there are no bowls.

We can think of all of these various forms of scene guidance as constituting a Bayesian "prior probability" that tells you how likely it is that any given object in the scene is the target (Ehinger et al., 2009).

FURTHER DISCUSSION of the Bayesian approach can be found in Chapters 4 (page 122), 5 (page 166), and 6 (page 204).

The Binding Problem in Visual Search

We will return to complicated stimuli like scenes later in this chapter. First, we need to step back and consider what selective attention does for us. One answer, championed by Anne Treisman (1996), is that selective attention allows us to solve the **binding problem**. This problem is illustrated in **Figure 7.12**. A quick glance tells us that we're looking at *pluses* whose components are brown and green and vertical and horizontal. However, if we need to find the two green-vertical, brown-horizontal items, we will need to search, directing attention to the individual items (Wolfe and Bennett, 1997). In the language of Treisman's **feature integration theory** (Treisman and Gelade, 1980), the basic features of color and orientation are available in a **preattentive stage** of processing, but we don't know how those features are bound together until we attend to a specific object. Looking back at Figure 7.6C, the problem with *T*s and *L*s is that they both have vertical and horizontal features. It is the relationship of those features to each other that's critical. To recognize an object, you must "bind" its features.

The idea of guided search, mentioned earlier, fits into this framework. We can use some preattentive feature information to guide the choice of what should be attended and bound next. If we're searching for a *little, brown*

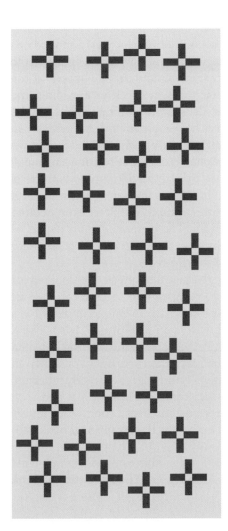

Figure 7.12 A conjunction search with a binding problem. In this image it is hard to find the green verticals (there are two of them), because all of the items have the features brown and green and vertical and horizontal.

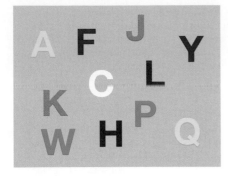

Figure 7.13 Illusory conjunctions. Look at this figure quickly, and then try to recall the colors of the letters. You may know what colors were there and you may remember many of the letters, but you are quite likely to pair a color and a letter incorrectly.

illusory conjunction An erroneous combination of two features in a visual scene—for example, seeing a red *X* when the display contains red letters and *X*s but no red *X*s.

rapid serial visual presentation (RSVP) An experimental procedure in which stimuli appear in a stream at one location (typically the point of fixation) at a rapid rate (typically about 8 per second).

attentional blink (AB) The tendency not to perceive or respond to the second of two different target stimuli amid a rapid stream of distracting stimuli if the observer has responded to the first target stimulus 200–500 milliseconds before the second stimulus is presented.

mouse, we should guide our attention to little stuff and brown stuff and not devote attention to shiny, red or large, square things. Even before attention can enable binding, the mere presence of the right collection of unbound features might, in some cases, very quickly give us a pretty good idea that there is a mouse (or at least an animal) present (Li et al., 2002), but full object recognition is going to require attention.

If attention is needed to bind features correctly, what happens if we don't have enough time to complete the job? We'll see something, but what? DON'T look at **Figure 7.13** yet. It is a demonstration of part of the answer. Now, what you must do is look quickly at the figure, and then look away and write down as many of the letters and their colors as you can. Try that now.

If you compare your list to the actual figure, you may find that you matched the wrong color to a letter. For example, you might be quite sure that you saw a green *H*. If so, you have experienced an **illusory conjunction**, a false combination of the features from two or more different objects (A. M. Treisman and Schmidt, 1982). You are unlikely to think that you have seen a blue *H* or a green *T*, because neither the color blue nor the letter *T* is present in the figure. We conjoin only those features that are actually in the display. When we can't complete the task of binding, we do the best we can with the information we have.

Attending in Time: RSVP and the Attentional Blink

So far in this chapter, we've concentrated on attentional selection in space. Let's consider what happens if you search in time rather than in space. Imagine the following situation: You're looking at a stream of letters that all appear at the same location in space. Showing the stimuli in this way is known as **rapid serial visual presentation** (**RSVP**). You're trying to decide whether there's an *X* in the stream of letters. How fast can the characters be presented and still permit you to do the task with high accuracy? With fairly large, clearly visible stimuli, we can reliably pick an *X* out of letters when the characters are appearing at a rate of 8–10 items per second. The task does not need to be limited to simple characters. If we're watching a stream of photographs flash by at this rate, we can monitor that stream for the appearance of a picnic photograph. We don't even need to know which particular picnic we're looking for. The general idea of "picnic" is adequate for the task (Potter, 1976). You can view scenes in an RSVP sequence yourself in **Web Activity 7.3: The RSVP Paradigm**.

Returning to simple letters, let's change the task a bit. Instead of looking for one target in a stream of letters, now we're looking for two. We can call the first "T1" (for "target number 1") and call the second "T2." In this example, T1 is a white letter in a stream of black letters, and T2 is an *X* (**Figure 7.14A**). The *X* will be present in 50% of the trials. The critical variable is the interval between T1 and T2, and the somewhat surprising result of the experiment is shown in **Figure 7.14B**. If T2 appears 200–500 ms after T1 and if T1 is correctly reported, we are very likely to miss T2. (Note that each frame in Figure 7.14A and each position on the x-axis in Figure 7.14B represents 100 ms of time, since letters appear every 100 ms.) This phenomenon is known as the **attentional blink (AB)** (Shapiro, 1994); it is as if our ability to visually attend to the characters in the RSVP sequence is temporarily knocked out, even though our eyes remain wide open. You'll find more on this topic in **Web Activity 7.4: The Attentional Blink and Repetition Blindness**.

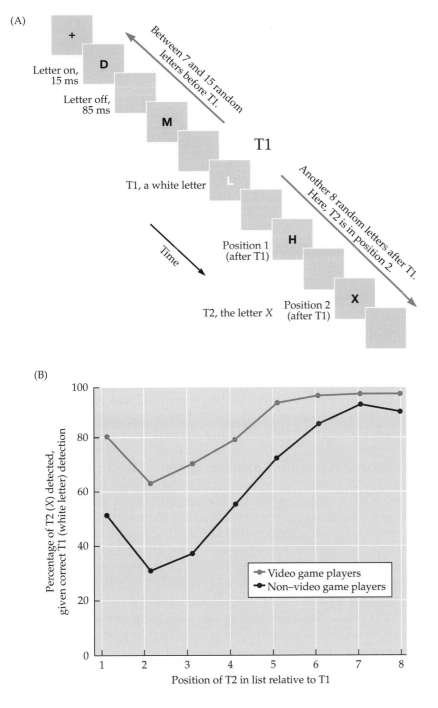

Figure 7.14 The attentional blink (AB) in video game and non–video game players. (A) In this AB task, observers try to report two targets: a white letter (T1), and an *X* (T2) coming in the stream after that white letter. Letters appear every 100 ms. T2 can appear in various positions in the list after T1. Here T2 is in position 2. (B) If the *X* appears within 500 ms (positions 1–5 after T1), detection is impaired. That impairment is known as the attentional blink. Video game players (blue) show less of a blink. (After Green and Bavelier, 2003.)

To show that missing T2 in this scenario is an attentional problem, we can do a control experiment in which participants report only T2. If participants are asked to monitor the RSVP stream for the T2 *X*, they pay no particular attention to the now irrelevant white letter, and T2 performance is uniformly good at all delays between T1 and T2.

Somehow the act of attending to T1 makes it very hard to attend to T2 if T2 appears 200–500 ms later in the stream. What is happening? Marvin Chun suggests the following metaphor: Imagine you're fishing with a net in a less-than-pristine stream, with boots and tires and the occasional fish floating or swimming by.

(A) (B) (C)

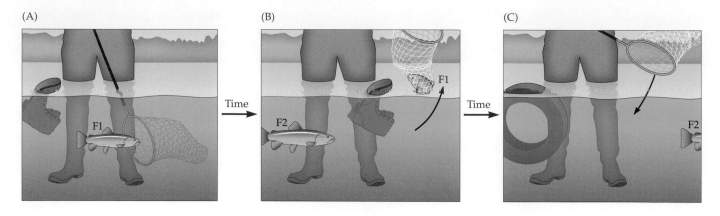

Time Time

Figure 7.15 Marvin Chun's fishing metaphor for attentional blink. (A) You can see all the stuff in the river as it drifts by (e.g., the boot and the fish). (B) You commit to fishing out fish number 1 (F1). The boot drifts by, and fish 2 (F2) appears. (C) Because you're tied up with F1, you will not be able to fish out F2, and that second fish swims by—detected perhaps, but uncollected.

You can monitor the stream and identify each item as it passes—boot, tire, boot, fish, boot, and so on. You can also dip your net in and catch a fish (**Figure 7.15A**). Once you have a fish in the net, however, it takes some time before you can get the net back into the water to catch fish number 2. As a result, you might miss fish 2 if it swims by too soon after you've caught fish 1 (**Figure 7.15B, C**) (Chun and Potter, 1995).

Looking back at Figure 7.14B, notice that performance is quite good if T2 appears immediately after T1. In Chun's metaphorical account, this would be a case in which one scoop nets two fish. This metaphor illustrates the idea that two processes are at work. Notice the interesting difference between the role attention plays here and the role it plays in the spatial example of visual search. In search, there is a capacity limit: you just don't seem to be able to recognize more than one object at a time. In attentional blink, though, the problem is probably not the size of the metaphorical net. The problem is that, once attention has dipped that net into the river, there is a temporary inhibition (Olivers and Meeter, 2008) or a temporary loss of control (Di Lollo et al., 2005) that makes it impossible to coordinate a second dip for several hundred milliseconds.

Figure 7.14B shows data from two groups of participants who performed differently on the AB task. Interestingly, the group that shows a smaller AB consists of players of "first-person shooter" video games. Indeed, those gamers seem to do better on a range of attentional tasks (C. S. Green and Bavelier, 2003). Why? A variety of factors make some people less subject to the blink (Willems and Martens, 2016). It could be that people who choose to play these video games have better attentional resources. It could also be that the games themselves enhance attention. To test this idea, Green and Bavelier (2003) conducted a study with two groups of non–video game players. One group got experience with a first-person shooter game, and the other group played the game Tetris. The first-person shooter group improved on attentional tasks; the Tetris group did not. Of course, this is not an endorsement of violent video games, but it does suggest that attentional abilities can be changed by training and that those first-person shooter video games produced change for reasons that remain to be worked out. In **Web Activity 7.4: The Attentional Blink and Repetition Blindness**, you can experience a related but not identical effect.

Effects like the AB are important because they tell us something about the time required for acts of attention and/or selection. From these RSVP experiments alone, we can see that there are several "speed limits" in our mental life. The single-target RSVP experiments tell us that if we are just watching a stream of stimuli over time, we can speed along at a rate of many images per second (perhaps as many as 75 per second; Potter et al., 2014). A much slower rate describes the speed with which we can act on items, even if we are just grabbing them to report about their presence. Here, the RSVP data suggest a speed limit of 2–5 items per second.

The Physiological Basis of Attention

In an oft-quoted passage, William James declared, "Everyone knows what attention is." This great nineteenth-century psychologist went on to say, "It is the taking possession by the mind, in clear and vivid form, of one out of what seem several simultaneously possible objects or trains of thought" (James, 1890, Vol. 1, pp. 403–404). That seems fair enough, but what does it mean for the mind to take possession of a possible object? If we try to get specific, we discover that this attention that everyone "knows" can be rather difficult to pin down. In part, it is difficult to know what attention does because attention performs a variety of tasks, as already discussed. But we also need to deal with the physiological question of what the brain is actually doing when it selects one location in space, or one object, or one moment in time, for further processing (Nobre and Kastner, 2014). Let's consider some of the neural possibilities.

Attention Could Enhance Neural Activity

If we are asked to attend to one location in the visual field, as in a Posner cueing task (see Figure 7.3), the neurons that respond to stimuli in that part of the field will become more active. This will be true even in the first stages of visual cortical processing, since those stages are influenced by attention (**Figure 7.16**) (Brefczynski and DeYoe, 1999; Gandhi, Heeger, and Boynton, 1998; Haenny and Schiller, 1988; McMains and Somers, 2004). As we progress further into the visual areas of the cortex, even larger attentional effects are seen (Reynolds and Chelazzi, 2004). In fact, the effects seen at the early stages in the cortex are quite possibly the results of feedback from these later stages of processing (Martinez et al., 1999). That feedback may be a very important part of visual processing (Ahissar and Hochstein, 2004; Di Lollo, Enns, and Rensink, 2000).

Subject A

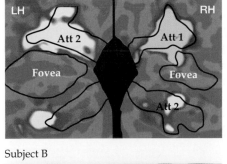

Subject B

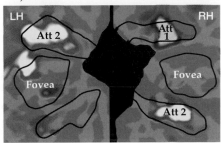

Figure 7.16 Spotlights of attention in the human brain. These fMRI images of human visual cortex (striate and some extrastriate) show activity in the brain while participants paid attention to one stimulus (Att 1) or two stimuli (Att 2). The stimuli were outside the fovea, so the regions of activity don't include the fovea. (From McMains and Somers, 2004.)

Figure 7.17 Attentional selection. First, attend to the red items and notice the rough oval that they form. Next, without moving your eyes, switch attention to the blue items or the horizontal items. Different aspects of the picture appear more prominent as you shift the property that you select to attend to.

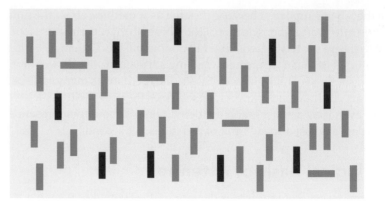

Attention Could Enhance the Processing of a Specific Type of Stimulus

The mechanisms of attention described in the previous section might suffice if we want to keep watch "out of the corner of the eye" by enhancing activity in a specific region of visual cortex. But imagine picking pennies out of a change bowl (a real-world visual search task). Somehow the wish to find pennies makes the pennies more salient. If we switched to quarters, the pennies would recede in salience and the quarters would rise. In this case, we are attending not on the basis of spatial location, but on the basis of a stimulus property.

You can experience this attentional shift in the salience of different stimulus attributes in **Figure 7.17**. Without moving your eyes, select the red items and notice how an oval emerges with no change in the stimulus. Similarly, you can select the blue items or the horizontal items. Each act of selection seems to alter what you see, even as the stimulus remains physically unchanged. In **Figure 7.18**, you can see attention change the apparent brightness and/or color of a stimulus (Tse, 2005).

Attentional selection can also activate parts of the brain that are specialized for the processing for one or another type of stimulus. Recall from Chapter 4 that fMRI has shown that the **fusiform face area** (**FFA**) is especially important in the processing of faces (Kanwisher, McDermott, and Chun, 1997) while the **parahippocampal place area** (**PPA**) is especially important in the processing of places (Epstein et al., 1999) (**Figure 7.19**). If participants view an image of a face superimposed on an image of a house (**Figure 7.20**), the FFA becomes more active when the participant is attending to the face, and the PPA becomes more active when the participant is attending to the house (O'Craven and Kanwisher, 2000).

> **FURTHER DISCUSSION** of FFA and PPA can be found in Chapter 4 on page 126.

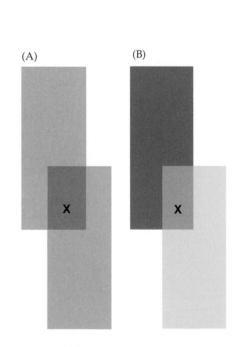

Figure 7.18 Attentional modulation of appearance. (A) Look at the X and notice that when you attend to one rectangle or the other, that one appears darker. (B) Here, if you attend to the pink rectangle, the overlapping area looks pink. It changes to blue if you attend to the blue rectangle. (After Tse, 2005.)

Attention and Single Cells

We have been talking about areas of the brain. On a finer scale, we can ask how attention might change the responses of a single neuron. **Figure 7.21** shows one set of possibilities. Suppose a cell responded to a range of different orientations but was maximally responsive to vertical lines (see Chapter 3). Attention might make the cell more responsive across the board (Figure 7.21A). This sort of **response enhancement** has been seen in visual cortex cells, but simple response enhancement seems like a rather indiscriminate change. Alternatively, a cell

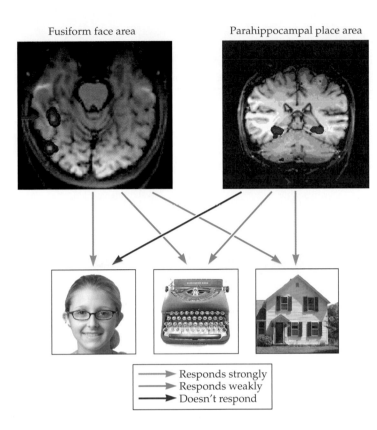

Fusiform face area

Parahippocampal place area

Responds strongly
Responds weakly
Doesn't respond

Figure 7.19 Functional MRI reveals that different pieces of the cortex are activated by faces and by places. This is true even when both stimuli are present at the same time (as in Figure 7.20) and the observer merely alters his mental set from faces to places. (MRIs courtesy of Nancy Kanwisher.)

fusiform face area (FFA) A region of extrastriate visual cortex in humans that is specifically and reliably activated by human faces.

parahippocampal place area (PPA) A region of extrastriate visual cortex in humans that is specifically and reliably activated more by images of places than by other stimuli.

response enhancement An effect of attention on the response of a neuron in which the neuron responding to an attended stimulus gives a bigger response.

sharper tuning An effect of attention on the response of a neuron in which the neuron responding to an attended stimulus responds more precisely. For example, a neuron that responds to lines with orientations from −20 degrees to +20 degrees might come to respond to ±10-degree lines.

might become more precisely tuned. In the example in Figure 7.21B, **sharper tuning** would mean that attention could make it easier for the neuron to find a weak vertical signal amid the noise of other orientations (as seems to happen when we attend to the horizontal bars in Figure 7.17). Lu and Dosher (1998) carried out elegant psychophysical experiments showing that attention does make it possible to exclude noise in this way, though some efforts to find physiological evidence for sharper tuning have found only response enhancement (Treue and Trujillo, 1999).

Figure 7.20 These images combine faces and houses. In both cases you can use attention to enhance the perception of one or the other. As you switch your attention from one type of object to the other, you also change the activation of different parts of the brain, as shown in Figure 7.19. (Left image from Downing, Liu, and Kanwisher, 2001.)

Figure 7.21 Three ways that the response of a cell could be changed as a result of attention: (A) enhancement, (B) sharper tuning, (C) altered tuning. In each row, the red line shows the response of a single cell to lines of different orientations, without attention (left column) and with attention (right column).

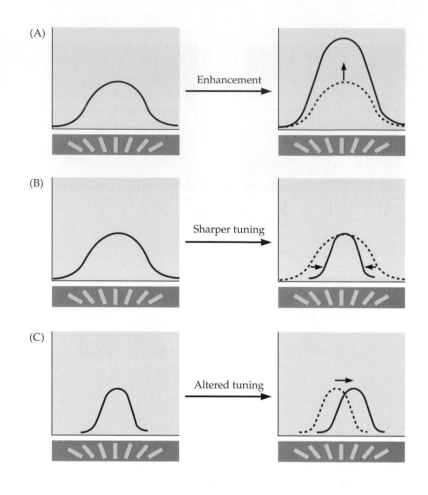

A more radical possibility is that attention changes the preferences of a neuron. As illustrated in Figure 7.21C, a cell that was initially tuned to vertical lines might come to respond better to a different orientation under the influence of attention. The best evidence for a change in the fundamental preferences of a neuron comes from studies of its preferences in space—that is, the size and shape of a neuron's receptive field (Moran and Desimone, 1985). **Figure 7.22** shows just such a change in a specific area of monkey cortex. When the monkey attends to one stimulus, the cell's sensitivity is enhanced around that location. When attention is shifted to another location, the receptive field shifts too (Womelsdorf et al., 2006).

If cells are restricting their processing to the object of attention, then sensitivity to neighboring items might be reduced as resources are withdrawn from them. This prediction is borne out: mapping the effects of attention reveals inhibition surrounding the object of attention (Mounts, 2000).

The three hypotheses about the microcircuitry of attention discussed here are not mutually exclusive. Different neurons perform different parts of the task of attending, and each subtask may require a different type of change in neuronal responses. As a hypothetical example, simple response enhancement from one neuron might be the "command" that causes another neuron to sharpen its tuning and/or to change the shape of its receptive field. In fact, these may not even be different functions, say John Reynolds and David Heeger (2009). Reynolds and Heeger's "normalization" theory says that the current response of a neuron is the product of that neuron's built-in receptive field and the effects of attention.

(A)   (B)

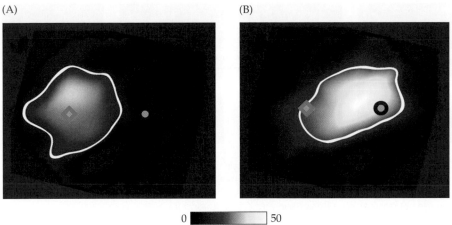

0 ▮▮▮▮▮▮▮ 50
Spikes/s

Figure 7.22 Each of these images is a receptive-field map of the responses of one cell in a monkey. In this experiment, the investigators flashed little spots of light at different locations and measured the responses of the cells. Brighter, whiter locations are areas of greater response. The only difference between (A) and (B) is that in (A) the monkey was attending to the location marked by the diamond, while in (B) it attended to the location of the circle. This change in attention caused the receptive field of the cell to shrink-wrap itself around the attended stimulus location. (From Womelsdorf et al., 2006.)

This product must then be "normalized" by neural suppression. Otherwise the numbers (or the level of excitation of the cell) can get too big. The results of this single process of multiplying and dividing can look like response enhancement, like sharper tuning, or like changes in receptive-field size and shape—all depending on the specific stimuli that are used in the experiment. For present purposes, the main message is that attention can change the activity of single cells.

Attention May Change the Way Neurons Talk to Each Other

We have discussed how attention can modulate the activity of a neuron and of an area of the brain. Now let us think about how attention might modify the interactions between neurons and/or areas. For example, how might the brain implement a solution to the binding problem? More specifically, if different brain areas perform different tasks such as processing faces or places or color or orientation, how might those areas be coordinated if, for instance, we want to think about how the windows and door of some red house look like two eyes and a mouth? One possibility is that this binding and coordination of areas involves synchronizing the temporal patterns of activity in those areas (Singer, 1999). One role of attention appears to be to control what is synchronized with what. For instance, Baldauf and Desimone (2014) showed that attention to faces or places could change whether FFA or PPA were synchronized with a third brain area. More locally, within a brain area, attention may serve to desynchronize neurons. If neurons are synchronized, it is as if they are all doing more or less the same thing. A group of properly desynchronized neurons can more accurately represent a stimulus if different neurons contribute different bits of information (Cohen and Maunsell, 2009). We can imagine a set of synchronized neurons saying, in effect, "that is a face" while other neurons, roused into desynchronized action by attention, are working on different aspects of recognition: "Hey, that is mom's face. Expression looks angry. We better check with memory and find out if we forgot to take out the trash."

Disorders of Visual Attention

What would happen if you could no longer pay attention? A complete inability to attend would be devastating. Because we cannot recognize objects or find what we're looking for without attention, complete inattention would be something

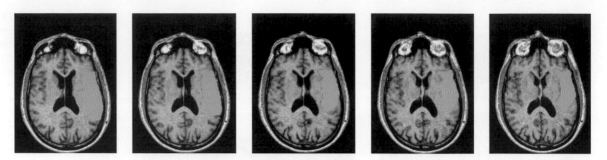

Figure 7.23 Five "slices" through the brain of a patient with neglect (magnetic resonance imaging viewed as though from above). The damage, shown here in yellow, includes the right parietal and frontal lobes. The patient neglects the left side of space. (Image courtesy of Lynn Robertson and Krista Schendel.)

visual-field defect A portion of the visual field with no vision or with abnormal vision, typically resulting from damage to the visual nervous system.

parietal lobe In each cerebral hemisphere, a lobe that lies toward the top of the brain between the frontal and occipital lobes.

neglect In reference to a neurological symptom, in visual attention: 1. The inability to attend or respond to stimuli in the contralesional visual field (typically, the left field after right parietal damage). 2. Ignoring half of the body or half of an object.

near to functional blindness. Brain damage that produces a deficit this severe is very rare. More common is the attentional equivalent of a **visual-field defect**. As you may recall, a person who is unfortunate enough to lose primary visual cortex in the right hemisphere will be blind on the opposite (left) side of visual space. Suppose, however, that the lesion is in the right **parietal lobe**. People with this sort of lesion (**Figure 7.23**) are not blind on their left side but have problems directing attention to objects and places there. These problems manifest themselves in a curious set of clinical symptoms, including *neglect* and *extinction*.

Neglect

Patients with **neglect** behave as if part of the world were not there. Asked to describe what he is seeing, a patient experiencing neglect of the left visual field will tend to name objects to the right of fixation and ignore objects on the left. A "line cancellation test" is a more systematic way to assess this problem. The patient is given a piece of paper full of lines and asked to draw an intersecting line through each one. He might produce something like the drawing in **Figure 7.24**: the lines on one side (the right, in this case) are crossed out, but those on the other side (here, the left) are overlooked. **Figure 7.25** shows what might result if a patient experiencing neglect of the left visual field were asked to copy a picture. Again, the right side is reproduced fairly faithfully, but the left side is missing. Such a patient might also eat only what's on the right side of his dinner plate or shave only the right side of his face.

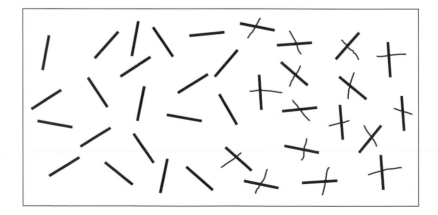

Figure 7.24 A patient with neglect could produce this sort of result if asked to cross out all the lines. The patient might neglect the lines in the left side of the image following damage to the right parietal lobe.

(A) (B)

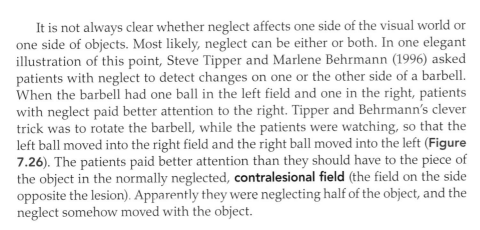

Figure 7.25 In copying a drawing like the one in (A), a patient with neglect often omits one side of the object, as in (B).

It is not always clear whether neglect affects one side of the visual world or one side of objects. Most likely, neglect can be either or both. In one elegant illustration of this point, Steve Tipper and Marlene Behrmann (1996) asked patients with neglect to detect changes on one or the other side of a barbell. When the barbell had one ball in the left field and one in the right, patients with neglect paid better attention to the right. Tipper and Behrmann's clever trick was to rotate the barbell, while the patients were watching, so that the left ball moved into the right field and the right ball moved into the left (**Figure 7.26**). The patients paid better attention than they should have to the piece of the object in the normally neglected, **contralesional field** (the field on the side opposite the lesion). Apparently they were neglecting half of the object, and the neglect somehow moved with the object.

contralesional field The visual field on the side opposite a brain lesion. For example, points to the left of fixation are contralesional to damage in the right hemisphere of the brain.

extinction In reference to visual attention, the inability to perceive a stimulus to one side of the point of fixation (e.g., to the right) in the presence of another stimulus, typically in a comparable position in the other visual field (e.g., on the left side).

Extinction

The phenomenon of **extinction** is related to neglect; it might even be neglect in a milder form (Driver, 1998). A neurologist might test for neglect by having a patient fixate on her (the neurologist's) nose. She might then hold up a fork in the patient's good (in this case, right) visual field and ask, "What do you see?" "A fork," would come the reply. Next the neurologist might present a spoon in the bad (left) field. A patient with left-visual-field neglect would be nonplussed, but a patient with extinction would be able to report the presence of the spoon. However, if the neurologist were to hold up a fork in one hand and a spoon in the other, the patient would report only the object in the good field. The other object would be perceptually "extinguished."

In neglect, the patient may be entirely unable to deploy attention to the contralesional side of the world or the object. In extinction, the patient may be able

Step 1 Step 2 Step 3

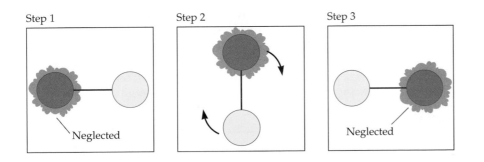

Figure 7.26 Tipper and Behrmann's (1996) experiment. Step 1: The patient neglected the left side of the barbell. Step 2: The barbell was rotated through 180 degrees. Step 3: The neglect rotated with the object, indicating that, in this case, the neglect was relative to the object, not to the whole scene.

ipsilesional field The visual field on the same side as a brain lesion.

attention deficit hyperactivity disorder (ADHD) A quite common childhood disorder that can continue into adulthood, symptoms of which include difficulty focusing attention and problems controlling behavior.

to deploy attention to an object in the contralesional field if it is the only salient object. However, if there is competition from a similar object in the **ipsilesional field** (the same side as the lesion), then the two objects compete for attention and the ipsilesional object wins. Objects are always competing for our attention, but as a general rule it is no great matter for us to redeploy attention from one object to the next. In extinction, the object that loses the competition is far less likely to attract attention than is the case normally. To learn what happens when the parietal lobe is damaged on both sides of the brain, see **Web Essay 7.1: Balint Syndrome.**

■ Sensation & Perception in Everyday Life ■

Selective Attention and Attention Deficit Hyperactivity Disorder (ADHD)

Neglect and extinction are relatively rare consequences of damage to the nervous system. There are much more common disorders of attention. **Attention deficit hyperactivity disorder** (**ADHD**) is the best known of these. Recall that, early on in this chapter, we said that attention was not a single thing but a name for a family of processes that restrict or bias our mental activities. That is demonstrably true, but at the same time, we have the intuition that there is some general attentional resource that is being summoned when our mother or our teacher or our significant other says, "Pay attention!" Some people seem to have more difficulty "paying attention" in this sense than others. If that difficulty is severe enough, they may be diagnosed with ADHD, which is diagnosed in North American children more than any other behavioral disorder. It is characterized by three kinds of symptoms: impulsivity (an inability to control behavior), hyperactivity, and of most interest to us, inattentiveness. An inattentive child or adult might fail to carry out a set of instructions or tasks (like homework). He might have problems organizing his activities and be easily distracted or forgetful. He might seem not to listen when spoken to (Feldman and Reiff, 2014; Volkow and Swanson, 2013).

How does the sort of attention that is disrupted in ADHD relate to the attentional processes that we have been discussing here? For instance, if you have trouble organizing a task, might you have trouble organizing a visual search? Mullane and Klein (2008) analyzed the results of a number of different studies of this question. They found that there were differences between observers with and without a diagnosis of ADHD but that these differences were fairly subtle. Doing search tasks like those shown in Figure 7.6, ADHD observers produced a pattern of results that was qualitatively similar to the pattern shown at the bottom of Figure 7.6. Feature searches were highly efficient; this was basically the same in ADHD and non-ADHD observers. Inefficient searches were a little more inefficient in ADHD observers, but the difference was not dramatic. ADHD and non-ADHD observers seem to search in pretty much the same manner. ADHD is a disorder with significant attentional components, but the major components of ADHD seem to lie outside of the realm of visual spatial attention.

Perceiving and Understanding Scenes

We said at the beginning of this discussion of attention that we need attention in order to deal with the vast amount of information in the visual scene in front of our eyes. The rest of this chapter is devoted to the problem of scenes; how we understand them and what it is that we are actually *seeing* at any moment in time.

Two Pathways to Scene Perception

Let's go back to the two-pathway idea introduced at the beginning of this chapter (Wolfe et al., 2011). Visual experience can be thought of as a combination of the work of a selective and a nonselective pathway (**Figure 7.27**). The initial stages of vision (Figure 7.27A, and as described in the preceding chapters) are shared by both pathways. The spotlight of attention is associated with the selective pathway (Figure 7.27B). Specific locations or objects are selected for the processing that allows for binding and object recognition. The visual world outside the current spotlight is brought to you via the nonselective pathway (Figure 7.27C). What do you see away from the current focus of attention?

The Nonselective Pathway Computes Ensemble Statistics

Look at **Figure 7.28**. You very rapidly know several things about this school of fish. You know that the school oriented to the right, perhaps slightly up from horizontal. You know the average size and color of the fish. You also know something about the distribution of orientations, sizes, and colors. That is, you know that a range of fish orientations is present. They are not all pointed in exactly the same direction. To know these things, you are computing

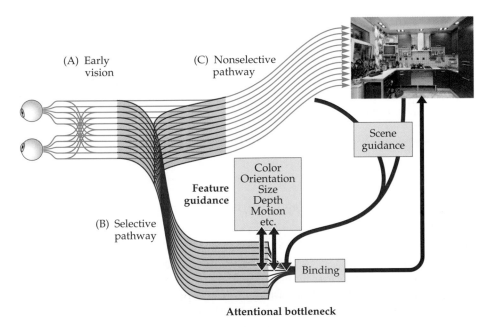

Figure 7.27 Two pathways from the world to our perception of the world. (A) Early stages of the visual system feed two pathways: (B) a selective pathway, with a bottleneck governed by selective attention, and (C) a nonselective pathway that is not subject to this attentional bottleneck. The selective pathway permits the recognition of one or a very few objects at one time. The nonselective pathway contributes information about the distribution of features across the scene, as well as information about the rough gist of the scene. (After Wolfe et al., 2011.)

Figure 7.28 Some "fishy" ensemble statistics. In a glance you can tell that these fish are oriented roughly horizontally as a group, even though you cannot tell, in that glance, which specific fish might be oriented exactly horizontally. Similarly, you know in a glance that some fish are more tilted and some are small. Selective attention is required to determine whether any one fish is both strongly tilted and small.

ensemble statistics The average and distribution of properties like orientation or color over a set of objects or over a region in a scene.

ensemble statistics (Alvarez, 2011). Ensemble statistics represent knowledge about the properties of a group (ensemble) of objects or, perhaps we should say, an ensemble of proto-objects. Our estimates of these statistics are surprisingly accurate (Chong and Treisman, 2003; Chubb and Landy, 1994).

These are *ensemble* statistics because we know them without knowing the properties of the individual fish. For example, you would have to search to find a fish that was pointed exactly horizontally, even though that fish's orientation contributes to the estimate of the ensemble orientation. Features are not bound in ensemble statistics. You would have no idea, without attentional scrutiny, if the most strongly tilted fish were also the smallest. You know there are smaller fish and more tilted fish, but appreciating conjunctions of those features requires the *selective* pathway.

> **FURTHER DISCUSSION** of our ability to perceive the characteristics of a group of objects can be found in Chapter 4 on page 114 (Figure 4.19).

The Nonselective Pathway Computes Scene Gist and Layout—Very Quickly

As was mentioned earlier in our discussion of attending in time, people can monitor a stream of images for one particular image or type of image at rates of one image every 100 ms (see Figure 7.14). In fact, in some cases you don't need as much as 100 ms. Holle Kirchner and Simon Thorpe (2006) presented two side-by-side scenes to observers and found that the observers could reliably move their eyes to fixate whichever scene included an animal (any animal) in as little as 120 ms. The fact that most of that 120 ms was taken up in generating the eye movement implies that the processing of the scene was really fast. Michelle Greene and Aude Oliva (2009) presented single scenes very fast, followed by masking stimuli. They found that people could differentiate between natural and urban scenes with just 19 ms of exposure to a scene. Global properties that described

(A)

(B)

Figure 7.29 How are ensemble statistics related to scene perception? (A) It is quite clear that the little patches of spatial frequency (Gabor patches) are roughly vertical on the top and horizontal on the bottom. You rapidly extract these ensemble statistics, though it would take you longer to determine whether any one little patch was actually vertical or horizontal. (B) Similarly, you rapidly see the vertical trees and horizontal line of the field, but analysis of any one tree would require attention. (A from Brady, Shafer-Skelton, and Alvarez, 2017.)

the **spatial layout** of the scene (e.g., was it a navigable or non-navigable space?) could be extracted a bit more quickly than could basic categories like "desert" or "lake," but all of these could be appreciated within about 50 ms. It probably takes 20–50 ms to recognize just one object, so observers are certainly not recognizing scenes by recognizing a string of objects and putting them together. What are they doing?

An interesting potential answer comes from the work of Aude Oliva and Antonio Torralba (2001). Look at **Figure 7.29A**. In a glimpse, it is clear that the field is divided in two with a roughly vertical top and a roughly horizontal bottom. You get that from the ensemble statistics as in Figure 7.28; it will take you longer to use your selective pathway to determine whether any one item is actually vertical or horizontal. Now look at **Figure 7.29B**. Again, in a glimpse, it is clear that the upper part of the image contains a lot of vertical *stuff* and a horizontal line divides the image. Oliva and Torralba argued that the same processes that allowed you to process all the local spatial frequency components could also allow you to distinguish beaches from city streets from bedrooms, and so forth. There was a straight line from ensemble statistics to the gist of a scene. Thus, wide-open scenes like beaches, fields, parking lots, and so on tend to have a lot of strong horizontal components corresponding to the horizon. Oliva and Torralba called this dimension "openness" and defined a number of other dimensions, including "naturalness" (versus "man-made") and "roughness." They could measure the amount of each of these dimensions by examining the local spatial frequency components that made up the stimulus.

When Oliva and Torralba measured the properties of thousands of scenes, they observed something very useful: scenes with the same meaning tended to be neighbors in the space defined by their scene dimensions. Suppose we

spatial layout The description of the structure of a scene (e.g., enclosed, open, rough, smooth) without reference to the identity of specific objects in the scene.

define a simple two-dimensional space using the dimensions of openness and expansion. **Figure 7.30** graphs a set of man-made scenes using these two dimensions. Look at how the scenes organize themselves. The frontal views of buildings fall in the upper right (low openness, low expansion). Highways fall in the lower left (high openness, high expansion). The rules that make this arrangement don't include anything about buildings or highways, just sine waves. Nevertheless, scenes with the same gist tend to cluster together. This chapter's Scientists at Work examines whether humans use ensemble information to get the gist of a scene.

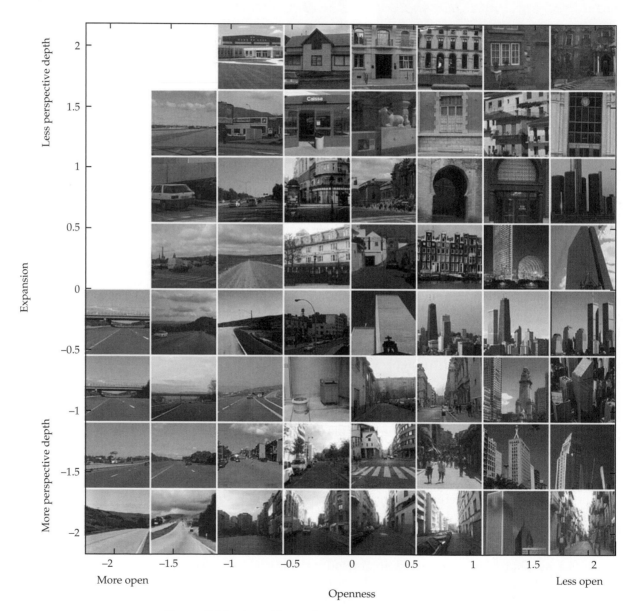

Figure 7.30 Spatial layout from global information. In this collection of urban scenes, the x-axis represents a measure of "openness," from panoramic scenes to vertically structured scenes, derived from spatial frequency information. The y-axis represents "expansion" (capturing a sense of depth from perspective). Scenes with the same meaning cluster together in this space. (Courtesy of Aude Oliva.)

■ Scientists at Work ■

Do Ensembles Make Gists?

■ **Question** Is the ability to rapidly understand a meaningful gist of a scene really based on the ability to process local spatial frequencies and orientations?

■ **Hypothesis** Ensemble processing is the basis for scene gist, but it is not the basis for object recognition.

■ **Test** First, the researchers used a computer algorithm to turn objects and scenes into textures that kept all the local spatial frequencies and orientations but, as you can see in **Figure 7.31**, made the stimuli hard or impossible to identify (Brady, Shafer-Skelton, and Alvarez, 2017). Next, they did a "priming" experiment: they showed observers a scene, object, or texture for 500 ms. Then, they showed an object for 100 ms and asked observers to name it.

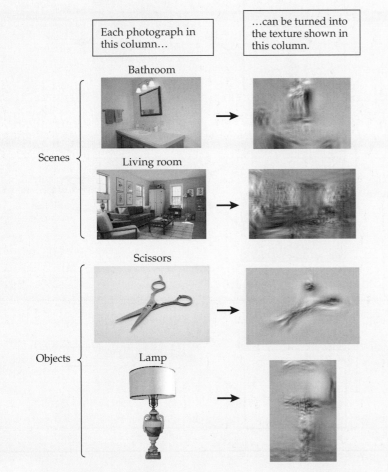

Each photograph in this column…

…can be turned into the texture shown in this column.

Scenes

Bathroom

Living room

Objects

Scissors

Lamp

Figure 7.31 A photograph of a scene or an object can be converted into a texture that has the same local mix of orientations and spatial frequencies but is no longer easily recognized. Stimuli and textures similar to those in the figure were used as "primes" in the Brady, Shafer-Skelton, and Alvarez (2017) experiment.

(Continued)

■ Scientists at Work (continued)

■ Results If the first stimulus (the "prime") was related to the second, observers responded more accurately than if the two stimuli were unrelated. So "scissors" and "bathroom" primed "comb," while "lamp" and "living room" did not. What about the unrecognizable textures? As shown in **Figure 7.32**, scene textures continued to prime while object textures did not.

■ Conclusion Since rapidly presented scene textures behave like rapidly presented scenes, the authors concluded that the basic gist of the scene is contained in the simple set of spatial frequencies and orientations. Recognizing an object, on the other hand, requires other, attention-demanding processes.

■ Future work How specific can a scene gist be? For example, with a bit of time, you can tell the difference between a sandy beach and a rocky beach, but is that sort of information present in the frequencies and orientations that make up the gist of "beach"?

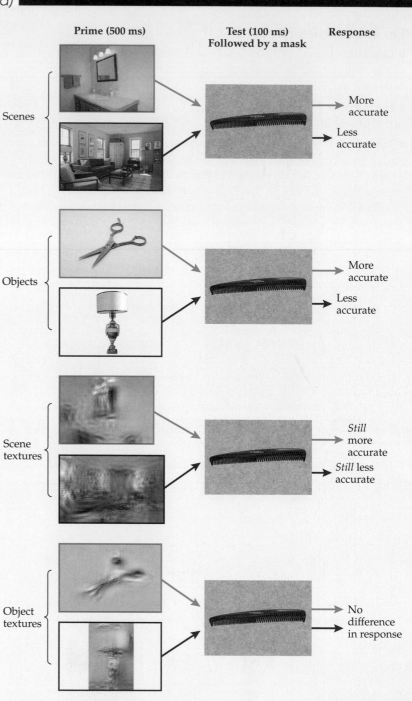

Figure 7.32 In the Brady, Shafer-Skelton, and Alvarez (2017) experiment, observers saw a prime (scene, object, or texture) for 500 ms. Then, for just 100 ms, they saw an object that they had to name. Blue conditions show when the prime and the test object were related (e.g., scissors → comb). Red shows when they were unrelated (e.g., lamp → comb). Observers were faster when primed by related objects or scenes. This still worked for the textures made from scenes, but not for the object textures, showing that a scene texture is like a scene.

Memory for Objects and Scenes Is Amazingly Good

The representation of scenes generated by information from the selective and nonselective pathways is very powerful. First, it gives rise to our perception of a world full of coherent objects in a coherent scene, even before we have a chance to attend to most of those objects. Second, it is easily stored in memory. Have a look at **Figure 7.33**. It contains photographs of 16 scenes. Spend about one second on each scene, and then flip the page to view **Figure 7.34**. There you will find another set of 16 scenes. Your job is to determine which 8 of the 16 in Figure 7.34 you saw in Figure 7.33. You probably won't need the answer key (it's in the figure). It is likely that you will correctly classify 14 or more of the images

Figure 7.33 Spend a second or two looking at each of these pictures. Then move on to Figure 7.34.

Figure 7.34 Without referring back to Figure 7.33, try to identify which of these pictures you already saw. Decide whether each picture is "old" or "new." You can check your answers on the grid to the left. The shaded squares show the locations of old pictures.

as "old" or "new." That's pretty quick learning of fairly complicated stimuli. Yet it is a mere fraction of what you could do if you had the time and we had the pictures. Roger Shepard (1967) conducted the original version of the test with 612 pictures and found that his observers were 98% correct. They were 90% correct when quizzed a week later. Standing, Conezio, and Haber (1970) got 85% accuracy after showing their observers 2500 pictures for 2 seconds apiece, and Standing (1973) later obtained similar results with 10,000(!) images.

In his studies, Standing used a diverse collection of scenes clipped from magazines of the time. Consider what might happen if we restricted the "scenes" to single objects (an apple, a backpack) or if we included other examples of these objects in the test set (Did I see *that* apple?) or, worse yet, if we used the same objects in different poses (Was that backpack lying down before?). Aude Oliva and her students (Brady et al., 2008) tried this with 2500 objects. When asked to pick between an old item and a new one, their observers got 92% correct if the new item was an object of a type that had not been seen before in the experiment. Amazingly, observers were still 88% correct at remembering which example of a category they had seen and 87% correct at remembering which state of a specific object they had seen, though some images were more memorable than others (Bylinskii et al., 2015).

But, Memory for Objects and Scenes Can Be Amazingly Bad: Change Blindness

From the findings just described, we could conclude that pictures can be understood very rapidly and that, given enough time—perhaps a few seconds—we can code them into memory in sufficient detail to be able to recognize them days later. But don't endorse that conclusion too quickly. In the 1990s, Ron Rensink and his colleagues introduced a different sort of picture memory experiment (Rensink, O'Regan, and Clark, 1997). They showed observers just one picture at a time. The observers would look at the picture for a while, and then it would vanish for 80 ms and would be replaced by a similar image. The observer's task was to determine what had changed. The two versions of the same image would flip back and forth, separated by a brief interval in which a blank screen was presented, until the observer spotted the change or time ran out. A static version of the task is illustrated in **Figure 7.35**. Try to find the differences between the two pictures in this figure. The answers are in **Figure 7.36**. You can also try detecting changes in some flicker movies in **Web Activity 7.5: Change Blindness**.

It may have taken you a while to discover all four changes in Figure 7.35. That's what happened in Rensink's experiment: participants took several seconds on average to find the changes, and some never managed the task at all in the time they were given. This phenomenon is known as **change blindness**. If the blank screen between the two images is removed, the changes are obvious because observers experience a kind of apparent-motion effect (see Chapter 8) when an object changes position, disappears, or changes color. But once we've taken

change blindness The failure to notice a change between two scenes. If the gist, or meaning, of the scene is not altered, quite large changes can pass unnoticed.

Figure 7.35 There are four differences between these two images. Can you find them?

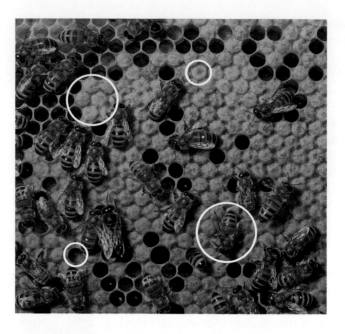

Figure 7.36 Here are the locations of the differences between the two images in Figure 7.35. When you go back to Figure 7.35 with this information, you will have no trouble seeing what was altered.

care of that low-level factor by inserting the blank screen, viewers can be quite oblivious to jet engines that vanish from airplanes, branches that jump from tree to tree, and boats that change color.

Actually, we can eliminate the need for a blank screen if the change is made while the eyes are moving. We are virtually blind during an abrupt (saccadic) eye movement. McConkie and Currie (1996) took advantage of this fact to make dramatic changes in a scene while an observer was just looking around. If they made the changes while the eye was in motion, observers often failed to notice.

FURTHER DISCUSSION FURTHER DISCUSSION of eye movements can be found in Chapter 8 starting on page 272.

It is not immediately obvious how these various facts can all be true of the same visual system. This is a topic of current controversy in the field. How can we remember thousands of objects after a mere second or two of viewing? And if we can do that, how can we fail to notice substantive change in a picture that is right in front of us? Does it make any sense that we remember the picture but seem oblivious to important details?

What Do We Actually See?

In the 1990s, Dan Simons and Dan Levin (1997) conducted a weird experiment on the streets of Ithaca, New York. One experimenter asked an unsuspecting passerby for directions. While the passerby was giving those directions, a couple of other people carried a door down the street and between the passerby and the experimenter. While the door was moving by, the experimenter ducked down, sneaked away, and was replaced by a second experimenter. Then the door was gone down the street, and the critical question was whether the passerby would return to giving instructions. In many cases, the passerby did just that, as if the change in experimenter had gone unnoticed. How could that be? Perhaps this change was undetected because it didn't change the gist of the scene. The passerby might think, "I'm giving instructions to a guy. Now there is this weird door. Now I'm giving instructions to a guy again" and simply never register that the *guy* changed. See "The Colour Changing Card Trick" in **Web Activity 7.5: Change Blindness** for another example, and see **Web Activity 7.6: The Attentional Bottleneck** for a much simpler version of change blindness that can be used in experiments.

To make this into a more convincing theory, it would help if we really understood what the "gist" of a scene might be. Gist is clearly more than the brief verbal description we might give if asked to "describe the gist." Look at **Figure 7.37**. Now look at **Figure 7.38** and decided which one of these two photographs is the same as Figure 7.37. You can probably do this quite easily, even though the gist descriptions of Figures 7.38A and B would be very similar: rowers in a boat on a sunny day. There is something about "gist" that we cannot trivially put into words. We have already suggested what that something might be. The nonselective pathway (see Figure 7.27) gives us some sort of texture of *ensemble statistics* across the entire visual field. Combining that rough representation with a stream of objects recognized by way of the selective pathway, we *infer* a coherent world, filled with recognized objects (Cohen, Dennett, and Kanwisher, 2016). This act of inference allows us to experience a full-color, in-focus, three-dimensional scene filled with clearly identifiable objects. We do not have a perceptual experience of a few objects, floating in a sea of ensemble statistics. We know, from the research described in other chapters, that this experience must be a construction of the mind, not an exact copy of the stimulus. We know from Chapter 2 that the world is decently focused only at the fovea and that high-resolution processing occurs only in the central 1 degree or so of the visual field. We will see in Chapter 8 that the scene before us is smeared across the retina three or four times each second as we move our eyes. We know from Chapter 6 that we're actually getting two slightly different copies of the scene from our two retinas, and that both copies are really two-dimensional.

Over and over in this book, we say that a particular aspect of perception is an inference, a guess about the world. Our conscious experience of the world is the mother of all inferences. This realization is hard for us to accept, because perception doesn't *feel* like an inference about what is. It feels like it must be showing us what's really out there. It feels like Truth. Phenomena like change blindness are important because they show us the gap between perception and reality. Experiments investigating change blindness show us that we don't see all of what *is* there. Rather, in some spots, we see what *was* there

Figure 7.37 Look at this picture for a couple of seconds. Describe it to yourself in a sentence. Then look at Figure 7.38.

(A)

(B)

Figure 7.38 Which of these two images is the one you saw in Figure 7.37? You probably know, even though your verbal description of the new image would be very similar to the description you gave for Figure 7.37. Apparently, the gist of a scene contains more than is captured by our usual verbal descriptions.

when we last paid attention, and even then we may not remember it perfectly (Irwin, Zacks, and Brown, 1990). In other spots we perceive what we think should be there (see **Web Essay 7.2: Boundary Extension**). Moreover, we may not perceive what we do not expect to see—what does not fit with the current inference. This failure to notice the unexpected is an example of **inattentional blindness**. The great example of inattentional blindness comes from another experiment of Dan Simons, this time in collaboration with Christopher Chabris. They had observers keeping track of ball movements in a basketball passing game. Many of these participants failed to notice an actor in a gorilla suit who wandered into the middle of the scene, waved, and wandered off (Simons and Chabris, 1999).

Outside the lab, the bottleneck between the world and our perception is not usually much of a problem, because the world is a pretty stable and predictable place—at least on a moment-to-moment basis. If you put your coffee mug down on the desk and turn your attention to the computer screen, the mug will be there when you choose to attend to it again. Only in the lab does the coffee mug vanish during an eye movement. This means that the physical world can serve as an "external memory" that backs up the perceptual world we create in our minds (O'Regan, 1992).

When the world does change, it usually changes in very predictable ways. If we've just driven past Second Avenue and then Third Avenue, we probably don't need to look at the next street sign to know that it says "Fourth Avenue." At a rate of about 20 objects per second, we can monitor the relevant items in this relatively stable world and be reasonably sure that we are up-to-date. And if something surprising does occur (a gorilla leaps into the middle of Fourth Avenue, for example), the event will probably be marked by a visual transient that grabs our attention so that we can update our internal representation pretty quickly and maintain our grasp on reality (Yantis, 1993). (See **Web Essay 7.3: Attentional Capture**.)

A certain amount of work needs to be done in order to induce us to miss gorillas. Still, we should not feel too complacent about our inference of the perceptual world. Let's end with two examples. In an odd version of the gorilla experiment, Drew, Vo, and Wolfe (2013) put the image of a gorilla in a CT image of a lung (**Figure 7.39**). Most radiologists, looking for small, white, round signs

inattentional blindness A failure to notice—or at least to report—a stimulus that would be easily reportable if it were attended.

of lung cancer, missed the big, black, shaggy gorilla. This shows, among other things, that experts are faced with the same attentional limits on perception as the rest of us. They have learned to do remarkable things with their visual systems, but the system is still the same system. Finally, let us consider eyewitness testimony. The basic assumption of eyewitness testimony is that you can report what *was* there, not what you inferred, guessed, hoped, or feared was there. Sadly, if unsurprisingly, we know that eyewitness testimony is subject to the same sorts of effects discussed here and that these factors are probably the cause of errors with real consequences (G. L. Wells and Olson, 2003). In an effort to illustrate this point, Chabris and Simons (2011) gave people the task of following a jogger down a track and found that those observers could easily fail to notice a very visible apparent beating that was occurring along their route. The researchers picked this particular scenario because of a real case in which a policeman reported that, as he chased a suspect, he never saw his colleagues beating another man. At the time, people didn't believe that he could have been so blind. Now you know that such a scenario is, at least, possible.

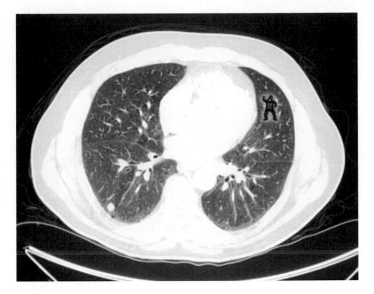

Figure 7.39 Radiologists tended to miss a gorilla in the lung, not because they were poor radiologists, but because even experts must perform their expert acts of attention and perception within the capacity limits of the human visual system. (From Drew, Vo, and Wolfe, 2013.)

Summary

1. Attention is a vital aspect of perception because we cannot process all of the input from our senses. The term *attention* refers to a large set of selective mechanisms that enable us to focus on some stimuli at the expense of others. Though this chapter talked almost exclusively about visual attention, attentional mechanisms exist in all sensory domains.

2. In vision, it is possible to direct attention to one location or one object. If something happens at an attended location, we will be faster to respond to it. It can be useful to refer to the "spotlight" of attention, though deployments of attention differ in important ways from movements of a spotlight.

3. In visual search tasks, observers typically look for a target item among a number of distractor items. If the target is defined by a salient basic feature, such as its color or orientation, search is very efficient and the number of distractors has little influence on the reaction time (the time required to find the target). If no basic feature information can guide the deployment of attention, then search is inefficient, as if each item needed to be examined one after the other. Search can be of intermediate efficiency if some feature information is available (e.g., if we're looking for a red car, we don't need to examine the blue objects in the parking lot).

4. Search for objects in real scenes is guided by the known features of the objects, by the salient features in the scenes, and by a variety of scene-based forms of guidance. For example, if you're looking for your can of soda, you will guide your attention to physically plausible locations (horizontal surfaces) and logically sensible places (the desk or counter, probably not the floor).

Go to the
Sensation & Perception
Companion Website at
oup.com/us/wolfe5e
for chapter overviews, activities, essays, flashcards, and other study aids.
Go to **DASHBOARD** for additional resources and assessments.

5. Attention varies over time as well as space. In the attentional blink paradigm, observers search for two items in a rapid stream of stimuli that appear at the point of fixation. Attention to the first target makes it hard to find the second if the second appears within 200–500 ms of the first. When two identical items appear in the stream of stimuli, a different phenomenon makes it hard to detect the second instance.

6. The effects of attention manifest themselves in several different ways in the brain. In some cases, attention is marked by a general increase in neural activity or by a greater correlation between activity in different brain areas. In other cases, attention to a particular attribute tunes cells more sharply for that attribute. And in still other cases, attention to a stimulus or location causes receptive fields to shrink so as to exclude unattended stimuli. It can also result in reduced correlation between neighboring cells as different cells begin to analyze different aspects of a stimulus. Many of these effects might be the result of a single, underlying normalization process.

7. Damage to the parietal lobe of the brain produces deficits in visual attention. Damage to the right parietal lobe can lead to neglect, a disorder in which it is hard to direct attention into the contralesional (in this case, the left) visual field. People with neglect may ignore half of an object or half of their own body.

8. Scene perception involves both selective and nonselective processing. Tasks like visual search make extensive use of selective processing to recognize specific objects. Nonselective processing allows observers to appreciate the mean and variance of features across many objects (or proto-objects). Thus, you know the average orientation of trees in the woods (vertical) before knowing whether any particular tree is oriented perfectly vertically. Using these ensemble statistics, even without segmenting the scene into regions and objects, the nonselective pathway can provide information about the gist of a scene (e.g., whether it's natural or man-made).

9. Picture memory experiments show that people can remember thousands of images after only a second or two of exposure to each. In contrast, change blindness experiments show that people can miss large changes in scenes if those changes do not markedly alter the meaning of the scene.

10. Our perceptual experience of scenes consists of nonselective processing of the layout and ensemble statistics of the scene, combined with selective processing of a very few objects at each moment. However, the final experience is an inference based on all of the preceding processing, not merely the sum of that processing. Usually this inference is adequate because we can rapidly check the world to determine whether the chair, the book, and the desk are still there. In the lab, however, we can use phenomena like inattentional blindness and change blindness to reveal the limits of our perception, and it is becoming increasingly clear that those limits can have real-world consequences.

8 Visual Motion Perception

■ Questions to Contemplate ■

Think about the following questions as you read this chapter. By the chapter's end, you should be able to answer and discuss them.

- Is motion a fundamental perceptual dimension?

- How is it that the world stands still when we move our eyes?

- What do beetles, flies, and humans have in common?

- How do the movies create the perception of objects in motion?

Like any self-respecting ladybug, the one in **Figure 8.1** flits around from leaf to leaf. At Time 1 it is on the lowermost leaf; at Time 2 it has moved to the middle leaf. Our visual system distinguishes the bug by a number of features, such as its shape, its location in space, and its color. Previous chapters have established these features as fundamental perceptual dimensions: characteristics of visual stimuli that are directly encoded by neurons fairly early in the visual system.

Is the ladybug's motion also a fundamental perceptual dimension? At first glance, we might think not. After all, motion is really just a change in an object's location over time. If we already have neural mechanisms set up to determine position, why go to the extra expense of adding more low-level machinery to process motion?

Though the added investment might seem unnecessary, consider this question from the position of the primordial vertebrates that "invented" the visual system we eventually inherited. Many bugs move pretty quickly, so if we depend on catching them for our supper, fast detection of their direction of motion will be important to our survival. Similarly, if other animals are trying to catch us for their supper, we need to be adept at detecting the motion of these predators, too. In Chapter 6 we saw that motion parallax is an important cue for depth perception. And from a more modern perspective, it would be hard to believe that hockey goalies, baseball

Sarah Holbrook, Untitled photograph from the *Driving Home* collection, 2013

batters facing knuckleball pitchers, and boxers trying to avoid being pummeled by their opponents could do their jobs without having a mechanism for very quickly determining and predicting the movements of pucks, balls, and fists.

Motion Aftereffects

In fact, we've already seen some strong indications that motion is a low-level perceptual phenomenon—in Chapter 3, where we learned that many cells in the primary visual cortex selectively respond to motion in one particular direction. A phenomenon called the waterfall illusion provides another piece of evidence that there is something special about motion. Here's how Robert Addams (1834) described this illusion after a visit to the waterfall of Foyers (**Figure 8.2**):

> Having steadfastly looked for a few seconds at a particular part of the cascade, admiring the confluence and decussation of the currents forming the liquid drapery of waters, and then suddenly directed my eyes to the left, to observe the face of the sombre age-worn rocks immediately contiguous to the water-fall, I saw the rocky surface as if in motion upwards, and with an apparent velocity equal to that of the descending water, which the moment before had prepared my eyes to behold that singular deception.

Time 1

Time 2

Figure 8.1 Motion is a change in position over time, as the movements of this ladybug demonstrate.

The "deception" that Addams described—which had also been noted by Aristotle (384–322 BCE)—was later dubbed the **motion aftereffect** (**MAE**). After viewing motion in a constant direction for a sustained period of time (at least 15 seconds or so), we see any stationary objects that we view subsequently (like the rocks around the waterfall) as moving in the opposite direction. This phenomenon may seem a lot like the color aftereffects we studied in Chapter 5, and that's no coincidence. Just as color aftereffects are caused by opponent processes for color vision, MAEs are caused by opponent processes for motion detection. We'll discuss these processes below.

We know that the monkey brain is very similar to the human brain, but it is always nice to establish converging evidence suggesting that results from monkey labs apply to human vision as well. In the case of motion perception, researchers have looked for this evidence using the motion aftereffect. As noted earlier, the existence of the MAE implies an opponent-process system much like the one that plays a role in color vision. Neurons tuned to different directions of motion generally do not respond to a stationary object, so they simply continue to fire at their spontaneous rate, and the spontaneous rates for upward- and downward-sensitive cells are normally balanced. That is, neurons sensitive to upward motion fire at about the same rate as neurons sensitive to downward motion, so the signals cancel out and no motion is perceived. But when we look at a waterfall for a prolonged period, the detectors sensitive to downward motion become adapted. When we then switch our gaze to a stationary object, such as the rocks next to the waterfall, the neurons sensitive to upward motion fire faster than the adapted downward-sensitive neurons, and we therefore perceive the rocks as drifting up.

Figure 8.2 The lower falls of Foyers.

motion aftereffect (MAE) The illusion of motion of a stationary object that occurs after prolonged exposure to a moving object.

You might wonder why *any* motion detectors would fire in response to a stationary rock, but as we will see in a bit, our eyes are constantly drifting around, so there is always a small amount of retinal motion to stimulate motion detectors at least slightly. You might also wonder what happens when we adapt to downward motion and then see something moving horizontally. Make a prediction, and then test your hypothesis using **Web Activity 8.1: Motion Aftereffects**.

Here's another experiment to try with this web activity: adapt for 15 seconds or so to rightward motion with your right eye open but your left eye closed, and then quickly switch eyes, closing your right eye and opening your left. You should experience an aftereffect that is only slightly reduced in magnitude compared with the aftereffect you get with both eyes open the whole time. What does this **interocular transfer** tell us about the locus of the MAE in the visual system? Could motion aftereffects be subserved by neurons in the retinas? What about neurons in the lateral geniculate nucleus (LGN)?

The fact that a strong MAE is obtained when one eye is adapted and the other tested means that the effect must be reflecting the activities of neurons in a part of the visual system where information collected from the two eyes is combined (Raymond, 1993). As we learned in Chapter 3, input from both eyes is not combined until the primary visual cortex (V1), where neurons show a preference for input from one eye or another but respond to some extent to stimuli in both eyes. Recent advances in functional imaging techniques may make it possible to locate the site of motion aftereffects even more precisely. The emerging evidence suggests that the MAE in humans is caused by the same brain region shown to be responsible for global-motion detection in monkeys: the **middle temporal area** of the cortex, an area commonly referred to as **MT** or V5. For example, David Heeger and colleagues (Huk, Ress, and Heeger, 2001), after controlling for the important effects of attention, demonstrated that the direction-selective adaptation produced a selective imbalance in the functional magnetic resonance imaging (fMRI) signal in human MT, providing evidence that MAEs are due to a population imbalance in area MT. Remarkably, more recent work shows that MAEs can occur even after very brief exposures—as little as 25 milliseconds—and that these can be explained by direction-selective responses of neurons in MT to subsequently presented stationary stimuli (Glasser et al., 2011).

> **FURTHER DISCUSSION** of the role of the primary visual cortex (V1) in combining input from both eyes can be found in Chapter 3 on page 81.

The waterfall illusion is just one of many motion illusions. Akiyoshi Kitaoka's art shows other powerful illusions of motion (see www.ritsumei.ac.jp/~akitaoka/index-e.html and **Web Essay 8.1: Perceiving Motion in Static Images**). Kitaoka's pictures are stationary on the page, but they can produce a strong illusion of motion if you allow your eyes to drift across them. How does this work? We don't yet have a consensus, but studies suggest that patterns like Kitaoka's *Rollers* elicit directional responses from neurons in monkey cortex that correspond closely to the directions perceived by humans (Conway et al., 2005).

Computation of Visual Motion

What are the minimum requirements for an effective motion detector? Because motion involves a change in position over time, a logical place to start is with two adjacent receptors (call them neurons A and B) separated by a fixed distance. Getting back to ladybugs, a bug (or a spot of light) moving from left to

interocular transfer The transfer of an effect (such as adaptation) from one eye to the other.

middle temporal area (MT) An area of the brain thought to be important in the perception of motion. Also called V5 in humans.

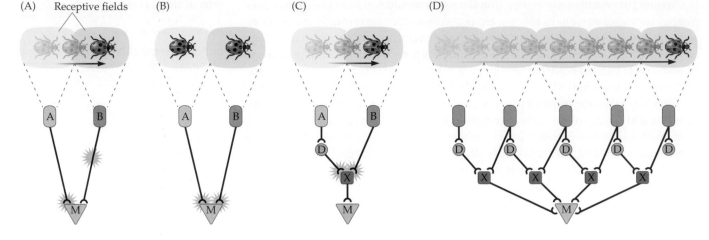

(A) Receptive fields   (B)   (C)   (D)

Figure 8.3 Constructing a neural circuit for the detection of rightward motion. See the text for details.

right would first pass through neuron A's receptive field, and then a short time later it would enter neuron B's receptive field (**Figure 8.3A**). In theory, a third cell that "listens" to neurons A and B should be able to detect this movement.

However, our motion detection cell (call it M) cannot simply add up excitatory inputs from A and B. Given such a neural circuit, M would fire in response to the moving bug, but it would also respond to two stationary bugs, one in each receptive field (**Figure 8.3B**). To solve this problem, we need two additional components in our neural circuit, as shown in **Figure 8.3C**. The first new cell, labeled D in the figure, receives input from neuron A and delays transmission of this input for a short period of time. Cell D also has a fast adaptation rate. That is, it fires when cell A initially detects light, but it quickly stops firing if the light remains shining on A's receptive field. Cells B and D are then connected to neuron X, a multiplication cell. This multiplication cell will fire only when both cells B and D are active. By delaying receptor A's response (D) and then multiplying it by receptor B's response (X), we can create a mechanism that is sensitive to motion (M). Note that in this scheme, for each B and D pair, there is one X neuron.

This mechanism would be direction-selective: it would respond well to motion from left to right, but not from right to left. A bug moving from cell B's receptive field into cell A's receptive field would cause B and D to fire in the wrong order, so X would not receive its two inputs simultaneously, and M would not fire. The mechanism would also be tuned to speed because when the bug moved at just the right speed, the delayed response from receptor A and the direct response from receptor B would occur at the same time and therefore reinforce each other. If the bug moved too fast or too slow, the outputs from B and D would be out of sync. This simple "bug" motion detector is based on a model initially developed by Werner Reichardt in the 1950s to explain how beetles and flies detect motion (Reichardt, 1986). Almost all models of human motion detection are, at their core, elaborations of Werner Reichardt's model adapted to the spatial-frequency filtering properties of the human visual system (see Chapter 3). Indeed, much of our current understanding about motion processing derives from studies of insects.

One elaboration, developed by Barlow and Levick (1965), uses what electrical engineers would call an "AND gate." Cell X fires if and only if *both* its inputs (B and D) are firing simultaneously, and it passes this message on to the motion detection cell M. The AND concept is almost certainly not correct, and a more elaborate version—developed by Adelson and Bergen (1985) and based on linear filters that delay, sum, and then are followed by nonlinearities—seems closer to the "truth." In **Web Activity 8.2: Motion Detection Circuit**, which presents a more elaborate version of this neural circuit, you can interactively move spots of light around and see how it works.

A more realistic circuit would include additional receptors to detect longer-range motion, as shown in **Figure 8.3D**. Here, the M cell fires continually as the bug moves across the fields of the five receptors at the top of the circuit. If you were the "circuit designer," how would you change the speed tuning of this circuit?

Apparent Motion

One possible objection to the Reichardt model is that it does not, in fact, require continuous motion in order to fire. An image of a bug that appears in A's receptive field, then disappears, and then reappears in B's receptive field a short time later will drive M to respond just as strongly as if the image had moved smoothly across the two receptive fields. Although it raises a valid concern, this observation turns out to be a virtue rather than a liability for the Reichardt model, because it provides an excellent explanation for a visual illusion, called apparent motion, that modern humans experience on a daily basis.

Apparent motion was first demonstrated by Sigmund Exner in 1875. Exner set up a contraption that would generate electrical sparks separated from each other by a very short distance in space and a very short period of time. Even though there were two separate sparks—that is, two different perceptual objects—observers swore that they saw a single spark moving from one position to another.

We in the twenty-first century experience apparent motion every time we watch television, go to a movie, or use a computer. You are probably aware that an animated cartoon is really a series of still drawings. Objects such as Daffy Duck (**Figure 8.4**) change positions each frame, and when the frames are

apparent motion   The illusory impression of smooth motion resulting from the rapid alternation of objects that appear in different locations in rapid succession.

Frame 1

Frame 2

Frame 3

Frame 4

Figure 8.4   Apparent motion on the screen. A series of still images played one after the other at a fast rate produces the apparent motion of cartoons, like this one of Daffy Duck impersonating Carmen Miranda, which includes these four stills in the Looney Tunes animation *Yankee Doodle Daffy*.

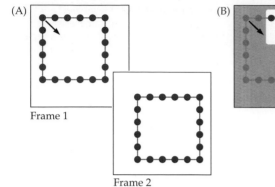

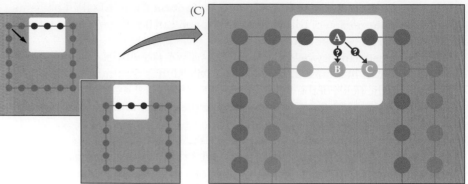

Figure 8.5 The correspondence problem. (A) The square moves down and to the right. (B) For a detector that "sees" just the contents of the white square, the motion is ambiguous. (C) What the detector sees is consistent with both motion straight down and motion down and to the right.

shown to us at a sufficiently fast speed (e.g., 30 frames per second), we perceive these position changes over time as motion. The Introduction section of **Web Activity 8.3: Types of Motion** shows the two frames in Figure 8.1 at a speed that makes it easy to infer motion. Live-action movies and television programs work in exactly the same way, except that the frames are still photographs rather than drawings.

The Correspondence Problem—Viewing through an Aperture

Although apparent motion turns out to be a win for our motion detection circuit, one of the classic perceptual "problems" that we've discussed over and over in this book remains an issue for the Reichardt model. We can illustrate this problem with the movies diagramed in **Figure 8.5**. Each movie has two frames that alternate back and forth. The only difference between the two frames is that the only object in the movie, the red square studded with small circles, has been shifted diagonally by a short distance. (These movies are animated in **Web Activity 8.3: Types of Motion**. Viewing the animations as you read this section will make the following discussion much clearer.)

If you view the first version of the movie (depicted in Figure 8.5A) on the website (click on "The Aperture Problem" and select "Movie 1"), you will clearly detect diagonal motion. This scenario appears to present no problem to our motion detector: the square moves down and to the right, and then back up and to the left, and detectors sensitive to these directions pick up and signal this movement. Now consider Movie 2 (depicted in Figure 8.5B), where we cover most of the square with a black "mask," leaving three of the circles viewable through a small window (an aperture—in the figure the mask is illustrated as transparent so that you can see what's behind it, but in the movie the mask is opaque). Beneath the mask, the square moves exactly as before, but if you view the movie, you will quite clearly perceive up-and-down, *not* diagonal, motion! (You will need to view the animation to appreciate the difference in the motion perceived in the two movies.)

The larger issue that these movies bring up is called the **correspondence problem** for motion detection. Consider the close-up view of the situation in Figure 8.5B, shown in Figure 8.5C. Here we superimposed the two frames, coloring the circles blue in their Frame 1 positions and green in their Frame 2 positions. The difficulty for our motion detection system is this: how does it know which

correspondence problem In reference to motion detection, the problem faced by the motion detection system of knowing which feature in Frame 2 corresponds to a particular feature in Frame 1.

circles in Frame 2 correspond to which circles in Frame 1? Because we have motion detectors for all directions, one detector will sense the diagonal motion implied by matching the circle labeled A in Figure 8.5C with the circle labeled C. But another detector will sense the vertical motion implied by matching circle A with circle B. These detectors compete to determine our overall perception. (You can see some other demonstrations of the correspondence problem in **Web Activity 8.4: Motion Correspondence**.)

> **FURTHER DISCUSSION** of correspondence as it relates to stereoscopic depth perception can be found in Chapter 6 starting on page 200.

An important example of the correspondence problem is known as the **aperture problem**. It gets its name from the fact that a different detector may win this competition when an object is viewed through an aperture than would win if we could see the whole object. Consider the demonstration illustrated in **Figure 8.6** and in Movie 5 of "The Aperture Problem" in **Web Activity 8.3: Types of Motion**. Here the object is a grating moving behind a window, which is referred to as the **aperture**. The motion direction of the grating is ambiguous—the grating could be moving up and to the left (perpendicular to the stripes, but diagonally overall) (Figure 8.6A), but it could also be moving just up (Figure 8.6B) or just to the left (Figure 8.6C). The motion component parallel to the grating cannot be inferred from the visual input (because there are no perpendicular contours or features on the grating). This means that a variety of contours of different orientations moving at different speeds can cause identical responses in a motion-sensitive neuron in the visual system. Without the aperture, there's no ambiguity and no problem. But when we view the grating through the aperture, the system appears to impose some kind of shortest-distance constraint, and thus the vertical-motion detector wins.

At this point you may be thinking it's rather silly to claim that an artificial situation such as the one we've set up here poses a broad challenge to the visual system. After all, how often is our view of a moving object limited to a small window as in the examples presented here? To understand the broader implications of the correspondence and aperture problems, consider the fact that every neuron in V1 has a limited receptive field. In other words, *every V1 cell sees the world through a small aperture*. Therefore, as **Figure 8.7** illustrates, none of the V1 cells (represented in the figure as gray triangles) can tell with certainty which visual elements correspond to one another when an object moves, even when no mask is present.

aperture problem The fact that when a moving object is viewed through an aperture (or a receptive field), the direction of motion of a local feature or part of the object may be ambiguous.

aperture An opening that allows only a partial view of an object.

(A)   (B)   (C)

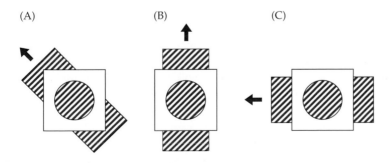

Figure 8.6 The aperture problem. The contents of the circle are the same in (A), (B), and (C), even though the physical motion is quite different.

Figure 8.7 Building a global-motion detector. See the text for details.

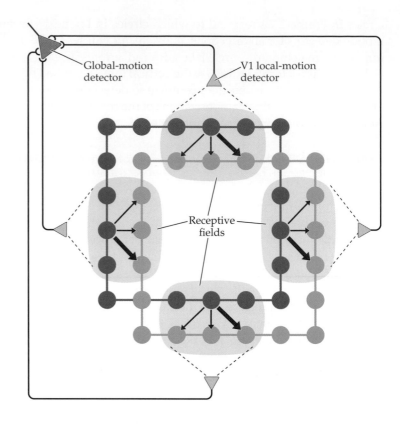

The solution to this problem is to have another set of neurons listen to the V1 neurons and integrate the potentially conflicting signals. As Figure 8.7 shows, only one direction—down and to the right—is consistent with what all four V1 cells are seeing here, and this is the direction we perceive when we see the object as a whole. If the neuron represented by the orange triangle in the figure has access to all the V1 cells detecting local-motion directions, it will be in a position to compare their outputs and find this common denominator. Of course, we haven't specified *how* this global-motion detector performs this comparison, but that question would lead us beyond the scope of this book.

As Duje Tadin from the University of Rochester points out, the aperture problem is like the Indian parable about the blind men and the elephant. In one version of this parable, the king asks six blind men to determine what an elephant looks like by feeling different parts of the elephant's body. The first blind man feels a leg and says the elephant is like a pillar; the second feels the tail and says the elephant is like a rope; the third feels the trunk and says the elephant is like a branch; the fourth feels the ear and likens the elephant to a fan; the fifth feels the belly and says the elephant is like a wall; and the sixth feels the tusk and says the elephant is like a solid pipe. The king explains to them, "You are all correct. The reason each of you is telling it differently is because each one of you touched a different part of the elephant. But, in fact the elephant has all the features you mentioned." In the aperture problem, each of the V1 cells is a blind man, and the correct answer comes from combining their responses.

Detection of Global Motion in Area MT

Though a discussion of how global-motion detectors work would be too broad for this text, we can say something about *where* the global-motion detectors are. We saw in Chapter 3 that lesions to the magnocellular layers of the LGN

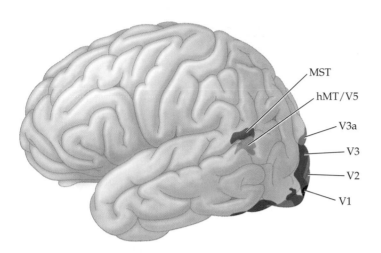

Figure 8.8 Motion-sensitive areas in the human brain. The middle temporal area (hMT/V5, green) and medial superior temporal area (MST, turquoise) are shown in relation to other visual areas (V1, V2, V3, and V3a). (After Heeger, 2006.)

MST

hMT/V5

V3a

V3

V2

V1

impair the perception of large, rapidly moving objects. Information from magnocellular neurons feeds into V1 and is then passed on to (among other places) the middle temporal area of the cortex, an area commonly referred to as MT in nonhuman primates, and then to the medial superior temporal area, MST. MT and MST are considered to be the hub for motion processing (Ilg, Vision Research, 2008). The human equivalent of MT has been localized using fMRI and variously labeled as hMT+, or V5 (**Figure 8.8**). Recent work suggests that this motion-sensitive area may have at least two separate maps located on the lateral surface at the temporal-occipital (TO) boundary. The vast majority of neurons in the MT are selective for motion in one particular direction, but they show little selectivity for form or color. But do these MT cells correspond to the orange neuron in Figure 8.7, which responds to large-scale motion of whole objects, or are they more like the low-level motion detectors represented by the gray triangles in Figure 8.7?

To find out, Newsome and Pare (1988) trained a group of monkeys to respond to correlated-dot-motion displays (**Figure 8.9**). In Figure 8.9A, all the dots (100%) are moving to the right. In Figure 8.9B, 50% of the dots have correlated motion (they are moving in the same direction), while the motion of the rest of the dots is uncorrelated (these dots are moving in random directions). In Figure 8.9C, only 20% of the dots have correlated motion. Just as in the aperture problem demonstration, no single dot in these displays is sufficient to determine the overall direction of correlated motion. So, to detect the correlated direction, a neuron must integrate information from many local-motion detectors. (Note that in the actual stimuli, all dots are the same color and no arrows are present.) You can get a much better feel for what Newsome and Pare's monkeys were

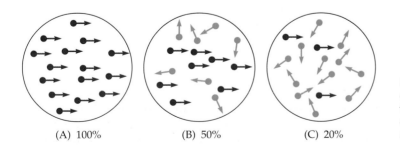

(A) 100%   (B) 50%   (C) 20%

Figure 8.9 The Newsome and Pare paradigm, initially described by Williams and Sekuler (1984). The observer's task is to identify the direction of motion of the correlated dots, shown in purple here. (In the actual stimuli the dots are not colored and there are no arrows.)

experiencing by visiting the "Correlated-Dot Motion" section of **Web Activity 8.3: Types of Motion**.

Once they were fully trained, the monkeys in Newsome and Pare's study could recognize the correlated-motion direction when only 2–3% of the dots were moving in this direction. The researchers then lesioned the monkeys' MT areas. Following the surgery, the monkeys needed about ten times as many correlated dots in order to correctly identify the direction of motion. However, the monkeys' ability to discriminate the orientation of stationary patterns was generally unimpaired. Interestingly, the monkeys' performance in the correlated-dot-motion task improved markedly during the weeks following the lesion, presumably because they learned to use other brain areas to discriminate motion.

Lesion studies have been central to our understanding of the specificity of brain areas. However, such studies are often less than completely compelling, because lesions (even "clean" chemical lesions, like those used by Newsome and Pare) may be incomplete or may influence other structures. To test the involvement of MT neurons in global-motion perception more directly, Newsome et al. trained a new group of monkeys to discriminate correlated-motion directions and then poked around in the monkeys' MT areas to find groups of neurons that responded to one particular direction (Salzman, Britten, and Newsome, 1990). Once they had found a group of neurons that responded, for example, to rightward motion, they showed the monkey a new set of stimuli and electrically stimulated the identified MT neurons. Remarkably, the monkeys showed a strong tendency to report motion in the stimulated neurons' preferred direction, even when the dots they were seeing were actually moving in the opposite direction! These results make a very strong case that the MT is critically involved in the processing of global motion.

Up to this point our discussion has focused on **first-order motion**—the change in position of **luminance-defined objects** over time. In the next section we describe another interesting motion phenomenon: **second-order motion**, in which **texture-defined objects**, also called **contrast-defined objects**, change position over time.

first-order motion The motion of an object that is defined by changes in luminance.

luminance-defined object An object that is delineated by differences in reflected light.

second-order motion The motion of an object that is defined by changes in contrast or texture, but not by luminance.

texture-defined object or **contrast-defined object** An object that is defined by differences in contrast, or texture, but not by luminance.

akinetopsia A rare neuropsychological disorder in which the affected individual has no perception of motion.

■ Sensation & Perception in Everyday Life ■

The Man Who Couldn't See Motion

Recall what it's like to experience a motion aftereffect. You stare at a waterfall and then shift your gaze to the cliff next to the falls. You know that the rocks are not moving, and you can see that they aren't actually going anywhere, yet you still experience an otherworldly sense of "disembodied" motion. (Review the phenomenon in **Web Activity 8.1: Motion Aftereffects** if you haven't tried it for a while.)

Now imagine the opposite experience: objects change position, and you are fully aware of these location shifts but you experience *no* perception of motion. As bizarre as it seems, this is exactly what happens in a rare neuropsychological disorder known as **akinetopsia**, described in the following case report (Horton and Trobe, 1999):

A 47-year-old man reported seeing streams of multiple, frozen images trailing in the wake of moving objects. As soon as motion ceased, the images collapsed into each other. He compared his vision to a scene lit by a flashing strobe, except that stationary elements were perceived normally. In fact, if nothing was in motion and he held perfectly still, his vision was entirely normal. The moment anything moved, however,

■ **Sensation & Perception in Everyday Life** *(continued)* ■

it left a stream of static copies in its path. For example, while out for an evening stroll, he saw a pack of identical dogs lined up behind his West Highland terrier. Driving was impossible because he was confused by multiple snapshots of cars, streets, and signs. Moving lights were followed by a long comet trail.

Another patient reported that when she watched her own arm moving, "passage of the limb would be reduplicated by multiple, fuzzy images, the way a cartoonist might draw motion."

Not surprisingly, akinetopsia appears to be caused by disruptions to V5, the area corre-

sponding to visual area MT. For the two patients described here, the disruptions were side effects of a prescription antidepressant drug, and their motion perception problems disappeared once they stopped taking the drug. In other cases, akinetopsia is brought on by direct trauma to area MT that is due to stroke or elective brain surgery (e.g., surgery to alleviate epileptic seizures). Patients in the latter category sometimes regain normal motion perception abilities several weeks after surgery, indicating that, as in Newsome's monkeys, the human brain can sometimes rearrange its connections so that different areas take over the MT's motion-processing functions.

Second-Order Motion

Second-order motion, illustrated in **Figure 8.10**, is an interesting phenomenon. The three frames in the figure look like collections of random black and white dots, which is what they are. But if you go to the website and look at the sequence of frames played as a movie, you will clearly perceive a set of leftward-moving stripes. (**Web Activity 8.3: Types of Motion** includes some additional frames that lead to the perception of an infinite loop in which the stripes move leftward off the edge of the movie and reappear on the right side.)

This movie is constructed from a combination of two patterns: a random collection of small white and black dots, and a series of wide white and black stripes. The patterns are overlaid and combined in such a way that dots covered by white bars are inverted (black dots turn white and vice versa), and dots covered by black bars are left alone. The frames of the movie are made by the process of shifting the bars to the left while the dots remain stationary. The resulting perception of movement is called second-order motion.

As in first-order apparent-motion displays, nothing actually moves in second-order motion. Even more incredibly, there is nothing *to* move in second-order

Frame 1   Frame 2   Frame 3

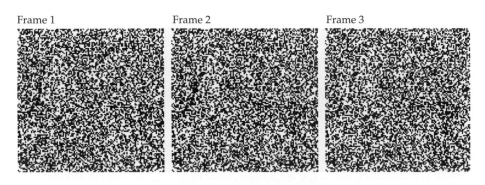

Figure 8.10 Second-order motion. If you try **Web Activity 8.3: Types of Motion**, you will quite clearly see stripes moving from right to left across the field of dots even though you cannot see the stripes in these static images. See the text for details.

Figure 8.11 Close-ups of one section of the frames in Figure 8.10, illustrating the changes from frame to frame.

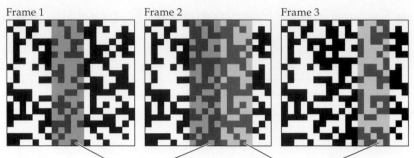

Frame 1   Frame 2   Frame 3

Inverted dots   Inverted dots

motion. As **Figure 8.11** shows, the only thing that changes in our second-order-motion movie is that strips of dots are inverted from one frame to another: from Frame 1 to Frame 2 the dots in the orange strip are inverted; then from Frame 2 to Frame 3 the dots in the blue strip are inverted. Just as random dot stereograms prove that matching discrete objects across the two eyes is not necessary for stereoscopic depth perception (see Chapter 6), second-order motion proves that matching discrete objects across movie frames is not necessary for motion perception.

Several lines of evidence suggest that the visual system includes specialized mechanisms for second-order motion. For example, Lucia Vaina and colleagues described one neurological patient who suffered brain damage that impaired the perception of first-order motion but not of second-order motion (Vaina and Cowey, 1996; Vaina et al., 1998). A second patient showed the opposite pattern: impaired second-order but spared first-order motion perception. These two patients had lesions in different brain areas, and together they demonstrate a **double dissociation** of function, which would not be possible if there were a single motion mechanism. Tim Ledgeway demonstrated a motion aftereffect for second-order motion and found that the second-order MAE transfers even more completely between eyes than does the first-order MAE (Ledgeway, 1994; Ledgeway and Smith, 1994).

Why did we evolve a motion detection system for something as esoteric as second-order motion? It turns out that second-order–like motion does occur in the real world, especially when an object is effectively camouflaged. This chapter's home page on the website shows a situation in which something like second-order motion makes an otherwise invisible object spring to life. (See also **Web Essay 8.2: Beyond Second-Order Motion**.)

Motion Induced Blindness (MIB)

While it may seem hard to believe, motion can make you temporarily blind! Bonneh, Cooperman, and Sagi (2001) discovered that if you carefully fixate a central target, stationary targets in the periphery will simply disappear, as if erased, when a global moving pattern is superimposed. You can check out this remarkably compelling illusion at www.michaelbach.de/ot/mot-mib.

While there is no clear explanation, MIB seems to be somewhat related to the well-known Troxler effect, in which an unchanging target in peripheral vision will fade and disappear if you steadily fixate a central target. This effect can be observed under conditions in which the retinal image is stabilized (or relatively stabilized when the target is in the periphery) so that the involuntary eye movements that occur during fixation (discussed below) do not move the target onto new receptive fields. The result is that the target is effectively not changing, and the underlying neurons become adapted.

double dissociation The phenomenon in which one of two functions, such as first- and second-order motion, can be damaged without harm to the other, and vice versa. See also Chapter 4.

Using Motion Information

Now that we know something about how the motion perception system works under the hood, let's consider some ways we might use motion information to interpret the world around us.

Going with the Flow: Using Motion Information to Navigate

For sighted people, getting around is easy. Our vision effortlessly guides our motion through space, whether we're walking or driving, so that we usually reach a destination quite safely. Indeed, safe navigation is one of the primary functions of the visual system. What information does the visual system use to help us navigate our way across a busy intersection? Or consider the challenge that confronts a pilot landing an airplane at high speed. In an attempt to improve World War II pilots' performance in such situations, J. J. Gibson (1957), who was working for the US Army at the time, developed an influential theory about the **optic array**, the collection of light rays that interact with objects in the world in front of a viewer. Some of these rays strike our retinas, enabling us to see. Gibson argued that when we move through our environment, we experience patterns of **optic flow** that our visual systems use to determine where we're going.

Consider a pilot coming in to land her plane. As the plane approaches the ground, the optic array will expand outward, in a pattern known as radial expansion (**Figure 8.12**). The pilot's heading—the specific point at which she is aiming her plane—will always be the center, or **focus of expansion**, of the optic array. As indicated in the figure, the focus of expansion is the one place in the visual field that will be stationary, so if the pilot's visual system can locate this stationary point, it can determine the heading. (For a relevant demonstration, see **Web Activity 8.3: Types of Motion**.)

Gibson was able to derive a number of optic flow heuristics that the visual system might use to navigate around the world. At the most basic level, the mere presence of optic flow indicates locomotion, and a lack of flow is a signal that you are stationary. If you have ever been sitting in a stationary train at a busy railroad station when the train beside you moves, you may have experienced a situation in which optic flow alone gives you the illusion that you (rather than the neighboring train) are in motion. Outflow (flow toward the periphery, as depicted in Figure 8.12) indicates that you are approaching a particular destination; inflow indicates retreat (assuming that your head is facing forward). And the focus of expansion, mentioned already, or focus of constriction if you're looking forward while driving in reverse, tells you where you're going to or coming from.

Are humans actually able to make use of optic flow information? Laboratories like Bill Warren's have used elaborate computer-generated displays of moving dots and lines to simulate optic flow information, and they have made a good deal of progress in understanding both the utility and complexity of optic flow information. For example, Warren, Morris, and Kalish (1988) demonstrated that humans could estimate their direction of heading to within about 1 or 2 degrees, using as their sole guide the pattern of optic flow simulated by the moving dots, even when the display contained only a very small number of dots.

Of course, the nice clean optic flow pattern diagramed in Figure 8.12 occurs only if the head and eyes remain fixed and pointed straight ahead. As soon as gaze shifts to one side, a new radial component is introduced to the optic flow. However, Warren showed that observers were able to discount these radial components, both when the observers moved their own eyes and when the computer-generated display mimicked the radial flow caused by an eye movement (W. H. Warren and Hannon, 1990). If the radial shift is relatively slow, observers

optic array The collection of light rays that interact with objects in the world that are in front of a viewer. The term was coined by J. J. Gibson.

optic flow The changing angular positions of points in a perspective image that we experience as we move through the world.

focus of expansion The point in the center of the horizon from which, when we're in motion (e.g., driving on the highway), all points in the perspective image seem to emanate. The focus of expansion is one aspect of optic flow.

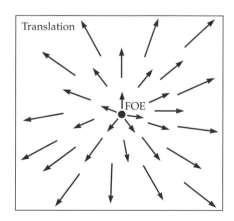

Figure 8.12 The optic flow field produced by movement forward in space. FOE = focus of expansion. (After W. H. Warren and Saunders, 1995.)

time to collision (TTC) The time required for a moving object (such as a cricket ball) to hit a stationary object (such as a batsman's head). TTC = distance / rate.

tau (τ) Information in the optic flow that could signal time to collision (TTC) without the necessity of estimating either absolute distances or rates. The ratio of the retinal image size at any moment to the rate at which the image is expanding is tau, and TTC is proportional to tau.

can compensate for simulated eye movements just as readily as they do for real eye movements; but with faster simulated eye movement speeds, performance breaks down (Royden, Banks, and Crowell, 1992). This result implies that the visual system can make use of the copies of eye muscle signals when it is processing optic flow information. We'll discuss this notion later, in the section titled "Saccadic Suppression and the Comparator."

Avoiding Imminent Collision: The Tao of Tau

In cricket, as in so much of life, the object is to keep your eye on the ball and to stay out of trouble. Indeed, much of our visual apparatus may be designed to do just that. The batsman shown in **Figure 8.13** evidently did not keep his eye on the ball. Luckily, accidents like this are not too common, because cricketers are extremely good at judging precisely when a tiny ball, hurtling toward them at speeds approaching 100 miles per hour, is about to collide with their head (Regan, 1991). What visual information do we use to avoid imminent collisions, or to achieve collision when catching or batting a ball? To rephrase somewhat more precisely, how do we estimate the **time to collision (TTC)** of an approaching object?

Consider a small, red cricket ball, thrown by a large, rather angry-looking man (on the other team), that bounces off the ground about 10 feet way from you. At this distance, if the ball hurtles toward the bridge of your nose at a constant rate of 50 feet per second, it will collide with your face in 0.20 second (TTC = distance / rate = 10 / 50). The most direct way to estimate TTC would therefore be to estimate the distance and speed of the ball. However, determining absolute distances in depth is a tricky proposition, as we saw in Chapter 6, and humans are far better at judging TTC than would be predicted on the basis of their ability to judge distance.

In an attempt to reconcile this apparent discrepancy, D. N. Lee (1976) and others have pointed out that there is an alternative source of information in the optic flow that could signal TTC without the need for absolute distances or rates to be estimated. Lee called this information source **tau (τ)**. Here's how tau works: As the ball approaches your nose, the image of the ball on your retina will grow larger (if you don't believe this, have someone throw a ball—preferably a soft one—at your face and see for yourself). The ratio of the retinal image size at any moment to the rate at which the image is expanding is tau, and TTC is proportional to tau. The great advantage of using tau to estimate TTC is that it relies solely on information available directly from the retinal image; all you need to do is track the visual angle subtended by the cricket ball as it approaches your eye.

Do we actually make use of tau? The jury is still out. It is clear that estimating the time to imminent collision is critically important to animals and humans, and almost every species tested will attempt to avoid a simulated collision. There is also evidence that certain neurons in the visual systems of pigeons and locusts respond to objects on a collision course with them and can signal a particular time to collision (Rind and Simmons, 1999; Wang and Frost, 1992). Interestingly, a looming object on a collision path with an observer captures his attention, whereas a looming object on a near-miss path does not, even when the observer is not aware of any difference between collision and near-miss objects (Lin, Murray, and Boynton, 2009). However,

Figure 8.13 This batsman has just been hit by a very hard cricket ball.

Tresilian (1999) concluded that tau is just one of a number of different sources of visual information that can be used to judge the time to collision.

Something in the Way You Move: Using Motion Information to Identify Objects

The fact that we use motion information to guide us as we move through our environment is not all that surprising. What may be less obvious is that motion can also help inform us about the nature of objects. More than 40 years ago, Gunnar Johansson (1975) recognized that there might be something special about the motion of animals and people—**biological motion**—that helps us identify both the moving object and its actions.

Consider the tennis player in **Figure 8.14A**. It's clear from the contours of her body that she's just smashed an innocent little tennis ball in the direction of her opponent. **Figure 8.14B** shows the same tennis player in the dark. All we can see are the little lights attached to her ankles, knees, hips, elbows, wrists, and shoulders. There's not very much in the static pattern of the lights to inform us that the contour is a human (let alone a woman), or that she/it is engaged in athletic activity. What Johansson discovered, though, is that when the lights move, their motion gives the viewer an immediate and very compelling impression of a live human in action. Once again, you really need to see this to appreciate it, so watch the classic "dot walker" movie, Image 3 in **Web Activity 8.3: Types of Motion**.

Importantly, the mechanisms that analyze biological motion obey different rules for integrating motion over space and time than do mechanisms for other forms of complex motion (Neri, Morrone, and Burr, 1998). There is even evidence that observers can use biological motion to identify whether a set of moving lights is attached to a male or female walker. How do they do that? As we walk, when the right leg is in front of the left leg, the right shoulder is behind, and vice versa. If we draw one line connecting the left shoulder with the right hip

biological motion The pattern of movement of living beings (humans and animals).

(A)   (B)

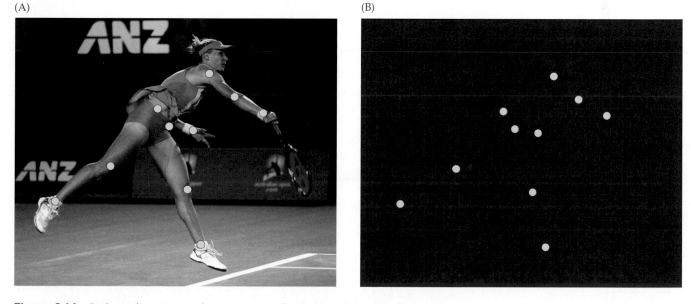

Figure 8.14 Biological motion can be seen compellingly when lights attached to a moving human (A) are viewed in total darkness (B). You can experience biological motion in **Web Activity 8.3: Types of Motion**.

and another connecting the right shoulder with the left hip, the intersection of the two lines is the center of the walker's motion. Because males typically have broader shoulders and narrower hips than females, the average male's center of motion is higher than that of females. James Cutting et al. suggested that observers use estimates of the center of motion as a cue to the walker's gender (Barclay, Cutting, and Kozlowski, 1978). Other studies (e.g., Mather and Murdoch, 1994) suggest that, in certain views, the amount of body sway might provide an even more salient gender cue.

Biological motion appears to play an important role in how we interpret human actions. For example, studies of biological motion with two "actors" either dancing or fighting show that we are much more efficient in discriminating biological motion of a human when two humans are acting in synchrony (e.g., fighting or dancing) than when they are out of sync. We can think of this phenomenon as proof of the old adage that "it takes two to tango" (Neri, Luu, and Levi, 2006). You should check out Niko Troje's wonderful site on biological motion at www. biomotionlab.ca/demos.

Eye Movements

Our eyes are constantly moving. When they move, the image on the retina moves, too. So how does our brain figure out which motions on the retina belong to real moving objects and which are caused by our own eye and head movements? Let's try a simple experiment: Place a blank piece of paper on the desk in front of you, and draw a small black dot right in the center of the paper. Close your left eye and focus your right eye's gaze on the dot; then position a pencil so that it is near the bottom right corner of the paper. Keeping your eye trained on the dot, move the pencil slowly across the sheet to the left side, as shown in **Figure 8.15A**. What did you perceive? The image of the pencil just swept across your retina from right to left, so assuming that your rightward-motion detectors are functioning correctly, you should have perceived movement in this direction. (You may have thought that the word *rightward* in the previous sentence was a typo, but technically the image sweeps across the retina in the opposite direction

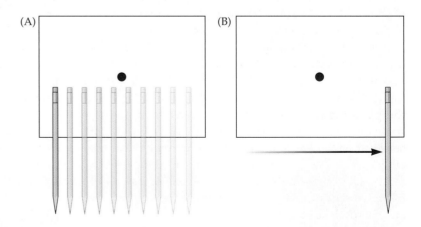

Figure 8.15 Studying eye movements. (A) Fixing our gaze on the dot while the pencil moves to the left causes the pencil to generate motion across the retina, and we perceive movement of the pencil in this direction. (B) Fixating our gaze on the pencil while it moves to the right causes the dot to generate motion in the same direction across the retina, but we do not perceive movement of the dot.

from the actual movement, since the right side of the world projects to the left side of the retina and vice versa. To avoid confusion, we'll ignore this inconvenient bit of physics for now and pretend that images move on the retina in the same direction that the objects in the world are moving. **Web Activity 8.5: Eye Movements** provides illustrations of these phenomena that honor physics.

Now try a slightly different demonstration. Start with the pencil near the bottom left corner of the paper, fixate the eraser, and track it with your eye as you move it back across the sheet of paper to the right corner (**Figure 8.15B**). Congratulations! You have just executed a type of eye movement called **smooth pursuit**, which kept the pencil's image stationary on the retina while the pencil was in motion. But think about what happened to the image of the dot just above your pencil. When the pencil was on the left side of the page, the dot was to the right of your fixation point. As you tracked the pencil, the dot shifted to the center of your retina, and then it slid to the left of your fixation point once the pencil reached the right side of the paper. However, you should *not* have perceived the dot to be moving in this case, even though the image of the dot made essentially the same journey across your retina that the image of the pencil did in Figure 8.15A.

We hope you've convinced yourself that the retinal image movement of the pencil when you keep your gaze centered on the dot (see Figure 8.15A) is essentially the same as the retinal image movement of the dot when you keep your gaze centered on the pencil (see Figure 8.15B). The question is, Why do we perceive motion of the pencil in the first case but perceive that the dot is stationary in the second case? The reason is that in one case there's an eye movement. Think about how the visual system might accomplish this balancing act while we back up and describe eye movements in a bit more detail. (By the way, you may want to save the piece of paper with the dot for another exercise later in this chapter.)

Physiology and Types of Eye Movements

As **Figure 8.16A** shows, six muscles are attached to each eye, arranged in three pairs. These muscles are controlled by an extensive network of structures in the brain. One way to get some inkling of the role of these brain structures is to stimulate them with small electrical signals and observe the movements of the eyes. For example, if a cell in the **superior colliculus** (**Figure 8.16B**) of a monkey is stimulated, the monkey's eyes will move by a specific amount in a specific direction. Every time that cell is stimulated, the same eye movement will result. Stimulating a neighboring cell will produce a different eye movement (Stryker and Schiller, 1975). (The superior colliculus also gets some input directly from retinal ganglion cells; this input presumably helps with the planning of eye movements.) By contrast, in response to stimulation of some of the cells in the frontal eye fields (Figure 8.16B) (and, indeed, certain superior colliculus cells, too), the monkey will move its eyes to fixate a specific spot in space. Depending on where the eyes start, this adjustment may require an eye movement up, down, left, or right. In this case, it is the destination and not the movement that is coded (Mays and Sparks, 1980; Schiller and Sandell, 1983).

This description merely scratches the surface of a motor system that is not only very complex, but very active. For example, even when we try to hold our eyes completely stationary, they continue to execute small but important movements. Specifically, there are involuntary eye drifts and small jerks called **microsaccades**; if the eye muscles are temporarily paralyzed—say, as a result

smooth pursuit A type of voluntary eye movement in which the eyes move smoothly to follow a moving object.

superior colliculus A structure in the midbrain that is important in initiating and guiding eye movements.

microsaccade An involuntary, small, jerk-like eye movement.

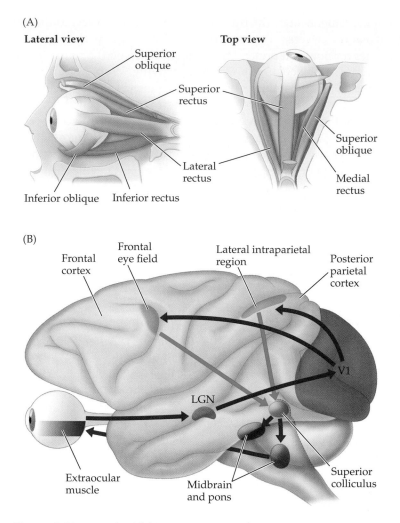

(A)

Lateral view

Superior oblique

Superior rectus

Lateral rectus

Inferior oblique   Inferior rectus

Top view

Superior oblique

Medial rectus

(B)

Frontal cortex

Frontal eye field

Lateral intraparietal region

Posterior parietal cortex

V1

LGN

Extraocular muscle

Midbrain and pons

Superior colliculus

Figure 8.16 Muscles of the eye. (A) Six muscles—arranged in three pairs (superior and inferior oblique, superior and inferior rectus, and medial and lateral rectus)—are attached to each eye. (B) Brain circuits for visually guided saccades. (B after Wurtz, 2008.)

of taking curare (it's amazing what some people will subject themselves to in the name of science!) (Matin et al., 1982)—the entire visual world gradually fades from view. As noted above, small peripheral targets may fade and disappear during steady fixation—an illusion known as the Troxler effect. In normal viewing, image velocities are often fast enough to prevent fading without the need for microsaccades (Kowler and Collewijn, 2010). So what are microsaccades good for? Recent work suggests that they may be important for very fine spatial judgments, such as threading a needle, because they precisely move the eye to nearby regions of interest (Ko, Poletti, and Rucci, 2010); for compensating for the very rapid falloff of acuity even a few minutes outside the fovea (Poletti, Listorti, and Rucci, 2013); and for changing the spatiotemporal pattern of information that arrives at the retina, in order to redistribute spatial information across temporal frequencies (Rucci and Victor, 2015). Other recent work suggests that microsaccades are directed toward objects we are attending (Hafed and Clark, 2002; Engbert and Kliegl, 2003)—thus playing an important role in attention.

Figure 8.17 A classic scan path (right) showing the pattern of eye movements during inspection of the picture of the girl on the left. (From Yarbus, 1967.)

In addition to involuntary eye movements, there are three types of voluntary eye movements. Most obvious, perhaps, are the previously discussed smooth-pursuit movements that we make when tracking a moving object. Observing these smooth-pursuit eye movements in patients is often used by doctors as a simple screening for neurological impairments, and they can even help distinguish individuals with schizophrenia from others (Benson et al., 2012). **Vergence** eye movements occur when we rotate our eyes inward (converging the eyes) or outward (diverging the eyes) to focus on a near or far object. The third type of voluntary movement is the **saccade**: a fast jump (up to 1000 degrees per second) (Bahill and Stark, 1979) of the eye that shifts our gaze from one spot to another. We can decide to make a saccade deliberately, but whether we're thinking about it or not, we will make three or four saccades every second of every minute of every waking hour of the day. That's something like 3 saccades × 60 seconds × 60 minutes × 16 hours = 172,800 saccades per day—and that doesn't include the saccades we make during our dreams in rapid-eye-movement (REM) sleep (Maquet et al., 1996).

When we view a scene, our saccades are not random. We tend to fixate the "interesting" places in the image. Thus, the eyes are more likely to make saccades in response to contours than to broad featureless areas of an image (**Figure 8.17**). *Interesting* also has a richer semantic meaning: We make eye movements that are based on the content of a scene and on our specific interests in that scene (Yarbus, 1967). Our pattern of eye movements as we enter the cafeteria will be different if we're looking for lunch than if we're looking for love.

There are also **reflexive eye movements**—for example, when the eyes move to compensate for head and body movement while maintaining fixation on a particular target. These are known as vestibular eye movements and operate via the vestibulo-ocular reflex (VOR) (see Chapter 12). **Optokinetic nystagmus (OKN)** is another reflexive eye movement in which the eyes will involuntarily track a continually moving object, moving smoothly in one direction (e.g., right) in pursuit of the object moving in that same direction, and then snap back. The

vergence A type of eye movement in which the two eyes move in opposite directions; for example, both eyes turn toward the nose (convergence) or away from the nose (divergence).

saccade A type of eye movement, made both voluntarily and involuntarily, in which the eyes rapidly change fixation from one object or location to another.

reflexive eye movement A movement of the eye that is automatic and involuntary.

optokinetic nystagmus (OKN) A reflexive eye movement in which the eyes will involuntarily track a continually moving object.

saccadic suppression The reduction of visual sensitivity that occurs when we make saccadic eye movements. Saccadic suppression eliminates the smear from retinal image motion during an eye movement.

presence of OKN in response to moving stripes has often been used as a measure of visual acuity in infants.

Eye Movements and Reading

If you are reading this chapter, then your eyes are doing a lot of moving! Reading English involves fixating for roughly a quarter of a second and then making a saccade of about 7–9 letter spaces—over and over again. We make saccades in order to bring the text onto our foveas, because print that's too far from our fixation cannot be read, in part because of visual crowding (see Chapter 3 and Levi, 2008). Interestingly, readers of English are able to gain information from up to 15 characters to the right of fixation, but only 3–4 characters to the left. Thus, the perceptual span is asymmetrical. Readers of Hebrew (which is read from right to left) have the reverse asymmetry. Readers of both Hebrew and English can switch this asymmetry depending on which language they're reading (Rayner, 1978), so the asymmetry is attentional, not a product of limitations imposed by the visual system.

As we discuss next, there is no information processing during saccades, so while we're reading, all of the information processing must take place during the fixations. Interestingly, such processing occurs during only a small fraction of each fixation. "Disappearing text" experiments (in which the words actually disappear off of the computer screen while participants are reading) reveal that if a word remains on the screen for only 50 milliseconds after it is first fixated, reading proceeds normally (Rayner et al., 2003). There are many other interesting aspects of eye movements in scene perception and in visual search and attention (see Chapter 7).

Saccadic Suppression and the Comparator

Now let's return to the tricky problem of discriminating motion across the retina that is due to eye movements versus object movements. Let's do one more demonstration using that white piece of paper with the dot in the middle: Close your left eye again and gaze just to the left of the dot; then execute some saccades, shifting your eye back and forth to the right and then to the left of the dot. The dot will be moving across your retina, but you should not experience any perception of movement. Now, with your left eye still closed, fixate the dot, place your right index finger on the right side of your right eye socket, and gently "jiggle" your eyeball. *Now* the dot (as well as the paper and the desk the paper is sitting on) *should* appear to move back and forth! What's going on here?

Part of the answer is thought to be **saccadic suppression**. When we make a saccade, the visual system essentially shuts down for the duration of the eye movement (visual activity is suspended in a similar way when we blink). To be a bit more precise, the visual system does not shut down altogether. Saccadic suppression acts mainly to suppress information carried by the magnocellular pathway.

To observe saccadic suppression, you need to find a mirror. As you look at yourself in the mirror, fixate first one eye and then the other. You will notice that you do not see the saccadic eye movements that you must be making. If you're concerned that the saccades might be too small to see, find a friend to help you. Have this person stand in front of you and move his or her fixation from one of your eyes to the other. You will have no trouble seeing your friend's saccades, even though you are quite blind to your own.

Although saccadic suppression eliminates the smear of the moving world during a saccade, it seems as if we should still be disturbed by the sudden displacement of the objects in front of us. In any case, no suppression takes place when we execute smooth-pursuit eye movements, as in the earlier exercise with the pencil. Although many scientists believe suppression to be an active process, others argue that saccadic suppression is little more than masking and that the magnocellular pathway (see Chapter 3) is not suppressed during saccades (Castet, Jeanjean, and Masson, 2001).

By sending out two copies of each order to move the eyes, the motor system is thought to solve the "problem" of why an object moving across the retina may appear stationary. One copy goes to the eye muscles; another (often referred to as the **efference copy** or the **corollary discharge signal**) goes to an area of the visual system that has been dubbed the **comparator** (**Figure 8.18**). The comparator can then compensate for the image changes caused by the eye movement, inhibiting any attempts by other parts of the visual system to interpret the changes as object motion. When we jiggle the eyeball with a finger, no signal is sent from the eye muscles to the comparator (the eye muscles are not what move the eye in this case), so the visual input is interpreted as our world being rocked. (For interactive demonstrations of the similarities and differences between eye movements and object movements, see **Web Activity 8.5: Eye Movements**.) While a lot of work has been dedicated to the analysis of extraretinal signals during smooth pursuit, visual stability during saccades remains a matter of active research, and attention seems to play an important

efference copy or **corollary discharge signal** The phenomenon in which outgoing (efferent) signals from the motor cortex are copied as they exit the brain and are rerouted to other areas in the sensory cortices.

comparator An area of the visual system that receives one copy of the command issued by the motor system when the eyes move (the other copy goes to the eye muscles). The comparator compares the image motion signal with the eye motion signal and can compensate for the image changes caused by the eye movement.

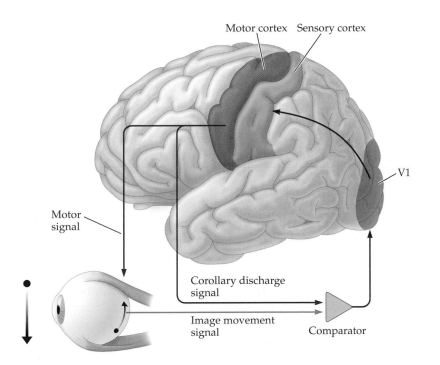

Figure 8.18 The comparator. The brain sends two copies (red lines) of each command to move the eyes. One copy (the motor signal) goes directly to the extraocular muscles; the other (known as the efference copy or the corollary discharge signal) goes to the comparator, which compares the image motion signal with the eye motion signal and can compensate for image changes produced by the eye movement.

(A) Receptive fields relative to a point of fixation

Figure 8.19 Receptive field updating. Receptive fields (ovals) are generally considered to be fixed in space, relative to the fixation point (stars) (A), so if the eyes move to a new fixation point, the receptive fields should shift in "lockstep" so that they maintain the same positions relative to the fovea (B). Shifting fixation from the sculpture on the bow of the boat (A) to the roof of the boat (B) results in a lockstep shift of the receptive fields. Recent work suggests that receptive fields of neurons in the frontal eye fields shift toward the target location (C).

(B) Receptive fields shift with the point of fixation

(C) Receptive fields transiently remap toward the new point of fixation

role (Cavanagh et al., 2010; Poletti, Listorti, and Rucci, 2010; Schutz, Braun, and Gegenfurtner, 2011; Gegenfurtner, 2016).

Updating the Neural Mechanisms for Eye Movement Compensation

How does the brain compensate for eye movements in order to preserve the stability of our visual world? Well over a century ago, Hermann von Helmholtz suggested that since the brain generates the neural signals for saccadic eye movements, it can perceptually compensate for them (by using the efference copy described above). One way this compensation could occur is through the "remapping" of visual receptive fields. We've discussed the receptive field—the region in space in which a visual stimulus causes a neuron to change its firing rate—at many points in the book (see Chapters 2–7). Receptive fields are generally considered to be fixed in space relative to the fixation point (star in **Figure 8.19A**), so if the eyes move to a new fixation point, the receptive fields (ovals in Figure 8.19) should shift in "lockstep" so that they maintain the same positions relative to the fovea (**Figure 8.19B**). Shifting fixation from the sculpture on the bow (Figure 8.19A) to the roof of the boat (Figure 8.19B) results in a lockstep shift of the receptive fields. However, the receptive fields of some neurons in the parietal cortex actually shift to the new locations before the saccade. Duhamel, Colby, and Goldberg (1992) referred to this anticipatory shift as predictive remapping or updating. A key assumption about this spatial-updating hypothesis is that the neural representation of the visual field is rigidly translated just prior to the eye movement. However, a recent study suggests a different view, illustrated in **Figure 8.19C**. Zirnsak et al. (2014) found that the receptive fields of neurons in the frontal eye fields shift transiently toward the target location. In this view, the receptive field shifts do not predict the retinal displacements produced by saccades, but rather reflect the fact that space is perceived to be compressed just before a saccade (Ross et al., 2001).

Development of Motion Perception

Sensitivity to visual motion does not develop all at once. Some aspects of motion perception are already evident at birth. For example, reflexive eye movements to moving targets (OKN) are present in newborns (as long as the targets are sufficiently large), and physiological studies show that neurons in V1 have adult-like sensitivity to motion direction. On the other hand, sensitivity to global motion, which is thought to reflect processing in area MT, appears to develop more slowly, reaching maturity at about 3–4 years of age, while sensitivity to motion-defined form and biological motion takes even longer (Freire et al., 2006; Parrish et al., 2005).

■ Scientists at Work ■

Guess Who's Coming to Dinner

■ **Question** How does a stationary praying mantis spot its moving dinner?

■ **Hypothesis** The praying mantis, *Sphodromantis lineola*, is a predator that stays stationary for long periods of time while waiting to ambush its fast-moving prey (a bug). This behavior is different from that of other insects that are constantly in motion, leading to the hypothesis that the praying mantis's motion detection system might be different from that of other insects.

■ **Test** The researchers (Nityananda et al., 2015) evaluated the mantis optomotor response to drifting gratings with different spatial and temporal frequencies and contrasts. On each trial a researcher, who was unaware of the stimulus direction, coded whether the mantis turned its body to the left or to the right. After the session, these responses were compared with the actual direction of the drifting grating on each trial. This enabled the researchers to generate psychometric functions showing the probability of eliciting an optomotor response as a function of stimulus contrast and to estimate the mantis threshold for each spatial and temporal frequency.

■ **Results** The contrast sensitivity of the mantis is dependent on both the spatial and temporal frequencies present in the stimulus rather than on object velocity (**Figure 8.20**).

■ **Conclusions** Praying mantis sensitivity to motion differs from that of humans and bees, but it is similar to that of hoverflies

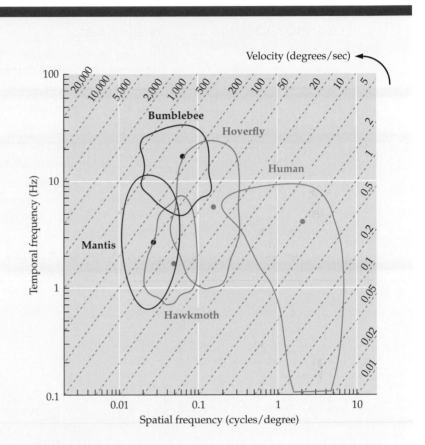

Figure 8.20 Contour isolines bounding the spatiotemporal frequencies where mantis sensitivity is half of its maximum value, and similar isolines for other species. Colored dots indicate the maximum sensitivity for each species.(After Nityananda et al., 2015.)

and hawkmoths in that it allows them to respond to stimuli at low and high velocities. This may be especially useful in enabling a stationary mantis to spot a fast-moving bug and catch it for dinner!

■ **Future work** It would be interesting to compare the properties of the early neuronal mechanisms of the praying mantis to their behavior, as measured here, to determine the specific mechanisms that underlie their sensitivity.

Summary

1. Like color or orientation, motion is a primary perceptual dimension that is coded at various levels in the brain. Motion information is used to determine where objects are going and when they're likely to get there.

2. We can build a simple motion-detecting circuit by using linear filters that delay and sum information (and are followed by nonlinearities).

3. V1 neurons view the world through a small window, leading to the well-known aperture problem (that is, a V1 neuron is unable to tell which elements correspond with one another when an object moves through its receptive field).

4. Strong physiological and behavioral evidence suggests that the middle temporal area (MT) is involved in the perception of global motion.

5. Aftereffects for motion, like those for orientation or color, can provide important insights into the underlying mechanisms of perception in humans.

6. Luminance-defined (first-order) motion and contrast- or texture-defined (second-order) motion appear to be analyzed by separate systems.

7. The brain has to figure out which retinal motion arises in the world, and which arises because of eye movements. Moreover, the brain must suppress the motion signals generated by our eye movements, or the world will be pretty "smeared."

8. Motion information is critically important to us for navigating around our world, avoiding imminent collision, and recognizing the movement of animals and people.

9 Hearing: Physiology and Psychoacoustics

■ Questions to Contemplate ■

Think about the following questions as you read this chapter. By the chapter's end, you should be able to answer and discuss them.

- What are the physical and psychological qualities of sound?

- How is sound energy turned into neural firing for the brain to interpret?

- How does the brain encode pitch and loudness?

- How is hearing loss caused, and what can be done about it?

Are humans really visual animals? We are reminded of the importance of vision whenever we close our eyes or awaken in the night, because so much of what we sense and know about our environment is suddenly gone. In contrast, most people never get such reminders of the importance of hearing. Ears are always open, and we can hear perfectly well in the dark. When we enter a dark place, we don't need to wait half an hour to be able to hear the soft sounds that tell us we're not alone. We can hear things when our nose is not pointed at the source of the sound, and we can even hear around obstacles and corners. For better or worse, we can often hear through barriers that light cannot penetrate. For all these reasons, it is easy to take hearing for granted.

Try to imagine a world, though, where nothing makes a sound. You watch a movie or online video, and the sound is always off. A person cries out, and you don't help because you cannot hear the cry. Without hearing, the world is a more dangerous place. You are relatively isolated by day and nearly totally isolated by night when your sense of vision is compromised by darkness.

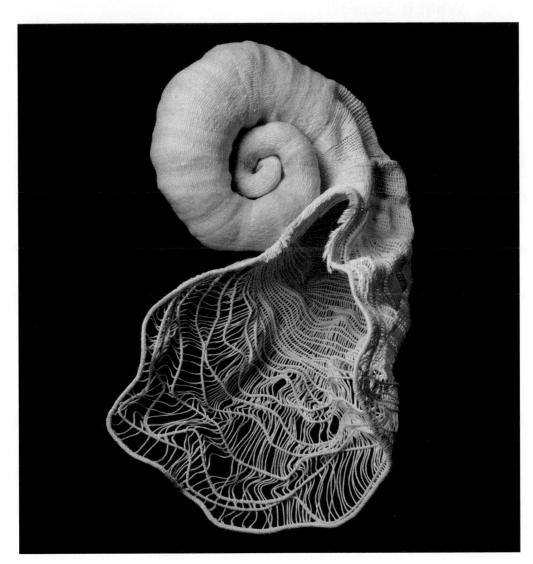

Carol Shaw-Sutton, *The White Sound*, 2009

The Function of Hearing

The next three chapters are all about hearing. In this chapter we cover the basics: the nature of sound, the anatomy and physiology of the auditory system, and how we perceive the two fundamental sound qualities—loudness and pitch. We conclude this chapter by looking at some of the ways in which hearing can be impaired and what we can do to avoid and overcome these impairments. In Chapter 10, we will move on to discuss some of the ways we use acoustic information to learn about our surroundings. Then, in Chapter 11, we will cover the higher-level auditory functions that we use when we're listening to speech and music.

Many fundamental principles in hearing apply to all of the senses. However, each sense developed at different periods in our evolutionary history and in response to different environmental challenges. So, although you should find that much of what you've learned thus far will help you to understand hearing, you will also be impressed by ways biology has provided some very different (and very clever) solutions to the challenges of sensing and interpreting sound.

(A)

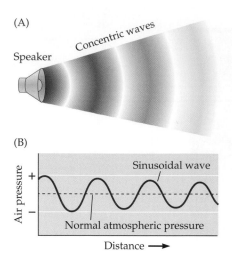

Speaker

Concentric waves

(B)

Air pressure

Sinusoidal wave

Normal atmospheric pressure

Distance ⟶

Figure 9.1 The pattern of pressure fluctuations of a sound stays the same as the sound wave moves away from the source (A), but the amount of pressure change decreases with increasing distance (B).

amplitude or **intensity** In reference to sound, the magnitude of displacement (increase or decrease) of a pressure wave. Amplitude is perceived as *loudness*.

frequency In reference to sound, the number of times per second that a pattern of pressure change repeats. Frequency is perceived as *pitch*.

hertz (Hz) A unit of measure for frequency; 1 hertz equals 1 cycle per second.

What Is Sound?

Sounds are created when objects vibrate. The vibrations of an object (the sound source) cause molecules in the object's surrounding medium (for humans, usually the Earth's atmosphere) to vibrate as well. This vibration causes pressure changes in the medium (**Figure 9.1**). These pressure changes are best described as waves, and they are similar to the waves on a pond caused by dropping a rock into the water. Water molecules displaced by the rock do not themselves travel very far, but the *pattern* of displacement will move outward from the source until something (the shore, a boat, a swimming duck, or anything else) gets in the way. Although the patterns of pond and sound waves do not change as they spread out, the initial amount of pressure change is dispersed over a larger and larger area as the wave moves away, so the wave becomes less prominent as it moves farther from its source.

Sound waves travel through different media at different speeds, moving faster through denser substances. For example, the speed of sound through air is about 340 meters per second, depending on the humidity level (sounds travel a bit faster on muggy days), but the speed of sound through water is about 1500 meters per second. Light waves move through air almost a million times faster than sound waves do. This is why you see lightning before hearing thunder—the difference is almost 5 seconds (4¾) per mile.

Basic Qualities of Sound Waves: Frequency and Amplitude

As we've seen, sound waves that we hear are simply fluctuations in air pressure across time. The magnitude of the pressure change in a sound wave—the difference between the highest pressure and the lowest pressure of the wave—is called the **amplitude** or **intensity** (**Figure 9.2**). Pressure fluctuations may be very close together or spread apart over longer periods. For light waves, we usually describe the pattern of fluctuations by measuring the distance between peaks in the waves—that is, the "wavelength." Sound waves also have wavelengths, but we describe their patterns by noting how quickly the pressure fluctuates; this rate of fluctuation is known as the **frequency** of the wave (see Figure 9.2). To see an example of frequency, dangle a thread in front of a stereo. As the speaker creates fluctuations in air pressure, the thread waves back and forth. The tempo of this waving is the thread's frequency. Sound wave frequencies are measured by these back-and-forth cycles, and the unit of measure is called a **hertz (Hz)**, where 1 cycle per second equals 1 Hz. For example, the pressure in a 500-Hz wave goes from its highest point down to its lowest point and back up to its highest point 500 times every second.

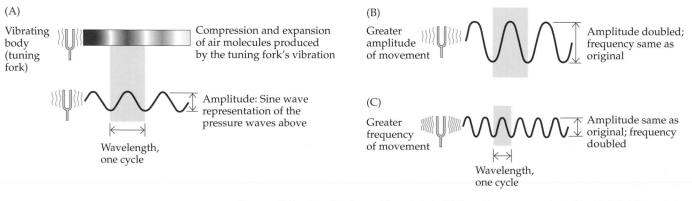

Figure 9.2 Amplitude and frequency. (A) Sound waves are described by the frequency and amplitude of pressure fluctuations. Changes in amplitude (B) and frequency (C) are shown for sine waves, the simplest kind of sound wave.

Figure 9.3 Humans can hear frequencies that range from about 20 to 20,000 Hz across a very wide range of intensities, or sound pressure levels (dB SPL, where dB = decibels).

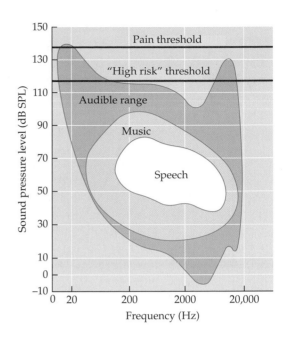

Just as the amplitude and wavelength of light waves correspond to perceptual qualities in vision (brightness and color, respectively), the amplitude and frequency of sound waves are closely related to auditory characteristics. Amplitude is associated with the perceptual quality of **loudness**: the more intense a sound wave is, the louder it will sound. Frequency is associated with **pitch**: low-frequency sounds correspond to low pitches (e.g., low notes played by a tuba), and high-frequency sounds correspond to high pitches (e.g., the high notes from a piccolo). We will have much more to say about the relationships between amplitude and loudness and between frequency and pitch later in this chapter.

In Chapter 2, you learned how visible light makes up only a small portion of the much broader range of electromagnetic energy; similarly, human hearing uses a limited range of the frequencies present in environmental sounds. If you are relatively young and you've been careful about your exposure to loud sounds, you may be able to detect sounds that vary from about 20 to 20,000 Hz (**Figure 9.3**). Some animals hear sounds that have lower and higher frequencies than those heard by humans. In general, larger animals are better at hearing low frequencies, and smaller animals are better at using high frequencies. Elephants hear vibrations at very low frequencies that help them detect the presence of large animals, such as other elephants. Dogs can be called with whistles that emit sounds at frequencies too high for humans to hear, and the sonar systems used by some bats use sound frequencies above 60,000 Hz.

Humans hear across a very wide range of sound intensities. The intensity ratio between the faintest sound humans can detect and the loudest sounds that do not cause serious damage to human ears is more than one to a million. To describe differences in amplitude across such a broad range, sound levels are measured on a logarithmic scale using units called **decibels** (**dB**). Decibels define the difference between two sounds in terms of the ratio between sound pressures. Each 10:1 sound pressure ratio is equal to 20 dB, so a 100:1 ratio is equal to 40 dB. The equation for defining decibels is

$$dB = 20 \log(p/p_0)$$

The variable p corresponds to the pressure (intensity) of the sound being described. The constant term p_0 is a reference pressure and is typically defined in auditory research contexts to be 0.0002 dyne per square centimeter (dyne/cm^2), and levels are defined in terms of dB SPL (sound pressure level). The level 0.0002 dyne/cm^2 is close to the minimum pressure that can be detected at frequencies for which hearing is most sensitive, and decibel values greater than zero describe the ratio between a sound being measured and 0.0002 dyne/cm^2. The range of human hearing extends from 0 to more than 120 dB SPL, and as shown in **Table 9.1**, this decibel range corresponds to a ratio of greater than 1,000,000:1.

loudness The psychological aspect of sound related to perceived intensity (amplitude).

pitch The psychological aspect of sound related mainly to the fundamental frequency.

decibel (dB) A unit of measure for the physical intensity of sound. Decibels define the difference between two sounds as the ratio between two sound pressures. Each 10:1 sound pressure ratio equals 20 dB, and a 100:1 ratio equals 40 dB.

■ **Table 9.1** ■

Decibel levels that correspond to different sound pressure ratios

Ratio relative to 0.0002 dyne/cm^2 (p_0)	dB
1	0
2	6
4	12
8	18
10	20
20	26
50	34
100	40
1000	60
10,000	80
100,000	100
1,000,000	120

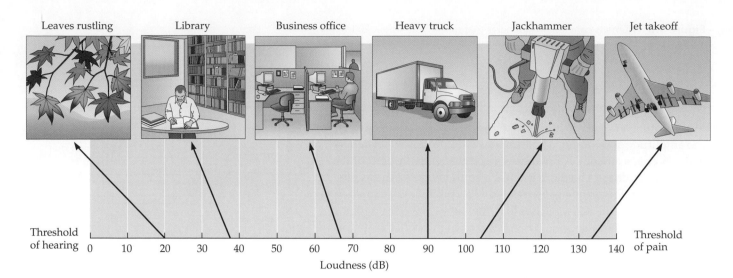

Threshold of hearing

Loudness (dB)

0 10 20 30 40 50 60 70 80 90 100 110 120 130 140

Threshold of pain

Figure 9.4 Sounds that we hear in our daily environments vary greatly in intensity.

Using a reference value such as p_0 is common to many measuring systems. For example, 0°C (32°F) is defined as the temperature at which water freezes, and 100°C (212°F) is the temperature at which water boils. If the pressure of the sound that you're measuring (p) is equal to 0.0002 dyne/cm^2, then dB = 20 log(1). Because the log of 1 is 0, a sound pressure that low would be equal to 0 dB SPL. But 0 dB SPL is not silence; sounds with amplitudes even smaller than p_0 have negative decibel levels, just as substances colder than the freezing point of water have negative Celsius temperatures.

An important thing to remember about logarithmic scales such as decibels is that relatively small decibel changes can correspond to large physical changes. For example, there is a roughly 44 dB difference between a heavy truck and a jet taking off, but the sound pressure level of the jet is 158 times as great as the truck (**Figure 9.4**).

Sine Waves and Complex Sounds

In Chapter 1 you were introduced to one of the simplest kinds of sounds: a **sine wave**, which is often called a **pure tone**. Any sound, even those as complex as the sounds produced by musical instruments, human speech, and city traffic, can be described as a combination of sine waves. (See **Web Activity 9.1: What We Hear**.)

A complex sound is best described in a **spectrum** (plural *spectra*) that displays how much energy, or amplitude, is present at multiple frequencies, as shown in **Figure 9.5**. Many common sounds have **harmonic spectra**, illustrated in **Figure 9.6**. These are typically caused by a simple vibrating source, such as the string of a guitar or the reed of a saxophone. Each frequency component in such a sound is called a harmonic. The first harmonic, called the **fundamental frequency**, is the lowest-frequency component of the sound. All the other harmonics have frequencies that are integer multiples of the fundamental.

The shape of the spectrum (spectral shape) is one of the most important qualities that distinguish different sounds. The properties of sound sources determine the spectral shapes of sounds, and these shapes help us to identify sound sources. For example, Figure 9.6 illustrates spectra from three musical instruments. Each instrument is producing a note with the same fundamental frequency (262 Hz, which corresponds to the note C$_4$, or middle C) and the same harmonics (524 Hz, 786 Hz, 1048 Hz, and so on). However, the shapes of the spectra (the patterns of amplitudes for each harmonic) vary. **Timbre** (pro-

sine wave or **pure tone** The waveform for which variation as a function of time is a sine function.

spectrum A representation of the relative energy (intensity) present at each frequency.

harmonic spectrum The spectrum of a complex sound in which energy is at integer multiples of the fundamental frequency.

fundamental frequency The lowest-frequency component of a complex periodic sound.

timbre The psychological sensation by which a listener can judge that two sounds with the same loudness and pitch are dissimilar. Timbre quality is conveyed by harmonics and other high frequencies.

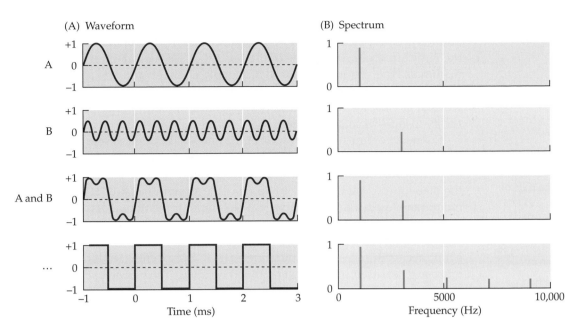

Figure 9.5 A spectrum displays the amplitude for each frequency present in a sound wave. Each signal is shown as a waveform (A) and as a spectrum (B).

nounced "tamber," like "amber") is a term used to describe the quality of a sound that depends, in part, on the relative energy levels of harmonic components.

We will return to harmonics, timbre, and other aspects of complex sounds in Chapter 10. In this chapter we'll stick mainly to the story of how the auditory system processes simple sounds such as sine wave tones.

Basic Structure of the Mammalian Auditory System

Now that you know what sound is, we can examine how sounds are detected and recognized by the auditory system. The sense of hearing has evolved over millions of years to be able to do some amazing things. We are about to describe quite a few anatomical structures that are essential to understanding how sequences of tiny air pressure changes are turned into meaningful sound perception. The discussion may occasionally be a bit confusing, but if you consult the figures and **Web Activity 9.2: Structure of the Auditory System** often, you will soon know the parts and how they fit together.

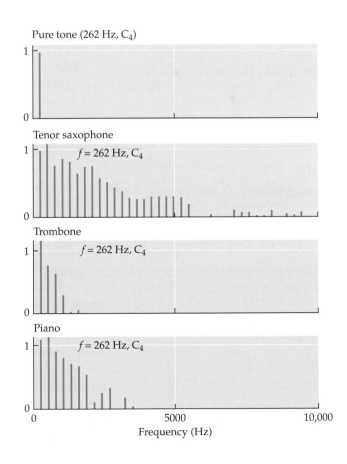

Figure 9.6 Harmonic sounds with the same fundamental frequency can sound different because amplitudes of individual frequency components are different, resulting in different spectral shapes. For example, different musical instruments playing the same note (the same fundamental frequency, abbreviated f) sound different. C_4 = middle C.

Outer Ear

Sounds are first collected from the environment by the **pinna** (plural *pinnae*), the curly structure on the side of the head that we typically call an ear. Only mammals have pinnae, and they vary wildly in shape and size across species and vary less dramatically across individuals within species (**Figure 9.7**). As we will see in Chapter 10, the shape of the pinnae plays an important role in our ability to localize sound sources.

Sound waves are funneled by the pinna into and through the **ear canal**, which extends about 25 millimeters (mm) into the head (**Figure 9.8**). The length and shape of the ear canal enhance sound frequencies between about 2000 and 6000 Hz, but the main purpose of the canal is to protect the structure at its end, the **tympanic membrane** (eardrum), from damage. The tympanic membrane is a thin sheet of skin that moves in and out in response to the pressure changes of sound waves.

It is a common myth that puncturing your eardrum will leave you deaf. While a ruptured eardrum can be excruciating, in most cases a damaged tympanic membrane will heal itself, just as other parts of the skin do. You probably know someone who has had tubes placed through tympanic membranes to remedy ear infections. Nevertheless, it is possible to damage the tympanic membrane beyond repair, so it's a good idea to follow your mother's advice to not stick things in your ear.

Middle Ear

Together, the pinna and ear canal make up a division of the auditory system called the **outer ear** (see Figure 9.8). The tympanic membrane is the border between the outer ear and the **middle ear**, which consists of three tiny bones, the **ossicles**, that amplify sound waves. The first ossicle, the **malleus**, is connected to the tympanic membrane on one side and to the second ossicle, the **incus**, on the other. The incus is connected in turn to the third ossicle, the **stapes**, which transmits the vibrations of sound waves to the **oval window**, another membrane, which forms the border between the middle ear and the **inner ear**.

The ossicles are the smallest bones in the human body, and they amplify sound vibrations in two ways. First, the joints between the bones are hinged in ways that make them work like levers: a modest amount of energy on one side of the fulcrum (joint) becomes larger on the other. This lever action increases the amount of pressure change by about a third. The second way the ossicles increase the energy transmitted to the inner ear is by concentrating energy from a larger to a smaller surface area. The tympanic membrane, which moves the malleus, is about 18 times as large as the oval window, which is moved by the stapes (see Figure 9.8). Therefore, pressure on the oval window is magnified 18 times relative to the pressure on the tympanic membrane. This is the same principle that makes stiletto heels a danger to wood floors (think of the tympanic membrane as the heel of the foot and the oval window as the tip of the stiletto), in contrast to the way snowshoes keep feet on top of the snow.

Amplification provided by these physical properties (leverage and different surface areas) is essential to our ability to hear faint sounds, because the inner ear, as we will see in a moment, is made up of a collection of fluid-filled chambers. Because it takes more energy to move liquid than it does to move air, this fluid creates a mismatch. If sound waves were transmitted to the oval window directly, many would simply bounce back without moving the oval window and the liquid behind it at all.

Ossicles play an important role for loud sounds, too. The middle ear has two muscles: the **tensor tympani** (attached to the malleus) and the **stapedius** (attached to the stapes) (see Figure 9.8). As might be expected because they are attached

pinna The outer, funnel-like part of the ear.

ear canal The canal that conducts sound vibrations from the pinna to the tympanic membrane and prevents damage to the tympanic membrane.

tympanic membrane The eardrum; a thin sheet of skin at the end of the outer ear canal. The tympanic membrane vibrates in response to sound.

outer ear The external sound-gathering portion of the ear, consisting of the pinna and the ear canal.

middle ear An air-filled chamber containing the middle bones, or ossicles. The middle ear conveys and amplifies vibration from the tympanic membrane to the oval window.

ossicle Any of three tiny bones of the middle ear: malleus, incus, and stapes.

malleus The most exterior of the three ossicles. The malleus receives vibration from the tympanic membrane and is attached to the incus.

incus The middle of the three ossicles, connecting the malleus and the stapes.

stapes The most interior of the three ossicles. Connected to the incus on one end, the stapes presses against the oval window of the cochlea on the other end.

oval window The flexible opening to the cochlea through which the stapes transmits vibration to the fluid inside.

inner ear A hollow cavity in the temporal bone of the skull, and the structures within this cavity: the cochlea and the semicircular canals of the vestibular system.

tensor tympani The muscle attached to the malleus. Tensing the tensor tympani decreases vibration.

stapedius The muscle attached to the stapes. Tensing the stapedius decreases vibration.

Figure 9.7 The size and shape of pinnae vary greatly among mammals.

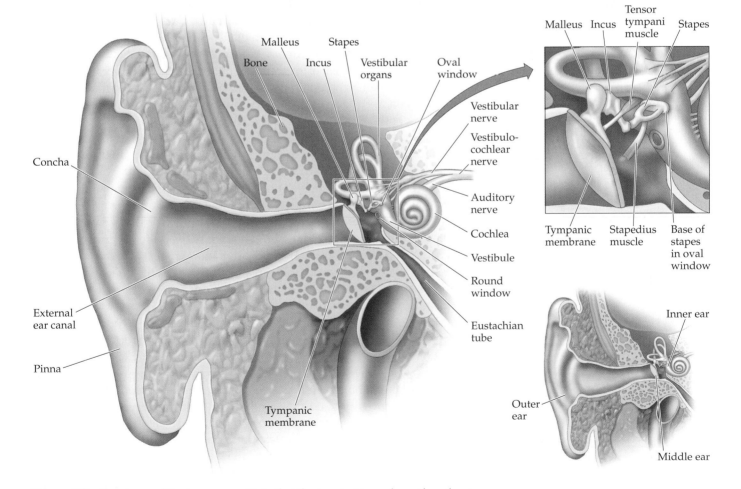

Figure 9.8 Structures of the human ear. Note that the tympanic membrane has about 18 times as much surface area as the oval window beneath the stapes.

acoustic reflex   A reflex that protects the ear from intense sounds, via contraction of the stapedius and tensor tympani muscles.

cochlea   A spiral structure of the inner ear containing the organ of Corti.

tympanic canal   One of three fluid-filled passages in the cochlea. The tympanic canal extends from the round window at the base of the cochlea to the helicotrema at the apex. Also called *scala tympani*.

vestibular canal   One of three fluid-filled passages in the cochlea. The vestibular canal extends from the oval window at the base of the cochlea to the helicotrema at the apex. Also called *scala vestibuli*.

middle canal   One of three fluid-filled passages in the cochlea. The middle canal is sandwiched between the tympanic and vestibular canals and contains the cochlear partition. Also called *scala media*.

helicotrema   The opening that connects the tympanic and vestibular canals at the apex of the cochlea.

Reissner's membrane   A thin sheath of tissue separating the vestibular and middle canals in the cochlea.

basilar membrane   A plate of fibers that forms the base of the cochlear partition and separates the middle and tympanic canals in the cochlea.

cochlear partition   The combined basilar membrane, tectorial membrane, and organ of Corti, which are together responsible for the transduction of sound waves into neural signals.

round window   A soft area of tissue at the base of the tympanic canal that releases excess pressure remaining from extremely intense sounds.

to the smallest bones in the body, the tensor tympani and the stapedius are the smallest muscles in the body. Their main purpose is to tense when sounds are very loud. They restrict movement of the ossicles and thus muffle pressure changes that might be large enough to damage the delicate structures in the inner ear. Unfortunately, this **acoustic reflex** follows the onset of loud sounds by about one-fifth of a second. So, while muscles help in environments that are loud for sustained periods, the acoustic reflex cannot protect against abrupt loud sounds, such as the firing of a gun. Muscles of the middle ear are also tensed during swallowing, talking, and general body movement, helping to keep the auditory system from being overwhelmed by sounds generated by our own bodies.

Inner Ear

The inner ear is an impressive feat of evolution. It is here that the minute changes in sound pressure available in the environment are translated into neural signals that inform the listener about the world. The function of the inner ear with respect to sound waves is roughly analogous to that of the retina with respect to light waves in vision: it translates the information carried by the waves into neural signals.

COCHLEAR CANALS AND MEMBRANES   The major structure of the inner ear is the **cochlea** (from the Greek *kochlos*, "snail"), a tiny coiled structure embedded in the temporal bone of the skull (see Figure 9.8). Rolled up, the cochlea is the size of a baby pea, about 4 mm in diameter in humans. Uncoiled, it would be a tube almost ten times as long—about 35 mm or 1.4 inches. The cochlea is filled with watery fluids in three parallel canals (**Figure 9.9**): the **tympanic canal** (or scala tympani), the **vestibular canal** (or scala vestibuli), and the **middle canal** (or scala media). The tympanic and vestibular canals are connected by a small opening, the **helicotrema**, and these two canals are effectively wrapped around the middle canal. Think of the tympanic and vestibular canals as one long, skinny balloon (the kind clowns use to make hats and animals), blown up and folded back on itself. The middle canal is another long balloon that is sandwiched, lengthwise, between the two halves of the first balloon.

The three canals of the cochlea are separated by two membranes (see Figure 9.9): **Reissner's membrane** between the vestibular canal and the middle canal, and the **basilar membrane** between the middle canal and the tympanic canal. Strictly speaking, the basilar membrane is not really a membrane, because it is not a thin, pliable sheet like the tympanic membrane, the oval window, or Reissner's membrane. Instead, it is a plate made up of stiff fibers. The basilar membrane forms the base of the **cochlear partition**, a complex structure through which sound waves are transduced into neural signals.

Vibrations transmitted through the tympanic membrane and middle-ear bones cause the stapes to push and pull the flexible oval window in and out of the vestibular canal at the base of the cochlea. This movement of the oval window causes waves of pressure changes, called traveling waves, to flow through the fluid in the vestibular canal, in much the same way that the membrane of a loudspeaker moves air to create sound waves. Because the cochlea is a closed system, changes in pressure cannot spread out in all directions. Instead, a displacement, or "bulge," forms in the vestibular canal and extends from the base of the cochlea down to the apex (look ahead to Figure 9.12). If sounds are extremely intense, any pressure that remains at the apex passes through the helicotrema and back to the cochlear base through the tympanic canal, where it is relieved by stretching yet another membrane, called the **round window** (see Figure 9.9).

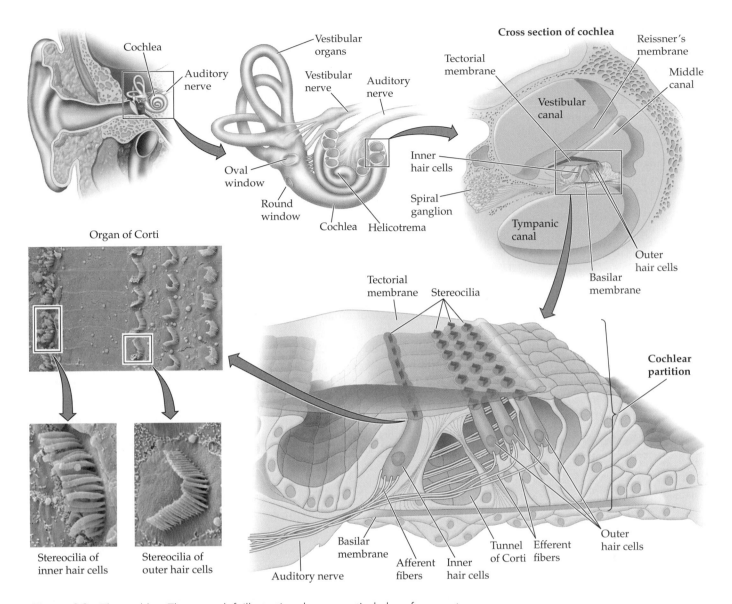

Figure 9.9 The cochlea. The upper left illustration shows a vertical plane from ear to ear. The remaining illustrations show cross sections of the cochlea at successively greater levels of detail. Note the three canals of the cochlea: vestibular, middle, and tympanic (upper right). When vibrations enter the cochlea, the tectorial membrane (lower right) shears across the organ of Corti. The top photomicrograph shows real hair cells: the single row of inner hair cells (left) and the three rows of outer hair cells (right). (Micrographs courtesy of Vijaya Prakash Krishnan Muthaiah.)

Because the vestibular and tympanic canals are wrapped tightly around the middle canal, when the vestibular canal bulges out, it puts pressure on the middle canal. This pressure has the effect of displacing the basilar membrane (which, recall, lies at the bottom of the middle canal), pushing down when the vestibular-canal bulge is created.

THE ORGAN OF CORTI Movements of the cochlear partition are translated into neural signals by structures in the **organ of Corti**, which extends along the top of the basilar membrane (see Figure 9.9). The organ of Corti is made up of a scaffold of cells that support specialized neurons called **hair cells**. Axons and

organ of Corti A structure on the basilar membrane of the cochlea that is composed of hair cells and dendrites of auditory nerve fibers.

hair cell Any cell that has stereocilia for transducing mechanical movement in the inner ear into neural activity sent to the brain. Some hair cells also receive inputs from the brain.

auditory nerve A collection of neurons that convey information from hair cells in the cochlea to the brain stem (afferent neurons) and from the brain stem to the hair cells (efferent neurons).

stereocilium Any of the hairlike extensions on the tips of hair cells in the cochlea that, when flexed, initiate the release of neurotransmitters.

tectorial membrane A gelatinous structure, attached on one end, that extends into the middle canal of the cochlea, floating above inner hair cells and touching outer hair cells.

dendrites of **auditory nerve** fibers terminate at the bases of hair cells. Hair cells in each human ear are arranged in four rows that run down the length of the basilar membrane: one row of about 3500 inner hair cells and three rows with a total of about 10,500 outer hair cells.

Inner and outer hair cells provide the foundations for minuscule hairlike bristles called **stereocilia** (singular *stereocilium*). On an inner hair cell, stereocilia are arranged as if posing for a group photo, in several nearly straight rows with the shorter stereocilia in front and the taller ones peering over their shoulders in the back. On an outer hair cell, stereocilia stand in rows that form the shape of a *V* or *W* (see Figure 9.9).

The **tectorial membrane** extends atop the organ of Corti. Like the basilar membrane, it isn't really a membrane. Rather, it is a gelatinous flap that is attached on one end and rests atop the outer hair cells on the other end. Taller stereocilia of outer hair cells are embedded in the tectorial membrane, and the stereocilia of inner hair cells are nestled against it. Because the tectorial membrane is attached on only one end, it shears across the width of the cochlear partition whenever the partition moves up and down. This shearing motion causes the stereocilia of both inner and outer hair cells to bend back and forth (**Figure 9.10**).

INNER AND OUTER HAIR CELLS Like photoreceptors in the retina, hair cells are specialized neurons that transduce one kind of energy (in this case, sound pressure) into another form of energy (neural firing). Hair cells in the vestibular organs also report head movements to the brain, as you will learn in Chapter 12. Deflection of a hair cell's stereocilia causes a change in voltage potential that initiates the release of neurotransmitters, which in turn encourages firing by auditory nerve fibers that have dendritic synapses on hair cells (Eggermont, 2017). However, it is the differences between photoreceptors and hair cells that are the most interesting.

While the retina has almost 100 million photoreceptors, the cochlea has only about 14,000 hair cells. Although outnumbered, stereocilia of hair cells blow away the competition when it comes to speed and sensitivity. Listeners can detect differences between onsets of two sounds as small as 1 millisecond (ms) (Zera and Green, 1993), and they can detect gaps between sounds as brief

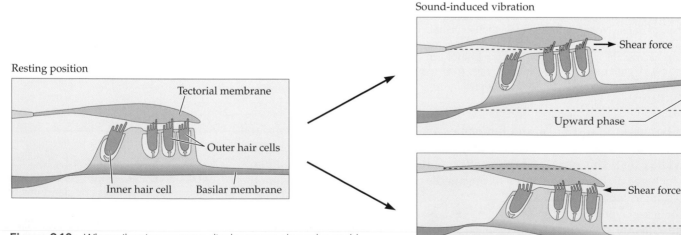

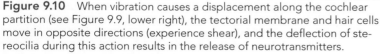

Figure 9.10 When vibration causes a displacement along the cochlear partition (see Figure 9.9, lower right), the tectorial membrane and hair cells move in opposite directions (experience shear), and the deflection of stereocilia during this action results in the release of neurotransmitters.

as 2–3 ms (Schneider and Hamstra, 1999). In contrast, when we watch a movie, pictures shown at 24 frames per second (over 40 ms apart) appear continuous to the visual system. Hair cells are not only extremely fast, but also extremely sensitive. It may take 30 minutes for our eyes to fully adjust to a dark theater, but our ears are always ready for the slightest sound.

Recall that the shortest stereocilia are in front of slightly taller stereocilia that are in front of still-taller stereocilia (**Figure 9.11**). Each stereocilium is connected to its neighbor by a tiny filament called a **tip link**, so the stereocilia connected by tip links bend together as a set when deflected by the shearing motion of the tectorial membrane. Because what happens next is very difficult to observe—tiny parts of tiny structures atop single hair cells—what follows is only a current hypothesis. When a stereocilium deflects, the tip link pulls on the taller stereocilium in a way that opens an ion pore somewhat like opening a gate for just a tiny fraction of a second. This action permits potassium ions (K^+) to flow rapidly into the hair cell, causing rapid depolarization (see Figure 9.11B and C). In turn, depolarization leads to a rapid influx of calcium ions (Ca^{2+}) and initiation of the release of neurotransmitters from the base of the hair cell to stimulate dendrites of the auditory nerve (Fettiplace and Hackney, 2006; Hudspeth, 1997).

tip link A tiny filament that stretches from the tip of a stereocilium to the side of its neighbor.

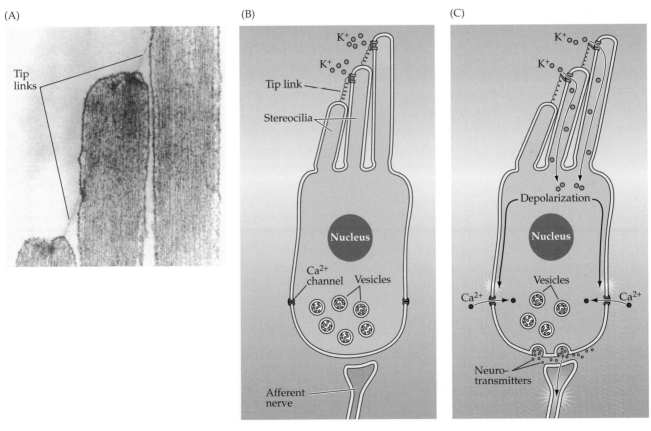

Figure 9.11 Stereocilia regulate the flow of ions into and out of hair cells. (A) This photomicrograph shows the threadlike tip links that connect the tip of each shorter stereocilium to its taller neighbor. (B, C) Bending the stereocilia atop a hair cell opens the ion pores, permitting a rapid influx of potassium ions (K^+) into the hair cell, and this depolarization opens channels that allow calcium ions (Ca^{2+}) to enter the base of the hair cell, causing the release of neurotransmitters into the synapse between the hair cell and an afferent auditory nerve fiber. (A courtesy of A. J. Hudspeth.)

place code Tuning of different parts of the cochlea to different frequencies, in which information about the particular frequency of an incoming sound wave is coded by the place along the cochlear partition that has the greatest mechanical displacement.

The opening of ion pores that results from the direct connection between stereocilia via tip links is known as mechanoelectrical transduction, which is responsible for both the extreme speed and the sensitivity of hair cells. Unlike the case in vision, depolarization in hearing does not await a cascade of biochemical processes such as those in photoactivation. Mechanoelectrical transduction is also extremely sensitive: ion pores open when deflection is as little as 1 nanometer (nm), roughly the diameter of a single atom.

The firing of the auditory nerve fibers finally completes the process of translating sound waves into patterns of neural activity.

Here's a brief summary of the whole process: An air pressure wave is funneled by the pinna through the ear canal to the tympanic membrane, which vibrates back and forth in time with the sound wave. The tympanic membrane vibrates the malleus, which vibrates the incus, which vibrates the stapes, which pushes and pulls on the oval window. The movement of the oval window causes pressure bulges to move down the length of the vestibular canal, and these bulges in the vestibular canal displace the middle canal up and down. This up-and-down motion forces the tectorial membrane to shear across the organ of Corti, moving the stereocilia atop hair cells back and forth. The pivoting of the stereocilia initiates rapid depolarization (followed by equally fast hyperpolarization) that results in spurts of neurotransmitter released into synapses between the hair cells and dendrites of auditory nerve fibers. These neurotransmitters initiate action potentials in the auditory nerve fibers that are carried to the brain. And that's all there is to it!

CODING OF AMPLITUDE AND FREQUENCY IN THE COCHLEA   Now that we know more about how ears work, we can return to the two fundamental characteristics of sound waves, amplitude and frequency, and learn how they are encoded by the cochlea.

If the amplitude of a sound wave is increased, the tympanic membrane and oval window move farther in and out with each pressure fluctuation. The result is that the bulge in the vestibular canal becomes bigger, which causes the cochlear partition to move farther up and down, which causes the tectorial membrane to shear across the organ of Corti more forcefully, which causes the hair cells to pivot farther back and forth, which causes more neurotransmitters to be released, which causes the auditory nerve fibers to fire action potentials more quickly. Thus, sound wave amplitude is conveyed in much the same way as light wave amplitude: the larger the amplitude, the higher the firing rate of the neurons that communicate with the brain. (We will discuss some complications of this simple explanation later in the chapter.)

Coding for frequency is a bit trickier. Earlier we said that the cochlear partition is displaced up and down in different places along the basilar membrane that correspond to different frequencies in the sound wave. This statement is true as far as it goes, but it does not tell the whole story, because different parts of the cochlear partition are displaced to different degrees by different sound wave frequencies. High frequencies cause the largest displacements closer to the oval window, near the base of the cochlea. Lower frequencies cause displacements farther away and nearer the apex. In other words, different places on the cochlea are "tuned" to different frequencies. This tuning is known as the **place code** for sound frequency.

Cochlear tuning to frequency is caused, in large part, by differences in the structure of the basilar membrane along the length of the cochlea (**Figure 9.12**). The cochlea narrows from base to apex, but the basilar membrane inside actually widens toward the apex. In addition, the basilar membrane is thick at the base and becomes thinner as it widens. While the basilar membrane gets thinner and

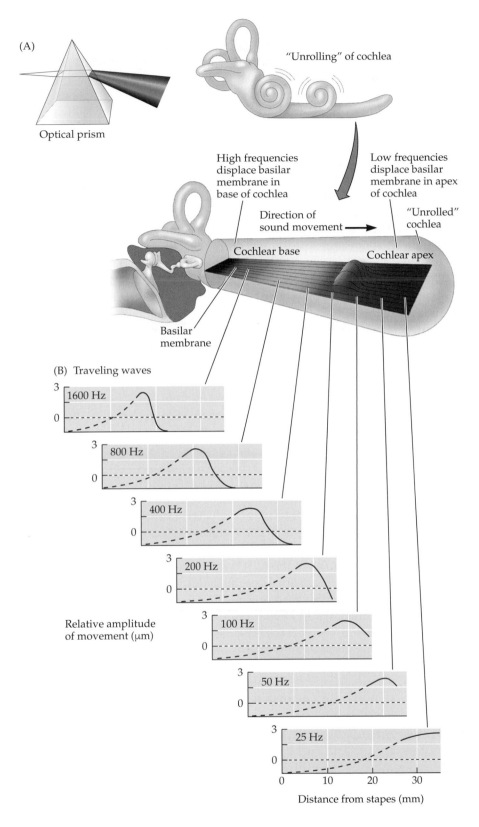

(A)

Optical prism

"Unrolling" of cochlea

High frequencies
displace basilar
membrane in
base of cochlea

Low frequencies
displace basilar
membrane in apex
of cochlea

Direction of
sound movement ⟶

"Unrolled"
cochlea

Cochlear base

Cochlear apex

Basilar
membrane

(B) Traveling waves

1600 Hz

800 Hz

400 Hz

200 Hz

Relative amplitude
of movement (µm)

100 Hz

50 Hz

25 Hz

Distance from stapes (mm)

Figure 9.12 The cochlea is like an acoustic prism in that its sensitivity spreads across different sound frequencies along its length. The narrower end of the basilar membrane toward the base is stiffer and most sensitive to higher frequencies. The wider, more flexible end toward the apex is most sensitive to lower frequencies. Here the cochlea is illustrated as if it were uncoiled (A), and the shapes of the traveling waves for different frequencies of vibration are shown (B).

wider along its length, the cochlea separates frequencies like an acoustic prism. Higher frequencies affect the narrower, stiffer regions of the basilar membrane near the base more, and lower frequencies cause greater displacements in the wider, more flexible regions near the apex.

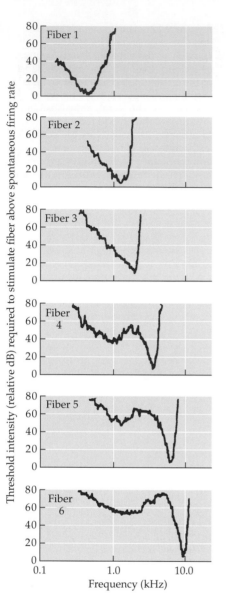

Figure 9.13   Threshold tuning curves for six auditory nerve fibers, each tuned to a different frequency. Curves define the lowest intensity necessary for the neuron to fire above its spontaneous rate at each frequency. The characteristic frequency for each of these six nerve fibers is at the lowest point of the tuning curve.

When you look at displacements from sounds of difference frequencies along the basilar membrane in Figure 9.12B, they are labeled as traveling waves. This is because the displacement really does travel from base to apex—faster near the base where the basilar membrane is narrower, and slower toward the wider apex. Because it takes time for the traveling wave to travel down the basilar membrane, high-frequency regions (base) are stimulated earlier than lower-frequency regions. This fact will become important when, in Chapter 10, you learn about how you know from what direction sounds are coming.

In addition to this passive, structural way of being tuned to frequency, the cochlea has processes that actively sharpen tuning. Remember that there are two different types of hair cells: inner and outer. Over 90% of the **afferent fibers** in the auditory nerve—fibers that take information *to* the brain—synapse on the 3500 inner hair cells (5–30 auditory nerve fibers listen to each inner hair cell). If the inner hair cells are conveying almost all the information about sound waves to the brain, then what do the 10,500 outer hair cells do? It turns out that most of the nerve fibers that synapse with the outer hair cells are **efferent fibers**, conveying information *from* the brain. These efferent fibers play a special role in determining what kind of information is sent on to the brain by the afferent fibers (Fettiplace and Hackney, 2006).

The Auditory Nerve

Now that we've covered the mechanics of how the auditory system translates air pressure changes into auditory nerve firing, let's discuss what we know about auditory nerve (AN) fibers. More specifically, we'll consider the type of information conveyed by afferent AN fibers from the cochlea to the brain.

Remember that sounds with different frequencies displace different regions of the cochlear partition. Inner hair cells, which provide most of the information to the brain via AN fibers, are lined up single file along the length of the basilar membrane. Put these two pieces of information together, and we can infer that the responses of individual AN fibers to different frequencies should be related to their place along the cochlear partition. Sure enough, when scientists record from individual AN fibers in animals, they find that different fibers selectively respond to different sound frequencies.

This frequency selectivity is clearest when sounds are very faint: at very low intensity levels (even less than 0 dB), an AN fiber will increase firing to only a very restricted range of frequencies. **Figure 9.13** shows **threshold tuning curves** for several AN fibers. To graph one of these curves, a researcher inserts an electrode very close to a single AN fiber and then measures how intense the sine waves of different frequencies must be for the neuron to fire faster than its normal, spontaneous firing rate. The frequency that increases the neuron's firing rate at the lowest intensity (the lowest point on the threshold tuning curve) is called the neuron's **characteristic frequency** (**CF**).

The sharp tuning measured from outputs of inner hair cells depends greatly upon the unsung heroes of the basilar membrane, the outer hair cells. From **Figure 9.14**, you can see how outer hair cells are required for threshold tuning curves to be focused on a narrow range of frequencies. Outer hair cells make

afferent fiber   A neuron that carries sensory information to the central nervous system.

efferent fiber   A neuron that carries information from the central nervous system to the periphery.

threshold tuning curve   A graph plotting the thresholds of a neuron in response to sine waves with varying frequencies at the lowest intensity that will give rise to a response.

characteristic frequency (CF)   The frequency to which a particular auditory nerve fiber is most sensitive.

parts of the cochlear partition stiffer in ways that make the responses of inner hair cells more sensitive (Dong and Olson, 2013) and more sharply tuned to particular frequencies (Eggermont, 2017).

Up to this point, the way the ear transduces acoustic energy at different frequencies into a pattern of neural responses seems fairly straightforward. A low-intensity sine wave tone with a certain frequency will cause certain AN fibers to increase their firing rates, while other AN fibers continue to fire at their spontaneous rates. As long as the brain knows which AN fibers have which characteristic frequencies, it can interpret the pattern of firing rates across all the AN fibers to determine the frequency of any tone (as long as it is within the range of frequencies picked up by the human cochlea).

Unfortunately, it's not quite this simple. Almost all sounds in the environment are more complex than single sine waves, and most sounds we hear are also much louder than the very quiet sound waves used to measure threshold tuning curves. So although the previous paragraph captures the gist of how AN fibers code for sound frequencies, we have to do a bit more work to understand how higher-intensity, complex sounds are encoded in the auditory nerve. We will consider two of the specific complications we have to deal with. Then, we'll look at one additional mechanism, related to timing rather than place, that the auditory system uses to convey low-frequency components of sound waves.

TWO-TONE SUPPRESSION   The rate at which an AN fiber responds changes when energy is introduced at nearby frequencies. In particular, when a second tone of a slightly different frequency is added, the rate of neural firing for the first tone actually decreases—a phenomenon called **two-tone suppression (Figure 9.15)**. Suppression effects are particularly pronounced when the second (suppressor) tone has a lower frequency than the first tone. In other words, if we're recording from an AN fiber whose CF is 8000 Hz and we use an 8000-Hz test tone, a 1000-Hz suppressor tone has a greater effect on the neuron's firing rate than a 15,000-Hz suppressor tone has. You can see how understanding the response of the whole auditory nerve to complex sounds (that is, frequency combinations) is more complicated than simply adding up the responses of individual AN fibers to individual pure tones.

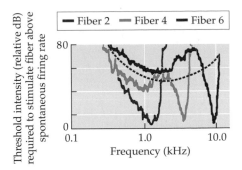

Figure 9.14   Outer hair cells improve both sensitivity and frequency selectivity. Three threshold tuning curves show responses when hair cells are active, and the dashed line shows what the rightmost tuning curve would look like if outer hair cells were not active. Higher-intensity tones would be required to excite the AN fiber, and the fiber would be less selective in frequencies to which it would fire.

two-tone suppression   A decrease in the firing rate of one auditory nerve fiber due to one tone, when a second tone is presented at the same time.

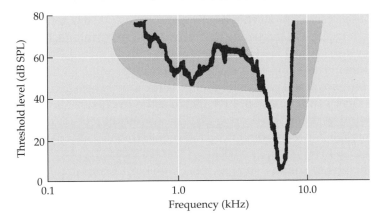
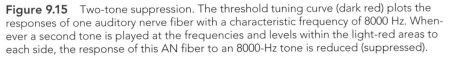

Figure 9.15   Two-tone suppression. The threshold tuning curve (dark red) plots the responses of one auditory nerve fiber with a characteristic frequency of 8000 Hz. Whenever a second tone is played at the frequencies and levels within the light-red areas to each side, the response of this AN fiber to an 8000-Hz tone is reduced (suppressed).

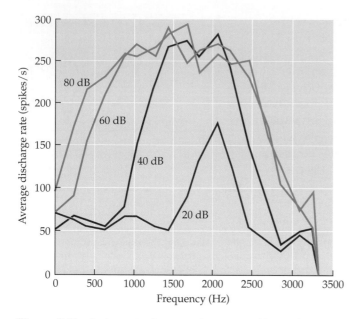

Figure 9.16 Isointensity functions for one AN fiber with a characteristic frequency of 2000 Hz. Tones of varying frequencies are presented at 20, 40, 60, and 80 dB. The neuron fires vigorously to a wider range of frequencies (mostly lower) when intensity is increased. Note that the 20-dB curve resembles an upside-down threshold tuning curve (compare with Figure 9.13) because 20 dB is almost as low as the intensities at which thresholds are measured.

isointensity curve A map plotting the firing rate of an auditory nerve fiber against varying frequencies at varying intensities.

rate saturation The point at which a nerve fiber is firing as rapidly as possible and further stimulation is incapable of increasing the firing rate.

rate-intensity function A graph plotting the firing rate of an auditory nerve fiber in response to a sound of constant frequency at increasing intensities.

RATE SATURATION Sounds that matter most to listeners—most conversational speech, for example—are usually heard at intensities, such as 60 or 70 dB, over 1000 times greater than the threshold for just detecting sounds. Are AN fibers as selective for their characteristic frequencies at levels well above threshold as they are for the barely audible sounds used to chart threshold tuning curves?

To answer this question, we can look at **isointensity curves**, which we chart by measuring an AN fiber's firing rate to a wide range of frequencies, all presented at the same intensity level. **Figure 9.16** shows a family of isointensity curves for one AN fiber with a CF of 2000 Hz. The bottom curve shows the average firing rate (number of action potentials per second) of the neuron in response to 20-dB tones with frequencies between 50 and 3300 Hz. The other curves track firing rates for 40-dB, 60-dB, and 80-dB tones over the same frequency range.

We learn from these curves that for relatively quiet, 20-dB sounds (this is about the sound level of leaves rustling in the wind), the neuron is still quite narrowly tuned, firing much faster in response to its CF (2000 Hz) than to neighboring frequencies. At 80 dB, however, the neuron appears to fire at about the same rate for any frequency in the range of 800–2500 Hz. In other words, frequencies such as 1000 Hz, to which the AN fiber had almost no response at low intensity levels, evoke quite substantial responses when intensity is increased.

The phenomenon behind this broadening of frequency selectivity is called **rate saturation**. Remember that AN fibers fire in response to the displacement of stereocilia on hair cells. The farther stereocilia pivot, the faster AN fibers linked to that hair cell fire. For a 20-dB tone at 1000 Hz, the stereocilia on the hair cell feeding the AN fiber featured in Figure 9.16 will not bend at all, so the fiber's firing rate remains at its resting level. The firing rate rises above this resting level when the frequency of the 20-dB tone is increased to 1700 Hz, and it reaches its highest level at the AN fiber's characteristic frequency, 2000 Hz.

When the intensity is increased to 40 dB, however, the bulge in the vestibular canal is so large that stereocilia start displacing even to a 1000-Hz tone (see Figure 9.16). If we increase the frequency to 1250 Hz, the firing rate increases, and it increases even more at 1500 Hz. The problem is that at about 1500 Hz, the fiber's firing rate maxes out (saturates). Stereocilia are pivoting as much as they can at this point, so increasing the frequency of the tone has no additional effect on the AN fiber's firing rate until we increase the frequency above the fiber's CF and the firing rate starts dropping again. For 80-dB tones, the fiber is maxed out at a range between even lower and higher frequencies relative to the CF of 2000 Hz.

For moderately intense sounds, such as speech, the brain cannot rely on a single AN fiber to determine the frequency of the tone. For example, we can't use the rule "if an AN fiber with a characteristic frequency of 2000 Hz is firing very fast, the sound must be 2000 Hz" because, as Figure 9.16 illustrates, this neuron will also fire at its maximum rate to a 1000-Hz tone if the sound wave has a large-enough amplitude.

One way the auditory system gets around this problem is to use AN fibers with different spontaneous firing rates. **Figure 9.17** shows **rate-intensity functions** for six fibers, all of which listen to the same hair cell (remember that dendrites from 5–30 auditory neurons are synapsing with each inner hair cell). To plot these curves, the intensity level of a tone at the AN fiber's CF is slowly raised from 0 dB up to 90 dB. As you can see, the resting rates of some fibers (whose functions are plotted in red) are less than 10 spikes per second. These neurons are **low-spontaneous fibers**. The blue lines plot firing rates for **high-spontaneous fibers**, which fire 30 or more times per second, even in silence. **Mid-spontaneous fibers** have resting rates between these levels.

High-spontaneous AN fibers are somewhat analogous to rods in the retina: they are especially sensitive to low levels of sound, responding at rates above resting level even when decibel levels are quite low. The trade-off is that the firing rates of these fibers quickly reach saturation, so their frequency selectivity is relatively poor when intensity is relatively high. Low-spontaneous fibers are more like cones, requiring more energy (higher-intensity sound waves) to start responding, but retaining their frequency selectivity over a broader range of intensity.

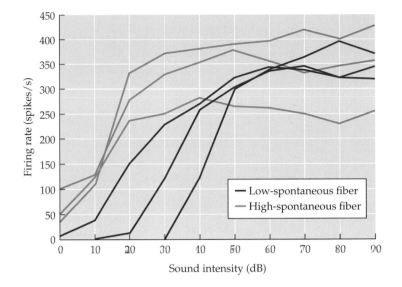

Figure 9.17 Firing rate plotted against sound intensity for six auditory nerve fibers: three low-spontaneous and three high-spontaneous. Firing rates for all six neurons increase with increasing sound level. Low-spontaneous neurons require higher-intensity sounds before they begin to fire, and they continue to increase firing rate to higher sound levels.

In addition to having different AN fibers with different spontaneous rates, the auditory system can accurately determine the frequency of incoming sound waves by integrating information across many AN fibers and using the *pattern* of firing rates across all these fibers. Remember that in the visual system, we use the pattern of firing across only three types of cones to calculate the wavelength of light. The auditory system uses the same principle, but it has some 14,000 AN fibers in each ear to discern acoustic frequency. Consequently, the frequency sensitivity of the human auditory system as a whole is exquisite across a wide range of intensity levels, despite the coarse selectivity of individual AN fibers.

THE TEMPORAL CODE FOR SOUND FREQUENCY In addition to the cochlear place code, the auditory system has another way to encode frequency. As **Figure 9.18** illustrates, many AN fibers tend to fire action potentials at one particular point in the phase of a sound wave—a phenomenon called **phase locking**. Phase locking may occur because AN fibers fire when the stereocilia of hair cells move in one direction (e.g., as the basilar membrane moves up toward the tectorial membrane) but do not fire when the stereocilia move in the other direction. Recall from our discussion of mechanoelectrical transduction in stereocilia that the encoding of time is extremely accurate.

The existence of phase locking means that the firing pattern of an AN fiber carries a **temporal code** for the sound wave frequency. For example, if the AN fiber fires an action potential 100 times per second, then downstream neurons listening to the AN fiber can infer that the sound wave includes a frequency component of 100 Hz.

While reliable for lower frequencies, temporal coding becomes inconsistent for frequencies higher than 1000 Hz and is virtually absent above 4000 or 5000 Hz. In large part, this inconsistency is due to the refractory period of the AN fiber. For high frequencies, fibers simply cannot produce action potentials quickly

low-spontaneous fiber An auditory nerve fiber that has a low rate (less than 10 spikes per second) of spontaneous firing. Low-spontaneous fibers require relatively intense sound before they will fire at higher rates.

high-spontaneous fiber An auditory nerve fiber that has a high rate (more than 30 spikes per second) of spontaneous firing. High-spontaneous fibers increase their firing rate in response to relatively low levels of sound.

mid-spontaneous fiber An auditory nerve fiber that has a medium rate (10–30 spikes per second) of spontaneous firing. The characteristics of mid-spontaneous fibers are intermediate between those of low- and high-spontaneous fibers.

phase locking Firing of a single neuron at one distinct point in the period (cycle) of a sound wave at a given frequency. (The neuron need not fire on every cycle, but each firing will occur at the same point in the cycle.)

temporal code Tuning of different parts of the cochlea to different frequencies, in which information about the particular frequency of an incoming sound wave is coded by the timing of neural firing as it relates to the period of the sound.

Figure 9.18 Phase locking. The histogram (bottom) shows neural spikes for an AN fiber in response to the same low-frequency sine wave (top) being played many times. Note that the neuron is most likely to fire at one particular phase of each cycle of the sine wave. This phase locking provides a temporal code to sound frequency.

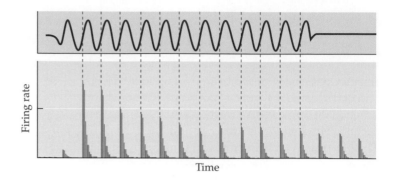

Firing rate

Time

volley principle The idea that multiple neurons can provide a temporal code for frequency if each neuron fires at a distinct point in the period of a sound wave but does not fire on every period.

cochlear nucleus The first brain stem nucleus at which afferent auditory nerve fibers synapse.

enough to fire on every cycle of the sound. However, multiple neurons could, in principle, encode higher frequencies as a group. For example, four neurons could each fire only once every fourth cycle of a 2000-Hz sound. If the four neurons "took turns," each would have to fire only 500 times per second to fully encode the 2000-Hz sound in their combined temporal pattern. This idea has a long history (Wever, 1949), and it is referred to as the **volley principle** (**Figure 9.19**). According to this hypothesis, neurons sustain a temporal pattern of firing much like the pattern of Revolutionary War–era soldiers firing guns from the front line of a formation while the second and third lines took time to reload.

When it comes to temporal coding, neurons along the full length of the cochlea can participate. Even AN fibers with relatively high-frequency CFs encode lower-frequency energy in the temporal pattern of their responses. For example, if you are listening to a fairly loud sound that is a combination of 200- and 8000-Hz sine wave tones, a neuron near the base of the cochlea that becomes wildly excited by the 8000-Hz component of the sound will also tend to be phase-locked to the 200-Hz component. This neuron thus carries information about both the high-frequency component (via place coding, because the brain knows the neuron's CF) and the low-frequency component (via temporal coding).

Auditory Brain Structures

The nerve fibers that make up the auditory nerve share cranial nerve VIII with nerve fibers for the vestibular system (which is discussed in Chapter 12); this is why cranial nerve VIII is known not only as the auditory nerve, but also as the vestibulocochlear nerve. All AN fibers initially synapse in the **cochlear nucleus** (**Figure 9.20**). The cochlear nucleus contains many different types of specialized neurons. Some of these are especially sensitive to onsets of sound at particular frequencies. Some are sensitive to the coincidence of onsets across many frequencies (they fire when multiple frequencies initially begin but stop firing if the

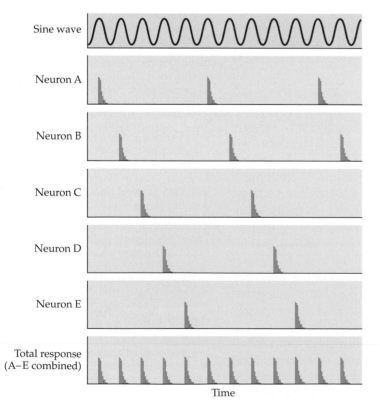

Sine wave

Neuron A

Neuron B

Neuron C

Neuron D

Neuron E

Total response (A–E combined)

Time

Figure 9.19 The volley principle. Even if one neuron cannot fire in response to every cycle of a higher-frequency tone, multiple AN fibers together can provide a temporal code for frequency if different neurons (A, B, C, D, E) fire at different periods of the sine wave.

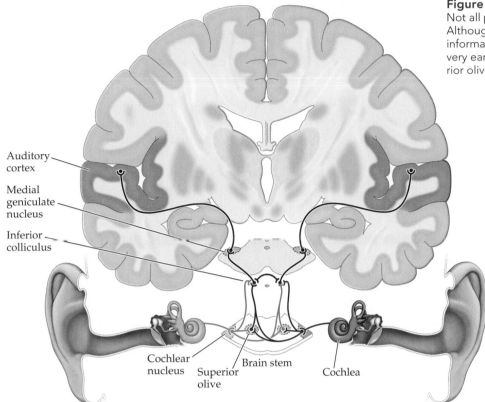

Figure 9.20 Pathways in the auditory system. Not all pathways are shown in this schematic. Although there are two parallel pathways, information from both ears comes together very early in the auditory system, at the superior olives.

Labels on figure:
Auditory cortex
Medial geniculate nucleus
Inferior colliculus
Cochlear nucleus
Superior olive
Brain stem
Cochlea

sound continues playing). Some cochlear nucleus neurons use lateral inhibition to sharpen the tuning to one frequency by suppressing nearby frequencies—a mechanism reminiscent of that used by retinal ganglion cells to respond to spots of light instead of broad fields of light. Others respond in exactly the same way as the AN fibers that feed them. Some neurons appear to serve as little more than quick relays from the cochlea to the **superior olive**, another brain stem nucleus.

As Figure 9.20 shows, some of the neurons that project from the cochlear nuclei to the superior olives cross over to the opposite side of the brain. Thus, unlike the visual system, where inputs from each visual field remain separate until they have extended a fair distance in the visual cortex, signals from both cochleas reach both sides of the brain after only a single synapse. As we will see in Chapter 10, this direct relay of information across both ears is essential to using tiny differences between the two ears to detect the direction of a sound.

Neurons from the cochlear nucleus and superior olive travel up the brain stem to the **inferior colliculus**. Most (but not all) of the input to each inferior colliculus comes from the opposite (contralateral) ear; that is, the left inferior colliculus listens mostly to the right ear, and vice versa.

The **medial geniculate nucleus** of the thalamus is the last stop in the auditory pathway before the cerebral cortex. Like the lateral geniculate of the visual system, there are many more neurons that project from the cortex to the medial geniculate (efferent neurons) than project from the medial geniculate to the cortex (afferent neurons). These efferent connections, some of which presumably convey information back to lower stages of the auditory system, provide further anatomical evidence that sensory systems are two-way streets, in which feedback from the brain is tightly integrated with sensory information flowing up to the brain.

superior olive   An early brain stem region in the auditory pathway where inputs from both ears converge.

inferior colliculus   A midbrain nucleus in the auditory pathway.

medial geniculate nucleus   The part of the thalamus that relays auditory signals to the temporal cortex and receives input from the auditory cortex.

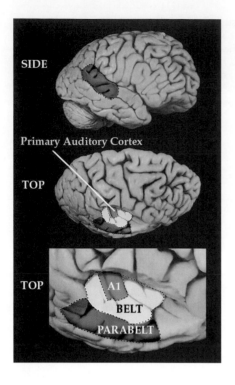

Figure 9.21 The first stages of auditory processing begin in the temporal lobe in areas within the Sylvian fissure. The top picture is from the side of the brain, and the lower two pictures are looking down at the brain with the parietal cortex cut away. Primary auditory cortex (A1) is in the center. It is surrounded by belt regions, and parabelt regions extend past the belt to the front and side. (From Brugge and Howard, 2002.)

All structures of the auditory system, beginning with the basilar membrane and continuing through the cochlear nucleus, superior olive, inferior colliculus, and medial geniculate nucleus, show a consistent organizational pattern in which neurons are aligned based on the frequencies to which they are most sensitive. That is, neurons most responsive to low-frequency energy lie on one edge of each structure, neurons responding to high frequencies lie on the other edge, and neurons responding to other frequencies are spread out in an orderly fashion in between. The pervasiveness of this **tonotopic organization** pattern reflects both the early mechanical properties of transduction and the importance of the frequency composition of sounds for auditory perception.

Primary auditory cortex is often referred to as **A1**, just as primary visual cortex is called V1. Tonotopic organization is less consistently maintained in A1 (Bandyopadhyay, Shamma, and Kanold, 2010; Rothschild, Nelken, and Mizrahi, 2010). Neurons from A1 project to the surrounding **belt area** of cortex, and neurons from this belt synapse with neurons in the adjacent **parabelt area** (**Figure 9.21**). Just about any sound will cause activation in some part of A1. In the belt and parabelt areas, referred to as secondary or associational auditory areas, simple sounds such as sine waves elicit less activity, particularly if the stimuli don't change much over time. Thus we see that, as in other sensory systems, processing proceeds from simpler to more complex stimuli as we move farther along the auditory pathway. We also find greater evidence of cross-modal processing (e.g., combining sound and light information), particularly in parabelt areas.

Comparing the overall structure of the auditory and visual systems shows that a relatively large proportion of the processing in the auditory system is done before A1. By contrast, as you learned in Chapter 3, the majority of the most important visual processing occurs in cortical areas V1 and beyond. Auditory capabilities that may be most important to humans, listening to speech and music, are subserved almost entirely by cortical areas. We will return to the role of the cortex in auditory processing when we discuss speech and music perception in Chapter 11.

Basic Operating Characteristics of the Auditory System

Up to this point we have discussed the anatomy of the auditory system and the physiology of how the system encodes the two basic physical attributes of sound waves: amplitude (intensity) and frequency. We've learned this through direct observation of anatomical structures. Scientists examine basilar membranes, record auditory nerve fibers, dissect various brain structures, and so on.

We turn now to the findings of researchers who have approached the auditory system from a different perspective. Instead of playing a sound and trying to determine how neurons respond, we can instead play the sound and ask actual human listeners—each of whom is the sum total of a great many neurons—what they hear. When human listeners are asked to report their auditory sensations, their answers are due partly to the acoustic properties of the sound signal and partly to their own psychological characteristics. This method of investigation is thus called **psychoacoustics**.

tonotopic organization An arrangement in which neurons that respond to different frequencies are organized anatomically in order of frequency.

primary auditory cortex (A1) The first area within the temporal lobes of the brain responsible for processing acoustic information.

belt area A region of cortex, directly adjacent to the primary auditory cortex (A1), with inputs from A1, where neurons respond to more complex characteristics of sounds.

parabelt area A region of cortex, lateral and adjacent to the belt area, where neurons respond to more complex characteristics of sounds, as well as to input from other senses.

psychoacoustics The branch of psychophysics that studies the psychological correlates of the physical dimensions of acoustics in order to understand how the auditory system operates.

Scientists who study psychoacoustics (psychoacousticians) are always careful to distinguish between the physical characteristics of sounds and the impressions of these sounds for listeners. As we noted earlier, whereas frequency, measured in hertz, is a physical description of the spectral composition of a sound, the subjective attribute of frequency for listeners is *pitch*. Sounds are measured with respect to frequency, but listeners hear pitch. Similarly, the intensity of sound is measured as sound pressure in decibels, but listeners hear *loudness*. If the auditory system operated exactly the same as electronic measuring devices, we could use the terms *frequency* and *pitch* and the terms *intensity* and *loudness* interchangeably. As we will see, however, biological auditory systems do not work exactly as electronic measuring devices work. For example, one sound wave may be heard as quite a bit louder than another, even though the two waves have exactly the same amplitude. Careful study of the differences between the responses of electronic devices (sound-level meters and spectrum analyzers) and biological listening devices (human beings) provides great insight into how the human auditory system works.

Intensity and Loudness

The bottom curve in **Figure 9.22** shows the human **audibility threshold**, which graphs the lowest sound pressure level that can be reliably detected across the frequency range of human hearing (20–20,000 Hz). Note that the best (lowest) absolute thresholds for human hearing are between 2000 and 6000 Hz (2–6 kilohertz [kHz]). Remember that these frequencies are enhanced by the physical properties of the ear canal. Thresholds rise on both sides of this range, meaning that higher- and lower-frequency sound waves must have larger amplitudes in order to be heard.

The other lines in Figure 9.22 are **equal-loudness curves** (Suzuki and Takeshima, 2004). We obtain these curves by asking listeners to equate the loudness of sounds with different frequencies. The starting point for each curve is always 1000 Hz, so the curve marked 40 shows the amplitude necessary to make tones at other frequencies sound exactly as loud as a 1000-Hz, 40-dB tone; the curve marked 60 represents the decibel levels necessary to match a 1000-Hz, 60-dB tone; and so on. As the figure shows, the same pattern of frequency-dependent sensitivity that we see in the audibility threshold curve extends to sounds above threshold. (See **Web Activity 9.3: Equal-Loudness Curves**.)

audibility threshold The lowest sound pressure level that can be reliably detected at a given frequency.

equal-loudness curve A graph plotting sound pressure level (dB SPL) against the frequency for which a listener perceives constant loudness.

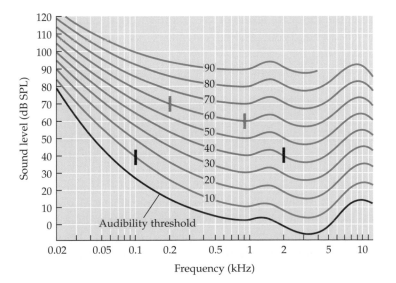

Figure 9.22 The lowest curve (red) illustrates the threshold for hearing sounds at varying frequencies. The curves labeled 10, 20, 30, and so on are equal-loudness curves. For a single contour, tones of different frequencies have different physical intensities, but they sound equally loud. (After Suzuki and Takeshima, 2004.)

The two orange tick marks in Figure 9.22 indicate that a 200-Hz tone presented at 70 dB sounds about as loud as a 900-Hz tone presented at 60 dB (that is, both points fall on the equal-loudness curve marked 60), whereas a 2000-Hz tone presented at 40 dB sounds much louder than a 100-Hz tone presented at the same level (purple tick marks). These observations demonstrate the inequality of sound pressure level and loudness: equal-amplitude sounds can be perceived as softer or louder than each other, depending on the frequencies of the sound waves.

Another way to track the relationship between amplitude and loudness is to pick one frequency, steadily raise the intensity of the sound, and ask a listener to judge how the loudness increases. Experiments of this type show, once again, that the relationship between intensity and loudness is far from perfect. Doubling the perceived loudness of a sound requires more than a doubling in the amount of acoustic energy present in a sound wave, especially above 40 dB. The same kind of relationship holds in vision: the number of photons must be more than doubled to double the perceived brightness of a light.

The loudness of a sound also depends on its duration. Within limits, longer sounds are heard as being louder. Again, the same thing happens in vision: flashes of light appear brighter when they last longer. The reason for this general phenomenon is that the perception of loudness or brightness depends on the summation of energy over a brief, but noticeable, period of time—a process called **temporal integration**. For hearing, temporal integration occurs over an interval of 100–200 ms. So if a sound is presented for less than 100 ms, it will be perceived as softer than a sound with the same amplitude and frequency presented for 300 ms. However, there will be little difference in loudness perception if the duration of the sound is increased from 300 to 1000 ms or longer.

In addition to studying absolute loudness judgments, psychoacousticians are interested in how proficient humans are at discriminating between the loudness levels of two sounds. There are several different ways to measure the smallest differences in intensity that can be detected, and many measures show sensitivity to changes of less than 1 dB. This ability is quite impressive, given the wide range of sound intensities (from 0 to over 100 dB) that humans can perceive and the fact that, unlike the visual system, the auditory system is always sensitive to this entire range (remember that, to achieve maximum visual sensitivity, we need time to adapt to lower or higher ambient light levels). Although the ability to discriminate between subtle loudness differences might not seem all that important to survival, we will see in Chapter 10 how the auditory system uses differences between the intensity levels of sounds reaching the left and right ears to determine *where* sound sources are located.

For a time, it was difficult to understand how listeners could be sensitive to such small differences in loudness over such a large range. Sound wave intensity is generally signaled by the firing rate of auditory nerve fibers: larger intensities (loud sounds) correspond to higher firing rates, and smaller intensities (quiet sounds) correspond to lower firing rates. You should recall that the intensities required to fire (thresholds) vary from one AN fiber to the next. For example, one fiber might selectively respond to the range of amplitudes between 0 and 25 dB, another might span the range of 15–40 dB, a third might cover 38–65 dB, and so on (see Figure 9.17). A full population of neurons with different thresholds can then encode a much broader range of intensities than is possible with any single neuron. In addition, remember that neurons become responsive to a broader range of frequencies when intensity is higher (see Figure 9.16). One result is that, as sounds become more intense, many more AN fibers become excited.

temporal integration The process by which a sound at a constant level is perceived as being louder when it is of greater duration. The term also applies to perceived brightness, which depends on the duration of light.

■ Scientists at Work

Why Don't Manatees Get Out of the Way When a Boat Is Coming?

■ **Question** Manatees, also known as sea cows (**Figure 9.23A**), are loved by children and adults alike. Sadly, about 100 manatees are killed each year when struck by motorboats. Why does it seem that manatees cannot hear boat motors and get out of the way?

■ **Hypotheses** Manatees either do not hear very well or cannot hear the particular sounds made by boat motors.

■ **Test** Train manatees to listen for sounds at different frequencies and respond when they hear (or do not hear) a sound (Gerstein, 2002) (**Figure 9.23B**).

■ **Results** Manatees have quite good hearing, generally better than that of humans underwater. Manatees, however, are not very good at hearing low frequencies (**Figure 9.23C**).

■ **Conclusion** Laws that require boaters to slow down in manatee zones result in motors running slower and producing softer sounds with lower frequencies. This may not have the desired effect of saving manatees. On the contrary, creating lower-frequency sounds is a good way to sneak up on a manatee without being heard.

■ **Future work** Driving boats faster is not a solution, because even if the manatees can hear faster boats better, they still need time to get out of the way. Instead, boats should have manatee alerting devices that project a band of sound in front of the boats as they move, and this sound should comprise one or more of the higher frequencies that manatees hear very well (Florida Atlantic University, 2017).

(A)
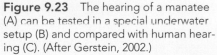

(B)

(C)
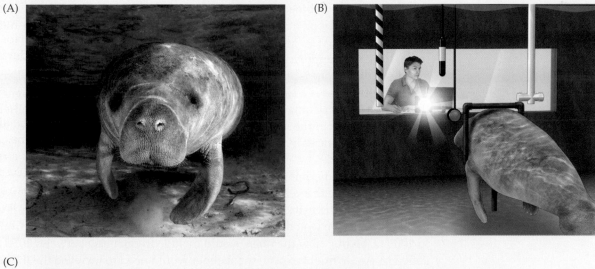

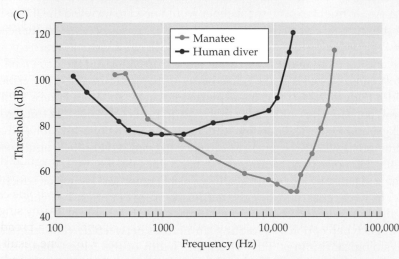

Figure 9.23 The hearing of a manatee (A) can be tested in a special underwater setup (B) and compared with human hearing (C). (After Gerstein, 2002.)

masking Using a second sound, frequently noise, to make the detection of another sound more difficult.

white noise Noise consisting of all audible frequencies in equal amounts. White noise in hearing is analogous to white light in vision, for which all wavelengths are present.

critical bandwidth The range of frequencies conveyed within a channel in the auditory system.

Frequency and Pitch

The tonotopic organization of the auditory system, from basilar membrane to primary auditory cortex, is a very big hint that frequency composition is a fundamental determinant of how we hear sounds. More than anything else, psychoacousticians have studied how listeners perceive pitch, the psychological counterpart to frequency. As is the case with intensity and loudness, the frequency of a sound is related to, but not perfectly correlated with, the perceived pitch of the sound. For any given frequency increase (e.g., 50 Hz), listeners will perceive a greater rise in pitch for lower frequencies than they do for higher frequencies. Consequently, listeners perceive a greater pitch difference when a tone shifts from 500 to 1000 Hz than when a tone shifts from 5000 to 5500 Hz.

Research done using pure tones (each composed of a single sine wave) indicates that humans are remarkably good at detecting very small differences in frequency. For example, listeners can discriminate between tones of 1000 and 1001 Hz—a difference of only one-tenth of 1%! Pitch discrimination at the lower and higher ends of the auditory system's frequency range is not quite as good, but it is still impressive.

Psychoacousticians also use **masking** experiments to investigate frequency selectivity. In the research described in the previous paragraph, listeners always hear only one sound frequency at a time. In a masking experiment, multiple frequencies are combined, and we see how well listeners can pick out certain components. We look at how effective one sound—the masker—is at hiding another sound.

In the classic approach to measuring frequency selectivity using masking, a single sine wave tone is placed in the middle of a band of acoustic noise (Fletcher, 1940). **White noise** is a signal that includes equal energy of every frequency in the human auditory range (20–20,000 Hz), just as white light includes light rays of all frequencies in the visible spectrum. A more limited band of noise might include all frequencies in the range of 500–1500 Hz; an even smaller band could span 500–510 Hz.

In a typical experiment, we might start with a 2000-Hz sine wave test tone presented along with a very narrow band of noise—say, 1975–2025 Hz. We would then adjust the intensity of the test tone until listeners could just hear it over the noise. Next we would increase the bandwidth of the noise, perhaps from 50 to 100 Hz, so that now the noise would include frequencies between 1950 and 2050 Hz. As we might expect, the listener would need to increase the intensity of the test tone to be able to hear it over this broader range of noise frequencies.

If we keep widening the bandwidth, however, we will eventually reach a point at which adding more frequencies to the noise stops affecting the detectability of the test tone. The size of the noise band at this point is called the **critical bandwidth** (**Figure 9.24A**). For the experimental data plotted in **Figure 9.24B**, the critical bandwidth is 400 Hz. In this case, to pick out a 2000-Hz tone from the background noise, listeners must increase the intensity of the tone when the bandwidth is widened from 50 to 100 Hz and from 200 to 400 Hz, but going from a 400-Hz noise band to an 800-Hz band does *not* require the listener to make the test tone any louder. In fact, the 400-Hz noise band is just as effective a masker as white noise covering the entire spectrum of human hearing.

Results from the masking paradigm have helped cement the role of place coding in pitch perception by revealing similarities between perceptual effects and physiological findings. First of all, the width of the critical bandwidth changes depending on the frequency of the test tone, and these widths correspond to the physical spacing of frequencies along the basilar membrane. For

(A)

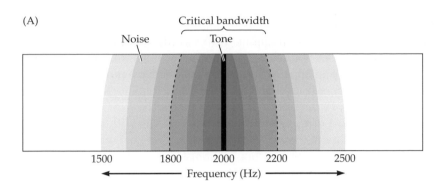

(B)

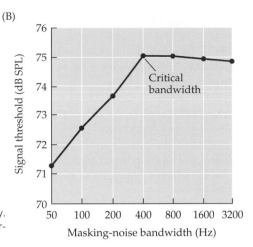

Figure 9.24 Critical bandwidth and masking. (A) To measure the width of a critical band, participants listen for a tone in the center of a band of noise of constant intensity. It is harder to detect the tone as the band of noise widens up to a point, after which further widening has no effect on detecting the tone. This point defines the critical bandwidth. (B) For this plot of bandwidth data, a 2000 Hz tone was used. The bandwidth of the noise had no effect on detection of the tone when it exceeded 400 Hz, so 400 Hz is the width of the critical band at 2000 Hz. (B adapted from Schoonevelt and Moore, 1989 with the permission of the Acoustical Society of America.)

example, we know that a greater proportion of the basilar membrane vibrates in response to low frequencies, and higher-frequency ranges vibrate smaller portions of the membrane. Correspondingly, masking studies show that the critical bandwidths for low frequencies are smaller than the critical bandwidths for high frequencies because the spacing between low frequencies is larger on the basilar membrane.

Another important finding is that masking effects are asymmetrical. Masking sounds at frequencies lower than that of the test tone are more effective—a phenomenon called the upward spread of masking. This phenomenon may seem counterintuitive, but a look back at Figure 9.12 shows how displacement of the basilar membrane (the traveling wave) extends from the high-frequency base to the low-frequency apex. Displacement for low-frequency energy sounds toward the apex leaves a trail of displacement across high-frequency regions toward the base. From two-tone suppression experiments, we also learned that suppression is greater if the suppressor tone is below an AN fiber's characteristic frequency than if the suppressor tone is above the fiber's characteristic frequency (see Figure 9.15).

Hearing Loss

Roughly 30 million Americans suffer some form of hearing impairment. When we talk about hearing loss, we typically do not mean the total loss of all hearing (deafness), but rather the elevation of sound thresholds. For example, frequencies that used to be audible at 20 dB may become inaudible unless they are presented at 40 or 60 dB. Of course, in the end we do not just need to detect sounds; the term *hearing* really refers to using spectral and temporal differences between sounds in order to learn something about events going on in the environment. As we will see, common forms of hearing loss can affect the ability to interpret sounds, even when the sounds are loud enough to be detectable.

Hearing can be impaired by damage to any of the structures along the chain of auditory processing from the outer ear all the way up to the auditory cortex. The simplest way to introduce some hearing loss is to obstruct the ear canal, thus inhibiting the ability of sound waves to exert pressure on the tympanic membrane. Many people do this on purpose by wearing earplugs. A less intentional

conductive hearing loss   Hearing loss caused by problems with the bones of the middle ear.

otitis media   Inflammation of the middle ear, commonly in children as a result of infection.

otosclerosis   Abnormal growth of the middle-ear bones that causes hearing loss.

sensorineural hearing loss   Hearing loss due to defects in the cochlea or auditory nerve.

hearing loss can be created by the excessive buildup of earwax (cerumen) in the ear canal. This problem is easy for clinicians to remedy, as long as the effort to clear out the ear canal does not damage the tympanic membrane.

Another type of hearing impairment, called **conductive hearing loss**, occurs when the middle-ear bones lose (or are impaired in) their ability to freely convey (conduct) vibrations from the tympanic membrane to the oval window. Such impairment occurs most often when the middle ear fills with mucus during ear infections—a condition known as **otitis media**. The oval window usually still vibrates under these conditions, but without the amplifying power of the ossicles, hearing thresholds can be raised by as much as 50 dB (that is, sounds need to be 50 dB louder in order to be heard). Thankfully, for the millions of young children who suffer ear infections, normal hearing returns after mucus is absorbed back into surrounding tissues; however, this reabsorption can take up to several months. A more serious type of conductive loss, **otosclerosis**, is caused by abnormal growth of the middle-ear bones, most typically around the oval window next to the stapes. Surgery can free the stapes from these bone growths and improve hearing.

By far the most common, and most serious, form of auditory impairment is **sensorineural hearing loss**, which most commonly occurs inside the cochlea and sometimes as a result of damage to the auditory nerve. Disorders such as diabetes as well as bacterial and viral infections can cause hearing loss (Eggermont, 2017). In other patients, hearing loss can be present at birth, or it can appear during adolescence or early adulthood and progressively worsen over one or more decades. Mutations in over 150 different genes have already been linked to hereditary hearing loss in humans.

Sensorineural loss is caused in two general ways: metabolic and sensory (Vaden Matthews, Eckert, and Dubno, 2017). Metabolic losses are caused by changes in the fluid environment of the cochlea that decrease the activity of hair cells. Sensory losses are caused by injury to hair cells. For example, certain antibiotics and cancer drugs are ototoxic, meaning that they kill hair cells directly. Physicians are well aware of these dangers and typically avoid using such drugs, but sometimes a patient faces the decision of life with deafness versus no life at all.

The major cause of sensory hearing loss is damage to the hair cells by excessive exposure to noise (Eggermont, 2017). Those exquisitely fast and sensitive hair cells are also very vulnerable to damage from excessive sound levels. It is widely accepted that damage to outer hair cells, the ones that make inner hair cells more sensitive and more sharply tuned (see Figure 9.14), has significant responsibility for noise-induced hearing loss. Damage to inner hair cells also occurs. With fewer inner hair cells, the neuronal firing pattern described by the volley principle for temporal coding of frequency would become more difficult to maintain, because there would be fewer neurons available to take turns firing (Sayles and Heinz, 2017).

It is fairly well known that shooting a gun without ear protection can cause hearing loss. At least since 1886, when Scottish surgeon Thomas Barr tested the hearing of Glasgow boilermakers, we have known that extended exposure to loud sounds such as the noise of factory equipment also causes hearing loss (Keats, 2014). It is no coincidence that so many aging rock stars and race car drivers wear hearing aids. (It is ironic, but wise, that many heavy-metal music fans now wear ear protection at concerts.) And evidence suggests that cumulative exposure to even everyday noises present in the environments of industrialized countries can cause hearing loss. In one study (Goycoolea et al., 1986), middle-aged and elderly residents of Easter Island who stayed almost exclusively on their quiet

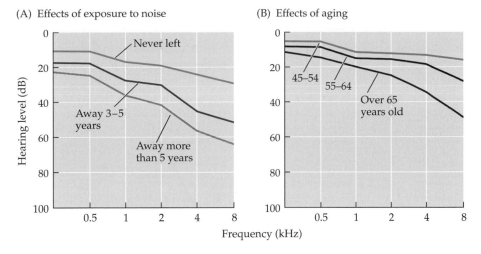

Figure 9.25 Environmental noise affects hearing. (A) The more people are exposed to noise in their environment, the more their hearing deteriorates. Easter Island residents who spent more years off of the relatively quiet island had relatively worse hearing. (B) Hearing becomes less sensitive with age, particularly for high frequencies. (After Goycoolea et al., 1986.)

island their whole lives were compared with other Easter Islanders, who made more frequent trips to the noisier outside world. As **Figure 9.25A** shows, the more time people spent off the island, the more hearing loss they experienced.

Unfortunately, it is not yet possible to state exactly how much exposure to sounds is safe. Readers of this textbook are especially likely to become the listeners from whom we learn what levels are unsafe. This is because of the use of personal listening devices (PLDs) delivering sounds directly to eardrums via earbuds. Right now, there is extensive debate concerning the contribution of PLDs to hearing loss, in part because consequences may be years down the road. At present, we know that use of PLDs and hearing loss are clearly correlated (Ivory, Kane, and Diaz, 2014).

Hearing loss is a natural consequence of aging for many people, and it is difficult to separate a person's age from the amount of exposure to noise. Typically, age-related hearing loss first affects the perception of high frequencies (**Figure 9.25B**). The 20- to 20,000-Hz frequency range for human hearing really applies only to young people; by the time most of us reach college age, we may have already lost some ability to hear frequencies above 15,000 Hz. The decrease in the ability to hear higher-frequency sounds continues throughout life, with the highest audible frequency becoming lower and lower as we grow older. Fortunately, many of the sounds that people care most about, including speech and music, are composed predominantly of lower frequencies.

Treating Hearing Loss

The earliest devices for helping people with hearing loss were simple horns. The small end of the horn would be held at the entry to the ear canal, and the wide end would be used to funnel more acoustic energy toward the listener's ear. Although effective, these horns were obviously somewhat cumbersome. Electronic hearing aids are much more convenient, but they must be designed to do more than simply amplify all sounds, because extremely loud sounds (above 100 dB) are just as annoying (or painful) for impaired listeners as they are for listeners with normal hearing. For a person who cannot hear sounds until their intensity is

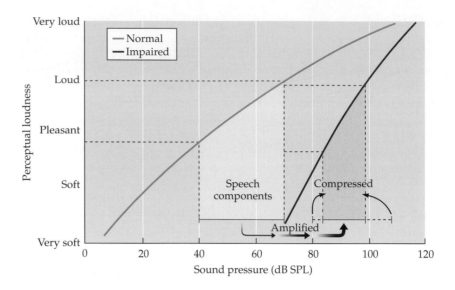

Figure 9.26 When hearing thresholds are increased by impairment, a sound must have more energy to be heard, but loudness increases faster than it does with healthy ears. When a hearing aid is used to increase the intensity of sounds, all variation in sound levels must be compressed into a smaller range of intensity because very loud sounds can be just as painful for listeners with hearing impairment as they are for listeners with healthy hearing. (After C. D. Geisler, 1998.)

at least 70 dB, compared with about 0 dB for healthy hearing, sounds that could normally vary between 0 and 100 dB must be squeezed between 70 and 100 dB (**Figure 9.26**). Nearly all modern hearing aids use some means to amplify the signal while also compressing intensity differences to keep the highest intensities within a comfortable listening level.

Hearing aids can also be tuned to provide the greatest amplification only for frequencies in the region of greatest loss (for most people, higher frequencies will need to be amplified more). An additional method is to move energy from frequency regions in which hearing is poor (usually high frequencies) into regions where hearing is normal (Alexander, 2016). Because the lower-frequency region is already being used for lower-frequency sounds, this strategy requires squeezing together some lower-frequency sounds to make room for the high-frequency sound that is being moved down.

One advantage of the old horns over electronic hearing aids was that they permitted listeners to direct their hearing toward the sound source they were most interested in. We may think about hearing aids as amplifying the voice to which one is listening, but they also amplify all the other sounds in the environment. The background noise in a car, or even the sound of a refrigerator, can become loud enough to compete with the sound of a person's voice. When the entire range of hearing is compressed from a range of 100 dB to only 30 dB, a 10-dB difference between the rumbling of the car's engine and the voice of the person in the passenger seat becomes compressed into only a 3-dB difference.

Hearing aids are gradually improving, and they have provided relief to millions of Americans, including former presidents Ronald Reagan and Bill Clinton. However, despite researchers' many clever innovations for improving the signal that arrives at the tympanic membrane, damage to the mechanisms that transduce sound waves into neural signals is proving difficult or impossible to overcome completely. By analogy to vision, the best eyeglasses, contact lenses, or even laser surgery cannot change an image enough to overcome retinal degeneration. The best advice is to never need a hearing aid. Protect your ears by avoiding exposure to loud sounds and by using hearing protection such as earplugs or earmuffs when necessary. If someone else can sing along to the song you're listening to on your personal media player, turn it down!

Using versus Detecting Sound

Even the best hearing aids serve mostly to amplify sounds for frequencies where thresholds are elevated. However, the ability to detect sounds is not the same as the ability to listen to and use sounds. The audiogram, our measure of the softest detectable tones at different frequencies, is not a perfect predictor of listeners' abilities to use sounds. Understanding speech or enjoying music, especially when there is background noise, can be good with poor audiograms and weak with normal audiograms.

A great deal of recent research activity concerns what is called hidden hearing loss. Hickox and Liberman (2014) showed how exposure to moderately high levels of noise changes the ability of mice to use sound even when their ability to detect sounds remains normal. This hidden hearing loss has been shown to occur following only one week of exposure to 84-dB noise (Maison, Usubuchi, and Liberman, 2013). Even brief periods of exposure to loud noise result in a loss of synapses between AN fibers and hair cells (**Figure 9.27**). Unlike damage to hair cells, which results in decreased sensitivity, loss of synapses results in a loss of connectivity. It has been hypothesized that hidden hearing loss might explain some of the difficulties that human listeners have in noisy situations even when their audiograms are normal (Bharadwaj et al., 2014). Unfortunately, improving the ability of listeners to detect sounds is unlikely to improve the ability of people with hidden hearing loss to use sounds.

Before noise exposure   After noise exposure

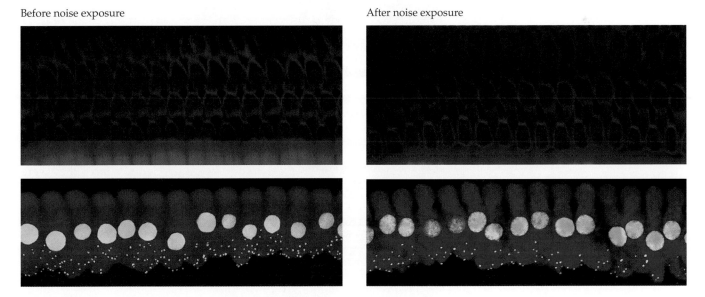

Figure 9.27 Following exposure to loud sounds, listeners can have difficulty using sounds even when hair cells appear to be undamaged. This is because some of the synapses between hair cells and neurons in the auditory nerve are lost. The top (purple) photos are of healthy hair cells before and after exposure to noise. The bottom photos show synapses highlighted as small yellow dots. There are fewer synapses following noise exposure (right) as compared to before noise exposure. (Courtesy of Vijaya Prakash Krishnan Muthaiah.)

■ Sensation & Perception in Everyday Life ■

Electronic Ears

Modern medical science and engineering are providing some degree of hearing to many people who are deaf. Cochlear prosthetics, more commonly known as cochlear implants (**Figure 9.28A**), are tiny flexible coils with about two dozen miniature electrode contacts along their length. Surgeons delicately thread these electrode arrays through the round window as far toward the apex of the cochlea as possible. The electrode array is connected to a tiny radio receiver under the scalp, and signals are transmitted from a small microphone device on the outside of the head behind the ear (**Figure 9.28B**). Signals coming in from the microphone activate the miniature electrodes at appropriate positions along the cochlear implant, which in turn stimulates associated auditory nerve fibers.

Although cochlear implants are a modern medical miracle, they cannot provide hearing that approaches what nature provides. We are not surprised, however, that a handful of electrodes cannot replace the function of 14,000 hair cells. Some people benefit more than others from implants, and many adults with electrical hearing converse flawlessly over the phone. Young children, receiving implants as young as age 1 or 2, do best of all because young brains are particularly plastic. Children's brain circuitry develops to get the most information possible from their electronic ears.

(A)

(B)

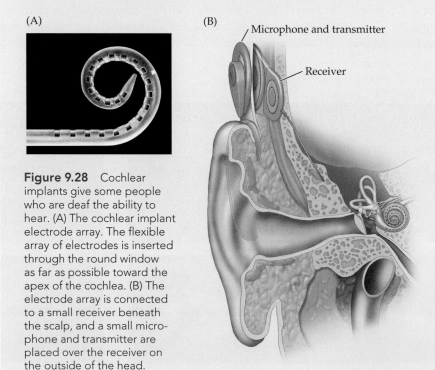

Figure 9.28 Cochlear implants give some people who are deaf the ability to hear. (A) The cochlear implant electrode array. The flexible array of electrodes is inserted through the round window as far as possible toward the apex of the cochlea. (B) The electrode array is connected to a small receiver beneath the scalp, and a small microphone and transmitter are placed over the receiver on the outside of the head.

Summary

1. Sounds are fluctuations of pressure. Sound waves are defined by the frequency, intensity (amplitude), and phase of fluctuations. Sound frequency and intensity correspond to our perceptions of pitch and loudness, respectively.

2. Sound is funneled into the ear by the outer ear, made more intense by the middle ear, and transformed into neural signals by the inner ear.

3. In the inner ear, cilia on the tops of inner hair cells pivot in response to pressure fluctuations in ways that provide information about frequency and intensity to the auditory nerve and the brain. Auditory nerve fibers convey information through both the rate and the timing patterns with which they fire.

4. Different characteristics of sounds are processed at multiple places in the brain stem before information reaches the cortex. Information from both ears is brought together very early in the chain of processing. At each stage of auditory processing, including primary auditory cortex, neurons are organized in relation to the frequencies of sounds (tonotopically).

5. Humans and other mammals can hear sounds across an enormous range of intensities. Not all sound frequencies are heard as being equally loud, however. Hearing across such a wide range of intensities is accomplished by the use of many auditory neurons. Different neurons respond to different levels of intensity. In addition, more neurons overall respond when sounds are more intense.

6. Series of channels (or filters) process sounds within bands of frequency. Depending on frequency, these channels vary in how wide (many frequencies) or narrow they are. Consequently, it is easier to detect differences between some frequencies than between others. When energy from multiple frequencies is present, lower-frequency energy makes it relatively more difficult to hear higher frequencies.

7. Hearing loss is caused by damage to the bones of the middle ear, to the hair cells in the cochlea, or to the neurons in the auditory nerve. Although hearing aids are helpful to listeners with hearing impairment, there is only so much that can be done to help after damage to hair cells that cannot be repaired.

Go to the
Sensation & Perception
Companion Website at
oup.com/us/wolfe5e
for chapter overviews, activities, essays, flashcards, and other study aids.
Go to **DASHBOARD** for additional resources and assessments.

10 Hearing in the Environment

■ Questions to Contemplate ■

Think about the following questions as you read this chapter. By the chapter's end, you should be able to answer and discuss them.

- How does your auditory system use tiny differences in time, amplitude, and frequency to make you aware of your world day and night?

- How do we define the characteristics of complex natural sounds about which you depend the most?

- How can you separate the many sounds in your environment when they all overlap one another when entering your ears?

The auditory system's ability to transform tiny air pressure changes into a rich perceptual world is an amazing wonder of bioengineering. From the funneling of sound waves by the pinnae, to the mechanics of middle-ear bones, to the traveling wave creating tiny perturbations of the basilar partition and hair cells, to the sophisticated neural encoding in the brain stem and cerebral cortex—some remarkable mechanisms have evolved to interpret acoustic information about the world around us.

Research that reveals these inner workings of the auditory system typically uses very simple stimuli under constrained situations—often isolated pure tones heard through headphones by listeners sitting in an otherwise perfectly quiet laboratory. Although these methods are invaluable for understanding how the auditory system functions, this is obviously not the way we experience sounds in our daily lives. In this chapter we get "outside the head" to investigate how hearing helps us learn about the real world.

We start by looking at how it is possible to determine the location of a sound source. In many respects, sound localization parallels visual depth perception, which you learned about in Chapter 6. We next turn from *where* to *what*, how

Nick Cave, *Soundsuit*, 2011

perceptual aspects of complex sounds are composed of simpler sounds in much the same way that visual representations of objects are built up from simple features (see Chapter 4). The third part of the chapter deals with auditory scene analysis, where we will see why some sounds group together, while separating from others, in ways that resemble the Gestalt principles introduced in Chapter 4. We see how the auditory system seamlessly fills in gaps to form a complete and coherent "picture" of our auditory environment in an auditory analog of how the visual system deals with occlusion (see Chapter 6). Finally, we explore how auditory attention has much in common with visual attention that you learned about in Chapter 7, while also serving a special role in keeping us ever vigilant for surprises in the world.

Sound Localization

Suppose you were out camping in your local state park one mild summer night, enjoying the last embers of your campfire, when suddenly an owl began hooting somewhere in front of you. You would instantly know whether the owl was perched to the left, to the right, or directly behind the fire pit. Moreover, if you were willing to leave the comfort of the fire, and if the owl were cooperative enough to sit still and keep hooting, you could easily walk to the exact source of the sound even though you wouldn't be able to see the owl until you were very close to it.

When you think about it a bit, you will realize that this feat of auditory localization is quite different from determining the location of a visual object. If you could see the owl in front of you, you would know that it was to the left or the right of your fovea because its image would appear on the right or left side of your retina (**Figure 10.1**). But the owl's hoots enter your ears in exactly the same place (funneled through the pinnae into the middle and inner ear) regardless of where the owl is.

You may recall that we face a similar dilemma when trying to determine how far away a visual object is. As we saw in Chapter 6, visual depth percep-

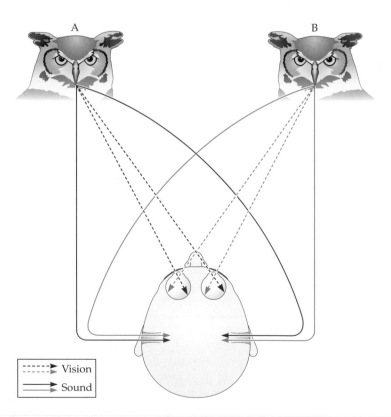

Figure 10.1 The position of the owl is easily encoded by the visual system because the owl's image falls on different parts of the retina (and thus activates different receptors) depending on whether it is to the left (A) or to the right (B) of the observer. In the auditory system, however, the same receptors are activated regardless of the owl's position.

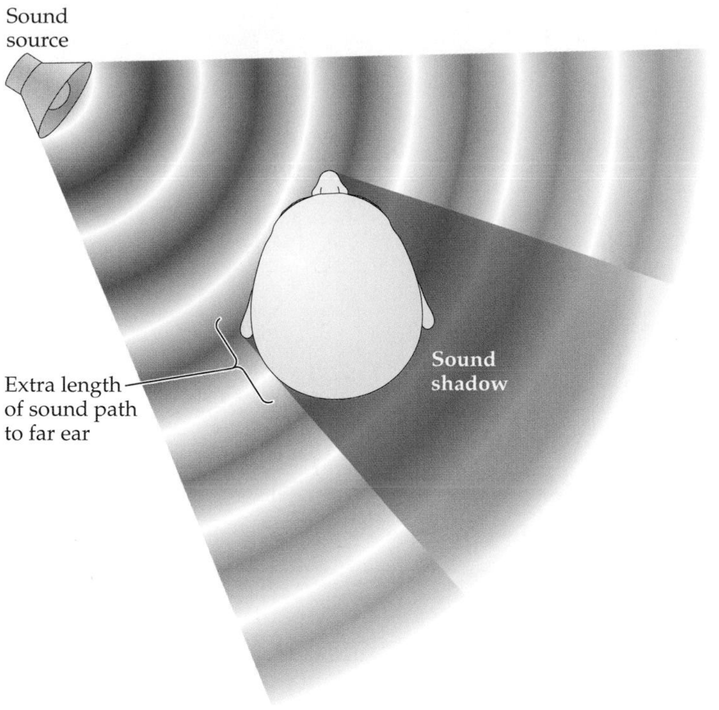

Sound source

Extra length of sound path to far ear

Sound shadow

Figure 10.2 The two ears receive slightly different inputs when the sound source is located to one side or the other. For frequencies greater than 1000 hertz, the head blocks some of the energy from reaching the opposite ear, creating a sound shadow.

tion involves processing and integrating a set of "cues"—stimulus aspects that provide indirect evidence about how far away an object is. The auditory system uses a similar approach to determine the location in space from which a sound is coming. (See **Web Activity 10.1: Auditory Localization Cues.**)

Even more than having two eyes turned out to be important for determining visual depth relations, having two ears is critical to determining auditory locations. For most positions in space, the sound source will be closer to one ear than to the other. Thus, there are two potential types of information for determining the source of a sound (**Figure 10.2**). First, even though sound travels fast, the pressure waves do not arrive at both ears at the same time. Sounds arrive sooner, albeit very slightly, at the ear closer to the source. Second, the intensity of a sound is greater at the ear closer to the source. These are our first two auditory localization cues.

Interaural Time Difference

Let's first consider what we can learn from the **interaural time difference** (**ITD**). If the source is to the left, the sound will reach the left ear first. If it's to the right, it will reach the right ear first. Thus, we can tell whether a sound is coming from our right or left by determining which ear receives the sound first. The term that is used to describe locations on an imaginary circle extending around us in a horizontal plane—front, back, left, and right—is **azimuth** (**Figure 10.3**).

A more detailed analysis of the ITD can tell us even more. See if you can answer the following questions: Where would a sound source need to be located to produce the maximum possible ITD? What location would lead to the minimum possible ITD, and what would the ITD be in this case? Finally, what would happen at intermediate locations? **Figure 10.4** illustrates the answers to these questions. The ITDs for sounds coming from various angles are represented by colored circles. Red circles indicate positions from which a sound will reach the right ear before the left ear; blue circles show positions from which a sound

interaural time difference (ITD)
The difference in time between arrivals of sound at one ear versus the other.

azimuth The angle of a sound source on the horizontal plane relative to a point in the center of the head between the ears. Azimuth is measured in degrees, with 0 degrees being straight ahead. The angle increases clockwise toward the right, with 180 degrees being directly behind.

Figure 10.3 Interaural time differences for sound sources varying in azimuth from directly in front of listeners (0 degrees) to directly behind (180 degrees). How much variation there is in the time it takes for a sound to reach each ear depends on where a sound comes from in space. (Data from Fedderson et al., 1957.)

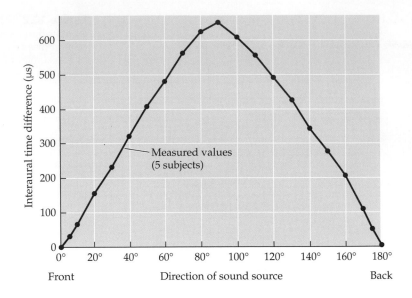

will reach the left ear first. The size and brightness of each circle represent the magnitude of the ITD.

As Figure 10.4 shows, ITDs are largest, about 640 microseconds (millionths of a second, abbreviated μs) when sounds come directly from the left or directly from the right, although this value varies somewhat, depending on the size of your head. A sound coming from directly in front of or directly behind the listener produces an ITD of 0; the sound reaches both ears simultaneously. For intermediate locations, the ITD will be somewhere between these two values. Thus, a sound source located at an angle of 60 degrees will always produce an ITD of 480 μs, and a sound coming from –20 degrees will always produce an ITD of –200 μs. That might not seem like much of a time difference, but listeners can actually detect interaural delays of as little as 10 μs for tones around 1000 hertz (Hz) (Brughera, Dunai, and Hartman, 2013) (**Figure 10.5**), which is good enough to detect the angle of a sound source to within 1 degree.

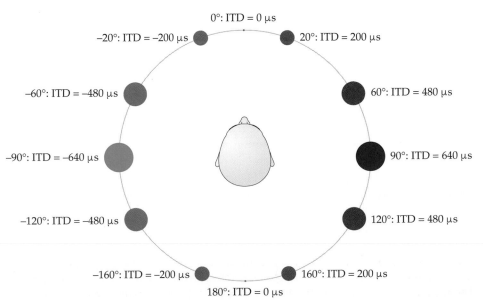

Figure 10.4 Interaural time differences for different positions around the head. Blue indicates locations from which sound reaches the left ear first; red indicates locations from which sound reaches the right ear first. (Data from Fedderson et al., 1957.)

Figure 10.5 Listeners can detect very brief differences in timing between the two ears. At the best frequencies, around 1000 Hz, differences as small as 10 µs can be detected by some listeners. (After Brughera, Dunai, and Hartman, 2013.)

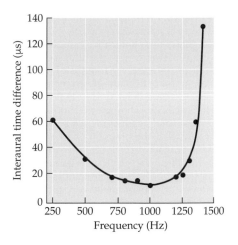

THE PHYSIOLOGY OF ITDS   The portion of the auditory system responsible for calculating ITDs obviously needs to receive input from both ears. As we saw in Chapter 9, binaural input enters almost every stage of the auditory nervous system after the auditory nerve (see Figure 9.20). As information moves upward through the system, however, with every additional synapse, the timing between the two ears is likely to become less precise. The **medial superior olives (MSOs)** are the first places in the auditory system where inputs from both ears converge (**Figure 10.6**), and sure enough, firing rates of neurons in the MSOs increase in response to very brief time differences between inputs from the two ears of cats (T. C. Yin and Chan, 1990).

How do these MSO neurons discover such tiny delays across the two ears? A single neural spike lasts about 1 millisecond (ms), and 10 µs is only 1/100 of 1 ms. About 70 years ago Jeffress (1948) hypothesized an ingenious way this could be possible. If an array of inputs from both ears formed a "ladder," then small differences between the lengths of axons could provide a way to delay input from one ear compared with the other; inputs would arrive at the MSO at the same time only when input to one ear was delayed relative to the other (**Figure 10.7A**). Unfortunately, anatomical and physiological evidence for this clever idea has been elusive (Joris, Smith, and Yin, 1998), so most researchers have become quite skeptical.

Very recent findings (Sayles et al., 2017) suggest that the brain takes advantage of the traveling wave to use frequency differences to measure time. Recall from the last chapter that the traveling wave really does travel along the basilar membrane, and this travel takes time. For the ear that the sound reaches first, the traveling wave reaches a lower frequency further down the cochlea compared with the ear to which the sound arrives slightly later. The result is that tiny time differences between the ears result in the traveling wave being at different places (frequencies) along the basilar membrane. Mark Sayles and colleagues (Sayles et al., 2017) recorded frequency tuning of neurons in the MSO and found evidence

medial superior olive (MSO)   A relay station in the brain stem where inputs from both ears contribute to detection of the interaural time difference.

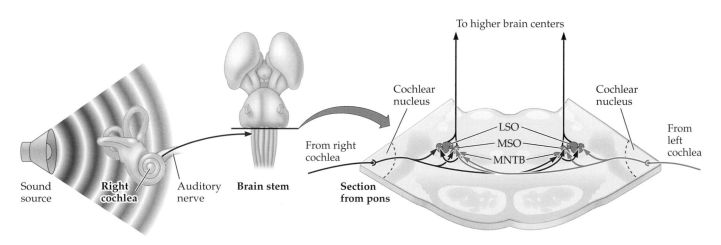

Figure 10.6   After only a single synapse in the cochlear nucleus, information from each ear travels to both the medial superior olive (MSO) and the lateral superior olive (LSO) on each side of the brain stem. MNTB = medial nucleus of the trapezoid body.

Figure 10.7 Models for the way neurons in the medial superior olive (MSO) can detect time difference between two ears. (A) It was long thought that differences between the lengths of neural axons coming from the two ears might provide a time delay to detect tiny time differences used to localize sounds. (B) The most recent evidence suggests that, instead, the brain takes advantage of the time it takes for the traveling wave to travel from high to low frequencies in the cochlea. Then, the brain uses small differences in frequencies across the two ears to measure time.

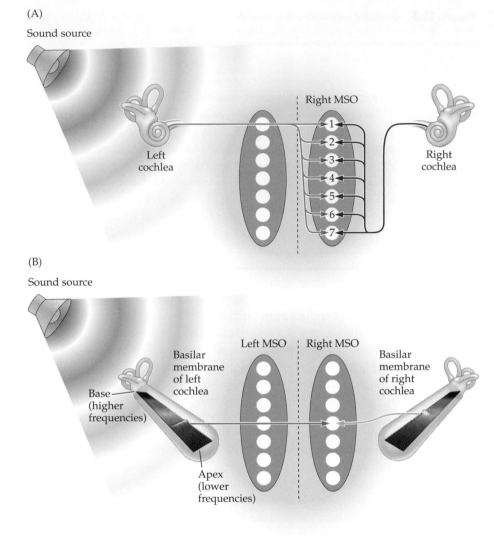

(A)

Sound source

Left cochlea

Right MSO

Right cochlea

(B)

Sound source

Base (higher frequencies)

Basilar membrane of left cochlea

Left MSO

Right MSO

Basilar membrane of right cochlea

Apex (lower frequencies)

that neurons were, in fact, tuned to capture slight frequency differences across the ears (**Figure 10.7B**). Perhaps, one might consider ITDs to really be interaural frequency differences (IFDs).

Interaural Level Difference

The second cue to sound localization is the **interaural level difference (ILD)** in sound intensity. Sounds are more intense at the ear closer to the sound source because the head partially blocks the sound pressure wave from reaching the opposite ear. The properties of the ILD relevant for auditory localization are similar to those of the ITD:

- Sounds are more intense at the ear that is closer to the sound source, and they are less intense at the ear farther away from the source.

- The ILD is largest at 90 and –90 degrees, and it is nonexistent at 0 degrees (directly in front) and 180 degrees (directly behind).

- Between these two extremes, the ILD correlates with the angle of the sound source, but because of the irregular shape of the head, the correlation is less precise than it is with ITDs.

interaural level difference (ILD) The difference between levels (intensities) of sound at one ear versus the other.

Figure 10.8 Interaural level (intensity) differences for tones of different frequencies presented at different positions around the head. Note that the biggest differences are for frequencies greater than 1000 Hz, at which point the head creates a sound shadow. The curves are not symmetrical toward the front and back, because of filtering characteristics of the pinnae. (Data from Fedderson et al., 1957.)

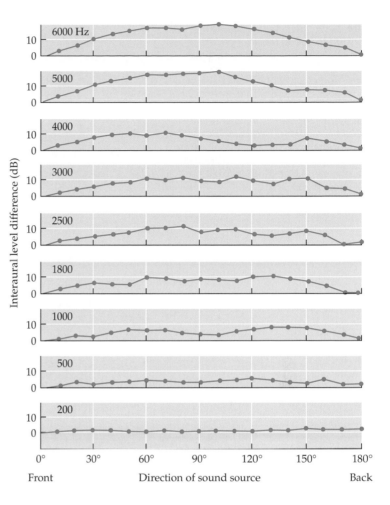

Although the general relationship between ILD and sound source angle is almost identical to the relationship between ITD and angle, there is an important difference between the two cues: the head blocks high-frequency sounds much more effectively than it does low-frequency sounds. This is because the long wavelengths of low-frequency sounds "bend around" the head in much the same way that a large ocean wave crashes over a piling near the shore. Thus, as shown in **Figure 10.8**, ILDs are greatest for high-frequency tones, and ILD cues work really well to determine location as long as the sounds have higher-frequency energy. ILDs are greatly reduced for low frequencies, becoming almost nonexistent below 1000 Hz. Our inability to localize low frequencies is the reason it does not matter where in a room you place the low-frequency subwoofer of your stereo system.

THE PHYSIOLOGY OF ILDS Neurons that are sensitive to intensity differences between the two ears can be found in the **lateral superior olives (LSOs)** (see Figure 10.6), which receive both excitatory and inhibitory inputs. Excitatory connections to each LSO come from the ipsilateral ear—that is, excitatory connections to the left LSO originate in the left cochlea, and excitatory connections to the right LSO come from the right cochlea. Inhibitory inputs come from the contralateral ear (the ear on the opposite side of the head) via the medial nucleus of the trapezoid body (MNTB).

Neurons in the LSOs are very sensitive to differences in intensity across the two ears because excitatory inputs from one ear (ipsilateral) and inhibitory inputs from the other ear (contralateral) are wired to compete. When the sound is more intense at one ear, connections from that ear are better both at exciting LSO neurons on that side and at inhibiting LSO neurons on the other side.

Cones of Confusion

If you examine Figures 10.4 and 10.8 for a bit, you should see a potential problem with using ITDs and ILDs for sound localization: An ITD of −480 μs arises from a sound source that is located at either an angle of −60 degrees from the line of sight (10 o'clock in Figure 10.4) or an angle of −120 degrees (8 o'clock). Adding information from intensity differences does not help us here, because the ILDs for these two angles are also identical. If we also consider the elevation of a sound source (how far above or below our head the sound source is—a factor we've been ignoring up to now), we find that a given ITD or ILD could arise from any

lateral superior olive (LSO) A relay station in the brain stem where inputs from both ears contribute to detection of the interaural level difference.

Figure 10.9 Elevation adds another dimension to sound localization. (A) Cones of confusion. (B) Interaural time differences (ITDs) are plotted here across azimuth and elevation. A sound with zero azimuth and elevation is directly in front of a listener's head. All of the locations in space that share the same color provide the exact same ITDs. Red contours plotted beneath the colored surface illustrate how all the locations on the red line give rise to the same ITD. (B after Wightman and Kistler, 1998.)

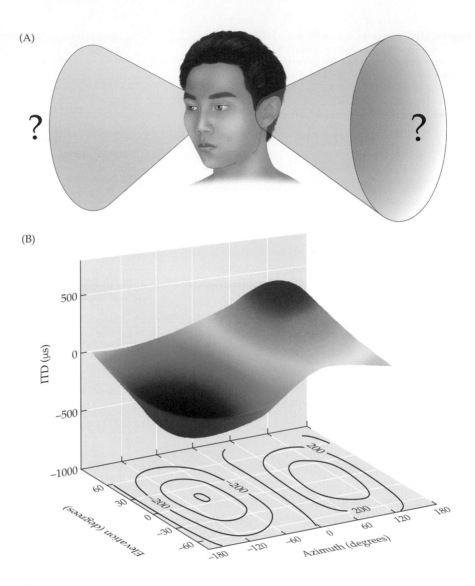

point on the surface of a **cone of confusion** that extends perpendicularly from the left or right ear (**Figure 10.9**).

Although many books speak of a single cone of confusion, actually an infinite number of cones are nested inside one another. In fact, the widest "cone" is really a disk extending from directly in front of you, up to directly over your head, back to directly behind your head, and continuing to directly below you. As strange as it may seem, this disk is the most confusing of the cones. Cones of confusion are real perceptual phenomena, not just theoretical problems for the auditory system. In the real world, thankfully, we need not hold our heads in a fixed position. As soon as you move your head, the ITD and ILD of a sound source shift, and only one spatial location will be consistent with the ITDs and ILDs perceived before and after you move your head (**Figure 10.10**).

Pinnae and Head Cues

Another reason why cones of confusion are not major practical problems for the auditory system is that time and intensity differences are not the only cues

cone of confusion A region of positions in space where all sounds produce the same time and level (intensity) differences (ITDs and ILDs).

(A)

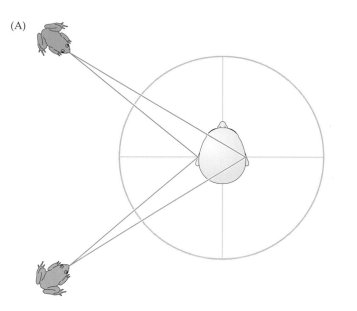

(B)

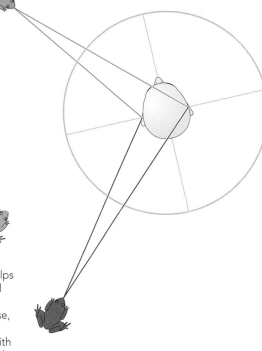

Figure 10.10 Evaluating ITDs and ILDs from two different head positions helps in sound localization. (A) At first, a sound source coming from the blue frog will lead to an ITD and an ILD that would also be consistent with a sound coming from the green frog. (B) If the listener's head is rotated slightly counterclockwise, the ITD/ILD will no longer be consistent with the location of the green frog. There will still be an ambiguity, however. Now the ITD/ILD will be consistent with the red frog as well as the blue frog. But only the blue location is consistent with both the first and the second sets of ITDs and ILDs.

for pinpointing the location of sound sources. Take a look at one of your pinnae (or, more realistically, take a look at a friend's pinna). You'll see that the shape of the pinna is quite complex, with lots of idiosyncratic nooks and crannies (**Figure 10.11**). Remember that the pinnae funnel sound energy into the ear

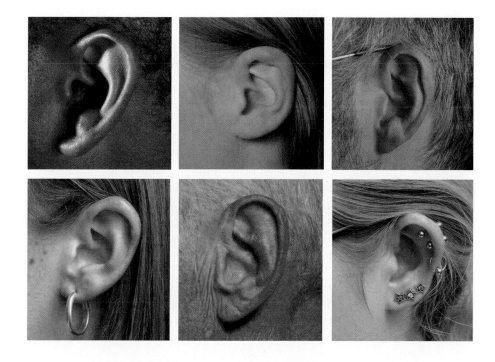

Figure 10.11 Pinna shapes vary quite a lot among people. Listeners learn how their personal pinnae affect how they hear sounds from different places in the environment.

canal. Because of their complex shapes, the pinnae funnel certain sound frequencies more efficiently than others. In addition to pinnae, the size and shape of the rest of the body, especially the upper torso, affect which frequencies reach the ear most easily. Because of these effects, the intensity of each frequency varies slightly according to the direction of the sound. This variation provides us with another auditory localization cue.

Here's a simple example to illustrate how the effects of pinnae and upper body shapes are measured. Suppose you're in an anechoic room, a room in which the walls are padded so that very little sound enters from the outside and very little sound bounces (reverberates) off the walls. The room is full of speakers at many locations—up, down, and all around you. Tiny microphones are inserted inside your auditory canals, right next to your eardrums. Now you can measure just how much energy from different frequencies actually reaches your eardrums from different locations. **Figure 10.12A** shows the measurements at the eardrum in a similar experimental setup—in this case for sounds played over a speaker 30 degrees to the left of a listener and 12 degrees up from the listener's head. Although the amounts of energy at all frequencies were equally intense coming from the speaker, you can see that the amounts of energy were *not* equally intense at the eardrum. Some frequencies (e.g., 5000 Hz) had higher intensity when they arrived at the eardrum; others (e.g., 800 Hz) had less intensity.

These changing spectral shapes across changes in elevation provide cues to auditory localization. Figure 10.9 showed how relative intensities of different frequencies change depending on azimuth and illustrated that those curves are not symmetrical toward the front and back, because of the filtering characteristics of the pinnae. For the final piece of the puzzle, look at **Figure 10.12B**, which shows the sound recorded by in-ear microphones when the speaker is moved up and down in elevation. As you can see, the relative intensities of different frequencies continuously change with changes in elevation as well as in azimuth. The sum total of these intensity shifts can be measured and combined to determine the **directional transfer function** (usually referred to by its acronym, **DTF**) for an individual.

The importance of the DTF in sound localization is easily understood if we consider the difference between hearing a concert live and listening to music through a set of headphones. In person, we perceive the sound of the French horns as coming from one side of the orchestra and the sound of the flutes as coming from the other side. But when we wear headphones (especially the type inserted directly inside the auditory canals), sounds are delivered directly to the eardrums, bypassing the pinnae. Auditory engineers can use multiple microphones to simulate the ITDs and ILDs that result from the musicians' different locations (the Beatles were early users of this type of technology), but DTFs are not simulated. As a result, you may be able to get some sense of direction when listening to a concert through headphones, but the sounds will seem to come from inside your skull, rather than from out in the world. The situation is akin to that of visual depth perception. Pictorial cues can give a limited sense of depth, but to get a true perception of three-dimensionality, we really need binocular-disparity information that we normally get only when we're seeing real objects.

Actually, just as stereoscopes can be designed to simulate binocular disparity, it is possible to simulate DTFs. Instead of using two camera lenses in place of two eyes, two microphones are placed near the eardrums as described earlier. Then the sound source, such as a concert, is recorded from these two microphones.

directional transfer function (DTF)
A measure that describes how the pinna, ear canal, head, and torso change the intensity of sounds with different frequencies that arrive at each ear from different locations in space (azimuth and elevation).

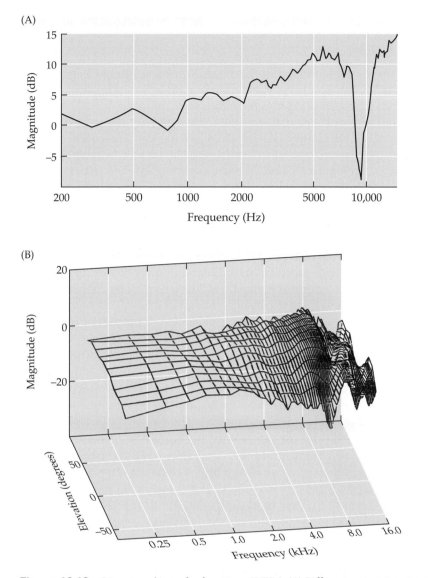

Figure 10.12 Directional transfer functions (DTFs). (A) Differences in intensity at the eardrum for sounds of varying frequency are plotted in this DTF for a single point in space. (B) The series of DTFs plotted here is for the same azimuth but at different elevations. (A from Kistler and Wightman, 1992; B from Wightman and Kistler, 1993.)

When this special stereo recording, called a binaural recording, is played over headphones, the listener experiences the sounds as if they were back out in the world where they belong. Unfortunately, however, every set of pinnae is different (see Figure 10.11), so for this simulation to work, every listener needs his or her individual recordings.

Just as heads (and their corresponding ITDs and ILDs) grow to be larger, ears grow and change during development. It is hypothesized that listeners learn about the way DTFs relate to places in the environment through their experience listening to sounds, while other sources of information, such as vision, provide feedback about location (Wightman and Kistler, 1998). This learning through experience suggests that children may update the way they use DTF information during development.

■ Scientists at Work

Vulcan Ears

■ **Questions** After their heads stop growing, can adults adjust to changing pinnae? Do people with radical piercings or large holes caused by stretching have a difficult time localizing sounds (**Figure 10.13A**)? If you are a boxing fan, you might ask if Evander Holyfield could localize sounds as well following his fight with Mike Tyson (**Figure 10.13B**).

■ **Hypothesis** Even after becoming full-grown adults, people can still adjust to changing ears when localizing sound.

■ **Test** Artificially change the shape of adult ears by inserting plastic ear molds and test whether listeners can still localize sounds as well as they could before the molds were inserted (Hofman, Van Riswick, and Van Opsal, 1998).

■ **Results** Listeners immediately became much poorer at localizing sounds. But by 6 weeks of living with these molds in their ears, the listeners' localization abilities

had greatly improved. Somewhat surprisingly, these listeners also remained quite good at localizing with their "old ears" when the molds were removed.

It would be interesting to know how well Leonard Nimoy (who played Spock in the original *Star Trek* series) could localize sounds with his Vulcan ear molds (**Figure 10.13C**). The experience of listeners in the Hofman et al. study suggests that switching between human and Vulcan pinnae every day may have become just a normal part of Nimoy's auditory life.

■ **Future work** Unfortunately, there are some limits to the ability to adjust to growing or remolded pinnae. Larger ears help older adults use lower-frequency cues; however, this improved ability to use low frequencies is insufficient to offset the effects of age-related hearing loss, and older individuals are poorer at localizing elevation (Otte et al., 2013). How can older adults with poorer hearing retain more of their ability to localize (and attend to) sounds?

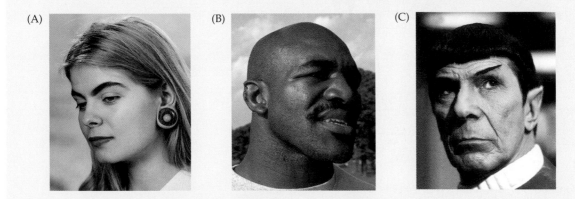

Figure 10.13 Listeners with stretched (A), bitten (B), or pointed (C) pinnae initially experience difficulty localizing sounds but soon adjust to the new shape of their pinnae.

Auditory Distance Perception

How do listeners know how far away a sound is? Although it is important to know what direction a sound is coming from, none of the cues we've discussed so far (ITD, ILD, DTF) provide much information concerning the distance between a listener and a sound source that is much more than an arm's length away. At the risk of ruining a good story, begin by knowing that listeners are not nearly as good at judging auditory distance as they are at judging direction. Listeners are best at judging the distance to a sound source when it is about 1 meter away. Closer than that, listeners overestimate distance, while they underestimate distance to the source when it is farther than 1 meter (Kolarik et al., 2016). In addition to underestimates and overestimates, auditory perception of distance is relatively sloppy compared with visual perception of distance—about twice as variable for hearing as for vision (Anderson and Zahorik, 2014).

The simplest cue for judging the distance of a sound source is the *relative intensity* of the sound. Because sounds become less intense with greater distance, listeners have little difficulty perceiving the relative distances of two identical sound sources. For example, if you hear a pair of croaking bullfrogs, the louder croaks should be coming from the closer frog. Unfortunately, this cue suffers from the same problem as relative size in depth perception. Interpreting the cue requires one to make assumptions about the sound sources that may turn out to be false (e.g., the softer-sounding frog might be very close, with its croaks muffled by surrounding vegetation). In Figures 6.8 and 6.9, you saw lots of rabbits when learning about the use of relative size in visual depth perception, and the problem in hearing is much the same. At the end of this section, we will return to the challenge of figuring out just how loud (big) a sound is perceived to be when distance changes. But first, we will continue to consider distance perception.

The effectiveness of relative intensity decreases quickly as distance increases, because sound intensity decreases according to the **inverse-square law (Figure 10.14)**. When sound sources are close to the listener, a small difference in distance can produce a relatively large intensity difference. For example, a sound that is 1 meter away is more intense by 6 decibels (dB) than a sound that is 2 meters away. But the same 1-meter difference between sound sources 39 and 40 meters away produces an intensity change of only a fraction of 1 dB. The inverse-square law helps you to understand why listeners are fairly good at using intensity differences to determine distance when sounds are presented within 1 meter of the head (Brungart, Durlach, and Rabinowitz, 1999), but listeners tend to consistently underestimate the distance to sound sources farther away, and the amount of underestimation grows as distance becomes longer (Zahorik, 2002).

Intensity works best as a distance cue when the sound source or the listener is moving. If a croaking frog starts hopping toward you, you will know it because its croaks will become louder and louder. Listeners also get some information about how far away a source is when they move through the environment. This is because, in a manner akin to motion parallax in the perception of visual depth,

inverse-square law A principle stating that as distance from a source increases, intensity decreases faster such that decrease in intensity is equal to the distance squared. This general law also applies to optics and other forms of energy.

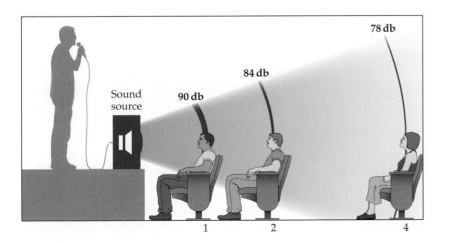

Figure 10.14 The intensity of a sound drops very quickly with greater distance from the sound source. Level decreases by half every time distance is doubled. (Recall that a 6-dB difference is a factor of 2 in sound pressure.) This relationship, which also holds for light energy, is called the inverse-square law.

sounds that are farther away do not seem to change direction in relation to the listener as much as nearer sounds do.

Another possible cue for auditory distance is the *spectral composition* of sounds. The sound-absorbing qualities of air dampen high frequencies more than low frequencies, so when sound sources are far away, higher frequencies decrease in energy more than lower frequencies as the sound waves travel from the source to the ear. Thus, the farther away a sound source is, the "muddier" it sounds. This change in spectral composition is noticeable only for fairly large distances, greater than 1000 meters. You experience the change in spectral composition when you hear thunder from near your window or from far away: you hear thunder as a loud "crack" nearby, but thunder from farther away sounds more like a "boom." Note that this auditory cue is analogous to the visual depth cue of aerial perspective (see Chapter 6; aerial perspective involves the fact that more-distant objects look more blurry).

A final distance cue stems from the fact that, in most environments, the sound that arrives at the ear is some combination of direct energy (which arrives directly from the source) and reverberant energy (which has bounced off surfaces in the environment). The *relative amounts of direct versus reverberant energy* inform the listener about distance because when a sound source is close to a listener, most of the energy reaching the ear is direct, whereas reverberant energy provides a greater proportion of the total when the sound source is farther away. Suppose you're attending a concert. The intensities of the musician's song and your neighbor's whispered comments might be identical, but the singer's voice will take time to bounce off the concert hall's walls before reaching your ear, whereas you will hear only the direct energy from your neighbor's whispers (**Figure 10.15**). (See **Web Essay 10.1: Reverberations and the Precedence Effect**.)

Direct energy
----→ Reverberant energy

Figure 10.15 The relative amounts of direct and reverberant energy coming from the listener's neighbor and the singer will inform the listener about the relative distances of the two sound sources.

As it happens, reverberations appear to be important for judging the loudness of sounds. You do not judge that a coyote is howling softly just because it is far away, so how do you estimate how loud the howls really are? Recall that the sound to which you are listening rapidly decreases in energy, following the inverse-square law. However, reverberations do not fall off so quickly, because the surfaces that sounds bounce off do not move when the sound source becomes closer or farther away. Following a clever set of experiments that allowed them to disentangle listeners' use of direct sound energy and reverberant energy, Zahorik and Wightman (2001) suggested that listeners maintain constant perceptions of loudness across changing distances by scaling direct energy relative to reverberant energy.

Spatial Hearing When Blind

Many studies have shown that severe loss of vision can result in improved auditory perception of localization of sounds in space (Kolarik et al., 2016). There is even evidence that regions of occipital (visual) cortex are recruited to process auditory input when visual inputs are no longer available (Voss and Zatorre, 2012). The most impressive demonstration of enhanced auditory perception of the spatial environment by visually impaired listeners is echolocation. You likely know about echolocation by bats and dolphins; they produce sounds in air or water and use the sounds that bounce back at them to gain information about their environments. Did you know that humans can do it, too? Some blind people learn to make clicks with their mouths and to use returning echoes to sense obstacles and even particular objects in their environment. Expert human echolocators can distinguish sizes and shapes of objects, as well as differences between the materials that comprise those objects (Thaler and Goodale, 2016). Measurement of human brain activity using fMRI has shown that visual regions of the brain are especially recruited to the task engaged by echolocation experts (**Figure 10.16**) (Thaler, Arnott, and Goodale, 2011).

Echolocation expert

Control participant

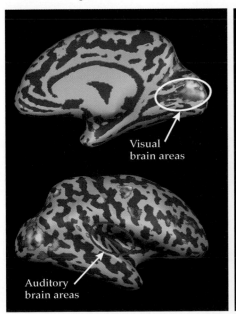
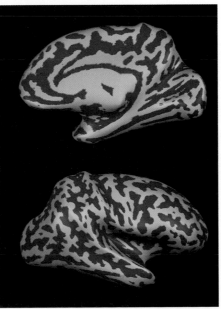

Visual brain areas

Auditory brain areas

Figure 10.16 The brain on the left belongs to an echolocation expert who had lost vision very early in life. The brain on the right belongs to a nonexpert. When listening to sounds such as clicks and echoes, brain regions typically associated with vision become very active only in the brain of the echolocation expert. (From Thaler, Arnott, and Goodale, 2011.)

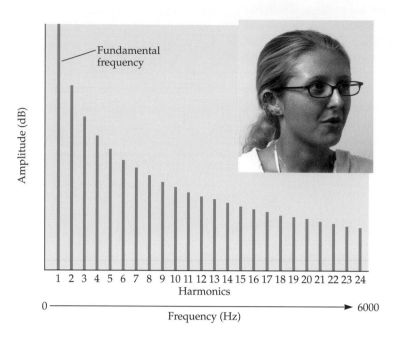

Figure 10.17 Many environmental sounds, including voices, are harmonic. The lowest frequency of a harmonic sound is the fundamental frequency, and there are peaks of energy at integer multiples of the fundamental.

fundamental frequency The lowest-frequency component of a complex periodic sound.

Complex Sounds

Simple sounds like sine waves and bands of noise are very useful for exploring the fundamental operating characteristics of auditory systems, just as sine wave gratings and single-wavelength light sources are essential tools for vision researchers. But pure sine wave tones, like pure single-wavelength light sources, are rare in the real world, where objects and events that matter to listeners are more complex, more interesting, and therefore more challenging for researchers to study.

Harmonics

Many environmental sounds, including the human voice and the sounds of musical instruments, have harmonic structure (**Figure 10.17**). In fact, harmonic sounds are among the most common types of sounds in the environment. The lowest frequency of a harmonic spectrum is the **fundamental frequency**. With natural vibratory sources (as opposed to pure tones created in the laboratory), there is also energy at frequencies that are integer multiples of the fundamental frequency. For example, a female speaker may produce a vowel sound with a fundamental frequency of 250 Hz. Her vocal cords will produce the greatest energy at 250 Hz, less energy at 500 Hz, less still at 750 Hz, even less at 1000 Hz, and so on. In this case, 500 Hz is the second harmonic, 750 is the third, and 1000 is the fourth. For harmonic complexes, the perceived pitch of the complex is determined by the fundamental frequency, and the harmonics (often called overtones by musicians) add to the perceived richness of the sound.

The auditory system is acutely sensitive to the natural relationships between harmonics. In fact, if the first harmonic (fundamental frequency) is removed from a series of harmonics, as shown in **Figure 10.18**, and only the others (second, third,

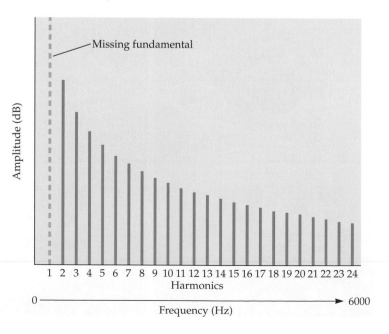

Figure 10.18 If the fundamental (lowest frequency) of a harmonic sound is removed, listeners still hear the pitch of this "missing fundamental."

fourth, and so on) are presented, the pitch that listeners hear corresponds to the fundamental frequency—even though it is not part of the sound! Listeners hear the *missing fundamental*. (See **Web Activity 10.2: The Missing-Fundamental Effect**.) It is not even necessary to have all the other harmonics present in order to hear the missing fundamental; just a few will do (**Figure 10.19A**).

The most straightforward explanations of the missing-fundamental effect involve the temporal code for pitch discussed in Chapter 9. One thing that all harmonics of a fundamental have in common is fluctuations in sound pressure at regular intervals corresponding to the fundamental frequency. For example, the waveform for a 500-Hz tone has a peak every 2.0 ms (**Figure 10.19B**). The waveforms for 750- and 1000-Hz tones have peaks every 1.3 and 1.0 ms, respectively (**Figure 10.19C, D**). As shown in **Figure 10.19E**, these three waveforms come into alignment every 4 ms, which, conveniently, happens to be the period of the fundamental frequency for these three harmonics: 250 Hz. Indeed, *every harmonic of 250 Hz will have an energy peak every 4 ms*. Some neurons in the auditory nerve and cochlear nucleus will fire action potentials every 4 ms to the collection of waves shown in Figure 10.19E, providing an elegant mechanism to explain why listeners perceive the pitch of this complex tone to be 250 Hz, even though the tone has no 250-Hz component.

Timbre

Loudness and pitch are relatively easy to describe, because they correspond fairly well to simple acoustic dimensions (amplitude and frequency, respectively). But the richness of complex sounds like those in our world depends on more than simple sensations of loudness and pitch. For example, a trombone and a tenor saxophone might play the same note (that is, their two notes will have the exact

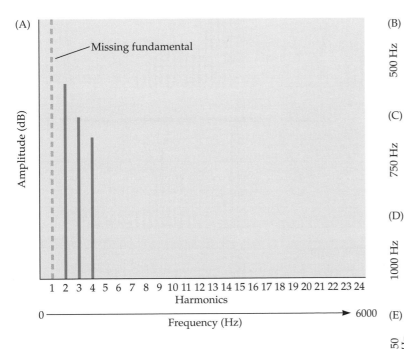

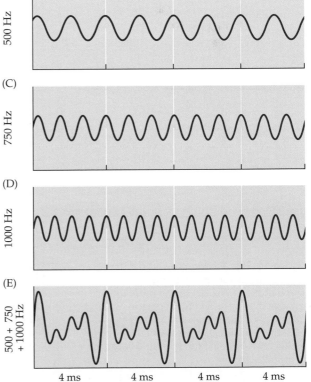

Figure 10.19 When only three harmonics of the same fundamental frequency are presented (B–D), listeners still hear the pitch of the missing fundamental frequency (A) because the harmonics share a common energy fluctuation every 4 ms, the period of a 250-Hz signal (E).

timbre The psychological sensation by which a listener can judge that two sounds with the same loudness and pitch are dissimilar. Timbre quality is conveyed by harmonics and other high frequencies.

same fundamental frequency) at exactly the same loudness (the sound waves will have identical intensities), but we would have no trouble discerning that two different instruments were being played. The perceptual quality that differs between these two musical instruments, as well as between vowel sounds such as those in the words *hot*, *heat*, and *hoot*, is known as **timbre**. (See **Web Activity 10.3: Timbre**.)

What exactly is timbre? You won't find a good answer to this question in the dictionary, because the official definition of *timbre* is "the quality that makes listeners hear two different sounds even though both sounds have the same pitch and loudness" (American Standards Association, 1960). However, differences in timbre between musical instruments or vowel sounds can be estimated closely by comparison of the extent to which the overall spectra of two sounds overlap (Plomp, 1976). Perception of visual color depends on the relative levels of energy at different wavelengths (see Chapter 5), and very similarly, perception of timbre is related to the relative energies of different acoustic spectral components (**Figure 10.20**). For example, the trombone and tenor saxophone notes whose spectra are plotted in Figure 10.20A share the same fundamental frequency (middle C, 262 Hz). However, notice that the trombone's third (786-Hz) component is stronger than its fourth (1048-Hz) component, whereas for the saxophone, the relationship between the energies of these two components is reversed.

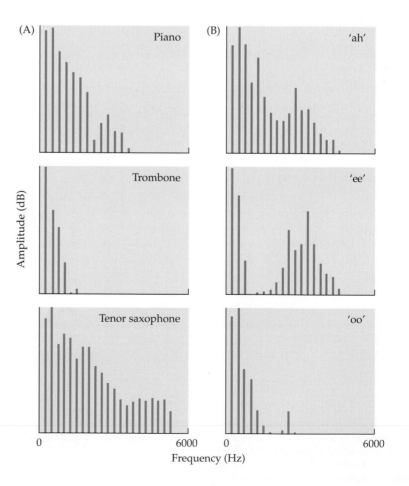

Figure 10.20 Timbre. (A) Three different musical instruments playing the same note (middle C, 262 Hz) sound different because they have different spectral shapes. (B) Three vowels produced by the same female talker, also with a fundamental frequency of 262 Hz, sound very different to listeners.

■ Sensation & Perception in Everyday Life ■

Auditory "Color" Constancy

Once we take off our headphones and get on out into the world, listening environments can dramatically alter the sounds that arrive at our ears. We already learned about the importance of reverberation energy for perception of distance and loudness of sounds. Even the way you decorate can change sounds on their way to your ears. Higher frequencies are reinforced by hard surfaces such as tile floors and concrete walls, but they are dampened by soft surfaces such as thick carpet and curtains. This is much like the problem of color constancy that you learned about in Chapter 5. In vision, the goal is to perceive the same colors even though the spectrum of illumination can be quite different depending on the type of lighting (sunlight, fluorescent, LED, and so on). In hearing, surfaces in the environment reflect and absorb energy at different frequencies in ways that change the spectral shape that finally arrives at your ears.

Kiefte and Kluender (2008) used the different spectral shapes of the vowel sounds 'ee' and 'oo' to learn how hearing calibrates for changes in the listening environment. They took advantage of the fact that the spectra for 'ee' and 'oo' differ in two important ways (**Figure 10.21A**). First, the vowel sound 'ee' has a relatively flat spectrum with almost as much energy in high frequencies as in low frequencies (upper left in the figure). In contrast, energy in 'oo' is dominated by low frequencies with less and less energy as frequency increases (lower right). We can say that the "tilt" of the 'ee' spectrum is much flatter than the tilt of 'oo.' Second, the sounds 'ee' and 'oo' also differ in where peaks are present in their spectra. The second peak in the 'ee' spectrum is at a higher frequency than the second peak in the 'oo' spectrum. Listeners use both tilt and the frequency of this second peak to tell 'ee' from 'oo' (**Figure 10.21B**) (Kiefte and Kluender, 2005).

To learn how the auditory system adjusts for listening context, Kiefte and Kluender (2008) created stimuli that enabled them to separately measure how much tilt and second-peak frequency contribute to the perception of these vowels. Then they had listeners identify vowels after hearing a sentence like "You will now hear the vowel," but with an interesting twist. They created some sentences so that the overall tilt of the sentence was the same as the tilt of the following vowel, either 'ee'-like or 'oo'-like. To other sentences they added a peak in the spectrum, all the way through the sentence, that matched the frequency of the second peak in the vowel ('ee' or 'oo') that listeners would identify. Listeners heard the very same vowels in dramatically different ways depending on which type of manipulated sentence preceded the vowels. When tilt was the same for both the preceding sentence and the vowel, listeners used only the frequency of the second peak to identify the vowel (**Figure 10.21C**). When the second peak was present all the way through the preceding sentence, listeners relied mostly on tilt to identify the vowel (**Figure 10.21D**).

(Continued)

■ Sensation & Perception in Everyday Life *(continued)* ■

Listeners calibrate for reliable spectral characteristics of a listening context much as observers calibrate for the spectral composition of illuminating light when perceiving color (Alexander and Kluender, 2010; Stilp et al., 2010). When the brain interprets spectral tilt as a consequence of the

environment in which a sound is heard (concrete versus curtains), listeners ignore tilt and use only the second peak. Conversely, when there seems to always be energy around the second peak in a listening environment, listeners use mostly tilt to decide which vowel they heard.

Figure 10.21 Listeners use both spectral tilt and the frequencies of spectral peaks to identify vowels. (A) Spectra of natural 'ee' and 'oo' are shown in the upper left and lower right, respectively. The vowel 'ee' has a relatively flat spectrum, and 'oo' has a tilted spectrum, such that there is much less energy at higher frequencies. The second spectral peak is lower in frequency for 'oo' than for 'ee.' Experimentally manipulated vowel sounds are also shown—with the tilt of 'ee' and second peak of 'oo' in the upper right, and the tilt of 'oo' and second peak of 'ee' in the lower left. Dotted lines illustrate spectral tilt. (B) Listeners use both tilt and frequency of the second peak to identify vowels. Lighter areas correspond to sounds that listeners hear as 'ee'; darker areas represent sounds that they hear as 'oo.' (C) Upon hearing a vowel after a sentence that has the same tilt as the vowel, listeners use only the frequency of the second peak to identify the vowel. (D) However, when the preceding sentence includes a peak at the same frequency as the second peak in the vowel, listeners use mostly tilt to identify the vowel.

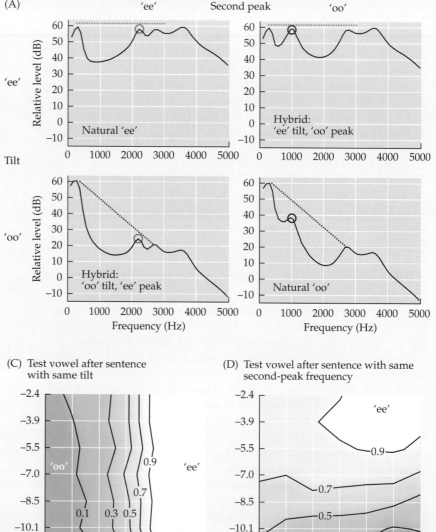

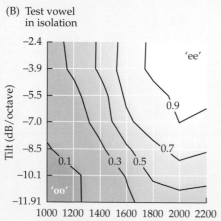
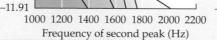
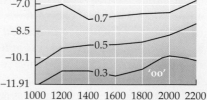

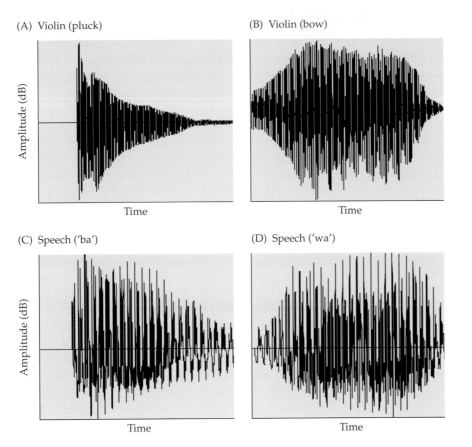

(A) Violin (pluck)

(B) Violin (bow)

(C) Speech ('ba')

(D) Speech ('wa')

Figure 10.22   We use the onsets of sounds (attacks) to identify them. The attack is quite different when a violin string is plucked (A) versus bowed (B). Similarly, different speech sounds, such as 'ba' (C) and 'wa' (D), have different attacks.

Attack and Decay

Another very important quality of a complex sound is the way it begins (the **attack** of the sound) and ends (the sound's **decay**) (**Figure 10.22**). Our auditory systems are very sensitive to attack and decay characteristics. For example, important contrasts between speech sounds in the words *bill* and *will* or the words *chip* and *ship* relate to differences in how quickly sound energy increases at the onset (the rate of attack).

The same musical instrument can have quite different attacks, from the rapid onset of a plucked violin string to the gradual onset of a bowed string (Figure 10.22A, B). How quickly a sound decays depends on how long it takes for the vibrating object creating the sound (e.g., the violin string) to dissipate energy and stop moving. One of the more challenging aspects of designing music synthesizers that could mimic real musical instruments was learning how to mimic the attacks and decays of the instruments.

To appreciate the importance of attack and decay in sound quality, explore **Web Activity 10.3: Timbre**, where you can hear a normal piano note and then hear the piano note played backward. The sound of a piano note is caused by a small hammer hitting a string. The amplitude of the resulting sound increases very quickly before more gradually dissipating. If a recording of a piano note is played backward, the sound no longer even remotely resembles that of a piano. Instead, the backward piano note sounds more like the same note played on an accordion.

attack   The part of a sound during which amplitude increases (onset).

decay   The part of a sound during which amplitude decreases (offset).

Auditory Scene Analysis

The acoustic environment can be a busy place. In most natural situations, the sound source that one is listening to is not the only source present. Consider, for example, conversing with a friend at a party where many other people are talking, music is playing, chips are being munched, the door is being opened and closed, and so on. Now consider simpler environments, such as those you choose for studying. To read this chapter, you probably chose the spot where you are right now because it was relatively quiet, but stop and listen carefully. Is a heater, air conditioner, computer, refrigerator, or some combination of these devices humming in the background? Can you hear people talking somewhere in the vicinity? Are chair legs sliding across floors? Places with only a single sound source are very uncommon. Indeed, there are few truly quiet places outside the laboratories of hearing scientists and the testing chambers of audiologists.

Environments with multiple sound sources are the rule, not the exception. How does the auditory system sort out these sources? Note that the visual system also has to contend with a busy world, but eyes can be directed to any part of the scene that is of interest to the visual system. Moreover, the rods and cones on the right side of the retina always see the objects on the left, politely leaving the receptors on the other side of the retina to collect data about objects on the right. For an auditory scene, the situation is greatly complicated by the fact that all the sound waves from all the sound sources in the environment are summed together in a single complex sound wave (**Figure 10.23**). You can move your ears around all you want, but everyone's voice at the party still has to be picked up by the same two sets of cochlear hair cells. Separating different sounds from

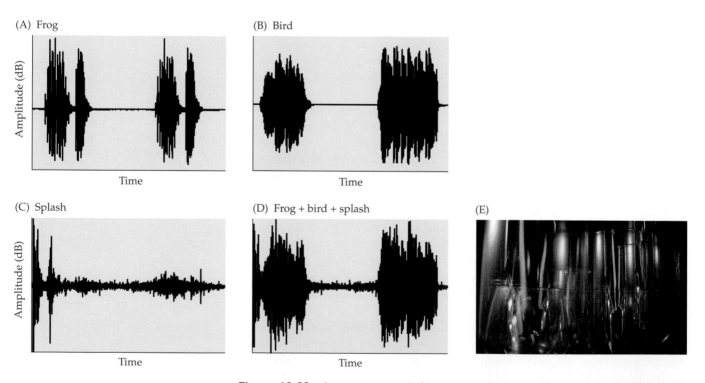

(A) Frog

(B) Bird

(C) Splash

(D) Frog + bird + splash

(E)

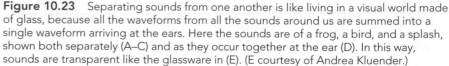

Figure 10.23 Separating sounds from one another is like living in a visual world made of glass, because all the waveforms from all the sounds around us are summed into a single waveform arriving at the ears. Here the sounds are of a frog, a bird, and a splash, shown both separately (A–C) and as they occur together at the ear (D). In this way, sounds are transparent like the glassware in (E). (E courtesy of Andrea Kluender.)

one another is like living in a world in which everything is made of glass: it is difficult to distinguish separate objects, because they all merge into a single combination of shapes, as Figure 10.23E illustrates.

Somehow, however, the auditory system contends quite well with the situation: our perception is typically of a world with easily separable sounds. We can understand the conversation of a dance partner at a party, and we can pick out a favorite instrument in the band. This distinction of auditory events or objects in the broader auditory environment is commonly referred to as **source segregation** or **auditory scene analysis**.

Spatial, Spectral, and Temporal Segregation

The auditory system uses a number of strategies to segregate sound sources. One of the most obvious strategies is spatial separation between sounds. Sounds that emanate from the same location in space can typically be treated as if they arose from the same source. Moreover, in a natural environment in which sound sources move, a sound that is perceived to move in space can more easily be separated from background sounds that are relatively stationary. Listeners move too, so if a sound stays in the same place relative to the path of a listener, it will be easier for that sound to be sorted out from other sounds.

In addition to being sorted by location, sounds can be segregated on the basis of their spectral or temporal qualities. For example, sounds with the same pitch or similar pitches are more likely to be treated as coming from the same source and to be segregated from other sounds. Being familiar with particular sounds is also helpful, and everyone has the experience of being distracted by someone saying one's name even in a crowded room full of voices. As you learn about the ways listeners make sense of the cascade of sounds surrounding them, you will see that both the physical properties of sounds and the experiences within one's head work together (Kondo et al., 2017).

Sounds that are perceived to emanate from the same source are often described as being part of the same "auditory stream," and dividing the auditory world into separate auditory objects is known as **auditory stream segregation** or auditory scene analysis. The challenge of sorting out the sound to which one is listening from all the competing sounds in the environment is common across all animals that hear, and variants of the examples that follow have been demonstrated to exist not only for humans, but also for birds, fishes, frogs, and nonhuman mammals (Itatani and Klump, 2017).

Perhaps the simplest example of auditory stream segregation involves two tones with similar frequencies that are alternated (**Figure 10.24A**). (See **Web Activity 10.4: Auditory Stream Segregation.**) This sequence sounds like a single coherent stream of tones that warble up and down in frequency. But if the alternating tones are markedly different in frequency (**Figure 10.24B**), two

source segregation or **auditory scene analysis** Processing an auditory scene consisting of multiple sound sources into separate sound images.

auditory stream segregation The perceptual organization of a complex acoustic signal into separate auditory events for which each stream is heard as a separate event.

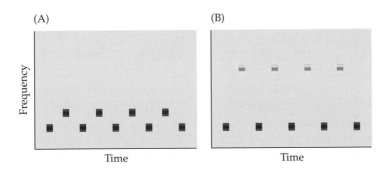

Figure 10.24 When tones that are close in frequency occur in rapid succession, they are heard as a single warbling stream (A), but when successive, rapidly alternating tones have very different frequencies, they are heard as two separate streams (B).

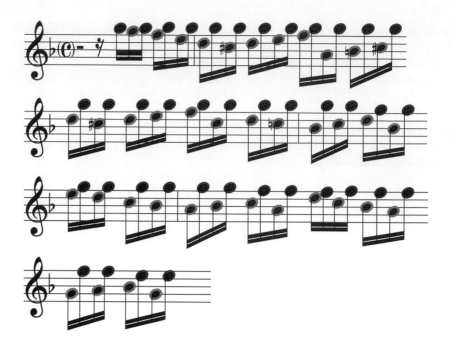

Figure 10.25 This musical sequence from J. S. Bach's *Toccata and Fugue in D Minor* utilizes the stream segregation principles "discovered" by auditory researchers in the twentieth century. When played in rapid succession, the higher notes (red) are heard as one melody separate from the lower notes (blue).

streams of tones are heard—one higher in pitch than the other (G. A. Miller and Heise, 1950).

Auditory stream segregation is a powerful perceptual phenomenon that is not limited to simple tones in the laboratory. Before stream segregation was "discovered" by auditory scientists, the composer Johann Sebastian Bach exploited these auditory effects in his compositions (**Figure 10.25**). The same instrument, such as a pipe organ, would rapidly play interleaved sequences of low and high notes. Even though the musician played a sequence in the order H1-L1-H2-L2-H3-L3, listeners heard two melodies—one high (H1-H2-H3) and one low (L1-L2-L3). This bit of knowledge about auditory perception was known not only to Bach, but also to other Baroque composers of the seventeenth and early eighteenth centuries.

When thinking about auditory scene analysis, it is sometimes useful to describe effects using Gestalt principles such as those elucidated for vision in Chapter 4. The examples of auditory stream segregation presented in this section can be described as applications of the Gestalt principle of **similarity** (see Figure 4.20A): sounds that are similar to each other tend to be grouped together into streams.

Grouping by Timbre

When a sequence of tones that have increasing and decreasing frequencies is presented (**Figure 10.26A**), tones that deviate from the rising/falling pattern are heard to "pop out" of the sequence (Heise and Miller, 1951). What happens when two patterns overlap in frequency—one increasing and then decreasing in frequency, and one decreasing and then increasing in frequency (**Figure 10.26B, C**)? If the tones are simple sine waves, two streams of sound are heard without overlapping pitches (Figure 10.26B); one stream includes all the high tones, and one includes all the low tones. However, if harmonics are added to one of the

similarity Gestalt grouping rule stating that the tendency of two sounds to group together will increase as the acoustic similarity between them increases.

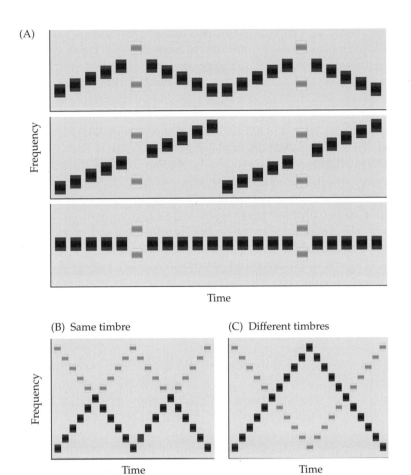

(A)

Frequency

Time

(B) Same timbre

(C) Different timbres

Frequency

Time   Time

Figure 10.26 Timbre affects how sounds are grouped. (A) Individual tones (green) "pop out" of a stream if they do not fit the patterns of rising or falling frequency for the other tones (red). (B, C) Sounds that share the same timbre group together. When sounds in a succession all share the same timbre (B), they are heard as streams according to similar frequency. But if sounds have different timbres (C), they will separate according to timbre, even if their frequencies cross another pattern with a different timbre.

sequences, thus creating a richer timbre, two overlapping patterns are heard as distinct (Figure 10.26C) (van Noorden, 1975).

Auditory stream segregation based on groups of notes with similar timbres can be seen as another example of the Gestalt principle of similarity at work. As Figure 10.20 illustrated, timbres are very different for pianos, trombones, and saxophones. Grouping by timbre is particularly robust because sounds with similar timbres usually arise from the same sound source. This principle is the reason why listeners are able to pick out the melody played on a single instrument—a trombone, for example—even when another instrument, such as a saxophone, plays a different or even opposite sequence of notes (Wessel, 1979).

Neural processes that give rise to stream segregation can be found throughout the auditory system, from the first stages of auditory processing to the primary auditory cortex (A1) to secondary areas of the auditory cortex, such as the belt and parabelt areas (J. S. Snyder and Alain, 2007). The brain stem shows neural evidence of stream segregation based on simple cues such as frequencies of tones, but segregation based on more sophisticated perceptual properties of sounds is more likely to take place in the cortex.

Grouping by Onset

In addition to timbre, sound components that begin at the same time, or nearly the same time, such as the harmonics of a music or speech sound, will also tend to be heard as coming from the same sound source. One way this phenomenon helps us is by grouping different harmonics into a single complex sound.

common fate Gestalt grouping rule stating that the tendency of sounds to group together will increase if they begin and/or end at the same time.

Frequency components with different onset times are less likely to be grouped. For example, if a single harmonic of a vowel sound begins before the rest of the harmonics of the vowel, that lone harmonic is less likely to be perceived as part of the vowel than if the onsets are simultaneous (C. J. Darwin, 1984).

R. A. Rasch (1978) showed that it is much easier to distinguish two notes from one another when the onset of one precedes the onset of the other by at least 30 ms. He noted that musicians playing together in an ensemble such as a string quartet do not begin playing notes at exactly the same time, even when the musical score instructs them to do so. Instead, they begin notes slightly before or after one another, and this staggered start probably helps listeners pick out the individual instruments in the group. Part of the signature style of the Rolling Stones has been to carry this practice to an extreme. Members of the group sometimes begin the same beat with such widely varying onsets that it is unclear whether they are playing together or not.

Grouping of sounds with common onsets is consistent with the Gestalt principle of **common fate**. Consider the consequences of dropping a bottle on a hard surface and listening for whether the bottle breaks. When any object bounces, each bounce results in a set of overtones that relate to the size, shape, and material of the object. If the dropped bottle does not break (**Figure 10.27A**), this pattern of overtones repeats as a group, and the intensity of the sounds decreases with every additional bounce. But if the bottle breaks upon landing (**Figure 10.27B**), individual shards of the bottle will have different spectral compositions, each shard being its own resonator. Onsets of the overtones for different shards will

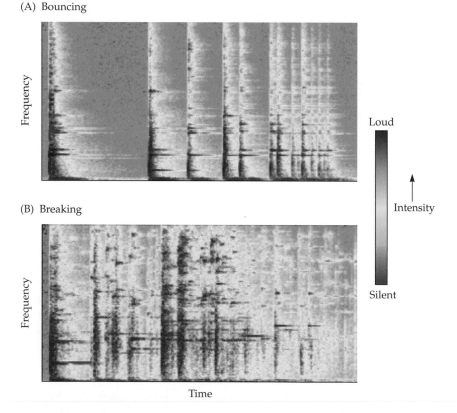

Figure 10.27 Spectrograms of a bottle bouncing (A) or breaking (B). When the bottle breaks, there are multiple patterns of onsets for multiple pieces of glass. Listeners can use patterns of onsets to accurately determine whether or not the bottle broke.

differ because the pieces bounce independently until they bounce no more. Thus, even when the initial burst of noise is removed from the sound of the bouncing and breaking bottles, listeners can use patterns of onsets to accurately determine whether the bottle broke (W. H. Warren and Verbrugge, 1984).

When Sounds Become Familiar

In addition to the simple Gestalt principles that we've already discussed, listeners make use of experience and familiarity to separate different sound sources. When you know what you're listening for, it's easier to pick out sounds from a background of other sounds. An obvious example is how quickly you recognize someone saying your name even though there are many other sounds, including other voices, in the room.

You might be surprised to learn how quickly you can come to recognize a completely new sound once you've heard it a few times. Sounds in the environment, such as bird calls, often occur more than once. To test how much experience listeners need in order to benefit from familiarity, McDermott, Wroblewski, and Oxenham (2011) created complex novel sounds by combining natural sound characteristics in ways that listeners had never heard before. They repeatedly played these sounds at the same time and intensity as a background of other novel sounds that did not repeat, as shown in **Figure 10.28**. Although listeners could not segregate a sound from its background when they listened to a single instance, they could nonetheless segregate and identify the sound when it repeated. Listeners needed only a few repetitions to perform well above chance, even though they had never heard the complex sounds before they came to the laboratory.

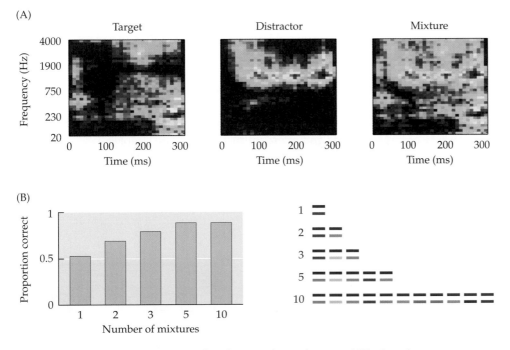

Figure 10.28 Listeners' task is to identify a novel complex sound (A) when that target and a distractor overlap in one combined sound (mixture). (B) When a new complex sound (red) is repeatedly played at the same time as different sounds (not red) just a few times, listeners quickly become familiar enough with the repeated sound that they can pick it out from other sounds in the background. (A from McDermott, Wroblewski, and Oxenham, 2011; B after McDermott, Wroblewski, and Oxenham, 2011.)

good continuation Gestalt grouping rule stating that sounds will tend to group together as continuous if they seem to share a common path, similar to a shared contour for vision.

An important part of learning new sounds is experiencing how changes along different dimensions of sounds, such as timbre and attack/decay, tend to co-occur. Christian Stilp and colleagues (Stilp, Rogers, and Kluender, 2010; Stilp and Kluender, 2012, 2016) have shown that listeners quickly learn how different dimensions of novel sounds tend to occur together even when the listeners are distracted while drawing on an Etch A Sketch. Listeners became so attuned to combinations of sound qualities that they could not even hear deviations from experienced patterns unless differences became very large. You may have had similar visual experiences when a very close friend complained that you did not notice a new haircut or glasses. You were so accustomed to the combination of facial features that you did not even detect the change in one of them.

Continuity and Restoration Effects

As already discussed, the sound we're trying to listen to at any given time is usually not the only sound in the environment. In addition to dealing with overlapping auditory streams, we also often have to deal with the total masking of one sound source by another for brief periods. Suppose you're listening on your cell phone as a friend gives you directions to the restaurant where you're to meet for lunch. A car may honk, a baby may cry, or your cell phone may produce a short burst of static, but if you're paying attention and the interruption is not too long, you will probably be able to "hear through" the interruption. This effect is consistent with the Gestalt principle of **good continuation** (see Figure 4.16A): the continuous auditory stream is heard to continue behind the masking sound. Auditory researchers have labeled these phenomena "continuity effects" or "perceptual restoration effects"—the latter label arising because the auditory system appears to restore the portion of the continuous stream that was blocked out by the interrupting sound (R. M. Warren, 1984). In this sense, auditory restoration is analogous to the visual system's filling in the portions of a background object that is sitting behind an occluding object.

> **FURTHER DISCUSSION** of Gestalt grouping rules as they pertain to vision can be found in Chapter 4 on pages 111–115.

Continuity effects have been demonstrated in the laboratory with a wide variety of target sounds and interrupting sounds. The simplest version of such an experiment is to delete portions of a pure tone and replace them with noise (**Figure 10.29A**). The tone will sound continuous if the noise is intense enough to have masked the tone, had it been present (R. M. Warren, 1984).

Figure 10.29 When a sound is deleted and replaced with a loud noise, listeners will hear the sound as if it continues through the noise. This is true when a tone maintains the same frequency (A) and when the tone steadily increases or decreases in frequency (B).

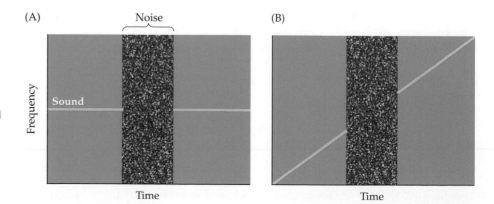

How do we know that listeners really hear a sound as continuous in experiments such as this? One of the best ways to determine what people really perceive is to use a signal detection task. Kluender and Jenison (1992) used signal detection methodology with a slightly more complex version of the continuity effect (**Figure 10.29B**). In their experiments, listeners heard tone *glides*, in which a sine wave tone varies continuously in frequency over time (the resulting sound is similar to that of a slide whistle). When intense noise is superimposed over part of the glide, listeners report hearing the glide continue behind the noise. (See **Web Activity 10.5: Continuity and Restoration Effects**.) Kluender and Jenison created stimuli in which the middle portion of the glide either was present with the noise or was completely removed. In trials in which the noise was shortest and most intense, the signal detection measure of discriminability (*d'*) dropped to 0. For these trials, perceptual restoration was complete: listeners had no idea whether or not the glide was actually present with the noise.

The compelling nature of perceptual restoration suggests that at some point the restored missing sounds are encoded in the brain as if they were actually present in the signal. Imaging studies of humans, who can report when they do and do not hear the tone through the noise, show metabolic activity in A1 that is consistent with what listeners report hearing, whether or not the tone is present (Riecke et al., 2007, 2009). Macaque monkeys also hear tones being restored even when interrupted by noise (Petkov, O'Connor, and Sutter, 2003), and neurons in A1 of monkeys show the same responses to real and restored tones (Petkov, O'Connor, and Sutter, 2007). These data from the auditory cortex cannot tell us whether the glides were restored in the cortex or at a point earlier in auditory processing. However, they make it easier to understand why perceptually restored sounds really sound present.

Restoration of Complex Sounds

Complex sounds such as music and speech can also be perceptually restored. When DeWitt and Samuel (1990) played familiar melodies with notes excised and replaced by noise, listeners perceived the missing notes as if they were present. Restoration was so complete that listeners could not report which notes had been removed and replaced with noise. The researchers also tested whether familiarity of the melodies mattered. Just as you might expect, listeners were much less likely to "hear" a missing note in an unfamiliar melody.

Just in case you think only human listeners care about melodies, listen up. Seeba and Klump (2009) trained European starlings (**Figure 10.30**) to peck when they heard a difference between two parts of starling song, called motifs. Then the starlings heard intact motifs and, for comparison, interrupted motifs with short snippets filled with either noise or silence. They were more likely to peck, indicating a difference between an intact and an interrupted motif, when silence filled the gap. This observation suggests that the starlings restored the missing bits of motifs when noise was inserted into the gap. Not all starling songs are equal, however. In the same set of experiments, the researchers used bits of song that were either familiar to the starling in the experiment (the bird's own song or the song of a cage mate) or unfamiliar (from starlings the subject had never heard). Just like humans listening to familiar and unfamiliar melodies, starlings are more likely to restore missing bits of a familiar song.

Figure 10.30 European starlings perceptually restore bits of starling songs and are more likely to restore song parts when familiar with the starling that produced them.

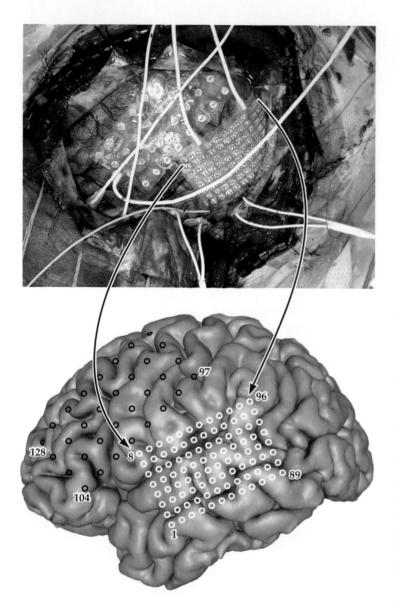

Figure 10.31 Prior to performing brain surgery to remove a tumor or to reduce effects of very severe epilepsy, neurosurgeons often place electrodes directly on the surface of the brain to localize regions of neural activity. Before surgery, researchers can take advantage of these electrodes to record responses to experimental materials. The electrode grid shown here is similar to that used in the Leonard et al. (2016) study. (Courtesy of Rick L. Jenison and Richard A. Reale.)

Perceptual restoration in speech is even more compelling than restoration of music. R. M. Warren and Obusek (1971) played the sentence "The state governors met with their respective legi*latures convening in the capital city" with the first *s* in *legislatures* removed and replaced by silence, a cough, a burst of noise, or any of a few other sounds. Despite the missing *s*, listeners heard the sentence as if it were intact and complete. Even when listeners were explicitly warned that a small part of the sentence had been removed and replaced with silence or another sound, they were unable to accurately report where the sentence had been changed, except when the missing *s* had been replaced with silence.

Listening to familiar melodies and to real speech sentences, as opposed to simple sounds such as sine waves and tonal glides, permits listeners to use more than just auditory processing to fill in missing information. Clearly, these "higher-order" sources of information are used for listening to sources in the face of other acoustic clutter. Consider words that vary by only a single sound, such as *novel* versus *nozzle*. When the single sound that changes the word ('v' versus 'z' in this example) is replaced by noise (as in 'no#el'), listeners can report which of the two alternatives they "heard." What is happening in the brain? Matthew Leonard and colleagues (Leonard et al., 2016) found answers when they measured the activity of thousands of neurons recorded by electrodes placed on the surface of the brains of patients who were awaiting brain surgery (**Figure 10.31**). First, they recorded brain responses to the intact-word sounds 'novel' and 'nozzle.' Then they played the sounds of the words with noise replacing 'v' and 'z,' that is, 'no#el.' Listeners would report which word they heard when they listened to 'no#el,' and the researchers could predict which word the listeners would report by looking at whether brain activity in response to 'no#el' was more like activity in response to 'novel' or to 'nozzle.' The brain had filled in the missing sound so well that the response to a word missing a sound looked like the response to an intact word.

Auditory Attention

Have you ever been so engrossed by a task, such as reading this book, that you didn't even hear someone calling your name? At other times, maybe also while reading this book, have you ever noticed that it took only the barest distraction to draw your attention away? We said a lot about visual attention in Chapter 7;

we will not delve so deeply into auditory attention, but there are some parallels to the visual case. Auditory attention can also differ from visual attention in ways that reflect the differences between senses. You just learned about how the auditory system is exquisitely fast and sensitive. In Chapter 9, we pointed out that hearing works great at a distance, in the dark, and around obstacles. These facts make hearing our primary sense for being vigilant in our surroundings—your first line of defense in a sensory world.

We see the auditory system playing the role of sentinel in the **acoustic startle reflex**. Just like its name implies, this is the very rapid bodily movement that arises following a loud, abrupt sound. This reflex is very fast: muscle twitches may follow the sound by as little as 10 ms (Musiek, 2003). Because the transmission time between ear (sound) and spinal cord (movement) is so brief, there can be no more than a few brain stem neurons between them. Being afraid increases acoustic startle (Davis, 2006). Directors of horror movies seem to know this, as they gradually ramp up your anxiety before the big event, and then the surprise is usually loud.

The acoustic startle reflex is unselective—almost any loud sound will do. In other cases, auditory attention is selective—it is picking one sound source out of several. Many sounds occur at the same time in natural environments, with all of the sounds becoming merged at the ears. This makes listening to only one sound among many a serious challenge. This problem has much in common with the selective visual attention that you learned about in Chapter 7.

Effects of attending to a particular sound source can be so strong that we completely miss out on hearing other sounds in a kind of inattentional deafness. Skilled musicians were no better than untrained listeners at noticing an electronic guitar improvisation that was mixed in with Richard Strauss's *Thus Spoke Zarathustra* (theme music from the sci-fi classic *2001: A Space Odyssey*) when both groups were asked to count (and, thus, to attend to) the number of timpani beats (Koreimann, Gula, and Vitouch, 2014). From this example, you see that task-specific "goals" can affect auditory attention in ways that may not be explained by only physical characteristics of sounds (Kaya and Elhilali, 2017). This inattentional deafness has its limits, because listeners had less trouble noticing the guitar when it was made sufficiently loud.

While inattentional deafness might seem to be a bad thing, it really represents an extreme example of auditory processes that help us to listen in our acoustically crowded world. Imagine yourself in a room full of people who are speed dating in their searches for true love (**Figure 10.32**). You earnestly focus on the person who you are sizing up, but many other voices compete with the one voice you are trying to understand. Listeners can use the acoustic characteristics of a talker to track what that voice is saying despite the clutter of other voices. While we might think that this relies on being familiar with a talker or actively concentrating on that voice, this may not be necessary (Bressler et al., 2014). It appears that the brain does this automatically, following principles like those for auditory stream segregation described earlier in the "Spatial, Spectral, and Temporal Segregation" section.

Suppose that, after sharing a brief exchange on favorite colors, you require no more time with the person to whom you've been listening. You begin to tune in to a neighboring conversation without moving away just yet from your currently assigned dating candidate. This requires shifting attention. There are several points to be made about this situation. First, there is a cost to moving to the next sound source: listeners become less accurate in understanding what they hear when they have to switch between talkers (Lawo and Koch, 2014). Second, your ability to look at one person while attending to a different conversation illustrates the

acoustic startle reflex The very rapid motor response to a sudden sound. Very few neurons are involved in the basic startle reflex, which can also be affected by emotional state.

Figure 10.32 The organizers of this speed-dating event couldn't seat potential couples so close together if we didn't have the ability to attend to one voice among many. Note that although each of these individuals appears to be attending to the person across the table, any of them could actually be attending to one of the other conversations.

flexibility of your attentional apparatus. Finally, if you are attending to another conversation, really embarrassing things can happen when you realize that your partner has stopped speaking and is waiting for a response to a question to which you have not attended. You can switch attention back and forth between streams, but you cannot fully process two streams of speech any more than you can read two sentences at the same time (see Figure 7.1).

Summary

1. Listeners use small differences, in time and intensity, across the two ears to learn the direction in the horizontal plane (azimuth) from which a sound comes.

2. Time and intensity differences across the two ears are not sufficient to fully indicate the location from which a sound comes. In particular, they are not enough to indicate whether sounds come from the front or the back, or from higher or lower (elevation).

3. The pinna, ear canal, head, and torso alter the intensities of different frequencies for sounds coming from different places in space, and listeners use these changes in intensity across frequency to identify the location from which a sound comes.

4. Perception of auditory distance is similar to perception of visual depth because no single characteristic of the signal can inform a listener about how distant a sound source is. Listeners must combine intensity, spectral composition, and relative amounts of direct and reflected energy of sounds to estimate distance to a sound source.

5. Many natural sounds, including music and human speech, have rich harmonic structure with energy at integer multiples of the fundamental frequency, and listeners are especially good at perceiving the pitch of harmonic sounds.

6. Important perceptual qualities of complex sounds are timbre (conveyed by the relative amounts of energy at different frequencies) and the onset and offset properties of attack and decay, respectively.

7. Because all the sounds in the environment are summed into a single waveform that reaches each ear, a major challenge for hearing is to separate sound sources in the combined signal. This general process is known as auditory scene analysis. Sound source segregation succeeds by using multiple characteristics of sounds, including spatial location, similarity in frequency and timbre, onset properties, and familiarity.

8. In everyday environments, sounds to which a person is listening often are interrupted by other, louder sounds. Perceptual restoration is a process by which missing or degraded acoustic signals are perceptually replaced.

9. Auditory attention has many aspects in common with visual attention. It is a balance between being able to make use of sounds one needs to hear in the midst of competing sounds and being on alert for new auditory information.

11 Music and Speech Perception

■ Questions to Contemplate ▬▬▬

Think about the following questions as you read this chapter. By the chapter's end, you should be able to answer and discuss them.

- How are musical sounds described? What are the differences and similarities in the descriptions of musical sounds and other sounds?

- How is perception of music and speech different from perception of other sounds?

- What are the differences and similarities in the descriptions of speech sounds and other sounds?

- In what ways is experience important for perception of music and speech?

- After gaining a richer appreciation for what ears do for you, if you had to give up one sensory system, why would you choose *not* to give up hearing?

Sounds from musical instruments and human vocal tracts obey the same laws of physical acoustics as all other sounds. Guitar strings and human vocal folds are vibratory structures, with similarities to rubber bands and suspension bridges. Trombones and vocal tracts act as resonators following the same laws as empty bottles and hollow logs. In this sense, spoken words and musical notes are nothing more than very familiar, complex sounds.

In other ways, however, music and speech can be distinguished from most other environmental sounds. Much as visual art, such as paintings and sculpture, is created to attract the eye, music and speech are created with ears in mind. Both

Michael Cheval, *Sounding Silence*, 2008

music and speech serve to communicate, and both can convey emotion and deeper meanings. In song, music and speech conspire to move the listener. Although dogs, birds, and whales share acoustic messages and even sing to one another, there is no question that the depth and breadth of human communication by music and language has no rival in the acoustic world. In this chapter we explore these communicative aspects of hearing: music and speech.

Music

People have been using music as a way to express themselves and influence the thoughts and emotions of others for a very long time. The oldest discovered

pitch The psychological aspect of sound related mainly to perceived frequency.

musical instruments—flutes carved from vulture bones—are at least 30,000 years old (Conard, Malina, and Münzel, 2009). You probably know of the great ancient Greek scholar Pythagoras (ca. 580–ca. 500 BCE) from the Pythagorean theorem in high school geometry. To say that Pythagoras was obsessed with numbers would be an understatement. And the numbers that he and his followers cared about most were those found in musical scales. They were convinced that the musical intervals they found most pleasing should provide the greatest insights not only to mathematics, but to the universe as a whole. Although music may not actually explain the known universe, we all appreciate how important music is to culture and, perhaps, to one's personal cultural identity.

Musical Notes

From Chapter 9 you know that one of the most important characteristics of any acoustic signal is frequency. You also know that brain structures for processing sounds are tonotopically organized to correspond to frequency. The psychological quality of perceived frequency is **pitch**. When you imagined pitch while reading Chapter 9, you probably imagined musical pitch. **Figure 11.1** illustrates the extent of the frequency range of musical sounds in relation to human hearing.

TONE HEIGHT AND TONE CHROMA   Musical pitch is one of the characteristics of musical notes, the sounds that constitute melodies. A very important

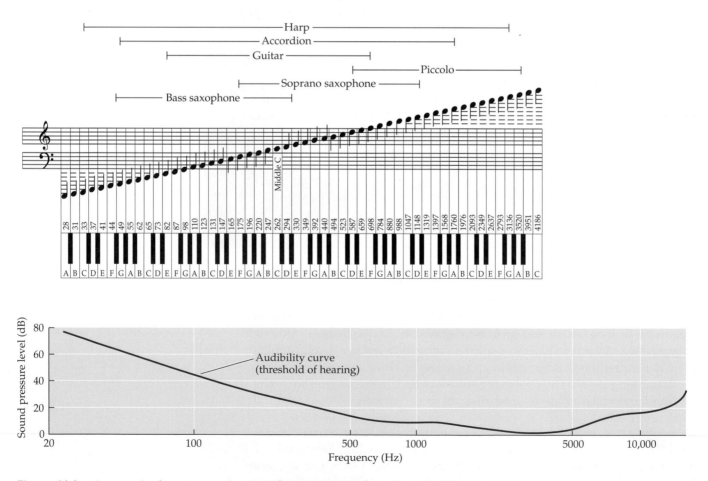

Figure 11.1   The sounds of music extend across a frequency range from about 25 to 4200 hertz (Hz).

concept in understanding musical pitch is the **octave**. When we described pitch (or psychoacoustic pitch) in Chapter 9, it seemed clear that the nearer any two sounds were in frequency, the nearer they were in pitch. Here's where octaves come in. When one of two periodic sounds is double the frequency of the other, those two sounds are one octave apart. For example, middle C (C_4) has a fundamental frequency of 261.6 hertz (Hz). Notes that are one octave below and above middle C are 130.8 Hz (C_3) and 523.2 Hz (C_5), respectively. Not only do these three sounds have the same names on the musical scale (C), but they also sound similar. In fact, C_3 (130.8 Hz) sounds more similar to C_4 (261.6 Hz) than to a sound with a closer frequency—for example, E_3 (164.8 Hz)! Clearly there is more to musical pitch than just frequency.

The preceding example illustrates the concept of "just intonation," in which frequencies of sounds are in simple ratios with one another (e.g., 2:1 for an octave). But in typical Western music, the frequencies of notes are adjusted slightly from simple ratios so that combinations of notes will sound equally good when played in higher- or lower-frequency ranges (keys). The set of notes (scale) used commonly in Western music is called "equal temperament."

Because of octave relations, musical pitch is typically described as having two dimensions. The first is **tone height**, which relates to frequency in a fairly straightforward way. The second dimension, related to the octave, is **tone chroma** (*chroma* is the Greek word for "color"). We can visualize musical pitch as a helix. Frequency and tone height increase with increasing height on the helix, as shown in **Figure 11.2**. The circular laps around the helix correspond to changes in tone chroma. At the same point along each lap around the helix, a specific sound lies on a vertical line, and all sounds along that line share the same tone chroma and are separated by octaves. (See **Web Activity 11.1: Notes, Chords, and Octaves**.)

In your early years of schooling, you probably learned to sing the notes of the musical scale: do, re, mi, fa, sol, la, ti, do. Perhaps you even tested how many times you could sing the scale at increasingly higher pitches. In that case, you were actually singing your way up the musical helix. Your pitch traveled a full turn upward with each repetition of a particular note—for example, do or re.

In Chapter 9 you learned that both a place code and a temporal code can be used in the perception of pitch. Neurons in the auditory nerve convey frequency information both by their location in the cochlea (place) and by the timing of their firing (temporal). For frequencies greater than 5000 Hz, temporal coding does not contribute to the perception of pitch, and pitch discrimination becomes appreciably worse because only place coding can be used. Most musical instruments generally produce notes that are below 4000 Hz. Could tone chroma somehow be related to the temporal encoding of pitch (Moore, 2003)? We do not know. We do know that a sequence of pure tones with frequencies greater than 5000 Hz does not convey a melody very well (Attneave and Olson, 1971), and listeners have great difficulty perceiving octave relationships between tones when one or both tones have a frequency greater than 5000 Hz (Ward, 1954).

CHORDS Music is further defined by richer, complex sounds called **chords**, which are created when three or more notes are played simultaneously. (The simultaneous playing of two notes is called a dyad.) The major distinction between chords is whether they are consonant or dissonant. Perceived to be most pleasing, *consonant* chords are combinations of notes in which the ratios between the note frequencies are simple. This is why Pythagoras was so taken

octave The interval between two sound frequencies having a ratio of 2:1.

tone height A sound quality corresponding to the level of pitch. Tone height is monotonically related to frequency.

tone chroma A sound quality shared by tones that have the same octave interval.

chord A combination of three or more musical notes with different pitches played simultaneously.

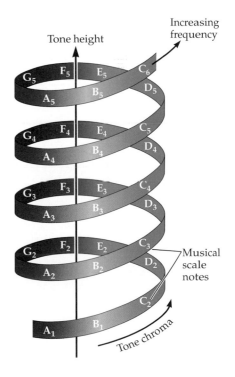

Figure 11.2 This helix illustrates the two characteristics of musical pitch: tone height and tone chroma.

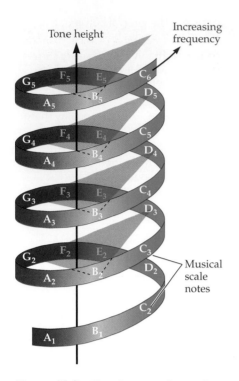

Tone height

Increasing frequency

Musical scale notes

Figure 11.3 Chords are made up of three or more notes and can be played with different tone heights while their chromatic relationships are maintained. Here, the G-major chord (purple shading) is shown being played at different heights.

by the relationship between pleasantness and mathematics. You already know one of the consonant relationships, the octave, in which the frequencies of the two notes are in the simple ratio of 2:1. Other major consonant intervals are the perfect fifth (3:2) and the perfect fourth (4:3). *Dissonant* intervals are defined by less elegant ratios. For example, the minor second (16:15) and the augmented fourth (45:32) do not sound very pleasing. Indeed, during the Middle Ages the augmented fourth was called the "devil in music" (Seay, 1975).

Because chords are defined by the ratios of the note frequencies combined to produce them, they are named the same no matter what octave they're played in. For example, the G-major chord consists of G, B, and D, and it can be played as $G_2 + B_2 + D_3$, $G_4 + B_4 + D_5$, $G_6 + B_6 + D_7$, or in any other octave, provided the ratios remain the same. Note that in the musical helix in **Figure 11.3**, the relationships between the notes of the chord on the helix stay the same, as in Figure 11.2; the only thing that changes is the pattern's height.

CULTURAL DIFFERENCES   Musical scales and intervals vary widely across cultures. Although potent relationships between notes such as octaves are relatively universal, different musical traditions use different numbers of notes and spaces between notes within an octave. All of our discussion has concerned the heptatonic (seven-note) scale. Another common scale, pentatonic, has five notes per octave, and you've heard this scale in gospel, jazz, rock, and blues music, among other North American genres. The pentatonic scale is traditional in many other parts of the world, especially Asia.

You may be aware that Asian languages such as Mandarin (a Chinese language), Thai, and Vietnamese are tone languages, giving a singsongy impression to some English listeners. Speakers of tone languages use changes in voice pitch (fundamental frequency) to distinguish different words in their language. For example, the Mandarin word *ma* means "horse" or "mother" depending on how voice pitch rises or falls.

It appears that language may affect the types of musical scales people use. Changes in pitch direction are larger and more frequent in spoken tone languages such as Mandarin, Thai, and Vietnamese than in English, French, and German. Parallel acoustic differences are found between the pentatonic music of China, Thailand, and Vietnam and the heptatonic music of Western cultures. Pitch changes in Asian music are larger and occur more often (Han et al., 2011).

In scales for which fewer notes comprise an octave, notes may be more loosely tuned than are notes in the heptatonic Western scale. When there are fewer notes to distinguish, a wider range of pitches can qualify for a given note. For example, the Javanese *sléndro* and *pélog* scales have fewer than seven notes within an octave, and there is greater variation in a note's acceptable frequencies.

Because people around the world have very different listening experiences, you might expect them to hear musical notes in different ways. Indeed, when Javanese and Western musicians hear intervals between notes, their estimates of the intervals vary according to how well those notes correspond to Javanese and Western scales, respectively (Perlman and Krumhansl, 1996). Furthermore, infants seem equipped to learn whatever scale is used in their environment. Lynch and Eilers (1990) tested the degree to which 6-month-old infants noticed inappropriate notes within both the traditional Western scale and the Javanese *pélog* scale. The infants appeared to be equally good at detecting such "mistakes" within both Western and Javanese scales, but adults from Florida were reliably better at detecting deviations from the Western scale.

Figure 11.4 A researcher (right) plays different sounds for a Tsimane' man who lives in the Amazon rain forest in Bolivia. The man is being asked about which musical chords, if any, he prefers over others. (From McDermott et al., 2016; courtesy of Alan Schultz.)

Even the basic principles about musical intervals are not as fixed in stone as Pythagoras thought. Remember the "devil in music," the augmented fourth, that is so dissonant that it sounds unpleasant? Deep in the Amazon rain forest of Bolivia, and largely untouched by Western civilization, live the Tsimane' villagers. As shown in **Figure 11.4**, researchers made their way through the rain forest to test what Tsimane' people like in their music (McDermott et al., 2016). While they have no difficulty hearing the difference between consonant and dissonant chords, they have no preference for consonant, dissonant, or even vocal harmonies. City folk in La Paz, however, have the same preferences as most other Westerners. While we cannot know whether this is a cause or an effect, you may find it interesting that Tsimane' people do not sing in groups.

ABSOLUTE PITCH You may have heard that some people are "gifted" with **absolute pitch** (**AP**), which is often referred to as "perfect pitch." AP is a rare ability of some listeners to accurately name or recreate particular notes in isolation. In this way, *absolute* is used to distinguish AP from the use of *relative pitch*, the way most people identify notes relative to one another. AP relates specifically to musical notes, because people with AP share the same basic sense of hearing as other people. Their auditory systems are no more sensitive than normal, and they are no better than usual at detecting differences between sounds.

Absolute pitch is very rare, occurring in less than one in 10,000 people (Takeuchi and Hulse, 1993). Among musicians, this rare skill is often considered to be highly desirable. Many believe that Ludwig van Beethoven had AP, and it appears fairly certain that Wolfgang Mozart had AP by the time he was only 7 years old (Deutsch, 2013).

Researchers disagree on how some people come to have AP. One idea is that people might acquire AP following a great deal of practice; however, it is very difficult for adults to acquire AP even through a great deal of practice (Brady, 1970). Others have suggested that in contrast to learning AP, some people are born with it (Athos et al., 2007), and this is consistent with the fact that AP appears to run in families (Theusch, 2009). However, children in the same family share more than genetics. In a home in which one child receives music lessons, it is likely that siblings also receive music lessons. There is variation

absolute pitch (AP) A rare ability whereby some people are able to very accurately name or produce notes without comparison to other notes.

in AP, and this variation presents a challenge for identifying possible genetic components. Most traits that are influenced by genetics, such as height, show variation—they are not all or none—and variation in expertise also occurs for skills that are learned. The best explanation for AP might be that it is acquired through experience but the experience must occur at a young age. In studies measuring abilities across many people, the age at which musical training begins is well correlated with future possession of AP (Deutsch et al., 2011; Lee and Lee, 2010).

Absolute pitch might not be so absolute, and adults with AP might be more flexible in their listening than typically thought. After first testing the identification of notes by listeners with AP, Hedger, Heald, and Nusbaum (2013) had their participants listen to Johannes Brahms's Symphony No. 1 in C minor and asked them to pay close attention to individual melodies. What the researchers did not tell their listeners was that, during the first part of the piece, they very gradually "detuned" the music by making all the notes a bit lower (flat) before playing the music at these lower frequencies for a while longer. After the musical passage was complete, AP listeners were more likely to judge flat notes as being in tune and to judge in-tune notes as being mistuned. While it may be very difficult to train adults to become AP listeners, perception of musical notes by adults with AP can be shifted by musical experience. Absolute pitch is apparently not as absolute as some people thought.

■ Sensation & Perception in Everyday Life ■

Music and Emotion

An ear can break a human heart
As quickly as a spear
We wish the ear had not a heart
So dangerously near

— Emily Dickinson, "The Saddest Noise, the Sweetest Noise"

Listening to music affects people's moods (Eich, 1995; Pignatiello, Camp, and Rasar, 1986) and emotions (Sloboda, 1999). When listeners hear pleasant-sounding chords preceding a word, they are faster to respond that a word such as *charm* is positive, and they are slower to respond that a word such as *evil* is negative (Sollberger, Reber, and Eckstein, 2003). Given the powerful effects of music on mood and emotion, some clinical psychologists practice music therapy, through which people sing, listen, play, and move to music in efforts to improve mental and physical health.

Music has deep physiological effects. Music can promote positive emotions, reduce pain, and alleviate stress, and it may even improve resistance to disease (Gangrade, 2011; Roy, Peretz, and Rainville, 2007). Evidence across many studies suggests that music can have a positive impact on pain, anxiety, mood, and overall quality of life for patients with cancer (Archie, Bruera, and Cohen, 2013). When people listen to highly pleasurable music, they experience changes in heart rate, muscle electrical activity, and respiration, as well as increases in blood flow to brain regions that are thought to be involved in reward and motivation (Blood and Zatorre, 2001). Music is a powerful human invention indeed.

Making Music

Notes or chords can form a **melody**, a sequence of sounds perceived as a single coherent structure. The notes of a familiar melody, such as "Twinkle, Twinkle, Little Star" (also known as "Now I Know My ABCs," "Baa Baa Black Sheep," and Variation K. 265 [300e] by Wolfgang Amadeus Mozart), "belong together" perceptually because they form this melody. Note that a melody is defined by its contour—the pattern of rises and declines in pitch—rather than by an exact sequence of sound frequencies (Handel, 1989).

You've already learned one simple way in which melody is not a sequence of specific sounds: shift every note of a melody by one octave, and the resulting melody is the same. When you sing with other people possessing higher or lower voices, they sing the same melody at very different pitches. Even within a single octave, the same melody can be heard from different notes if the steps between notes stay the same.

In addition to varying in pitch, notes and chords vary in duration. The average duration of a set of notes in a melody defines the music's **tempo**. Any melody can be played at either a fast or a slow tempo. But the relative durations within a sequence of notes are a critical part of the melodies themselves. If the notes of a given sequence are played with different relative durations, we will hear completely different melodies (**Figure 11.5**).

RHYTHM   In addition to varying in speed, music varies in rhythm. The fact that music has rhythm should go without saying. After all, how else would we dance to it? Less obvious, perhaps, is that many—or even most—activities have rhythm. Walking and galloping have rhythm. So do finger tapping, waving, and swimming. Perhaps it is the very commonness of rhythm that causes us to hear nearly all sounds as rhythmic, even when they're not!

Over a century ago, Thaddeus Bolton (1894) conducted experiments in which he played a sequence of identical sounds perfectly spaced in time; they had no rhythm. Nevertheless, his listeners readily reported that the sounds occurred in groups of two, three, or four. Moreover, they reported hearing the first sound of a group as accented, or stressed, while the remaining sounds were unaccented, or unstressed. You've probably had a similar experience while riding in a train

melody   A sequence of notes or chords perceived as a single coherent structure.

tempo   The perceived speed of the presentation of sounds.

Figure 11.5   The pattern of increasing and decreasing pitches can remain the same, but the melody will change if notes have different durations. Here, three series of notes with the same melody contour are shown with notes that differ only in duration.

syncopation Any deviation from a regular rhythm.

or car. Even though a train travels over junctions in the rails at nearly equal intervals, you hear the sound as "CLICK click CLICK click." When you ride in a car at a steady speed, you hear "THUMP thump THUMP thump" as your tires roll over cracks in a concrete road.

As Bolton's studies show, listeners are predisposed to grouping sounds into rhythmic patterns. Several qualities contribute to whether sounds will be heard as accented (stressed) or unaccented (unstressed). Sounds that are longer, louder, and higher in pitch all are more likely to be heard as leading their groups (Woodrow, 1909). The timing relationship between one sound and the others in a sequence also helps determine accent. For example, we are more likely to hear a series of three sounds as "Aaa Aaa Aaa" than as "aAa aAa aAa."

Listeners prefer, or at least expect, sequences of notes to be fairly regular, and this tendency provides opportunities for composers to get creative with their beats. One way to be creative in deviating from a bland succession of regular beats is to introduce **syncopation**. Syncopation is any deviation from a regular rhythm, for example, by accenting a note that is expected to be unaccented or not playing a note (replacing it with a rest) when a note is expected. Syncopation has been used for centuries and can be found in compositions by all the great composers, including Bach, Beethoven, and Mozart. College students may be more familiar with syncopation from jazz, reggae, and ska.

One particularly interesting example of syncopation is syncopated auditory polyrhythms. When two different rhythms are overlapped, they can collide in interesting ways. For example, if one rhythm is based on 3 beats (AaaAaaAaaAaa) and the other on 4 (BbbbBbbbBbbb), the first accented sound for both rhythms will coincide only once every 12 beats. Across the 11 intervening beats, the two rhythms will be out of sync. When we listen to syncopated polyrhythms, one of the two rhythms becomes the dominant or controlling rhythm, and the other rhythm tends to be perceptually adjusted to accommodate the first (**Figure 11.6**). In particular, the accented beat of the subordinate rhythm shifts in time (Handel and Oshinsky, 1981). Thus, syncopation is the perception that beats in the subordinate rhythm have actually traveled backward or forward in time!

These findings reveal that rhythm is, in large part, psychological. We can produce sequences of sounds that are rhythmic and are perceived as such. But we also hear rhythm when it does not exist, and notes effectively travel in time to maintain the perception of consistent rhythm.

Given the psychological nature of rhythm, at least with respect to syncopation, you might be wondering if the classic intervals of musical notes themselves are predestined or the result of experience. The durations of notes in Western musical notation are at very tidy intervals. A sixteenth note (♪) is half as long as an eighth note (♪), which is half as long as a quarter note (♩), which is half as long as a half note (♩), which is half as long as a whole note (o). Just as octaves are defined by doubling frequency, musical notes represent doubling of duration.

Let's return to our Bolivian friends the Tsimane'. We do not have Tsimane' notes to look at, but we can ask whether they prefer certain rhythms more than

Figure 11.6 When two rhythms are played together and one rhythm (in this case Aaa) is dominant, listeners tend to perceive the timing of beats in the nondominant rhythm (Bbbb) adjusted to conform with the dominant rhythm.

A̲a a A a a A a a A a a A̲a a A a a A a a A a a A̲a a

B b b b B b b b B b b b B̲ b b b B b b b B b b b B̲ b b b
    ←   →   ←   →

others. Tsimane' listeners do gravitate toward the simple rhythms that follow simple doubling of intervals (such as 1:1:1, 1:1:2, 1:2:1, 2:1:1, 1:2:2, 2:1:2, and 2:2:1). However, Tsimane' listeners are much less inclined toward other fairly simple rhythms (for example, 1:1:3, 1:2:3, or 2:2:3) that do not involve doubling, when compared to US listeners (Jacoby and McDermott, 2017). This is true even when the listeners from the United States have no musical training.

MELODY DEVELOPMENT Like rhythm, melody is essentially a psychological entity (Handel, 1989). There is nothing about the particular sequence of notes in "Twinkle, Twinkle, Little Star" that makes them a melody. Rather, it is our experience with a particular sequence of notes or with similar sequences that helps us perceive coherence.

Studies of 8-month-old listeners reveal that learning of melodies begins quite early in life. Saffran et al. (1999) created six simple and deliberately novel "melodies" composed of sequences of three tones. Infants sat on their parents' laps while hearing only 3 minutes of continuous random repetitions of the melodies. Next, infants heard both the original melodies and a series of new three-tone sequences. These new sequences contained the same notes as the originals, but one part of the sequence was taken from one melody and another part from another melody. Because the infants responded differently to the new melodies, we can deduce that they had learned something about the original melodies.

This ability to learn new melodies is not limited to simple sequences of tones. In a study with 7-month-old infants, parents played a recording of two Mozart sonata movements to their infants every day for 2 weeks (Saffran, Loman, and Robertson, 2000). After another 2 weeks had passed, the infants were tested in a laboratory to see whether they remembered the movements. Infant listeners responded differently to the original movements than to similar Mozart movements introduced to them for the first time in the laboratory.

Speech

Most people who listen to speech also produce speech. Talkers speak so that they can be understood, and the relationship between the production and perception of speech is an especially intimate one. Therefore, it is important to know some things about speech production before trying to understand speech perception.

Humans are capable of producing an incredible range of distinct speech sounds (the 5000 or so languages across the world use over 850 different speech sounds) (Maddieson, 1984). If you've ever heard Kenny Muhammad, the "Human Orchestra," you've experienced the unrivaled versatility of human sound production. This flexibility arises from the unique structure of the human **vocal tract** (Lieberman, 1984) (**Figure 11.7**). Unlike that of other animals, the human larynx is positioned quite low in the throat. One notorious disadvantage of such a low larynx is that humans choke on food more easily than any other animal does. The fact that these life-threatening anatomical liabilities were evolutionarily trumped by the survival advantage of oral communication is a testament to the importance of language to human life.

Speech Production

The production of speech has three basic components: respiration (lungs), phonation (vocal folds), and articulation (vocal tract) (see Figure 11.7). Speaking fluently requires an impressive degree of coordination among these components.

vocal tract The airway above the larynx used for the production of speech. The vocal tract includes the oral tract and nasal tract.

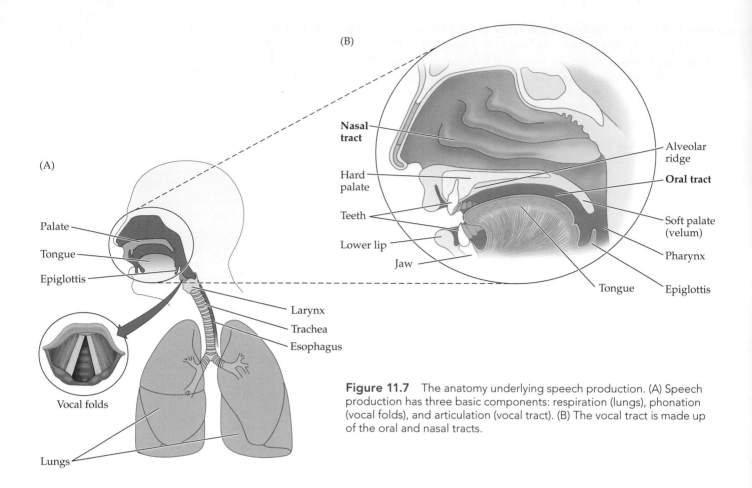

(B)

Nasal tract

Hard palate

Teeth

Lower lip

Jaw

Alveolar ridge

Oral tract

Soft palate (velum)

Pharynx

Tongue

Epiglottis

(A)

Palate

Tongue

Epiglottis

Larynx

Trachea

Esophagus

Vocal folds

Lungs

Figure 11.7 The anatomy underlying speech production. (A) Speech production has three basic components: respiration (lungs), phonation (vocal folds), and articulation (vocal tract). (B) The vocal tract is made up of the oral and nasal tracts.

RESPIRATION AND PHONATION To initiate a speech sound, air must be pushed out of the lungs, through the trachea, and up to the larynx. The diaphragm flexes to draw air into the lungs, and elastic recoil forces air back out. At the larynx, air must pass through the two vocal folds, which are made up of muscle tissue that can be adjusted to vary how freely air passes through the opening between them. These adjustments are described as types of **phonation**.

The rate at which vocal folds vibrate depends on their stiffness and mass. Consider guitar strings as an analogy. Just like guitar strings, vocal folds become stiffer and vibrate faster as their tension increases, creating sounds with higher pitch. The pitch of a guitar string also depends on its thickness or mass. Thinner guitar strings vibrate more quickly and create higher-pitched sounds. Similarly, children, who have relatively small vocal folds, have higher-pitched voices than adults do. Adult men generally have lower-pitched voices than women have, because one of the effects of testosterone during puberty is to increase the mass of the vocal folds. By varying the tension of vocal folds (stiffness) and the pressure of airflow from the lungs, individual talkers can vary the fundamental frequency of voiced sounds.

If we were to measure the sound right after the larynx, we would see that vibration of the vocal folds creates a harmonic spectrum, described in Chapter 10 and illustrated in **Figure 11.8A**. If we could listen to just this part of speech, it would sound like a buzz. The first harmonic corresponds to the actual rate of physical vibration of the vocal folds—the fundamental frequency. Talkers can

phonation The process through which vocal folds are made to vibrate when air pushes out of the lungs.

make interesting modifications in the way their vocal folds vibrate—creating breathy or creaky voices, for example—and singers can vary vocal-fold tension and air pressure to sing notes with widely varying frequencies. However, the really extraordinary part of producing speech sounds occurs above the larynx and vocal folds.

ARTICULATION   The area above the larynx—the oral tract and nasal tract combined—is referred to as the vocal tract (see Figure 11.7B). Humans have an unrivaled ability to change the shape of the vocal tract by manipulating the jaw, lips, tongue body, tongue tip, velum (soft palate), and other vocal-tract structures. These manipulations are referred to as **articulation**. As you will recall from Chapter 9, changing the size and shape of the space through which sound passes increases and decreases energy at different frequencies. We call these effects "resonance characteristics," and the spectra of speech sounds are shaped by the way people configure their vocal tracts as resonators. **Figure 11.8B** illustrates the filtering effects of the vocal tract for the vowel sound 'eh,' as in *wet*. **Figure 11.8C** portrays the net result of passing the periodic energy from the larynx through the vocal tract.

Peaks in the speech spectrum are referred to as **formants**, and formants are labeled by number, from lowest frequency to highest (F_1, F_2, F_3, and so on). These concentrations in energy occur at different frequencies, depending on the length of the vocal tract. For shorter vocal tracts (in children and smaller adults), formants are at higher frequencies than they are for longer vocal tracts. Because frequencies for each peak change depending on who's talking, listeners must use the relationships between formant peaks to perceive speech sounds (Kluender, Stilp, and Kiefte, 2013; Llanos, Jiang, and Kluender, 2014). Only the first three formants are depicted in Figure 11.8C. For the most part, we can distinguish almost all speech sounds on the basis of energy in the region of these lowest three formants. However, additional formants do exist, at higher frequencies with lower amplitudes.

In Chapters 9 and 10, many of the sounds that we discussed had constant frequency spectra. That is, if a sound started with a 50-decibel (dB), 100-Hz component and a 60-dB, 200-Hz component, these frequencies continued at these amplitudes for the duration of the sound. One of the most distinctive characteristics of speech

articulation   The act or manner of producing a speech sound using the vocal tract.

formant   A resonance of the vocal tract. Formants are specified by their center frequency and are denoted by integers that increase with relative frequency.

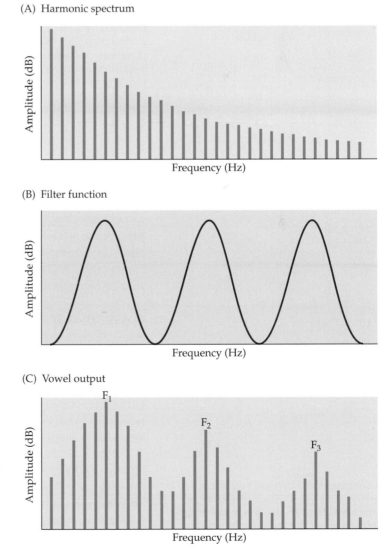

(A) Harmonic spectrum

(B) Filter function

(C) Vowel output

Figure 11.8   The spectrum of sound coming from the vocal folds is a harmonic spectrum (A). After passing through the vocal tract, which has resonances based on the vocal tract's shape at the time (B), there are peaks (formants; here F_1, F_2, and F_3) and troughs of energy at different frequencies in the sounds that come out of the mouth (C).

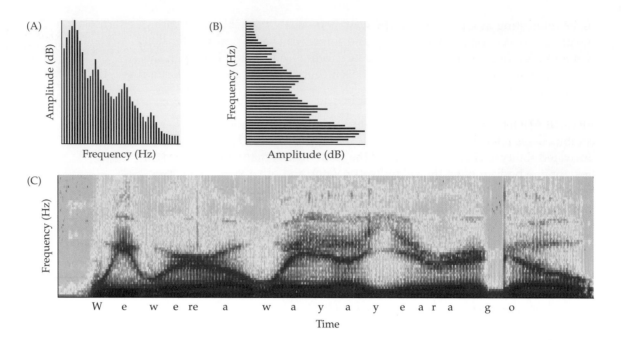

Figure 11.9 For sounds that do not vary over time, frequency spectra can be represented by graphs that plot amplitude on the y-axis and frequency on the x-axis (A). To graphically show sounds whose spectra change over time, we rotate the graph so that frequency is plotted on the y-axis (B); then we plot time on the x-axis (C), with the amplitude of each frequency during each time slice represented by color (redder showing greater intensity). The spectrogram in (C) shows the acoustic signal produced by a male uttering the sentence "We were away a year ago."

sounds is that their spectra change over time. To represent this third dimension (time) in addition to the dimensions of frequency and amplitude represented in frequency spectra of static sounds, auditory researchers use a type of display called a **spectrogram**. In a sound spectrogram, frequency is represented on the y-axis, time is tracked on the x-axis, and amplitude is indicated by the color of any point on the graph (**Figure 11.9**). Formants show up clearly in spectrograms as bands of acoustic energy that undulate up and down, depending on the speech sounds being produced.

CLASSIFYING SPEECH SOUNDS   Speech sounds are most often described in terms of articulation. This is because in the early days of studying speech, people did not have electronic recording or the ability to analyze sounds. Instead, they paid close attention to their own vocal tracts and described speech sounds in terms of the articulations necessary to produce them. You will get the most out of the following discussion if you "sing along" just as these early speech researchers did, producing the speech sounds yourself and feeling the various articulatory maneuvers necessary to speak them.

Vowel sounds are all made with a relatively open vocal tract, and they vary mostly in how high or low and how far forward or back the tongue is placed in the oral tract, along with whether or not the lips are rounded. We produce the 'ee' sound in the word *beet* by placing the tongue up and forward, the 'aw' in *bought* by moving the tongue down and back, and the 'oo' in *boot* by moving the tongue up and back while rounding the lips (**Figure 11.10**).

spectrogram   In reference to sound analysis, a three-dimensional display that plots time on the horizontal axis, frequency on the vertical axis, and amplitude (intensity) on a color or gray scale.

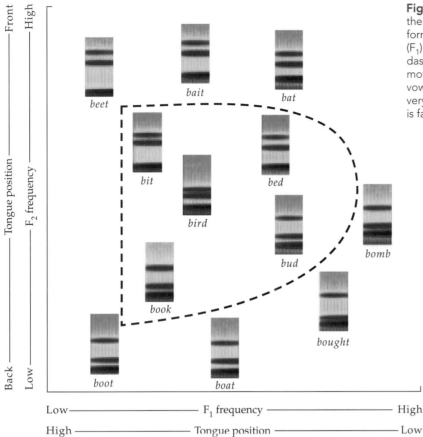

Figure 11.10 Vowel sounds of English, showing how the frequencies of the first formant (F_1) and second formant (F_2) relate to how high or low the tongue is (F_1) and how far forward or back the tongue is (F_2). The dashed line illustrates limits on how far the tongue moves when vowels are produced. For example, the vowels 'ee' and 'oo' are produced with the tongue very high in the mouth. In the case of 'ee,' the tongue is far forward, but for 'oo,' the tongue is far back.

We produce consonants by obstructing the vocal tract in some way, and each consonant sound can be classified according to three articulatory dimensions:

1. *Place of articulation* (see Figure 11.7B). Airflow can be obstructed
   - At the lips (bilabial speech sounds: 'b,' 'p,' 'm')
   - At the alveolar ridge just behind the teeth (alveolar speech sounds: 'd,' 't,' 'n')
   - At the soft palate (velar speech sounds: 'g,' 'k,' 'ng')

2. *Manner of articulation*. Airflow can be
   - Totally obstructed (stops: 'b,' 'd,' 'g,' 'p,' 't,' 'k') **(Figure 11.11)**
   - Partially obstructed (fricatives: 's,' 'z,' 'f,' 'v,' 'th,' 'sh')
   - Only slightly obstructed (laterals: 'l,' 'r'; and glides: 'w,' 'y')
   - First blocked, and then allowed to sneak through (affricates: 'ch,' 'j')
   - Blocked at first from going through the mouth, but allowed to go through the nasal passage (nasals: 'n,' 'm,' 'ng')

3. *Voicing* (see Figure 11.11). The vocal folds may be
   - Vibrating (voiced consonants, which can be felt by a finger on the throat: 'b,' 'm,' 'z,' 'l,' 'r')
   - Not vibrating (voiceless consonants: 'p,' 's,' 'ch')

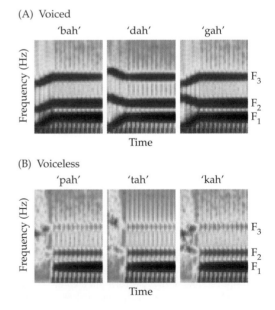

Figure 11.11 English stop consonants may be (A) voiced, as in 'bah,' 'dah,' and 'gah,' or (B) voiceless, as in 'pah,' 'tah,' and 'kah.' The main articulatory difference between voiced and voiceless stop consonants is that, for the latter, talkers delay vibration of the vocal folds by about 1/20 of a second after opening the vocal tract to begin the sound.

coarticulation The phenomenon in speech whereby attributes of successive speech units overlap in articulatory or acoustic patterns.

These speech sounds from English are only a small sample of the sounds used by languages around the world. Most languages use fewer consonants and vowels than are used in English. Some sounds are quite common across languages, and others, such as English 'th' and 'r,' are fairly uncommon around the world. When many or most languages include particular speech sounds, often the reason is that the differences between them are particularly easy to perceive. Humans must sometimes communicate in difficult environments where the listener is far away or there are many competing sounds. To be effective, speech sound repertoires of languages have developed over generations of individuals to include mainly sounds that are relatively easy to tell apart.

In addition to using relatively easily distinguishable sounds, another way speech provides effective communication is by signaling all distinctions between vowels and consonants with multiple differences between sounds. Because more than one acoustic property can be used to tell two sounds apart, distinctions are signaled redundantly, and this redundancy helps listeners. The speech signal is so redundant that if we remove all energy below 1800 Hz, listeners will still perceive speech nearly perfectly, and the same is true if we remove all energy above 1800 Hz (**Figure 11.12**). You may already know this all too well if you have lived in an apartment or mobile home with thin walls. Even though walls stop energy at higher frequencies, you may learn far more about your neighbors than you wish from their conversations on the other side.

Speech Perception

Speech production is very fast. In casual conversation we produce about 10–15 consonants and vowels per second, and if we're in a hurry, we can double this rate. To achieve this acoustic feat, our articulators (tongue, lips, jaw, and so on) must do many different things very quickly. However, articulators can move only so fast, and mass and inertia keep articulators from getting all the way to the position for the next consonant or vowel. Experienced talkers also adjust their production in anticipation of where articulators need to be next. In these ways, production of one speech sound overlaps production of the next. This overlap of articulation in space and time is called **coarticulation**. As we turn from speech production to speech perception, we will find that although coarticulation does not cause much trouble for listeners understanding speech, it has made it harder for speech perception researchers to explain how we do it.

Figure 11.12 Because the speech signal has so many redundant acoustic characteristics, listeners can understand speech when all energy either below or above 1800 Hz is removed. The green line shows performance when energy above different frequencies (high pass) is available to listeners, and the red line shows performance when energy below different frequencies (low pass) is present. The red line shows intelligibility when the cutoff is above the given x value, and the green line shows intelligibility when the cutoff is below the given x value. Notice that intelligibility is excellent when all energy is removed below about 1500 Hz (green) and also when all energy is removed above about 2000 Hz (red). (After Fletcher and Galt, 1950.)

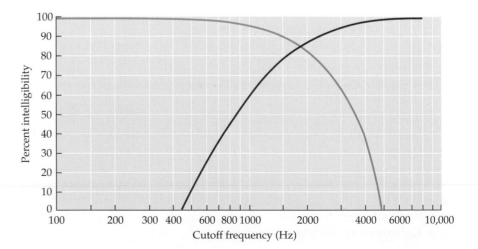

Figure 11.13 Spectrograms of 'd' sounds (center column), along with stop-consonant cousins 'b' (left) and 'g' (right). Changes in formants across time (formant transitions) for these sounds differ dramatically depending on the following vowels: 'ah' (top row), 'oo' (middle), and 'ee' (bottom).

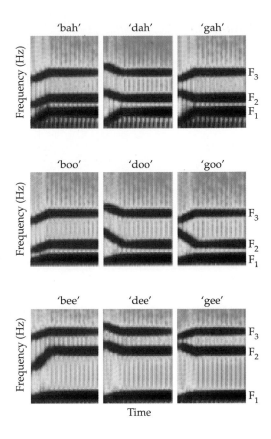

COARTICULATION AND LACK OF INVARIANCE   To get a better sense of what coarticulation is, say the word *moody* a few times, and note the activity of your tongue as you form the 'd' sound. You will find that it starts in the back of your mouth, where it must be to form the 'oo' vowel sound. Then it touches the alveolar ridge just behind the teeth to form the 'd.' And finally it ends up toward the front of the mouth to form the 'ee.' Now say the nonsense word *eedoom*. Reversing the vowel sounds means sending the tongue on the opposite journey, from front to alveolar ridge to back. As a result of the very different path taken by the tongue in these two utterances, the acoustic qualities of the 'd' in the two utterances are quite different depending upon the context of preceding or following tongue movements.

This context sensitivity is a signature property of speech. One might expect context sensitivity to cause a significant problem for speech perceivers, because it means there are no "invariants" that we can count on to uniquely identify different speech sounds. For 'b,' 'd,' and 'g' in **Figure 11.13**, notice that the shape of the first formant (F_1) is pretty much the same for all three consonants when they precede the same vowel. F_1 is helpful in telling 'b,' 'd,' and 'g' apart from other speech sounds, but it does not help much in telling these sounds apart from one another. An F_1 like that shown in Figure 11.13 is necessary for a sound to be 'b,' but it is not sufficient to inform the listener that the sound is 'b,' and not 'd' or 'g.' F_2 is very important for telling 'b' from 'd' from 'g,' but what F_2 tells the listener depends on the quality of F_3 and the nature of the following vowel.

Explaining how listeners understand speech despite all this variation has been one of the most significant challenges for speech researchers. Context sensitivity due to coarticulation also presents one of the greatest difficulties in developing computer recognition of speech. We cannot program or train a computer to recognize a speech sound—consonant or vowel—without also taking into consideration which speech sounds precede and follow that sound. And we cannot identify those preceding and following sounds without also taking into consideration which sounds precede and follow them, and so on. As it happens, this is pretty much what computers do to "understand" speech; they store millions of slices of every speech sound preceded and followed by slices of nearly every other speech sound.

CATEGORICAL PERCEPTION   If it is challenging to get computers to recognize speech, why do children acquire this ability so early and easily? *Something* in the acoustic signal must lead them to perceive the 'd' in *deem, doom,* and *dam* as the same consonant. Shortly after World War II, researchers invented machines that could produce speechlike sounds, and they started testing listeners to try to determine exactly what the acoustic cues were that enabled them to distinguish different speech sounds. They found, for example, that by varying the transitions of F_2 and F_3, they could produce sounds that listeners reliably reported hearing as 'bah,' 'dah,' or 'gah' (**Figure 11.14**). (See **Web Activity 11.2: Categorical Perception**.)

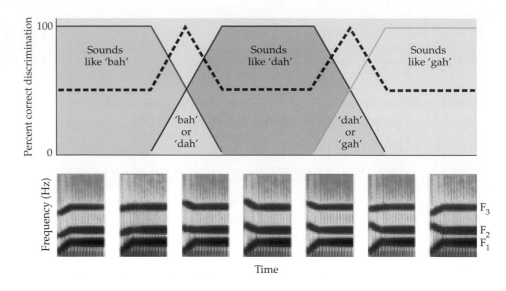

Figure 11.14 The sound spectrograms at the bottom of this figure indicate auditory stimuli that change smoothly from a clear 'bah' on the left through 'dah' to a clear 'gah' on the right. Perception, however, does not change smoothly. All the sounds on the left sound like a 'bah' (blue curve) until we reach a sharp 'bah'-'dah' border. Listeners are much better at discriminating a 'bah' from a 'dah' than at discriminating two 'bah's or two 'gah's. The dashed black line indicates discrimination performance. The same is true for 'dah' (red curve) and 'gah' (green curve).

These researchers knew that making small, incremental changes to simple acoustic stimuli such as pure tones leads to gradual changes in people's perception of these stimuli. For example, tones sound just a little higher in pitch with each small step in frequency. Surprisingly, speech sounds were not perceived in this way. When researchers started with a synthesized 'bah' and gradually varied the formant transitions moving toward 'dah' and then 'gah,' listeners' responses did not gradually change from 'bah' to 'bah'-ish 'dah' to 'dah' to 'dah'-ish 'gah' to 'gah' (Liberman et al., 1957). Instead, listeners identified these sounds as changing abruptly from one consonant to another.

Furthermore, listeners appeared incapable of hearing that much of anything was different when two sounds were labeled as the same consonant. In this second part of the experiments, researchers played pairs of synthesized speech sounds and asked listeners to tell them apart. Listeners performed almost perfectly when detecting small differences between two sounds if one was 'bah' and the other was 'dah.' But if both sounds were 'bah' or both were 'dah,' performance dropped to nearly chance levels (dashed line in Figure 11.14), even though the differences in formant transitions in the first and second pairs of stimuli were equally large.

This pattern of results has come to be called **categorical perception**. As illustrated in Figure 11.14, three qualities define categorical perception. The first two were just described: a sharp labeling (identification) function and discontinuous discrimination performance. The third definitional quality of categorical perception follows from the first two: researchers can predict discrimination performance on the basis of labeling data. In short, listeners report hearing differences between sounds only when those differences would result in different labels for the sounds, so the ability to discriminate sounds can be predicted by how listeners label the sounds.

categorical perception For speech as well as other complex sounds and images, the phenomenon by which the discrimination of items is no better than the ability to label items.

'Dah'

'Gah'

'Bah'

1. A videotape shows a person repeating the sound 'Gah.'

2. An audio track plays the sound 'Bah.'

3. The subject hears the sound 'Dah.'

Figure 11.15 The motor theory was bolstered by, among other things, a somewhat peculiar finding by McGurk and MacDonald (1976). Experimental participants were shown a video of a person saying the syllable 'gah' over and over. The audio track, however, was playing the sound 'bah' repeatedly. Incredibly, participants consistently reported hearing a third syllable, 'dah,' even if they knew how they were being fooled (because they heard 'bah' when they closed their eyes). (This effect really has to be experienced to be believed; try it now in **Web Activity 11.3: The McGurk Effect**.)

HOW SPECIAL IS SPEECH? Categorical perception of speech sounds is not limited to the 'bah'/'dah'/'gah' dimension; it has been shown for many different contrasts between sounds in English, as well as other languages. These findings, along with the failure to find invariants that distinguish speech sounds from each other, led many speech researchers to suspect that humans had evolved special mechanisms just for perceiving speech. One very influential version of the "speech is special" idea, called the "motor theory" of speech perception (Liberman and Mattingly, 1985; Liberman et al., 1967), held that processes used to produce speech sounds can somehow be run in reverse to understand the acoustic speech signal (**Figure 11.15**).

Over time, however, a number of problems with the motor theory cropped up. First, it turns out that speech production is at least as complex as speech perception, if not more so. Every aspect of the acoustic signal relates to a particular aspect of the vocal tract. So if the acoustic signal is complex, this complexity must be the result of complexity in production. Trying to explain speech perception by reference to production is at least as difficult as explaining speech perception on the basis of acoustics alone.

A second reason to doubt that processes for perceiving speech are unique to humans is that numerous demonstrations have shown that nonhuman animals can learn to respond to speech signals in much the same way that human listeners do (Kluender, Lotto, and Holt, 2005; Kluender et al., 1998). For example, Japanese quail (**Figure 11.16A**) can be taught to tell 'd' from 'b' and 'g' across the same sort of acoustic variation depicted in Figure 11.13 (Kluender, Diehl, and Killeen, 1987). Chinchillas (**Figure 11.16B**) have also shown classic categorical-perception effects (Kuhl, 1981; Kuhl and Miller, 1978).

Furthermore, we now know that categorical perception, one of the definitional characteristics of speech that was thought to be so unusual as to require a special processing mechanism, is not at all limited to speech sounds. Other types of auditory stimuli, such as musical intervals (Smith et al., 1994), are also perceived

(A)

(B)

Figure 11.16 Speech perception by nonhumans. (A) Japanese quail can learn to tell 'd' from 'b' and 'g' preceding different vowels just as humans do. (B) Chinchillas have shown categorical perception of sounds varying from 'dah' to 'tah.' (A courtesy of Keith R. Kluender; B courtesy of Annie Huyler, Pioneer Valley Chinchillas.)

categorically, as are visual stimuli such as familiar objects (Newell and Bülthoff, 2002), human faces (Levin and Beale, 2000), and facial expressions (De Gelder, Teunisse, and Benson, 1997). People even perceive differences between familiar animals categorically (R. Campbell et al., 1997) (**Figure 11.17**), and monkeys learn to perceive images of cats versus dogs categorically (Freedman et al., 2001).

COARTICULATION AND SPECTRAL CONTRAST Contemporary research has turned increasingly to investigating how speech perception is explained by general ways that hearing, and perception more broadly, works. For example, the perception of coarticulated speech appears to be at least partially explained by some fundamental principles of perception that you've already read about. Let's turn again to our example of stop consonants such as 'b' and 'd.' Two of the acoustic features that contribute to the perception of 'b,' as contrasted with the perception of 'd,' are the onset frequency and trajectory of the second formant (F_2). Because of coarticulation, production of one speech sound always affects production of the next sound; formants for one sound always are more like (assimilate to) the sounds that precede and follow. The onset of

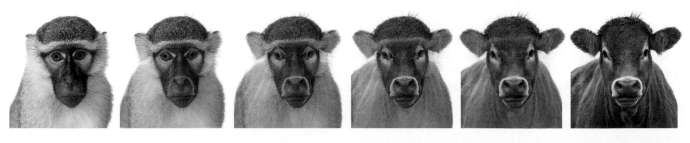

Figure 11.17 People categorically perceive changes between images of familiar animals such as monkeys and cows. The labels that observers use shift abruptly between "monkey" and "cow" when they identify images like those in the series shown here. Observers also are better at discriminating two images when they label one as "monkey" and one as "cow." (After R. Campbell et al., 1997.)

F_2 varies depending on whether 'bah' or 'dah' follows vowels such as 'ee' (higher) or 'oo' (lower).

Perception of the syllables 'bah' and 'dah' works in a way that nicely fits the facts of coarticulation. The very same F_2 onset is heard as 'dah' following 'oo' and as 'bah' following 'ee' (**Figure 11.18**). Why does perception work this way? Because coarticulation always causes a speech sound to become more like the previous speech sound, auditory processes that enhance the contrast between successive sounds undo this assimilation. Listeners are more likely to perceive 'bah' (low F_2) when preceded by the vowel sound 'ee' (high F_2), and to perceive 'dah' (high F_2) when preceded by 'oo' (low F_2). Preceding sounds do not even have to be speech sounds. If, instead of playing 'ee' and 'oo' before syllables varying from 'bah' to 'dah,' we present only a single small band of energy at the frequencies where F_2 would be in 'ee' or 'oo,' perception of the following syllable changes just as it does with the full 'ee' or 'oo' vowel sound (Coady, Kluender, and Rhode, 2003). The onset of F_2 for 'bah' and 'dah' is perceived relative to whether the preceding energy is lower or higher in frequency. We perceive syllables such as 'bah' and 'dah' in terms of the relative change in the spectrum—how the onsets contrast with the energy that precedes them (Alexander and Kluender, 2009).

You've encountered contrast effects several times before in this book—for example, brightness contrast in Chapter 2. Remember that melodies are defined by *changes* between adjacent notes, and not by the exact notes in particular. While learning about vision, you saw many examples of contrast. Contrast plays a large role in the perception of brightness, color, and size, as well as line orientation, position, curvature, depth, and spatial frequency. Here, spectral contrast helps listeners perceive speech, despite the lack of acoustic invariance due to coarticulation.

USING MULTIPLE ACOUSTIC CUES

What do speech sounds, musical intervals, and faces all have in common? They are all stimuli that people have a great deal of experience perceiving. We spend a large chunk of our waking lives listening to speech and identifying people by their faces. Another thing that makes distinguishing between individual speech sounds and individual faces similar is that many small differences must be used together in order to discriminate different speech sounds and different faces (e.g., small changes in formant transitions and small changes in nose shape). At the same time, other stimulus differences must be ignored so that multiple instances of the same speech sound or multiple images of the same face can be classified properly (e.g., acoustic variation introduced when different speakers utter the same speech sound, or image variation introduced when a face is viewed from different angles).

To the extent that perception depends heavily on experience, speech is special because (1) humans have evolved unique anatomical machinery for producing it and (2) we spend a great deal of time practicing the perception of speech. The fact that there are no acoustic invariants for distinguishing speech sounds is really no different from many comparable situations in visual perception. For example, we saw in Chapter 6 that one particular cue for depth perception may fail us, but by taking multiple cues into account, we rarely make large mistakes when calculating distance relations.

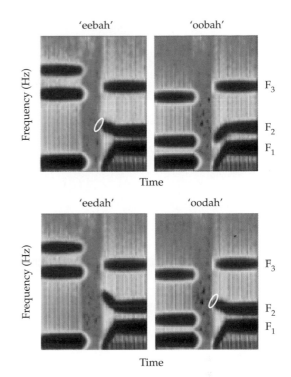

Figure 11.18 Because of coarticulation, consonant sounds such as 'bah' and 'dah' are acoustically very different, depending on the preceding vowel. Here, 'bah' is shown following 'ee' (top left) and 'oo' (top right), and 'dah' is shown following the same vowels (bottom). Note that F_2 in 'eebah' (top left) is acoustically identical to F_2 in 'oodah' (bottom right). Listeners hear the same consonant sound as 'b' following 'ee' and as 'd' following 'oo' because of the contrast between the spectrum of 'ee' and 'oo' and the spectrum of the following consonant.

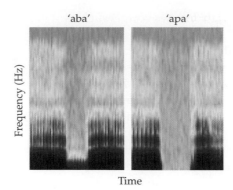

'aba'   'apa'

Frequency (Hz)

Time

Figure 11.19 The simple distinction between 'aba' (left) and 'apa' (right) includes at least 16 acoustic differences. Some differences that are easy to see include duration of the first vowel, duration of the interval between syllables, and the presence of low-frequency energy in the middle of 'aba.'

The comparison with face recognition may be even more apt. Caitlin's nose may be quite similar to Sara's nose, Caitlin's eyes may be exactly as far apart as Hannah's eyes, and Caitlin's mouth may be shaped just like Emily's mouth. But given enough experience with all four faces (and enough experience with face recognition in general), we can use the pattern of facial features to pick Caitlin out from a lineup every time—even if she's covering her mouth with her hand. Turning to speech perception, utterances of the syllables 'aba' and 'apa' can be distinguished from each other by at least 16 different characteristics of the acoustic signal (**Figure 11.19**) (Lisker, 1986). Listeners can make use of their experience with the co-occurrence of these multiple acoustic differences to understand speech.

To sum up, we don't need individual acoustic invariants to distinguish speech sounds; we just need to be as good at pattern recognition for sounds as we are for visual images. And one of the things that the billions of neurons in the brain do best is integrating multiple sources of information to recognize patterns (Kluender and Alexander, 2008).

■ Scientists at Work

Tickling the Cochlea

■ **Question** What speech sounds are most important? When reading, th* b*s*c d*m*nstr*t**n *s th*t t*xt *s st*ll m*r* *r l*ss l*g*bl* wh*n th* v*w*ls h*v* b**n r*m*v*d. Many experiments have been conducted to learn whether consonants, vowels, or combinations between consonants and vowels are most essential for understanding spoken language. The answer has been unclear. How much can we learn about understanding speech if we go back to what we learned about the basilar membrane within the cochlea in Chapter 9?

■ **Hypothesis** The most important parts of the speech signal are those that change patterns of vibration across the basilar membrane the most.

■ **Test** Replace portions of sentences, for either 80 or 112 milliseconds, with noise during selected intervals. For some selected intervals, the pattern of stimulation along the basilar membrane did not change a lot (low change). Other intervals were selected because the

pattern of stimulation changed a lot (high change). Finally, intervals were selected because they fell in between a little and a lot.

■ **Results** We can predict how well listeners will understand speech by measuring nothing more than the amount of change occurring along the length of the basilar membrane in the cochlea (**Figure 11.20**) (Stilp and Kluender, 2010).

■ **Conclusion** Listeners are better at understanding sentences when intervals spanning less change in the pattern of stimulation along the basilar membrane are replaced by noise.

■ **Future work** The knowledge that the most important part of understanding speech is how the input changes across time can be used to increase the information conveyed by cochlear implant electrodes to listeners with hearing impairments (Stilp et al., 2016).

■ Scientists at Work *(continued)* ■

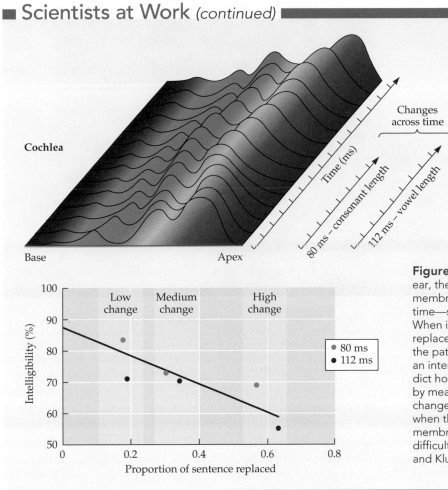

Figure 11.20 When speech sounds enter the ear, the pattern of stimulation along the basilar membrane changes nearly continuously across time—sometimes a lot and sometimes less. When intervals of sentences are removed and replaced with noise on the basis of how much the pattern of stimulation changes throughout an interval (80 or 112 ms), the best way to predict how well listeners will understand speech is by measuring how much the basilar membrane changes shape. When noise replaces an interval when the pattern of stimulation along the basilar membrane changes more, people have more difficulty understanding the speech. (After Stilp and Kluender, 2010.)

Learning to Listen

In our discussion of vision earlier in the book, we saw that experience is incredibly important for visual perception, particularly the higher-level perception of objects and events in the world. Experience is every bit as important for auditory perception, especially for the perception of speech. And unlike vision, experience with speech begins very early in development. In fact, babies gain significant experience with speech even before they're born!

Measurements of heart rate as indicators of the ability to notice change between speech sounds have revealed that late-term fetuses can discriminate between different vowel sounds (Lecanuet et al., 1986). Prenatal experience with speech sounds appears to have considerable influence on subsequent perception. For one thing, a newborn prefers hearing her mother's voice over other women's voices (DeCasper and Fifer, 1980). When 4-day-old infants in Paris were tested, they preferred hearing French instead of Russian (Mehler et al., 1988). Perhaps most amazingly, newborns prefer hearing particular children's stories that were read aloud by their mothers during the third trimester of pregnancy (DeCasper and Spence, 1986).

BECOMING A NATIVE LISTENER   As we have seen, speech sounds can differ in many ways. Acoustic differences that matter critically for one language may

Figure 11.21 How we hear speech sounds depends on our experience with the speech sounds of our first language. Because of experience with one language, it is often difficult to perceive and produce distinctions in a new language. For example, most Japanese people learning English as a second language have trouble distinguishing between 'l' and 'r,' both when they listen and when they speak.

be irrelevant or even distracting in another language. For example, the English language makes use of the distinction between the sounds 'r' and 'l,' whereas these two sounds are both very similar to only one sound (called a "flap") in Japanese. As another example, Spanish is one of many languages that uses only the five vowel sounds 'ee' (as in *beet*), 'oo' (as in *boot*), 'ah' (as in *bomb*), 'ay' (as in *bake*), and 'oh' (as in *boat*), whereas English employs up to ten additional vowel sounds.

As anyone who has spoken to a native Japanese speaker in English knows, the 'r'/'l' distinction is very difficult for Japanese people to pick up when they learn English as a second language (**Figure 11.21**). Because the difference between 'l' and 'r' is irrelevant to native Japanese speakers when they're learning their native language, it is adaptive for them to learn to ignore it, thus allowing them to focus on speech sound distinctions that are important in Japanese. When people have spent most of their lives listening to Japanese and not hearing the difference between 'r' and 'l,' we are not surprised that they have difficulty learning to produce the 'r' and 'l.' By the same token, a native Spanish speaker who complains that your dog just "beat" him is probably not claiming that Rover threw a punch; rather, the difference between 'ee' and 'ih' is less perceptible to the Spanish speaker, because both of these English sounds are similar to the Spanish 'ee.'

Interestingly, studies show that infants begin filtering out irrelevant acoustic differences long before they begin to utter speech sounds (even before their babbling stage). One study found that by 6 months of age, infants from Seattle were more likely to notice acoustic differences that distinguish two English vowels than to notice equivalent differences between Swedish vowels, and infants from Stockholm were more likely to notice the differences between two Swedish vowels than the differences between two English vowels (Kuhl et al., 1992). Tuning of perception for consonants appears to take a bit longer to develop, but by the time infants are 1 year old, they have also begun to ignore, just as their parents do, consonant distinctions not used in their native language (**Figure 11.22**).

Of course, it is possible, with much training, to learn to perceive and produce speech sound distinctions that you've spent most of your life ignoring. As you might expect, the longer a person uses only her first language, the longer it takes to learn to produce and perceive sounds from a second language (Flege, Bohn, and Jang, 1997; Imai, Flege, and Wayland, 2002). Many studies have been aimed at determining what makes new distinctions hard or easy for second-language learners to pick up. Learning is most difficult when both of the sounds in the second language are similar to a single sound in the first language (e.g., 'r' and 'l' for Japanese speakers learning English). Learning is easier if the two new sounds are both unlike any sound in the native language. For example, native English listeners have no problems distinguishing click sounds from Zulu because Zulu clicks are so unlike any English sounds (Best, McRoberts, and Sithole, 1988). Learning also is easier if two new sounds from a new language differ in the same way that two sounds from the first language differ.

Picking up on distinctions in a second language is easiest if the second language is learned at the same time as the first. This is why language immersion programs are becoming popular in preschool and elementary curriculums of multicultural countries such as the United States. The small downside to this strategy is that kids learning multiple languages at the same time usually take a little longer to master each of the languages than do children learning only a single language (Bialystok and Hakuta, 1994). This is a natural consequence of having to learn not one but two sets of rules about when to ignore and when to pay attention to speech sound differences (as well as learning two vocabularies, two sets of grammatical rules, and so on). On the upside, these children catch up to speak more than one language fluently for the rest of their lives.

LEARNING WORDS   Thus far in this chapter, we've learned many things about the nature and complexity of speech sounds and about how listeners perceive consonants and vowels. But the whole point of producing and perceiving these speech sounds is to put them together to form words, which are the units of language that convey meaning. How do novice language learners (infants) make the leap from streams of meaningless speech sounds to the meaningful groups of speech sounds that we call words?

First, let's state the obvious. Just like strings of musical notes, no string of speech sounds is inherently meaningful. The string 'd'-'aw'-'g' becomes meaningful to English-speaking infants, but to French-speaking, Spanish-speaking, and German-speaking infants this string remains completely meaningless because their parents refer to their furry house companions as *chien*, *perro*, and *Hund*, respectively. Infants in different places in the world must learn the words that are specific to their native languages.

We've already seen how a series of consonants and vowels within a single word tend to "run into" one another because of coarticulation. It turns out that the situation is not much better for a series of words forming a sentence. This fact is easily seen in **Figure 11.23**: without the letters at the bottom of the figure, you would have no idea where the spoken word *where* ends and *are* begins.

Interestingly, our perception usually seems at odds with this acoustic reality. When we listen to someone talking to us in our native language, individual words seem to stand out quite clearly as separate entities. But listening to someone

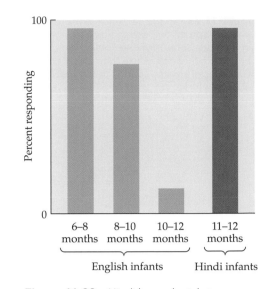

Figure 11.22   Hindi has a dental stop consonant produced with the tongue tip touching the teeth and a retroflex stop consonant that requires the tongue to bend up and back in the mouth. Adult speakers of English hear both of these sounds as 't' because they are similar to the English 't.' When Werker and Tees (1984) tested infants from English-speaking families in Vancouver, the youngest (6–8 months old) reliably responded to the difference between these two Hindi sounds. By 1 year of age, however, the infants were mimicking their parents' behavior by ignoring the distinction between the two sounds.

Figure 11.23 In the sentence "Where are the silences between words?" we can see that there are no breaks between the sounds of one spoken word and the sounds of the next. Infants can use their experience with particular sequences of speech sounds to learn about boundaries between words.

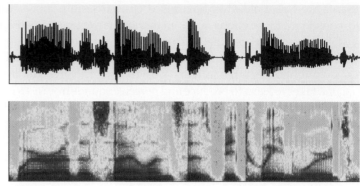

Where are the s i l en c e s be t w een wo rd s ?

speak in a different language is often a very different experience. Listen to the Chinese and Arabic speakers in **Web Activity 11.4: Word Breaks**. Unless you have experience with these languages, it probably sounds as if they include lots of really long words—some as long as whole English sentences. It may also seem as if people in these cultures speak much faster than English speakers do. Native Chinese and Arabic speakers probably say the same things about the English language and English speakers. This is the situation faced by infants the world over.

To study how infants learn words from the continuous streams of speech that they encounter in their environment, Saffran, Aslin, and Newport (1996) invented a novel language. Each of the words of this new language had three syllables—for example, *tokibu*, *gopila*, *gikoba*, and *tipolu*. Next they created randomized sequences of these novel words, with words running together just as they do in fluently produced sentences (**Figure 11.24**). A sample would sound like "tokibugopilagikobatipolugopilatokibutipolugikoba." Eight-month-old infants listened to a 2-minute sequence such as this while sitting on their parents' laps. After this brief period of learning, infants heard either "tupiro" (one of the novel words) or "pabiku" (a new combination of the same syllables used to produce the "real" novel words). The infants listened longer to the nonwords than to the words, indicating that after just 2 minutes of exposure, they had already begun to learn the words in this new "language." How did they do it?

Saffran and her colleagues suggest that the infants in their study learned the words by being sensitive to the statistics of the sequences of sounds that they heard in the first part

(A)

> tokibugopilagikobatipolutokibu
> gopilatipolutokibugikobagopila
> gikobatokibugopilatipolugikoba
> tipolugikobatipolugopilatipolu
> tokibugopilatipolutokibugopila
> tipolutokibugopilagikobatipolu
> tokibugopilagikobatipolugikoba
> tipolugikobatipolutokibugikoba
> gopilatipolugikobatokibugopila

(B)

> tokibugopilagikobatipolutokibu
> gopilatipolutokibugikobagopila
> gikobatokibugopilatipolugikoba
> tipolugikobatipolugopilatipolu
> tokibugopilatipolutokibugopila
> tipolutokibugopilagikobatipolu
> tokibugopilagikobatipolugikoba
> tipolugikobatipolutokibugikoba
> gopilatipolugikobatokibugopila

Figure 11.24 Eight-month-old infants can learn to pick out words from streams of continuous speech based on the extent to which successive syllables are predictable or unpredictable. While sitting on their parents' laps, infants heard 2-minute sequences of syllables (A). In the second part of the experiment, infants were familiar with three-syllable sequences that they had heard before ("tokibu," "gopila," "gikoba," "tipolu") (B), but they noticed that they had never heard other syllable combinations ("poluto," "bugopi," "kobati").

of the experiment. In the real world of language, words are simply sequences of speech sounds that tend to occur together. Other sequences occur together less often. For example, think about the sequence 'p'-'r'-'ih'-'t'-'ee'-'b'-'ay'-'b'-'ee.' An infant will hear the sounds making up the word *pretty* in many different contexts ("pretty dress," "pretty good," and so on) and the sounds making up the word *baby* in other contexts (e.g., "good baby," "baby doll"). In contrast, the sequence 't'-'ee'-'b'-'ay' will almost never be heard in any other context, because no English words have this sequence of syllables. Saffran (2001, 2002) suggests that infants learn to pick words out of the speech stream by accumulating experience with sounds that tend to occur together; these are words (at least to babies). For example, infants eventually split the "word" *allgone* into two as they acquire more linguistic experience. When sounds that are rarely heard together occur in combination, that's a sign that there is a break between two words.

Speech in the Brain

Our earliest understanding of the role of cerebral cortex for the perception of speech and music was gained through unfortunate "natural" experiments in which people had lost their ability to understand speech following stroke or other brain injuries. However, it is difficult to draw strong conclusions about brain processes from brain injuries. Brain damage from stroke follows patterns of blood vessels, not brain function. Damage from stroke might cover just part of a particular brain function, leaving some of the function undamaged; or damage could cover a wide region that includes some or all of a particular brain function, as well as all or part of other functions. Performance following brain damage, along with later experimental findings, has taught us that different hemispheres of the brain are better at doing some types of tasks. For most people, the left hemisphere is dominant for language processing. The development of techniques for brain imaging, such as positron emission tomography (PET) and functional magnetic resonance imaging (fMRI), has made it possible for us to learn more about how speech is processed in the brain.

As we would expect on the basis of what we learned in Chapter 9, hearing sounds of any kind activates the primary auditory cortex (A1). Further, we learned that the processing of complex sounds relies on additional areas of cortex adjacent to A1. These nearby areas of auditory cortex, called belt and parabelt areas, as shown in Figure 9.21 and **Figure 11.25**, often are referred to as secondary or association areas. As one might expect, we see these areas activated when listeners hear speech and music. Even at this relatively early level of cortical processing, some areas are already more responsive to speech versus music versus other commonly heard natural sounds (Norman-Haignere, Kanwisher, and McDermott, 2015). This sorting of responsiveness to sounds appears to be pretty much the same for both hemispheres.

Because we know that language is typically lateralized to one hemisphere—usually the left side for right-handed people—processing of speech should become more lateralized at some point because perceiving speech is part of understanding language. One challenge for researchers is to create stimuli that have all the complex properties of speech without being heard as speech. We already learned that listeners are very good at understanding speech even under adverse circumstances when some parts of the signal are missing or distorted, so this capability makes it pretty difficult to construct stimuli that are complex like speech without being heard as speech.

Rosen et al. (2011) developed a particularly clever way to tease apart cortical responses to acoustic complexity from responses to speech per se. As **Figure 11.26**

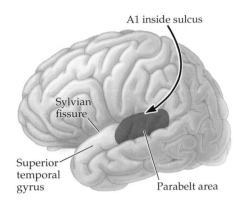

Figure 11.25 The superior temporal gyrus extends along the upper surface of each temporal lobe. Primary auditory cortex (A1) and the adjacent belt area are hidden inside the Sylvian fissure, with only the parabelt area exposed toward the posterior superior temporal gyrus. Portions of the superior temporal gyri (left and right) are active when we listen to complex sounds.

Figure 11.26 Stimuli created to measure cortical responses to acoustic complexity versus responses to speech. (A) This spectrogram represents an intact intelligible sentence with natural changes in frequency and amplitude. (B–E) In these spectrograms, the same sentence is now unintelligible because either frequency changes were removed (B) or amplitude changes were removed (C). The spectrogram in (D) has frequency changes from (A) but amplitude changes from (E). While (D) is equal to (A) in acoustic complexity, it is unintelligible because of the mismatch between changes in amplitude and frequency. (After Rosen et al., 2011.)

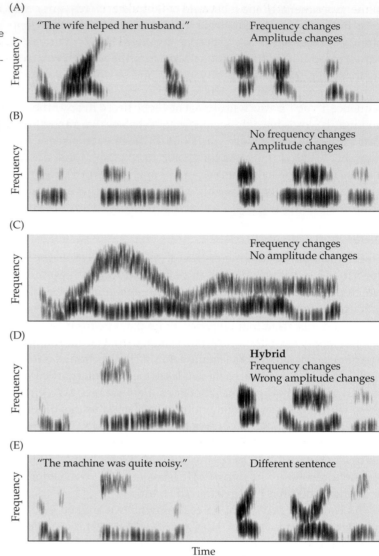

shows, they began with complete sentences that included natural changes in both amplitude and frequency (Figure 11.26A), although they replaced voicing vibration with noise. Although using noise made the sentences sound whispered, they were perfectly intelligible. Next the researchers took away changes in frequency, leaving behind only changes in amplitude (Figure 11.26B). Then they took away changes in amplitude, leaving only changes in frequency (Figure 11.26C). Finally, to match the amount of acoustic complexity in speech, they created hybrid "sentences" by adding the amplitude changes of one sentence (Figure 11.26E) to the frequency changes in another (Figure 11.26A). These hybrids (Figure 11.26D) were just as complex as the sentence in Figure 11.26A, but they were completely unintelligible. The researchers played these four types of sentences (Figure 11.26A–D) to listeners while their brains were being scanned using PET.

As **Figure 11.27** illustrates, neural activity in response to unintelligible hybrid "sentences" (see Figure 11.26D) was found bilaterally, with a little more activity along the superior temporal gyrus running along the top of the right temporal lobe. Responses in the left superior temporal gyrus became dominant only when sentences were intelligible because amplitude and frequency changes coincided properly (see Figure 11.26A). From these findings, it appears that language-dominant hemisphere responses depend on listeners using speech for linguistic understanding and are not due to acoustic complexity alone.

A great deal of research is being conducted to further our understanding of how speech is processed in the brain on its way to becoming part of words and sentences. For now, the evidence suggests that as sounds become more complex, they are processed in more anterior and ventral regions of the superior temporal cortex farther away from A1 (Patterson and Johnsrude, 2008; Uppenkamp et al., 2006). When speech sounds become more clearly a part of language, they are processed more anteriorly (forward) in the left temporal lobe. This much appears true; however, this back-to-front path may not be all there is to speech perception in the brain. Other brain regions are likely involved.

What could we learn if we could actually place electrodes right on top of the brain? Prior to performing brain surgery to remove a tumor or to reduce effects of very severe epilepsy, neurosurgeons often place electrodes directly on the surface of the brain to localize regions of neural activity. Back in Chapter 10, you were first introduced to an electrode grid placed over a region of left superior posterior temporal lobe (see Figure 10.31). Mesgarani et al. (2014) played 500 sentences spoken by 400 different people to six human participants while recording directly on the surface of their superior temporal gyri. At different single electrodes, responses were selective for certain classes of speech sounds such as fricatives, stop consonants, or vowels. In some cases, responses were even more selective. For example, responses to stop consonants might be selective for only voiceless stops ('p', 't', 'k') or for one place of articulation (e.g., 'd') versus others ('b' and 'g').

Chang et al. (2010) played a series of synthesized syllables varying incrementally from 'bah' to 'dah' to 'gah,' much like those in Figure 11.14, to patients who were awaiting surgery. The researchers found that, across populations of thousands of neurons recorded by their surface electrodes, neural responses were much like listening data for the same syllables. Neural responses were very similar for pairs of stimuli that listeners would label as the same, as 'bah' or 'dah' or 'gah'; responses were quite distinct for pairs of syllables that were acoustically separated by the same extent but were labeled as different, as 'bah' and 'dah' or as 'dah' and 'gah.'

As with perception in general, cortical organization depends critically on experience, and the perception of speech sounds is tremendously experience-dependent. Because we know that English and Hindi speakers hear sounds like 'd' differently, we know that the way listeners discriminate 'bah' and 'dah' depends on experience. Chang et al. (2010) have revealed places in the left temporal lobe where experience with English 'b' and 'd' shapes neural activity.

Earlier while discussing music, we mentioned languages such as Mandarin that make great use of pitch changes in distinguishing one word from another. In English and most other languages, pitch is used, too. For example, when you say the noun *contract*, 'CON' has a higher pitch than 'con' in the verb *contract*. Areas in the cortex that are especially responsive to these pitch changes are intermingled among areas responsive to 'bah' versus 'dah' versus 'gah,' and these are intermingled with areas that are more responsive to some talkers than to others (Tang, Hamilton, and Change, 2017).

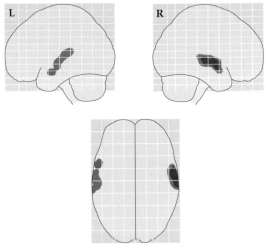

Figure 11.27 Substantial neural activity was observed in both left and right superior temporal lobes (red) when listeners heard hybrid sentences such as the one shown in Figure 11.26D, for which amplitude and frequency changes came from different sentences. An increase in activity in only the language-dominant left anterior superior temporal lobe (purple) was evident when the sentences were intelligible (Figure 11.26A), with matching amplitude and frequency changes. (After Rosen et al., 2011.)

Cortical processes related to speech perception can be distinguished from brain processes that contribute to the perception of other complex sounds in two other ways. Listeners have a wealth of experience simultaneously hearing speech and viewing talkers' faces, and the McGurk effect (see Figure 11.15) is evidence of the profound effects that visual cues can have on the way speech sounds are perceived. Reale et al. (2007) also used grids of electrodes on the surface of posterior temporal cortex (see Figure 10.31) in their experiments investigating cortical processing of audio and visual speech. They found that neural responses to auditory speech stimuli in the language-dominant hemisphere were influenced substantially by simultaneous viewing of the lower half of the face of a person either producing audible speech or carrying out a meaningless mouth motion.

Because visual information combines with auditory experience when we're perceiving speech, you may wonder what happens for people who are deaf. Zatorre (2001) studied a group of people with cochlear implants who previously had been deaf. These listeners exhibited increased brain activity in the visual cortex when listening to speech. Zatorre hypothesized that this activation of visual areas of the brain is the result of increased experience and ability with lip-reading for these previously deaf individuals.

Finally, whenever people talk, they both hear the sounds they're producing and experience the movements of speech production in their own vocal tracts. People have a lot of experience with the simultaneous activities of producing and perceiving our own speech, so one might expect to find brain regions where these related activities combine. As it happens, there are areas of the motor cortex (see Figure 1.21) that become active when listening to speech. As you might have anticipated from what you learned about the motor theory of speech perception, discovery of these areas of activity was taken by some investigators to be evidence that speech sounds are processed with reference to the motor activities engaged to produce them. This was a very controversial idea because motor theory had been abandoned by most investigators, so alternative explanations were developed (Lima, Krishnan, and Scott, 2016). While it is too soon to know exactly what the motor cortex is up to when a person is listening to speech, we have learned that responses in motor cortex and responses in the temporal lobe are organized similarly, and these responses are very different from brain responses recorded when people are talking (Cheung et al., 2016). (See **Web Essay 11.1: Studying Brain Areas for Language Processing**.)

Summary

1. Musical pitch has two dimensions: tone height and tone chroma. Musical notes are combined to form chords. Notes and chords vary in duration and are combined to form melodies.

2. Melodies are learned psychological entities defined by patterns of rising and falling musical pitches, with different durations and rhythms.

3. Rhythm is important to music, and to auditory perception more broadly. The process of perceiving sound sequences is biased to hear rhythm.

4. Humans evolved to be able to produce an extremely wide variety of sounds that can be used in languages. The production of speech sounds has three basic components: respiration, phonation, and articulation. Speech sounds vary in many dimensions, including intensity, duration, periodicity, and noisiness.

5. In terms of articulation and acoustics, speech sounds vary according to other speech sounds that precede and follow (coarticulation). Because of coarticulation, listeners cannot use any single acoustic feature to identify a vowel or consonant. Instead, listeners must use multiple properties of the speech signal.

6. In general, listeners discriminate speech sounds only as well as they can label them. This is categorical perception, which also has been shown for the perception of many other complex familiar auditory and visual stimuli.

7. How people perceive speech depends very much on their experience with speech sounds within a language. This experience includes learning which of the many acoustic features in speech tend to co-occur. Because of the role of experience in how we hear speech, it is often difficult to perceive and produce new speech sounds from a second language following experience with a first language.

8. One of the ways that infants learn words is to use their experience with the co-occurrence of speech sounds.

9. Speech sounds are processed in both hemispheres of the brain much as other complex sounds are, until they become part of the linguistic message. Then, speech is further processed in anterior and ventral regions, mostly in the left superior temporal cortex, but also in posterior superior temporal cortex.

Vestibular Sensation

■ Questions to Contemplate ■

Think about the following questions as you read this chapter. By the chapter's end, you should be able to answer and discuss them.

- If you had to give up one sensory system, why would you *not* give up vestibular function?

- Can you identify at least four functional roles played by the vestibular system?

- Why can it be claimed that our tilt sense—often referred to as graviception—is among the most fundamental sensory modalities?

- Can you list at least three vestibular modalities?

- Is it good that most contributions of the vestibular system are not usually consciously experienced?

- What does the vestibular system have to do with the motion sickness sometimes experienced with virtual reality?

Remember when you were a child and you used to spin around until you were dizzy and couldn't walk straight? Perhaps you even fell. Why were you dizzy? The sensations did not arise from one of the five senses that Aristotle recognized—vision, hearing, touch, taste, or smell. Your dizziness arose from contributions of your **vestibular organs** to your vestibular sense, which is also sometimes called your equilibrium sense.

The vestibular organs are a set of specialized sense organs located in the inner ear right next to the cochlea. Vestibular organs sense motion of the head, as well as the orientation of gravity, and make a predominant contribution to

vestibular organs The set of five sense organs—three semicircular canals and two otolith organs—located in each inner ear that sense head motion and head orientation with respect to gravity.

F. Scott Hess, *Dancing at the Edge of Time*, 2015

our sense of tilt and our sense of self-motion. Taken together, the senses of tilt and self-motion comprise our sense of **spatial orientation**.

FURTHER DISCUSSION of the cochlea can be found in Chapter 9 on page 290.

You may be asking, "Wait a minute, why didn't I learn about the **vestibular system** and equilibrium when I first learned about the five senses?" Good question. Perhaps you should have. The vestibular "sixth sense" provides fundamental contributions that are often overlooked. For example, the vestibular system contributes to clear vision when we move, and it helps us maintain balance when we stand. And it is so crucial that some patients even report cognitive deficits when it fails. Yet despite these essential contributions, the vestibular system toils in anonymity. Much of the time, we remain unaware of it until it stops working properly.

The fundamental nature of the vestibular system is emphasized by the fact that the vestibular organs appeared very early in evolutionary history and have

spatial orientation A sense consisting of three interacting modalities: perception of linear motion, angular motion, and tilt.

vestibular system The vestibular organs as well as the vestibular neurons in cranial nerve VIII and the central neurons that contribute to the functional roles that the vestibular system participates in.

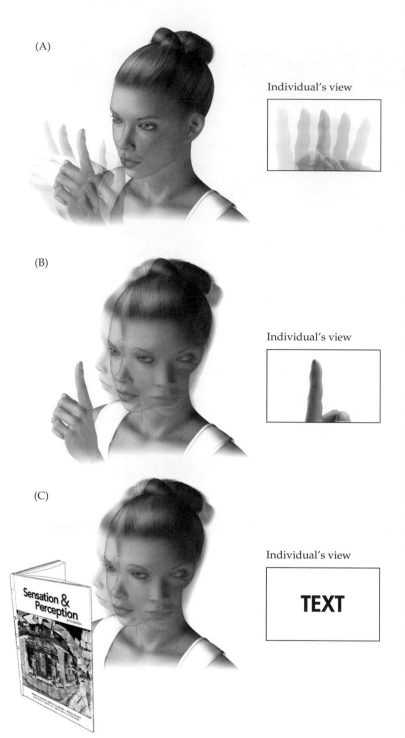

(A)

Individual's view

(B)

Individual's view

(C)

Sensation & Perception

Individual's view

TEXT

Figure 12.1 Demonstration of the vestibulo-ocular reflex. (A) As your fingertip moves faster and faster in front of your face, the fingertip begins to blur. (B) When you shake your head back and forth as if to say "no," the fingertip remains clearer. (C) Text also remains clearer during head shaking.

remained relatively unchanged. The vertebrate fossil record shows the presence of distinct vestibular organs in fish at least 400 million years ago. The system is not only ancient but largely automatic: vestibular perception is often relegated to the attentional background, and many responses evoked by the vestibular system are reflexive. Though we are all aware of the normal function of our eyes and ears, only when we experience problems such as dizziness, vertigo, spatial disorientation, imbalance, blurred vision, and/or illusory self-motion are we likely to become acutely aware of our vestibular sense.

Obviously, we can no longer ask Aristotle—who is credited with first cataloging our sensory systems—why he did not include equilibrium or our vestibular sense among the specialized sensory systems, but we can speculate. It certainly is not because **vertigo** was unknown, since Aristotle himself described the vertiginous effects of alcohol. One explanation may be that it was not until the nineteenth century that scientists understood that the vestibular system is a specialized set of sense organs. Until then, the vestibular system had been considered an entrance to the cochlea. In fact, the name *vestibular* records this error for posterity because *vestibule* means "entrance." But this explanation is not entirely satisfactory, since Aristotle had cataloged other senses without detailed anatomical or physiological knowledge. (See Wade, 2000, for a historical review of vestibular knowledge prior to the nineteenth century.)

Another explanation may be the inconspicuous nature of our vestibular sense. In fact, as we'll see, many responses evoked by the vestibular system are reflexive. For example, the vestibular system helps us see clearly by reflexively rotating the eyeballs in the sockets to compensate for head rotation—thereby helping to keep visual images stable on the retina. This reflex is called the **vestibulo-ocular reflex** (**VOR**).

To demonstrate this to yourself, move your hand a few inches back and forth in front of your face (**Figure 12.1A**). Start slowly and then speed up the movement. Focus on a fingertip and notice that it starts to appear more and more blurry as your hand moves at a higher frequency. This exercise demonstrates the limits of smooth pursuit, a form of visual tracking that you learned about in

vertigo A sensation of rotation or spinning. The term is often used more generally to mean any form of dizziness.

vestibulo-ocular reflex (VOR) A short-latency reflex that helps stabilize vision by counterrotating the eyes when the vestibular system senses head movement.

Chapter 8. Now hold your hand in front of your face and shake your head from side to side as if to say "no" (**Figure 12.1B**). Again, start slowly and gradually increase the speed. At higher frequencies of head rotation, you should notice that each fingertip stays in focus more readily when you move your head than when you move your hand. You can compensate for head movement more readily than hand movement, because of a VOR that we will discuss in more detail later in this chapter.

Before we move on, there's one more lesson to draw from this VOR example. Rotate your head back and forth while you read this text (**Figure 12.1C**). Until now, because you were asked to attend to vision, you probably were focused on visual perception and didn't explicitly perceive your head rotation. In fact, your head often moves around, but you do not typically perceive your head motion, because the vestibular system usually performs its job automatically—with little, if any, conscious awareness. But now that we've called your attention to it, as you continue to shake your head, you can perceive your head rotating, can't you? Thus, it is not that you are unable to perceive vestibular stimulation, but rather that vestibular stimulation is almost always relegated to the attentional background (discussed in Chapter 7).

Vestibular Contributions

The vestibular system provides the sensory foundation for spatial orientation, which includes perception of translation, rotation, and tilt. The vestibular system also makes crucial contributions to **balance** but does not provide the sensory foundation for balance; **kinesthesia** does (see Chapter 13). While blind individuals and those without vestibular systems can stand, individuals lacking kinesthesia typically cannot stand. In addition, the vestibular system helps stabilize our eyes during head motion. In this role, the vestibular system makes crucial contributions to clarity of sight but does not provide the sensory foundation; our eyes and visual system do (see Chapters 2–8). The vestibular system also helps maintain blood flow to the brain via contributions to cardiac (heart) regulation but is not foundational there either; somatosensation is (see Chapter 13).

Also, as will be discussed in detail later in this chapter, our vestibular sense is active, not passive. By this we mean that our vestibular sense (**Figure 12.2**) combines information flowing from our brain to our muscles with information flowing inward to the brain from various sensory systems, especially the kinesthetic, visual, and vestibular systems. For example, signals that tell our muscles to rotate our head provide information about head rotation just as vestibular signals do. Information from these various sources is combined to help improve our vestibular sense. More generally, **active sensing** balances information derived from **efferent commands** flowing outward from the brain to the periphery (e.g., to muscles) with information from various **afferent signals** flowing from sensors inward to the brain.

In summary, the vestibular system contributes to our sense of equilibrium, which is composed of many fundamental reflexes and perceptual modalities (see Figure 12.2). The breadth of the vestibular system's contributions is pretty amazing (some might say it provides a "dizzying" array of contributions). When combined, these various perceptual and reflexive roles are referred to as our sense of equilibrium because they involve a balance of influences and/ or a balance of forces—matching definitions of *equilibrium* you might find in a dictionary.

balance The neural processes of postural control by which weight is evenly distributed, enabling us to remain upright and stable.

kinesthesia Perception of the position and movement of our limbs in space.

active sensing Sensing that includes self-generated probing of the environment. Besides our vestibular sense, other active human senses include vision and touch. Animal active sensing includes the use of echoes by whales and bats, the use of electrical signals by some fishes, and the use of whiskers/antennae by fishes, insects, and nocturnal rodents.

efferent commands Information flowing outward from the central nervous system to the periphery. A common example is motor commands that regulate muscle contraction. The copy of such motor commands is often called an efferent copy.

afferent signals Information flowing inward to the central nervous system from sensors in the periphery. Passive sensing would rely exclusively on such sensory inflow, providing a traditional view of sensation.

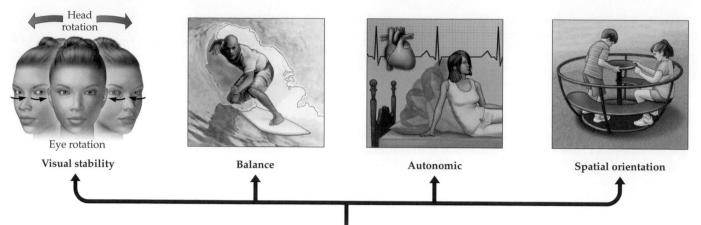

Head
rotation

Eye rotation

Visual stability

Balance

Autonomic

Spatial orientation

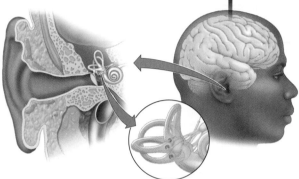

Figure 12.2 Our vestibular sense is composed of multiple reflexes and multiple perceptual modalities that originate (at least in part) in the vestibular organs in the inner ear. Vestibular reflexes include compensatory eye movements, called vestibulo-ocular reflexes, that rotate our eyes to help compensate for head motion; balance reflexes that help us stand; and even some autonomic reflexes that help maintain blood flow to our brain when we rise to a standing position. Spatial orientation includes perception of rotation, perception of translation, and perception of tilt, which are all "practiced" on playgrounds every day.

Evolutionary Development and Vestibular Sensation

Knowing up from down is crucial for us as humans, and this sensation provides a "stable permanent framework of the environment" for many perceptual processes that provides an "underlying and ceaseless awareness of what is permanent in the world" (Gibson, 1966). As just one example, the receptive field orientation of simple visual cortical neurons (see Chapter 3) is impacted by **graviception** (Tomko, Barbaro, and Ali, 1981). The fundamental nature and importance of this modality is even captured by the words we use to describe actions that define us as human (e.g., *stand up*). But tilt sensation, sometimes referred to as graviception, is not limited to humans. All mammals, including the platypus and all four species of echidna, have vestibular labyrinths that include otolith organs. In fact, all vertebrates, including fishes, amphibians, non-avian reptiles, and birds, have vestibular organs. Even the dinosaurs had vestibular organs. While crustaceans (e.g., crabs) and invertebrates (e.g., jellyfishes) don't have vestibular organs, some have dedicated graviceptors, and plants sense gravity (how else could trees grow up?) (**Figure 12.3**). Going farther back along the evolutionary chain, even some bacteria need to know up from down. In summary, from an evolutionary perspective, graviception has been around a long time.

The above facts suggest that vestibular sensation is fundamental. But, relative to the vestibular organs of all other vertebrates, the human vestibular organs include the unique feature that the vertical canals are relatively larger than in other species. Larger canals contribute to higher sensitivity, which is believed to yield enhanced head and eye stabilization when we run (Spoor, Wood, and Zooneveld, 1994). This is believed to have contributed to enhanced exercise

graviception The physiological structures and processes that sense the relative orientation of gravity with respect to the organism.

(A)   (B)

Figure 12.3 Even plants and invertebrates, like jellyfishes, sense gravity. (A) Jellyfishes have what are called statoliths, which include calcium crystals that stimulate cilliated mechanoreceptors that are analogs to otoconia and hair cells of the otolith organs. (B) While plants don't have organs analogous to the otoliths, they too need to sense gravity for a root to grow downwards and a shoot to grow upwards.

capacity (Bramble and Lieberman, 2004), which, in turn, is believed to have contributed to larger human brains (Raichlen and Gordon, 2011). Who knew the vestibular system was so important?

Modalities and Qualities of Spatial Orientation

Our perception of spatial orientation includes three sensory modalities: the senses of **angular motion**, **linear motion**, and **tilt**. Why do we call these "modalities," as though they were different senses, rather than calling them "qualities"? For example, vision and hearing are different *modalities*, but we would say that color and brightness are different *qualities*, not different modalities. The key lies in the energy **transduced**. Color and brightness are different interpretations of the same energy (light)—hence, *qualities*. Seeing and hearing involve different types of energy—light and pressure waves, respectively. As with seeing and hearing, perceiving angular motion, linear motion, and tilt requires that three different stimuli—angular acceleration, linear acceleration, and gravity, respectively—be transduced.

Sensing Angular Motion, Linear Motion, and Tilt

These three stimulation energies are sensed by two types of vestibular sense organs: the semicircular canals and the otolith organs. The **semicircular canals** sense **angular acceleration**, which is a change in angular velocity; this signal makes a predominant contribution to our sense of angular motion. To experience your sense of angular motion, simply close your eyes and rotate your head from side to side as if to say "no." Because of contributions from your vestibular system, you should experience a perception of angular velocity that roughly matches the true angular velocity of your head.

The **otolith organs** transduce both **linear acceleration**, which is a change of linear velocity, and **gravity**. The otolith organs provide a predominant

angular motion   Rotational motion like the rotation of a spinning top or swinging saloon doors that rotate back and forth.

linear motion   Translational motion like the predominant movement of a train car or bobblehead doll.

tilt   To attain a sloped position like that of the Leaning Tower of Pisa.

transduce   To convert from one form of energy to another (e.g., from light to neural electrical energy, or from mechanical energy to neural electrical energy).

semicircular canal   Any of three toroidal tubes in the vestibular system that sense angular motion.

angular acceleration   The rate of change of angular velocity. Mathematically, the integral of angular acceleration is angular velocity, and the integral of angular velocity is angular displacement. Angular acceleration, angular velocity, and angular displacement all mathematically represent angular motion.

otolith organ   Either of two mechanical structures (utricle and saccule) in the vestibular system that sense both linear acceleration and gravity.

linear acceleration   The rate of change of linear velocity. Mathematically, the integral of linear acceleration is linear velocity, and the integral of linear velocity is linear displacement, which is also referred to as "translation." Linear acceleration, linear velocity, and linear displacement all mathematically represent linear motion.

gravity   A force that attracts a body toward the center of the Earth.

contribution to your sense of head tilt and a predominant contribution to your sense of linear motion, which is also referred to as your sense of translation. To experience your sense of tilt, simply pitch your head forward as if to say "yes" and hold it there for several seconds; then pitch your head backward and hold it there. You should experience a perception of head tilt. Relatively pure linear motion is more difficult to achieve passively, but the experience of riding in a car, train, or bus provides an example. Try the following when you are a passenger in a vehicle. With your eyes closed, pay attention to your sense of motion as the driver backs the car out of the garage, brings the car to a stop, and then begins to accelerate forward. Initially, you should perceive backward translation (backward linear motion). You should also perceive the cessation of translation as the car comes to a stop, and then forward translation as the car accelerates forward.

Two different types of sense organs—the semicircular canals and the otolith organs—establish at least two sensory modalities. But if we have only two types of sense organs, why do we say there are three modalities? As noted, the otolith organs transduce both gravity and linear acceleration. Perception of tilt results from the brain's estimate of orientation with respect to gravity, and perception of linear motion results from the brain's estimate of linear acceleration. Personal experience suggests that tilt perception is fundamentally different from translation perception; these do not seem to be different sensory qualities like color and brightness.

Why is this so? This key question leads to the fundamental rationale for two modalities arising from otolith signals. Classical physics teaches that gravity and linear acceleration are distinct from one another. Though Einstein hypothesized that gravity and linear acceleration have equivalent effects, he did not assert that

sensory conflict Sensory discrepancies that arise when sensory systems provide conflicting information. For example, vision may indicate that you are stationary while the vestibular system tells you that you are moving (or vice versa).

■ Sensation & Perception in Everyday Life ■

The Vestibular System, Virtual Reality, and Motion Sickness

What does the vestibular system have to do with motion sickness experienced by some virtual reality gamers (**Figure 12.4**)? As noted earlier, visual cues combine with vestibular cues to yield our equilibrium sense. The brain learns to associate certain combinations of these cues. For example, if I rotate my head to the right, the vestibular system senses that head rotation and my eyes see relative rotation of the visual field to the left. I don't expect relative motion of the visual field when my head is still (and vice versa). Any imperfections in these visual-vestibular interactions yield discrepancies relative to the normal sensory interactions that are expected by the brain. Such sensory discrepancies, often called **sensory conflict**, cause motion sickness. For example, when we are engaged with virtual reality, there is an inherent delay between sensing a head motion and the resultant virtual visual scene motion, because the calculations needed to move the image on the display cannot be performed instantaneously. When this delay is long enough, the brain senses discrepancies between the virtual visual motion experienced and the visual motion that would normally accompany the sensed head motion. This can (and often does) lead to motion sickness.

Figure 12.4 Virtual reality is becoming more popular. Motion sickness, believed to be due to a mismatch between vestibular and visual cues, has limited the adoption of virtual reality as a standard visual display.

they were the same. In fact, the brain does its best to separate the signals from the otolith organs into signals representative of gravity and signals representative of linear acceleration. (See **Web Essay 12.1: Gravity versus Linear Acceleration** for more on this equivalence of gravity and linear acceleration.) Therefore, we assert three interacting sensory modalities—a **sense of angular motion**, a **sense of linear motion**, and a **sense of tilt**—paralleling the three different sources of stimulation energy—angular acceleration, linear acceleration, and gravity (Guedry, 1974; Young, 1984).

Basic Qualities of Spatial Orientation: Amplitude and Direction

Each of our three spatial orientation modalities includes two qualities: **amplitude** and **direction**. As an example of amplitude, the speed of our perceived motion can be large (as in a jet just before takeoff) or small (as for a baby crawling). As an example of direction, perceived linear motion might be forward, up, or to the left.

AMPLITUDE   For linear motion we can perceive translation having high velocity (think of a car passing you on the freeway) or low velocity (think of a car inching forward in a traffic jam). Similarly, we can perceive rotational velocity with high amplitude (think of vigorously shaking your head) or low amplitude (think of the slow rotation of minute or hour hands on a clock). Finally, tilt amplitude is also important. Tilt amplitudes can be small (as when you gently nod your head) or large (as when you lie down or hang upside down).

DIRECTION   To help clearly classify direction, we first define a simple Cartesian coordinate system that moves with the head (**Figure 12.5**). Since the physical space that we move in is three-dimensional, we need three axes. In our coordinate system, the x-axis always points forward, the y-axis always points out the left ear, and the z-axis always points out the top of the head.

sense of angular motion   The perceptual modality that senses rotation.

sense of linear motion   The perceptual modality that senses translation.

sense of tilt   The perceptual modality that senses head inclination with respect to gravity.

amplitude   In reference to vestibular sensation, the size (increase or decrease) of a head movement (with angular velocity, linear acceleration, tilt, etc.).

direction   The line one moves along or faces, with reference to the point or region one is moving toward or facing.

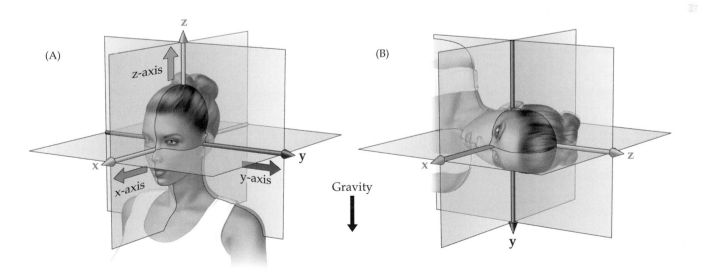

Figure 12.5 Movement of the head can be described in terms of a simple fixed coordinate system. (A) The x-axis always points forward relative to the current orientation of the head, the y-axis always points out the left ear, and the z-axis always points out the top of the head. As (B) illustrates, this coordinate system always moves with the head.

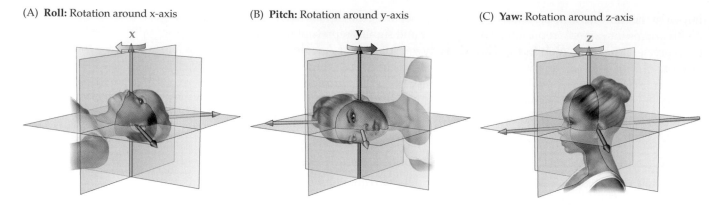

(A) **Roll:** Rotation around x-axis

(B) **Pitch:** Rotation around y-axis

(C) **Yaw:** Rotation around z-axis

Figure 12.6 Rotating bodies can move in three directions. The head can turn with a pure roll velocity around the x-axis (A), a pure pitch velocity around the y-axis (B), or a pure yaw velocity around the z-axis (C).

Three directions define our sense of angular motion. That is, the head can rotate in three independent ways, which can be represented (1) with a roll angular velocity (**Figure 12.6A**); (2) with a pitch angular velocity, as when you nod "yes" (**Figure 12.6B**); and (3) with a yaw angular velocity, as when you shake your head "no" (**Figure 12.6C**). These three angular motions can be combined to represent any three-dimensional head rotation.

There are also three directions for our sense of linear motion. Imagine (1) stepping forward or backward along the x-axis (**Figure 12.7A**), (2) sliding from right to left along the y-axis (**Figure 12.7B**), and (3) translating up or down along the z-axis (**Figure 12.7C**), which can also be combined to represent any three-dimensional linear motion.

Finally, each orientation has two tilt directions. For example, when you are upright, you might experience a pitch tilt forward or backward (**Figure 12.8A**). Or you might experience a roll tilt to the left or right (**Figure 12.8B**). What happened to the third dimension? The third rotation direction would be a yaw rotation, but this would not yield a change in the tilt of the head with respect to gravity

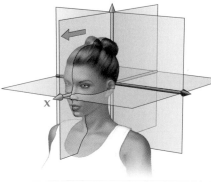

(A) Positive x-axis translation

(B) Positive y-axis translation

(C) Positive z-axis translation

Figure 12.7 Translating bodies can move in three directions. The head can translate forward and backward along the x-axis (A), left and right along the y-axis (B), or up and down along the z-axis (C).

(A) Pitch tilt (B) Roll tilt

Gravity

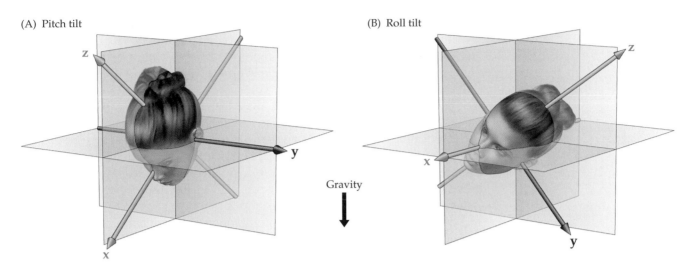

Figure 12.8 Tilting bodies can move in two directions. When you are initially upright with respect to gravity, there are two directions of tilt. You can pitch-tilt forward or backward (A), or you can roll-tilt to the left or right (B).

(see Figure 12.6C). When head rotations align with gravity, there is no change in head tilt. So there are three directions for angular velocity and translation, but only two directions for tilt.

The Vestibular Periphery

In this section we look at where and how motion signals are transduced by the vestibular organs. The vestibular organs are about the size of a large pea and can be found in the inner ear right next to the cochlea (**Figure 12.9A**). They respond primarily to head motion—both linear and angular—and head tilt

Figure 12.9 The vestibular labyrinth. (A) The vestibular organs occupy a membranous, fluid-filled sac that is in a cavity in the temporal bone, near the cochlea, and is the nonhearing part of the inner ear. (B) The vestibular organs consist of three semicircular canals (anterior, posterior, and horizontal) and two otolith organs (utricle and saccule) on each side of the head. The vestibular organs are innervated by the vestibular nerve, which joins the auditory nerve to form cranial nerve VIII, called the vestibulocochlear nerve (see Figure 1.20).

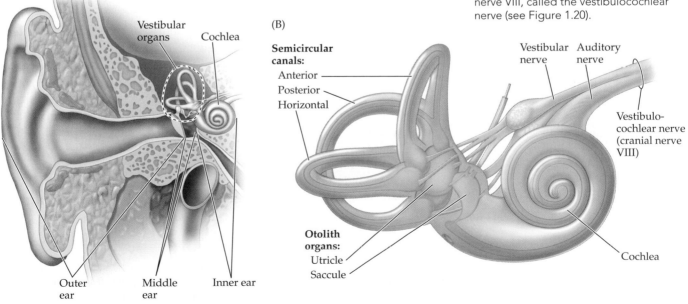

(A)

Vestibular organs   Cochlea

Outer ear   Middle ear   Inner ear

(B)

Semicircular canals:
Anterior
Posterior
Horizontal

Vestibular nerve   Auditory nerve

Vestibulo-cochlear nerve (cranial nerve VIII)

Otolith organs:
Utricle
Saccule

Cochlea

with respect to gravity. Each inner ear has one vestibular labyrinth, and each vestibular labyrinth includes five sense organs (**Figure 12.9B**): three semicircular canals that sense rotational motion, and two otolith organs that sense gravity and linear acceleration. (See **Web Activity 12.1: A Guided Tour of the Vestibular System**.)

Note that neither the otolith organs nor the semicircular canals respond to constant **velocity**. Rather, they respond to *changes* in velocity—called **acceleration**. The sensitivity of the vestibular system to acceleration—angular acceleration for the semicircular canals and linear acceleration for the otolith organs—demonstrates that the vestibular system is principally sensitive to *changes* in motion. Constant motion, whether angular or linear, does not result in vestibular signals that directly indicate motion.

As you will see again later, the otolith organs transduce both linear acceleration and gravity into a single neural signal sent to the brain. In fact, as Einstein asserted, no device can tell the difference between gravity and linear acceleration. Separating the otolith measurement of gravity and linear acceleration into an estimate of gravity and an estimate of linear acceleration is not easy and must be important, since the brain expends energy and effort to do so (Angelaki et al., 1999; Merfeld, Zupan, and Peterka, 1999). (See **Web Essay 12.2: Canal-Otolith Integration** for more on how the brain distinguishes gravity from linear acceleration.)

Hair Cells: Mechanical Transducers

Hair cells, which you read about in Chapter 9 when you began to learn about hearing (see Figure 9.9), act as **mechanoreceptors** in each of the five vestibular organs. Head motion causes hair cell stereocilia to deflect. Stereocilia deflection causes a change in the hair cell voltage, which alters neurotransmitter release, which, in turn, evokes action potentials in those vestibular-nerve fibers that have one or more synapses on the hair cell. These afferent neurons carry the action potentials to the brain.

Let's consider vestibular hair cell responses in a bit more detail. In the absence of stimulation, vestibular hair cells have a negative voltage and release neurotransmitter at a constant rate, evoking a constant rate of action potentials in the afferent neurons (**Figure 12.10A**). Changes in hair cell voltage—called the **receptor potential**—are proportional to the bending of the hair cell bundles and control the rate at which hair cells release neurotransmitter to the afferent neurons. When a hair cell bends toward the tallest stereocilia (**Figure 12.10B, C**), the hair cell voltage becomes less negative. This voltage change is also called a depolarization because the hair cell becomes less polarized than the negative resting potential (see Figure 12.10A). The hair cell depolarization increases the release of neurotransmitter, causing an increase in the action potential rate (called excitation). On the other hand, if the hair cell is bent away from the tallest stereocilia, the cell potential becomes more negative (hyperpolarizes), causing a decrease in the release of neurotransmitter and a decrease in the action potential rate (called inhibition). In summary, the rate of action potentials transmitted by afferent neurons increases or decreases following the hair cell receptor potential.

> **FURTHER DISCUSSION** of the receptor potential of hair cells can be found in Chapter 9 on pages 292–294.

Thinking back to the fact that amplitude is one quality of our vestibular sense, we can begin to see how amplitude is encoded, since the rate of action potentials

velocity   The speed and direction in which something moves. Mathematically, velocity is the integral of acceleration. In words, linear velocity is distance divided by time to traverse that distance; angular velocity is rotation angle divided by time to traverse that angle.

acceleration   A change in velocity. Mathematically, acceleration is the derivative of velocity. In words, linear acceleration indicates a change in linear velocity; angular acceleration indicates a change in angular velocity.

hair cell   Any cell that has stereocilia for transducing mechanical movement in the inner ear into neural activity sent to the brain; some hair cells also receive inputs from the brain.

mechanoreceptor   A sensory receptor that responds to mechanical stimulation (pressure, vibration, or movement).

receptor potential   A change in voltage across the membrane of a sensory receptor cell (in the vestibular system, a hair cell) in response to stimulation.

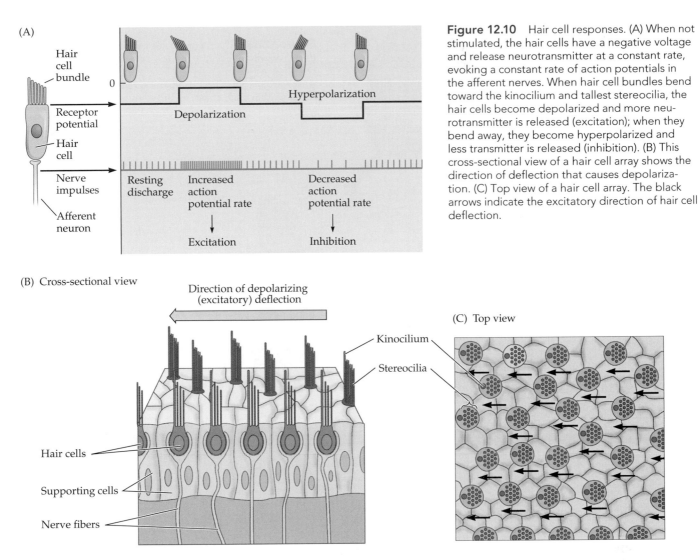

(A)

Hair cell bundle

0

Receptor potential

Hair cell

Nerve impulses

Afferent neuron

Hyperpolarization

Depolarization

| Resting discharge | Increased action potential rate | Decreased action potential rate |

Excitation   Inhibition

Figure 12.10 Hair cell responses. (A) When not stimulated, the hair cells have a negative voltage and release neurotransmitter at a constant rate, evoking a constant rate of action potentials in the afferent nerves. When hair cell bundles bend toward the kinocilium and tallest stereocilia, the hair cells become depolarized and more neurotransmitter is released (excitation); when they bend away, they become hyperpolarized and less transmitter is released (inhibition). (B) This cross-sectional view of a hair cell array shows the direction of deflection that causes depolarization. (C) Top view of a hair cell array. The black arrows indicate the excitatory direction of hair cell deflection.

(B) Cross-sectional view

Direction of depolarizing (excitatory) deflection

(C) Top view

Kinocilium

Stereocilia

Hair cells

Supporting cells

Nerve fibers

is proportional to the receptor potential, which in turn is proportional to the amount of hair cell deflection, which in turn is proportional to the amplitude of the motion.

The fact that the hair cells respond oppositely for deflections in opposite directions (see Figure 12.10A) is also crucial for the coding of vestibular stimuli. For example, as we'll discuss in detail in the following section, a yaw rotation to the left will increase the hair cell receptor potential for a hair cell located in the horizontal canal of the left ear, and a yaw rotation to the right will decrease the receptor potential for that same hair cell. A similar general principle applies for the otolith organs: acceleration in one direction increases the receptor potentials of some hair cells, while acceleration in the opposite direction decreases those receptor potentials.

Semicircular Canals

Each inner ear has three semicircular canals—horizontal (or lateral), anterior (or superior), and posterior (**Figure 12.11**) (the anterior and posterior canals are sometimes called the vertical canals). These canals are roughly orthogonal to one another. The name *semicircular canal* loosely reflects the gross anatomy of this structure, which has the circular shape of an incomplete toroid or doughnut.

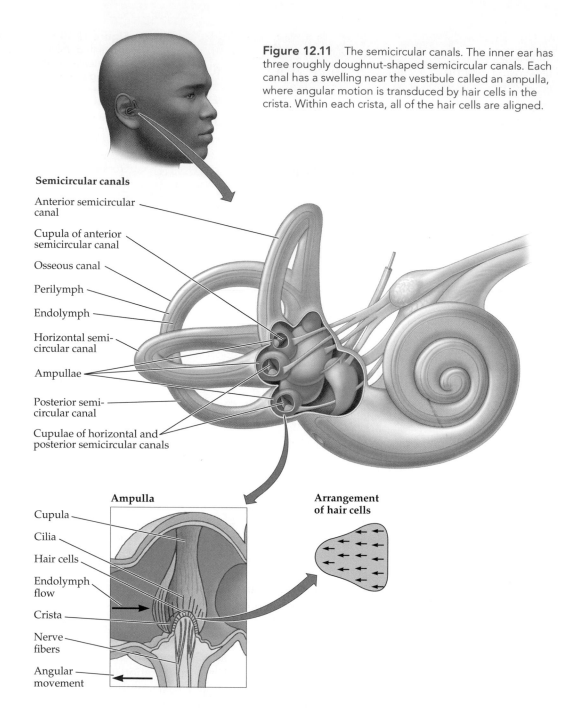

Figure 12.11 The semicircular canals. The inner ear has three roughly doughnut-shaped semicircular canals. Each canal has a swelling near the vestibule called an ampulla, where angular motion is transduced by hair cells in the crista. Within each crista, all of the hair cells are aligned.

Semicircular canals

Anterior semicircular canal

Cupula of anterior semicircular canal

Osseous canal

Perilymph

Endolymph

Horizontal semi-circular canal

Ampullae

Posterior semi-circular canal

Cupulae of horizontal and posterior semicircular canals

Ampulla

Cupula

Cilia

Hair cells

Endolymph flow

Crista

Nerve fibers

Angular movement

Arrangement of hair cells

Specifically, about three-fourths of a toroid is formed by a bony tube approximately 15 millimeters (mm) long, with a cross section about 1.5 mm in diameter. This space—called the osseous (meaning "bony") canal because it is a canal carved out of the mastoid bone—is colored tan in the figure and is filled with a fluid called perilymph. The remaining length of the toroid passes through the vestibule, which is opened up in the figure to allow a glimpse inside. A second, smaller toroid, appearing bluish in the figure, is found inside the larger toroid. This smaller toroid is formed by a membrane filled with a fluid called endolymph, and in cross section it has a diameter of about 0.3 mm, which is just a little thicker than a very thick human hair.

The cross section for each canal swells substantially near where the canals join the vestibule. Each swelling is called an **ampulla** (plural *ampullae*) (see Figure 12.11). Within the endolymph space of each ampulla, the angular-motion detectors are assembled into a sensory epithelium called the **crista** (plural *cristae*). Each crista consists of a small ridge, which has an epithelium made up of about 7000 hair cells and is innervated by about 4000 nerve fibers. The kinocilium and stereocilia (singular *stereocilium*) of each hair cell project into a jellylike cupula (plural *cupulae*) that forms an elastic dam extending to the opposite wall of the ampulla, with endolymph on both sides of the dam.

When the head rotates, the inertia of the endolymph causes it to lag behind the motion of the head (Breuer, 1874; Brown, 1874; Mach, 1875/2001), leading to deflection of the cupula and thereby to tiny deflections of the stereocilia in the crista. As mentioned earlier, such deflections evoke voltage changes in the hair cells, which in turn cause changes in the firing rate of afferent neurons (see Figure 12.10A). For each individual semicircular canal, all of the hair cells are aligned (see Figure 12.11). Thus, rotations in one direction yield increases in the receptor potential of all hair cells in that semicircular canal, as well as concomitant increases in the action potential rate for all neurons that innervate that semicircular canal. Rotations in the opposite direction yield decreases in the hair cell receptor potentials and concomitant decreases in the rate of action potentials.

The three semicircular canals are maximally sensitive to rotations in different planes, thus yielding direction coding for head rotation. Specifically, each canal is maximally sensitive to rotations about the axis perpendicular to it, and insensitive to rotations about axes that fall in its plane (**Figure 12.12**). Think of each canal as a wheel that can spin about the axle. The canal is maximally sensitive to rotations that match the normal rotation of a wheel and insensitive to rotations in other planes.

HOW AMPLITUDE IS CODED IN THE SEMICIRCULAR CANALS   In the absence of any rotation, many afferent neurons from the semicircular canals respond with a nearly constant rate of action potentials (see Figure 12.10A); canal afferent firing rates at rest average nearly 100 action potentials ("spikes") per second (Goldberg and Fernandez, 1971), a rate that is high relative to spontaneous rates for nerve fibers for other sensory systems. For comparison, recall from Chapter 2 that retinal ganglion cells fire spontaneously at a rate of about one spike per second in the dark.

The relatively high spontaneous firing rate of vestibular afferent neurons allows these neurons to decrease the firing rate for rotations in one direction and increase the firing rate for rotations in the opposite direction. In addition, the semicircular canals are organized as

ampulla   An expansion of each semicircular-canal duct that includes that canal's cupula, crista, and hair cells, where transduction occurs.

crista   Any of the specialized detectors of angular motion located in each semicircular canal in a swelling called the ampulla.

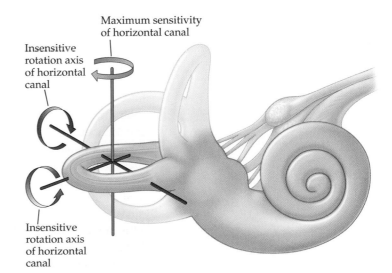

Figure 12.12   Each semicircular canal is maximally sensitive to rotations perpendicular to the canal plane. Thinking of each semicircular canal as a wheel, we can see that the canals are maximally sensitive to rotations that align with the rotation axis (green) and are insensitive to rotations that fall in the plane of the semicircular canal (e.g., red and blue).

Maximum sensitivity of horizontal canal

Insensitive rotation axis of horizontal canal

Insensitive rotation axis of horizontal canal

Figure 12.13 The semicircular canals function in pairs that have a push-pull relationship. (A) Bilateral stimulation of the horizontal semicircular canals as the head turns to the right (a yaw head rotation as shown in Figure 12.6C). This yaw rotation produces relative movement of the endolymph in the horizontal semicircular canals on both sides of the head. The movement of the fluid bends the hair cell bundles toward the tallest stereocilia on the right side, which depolarizes these hair cells and increases the rate of action potentials for neurons from the right side. The hair cell bundles move away from the tallest stereocilia on the left, hyperpolarizing the hair cells and decreasing the rate of action potentials for left-side neurons. This response—an increase on one side coupled with a decrease on the other side—is often called a push-pull response. The two horizontal canals form one push-pull pair. (B) The axis of maximum sensitivity for the right horizontal canal. (C) The right anterior canal and the left posterior canal form another pair. Note that the maximum-sensitivity axes for the right anterior and left posterior canals are parallel. This means that they maximally respond to rotations around the same axis. The push-pull nature of this canal pair is a consequence of the opposite directions of their maximum-sensitivity rotations, as shown by the green arrows.

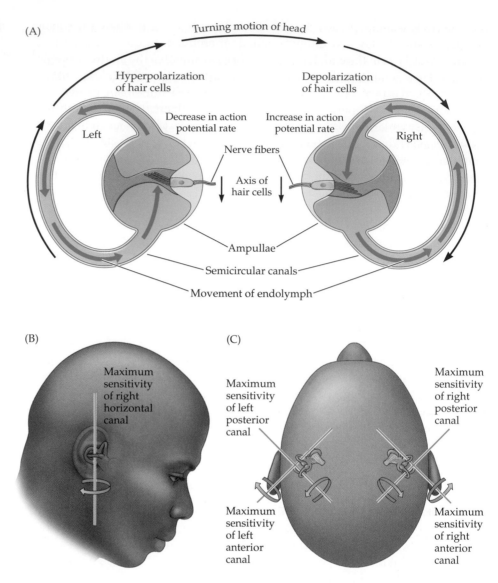

functional pairs in what is called a push-pull arrangement. The two horizontal canals—one on the right side of the head and one on the left—lie roughly in the same plane and form one of the three functional canal pairs (**Figure 12.13A, B**) (Curthoys, Blanks, and Markham, 1977; V. J. Wilson and Melvill Jones, 1979). The horizontal-canal afferent neurons on the right all increase their firing rate for yaw head turns to the right (shaking "no") while those on the left decrease their firing rate. For head turns to the left, the pattern is reversed, with left-canal afferent neurons increasing their firing rate and right-canal neurons decreasing their firing rate. The anterior and posterior canals are minimally sensitive to these yaw rotations.

In contrast to the horizontal-canal arrangement, the mirror symmetry of the semicircular canals in the left and right ears yields functional pairs that involve different vertical canals (**Figure 12.13C**); the maximum-sensitivity axis of the anterior semicircular canal on one side roughly parallels the maximum-sensitivity axis of the posterior semicircular canal on the opposite side. So the right anterior and left posterior canals form one canal pair, as do the left anterior and right posterior canals. These canal pairs work in a push-pull manner like that previously described for the horizontal canals.

The change in the firing rate is larger for large changes in the angular velocity of the head than for small changes (Goldberg and Fernandez, 1971). Since the change in the firing rate is proportional to angular velocity, we can think of the canals as somewhat similar to the speedometer in a car, with the change in neural activity proportional to the angular velocity of the head. As a specific example, if the afferent neurons from a horizontal canal suddenly change their firing rate, we know that the rotation includes a change in the velocity component aligned with the sensitive axis of that horizontal canal. The same is true for the other canals.

HOW DIRECTION IS CODED IN THE SEMICIRCULAR CANALS   As previously discussed, the three semicircular canals are maximally sensitive to rotations in different planes; the result is direction coding of head rotations. Specifically, the head can rotate about any arbitrary rotation axis made up of roll, pitch, and yaw rotational velocity components. Each canal transduces the component of head velocity perpendicular to its plane. The brain then combines these signals to sense the rotation direction of the head movement.

SEMICIRCULAR-CANAL DYNAMICS   If you suddenly begin to rotate at a constant velocity, the semicircular canals sensitive to that rotation will respond by causing a sudden change in afferent neural activity. But as the rotation continues at a constant velocity, the afferent neural activity will decay back to near zero after about 15 seconds. If you then suddenly decelerate to a stop, the canals will show a large response in the opposite direction (**Figure 12.14**). The afferent

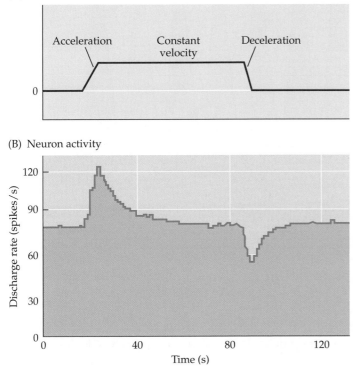

Figure 12.14   Response of a semicircular-canal neuron to constant-velocity rotation. (A) The stimulus is a rotation that first accelerates to a constant angular velocity, then maintains that velocity, and then decelerates the head to a stop. (B) During the initial acceleration, the cupula deflects, causing the neuron activity to increase. During the constant angular velocity, the cupula returns to its nondeflected position, so the neuron activity returns to the baseline rate after about 15 seconds of constant-velocity rotation. During deceleration, the cupula is deflected in the opposite direction, causing a transient decrease in the firing rate. (After Goldberg and Fernandez, 1971.)

oscillatory   Referring to back-and-forth movement that has a constant rhythm.

sinusoidal   Referring to any oscillation, such as a sound wave or rotational motion, whose waveform is that of a sine curve. The period of a sinusoidal oscillation is the time that it takes for one full back-and-forth cycle of the motion to occur. The frequency of a sinusoidal oscillation is defined as the numeral 1 divided by the period.

neural activity will then decay with a time course similar to that during the constant-velocity rotation (Goldberg and Fernandez, 1971).

What happens for more natural head rotations—like the **oscillatory** back-and-forth movement when you shake your head "no"? (If you don't have a solid understanding of frequency analysis, now may be a good time to review the "Fourier Analysis" section in Chapter 1. See also **Web Activity 12.2: Sinusoidal Motion**.) **Figure 12.15A** shows a **sinusoidal** motion trajectory at a frequency of 0.05 hertz (Hz)—a repeating back-and-forth motion that takes 20 seconds to complete (like slowly shaking your head). **Figure 12.15B** shows the oscillatory neural response in an afferent neuron evoked by that sinusoidal motion. The firing rate increases and decreases as the angular velocity of the head increases

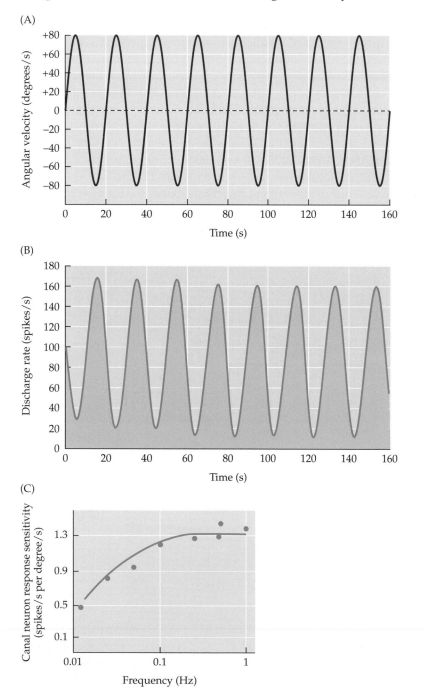

Figure 12.15 Sinusoidal motion trajectories. Stimulus (A) and response (B) for a single semicircular-canal afferent neuron at 0.05 Hz. Note that the neural firing rate increases and decreases nearly in tandem with the oscillating stimulus. (C) Repeating the sensitivity calculation at different stimulus frequencies shows that the sensitivity of the neuron changes with frequency. For this semicircular-canal neuron, the response sensitivity averaged about 1.3 spikes/second per degree/second for frequencies above 0.1 Hz. The response sensitivity decreases substantially for frequencies below about 0.1 Hz. (After Fernandez and Goldberg, 1971.)

or decreases; that is, the change in firing rate has the same frequency as the head velocity. We can calculate an estimate of afferent neuron sensitivity by taking the peak-to-peak amplitude of the change in the firing rate (from Figure 12.15B) and dividing it by the peak-to-peak velocity (from Figure 12.15A). The maximum firing rate is about 170 spikes/second; the minimum, about 10 spikes per second. So the peak-to-peak amplitude of the change in the firing rate is about 160 spikes/second. The peak-to-peak amplitude of the change in motion is 160 degrees/second (80 degrees/second to the left and 80 degrees/second to the right). The result is a sensitivity of about 1 spike/second per degree/second of motion. Experimentally, this process is often repeated at several different head rotation frequencies, yielding a number representing the neural sensitivity at each frequency tested.

Semicircular canals are not equally sensitive to all frequencies of rotation. **Figure 12.15C** shows a plot of response sensitivity as frequency is varied for a typical neuron innervating a semicircular canal; this plot indicates how the magnitude of the canal afferent firing rate changes with head rotation frequency. The data show that the amplitude of the canal afferent neuron's response is nearly constant for rotation frequencies above about 0.1 Hz. But when the frequency is less than about 0.1 Hz, the neuron responds less and less. For example, the response sensitivity at a frequency of 0.02 Hz (one cycle in 50 seconds) is only about 0.5 spike/second per degree/second—more than a 50% reduction from that observed at 1 Hz (one cycle in 1 second).

WHY SINE WAVE MOTIONS?   Now that we have described canal afferent responses to sinusoidal motion in some detail, you may wonder why anyone would care. We rarely experience perfect sinusoidal motion in the real world; we experience complex motions that vary with time. What do responses to sinusoidal motion at different frequencies tell us about how we sense motion?

One answer is that, although "pure" sine wave motions may be rare in the real world, patterns of oscillatory motions that have a predominant frequency are quite common: think again of shaking your head to say "no" or nodding your head to say "yes." More generally, **Fourier analysis** tells us that any complex motion can be broken down into some number of single-frequency components. Therefore, if we know responses to single frequencies, we know a good deal about responses to more complex motion.

> **FURTHER DISCUSSION** of Fourier analysis in vision can be found in Chapter 3 on page 70.

Otolith Organs

As we mentioned earlier, the sensing of gravity and linear acceleration relies on two structures in each ear called the otolith organs: the **utricle** (or utriculus) and the **saccule** (or sacculus). Each of these organs consists of a small, oval-shaped, fluid-filled sac that is about 3 mm long in the longest direction and includes an area called the **macula** (plural *maculae*), which is where actual sensory transduction occurs (**Figure 12.16A**). Each human utricular macula contains about 30,000 hair cells; each saccular macula, about 16,000. The utricular and saccular maculae are innervated by about 4000 neurons each. Each macula is roughly planar and is primarily sensitive to shear forces—forces parallel to the macular plane. Perpendicular forces have little influence on neural response. Small movements caused by parallel shear forces, due to gravity and/or linear acceleration, deflect the hair cells and produce changes in the firing rate of afferent neurons.

Fourier analysis   A mathematical procedure by which any signal—in this case motion trajectories as a function of time—can be separated into component sine waves at different frequencies. Combining these sine waves will reproduce the original motion trajectory.

utricle   One of the two otolith organs. A saclike structure that contains the utricular macula. Also called *utriculus*.

saccule   One of the two otolith organs. A saclike structure that contains the saccular macula. Also called *sacculus*.

macula   Any of the specialized detectors of linear acceleration and gravity found in each otolith organ.

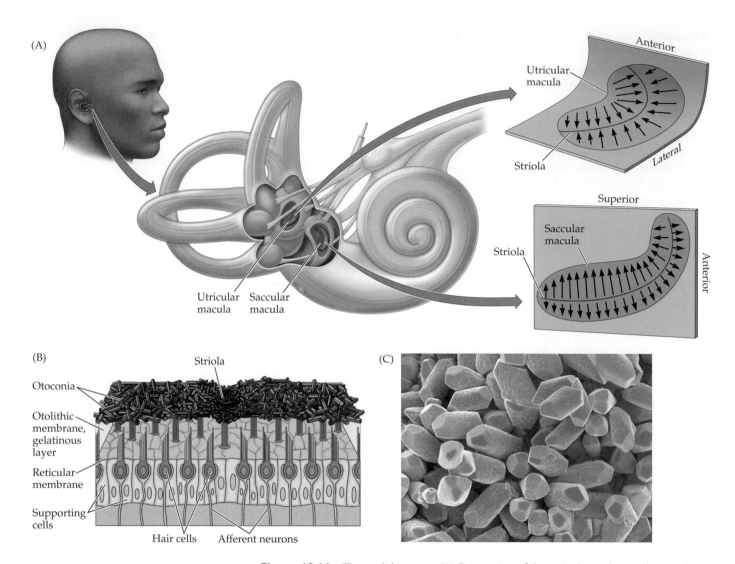

Figure 12.16 The otolith organs. (A) Orientation of the utricular and saccular maculae in the head. The saccules are oriented more or less vertically; the utricles, more or less horizontally. The striola is a structural landmark that divides each otolith organ. The tallest stereocilia point toward the striola in the utricular macula and away from it in the saccular macula, as the arrows indicate. Because hair cells depolarize if they deflect toward the tallest stereocilia and hyperpolarize if they deflect away from them, the arrows also show the movement direction that causes maximal neural excitation at each location on the maculae. Note that, given one utricle and one saccule on each side of the head, there is a continuous representation of all directions for sensing gravity and linear acceleration. (B) Cross section of the macula of an otolith organ. Hair bundles project into a gelatinous layer. (C) The otoconia shown in this scanning electron micrograph come from the utricular macula of a cat. Crystals are between 0.5 and 10 micrometers long.

otoconia Tiny calcium carbonate stones in the ear that provide inertial mass for the otolith organs, enabling them to sense gravity and linear acceleration.

The cilia of the otolith hair cells are encased in a gelatinous structure (**Figure 12.16B**) that contains calcium carbonate crystals called **otoconia** (singular *otoconium*) (**Figure 12.16C**). There are literally millions of these otoconia in the utricle and saccule. These small stones give the otolith organs their name: *oto* means "ear," and *lithos* means "stone" in Greek, so *otolith* translates as "ear stone." The otoconia are denser than the surrounding fluid. Like any dense object, they are pulled by both gravitational force and inertial force due to linear acceleration. The resulting displacement of the otoconia drags the gelatinous layer, thereby moving the hair cell stereocilia, leading to changes in the hair cell receptor potential, which in turn cause changes in the rate of action potentials in the afferent neurons.

HOW AMPLITUDE IS CODED IN THE OTOLITH ORGANS   As in the semicircular canals, one aspect of amplitude coding in the otolith organs can be found in the response of a single neuron or single hair cell. Recall that (1) hair cell receptor potentials increase when hair bundle tips move toward the largest stereocilia, (2) receptor potentials decrease for movements in the opposite direction (see Figure 12.10A), and (3) the direction of rotation is coded by excitation from a semicircular canal on one side and inhibition from the other side.

Similar mechanisms are at work in each otolith organ macula. Populations of hair cells on each macula have their stereocilia oriented in opposite directions (see Figure 12.16A). Both the utricle and the saccule include a central band called the striola (plural *striolae*). On opposite sides of the striola, hair cells are oriented in opposite directions. Remember that movement toward the tallest stereocilia excites the hair cells, and movement in the opposite direction inhibits the hair cells. Since the neuronal response arises from synapses to the hair cells, tilts (or linear accelerations) in opposite directions cause opposite changes in firing rate (**Figure 12.17**). So a tilt or an acceleration that maximally excites a hair cell and afferent neuron on one side of the striola will maximally inhibit a hair cell and afferent neuron on the opposite side.

Larger accelerations (or larger gravitational shear forces) move the otolith organs' otoconia more. This movement, in turn, leads to greater deflection of the hair cell bundles, which causes larger changes in the hair cell receptor potentials. The receptor potential evoked in a given hair cell is proportional to the component of gravity or linear acceleration that is aligned with the sensitive axis of that hair cell. Larger changes in the hair cell receptor potential lead to larger changes in the rate of action potentials sent to the brain via afferent neurons.

HOW DIRECTION IS CODED IN THE OTOLITH ORGANS
Direction coding in the otolith organs arises, in part, from their anatomical orientation. The plane of the utricular macula is horizontal; the plane of the saccular macula, vertical (see Figure 12.16A). The maculae are exquisitely sensitive to gravity and linear acceleration

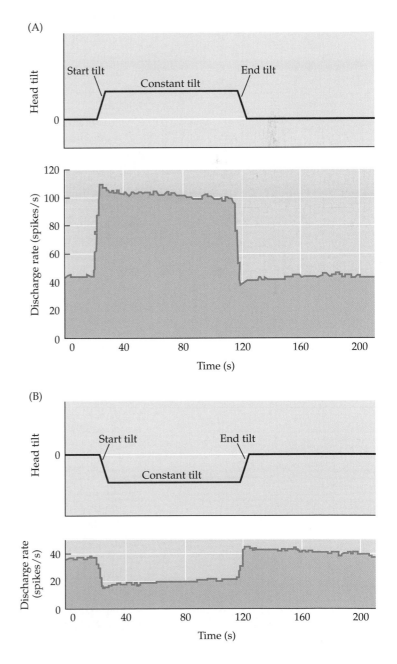

Figure 12.17 Activity of a vestibular neuron innervating the utricle (an otolith organ). (A) A change in head tilt is the stimulus (top). As shown in the histogram of the discharge rate (bottom), the neuron's activity increases in response to tilt in a particular direction. (B) The same neuron decreases its activity in response to tilt in the opposite direction. (After Goldberg and Fernandez, 1976.)

in the plane of the macula and insensitive to gravity and acceleration perpendicular to the macula. Therefore, with the head near upright, the utricle will be sensitive primarily to any Earth-horizontal linear acceleration, while the saccule will be sensitive to vertical linear acceleration.

The other component of direction coding arises from variations in the orientation of the hair cells (Figure 12.16A, far right). Different hair cells respond maximally to different movement directions, with the direction of maximal sensitivity varying systematically across the plane of each macula. For example, hair cells in one region of the utricular macula will be maximally sensitive to forward-backward acceleration, while cells in another region will be maximally sensitive to side-to-side linear acceleration. In between, cells will maximally respond to linear acceleration that has both forward-backward and side-to-side components.

Spatial Orientation Perception

Long after it was known that we see with our eyes and hear with our ears, the primary source for our perception of spatial orientation remained a mystery. In fact, in the eighteenth century, gross fluid shifts in the head were accepted as an explanation for the source of our sense of spatial orientation. Once it was established that this sense degrades when the vestibular system is damaged, it became clear that the vestibular system provides crucial information regarding spatial orientation. For example, when patients with vestibular loss are moved in the dark, they have a much more difficult time correctly perceiving their motion than do people with normal vestibular function.

Today, three different techniques are frequently used to investigate spatial orientation perception: thresholds, magnitude estimation, and matching. For a vestibular threshold study, a helpful question is, What is the minimum motion (the threshold) required for correctly perceiving the direction we are moved? Note that this is different from simply reporting *whether* we've moved, since vibration can provide a motion cue without informing us about the direction of the motion. The vestibular system tells us more than whether motion is present or not; it actually informs us of the direction of motion—for example, whether we moved to the left or to the right.

In a magnitude estimation study, participants might be asked to give verbal reports of how much they tilted, rotated, or translated, using physical units like the number of degrees they rotated. Alternatively, magnitude estimation may utilize arbitrary scaling. For example, participants may be trained to rotate a knob in proportion to their perceived velocity or provide a verbal indicator of their velocity on a scale of 1–10.

In a matching task, participants might be asked to align a visual line with perceived Earth-vertical (Which way is "down"?). In such a task, called the "subjective visual vertical" task, the investigator could produce a vestibular stimulus by tilting the participant. That participant would be provided with a visible line in otherwise dark surroundings and with the ability to rotate the line to the perceived Earth-vertical. Alternatively, haptic sensation, which you will learn more about in Chapter 13, could be utilized instead of vision. For this technique, participants might be asked to use their sense of limb position to align a bar that they hold—but cannot see—with perceived vertical.

FURTHER DISCUSSION of similar matching tasks in connection with the sense of touch can be found in Chapter 13 on pages 454–455.

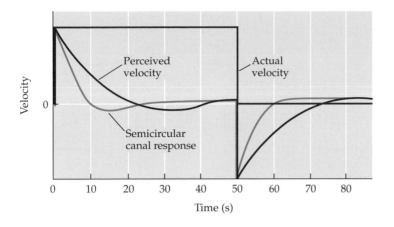

Figure 12.18 The red line on this graph shows the angular velocity of a person who began at rest with eyes closed, was suddenly rotated at a constant speed for 50 seconds, and then was abruptly returned to rest. Initially, the participant's estimate of angular velocity was accurate (purple line at time 0), but then the perceived velocity dropped to near 0 after nearly 30 seconds. When stopped, the participant perceived an abrupt velocity in the opposite direction, which mimicked the initial perception but in the opposite direction. For comparison, we show a representation of the canal response in blue, similar to that shown in Figure 12.14. Note the faster return to baseline for the canal response. (After Young, 1984.)

Rotation Perception

If you are spun on a barstool in the dark at a nearly constant velocity, you will initially perceive an angular velocity that is roughly the same as the actual rotation. However, if the constant-velocity rotation lasts more than a second or two, you will perceive that you are slowing down (**Figure 12.18**). If the constant-velocity rotation continues for more than 30 seconds or so, you will perceive that you are no longer rotating.

This description may remind you of the way the response of the semicircular canals decays during constant-velocity rotation (see Figure 12.14), and it is another example of how the vestibular system is attuned to *changes* in motion. Interestingly, though, the time course of the perceptual decay is more gradual than that of the semicircular-canal signal sent to the brain. This effect is sometimes called **velocity storage** because the perception of rotation persists after the afferent signal from the semicircular canals has dissipated. The velocity storage phenomenon is interesting and important because it shows that the brain has improved on the incoming sensory information to yield a rotation perception that—while far from perfect—is closer to the actual rotation than if the perception simply followed the time course of the semicircular-canal afferent signal (Bertolini et al., 2011).

Later, if you are abruptly brought to a stop following extended rotation, you will perceive an angular velocity opposite the one you experienced while rotating (see Figure 12.18). This rotation illusion is one that many of us played with as children when we would spin ourselves for a while and then suddenly stop spinning and try to stand or walk. (And some amusement park junkies still play with this illusion, as you'll see at the end of this chapter!) The **dizziness** and **imbalance** that we experienced when we stopped rotating were due to an illusion of self-rotation caused by the semicircular-canal response. (You can view examples of this by searching YouTube for "people spinning and falling".)

One can develop an intuitive understanding of the reason for this illusion by considering the analogy of riding in a car. When you're riding at a constant velocity, you and the car are moving together. But when the car suddenly stops, you are thrown forward because you have momentum and keep moving even though the car has stopped. When you're rotating at a constant velocity, there is little or no hair cell deflection, because the endolymph and cupula are moving together. When the rotation is suddenly halted, however, the cupula stops moving quickly but the endolymph has momentum and tends to keep moving. The hair cells are therefore deflected, and the direction of the hair cell response is opposite the one measured when the constant-velocity rotation began.

velocity storage Prolongation of a rotational response by the brain beyond the duration of the rotational signal provided to the brain by the semicircular canals; typically yielding responses that are nearer the actual rotational motion than the signal provided by the canals.

dizziness A commonly used lay term that nonspecifically indicates any form of perceived spatial disorientation, with or without instability.

imbalance Lack of balance; unsteadiness; nearly falling over.

Figure 12.19 Mean velocity threshold as a function of frequency for seven participants. Threshold velocity was the peak velocity achieved during a single cycle of sinusoidal acceleration at which participants correctly recognized the direction of motion most of the time. The plotted curve shows a model fit to the data. The inset shows the angular acceleration, angular velocity, and angular displacement for a single cycle of sinusoidal acceleration at 0.5 Hz. For the example shown, the peak magnitude of the acceleration is 1.57 degrees/second^2, the peak velocity is 1 degree/second, and the peak displacement is 1 degree. (After Grabherr et al., 2008.)

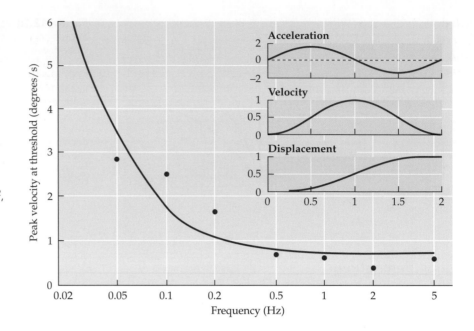

How sensitive are we to rotation? Direction recognition thresholds for yaw rotation have been measured for rotational motion frequencies ranging from 0.05 Hz (one back-and-forth cycle of yaw acceleration in 20 seconds) to 5 Hz (five back-and-forth cycles of yaw acceleration in 1 second). For frequencies above 1 Hz (one back-and-forth acceleration cycle in 1 second), direction recognition thresholds are roughly constant; your head has to be moving at a speed of just a little below 1 degree per second, which at 5 Hz corresponds to a head angular displacement of just 0.1 degree or just 0.02 of a minute on a clockface! Clearly, we are very sensitive to rotation. For frequencies below 0.5 Hz (one back-and-forth oscillation in 2 seconds), thresholds increase with decreasing frequency (**Figure 12.19**). The important point here is to recognize that rotation thresholds vary as the frequency of the angular acceleration stimulus varies. (Recall that hearing thresholds also changed with frequency [see Figure 9.22], though the causes of the variations with frequency are different for the two modalities.)

Translation Perception

When participants are passively translated short distances while seated in a chair in the dark and then asked, while still seated in the chair, to use a joystick to actively move the chair to reproduce the distance that they had been passively translated, they do so accurately. But even though not asked to do so, they also reproduce the *velocity* of the passive-motion trajectory (Berthoz et al., 1995). The unrequested replication of velocity suggests that the brain remembers and replicates the velocity trajectory. Earlier we said that the otolith organs transduce linear acceleration, which is the change in linear velocity. Therefore, replication of the velocity trajectory means that the brain also seems to **mathematically integrate** the acceleration signal provided by the otolith organs to yield a perception of linear velocity. This apparent calculation suggests that while otolith organs sense linear acceleration, our brains turn this information into a perception of linear velocity.

As for yaw rotation, direction recognition thresholds for side-to-side (y-axis) translation have been measured for motion frequencies ranging from 0.05 Hz (one back-and-forth cycle of acceleration in 20 seconds) to 5 Hz (five back-and-forth cycles of acceleration in 1 second). For frequencies above 1 Hz (one back-and-

mathematical integration Computing an integral—one of the two main operations in calculus (the other, the inverse operation, is differentiation). Velocity is the integral of acceleration. Change of position is the integral of velocity.

forth cycle in 1 second), direction recognition thresholds are roughly constant. To sense translation direction correctly, your head has to be moving at least at a speed of 5.0 mm per second, which at 5 Hz corresponds to a head angular displacement of just 0.5 mm! Clearly, we are also very sensitive to translation. As for yaw rotation, for frequencies below 0.5 Hz (one back-and-forth oscillation in 2 seconds), thresholds increase with decreasing frequency (Valko et al., 2012).

Tilt Perception

How well do we perceive our tilt when we are slanted away from true Earth-vertical? For tilt angles less than 90 degrees—that is, body orientations between standing up (0 degrees) and lying down (90 degrees)—we are pretty good, according to a variety of magnitude estimation techniques. Observers produce reliable and consistent answers if they indicate their perceived tilt verbally or if they align a handheld probe with perceived vertical (**Figure 12.20**).

We are not perfect, though. Some consistent errors appear, especially in the subjective visual vertical task described near the beginning of the "Spatial

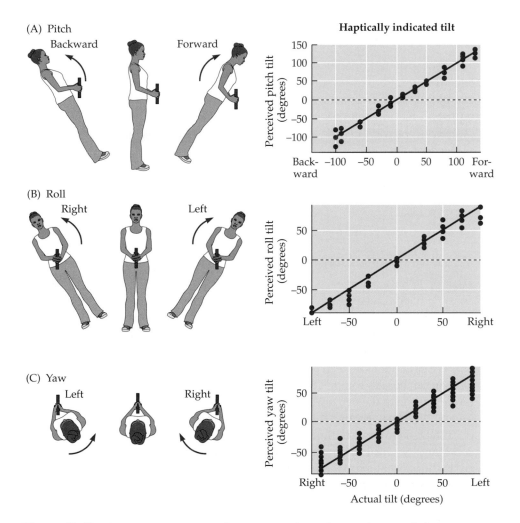

Figure 12.20 Participants are generally pretty good at indicating how much they are tilted. Data points show tilt perception provided by participants using a handheld haptic indicator (shown schematically at left) for static pitch (A), roll (B), and yaw (C) tilts. Perceived tilt roughly reflects the actual tilt (solid lines) for all three tilt directions. (After Bortolami et al., 2006.)

Orientation Perception" section of this chapter. Back in 1861, Hermann Rudolf Aubert found that when he roll-tilted his head to the left or right while looking at a vertical streak of light, the vertical line appeared to tilt in the direction opposite his head tilt. For tilt angles less than 90 degrees, the illusory tilt error is typically about 10 degrees, but the apparent tilt of the visual line can be as large as 45 degrees when the head is tilted 135 degrees. You can investigate this illusion in a completely dark room by leaving the door open just a crack—just enough to see a line of light in the doorway without illuminating the room at all—while you hold your head in a tilted position. Does the line appear to tilt when your head is tilted? Does it move in the direction of your tilted head or in the opposite direction?

Thresholds for recognizing the direction of tilt show that normal individuals correctly report the direction of a static tilt when tilted about 1 degree off vertical in the dark. This sensitivity serves our ability to stand upright, because the farther we are tilted from upright, the more difficult standing up is. For example, the amount of muscular effort required to maintain posture roughly doubles if we are tilted 2 degrees instead of 1 degree, so just imagine the effort of trying to stand tilted 20 degrees away from upright!

Sensory Integration

The senses do not operate independently. Instead, the brain combines signals from different sensory systems via neural processes of **sensory integration**. For example, visual cues influence sound localization—an effect used by ventriloquists. Vestibular signals combine with information from numerous sensory systems to provide us with an understanding of the position and movements of the head and body.

> **FURTHER DISCUSSION** of a remarkable example of sensory integration—the McGurk effect on speech perception—can be found in Chapter 11 on page 365.

Visual-Vestibular Integration

Most of us have experienced illusions of self-motion caused by moving visual cues. Perhaps you've perceived self-motion while watching an IMAX movie. Or perhaps you've felt as if you were moving backward when you were stationary but the car (or train or bus) next to you began to move forward. Or perhaps you felt unsteady when standing on a bridge looking at the water flowing beneath. All of these situations can lead to perceptions of illusory self-motion called **vection**. Vection can be very compelling. For example, drivers stopped in traffic often press harder on the brake pedal when they perceive that they and their stationary car are moving, even though it is the cars around them that are moving.

To consider how vection contributes to spatial orientation, imagine a person standing upright while viewing the inside of a sphere rotating about an Earth-horizontal axis (**Figure 12.21A**). At first, subjective perceptions match reality; humans initially perceive that they are stationary and that the sphere is rotating. But if they continue to observe the rotating visual display for 10 seconds or so, they usually begin to perceive that they're rotating in the direction opposite the sphere rotation (**Figure 12.21B**). This illusory rotational vection demonstrates the crucial contributions of vision to our sense of self-rotation. In fact, signals related to vision converge with the semicircular-canal signals in the vestibular nuclei, which is the first place in the brain that vestibular information reaches.

sensory integration The process of combining different sensory signals. Typically, combining several signals yields more accurate and/or more precise information than can be obtained from individual sensory signals. This is *not* the mathematical process of integration learned in calculus (e.g., the integral of acceleration is velocity).

vection An illusory sense of self-motion caused by moving visual cues when one is not, in fact, actually moving.

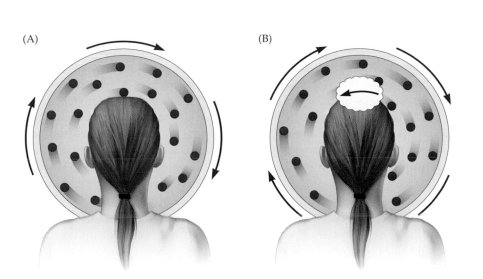
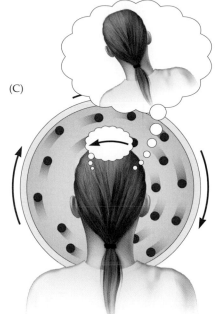

(A) (B) (C)

Figure 12.21 Rotational vection. An individual views a visual display rotating in roll. For demonstration purposes, the visual display is shown here as transparent. (A) Initially, the individual correctly senses that she is stationary and the visual display is rotating. (B) The individual begins to perceive vection, a sense of self-rotation in the direction opposite the rotation of the visual display. (C) Roll vection is often accompanied by an illusion of roll tilt that is induced by the perceived roll rotation. The direction of the perceived tilt is consistent with the tilt direction that would occur if the individual were truly rotating in roll. (After Young, Shelhamer, and Modestino, 1986.)

(**Web Essay 12.2: Canal-Otolith Integration** discusses a similar interaction of signals from the semicircular canals and otolith organs.)

Paradoxically, individuals experiencing such rotational vection almost never report that they are tumbling head over heels as they would if they truly were rotating to the extent that they perceive. In fact, individuals typically experience a simultaneous illusory sensation of tilt that gradually builds up to a relatively constant level (**Figure 12.21C**). These perceptions—experienced as a sensation of motion without getting anywhere—are contradictory, since we cannot be rotating relative to gravity (as suggested by the visual cues) while also maintaining a constant orientation with respect to gravity (as indicated by the otolith organs). In addition to exemplifying sensory integration, this sensation of motion without getting anywhere demonstrates that our sense of spatial orientation is not constrained to combinations of motion and orientation that are physically possible.

In this example, the role played by the vestibular system is to put the brakes on visually induced vection. Individuals suffering from severe vestibular damage generally report greater vection than do normal individuals. Astronauts experiencing rotational vection in space—in the absence of gravitational signals—report a head-over-heels tumbling sensation that is absent on Earth. These findings are explained by the fact that neither the individuals with vestibular damage nor the astronauts receive normal gravitational cues from the otolith organs to contradict their visual rotational cues. (**Web Essay 12.3: Space Motion Sickness** discusses another aspect of spaceflight that many astronauts experience.) Since illusory motion is greater when there are no otolith cues to contradict the visual cues, we can infer that, under normal circumstances, information from the vestibular system is combined with visual information to yield a "consensus" about our sense of spatial orientation.

Active Sensing

Our sensory systems are simultaneously activated as the result of our own actions and changes in the external world. Indeed, most of our sensory experiences are gained by active exploration of the world resulting from locomotion, eye movements, touching, and other interactive activities. Our brain's ability to distinguish sensory events that are self-generated, sometimes called **sensory reafference**, from those that arise externally, sometimes called **sensory exafference**, is essential for perceptual stability and accurate motor control. For example, when our eyes move, the image of the world moves across our retinas; yet we do not perceive the image of the world as moving.

In order to avoid responding to sensory inputs that arise from self-generated actions, the sensory system needs to know what the motor system has done. Based on their observations, Von Holst and Mittelstaedt (1950) proposed the

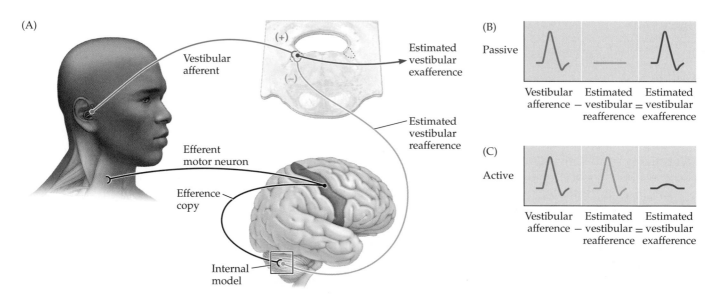

sensory reafference   Change in afference caused by self-generated activity. For the vestibular system, vestibular afference evoked by an active self-generated head motion would yield sensory reafference.

sensory exafference   Change in afference caused by external stimuli. For the vestibular system, vestibular afference evoked by passive head motion would yield sensory exafference.

Figure 12.22   Simplified representation of the active vestibular sensing network. (A) When a command is sent to the neck muscle to rotate the head via efferent motor neurons, a copy of those motor command signals—called an efference copy—is sent in parallel to the brain. This signal is processed by a neural network, called an internal model, that predicts the expected vestibular afference due to the self-generated motion, which is called estimated vestibular reafference. This estimated reafference is subtracted from the signals from the vestibular afferent neurons to yield estimated vestibular exafference, the component of the afferent signal that is not due to self-generated motion. (B) When the head undergoes passive rotation, the head rotation is accurately encoded by the vestibular afference (blue). No neck motor command is generated during passive rotation, so the passive expected vestibular reafference signal is flat, corresponding to no self-generated motion. The difference between these yields estimated vestibular exafference, which, for passive motion, is identical to the vestibular afferent signal. (C) When the head is actively rotated, the head rotation is accurately encoded by the vestibular afference. In this case, a neck motor command is generated to evoke the passive rotation, so a motor command is sent to the neck muscles and a copy is sent to an internal model that predicts the vestibular afference anticipated for the active head rotation being generated. For some vestibular nuclei neurons, the difference between the vestibular afference and the estimated reafference yields estimated exafference, which is nearly flat. (B, C after Cullen, 2011.)

principle of reafference. In today's version of this principle (**Figure 12.22A**), a copy of motor commands, called an efference copy, is generated to help the brain predict the expected sensory results of motor commands. This predicted sensory activity is called sensory reafference, and the brain's estimate of sensory reafference is subtracted from the sensory afferent signal to eliminate reafferent information. In certain model systems, including the electrosensory systems of electric fish, self-generated sensory information is selectively suppressed at the level of afferent fibers.

Signals from the vestibular afferent neurons do not distinguish between active and passive head movements; vestibular afferent neurons respond identically to self-generated and externally applied self-motion (**Figure 12.22B, C**). But differential processing of vestibular signals is evident at the next stage of processing in the vestibular nuclei. The modulation of some vestibular nuclei neurons, which receive direct inputs from the vestibular afferents, is dramatically attenuated in response to vestibular inputs that result from self-generated movements. The dramatic difference between the responses of these vestibular nuclei neurons demonstrates a clear example of active sensing, since this brain signal directly depends upon whether the motion is self-generated (active) or not (passive). We emphasize that this distinction between self-generated neural activity and externally generated neural activity arises at the first central synapse in the vestibular nuclei for those vestibular pathways that contribute to balance and perception. This shows that this distinction occurs very early in the processing of some vestibular information, which suggests that the ability to distinguish between self-generated and externally generated neural activity is fundamental.

Reflexive Vestibular Responses

As mentioned earlier, some crucial contributions of the vestibular system are automatic, or reflexive, doing their work outside of conscious awareness. For example, there is a set of automatic responses called vestibulo-ocular reflexes—VORs for short. We started the chapter with one of these. Remember looking at your finger as you shook your head? (If not, now might be a good time to go back and try this demonstration again; see Figure 12.1.) This task illustrates how the VOR contributes to visual stability by counterrotating the eyes in the head during head motion sensed by the vestibular system.

There is also a set of vestibulo-autonomic reflexes that contribute to autonomic responses like those that regulate blood pressure and help maintain adequate blood flow to the brain. Other vestibulo-autonomic reflexes lead to motion sickness. Finally, vestibulo-spinal reflexes contribute to postural control via the **balance system**. To demonstrate vestibular contributions to balance, try standing on one foot with your eyes closed. (When you start to feel unsteady, immediately open your eyes and put both feet on the ground!) Most healthy people with a normal balance system—including normal vestibular function—can do this for at least 5 seconds and often much longer. Patients without vestibular function, however, cannot stand on one foot in the dark for more than an instant.

Vestibulo-Ocular Responses

The angular VOR, the eye rotation that helps compensate for angular rotations of the head, is a robust reflex. In fact, this reflex is so robust that it is a standard part of clinical examinations of vestibular function. Furthermore, the VOR is certainly among the best-studied reflexes, dating as far back as the late 1700s with reports by William Charles Wells (1792).

balance system The sensory systems, neural processes, and muscles that contribute to postural control. Specific components include the vestibular organs, kinesthesis, vestibulo-spinal pathways, skeletal bones, and postural control muscles. Because of the vestibular system's crucial contributions to balance, some even informally refer to the vestibular system as the "balance system" and the vestibular organs as the "balance organs." But the balance system is much more than just the vestibular system, and the vestibular system contributes to much more than just balance.

The angular VOR is the compensatory eye rotation evoked by the semicircular canals when they sense head rotation. For example, when the head rotates (yaws) to the left, the reflex pathways cause the eyes to rotate to the right with respect to the head, to compensate—at least in part—for the head turn. When observing the eyes, we see this eye rotation as movement of the pupils to the right. Of course, since the eyeball is roughly a spherical ball, it is really rotating in the eye socket, not moving laterally.

Recall that six ocular muscles—called oculomotor muscles—rotate the eyeball (see Figure 8.16). Muscles can only pull; they cannot push. Muscles are paired to pull in opposite directions and are therefore called agonist-antagonist muscle pairs. For example, moving the left eye horizontally requires a coordination of the lateral rectus that pulls the eye to the left and the medial rectus that pulls the eye to the right. To make an eye movement to the right, the lateral rectus is inhibited and thus relaxes its pull, while the medial rectus is excited and thus increases its pull. The six oculomotor muscles are organized in three pairs that rotate the eye in each of three directions. (See **Web Activity 12.3: Observing Torsional Eye Movement.**) Eye movements result from a coordinated inhibition and excitation of the eye muscles.

When the VOR is working effectively, it actively rotates the eyes in the head such that the rotation of the eyes roughly compensates for the rotation of the head in space. **Figure 12.23** demonstrates this with a simple example. In Figure 12.23A, the eyes rotate with the head; they do not counterrotate in the head. In Figure 12.23B, the eyes counterrotate in the head, which helps stabilize the visual field on the retina. If the eyes do not counterrotate in the head, the retinal image tends to blur during head rotation. (Remember how your fingers blurred when you rapidly moved them back and forth?) The counterrotation of the eye in the head helps reduce this blur by reducing the motion of the image of an object across the retina. Note that because of eye counterrotation, the actual rotation of the eyes with respect to the external world is much less than that of the head.

 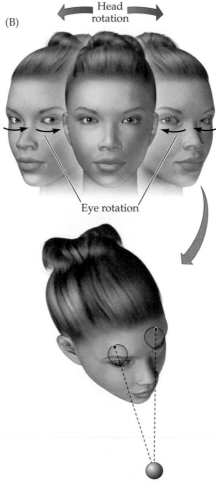

Figure 12.23 Contribution of the angular VOR to visual stability. (A) When the eyes do not counterrotate, the image of the object moves across the retina during head rotation, causing blurred vision. (B) When the eyes counterrotate during head rotation—with the amount of eye rotation roughly equal to the amount of head rotation—the image of an object can remain stationary on the retina even during head rotation. Because the eyes counterrotate in the head in (B) but not in (A), they continue to look at you in (B) but not in (A). This effect demonstrates how the angular VOR contributes to visual acuity, by helping to keep object images stationary on the retina, thereby reducing blurring.

The most direct neural path for the VORs consists of an arc of three neurons that yields reflexive eye responses with a latency of less than 10 milliseconds between the start of head motion and the eye movement. (That is really fast. Try doing anything else in less than 10 milliseconds!) The first neurons in the arc are the afferent neurons (bottom right in **Figure 12.24**); these neurons transmit

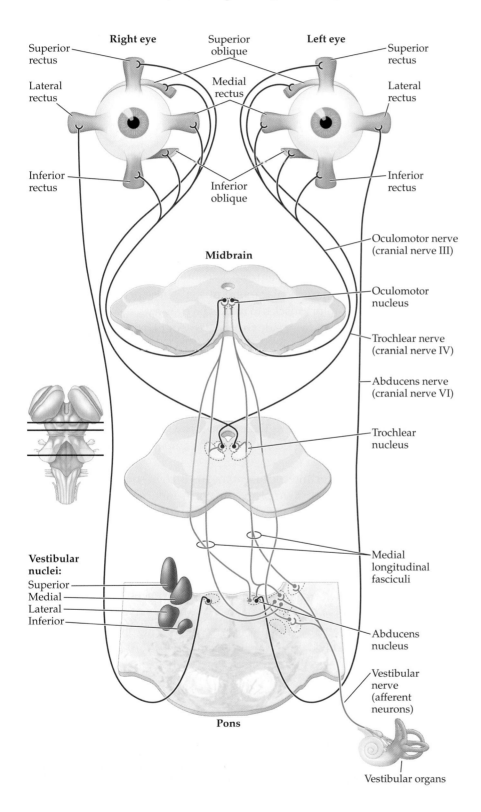

Figure 12.24 Neural pathways for the three-neuron arc of the angular VOR. Each type of neuron is depicted using a different color. Each of the vestibular afferent neurons (blue)—one branch for each of the three canals—projects to one of three vestibular nuclei: superior, medial, or lateral. Neurons that connect afferent to efferent neurons, called interneurons (green), project from the vestibular nuclei to the three ocular motor nuclei: abducens, trochlear, and oculomotor. (Only the *oculomotor* nucleus, which is one of the three *ocular motor* nuclei, is shown.) The six efferent oculomotor neurons (red) project from these three ocular motor nuclei to the six oculomotor muscles: inferior oblique, superior oblique, inferior rectus, superior rectus, lateral rectus, and medial rectus. Recall that you previously were introduced to the oculomotor muscles in Figure 8.16.

Figure 12.25 VOR responses in the dark at three frequencies. The stimulus (sinusoidal head rotation; top row) is shown for (A) 0.01 Hz, (B) 0.05 Hz, and (C) 1.0 Hz. Sinusoidal motion evokes an oscillatory VOR (bottom row), which opposes the head rotation such that head rotations to the right are accompanied by eye rotations to the left. If the VOR were perfect, it would have the same peak amplitude (labeled "A" in the figure) as the head rotation, meaning that the eye rotated at the same velocity as the head rotation. However, the peak compensatory eye velocity shown for 0.05 and 1.0 Hz in the dark is about 70% of the peak head velocity. We would say that this has a gain of about 0.7, where gain is a dimensionless ratio of the eye velocity divided by the head velocity. A gain of 0 would indicate that the eyes did not rotate with respect to the head, as in Figure 12.23A. A gain of 1 would indicate that the eyes were counterrotating with the same amplitude as the head motion, as suggested by Figure 12.23B. The remaining 30% is usually made up by visual contributions. At lower frequencies, the VOR is smaller; for example, at 0.01 Hz it is only about 50% of the peak head velocity (a gain of about 0.5).

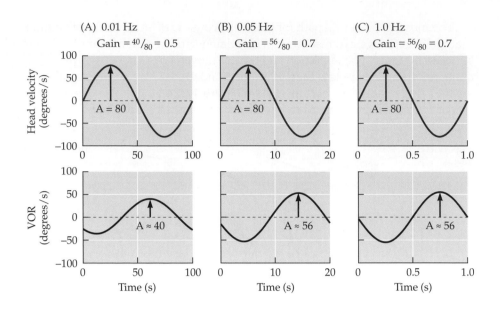

information from the vestibular periphery to the vestibular nuclei. There, the afferent neurons synapse on interneurons. The interneurons synapse on efferent oculomotor neurons in the ocular motor nuclei. These oculomotor neurons synapse with the oculomotor muscles to rotate the eyes with respect to the head.

As you rotate your head from side to side, the angular VOR has properties similar to the characteristics that were discussed earlier for the semicircular canals, as illustrated in **Figures 12.25** and **12.26**. The VOR demonstrates a constant, relatively high amplitude at high frequencies, but it gets smaller and smaller as the frequency drops below about 0.05 Hz (Figure 12.25). Though the frequency characteristics of the VOR and canal afferents are qualitatively similar, there is an interesting difference. As Figure 12.26 shows, the response of canal afferent neurons declines for frequencies below 0.2 Hz. In comparison, the VOR declines for frequencies below 0.05 Hz.

That difference is interesting because it means that, in some sense, the VOR response is more accurate than a simple reading of its input signal would provide. This effect is analogous to what we saw earlier for rotation perception (see Figure 12.18) and is called velocity storage. It shows that the brain is not simply a relay station that passes sensory information to the muscles that yield the reflexive action. Instead, the brain helps shape the reflexes to be as effective as possible, given the available sensory information. In this specific case, central processing increases the effective VOR frequency range (Raphan, Matsuo, and Cohen, 1977; Robinson, 1977; Merfeld et al., 1993).

We also have a translational VOR that is evoked when the otolith organs sense head translation, especially high-frequency head translation. This translational VOR helps us keep our eyes pointed at an object when the head translates in one direction or the other.

Vestibulo-Autonomic Responses

The vestibular system also makes contributions to responses of the **autonomic nervous system**. Perhaps the most vivid of these responses is motion sickness, a vestibulo-autonomic ordeal that many of us wish we had never experienced. Severe symptoms of motion sickness include nausea and vomiting. Motion

autonomic nervous system The part of the nervous system that is responsible for regulating many involuntary actions and that innervates glands, heart, digestive system, etc.

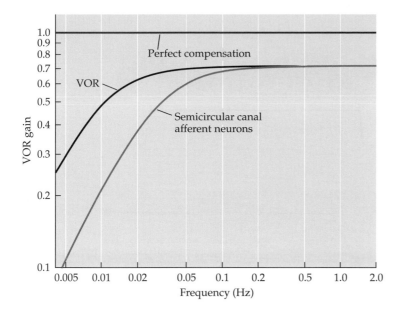

Figure 12.26 Dynamics of the VOR (black curve) are such that the response has a nearly constant gain—roughly a gain of 0.7, as calculated in Figure 12.25—at frequencies between about 0.05 and 2.0 Hz. In fact, while not shown in this figure, the VOR gain remains nearly constant for frequencies up to 25–30 Hz (Huterer and Cullen, 2002; R. Ramachandran and Lisberger, 2005). Perfect compensation—having a gain of 1—is shown in red. See Figure 12.25 for examples of how this gain is calculated at each frequency. Below 0.05 Hz, the gain of the VOR decreases. For comparison, the normalized frequency response of semicircular-canal neurons that we saw in Figure 12.15 is indicated by the green curve. Since the green curve represents the information provided to the brain and the black line represents the VOR response at different frequencies, the difference between the black and green curves represents neural compensation performed by the brain.

sickness typically results when there is a disagreement between the motion and orientation signals provided by the semicircular canals, otolith organs, and vision (Oman, 1990; Reason and Brand, 1975). For example, if you are below deck on a boat, your vestibular system will accurately record the motion of the boat while vision suggests no relative motion of the world, since you and the boat are moving together.

What is this response good for? One of several hypotheses is that it is a defense against some classes of poisons (M. Treisman, 1977). If you have been poisoned, you want to get rid of the poison before it gets rid of you. But how do you know if you have been poisoned? If the poison is a neurotoxin, disruption of the sensory systems is a good hint. How do you know that your senses have been disrupted? One way is to check whether senses that normally agree with one another have stopped doing so. Normally, if you move, your visual system and your vestibular system both register that fact. If the vestibular system says one thing and the visual system says another, the brain may decide that it is time to rid the body of a possible cause of the disagreement. This response could be a lifesaver if you just ate a bad mushroom. It is less desirable when you have to pull out the motion sickness bag during turbulence at 35,000 feet.

Other vestibulo-autonomic responses are less spectacular and generally take the form of compensatory contributions (Yates et al., 2014). For example, consider the problem of regulating blood pressure. The heart pumps blood throughout the body, but maintaining oxygenation of the brain via blood flow is especially critical because you will black out in just a few seconds if your brain does not receive adequate oxygen. Gravity pulls blood downward, so in the normal upright posture your heart has to work to maintain blood flow to the brain. When you're lying down, it takes much less work to pump blood to the brain. Now suppose you rapidly stand up. The cardiovascular system has to suddenly change the regulation of blood flow to maintain adequate oxygen supply to the brain. If these mechanisms fail, you will experience light-headedness or, in extreme cases, blackout. By informing the relevant parts of the autonomic nervous system about the position and motion of the head, the vestibular system contributes to the regulation of blood flow to the brain. As a result, one consequence of destructive

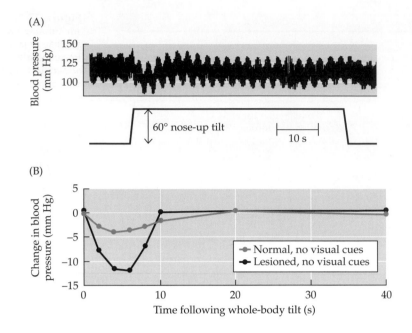

Figure 12.27 Vestibular influences on blood pressure. (A) The trace represents blood pressure in the head versus time in response to a nose-up tilt in an individual with a lesioned vestibular system. In the absence of vestibular contributions, a transient decrease in blood pressure can be observed immediately after the tilt. (B) Change in blood pressure is much greater for the individual without a functional vestibular system (lesioned) than for the individual with a normal vestibular system, demonstrating that the vestibular system helps maintain more constant blood pressure during whole-body tilts. (After Yates and Miller, 1998.)

lesions of the vestibular organs is that blood pressure regulation during whole-body tilts becomes much less stable (**Figure 12.27**).

Vestibulo-Spinal Responses

In the early 1800s, the French physiologist Jean Pierre Flourens reported abnormal head movements in pigeons after he had cut individual semicircular canals. The head movements he reported were in the plane of the lesioned canal. These studies demonstrated the presence of what we today consider to be the vestibular influences on posture control, and they initiated the formal study of vestibular influences on balance.

Vestibular reflexes keep us from falling over. Without vestibulo-spinal reflexes our balance (**Figure 12.28**) would be severely degraded. We would be unable to stand in the dark. Part of the reason is that when we stand, we are inherently unstable. As two-legged creatures, we can be thought of as being composed of a series of inverted pendulums—pendulums in which the mass is above the pivot point. A pencil or broom balanced on your palm demonstrates a simple inverted pendulum. One of these challenging tasks can be mastered with practice, but imagine trying to stabilize a series of at least four brooms or pencils on top of one another. At its essence, this is the task faced by our balance system, which works to keep the head, torso, thighs, and calves—each an inverted pendulum—upright with respect to gravity.

A thorough discussion of the dynamics of the entire posture control system is beyond the scope of this book. To study the postural system experimentally, investigators have simplified the dynamics by strapping the head and body to

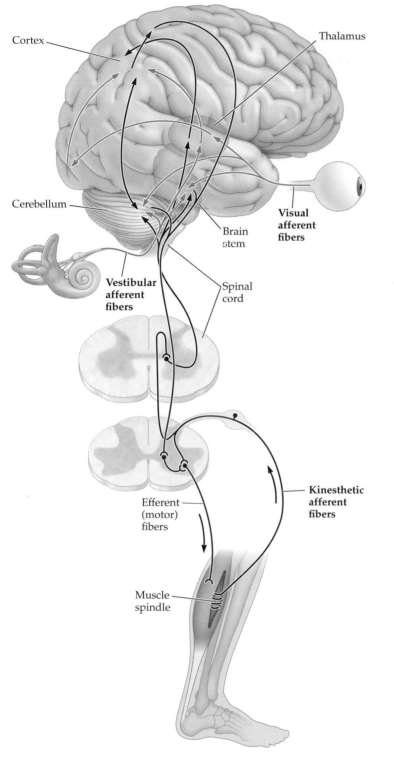

Figure 12.28 The balance system, illustrated here, is often confused with the vestibular system. Our kinesthetic, vestibular, and visual senses all make fundamental contributions to balance. Patients without kinesthesia typically cannot stand. If you ever tried to walk after spinning in circles, you probably recognized the contributions of the vestibular system to balance. And Figure 12.21 illustrated how visual cues can lead to tilt illusions, which contribute to imbalance that can lead to falls. These kinesthetic (purple), vestibular (blue), and visual (orange) sensory cues are then transmitted via the brain stem, cerebellum, thalamus, and cortex, eventually yielding motor signals (red) that descend via the spinal cord to our postural muscles. Our balance system is called a closed-loop system because sensory signals contribute to muscle signals, which yield movements that are sensed by the sensory systems, which contribute to muscle signals … (ad infinitum). To help minimize any confusion between the balance system and the vestibular system, perhaps now is a good time to refer back to Figure 12.2, which shows that the vestibular system contributes to balance and that balance is one of four fundamental contributions of the vestibular system.

a rigid board that converts the complex multijoint body into a single inverted pendulum pitching forward and backward about the ankle joint (**Figure 12.29**). When the foot plate that the participant stands on is gently rocked forward and backward while the participant's eyes are closed, normal participants demonstrate body sway that is not substantially greater than the amplitude of the applied

Figure 12.29 The contributions of the vestibular system to balance are demonstrated by the comparison of postural responses of individuals with normal vestibular function to responses of individuals suffering severe bilateral vestibular loss. Participants were asked to maintain themselves upright in the presence of small, angular displacements of their feet that were designed to challenge their balance control. For the purposes of illustration, a platform tilt of 20 degrees is shown; in typical experiments the tilt would be much smaller (otherwise the participants might fall off!). (A) The values on the y-axis (the gain) represent the amplitude of the participant's response divided by the amplitude of displacement. (*Gain* in this context is defined as tilt of the participant divided by tilt of the platform.) (B) If the participant did the task perfectly, the result would be a gain of 0 (0/θ). If the participant remained perpendicular to the platform, the gain would be 1 (θ/θ). If the participant tilted more than the platform, the gain would be greater than 1. The response gains for normal individuals were always near or below 1. On the other hand, individuals with vestibular loss had response gains that often exceeded 1, indicating that their body tilt exceeded the platform tilt disturbance. Individuals with vestibular loss exhibited much greater sway than normal individuals, clearly demonstrating the fundamental contributions of the vestibular system to balance control. (After Peterka, 2002.)

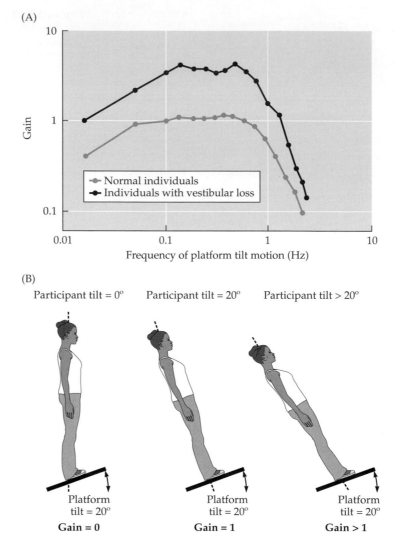

(A)

Gain

Frequency of platform tilt motion (Hz)

Normal individuals
Individuals with vestibular loss

(B)

Participant tilt = 0°   Participant tilt = 20°   Participant tilt > 20°

Platform tilt = 20°   Platform tilt = 20°   Platform tilt = 20°

Gain = 0   **Gain = 1**   **Gain > 1**

spatial disorientation Any impairment of spatial orientation. More specifically, any impairment of our sense of linear motion, angular motion, or tilt.

rocking movement, shown in Figure 12.29A as a gain of less than or equal to 1. This indicates that the vestibular system is helping to compensate for the applied-movement disturbance. The vestibular system measures the movement of the head and sends commands to the postural control system that help reduce the amount of body sway. In contrast, patients with severe vestibular loss demonstrate body sway that exceeds the amplitude of the disturbance, as seen by the gain in Figure 12.29A exceeding 1 across a broad range of frequencies. This difference between postural responses of people with normal vestibular function and those of patients with vestibular loss is a clear indication of the importance of the vestibular system to balance and posture control. A little later in the chapter, we'll discuss mal de debarquement syndrome, an unusual disorder that causes imbalance and/or **spatial disorientation**.

The vestibulo-spinal response can be thought of as a whole family of reflexes (**Figure 12.30**). In the vestibular nuclei, the primary afferent neurons synapse on descending interneurons that carry information through the lateral and medial vestibulo-spinal tracts. How far these neurons carry information down the spinal cord depends on their contribution to the balance system. If the interneuron synapses onto a neuron that controls a leg muscle, the information is transmitted

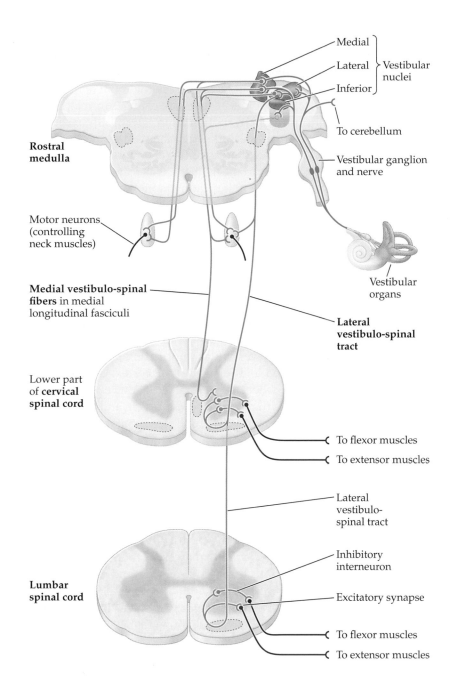

Medial
Lateral — Vestibular nuclei
Inferior

To cerebellum

Vestibular ganglion and nerve

Rostral medulla

Motor neurons (controlling neck muscles)

Vestibular organs

Medial vestibulo-spinal fibers in medial longitudinal fasciculi

Lateral vestibulo-spinal tract

Lower part of **cervical spinal cord**

To flexor muscles
To extensor muscles

Lateral vestibulo-spinal tract

Inhibitory interneuron

Lumbar spinal cord

Excitatory synapse

To flexor muscles
To extensor muscles

Figure 12.30 Neural pathways for vestibulo-spinal reflexes. Most vestibular afferent neurons (blue) synapse in one of the vestibular nuclei, but some project to the cerebellum. From the vestibular nuclei, descending interneurons (green) carry the information via vestibulo-spinal tracts downward through the brain stem and spinal cord until they synapse on efferent neurons (red) that activate the muscles that control balance. (After Netter, 1983.)

beyond the bottom of the spinal cord. If the information contributes to postural control of the head, it is transmitted only as far as the neck.

Spatial Orientation Cortex

We have visual cortex and auditory cortex. Do we have vestibular cortex? Some areas of the cortex certainly do respond to vestibular input, but these areas tend to include a variety of sensory and motor signals. There does not appear to be an area of the cortex exclusively dedicated to vestibular signals. This is not shocking, since we learned earlier that perception of body motion and tilt result from multisensory convergence, including predominant contributions by the vestibular system and vision.

It may be that there is simply no good reason for the cortex to process vestibular information in isolation when other sensory information is available. For example, the visual system is responsive to constant-velocity visual motion—like that experienced during rotation in the light as you see the room spin around you—while the vestibular system responds primarily to changes in velocity and is relatively insensitive to constant-velocity motion. More specifically, recall that when rotated at a constant velocity in the dark, after about 30 seconds humans perceive that they are not rotating (see Figure 12.18). Therefore, when you are rotating with a nearly constant velocity in the light, it seems reasonable that your brain would utilize the visual information indicating motion to better estimate self-motion. It thus makes sense that areas of the cortex related to the perception of tilt and self-motion demonstrate a convergence of visual and vestibular information, as well as information from other sensory systems that contribute to spatial orientation.

Vestibular Thalamocortical Pathways

Vestibular information reaches the cortex via what are called the thalamocortical pathways (**Figure 12.31**). This means simply that the vestibular information, like most other sensory information, reaches the cortex via the thalamus. Neurons from the vestibular nuclei carry vestibular information to the thalamus, where that information is processed and relayed to the cortex. Compare this, for example, to the visual system, where the retinal ganglion cells synapse in the lateral geniculate nucleus of the thalamus (see Figure 3.16 and "The Lateral Geniculate Nucleus" section in Chapter 3). There the information is processed and passed on to visual cortex.

Evidence suggests that the temporo-parieto-insular cortex is involved in spatial orientation perception. This area of the cortex receives input from both the semicircular canals and the otolith organs. Furthermore, immediately after this part of the cortex is lesioned by a stroke, many patients report illusory tilts and/or illusory translation. Though more rare, rotational vertigo—an illusory sense of spinning—is reported by some of these patients.

Though more direct vestibular projections may exist, there is a vestibular pathway that leads to the hippocampus through the cortex, and neurons in the hippocampal formation respond to vestibular stimuli (Horii et al., 2004). These include "head direction cells," a set of neurons that tend to spike vigorously when an animal's head is pointed toward a specific direction (Taube, 2007).

Cortical Influences

The areas of the cortex that receive projections from the vestibular system also project back to the vestibular nuclei. The existence of these pathways suggests that feedback from areas of the cortex that respond to vestibular stimulation likely modulates low-level vestibular processing in the brain stem. A specific role for these projections has not been proven, but it is known that higher cognitive knowledge can affect both perceptions and reflexive responses. For example, imagining whether an unseen visual target rotates with you alters the VOR evoked by rotation. As is appropriate, the VOR is suppressed when participants imagine that the target moves with them but is relatively large when participants imagine that the target is Earth-fixed (Barr, Schultheis, and Robinson, 1976).

As another example of higher-order cortical influences, knowledge of the motion capabilities of a specific device can influence motion perceptions (Rader, Oman, and Merfeld, 2011; Wertheim, Mesland, and Bles, 2001). For example, if you were blindfolded and then taken to a merry-go-round that you had never

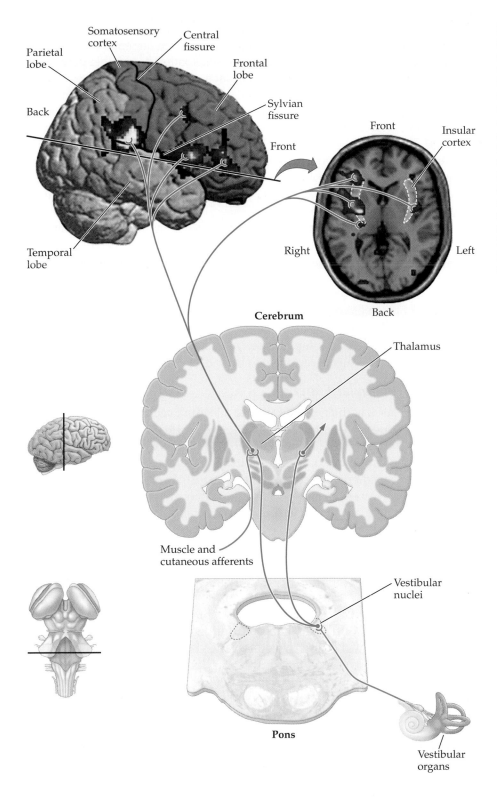

Figure 12.31 Ascending vestibular (thalamocortical) pathways pass from the vestibular nuclei to the thalamus on their way to the cortex. The brain is viewed from the right side. Cortex activation patterns shown at the top are PET (positron emission tomography) scans (the one on the left is colorized) obtained during stimulation of the vestibular system on the right side. Red and yellow indicate activation, which occurs in the temporo-parieto-insular areas of both hemispheres. Unlike activation in most other sensory systems, much of the vestibular activation is not visible on the outermost surface of the cortex but is found deeper in the brain, in the insular cortex. (Brain images from Dieterich and Brandt, 2008; courtesy of Marianne Dieterich.)

ridden before, your perception of tilt and motion might differ from what you would experience if you were riding a merry-go-round that you had ridden many times before. The vestibular stimuli might be the same, but your knowledge and expectations—both of which are higher-level functions—would be different and could alter your spatial orientation perceptions.

FIGURE 12.32 Some symptoms of vestibular dysfunction, like imbalance causing falls, mirror the effects of alcoholic beverages. This button highlights how the symptoms of vestibular disorders could be misinterpreted.

When the Vestibular System Goes Bad

We have learned that the vestibular system makes fundamental contributions to our sense of spatial orientation and also contributes to a number of reflexive responses. What happens when the vestibular system fails? Reflecting the widespread influence of the vestibular system, the bad news is that a lot of problems develop (Baloh and Halmagyi, 1996). Many patients develop spatial disorientation. Many experience imbalance. Many cannot see clearly unless they make an effort to hold their heads absolutely still. Many develop motion sickness that can lead to nausea or even vomiting. Some even develop cognitive problems. Because we are usually unaware of the vestibular system's contributions, it is possible to misinterpret the actions of people suffering from vestibular disorders (**Figure 12.32**).

The good news is that most patients partially adapt to the situation. For example, many patients quickly learn to curtail activities that lead to problems. This strategy is effective, but curtailing one's lifestyle is not an entirely satisfactory solution. Fortunately, in addition, most patients also learn to utilize other sensory information. As with the exquisite sense of hearing that is sometimes reported in blind patients, other sensory systems fill in to help reduce behavioral deficits caused by vestibular problems. This adaptation, coupled with physical rehabilitation and a curtailing of motion-related activities, yields an altered lifestyle that helps patients acclimate to their disability.

Falls and Vestibular Function

Fall risk increases with age, and falls are a leading cause of accidental death. Moreover, balance data correlate with falls, and vestibular dysfunction impacts balance (e.g., Horak, Nashner, and Diener, 1990). Recent data show that higher roll tilt thresholds in the dark are significantly correlated with failure to complete the vestibular condition of a standard balance test (Bermúdez Rey et al., 2016). Furthermore, an analysis of more than 5000 Americans showed that failure to complete this same balance test condition was correlated with substantially higher odds of having fallen in the past year (Agrawal et al., 2009). These findings together indicate that substandard vestibular sensation, including declines with age, might contribute to the death of 50,000 Americans each year (Bermúdez Rey et al., 2016).

Mal de Debarquement Syndrome

Most travelers feel a little unbalanced after disembarking from a large ship following an extended cruise. This imbalance is sometimes accompanied by motion sickness and by swaying, rocking, or tilting perceptions. You may have experienced these sensations after spending just a few hours on a boat. After disembarking, as you lay in your bed, you may have felt the gentle rocking of the waves, even though you knew you were perfectly still. These symptoms are bothersome but typically dissipate within a few hours. It is generally believed that these perceptions are an aftereffect of adaptation. Specifically, you adapt to the rocking motion experienced while on the boat. This adaptation—"getting your sea legs"—is appropriate while you're on board the boat, but it is inappropriate once you're back on land, leading to transient perceptions of disorientation, imbalance, and rocking that appear when you first disembark and then dissipate as you readapt to firm ground.

Relatively rarely, people are unable to readily readapt, and the condition sometimes leads to a clinical syndrome called mal de debarquement syndrome (meaning "disembarking sickness"). For these patients, the symptoms of spatial

■ Scientists at Work ■

Vestibular Aging

■ **Question** How does vestibular function vary with age?

■ **Hypothesis** Vestibular thresholds will increase as part of the aging process.

■ **Test** Direction discrimination thresholds (the smallest motion that individuals can reliably perceive, discussed at length in Chapter 1) were measured in 105 people between the ages of 18 and 80 (Bermúdez Rey et al., 2016; **Figure 12.33**). Each was strapped into a chair that moved within a completely dark room. For the z-translation curve in the graph, in which perceptual thresholds are plotted versus age, participants were translated along their z-axis either upward or downward, with each movement taking 1 second. The participants performed a forced-choice perceptual task in which they were required to respond "up" or "down." Thresholds were determined by fitting a psychometric function—like that shown in Figure 1.6—to each participant's perceptual responses.

■ **Results** Thresholds for up/down z-axis translations were constant between the ages of 18 and 40 but increased at a rate of 84% on average every 10 years above the age of 40. Four other motions (including y-translation, yaw rotation, and roll tilts at motion durations of 1 second and 5 seconds) yielded similar degradation patterns with age.

■ **Conclusion** Vestibular thresholds showed no evidence of aging prior to the age of about 40. After age 40, vestibular thresholds increased relatively rapidly. For example, the z-axis translation thresholds shown in Figure 12.33B roughly doubled between the ages of 42 and 54 and continued to increase at the same rapid rate above age 54.

■ **Future work** Might this degradation in vestibular function be a contributor to the increased risk of falling as we age? How would you design a study to investigate this question?

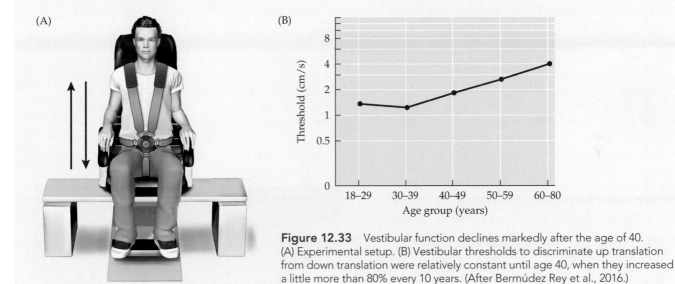

(A)   (B)

Figure 12.33 Vestibular function declines markedly after the age of 40. (A) Experimental setup. (B) Vestibular thresholds to discriminate up translation from down translation were relatively constant until age 40, when they increased a little more than 80% every 10 years. (After Bermúdez Rey et al., 2016.)

---

disorientation, imbalance, and rocking last a month or more after they disembark (Dai et al., 2017). In extreme cases, the symptoms can last for years and can be very debilitating. It remains a mystery why some individuals are unable to readapt when they leave the ship.

Ménière's Syndrome

Imagine suddenly experiencing dizziness, imbalance, and spatial disorientation so severe that either you have to lie down (quickly!) or you fall down. Imagine that severe motion sickness ensues and leads to repeated vomiting. Now imagine that these symptoms can occur suddenly and more or less unexpectedly at any time. This is the plight experienced by some patients suffering from Ménière's syndrome, named after Prosper Ménière, the French physician who first described the syndrome in 1861.

Ménière's syndrome afflicts about one in 500 people. It may strike at any age, but typically the syndrome first occurs in mid adulthood. Other symptoms include tinnitus (an illusory ringing sound), hearing loss, and a feeling of pain or fullness in the ear—making this an inner-ear disorder and not just a vestibular disorder.

The vestibular symptoms of dizziness, imbalance, and disorientation are so debilitating that patients often are incapacitated when experiencing a Ménière's

■ Sensation & Perception in Everyday Life

Amusement Park Rides—Vestibular Physics Is Fun

The canals are not very good transducers of low-frequency rotations—an effect that amusement park rides use to great advantage. What makes playground and amusement park rides fun? Clearly these are designed to be sensory experiences. Certainly hearing, taste, and smell are not the predominant sensory contributors, and while vision may play a role in the overall experience, most of these rides do not require vision to create the sensations people feel. In fact, some roller coaster patrons enjoy the experience more with their eyes closed! Playground and amusement park rides are designed, in large part, to stimulate the vestibular system. In fact, much of the enjoyment from a good amusement park ride derives from tricking the vestibular system in some way; typically, the designer of a good amusement park ride is playing with one or more of the fundamental characteristics of the vestibular system.

As a first example, let's consider the simple child-powered merry-go-round found in playgrounds (see Figure 12.2). These devices typically have a great deal of mass, especially compared with the mass of the children. The large device mass means that it takes a substantial amount of time—say 10 seconds or more—for it to speed up or slow down. Such gradual changes have low-frequency components that trick the semicircular canals into incorrectly sensing angular velocity. At the same time, the combination of both the radius from the rotation axis at the center of the ride to the edge and the angular velocity at the edge yield a centripetal acceleration with low-frequency components that is sensed by the otolith organs. Low-frequency accelerations trick the brain into perceiving self-tilt even in the absence of actual tilt. This divergence of perception from reality is the definition of an illusion. Such illusions seem to yield at least some of the fun experienced when riding playground and amusement park rides but can also lead to motion sickness.

Now let's consider the roller coaster (**Figure 12.34**). Although part of the fun of a roller coaster comes from the thrill of moving at a high speed, the twists and turns of a roller coaster minimally change the speed of the carriage. These twists and turns are there primarily to yield vestibular stimulation well beyond that typically experienced in normal life. Usually, the turns are located where the carriage travels with nearly maximal speeds—thereby yielding high angular velocities transduced by semicircular canals and high linear accelerations transduced by the otolith organs. These extreme vestibular stimuli add to the thrill experienced during roller coaster rides.

Figure 12.34 Many, but not all, enjoy the thrill of vestibular stimuli. Much of the thrill experienced while riding a roller coaster is due to vestibular stimulation.

attack. Furthermore, the concern that these symptoms might return at any time can be terrifying; some patients become afraid to leave their homes even when they are symptom-free. Making matters worse, although the vestibular system is known to be the source for the spatial disorientation suffered, the specific cause of the symptoms remains elusive. While some think that excess fluid in the inner ear causes Ménière's syndrome, others think that several different inner-ear disorders yield this constellation of symptoms.

Treatments of the disease include medications to lower pressure in the inner ear, implanted devices that provide transtympanic micropressure pulses, and sometimes procedures that destroy the vestibular apparatus. Stop for a moment and imagine that! The transient Ménière's syndrome symptoms are so severe that patients (and their physicians) are willing to induce a permanent disability just to be rid of the symptoms. For those of us lucky enough to have never experienced severe vestibular problems, this provides a small hint at how disabling the symptoms can be when the vestibular system malfunctions, as well as a glimpse at the fundamental contributions provided by the vestibular system.

Summary

1. The vestibular organs are the inner-ear organs that sense head motion and gravity and contribute to our equilibrium sense.

2. The vestibular organs include three semicircular canals (horizontal, anterior, and posterior), which sense angular motion, and two otolith organs (utricle and saccule), which sense both gravity and linear acceleration.

3. Vestibular hair cells are the mechanoreceptors that convert both orientation with respect to gravity and head motion into signals that are sent to the brain.

4. Spatial orientation includes three perceptual modalities: linear motion, angular motion, and tilt. Direction and amplitude are qualities that define each of these three perceptual modalities.

5. We are exquisitely sensitive to head motion even in the dark, recognizing the directions of rotation, linear motion, and tilt at very low thresholds.

6. We do not have vestibular perception isolated from the other senses. Spatial orientation perception uses information from multiple sensory systems—with the vestibular and visual systems making predominant contributions.

7. The brain processes the vestibular information to yield perceptions that differ substantially from the signals found on the afferent neurons.

8. In addition to their contributions to spatial orientation perception, the vestibular organs contribute to postural, vestibulo-autonomic, and vestibulo-ocular reflexes. Vestibular-evoked postural reflexes help us maintain balance. Vestibular-autonomic reflexes help regulate blood flow, especially to the brain. Vestibulo-ocular reflexes are compensatory eye movements that helps us see clearly even when the head moves.

9. Vestibular problems are widespread, and treatments are limited. For Ménière's syndrome patients, for example, the symptoms may become so disabling that patients accept treatments that yield permanent disability just to be rid of the symptoms.

Go to the
Sensation & Perception
Companion Website at
oup.com/us/wolfe5e
for chapter overviews, activities,
essays, flashcards, and other
study aids.
Go to **DASHBOARD** for
additional resources and
assessments.

13

Touch

■ Questions to Contemplate ■

Think about the following questions as you read this chapter. By the chapter's end, you should be able to answer and discuss them.

- If you had to give up one sensory modality, why would you *not* give up the sense of touch?

- What physical stimuli trigger this sense?

- What are the limitations of touch perception without movement?

- If someone strokes your arm, you might feel it as pleasant, informative, or painful—what would determine the perceptual result?

- Should babies be petted, like cats and dogs?

touch The sensations caused by stimulation of the skin, muscles, tendons, and joints.

tactile Referring to the result of mechanical interactions with the skin.

kinesthesia Perception of the position and movement of our limbs in space.

proprioception Perception mediated by kinesthetic and internal receptors.

et's start with the basic question about how the touch system is activated by physical stimulation. By its most narrow definition as a sense, the term **touch** is used to refer to the sensations caused by mechanical displacements of the skin. These displacements occur when you are poked by your 4-year-old nephew, licked by your dog, or kissed by your significant other. They occur any time you grasp, wield, or otherwise make contact with an object. We will use the term **tactile** (the adjective form of *touch*) to refer to these mechanical interactions and will expand the definition of *touch* to include the perception of temperature changes (thermal sensation); the sensation of pain, which occurs when our body tissues are damaged (or potentially damaged) in some way; itchiness; pleasant effects of stroking; and the internal sensations arising from muscles, tendons, and joints that inform us of the positions and movements of our limbs in space, technically called **kinesthesia**. Several other terms arise in connection with the sensory modality of touch, varying in inclusiveness. **Proprioception** (from the

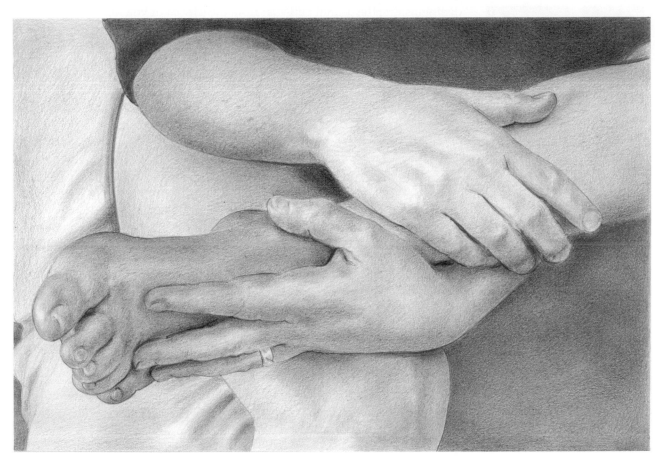

Nancy Haver, *Graphite Drawing of Hands*, 2004

Latin for "one's own") incorporates sensory input from locations internal to the body, such as your stomach, along with kinesthesia. **Somatosensation** (*soma* is the Greek word for "body") further encompasses the input from touch receptors in the skin as well as the proprioceptive system. As was noted in Chapter 12, the vestibular system adds to proprioceptive information in controlling balance and to somatosensation in controlling the autonomic nervous system.

It is difficult to conceive of our species surviving without a sense of touch. Pain serves as a sophisticated warning system that tells us when something might be internally wrong or when an external stimulus might be dangerous, enabling us to defend our bodies as quickly as possible (e.g., by rapidly moving away from the noxious stimulus). Temperature sensations enable us to seek or create a thermally safe environment. Mechanical sensations play an important role in our intimate sexual and reproductive activities, and they provide a powerful means of communicating our thoughts and emotions nonverbally.

On a more fundamental level, touch is important because we can use it to identify and manipulate objects that cannot be seen or heard. Blindfold yourself for at least 10 minutes and try doing some routine tasks, like making a sandwich, getting dressed, or taking a shower. The first thing you will notice while doing this exercise is just how much our species normally relies on vision to inform us about the world around us. But you should also discover that touch can substitute for vision to a surprising degree: You probably won't have as much trouble

somatosensation Collectively, sensory signals from the skin, muscles, tendons, joints, and internal receptors.

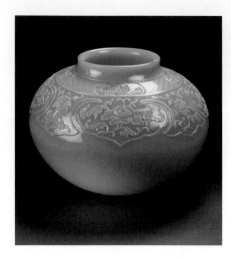

Figure 13.1 Ceramic jar from the Qing period, China, mid-eighteenth century.

distinguishing the peanut butter jar from the jelly jar as you might think. And if you pay attention, you will find that you don't actually use vision, or any sense other than touch, very much at all for some tasks (e.g., buttoning your shirt, brushing your teeth, opening that jar of peanut butter).

There is one more thing you may become acutely aware of during your experiment with the blindfold: Our eyes and ears can perceive signals from objects that are far from the body, but we must almost always be in direct contact with an object to perceive it by touch (exceptions to this rule include a jackhammer, whose vibrations on the street outside we can feel, and the sun, from which we feel warmth even though it is millions of miles away). Therefore, to use touch to learn about the world, we must act. If we want to know the weight of a beautiful Chinese jar like the one in **Figure 13.1**, we pick it up. We might also run our fingers along its raised contours, cup its rounded shape between our hands, or press it to our forehead to feel its coolness. In sum, touch involves action, arguably to a greater degree than any of our other senses do. For further discussion of how the sight of an object might invite you to touch it, see **Web Activity 13.1: Need for Touch**.

Touch Physiology

The sites of our sensing equipment for vision, audition, olfaction, and gustation are all located in organs (the eyes, ears, nose, and mouth, respectively) that are more or less dedicated to sensory processing. Some other animals have analogous appendages: antennae. You might think that, for touch, humans do not have a readily apparent sense organ. To the contrary, the site of touch sensing includes the most obvious organ of all!

Touch Receptors

In fact, the human sense of touch is mostly housed in what is actually the largest and heaviest of the sense organs, the skin, which covers an area of approximately 1.8 square meters (19.3 square feet) and weighs about 4 kilograms (almost 9 pounds). Touch receptors are embedded all over the body, in both hairless and hairy skin. They are also found within our mouths and our muscles, tendons, and joints. Just as the eye has its rods and three types of cones, the sense of touch has multiple types of receptors. These receptors form the basis for multiple "channels," specialized information-processing subsystems that each contribute to the overall perceptual experience. For example, if we wrap our fingers around a cube of ice, different channels convey information about its temperature, its shape, and its texture. Specialized receptors also respond to painful pinches and pleasant stroking. We will discuss the receptors for various channels in detail within the sections that follow (see also **Web Activity 13.2: Somatosensory Receptors**).

TACTILE RECEPTORS Although the external quality of the skin varies across different parts of the body (it is thicker in some parts and thinner in others, smoother in some regions and coarser in others, and so on), most skin includes tactile receptors called **mechanoreceptors** because they respond to mechanical stimulation or pressure. The tactile receptors are embedded in both the outer layer, called the **epidermis**, and the underlying layer, known as the **dermis**. A tactile receptor consists of a "nerve fiber" and an associated expanded ending. The nerve fiber of a receptor is composed of its axon and myelin sheath, if present. All tactile nerve fibers fall into a myelinated class called **A-beta fibers**,

mechanoreceptor A sensory receptor that responds to mechanical stimulation (pressure, vibration, or movement).

epidermis The outer of two major layers of skin.

dermis The inner of two major layers of skin, consisting of nutritive and connective tissues, within which lie the mechanoreceptors.

A-beta fiber A wide-diameter, myelinated sensory nerve fiber that transmits signals from mechanical stimulation.

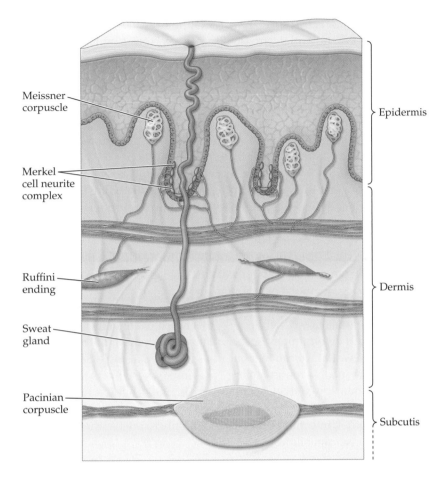

Figure 13.2 A cross section of hairless skin of the human hand, schematically demonstrating the locations of the four types of tactile receptors—Meissner corpuscles, Merkel cell neurite complexes, Ruffini endings, and Pacinian corpuscles—and illustrating the two major layers of human skin—the epidermis and the dermis. The subcutis, which underlies these outer two layers as shown here, is not usually included in the formal definition of "skin." (After R. S. Johansson and Vallbo, 1983.)

which have relatively wide diameters that permit very fast neural conduction. The fiber of a tactile mechanoreceptor extends from its terminal at the expanded ending all the way to the dorsal root of the spinal cord, and it can sometimes be very long (stretching from the sole of your foot to your backbone, for example).

The four populations of tactile receptors that are found in the **glabrous** (hairless) skin on the palms are shown in **Figure 13.2**. The nerve fibers of the various types are assumed to terminate in different expanded endings, and the receptors have come to be named after the anatomists who first described these endings: **Meissner corpuscles**, **Merkel cell neurite complexes**, **Pacinian corpuscles**, and **Ruffini endings**. The endings of Meissner and Merkel receptors are located at the junction of the epidermis and dermis, whereas the Pacinian and Ruffini receptors are embedded more deeply in the dermis and underlying subcutaneous tissue. The specific kind of expanded ending for each type of nerve fiber has provoked considerable controversy among tactile scientists for over a century now, because observing the physical connections directly has proved extremely difficult.

The four types of mechanoreceptors can be independently classified according to two attributes describing how they function:

1. *Size of the receptive field.* Receptors are activated when stimulation is applied to a particular area of the body, which constitutes the receptors' *receptive field* (recall that the same term is used for the receptors of other sensory systems). The size of the receptive field is the extent of the body area that elicits a receptor response.

glabrous In reference to skin, lacking hair.

Meissner corpuscle A specialized nerve ending associated with fast-adapting (FA I) fibers that have small receptive fields.

Merkel cell neurite complex A specialized nerve ending associated with slowly adapting (SA I) fibers that have small receptive fields.

Pacinian corpuscle A specialized nerve ending associated with fast-adapting (FA II) fibers that have large receptive fields.

Ruffini ending A specialized nerve ending associated with slowly adapting (SA II) fibers that have large receptive fields.

2. *Rate of adaptation (fast versus slow).* A fast-adapting (FA) receptor responds with bursts of action potentials, first when its preferred stimulus is applied and then again when the stimulus is removed. It does not respond during the steady state between stimulus onset and offset. In contrast, a slowly adapting (SA) receptor remains active throughout the period during which the stimulus is in contact with its receptive field.

> **FURTHER DISCUSSION** of receptive fields as they relate to vision can be found in Chapter 2 on pages 53–56, and throughout Chapter 3.

These two dimensions lead to a second set of labels, listed in **Table 13.1**. Each type of tactile fiber is particularly sensitive to certain features of mechanical stimulation, rendering it suitable for particular types of functions, as shown in **Table 13.2**.

- Slowly adapting type I (SA I) fibers respond best to steady downward pressure, as when we push our fingers against fine spatial details, and very-low-frequency vibrations of less than about 5 Hertz (Hz = cycles per second). They are especially important for texture and pattern perception. Some activities particularly dependent on this touch channel include reading Braille and determining the location and orientation of the slot on the head of a screw that we can feel but not see. When a single SA I fiber is stimulated, people report feeling "pressure." These fibers are assumed to terminate in Merkel cell neurite complexes, but it is not as yet clear whether these endings play a direct role in generating the afferent response or whether, in contrast, they function only to enable the fiber itself to develop response capabilities.

- Slowly adapting type II (SA II) fibers in the skin (as well as in all fibrous tissues in the body) respond to sustained downward pressure and particularly to lateral skin stretch, which occurs, for example, when we grasp an object. When you reach out for your coffee cup, the SA II fibers help determine when your fingers are shaped properly for picking up the cup. SA II fibers terminating in the folds of skin around the nails convey forces on the fingertips as they interact with objects (Birznieks et al., 2009). Scientists have shown that when a single SA II fiber is stimulated, people experience no tactile sensation at all; for stimulation to be detectable, more than one SA II fiber must be stimulated. Although SA II fibers in the skin are assumed to terminate in Ruffini endings, recent research has questioned whether these expanded terminals are as numerous as traditionally believed.

◼ Table 13.1 ◼

Response characteristics of the four mechanoreceptor populations

Adaptation rate	Size of receptive field	
	Small	Large
Slow	SA I (Merkel)	SA II (Ruffini)
Fast	FA I (Meissner)	FA II (Pacinian)

Note: FA I = fast-adapting type I; FA II = fast-adapting type II; SA I = slowly adapting type I; SA II = slowly adapting type II. The terminal ending associated with each type of tactile nerve fiber is shown in parentheses.

■ Table 13.2 ■

Mechanoreceptors: Feature sensitivity and associated function

Mechanoreceptor	Maximum feature sensitivity	Primary function(s)
SA I	Sustained pressure, very low frequency (< ~5 Hz) Spatial deformation	Texture perception Pattern/form perception
SA II	Sustained downward pressure (low sensitivity to vibration across frequencies) Lateral skin stretch	Finger position
FA I	Temporal changes in skin deformation (~5–50 Hz) Skin slip	Low-frequency vibration detection Stable grasp
FA II	Temporal changes in skin deformation (~50–700 Hz)	High-frequency vibration detection Fine texture perception

- Fast-adapting type I (FA I) fibers respond best to low-frequency vibrations from about 5 to 50 Hz. If your coffee cup is heavier than you expected and begins to slip across your fingers, this motion across the skin will cause just such vibrations, and FA I fibers will help you correct your grip before your coffee spills all over you. When a lone FA I fiber is stimulated, people report a very localized sensation that they describe as "wobble" or "flutter." These fibers are assumed to terminate in Meissner corpuscles.

- Fast-adapting type II (FA II) fibers respond best to high-frequency vibrations from about 50 to 700 Hz (the highest frequency tested to date). Such vibrations occur whenever an object first makes contact with the skin, as, for example, when a mosquito lands on your arm. Such vibrations are also generated when an object that you're holding contacts another object, so FA II fibers help you determine how hard you're tapping your pencil on your desk as you try to cram all this information into your brain. When a single FA II fiber is stimulated, people report a more diffuse sensation in the skin that corresponds to a "buzz." These fibers have been shown to terminate in Pacinian corpuscles.

The four types of mechanoreceptors are always working together to inform us about every individual object we touch. The SA I and FA I fibers, in particular, are analogous to cones and rods, respectively, in their functions: one affording acuity and the other sensitivity to low-intensity stimulation. K. O. Johnson (2002) gives the example of opening a door with a key. Feeling the shape of your key in your pocket requires the SA I (and maybe also the FA I) channel. Shaping your fingers to grasp the key involves the SA II channel. As you insert the key into the lock, your grip force increases so that the key does not slip, thanks to your FA I channel. Finally, your FA II channel tells you when the key has hit the end of the keyhole.

The majority of research on touch receptors has concentrated on the hairless parts of the body, but more recent research acknowledges the importance of hairy skin, such as the forearm, for touch perception. Understandably, this area of study has focused on mammals with more hair than humans have, such as cats. The mechanoreceptors in hairy skin exhibit a variety of endings and associated fiber types, as with hairless areas, but additional receptors are found near the follicles of the hair itself. In humans, hairy skin appears to play a unique and important role in pleasant touch, to be discussed below.

Figure 13.3 A muscle spindle embedded in main (extrafusal) muscle fibers contains inner (intrafusal) fibers. When the inner fibers contract, a sensory response from the spindle is sent back to the central nervous system, conveying information about muscle length and thus regulating muscle tension.

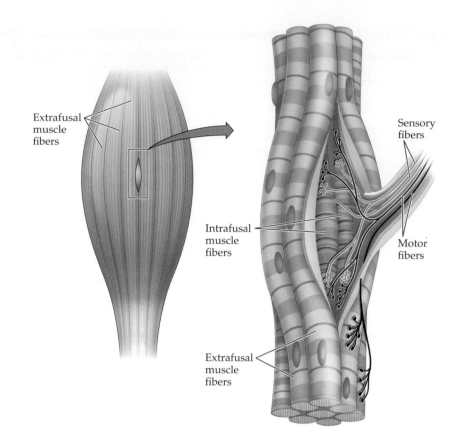

Extrafusal muscle fibers

Sensory fibers

Intrafusal muscle fibers

Motor fibers

Extrafusal muscle fibers

KINESTHETIC RECEPTORS In addition to the tactile mechanoreceptors in the skin, other types of mechanoreceptors lie within muscles, tendons, and joints. These are collectively referred to as **kinesthetic** receptors, and they play an important role in sensing where our limbs are and what kinds of movements we're making (Clark and Horch, 1986; L. A. Jones, 1999). The angle formed by a limb at a joint is perceived primarily through muscle receptors called muscle spindles (**Figure 13.3**), which convey the rate at which the muscle fibers are changing in length. Receptors in the tendons, called Golgi tendon organs, provide signals about the tension in the muscles attached to the tendons, and receptors directly in the joints themselves come into play particularly when a joint is bent to an extreme angle.

The importance of kinesthetic receptors is graphically illustrated by the striking case of a neurological patient named Ian Waterman (read *Pride and a Daily Marathon* [1991] by Jonathan Cole for more about this interesting individual; video content has also been posted online). The cutaneous nerves that connected Waterman's kinesthetic and other mechanoreceptors to his brain were destroyed by a viral infection when he was 19 years old. Lacking kinesthetic senses, Waterman is now completely dependent on vision to tell him about the positions of his limbs in space. If the lights are turned off, he cannot tie his shoes, walk up or down stairs, or even clap his hands, because he has no idea where his hands and feet are! Caught in an elevator when the lights went out, he was unable to remain standing and could not rise again until the illumination returned. (For additional details about Waterman's challenges, and the amazing degree to which he has compensated for his lack of kinesthetic receptors, see **Web Essay 13.1: Living without Kinesthesis**.)

kinesthetic Referring to perception involving sensory mechanoreceptors in muscles, tendons, and joints.

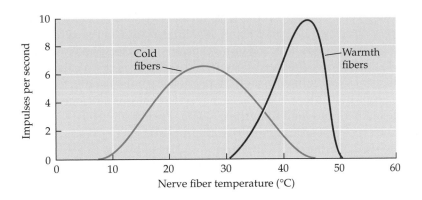

Figure 13.4 Thermal receptivity functions, showing the response of warmth and cold fibers to different temperatures. (After Guyton, 1991.)

THERMORECEPTORS **Thermoreceptors** located in both the epidermal and dermal layers of the skin inform us about changes in skin temperature. There are two distinct populations of thermoreceptors (**Figure 13.4**): **Warmth fibers** fire when the temperature of the skin surrounding the fibers rises. **Cold fibers** (which outnumber warmth fibers by a ratio of about 30:1) fire in response to decreases in skin temperature. The neural fibers that mediate cold and warmth include unmyelinated, and hence relatively slowly conducting, **C fibers** and faster-conducting, myelinated **A-delta fibers**. Both types are smaller in diameter than those coming from the mechanoreceptors in the skin—the wider-diameter fibers known as type A-beta—and they lack specialized endings.

Our bodies are constantly working to regulate their internal temperature, so under normal conditions the skin is kept between 30°C and 36°C (86°F and 96°F), and neither cold nor warmth fibers respond much while skin temperature remains within this range. If you bundle up in your long underwear and snowsuit but then sit inside in front of the fire, your skin temperature will probably rise above 36°C, and your warmth fibers will begin to fire. If you then take the snowsuit off and walk out into the snow, your skin temperature will rapidly begin to fall, and as soon as it goes below 30°C, your cold receptors will start firing.

Thermoreceptors also kick into gear when we make contact with an object that is warmer or colder than our skin. Objects in the environment are typically cooler than 30°C, so it is usually the cold fibers that tell us about the object. For example, steel conducts heat more efficiently than stone. Your cold fibers will thus fire less rapidly and for a shorter period of time when you touch a steel object than when you touch a stone object (because the steel object will warm more quickly to match your skin temperature). If you've had prior experience with steel and stone, you can make use of the different thermoreceptor responses to make this distinction. As we will see in the following discussion of pain, receptors that respond to extreme temperature changes also respond to foods that we associate with thermal sensations, like chili (warmth) and menthol (cold).

NOCICEPTORS Pain is the realm of touch that has the dubious honor of being home to the sensations we like the least. We may find some visual stimuli revolting and some olfactory or gustatory stimuli disgusting, but of all the sensations, it is pain that we take the most drastic actions to avoid. Pain itself is the unpleasant sensory and emotional consequence of signals from **nociceptors**, touch receptors that have bare nerve endings and that respond to various forms of tissue damage or to stimuli that have the potential to damage tissue (including extreme skin temperatures lower than 15°C [59°F] or higher than 45°C [113°F]). (Pain receptors are also found in internal organs, but we will confine this discussion to touch.)

thermoreceptor A sensory receptor that signals information about changes in skin temperature.

warmth fiber A sensory nerve fiber that fires when skin temperature increases.

cold fiber A sensory nerve fiber that fires when skin temperature decreases.

C fiber A narrow-diameter, unmyelinated sensory nerve fiber that transmits pain and temperature signals.

A-delta fiber An intermediate-sized, myelinated sensory nerve fiber that transmits pain and temperature signals.

nociceptor A sensory receptor that responds to painful input, such as extreme heat or pressure.

Like thermoreceptors, nociceptors lack specialized endings and can be divided into two types by their nerve fibers. Myelinated A-delta fibers respond primarily to strong pressure or heat, and unmyelinated C fibers respond to intense stimulation of various sorts: pressure, heat or cold, or noxious chemicals. Many painful events seem to occur in two stages: a quick, sharp burst of pain, followed by a throbbing sensation. These two stages may reflect the onset of signals first from the A-delta fibers and then from the C fibers (Price et al., 1977).

How do nociceptive neurons detect that thermal and chemical stimulation that produces pain? A critical role appears to be played by a set of thermally sensitive transient receptor potential (thermoTRP) ion channels, which regulate the flow of charged atoms and molecules across the membrane of a cell (Julius, 2013). **Figure 13.5** illustrates the range of temperatures associated with various TRP channels also activated by natural foodstuffs, which span from noxious cold to noxious heat. Chili pepper and wasabi mustard (sushi, anyone?) are two foods that, at extreme levels, lead to pain. Each is associated with a thermoTRP channel (TRPV1 and TRPA1, respectively). When we say that food like chili feels hot, we are implicitly recognizing that the TRPV1 channel responds to intense thermal heat as well as spiciness. Mice lacking the TRPV1 channel are insensitive to heat at levels that normally cause pain. TRPV1 is also implicated as a channel for the induction of itch, which might cause you to wonder whether losing this channel would be such a bad thing (Ross, 2011)! Conversely, there is a TRP channel (TRPM8) associated with the sensation of noxious cold, and lack of this channel makes animals insensitive to a painfully cold surface contacting the skin. Identifying the specialized roles for thermoTRP channels in pain perception has added evidence to the idea that nociceptive neural fibers act as "labeled lines," conveying a particular type of noxious stimulation to the brain.

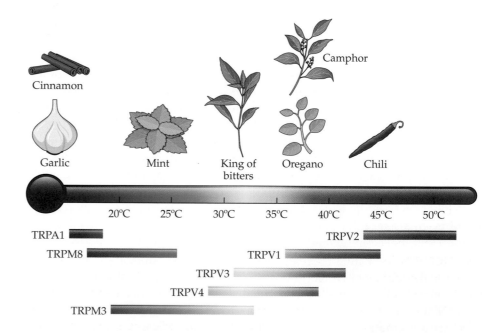

Figure 13.5   Natural plant compounds activate TRP channels that operate across distinct ranges of thermal stimulation (thermoTRPs), as shown. These channels operate in normal thermal sensation and at extremes of painful cold and painful hot. (From Latorre et al., 2009; after Ferrandiz-Huertas et al., 2014.)

It might seem that feeling pain has no upside, but consider what would happen if we had no nociceptors. We wouldn't be able to sense dangerously sharp or hot objects. Lacking alarms, we might soon lack fingers! Some diseases, such as Hansen's disease (leprosy) and diabetes, are characterized by the loss of pain sensation and provide real-life examples of the consequences. The case of "Miss C," reported by Melzack and Wall (1988), shows what can happen to people born with insensitivity to pain. Not only did Miss C lack pain sensation, but she did not sneeze, cough, gag, or protect her eyes reflexively. She suffered childhood injuries from burning herself on a radiator and biting her tongue while chewing food. As an adult, she developed problems in her joints that were attributed to lack of discomfort, for example, from standing too long in the same position. She died at age 29 from infections that could probably have been prevented in someone who was alerted to injury by painful sensations.

PLEASANT TOUCH RECEPTORS   The traditional way of classifying different bodily sensations, introduced at the beginning of this chapter, is in terms of tactile, thermal, pain, and itch experiences. Collectively, these classic sensations are known as discriminative touch. A fifth component, discovered more recently, is named "pleasant" or "emotional" touch (McGlone et al., 2007). The emotional properties of nonpainful bodily touch appear to be mediated in large part by a class of unmyelinated (and thus, relatively slow) peripheral C fibers known as **C tactile (CT) afferents** that are not related to either pain or itch. This type of C fiber preferably responds to mechanical stimulation in the form of slowly moving (1–10 centimeters/second), lightly applied forces (like petting!). Researchers believe that CT afferents are located only in hairy skin.

The optimal stroke rates to produce firing in CT afferents correspond to speeds of stroking that people select as more pleasant (Perini et al., 2015). People also produce speeds in these ranges when stroking the arm of a loved adult or a baby, but not when petting an artificial arm (Croy et al., 2016). Optimal stroke speeds for the CT afferents also elicit activity in smile muscles that is not evident at other speeds (Pawling et al., 2017).

Isolating attributes of the pleasant touch system is rather difficult because, ordinarily, stimulation of the CT fibers also induces responses from the myelinated A-beta fibers that respond to general mechanical stimulation. This isolation has been made possible, however, by studies of individuals who lack A-beta fibers because of a rare disorder. One such individual, GL, feels no sensation of touch below the nose and cannot feel pleasant touch either, when stimulated on hairless skin. Yet when stroked on hairy skin with a brush, she can detect and coarsely localize the source, which she finds vaguely pleasant (Björnsdotter et al., 2009; Olausson et al., 2008).

It has been suggested that the CT afferent units form part of a neural subsystem that integrates the body with its sensory and social environment, inducing emotional, hormonal, and behavioral responses to skin-to-skin contact. The importance of parental skin contact for the welfare of premature infants has been demonstrated by analyzing hormones related to well-being and stress. During contact by mothers and fathers, levels of oxytocin (a hormone associated with childbirth and social bonding) increase, and levels of cortisol (a stress-related hormone) decrease, as do measures of anxiety (Cong et al., 2015). Fairhurst et al. (2014) stroked infants with a soft brush at a preferred speed for pleasant touch of 3 centimeters (cm) per second, or at faster or slower speeds (30 cm/second and 0.3 cm/second, respectively) (**Figure 13.6**). They found that during periods of stroking at the moderate speed, infants' heart rates declined, whereas at speeds

C tactile (CT) afferent   A narrow-diameter, unmyelinated sensory nerve fiber that transmits signals from pleasant touch.

Figure 13.6 Baby being stimulated by brushstrokes and resulting change in heart rate for three different speeds of stroking. (After Fairhurst et al., 2014.)

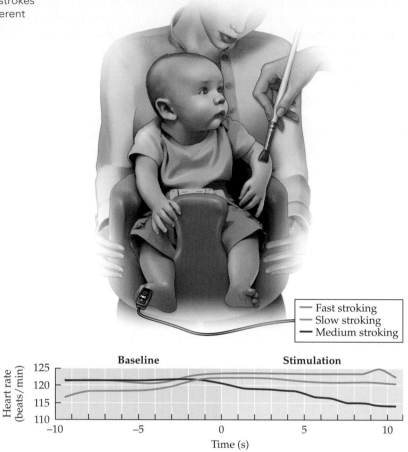

slower or faster, they slightly increased. Individual infants' responsiveness to optimal brush stroking was correlated with how much their parents liked to give, receive, and observe touch, as measured by a social touch scale.

From Skin to Brain

Initially the axons of various tactile receptors are combined into single nerve trunks, in much the same way that retinal ganglion axons converge in the optic nerve (see Chapter 2) and cochlear hair cells converge in the auditory nerve (see Chapter 9). This analogy omits important differences, however: First, whereas there are only two optic nerves and two auditory nerves, there are a number of somatosensory nerve trunks, arising in the hands, arms, feet, legs, and other areas of the skin. Second, the tactile nerves must carry their messages considerably farther. Because the receptors for sights, sounds, tastes, and smells are all located in the skull, the pathways that deliver information from these receptors to the brain are connected directly to the brainstem, rather than to nerves that have to travel up the spinal cord. Touch messages, on the other hand, must travel as far as 2 meters (6.6 feet) to get from the skin and muscles of the feet to the brain.

To cross this distance, the information must move up through the spinal cord. The cord is far more than a handy transmission pipe; its neural structure makes important contributions to the perceptual outcomes of touch. As described thus far, the nerve fibers arising from the skin might seem to constitute **labeled lines**; that is, each fiber type codes a particular touch sensation. Beyond the

labeled lines A theory of sensory coding in which each nerve fiber carries a particular stimulus quality.

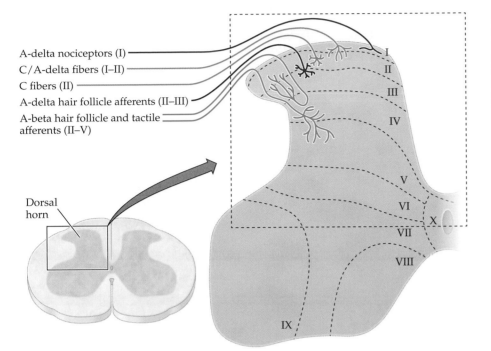

A-delta nociceptors (I)
C/A-delta fibers (I–II)
C fibers (II)
A-delta hair follicle afferents (II–III)
A-beta hair follicle and tactile afferents (II–V)

Dorsal horn

Figure 13.7 Neural projections to the dorsal horn of the spinal cord, based on the cat, rat, and monkey. The horn is divided into layers (laminae—of which layer II is the substantia gelatinosa). Afferent types terminate within the horn in a regular pattern, as shown. (After Todd, 2010.)

peripheral neural layer, however, the lines become interconnected, making it possible for complex patterns to emerge. The spinal cord is the site at which this cross communication is initiated.

The cell bodies associated with the tactile neural fibers are bundled into a cascade of ganglia, lumpy bodies that lie just outside the cord. The axons themselves enter the spinal cord at the **dorsal horn**, which is toward the back of the spinal column. The horn is organized into multiple layers, or laminae, as shown in **Figure 13.7**. Every skin mechanoreceptor projects into the horn, although that may not be its only projection. The inputs to the cord are organized **somatotypically**. Somatotopy is analogous to the topographical spatial representation of events on the retina found in vision (see Chapter 3); adjacent areas on the skin are ultimately connected to adjacent areas within a region of the cord. What may be surprising is that these inputs constitute only a small part of the neural structure of the dorsal horn, as most of its neurons lie entirely within the spinal cord and serve as local connections, like the intermediate layers of the retina. In a review of dorsal horn function, Abraira and Ginty (2013) propose that it is this connectivity that provides the sense of touch with its rich canvas of effects, from caresses to pokes.

Once in the spinal cord, touch information proceeds upward toward the brain via two major pathways, as shown in **Figure 13.8**. The evolutionarily older **spinothalamic pathway** (Figure 13.8A) is the slower of the two and carries most of the information from thermoreceptors and nociceptors. The **dorsal column–medial lemniscal (DCML) pathway** (Figure 13.8B) includes wider-diameter axons and fewer synapses and therefore conveys information more quickly to the brain. Tactile and kinesthetic information carried along this pathway is used for planning and executing rapid movements, where quick feedback is a must. The DCML pathway not only includes fibers ascending directly from the mechanoreceptors, but also is densely populated by fibers from neurons originating in the dorsal horn, presumably conveying the output of the neural activity within the spinal cord.

dorsal horn A region at the rear of the spinal cord that receives inputs from receptors in the skin.

somatotypical Referring to normal somatosensation.

spinothalamic pathway The route from the spinal cord to the brain that carries most of the information about skin temperature and pain.

dorsal column–medial lemniscal (DCML) pathway The route from the spinal cord to the brain that carries signals from skin, muscles, tendons, and joints.

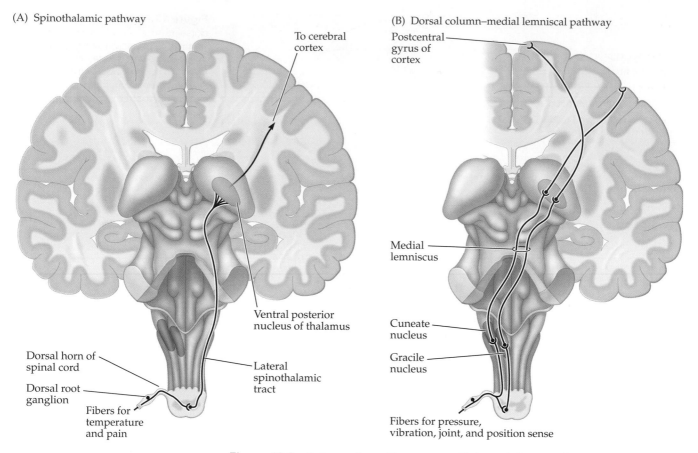

(A) Spinothalamic pathway

To cerebral cortex

Ventral posterior nucleus of thalamus

Dorsal horn of spinal cord

Dorsal root ganglion

Fibers for temperature and pain

Lateral spinothalamic tract

(B) Dorsal column–medial lemniscal pathway

Postcentral gyrus of cortex

Medial lemniscus

Cuneate nucleus

Gracile nucleus

Fibers for pressure, vibration, joint, and position sense

Figure 13.8 Pathways from skin to cortex. (A) Spinothalamic pathway. (B) Dorsal column–medial lemniscal pathway. (After Levine, 2000.)

Neurons in the DCML pathway first synapse in the cuneate and gracile nuclei, near the base of the brain (see Figure 13.8B). Activity is then passed on to neurons that synapse in the ventral posterior nucleus of the thalamus. Recall from Chapters 3 and 9 that the visual and auditory pathways also pass through the thalamus, each synapsing in its own modality-specific nucleus. Because this portion of the brain is largely shut down when we are asleep, the brain does not register (and therefore does not attempt to respond to) the relatively gentle touch sensations that occur, for example, when we roll over in our sleep.

From the thalamus, much of the touch information is carried up to the cortex (**Figure 13.9**) into **somatosensory area 1 (S1)**, located in the parietal lobe just behind the postcentral gyrus. In terms of its position in the transmission chain from the periphery to the brain, S1 is analogous to V1 in vision (see Chapter 3). With respect to responses of cells in S1 to spatial patterns, the analogy is closer to what happens in the retina. When monkeys scan raised-dot patterns with their fingertips, receptive fields found in S1 tend to take the form of an excitatory region with adjacent inhibitory areas, resembling the ON-center retinal ganglion cells (DiCarlo, Johnson, and Hsiao, 1998). Neurons in S1 communicate with **somatosensory area 2 (S2)**, which lies in the upper bank of the lateral sulcus, and with other cortical areas. The motor areas of the cortex, which control movements of body parts, are located just in front of the central sulcus. This adjacency enhances communication between the somatosensory and motor control systems.

somatosensory area 1 (S1)
The primary receiving area for touch in the cortex.

somatosensory area 2 (S2)
The secondary receiving area for touch in the cortex.

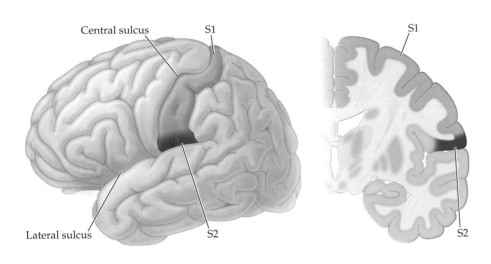

Figure 13.9 Primary somatosensory receiving areas in the brain. S1 includes multiple areas identified by the famous anatomist Brodmann on the basis of their cellular structure: 1, 2, 3a, and 3b. (Brodmann areas are not shown in this figure.) S2 lies within the lateral sulcus.

Touch sensations that result from stimulation of the skin are spatially represented in S1, and to some extent beyond, **somatotopically**. Similar to the skin's projection to the spinal cord, adjacent areas on the skin have a connection to adjacent areas in the brain (**Figure 13.10A**). As a result, the somatosensory cortex is organized into a spatial map (or as we will see below, multiple maps) of the layout of the skin. Each map has been called a sensory **homunculus** (plural *homunculi*) (**Figure 13.10B**) and actually has a twin homunculus because there are corresponding spatial maps in the left and right hemispheres.

somatotopic Referring to spatial mapping in the somatosensory cortex in correspondence to spatial events on the skin.

homunculus A maplike representation of regions of the body in the brain.

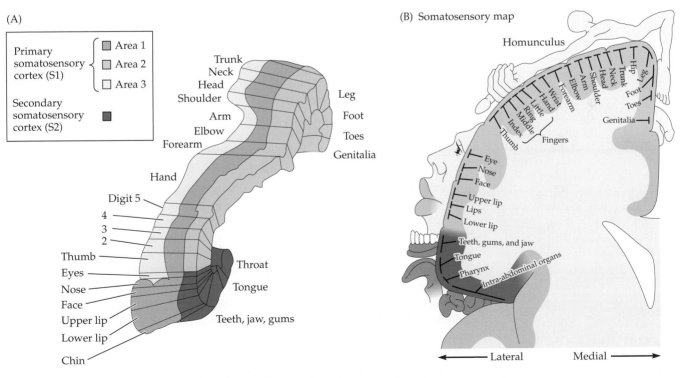

Figure 13.10 The sensory homunculus, showing brain regions that respond to stimulation of different parts of the body. (A) Multiple maps exist in primary and secondary somatosensory areas, three of which are shown within S1 and one within S2. (B) A schematic of the relative distribution of body parts in S1, as originally derived by Penfield and Rasmussen (1950).

body image   The impression of our bodies in space.

phantom limb   Sensation perceived from a physically amputated limb of the body.

The sensory homunculus is derived largely from the work of Canadian neurosurgeon Wilder Penfield, who charted the somatotopic map with the aid of patients undergoing brain surgery to alleviate epilepsy. Because there are no pain receptors in the brain, the patients did not need to be anesthetized and could remain responsive. During the operation, Dr. Penfield systematically stimulated different parts of a patient's somatosensory cortex with an electrode. As the probe was moved from one location in S1 to another, the patient reported feeling sensations in the arms, legs, face, and so on. The correspondence between the stimulation and the sensation gave rise to a map of the body in the brain (see **Web Activity 13.3: The Sensory Homunculus**). In fact, the brain contains multiple sensory maps of the body. Separate maps are now known to exist in the different subareas of S1, and additional maps exist in secondary areas, as shown in Figure 13.10A.

Like the retinotopic map in V1 (see Figure 3.16), Penfield's somatotopic map in S1 is distorted. The thumb, for example, grabs a big piece of real estate relative to its size. In contrast, sensations from the leg are processed in a relatively small portion of S1. In the visual system, the foveal area is overrepresented in V1 (cortical magnification; see Chapter 3) because there are many more photoreceptors in the fovea than in peripheral parts of the retina. Similarly, a larger chunk of S1 is dedicated to processing information from the lips than from the neck because tactile receptors are much more heavily concentrated in the lips than they are in the neck.

The distortion in the brain's map is echoed in how people perceive their own bodies, or their **body image**. Fuentes, Longo, and Haggard (2013) had people draw maps of their own bodies on a computer, by clicking on locations of body parts relative to the on-screen image of a head. People's body image proves to be systematically distorted toward top-heaviness, with expanded shoulders and upper arms but reduced-size lower arms and legs (**Figure 13.11**). The body representation can be changed by experience, even by something as mundane as wielding a tool (**Figure 13.12**). After blindly wielding a tool to retrieve objects arranged on the floor, wielders were asked to indicate the location of their elbow and wrist under an occluding box, thereby indicating the subjective length of the forearm. Like Pinocchio's nose after lying, it grew! For a tool 100 cm in length, the increase in perceived arm length amounted to over 1 cm, suggesting that about 1% of the tool had been incorporated into the mental representation of the arm (Canzoneri et al., 2013).

The body image changes with direct transformation of the body itself, as was shown by the results of a surgical procedure to elongate arms shortened by dwarfism (Cimmino et al., 2013). Within 6 months, the patient's body image of her upper limbs changed from being shortened to being congruent with normal controls, while the lower portion of her body image remained unchanged. (See **Web Activity 13.4: The Rubber Hand Illusion** for an experience of displacing your body image, and see **Web Essay 13.2: Body Image** to see how the impression we have of our bodies in space [body image] is highly changeable.) The relatively tight correspondence between body parts and areas of S1 can have unfortunate side effects in cases of limb amputation. If an amputee's left arm is missing, obviously no mechanoreceptors are sending touch signals from that arm. However, sporadic activity can continue in the area of the amputee's right S1 corresponding to the arm, leading to the perception of a **phantom limb**. At times, individuals may perceive their phantom limbs to be in uncomfortable positions, leading to persistent (and very real) pain.

The psychologist Vilayanur Ramachandran made the astonishing observation that amputees often report feeling sensations in their phantom arms and hands

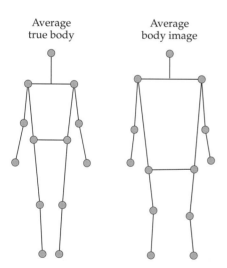

Average true body   Average body image

Figure 13.11   Shape of the body as determined from locations of parts (dots) for people's true body (left) and locations they report relative to the head, which form their body image (right). Multiple maps are averaged by scaling each one relative to the person's body height. (From Fuentes et al., 2013.)

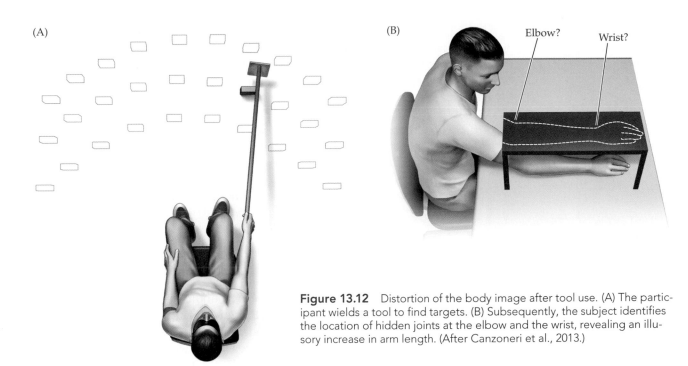

Figure 13.12 Distortion of the body image after tool use. (A) The participant wields a tool to find targets. (B) Subsequently, the subject identifies the location of hidden joints at the elbow and the wrist, revealing an illusory increase in arm length. (After Canzoneri et al., 2013.)

when their faces or remaining limbs are touched (**Figure 13.13**). The source of this somatosensory confusion can be traced to an idiosyncrasy in the homunculus. Note in Figure 13.10 that the area responding to the face is located (somewhat arbitrarily) adjacent to the area responding to the hand and arm. Apparently the hand and arm areas of S1 are, to some extent, "invaded" by neurons carrying information from touch receptors in the face. However, other parts of the brain listening to the hand and arm areas are not fully aware of these altered connections, and therefore they attribute activity in these areas to stimulation from the missing limb. (You can read more about Ramachandran's fascinating studies on phantom limbs in **Web Essay 13.3: Phantom Limbs**.)

Projections from S1 form the basis for further analysis of objects and surfaces by the cortex of the brain. The results of some recent studies suggest that, like vision (see Chapter 4), the sense of touch may show a division between *what* and *where* systems in higher cortical centers. A patient studied by Reed, Caselli, and Farah (1996) showed an impairment in her ability to recognize objects by touch (*what*), but she showed no deficit in her spatial ability (*where*). Another patient could locate and manipulate objects by touch without recognizing them (Rossetti, Rode, and Boisson, 1995). Activation of the brain, observed with fMRI (see Chapter 1), has been found in different areas, depending on whether the task is to locate an object or to recognize it tactually. And, as in vision, there is relatively more dorsal activation for locating objects and more ventral activation for recognizing objects (Reed, Klatzky, and Halgren, 2005; Reed, Shoham, and Halgren, 2004).

Thus far we have described the path of discriminative touch to the brain; pleasant touch appears to follow a different trajectory. Whereas primary somatosensory cortex is activated by the physical aspects of the stimulus (e.g., by the pressure it produces on the skin or a change in skin temperature), the CT system is associated with another brain area, the insula, which is thought to play a role in regulating the body and linking sensory to emotional systems. When GL,

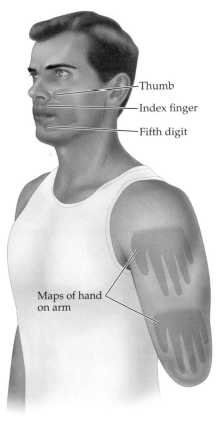

Figure 13.13 Phantom limbs may be perceived on the face and stump subsequent to amputation. Amputees report feeling the amputated hand when their face or remaining limbs are stimulated. (After V. S. Ramachandran, 1993.)

who has CT fibers but lacks input from tactile mechanoreceptors, was stimulated by brushing hairy skin, brain activation was found in the insula but not the somatosensory areas (Björnsdotter et al., 2009). Another area of the frontal lobes known to be involved in emotion—the orbitofrontal cortex—is also activated by pleasant mechanical stimulation (S. T. Francis et al., 1999). As described in Chapter 15, both insula and orbitofrontal cortex receive direct projections from the taste receptors, and as we will find later in this chapter, the insula plays a role in social connectedness and the relief we get from scratching an itch!

FURTHER DISCUSSION of the orbitofrontal cortex in the context of olfaction and taste can be found in Chapters 14 (page 499) and 15 (page 517), respectively.

Lest you conclude that the neural organization of our brains for touch is permanent and unchanging, consider an experiment performed by Pascual-Leone and Hamilton (2001). These neuroscientists deprived normal, sighted volunteers of visual stimulation by having them wear a blindfold for 5 days. On each day the volunteers participated in an fMRI study during which pairs of Braille patterns were presented to the right index finger. Participants were required to judge whether the two patterns within each pair were the same or different. Brain imaging found that on the first day, the Braille task activated only S1 on the left side of the brain (which, because of the neural pathways from the skin, is activated by touching the right side of the body). But as the days progressed, the amount of activation declined in S1 while increasing in V1. Apparently area V1, which we think of as dedicated to vision, took over processing the spatial patterns introduced through the sense of touch. This change in V1 was transient: removing the blindfold resulted in a full return to the neural functioning that had been observed before blindfolding.

Such results reveal the remarkable **neural plasticity** of the somatosensory system. Plasticity is a recurring theme in sensory systems. We saw something very similar at the end of Chapter 3 in the discussion of visual development and strabismus, in which abnormal experience alters the wiring of the visual system. Note that the example we're discussing here shows that plasticity is a property of the adult brain and is not limited to the immature nervous system.

The philosopher William Molyneaux was probably not thinking about neural plasticity when, in 1688, he posed the question to John Locke about whether a blind person who was suddenly able to see would recognize objects previously known only by touch. Medical interventions eventually made it possible to answer this question by providing sight to congenitally blind individuals. It was demonstrated that although visual objects are not connected immediately to their touched equivalents, only a few days of visual experience are needed to make the connection (Held et al., 2011). This surprising finding, given the individuals' long-term experience without vision, underscores the plastic nature of the perceptual system.

The pathways from the skin to the brain tell just one part of the story of the transmission of signals in touch. Downward pathways from the brain can alter the sensations that stimulating the periphery produces. Some of the most surprising effects of these downward pathways relate to the feeling of pain, which we discuss next.

neural plasticity   The ability of neural circuits to undergo changes in function or organization as a result of previous activity.

Pain

We tend to think of pain as an inevitable consequence of stress on or damage to our bodies, flowing from sensory levels to the conscious feeling of "ouch." The scientific study of pain, however, reveals it to be a highly subjective state with distinguishable components. What we think of as pain arises at multiple levels— sensory, emotional, and cognitive—which interact to create a conscious experience.

MULTIPLE LEVELS OF PAIN   Pain sensations are triggered by the nociceptors (described earlier in this chapter). Neurons carrying nociceptive signals arrive at the dorsal horn of the spinal cord in its outermost layers, particularly the second, called the **substantia gelatinosa** (see Figure 13.7). Neurons there receive information *from* the brain, and they form synapses with the neurons that are conveying sensory information from nociceptors *to* the brain (see Figure 13.8). According to the very influential **gate control theory** (Melzack and Wall, 1988), the bottom-up pain signals from the nociceptors can be blocked via a circuit located in the spinal cord. Neurons in the dorsal horn actively inhibit pain transmission, and what is transmitted to somatosensory areas in the brain is the combined output of pain excitation from the nociceptors and this inhibition. The inhibitory neurons in the dorsal horn receive input signals from two quite disparate sources: the large-diameter A-beta fibers coming from the skin, which respond to benign touch rather than pain, and the top-down pathways from the brain. Gate control theory gets its name from the idea that the transmission of the pain acts like a gate that is pushed open by excitatory pain signals but closed by inhibitory inputs. The theory is supported by the identification of neural circuits that could act as the mechanism to open and close the gate (Peirs and Seal, 2016).

Pain signals arising at S1 and S2 don't tell the whole story, however. Imaging methods identify other areas of the brain that correspond to the emotional aspects of painful experiences. The complex cluster of brain areas that responds to the emotion and discriminative aspects of noxious touch are shown in **Figure 13.14**. Among those we have previously discussed are the thalamus and insula.

substantia gelatinosa   A region of interconnecting neurons in the dorsal horn of the spinal cord.

gate control theory   A description of the pain-transmitting system that incorporates modulating signals from the brain.

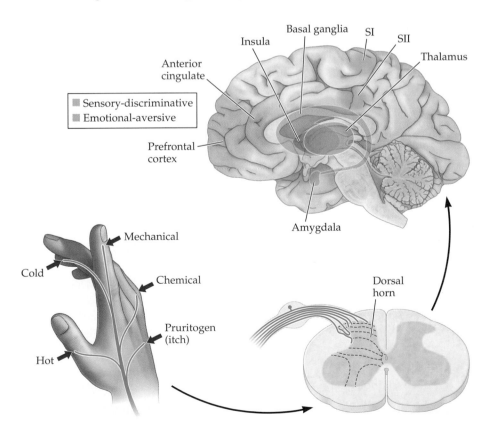

Figure 13.14 Organization of pain circuits. Nociceptive and tactile afferents project to the dorsal horn of the spinal cord and from there to brain centers that process sensory-discriminative or emotional-aversive touch. (After Peirs and Seal, 2016.)

anterior cingulate cortex (ACC)
A region of the brain associated with the perceived unpleasantness of a pain sensation.

Another area, **anterior cingulate cortex (ACC)**, responds differentially to hypnotic suggestions of increased or decreased pain unpleasantness, while S1 and S2 consistently respond to the painful stimulation regardless of suggestions to the contrary (Rainville et al., 1997). Another region involved in pain circuitry is the prefrontal cortex, an area concerned with cognition and executive control that may represent what Price (2000) called "secondary pain affect," the emotional response associated with long-term suffering that occurs when painful events are imagined or remembered.

It may seem odd to associate pain with laughter, but at least some of the response people have to tickling seems to depend on nociceptors (Zotterman, 1939). And, just as signals from the brain can control pain perception, they appear to come into play when we try to tickle ourselves. Self-induced tickling not only produces less laughter, it also produces less activity in the somatosensory cortex, because of canceling signals from other brain areas that know where the tickling stimulation is coming from (S.-J. Blakemore, Wolpert, and Frith, 1998).

Some people may claim that itchiness is as great a pain as pain itself. In one extreme case, Mary Ellen Nilsen, over a period of a year after experiencing an outbreak of shingles (the same virus that causes chicken pox), scratched her scalp so intensively that she broke through the bone and damaged brain tissue. Pain and itch are closely connected in a neural sense as well as a perceptual one. Some itch fibers respond to both pain and itch, whereas others, called pruriceptors, are itch-selective. The separation of pain and itch was shown by mice whose itch neurons in the spinal cord were eliminated. They didn't scratch, even when injected with stuff that drove normal mice into scratching frenzies; the animals' response to pain, in contrast, was unaffected (Sun et al., 2009).

As for scratching, despite what you may have been told about "making it worse," it beneficially decreases activation at itch sites as early as the spinal cord (S. Davidson et al., 2009), acting as a form of gate control. At the level of the brain, scratching regulates responses of the anterior cingulate cortex and the insula, which, you may recall, respectively respond to emotional pain and pleasant touch (Papoiu et al., 2014). And unlike tickling, which is more effective when done by someone else, scratching yourself is more pleasurable and itch-relieving than being scratched (Papoiu et al., 2014).

■ Scientists at Work

Tickling Rats

■ **Question** Are there specialized neural mechanisms for tickle? Where might they be found?

■ **Hypothesis** Although no dedicated sensory afferent has been found to carry a tickle signal, there might be specific responses in the somatosensory cortex regions representing the tickled body part.

■ **Test** The researchers tickled rats on their trunk (tummy) or, alternatively, touched them gently there (**Figure 13.15A**). They assessed behavioral responses that might indicate the sensation of tickle and also recorded the activity in the somatosensory area that represents the trunk (Ishiyama and Brecht, 2016).

■ **Results** Tickled rats produced laugh-like vocalization and made *Freudensprünge* (jumps of joy). They chased after the experimenter's

■ Scientists at Work (continued)

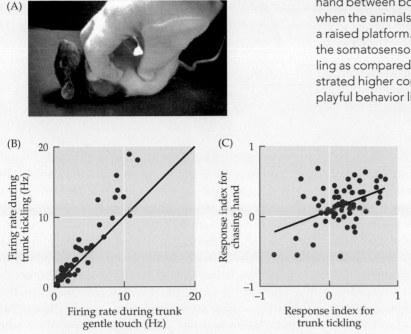

(A)

(B)

(C)

Figure 13.15 Tickling rats. (A) Rat being tickled. (B) Firing rate in somatosensory cortex for tickle versus gentle touch; note that tickle is generally higher. (C) Measure of play behavior in relation to neural response to tickle, for individual rats; note the positive relationship. (A from Ishiyama and Brecht, 2016; B after Ishiyama and Brecht, 2016.)

hand between bouts of tickling. Tickling was ineffective when the animals were stressed by bright light or placed on a raised platform. Most critically, cells in the trunk area of the somatosensory cortex fired at higher rates during tickling as compared with gentle touch, and rats that demonstrated higher cortical firing rates also exhibited more playful behavior like hand chasing (**Figure 13.15B, C**).

■ **Conclusion** The somatosensory cortex of the rat plays a privileged role in the processing of tickle sensations. The results connect tickling sensations to play and social interaction and, in doing so, provide support for the idea that the primary receiving area for touch in the brain also plays a role in emotional responses.

■ **Future work** Given how much the rats seem to enjoy being tickled by humans, do you think they would seek out a tickling machine? If not, what would this suggest to you about tickling as a form of social interaction?

MODERATING PAIN Pain experiences are the complex result of sensory signals interacting with many other factors that have moderating effects. Damping of pain sensations (without losing consciousness) is called **analgesia**. Responses to noxious stimulation can be affected by analgesic drugs, of course, but perhaps more surprising are the attenuating effects of anticipation, religious belief, prior experience, or excitement. Studies also highlight the importance of interpersonal and broader social influences on the emotional component of pain.

Pain can be moderated to some extent by benign counterstimulation—for example, rubbing the skin near a stubbed toe. This results from interactions at the level of the spinal cord between the large-diameter fibers and the nociceptors, as described by the gate control model. Although it won't work for all types of pain, crossing your fingers eliminates the pain induced by the thermal grill illusion, where a pattern of warm-cold-warm across the middle fingers of the hand makes you feel like the middle (cold) finger is burning (Marotta et al., 2015)!

A more drastic measure is counterirritation or "diffuse noxious inhibitory control"—extreme pressure, cold, or other noxious stimulation applied to another site distant from the source of the pain. For example, pain from electrically stimulating a tooth can be reduced by noxious stimulation of the hand (Motohashi and Umino, 2001). Painful stimulation can also suppress the sensation of itch, although you might prefer the itchiness. As with the gate control model of pain regulation, the explanation involves inhibitory interactions in the spinal cord, as shown in **Figure 13.16**.

analgesia Decreasing pain sensation during conscious experience.

Figure 13.16 Pain and itch stimulation are initially transmitted by separate "labeled lines." In the spinal cord, pain neurons connect to an itch-inhibiting neuron, with the result that painful stimulation inhibits itch. (After Ma, 2010.)

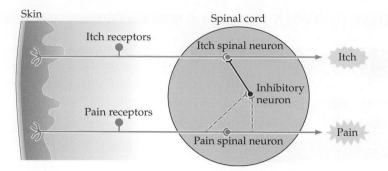

There are many stories of soldiers in battle who did not feel painful wounds until the stress was over. The analgesic effect in such cases is probably caused by **endogenous opiates**, chemicals released by the body that block the release or uptake of neurotransmitters necessary to transmit pain sensations to the brain. Differences between individuals with respect to pain responsiveness (that is, pain "thresholds") may reflect differences in their baseline levels of these substances, although other causes have been implicated, such as genetically caused differences in nociceptive pathways. Externally produced substances such as morphine, heroin, and codeine are similar in chemical structure to these endogenous opiates, and thus they have similar analgesic effects. Other drugs, such as acetaminophen and ibuprofen, alleviate pain at its source by counteracting chemicals that would otherwise start the nociceptors firing.

What about pain reduction by a simulated intervention? The **placebo effect** is the reduction of pain when people merely think they are being treated, for example, when they take a surrogate for an analgesic drug. The subjective reduction of pain by placebos is well documented, and imaging of the spinal cord with fMRI reveals that placebos actually inhibit nociceptive processing as early as the dorsal horn (Eippert et al., 2009). Placebos can have positive effects as well: imaging of the brains of people who self-administered an inert nasal spray that they were told would heighten their responses to pleasant touch showed increased activation under pleasant touch in the same areas that were attenuated by analgesic placebos under painful stimulation (Ellingsen et al., 2013). The locations of these effects encompassed emotional areas as well as somatosensory cortex.

Research has shown that contact with those we love reduces brain activation in areas that regulate our emotions and bodily arousal responses to the threat of painful stimulation. In an fMRI study by Coan, Schaefer, and Davidson (2006), women experienced the threat of electric shock under three conditions. A woman could hold her husband's hand, the hand of a male with whom she was unacquainted, or no hand at all. The neural pain response was reduced by touching another's hand, and this effect increased with the closeness of the relationship. Broader social influences on pain have also been found. For example, reports of painful strains of the arm from tasks requiring repetitive motion spread rapidly in Australia during the 1980s—like a contagious disease—but they were communicated by workers who did nothing more than talk to one another about their experiences. The cross talk could have had multiple effects in this example, both heightening people's sensitivity to their suffering and providing a name for it.

endogenous opiate A chemical released by the body that blocks the release or uptake of neurotransmitters necessary to transmit pain sensations to the brain.

placebo effect Decreasing pain sensation when people think they're taking an analgesic drug but actually are not.

hyperalgesia An increased or heightened response to a normally painful stimulus.

PAIN SENSITIZATION Nociceptors provide a signal when there is impending or ongoing damage to the body's tissue. This is called "nociceptive" pain. When pain surpasses normal expectations, the experience is **hyperalgesia**. An increased or heightened pain response to a normally painful stimulus is called "inflammatory," and it usually goes away once the tissue heals, although chronic pain can persist after healing. Pain can also arise in the absence of immediate trauma, because of damage to or dysfunction of the nervous system. The resulting pain is called "neuropathic." Some neuropathic pain reflects changes in the sensory fibers at the skin that do not normally produce pain but now become pain inducers (a phenomenon known as allodynia); other neuropathic pain arises from changes in the dorsal horn of the spinal cord. The mechanisms by which neuropathic pain arises are increasingly understood at the cellular and molecular levels. An important implication of this research is that no single medication will alleviate all types of pain.

Tactile Sensitivity and Acuity

Now that we've covered the physiological substrate of the touch system, we can turn to the psychological and psychophysical aspects. How sensitive are we to mechanical stimulation? What are the limits on tactile acuity in space and time? Put a bit differently, what are the smallest details that we can feel?

How Sensitive Are We to Mechanical Pressure?

To measure the minimum pressure that can be reliably sensed by a particular region of skin, we need a way to present well-defined amounts of pressure over and over again. In the nineteenth century, Max von Frey (1852–1932) developed an elegant and simple way to do this using carefully calibrated stimuli, including horse and human hairs. Modern researchers typically use nylon monofilaments (e.g., fishing lines) of varying diameters. The smaller the diameter, the less force the line applies to the skin before it buckles.

To replicate von Frey's method yourself, touch different parts of your skin with a hair from your head and a bristle from a hairbrush to reveal the relative skin sensitivity to these two different forces. With the thinner hair, you will probably find that you can feel it on the more sensitive areas, such as your lips and perhaps some parts of your hand. You probably will not feel it pushing into your thigh or upper arm. With the bristle, however, you should discover that your skin is sensitive to mechanical pressure all over, but not uniformly so. For example, if you explore the skin on the back of your hand, you should be able to convince yourself that there are spots of greater and lesser sensitivity (Geldard, 1972).

Data from more controlled pressure sensitivity studies reveal that thresholds vary across different sites of the body (a high threshold means that that part of the body is less sensitive). In general, tactile pressure sensitivity is highest on the face, followed by the trunk and upper extremities (arms and fingers) and then the lower extremities (thigh, calf, and foot) (Weinstein, 1968). The pattern for males and females is very similar, except that women tend to be more sensitive to pressure than men. Sensitivity to temperature changes, as well as to pain, also varies markedly as a function of body site.

Another approach to measuring sensitivity is to ask what the smallest raised element is that we can feel as an otherwise completely smooth surface is passed over the skin. Like the storied princess who detected a pea under a pile of mattresses, we appear to be very sensitive to the pressure difference caused by a raised dot on a smooth surface. At a criterion of 75% detection, people can detect a dot only 1 micrometer high—that's a millionth of a meter, or 39 millionths of an inch! The dot seems to trigger detection by the FA I receptors, which also help us detect and correct for an object slipping as we grasp it. Even more impressive,

Figure 13.17 Results of an experiment measuring the minimal (threshold) amplitude of vibration at the fingertip that people can detect, as a function of the vibratory frequency. As labeled on the y-axis, the threshold is measured on a decibel (dB) scale relative to a reference vibration (see Chapter 9). The experimentally obtained function, portrayed by the solid line, is believed to reflect the contribution of three different mechanoreceptor populations (SA I, FA I, and FA II), which are shown as different-colored segments. Each population is assumed to control the threshold in the limited frequency range where it is most sensitive. For comparison, the dashed lines in each color show the vibratory threshold for the corresponding mechanoreceptor population across the entire range of frequencies tested. These lines cannot be obtained from the experiment portrayed here but, rather, are based on the results of neurophysiological studies of single-unit mechanoreceptor responses. Researchers have proposed that SA I units mediate our threshold for vibrations below about 5 Hz; FA I fibers, for frequencies from about 5 to 50 Hz; and FA II units, for frequencies above about 50 Hz. (After Löfvenberg and Johansson, 1984.)

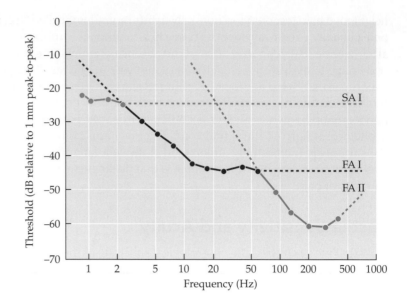

when a texture that is made of many raised dots only a very small fraction of a micrometer high moves across the skin, the resulting vibrations trigger the FA II receptors deep within the skin, enabling us to distinguish the dots from a perfectly smooth surface (LaMotte and Srinivasan, 1991). How sensitive the skin is measured to be depends on the measuring sensitivity, it appears, as much as the skin. Recent techniques have allowed wrinkles scaled in nanometers (nm = billionth of a meter) to be manufactured, and the smallest wrinkle heights that can be detected by rubbing the surfaces approximate 10 nm (Skedung et al., 2013)!

People are also sensitive to changes in pressure over time—that is, to tactile vibration. **Figure 13.17** shows absolute vibratory threshold (the minimum amount that a vibrating stimulus displaces the skin in order to be detected) as a function of the frequency presented to the fingertip (Löfvenberg and Johansson, 1984). In this study, people could detect the presence of vibrations from below about 5 Hz up to about 400 Hz, the highest frequency that was tested. Other studies have confirmed that people can detect vibrations up to 700 Hz (Verrillo, 1963), the highest frequency tested to date.

Although people can detect vibrations over a wide frequency range, they are not equally sensitive to all frequencies, as Figure 13.17 clearly shows. Since the various mechanoreceptor populations are sensitive to different frequencies, the overall psychophysical function for the detection of vibration reflects the contributions of different mechanoreceptor populations at different levels of vibration. Take a look at the corresponding vibration sensitivities of SA I, FA I, and FA II mechanoreceptor populations from less than 5 to 400 Hz, also shown in Figure 13.17. The SA I units would seem to mediate our absolute vibratory thresholds for frequencies below about 5 Hz; the FA I fibers, for frequencies from about 5 to 50 Hz; and the FA II units, for frequencies above about 50 Hz.

How Finely Can We Resolve Spatial Details?

Pressure detection is the tactile equivalent of detecting a spot of light, where the basic question is whether you can see or feel anything at all. For the tactile equivalent of visual acuity (can you make out the pattern of what you see or feel?), try measuring your **two-point touch threshold**. As the name suggests,

two-point touch threshold The minimum distance at which two stimuli (e.g., two simultaneous touches) are just perceptible as separate.

this is the smallest separation at which we can tell that we're being touched by two points and not just one. This experiment is best done with a partner, although it will work to some degree if you test yourself. A compass (the kind that draws circles) is a useful stimulator, but you can use anything that enables you to vary the separation between two points, such as a bent paper clip. Pick one of your own or your partner's body regions and see if you can distinguish between a single point and two points. Then repeat the procedure with different separations of the two points (e.g., 0.5, 2, and 4 cm) and at different places on the skin (**Figure 13.18**).

Like sensitivity to pressure, spatial acuity varies across the body. Systematic studies of two-point touch thresholds as a function of body site demonstrate that the extremities (hands, face, feet) show the highest acuity (Mancini et al., 2014; Weinstein, 1968) (**Figure 13.19**). On the fingertips we are capable of resolving a separation of only about 1 millimeter (mm) (Loomis, 1981). These results place tactile acuity somewhere between vision and audition: it is worse than visual acuity, but better than auditory spatial resolution.

We've looked at the two-point threshold for spatial acuity with pressure stimulation, but how about for pain? A stumbling block on measuring this threshold is the difficulty of constructing pinpoint-sized painful stimuli that people can be asked to differentiate. By delivering very small pulses of radiant heat, the laser has made it possible to determine the threshold distance between two pain locations that could be resolved as distinct (Mancini et al., 2014). Figure 13.19 compares the two-point threshold between pain and touch at various body sites. The glabrous (hairless) skin of the hand and forehead shows the greatest sensitivity (lowest threshold) for both: At this location, pain acuity is nearly at the level of tactile acuity. On the hairy skin of the arm, however, pain and touch diverge. For example, the shoulder is more spatially sensitive than the forearm to pain, but the reverse is found for tactile stimulation.

Note the general correspondence between the pattern of two-point touch thresholds across the body in Figure 13.19 and the relative distortion of different

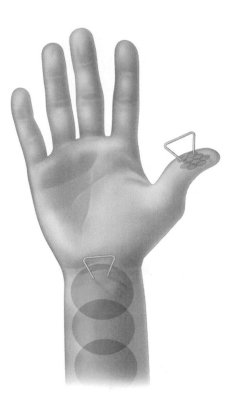

Figure 13.18 Two-point touch thresholds are determined primarily by the concentration and receptive-field sizes of tactile receptors in an area of the skin. The triangles represent point stimulators, and the circles represent the areas of skin that would respond to a single stimulation.

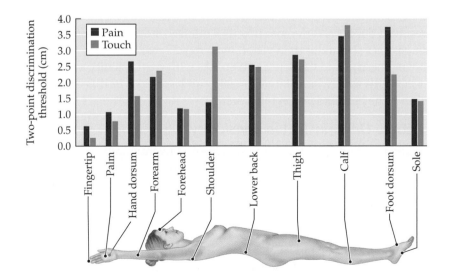

Figure 13.19 The two-point discrimination threshold for pain and touch. The threshold is the minimal separation between two stimulated points on the body needed to perceive them as separate. (After Mancini et al., 2014.)

body parts in the sensory homunculus of Figure 13.10. This match is not coincidental. The determination that two closely spaced points instead of just one are touching your skin requires that your brain receive two separate signals. This means that at the skin there must be a sufficient concentration of receptors, each with a small enough receptive field that the two contact points will elicit different responses. An additional constraint is that as the signals are sent to the cortex, they must not converge. A chunk of cortical real estate large enough to receive them separately is necessary. In short, the two-point threshold is low (that is, the ability to discern two very close points as separate is high) only when the density of receptors is relatively high, the receptive fields are small, and cortical convergence does not occur. Tactile spatial acuity thresholds are mediated by the SA I (and possibly FA I) tactile receptors, which have relatively small receptive fields and high receptor densities. (See **Web Activity 13.5: Two-Point Touch Thresholds**.) Where pain and tactile sensitivity differ, as in the relative acuity of the shoulder versus the forearm seen in Figure 13.19, the patterns follow the density of the receptor populations for touch versus pain in those regions of the body.

Although useful, the traditional two-point touch test has some drawbacks, as you may see when you try your own experiment. Even if the two stimulated points feel like one, it is not quite the same as stimulating the skin with a single continuous contact. Therefore, asking people whether they are really being touched by one point or two yields quite a different answer than does asking them if it *feels like* one point or two, especially in sensitive areas such as the fingertip. Alternatives that are more objective have been suggested, including judging whether an edge has a gap or indicating how a grating (a surface with alternating grooves and ridges) that is applied to the skin is oriented—along versus across the finger (Craig and Johnson, 2000).

How Finely Can We Resolve Temporal Details?

It is somewhat more difficult to perform your own measures of how well people can resolve fine temporal differences in tactile stimulation. Various psychophysical methods have been used to address this question. A common method requires participants to decide whether two tactile pulses delivered to the skin appear to be either simultaneous or successive in time. With this method, participants can resolve a temporal difference of only 5 milliseconds (ms) (Gescheider, 1974). Touch proves to be better than vision (which is 25 ms) but worse than audition (0.01 ms) (Sherrick and Cholewiak, 1986). As with spatial acuity, you will notice that touch falls somewhere between vision and audition; in this case, however, audition is the best and vision the worst.

Do People Differ in Tactile Sensitivity?

If you are a sighted person reading this book conventionally, your tactile sensitivity in 10 years is likely not to be what it is today; a decline with age is to be expected. Studies of blind people who read Braille reveal an exciting exception to this trend, however: Legge and colleagues (2008) tested the ability of blind and sighted people to identify raised three-dot patterns derived from Braille symbols, displayed at different scales. They found that sighted adults lost about 1% per year in their acuity levels between their teens and their 80s, but blind Braille readers showed essentially no age-related decline (**Figure 13.20**). There is an unfortunate implication of this trend for people who lose their sight late in life (a sizable proportion of the blind population). The zero point on the left vertical axis in Figure 13.20 is set to the standard spacing between Braille dots;

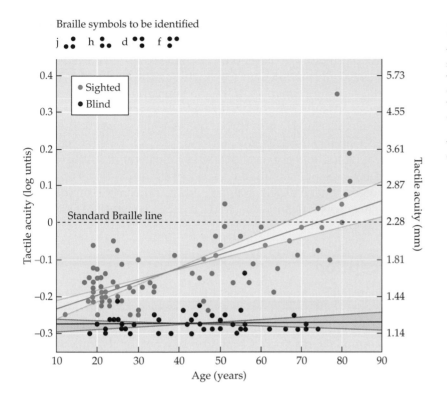

Braille symbols to be identified

j •ː h •ˑ d •• f ••

Figure 13.20 Tactile acuity versus age. Acuity is measured by the accuracy of symbol identification when using the index finger, across different scales. The left vertical axis uses a log measure, where the spacing of dots in a standard Braille character is set to zero (dashed line). On the right vertical axis, the measure is the distance between dot centers within the identified characters in millimeters (mm). The bands around the lines that are fit to the data represent 95% confidence intervals. (After Legge et al., 2008.)

once the necessary font size passes above it (at around 74 years of age), fingertip sensitivity is not sufficient to read Braille.

Another factor that affects your tactile sensitivity is, apparently, your genes. Both tactile spatial acuity and vibratory sensitivity are more correlated in identical than in nonidentical twins, pointing to a genetic contribution (Frenzel et al., 2012). The same study asked whether genes that influence one sense organ that responds to pressure, the skin, might also influence another, the ear. They found that hearing acuity was significantly correlated with both tactile spatial acuity and the threshold for warmth; moreover, individuals who had genetic mutations leading to early deafness showed reduced spatial and vibratory sensitivity in touch. Thus, common genes appear to be expressed in multiple sensory forms.

In contrast to the reduced sensitivity associated with early deafness, individuals diagnosed with autism spectrum disorder display heightened sensitivity to a broad range of touch stimulation: thermal and vibratory, and in glabrous and hairy skin. These responses are so intense that they have been described as overwhelming (Tomchek and Dunn, 2007). A possible genetic basis for this sensitivity has been identified by modifying the genes of mice so that they affect their processing of touch afferents (Orifice et al., 2016). Relative to controls, the modified mice were more sensitive to an air puff on the skin but, conversely, showed less discrimination between textures when exploring them with the hairless skin on their paws—which they were induced to do because their whiskers had been removed. In conjunction with these sensory deficits, the genetically modified mice showed deficits in social behaviors. They explored the world around them less and failed to habituate to repeated noise, indicators of anxiety. They constructed nests of lower quality and didn't approach another mouse any more than an empty cup, indicators that they were less sociable. These social deficits appear to be specific to animals whose touch is altered

haptic perception   Knowledge of the world that is derived from sensory receptors in skin, muscles, tendons, and joints, usually involving active exploration.

early in development. This was shown by comparing the genetically modified strain to a set of controls in which corresponding somatosensory abnormalities were chemically induced during adulthood. While the controls showed similar alteration to the genetically modified mice on tactile sensitivity tests, they were not afflicted by the same anxiety and social nonresponsiveness. The specificity of these latter effects to mice whose sensory systems were affected at birth suggests that the altered sensations of early experience played a critical role in engendering the deficits in personality (or should we say, "mouseness") observed in the adult. A counterpart to these results can be found in humans with autism spectrum disorders, who show multimodal sensory abnormalities. The mouse genetic model suggests that a developmental pathway encompassing not only touch, but multiple sensory modalities, could contribute to the social phenomena associated with the condition.

Haptic Perception

With the physiology and basic psychophysics of the touch system now under our belts, we can turn to questions about how we use the information gathered by our thermoreceptors, muscle spindle fibers, Pacinian corpuscles, and so on. The term **haptic perception** refers to perceptual processing of inputs from multiple sensory subsystems, including those in skin, muscles, tendons, and joints. Haptic perception is usually active and information-seeking: the perceiver explores the world rather than passively receiving it.

Perception for Action

As mentioned earlier, touch relies on action to get information from the world. Expanding on this point a bit more, we can say that touch is active in two complementary ways. Using our hands to actively explore the world of surfaces and objects outside our bodies is *action for perception*. Using sensory input to prepare us to interact with objects and surfaces around us involves *perception for action*. Preparation for action starts well before contact. Vision allows us to plan the approach to manipulation, slowing our reach to a slippery object, for example. This advance planning is evidenced by fMRI imaging not only in visual areas of the brain, but in somatosensory areas as well: area S2 responds differently to objects that *look* slippery (have glossy surfaces) versus rough (matte surfaces), and the differences mimic those found when smooth and rough objects are touched. These results suggest an information-processing network that proceeds from visual analysis to somatosensory areas, preparing people for the expected consequences of action before an object is even touched (Sun et al., 2016).

Once we touch an object, somatosensation controls our impressive ability to grasp and manipulate it. In our discussion of kinesthetic receptors, we talked about how the loss of these internal tactile receptors leads to a devastating inability to know (without looking) where our limbs are positioned. Westling and Johansson (1984) showed that mechanoreceptors in the skin also play critical roles when we're interacting with objects (**Figure 13.21**). After these investigators anesthetized the skin on volunteers' hands, the volunteers could no longer maintain a stable grasp of objects that they could see perfectly well. Feedback from the mechanoreceptor populations in the skin appears to provide crucial information about when an object is about to slip on the skin. You may know this yourself from trying to unlock a door when your fingers are very cold!

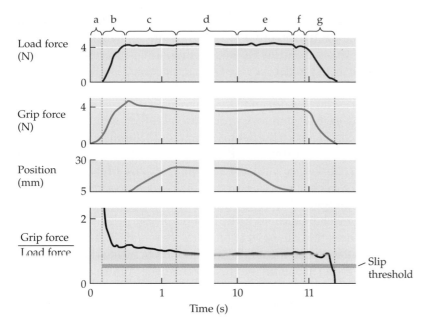

Figure 13.21 Force and position during lifting, grasping, and replacing a cube. Region a = grasping; b and c = lifting; d = holding; e = lowering; f and g = releasing. The load force (in newtons [N]) is in the gravitational direction, the grip force is imposed by the fingers pinching the cube, and the position is the height of the cube relative to its starting position on the table. The ratio of grip force to load force is set such that it just prevents the cube from slipping. (After Westling and Johansson, 1984.)

Action for Perception

Let's now consider the action-for-perception side of haptic processing. Lederman and Klatzky (1987) coined the term **exploratory procedure** for a particular way of feeling an object in order to learn about one or more of its properties (**Figure 13.22**). Each exploratory procedure is optimal for obtaining precise details about one or two specific properties. For example, to find out how rough an object is, the best exploratory procedure is lateral motion—moving the fingers back and forth across the surface. This is the exploratory procedure that people freely choose when they wish to learn about roughness, and research indicates that it is also

exploratory procedure A stereotyped hand movement pattern used to touch objects in order to perceive their properties; each procedure is best for determining one (or more) object properties.

Lateral motion: texture

Pressure: hardness

Static contact: temperature

Unsupported holding: weight

Enclosure: global shape, volume

Contour following: global shape, exact shape

Figure 13.22 Exploratory procedures described by Lederman and Klatzky, and the object properties associated with each procedure. (After Lederman and Klatzky, 1987.)

the one that works best. A closer look within these general patterns reveals that people fine-tune exploration according to expectations and goals. People apply more force and move more quickly when discriminating surfaces by roughness than when they are merely told to explore (Tanaka et al., 2014). When they expect to probe a soft surface, they move more quickly, but less forcefully, than when they expect a rigid surface (Kaim and Drewing, 2009).

To explain why each exploratory procedure is linked to a specific object property, we must consider both the neural structures that transduce information and the processes that operate on that information. Why do we rub, for example, in order to perceive surface roughness? The answer is that relevant receptors become more active. For roughness, two neural populations are relevant. K. O. Johnson and his colleagues (K. O. Johnson, 2002) have shown that the activity of slowly adapting mechanoreceptors (the SA I fibers) is a principal basis for the perception of surfaces that are at least moderately rough; these receptors are ten times as responsive when there is relative motion between the skin and the surface (rubbing) as when the fingers rest against the surface. When surface variations are very fine, the mechanoreceptors responsive to high-frequency vibrations (the FA II fibers) appear to encode surface roughness; again, stroking with the fingers is needed to set up the vibration (see Hollins, 2002).

The activity of the receptors is sent on for processing that further differentiates coarse and fine textures. As your finger sweeps across a coarsely varying surface like rough sandpaper, the pattern of force varies with the hills and troughs on the object's surface, providing a spatial map of the variations in skin deformation that is sensed by the SA I fibers. This map is passed on to higher-level neural structures, which integrate the lower-level information into an overall measure of the amount of variation that the brain then uses to estimate the roughness of the surface. Whereas coarse textures are perceived over space, fine textures are processed as pressure variation over time. Now the skin may act less like a map and more like the ear. Just this argument was made by Saal, Wang, and Bensmaia (2016), using data like that shown in **Figure 13.23**. Figure 13.23A shows that FA II afferents fire in synchrony with vibrating pressure applied to the skin. Figure 13.23B shows a similar pattern produced when the skin rubs a fabric texture. The analogy between hearing and tactile texture perception becomes even more compelling when we see that the equivalent of a sound spectrogram can be obtained for fabrics passed over the fingertip, in this case showing the frequency of oscillation on the skin rather than sound waves acting on the tympanic membrane (Figure 13.23C, D). Different fabrics, like instruments, produce different "timbres."

> **FURTHER DISCUSSION** of timbre can be found in Chapter 10 on pages 331–332 and **Web Activity 10.3: Timbre**.

The What System of Touch: Perceiving Objects and Their Properties

Chapter 4 described the processes that underlie visual object recognition. We need somatosensation to control simple actions such as standing or grasping and to warn of danger through pain, but how much value does the sense of touch have as an object recognition system? You know that touch alone can function quite well to identify objects if you have ever gotten out of bed in the dark to use the bathroom. And the next time you get dressed, try to keep your gaze constantly focused on your hands as you button your shirt. This simple exercise

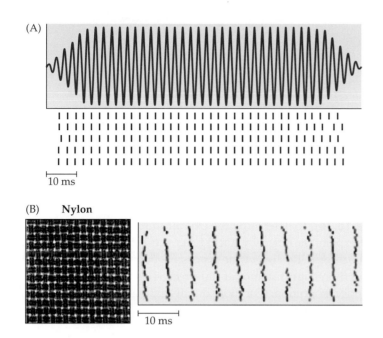

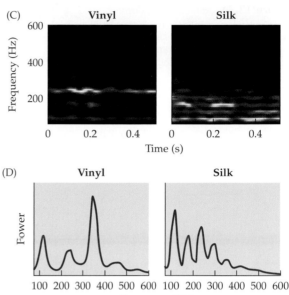

Figure 13.23 Effects of vibration on the skin from a controlled stimulus and rubbing fabric. (A) Trace of a vibrating stylus pressing on the skin at a rate of 400 Hz. Just below it are points in time where an FA II afferent fired as the skin was vibrated; each row depicts firing to a different presentation of the stimulus. All presentations produce a firing pattern that is directly coupled with the vibration over time. (B) Similarly synchronized firing of FA II afferents for a nylon patch (illustrated at left). (C) The spectrogram (frequency versus time) obtained from measurement of skin oscillation as a fabric (vinyl or silk) is scanned over the skin at 80 Hz. (D) The power at different frequencies in the spectrograms for the two fabrics; vinyl and silk demonstrate distinct fabric "timbres." (A, D after Saal, Wang, and Bensmaia, 2016; B, C from Saal, Wang, and Bensmaia, 2016.)

should convince you that even when you can use vision, you sometimes rely on touch to recognize objects and their parts. On the other hand, object recognition by touch has its limits: the designers of coins know that it is imperative to be able to tell one from another in your pocket, but the Susan B. Anthony dollar nonetheless failed, because it felt too similar to the quarter.

PERCEIVING MATERIAL VERSUS GEOMETRIC PROPERTIES People can perform haptic object recognition very well. Klatzky, Lederman, and Metzger (1985) asked people to identify each of 100 common objects (e.g., a fork, a brush, a paper clip) placed in their hands. Not only did people perform almost perfectly without looking at the objects, but they also generally responded in less than about 2 seconds. However, the information used in haptic object recognition is quite different from that used in visual object recognition. Consider the difference between material properties—those that do not depend on the structure of a particular object, like its surface roughness—and geometric properties like size and shape. In haptic perception, the observer is in contact with the object being observed, so material properties of the object (is it soft? cold? fuzzy?) are easy to perceive, and they play a crucial role in the recognition process. In vision there is no physical contact, so thermal and textural properties of objects are much more difficult to perceive.

Therefore, the geometric properties of objects are the most important for visual recognition. Indeed, sparse line drawings may be quite easy to recognize visually, but they are hard to recognize when presented haptically as raised

Figure 13.24 Examples of common objects that are easy to recognize visually in two-dimensional form but that when raised for haptic presentation are not easily recognized by touch. (After Lederman et al., 1990.)

contours (**Figure 13.24**). To determine the overall shape of an object haptically, we usually must explore the object by tracing along its contours with our fingers. Integrating tactile information over time is possible but not very efficient, which is why the instantly recognizable material properties tend to be much more important in haptic recognition. (For more on this topic, see **Web Activity 13.6: Haptic Object Recognition**.)

THE ILLUSORY GEOMETRY OF CURVATURE   At least for the geometric property of curvature, what we perceive by touch is something of an illusion. As we learned in Chapter 4, perceptual illusions like illusory contours don't arise by accident; they are the result of the heuristics and algorithms that perceptual systems use to interpret sensory data. Illusory contours can be found in touch as well as with vision; they arise from the way haptic perceptual systems interpret data from exploratory procedures. Take a look at **Figure 13.25A**, which depicts the kind of curved contour you might feel on a computer mouse. As shown in **Figure 13.25B**, running your finger over this curve would change both its height in space and the slant of the surface pressing against your finger at the contact location. Using a clever mechanical device, researchers were able to simulate these effects as in **Figure 13.25C** or manipulate the two cues independently (slant in **Figure 13.25D**, height in **Figure 13.25E**), in order to determine which cue produces the perception of a curved surface (Wijntjes et al., 2009). They found that discrimination between levels of curvature relied almost entirely on the momentary variation in slant, rather than the up-and-down movement of the finger. In fact, it is possible to produce the illusion of a curved surface simply by changing the slant of the surface against the finger as it makes a horizontal pass, without lifting it up and down.

FURTHER DISCUSSION of illusory contours in vision can be found in Chapter 4 on pages 110–111.

If the orientation of the surface contacting the finger is what matters for curvature perception, one might ask whether simply passing a surface below someone's finger, without allowing active exploration, would be sufficient for the person to perceive that it is curved. The surprising result of such a manipulation is that the minimal amount of curvature needed to perceive a surface as not flat is actually less in a passive condition than an active one (Cheeseman, Norman, and Kappers, 2016). This finding may reflect an inhibitory circuit that has been identified in monkeys, by which commands to move the arm suppress inputs from the peripheral tactile afferents (Chapman, Jiang, and Lamarre, 1988). If the inhibitory process holds for humans, then the ability to feel the surface

(A)

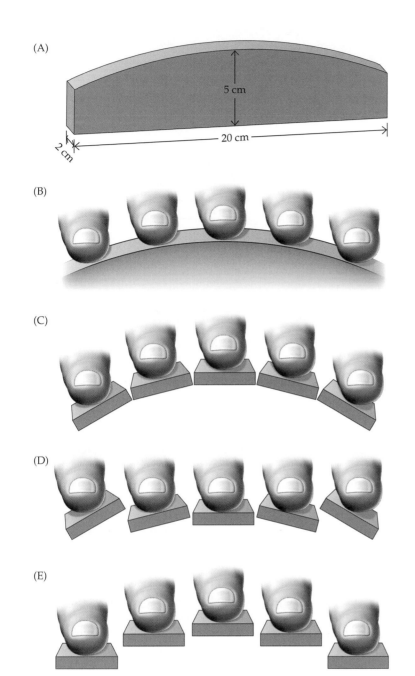

Figure 13.25 Illusory contours in touch. (A) A physical curved surface; (B) position and height as a fingertip explores the surface; (C) equivalent changes to those in (B) but induced by a platform that rotates and changes height depending on spatial position; (D) a curve induced entirely by rotation of the platform; (E) a curve induced entirely by height changes in the platform. (After Wijntjes et al., 2009.)

orientation underlying curvature perception is reduced when people move their arms to explore.

HAPTIC SEARCH As we saw in Chapter 7, a number of so-called preattentive features in the visual domain are presumed to be critical in the visual object recognition process. These features can be identified by the extent to which they "pop out" in a visual search task. For example, if you are searching for a red object, you will be equally fast at finding it regardless of how many green objects are presented along with it. This result implies that the "redness" of an object is available to recognition processes before attentional mechanisms examine the objects in the display and integrate the various features of each one.

(A)

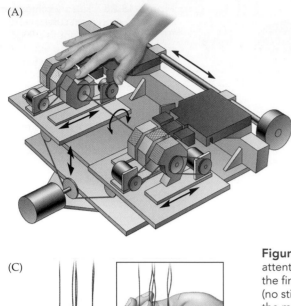

(B)

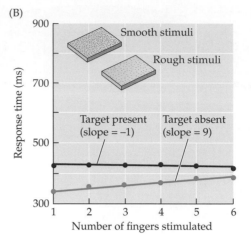

(C)

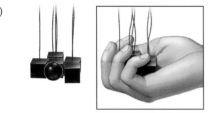

Figure 13.26 An experiment investigating whether touch supports pre-attentive feature detection. (A) The apparatus used to display targets to the fingertips. The rotating drums bring either a stimulus patch or a cutout (no stimulus) to the upper surface, and then they rise as a whole to contact the middle three fingers of both hands (only one hand is shown). (B) The amount of time required to detect a rough target among smooth distractors as a function of the number of fingers stimulated. (C) A three-dimensional version, where a target object (sphere among cubes in the example shown) is detected among objects grasped in the hand (inset). (A, B after Lederman and Klatzky, 1997; C after Plaisier, Bergmann Tiest, and Kappers, 2009.)

Does the sense of touch also support preattentive feature detection? To find out, Lederman and Klatzky (1997) constructed a set of surfaces something like a tactile slot machine with one key for each of six fingers. The subject's right hand is shown in **Figure 13.26A**. Stimulus patches were mounted around the planar edges of each of six stimulus wheels. On each trial, the wheels were rotated until the desired stimulus patches were facing upward to form the haptic display. The entire display was then moved up to contact different combinations of the middle three fingertips of each hand. Using this apparatus, Lederman and Klatzky found that a number of haptic features do indeed pop out. As **Figure 13.26B** shows, participants in these experiments were just as fast at detecting a rough surface when there was no smooth surface in the tactile "display" as when there were as many as five smooth surfaces. Similarly, a hard surface popped out of a group of soft surfaces, a cool surface popped out of warm surfaces, and a surface with an edge popped out of perfectly flat surfaces.

Plaisier, Bergmann Tiest, and Kappers (2009) developed a three-dimensional version of the haptic search paradigm in which clusters of objects were grasped in the hand, as shown in **Figure 13.26C**. Objects with different shapes had corresponding differences in the locations of edges, surface curvature, surface area, and height-to-width ratio. By means of a single grasp, participants exhibited highly efficient search when targets and distractors differed in the type of shape; for example, a cube grasped within a handful of spheres tended to pop out.

However, not every haptic difference supports efficient search. For example, response times increased with the number of distractors when the task was to find a target with a horizontally oriented edge among distractors having vertical edges. Note that horizontal targets do pop out of vertical distractors in visual search tasks. This distinction fits nicely with the previous observation that haptic recognition relies extensively on material properties but that the tactile system does not appear to be set up to efficiently differentiate object contours by their spatial layout.

PERCEIVING PATTERNS WITH THE SKIN   Even if pattern perception by touch is not terribly efficient, it can be done, especially if the patterns are small enough to be perceived by a single fingertip. Loomis (1990) suggested that, to some extent, touch acts like blurred vision when the fingertip explores a raised pattern. (Note the contrast with the previous argument, that the skin acts like an ear when perceiving a fine texture!) He tested people's ability to identify a set of patterns including Braille symbols, English and Japanese letters, and geometric forms—a few of which are shown in **Figure 13.27**. Sometimes the patterns were presented to the fingertips as raised elements. Other times they were presented visually behind a blurring screen that matched the resolution of the eye with the more limited acuity of fingertip skin. Interestingly, Loomis found very similar patterns of visual and tactile confusion errors—that is, responses in which one pattern was confused for another. This finding suggests that a common decision process operates on both haptically and visually perceived patterns.

In the Braille alphabet, shown in the first row of Figure 13.27, each letter is formed by raising some of the dots in a 2 × 3 array. For the letter *A*, for example, a single dot is raised in the top left position; and for the letter *Q*, all dots except for the one in the lower right position are raised. This design reflects a compromise between the skin's acuity and its "field of view," the area of skin that we can take in all at once. It would be nice to include more than six dots in the array, but because of the spatial blurring imposed by the skin, denser patterns would be difficult to resolve and discriminate (remember that two-point touch thresholds on the fingertips are about 1 mm). Spreading a greater number of dots across a larger contact area would not work either, because then the pattern would extend beyond the fingertip. Unfortunately, people are unable to "read" more than one finger at a time, suggesting that our tactile field of view is very narrow.

TACTILE AGNOSIA   Just as lesions in the temporal lobe can produce visual agnosia (see Chapter 5), lesions of the parietal lobe can produce **tactile agnosia**, an inability to identify objects by touch. In making a diagnosis of tactile agnosia, the neurologist needs to be able to eliminate other possibilities. Is the problem impaired motor control, which would prevent the exploratory procedures needed to effectively learn about an object's properties? Or might the problem be a higher-level cognitive dysfunction, such as a loss of access to object names?

We already described a patient who could not recognize objects by touch but could locate them. She had tactile agnosia with her right hand, due to a lesion in the left inferior parietal region of her brain, but the deficit did not extend to her left hand. Reed and Caselli (1994) documented that, although the patient could not recognize objects such as a key chain or a combination lock with her right

tactile agnosia The inability to identify objects by touch.

frame of reference The coordinate system used to define locations in space.

egocenter The center of a reference frame used to represent locations relative to the body.

hand, she could easily recognize these objects visually or with her left hand, ruling out a general loss of knowledge about objects. Other capabilities were normal in both hands, including sensory threshold levels and the movements with which objects were explored. The patient could also discriminate between objects with differing weight and roughness using either hand. And she could answer questions about the haptic properties of named objects, such as whether an orange was harder than an apple, indicating that she had the ability to remember and imagine how objects felt.

Thus, the patient could acquire information with her impaired hand about an object's properties (e.g., its weight and roughness), and she had intact haptic knowledge about objects she had encountered in the past. What she lacked was a connection between these two components of object identification. That is, either she was unable to integrate the perceived properties into a coherent object representation, or she was unable to match perceived representations to stored representations in memory.

The Where System of Touch: Locating Objects

As with other sensory modalities, knowing *what* a haptic stimulus might be is only part of the perceptual problem. We also need to know *where* that stimulus is located, because we often want to do something with it. If you are already touching an object, you obviously know where it is (a tree limb that you bump your head on is in the air; one that you stumble over has fallen to the ground). If you are not yet touching the object but can see it, your sense of vision can work out where the object is and guide your reaching behavior. But what about groping for the snooze button on your alarm clock when your eyes have not yet opened for the day? As mentioned already, there is evidence that touch, like vision, has a specialized neural pathway for dealing with questions of where objects are located, as compared with knowing what they are like.

HAPTIC OBJECT LOCALIZATION Like visual and auditory localization, haptic object localization first requires that we establish a **frame of reference**. For vision, the center of the reference frame—the **egocenter**—is located near the bridge of the nose, between the two eyes; the auditory egocenter is at a point smack in the middle of the head (between the two ears). One way to pinpoint your haptic egocenter is to place your left index finger on top of the edge of a desk or table in a natural position on the left side of your body, close your eyes, and try to match this location by placing your right index finger on the bottom of the desk. If you do this many times, you may find that you consistently go too far to the left. Conversely, if you try to match the location of your right index finger with your left, you will be more likely to err too far to the right. **Figure 13.28** shows a version of this task using a stylus in each hand instead of the index finger. A careful analysis of errors in a task of this type led Haggard et al. (2000) to conclude that there is, in fact, no single, fixed frame of reference for the haptic perception

(A) Top view

(B) Front view

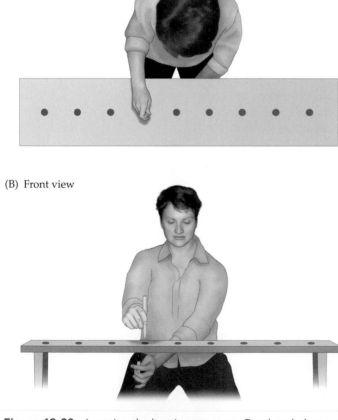

Figure 13.28 Locating the haptic egocenter. One hand places a stylus on the target on the upper table surface, and the other hand attempts to match up underneath the table in the corresponding location. (After Haggard et al., 2000.)

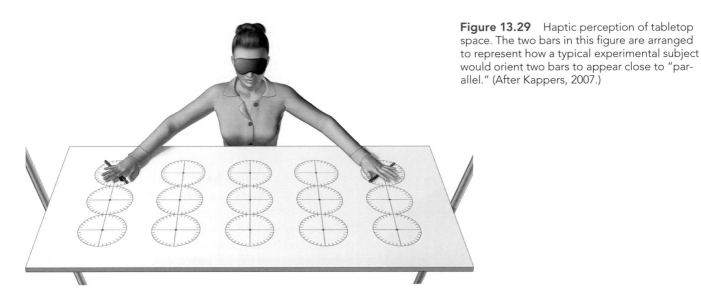

Figure 13.29 Haptic perception of tabletop space. The two bars in this figure are arranged to represent how a typical experimental subject would orient two bars to appear close to "parallel." (After Kappers, 2007.)

of locations. In the case of the index finger reaching task, the egocenter appears to be located at the shoulder of the arm doing the reaching. In other tasks, the egocenter may move to other positions on the body.

Although you might think you're pretty accurate at determining how external objects are oriented in haptic space, research has shown that people make surprisingly large and systematic errors. Try the following task, which is an informal demonstration of the experiment illustrated in **Figure 13.29** (Kappers, 2007). Have a friend place two pencils in front of you within reach, one far off to your left and the other far off to your right. Position your hands in a natural way on both pencils. The orientation of the left pencil should be fixed so that its length lies crosswise to the fingers of your left hand. The right pencil should be set in a random position beneath your right hand. Rotate the right-hand pencil until it feels parallel to the left-hand pencil. Now have a look at how the two pencils are aligned with respect to each other. Are they physically parallel?

In the actual experiment (Kappers, 2007), the rods at the two positions illustrated in Figure 13.29 were rotated to orientations differing by 40 degrees on average! Although individuals varied in their susceptibility to spatial errors in this haptic parallelism task (errors for the positions shown ranged from 8 to as much as 91 degrees), the average trends were quite consistent. Participants tended to judge what was parallel by weighting their orientation judgments with respect to two different spatial frames of reference: one was egocentric (with reference to the body, and commonly centered on the hand); the other was allocentric (with reference to external space).

Tactile Spatial Attention

Although the last 50 years or so have produced a considerable amount of research on visual and auditory attention, only more recently have scientists begun to investigate the nature of the processes that underlie tactile attention. In this section we focus on tactile spatial attention.

FURTHER DISCUSSION of attention as it relates to visual perception can be found in Chapter 7.

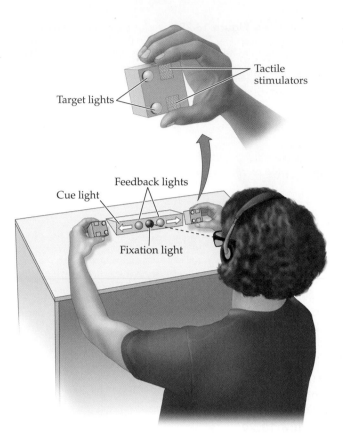

Target lights

Tactile stimulators

Feedback lights

Cue light

Fixation light

Figure 13.30 Studying competition between sensory modalities. In each hand the subject holds a cube that has vibrotactile stimulators and lights, either of which can signal the required response. The arrows near the feedback lights are used to direct attention. (After Spence, Pavani, and Driver, 2000.)

endogenous In reference to spatial attention, a form of top-down (knowledge-driven) control in which attention is voluntarily directed toward the site where the observer anticipates a stimulus will occur.

exogenous In reference to spatial attention, a form of bottom-up (stimulus-driven) attention reflexively (involuntarily) directed toward the site at which a stimulus has abruptly appeared.

When people anticipate being touched in a particular location, they can voluntarily direct their attention to that location. Attention that is directed in this way is known as **endogenous** (or top-down) control, in contrast to reactive **exogenous** (or bottom-up) processing. In one study (Spence, Pavani, and Driver, 2000), participants were asked to indicate whether a sustained force or a series of pulses was delivered to a fingertip (**Figure 13.30**). The stimulated fingertip could be on the left or the right hand. A visual precue, in the form of an arrow, predicted which hand would receive the stimulation. If people could make use of this precue to direct attention to the predicted hand, it was expected that they would be faster at deciding whether the stimulus was sustained or pulsed. And indeed, this was the case: the precue sped up responses relative to a no-cue control. Occasionally, however, the precue directed the participant's attention to the wrong hand, and on such trials people responded more slowly than in the no-cue condition. These effects are analogous to attentional cueing effects in vision and audition, showing that tactile attention is likewise a limited resource that must be allocated in one way or another.

The sense of touch also demonstrates the attentional phenomena of change blindness and inattentional blindness, described in Chapter 7. In a study mimicking the flicker paradigm used in visual change blindness, Gallace, Tan, and Spence (2007) stimulated participants with vibrations at two or three sites on the body and asked them to detect when the number of vibrations changed from one presentation to the next. When the second presentation was preceded by a brief period in which multiple sites were stimulated, the ability to detect a change decreased dramatically. Even a single irrelevant vibratory stimulus, called a "mudsplash," between the two vibratory patterns substantially decreased the ability to detect differences between them. An analog to inattentional blindness has also been demonstrated, where people fail to detect a vibration on the hand while attending to a demanding visual search task—it's called inattentional numbness, of course (Murphy and Dalton, 2016).

Social Touch

As we learned in the discussions of pleasant touch and autism, influences of touch extend beyond perception and action to encompass social interaction. Many words describing interpersonal responses refer to haptic properties, as when we describe someone as "warm," "cold," "hard," or even "a soft touch." Work of Inagaki and Eisenberger (2013) suggests that these verbal connections are not just metaphoric. After reading loving messages from others with whom they had close relationships, people felt physically warmer, and conversely, holding a heated pack led to heightened feelings of social connection. Brain imaging further revealed that activation by physical warmth and activation by loving messages were found in common brain areas, particularly the insula, an area that we have seen is associated with positive touch-related experiences. Affectionate touch between adults promotes the health of the individuals and their relationship (Jakubiak and Feeney, 2016).

The connection between physical and social warmth may be the result of past experience with a caregiver, but it may also have a genetic component. It has been found, in fact, that touch affects social interactions through individual characteristics that we think of as genetically determined, like personality. Work in the field of *epigenetics* has led to a model describing how the expression of genes related to social interaction is controlled by touch in the rat. Mother rats who lick and groom their pups produce offspring who tend to lick and groom their own pups as well. "Aha!" we might say, there must be a licking-and-grooming gene that is passed from one generation to the next. But to complicate matters, if pups from attentive and remote rat moms are switched at birth, as in the old fable, they "inherit" the behaviors of their adoptive, rather than biological, mothers (D. Francis et al., 1999). Their maternal behavior is governed not by their genetic makeup, but by the grooming behavior they have experienced.

Have the pups learned from their experience, then, to lick and groom? The mechanism for passing on the behavior is not what we normally think of as learning by association. There is instead an epigenetic process that turns licking-and-grooming genes off or on, according to the pup's experience with the same behaviors, by regulating neuroendocrine systems (Champagne, 2008). Complex behaviors are transmitted from one rat generation to the next by regulation of the genes, not control of their component DNA. Evidence for a similar mechanism in humans has been obtained (McGowan et al., 2009).

The rat mother's contact has consequences well beyond the maternal care exhibited by the offspring when they in turn have pups. Offspring of licking-and-grooming mothers turn out to be less timid than those of remote mothers.

Interactions between Touch and Other Modalities

Touch does not occur only in the absence of other sensory input, of course. We commonly touch objects that we see, and we hear the consequences of contact. How does the perceptual system as a whole deal with signals from multiple modalities? Sometimes they compete, and sometimes the whole is an integrated combination of the different inputs.

Competition can arise when resources are limited—that is, when attention comes into play in a particular task. Do the different modalities compete among one another for attentional resources as well? Consider the fact that the pressure stimulus of your posterior on your seat seems to have lost out to this visual text in the current competition for your attention (until now, that is). In the lab, Spence, Nicholls, and Driver (2001) did a cross-modal version of the same sort of endogenous cueing experiment that was described previously (see Figure 13.30): They led participants to expect a stimulus to be presented via one modality and then sometimes presented it in a different modality. The participants were instructed to indicate with a foot pedal whether a target stimulus appeared on their left or right side. The stimulus could be noise from a loudspeaker (audition), a red circle at the location of the loudspeaker (vision), or a rod pressing the finger while it touched the loudspeaker (touch); and a cue could direct attention toward any of the three modalities.

Again, responses were faster when the cue was valid and slower when it was invalid. Interestingly, the greatest cost for an invalid cue occurred when observers expected a tactile stimulus but a visual or auditory stimulus was presented instead. This result may imply that the sense of touch has a particularly restricted attentional channel—that once attention is focused on the touch modality, it is relatively difficult to reallocate it. Or it may be that visual attention and auditory attention are shared to some extent, because expectancies in those modalities could be directed to a common location in external space, whereas the expectancy for touch was directed to a location on the body.

In contrast to attentional competition, intersensory integration can occur when different modalities receive information about the same object. Suppose, for example, that you're touching sandpaper. The roughness you feel also depends on the roughness you see. Participants in an experiment by Lederman, Thorne, and Jones (1986) saw one sandpaper surface and felt another but were told the two surfaces were one and the same. When they were asked about how closely packed the elements in the surface were, they were more strongly influenced by vision. When asked about the roughness of the surface, however, touch became more important and vision less important.

In some circumstances, one modality may appear to dominate. In a classic study pitting vision against touch, Rock and Victor (1964) had people grasp a square while looking at it through a distorting lens. What these participants felt was pretty much what they saw: a rectangle. That is, feeling that the sides of the shape were equal in length had essentially no influence. But dominance by one modality over the other is not the rule. A more general model is that people integrate the signals from two modalities, producing a weighted average. That is, they use x percent of the information from one modality and $(100 - x)$ percent from the other. The relative weighting reflects the quality of the signal from each modality.

Ernst and Banks (2002) demonstrated such integration with an apparatus that simultaneously created touch and sight of the same virtual display. The display consisted of a plane with a raised bar across the middle (**Figure 13.31**). The virtual visual display was produced with stereo glasses and an appropriate pair of random dot stereograms, one presented to each eye (see Figure 6.35), creating the visual illusion of a bar stepping up from a plane. The corresponding virtual touch display was created with a device that generated forces that pushed back on the hand whenever contact was made with the simulated surface. When the bar heights presented to the two modalities did not match (the touched bar was higher than the viewed bar, or vice versa), the perceived height of the bar was a weighted compromise between them, with vision more strongly weighted than touch. When the investigators made the information from vision less reliable by randomly changing the apparent height of some of the surface dots, the weight assigned to touch increased, and it played a greater role in determining the perceived height of the bar.

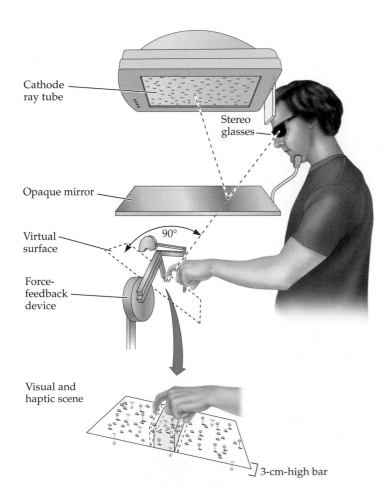

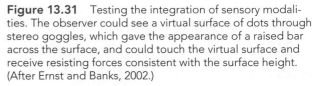

Figure 13.31 Testing the integration of sensory modalities. The observer could see a virtual surface of dots through stereo goggles, which gave the appearance of a raised bar across the surface, and could touch the virtual surface and receive resisting forces consistent with the surface height. (After Ernst and Banks, 2002.)

Multiple modalities may collaborate by signaling different, but complementary, sources of information about an object. Our discussion of object perception emphasized that vision and touch are intrinsically complementary: one is well suited to convey an object's geometry; the other, its material. Perhaps the philosopher Molyneaux had this complementarity in mind when he asked his famous question about whether a blind person who gained sight would recognize familiar objects with this new sense. (For a rather different way in which the modalities cooperate see **Web Essay 13.4: Lego Blocks Front and Back**.)

■ Sensation & Perception in Everyday Life ■

Haptic Simulation for Surgical Training

How do surgeons learn to perform procedures? Like the old joke that asks, "How do I get to Carnegie Hall?" the answer is practice, practice, practice. It has been estimated that several hundred surgeries are needed for surgeons to become proficient in laparoscopic procedures, the minimally invasive technique that has replaced open surgery for many medical problems (Vickers et al., 2009). In order to enable surgeons to train without affecting a human patient along the way, medical simulators that combine virtual touch and vision have been developed. The simulator incorporates a handheld device that senses the forces the surgeon is applying during a virtual operation and delivers forces and vibrations that provide surgical "feel," based on a computer model of the tissue and surgical implement.

To illustrate the complexity of this problem, think about a simulator for training in oral surgery. The model must convey the bouncing contact between the tool and the rigid teeth, with their complex surfaces; the way the soft tissue deforms and stiffens as it is probed by the tool tip; the sudden release of pushing force at a point of puncture; as well as adverse events like tissue tearing. Underlying these features are complex physical models. Another technical achievement is the haptic interface that senses the forces applied by the operator and delivers the computational results back to the handheld controller. Several commercial force-feedback products are in the marketplace for this purpose.

Despite the challenges, virtual visual-haptic training devices have been developed for palpation of the body, extracting cerebrospinal fluid, dental procedures, endoscopy (examining the interior of a hollow organ or body cavity), bone drilling, removing foreign bodies from the eye, and more. While such surgical trainers are on the increase, a more elusive problem is adding haptic feedback to real surgical procedures where the surgeon controls a robot to perform laparoscopic surgery and the sense of touch therefore provides no direct information about the effects on the patient's body. The race is on for haptic devices to add virtual touch to robotic-assisted surgery (**Figure 13.32**).

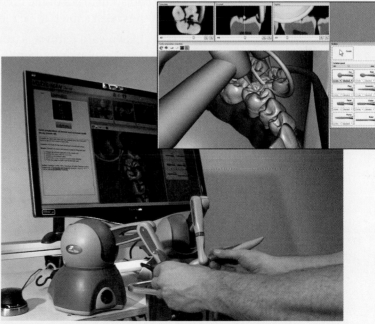

Figure 13.32 The Voxel-Man dental simulator and an inset showing a close-up of the screen during an interaction. (Photos courtesy of Voxel-ManGroup.)

Summary

1. The sense of touch produces a number of distinct sensory experiences. Each type of experience is mediated by its own sensory receptor system(s). Touch receptors are responsive not only to pressure, but also to vibration, changes in temperature, and noxious stimulation. The kinesthetic system, which also contributes to our sense of touch, is further involved in sensing limb position and the movement of our limbs in space. Pleasant or emotional touch is another form of sensory specialization.

2. Four classes of pressure-sensitive (mechano-) receptors have been found within hairless skin, and another five classes within hairy skin. The organs used to sense limb position and movement (namely, our muscles, tendons, and joints) are more deeply situated within the body. Thermoreceptors respond to changes in skin temperature that occur, for example, when we contact objects that are warmer or cooler than our bodies. Nociceptors signal tissue damage (or its potential) and give rise to sensations of pain. TRP channels have been found that respond to thermal pain and hot and cold tastes.

3. The pathways from touch receptors to the brain are complex. Two major pathways have been identified: a fast one (the dorsal column–medial lemniscal pathway), which carries information from mechanoreceptors, and a slower one (the spinothalamic pathway), which carries thermal and nociceptive information. Both enter the dorsal horn of the spinal cord, which itself has dense neural connectivity. The pathways project to the thalamus and from there to the primary somatosensory area, located in the parietal lobe just behind the central sulcus. This area contains several somatotopically organized subregions, in which adjacent areas of the body project to adjacent areas of the brain. The neural organization of the brain for touch has been shown to be remarkably plastic, even in adults.

4. Downward pathways from the brain play an important role in the perception of pain. According to the gate control theory, signals along these pathways interact at the spinal cord with those from the periphery of the body. Such interactions can block the pain signals that would otherwise be sent forward to the brain. The sensation of pain is further moderated by areas in the cortex.

5. Investigators have measured sensitivity to mechanical force by applying nylon hairs of different diameters to the skin. They determine spatial acuity of the skin by measuring the two-point touch threshold, and more precisely by discriminating the orientation of gratings applied to the skin. Tactile pressure sensitivity and spatial acuity vary with body site because of varying concentrations of different types of mechanoreceptors; similar (but not identical) variations are found with pain. The minimum depression of the skin needed to feel a stimulus vibrating at a particular rate (frequency) provides a measure of vibration sensitivity.

6. The sense of touch is intimately related to our ability to perform actions. Signals from the mechanoreceptors are necessary for simple actions such as grasping and lifting an object. Conversely, our own movements determine how touch receptors respond and, hence, which properties of the concrete world we can feel. Touch is better adapted to feeling the material properties of objects than it is to feeling their geometric features (e.g.,

shape), particularly when an object is large enough to extend beyond the fingertip.

7. Like other sensory modalities, touch gives rise to internal representations of the world, which convey the positions of objects using the body as a spatial reference system. Touch-derived representations are inputs to higher-level functions like allocation of attention and integration with information from other modalities.

8. The psychological study of touch is useful for a number of applications. Virtual touch environments that transmit forces to the touch receptors can provide a basis for training people to perform remote operations like surgery and perhaps, in the future, will convey the illusion of touched objects over the Internet.

14

Olfaction

■ Questions to Contemplate ■

Think about the following questions as you read this chapter. By the chapter's end, you should be able to answer and discuss them.

- If you had to give up one sensory modality, why would you *not* give up the sense of smell?

- How is odor liking and perception influenced by experience?

- What are some of the physical and psychological factors that influence olfactory sensitivity and perception?

- Is there any scientific basis to aromatherapy? If so, what is it?

- What are some ways in which olfaction is not like any of our other senses?

The story of the next two chapters begins at the dawn of life itself. When single-celled organisms first appeared on Earth, their basic purpose in life was to take in some substances (food) and avoid others (toxins). As these organisms evolved into multicellular creatures, detecting chemicals in the environment continued to be crucial for survival. Systems to detect and analyze environmental molecules were thus the first senses to evolve. Today, from the most complex of life-forms to the simplest, the basic principles—to approach chemicals that elicit pleasure and/or aid survival and to avoid chemicals that elicit aversion and/or hasten demise—remain the primary functions of the chemical senses.

Humans have two main chemical detection systems: one for molecules floating in the air, and another for molecules that enter our mouths. The technical names for these two systems are **olfaction** and **gustation**, respectively. The former, more commonly known as "smell," is the subject of this chapter. Gustation, which you probably know as "taste," will be explored in Chapter 15. Another chemical-sensing system that is important for our experiences of both

olfaction The sense of smell.

gustation The sense of taste.

Stephen Hanson, *Sunday Roast*, 2017

smells and tastes is the trigeminal system, innervated by the trigeminal nerve. The trigeminal system enables us to feel gustatory and olfactory experiences, like burning and cooling, and you will learn more about this system in Chapter 15. Our sense of smell is critically involved in our experience of food. The reason is because there are two routes through which we perceive odors. First we have **orthonasal olfaction**, which occurs when we sniff odorant molecules through our nostrils and they travel up our nose and onto the olfactory epithelium—as happens when we smell a rose. Orthonasal olfaction is the primary topic of this chapter. The second route is called **retronasal olfaction**, which occurs when we exhale in odorant molecules in our mouth and they travel up from the back of our mouth into our upper nasal cavity and onto the olfactory epithelium. Retronasal olfaction occurs when we are eating and drinking, and it produces the sensation of "flavor." You will learn more about retronasal olfaction and our experience of flavor in Chapter 15.

orthonasal olfaction Sniffing in and perceiving odors through our nostrils, which occurs when we are smelling something that is in the air.

retronasal olfaction Perceiving odors through the mouth while breathing and chewing. This is what gives us the experience of flavor.

Olfactory Physiology

Every day we inhale at least 23,000 times and with each breath comes the opportunity to experience the world around us through smell. But what is it that we are experiencing?

Odors and Odorants

odor The translation of a chemical stimulus into the sensation of an odor percept. For example, "The cake has a chocolate odor."

odorant A molecule that is defined by its physicochemical characteristics and that can be translated by the nervous system into the perception of a smell. For example, "You smelled the odorant methyl salicylate, which has the odor of wintergreen mint."

Olfactory sensations are called **odors**. The stimuli for odors are chemical compounds called odorants. An analogy can be made with vision, where wavelengths of light are stimuli and colors are the visual sensations. However, not every chemical is an **odorant**. To be smelled, odorant molecules must be volatile (able to float through the air), small (between 25 and 300 daltons), and hydrophobic (repellent to water). **Figure 14.1A** shows the chemical structures of two odorant molecules. Not all molecules that would seem to meet the basic requirements for being odorants have a smell to us. Two examples are natural gas (methane) and a by-product of methane, carbon monoxide (**Figure 14.1B**). Our evolutionary ancestors would have had no reason to detect these substances, which are not dangerous in the concentrations found in nature. But because the buildup of carbon monoxide in enclosed spaces such as homes with gas furnaces can be fatal, gas companies add a compound (tertiary-butyl mercaptan) that we smell as rotten eggs, to act as a warning signal when a stove's pilot light goes out. We also can't smell the molecules that make up the air we breathe, such as oxygen, helium, and nitrogen.

(A)   Menthol   2-Isobutyl-3-methoxypyrazine
(green bell pepper)

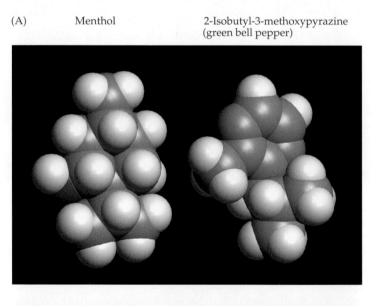

(B)   Methane   Carbon monoxide

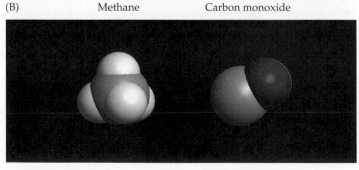

Figure 14.1 Odorants. (A) Most small, volatile, and hydrophobic molecules activate the sense of smell, (B) but there are notable exceptions to the rule, such as methane and carbon monoxide.

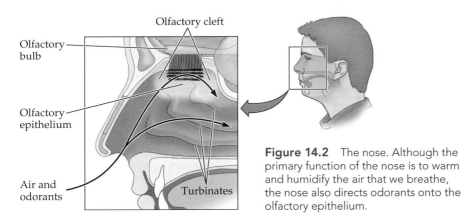

Olfactory cleft

Olfactory bulb

Olfactory epithelium

Air and odorants

Turbinates

Figure 14.2 The nose. Although the primary function of the nose is to warm and humidify the air that we breathe, the nose also directs odorants onto the olfactory epithelium.

The Human Olfactory Apparatus

Unlike the visual and auditory systems, but like the systems of touch and taste, the human olfactory system is tacked onto an organ that serves another purpose. The primary function of the nose (**Figure 14.2**) is to filter, warm, and humidify the air that we breathe. But the inside of the nose has small ridges called turbinates that add turbulence to incoming air, causing a small puff of each breath to rise upward, pass through a narrow space called the **olfactory cleft**, and settle on a yellowish patch of mucous membrane called the **olfactory epithelium (Figure 14.3)**. Notably, our two nostrils take in different amounts of air, and this **nasal dominance** alternates between our nostrils throughout the day. This means that, as a function of the amount of air inhaled, the two nostrils continuously vary in their sensitivities to odorants.

olfactory cleft A narrow space at the back of the nose into which air flows and where the olfactory epithelium is located.

olfactory epithelium A secretory mucous membrane in the nose whose primary function is to detect odorants in inhaled air. Located on both sides of the upper portion of the nasal cavity and the olfactory clefts, the olfactory epithelium contains three types of cells: olfactory sensory neurons, basal cells, and supporting cells.

nasal dominance The asymmetry characterizing the intake of air by the two nostrils, which leads to differing sensitivity to odorants between the two nostrils. Nasal dominance alternates nostrils throughout the day, but there is no predictability for when the nostrils alternate.

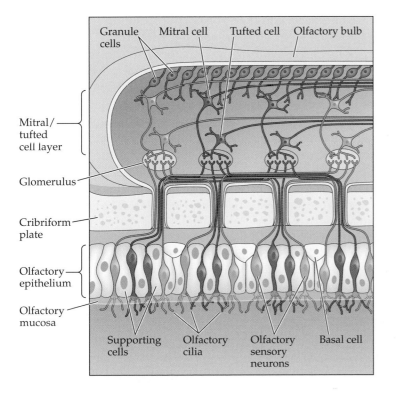

Granule cells

Mitral cell

Tufted cell

Olfactory bulb

Mitral/tufted cell layer

Glomerulus

Cribriform plate

Olfactory epithelium

Olfactory mucosa

Supporting cells

Olfactory cilia

Olfactory sensory neurons

Basal cell

Figure 14.3 The "retina of the nose." The olfactory epithelium contains three types of cells: olfactory sensory neurons (OSNs), basal cells, and supporting cells. The OSNs are located within a watery mucous layer on the epithelium; the hairlike olfactory cilia of the OSN dendrites project through the mucus and are the receptor sites for odorant molecules. The different colors of the OSNs in this illustration indicate the glomeruli onto which they converge. All blue OSNs connect to blue glomeruli, all purple to purple, and so on. This schematic illustrates the fact that different OSNs expressing the same receptors converge on the same type of glomerulus, no matter where they are in the olfactory epithelium.

Figure 14.4 A fluorescence image of an olfactory sensory neuron (lower right), with a schematic graph (upper right) of an action potential sequence following the application of odorant. The OSN collects odorant molecules via receptors on the cilia of its dendrites and sends action potentials to the brain through its axon. Note that pA = picoamperes (10^{-12} amperes). (Fluorescence image courtesy of C. Balmer and A. LaMantia.)

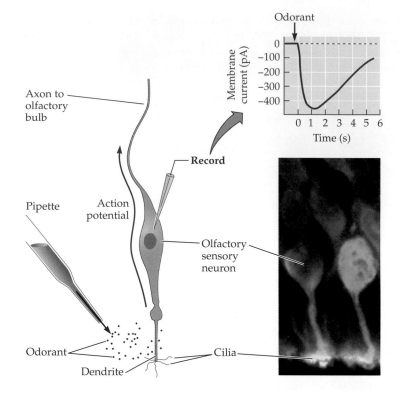

supporting cell One of the three types of cells in the olfactory epithelium. Supporting cells provide metabolic and physical support for the olfactory sensory neurons.

basal cell One of the three types of cells in the olfactory epithelium. Basal cells are the precursor cells to olfactory sensory neurons.

olfactory sensory neuron (OSN) One of three cell types—the main one—in the olfactory epithelium. OSNs are small neurons located within a mucous layer in the epithelium. The cilia on the OSN dendrites contain the receptor sites for odorant molecules.

cilium Any of the hairlike protrusions on the dendrites of olfactory sensory neurons. The receptor sites for odorant molecules are on the cilia, which are the first structures involved in olfactory signal transduction.

odorant receptor (OR) The region on the cilia of olfactory sensory neurons where odorant molecules bind.

glomerulus Any of the spherical conglomerates containing the incoming axons of the olfactory sensory neurons. Each OSN converges onto two glomeruli (one medial, one lateral).

The olfactory epithelium is the "retina of the nose." We have an olfactory epithelium at the back of each nasal passage, about 2¾ inches up from the nostril. Each epithelium measures about 1–2 square inches (depending on the size of the nose) and contains three types of cells: **supporting cells**, **basal cells**, and **olfactory sensory neurons** (**OSNs**). (See **Web Activity 14.1: Olfactory Anatomy.**)

OSNs (**Figure 14.4**) are small neurons that have **cilia** (singular *cilium*) protruding from the mucus covering the olfactory epithelium. These cilia are at the end of the OSN dendrite and have **odorant receptors** (**ORs**) on their tips. Note that OSNs are bipolar neurons and have one axon and one dendrite.

The basic rule of olfactory sensory physiology is "one to one to one": each OSN expresses only one type of OR, and all OSNs expressing the same type of OR project to the same type of **glomerulus** (singular *glomeruli*) (see Figure 14.3). The interaction between an odorant and the OR stimulates a cascade of biochemical events, ultimately producing an action potential that is transmitted along the axon of the OSN to the olfactory bulb (Schild and Restrepo, 1998). To initiate an action potential, about seven or eight odorant molecules must bind to a receptor, and it takes about 40 of these nerve impulses for a smell sensation to be reported.

You might be wondering how many odors we can detect. The latest findings suggest that the answer is over one trillion (Bushdid et al., 2014)! Although this number remains controversial (Gerkin and Castro, 2015), it seems likely that we can detect any and all "smellable" molecules. This means that our sense of smell is far better than formerly believed, and we can detect far more odors than the number of colors we can see (up to about 7.5 million) and the number of tones we can hear (approximately 340,000). Given that the universe of smell is right under our nose, can we actually perceive the scent of a trillion odors? The answer is "no"—for various reasons. Beyond the fact that we couldn't possibly live long enough—a trillion seconds is about 32,000 years—there are other, more mundane constraints, as you will discover throughout this chapter.

There has been disagreement over how many OSNs humans possess, because the number of OSNs in the human olfactory epithelia has never actually been counted. Therefore, the number arrived at has been extrapolated from research in other mammals. Until recently it was believed that we had about 20 million OSNs, split between the epithelia of our right and left nostrils. However, current research in rodents (Lam and Mombaerts, 2013) and micrographs of the human epithelia (Holbrook et al., 2011) suggest that the number of OSNs is between 5 and 10 million and that there are more OSNs expressing the same OR than previously thought (personal communication Charles Greer, June 4, 2013). More research may soon clarify this issue. Whatever the exact number of OSNs, we know that vision is the only sensory system that has more sensory neurons than olfaction. Despite this large number we are not the extreme sniffers of the animal kingdom. Dogs have at least 100 times more OSNs than humans. Humans can likely smell the same number of scents as dogs (the bloodhounds aren't talking, so we can't be sure), but dogs can sense odors at concentrations nearly 100 million times lower than the concentrations that humans can detect (Krestel et al., 1984; Willis et al., 2004). Other super smellers include pigs, which can smell the scent of truffles (the mushroom, not the chocolate) under 6 inches of soil, and salmon, which use smell to find the waters of their birth from hundreds of miles away (Dittman and Quinn, 1996). But the most extreme sniffer of all appears to be the African elephant, with approximately 2000 functional ORs (more than five times as many functional ORs as humans) and the longest nose in the animal kingdom (Niimura et al., 2014). Their incredible proboscis allows them to distinguish, with just a whiff, two ethnic groups with whom they share their habitat: the Masai whom they fear—to show their virility, young Masai men spear them—and the Kamba whom they ignore—the Kamba are farmers and do not bother the elephants (Bates et al., 2007).

It has long been assumed that humans are not very good at using their noses. But, despite comparatively few OSNs, human olfactory ability is actually very good. In one study, humans were able to follow a 10-meter-long scent track of chocolate aroma while on all fours in an open grass field (Porter et al., 2007), and the tracking pattern that they used was strikingly similar to that of a dog (**Figure 14.5**). Another recent study showed that humans, like homing pigeons, could use odors located at different places in a room to form a spatial map and navigate to various points in the room (Jacobs et al., 2015). Moreover, whether humans are worse at odor detection than other animals seems to depend on the odorant in question. In a recent test using six sulphur-containing compounds,

(A)

(B)

Figure 14.5 Tracking scents. (A) The path (red) of a dog following the scent trail (yellow) of a pheasant dragged through a field. (B) The path (red) of a human following a scent trail (yellow) of chocolate essential oil through a field. (From Porter et al., 2007.)

humans were able detect two of the compounds more acutely than mice, whereas mice were better than humans at detecting the other four (Sarrafchi et al., 2013; McGann, 2017). The absolute size of the **olfactory bulb** in humans is also much greater than the olfactory bulb of the mouse (**Figure 14.6A**), even though two hundred times more of a mouse's brain is devoted to the sense of smell. In fact, the number of neurons in the olfactory bulb is relatively conserved across mammals compared to the variability of other physical features, such as size and weight, in these same species. (**Figure 14.6B**). Therefore, absolute differences in the neural hardware for olfaction across species is much less than previously assumed. A re-examination of the literature has revealed that the belief that humans are poor smellers was proclaimed because the pressures of nineteenth-century religion and philosophy superseded scientific evidence, and the truth is that humans are very good smellers after all (McGann, 2017).

The axon on the ends of OSNs opposite the dendrite and cilia passes through the tiny sieve-like holes of the **cribriform plate**, a bony structure at the level of the eyebrows that separates the nose from the brain. A hard blow to the front or back of the head can cause the cribriform plate to be sharply jarred or fractured, slicing off the fragile olfactory axons and consequently inducing **anosmia** ("smell blindness"), the total absence of a sense of smell. Stem cells in the olfactory epithelium can form new OSNs; indeed, all of our OSNs die and regenerate about once every 28 days. However, fractured cribriform plates typically scar over, preventing the new OSN axons from passing through to the brain, thereby crippling the sense of smell for life.

(A)

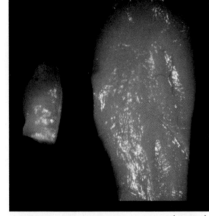

2 mm

Figure 14.6 Olfactory bulbs. (A) Comparison of the mouse and human olfactory bulb. (B) The number of olfactory bulb neurons differs across mammalian species but is much less variable than the differences in other physical features across those same species. (A from McGann, 2017; B after McGann, 2017.)

(B)

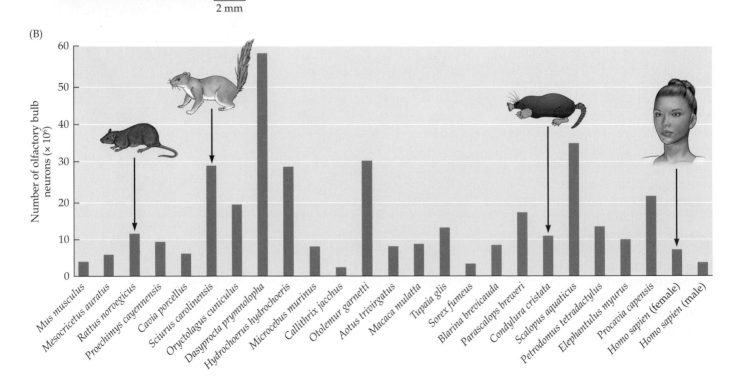

▪ Sensation & Perception in Everyday Life ▬

Anosmia

Anosmia ("smell blindness") is the total absence of a sense of smell. Hyposmia is a significantly reduced sense of smell. Smell loss is much more prevalent than most people think. From a survey by the National Institutes of Health (NIH) in 1994, it was conservatively estimated that one in every 100 people suffers from anosmia. However, more recent estimates indicate that as many as 14 million Americans over the age of 55 have a severely compromised sense of smell. When younger adults are included, it appears that about one in 20 Americans may have some olfactory dysfunction. However, compared with loss of vision or hearing, olfactory loss is paid little attention by both the medical and the general communities. The American Medical Association values the loss of smell as 1–5% of what a person's life is worth, whereas loss of vision is valued at 85%. In a questionnaire administered to students at the University of Pennsylvania, loss of the sense of smell was ranked equal to loss of one's big toe (Wrzesniewski, McCauley, and Rozin, 1999).

Despite general indifference to smell loss, anosmia can cause great suffering. Indeed, it has been reported that although the trauma of being blinded is initially worse than losing one's sense of smell, after one year blind people begin to cope better, whereas those with anosmia are faring worse, and deterioration in their quality of life typically becomes progressively more extensive with time (Herz, 2007). The reason is that losing our sense of smell affects almost every aspect of our lives. The consequences of smell loss are most obvious in our enjoyment of food and drink and the experience of flavor. But anosmia can also lead to serious health consequences, as people cannot detect food poisoning that doesn't have visual cues, and they cannot perceive smoke or the scent used to signal an accumulation of carbon monoxide. Anosmia also affects people's ability to function socially and to be intimate in sexual relationships. It impairs cognitive and spatial ability, eliminates some of our most significant memories, alters our sense of self, and can profoundly disturb emotional health. People who lose their sense of smell often fall into clinically depressive states, and because the lack of olfactory stimulation leads to progressive emotional deterioration, the depression that results can become dangerous. There is also a notable connection between depression and olfaction in people without anosmia. People suffering from depression have impaired performance on tests of olfactory perception, and they exhibit reduced olfactory bulb volume and activity in neurological regions associated with odor processing (Croy et al., 2014; Negoias et al., 2010). However, once they have recovered from a period of depression, their olfactory perception returns to normal. Unfortunately, if anosmia is not treatable, a prognosis of worsening depression is likely.

Being born anosmic is quite rare and affects less than 0.06% of the population. The most common cause of anosmia is sinus infection, followed by nasal polyps. Chronic sinusitis and allergies can also lead to anosmia. In these cases anosmia is due to blocked nasal passages, which prevent odorants from interacting with the olfactory receptors. Usually when these conditions are cured, the person regains normal smell

(Continued)

olfactory bulb   A blueberry-sized extension of the brain just above the nose, where olfactory information is first processed. There are two olfactory bulbs, one in each brain hemisphere, corresponding to the right and left nostrils.

cribriform plate   A bony structure riddled with tiny holes that separates the nose from the brain at the level of the eyebrows. The axons from the olfactory sensory neurons pass through the holes of the cribriform plate to enter the brain.

anosmia   The total inability to smell, most often resulting from sinus illness or head trauma.

■ Sensation & Perception in Everyday Life *(continued)*

function. Less commonly—about 30% of cases—anosmia is caused by head injury, which can occur in sports like football or boxing or through car or bicycle accidents. In these situations smell loss is usually permanent. Nevertheless, there is some very encouraging recent evidence that suggests that repeated sniffing of various odorants can result in some improvement in the ability to detect those compounds among patients whose traumatic injury was sustained within two years. The explanation is unclear but may be due to active sniffing stimulating olfactory bulb neurogenesis (Jiang, Twu, and Liang, 2017).

Many everyday toxins, including gasoline and hairdressing chemicals, can cause either temporary or permanent smell dysfunction (Smith, Davidson, and Murphy, 2009). Certain medications can also cause smell loss or disturbance—particularly those used in chemotherapy. In fact, many common drugs, including antibiotics, antidepressants, and even some antihistamines, can impair olfactory function (Doty and Bromley, 2004). Long-term excessive alcohol consumption also reduces olfactory function (Rupp et al., 2003). By contrast, marijuana may have ameliorating effects, as we'll discuss shortly.

Smell function also declines with age; however, the decrease in function is gradual and there is wide individual variability in severity. Notably, loss of smell among the elderly who live alone can lead to missed meals and poor nutrition. The symptoms of malnourishment can be misinterpreted as dementia, and people may be presumed to be cognitively impaired when they are "only" experiencing the normal olfactory dysfunction of aging. Fortunately, when a healthy diet is implemented in these instances, signs of cognitive impairment go away. However, it is also the case that smell loss is the first warning sign of several neurological disorders—in particular, Alzheimer's disease (AD) and Parkinson's disease (PD)—and olfactory symptoms often appear years before any other signs of the illness are present. If you know someone over 40 who has suddenly started having trouble identifying familiar smells, you may want to recommend a visit to a neurologist. The earlier AD and PD can be diagnosed, the better treatment outlook and prognosis are. Several tests can be administered to assess smell loss. The most common are the University of Pennsylvania Smell Identification Test (UPSIT) and Sniffin' Sticks. The UPSIT is a 40-item scratch-and-sniff multiple-choice test that measures detection and identification. Sniffin' Sticks involve three olfactory tests to evaluate threshold detection, odor discrimination, and odor identification.

Many smell and taste clinics throughout the country administer simple tests to determine the causes and treatment possibilities for olfactory loss and dysfunction. However, currently there is no equivalent of a hearing aid or glasses for the nose; therefore, if smell loss cannot be treated by addressing the underlying condition (e.g., sinus infection, medication use), it is likely to be permanent.

Neurophysiology of Olfaction

In someone with a healthily functioning sense of smell, the OSN axons pass through the cribriform plate, and form the **olfactory nerve** (cranial nerve I), as they enter the olfactory bulb (**Figure 14.7**). We have two olfactory bulbs, one in each brain hemisphere. Unlike the other senses we've studied so far, olfaction is **ipsilateral**, meaning that the right olfactory bulb gets information from the right nostril, and the left olfactory bulb gets information from the left nostril.

The synthetic chemical methyl salicylate, $C_8H_8O_3$, has an odor that we identify as wintergreen mint. Like other odorants, methyl salicylate can activate several different types of ORs, and it does so with different degrees of "weighting" depending on the receptor's affinity to the wintergreen molecule. Humans have between 350 and 400 different types of functioning ORs. Most of these receptors won't be activated by methyl salicylate; a few will be weakly activated, and one or two will be strongly activated (this will become clearer as you read the following sections).

The first relay for the OSNs in the brain is in the olfactory bulb, where the sensory nerve endings gather together to form tiny spheres called glomeruli.

olfactory nerve The first cranial nerve. The axons of the olfactory sensory neurons bundle together after passing through the cribriform plate to form the olfactory nerve, which conducts impulses from the olfactory epithelium in the nose to the olfactory bulb. Also called *cranial nerve I.*

ipsilateral Referring to the same side of the body (or brain).

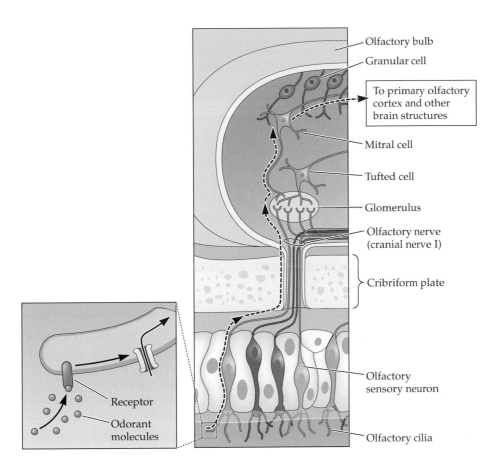

Figure 14.7 The pathway of olfactory perception, from odorant molecule to the olfactory bulb.

Molecular genetic studies in mice have shown that all neurons expressing a particular OR type, no matter where they are on the nasal epithelium, send their axons to the same glomerulus pair (consisting of one medial and one lateral glomerulus) in the olfactory bulb (Mombaerts et al., 1996). The distinct pattern of OR activation for a specific odorant is then translated into a specific pattern of spatial activity across the glomeruli. Methyl salicylate, for example, will activate a particular set of ORs and consequently produce a pattern of glomerular activity that is unique to it. The compounds of rose aroma will initiate a different activity pattern, and so on. The specific pattern of glomeruli activity is then interpreted by the brain as indicating a specific odor.

However, this relatively simple picture is complicated by the fact that each glomerulus may receive axons from several different receptor types. Moreover, our personal experience with an odor can actually change the pattern of activity that is produced by the glomeruli in the olfactory bulb. For example, if you liked methyl salicylate (wintergreen) mints but one day became ill after eating them, causing you to thereafter find the scent very unpleasant (illustrating what is known as a learned taste aversion, which will be discussed further toward the end of this chapter), the pattern of activity produced by the scent of methyl salicylate in the olfactory bulb would thereafter be different from what it was when you liked wintergreen mints. Astonishingly, what this means is that there is no fixed code for odor perception; rather, our personal experience with an odor determines how it will be processed by the olfactory system, even at very early levels (Wilson, Best, and Sullivan, 2004).

juxtaglomerular neurons The first layer of cells surrounding the glomeruli. They are a mixture of excitatory and inhibitory cells and respond to a wide range of odorants. The selectivity of neurons to specific odorants increases in a gradient from the surface of the olfactory bulb to the deeper layers.

tufted cells The next layer of cells after the juxtaglomerular neurons. They respond to fewer odorants than the juxtaglomerular neurons, but more than neurons at the deepest layer of cells.

mitral cells The deepest layer of neurons in the olfactory bulb. Each mitral cell responds to only a few specific odorants.

granular cells Like mitral cells, granular cells are at the deepest level of the olfactory bulb. They comprise an extensive network of inhibitory neurons, integrate input from all the earlier projections, and are thought to be the basis of specific odorant identification.

olfactory tract The bundle of axons of the mitral and tufted cells within the olfactory bulb that sends odor information to the primary olfactory cortex.

primary olfactory cortex or **piriform cortex** The neural area where olfactory information is first processed. It comprises the amygdala, parahippocampal gyrus, and interconnected areas, and it interacts closely with the entorhinal cortex.

amygdala-hippocampal complex The conjoined regions of the amygdala and hippocampus, which are key structures in the limbic system. This complex is critically involved in the unique emotional and associative properties of olfactory cognition.

entorhinal cortex A phylogenetically old cortical region that provides the major sensory association input into the hippocampus. The entorhinal cortex also receives direct projections from olfactory regions.

Immediately surrounding each glomerulus is a mixed population of excitatory and inhibitory cells called **juxtaglomerular neurons**. These cells respond to a much wider range of odorants than the next layer of neurons that is composed of **tufted cells**, which themselves respond to more odorants than neurons in the deepest level of neurons in the olfactory bulb, called **mitral cells** that respond to just a few specific odorants. In other words, the selectivity of neurons to a specific odorant is increasingly sharpened in a gradient from the surface of the olfactory bulb to the deeper layers. The mechanisms that determine the response profiles to specific odorants are still unknown, but it seems that this increasing fine tuning through neuronal layers is important for helping the brain distinguish between similar odors (Kikuta et al., 2013). Furthermore, at the deepest level of the olfactory bulb, **granular cells**, an extensive network of inhibitory neurons, integrate input from all the earlier projections and are thought to function as higher-order feature detectors—capable of detecting and learning specific combinatorial patterns of mitral and tufted cell activation and thus responding specifically to different odorants (Koulakov and Rinberg, 2011). Axons of the mitral and tufted cells of each bulb combine and form the **olfactory tract**, one in each hemisphere of the brain, that conveys odor information ipsilaterally to the **primary olfactory cortex**, also known as the **piriform cortex**. The primary olfactory cortex comprises the amygdala, the parahippocampal gyrus, and the interconnected areas known as the **amygdala-hippocampal complex**, and it intimately interacts with the **entorhinal cortex** (Figure 14.8).

Though they number in the millions, OSNs converge onto a relatively small number of glomeruli. The mouse, whose brain and OR physiology are much more devoted to olfaction than are those of humans, has 3600 glomeruli (Richard, Taylor, and Greer, 2010). It was therefore speculated that humans, with far fewer functioning ORs, would have about 700 glomeruli. However, immunohistochemistry research from Charles Greer's laboratory at Yale University has revealed that humans have as many as 6000 glomeruli—nearly twice as many

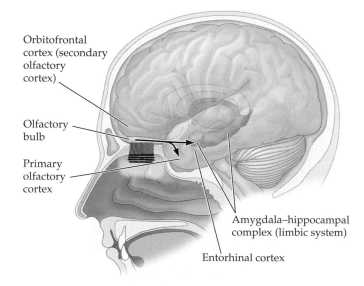

Orbitofrontal cortex (secondary olfactory cortex)

Olfactory bulb

Primary olfactory cortex

Amygdala–hippocampal complex (limbic system)

Entorhinal cortex

Figure 14.8 A cross-sectional view of the neural organization of olfaction. Olfactory information is transmitted from the olfactory bulb to the primary olfactory cortex comprising the amygdala-hippocampal complex of the limbic system in the first stages of olfactory processing. The orbitofrontal cortex is considered to be the secondary olfactory cortex and is responsible for conscious odor perception.

as the mouse for only a third the number of receptors (Maresh et al., 2008). This discovery was quite a surprise and suggests that using the mouse olfactory system as a model for humans, which has been the traditional approach, may not be as useful as once thought.

The central brain structures that process olfactory information are all part of a network of structures known as the **limbic system** that is involved in many aspects of emotion and memory. As we will see later, these connections are key to the unique associative learning and emotional properties of olfaction. It may be surprising, but paleontological research has shown that mammalian brain evolution was precipitated by an increase in olfactory ability (Rowe, Macrinin, and Luo, 2011). That is, the first structures in mammalian brains to increase in size and complexity were those associated with the sense of smell. It is theorized that increased olfactory capacity enabled our 200-million-year-old predecessors to hunt at night, giving them the evolutionary edge they needed to develop further and eventually evolve our current brains, which, ironically, along the way traded off olfactory advantages for vision (see discussion of pseudogenes in the next section).

Olfactory sensory neurons are different from all other sensory receptor cells in that they are not mediated by a protective barrier and instead make direct contact with the brain. By contrast, visual receptors are protected by the cornea, receptors for hearing are protected by the eardrum, and taste buds are buried in papillae. One consequence of the fact that the olfactory sensory neurons are direct conduits into the brain is that many drugs can be inhaled.

In spite of their direct linkage into the brain, OSN axons are among the thinnest and slowest in the body. Therefore, even though the nose connects directly to the brain, the time it takes to process a sensation (in this case an odor) is long, compared with our other sensory experiences. The lag time between sniffing and the brain's registering a scent varies, averaging approximately 400 milliseconds (ms), almost half a second; compare this with the 45 ms it takes for the visual cortex to register an image presented to the retina. This half-second duration for odor registration does not take into account the time it takes to react to a scent, which effectively doubles the perceptual time, making olfaction a particularly slow sense. You have probably observed that smells seem to emerge gradually, rather than flashing into your awareness.

FURTHER DISCUSSION of how long it takes the brain to register a sound or a touch can be found in Chapter 9 (page 304) and Chapter 13 (page 444), respectively.

These distinctions bring up the subtle differences between sensation and perception in olfaction. Sensation occurs when an odor is neurally registered; perception occurs when we become aware of detecting a scent. Odor clearance is also slow, and you may have noticed that odors tend to linger. This is due both to ambient air currents (e.g., a breeze versus still air) and the time it takes ORs to clear an odorant. The relatively slow speed and lingering features of olfaction have been the central obstacles for developing effective "smell-o-vision" and olfactory virtual-reality technologies. (See **Web Essay 14.1: Smell-O-Vision**.)

The Genetic Basis of Olfactory Receptors

In 1991, molecular biologists Linda Buck and Richard Axel (who were rewarded with a Nobel Prize in 2004 for their efforts) showed that the mammalian genome contains at least 1000 different odorant receptor genes, depending on the species (elephants have the most), each of which codes for a single type of OR. The OR

limbic system The group of neural structures that includes the olfactory cortex, the amygdala, the hippocampus, the piriform cortex, and the entorhinal cortex. The limbic system is involved in many aspects of emotion and memory. Olfaction is unique among the senses for its direct connection to the limbic system.

Figure 14.9 Olfactory receptor (OR) genes. Comparison of the number of OR genes in selected mammalian species. Note that these are rough estimates. (After Niimura, Matsui, and Touhara, 2014.)

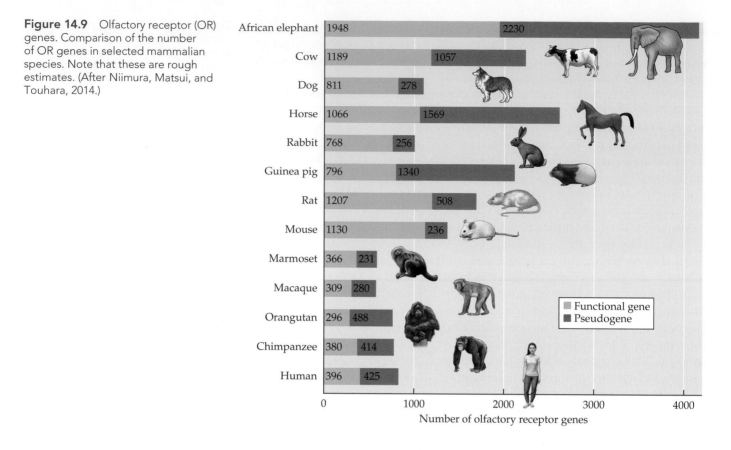

genome is the largest gene family known in mammals. All mammals appear to have pretty much this same set of genes, but some OR genes in each species are nonfunctional "pseudogenes": the genes are present on the chromosomes, but the proteins coded for by the genes do not get produced. The latest figures suggest that dogs have 811 functional OR genes (Niimura, Matsui, and Touhara, 2014); therefore, about 25% of their OR genes are pseudogenes. In humans, the OR genome contains less than 1000 genes, and the proportion of pseudogenes is 52% (**Figure 14.9**). That is, in contrast to the number of neurons in the olfactory bulb, where there is relative consistency across mammalian species, the proportion of functional OR genes differs considerably across mammals. Importantly, it has been suggested that the large number of pseudogenes in humans may operate as a regulatory network that affects what genes are turned on or off depending upon the olfactory environment (Cadiou et al., 2014).

Some researchers have suggested that the high proportion of OR pseudogenes in humans is the result of an evolutionary trade-off between vision and olfaction. In a cross-primate comparison, Gilad and colleagues (2007) observed that in nonhuman apes, such as gorillas, the proportion of pseudogenes is approximately 36%. In old world monkeys, like baboons, the proportion of OR pseudogenes is about 32%, but most New World species (e.g., squirrel monkeys) have a lower proportion of OR pseudogenes (about 18%). The one New World exception is the howler monkey, which also has about 31% OR pseudogenes. It turns out that the howler monkey has something in common with Old World monkeys that other New World monkeys do not: trichromatic color vision. Brains can get only so big, therefore to free up the brain space necessary to house evolving visual analysis tools (including trichromatic vision), human ancestors may have dropped the ability to analyze the odorants detected by certain OR genes, and those then became pseudogenes. Note however, that in another study researchers who conducted a cross-species comparison did *not* conclude that trichromatic color vision was related to a decreased number of functional OR genes (Matsui, Go, and Niimura, 2010). At this point we don't know whether or how color vision and OR genes are evolutionary connected, or if fewer ORs exerts any important cost. This is another example of how the full story of olfaction is not yet known and therefore competing theories for the same phenomena exist.

We don't have a precise percentage of pseudogenes for humans, because there is enormous diversity in the repertoire of functional odorant receptor genes among different people; the range of functional ORs seems to be between 350 and 400. In olfaction everybody actually has a unique nose (McRae et al., 2013; Menashe et al., 2003). Thus, one person may express 358 ORs while another expresses 388, but both have a "normal" sense of smell. This number reflects both which genes are expressed as functional receptors and how many copies of a specific receptor a person may have. The more copies of a specific receptor you have, the more sensitive you will be to certain odorants (that is, certain specific chemicals will smell stronger to one person than they do to another because of the number of receptor copies they have), and whether you have a pseudogene or a functional gene for a given receptor also alters odor perception (Keller et al., 2007). For example, people who "hate" the aroma of cilantro (also known as coriander) have a nonfunctional gene for detecting the herbal floral component of this aroma and therefore only detect the soapy note (Kurz, 2008). Most recently the genes associated with the OR expression that determine our sensitivity to four more food-relevant odors—banana, beer, blue cheese, and violets—were identified (McRae et al., 2013). However, as of now, the specific genetic basis for our perception of most other aromas is unknown.

The number of particular receptors people express influences their liking for an odor, because having more receptors leads to a more intense smell, and strong scents in general tend to be perceived as less pleasant than the same scents at a lower intensity (see the "Olfactory Hedonics" section of this chapter). We see this relationship with intensity in all our senses. Very bright lights and loud sounds are inherently more unpleasant than moderate-intensity lights and sounds, and our relative sensitivity to light and sound will affect how much each of us can tolerate (see Chapters 5 and 9 for more detail). Having few receptors of a given type can lead us to perceive a scent weakly, and if we like an aroma, we may expose ourselves to more of it to get the same punch as someone with more ORs that are sensitive to that odorant would.

When it comes to food, the more intense our perception of the retronasal aroma of the food, the less we tend to consume of it (Ruijschop et al., 2008). For example, if our OR expression for the odorant that contributes to the banana aroma in banana cream pie is low, we may eat more pie than someone who can perceive the banana aroma strongly, and this may lead us to consume more dessert than we might have intended. These findings demonstrate the subtle but important ways by which OR variation can influence our food choices as well as our food intake. It should, however, be noted that many psychological factors mediate our food consumption as well as our odor preferences (see "Olfactory Hedonics" later in this chapter). Therefore, our genetic makeup cannot predetermine our response to any given odorant or food.

Other factors can also increase our sensitivity to odors temporarily. For example, even though heavy alcohol consumption (e.g., three drinks per hour) impairs olfactory sensitivity, having only one drink (blood alcohol level less

trigeminal nerve The fifth cranial nerve, which transmits information about the "feel" of an odorant (e.g., mint feels cool, cinnamon feels warm), as well as pain and irritation sensations (e.g., ammonia feels burning). Also called *cranial nerve V*.

than 0.06%) improves olfactory acuity (Endevelt-Shapira et al., 2014). This may be a good reason to drink moderately while dining—with one glass of wine the flavor aromatics of your meal will be enhanced, but the more you pour, the less flavor you'll perceive. Another popular recreational drug, marijuana, also boosts olfaction. It was recently found that activating endocannabinoid receptors (the receptors that respond to the active component in marijuana) in the brains of fasted mice increased their smell sensitivity and induced the mice to eat more (Soria-Gomez et al., 2014). Extrapolating to humans, the reason for the "munchies" with a marijuana buzz may be that flavor (through smell) is intensified, and thus what we eat tastes richer and is more alluring. We get a whiff of pizza and are immediately seduced. Indeed, stimulating appetite is one of the main reasons marijuana is prescribed for patients undergoing chemotherapy. Although this may seem like a contradiction to what was just mentioned about greater flavor intensity decreasing food consumption, the cannabinoid effects observed were in fasted mice, not those who had recently eaten. It may also be that the munchies we experience are due to being less aware of our internal physical/homeostatic states when we're under the influence. That is, we may not be feeling whether our stomachs are hungry or full; we may just be savoring the newfound flavor intensity of pepperoni pizza. This "munchies" theory is currently speculative and based on anecdote in humans, but it illustrates the multiple, sometimes contradictory, and as yet unknown ways that odor perception can affect our food intake. Stay tuned.

The Feel of Scent

As mentioned at the start of this chapter, our experience of odors often has a feel to it, as well as a smell. This is because most odorants stimulate the somatosensory system to some degree through polymodal nociceptors (touch, pain, and temperature receptors) inside the nose. For example, menthol feels cool and ammonia feels burning. These sensations are mediated by the **trigeminal nerve** (cranial nerve V), which responds to stimuli in and around the mouth, nose, and eyes (**Figure 14.10A**). In many cases it is impossible to distinguish between the sensations traveling up cranial nerve I from olfactory receptors and those traveling up cranial nerve V from somatosensory receptors. For example, the nasal cooling (cranial nerve V) and specific scent (cranial nerve I) associated with the smell of peppermint fuse to produce a holistic sensory experience. Trigeminal stimulation accounts for why our eyes tear when we chop onions (as

(A)

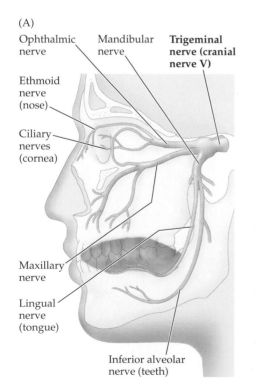

Ophthalmic nerve

Mandibular nerve

Trigeminal nerve (cranial nerve V)

Ethmoid nerve (nose)

Ciliary nerves (cornea)

Maxillary nerve

Lingual nerve (tongue)

Inferior alveolar nerve (teeth)

(B)

Figure 14.10 The trigeminal nerve's role in the perception of odors. (A) The trigeminal nerve carries information from somatosensory receptors in the nose and other areas of the face to the thalamus and then on to the somatosensory cortex. (B) Your eyes tear when you chop onions because of stimulation of the trigeminal nerve.

in **Figure 14.10B**) and why we sneeze when we sniff pepper. High levels of trigeminal stimulation can produce a severe burning sensation, and trigeminal activity has been linked to the facial and head pain felt in migraine headaches. Smelling salts (made from ammonia combined with eucalyptus oil) revive us because of their trigeminal activation.

> **FURTHER DISCUSSION** of the trigeminal nerve can be found in Chapter 15 on page 533.

From Chemicals to Smells

Now that we know something about the physiological basis of olfaction, we can ask the following crucial question: How does the biochemical interaction between an odorant and an OR, and subsequent neurological processing in the olfactory bulbs and later brain structures, result in the psychological perception of a scent such as wintergreen mint? Buck and Axel's seminal discovery of olfactory receptor genes prompted an explosion of research surrounding this question over the past two decades, but a fully comprehensive theory of how we perceive scents has still not been realized.

Theories of Olfactory Perception

At present, the best-accepted biochemical theory (first proposed in its modern form in the 1950s by the British scientist John Amoore) is based on the match between the shapes of odorants and odorant receptors. It was dubbed "shape theory" but is better denoted as shape-pattern theory. In a nutshell, **shape-pattern theory** contends that odorant molecules have different shapes and olfactory receptors have different shapes, and an odorant will be detected by a specific OR to the extent that the odorant's molecules fit into the OR (**Figure 14.11**). Gordon Shepherd at

shape-pattern theory The current dominant biochemical theory for how chemicals come to be perceived as specific odors. Shape-pattern theory contends that different scents—as a function of the fit between odorant shape and OR shape—activate different arrays of olfactory receptors in the olfactory epithelia. These various arrays produce specific firing patterns of neurons in the olfactory bulbs, which then determine the particular scent we perceive.

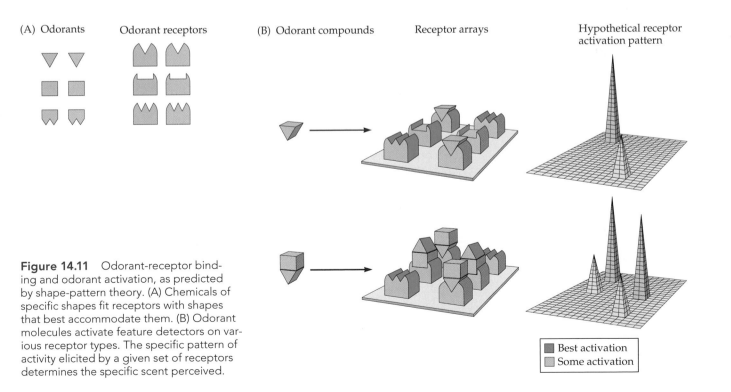

Figure 14.11 Odorant-receptor binding and odorant activation, as predicted by shape-pattern theory. (A) Chemicals of specific shapes fit receptors with shapes that best accommodate them. (B) Odorant molecules activate feature detectors on various receptor types. The specific pattern of activity elicited by a given set of receptors determines the specific scent perceived.

vibration theory An alternative to shape-pattern theory for describing how olfaction works. Vibration theory proposes that every odorant has a different vibrational frequency and that molecules that produce the same vibrational frequencies will smell the same.

specific anosmia The inability to smell one specific compound amid otherwise normal smell perception.

Yale University and his students pioneered the idea that when a given odorant is sniffed, a particular pattern is generated across the glomeruli. Differences in those spatial patterns provide the basis for the array of odors that we perceive.

The most recent molecular research suggests that scents are detected by means of a combinatorial code, where one odorant may bind to several different receptors and one receptor may bind several different odorants to varying degrees (see Figure 14.11). This means that different scents activate different arrays of olfactory receptors in the olfactory epithelia, producing specific glomerular activity in the olfactory bulb. The specific pattern of glomerular activity in the olfactory bulb then determines the particular scent we perceive. That is, different patterns are elicited for the perception of rose, mint, urine, and skunk (for example), and the various patterns for specific scents turn out to be highly consistent across individuals (Zou, Li, and Buck, 2005). This theory was implied in the section "Neurophysiology of Olfaction" above. However, there are also alternative explanations of how olfaction works, because shape-pattern theory has problems explaining how molecules with very different shapes can produce very similar smells. For example, both the single chemical phenylethyl alcohol and a chemical mixture composed of over 1000 different chemicals can produce a scent we call "rose."

The strongest alternative to shape-pattern theory is **vibration theory**, championed most recently by Luca Turin (Franco et al., 2011; Turin, 1996; Turin et al., 2015). In essence, vibration theory proposes that, because of atomic structure, every odorant has a different vibrational frequency, and molecules that produce the same vibrational frequencies have the same smell. Turin reported that various chemicals that have predictably similar vibrations because of their molecular composition also have similar smells. For example, all citrus odors fall into the same vibrational-frequency class. Indeed, recent work has shown that fruit flies are capable of distinguishing between two molecules that are identical in shape but have different vibrational frequencies (Franco et al., 2011).

A number of researchers have argued against the vibration theory (e.g., Block et al., 2015; Keller and Vosshall, 2004), while others are currently trying to bridge the gap and have shown that receptors influence the vibrational properties of odorants (Reese et al., 2016). Nevertheless, vibration theory has problems explaining various aspects of odor perception, in particular, specific anosmias and the different scents produced by stereoisomers, which shape-pattern theory can explain.

A **specific anosmia** is the inability to smell one specific compound amid otherwise normal smell perception. Specific anosmias are due to faulty odorant-receptor interactions, or the lack of (or different variants of) specific ORs, not odorant vibrations. Most specific anosmias are to steroidal musk compounds, and the condition appears to be genetic. The most studied specific anosmia is an inability to smell the compound androstenone, which is found in armpit sweat and pork. A significant proportion of the population has a specific anosmia to androstenone; estimates range between 11% and 75%, but between 20% and 40% is more typical (Bremner et al., 2003). Interestingly, among those who can smell androstenone, the majority find it to be unpleasant and "urinous," while the rest describe it as a "sweet musky-floral" scent. A cloning study of human olfactory receptors showed that the variability in detection of the odorant androstenone, as well as its perceived pleasantness, is due to genetic differences in OR expression between individuals (Keller et al., 2007). Similarly, the different anosmia rates obtained for androstenone in different studies most likely reflect the fact that the gene governing the ability to smell androstenone varies randomly within any given sample of participants.

FURTHER DISCUSSION of specific sensory deficits amid otherwise normal perception—in this case vision (agnosias)—can be found in Chapter 4 on page 104.

Nonmusk odorants for which specific anosmias have been found include the sulfur compound in asparagus—this is the "funny" smell in urine that some people detect after eating it—but in addition to variation in the ability to smell this compound, the amount of the compound that is excreted in urine varies genetically among individuals. Therefore, if you don't smell something funny after eating asparagus, it may be because you don't excrete the sulfur metabolite, not because you're missing the receptor to detect the odorant (Pelchat et al., 2011). If you really want to check whether you're among the approximately 6% of Americans who are anosmic to asparagus pee, you'll need to take a sniff after a friend who can smell it in her own urine and ate asparagus with you goes to the bathroom. Approximately 10% of the population is anosmic to the scent of freesia flowers, and sensitivity to the sweaty-sock aroma of isovaleric acid also varies vastly among people, with about 6% of the population unable to detect it at all (Vockley and Ensenauer, 2006). These examples all illustrate how individual genetic variability in receptor expression determines each of our own unique olfactory experiences. Although the differences in perception may be small, as stated before, unless you have an identical twin, everyone has a different nose. This complication, that the same stimulus is perceived differently by different individuals, is not unique to olfaction. People who are colorblind perceive the same visual stimulus differently from standard observers; however, in olfaction the difference between individuals is much more complex.

Vibration theory cannot explain the presence of specific anosmias or why the same odorant produces different scent sensations in different people, but shape-pattern theory can: these phenomena could arise from differing odorant-receptor interactions or the absence of or variance in certain receptors. Another mark in favor of shape-pattern theory comes from the study of stereoisomers. **Stereoisomers** are molecules that are mirror-image rotations of one another, and although they contain all the same atoms, they can smell completely different. For example, D-carvone (the right-handed isomer) smells like caraway (**Figure 14.12A**), and L-carvone (the left-handed isomer) smells like spearmint (**Figure 14.12B**). According to shape-pattern theory, this difference arises because the rotated molecules do not fit the same receptors (as if you were trying to put your right hand into your left-hand glove); thus, different receptors are activated for these two molecules, causing different scents to be perceived. Vibration theory cannot explain why stereoisomers smell different, because the vibrations of stereoisomers should be the same. More direct evidence for shape-pattern theory comes from in vitro experiments using cloned olfactory receptors, which have revealed chemical-receptor interactions

stereoisomers Isomers (molecules that can exist in different structural forms) in which the spatial arrangements of the atoms are mirror-image rotations of one another, like a right and left hand.

(A) D-carvone   (B) L-carvone

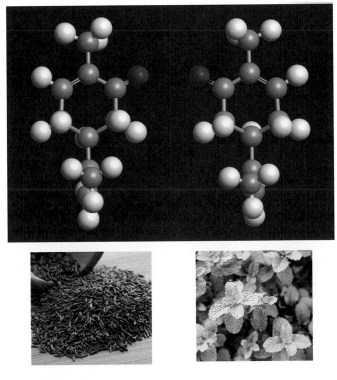

Figure 14.12 The stereoisomers D-carvone (A) and L-carvone (B) contain the same atoms, yet they smell completely different: D-carvone smells like caraway; L-carvone, like spearmint. Shape-pattern theory can account for this fact.

that show specific odorants binding with specific receptors. A new effort from the shape-pattern camp called the DREAM Olfaction Prediction Challenge is using a crowd-sourced competition to develop software that can predict what scent we will perceive based on an odorant's molecular makeup. The results so far suggest that the best algorithm can reasonably predict what a large group of people will say a certain molecule smells like—for example, molecules with sulfur groups tend to produce a "garlicky" smell—but is still quite poor at determining how any given individual will describe specific chemicals (Keller et al., 2017)—again underscoring the idiosyncratic nature of olfactory perception.

In any event, a fully realized explanation for odor perception has yet to be determined. The benefit of scientific controversy is that it motivates continued research to solve the problem. Stay tuned.

The Importance of Patterns

You may have noticed a potential discrepancy in how we've accounted for odor perception. As already noted, we can detect an infinite number of odors, yet our genes code for only about 1000 olfactory receptors, and 600–700 of them are nonfunctional. How can we detect so many different scents? To start to see the way out of this conundrum, recall that, in vision, we can tell the difference between thousands of different colors, even though we have only three types of cones. Each type of olfactory receptor responds to the structure of certain molecules only. However, a molecule may have features that stimulate several different receptors. Moreover, each receptor appears to have various feature detectors that contribute to further specificity in OR activation. Thus, in addition to differences in OR activation, a different set of feature detectors is activated when we smell chocolate or wintergreen or rose.

As with color detection, we detect odors by the pattern of activity across various different receptor types. The intensity of an odor also changes which receptors (and hence patterns) will be activated, which is why weak and strong concentrations of an odorant do not smell quite the same. The fact that receptor activation is affected by odorant concentration likely explains why dogs with many more functional receptors than we have can perceive odorants of considerably lower concentrations. The timing of olfactory receptor activation also seems to be important; an odorant that activates several receptors will also stimulate them in a specific temporal sequence and at a particular rate. Another odorant might stimulate the same receptors but in a different order and rate, and the difference leads to the perception of different scents (**Figure 14.13**). Thus, the perception of different odors can be due to different OR firing patterns, or to firing of the same receptors at a different rate and/or in a different sequence.

The flip side of the pattern perception mechanism is that if two odorants, one molecularly simple and the other complex, activate the same receptors in the same way, we end up smelling the same thing. For example, the feature detectors for the single-molecule odorant phenylethyl alcohol (which is artificial rose scent) and for the odorants of a real live rose (whose scent is composed of more than 1000 different molecules) might both result in the same basic pattern of OR activation and hence the same perception of "rose" (this phenomenon should be reminiscent of metamers in color vision, discussed in Chapter 5).

Patterns are also important for odor processing at early stages in the olfactory cortex. Specific patterns of activity are produced by specific odors in the piriform cortex, and odors that are perceived as smelling similar produce similar patterns. For example, "minty" odors like wintergreen and spearmint produce patterns of activity that have a lot of overlap, but the pattern produced by a "cit-

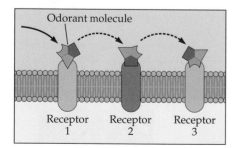

Figure 14.13 The hypothetical role of OR activation timing and order. A single molecule binds first to receptor type 1, then a split second later to receptor type 2, and then to receptor type 3. Brains are especially well suited to recognizing patterns of responses such as this, so the number of odors we can recognize greatly exceeds the number of receptor types available.

rus" odor like lemon does not overlap with the pattern elicited by wintergreen. The fact that configural representations of odors (e.g., citrusy, minty) occur in the piriform cortex suggests that the piriform cortex is the olfactory analog of visual associative areas in the ventral temporal cortex. Notably, however, these areas differ dramatically in their connectivity to emotion and language. The piriform cortex is densely connected to limbic areas that process motivation and emotion but is poorly connected to areas that process language—which is one reason why odors are so hard to name (see "Identification" below). Moreover, distinctive patterns of activity by specific categories of odors are *not* seen farther downstream in olfactory processing, such as in the amygdala or orbitofrontal cortex (J. D. Howard et al., 2009). Patterns may be lacking in these regions of the brain because at these stages of processing, personal and emotional associations mediate activity patterns.

Is Odor Perception Synthetic or Analytical?

Just as we rarely hear pure tones outside of auditory perception experiments, we rarely smell "pure odorants" outside of an olfactory perception lab. Almost all of the olfactory stimuli that we encounter in the real world are mixtures, like the 1000-molecule rose scent emanating from a flower bed that we discussed in the previous section. How do we process the components in an odorant mixture? There are two broad possibilities: analysis and synthesis. Auditory mixtures provide the classic example of analysis. A high note and a low note played simultaneously on a piano each can be analyzed out of the mix and perceived separately (**Figure 14.14A**). Color mixtures provide the classic example of synthesis. If we mix red and green lights, the resulting color that we see is yellow (**Figure 14.14B**). Red and green cannot be analyzed out, because the two lights have been synthesized into something else. Is olfaction (**Figure 14.14C**) an analytical or a synthetic sense?

It seems that the answer is both—olfactory perception can be both analytical and synthetic, although the synthetic aspect is what we are more likely to perceptually experience. The analytical qualities of olfaction are evident in **binaral rivalry**. As you read in Chapter 6, when a different object is presented to each eye simultaneously, you don't see a blend of the two objects; rather, binocular rivalry occurs, and you see the two objects alternating. A similar phenomenon

binaral rivalry Competition between the two nostrils for odor perception. When a different scent is presented to each nostril simultaneously, we perceive each scent to be alternating back and forth with the other, and not a blend of the two scents.

(A) Auditory mixture: analysis   (B) Color mixture: synthesis   (C) Olfactory mixture: analysis and synthesis

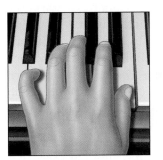
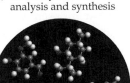

Figure 14.14 The roles of analysis and synthesis in sensory perception. We can separately perceive the three tones of the musical chord being played in (A), but not the high- and medium-wavelength light rays mixing in the center of (B). When we mix odorants (C), we perceive the mixture primarily synthetically, but some degree of analytical perception is possible. Analytical ability varies with prior training and with the odorants that constitute the mixture.

occurs in hearing when discrepant sounds are presented to each ear (see Chapter 10). It was recently found that binaral rivalry in olfaction also occurs: when two different odors are presented, one to each of our nostrils, we alternate in our ability to smell one odor or the other (Zhou and Chen, 2009). Researchers presented a rose scent to one nostril and simultaneously an odor that smelled like marker pens to the other nostril and found that the participants alternated back and forth between saying that they smelled "markers" or "rose." The marker scent was perceived as more intense, and it was usually perceived first, which also occurs in binocular rivalry, where the "stronger" image tends to dominate. What's interesting is that this rivalry seems to occur in both the nose and the brain. When the same participants were later presented with a scent mixture of both rose and markers to both nostrils simultaneously, most of them also reported smelling first markers and then rose and then markers again, and so on. This observation suggests that odor rivalry is occurring in the brain as well as in the nostrils, or perhaps only in the brain.

New research regarding the analytical component of odor perception has also suggested that as in vision, where we have additive and subtractive color primaries (red, green, blue or cyan, magenta, yellow), odor perceptions fall into categories or perceptual clusters and there may be ten of them (Castro, Ramanathan, and Chennubhotla, 2013). Researchers recently reported that using sophisticated statistical analysis applied to 144 diverse odorants, they could categorize all of the odorants into one of ten perceptual categories, loosely labeled as follows: fragrant, woody/resinous, chemical, fruity (not lemon), lemony, sickening/sour, minty, sweet, nutty, and sickening/sulfurous. This is not a new idea, and in the 1950s John Amoore (who, as mentioned earlier, first proposed the shape theory for odor perception) hypothesized that there were seven odor primaries: sweaty, spermous, fishy, malty, urinous, musky, and camphoraceous (like mothballs). Amoore's work was based largely on studying specific anosmias, but independent support for his theory was never found—until now? Note that the primaries most recently discovered are somewhat different from those described by Amoore, so though tantalizing, the existence of odor primaries should be considered tentative until further convergent evidence is obtained. Wait for further research.

Although we are capable of discriminating thousands of different odors, intuition tells us that most mixtures are perceived as unitary wholes. For example, the smell of bacon is very distinctive, and most people would perceive it to be a unitary sensation. But, as with natural rose aroma, there is no single "bacon" odorant, and the sensation we recognize as bacon is made up of a combination of many different volatile chemicals. To test the synthetic/analytical nature of olfactory perception, Laing and his colleagues (Laing and Francis, 1989; Laing and Glemarec, 1992) conducted a series of experiments in which they asked untrained participants, participants who had received preliminary "odor training," and experienced perfumers and flavorists to identify the constituents of mixtures containing between one and five common odorants. The average discrimination rate from all the participants combined was no more than three components in a five-component mixture. However, the more training the participants had, the better they did. With more than five components in a mixture, though, even professional perfumers' analytical ability breaks down. Thus, it appears that olfaction is primarily a synthetic sense but that a certain amount of analytical ability can be developed.

The predominantly synthetic quality of odor mixture perception was also supported by a recent experiment demonstrating the existence of **olfactory white**. Like white noise, where various mixtures of many different frequencies

olfactory white   The olfactory equivalent of white noise or the color white. When at least 30 odorants of equal intensity that span olfactory physiochemical and psychological (perceptual) space are mixed, they produce a resultant odor perception that is the same as that of every other mixture of 30 odorants meeting the same span and equivalent intensity criteria, even though the various mixtures do not share any common odorants.

are perceived as sounding like the same kind of meaningless buzz, or like white in vision, where mixtures of many different wavelengths produce the perception of "white," olfactory white is produced by many different odors.

Researchers in Israel found that when at least 30 odorants that span olfactory, physiochemical, and psychological (perceptual) space that are of equal intensity are mixed, they produce an odor perception that is the same as the perception produced for every other mixture of 30 odorants meeting the same span and intensity criteria, even though the various mixtures do not share any common odorants (Weiss et al., 2012). That is, three different mixtures of 30 different odorant molecules actually smell the same if the contributing odorants have the same intensity and are distributed across the range of olfactory stimulus space. The more odorants in the mixture the more indistinguishable the mixtures become, and 30 seems to be the tipping point. The scent of this "olfactory white" is variously described (to some it smells floral), but it is consistently rated as being of neutral pleasantness. You may now be wondering why complex odorant mixtures that produce the perceptions of "bacon" or "rose" do not instead all smell the same. The answer is that the component odorant molecules in "bacon" and "rose" aroma do not span the range of olfactory space, nor are they of equal intensity; rather, the odorants with dominant intensities and certain blends stand out, thus producing the specific perceptions of rose, bacon, coffee, and indeed many of the specific odor sensations we can perceive. Notably, this exciting new finding suggests an underlying commonality between olfaction, vision, and audition—a uniform perceptual experience can arise from large mixtures.

FURTHER DISCUSSION of color mixture synthesis can be found in Chapter 5 on pages 144–145.

The Power of Sniffing

When you smell something passively, you are breathing in air containing odorant molecules and detecting those molecules. By contrast, when you sniff, you are consciously and forcibly inhaling bursts of air into your nostrils. Sniffing increases the ability to detect odorants. Sniffing also produces greater activation in some parts of the brain, such as the cerebellum, than passive inhalation does. Exciting new research is currently exploring how active sniffing may enable severely physically disabled people to communicate with the outside world and to move independently. Locked-in syndrome is a terrible neurological condition characterized by completely intact cognition and mentality but total physical paralysis such that afflicted people are literally locked in their own bodies. Brain-computer interfaces would be an ideal solution for such individuals, and they have begun to be implemented with some success.

Until recently, it was believed that control over eye blinks was the only physical capability individuals with locked-in syndrome had, but active sniffing has now been discovered to be preserved in these individuals as well. Taking advantage of this intact physical function, researchers recently showed that locked-in patients can be successfully trained to control text-writing software and meaningfully communicate with loved ones by using precise, deliberate sniffing—changing sniff magnitude, duration, onset, and offset. Using the same type of sniff technology, quadriplegic patients have also been trained to move their wheelchairs in complex circuits by using their nose alone (Plotkin et al., 2010). This may be the dawn of a nasally powered world.

Odor Imagery

One area where olfaction and our other senses diverge is imagery. We know that visual and auditory imagery is easy and readily accessible and, though in somewhat different ways, imagery is also evident in touch (shivers, tingles, phantom limbs) and taste (e.g., the sour salivation reaction). By contrast, humans appear to have little or no ability to conjure "odor images." For example, you can probably see the visual image of a Hershey's chocolate kiss in your mind's eye right now (you might even start salivating). But can you really reproduce the smell of chocolate in your "mind's nose"? Brain-imaging studies (e.g., Kosslyn et al., 1995) have shown that many of the parts of the brain that would be involved in actually seeing the kiss are also involved in visually imaging it; with olfaction, however, similar studies suggest that the degree of overlap between smelling an odor and "imaging" it is much weaker (Djordjevic et al., 2005). Dreams with olfactory sensations are also very rare (Carskadon et al., 1989; Zadra, Nielsen, and Donderi, 1998).

Animals, such as rodents, that rely predominantly on smell as the sense by which they negotiate the world may well think and dream in odors. However, because we do not think in odor terms, it is not necessary to have stored representations of olfactory experiences. Nevertheless, recent functional neuroimaging research suggests that although odor imagery among average people is very weak, expert perfumers may be able to acquire the ability to image odors through training. Functional magnetic resonance imaging (fMRI) showed that perfumers produced activation in their piriform cortex when asked to image odors, and the greater their perfumery experience, the more their brains appeared to be reorganized to accommodate this task (Plailly, Delon-Martin, and Royet, 2011). This is another example of how the olfactory system is extremely flexible and capable of neural reorganization on the basis of experience and learning.

Olfactory Psychophysics, Identification, and Adaptation

The subfield of psychology called **psychophysics** was introduced in Chapter 1. The goal of the psychophysicist is to quantify the psychological experience of our sensory world. In this section some of the nuts-and-bolts questions addressed by olfactory psychophysics are discussed, and then we'll go on to consider how we identify and adapt to odors.

Detection, Discrimination, and Recognition

Although we can theoretically detect over a trillion odors, a number of factors limit our detection ability in reality. A main factor has to do with how much stimulation is required before we perceive something. As with other senses, there are many other reasons for variability in detection. For instance, odorant molecules with longer carbon chains, such as vanillin, are easier to detect (have lower detection thresholds) than those with shorter carbon chains, such as acetone (otherwise known as nail polish remover). Other limitations have to do with individual difference factors, as you will see soon in the "Individual Differences" section.

The ability to detect an odorant can also be manipulated by experience. Serendipitous observation revealed that through repeated testing, sensitivity to androstenone (the steroidal musk compound that many people have a specific anosmia for, discussed above in the section "Theories of Olfactory Perception") can be induced in about half of the people who are initially unable to detect it (Wysocki et al., 1989). That is, a proportion of the people who are anosmic to this

psychophysics The science of defining quantitative relationships between physical and psychological (subjective, perceptual) events.

particular chemical develop an ability to smell androstenone through repeated exposure in their olfactory environment. Other studies have shown that increased sensitivity to some common odorants, such as benzaldehyde (cherry-almond aroma) and Citralva (lemon-orange scent), can be induced through repeated exposure to these chemicals, particularly among females (Dalton et al., 2002; Diamond et al., 2005), and overall olfactory detection abilities appear to be enhanced simply by odor exposure. In a recent study, exposure to four familiar odors at least twice a day for 12 weeks enhanced general odor detection ability among children (Mori et al., 2015). A review of research on smell loss in adults, due to various causes, also suggests that intensive training and exposure to odors can lead to some olfactory recovery (Reichert and Schöpf, 2017). It is currently unclear how these enhancements occur, but possible explanations include "turning on" genes through experience. We know from other areas of biology that genes can be turned on by environmental factors, and because each olfactory receptor is coded for by a specific gene, it is conceivable that the receptors for detecting chemicals can be activated through repeated presentation. Neuroplasticity and modulation from the environment and experience appear to be basic principles in olfaction.

Odor detection is also influenced by attention. Neuroimaging research has shown that paying attention to odors alters brain activity and increases odor detection ability (Plailly et al., 2008; Zelano et al., 2005). We use more of our brain and can smell more acutely when we consciously focus on smelling than when we don't. It would make sense that a combination of learning to pay greater attention to odors as a consequence of odor training coupled with some physiological alterations such as increased sensitization of OR genes, is responsible for enhanced odor detection after odor training.

A healthy person can discriminate—tell the difference between—a huge number of odors. Note, however, that discrimination is not the same thing as recognition, the ability to remember whether or not we've smelled an odor before. We need up to three times as many odorant molecules to recognize an odor as we do to simply detect its presence. You've probably experienced this phenomenon yourself: you register that you smell something before you know what the smell is. Interestingly, we don't need to know what a smell is, or be able to name it, in order to recognize it or even to have a memory triggered by it. The only requirement is that we have previously encountered the scent and have a past experience with it (Cleary et al., 2010; Herz and Cupchik, 1992). This is different from other sensory experiences among cognitively healthy adults. For example, we wouldn't be able to say that we recognize, respond appropriately to, or have a memory elicited by something that we see without having some kind of label for it, even if the label is very vague or idiosyncratic, such as "food" or "uncle's weird hat." Brain-damaged patients with visual agnosia are the exception in that they often know how to use an object even if they don't know what it's called.

Another interesting feature of odor recognition is its durability. In controlled experiments, a 30-second delay between odor presentation and testing produces a precipitous drop in recognition accuracy, but what we remember after 30 seconds is very close to what we remember after 3 days, a month, or even a year (**Figure 14.15**) (Engen, Kuisma, and Eimas, 1973; Engen and Ross, 1973; Murphy et al., 1991; Rabin and Cain, 1984). Again, you probably recognize this phenomenon from your own life. If you smelled a certain perfume in a meaningful situation only once and then came upon that perfume again 20 years

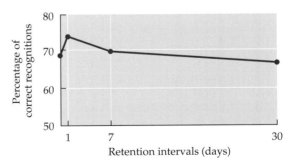

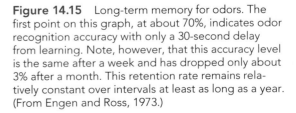

Figure 14.15 Long-term memory for odors. The first point on this graph, at about 70%, indicates odor recognition accuracy with only a 30-second delay from learning. Note, however, that this accuracy level is the same after a week and has dropped only about 3% after a month. This retention rate remains relatively constant over intervals at least as long as a year. (From Engen and Ross, 1973.)

staircase method A psychophysical method for determining the concentration of a stimulus required for detection at the threshold level. The staircase method is an example of a *method of limits*. A stimulus (e.g., odorant) is presented in an ascending concentration sequence until detection is indicated, and then the concentration is shifted to a descending sequence until the response changes to "no detection." This ascending and descending sequence is typically repeated several times, and the concentrations at which reversals occur are averaged to determine the threshold detection level of that odorant for a given individual. Also called *reverse staircase method*.

triangle test A test in which a participant is given three odorants to smell, of which two are the same and one is different. The participant is required to state which is the odd odor out. Typically, the order in which the three odorants are given (e.g., same, same, different; different, same, same; same, different, same) is manipulated and the test is repeated several times for greater accuracy.

later, you would likely say that the odor was familiar. Our memory for odors is even more resilient if the initial exposure is accompanied by emotion (Herz, 1997).

Psychophysical Methods for Detection and Discrimination

Researchers wanting to measure how perceptually sensitive people are to odors, or whether they can discriminate one odorant from another, use various psychophysical methods. A common olfactory technique for determining someone's odor detection threshold is called the **staircase method** (or the reverse staircase method), and it is an example of what are known as methods of limits (see Chapter 1). There are various versions of the staircase method. In a typical procedure, an odorant is presented in ever-increasing concentration increments until the participant reports being able to "smell something" for several repeats of a concentration. Then the odorant's concentration is decreased incrementally until the participant reports no detection. These reversals are repeated a number of times, and the odorant concentrations at the point where reversals occur are averaged to determine the approximate concentration needed for that person to detect the odorant (**Figure 14.16**). As a reversal point is reached, the increments by which an odorant's concentration is raised and lowered can be fine-tuned for precision. Staircase methods can be used to determine a general benchmark for someone's olfactory sensitivity. They can also be used to determine an individual's detection thresholds for a range of different odorants.

To determine whether someone can discriminate between two odorants, the most common psychophysical test used is called the **triangle test**. In a triangle test, a participant is given three odorants to smell, of which two are the same and one is different. The participant is required to state which is the odd odor out. Typically, the order in which the three odorants are given (e.g., same, same, different; different, same, same; same, different, same) is manipulated, and the test is repeated several times to establish accuracy.

Identification

Attaching a verbal label to a smell is a step beyond odor recognition. Olfaction has been called the mute sense because we are so often lost for words to describe our olfactory experiences (D. Ackerman, 1990). All of us have had the experience

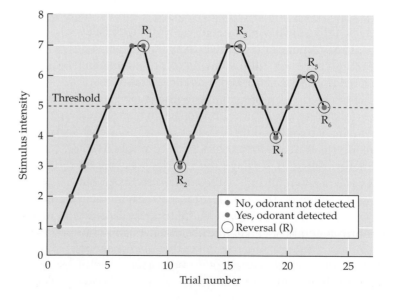

Figure 14.16 Staircase method. The odorant concentration at each of the reversal points is averaged to calculate the threshold concentration at which the odorant is detected.

of not being able to come up with the name of something we know; for example, what was the name of your fourth-grade teacher? This experience is known as the tip-of-the-tongue phenomenon. In the olfactory domain, suppose you take a sniff of something from a bottle that provides no visual clues to what it contains, and you immediately know that the scent is extremely familiar, but you just can't come up with the name for it. Borrowing from the verbal scenario, we call this experience the **tip-of-the-nose phenomenon** (Lawless and Engen, 1977), and it can be very frustrating.

There are some important differences between the tip-of-the-nose state and the tip-of-the-tongue state. For one, in the tip-of-the-tongue state even though we don't know the exact word we're looking for, we typically have some semantic information, such as its first letter, its general word configuration, the number of syllables in the word, and so on ("Starts with a *K*, two syllables, sounds like a sandwich roll … aha, my fourth-grade teacher was Mrs. Kaiser!"). By contrast, in the tip-of-the-nose state, we typically know nothing about the label we're searching for. Up until very recently anthropologists thought that in all languages there were fewer words that referred exclusively to our experience of smells than there were for any other sensation (Classen, Howes, and Synnott, 1994). In English, *aromatic, fragrant, redolent*, and *stinky* pretty much exhaust the list of adjectives that specifically describe olfactory stimuli and nothing else. Typically people use words referring to the perceived source of the scent, like *lemony*, or category terms, like *floral* or *fruity*, or commercial products we are familiar with. As you might expect, the more familiar we are with a scent, the easier it is for us to describe it. We also borrow terms from other senses (cake smells "sweet," grass smells "green," and so on). New evidence, however, suggests that though an impoverished olfactory vocabulary is still the case for most languages, at least one language is the exception to the rule. The language of the Jahai, a nomadic hunter-gatherer society living in the Malay Peninsula (the mountainous rain forest that runs between Myanmar, Malaysia, and Thailand), has specific and discrete words for a panoply of olfactory sensations, such as their word *pus* (pronounced "pa-oos"), which describes what dead branches and some types of fur and feathers smell like (Majid and Burenhult, 2014). In other words, the Jahai appear to be able to isolate basic olfactory properties the way we all isolate the color green from a leaf or a lime. It is not yet known why the Jahai have such an expanded olfactory vocabulary, but it is known that scents play a very important role in their daily life, so learning and establishing an exact vocabulary for olfactory experiences such as the scent of tiger versus monkey scat, or a poisonous versus nutritious mushroom, would assist much more with their survival than it would for us living in an industrial world.

It is not fully known why olfaction and language are generally so disconnected. Various possibilities include the fact that unlike what happens in other sensory systems, olfactory information does not need to be integrated in the thalamus prior to processing in the cortex, and it is argued that the thalamus has relevance for language. A large body of evidence further indicates that the majority of olfactory processing occurs in the right hemisphere of the brain, whereas language processing is known to be dominated by the left hemisphere (see Royet and Plailly, 2004, for a review). In addition, the association area for olfaction, the piriform cortex, is not anatomically linked to language-processing networks.

Intriguingly, convergent data from brain-imaging studies have also shown that conscious odor perception interferes with language processing. That is,

tip-of-the-nose phenomenon The inability to name an odor, even though it is very familiar. Contrary to the tip-of-the-tongue phenomenon, one has no lexical access to the name of the odor, such as first letter, rhyme, number of syllables, and so on, when in the tip-of-the-nose state. This is an example of how language and olfactory perception are deeply disconnected.

processing of odors and processing of words compete for the same cortical resources. This means that simultaneously presenting an odor and a word will lead to impaired word encoding such that naming something at the same time as smelling an odor is especially difficult. Likewise, processing words at the same time as smelling diminishes the perceptual quality of the odor and the odor smells weaker (Lorig, 1999; Parr, Heatherbell, and White, 2002; Walla et al., 2003; Walla, 2008). (See also **Web Essays 14.2: Olfactory Lateralization** and **14.3: Verbal-Olfactory Interactions**.) New research also suggests that olfaction can affect visual perception. When participants smelled an apple odor while they were exposed to a nearly subliminal (around critical flicker fusion frequency, which is the frequency at which an intermittent [flickering] light appears to be constantly visible) image of an apple, they detected the apple image faster than a picture of a banana. What's more, the presence of a congruent odor made the visual image appear to last for a longer time, even though it wasn't presented for longer (Zhou et al., 2017). In other words, odor input warps visual time. This is not science fiction!

Individual Differences

We do not all perceive all odors the same way or equally acutely. One of the reasons for these differences is individual variation in how many and which ORs are expressed in our olfactory epithelia (as discussed in "The Genetic Basis of Olfactory Receptors" earlier in this chapter). Genetic variability accounts for differences in perception among people with a "normal" sense of smell and those with a specific anosmia. However, there are two other major individual difference factors that affect our olfactory capabilities overall: age and sex.

Sex differences are reliably demonstrated in odor perception, with women typically outperforming men on all measures (e.g., detection, identification, discrimination) at all ages (Boesveldt et al., 2011; Doty and Cameron, 2009). During a woman's reproductive years, it seems, female superiority is mediated by hormonal fluctuations, with women being especially sensitive to odors during ovulation but no different from men during menses (Doty et al., 1981). However, a female advantage is also seen before puberty and after menopause; thus it has been speculated that endocrinologic effects exert an organizing influence on the nervous system during early development such that baseline sex differences in olfactory sensitivity persist throughout the life span (Doty and Cameron, 2009). Contrary to popular belief, however, research has shown that olfactory sensitivity is not heightened during pregnancy (Cameron, 2007; Hummel et al., 2002; Laska et al., 1996). Taste is another story, as we'll see in Chapter 15.

Our ability to detect odorants declines with age, because of a change in the proportion of cell regeneration to cell death in ORs. As we age, the number of odorant receptors that die off rises beyond the number that are regenerated (Kern et al., 2004). This ratio continues to worsen in favor of cell death as we grow older, such that after the age of 85 it is estimated that about 50% of that population has effectively become anosmic (Hummel et al., 2007; J. C. Stevens and Cain, 1987). Trigeminal perception declines with age as well and seems to be directly related to loss in olfactory function (Hummel et al., 2003). Sensitivity to tastants decreases as we get older too, but not all tastes suffer to the same extent; bitter seems to be least affected (Doty et al., 2016). These declines in chemosensory function explain the increased use of condiments among the elderly (especially salt, which may produce unhealthy outcomes).

Similar to detection, our ability to identify odors is best between our teenage years and our 40s, but when we are in our 50s, it starts to decline fairly precipitously, such that by age 65, about half of the population have noticeably impaired olfactory identification ability. For people age 80 or older, about 75% suffer from major impairments in odor identification (Doty et al., 1984) (**Figure 14.17**). A main reason for this sharp decline is that odor identification is strongly influenced by verbal and semantic processing. It is well established that as we continue to age in adulthood, our ability to name everything gets worse (Au et al., 1995). Because there is already a weak connection between language and olfaction, any increase in the vulnerability of our naming ability is most readily observed in olfactory identification. That is, these "senior moments" are most obvious with olfaction because it's always been harder to identify the scent in the spice jar that is "rosemary" than to say that the name of that guy in the movie is "Vin Diesel." Notably, however, people with higher education levels (more years of postsec-ondary schooling) have better odor identification ability as they age than people with less education (Boesveldt et al., 2011). The correlation is presumably due to an association between education and naming ability or verbal fluency—the more education you

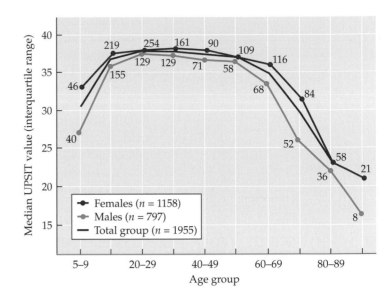

Figure 14.17 Changes in olfactory identification ability as a function of age. Our ability to correctly identify odors peaks in our 20s and stays relatively constant until our mid-50s, when it starts to decline. Males tend to have slightly lower scores than females at all ages. However, there is a great deal of individual variability, and a number of octoge-narians still have high function. (After Doty and Cameron, 2009.)

have, the better your vocabulary and verbal fluency—and this buffers the odor identification declines of aging. Notably, age-related declines in ability are not nearly as pronounced for odor detection and discrimination as they are for identification, because they rely much less on semantic processing (Hedner et al., 2010). It should be mentioned, though, that just as with hearing and vision, there is considerable individual variability in age-related declines in odor perception, and there are many octogenarians with excellent olfactory ability.

As mentioned earlier, the connection between naming and olfactory identifi-cation turns out to be very important in identifying certain neurological diseases at their earliest stages, in particular Alzheimer's disease (AD). This is because AD is a disease characterized by loss of memory, especially semantic memory (memory for the names of things and factual information), and because, as already explained, odor naming (compared with naming anything else) is most vulnerable to slight cognitive perturbations. Testing for such a deficit is crucial because the sooner people are correctly diagnosed with Alzheimer's disease and treated, the better their quality and duration of life will be. Parkinson's disease (PD) is also often foreshadowed by a loss of odor identification abilities, and the same benefits from early intervention apply (see this chapter's Scientists at Work box). (For reviews of olfactory impairment in AD and PD see Mesholam et al., 1998 and Ruan et al., 2012.)

In addition to differences between individuals, new evidence indicates that our ability to detect odors varies for each of us throughout the day. Researchers conducted a study with adolescents in which the influence of circadian rhythms was separated from the influence of how long someone had been awake, and found that both factors independently alter our sensitivity to smells. Specifi-cally, olfactory acuity was never best in the circadian phase that mapped onto the clock time between late morning to late afternoon (Herz et al., 2017a). In addition, the longer the teenagers had been awake, the worse their olfactory sensitivity became, and the deleterious effect of staying up late was most pronounced among females. After being awake for more than 15 hours, girls were substantially worse at detecting odors than they had been earlier in the day, and they were also significantly more affected than boys (Herz et al., 2017b). Other recent research has shown that sleep deprivation increases the brain's sensitivity to food aromas (Bhutani, Gottfried, and Khant, 2017). Together these findings have critical implications regarding the consequences of staying up late and snacking—lower olfactory acuity leads to less satisfaction from food and increased body mass index (BMI) overall (Aschenbrenner et al., 2008; Pastor et al., 2016), and when we are sleep deprived, the smell of doughnuts is especially enticing. Do we stand a chance?!

■ Scientists at Work

A New Test to Diagnose Parkinson's Disease

■ **Background and aim** Parkinson's disease (PD) is a neurodegenerative disorder characterized by various motor and cognitive disturbances. The motor symptoms are the result of degeneration of dopaminergic neurons in the basal ganglia. This degeneration produces deposits of a protein in the olfactory system that impedes odor perception. Importantly, olfactory loss can precede the observable motor symptoms in PD by years, and as with Alzheimer's disease, the sooner treatment can be started, the better the long-term outcome. In addition to having impaired odor detection, discrimination, and identification, people with PD perceive odors overall as less pleasant. Odor identification tests can differentiate people with PD from healthy peers, but these tests rely on cognitive ability and language, which can also become impaired in PD. Evaluating odor pleasantness requires only minimal effort and could be highly useful. The aim of this study was to determine whether a new tool called the New Test of Odor Pleasantness (NTOP) could distinguish people with PD from healthy controls and whether it would be suitable for use with PD patients.

■ **Test** Researchers asked 30 PD patients and 30 healthy control participants to perform two previously established olfactory perception tests and the NTOP, which involved smelling 32 odorants and then categorizing them for pleasantness.

■ **Results** Lower hedonic ratings on the NTOP were strongly correlated with lower identification scores on the other tests and successfully differentiated PD patients from controls. That is, the PD patients exhibited significantly lower pleasantness ratings than controls on the NTOP (**Figure 14.18**). Importantly, the PD patients also preferred taking the NTOP over the two other olfactory tests.

■ **Conclusions** The NTOP is a promising new tool for distinguishing individuals with PD from healthy controls, and it is well accepted in this patient group.

■ **Future work** Developing a pleasantness test that has fewer odorants and was therefore faster and more efficient to administer would be a beneficial avenue for further progress.

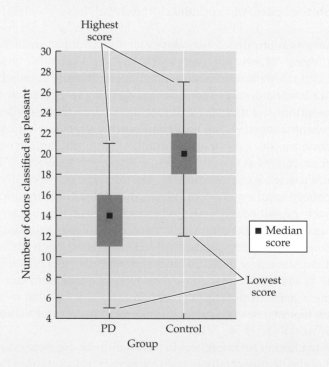

Figure 14.18 New Test of Odor Pleasantness. The boxplot shows the number of odors classified as pleasant by individuals in the Parkinson's disease (PD) group and in the control group. (After Pospichalova, Vodicka, and Kopal, 2016.)

Adaptation

Have you ever had the experience of noticing coworkers or classmates who seem to be pouring cologne over their head every morning, leaving you choking on the overpowering aroma? Can't they smell anything? Or perhaps you've noticed that, after using a perfume for a few months, you can't smell the fragrance in the bottle anymore. Or you've gone away on vacation and returned home to find that your house seems to have a "funny" smell that it didn't have when you left. What's going on? The answer has two parts: the first involves the nose, and the second involves the mind.

The sense of smell is a change detection system. When a new chemical comes along, your olfactory receptors fire in response to it, and you perceive a scent. For example, when you first enter a bakery, you notice the mouthwatering aromas of the cakes, cookies, pies, and danishes. But if you stand inside inspecting the pastries for a while, you may find that by the time you've picked out what cake you want for dessert, you can no longer smell it. What has happened is that the odorant molecules that make up the bakery aroma have bound to the corresponding olfactory sensory neurons in your nose. When this happens the ORs retreat into the cell body (Firestein, 2001). The receptors are therefore no longer physically available to respond to the bakery scent molecules. This response is a process in "receptor recycling." Specifically, an odorant binding to an OR causes the OR to be internalized into its cell body, where it becomes unbound from the odorant and is then recycled through the cell and emerges again in a number of minutes, if that same odorant doesn't block it. Receptor recycling is a mechanism common to all receptors in the class to which ORs belong: **G protein–coupled receptors (GPCRs)**.

> **FURTHER DISCUSSION** of parallels to visual adaptation can be found in Chapter 2 starting on page 46.

This process is called **receptor adaptation**. The precise length of time required for adaptation varies as a function of both the individual (Dalton, 2002) and the odorant (Pierce et al., 1996). On average it takes about 15–20 minutes of continual exposure to an odorant for the molecules to stop eliciting an olfactory response, but adaptation can also occur in less than a minute. Receptor adaptation can also be undone relatively quickly. Stepping outside the bakery for a few minutes gives unbound olfactory receptors a chance to accumulate on the cell surface again in the absence of the bakery aroma, so when you walk back in, you can enjoy the appetizing scents once more. The magnitude of adaptation is also affected by odor intensity (Kadohisa and Wilson, 2006). As the concentration of an odorant increases, the length of time for adaptation decreases. For example, it takes less time to adapt to the aroma wafting from an apple pie baking in the oven than to the scent emanating from a cool pie on the kitchen counter. This is because more molecules of apple pie aroma become volatile and are thus available to activate ORs when the pie is hot than when it is cold.

One way to prolong the effect of smelling a scent before adaptation kicks in is to dispense an odor intermittently. For example, bursts of air freshener alternated with no scent will draw out the time before your receptors are smothered by the air freshener molecules and duck for cover.

Dalton (1996) also showed that presumed danger can have an effect on adaptation rates. In one experiment, half the participants were told that an odor they were being exposed to was "healthful," while the other participants were told the odor was "hazardous." Twenty minutes after initial exposure, the

G protein–coupled receptor (GPCR) Any of the class of receptors that are present on the surface of olfactory sensory neurons. All GPCRs are characterized by a common structural feature of seven membrane-spanning helices.

receptor adaptation The biochemical phenomenon that occurs after continual exposure to an odorant, whereby receptors are no longer available to respond to the odorant and detection ceases.

participants smelling the supposedly healthful odor had adapted to it, whereas the participants who thought they were smelling a hazardous chemical actually became sensitized—they reported the smell as even more intense after 20 minutes than at the start of the experiment. However, when these participants were given a psychophysical test of odor detection, it was shown that they had adapted just as the people who were told that the odor was healthful had adapted. Fear of odor exposure can even make people perceive an odor that does not exist (Engen, 1972). For example, people who believe that a factory is emitting dangerous chemicals frequently complain that they can smell a malodor coming from the facility, regardless of what the factory produces or whether it is even operating.

New findings shed light on why psychological factors often supersede physical reality in odor perception. Recent research (Krusemark et al., 2013) has shown that when we are anxious, initially neutral odors become perceived as unpleasant and these now negative odors correspondingly elicit augmented responses in higher-order olfactory and emotional processing centers in the brain (orbitofrontal cortex and pregenual anterior cingulate cortex). Moreover, anxiety strengthens the connection between olfactory processing in the orbitofrontal cortex and emotional processing in the amygdala. This suggests that when we are worried that an odor may harm us, we perceive it as more unpleasant, and it elicits more-intense emotional processing, which potentiates further negative emotional responses to it. For example, if you smell an odor coming from a factory that you believe is producing dangerous chemicals, that odor will smell bad to you even though that same odor could be one you like in a different context. Emotional hypersensitivity can also create olfactory illusions, and you may believe that you are smelling the "bad" odor when you are merely seeing the factory, even when no odor at all is being emitted (Engen, 1972; Herz and Von Clef, 2001).

One of the benefits of olfactory adaptation is that it enables us to filter out stable background odors, and this filtering ability can be enhanced through active sniffing—taking deliberate, quick inhalations (Kepecs, Uchida, and Mainen, 2007). Sniffing makes OR neurons less responsive to stable odors and more responsive to new odorants (Verhagen et al., 2007). For example, if we're at a car dealership and think we smell something burning, we typically engage in active sniffing to (1) see if we're right and (2) determine which Subaru is smoldering. In vision and hearing, perceptual stimuli in the foreground can be segregated from stimuli in the background through spatial analysis of the scene. In olfaction, spatial analysis is compromised because background and foreground odors merge in the air. However, provided that background and foreground odors are at least briefly separated in time (new-car smell first and then the scent of burning plastic), sniffing enables us to separate components of an olfactory scene. Active sniffing for differences in odor intensity across space also helps us locate a new odor.

In some cases, exposure to one odorant can raise the odor detection threshold for a second, completely different odorant. For example, when you're picking out a perfume in a department store, your nose may become fairly useless at differentiating the fragrances after several samples, despite the salesperson's insistence that the perfumes are quite different from each other (**Figure 14.19**). This phenomenon is called **cross-adaptation**, and it is presumed to occur when components of the odors in question, or specific odorants, rely on similar sets of olfactory receptors. However, this simple explanation is complicated by the fact that most cross-adaptation relationships are nonreciprocal. For example, smelling pentanol (a chemical used in some paints) seems to have a strong cross-adapting effect on next smelling propanol (used as an antiseptic and solvent), whereas

cross-adaptation The reduction in detection of one odorant following exposure to a prior odorant. Cross-adaptation is presumed to occur because the components of the odors (or odorants) in question share one or more olfactory receptors for their transduction, but the order in which odorants are presented also plays a role.

Figure 14.19 Do these five fragrances smell the same? No, but because of olfactory cross-adaptation, as you go through smelling them, their differences are diminished.

smelling propanol first has only a small cross-adapting effect on then smelling pentanol (Cain and Engen, 1969). Furthermore, exposure to the first odorant can sometimes enhance sensitivity to the second odorant. (See **Web Activity 14.2: Odor Adaptation and Habituation**.)

Regardless of why they occur, cross-adaptation effects usually go away after a few minutes. Professional perfumers, who may have to smell hundreds of scents per day and thus don't have a few minutes to spare, use a trick of sniffing their bare arm or cotton shirtsleeve between smelling odorants; doing this effectively clears the nose even at a fast pace of odorant presentation. Nobody knows why this works, but it does. The next time you find yourself suffering from numb nose at a perfume counter, try it.

Cognitive Habituation

Receptor adaptation explains why you lose the delicious aroma of the bakery after you've been in the store for a while but can smell it again after a short break outside. If you took a job at a bakery, however, a different process would take place. This is the phenomenon that your friend who can't smell his own cologne is experiencing, and it's the reason why you don't smell the ambient scent of your own home unless you go out of town for a couple of weeks. It is a psychological effect called **cognitive habituation**.

In short, when we live with an odor, we cognitively habituate to it and no longer react to it, or we show a very diminished response to it. For example, textile workers exposed daily to acetone exhibited acetone detection thresholds that were eight times higher than those of a comparable group of control subjects. However, thresholds to another chemical (butanol), to which neither group had been regularly exposed, were no different for the two groups (Wysocki et al., 1997). We habituate (that is, our receptors adapt) to some degree to stimuli presented

cognitive habituation The psychological process by which, after long-term exposure to an odor, one no longer has the ability to detect that odor or has very diminished detection ability.

to all our senses (e.g., you stop hearing the ticktock of a grandfather clock after being in the room for a while), but attention can bring us out of habituation with every sense except smell. Unlike receptor adaptation, which can be undone in a few minutes, cognitive habituation requires weeks to reverse, even for pungent trigeminal stimulants like acetone (Dalton et al., 1997; Wysocki et al., 1997). For example, if you stopped wearing your cologne for 5 days, you would still not be able to smell it well when you used it again. But if you abstained for 2 weeks or more, you would.

Dalton (2002) suggested that at least three mechanisms could be involved—either singularly or in combination—in producing olfactory habituation. First, the olfactory receptors that are internalized into their cell bodies during odor adaptation may be more hindered after continual exposure and take much longer to recycle than they normally would. Second, from continual exposure, odorant molecules may be absorbed into the bloodstream and then transported to the olfactory receptors via nasal capillaries when we breathe out through the nose. As long as the odorant chemicals remain in the bloodstream, we will be constantly adapted (Maruniak, Silver, and Moulton, 1983). Finally, cognitive-emotional factors, like those demonstrated in the experiment in which participants were told that an odor was harmful and then did not adapt, may be involved (but in the reverse direction) in cognitive habituation.

Another feature of olfactory perception that highlights the importance of conscious perception is that we do not respond to odors while we're asleep (Carskadon and Herz, 2004). Unlike what happens with auditory stimuli, when trigeminally activating odorants such as menthol and pyridine (also a chemical component of smoke) were presented, even at high concentrations, to participants in slow-wave sleep; deep sleep) or REM sleep, they did not awaken or show any electroencephalogram (EEG) sleep pattern changes. More recently, it was found that exposing sleepers to artificial smoke during all stages of sleep had no effect on arousal frequency or EEG activity (Heiser et al., 2012). These findings underscore the need for auditory smoke detectors, and why our sense of smell cannot protect us from smoke inhalation and consequent catastrophes while we sleep. However, there is some evidence that odors presented during sleep can still modify our behavior. A recent study testing whether odors could be used to curb smoking found that using a conditioning procedure where a noxious odor was paired with the smell of cigarette smoke when the participants were awake did not have any effect on the number of cigarettes they later smoked (Arzi et al., 2014). However, the same conditioning procedure presented during REM and especially stage 2 sleep was able to significantly reduce the number of cigarettes smoked, and the effect lasted for several days. This was the case even though there were no arousals from sleep or EEG changes during the odor presentations and waking ratings of the pleasantness of cigarette smoke pre- and postconditioning were the same. This finding suggests that controlling addictive behavior may be best addressed using implicit (e.g., during sleep) rather than explicit (e.g., during wakefulness) strategies and that, because of their connectivity to emotion and reward centers in the brain, odors may be especially well suited for these procedures.

Olfactory Hedonics

odor hedonics The liking dimension of odor perception, typically measured by ratings of an odor's perceived pleasantness, familiarity, and intensity.

The most immediate and basic response we have to an odor is whether we like it or not. Such affective evaluations are known as **odor hedonics**. In tests of odor hedonic evaluation, people are typically asked to rate how pleasant, familiar, and intense a given odor is. These measures are then used to determine the hedonic value of a specific smell. It is obvious that perceived pleasantness is related to our liking for an odor. But how are familiarity and intensity related?

Familiarity and Intensity

As with many other facets of life, we tend to like odors that we've smelled many times before. That is, we tend to like familiar odors better than unfamiliar odors. Moreover, we often perceive pleasant odors as being more familiar than unpleasant odors, regardless of how truly familiar we are with them (Moskowitz, Dravnieks, and Klarman, 1976; Sulmont, Issanchou, and Koster, 2002). Thus, ratings of odor pleasantness and familiarity show a linear relationship with odor liking.

The perceived intensity of a given chemical is dependent both on how many molecules reach the ORs and how those molecules interact with the odorant receptors—how those ORs are activated. That is, the concentration of a chemical (how much is there) does not necessarily predict how intense it will smell. Intensity also has a more complex relationship to odor liking that is often represented by an inverted-U function, but this depends on the odorant. A rose scent, like phenylethyl alcohol, may be evaluated as more positive with increasing intensity, up to a point; then the function reverses, and as the scent becomes stronger, it is judged to be more disagreeable (**Figure 14.20A**). This is why an overdose of cologne is unpleasant. By contrast, a fishy odor, like trimethylamine, may be acceptable at low concentrations, but as intensity increases, its perception becomes steadily more negative (**Figure 14.20B**). Note also that individual differences in the number and type of receptors expressed may influence one's sensitivity (intensity perception) and hence the predisposition to experience the intensity of specific odorants along a pleasantness continuum.

Nature or Nurture?

An on-going debate in the field of olfaction is the degree to which hedonic responses to odors are innate or learned. Researchers on the innate side of the debate to various degrees claim that we are born with a predisposition to like or dislike various smells. In other words, rose is inherently a good smell and skunk is inherently a bad smell, the way bitter taste is inherently unpleasant to us and sweet inherently pleasant (see Chapter 15). In contrast, researchers taking the view that hedonic responses are learned hold that we are born merely with a predisposition to learn to like or dislike smells, and that whether a smell is liked or not is determined by the emotional value (good or bad) of the experiences that have been associated with it. That is, if we like rose and dislike skunk, the reason is that we have a good and a bad association, respectively, with these two scents. We need not have direct contact with a skunk to form such an association, though, because cultural learning gives us meanings for many unencountered stimuli.

If asked to take a position yourself, on the sole basis of your own personal experiences, it's pretty likely you would come down on the innate side of the debate. After all, who could like the smell of skunk, and who wouldn't like the smell

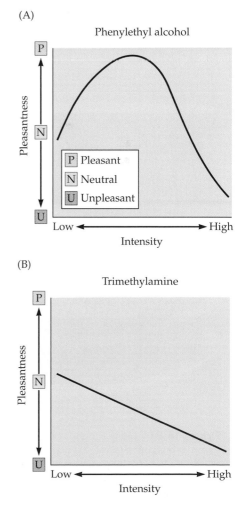

(A)

Figure 14.20 Pleasantness ratings of odorants plotted against intensity. (A) The relationship between odor intensity and pleasantness is often described by an inverted-U function, if the odorant is initially considered pleasant, as the synthetic rose scent (phenylethyl alcohol) usually is. (B) For an odorant that is initially considered tolerable (but not necessarily pleasant), such as fishy smelling trimethylamine, the relationship is typically described by a linear graph.

of a rose? In fact, however, a great deal of evidence suggests that odor hedonics are almost exclusively learned. A good place to start looking for such evidence is with infants. If odor preferences are innate, then newborns should display them. However, researchers have repeatedly found that infants and children often display very different preferences from those of adults. For instance, infants do not find the smells of sweat and feces unpleasant (Engen, 1982; M. Stein, Ottenberg, and Roulet, 1958), and toddlers typically do not hedonically differentiate between odorants that adults find either very unpleasant (e.g., butyric acid, which smells like dirty socks) or pleasant (e.g., amyl acetate, which smells like banana).

One difficulty with these types of studies is that the olfactory system is fully functional by the third month of gestation (6 months before the baby is born) (Schaal, Marlier, and Soussignan, 1995, 1998; Winberg and Porter, 1998), and odorant molecules do find their way into the womb. So it is difficult to know exactly how much exposure even a newborn infant has had to an odorant. But exposure to odors in utero has led to yet another line of evidence in support of the learned view of hedonics: Mennella and colleagues found that mothers who consumed distinctive-smelling volatiles (e.g., garlic, alcohol, and cigarette smoke) during pregnancy or breast-feeding had infants who showed greater preferences for these smells than did infants who had not been exposed to these scents (Mennella and Beauchamp, 1991, 1993; Mennella, Johnson, and Beauchamp, 1995). What we learn about odors prenatally and during infancy and early childhood can also go on to influence our food and flavor preferences in adulthood (Haller et al., 1999). This correlation suggests that it might be a good idea for women to eat lots of brussels sprouts and salmon and other healthful, flavorful foods during pregnancy and lactation.

Cross-cultural data provide further support for the idea that associative learning, and not hardwired responses, is responsible for olfactory preferences. No scientific studies to date have found cross-cultural agreement for hedonic responses to common everyday odors, either "good" or "bad" (Ayabe-Kanamura et al., 1998; Schleidt, Hold, and Attila, 1981). Anecdotal and observational examples also illustrate the many culturally polarized responses that we have to specific odors, especially food aromas. For example, Asians typically consider the smell of cheese to be disgusting, yet most Westerners consider it anything from comfort food to an extravagant indulgence. In contrast, many Japanese often enjoy a meal for breakfast called *nattō* (a fermented soybean dish) (**Figure 14.21**) that most Westerners wouldn't bring near their mouths (some say it smells like burning rubber). Both cheese and *nattō* are high in protein and similarly nutritious; the reason they are preferred, or not, has to do with the respective differences in the learned associations to their scents.

In case you're thinking that the examples of odors given so far aren't really that bad, and that there must be consensus on really horrid stenches, this also doesn't seem to be the case. Fecal smells are not high on most North Americans' "best smells list," but the Masai of Africa like to dress their hair with cow dung as a cosmetic color treatment. And in a study undertaken by the US military to create a stink bomb (to be used in place of tear gas to disband riots), it was impossible to find an odor (including "US Army-issue latrine scent") that was unanimously considered repellent across ethnic groups (Dilks, Dalton, and Beauchamp,

Figure 14.21 Many Japanese regularly eat *nattō* (right) for breakfast, but Westerners do not associate its smell with food. In contrast, cheese, which most Westerners enjoy, is considered disgusting by most Japanese.

1999). Laboratory studies directly aimed at testing the learning hypothesis have shown that a novel odor can be made to be perceived as good or bad as a function of the experiences (good or bad) that are associated with it (Herz, Beland, and Hellerstein, 2004). Note, however, that from an experimental perspective it is much easier to demonstrate that odor preferences can be learned than to prove that no odorants exist to which innate responses may be shown.

In an attempt to support the view that odor pleasantness has an innate basis, one study tested whether the physical and chemical structure of an odorant could predict to what degree it would be considered pleasant (Khan et al., 2007). The researchers found that the molecular structure of odorants could account for 30% of the variance in participants' responses (70% was not accounted for this way) and therefore argued that a portion of odor pleasantness perception may be innate. More recent research has shown that the more oxygen atoms there are in a chemical, the more pleasant it is perceived to be (Keller and Vosshall, 2016). Vanilla is one such example. This may reflect a direct chemical-perception relationship or may simply be coincident with the fact that vanillin is a component of most sweet foods, and since sweetness is innately pleasant (see Chapter 15), we have learned the connection between that pleasure and the corresponding scent—in this case vanilla. The problem is that it would actually be disadvantageous for us if our odor preferences were hardwired.

An Evolutionary Argument

Specialist animal species live in very specific habitats and thus have a limited number of food sources and predators. For such species, innate responses to particular odors are adaptive. California ground squirrels, for example, exhibit an instinctive defensive response the first time they are exposed to the odor of their natural predator, the Pacific rattlesnake, but they don't show the same response to the scent of Pacific gopher snakes, which are not their natural predators (**Figure 14.22**) (Coss et al., 1993; Poran and Coss, 1990). Generalist species (including humans, rats, and cockroaches), by contrast, can exploit many different habitats. For generalists, the available resources and potential predators can vary widely across environments, so it is not adaptive for these species to have predetermined olfactory responses to any particular odor. For example,

(A)

(B)

Figure 14.22 The California ground squirrel lives in a restricted habitat (A), so it has only a few natural predators, including the Pacific rattlesnake (B). Studies have shown that, unlike humans, specialist species such as the California ground squirrel show innate odor responses, in this case to avoid the scent of the animal that will try to eat them.

learned taste aversion The avoidance of a novel flavor after it has been paired with gastric illness. The smell, not the taste, of the substance is key for the learned aversion response in humans.

a certain odor in one locale may signal poisonous mushrooms, but in another environment that same odor may mean nutritious food.

Clear evidence that learning is a critical mechanism by which generalists acquire odor responses is shown by **learned taste aversions**. Rats and humans can be made to avoid a flavor by being made sick after consumption (see Chapter 15 for an explanation of the critical role of olfaction in flavor perception). For example, presenting a rat with a sweet-tasting, banana-smelling drink and then injecting the rat with lithium, which causes nausea, creates a conditioned avoidance of this flavor in the future. Similarly, a pioneering experiment in humans testing the phenomenon of learned taste aversions showed that children who had chemotherapy after ingesting a novel flavor of ice cream (dubbed "mapletoff") subsequently refused to eat mapletoff ice cream but had no problem enjoying a different novel-flavored ice cream (Bernstein, 1978).

Researchers have shown that in humans the conditioned aversion is to the smell, not the taste, of the substance (Bartoshuk and Wolfe, 1990; also see Miranda, 2012, for review). In rodents, although discrete taste aversion can occur (e.g., to the taste of saccharine; Moraga-Amaro, 2013), it is also clear that discrete (without a tastant) odor aversion learning can take place, especially when the odorant is consumed (e.g., scented water), and that a compound's odor is often the central feature of conditioned "taste" aversion (Capaldi et al., 2004; Chapuis et al., 2007). The long-term effects of learned taste aversion are clearly adaptive. If poison is ingested, it is best to learn to immediately avoid it, rather than having to repeat the mistake until it kills you.

The special importance of initial associations in odor learning was further shown in a recent fMRI study where it was found that the first association made to an odor is etched into the brain and produces a unique neural signature in the amygdala-hippocampal complex that predicts later memory for that odor association. However, after the first association is made to an odor, subsequent associations do not produce a new unique neural signature (Yeshurun et al., 2009). The bottom line is that the olfactory system of generalists does not come preprogrammed but, rather, is geared to very effectively learn the meaning of smells based on experience, especially first experiences.

Caveats

Although a great deal of evidence suggests that odor hedonics are learned, we must note two caveats. First, trigeminally irritating odorants may elicit pain responses, and all humans have an innate drive to avoid pain (although even this drive can be overcome by social and cultural influences, as attested by the popularity of chili peppers in many ethnic cuisines). Second, as has been mentioned several times, the potential variability in the receptor genes and pseudogenes that are expressed across individuals may influence odor intensity, and consequently the perceived pleasantness, of odors. For example, people who like the smell of skunk may exhibit this response in part because they are missing receptors for detecting some of the more pungent volatiles, whereas people who are particularly repulsed by this scent may be endowed with a greater number of receptors that are keenly attuned to the mercaptan and sulfide components of this bouquet. That is, detection of the full complement of chemicals that make up an odor (e.g., skunk, cilantro) and how strong or weak an odor is perceived to be play a role in its perceived (un)pleasantness. Recall that for many odors, an inverted-U function describes the relationship between liking and intensity (see Figure 14.20). Genetic differences in OR expression appear to extend to ethnicities as well (Menashe et al., 2003), which may help explain why it has been impossible to develop a universally effective stink bomb.

Associative Learning and Emotion: Neuroanatomical and Evolutionary Considerations

In the mid-1960s in Britain, adult respondents were asked to provide hedonic ratings for a battery of common odors (Moncrieff, 1966). A similar study was conducted in the United States in the late 1970s (Cain and Johnson, 1978). Included in both studies was the odorant methyl salicylate (wintergreen). In the British study, wintergreen was given one of the lowest pleasantness ratings; in the American study, it was rated as the most pleasant scent tested. There is a historical reason for this difference. In Britain, the smell of wintergreen is associated with medicine; in particular, wintergreen was added to analgesics used during World War II, a time that the adults in the 1966 study would not have remembered fondly. Conversely, in the United States the smell of wintergreen is mostly a candy smell, so it has sweet, positive connotations. As this example demonstrates, the key to olfactory associative learning is the experience when the odor is first encountered and, in particular, the emotional connotation of that experience (Bartoshuk, 1991; Engen, 1991; Herz, 2001).

When an odor is liked or disliked because of what it has been associated with in our past, we are also recalling a memory when we smell it. Many of our odor experiences, such as most Britons' and Americans' experiences with wintergreen, are too vague to conjure up specific memories, and only general associations (e.g., "a bad, medicinal smell" or "a happy, appetizing smell") and feelings of disliking or liking are registered. However, one of the most distinctive features of olfaction is its ability to elicit our most emotional and evocative personal recollections. For more information see "Sensation & Perception in Everyday Life: Odor-Evoked Memory and the Truth behind Aromatherapy" on page 503.

Neuroanatomy supports the proposition that our olfactory system is especially prepared to learn the affective significance of odors. The amygdala, which synapses directly with the olfactory nerve, is critical for emotional associative learning (M. Davis and Whalen, 2001). The **orbitofrontal cortex** (**OFC**), which is located behind our eyes at the very front of the frontal lobes (see Figure 14.8), is where we consciously experience and perceive odors. The OFC is considered to be the "secondary olfactory cortex," as well as the "secondary taste cortex" (Rolls, 2006) because it is where pleasure and displeasure from food are integrated. Indeed, the OFC has been identified as the neural locus for assigning affective value in general—that is, our hedonic response to a wide range of stimuli (R. J. Davidson, Putnam, and Larson, 2000). Notably, the right OFC plays a significant role in conscious olfactory perception (W. Li et al., 2010). This is important because the right hemisphere of the brain is dominant for emotional processing (R. J. Davidson, 1984) and odors are inherently hedonic—that is, emotional—stimuli (Herz, 2007). Furthermore, the most ancient part of the brain, the rhinencephalon—literally, the "nose brain"—which comprises the primary olfactory cortex and the specific structures of the limbic system, developed first from neural tissue that was dedicated only to processing odors. It wasn't until later in evolution that limbic structures such as the amygdala and hippocampus emerged. It is interesting to consider that our hedonic and emotional reactions to stimuli in general may have their origin in our sense of smell.

orbitofrontal cortex (OFC) The part of the frontal lobe of the cortex that lies behind the bone (orbit) containing the eyes. The OFC is responsible for the conscious experience of olfaction, as well as the integration of pleasure and displeasure from food. The OFC is also involved in many other functions, and it is critical for assigning affective value to stimuli—in other words, determining hedonic meaning. It is also referred to as the *secondary olfactory cortex* and the *secondary taste cortex*.

main olfactory bulb (MOB) The rounded extension of the brain just above the nose that is the first region of the brain where smells are processed. In humans we refer simply to olfactory bulb(s); in nonhuman animals with accessory olfactory bulbs, we distinguish between main and accessory.

accessory olfactory bulb (AOB) A neural structure found in nonhuman animals that is smaller than the main olfactory bulb and located behind it and that receives input from the vomeronasal organ.

vomeronasal organ (VNO) Found in nonhuman animals, it is a chemical-sensing organ at the base of the nasal cavity with a curved tubular shape. The VNO evolved to detect chemicals that cannot be processed by ORs, such as large and/or aqueous molecules, the types of molecules that constitute pheromones. Also called *Jacobson's organ.*

Almost all species of animals use smell or chemical communication for the most basic behaviors necessary for survival: recognizing kin, finding reproductively available mates, locating food, and determining whether an animal or object is dangerous (see the next section). Only in humans have visual and auditory information mostly replaced smell for imparting this kind of crucial knowledge about the world. Yet our olfactory system has retained some of its basic functions. The most immediate responses we have to odors are simple binary opposites: like or dislike, approach or avoid. Emotions convey similar messages: approach what is good, safe, and joyful; avoid what is bad, dangerous, or liable to cause grief. Thus, emotions and olfaction are functionally analogous. Both enable an organism to react appropriately to its environment, maximizing its chances for basic survival and reproductive success. Viewed in this context, the human emotional system can be seen as a highly evolved, abstract cognitive version of the basic behavioral motivations instigated by the olfactory system in animals (Herz, 2000, 2004).

The Vomeronasal Organ, Human Pheromones, and Chemosignals

In animals that rely on smell for survival, the olfactory system consists of two subdivisions: the **main olfactory bulb** (**MOB**) and the **accessory olfactory bulb** (**AOB**) (**Figure 14.23**). The AOB is attached to the back of the MOB. Just as each hemisphere of our brain has an olfactory bulb, in animals that possess them, each hemisphere has an MOB and AOB. Neurons from the MOB and the AOB do not interconnect, and the two systems function separately in the integration of specific chemicals. In order for the AOB to be activated, a structure different from the nose needs to be engaged. This structure is called the **vomeronasal organ** (**VNO**), sometimes also referred to as Jacobson's organ after the Danish anatomist who discovered it.

The VNO is found in some amphibians, most reptiles (but not birds), and many mammals, including New World primates. When a snake opens its mouth and appears to be licking the air, it is actually moving chemicals from the air into the vomeronasal organ. In mammals, the VNO is cigar-shaped and located at the base of the nasal cavity. The VNO can respond to some olfactory stimuli, but it responds primarily to chemicals that are too high in molecular weight to be detected by the olfactory sensory neurons, as well as to chemicals that are nonvolatile. It also detects chemicals dissolved in water (as opposed to only in air). Whether humans possess a functioning VNO has been the focus of much debate, but it is now generally accepted that although human embryos may have a VNO, this tissue is not neurally connected and disappears shortly after birth. Moreover, we do not have an AOB for VNO neurons to connect to in the brain.

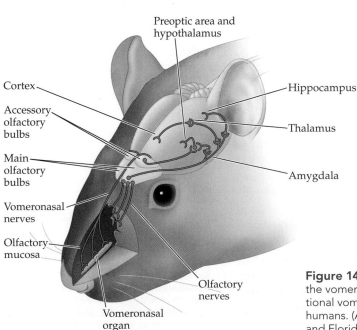

Figure 14.23 The olfactory system of a hamster, showing the location of the vomeronasal organ and accessory olfactory bulbs. Note that no functional vomeronasal organ or accessory olfactory bulbs have been found in humans. (After an illustration by Dr. Michael Meredith; © Michael Meredith and Florida State University Program in Neuroscience.)

In animals that possess a VNO, its primary function is to detect **pheromones**. Pheromones are not odors. They are chemicals that may or may not have a smell. The word *pheromone* is derived from the Greek *pherein*, meaning "to carry," and *hormon*, meaning "to stimulate." It was first coined in 1959 by Peter Karlson (a German biochemist) and Martin Lüscher (a Swiss entomologist) to describe a chemical substance that carries a message about the physiological or behavioral state of one insect to another, and that in turn leads to a specific reaction in the receiver insect. That is, pheromones are a means of chemical communication. Today, the more generalized definition of a pheromone is "a chemical compound produced by one animal that elicits a specific behavioral or physiological response in another animal of the same species."

Pheromones are most important for communication in the social insects, like ants, termites, and bees, but they also convey important information for many non-insect species, including primates. There are many examples of this form of chemical communication. Pheromones are used to identify territory. For example, a tiger will rub a tree with glands from its cheeks to claim it—just as a cat rubs your leg with its eyebrow and rump glands to mark you as its territory! Pheromones also initiate alarm or defense reactions. When a honeybee stings us, the chemical released from the stinger (which happens to smell like banana) is a cue to other bees to join in—unfortunately for us. Most important, for many animals pheromones are critically involved in communication about reproductive behavior. They can provide signals to males about when a female is fertile and provide signals to females to initiate sexual behavior. For example, a male rhesus monkey will ignore a female rhesus in heat if his nose is blocked, and a female pig will not go into **lordosis** (the position necessary for impregnation) if she isn't exposed to the male pig pheromone androstenone.

Pheromones have two kinds of effects. The two types of pheromones that cause these effects are known as **releaser pheromones** and **primer pheromones**. Primer pheromone effects are slow and produce a physiological change in the recipient over time. For example, female rodents that are housed together will come into estrus at the same time after several cycles. Releaser pheromone effects are fast and always produce behavioral responses. The consequence of the banana aroma from a bee sting is one example. Sexual cues and behavioral responses to those cues, such as lordosis, are other examples of releaser pheromone effects. In contrast, primer pheromones may produce no behavioral consequences and may be noticeable only in terms of physiological changes.

The most frequently mentioned example of a primer pheromone effect in humans is known as the McClintock effect after the psychologist Martha McClintock, who identified this phenomenon in college while pursuing her undergraduate degree. The McClintock effect is shown when women who are in physical proximity (e.g., live together) over time start to have menstrual cycles that coincide. That is, women who move into college dormitories together at the beginning of the school term often find that by the end of the semester they're having their periods in sync with one another. However, recent research casts strong doubt that any human pheromones exist (Doty, 2010), and the McClintock effect has come under sharp criticism. Moreover, we do not have a functioning VNO or AOB, therefore it is unknown how pheromones could be processed. Since the existence of human pheromones is highly uncertain, a more impartial way to discuss human chemical communication is to use the term **chemosignal**. Here, *chemosignals* refers to chemicals emitted by humans that are detected by

pheromone A chemical emitted by one member of a species that triggers a physiological or behavioral response in another member of the same species. Pheromones are signals for chemical communication and may or may not have any smell.

lordosis The position that females of some species (e.g., pigs and rats) need to assume in order to be impregnated. It involves the downward curving of the spinal column and exposure of the genitals.

releaser pheromone A pheromone that triggers an immediate behavioral response among conspecifics.

primer pheromone A pheromone that triggers a physiological (often hormonal) change among conspecifics. This effect usually involves prolonged pheromone exposure.

chemosignal Any of various chemicals emitted by humans that are detected by the olfactory system and that may have some effect on the mood, behavior, hormonal status, and/or sexual arousal of other humans.

the olfactory system and that may have some effect on the mood or behavior of other humans.

The chemical androstadienone (AND) is a steroid derivative of the male sex hormone testosterone (it is chemically related to androstenone, which was mentioned earlier), and it is present in body fluids (e.g., sweat) at higher concentrations in males than in females. In several studies, AND has been observed to improve women's mood, but only when women are in the presence of men (Jacob, Hayreh, and McClintock, 2001; Lundstrom and Olsson, 2005). In the presence of a female experimenter, AND had no effect on female participants' mood. Another study with a male experimenter and female participants found that AND increased self-rated sexual arousal and cortisol (a stress and arousal hormone) levels (Wyert et al., 2007). Notably, however, the levels of AND that women were exposed to in these studies were a million times higher than the amount a normal man emits. Thus, the ecological validity of AND as an aphrodisiac chemosignal in a naturalistic setting is questionable. Moreover, a recent study examining the effect of both AND and estratetraenol (EST)—a steroid metabolized from the female sex hormone estradiol and a chemical of interest in the quest for human pheromones—found that neither chemical had any effects on judgments that heterosexual male and female participants made regarding the attractiveness of male or female faces or on how they categorized ambiguous gender-neutral faces—created by blending faces of men and women together—as either male or female (Hare et al., 2017). The authors thereby concluded that these chemicals have no effect on human social-sexual responses.

Nevertheless, some mysteries remain concerning the effects of human chemosignals. A study with professional exotic lap dancers found that the dancers earned almost twice as much in tips (averaging $335 a night versus $185) when they performed during the ovulatory phase of their menstrual cycles, compared with the menstrual phase of their cycles (G. Miller, Tybur, and Jordan, 2007). Moreover, dancers who were taking birth control pills (and were thus hormonally infertile) showed no change in tip earnings over time and also earned less overall than did dancers who were not using hormonal contraception (averaging $193 versus $276). Since the dancers all claimed they performed the same way every day and that their behavior to the patrons was consistent, the explanation offered is that the women were perceived as more attractive by the male patrons when they were most fertile, through some mechanism other than behavioral or visual cues. This other mechanism is proposed to be chemical. Another study found that when men smelled T-shirts that had been worn by ovulating women, their testosterone levels were higher than they were after they sniffed T-shirts worn by nonovulating women or a clean, unworn T-shirt (S. L. Miller and Maner, 2010). However, not all female chemosignals increase sexual desire. Indeed, chemicals present in the tears of women dampen the sexual desire of men (Gelstein et al., 2011). When men were exposed to a strip placed under their nose containing emotional tears from women, though they knew nothing about the source of the compound, a significant decrease was observed in self-rated sexual desire, rated sexual attractiveness of female faces, testosterone level, and brain activity associated with sexual arousal. Are the tears of a distressed woman a direct turnoff, or is the effect due to something else? The authors suggested that the drop in testosterone and sexual arousal may be a by-product of a drop in aggression, which is also manifested by lowered testosterone, and there are good evolutionary reasons to hope for a decrease in testosterone from potential aggressors when they are exposed to your tears. With that in mind, the authors

■ Sensation & Perception in Everyday Life ■

Odor-Evoked Memory and the Truth behind Aromatherapy

You have probably had the experience where an odor triggered a specific and special autobiographical memory. These occurrences are often referred to as Proustian memories after the literary anecdote described by Marcel Proust where the aroma of linden tea and a madeleine cookie suddenly triggered the recollection of a long-forgotten event (Proust, 1928). Proustian memories have been shown to differ from episodic memories triggered by other cues in several important ways.

Compared with visual and verbal cues, odors elicit more affective, old, rare, and evocative personal memoires, as well as greater activity in the amygdala, than memories elicited by verbal or visual representations of the same cue (Arshamian et al., 2013; Chu and Downes, 2000; Herz and Schooler, 2002; Herz et al., 2004; Hinton and Henley, 1993; Larsson and Willander, 2009; Rubin, Groth, and Goldsmith, 1984; Willander and Larsson, 2007; Zucco et al., 2012). Odors even evoke more emotional memories than musical or tactile cues (Herz, 1998). (See **Web Activity 14.3: Sensory Memory Cues**.)

Herz (1998, 2004) compared recollections stimulated by a familiar smell—for example, popcorn—with memories evoked by the sight of popcorn, the sound of popcorn popping, the feel of popcorn kernels, or simply the word *popcorn* (**Figure 14.24**). Consistently, memories that were triggered by odors were experienced as more emotionally intense, and participants felt more transported back to the original time and place of the event, than when memories were triggered by cues in any other modality.

The distinctive emotional features of odor-evoked memory are explained by the uniquely direct connection between the neural substrates of olfaction, emotion, associative learning, and memory (Cahill et. al., 1995). Only two synapses separate the olfactory nerve from the amygdala, a structure critical for the expression and experience of emotion and human emotional memory, and only three synapses separate the olfactory nerve from the hippocampus, involved in the selection and transmission of information in working memory, short-term and long-term memory transfer, and various declarative memory functions (Eichenbaum, 2001). The amygdala has also been shown to

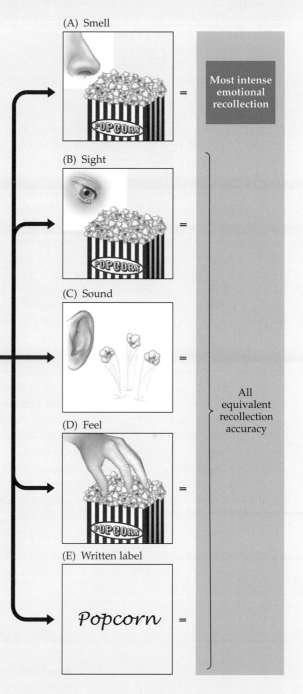

FIGURE 14.24 The smell (A), sight (B), sound (C), feel (D), and written label (E) of popcorn elicit memories that are equivalent in terms of their accuracy. However, odor-induced recollections are more intensely emotional, and this quality has earned odors a reputation as particularly good cues for memory.

(Continued)

■ Sensation & Perception in Everyday Life *(continued)* ■

play a major role in stimulus reinforcement association learning in primates (Jones and Mishkin, 1972; Wilson and Rolls, 2005), and neuroimaging studies in humans have shown a direct neurobiological correlation between recall of significantly emotional odor-evoked memories and activity in the amygdala (Arshamian et al., 2013; Herz et al., 2004; Vermetten et al., 2007).

Notably, although memories evoked by odors have many unique and special characteristics, they are not more accurate than memories elicited by other cues. Nevertheless, odors have earned the reputation of being the "best cues" to memory. Part of this can be explained by the same mechanisms that make eyewitness testimony so fraught. When there is a high degree of emotion experienced during recollection, people are much more confident that their memories are correct, even though they are often shown to be inaccurate (Herz, 1998). However, it is also the case that, as Proust experienced, odors can remind one of memories that might otherwise be forever forgotten. That is, odors may unlock memories whose only "mental tag" was the odor that was present when the memory was encoded. The reason for the special capacity of odors to do this may be twofold: (1) the low frequency by which certain odors are encountered, rendering minimal interference from multiple associations, and (2) resistance to being overwritten—there are very strong proactive interference effects in olfaction, so the first association you acquire to an odor is extremely hard to undo, and subsequent associations are very hard to make. Unfortunately, it is not possible to test whether odors can retrieve memories that would otherwise never be remembered,

but anecdote suggests that this may indeed be the one feature that makes odors "better" memory cues (Herz, 2007).

Odors that elicit specific emotional associations can also produce concomitant changes in behavior. For example, it has been shown that an odor that was associated with a frustrating experience led to reduced motivation and performance when later smelled (Epple and Herz, 1999; Herz, Shankler, and Beland, 2004), and odors that have acquired connotations of being energizing, such as peppermint, cinnamon, and grapefruit, can lead to heightened physical and mental performance when participants are later exposed to them (Raudenbush, Corley, and Eppich, 2001; Raudenbush et al., 2009). Proponents of **aromatherapy** contend that odors alter mood, performance, well-being, and the physiological correlates of emotion (e.g., heart rate, blood pressure, and sleep) in a drug-like automatic manner. There is, however, no evidence for pharmacological effects of odors in humans. Instead, so-called aromatherapeutic effects can all be explained by the emotions associated with the scent (Herz, 2009; 2016). The scent of peppermint can indeed make you feel invigorated, but only if you have uplifting and energizing associations to this aroma. It is also the case that the emotions elicited by an odor can have downstream effects on physiology and performance. Therefore, an odor associated with an arousing experience (e.g., peppermint) can increase your heart rate and may also make you run faster. However, if you have never smelled peppermint before, or if you dislike the scent, it will produce either no effect or a negative one (Herz, 2009).

aromatherapy   The manipulation of odors to influence mood, performance, and well-being as well as the physiological correlates of emotion such as heart rate, blood pressure, and sleep.

speculated that the effect would also be seen if the tears came from a man. In sum, chemicals present in human body fluids may modulate sexual arousal to some extent. These findings can be interpreted as illustrating a biological basis for olfactory influences on behavior, but they are also consistent with the view that through past associations, odors acquire meaning and then affect emotional and behavioral responses accordingly. Therefore, the scent of ovulating women may be arousing to men because of the men's past sexual experiences; and despite not having a clearly discernible odor, past associations with tears and their connection with sadness may explain why tears are the anti-Viagra. The degree to which perceptible odors and/or imperceptible chemical signals influence human sexuality is an ongoing field of research.

Summary

1. Olfaction is one of the two chemical senses; the other is taste (discussed in Chapter 15). To be perceived as a scent, a chemical must possess certain physical properties; however, even some molecules that have these characteristics cannot be smelled. Contrary to long standing beliefs that human olfactory capabilities are poor compared to that of other animals, recent research has shown that human odor detection is similar to many other mammalian species, and that how olfactory acuity is measured is a key factor. Human olfaction also has some unique physiological properties, one of which is that only 35% to 40% of the genes that code for olfactory receptors in humans are functional. Another unusual feature is that most odorants also stimulate the somatosensory system via the trigeminal nerve, and it is often impossible to distinguish the contribution of olfactory sensation from trigeminal stimulation.

2. Anosmia is the complete absence of a sense of smell. It is most frequently caused by sinus disease, which can usually be treated, enabling the return of normal olfactory function. However, if anosmia is caused by head trauma, it is likely to be permanent. Anosmia can lead to severe disturbances in an individual's quality of life. Gradual loss of olfaction is a normal consequence of aging; however, sudden olfactory loss can be the first sign of Alzheimer's or Parkinson's disease and should be investigated.

3. The dominant biochemical theory of odor perception—shape-pattern theory—contends that the fit between a molecule and an olfactory receptor (OR) determines which molecules are detected as scents and that specific odorants activate a combinatorial code of ORs, producing specific patterns of spatial and temporal neural activation for each perceived scent. However, this theory is not universally accepted, and alternate explanations exist (e.g., vibration theory).

4. Recently, researchers demonstrated closer connections between the visual system and olfaction than has ever before been thought to exist. Two examples are binaral rivalry and the discovery of "olfactory white." New evidence further suggests that smelling odors that are congruent with what we see alters visual perception. There is also a difference between active sniffing and passive inhalation of odors at both neurological and functional levels. Active sniffing may even have therapeutic applications for individuals suffering from extreme physical disabilities. Other therapeutic applications include treatments to regain olfactory function after loss and conditioning manipulations during sleep to help decrease addictive behaviors.

5. Although we can potentially detect over a trillion odors, almost all odors that we encounter in the real world are mixtures, and we are generally not very good at analyzing the discrete chemical components of scent mixtures. Olfaction is thus primarily a synthetic, as opposed to analytical, sense. However, analytical olfactory ability can be developed with training. True odor imagery is also weak (or nonexistent) for most people, but training, as in the case of odor experts (e.g., perfumers), appears to facilitate this ability.

6. The psychophysical study of smell has shown that various odorant intensity levels and various cognitive functions are required for odor detection,

discrimination, and recognition. Identification differs from odor recognition in that, in the former, one must come up with a name for the olfactory sensation. It is very difficult to name even very familiar odors, and as we age, this becomes even harder. This state is known as the tip-of-the-nose phenomenon—one of several indications that linguistic processing is highly disconnected from olfactory experience. However, new research has shown that at least one culture may possess an enhanced verbal connection with odors. Regardless, unlike the case with other sensory experiences, we do not need to access any semantic information about an odor in order to respond to it appropriately, as long as it is familiar.

7. Another important discrepancy between the physical experience and the psychological experience of odors is the difference between receptor adaptation and cognitive habituation. Receptor adaptation occurs after continual odorant exposure over a number of minutes, can be undone after a few minutes away from the odorant, and is explained by a basic biochemical mechanism. In contrast, cognitive habituation occurs after long-term exposure (e.g., in a living or work environment) to an odor, takes weeks away from the odor to undo, and has not been conclusively defined in terms of mechanism. Psychological influences can have strong effects on both perceived odor adaptation and habituation.

8. The most immediate and basic response we have to an odor is whether we like it or not; this is called hedonic evaluation. Odor hedonics are measured by pleasantness, familiarity, and intensity ratings. Pleasantness and familiarity are linearly related to odor liking; odor intensity has a more complex relationship with hedonic perception. Substantial evidence suggests that our hedonic responses to odors are learned and not innate, even for so-called stenches. That we have learned to like or dislike various odors rather than being born with hardwired responses is evolutionarily adaptive for generalist species such as humans. Qualifying factors for the learned-response proposition are odors that are highly trigeminally irritating (pain inducing) and the genetic variability in the number and types of receptors expressed across individuals, which may influence olfactory sensitivity and hence odor hedonic perception.

9. The key to olfactory associative learning is the emotional value of the context in which the odor is first encountered. If the emotional context is good, the odor will be liked; if it is bad, the odor will be disliked. Previously acquired emotional associations with odors also underlie validated aromatherapy effects. Emotional potency further distinguishes odor-evoked memories from memories triggered by other sensory cues. The neuroanatomy of the olfactory and limbic systems and their neuroevolutionary development illustrate how emotional processing and olfactory processing are uniquely and intimately interrelated.

10. Pheromones are chemicals emitted by individuals that affect the physiology and/or behavior of other members of the same species and may or may not have any smell. In all mammals that have been shown to use pheromones for communication, detection is mediated through the vomeronasal organ (VNO) and processed by the accessory olfactory bulb (AOB). Humans do not possess a functional VNO or AOB, and empirical evidence for human pheromones is lacking. Nevertheless, human chemosignals that are processed through the olfactory system appear to have some influence on hormonal status and social-sexual responses.

Taste

■ Questions to Contemplate

Think about the following questions as you read this chapter. By the chapter's end, you should be able to answer and discuss them.

- If you had to give up one sensory modality, why would you *not* give up the sense of taste?

- How are taste and flavor linked to survival?

- Why is the pleasure you experience from sweet special?

- Do we all live in the same taste world?

- Why do we love cookies?

na Garten (the Barefoot Contessa), one of my favorite cookbook authors, said, "You can be miserable before you have a cookie, and you can be miserable after you eat a cookie, but you can't be miserable while you are eating a cookie."

Why do we love cookies? Taste and smell are often grouped together as the chemical senses, and in terms of physiology, these two sensory systems are in some ways quite similar. But the chemicals we taste have already entered our mouths and are about to move even farther into our bodies. Thus, taste serves the most specific function of any of the senses: discerning which chemicals we need to ingest because they are nutritious, and which we need to spit out because they may be poisonous. Perhaps this is why something about our liking or disliking of tastes and flavors seems to be very different from the liking or disliking that one might associate with the color red or the sound of middle C on the piano. Nature has equipped us to care passionately about food because that passion holds the key to our survival.

Danielle Richard, *Girl with Melon*, 2009

Taste versus Flavor

Before delving any further into the gustatory system, we need to clear up a very old misunderstanding. According to the early Greeks, sensations perceived from foods and beverages in the mouth were **tastes**, and sensations perceived by sniffing were smells. In fact, however, food molecules are almost always perceived by both our taste and our olfactory systems. The molecules we taste are dissolved in our saliva and stimulate the taste receptors on our taste buds, as we'll discuss in this chapter. But when we chew and swallow foods, other molecules are released into the air inside our mouths and forced up behind the palate into the nasal cavity, where they contact the olfactory epithelium and stimulate our olfactory receptors (**Figure 15.1**). The brain then knits these **retronasal olfactory sensations** together with our taste sensations into a kind of metasensation that goes by the name **flavor**.

taste Sensations evoked by solutions in the mouth that contact receptors on the tongue and the roof of the mouth that then connect to axons in cranial nerves VII, IX, and X.

retronasal olfactory sensation The sensation of an odor that is perceived when chewing and swallowing force an odorant in the mouth up behind the palate into the nose. Such odor sensations are perceived as originating from the mouth, even though the actual contact of odorant and receptor occurs at the olfactory mucosa.

flavor The combination of true taste (sweet, salty, sour, bitter) and retronasal olfaction.

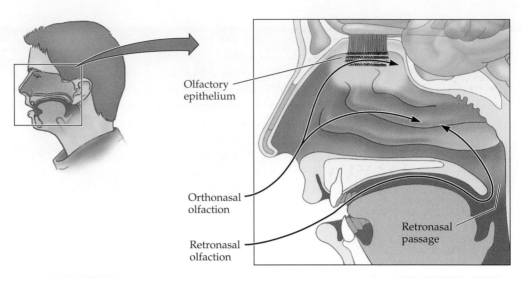

Olfactory
epithelium

Orthonasal
olfaction

Retronasal
olfaction

Retronasal
passage

Figure 15.1 Molecules released into the air inside our mouths as we chew and swallow food travel up through the retronasal passage into the nose, where they then move upward and contact the olfactory epithelium.

It is quite easy to prevent the airflow that carries odorants through the retronasal passage. Children do it all the time when they hold their noses while eating spinach. Try the following experiment now—but use a piece of chocolate if you're not crazy about spinach. Pinch your nose before putting the chocolate in your mouth, and then chew it and note the sensation, which will be almost pure taste (sweet with a bit of bitter). Then, swallow and release your nose. The volatile molecules responsible for the chocolate sensation will immediately flow up behind your palate and into the nasal cavity, and you will understand the difference between taste and flavor. You've probably noticed before that flavor is similarly impoverished when you have a stuffy nose. (**Web Activity 15.1: Taste without Smell** asks you to test this phenomenon with other stimuli.)

If you are a very careful observer, you will notice something else that happens when you do this retronasal olfaction demonstration: the sweetness of the candy will increase when you perceive the chocolate sensation. This results because some retronasal olfactory sensations enhance the taste of sweet. Our current understanding of this comes from increasing awareness that the central integration of retronasal olfaction and taste is complex, and we have yet to understand all of the rules.

Foods are also perceived by the somatosensory system via touch, temperature, and pain receptors in the tongue and mouth. Some of these sensations have protective functions: the burn of acid (which might damage your stomach if swallowed), the heat pain from scalding coffee, the pain of biting the tongue, and so on. Somatosensations also provide information about the nature of foods and beverages. For example, we get information about the fat content of foods from tactile sensations such as oily, viscous, thick, and creamy.

Localizing Flavor Sensations

You should have realized something else when you performed the chocolate experiment described in the previous section: even though you now know that the chocolate sensation originates from the olfactory receptors in your nose, you probably still perceived the flavor as coming entirely from your mouth. This perception is due in part to the tactile sensations evoked by chewing and swallowing, and in part to taste. Because you taste and feel the food only in your mouth (not in your nose), your brain localizes the sensations entirely to your mouth. Exceptions include foods such as horseradish, wasabi, and spicy mustard, which give off volatile chemicals that activate pain receptors all the way up through the retronasal passage. But these exceptions prove the rule: when we eat these foods, we experience the sensations as coming from our noses as well as our mouths.

Now consider the following curious case. A patient with normal olfaction but damaged taste and oral touch reported that she could smell lasagna, but when she ate it, it had no flavor. A similar effect was produced in a laboratory using a small amount of lidocaine and a large amount of blueberry yogurt. Participants in this study had their left **chorda tympani** (a branch of the facial nerve, one of the **cranial nerves** that carries information from taste receptors to the brain) anesthetized with the lidocaine while they tasted the yogurt. In this situation participants reported that the blueberry sensation—which is due entirely to retronasal olfaction—seemed to come only from the right side of the mouth. Moreover, the intensity of the blueberry sensation was reduced, and this intensity was reduced even further when both taste nerves were blocked (D. J. Snyder et al., 2001).

In both the patient and the experimental participants, the pathway from the mouth to the nasal cavity was completely intact. Why then were their lasagna and blueberry sensations reduced? This is another consequence of the central links between retronasal olfaction and taste. When the retronasal olfactory sensation of chocolate was added to sweetness, the sweetness went up; when taste was removed (by pathology or anesthetic), the retronasal olfactory sensations (lasagna, blueberry) went down.

Brain-imaging research by Dana Small (Small et al., 2005) was key to revealing characteristics of retronasal olfaction: the brain processes odors differently, depending on whether they come from the mouth or through the nostrils. This distinction makes good sense functionally because the significance of odors in the mouth is very different from that of odors sniffed from the outside world. Without the proper cues to tell us where an odorant is coming from, input from the olfactory receptors apparently cannot be routed to the proper brain area to connect the smell sensation with the food stimulus.

Some of the interactions between taste and retronasal olfaction have been understood by the food industry for many years (Sjöström, 1955). For example, if a company is marketing pear juice and wants to intensify the sensation of pear, it can add sugar. The increase in sweetness (a pure taste sensation) will increase the retronasal olfactory sensation of pear. Only more recently have we begun to focus on the reverse interaction: retronasal olfactory intensification of taste (see Bartoshuk and Klee, 2013). The commercial implications of this are obvious. The addition of the appropriate volatiles could allow a manufacturer to reduce the amount of sugar (or artificial sweetener) and salt. The scientific puzzle remains: do these complex interactions serve some biological purpose?

The pervasiveness of food additives such as carrageenan, guar gum, and other thickening agents shows that the food industry also has a good handle on how somatosensation affects food perception. And the ingredient lists of most processed foods include at least one artificial coloring, testifying to the importance of yet another sense, vision, in how we perceive foods.

chorda tympani The branch of cranial nerve VII (the facial nerve) that carries taste information from the anterior, mobile tongue (the part that can be stuck out). The chorda tympani exits the tongue with the lingual branch of the trigeminal nerve (cranial nerve V) and then passes through the middle ear on its way to the brain.

cranial nerves Twelve pairs of nerves (one for each side of the body) that originate in the brain stem and reach sense organs and muscles through openings in the skull.

■ Sensation & Perception in Everyday Life ■

Volatile-Enhanced Taste: A New Way to Safely Alter Flavors

Flavor dominates our lives. Flavor is created in the brain from the integration of retronasal olfaction and taste, but the rules governing that integration are not well understood. As noted earlier, the food industry has made considerable use of one of the rules: since the 1950s, they have added sugar to fruit to intensify the fruit flavors. It took a couple more decades before hints began to appear that the reverse was also true: some fruit flavors were shown to intensify sweet. At first this did not seem to be practical, because the effects were so small. However, a serendipitous finding during a tomato (botanically, a fruit) experiment offered a different point of view.

The tomato experiment was aimed at a problem food shoppers are well aware of: it's hard to find a good tomato in a supermarket. Recently, heirloom tomatoes have been finding their way into markets. Why would these tomatoes taste better? The answer is that intensive breeding to give tomatoes characteristics thought to be desirable (uniform ripening time, fruit size, and so on) have in some cases led to a deterioration in flavor. Heirloom tomatoes are genetically more diverse because they come from a time prior to the intensive breeding (**Figure 15.2A**). Thus some of them have the flavors remembered from those earlier days.

Collaboration between plant biologists and psychologists at the University of Florida led to an experiment utilizing 80 heirloom tomatoes grown on university farmland (Tieman et al., 2012). After harvesting, half went to a chemistry lab where the sugars, acids, and volatiles were measured; half went to a psychophysics lab where taste, flavor (i.e., retronasal olfaction), and preference were measured. Regression analyses identified the components responsible for the sensory properties of the tomatoes as well as how much they were liked. The solution to the problem turned out to be simple. Some tomato constituents correlated positively with liking; that is, the more of that constituent that was in the tomato, the more it was liked. Some did the reverse, and some did not matter. To make a better tomato, increase the constituents contributing to liking and decrease those contributing to disliking. Knowing what to aim for, crossbreeding will give us better tomatoes (**Figure 15.2B**).

The serendipitous result came from a mathematical analysis of the tomato data set. Multiple regression is used widely in the social sciences to examine various sources for a given effect; for example, an investigator might want to look at contributions to IQ from a variety of sources (age, health, income, education, and so on). Multiple regression was applied to the tomato data to see if any constituents other than the sugars were contributing to sweetness. The result was startling. A considerable amount of sweetness was coming from the volatiles. It was suddenly apparent that

(A)

(B)

Figure 15.2 Flavorful tomatoes. (A) Heirloom tomatoes come in a variety of shapes, sizes, and colors. (B) Garden gems tomatoes were created by Harry Klee using insights from the University of Florida tomato study (Tieman et al., 2012). (B courtesy of Harry Klee.)

■ Sensation & Perception in Everyday Life (continued)

small effects from individual volatiles were adding up such that a considerable amount of the sweetness of a given tomato was produced by the volatiles (perceived retronasally). In fact, increasing the concentrations of those volatiles could double the sweetness of a tomato.

The implications for sugar reduction are clear: adding the correct volatiles can reduce the amount of sugar needed to sweeten foods and beverages. However, the potential goes even further. There are other volatiles that can enhance salty and still more that can suppress bitter.

The discovery that plants use volatiles in this way is very new. Are these effects hardwired in the brain? Are they acquired somehow from experience? The original thinking about the volatiles that enhanced sweet was that these would be limited to fruity flavors, because we so often experience fruit and sweet together. However, one of the tomato volatiles that enhanced sweet was isovaleric acid, which smells like sweaty socks. Sweaty socks and sweet do not seem to be a combination that would be experienced together very often!

Much is yet to be learned. However, better tomatoes are surely right around the corner, with safe new ways to sweeten or salt foods and reduce unwanted bitter (e.g., bitter vegetables, medications) to follow.

Anatomy and Physiology of the Gustatory System

Taste perception consists of the following sequence of events (the structures involved are illustrated in **Figure 15.3**): Chewing breaks down food substances into molecules, which are dissolved in saliva. The saliva-borne food molecules flow into taste pores that lead to the **taste buds** housed in structures called **papillae** (singular *papilla*) that are located mostly on the tongue in a rough oval (if the olfactory epithelium is the retina of the nose, the tongue is the retina of the mouth). Taste buds, in turn, contain multiple **taste receptor cells**, each of which responds to a limited number of molecule types. When a taste receptor cell comes in contact with one of its preferred molecules, it produces action potentials that send information along one of the cranial nerves to the brain.

Papillae give the tongue its bumpy appearance and come in four major varieties: filiform, fungiform, foliate, and circumvallate. The last three of these contain taste buds.

Filiform papillae, the ones *without* any taste function, are located on the anterior portion of the tongue (the part we stick out when giving someone a raspberry) and come in different shapes in different species. In cats, they are shaped like tiny spoons with sharp edges. The filiform papillae on our tongues are not shaped like tiny spoons, which is why you will find lapping milk from a bowl considerably more difficult than your cat does.

Fungiform papillae, so named because they resemble tiny button mushrooms, are also located on the anterior part of the tongue. They are visible to the naked eye, but blue food coloring swabbed onto the tongue makes them particularly easy to see (blue food coloring stains filiform papillae much better than fungiform papillae, so the fungiform papillae appear as light circles against a darker blue background). Fungiform papillae vary in diameter, but the maximum is about 1 millimeter (mm). On average, about six taste buds are buried in the surface of each fungiform papilla. If we stain the tongues of many individuals, we see a large amount of variation (**Figure 15.4**). Some people have so few fungiform papillae that their stained tongues appear to

taste bud A globular cluster of cells that has the function of creating neural signals conveyed to the brain by the taste nerves. Some of the cells in a taste bud have specialized sites on their apical projections that interact with taste stimuli. Some of the cells form synapses with taste nerve fibers.

papilla Any of multiple structures that give the tongue its bumpy appearance. From smallest to largest, the papilla types that contain taste buds are fungiform, foliate, and circumvallate; filiform papillae, which do not contain taste buds, are the smallest and most numerous.

taste receptor cell A cell within the taste bud that contains sites on its apical projection that can interact with taste stimuli. These sites fall into two major categories: those interacting with charged particles (e.g., sodium and hydrogen ions) and those interacting with specific chemical structures.

filiform papillae Small structures on the tongue that provide most of the bumpy appearance. Filiform papillae have no taste function.

fungiform papillae Mushroom-shaped structures (maximum diameter 1 millimeter) that are distributed most densely on the edges of the tongue, especially the tip. Taste buds (an average of six per papilla) are buried in the surface.

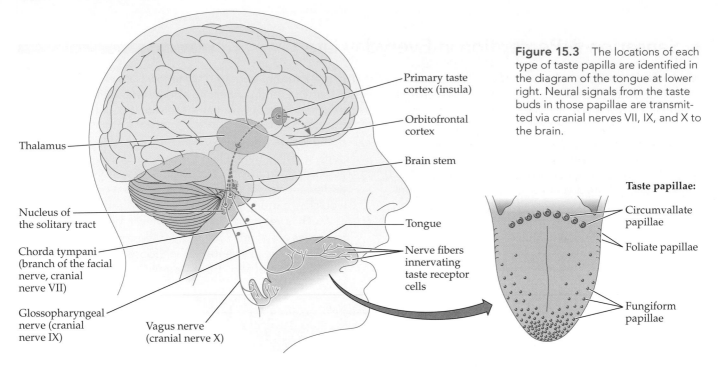

Figure 15.3 The locations of each type of taste papilla are identified in the diagram of the tongue at lower right. Neural signals from the taste buds in those papillae are transmitted via cranial nerves VII, IX, and X to the brain.

have polka dots on them. Other tongues—those of **supertasters**—have so many that there is little space between them.

Foliate papillae are located on the sides of the tongue at the point where the tongue is attached. Under magnification, they look like a series of folds. Taste buds are buried in the folds.

Finally, **circumvallate papillae** are relatively large, circular structures forming an inverted *V* on the rear of the tongue. These papillae look like tiny islands surrounded by moats. The taste buds are buried in the sides of the moats.

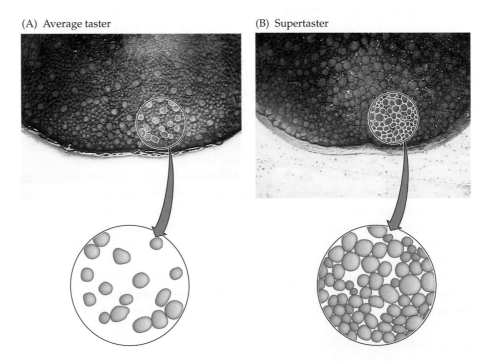

Figure 15.4 Examples showing typical variability in the density of fungiform papillae from one individual to the next. The circles show the 6-mm template area used for counting fungiform papillae on tongues stained with blue food coloring. (A) The tongue of this average taster has 16 fungiform papillae. In extreme cases, individuals may have as few as 5 fungiform papillae. (B) This supertaster's tongue (supertasters are discussed later in the chapter) has 60 fungiform papillae in that area.

Although most people don't realize this, there are also taste buds on the roof of the mouth where the hard and soft palates meet. To demonstrate these, wet your finger and dip it into salt crystals. Touch the roof of your mouth and move your finger back until you feel the bone end (the margin between the hard and soft palates). You will experience a flash of saltiness as you move the salt crystals onto the taste buds arrayed on that margin.

In sum, the taste buds are distributed in a line across the roof of the mouth and in papillae distributed in an oval on the tongue. Fungiform papillae make up the front of the oval, and foliate and circumvallate papillae make up its rear. Note that we have no subjective awareness of this distribution of taste buds. (See **Web Activity 15.2: Gustatory Anatomy** for an interactive overview of the system.)

Taste Myth: The Tongue Map

Edwin Boring is responsible for one of the best known "facts" about taste. In 1901, D. P. Hänig published a paper (in German) of work done in the laboratory of Wilhelm Wundt (Wundt's laboratory was the first dedicated to psychology). Hänig measured taste thresholds for bitter, sweet, salty, and sour all around the perimeter as well as at the base of the tongue. Hänig's paper was translated by Boring, a famous psychologist at Harvard, and described in his classic book, *Sensation and Perception in the History of Experimental Psychology*, published in 1942. Hänig provided tables of thresholds measured from five participants for each of the classic taste qualities. (Incidentally, Hänig listed his participants by name, a common practice of the era, which would violate our modern rules of participant confidentiality.) Boring calculated the reciprocals of those thresholds (1 / threshold). He called these transformed values "sensitivity" and plotted somewhat smoothed curves that seemed to show a picture of how the classic taste qualities varied across tongue locations (**Figure 15.5A**). In comparison, **Figure 15.5B** shows Hänig's actual data, unsmoothed and correctly labeled. Over the years, various authors have simply drawn a tongue map; one example is shown in **Figure 15.5C**.

THE MAP IS BOGUS Taste thresholds do vary across different tongue locations, but that variation is actually quite small. Boring plotted *relative*, not *absolute*, variation. His label "sensitivity" obscured this. The map shown in Figure 15.5C is one of many drawn to reflect the imagined tongue map as it became enshrined in texts. However, there is an even more profound error involved. Thresholds only reflect the lowest detectable taste concentrations; they do not predict taste intensities in the real world. One reason that taste thresholds fail to predict real-world perceived intensities has to do with characteristics of individual taste nerve fibers. Thresholds are determined by the most sensitive of the fibers. Real-world taste intensities are produced by the summation across fibers with varying thresholds.

Taste Buds and Taste Receptor Cells

Taste neurons are pseudounipolar: a single process exits the cell body and then splits into peripheral and central axons. The peripheral axons make up the nerves that project into the tongue (e.g., chorda tympani and glossopharyngeal nerves). The central axons project to the brain.

Each taste bud is a cluster of elongated cells, organized much like the segments of an orange. The tips of some of the cells—taste receptor cells—end in slender **microvilli** (singular *microvillus*) containing sites that bind to taste substances. In an earlier era, these microvilli were mistakenly thought to be tiny hairs; we now know that microvilli are extensions of the cell membrane.

supertaster An individual whose perception of taste sensations is the most intense. A variety of factors may contribute to this heightened perception; among the most important is the density of fungiform papillae.

foliate papillae Folds of tissue containing taste buds. Foliate papillae are located on the rear of the tongue lateral to the circumvallate papillae, where the tongue attaches to the mouth.

circumvallate papillae Circular structures that form an inverted V on the rear of the tongue (three to five on each side, with the largest in the center). Circumvallate papillae are mound-like structures, each surrounded by a trench (like a moat). These papillae are much larger than fungiform papillae.

microvilli Slender projections of the cell membrane on the tips of some taste bud cells that extend into the taste pore.

(A) Boring's figure

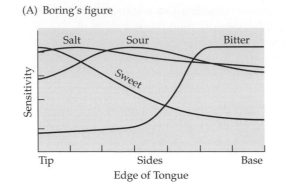

(B) Hänig's data plotted and labeled correctly

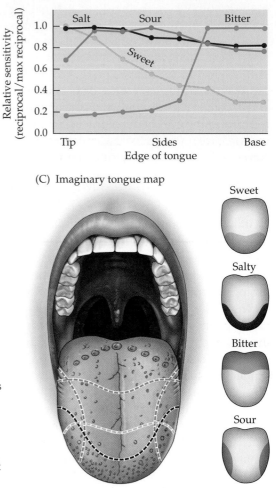

(C) Imaginary tongue map

Sweet

Salty

Bitter

Sour

Figure 15.5 Here's how the tongue map originated. (A) Boring's figure shows his version of Hänig's data. (B) Hänig's actual data are plotted and labeled more clearly. (C) One example of the imaginary tongue maps. (A after Boring, 1942; B after Hänig, 1901; C after Hoon et al., 1999.)

Some years ago, taste receptor cells were thought to have sites stimulated by taste stimuli at one end and synapses with peripheral taste axons at the other end. But more recent work shows that not all receptor cells synapse with taste nerve fibers. How is information from these receptor cells conveyed to the brain? Details of how this happens are beginning to emerge. Anatomically, taste bud cells fall into three different groups with different functions (**Figure 15.6**): Type I cells may primarily have housekeeping functions. Type II cells respond to sweet, bitter, or amino acid stimuli. These cells have G protein–coupled receptors (GPCRs) that wind back and forth seven times across the microvillus membrane. When a particular **tastant** molecule "key" is fitted into the "lock" portion of a GPCR on the outside of the membrane, the portion of the GPCR inside the cell starts a cascade of molecular events. These receptor cells do not have synapses; however, they secrete ATP (adenosine triphosphate, a neurotransmitter), which can activate taste axons. Type III cells do have synapses and appear to mediate sour taste. In addition, there appears to be communication among the cells in the taste bud. Salty taste is still a mystery. We do not yet know which taste receptor cells mediate salty and how they do it (Roper and Chaudhari, 2017).

tastant Any stimulus that can be tasted.

FURTHER DISCUSSION of the lock-and-key metaphor in relation to other sensory modalities can be found in Chapter 4 (pages 127–128) and Chapter 14 (shape-pattern theory, page 477).

Taste receptors have a limited life span. After a matter of days, they die and are replaced by new cells. This constant renewal enables the taste system to recover from a variety of sources of damage, and it explains why our taste systems remain robust even into old age. It appears that the nerve fibers are somehow able to select the cells with which they will synapse so that the message they convey remains stable, even though the receptor cells are continually replaced.

Extraoral Locations for Taste Receptors

When we think of taste receptors, we naturally think of the mouth. However, as far back as Ivan Pavlov, there was speculation about receptors that could sense chemicals in the gastrointestinal tract (commonly called the gut). The taste receptors in the mouth produce conscious sensations, while those in the gut play other roles (more about this in the discussion on "basic tastes" to follow).

The GPCRs that mediate sweet and bitter sensations have been found in an amazing array of places outside the mouth and gut. For example, in the upper airways, bitter compounds can cause cilia to beat and clear bacteria from airways (Lee et al., 2014). In the stomach, bitter compounds can slow absorption of toxins that are not successfully rejected at the mouth (Jeon et al., 2008).

FURTHER DISCUSSION of GPCRs in the context of olfaction can be found in Chapter 14 on page 491.

Taste Processing in the Central Nervous System

After leaving the taste buds through the cranial nerves, gustatory information travels through way stations in the medulla and thalamus before reaching the **insular cortex** (also referred to as the gustatory cortex) (**Figure 15.7**) (Pritchard and Norgren, 2004). Notice that taste projects ipsilaterally from the periphery to the cortex. A central injury (e.g., a stroke in an area mediating taste) will produce loss of taste on the tongue on the same side as the stroke (Pritchard, Macaluso, and Eslinger, 1999).

The functional separation of the taste qualities suggested to early investigators that there would likely be a gustotopic map in the cortex, but evidence for this has been elusive. Earlier studies stimulated the tongue with taste solutions while simultaneously recording electrical activity from individual neurons in the cortex. However, newer methods can give us a broader picture of neural activity; one of these methods is optical imagery of intrinsic signals (changes in tissue as a result of taste stimulation). Using this method, investigators mapped the gustatory cortex of rats and found "distinctive spatial patterns" with some overlap for the four classic taste qualities (Accolla et al., 2007).

The **orbitofrontal cortex** (**OFC**) receives projections from the insular cortex. Some orbitofrontal neurons are multimodal; that is, they respond to temperature, touch, and smell, as well as to taste, suggesting that the OFC may be an integration area.

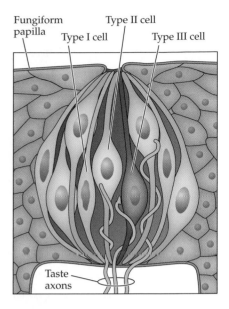

Figure 15.6 A taste bud buried in the tissue of a fungiform papilla has three types of cells. Type I cells have housekeeping functions. Type II cells are the receptor cells for sweet, bitter, and amino acid stimuli. They secrete ATP, which excites taste axons. Type III cells are excited by sour stimuli and transmit signals to the brain via synapses. (After Roper and Chaudhari, 2017.)

insular cortex The primary cortical processing area for taste—the part of the cortex that first receives taste information. Also called the *insula* or the *gustatory cortex*.

orbitofrontal cortex (OFC) The part of the frontal lobe of the cortex that lies behind the bone (orbit) containing the eyes. It is involved in many functions and is responsible for the conscious experience of olfaction, as well as the integration of pleasure and displeasure from food, and has been referred to as the *secondary olfactory cortex* and *secondary taste cortex*. It is also critical for assigning affective value to stimuli—in other words, determining hedonic meaning.

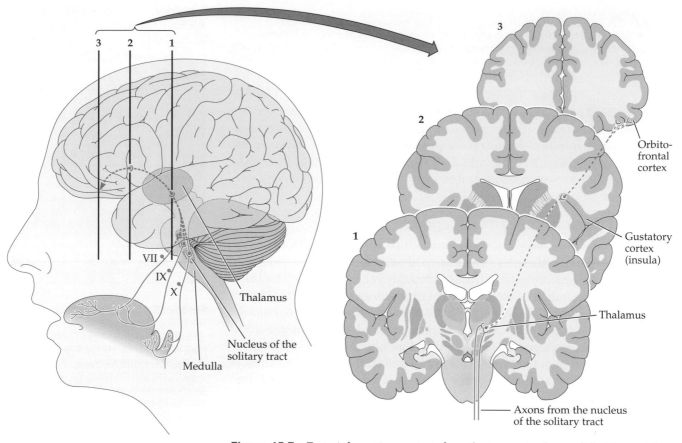

Figure 15.7 Taste information projects from the tongue to the medulla (via cranial nerves VII, IX, and X), then to the thalamus (shown in cross section 1 of the brain), then to the insula (cross section 2), and finally to the orbitofrontal cortex (cross section 3).

Inhibition plays an important role in the processing of taste information in the brain. One of the functions of this inhibition may be to protect our whole-mouth perception of taste in the face of injuries to the taste system. Our brains receive taste input bilaterally from three nerves. Damage to one of them diminishes its contribution to the whole; however, that damage also releases the inhibition that is normally produced by the damaged nerve. The result is that whole-mouth taste intensities are relatively unchanged. Unfortunately, this preserved whole-mouth perception comes at a cost in some cases. Localized taste damage is often accompanied by "phantom taste" sensations (recall the phantom limbs experienced by many limb amputees, described in Chapter 13), as if the release of inhibition permits even noise in the nervous system to be perceived as a taste.

Descending inhibition from the taste cortex to a variety of other structures may also serve other functions. For example, mouth injuries that lead to oral pain make it harder to eat. The inhibition of such pain perceptions by taste-processing parts of the brain would make eating easier and thus increase the likelihood of survival (because no matter how much the mouth hurts, we still have to eat). Consistent with this principle, patients with a serious oral pain disorder (burning mouth syndrome) were shown to have localized taste damage as well (Grushka and Bartoshuk, 2000). Furthermore, women who have taste damage are more likely to suffer from severe nausea and vomiting during pregnancy (Sipiora et al., 2000); and patients with cancer, whose chemotherapy and radiation therapy is known to damage the taste system, are more likely to experience coughing, gagging, hiccups, and oral pain. In all these cases, inhibitory signals from the taste cortex that normally help prevent eating-disruptive symptoms (oral pain, vomiting, hiccupping, and so on) may have been turned off because of the damage to the taste system.

The Four Basic Tastes?

We learned in Chapter 14 that we are able to distinguish many different odorants. Already in this chapter, however, we have seen that when olfaction is taken out of the equation, much of the complexity of the sensations evoked by foods vanishes. Thus we are led to believe that the number of basic taste qualities is quite small. In fact, the current universally accepted list includes only the four **basic tastes** previously mentioned in the "Taste Buds and Taste Receptor Cells" section of this chapter: **salty**, **sour**, **bitter**, and **sweet**. As we discuss these in the sections that follow, note that one of the most important features of these basic tastes is that our liking (or disliking) for them is hardwired in the brain; that is, we are essentially born liking or disliking these tastes. This is very different from the way we learn to like or dislike odors. Incidentally, the number of basic tastes has been the subject of argument that goes back even before Aristotle (see Bartoshuk, 1978). Various investigators have suggested adding to the list of basic tastes. The two most recent contenders (umami and fatty) are important because of their special association with learned preferences. There is no universal definition of "basic taste"; however, the authors of this text prefer to reserve *basic taste* for those sensations that produce hardwired affect, since that is arguably the characteristic of taste that most distinguishes it from the other senses. Some argue that any chemicals for which there are receptors in the mouth produce basic tastes. However, as we note below, receptors for chemicals are now known to be throughout the body, and we certainly would not argue that these mediate basic tastes. Umami and fatty appear to be examples of stimuli for which there are receptors that function to regulate the palatability of protein and fat (more on this later in the chapter).

For many years we have known that taste stimuli can be divided into two major groups: salty and sour, mediated by ion channels (small openings in the membranes of the microvilli), and bitter and sweet, mediated by protein receptors (which we now know to be GPCRs in the membranes of the microvilli).

Salty

Salts are made up of two charged particles: a cation (positively charged) and an anion (negatively charged). For example, common table salt is NaCl; the sodium is the cation (Na^+), and the chloride is the anion (Cl^-). The source of the salty taste is the cation (**Figure 15.8A**). Although all salts taste at least a little salty to humans, pure NaCl is the saltiest-tasting salt around. Sodium must be available in relatively large quantities in the body to maintain nerve and muscle function, and loss of too much body sodium leads to a swift death.

Our ability to perceive saltiness is not static. Gary Beauchamp and his colleagues showed that diet can affect the perception of saltiness (Bertino, Beauchamp, and Engelman, 1982). Fortunately for those on low-sodium diets, reduced sodium intake increases the intensity of saltiness over time. Individuals who are initially successful in reducing their sodium intake will find that foods they used to love may now taste too salty. This adjustment in perception helps them keep their sodium intake down.

Our liking for saltiness is not static either. Early experiences can modify salt preference. In 1978 and 1979, several hundred infants were fed soy formulas

basic taste Any of the four taste qualities that are generally agreed to describe human taste experience: sweet, salty, sour, bitter.

salty One of the four basic tastes; the taste quality produced by the cations of salts (e.g., the sodium in sodium chloride produces the salty taste). Some cations also produce other taste qualities (e.g., potassium tastes bitter as well as salty). The purest salty taste is produced by sodium chloride (NaCl), common table salt.

sour One of the four basic tastes; the taste quality produced by the hydrogen ion in acids.

bitter One of the four basic tastes, the taste quality, generally considered unpleasant, produced by substances like quinine or caffeine.

sweet One of the four basic tastes; the taste quality produced by some sugars, such as glucose, fructose, and sucrose. These three sugars are particularly biologically useful to us, and our sweet receptors are tuned to them. Some other compounds (e.g., saccharin, cyclamate, aspartame) are also sweet.

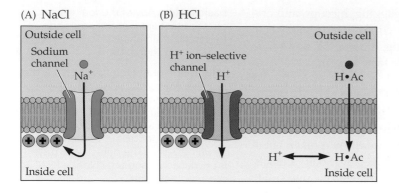

(A) NaCl

(B) HCl

Figure 15.8 Diagram of a taste receptor cell, illustrating the different receptor mechanisms for ionic stimuli (salty and sour). (A) Salty taste is produced by the cation in a salt. In NaCl, the sodium cation is admitted to the receptor cell by sodium channels. (B) Sour taste is produced by hydrogen ions (H^+), which can enter the cell in two ways (see the text for details). (After Chaudhari and Roper, 2010.)

that were accidentally deficient in chloride because of an error in formulation. Chloride deficiency has effects on human physiology that mimic the effects of sodium deficiency. Thus, the infants who were chloride-deficient offered an important way to study sodium deficiency in humans. The Centers for Disease Control and Prevention (CDC) in Atlanta monitored these infants, and a variety of studies were done to assess any potential damage. One of the consequences was that the salt preference of the children increased (L. J. Stein et al., 1996). Experiences during gestation can also affect salt preference. For example, college students whose mothers had experienced moderate to severe morning sickness during pregnancy showed an increased preference for salty snacks (Crystal and Bernstein, 1995). The exact mechanisms by which these abnormal metabolic events enhance salt preference are still not understood.

Sour

As you may remember from high school chemistry, a solution containing hydrogen ions (H^+) and hydroxide ions (OH^-) in equal proportions produces water (HOH, or H_2O). As the relative proportion of H^+ increases (decreasing the pH level), the solution becomes more *acidic*. Why do you need to be reminded of all this? Because sour taste is produced by hydrogen ions. Hydrogen ions enter the receptor cell through ion channels; however, an additional mechanism for sour taste allows undissociated acid molecules (intact molecules that have not split into two charged particles) to enter as well. The undissociated acid molecules dissociate inside the cell. Ultimately, the stimulus that triggers sour taste is the hydrogen concentration inside the receptor cell (**Figure 15.8B**) (DeSimone et al., 2011). For this reason, organic acids, which do not completely dissociate, are more sour than their pH values would suggest.

Some individuals like the sourness of acids in relatively low concentrations. Many adults enjoy pickles and sauerkraut, both of which get their sour tastes from acids. In addition, many children in particular like sour candies (Liem and Mennella, 2003). At high concentrations, however, acids will damage both external and internal body tissues.

Bitter

The Human Genome Project has revealed a multigene family responsible for about 25 different bitter receptors. They are named according to the rules established by the Gene Nomenclature Committee of the Human Genome Organisation (HUGO), an international organization of scientists involved in the Human Genome Project and other human genetic and genomic research. The bitter gene family is *TAS2R* ("TAS" stands for taste, with the "2" indicating bitter); numbers following the *R* indicate the particular gene that is a member of that family. The 25 bitter genes are located on three different chromosomes: 5, 7, and 12. The receptors these genes express (GPCRs) are designated without using italics (e.g., TAS2R# or T2R# where # is the number of the receptor).

These receptors face a formidable task. Wolfgang Meyerhof, one of the world's experts on bitter genes, estimates that there are thousands of bitter molecules (many coming from plants that protect themselves from predators by tasting bitter). How can only 25 bitter receptors handle the job? Part of the answer is that some of the T2 receptors respond only to specific compounds (e.g., the propylthiouracil [PROP] receptor), but others (bitter "generalists") respond to many compounds. The studies identifying the compounds that stimulate the bitter genes have been summarized on a website (bitterdb.agri.huji.ac.il/dbbitter.php). **Figure 15.9** shows some common bitter stimuli and the receptors they stimulate. For example, denatonium benzoate (marketed as Bitrex) is a very bitter compound that is sometimes added to dangerous household products to prevent children from ingesting them; Bitrex stimulates 8 bitter receptors. Limonin is a bitter compound that increases in oranges attacked by the HLB ("greening disease") bacteria—one of the reasons this disease is decimating the citrus industry; limonin stimulates only one bitter receptor. Quinine (which gives tonic water its bitter taste) stimulates 9 of the 25 bitter receptors.

Tonic water was originally formulated as a treatment for malaria; now, however, we know that tonic water does not contain enough quinine for that purpose. However, tonic water does contain enough quinine to taste very bitter, and for this reason lots of sugar was added to make the tonic water palatable. This approach works because sweet and bitter tastes inhibit one another; tonic water tastes much less bitter than the quinine content alone would, and it also tastes much less sweet than the sugar content alone would. Tonic water actually contains about the same amount of sugar as sodas.

Compound	Common name or use	1	3	4	5	7	8	9	10	13	14	16	38	39	40	41	42	43	44	45	46	47	48	49	50	60
Acesulfame K	Sweetener																	■								
Acetaminophen	Analgesic													■												
Caffeine	Stimulant					■			■		■							■			■					
Chloramphenicol	Antibiotic	■				■																				
Chlorpheniramine	Antihistamine			■		■			■		■			■	■	■										
Cyclamate	Sweetener	■																								
Denatonium benzoate	Bitrex			■			■		■	■				■				■			■					
Limonin	In citrus													■												
PROP	Genetic compound												■													
Quinine	Tonic water			■		■			■		■			■	■			■	■		■					
Saccharin	Sweetener																	■	■							
Sodium benzoate	Preservative											■														
Strychnine	Poison								■																	
Thiamine	Vitamin	■																								

Figure 15.9 Bitter receptors are designated by TAS2R#, where # is the number of the receptor. The receptor numbers are shown at the top of the table. Examples of common bitter compounds are listed at the left. A filled box indicates a receptor that responds to the bitter compound on the left. Receptors for which no stimulus is known, as yet, are shown in gray. Receptors 3, 5, 9, 49 and 50 are stimulated by compounds not included in the list shown here. (Data from Wiener et al., 2012.)

Although a great many different compounds taste bitter, we generally do not distinguish between the tastes of these compounds; we simply avoid them all. The diversity of receptors for bitterness enables species or even individuals in a given species to have varying responses to an array of bitter compounds. One of the most famous of these is "taste blindness" to phenylthiocarbamide (PTC) found in humans—a phenomenon we will revisit later in this chapter.

Although bitter taste usually signals poison, some bitter stimuli are actually good for us. For example, bitter compounds in some vegetables help protect against cancer. We would like to be able to "turn off" these bitter sensations to make it easier for people to eat their vegetables. In pursuit of this goal, Robert Margolskee, a pioneer in studies of bitter transduction, used his understanding of the bitter system to identify a substance that can inhibit some bitter sensations: adenosine monophosphate (AMP) (Ming, Ninomiya, and Margolskee, 1999). AMP may actually function as a natural bitter inhibitor in mother's milk. A number of compounds in milk, such as casein (milk protein) and calcium salts, taste bitter, and aversions to bitter tastes are present at birth. The presence of AMP in mother's milk may suppress those bitter tastes enough to allow milk to be palatable to babies who are particularly responsive to them (e.g., supertaster babies).

Bitter perception is also affected by hormone levels in women. Sensitivity to bitterness intensifies during pregnancy and diminishes after menopause (Duffy et al., 1998). These differences make sense in the context of the function of bitterness as a poison detection mechanism. Intensifying the perception of bitter early in pregnancy, when toxins exert their maximum effects, has clear biological value. Consistent with this correlation, some of the aversions common during pregnancy occur with foods or beverages that have bitter tastes (e.g., coffee).

Sweet

Glucose and fructose are simple sugars. When a molecule of glucose bonds to a molecule of fructose, sucrose is formed. Glucose is the principle source of energy in humans, as well as nearly every other living thing on Earth. Unfortunately, glucose often turns up in nature in the form of sucrose (e.g., in sugar cane, sugar beets, corn). When we consume sucrose, an enzyme breaks the molecule into its constituents, glucose and fructose. The glucose speeds away, providing energy to all the cells in our bodies. The fructose goes to the liver, where some of it is converted to glucose, but the rest of it has a variety of fates that are not necessarily good for us. High-fructose corn syrup (HFCS) is increasingly used as a sweetener. HFCS is made by breaking the sucrose in corn into glucose and fructose, but in addition to this, some of the glucose is converted to fructose. Why? Because fructose is sweeter than glucose. Since we love sweet, we love HFCS.

The biological function of sweet is different from that of bitter, and the way taste receptors are tuned supports that biological difference. Many different molecules taste bitter. Our biological task is not to distinguish among them but rather to avoid them all. Thus, we have multiple bitter receptors to encompass the chemical diversity of poisons, but they all feed into common lines leading to rejection. With regard to sweet, some biologically useless sugars have structures very similar to those of glucose. In this case, then, the task of the taste system is to tune receptors such that the biologically important sugars stimulate sweet taste but the others do not. Why aren't our sweet receptors tuned to glucose only? Perhaps because one of the best ways to get glucose is from the sucrose in nature.

Consistent with the biological purpose, only two GPCRs of the type II taste receptor cells are involved with sweet taste—T1R2 and T1R3. These two proteins combine to form a single receptor called a **heterodimer** (**Figure 15.10**). The

heterodimer A chain of two molecules that are different from each other.

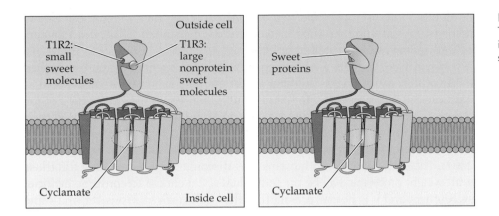

Figure 15.10 Structure of the T1R2-T1R3 heterodimer sweet receptor, showing binding sites for both large and small sweet molecules. (After Temussi, 2007.)

outer portions of the two proteins resemble the shape of Venus flytraps, large sweetener molecules can enter the "flytraps" to stimulate the receptor. A variety of other binding sites accommodate smaller molecules like sugars, saccharin, cyclamate, and aspartame. Initially, the T1R2-T1R3 heterodimer was thought to be responsible for all sweetness, but it introduced a new puzzle: No matter how the heterodimer is stimulated, the receptor produces only one signal. Therefore, we would expect all sweeteners—sugars and artificial sweeteners alike—to produce the same sweetness. However, artificial sweeteners like saccharin, cyclamate, and aspartame do not taste exactly like sugar; if they did, there would be no need to continually search for better artificial sweeteners. Some claim that artificial sweeteners produce additional tastes that account for the difference. For example, saccharin tastes bitter as well as sweet to many. But some of us (the author included) do not taste the bitterness of saccharin at all; we are quite convinced that it is the nature of the sweetness that differs. Genetic studies may offer some help here. The receptor T1R3 appears to be able to function alone to respond only to high concentrations of sucrose (Zhao et al., 2003). In addition, Margolskee and colleagues (Yee et al., 2011) have identified yet another mechanism in addition to the heterodimer that can mediate sweetness. Thus we can explain why many of us perceive differences between the sweetness of sucrose and those of artificial sweeteners.

Given that our taste system can produce sweet receptors so precisely tuned to the biologically useful sugars, what is going on with artificial sweeteners? Are these nonsugar molecules sweet because they accidentally stimulate the sweet heterodimer? We don't know. Are artificial sweeteners medically useful? Certainly they enable diabetics to enjoy a sweet taste without the dangers of sugar, but the early claims that artificial sweeteners would be a panacea for weight loss now appear wrong.

Saccharin was discovered in 1879 when the chemist Ira Remsen, working on coal tar derivatives, failed to wash up before dinner and subsequently noticed that the tar residue on his hands tasted sweet. Another artificial sweetener was discovered in 1937, by a graduate student working in what must have been a messy lab. When he tasted sweet while smoking a cigarette, he realized that some compound in the lab must be responsible. In this way, cyclamate was discovered. Cyclamate was very popular for a few years, but suspicions were raised that it was carcinogenic. Although those suspicions were challenged and cyclamate remains legal in a number of other countries, the Food and Drug Administration (FDA) banned it in the United States. Artificial sweeteners are attractive to dieters because their sweet taste comes with essentially no calories. Millions of dieters count on this property to help them watch their weight, but a 1986 epidemiological study showed that women who consumed artificial sweeteners actually gained weight (Stellman, 1988).

Also in 1986, John Blundell, an English expert on weight regulation, published a provocative article suggesting that aspartame (the artificial sweetener sold as NutraSweet) increases appetite (Blundell and Hill, 1986). Was the benefit of the reduced calories lost when individuals using aspartame actually increased their caloric intake in subsequent meals? Terry Davidson and Susan Swithers elaborated on this kind of thinking with studies using rats (T. L. Davidson and Swithers, 2004). The earlier work with humans was discounted by many; after all, those with weight problems may be the individuals who choose to consume artificial sweeteners and it is not surprising that they gain weight. However, the same criticism could not apply when the rats fed artificial sweeteners gained weight. Davidson and Swithers point to the fact that the "obesity epidemic" occurred over the same years as the introduction of low-calorie foods into the American market. They argue that the uncoupling of the sensory properties of these diet foods from their metabolic consequences disrupts regulation, leading to weight gain.

Are There More Than Four Basic Tastes? Does It Matter?

Historically, the qualitatively distinct sensations that characterize each sense were identified by introspection. As more and more sensory receptors were discovered, investigators sought to link specific receptors to these distinct sensations. However, it is worth remembering that not all responses to stimuli produce conscious sensations. Proteins and fats provide examples. Proteins and fats are large molecules. In fact, they are too large to stimulate either taste or olfaction. Fats do produce conscious sensations, but they are somatosensations (e.g., thick, oily, viscous, creamy). Both fat and protein are broken into their constituent parts by digestion, and some of those constituents stimulate receptors in the gut. This stimulation does not produce conscious taste sensations. Rather, this stimulation appears to contribute to the palatability of the foods containing proteins and fats through learning (see below).

Umami

Umami arose as a candidate for a fifth basic taste as part of advertising claims by manufacturers of **monosodium glutamate (MSG)**, the sodium salt of glutamic acid. Identified by Japanese chemists in the early 1900s, MSG was initially marketed as a flavor enhancer, said to suppress unpleasant tastes and enhance pleasant ones. Taste experts expressed skepticism. MSG manufacturers then went on to claim that MSG was a fifth basic taste, speculating that it signaled protein and thus played an important role in nutrition. Unfortunately, although having special receptors for proteins might be nutritionally helpful, as noted above, protein molecules are too large to stimulate taste or olfaction. A protein is a chain of amino acids; one of those amino acids is glutamic acid (which turns into glutamate by losing a hydrogen atom). Although a small amount of protein may be broken into its amino acids in the mouth, the primary site for this is the gut. Not surprisingly, the taste evoked by glutamate is not perceptible in most proteins. Glutamate does not produce a universally liked sensation, but we can learn to like glutamate.

Because glutamate is an important neurotransmitter, receptors for the molecule are common throughout the body. The argument that some of these receptors might have been harnessed by the taste system to signal umami

umami The taste sensation produced by monosodium glutamate.

monosodium glutamate (MSG) The sodium salt of glutamic acid (an amino acid).

gained respectability when neuroscientists Nirupa Chaudhari and Steve Roper identified a version of a glutamate receptor in rat taste papillae. There is now evidence for multiple receptors for umami, including a heterodimer made up of two G protein–coupled receptors: T1R1 and T1R3 (remember that T1R2 and T1R3 form the sweet heterodimer) (Roper and Chaudhari, 2017).

Robert Margolskee (whose pioneering studies focused on not only the bitter receptor but also the sweet receptor) was an early advocate for the importance of taste receptors in the gut. These receptors signal the brain that protein has been consumed. In this way, glutamate receptors can signal the brain that protein has been consumed, but the signal comes from the gut, not the mouth. Consistent with this finding, John Prescott (a cognitive psychologist who studies the chemical senses) showed that consuming a novel-flavored soup with MSG added to it produces a conditioned preference for the novel flavor, while simply holding the soup in the mouth does not (Prescott, 2004). Note that using glutamate receptors in the gut to signal protein makes biological sense. This allows many different proteins (that do not taste of umami) to evoke pleasure: not hardwired pleasure but, rather, learned pleasure.

Because glutamate is a neurotransmitter, concerns have been raised about its safety in the human diet. MSG became particularly notorious in the 1960s. First, it became associated with Chinese restaurant syndrome—a constellation of symptoms including numbness, headache, flushing, tingling, sweating, and tightness in the chest—that was reported by some individuals after consuming MSG (R. H. M. Kwok, 1968). Then, Dr. John Olney, a toxicologist, suggested that MSG might induce brain lesions, particularly in infants (Olney and Sharpe, 1969). In response to these concerns, MSG was removed from baby foods in the 1970s. The final conclusion (see Walker and Lupien, 2000) is that MSG in large doses may be a problem for some sensitive individuals, but apparently it does not present a serious problem for the general population.

Fat

Like protein, fat is a very important nutrient. Also like protein, fat molecules are too large to stimulate either taste or olfaction but are broken into their constituent parts by digestion in the gut. Fat molecules are made up of fatty acids attached to a support structure; a few fat molecules may be partially digested while still in the mouth, thus releasing fatty acids. Neurobiologist Tim Gilbertson (1998) discovered fatty acid receptors on the tongues of rats, and that suggested to some that these oral fatty acid receptors might contribute to fat regulation; however, we now know that fatty acid receptors are found throughout the gut. Thus nature uses a more general method to ensure that we love fat-containing foods. Anthony Sclafani (1997) (a learning theorist who is an expert on conditioned food preferences) showed that fat in the gut produces conditioned preferences for the sensory properties of the food containing the fat. Once we understand the role of conditioning in food preferences, we should have a healthy skepticism about the value of so-called diet foods. Mimicking the sensory properties of normal foods but reducing the caloric content disrupts normal regulatory mechanisms.

Genetic Variation in Bitter

In 1931, a chemist named Arthur Fox discovered that we do not all live in the same taste world (A. L. Fox, 1931). Fox was synthesizing the compound PTC when some spilled and flew into the air. A colleague nearby noticed a bitter taste, but Fox tasted nothing. A test of additional colleagues revealed a few more **nontasters**

nontaster (of PTC/PROP) An individual born with two recessive alleles for the *TAS2R38* gene and unable to taste the compounds phenylthiocarbamide (PTC) and propylthiouracil (PROP).

taster (of PTC/PROP) An individual born with one or two dominant alleles for the *TAS2R38* gene and able to taste the compounds phenylthiocarbamide (PTC) and propylthiouracil (PROP). PTC/PROP tasters who also have a high density of fungiform papillae are PROP supertasters.

like Fox who tasted little bitterness in the compound, but most were **tasters**; that is, they perceived it as bitter. The next year, Albert Blakeslee (a famous geneticist of the day) and Fox took PTC crystals to a meeting of the American Association for the Advancement of Science and set up a voting booth for attendees to register their perceptions. About one-third of those polled found the crystals to be tasteless, while two-thirds found them to be bitter. These proportions captured the imagination of many researchers, and for several years the *Journal of Heredity* sold papers impregnated with PTC for further studies. Family studies eventually confirmed that taster status is an inherited trait (e.g., the Dionne quintuplets were all found to be tasters in 1941). Nontasters carry two recessive alleles, whereas tasters have either one or two dominant alleles.

Initially, individuals were simply classified according to whether they could taste PTC, but eventually threshold studies came into vogue. In a threshold method invented specifically for PTC studies, participants were given eight cups, four containing water and four containing a given concentration of PTC. Correct sorting determined the threshold. The distribution of thresholds was bimodal, with nontasters showing very high thresholds and tasters showing low thresholds. This distribution varied by sex and race: women had lower thresholds than men, and Asians had lower thresholds than Caucasians.

In the 1960s, Roland Fischer shifted studies to a chemical relative of PTC that was safer to test—propylthiouracil (PROP)—and focused on the nutritional implications of the genetic variation in taster status (Fischer and Griffin, 1964). Fischer suggested that tasters were more finicky eaters: because bitter tastes are more intense to these individuals, they tend to dislike foods high in bitter compounds, such as many vegetables, that nontasters find more palatable. Fischer also related taster status to body type (e.g., weight) and health. Alcoholics and smokers were found to contain a lower proportion of tasters than would be expected by chance, presumably because unpleasant sensations (e.g., bitterness) produced by alcoholic beverages and tobacco act as deterrents. The effect of genetic variation in taste is even related to cancer risk, as will be described shortly.

In 2003, Dennis Drayna and his colleagues discovered the location of the gene that expresses PTC/PROP receptors (Kim et al., 2003). This gene is a member of the bitter family introduced earlier and is designated *TAS2R38*. Individuals with two recessive alleles are nontasters; those with either one or two dominant alleles are tasters.

Supertasters

By the 1970s, the "direct" psychophysical methods introduced by Harvard's S. S. Stevens led to a new look at genetic variation in taste. Instead of measuring thresholds—the dimmest sensations—investigators could look at suprathreshold taste and plot the psychophysical functions showing how perceived taste intensity varies with concentration. You may remember from Chapter 1 that Stevens and his students documented what is now known as Stevens's power law. It holds that perceived sensations rise as the stimulus raised to some power. Written as an equation, this is

$$S = I^b$$

where S is sensation, I is stimulus intensity (concentration of a solution if we're talking about taste, and we are), and b takes on different values for different sensory modalities (Stevens and Galanter, 1957). If we take the logarithm of each side of the equation above, we get $\log S = b \times \log I$, which is the formula for a straight line of slope b. Of special interest for our present purposes, b takes on

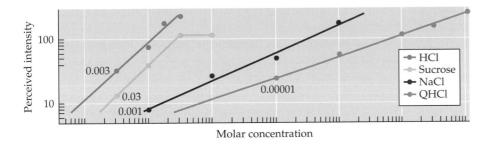

Figure 15.11 Psychophysical functions for sour (HCl), sweet (sucrose), salty (NaCl), and bitter (quinine hydrochloride, QHCl). The logarithm of the perceived taste intensity is plotted against the logarithm of the concentration. The lowest concentration of each tastant is indicated on the figure. The slopes (*b*) of the functions are as follows: HCl, 0.89; sucrose, 0.94 (for the lower portion); NaCl, 0.43; and QHCl, 0.32. (After Bartoshuk, 1975.)

different values for different taste qualities. For example, **Figure 15.11** shows plots of HCl (sour), sucrose (sweet), NaCl (salty), and QHCl (quinine hydrochloride, bitter). Note that the slope is highest for HCl and lowest for QHCl. That is, sourness grows much more rapidly with concentration than does bitterness.

Unfortunately, knowing how taste intensity grows with concentration does not permit comparisons of perceived taste intensity across individuals; *b* can be equal for two people even if one experiences taste intensities twice as great as the other. Fortunately, two of S. S. Stevens's students—Joseph Stevens and Lawrence Marks—made another fundamental discovery in this era. As we discussed in Chapter 1, humans are surprisingly good at **cross-modality matching** (Stevens, 1959) (see Figure 1.9). For example, we can match the loudness of a sound to the brightness of a light, and we can match both of these to the intensity of a taste. We can use this cross-modality matching to see if some individuals experience more intense sensations than others. First, we need to select a control modality that is not related to taste. As far as we know, our experiences of loudness or brightness are not related to our experiences of taste; either of these could be our control modality. For example, let's match our taste sensations to loudness. We can offer our participants a taste stimulus: a sweet soda (e.g., Coke or Pepsi). We give our participants a sound source that can be varied in loudness, and we instruct them to set the loudness such that it matches the sweetness of the beverage (this is cross-modality matching of loudness and sweetness). Some of our participants match the sweetness to a sound of 90 decibels (db) (the loudness of a train whistle). Others match it to a much weaker sound, 80 db (the loudness of a telephone dial tone). We know that 90 db is twice as loud as 80 db (every 10 db doubles loudness). Now we know that some participants perceive a beverage to be twice as sweet as another group. Those in the first group (who experience the more intense sweetness) are called supertasters.

What causes supertasting? There are probably several factors, but one of them is anatomy. If we look at the tongues of the subjects in our cross-modality matching experiment, we find that those who experienced the beverage as twice as sweet have the most fungiform papillae (and thus the most taste buds; see Figure 15.4B).

This association between supertasting and tongue anatomy causes more differences between supertasters and others. Supertasters experience the most intense sensations of oral burn (e.g., from chili peppers) and oral touch (from fats or thickeners in foods) because fungiform papillae are innervated by nerve fibers that convey burn and touch sensations as well as those that convey taste

cross-modality matching The ability to match the intensities of sensations that come from different sensory modalities. This ability allows insight into sensory differences. For example, a listener might adjust the brightness of a light until it matches the loudness of a tone.

sensations; the more fungiform papillae you have, the more nerve fibers that carry oral pain and oral touch.

In addition, because of central connections between taste and retronasal olfaction, those who experience the most intense taste sensations also perceive more intense retronasal olfaction and thus more intense flavor.

Pathology adds yet another source of variation in our oral sensations. Surprisingly, removing input from one of the taste nerves (by anesthesia or damage) can actually intensify whole-mouth taste sensations (Bartoshuk et al., 2012). This intensification results because inputs from the different taste nerves inhibit one another in the brain. Loss of input from one nerve releases others from that inhibition. In some cases, the result is actual intensification of whole-mouth taste. When damage is more widespread, not surprisingly, taste perception diminishes.

In sum, the intensities of our taste experiences result from genetic variation, pathology, and interactions among all of the cranial nerves innervating the mouth.

Health Consequences of Variation in Taste Sensations

With these insights, the potential links between responsiveness to PROP and health have become the focus of considerable interest. The new psychophysical methods permitted nutrition expert Valerie Duffy to show that variation in the sensory properties of foods and beverages affects food preferences and thus diet. Because diet is a major risk factor for a variety of diseases, genetic variation in taste plays a role in these diseases. For instance, some vegetables produce unpleasant sensations (e.g., bitter) to medium tasters and supertasters, leading these individuals to eat fewer of them. Reduced vegetable intake is a risk factor for colon cancer.

Sure enough, Duffy and her colleagues found that, in a sample of older men getting routine colonoscopies at a Department of Veterans Affairs hospital, those tasting PROP as most bitter had the most colon polyps, a precursor to colon cancer (Basson et al., 2003). On the other hand, fats can produce unpleasantly intense sensations in supertasters, leading them to eat fewer high-fat foods and thereby lowering their risk of cardiovascular disease (Duffy et al., 2004). These sensory links to behavior that affects health are not limited to diet. Fischer's early suggestion that nontasters are more likely to smoke and consume alcohol has proved correct (Duffy et al., 2004; Snyder et al., 2005).

More generally, variation in the sensory properties of foods and beverages is linked to health because that variation affects what we like to eat, and diet affects health. In addition to variation due to genetic differences, there is taste damage due to common pathologies. The pathways of the taste nerves from the tongue to the brain are vulnerable to damage. The chorda tympani taste nerve passes through the middle ear, where it is vulnerable to middle-ear infections (otitis media). The glossopharyngeal taste nerve is physically near the tonsils. A layer of muscle can protect the glossopharyngeal nerve during tonsillectomy, but that muscle is lacking in some individuals. Both the chorda tympani and the glossopharyngeal nerves can be damaged by head injuries even if they are relatively mild. Taste damage can have unexpected consequences because of inhibitory connections between taste nerves and between taste and other oral sensations. Individuals with histories of otitis media (usually in infancy or childhood), tonsillectomy, or head injury were found to weigh more in their 40s than those without those histories (Bartoshuk, 2012; Bartoshuk et al., 2013). Sensory testing revealed a likely scenario. The localized taste damage released inhibition on undamaged nerves such that whole-mouth taste, perception of touch (fats in foods), and retronasal olfaction all increased. These sensory changes were associated with enhanced palatability of high-fat foods, which could potentially lead to weight gain.

■ Scientists at Work ■

The Role of Food Preferences in Food Choices

■ **Question** Do our food preferences determine how much we weigh? Our diets have a great deal to do with risk for cardiovascular disease (i.e., heart attacks, strokes). A great deal of effort has been put into devising measures of dietary intake but this has proved difficult because of recall problems and biases (e.g., people who are overweight tend to underestimate fat intake). Duffy and her colleagues looked at this problem in a new way using a psychophysical measure of food preference (Duffy et al., 2007).

■ **Hypothesis** We are not very good at recalling what we eat accurately. However, we are good at describing what we like to eat. Thus our food preferences may be a good way to assess dietary risk.

■ **Test** Duffy recruited 422 men from a manufacturing company to participate in a health risk appraisal (HRA) survey. Their adiposity (e.g., waist circumference as well as body mass index [BMI], which is weight corrected for height) was assessed, they reported the number of times per week that they consumed high-fat foods, and they rated their liking for high-fat foods.

■ **Results** The degree to which these men liked high-fat foods correlated significantly with BMI and waist circumference; the frequency with which they ate high-fat foods did not. There are two reasons why an affective measure mapped onto adiposity better than

dietary recall did. First, memory experts know that it is harder to recall facts than it is to recall feelings. For example, think about how hard is it to remember how often you have consumed chocolate cake. Now think about how much easier it is to remember how much you like chocolate cake. Second, the investigators asked participants to rate their liking for high fat foods on a special rating scale. The key to that special scale was the context. Participants rated how much they liked high-fat foods in the context of all kinds of pleasures (e.g., enjoying music, spending time with friends, watching a favorite TV show). The pleasure from the non-food items served as a kind of standard which was not related to adiposity and thus could be assumed to be roughly equal to all participants. Thus the pleasure experienced by the heavier individuals from the high-fat foods could be seen as higher relative to the non-food pleasures.

■ **Conclusion** Jeremy Bentham, an eighteenth-century philosopher, argued for the primacy of pleasure in determining what we do. The pleasure associated with eating is an example of this. Food preferences can predict adiposity.

■ **Future work** Assessing food preferences is much easier than assessing dietary intake. Would you recommend adding food preference assessment to HRAs?

How Do Taste and Flavor Contribute to the Regulation of Nutrients?

Bentham said, "Nature has placed mankind under the governance of two sovereign masters, pain and pleasure. It is for them alone to point out what we ought to do, as well as to determine what we shall do." He would not have been surprised to learn that the pleasure associated with taste and flavor guides our food choices. Some species have few food choices to make; for example, koala bears eat primarily leaves from the eucalyptus tree. However, humans (and rats) are omnivores; we are confronted with an array of choices, and we must select safe foods and avoid poisons to survive. Paul Rozin coined the term *omnivore's dilemma* to describe this biological imperative (Rozin, 1981). Michael Pollan subsequently applied the term to the modern human's need to find a healthy diet amid the dizzying choices available to us today (Pollan, 2006). How does the pleasure associated with taste and flavor solve this dilemma?

Taste

The taste system responds to a small set of molecules that we encounter in nature. This precise tuning is consistent with the role of taste as a system for detecting nutrients and "antinutrients" (substances that are either helpful or harmful, respectively, to our bodies) before we ingest them.

Each of the four basic tastes is responsible for a different nutrient or antinutrient and has evolved according to its purpose. For example, the bitter taste subsystem is nature's poison detector. In terms of chemical structure, poisons are quite diverse. Thus, the bitter receptors must be diverse as well. On the other hand, given that we don't really care if we can discriminate among poisons (since we just want to avoid them all), we could hook all of those receptors up to a few common lines to the brain. As we saw earlier, this is exactly how the bitter subsystem is set up.

Similarly, the sour subsystem is configured to reject any highly acidic solution without distinguishing exactly what is causing the acidity of the solution to be so high. The other two taste subsystems enable us to detect, and therefore selectively ingest, foods that contain nutrients that our bodies need: sodium (salty) and sugars (sweet).

Some of the most impressive evidence for this hardwired affect with taste came from the work of Jacob Steiner on facial expressions in newborn infants (Steiner, 1973). Steiner found that infants responded with stereotyped facial expressions when sweet, salty, sour, and bitter solutions were applied to their tongues. Sweet evoked a "smilelike" expression followed by sucking (**Figure 15.12A**). Sour produced pursing and protrusion of the lips (**Figure 15.12B**). Bitter produced gaping, movements of spitting, and in some cases, vomiting movements. Even infants born without cerebral hemispheres (a condition known as anencephaly) showed the same facial expressions, suggesting that these expressions are mediated by very primitive parts of the brain.

The fact that the basic tastes provide both information and pleasure (affect) enables organisms to solve critical nutritional problems immediately, without having to learn (which takes time). The newborn baby can nurse because the sweet taste of mother's milk is pleasurable. The baby can also reject poisons because the bitter tastes they evoke are aversive. The athlete who sweats or the new mother who loses blood can replace lost sodium because the taste of salt is pleasant and often becomes more pleasant when salt is needed.

(A)   (B)

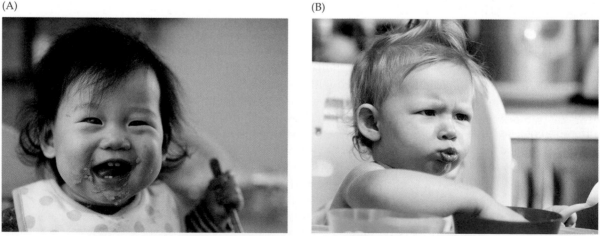

Figure 15.12 The two toddlers' facial expressions reveal the taste qualities that they're experiencing. (A) Sweet potato produces the typical smile associated with the acceptance of sweet. (B) Green apple produces the puckery face associated with sour.

Flavor

Taste affect guides us very effectively for the few nutrients discussed above. However, olfactory affect becomes critical when nutrients are not conveniently labeled by taste. When we eat foods, we experience retronasal olfactory stimulation. Specific features of the olfactory molecules interact with receptors tuned to them. All receptors of a given type project to individual glomeruli in the olfactory brain. The pattern across the glomeruli creates a picture of the chemical structure of a molecule (or a mixture of molecules). These pictures are stored in the brain and can be associated with positive or negative affect depending on the consequences of what we eat. If we get sick, the pictures acquire negative affect. If our brains judge the consequences as good (e.g., calories, positive mood states), the pictures acquire positive affect. Our like or dislike of foods is made up of the hardwired affect of taste along with the learned affect of retronasal olfaction.

This view of nutrient regulation owes much to the work of Paul Rozin, who debunked an important early idea: wisdom of the body. The phrase *wisdom of the body* dates back to a famous lecture by E. H. Starling (1923) and a subsequent book by Cannon (1939) on homeostasis, the body's ability to maintain constancy (e.g., the regulation of blood sugar by insulin). However, Curt Richter extended this thinking to behavior with his **specific hungers theory**; he suggested that animals can recognize a need for a specific nutrient, find and consume it, and so restore the body to its normal condition. The evidence for wisdom of the body at first looked impressive. For example, a 3½-year-old boy with an intense craving for salt died when his salt intake was restricted during a hospital stay. An autopsy revealed a tumor of his adrenal gland that had caused his body to lose sodium. His salt craving had enabled his body to retain enough sodium to keep him alive (Wilkins and Richter, 1940). Another source of support for specific hungers was a treatment for schizophrenia that was popular in the 1940s. At the time, some experts believed that the brain, which depends on glucose for fuel, could be forcibly rested if blood glucose were driven to very low values with insulin. Intense cravings for sweet were an unexpected by-product of the therapy. Subsequent laboratory studies confirmed that insulin injections produce increased liking for sweet. Richter concluded that ingestion of the nutrient reduces the craving and brings the body back into balance. Even more support for the idea of specific hungers seemed to come from the work of a pediatrician, Clara Davis. She allowed a group of 6-month-old infants to eat whatever they liked, to see if they would choose wisely (C. M. Davis, 1928). The infants thrived, leading Davis to conclude that, when allowed to choose among a variety of healthy foods, infants had the ability to select a healthy diet.

The specific hungers theory came to a screeching halt when investigators tried to extend it to vitamins. In one of the early studies, rats were fed a diet deficient in vitamin B_1, which made them sick. When humans are deficient in vitamin B_1, they also get sick; that deficiency disease is called beriberi. When the rats were offered a choice of remaining on the same diet or switching to a diet containing B_1, they immediately switched. But Rozin later conducted the experiment with a crucial control: he gave the control rats the choice of the original diet or a different diet that was also deficient in B_1. These rats also immediately switched to the different diet. Thus, the rats in the original study had not specifically sought B_1; they had simply learned to avoid the diet that made them ill (Rozin, 1967).

Rozin's work ended belief in specific hungers as an explanation of dietary regulation for anything beyond sugar and salt. In retrospect, we can see that the theory lacked an important ingredient. For craving to cause an animal to seek out and take in a needed nutrient, a sensory cue would have to be unambiguously associated

specific hungers theory The idea that deficiency of a given nutrient produces craving (a specific hunger) for that nutrient. Curt Richter first proposed this theory and demonstrated that cravings for salty or for sweet are associated with deficiencies in those substances. However, the idea proved wrong for other nutrients (e.g., vitamins).

Figure 15.13 In our evolutionary past, when food was scarce and we had to expend considerable physical effort to get it, specific hungers for sugar and salt were adaptive. In the current era, in which foods are plentiful and easily obtained, these specific hungers (combined with the profit motive for the food industry) lead many to consume too much junk food. The nutrients in vegetables are, alas, largely undetectable, so we cannot develop specific hungers for them.

with the nutrient. The saltiness of salt and the sweetness of sugar could serve as such cues, but the B_1 molecule does not produce a detectable cue in food (**Figure 15.13**).

We were left with a problem, though. How did Clara Davis's infants know how to select a healthy diet if specific hungers do not operate for all nutrients? It turned out that they were not selecting a healthy diet at all. They were simply eating a variety of the foods presented, because they got bored eating single foods. This phenomenon is called sensory-specific satiety (Rolls, 1986). Because all of the choices were healthy, all the infants needed to do was eat a variety. In the modern world, eating whatever we like will not produce good health, because too many of the available foods are not healthy. In fact, the specific hungers that are genuine can do us considerable harm; just think about our love for sweet and salty junk foods.

Rozin ended the belief that the brain was hardwired to tell us what to eat. But he offered us a much more flexible guide: learning. We come to like or dislike foods based on the consequences of consuming them. When the consequences are negative (e.g., nausea), we dislike the food and avoid it (conditioned aversion); when the consequences are positive (e.g., calories), we like the food and consume it (conditioned preference). As we saw in Chapter 14, olfactory likes and dislikes are not hardwired as those for taste are.

The association of negative or positive affect with an experience is called evaluative conditioning. The phenomenon has received remarkably little attention, given the powerful role that affect plays in our lives. The experience of value is important in our social worlds (e.g., in religion, politics) as well as in our food worlds. The classic paradigm of evaluative conditioning is the transfer of affect from a stimulus with positive (or negative) valence to a neutral stimulus. For example, Debra Zellner and Paul Rozin (1993) conducted an experiment ostensibly about preference for teas. Participants were asked to rate the palatability of a variety of teas; some had sugar added, some did not. Tested a second time, the teas that had originally been paired with sugar were rated as more positive.

Back to Ina Garten's cookie. Why are cookies so universally loved? They contain sugar, which we are hardwired to love, and they contain flavorings, which we have learned to love because they are paired with fat and starch that give us calories.

Is All Olfactory Affect Learned?

The evidence that all olfactory affect is learned is still provisional. The number of odorants tested on young children is limited by the difficulty of doing these experiments. Could there be a few odorants that, like taste, have hardwired affect? One suggestion makes considerable evolutionary sense. Certain odorants are derived from important nutrients in fruits and vegetables and are thus cues to those nutrients. Hardwired liking for these odorants would lead to a healthier diet (Goff and Klee, 2006).

Another reason to consider the possibility of hardwiring of the pleasure associated with some odorants is the evidence for hardwired olfactory aversions in some species. Once we consider the possibility that some odorants are innately disliked, it is reasonable to reevaluate the possibility that some are innately liked. The problem with innate aversion to odors is that studies claiming this must do a crucial control. Since pain and its milder cousin, irritation, are innately disliked, any odorant claimed to be innately disliked must be shown to lack irritation sensations. For example, consider sniffing ammonia. Ammonia has an odor, but it also burns the nose. The burn is mediated by the trigeminal nerve. With humans there is an easy way to identify an odorant that also stimulates the trigeminal nerve through the localization of sensation. If a pure odorant is introduced to just one nostril but both nostrils are stimulated, the odor cannot be localized to the appropriate nostril. If the odorant contains trigeminal stimulants, the sensation can be localized. There are no final answers yet. Stay tuned.

The Nature of Taste Qualities

Although we take for granted that sweet, salty, sour, and bitter are taste qualities, historically that was not always the case. Hermann von Helmholtz, a physician and physicist of note in the nineteenth century (see Chapter 1), taught that modality and quality should be distinguished; if two sensations are so different that there are no transitions between them, then they should be considered separate modalities. Two students of Helmholtz (Wilhelm Wundt and Frithiof Holmgren) in turn produced students (Friedrich Kiesow and Hjalmar Öhrwall) who saw Helmholtz's view differently. Kiesow saw the different taste sensations as analogous to colors and so concluded that different taste sensations are different qualities within the taste sense. On the other hand, Öhrwall saw taste qualities as independent of one another and so as separate modalities. The details of their research duels (see Bartoshuk, 1978) actually supported Öhrwall, but Kiesow obviously won the battle. One important factor was that Wundt's lab hosted a variety of prominent psychologists, among them many Americans. The proximity of Kiesow to Americans who wrote influential texts may have contributed to that victory.

Reminiscent of this old debate is a modern debate over how taste quality is coded. A major source of historical controversy in the taste literature revolved around whether tastes are coded mainly via **labeled lines**, in which each taste neuron unambiguously signals the presence of a certain basic taste, or via patterns of activity across many different taste neurons. We've seen examples of both types of coding in other senses. For example, color vision and olfaction use pattern coding. A single type of cone cannot tell us the wavelength of a light ray, but the pattern of activity across our three cone types can give us this information. Hearing, on the other hand, uses a mechanism more akin to the labeled-line approach: certain neurons always respond best to 5000-hertz (Hz) tones, others always respond best to 5100-Hz tones, and so on. Which scheme is used in the gustatory system?

labeled lines A theory of taste coding in which each taste nerve fiber carries a particular taste quality. Thus a fiber that responds best to sucrose but also responds with small responses to other stimuli carries only sweet.

FURTHER DISCUSSION of the coding of colors, sounds, and odors can be found in Chapters 5, 9, and 14, respectively.

Given what we've already learned about the functions of the four basic tastes, it is easy to construct an evolutionary argument for labeled-line coding. Recall that in olfaction, which uses pattern coding, mixtures of different compounds very often produce a new smell sensation; the components cannot be recognized. Such a coding system would be disastrous for the purpose of the taste system. For example, poisonous plants contain components with a variety of tastes. If bitterness were to synthesize with these other tastes, we would not be able to parse it out and thus avoid the poison. The functions of the four tastes are well served by their independence from each other. A final argument involves taste mixtures. Studies have shown that we are, in fact, very good at analyzing taste mixtures. For example, in tonic water, which contains a combination of quinine and sugar, we have no difficulty identifying its two components—bitter and sweet. In a pattern-coding theory, bitter and sweet would each be coded by a different pattern; combining those patterns would produce a new pattern and a new taste.

The historical controversy arose because initial research seemed to indicate that most neurons coming from taste buds responded to more than one of the four basic tastes. How could such a system code sweet, sour, salt, and bitter without confusion? Carl Pfaffmann initially concluded that taste qualities must be coded by a pattern across taste fibers, but he changed his mind. Additional research showed that much of the earlier confusion was noise (Pfaffmann, 1974a, 1974b).

Taste Adaptation and Cross-Adaptation

As we've seen throughout this book, all sensory systems show adaptation effects, in which constant application of a certain stimulus temporarily weakens subsequent perception of that stimulus. In taste, our constant adaptation to the salt in saliva affects our ability to taste salt; in addition, adaptation to certain components in one food can change the perception of a second food. (See **Web Essay 15.1: Water Tastes**.) You've experienced cross-adaptation yourself if you've ever noticed that a beverage like lemonade tastes too sour after you eat a sweet dessert. The sugar in the dessert adapts the sweet receptors so that the subsequent lemonade tastes less sweet and more sour than normal.

Pleasure and Retronasal versus Orthonasal Olfaction

There is still much that is not understood about the links between retronasal and orthonasal (through the nostrils) olfaction, including the pleasure or displeasure associated with these sensations. We know that we learn to like or dislike smells, but do we learn these preferences separately for retro- and orthonasal olfaction? Linda Bartoshuk (one of the authors of this book) recounts getting carsick on a childhood vacation while simultaneously eating chocolate-covered cherries. She now not only avoids the cherries, but also finds cherry-scented soaps disgusting as well. The distinction between retronasal and orthonasal olfaction has only emerged as important in recent years. We have much to learn in this area.

The Pleasure of the Burn of Chili Peppers

Capsaicin produces the burn associated with chili peppers. As you learned in Chapter 1, capsaicin stimulates both fibers that mediate warmth and those that mediate burn, but there is one important difference between the tongue and outer body skin: the tongue is more sensitive. For example, if you use chilis in cooking you have probably gotten capsaicin on your hands. Your hands may feel fine but if you lick your fingers you will feel burn. The thresholds for the burn of capsaicin are considerably lower on the tongue.

Many people experience pleasure from the burn of capsaicin, but we are not born liking this burn. Rozin (Rozin and Schiller, 1980) studied the acquisition of chili pepper preference in Mexico and found that the process depends on social influences. Chili is gradually added to the diet of young children beginning at about age 3, and the children observe their family members enjoying it. By age 5 or 6, children voluntarily add chili to their own food. At some point the chili is liked for its own sake.

A variety of arguments based on presumed health benefits have been introduced to account for our love of chili peppers. For example, some have argued that chilis kill microorganisms in food, thus acting as a preservative. Others have argued that chilis contain vitamins A and C, which give them adaptive value (in other words, the pain of the chili serves as a cue for the presence of the vitamins). The pleasure that some people experience from chilis has also been linked to the idea that the resulting burn leads to the release of endorphins, the brain's internal painkillers.

One of the most interesting features of the liking for the burn of chili peppers is its near total restriction to humans. Rozin has documented a few cases on record of animals showing a liking for chilis, but in all cases these were pets fed chili pepper by their human companions. When Rozin tried to produce liking for chilis in rats, he failed (Rozin, Gruss, and Berk, 1979). But one of Rozin's students, Bennett Galef (Galef and Wigmore, 1983), who is famous for the study of social interactions among rats, was finally able to get rats to like a diet seasoned with a mild level of cayenne pepper by exposing the rats to a "demonstrator" rat that had just eaten the diet. It seems that growing to like chili peppers is a social phenomenon for rats as well.

The burn that we experience from chili peppers is highly variable across individuals (**Figure 15.14**). The variability has two sources. First, as noted earlier, individuals with the largest number of fungiform papillae (supertasters) have the most fibers mediating pain, and thus they perceive the most intense oral burn from chilis. Second, capsaicin, the chemical that produces the burn in chilis, desensitizes pain receptors. This means that individuals who consume chilis quite often (once every 48 hours is sufficient) are chronically desensitized. Chili peppers produce considerably less burn to those who are desensitized.

Incidentally, you may see your favorite chilis rated in terms of Scoville units. For example, the jalapeño pepper you can buy in supermarkets is rated at 3,500–10,000 Scoville units while the habanero and scotch bonnet peppers (you may have to grow these yourself) are rated at 100,000–350,000 Scoville units. A Scoville unit is a strange sort of unit. It is the number of times you have to dilute the dry pepper until the burn can no longer be detected. If you would like your peppers described in terms of the content of capsaicin, you can express capsaicin in ppm (1 ppm equals 1 milligram per liter of water). However, since the burn of chili peppers is not the same for everyone, these units will not tell you how much the pepper will burn to you.

Desensitization can come to your rescue if you accidentally order a meal that proves to be overspiced for your palate. After the first mouthful, wait until the burn has subsided.

Figure 15.14 Do these images inspire fear or delight?

The mistake many diners make is to keep trying to eat. As long as the capsaicin continues to be applied, desensitization does not occur. Desensitization occurs during the decline of the burn (B. G. Green, 1993). Once the initial burn has faded, the rest of the meal can be consumed with relative comfort.

Capsaicin desensitization has important clinical value. The ancient Mayans used a concoction made of chilis to treat the pain of mouth sores. In the 1990s, Wolffe Nadoolman, then a medical student at Yale working in Bartoshuk's laboratory, created a similar remedy by adding cayenne pepper to a recipe for taffy. People with cancer often develop painful mouth sores from chemotherapy and radiation therapy, and if these patients suck on the capsaicin candies, capsaicin is brought into contact with the pain receptors stimulated by the sores. The pain receptors are then desensitized, and the pain is dramatically reduced (Berger et al., 1995). Although capsaicin can be used to reduce pain at any body site, the skin is a potent barrier that prevents capsaicin from contacting pain receptors. Thus, capsaicin remedies for disorders like arthritis are rarely very satisfactory. In the mouth, the mucous membrane permits capsaicin to easily contact pain receptors, so there, desensitization is fast and powerful.

In case you would like to try the candy, you can find the recipe in Berger et al. 1995, but you can also turn ordinary caramels into capsaicin caramels by melting a pound of them and adding 1/2 teaspoon of McCormick cayenne pepper. Why McCormick? The company was kind enough to tell us how much capsaicin is in their cayenne pepper so that we could make the candy contain 5–9 ppm capsaicin.

Summary

1. Flavor is produced by the combination of taste and retronasal olfaction (olfactory sensations produced when odorants in the mouth are forced up behind the palate into the nose). Flavor sensations are localized to the mouth, even though the retronasal olfactory sensations come from the olfactory receptors high in the nasal cavity.

2. Taste buds are globular clusters of cells (like the segments in an orange). The tips of some of the cells (microvilli) contain sites that interact with taste molecules. Those sites fall into two groups: ion channels that mediate responses to salts and acids, and G protein–coupled receptors that bind to sweet and bitter compounds as well as amino acids.

3. The tongue has a bumpy appearance because of structures called papillae. Filiform papillae (the most numerous) have no taste buds. Taste buds are found in the fungiform papillae (front of the tongue), foliate papillae (rear edges of the tongue), and circumvallate papillae (rear center of the tongue), as well as on the roof of the mouth.

4. Taste projects ipsilaterally from the tongue to the medulla, thalamus, and cortex. It projects first to the insula in the cortex, and from there to the orbitofrontal cortex, an area where taste can be integrated with other sensory input (e.g., retronasal olfaction).

5. Taste and olfaction play very different roles in the perception of foods and beverages. Taste is the true nutritional sense; taste receptors are tuned to molecules that function as important nutrients. Bitter taste is a poison detection system. Sweet taste enables us to respond to the sugars that are biologically useful to us: sucrose, glucose, and fructose. Salty taste enables us to identify sodium, a mineral crucial to survival because of its role in

nerve conduction and muscle function. Sour taste permits us to avoid acids in concentrations that might injure tissue.

6. Umami, the taste produced by monosodium glutamate, has been suggested as a fifth basic taste that detects protein. However, umami lacks one of the most important properties of a basic taste: hardwired affect. Some individuals like umami, but others do not. Taste receptors are not only in the mouth but also in the gut. Digestion breaks down proteins into their constituent amino acids, and the glutamate released stimulates gut glutamate receptors, leading to conditioned preferences for the sensory properties of the foods containing protein.

7. The importance of taste to survival requires that we be able to recognize each taste quality independently, even when it is present in a mixture. By coding taste quality with labeled lines in much the same way that frequencies are coded in hearing, nature has ensured that we have this important capability. These labeled lines are noisy. For example, acids are able to stimulate fibers mediating saltiness, as well as those mediating sourness. Thus, acids tend to taste both salty and sour.

8. Foods do not taste the same to everyone. The Human Genome Project revealed that we carry about 25 genes for bitter taste. The most studied bitter receptor responds to PROP and shows allelic variation in humans, leading to the designations "PROP nontaster" for those who taste the least bitterness and "PROP taster" for those who taste the most. In addition, humans vary in the number of fungiform papillae (and thus taste buds) they possess. Those with the most taste buds are called supertasters and live in a "neon" taste world; those with the fewest taste buds live in a "pastel" taste world. Psychologists discovered these differences by testing people's ability to match sensory intensities of stimuli from different modalities. For example, the bitterness of black coffee matches the pain of a mild headache to nontasters but resembles a severe headache to supertasters. The way foods taste affects palatability, which in turn affects diet. Poor diet contributes to diseases like cancer and cardiovascular disease.

9. For taste, unlike olfaction, liking and disliking are hardwired; for example, babies are born liking sweet and salty and disliking bitter. When we become deficient in salt or sucrose, liking for salty and sweet tastes, respectively, increases. Junk foods are constructed to appeal to these preferences. Liking the burn of chili peppers, on the other hand, is acquired and, with the exception of some pets, is essentially limited to humans. Taste buds are surrounded by pain fibers; thus supertasters perceive greater burn from chilis than do nontasters. In addition, fungiform papillae, structures that house taste buds, are innervated by touch fibers; thus supertasters perceive greater touch sensations from fats (e.g., creamy, viscous, thick) in foods.

Glossary

Numbers in brackets refer to the chapter(s) where the term is introduced.

A

A-beta fiber   A wide-diameter, myelinated sensory nerve fiber that transmits signals from mechanical stimulation. [13]

A-delta fiber   An intermediate-sized, myelinated sensory nerve fiber that transmits pain and temperature signals. [13]

abducens (VI) nerves   The sixth pair of cranial nerves, which innervate the lateral rectus muscle of the eyeballs. [1]

absolute metrical depth cue   A depth cue that provides quantifiable information about distance in the third dimension (e.g., his nose sticks out 4 centimeters in front of his face). [6]

absolute pitch   A rare ability whereby some people are able to very accurately name or produce notes without comparison to other notes. [11]

absolute threshold   The minimum amount of stimulation necessary for a person to detect a stimulus 50% of the time. [1]

absorb   To take up something—such as light, noise, or energy—and not transmit it at all. [2]

acceleration   A change in velocity. Mathematically, acceleration is the derivative of velocity. In words, linear acceleration indicates a change in linear velocity; angular acceleration indicates a change in angular velocity. [12]

accessory olfactory bulb (AOB)   A neural structure found in nonhuman animals that is smaller than the main olfactory bulb and located behind it and that receives input from the vomeronasal organ. [14]

accidental viewpoint   A viewing position that produces some regularity in the visual image that is not present in the world (e.g., the sides of two independent objects lining up perfectly). [4]

accommodation   The process by which the eye changes its focus (in which the lens gets fatter as gaze is directed toward nearer objects). [2, 6]

achromatopsia   An inability to perceive colors that is caused by damage to the central nervous system. [5]

acoustic reflex   A reflex that protects the ear from intense sounds, via contraction of the stapedius and tensor tympani muscles. [9]

acoustic startle reflex   The very rapid motor response to a sudden sound. Very few neurons are involved in the basic startle reflex, which can also be affected by emotional state. [10]

active sensing   Sensing that includes self-generated probing of the environment. Besides our vestibular sense, other active human senses include vision and touch. Animal active sensing includes the use of echoes by whales and bats, the use of electrical signals by some fishes, and the use of whiskers/antennae by fishes, insects, and nocturnal rodents. [12]

acuity   The smallest spatial detail that can be resolved at 100% contrast. [3]

adaptation   A reduction in response caused by prior or continuing stimulation. [3]

adapting stimulus   A stimulus whose removal produces a change in visual perception or sensitivity. [5]

additive color mixture   A mixture of lights. If light A and light B are both reflected from a surface to the eye, in the perception of color the effects of those two lights add together. [5]

aerial perspective or haze   A depth cue based on the implicit understanding that light is scattered by the atmosphere. More light is scattered when we look through more atmosphere. Thus, more distant objects are subject to more scatter and appear fainter, bluer, and less distinct. [6]

afferent fiber   A neuron that carries sensory information to the central nervous system. Compare *efferent fiber*. [9, 12]

afferent signals   Information flowing inward to the central nervous system from sensors in the periphery. Passive sensing would rely exclusively on such sensory inflow, providing a traditional view of sensation. See also *afferent fiber*. [12]

age-related macular degeneration (AMD)   A disease associated with aging that affects the macula. AMD gradually destroys sharp central vision, making it difficult to read, drive, and recognize faces. There are two forms of AMD: wet and dry. [2]

agnosia   A failure to recognize objects in spite of the ability to see them. Agnosia is typically due to brain damage. [4, 5]

akinetopsia   A rare neuropsychological disorder in which the affected individual has no perception of motion. [8]

amacrine cell   A retinal cell found in the inner synaptic layer that makes synaptic contacts with bipolar cells, ganglion cells, and other amacrine cells. [2]

ambiguous figure   A visual stimulus that gives rise to two or more interpretations of its identity or structure. [4]

amblyopia   A developmental disorder characterized by reduced spatial vision in an otherwise healthy eye, even with proper correction for refractive error. Also known as *lazy eye*. [3]

amplitude   In reference to vestibular sensation, the size (increase or decrease) of a head movement (e.g., angular velocity, linear acceleration, tilt). [12]

amplitude or intensity   In reference to hearing, the magnitude of displacement (increase or decrease) of a sound pressure wave. Amplitude is perceived as *loudness*. [9]

ampulla   An expansion of each semicircular-canal duct that includes that canal's cupula, crista, and hair cells, where transduction occurs. [12]

amygdala-hippocampal complex
The conjoined regions of the amygdala and hippocampus, which are key structures in the limbic system. This complex is critically involved in the unique emotional and associative properties of olfactory cognition. [14]

analgesia   Decreasing pain sensation during conscious experience. [13]

anamorphosis or anamorphic projection   Use of the rules of linear perspective to create a two-dimensional image so distorted that it looks correct only when viewed from a special angle or with a mirror that counters the distortion. [6]

angular acceleration   The rate of change of angular velocity. Mathematically, the integral of angular acceleration is angular velocity, and the integral of angular velocity is angular displacement. Angular acceleration, angular velocity, and angular displacement all mathematically represent angular motion. [12]

angular motion   Rotational motion like the rotation of a spinning top or swinging saloon doors that rotate back and forth. [12]

anisometropia   A condition in which the two eyes have different refractive errors (e.g., one eye is farsighted and the other not). [3]

anomia   An inability to name objects in spite of the ability to see and recognize them (as shown by usage). Anomia is typically due to brain damage. [5]

anosmia   The total inability to smell, most often resulting from sinus illness or head trauma. [14]

anterior cingulate cortex (ACC)   A region of the brain associated with the perceived unpleasantness of a pain sensation. [13]

aperture   An opening that allows only a partial view of an object. [8]

aperture problem   The fact that when a moving object is viewed through an aperture (or a receptive field), the direction of motion of a local feature or part of the object may be ambiguous. [8]

apparent motion   The illusory impression of smooth motion resulting from the rapid alternation of objects that appear in different locations in rapid succession. [8]

aqueous humor   The watery fluid in the anterior chamber of the eye. [2]

aromatherapy   The manipulation of odors to influence, mood, performance, and well-being as well as the physiological correlates of emotion such as heart rate, blood pressure, and sleep. [14]

articulation   The act or manner of producing a speech sound using the vocal tract. [11]

astigmatism   A visual defect caused by the unequal curving of one or more of the refractive surfaces of the eye, usually the cornea. [2]

attack   The part of a sound during which amplitude increases (onset). [10]

attention   Any of the very large set of selective processes in the brain. To deal with the impossibility of handling all inputs at once, the nervous system has evolved mechanisms that are able to bias processing to a subset of things, places, ideas, or moments in time. [7]

attention deficit hyperactivity disorder (ADHD)   a quite common childhood disorder that can continue into adulthood. Symptoms include difficulty focusing attention as well as problems controlling behavior. [7]

attentional blink   The tendency not to perceive or respond to the second of two different target stimuli amid a rapid stream of distracting stimuli if the observer has responded to the first target stimulus within 200–500 milliseconds before the second stimulus is presented. [7]

audibility threshold   The lowest sound pressure level that can be reliably detected at a given frequency. [9]

auditory nerve   A collection of neurons that convey information from hair cells in the cochlea to (afferent) and from (efferent) the brain stem. [9]

auditory stream segregation   The perceptual organization of a complex acoustic signal into separate auditory events for which each stream is heard as a separate event. [10]

autonomic nervous system   The part of the nervous system that is responsible for regulating many involuntary actions and that innervates glands, heart, digestive system, etc. [12]

azimuth   The angle of a sound source on the horizontal plane relative to a point in the center of the head between the ears. Azimuth is measured in degrees, with 0 degrees being straight ahead. The angle increases clockwise toward the right, with 180 degrees being directly behind. [10]

B

balance   The neural processes of postural control by which weight is evenly distributed, enabling us to remain upright and stable. [12]

balance system   The sensory systems, neural processes, and muscles that contribute to postural control. Specific components include the vestibular organs, kinesthesis, vestibulo-spinal pathways, skeletal bones, and postural control muscles. Because of its crucial contributions to balance, some even informally refer to the vestibular system as the "balance system" and the vestibular organs as the "balance organs." But the balance system is much more than just the vestibular system, and the vestibular system contributes to more than just balance. [12]

basal cell   One of the three types of cells in the olfactory epithelium. Basal cells are the precursor cells to olfactory sensory neurons. [14]

basic color terms   Color words that are single words (like "blue," not "sky blue"), are used with high frequency, and have meanings that are agreed upon by speakers of a language. [5]

basic taste   Any of the four taste qualities that are generally agreed to describe human taste experience: sweet, salty, sour, bitter. [15]

basilar membrane   A plate of fibers that forms the base of the cochlear partition and separates the middle and tympanic canals in the cochlea. [9]

Bayesian approach A way of formalizing the idea that our perception is a combination of the current stimulus and our knowledge about the conditions of the world—what is and is not likely to occur. The Bayesian approach is stated mathematically as Bayes' theorem—$P(A|O) = P(A) \times P(O|A)/P(O)$—which enables us to calculate the probability (P) that the world is in a particular state (A) given a particular observation (O). [4, 6]

belt area A region of cortex, directly adjacent to the primary auditory cortex (A1), with inputs from A1, where neurons respond to more complex characteristics of sounds. [9]

binaral rivalry Competition between the two nostrils for odor perception. When a different scent is presented to each nostril simultaneously, we perceive each scent to be alternating back and forth with the other, and not a blend of the two scents. [14]

binding problem The challenge of tying different attributes of visual stimuli (e.g., color, orientation, motion), which are handled by different brain circuits, to the appropriate object so that we perceive a unified object (e.g., red, vertical, moving right). [7]

binocular Referring to two eyes. [6]

binocular depth cue A depth cue that relies on information from both eyes. Stereopsis is the primary example in humans, but convergence and the ability of two eyes to see more of an object than one eye sees are also binocular depth cues. [6]

binocular disparity The differences between the two retinal images of the same scene. Disparity is the basis for stereopsis, a vivid perception of the three-dimensionality of the world that is not available with monocular vision. [6]

binocular rivalry The competition between the two eyes for control of visual perception, which is evident when completely different stimuli are presented to the two eyes. [6]

binocular summation The combination (or "summation") of signals from each eye in ways that make performance on many tasks better with both eyes than with either eye alone. [6]

biological motion The pattern of movement of living beings (humans and animals). [8]

bipolar cell A retinal cell that synapses with either rods or cones (not both) and with horizontal cells, and then passes the signals on to ganglion cells. [2]

bitter One of the four basic tastes; the taste quality, generally considered unpleasant, produced by substances like quinine or caffeine. [15]

blood oxygen level–dependent (BOLD) signal The ratio of oxygenated to deoxygenated hemoglobin that permits the localization of brain neurons that are most involved in a task. [1]

body image The impression of our bodies in space. [13]

C

C fiber A narrow-diameter, unmyelinated sensory nerve fiber that transmits pain and temperature signals. [13]

C tactile (CT) afferent A narrow-diameter, unmyelinated sensory nerve fiber that transmits signals from pleasant touch. [13]

cataract An opacity of the crystalline lens. [2]

categorical perception For speech as well as other complex sounds and images, the phenomenon by which the discrimination of items is no better than the ability to label items. [11]

change blindness The failure to notice a change between two scenes. If the gist, or meaning, of the scene is not altered, quite large changes can pass unnoticed. [7]

characteristic frequency (CF) The frequency to which a particular auditory nerve fiber is most sensitive. [9]

chemosignal Any of various chemicals emitted by humans that are detected by the olfactory system and that may have some effect on the mood, behavior, hormonal status, and/or sexual arousal of other humans. [14]

chord A combination of three or more musical notes with different pitches played simultaneously. [11]

chorda tympani The branch of cranial nerve VII (the facial nerve) that carries taste information from the anterior, mobile tongue (the part that can be stuck out). The chorda tympani exits the tongue with the lingual branch of the trigeminal nerve (cranial nerve V) and then passes through the middle ear on its way to the brain. [15]

chromophore The light-catching part of the visual pigments of the retina. [2]

cilium (pl. *cilia*) Any of the hairlike protrusions on the dendrites of olfactory sensory neurons. The receptor sites for odorant molecules are on the cilia, which are the first structures involved in olfactory signal transduction. [14]

circadian Referring to the biological cycle that recurs approximately every 24 hours, even in the absence of cues to time of day (via light, clocks, etc.). [5]

circumvallate papillae Circular structures that form an inverted V on the rear of the tongue (three to five on each side, with the largest in the center). Circumvallate papillae are moundlike structures, each surrounded by a trench (like a moat). These papillae are much larger than fungiform papillae. [15]

closure In reference to perception, closure is the name of a Gestalt principle that holds that a closed contour is preferred to an open contour. [4]

coarticulation The phenomenon in speech whereby attributes of successive speech units overlap in articulatory or acoustic patterns. [11]

cochlea A spiral structure of the inner ear containing the organ of Corti. [9]

cochlear nucleus The first brain stem nucleus at which afferent auditory nerve fibers synapse. [9]

cochlear partition The combined basilar membrane, tectorial membrane, and organ of Corti, which are together responsible for the transduction of sound waves into neural signals. [9]

cognitive habituation The psychological process by which, after long-term exposure to an odor, one no longer has the ability to detect that odor or has very diminished detection ability. [14]

cold fiber A sensory nerve fiber that fires when skin temperature decreases. [13]

color-anomalous A better term for the commonly used term *color-blind*. Most "color-blind" individuals can still make discriminations based on wavelength. Those discriminations are different from the norm—that is, *anomalous*. [5]

color assimilation A color perception effect in which two colors bleed into each other, each taking on some of the chromatic quality of the other. [5]

color constancy The tendency of a surface to appear the same color under a fairly wide range of illuminants. [5]

color contrast A color perception effect in which the color of one region induces the opponent color in a neighboring region. [5]

color space The three-dimensional space, established because color perception is based on the outputs of three cone types, that describes the set of all colors. [5]

column A vertical arrangement of neurons. Neurons within a single column tend to have similar receptive fields and similar orientation preferences. [3]

common fate Gestalt grouping rule stating that the tendency of sounds to group together will increase if they begin and/or end at the same time. [10]

comparator An area of the visual system that receives one copy of the command issued by the motor system when the eyes move (the other copy goes to the eye muscles). The comparator compares the image motion signal with the eye motion signal and can compensate for the image changes caused by the eye movement. [8]

complex cell A cortical neuron whose receptive field does not have clearly defined excitatory and inhibitory regions. [3]

computed tomography (CT) An imaging technology that uses X-rays to create images of slices through volumes of material (e.g., the human body). [1]

conductive hearing loss Hearing loss caused by problems with the bones of the middle ear. [9]

cone A photoreceptor specialized for daylight vision, fine visual acuity, and color. [2]

cone monochromat An individual with only one cone type. Cone monochromats are truly color-blind. [5]

cone of confusion A region of positions in space where all sounds produce the same time and level (intensity) differences (ITDs and ILDs). [10]

cone-opponent cell A cell type—found in the retina, lateral geniculate nucleus, and visual cortex—that, in effect, subtracts one type of cone input from another. [5]

congenital prosopagnosia A form of "face blindness" apparently present from birth, as opposed to "acquired prosopagnosia," which would typically be the result of an injury to the nervous system. [4]

conjunction search Search for a target defined by the presence of two or more attributes (e.g., a *red*, *vertical* target among *red* horizontal and blue *vertical* distractors). [7]

continuity constraint In stereopsis, the observation that, except at the edges of objects, neighboring points in the world lie at similar distances from the viewer. This is one of several constraints that have been proposed as helpful in solving the correspondence problem. [6]

contralateral Referring to the opposite side of the body (or brain). [3]

contralesional field The visual field on the side opposite a brain lesion. For example, points to the left of fixation are contralesional to damage in the right hemisphere of the brain. [7]

contrast The difference in luminance between an object and the background, or between lighter and darker parts of the same object. [2, 3]

contrast sensitivity function (CSF) A function describing how the sensitivity to contrast (defined as the reciprocal of the contrast threshold) depends on the spatial frequency (size) of the stimulus. [3]

contrast threshold The smallest amount of contrast required to detect a pattern. [3]

convergence The ability of the two eyes to turn inward, often used in order to place the two images of a feature in the world on corresponding locations in the two retinal images (typically on the fovea of each eye). Convergence reduces the disparity of that feature to zero (or nearly zero). [6]

cornea The transparent "window" into the eyeball. [2]

correspondence problem 1. In binocular vision, the problem of figuring out which bit of the image in the left eye should be matched with which bit in the right eye. The problem is particularly vexing when the images consist of thousands of similar features,

like dots in random dot stereograms. 2. In motion detection, the problem faced by the motion detection system of knowing which feature in Frame 2 corresponds to a particular feature in Frame 1. [6, 8]

corresponding retinal points Two monocular images of an object in the world are said to fall on corresponding points if those points are the same distance from the fovea in both eyes. The two foveas are also corresponding points. [6]

cortical magnification The amount of cortical area (usually specified in millimeters) devoted to a specific region (e.g., 1 degree) in the visual field. [3]

cranial nerves Twelve pairs of nerves (one for each side of the body) that originate in the brain stem and reach sense organs and muscles through openings in the skull. [1, 15]

cribriform plate A bony structure riddled with tiny holes that separates the nose from the brain at the level of the eyebrows. The axons from the olfactory sensory neurons pass through the tiny holes of the cribriform plate to enter the brain. [14]

crista Any of the specialized detectors of angular motion located in each semicircular canal in a swelling called the ampulla. [12]

criterion In reference to signal detection theory, an internal threshold that is set by the observer. If the internal response is above criterion, the observer gives one response (e.g., "yes, I hear that"). Below criterion, the observer gives another response (e.g., "no, I hear nothing"). [1]

critical bandwidth The range of frequencies conveyed within a channel in the auditory system. [9]

critical period A phase in the life span during which abnormal early experience can alter normal neuronal development. Critical periods are proposed for the development of binocular vision and development of a first human language. [3, 6]

cross-adaptation The reduction in detection of one odorant following exposure to a prior odorant. Cross-adaptation is presumed to occur because the components of the odors (or the odorants) in question share one or more olfactory receptors for their transduction, but the order in which odorants are presented also plays a role. [14]

cross-modality matching The ability to match the intensities of sensations that come from different sensory modalities. This ability allows insight into sensory differences. For example, a listener might adjust the brightness of a light until it matches the loudness of a tone. [1, 15]

crossed disparity The sign of disparity created by objects in front of the plane of fixation (the horopter). The term *crossed* is used because images of objects located in front of the horopter appear to be displaced to the left in the right eye, and to the right in the left eye. [6]

cue A stimulus that might indicate where (or what) a subsequent stimulus will be. Cues can be valid (giving correct information), invalid (incorrect), or neutral (uninformative). [7]

cultural relativism In sensation and perception, the idea that basic perceptual experiences (e.g., color perception) may be determined in part by the cultural environment. [5]

cycle For a grating, a pair consisting of one dark bar and one bright bar. [3]

cycles per degree The number of pairs of light and dark bars (cycles of a grating) per degree of visual angle. [1, 3]

Cyclopean Referring to stimuli that are defined by binocular disparity alone. Named after the one-eyed Cyclops of Homer's *Odyssey*. [6]

cytochrome oxidase (CO) An enzyme used to reveal the regular array of "CO blobs," which are spaced about 0.5 millimeter apart in the primary visual cortex. [3]

D

decay The part of a sound during which amplitude decreases (offset). [10]

decibel (dB) A unit of measure for the physical intensity of sound. Decibels define the difference between two sounds as the ratio between two sound pressures. Each 10:1 sound pressure ratio equals 20 dB, and a 100:1 ratio equals 40 dB. [9]

decoding The process of determining the nature of a stimulus from the pattern of responses measured in the brain or, potentially, in an artificial system like a computer network. The stimulus could be a sensory stimulus or it could be an internal state (e.g., the contents of a dream). [4]

deep neural network (DNN) A type of "machine learning" in artificial intelligence in which a computer is programmed to learn something (here object recognition). First the network is "trained" using input for which the answer is known ("that is a cow"). Subsequently, the network can provide answers from input that it has never seen before. [4]

dermis The inner of two major layers of skin, consisting of nutritive and connective tissues, within which lie the mechanoreceptors. [13]

deuteranope An individual who suffers from color blindness that is due to the absence of M-cones. [5]

dichoptic Referring to the presentation of two different stimuli, one to each eye. Different from *binocular* presentation, which could involve both eyes looking at a single stimulus. [6]

diffuse bipolar cell A bipolar retinal cell whose processes are spread out to receive input from multiple cones. [2]

diopter (D) A unit of measurement of the optic power of a lens. It is equal to the reciprocal of the focal length, in meters. A 2-diopter lens will bring parallel rays of light into focus at ½ meter (50 cm). [2]

diplopia Double vision. If visible in both eyes, stimuli falling outside of Panum's fusional area will appear diplopic. [6]

direction The line one moves along or faces, with reference to the point or region one is moving toward or facing. [12]

directional transfer function (DTF) A measure that describes how the pinna, ear canal, head, and torso change the intensity of sounds with different frequencies that arrive at each ear from different locations in space (azimuth and elevation). [10]

distractor In visual search, any stimulus other than the target. [7]

divergence The ability of the two eyes to turn outward, often used in order to place the two images of a feature in the world on corresponding locations in the two retinal images (typically on the fovea of each eye). Divergence reduces the disparity of that feature to zero (or nearly zero). [6]

dizziness A commonly used lay term that nonspecifically indicates any form of perceived spatial disorientation, with or without instability. [12]

doctrine of specific nerve energies A doctrine, formulated by Johannes Müller, stating that the nature of a sensation depends on which sensory fibers are stimulated, rather than how they are stimulated. [1]

dorsal column–medial lemniscal (DCML) pathway The route from the spinal cord to the brain that carries signals from skin, muscles, tendons, and joints. [13]

dorsal horn A region at the rear of the spinal cord that receives inputs from receptors in the skin. [13]

double dissociation The phenomenon in which one of two functions, such as first- and second- order motion, can be damaged without harm to the other, and vice versa. [8]

double-opponent cell A cell type, found in the visual cortex, in which one region is excited by one cone type, combination of cones, or color and inhibited by the opponent cones or color (e.g., R+/G–). Another adjacent region would be inhibited by the first input and excited by the second (thus, in this example, R–/G+). [5]

dualism The idea that the mind has an existence separate from the material world of the body. [1]

duplex In reference to the retina, consisting of two parts: the rods and cones, which operate under different conditions. [2]

E

ear canal The canal that conducts sound vibrations from the pinna to the tympanic membrane and prevents damage to the tympanic membrane. [9]

eccentricity The distance between the retinal image and the fovea. [2]

efference copy or corollary discharge signal The phenomenon in which outgoing (efferent) signals from the motor cortex are copied as they exit the brain and are rerouted to other areas in the sensory cortices. [8]

efferent commands Information flowing outward from the central nervous system to the periphery. A common example is motor commands that regulate muscle contraction. The copy of such motor commands is often called an efferent copy. See also *efferent fiber*. [12]

efferent fiber A neuron that carries information from the central nervous system to the periphery. Compare *afferent fiber*. [9, 12]

egocenter The center of a reference frame used to represent locations relative to the body. [13]

electroencephalography (EEG) A technique that, using many electrodes on the scalp, measures electrical activity from populations of many neurons in the brain. [1]

emmetropia The condition in which there is no refractive error, because the refractive power of the eye is perfectly matched to the length of the eyeball. [2]

end stopping The process by which a cell in the cortex first increases its firing rate as the bar length increases to fill up its receptive field, and then decreases its firing rate as the bar is lengthened further. [3]

endogenous In reference to spatial attention, a form of top-down (knowledge-driven) control in which attention is voluntarily directed toward the site where the observer anticipates a stimulus will occur. [13]

endogenous cue In directing attention, a cue that is located in (endo) or near the current location of attention [7]

endogenous opiate A chemical released by the body that blocks the release or uptake of neurotransmitters necessary to transmit pain sensations to the brain. [13]

ensemble statistics The average and distribution of properties like orientation or color over a set of objects or over a region in a scene. [7]

entorhinal cortex A phylogenetically old cortical region that provides the major sensory association input into the hippocampus. The entorhinal cortex also receives direct projections from olfactory regions. [14]

entry-level category For an object, the label that comes to mind most quickly when we identify it (e.g., "bird"). At the subordinate level, the object might be more specifically named (e.g., "eagle"); at the superordinate level, it might be more generally named (e.g., "animal"). [4]

epidermis The outer of two major layers of skin. [13]

equal-loudness curve A graph plotting sound pressure level (dB SPL)

against the frequency for which a listener perceives constant loudness. [9]

equilibrium In reference to the vestibular system, our vestibular sense comprised of spatial orientation perception—encompassing our perception of linear motion, angular motion, and tilt—combined with reflexive vestibular responses like posture, vestibulo-autonomic reflexes, and vestibulo-ocular reflexes. [12]

equiluminant Referring to stimuli that vary in color but not in luminance. [5]

esotropia Strabismus in which one eye deviates inward. [6]

Euclidean Referring to the geometry of the world, so named in honor of Euclid, the ancient Greek geometer of the third century BCE. In Euclidean geometry, parallel lines remain parallel as they are extended in space, objects maintain the same size and shape as they move around in space, the internal angles of a triangle always add to 180 degrees, and so forth. [6]

event-related potential (ERP) A measure of electrical activity from a subpopulation of neurons in response to particular stimuli that requires averaging many EEG recordings. [1]

exogenous In reference to spatial attention, a form of bottom-up (stimulus-driven) attention reflexively (involuntarily) directed toward the site at which a stimulus has abruptly appeared. [13]

exogenous cue In directing attention, a cue that is located out (*exo*) at the desired final location of attention. [7]

exotropia Strabismus in which one eye deviates outward. [6]

exploratory procedure A stereotyped hand movement pattern used to touch objects in order to perceive their properties; each procedure is best for determining one (or more) object properties. [13]

extinction In visual attention, the inability to perceive a stimulus to one side of the point of fixation (e.g., to the right) in the presence of another stimulus, typically in a comparable position in the other visual field (e.g., on the left side). [7]

extrastriate body area (EBA) A region of extrastriate visual cortex in humans that is specifically and reliably activated by images of the body other than the face. [4]

extrastriate cortex The region of cortex bordering the primary visual cortex and containing multiple areas involved in visual processing. [4]

F

familiar size A depth cue based on knowledge of the typical sizes of objects such as humans or pennies. [6]

feature integration theory Anne Treisman's theory of visual attention, which holds that a limited set of basic features can be processed in parallel preattentively, but that other properties, including the correct binding of features to objects, require attention. [7]

feature search Search for a target defined by a single attribute, such as a salient color or orientation. [7]

Fechner's law A principle describing the relationship between stimulus and resulting sensation that says the magnitude of subjective sensation increases proportionally to the logarithm of the stimulus intensity. [1]

feed-forward process A process that carries out a computation (e.g., object recognition) one neural step after another, without need for feedback from a later stage to an earlier stage. [4]

figure-ground assignment The process of determining that some regions of an image belong to a foreground object (figure) and other regions are part of the background (ground). [4]

filiform papillae Small structures on the tongue that provide most of the bumpy appearance. Filiform papillae have no taste function. [15]

filter An acoustic, electrical, electronic, or optical device, instrument, computer program, or neuron that allows the passage of some range of parameters (e.g., orientations, frequencies) and blocks the passage of others. [2, 3]

first-order motion The motion of an object that is defined by changes in luminance. [8]

flavor The combination of true taste (sweet, salty, sour, bitter) and retronasal olfaction. [15]

focal distance The distance between the lens (or mirror) and the viewed object, in meters. [2]

focus of expansion The point in the center of the horizon from which, when we're in motion (e.g., driving on the highway), all points in the perspective image seem to emanate. The focus of expansion is one aspect of optic flow. [8]

foliate papillae Folds of tissue containing taste buds. Foliate papillae are located on the rear of the tongue lateral to the circumvallate papillae, where the tongue attaches to the mouth. [15]

formant A resonance of the vocal tract. Formants are specified by their center frequency and are denoted by integers that increase with relative frequency. [11]

Fourier analysis A mathematical procedure by which any signal can be separated into component sine waves at different frequencies. Combining these sine waves will reproduce the original signal. [1, 12]

fovea A small pit located near the center of the macula and containing the highest concentration of cones, and no rods. It is the portion of the retina that produces the highest visual acuity and serves as the point of fixation. [2]

frame of reference The coordinate system used to define locations in space. [13]

free fusion The technique of converging (crossing) or diverging the eyes in order to view a stereogram without a stereoscope. [6]

frequency For sound, the number of times per second that a pattern of pressure change repeats. Frequency is perceived as *pitch*. [9]

functional magnetic resonance imaging (fMRI) A variant of magnetic resonance imaging that makes it possible to measure localized patterns of activity in the brain. Activated neurons provoke increased blood flow, which can be quantified by measuring changes in the response of oxygenated and deoxygenated blood to strong magnetic fields. [1]

fundamental frequency The lowest-frequency component of a complex periodic sound. [9, 10]

fundus The back layer of the retina: what the eye doctor sees through an ophthalmoscope. [2]

fungiform papillae Mushroom-shaped structures (maximum diameter 1 millimeter) that are distributed most densely on the edges of the tongue, especially the tip. Taste buds

(an average of six per papilla) are buried in the surface. [15]

fusiform face area (FFA) A region of extrastriate visual cortex in humans that is specifically and reliably activated by human faces. [4, 7]

G

G protein–coupled receptor (GPCR) Any of the class of receptors that are present on the surface of olfactory sensory neurons. All GPCRs are characterized by a common structural feature of seven membrane-spanning helices. [14]

ganglion cell A retinal cell that receives visual information from photoreceptors via two intermediate neuron types (bipolar cells and amacrine cells) and transmits information to the brain and midbrain. [2]

gate control theory A description of the pain-transmitting system that incorporates modulating signals from the brain. [13]

geon In Biederman's recognition-by-components model, any of the "geometric ions" out of which perceptual objects are built. [4]

Gestalt In German, literally "form." In reference to perception, a school of thought stressing that the perceptual whole could be greater than the apparent sum of the parts. [4]

Gestalt grouping rules A set of rules describing which elements in an image will appear to group together. The original list was assembled by members of the Gestalt school of thought. [4]

glabrous In reference to skin, lacking hair. [13]

global superiority effect The finding in various experiments that the properties of the whole object take precedence over the properties of parts of the object. [4]

glomerulus (sing. glomeruli) Any of the spherical conglomerates containing the incoming axons of the olfactory sensory neurons. Each OSN converges onto two glomeruli (one medial, one lateral). [14]

good continuation 1. In reference to vision, a Gestalt grouping rule stating that two elements will tend to group together if they seem to lie on the same contour. 2. In reference to hearing, a Gestalt grouping rule stating that sounds will tend to group together as continuous if they seem

to share a common path, similar to a shared contour for vision. [4, 10]

graded potential An electrical potential that can vary continuously in amplitude. [2]

granular cells Like mitral cells, granular cells are at the deepest level of the olfactory bulb. They comprise an extensive network of inhibitory neurons, integrate input from all the earlier projections, and are thought to be the basis of specific odorant identification. [14]

graviception The physiological structures and processes that sense the relative orientation of gravity with respect to the organism. [12]

gravity A force that attracts a body toward the center of the Earth. [12]

guided search Search in which attention can be restricted to a subset of possible items on the basis of information about the target item's basic features (e.g., its color). [7]

gustation The sense of taste. [14]

H

hair cell Any cell that has stereocilia for transducing mechanical movement in the inner ear into neural activity sent to the brain; some hair cells also receive inputs from the brain. [9, 12]

haptic perception Knowledge of the world that is derived from sensory receptors in skin, muscles, tendons, and joints, usually involving active exploration. [13]

harmonic spectrum The spectrum of a complex sound in which energy is at integer multiples of the fundamental frequency. [9]

helicotrema The opening that connects the tympanic and vestibular canals at the apex of the cochlea. [9]

hertz (Hz) A unit of measure for frequency. One hertz equals one cycle per second. [9]

heterodimer A chain of two molecules that are different from each other. [15]

heuristic A mental shortcut. [4]

high-spontaneous fiber An auditory nerve fiber that has a high rate (more than 30 spikes per second) of spontaneous firing; high-spontaneous fibers increase their firing rate in response to relatively low levels of sound. [9]

holistic processing Processing based on analysis of the entire object or scene and not on adding together a set of smaller parts or features. [4]

homologous regions   Brain regions that appear to have the same function in different species. [4]

homunculus   A maplike representation of regions of the body in the brain. [13]

horizontal cell   A specialized retinal cell that contacts both photoreceptor and bipolar cells. [2]

horopter   The location of objects whose images lie on corresponding points. The surface of zero disparity. [6]

hue   The perceptual attribute of colors that enables them to be classed as similar to red, green, or blue, or something in between. [2]

hyperalgesia   An increased or heightened response to a normally painful stimulus. [13]

hypercolumn   A 1-millimeter block of striate cortex containing two sets of columns, each covering every possible orientation (0–180 degrees), with one set preferring input from the left eye and one set preferring input from the right eye. [3]

hyperopia   Farsightedness, a common condition in which light entering the eye is focused behind the retina and accommodation is required in order to see near objects clearly. [2]

hyperpolarization   An change in membrane potential such that the inner membrane surface becomes more negative than the outer membrane surface. [2]

I

illuminant   The light that illuminates a surface. [5]

illusory conjunction   An erroneous combination of two features in a visual scene—for example, seeing a red X when the display contains red letters and Xs but no red Xs. [7]

illusory contour   A contour that is perceived even though nothing changes from one side of it to the other in an image. [4]

image   A picture or likeness. [2]

imbalance   Lack of balance; unsteadiness; nearly falling over. [12]

inattentional blindness   A failure to notice—or at least to report—a stimulus that would be easily reportable if it were attended. [7]

incus   The middle of the three ossicles, connecting the malleus and the stapes. [9]

inferior colliculus   A midbrain nucleus in the auditory pathway. [9]

inferotemporal (IT) cortex   Part of the cerebral cortex in the lower portion of the temporal lobe, important in object recognition. [4]

inhibition of return   The relative difficulty in getting attention (or the eyes) to move back to a recently attended (or fixated) location. [7]

inner ear   A hollow cavity in the temporal bone of the skull, and the structures within this cavity: the cochlea and the semicircular canals of the vestibular system canals. [9]

inner segment   The part of a photoreceptor that lies between the outer segment and the cell nucleus. [2]

insular cortex   The primary cortical processing area for taste—the part of the cortex that first receives taste information. Also called the *insula* or the *gustatory cortex*. [15]

interaural level difference (ILD)   The difference in level (intensity) between a sound arriving at one ear versus the other. [10]

interaural time difference (ITD)   The difference in time between a sound arriving at one ear versus the other. [10]

interocular transfer   The transfer of an effect (such as adaptation) from one eye to the other. [8]

inverse-square law   A principle stating that as distance from a source increases, intensity decreases faster such that decrease in intensity is equal to the distance squared. This general law also applies to optics and other forms of energy. [10]

ipsilateral   Referring to the same side of the body (or brain). [3, 14]

ipsilesional field   The visual field on the same side as a brain lesion. [7]

iris   The colored part of the eye, consisting of a muscular diaphragm surrounding the pupil and regulating the light entering the eye by expanding and contracting the pupil. [2]

isointensity curve   A map plotting the firing rate of an auditory nerve fiber against varying frequencies at varying intensities. [9]

J

just noticeable difference (JND) or difference threshold   The smallest detectable difference between two stimuli, or the minimum change in a stimulus that enables it to be correctly judged as different from a reference stimulus. [1]

juxtaglomerular neurons   The first layer of cells surrounding the glomeruli. They are a mixture of excitatory and inhibitory cells and respond to a wide range of odorants. The selectivity of neurons to specific odorants increases in a gradient from the surface of the olfactory bulb to the deeper layers. [14]

K

kinesthesia   Perception of the position and movement of our limbs in space. [12, 13]

kinesthetic   Referring to perception involving sensory mechanoreceptors in muscles, tendons, and joints. [13]

koniocellular   Referring to cells in the koniocellular layer of the lateral geniculate nucleus of the thalamus. *Konio* from the Greek for "dust" referring to the appearance of the cells. [5]

koniocellular cell   A neuron located between the magnocellular and parvocellular layers of the lateral geniculate nucleus. This layer is known as the koniocellular layer. [2, 3]

L

L-cone   A cone that is preferentially sensitive to long wavelengths; colloquially (but not entirely accurately) known as a "red cone." [5]

labeled lines   A theory of sensory coding in which each nerve fiber carries a particular stimulus quality. For example, a taste nerve fiber that responds best to sucrose but also responds with small responses to other stimuli carries only sweet. [13, 15]

lateral geniculate nucleus (LGN)   A structure in the thalamus, part of the midbrain, that receives input from the retinal ganglion cells and has input and output connections to the visual cortex. [3, 5]

lateral inhibition   Antagonistic neural interaction between adjacent regions of the retina. [2]

lateral superior olive (LSO)   A relay station in the brain stem where inputs from both ears contribute to detection of the interaural level difference. [10]

learned taste aversion The avoidance of a novel flavor after it has been paired with gastric illness. The smell, not the taste, of the substance is key for the learned aversion response in humans. [14]

lens The lens inside the eye that enables the changing of focus. [2]

lesion In reference to neurophysiology, 1. (n) A region of damaged brain. 2. (v) To destroy a section of the brain. [4]

limbic system The group of neural structures that includes the olfactory cortex, the amygdala, the hippocampus, the piriform cortex, and the entorhinal cortex. The limbic system is involved in many aspects of emotion and memory. Olfaction is unique among the senses for its direct connection to the limbic system. [14]

linear acceleration The rate of change of linear velocity. Mathematically, the integral of linear acceleration is linear velocity, and the integral of linear velocity is linear displacement, which is also referred to as "translation." Linear acceleration, linear velocity, and linear displacement all mathematically represent linear motion. [12]

linear motion Translational motion like the predominant movement of a train car or bobblehead doll. [12]

linear perspective A depth cue based on the fact that lines that are parallel in the three-dimensional world will appear to converge in a two-dimensional image. [6]

lordosis The position that females of some species (e.g., pigs and rats) need to assume in order to be impregnated. It involves the downward curving of the spinal column and exposure of the genitals. [14]

loudness The psychological aspect of sound related to perceived intensity (amplitude). [9]

low-spontaneous fiber An auditory nerve fiber that has a low rate (less than 10 spikes per second) of spontaneous firing; low-spontaneous fibers require relatively intense sound before they will fire at higher rates. [9]

luminance-defined object An object that is delineated by differences in reflected light. [8]

M

M ganglion cell A ganglion cell resembling a little umbrella that receives excitatory input from diffuse bipolar cells and feeds the magnocellular layer of the lateral geniculate nucleus. [2]

M-cone A cone that is preferentially sensitive to middle wavelengths; colloquially (but not entirely accurately) known as a "green cone." [5]

macula 1. In reference to vision, The pigmented region with a diameter of about 5.5 mm near the center of the retina. It is sometimes referred to as the macula lutea (from the Latin) because of its yellow appearance. 2. In reference to the vestibular system, any of the specialized detectors of linear acceleration and gravity found in each otolith organ. [2, 12]

magnetic resonance imaging (MRI) An imaging technology that uses the responses of atoms to strong magnetic fields to form images of structures like the brain. The method can be adapted to measure activity in the brain, as well (see *functional magnetic resonance imaging*). [1]

magnetoencephalography (MEG) A technique, similar to electroencephalography, that measures changes in magnetic activity across populations of many neurons in the brain. [1]

magnitude estimation A psychophysical method in which the participant assigns values according to perceived magnitudes of the stimuli. [1]

magnocellular layer Either of the bottom two neuron-containing layers of the lateral geniculate nucleus, the cells of which are physically larger than those in the top four layers. [3]

main olfactory bulb (MOB) The rounded extension of the brain just above the nose that is the first region of the brain where smells are processed. In humans we refer simply to olfactory bulb(s); in nonhuman animals with accessory olfactory bulbs, we distinguish between main and accessory. [14]

malleus One of the three ossicles. The malleus receives vibration from the tympanic membrane and is attached to the incus. [9]

masking Using a second sound, frequently noise, to make the detection of another sound more difficult. [9]

materialism The idea that the only thing that exists is matter, and that all things, including the mind and consciousness, are the results of interaction between bits of matter. [1]

mathematical integration Computing an integral—one of the two main operations in calculus (the other, the inverse operation, is differentiation). Velocity is the integral of acceleration. Change of position is the integral of velocity. [12]

mechanoreceptor A sensory receptor that responds to mechanical stimulation (pressure, vibration, or movement). [12, 13]

medial geniculate nucleus The part of the thalamus that relays auditory signals to the temporal cortex and receives input from the auditory cortex. [9]

medial superior olive (MSO) A relay station in the brain stem where inputs from both ears contribute to detection of the interaural time difference. [10]

Meissner corpuscle A specialized nerve ending associated with fast-adapting (FA I) fibers that have small receptive fields. [13]

melanopsin A photopigment, found in a class of photoreceptive retinal ganglion cells, that is sensitive to ambient light. [2, 5]

melody A sequence of notes or chords perceived as a single coherent structure. [11]

Merkel cell neurite complex A specialized nerve ending associated with slowly adapting (SA I) fibers that have small receptive fields. [13]

mesoptic Referring to the middle range of light intensities. [5]

metamers Different mixtures of wavelengths that look identical. More generally, any pair of stimuli that are perceived as identical in spite of physical differences. [5]

method of adjustment A method of limits in which the participant controls the change in the stimulus. [1]

method of constant stimuli A psychophysical method in which many stimuli, ranging from rarely to almost always perceivable (or rarely to almost always perceivably different from a reference stimulus), are presented one at a time. Participants respond to each presentation: "yes/no," "same/different," and so on. [1]

method of limits A psychophysical method in which the particular dimension of a stimulus, or the difference between two stimuli, is varied incrementally until the participant responds differently. [1]

metrical depth cue A depth cue that provides quantitative information about distance in the third dimension. [6]

microsaccade An involuntary, small, jerklike eye movement. [8]

microvilli Slender projections of the cell membrane on the tips of some taste bud cells that extend into the taste pore. [15]

mid-spontaneous fiber An auditory nerve fiber that has a medium rate (10–30 spikes per second) of spontaneous firing. The characteristics of mid-spontaneous fibers are intermediate between low- and high-spontaneous fibers. [9]

mid-level (or middle) vision A loosely defined stage of visual processing that comes after basic features have been extracted from the image (low-level, or early, vision) and before object recognition and scene understanding (high-level vision). [4]

middle canal One of three fluid-filled passages in the cochlea. The middle canal is sandwiched between the tympanic and vestibular canals and contains the cochlear partition. Also called *scala media*. [9]

middle ear An air-filled chamber containing the middle bones, or ossicles. The middle ear conveys and amplifies vibration from the tympanic membrane to the oval window. [9]

middle temporal area (MT) An area of the brain thought to be important in the perception of motion. Also called *V5* in humans. [8]

midget bipolar cell A small bipolar cell in the central retina that receives input from a single cone. [2]

mitral cell The deepest layer of neurons in the olfactory bulb. Each mitral cell responds to only to a few specific odorants. [14]

monocular Referring to one eye. [6]

monocular depth cue A depth cue that is available even when the world is viewed with one eye alone. [6]

monosodium glutamate (MSG) The sodium salt of glutamic acid (an amino acid). [15]

motion aftereffect (MAE) The illusion of motion of a stationary object that occurs after prolonged exposure to a moving object. [8]

motion parallax An important depth cue that is based on head movement. The geometric information obtained from an eye in two different positions at two different times is similar to the information from two eyes in different positions in the head at the same time. [6]

myopia Nearsightedness, a common condition in which light entering the eye is focused in front of the retina and distant objects cannot be seen sharply. [2]

N

nasal dominance The asymmetry characterizing the intake of air by the two nostrils, which leads to differing sensitivity to odorants between the two nostrils. Nasal dominance alternates nostrils throughout the day, but there is no predictability about when the nostrils alternate. [14]

Necker cube An outline that is perceptually bi-stable. Unlike the situation with most stimuli, two interpretations continually battle for perceptual dominance. [4]

negative afterimage An afterimage whose polarity is the opposite of the original stimulus. Light stimuli produce dark negative afterimages. Colors are complementary; for example, red produces green, and yellow produces blue. [5]

neglect As a neurological symptom, in visual attention: (1) The inability to attend or respond to stimuli in the contralesional visual field (typically, the left field after right parietal damage). (2) Ignoring half of the body or half of an object. [7]

neural plasticity The ability of neural circuits to undergo changes in function or organization as a result of previous activity. [13]

neuroimaging A set of methods that generate images of the structure and/or function of the brain. In many cases, these methods allow us to examine the brain in living, behaving humans. [1]

neurotransmitter A chemical substance used in neuronal communication at synapses. [1]

neutral point The point at which an opponent color mechanism is generating no signal. If red-green and blue-yellow mechanisms are at their neutral points, a stimulus will appear achromatic. (The black-white process has no neutral point.) [5]

nociceptor A sensory receptor that responds to painful input, such as extreme heat or pressure. [13]

nonaccidental feature A feature of an object that is not dependent on the exact (or accidental) viewing position of the observer. [4]

nonmetrical depth cue A depth cue that provides information about the depth order (relative depth) but not depth magnitude (e.g., his nose is in front of his face). [6]

nontaster (of PTC/PROP) An individual born with two recessive alleles for the *TAS2R38* gene and unable to taste the compounds phenylthiocarbamide (PTC) and propylthiouracil (PROP). [15]

O

occlusion A cue to relative depth order in which, for example, one object obstructs the view of part of another object. [6]

octave The interval between two sound frequencies having a ratio of 2:1. [11]

ocular dominance The property of the receptive fields of striate cortex neurons by which they demonstrate a preference, responding somewhat more rapidly when a stimulus is presented in one eye than when it is presented in the other. [3]

oculomotor (III) nerves The third pair of cranial nerves, which innervate all the extrinsic muscles of the eye except the lateral rectus and the superior oblique muscles, and which innervate the elevator muscle of the upper eyelid, the ciliary muscle, and the sphincter muscle of the pupil. [1]

odor The translation of a chemical stimulus into the sensation of an odor percept. For example, "The cake has a chocolate odor." [14]

odor hedonics The liking dimension of odor perception, typically measured by ratings of an odor's perceived pleasantness, familiarity, and intensity. [14]

odorant A molecule that is defined by its physicochemical characteristics, and that can be translated by the nervous system into the perception of a smell. For example, "You smelled the odorant methyl salicylate, which has the odor of wintergreen mint." [14]

odorant receptor (OR) The region on the cilia of olfactory sensory neurons where odorant molecules bind. [14]

OFF bipolar cell A bipolar cell that hyperpolarizes in response to an increase in light captured captured by the cones. [2]

OFF-center cell A cell that increases firing in response to a decrease in light intensity in its receptive-field center. [2]

olfaction The sense of smell. [14]

olfactory bulb A blueberry-sized extension of the brain just above the nose, where olfactory information is first processed. There are two olfactory bulbs, one in each brain hemisphere, corresponding to the right and left nostrils. [14]

olfactory cleft A narrow space at the back of the nose into which air flows and where the olfactory epithelium is located. [14]

olfactory epithelium A secretory mucous membrane in the human nose whose primary function is to detect odorants in inhaled air. Located on both sides of the upper portion of the nasal cavity and the olfactory clefts, the olfactory epithelium contains three types of cells: olfactory sensory neurons, basal cells, and supporting cells. [14]

olfactory (I) nerves The first pair of cranial nerves. The axons of the olfactory sensory neurons bundle together after passing through the cribriform plate to form the olfactory nerve, which conducts impulses from the olfactory epithelia in the nose to the olfactory bulb. [1, 14]

olfactory sensory neuron (OSN) One of three cell types—the main one—in the olfactory epithelium. OSNs are small neurons located beneath a mucous layer in the epithelium. The cilia on the OSN dendrites contain the receptor sites for odorant molecules. [14]

olfactory tract The bundle of axons of the mitral and tufted cells within the olfactory bulb that sends odor information to the primary olfactory cortex. [14]

olfactory white The olfactory equivalent of white noise or the color white. When at least 30 odorants of equal intensity that span olfactory physiochemical and psychological (perceptual) space are mixed, they produce a resultant odor perception that is the same as that of every other mixture of 30 odorants meeting the same span and equivalent intensity criteria, even though the various

mixtures do not share any common odorants. [14]

ON bipolar cell A bipolar cell that depolarizes in response to an increase in light captured by the cones. [2]

ON-center cell A cell that increases firing in response to an increase in light intensity in its receptive-field center. [2]

opponent color theory The theory that perception of color is based on the output of three mechanisms, each of them resulting from an opponency between two colors: red-green, blue-yellow, and black-white. [5]

optic array The collection of light rays that interact with objects in the world that are in front of a viewer. Term coined by J. J. Gibson. [8]

optic flow The pattern of apparent motion of objects in a visual scene produced by the relative motion between the observer and the scene. [6, 8]

optic (II) nerves The second pair of cranial nerves, which arise from the retina and carry visual information to the thalamus and other parts of the brain. [1]

optokinetic nystagmus (OKN) A reflexive eye movement in which the eyes will involuntarily track a continually moving object. [8]

orbitofrontal cortex (OFC) The part of the frontal lobe of the cortex that lies behind the bone (orbit) containing the eyes. The OFC is responsible for the conscious experience of olfaction, as well as the integration of pleasure and displeasure from food; and it has been referred to as the *secondary olfactory cortex* and the *secondary taste cortex*. The OFC is also involved in many other functions, and it is critical for assigning affective value to stimuli—in other words, determining hedonic meaning. [14, 15]

organ of Corti A structure on the basilar membrane of the cochlea that is composed of hair cells and dendrites of auditory nerve fibers. [9]

orientation tuning The tendency of neurons in striate cortex to respond optimally to certain orientations and less to others. [3]

orthonasal olfaction Sniffing in and perceiving odors through our nostrils, which occurs when we are smelling something that is in the air. [14]

oscillatory Referring to back-and-forth movement that has a constant rhythm. [12]

ossicle Any of three tiny bones of the middle ear: malleus, incus, and stapes. [9]

otitis media Inflammation of the middle ear, commonly in children as a result of infection. [9]

otoconia Tiny calcium carbonate stones in the ear that provide inertial mass for the otolith organs, enabling them to sense gravity and linear acceleration. [12]

otolith organ Either of two mechanical structures (utricle and saccule) in the vestibular system that sense both linear acceleration and gravity. [12]

otosclerosis Abnormal growth of the middle-ear bones that causes hearing loss. [9]

outer ear The external sound-gathering portion of the ear, consisting of the pinna and the ear canal. [9]

outer segment The part of a photoreceptor that contains photopigment molecules. [2]

oval window The flexible opening to the cochlea through which the stapes transmits vibration to the fluid inside. [9]

P

P ganglion cell A small ganglion cell that receives excitatory input from single midget bipolar cells in the central retina and feeds the parvocellular layer of the lateral geniculate nucleus. [2]

Pacinian corpuscle A specialized nerve ending associated with fast-adapting (FA II) fibers that have large receptive fields. [13]

panpsychism The idea that the mind exists as a property of all matter—that is, that all matter has consciousness. [1]

Panum's fusional area The region of space, in front of and behind the horopter, within which binocular single vision is possible. [6]

papilla (pl. *papillae*) Any of multiple structures that give the tongue its bumpy appearance. From smallest to largest, the papilla types that contain taste buds are fungiform, foliate, and circumvallate; filiform papillae, which do not contain taste buds, are the smallest and most numerous. [15]

parabelt area A region of cortex, lateral and adjacent to the belt area, where neurons respond to more complex characteristics of sounds, as well as to input from other senses. [9]

parahippocampal place area (PPA) A region of extrastriate visual cortex in humans that is specifically and reliably activated more by images of places than by other stimuli. [4, 7]

parallel search A search in which multiple stimuli are processed at the same time. [7]

parallelism A rule for figure-ground assignment stating that parallel contours are likely to belong to the same figure. [4]

parietal lobe In each cerebral hemisphere, a lobe that lies toward the top of the brain between the frontal and occipital lobes. [7]

parvocellular Referring to cells in the parvocellular layers of the lateral geniculate nucleus of the thalamus. *Parvo* from the Greek for "small" referring to the size of the cells. [5]

parvocellular layer Any of the top four neuron-containing layers of the lateral geniculate nucleus, the cells of which are physically smaller than those in the bottom two layers. [3]

perception The act of giving meaning to a detected sensation. [1]

period In reference to hearing, the time required for a full wavelength of an acoustic sine wave to pass by a point in space. [1]

phantom limb Sensation perceived from a physically amputated limb of the body. [13]

phase 1. A fraction of the cycle of the sine wave described in degrees (0° to 360°) or radians (0π to 2π). In reference to hearing, phase can be used to describe fractions of a period that relate to time. 2. The relative position of a grating. [1, 3]

phase locking Firing of a single neuron at one distinct point in the period (cycle) of a sound wave at a given frequency. (The neuron need not fire on every cycle, but each firing will occur at the same point in the cycle.) [9]

pheromone A chemical emitted by one member of a species that triggers a physiological or behavioral response in another member of the same species. Pheromones are signals for chemical communication and may or may not have any smell. [14]

phonation The process through which vocal folds are made to vibrate when air pushes out of the lungs. [11]

photoactivation Activation by light. [2]

photon A quantum of visible light or other form of electromagnetic radiation demonstrating both particle and wave properties. [2]

photopic Referring to light intensities that are bright enough to stimulate the cone receptors and bright enough to "saturate" the rod receptors (that is, drive them to their maximum responses). [5]

photoreceptor A light-sensitive receptor in the retina. [2]

pictorial depth cue A cue to distance or depth used by artists to depict three-dimensional depth in two-dimensional pictures. [6]

pinna (pl. *pinnae*) The outer, funnel-like part of the ear. [9]

pitch The psychological aspect of sound related mainly on the frequency of vibration. [9, 11]

place code Tuning of different parts of the cochlea to different frequencies, in which information about the particular frequency of an incoming sound wave is coded by the place along the cochlear partition that has the greatest mechanical displacement. [9]

placebo effect Decreasing pain sensation when people think they're taking an analgesic drug but actually are not. [13]

polysensory Referring to blending multiple sensory systems. [1]

positivism A philosophical position arguing that all we really have to go on is the evidence of the senses, so the world might be nothing more than an elaborate hallucination. [6]

positron emission tomography (PET) An imaging technology that enables us to define locations in the brain where neurons are especially active by measuring the metabolism of brain cells using safe radioactive isotopes. [1]

preattentive stage The processing of a stimulus that occurs before selective attention is deployed to that stimulus. [7]

presbyopia Literally "old sight." The age-related loss of accommodation, which makes it difficult to focus on near objects. [2]

primary auditory cortex (A1) The first area within the temporal lobes of the brain responsible for processing acoustic information. [9]

primary olfactory cortex or piriform cortex The neural area where olfactory information is first processed. It comprises the amygdala, parahippocampal gyrus, and interconnected areas, and it interacts closely with the entorhinal cortex. [14]

primary visual cortex (V1), area 17, or striate cortex The area of the cerebral cortex of the brain that receives direct inputs from the lateral geniculate nucleus, as well as feedback from other brain areas. [3]

primer pheromone A pheromone that triggers a physiological (often hormonal) change among conspecifics. This effect usually involves prolonged pheromone exposure. [14]

principle of univariance The fact that an infinite set of different wavelength-intensity combinations can elicit exactly the same response from a single type of photoreceptor. One photoreceptor type cannot make color discriminations based on wavelength. [5]

probability summation The increased detection probability based on the statistical advantage of having two (or more) detectors rather than one. [6]

projective geometry For purposes of studying perception of the three-dimensional world, the geometry that describes the transformations that occur when the three-dimensional world is *projected* onto a two-dimensional surface. For example, parallel lines do not converge in the real world, but they do in the two-dimensional projection of that world. [6]

proprioception Perception mediated by kinesthetic and internal receptors. [13]

prosopagnosia An inability to recognize faces. [4]

protanope An individual who suffers from color blindness that is due to the absence of L-cones. [5]

proximity A Gestalt grouping rule stating that the tendency of two features to group together will increase as the distance between them decreases. [4]

psychoacoustics The study of the psychological correlates of the physical dimensions of acoustics; a branch of psychophysics. [9]

psychophysics The science of defining quantitative relationships between physical and psychological (subjective, perceptual) events. [1, 14]

pupil The dark, circular opening at the center of the iris in the eye, where light enters the eye. [2]

Q

qualia (sing. *quale***)** In reference to philosophy, private conscious experiences of sensation or perception. [1, 5]

R

random dot stereogram (RDS) A stereogram made of a large number (often in the thousands) of randomly placed dots. Random dot stereograms contain no monocular cues to depth. Stimuli visible stereoscopically in random dot stereograms are Cyclopean stimuli. [6]

rapid serial visual presentation (RSVP) An experimental procedure in which stimuli appear in a stream at one location (typically the point of fixation) at a rapid rate (typically about eight per second). [7]

rate saturation The point at which a nerve fiber is firing as rapidly as possible and further stimulation is incapable of increasing the firing rate. [9]

rate-intensity function A graph plotting the firing rate of an auditory nerve fiber in response to a sound of constant frequency at increasing intensities. [9]

reaction time (RT) A measure of the time from the onset of a stimulus to a response. [7]

realism A philosophical position arguing that there is a real world to sense. [6]

receiver operating characteristic (ROC) curve In reference to studies of signal detection, the graphical plot of the hit rate as a function of the false-alarm rate. If these are the same, points fall on the diagonal, indicating that the observer cannot tell the difference between the presence and absence of the signal. As the observer's sensitivity increases, the curve bows upward toward the upper left corner. That point represents a perfect ability to distinguish signal from noise (100% hits, 0% false alarms). [1]

receptive field The region on the retina in which visual stimuli influence a neuron's firing rate. [2]

receptor adaptation The biochemical phenomenon, that occurs after continual exposure to an odorant, whereby receptors are no longer available to respond to the odorant and detection ceases. [14]

receptor potential A change in voltage across the membrane of a sensory receptor cell (in the vestibular system, a hair cell) in response to stimulation. [12]

recognition-by-components model Biederman's model of object recognition, which holds that objects are recognized by the identities and relationships of their component parts. [4]

reflect To redirect something that strikes a surface—especially light, sound, or heat—usually back toward its point of origin. [2]

reflectance The percentage of light hitting a surface that is reflected and not absorbed into the surface. Typically reflectance is given as a function of wavelength. [5]

reflexive eye movement A movement of the eye that is automatic and involuntary. [8]

refract 1. To alter the course of a wave of energy that passes into something from another medium, as water does to light entering it from the air. 2. To measure the degree of refraction in a lens or eye. [2]

refractive error A very common disorder in which the image of the world is not clearly focused on the retina. The most common refractive errors are: myopia, hyperopia, astigmatism and presbyopia. [2]

Reissner's membrane A thin sheath of tissue separating the vestibular and middle canals in the cochlea. [9]

relatability The degree to which two line segments appear to be part of the same contour. [4]

related color A color, such as brown or gray, that is seen only in relation to other colors. For example, a "gray" patch in complete darkness appears white. [5]

relative height As a depth cue, the observation that objects at different distances from the viewer on the ground plane will form images at different heights in the retinal image.

Objects farther away will be seen as higher in the image. [6]

relative metrical depth cue A depth cue that could specify, for example, that object A is twice as far away as object B without providing information about the absolute distance to either A or B. [6]

relative size A comparison of size between items without knowing the absolute size of either one. [6]

releaser pheromone A pheromone that triggers an immediate behavioral response among conspecifics. [14]

response enhancement An effect of attention on the response of a neuron in which the neuron responding to an attended stimulus gives a bigger response. [7]

retina A light-sensitive membrane in the back of the eye that contains photoreceptors and other cell types that transduce light into electrochemical signals and transmits them to the brain through the optic nerve. [2]

retinitis pigmentosa (RP) A progressive degeneration of the retina that affects night vision and peripheral vision. RP commonly runs in families and can be caused by defects in a number of different genes that have recently been identified. [2]

retronasal olfaction Perceiving odors through the mouth while breathing and chewing. This is what gives us the experience of flavor. [14]

retronasal olfactory sensation The sensation of an odor that is perceived when chewing and swallowing force an odorant in the mouth up behind the palate into the nose. Such odor sensations are perceived as originating from the mouth, even though the actual contact of odorant and receptor occurs at the olfactory mucosa. [15]

reverse-hierarchy theory A theory that fast, feed-forward processes can give your crude information about objects and scenes based on activity in high-level parts of the visual cortex. You become aware of details when activity flows back down the hierarchy of visual areas to lower-level areas where the detailed information is preserved. [4]

rhodopsin The visual pigment found in rods. [2]

rod A photoreceptor specialized for night vision. [2]

rod monochromat An individual with no cones of any type. In addition to being truly color-blind, rod monochromats are badly visually impaired in bright light. [5]

round window A soft area of tissue at the base of the tympanic canal that releases excess pressure remaining from extremely intense sounds. [9]

Ruffini ending A specialized nerve ending associated with slowly adapting (SA II) fibers that have large receptive fields. [13]

S

S-cone A cone that is preferentially sensitive to short wavelengths; colloquially (but not entirely accurately) known as a "blue cone." [5]

saccade A type of eye movement, made both voluntarily and involuntarily, in which the eyes rapidly change fixation from one object or location to another. [8]

saccadic suppression The reduction of visual sensitivity that occurs when we make saccadic eye movements. Saccadic suppression eliminates the smear from retinal image motion during an eye movement. [8]

saccule One of the two otolith organs. A saclike structure that contains the saccular macula. Also called *sacculus*. [12]

salience The vividness of a stimulus relative to its neighbors. [7]

salty One of the four basic tastes; the taste quality produced by the cations of salts (e.g., the sodium in sodium chloride produces the salty taste). Some cations also produce other taste qualities (e.g., potassium tastes bitter as well as salty). The purest salty taste is produced by sodium chloride (NaCl), common table salt. [15]

scatter To disperse something—such as light—in an irregular fashion. [2]

scene-based guidance Information in our understanding of scenes that helps us find specific objects in scenes (e.g., objects do not float in air, faucets are near sinks). [7]

scotopic Referring to light intensities that are bright enough to stimulate the rod receptors but too dim to stimulate the cone receptors. [5]

second-order motion The motion of an object that is defined by changes

in contrast or texture, but not by luminance. [8]

selective attention The form of attention involved when processing is restricted to a subset of the possible stimuli. [7]

semicircular canal Any of three toroidal tubes in the vestibular system that sense angular motion. [12]

sensation The ability to detect a stimulus and, perhaps, to turn that detection into a private experience. [1]

sense of angular motion The perceptual modality that senses rotation. [12]

sense of linear motion The perceptual modality that senses translation. [12]

sense of tilt The perceptual modality that senses head inclination with respect to gravity. [12]

sensitivity 1. The ability to perceive via the sense organs. 2. Extreme responsiveness to radiation, especially to light of a specific wavelength. 3. The ability to respond to transmitted signals. 4. In reference to signal detection theory, a value that defines the ease with which an observer can tell the difference between the presence and absence of a stimulus or the difference between Stimulus 1 and Stimulus 2. [1, 2]

sensorineural hearing loss Hearing loss due to defects in the cochlea or auditory nerve. [9]

sensory conflict Sensory discrepancies that arise when sensory systems provide conflicting information. For example, vision may indicate that you are stationary while the vestibular system tells you that you are moving (or vice versa). [12]

sensory exafference Change in afference caused by external stimuli. For the vestibular system, vestibular afference evoked by passive head motion would yield sensory exafference. Compare *sensory reafference*. [12]

sensory integration The process of combining different sensory signals. Typically, combining several signals yields more accurate and/or more precise information than can be obtained from individual sensory signals. This is *not* the mathematical process of integration learned in calculus (e.g., the integral of acceleration is velocity). [12]

sensory reafference Change in afference caused by self-generated activity. For the vestibular system, vestibular afference evoked by an active self-generated head motion would yield sensory reafference. Compare *sensory exafference*. [12]

serial self-terminating search A search from item to item, ending when a target is found. [7]

set size The number of items in a visual display. [7]

shape-pattern theory The current dominant biochemical theory for how chemicals come to be perceived as specific odors. Shape-pattern theory contends that different scents—as a function of the fit between odorant shape and OR shape—activate different arrays of olfactory receptors in the olfactory epithelia. These various arrays produce specific firing patterns of neurons in the olfactory bulbs, which then determine the particular scent we perceive. [14]

sharper tuning An effect of attention on the response of a neuron in which the neuron responding to an attended stimulus responds more precisely. For example, a neuron that responds to lines with orientations from −20 degrees to +20 degrees might come to respond to ±10-degree lines. [7]

signal detection theory A psychophysical theory that quantifies the response of an observer to the presentation of a signal in the presence of noise. Measures obtained from a series of presentations are sensitivity (*d′*) and criterion of the observer. [1]

similarity A Gestalt grouping rule stating that the tendency of two features to group together will increase as the similarity between them increases. For example, in hearing, the tendency of two sounds to group together will increase as the acoustic similarity between them increases. [4, 10]

simple cell A cortical neuron whose receptive field has clearly defined excitatory and inhibitory regions. [3]

simultagnosia An inability to perceive more than one object at a time. Simultagnosia is a consequence of bilateral damage to the parietal lobes (Balint syndrome). [7]

sine wave A simple, smoothly changing oscillation that repeats across space. Higher-frequency sine waves have more oscillations, and lower frequencies have fewer oscillations, over a given distance. 1. In reference to hearing, a waveform for which variation as a function of time is a sine function. Also called *pure tone*. 2. In reference to vision, a *pattern* for which variation in a property like brightness or color as a function of space is a sine function. [1, 9]

sine wave grating   A grating with a sinusoidal luminance profile as shown in Figure 3.4A. [3]

single-opponent cell   Another way to refer to cone-opponent cells, in order to differentiate them from double-opponent cells. [5]

sinusoidal   Referring to any oscillation, such as a sound wave or rotational motion, whose waveform is that of a sine curve. The period of a sinusoidal oscillation is the time that it takes for one full back-and-forth cycle of the motion to occur. The frequency of a sinusoidal oscillation is defined as the numeral 1 divided by the period. [12]

smooth pursuit   A type of voluntary eye movement in which the eyes move smoothly to follow a moving object. [8]

somatosensation   Collectively, sensory signals from the skin, muscles, tendons, joints, and internal receptors. [13]

somatosensory area 1 (S1)   The primary receiving area for touch in the cortex. [13]

somatosensory area 2 (S2)   The secondary receiving area for touch in the cortex. [13]

somatotopic   Referring to spatial mapping in the somatosensory cortex in correspondence to spatial events on the skin. [13]

somatotypical   Referring to normal somatosensation. [13]

sour   One of the four basic tastes; the taste quality produced by the hydrogen ion in acids. [15]

source segregation or auditory scene analysis   Processing an auditory scene consisting of multiple sound sources into separate sound images. [10]

spatial disorientation   Any impairment of spatial orientation. More specifically, any impairment of our sense of linear motion, angular motion, or tilt. [12]

spatial frequency   The number of cycles of a grating (e.g., changes in light and dark) per unit of visual angle (usually specified in cycles per degree). [1, 3]

spatial layout   The description of the structure of a scene (e.g., enclosed, open, rough, smooth) without reference to the identity of specific objects in the scene. [7]

spatial orientation   A sense consisting of three interacting modalities: perception of linear motion, angular motion, and tilt. [12]

spatial-frequency channel   A pattern analyzer, implemented by an ensemble of cortical neurons, in which each set of neurons is tuned to a limited range of spatial frequencies. [3]

specific anosmia   The inability to smell one specific compound amid otherwise normal smell perception. [14]

specific hungers theory   The idea that deficiency of a given nutrient produces craving (a specific hunger) for that nutrient. Curt Richter first proposed this theory and demonstrated that cravings for salty or for sweet are associated with deficiencies in those substances. However, the idea proved wrong for other nutrients (e.g., vitamins). [15]

spectral power distribution   The physical energy in a light as a function of wavelength. [5]

spectral reflectance function   The percentage of a particular wavelength that is reflected from a surface. [5]

spectral sensitivity   The sensitivity of a cell or a device to different wavelengths on the electromagnetic spectrum. [5]

spectrogram   In sound analysis, a three-dimensional display that plots time on the horizontal axis, frequency on the vertical axis, and amplitude (intensity) on a color or gray scale. [11]

spectrum   A representation of the relative energy (intensity) present at each frequency. [9]

spinothalamic pathway   The route from the spinal cord to the brain that carries most of the information about skin temperature and pain. [13]

staircase method   A psychophysical method for determining the concentration of a stimulus required for detection at the threshold level. The staircase method is an example of a *method of limits*. A stimulus (e.g., odorant) is presented in an ascending concentration sequence until detection is indicated, and then the concentration is shifted to a descending sequence until the response changes to "no detection." This ascending and descending sequence is typically repeated several times, and the concentrations at which reversals occur are averaged to determine the threshold detection level of that odorant for a given individual. Also called *reverse staircase method*. [14]

stapedius   The muscle attached to the stapes; tensing the stapedius decreases vibration. [9]

stapes   One of the three ossicles. Connected to the incus on one end, the stapes presses against the oval window of the cochlea on the other end. [9]

stereoacuity   A measure of the smallest binocular disparity that can generate a sensation of depth. [6]

stereoblindness   An inability to make use of binocular disparity as a depth cue. This term is typically used to describe individuals with vision in both eyes. Someone who has lost one (or both) eyes is not typically described as "stereoblind." [6]

stereocilium   Any of the hairlike extensions on the tips of hair cells in the cochlea that, when flexed, initiate the release of neurotransmitters. [9]

stereoisomers   Isomers (molecules that can exist in different structural forms) in which the spatial arrangements of the atoms are mirror-image rotations of one another, like a right and left hand. [14]

stereopsis   The ability to use binocular disparity as a cue to depth. [6]

stereoscope   A device for simultaneously presenting one image to one eye and another image to the other eye. Stereoscopes can be used to present dichoptic stimuli for stereopsis and binocular rivalry. [6]

Stevens's power law   A principle describing the relationship between stimulus and resulting sensation that says the magnitude of subjective sensation is proportional to the stimulus magnitude raised to an exponent. [1]

stimulus onset asynchrony (SOA)   The time between the onset of one stimulus and the onset of another. [7]

strabismus   A misalignment of the two eyes such that a single object in space is imaged on the fovea of one eye and on a nonfoveal area of the other (turned) eye. [3, 6]

structural description   A description of an object in terms of the nature of its constituent parts and the relationships between those parts. [4]

structuralism   A school of thought believing that complex objects or perceptions could be understood by analysis of the components. [4]

substantia gelatinosa   A region of interconnecting neurons in the dorsal horn of the spinal cord. [13]

subtraction method   In function magnetic imaging, brain activity is measured in two conditions: one with and one without the involvement of the mental process of interest. Subtracting the two conditions shows regions of brain specifically activated by that process. [4]

subtractive color mixture   A mixture of pigments. If pigments A and B mix, some of the light shining on the surface will be subtracted by A, and some by B. Only the remainder will contribute to the perception of color. [5]

superior colliculus   A structure in the midbrain that is important in initiating and guiding eye movements. [8]

superior olive   An early brain stem region in the auditory pathway where inputs from both ears converge. [9]

supertaster   An individual who experiences the most intense taste sensations. Some stimuli are dramatically more intense for supertasters than for medium tasters or nontasters. Supertasters also tend to experience more intense oral burn and oral touch sensations. A variety of factors may contribute to this heightened perception, among the most important is the density of fungiform papillae. [1, 15]

supporting cell   One of the three types of cells in the olfactory epithelium. Supporting cells provide metabolic and physical support for the olfactory sensory neurons. [14]

suppression   In vision, the inhibition of an unwanted image. Suppression occurs frequently in people with strabismus. [6]

surroundedness   A rule for figure-ground assignment stating that if one region is entirely surrounded by another, it is likely that the surrounded region is the figure. [4]

sweet   One of the four basic tastes; the taste quality produced by some sugars, such as glucose, fructose, and sucrose. These three sugars are particularly biologically useful to us, and our sweet receptors are tuned to them. Some other compounds (e.g., saccharin, cyclamate, aspartame) are also sweet. [15]

symmetry   A rule for figure-ground assignment stating that symmetrical regions are more likely to be seen as figure. [4]

synapse   The junction between neurons that permits information transfer. [1]

synaptic terminal   The location where axons terminate at the synapse for transmission of information by the release of a chemical transmitter. [2]

syncopation   Any deviation from a regular rhythm. [11]

T

tactile   Referring to the result of mechanical interactions with the skin.

tactile agnosia   The inability to identify objects by touch. [13]

target   The goal of a visual search. [7]

tastant   Any stimulus that can be tasted. [15]

taste   Sensations evoked by solutions in the mouth that contact receptors on the tongue and the roof of the mouth that then connect to axons in cranial nerves VII, IX, and X. [15]

taste bud   A globular cluster of cells that has the function of creating neural signals conveyed to the brain by the taste nerves. Some of the cells in a taste bud have specialized sites on their apical projections that interact with taste stimuli. Some of the cells form synapses with taste nerve fibers. [15]

taste receptor cell   A cell within the taste bud that contains sites on its apical projection that can interact with taste stimuli. These sites fall into two major categories: those interacting with charged particles (e.g., sodium and hydrogen ions), and those interacting with specific chemical structures. [15]

taster (of PTC/PROP)   An individual born with one or both dominant alleles for the *TAS2R38* gene and able to taste the compounds phenylthiocarbamide (PTC) and propylthiouracil (PROP). PTC/PROP tasters who also

have a high density of fungiform papillae are PROP supertasters. [15]

tau (τ)   Information in the optic flow that could signal time to collision (TTC) without the necessity of estimating either absolute distances or rates. The ratio of the retinal image size at any moment to the rate at which the image is expanding is tau, and TTC is proportional to tau. [8]

tectorial membrane   A gelatinous structure, attached on one end, that extends into the middle canal of the ear, floating above inner hair cells and touching outer hair cells. [9]

template   The internal representation of a stimulus that is used to recognize the stimulus in the world. Unlike its use in, for example, making a key, a mental template is not expected to actually look like the stimulus that it matches. [4]

tempo   The perceived speed of the presentation of sounds. [11]

temporal code   Tuning of different parts of the cochlea to different frequencies, in which information about the particular frequency of an incoming sound wave is coded by the timing of neural firing as it relates to the period of the sound. [9]

temporal integration   The process by which a sound at a constant level is perceived as being louder when it is of greater duration. The term also applies to perceived brightness, which depends on the duration of light. [9]

tensor tympani   The muscle attached to the malleus; tensing the tensor tympani decreases vibration. [9]

tetrachromatic   Referring to the rare situation (in humans, at least) where the color of any light is defined by the relationships of four numbers—the outputs of those four receptor types. [5]

texture gradient   A depth cue based on the geometric fact that items of the same size form smaller images when they are farther away. An array of items that change in size smoothly across the image will appear to form a surface tilted in depth. [6]

texture segmentation   Carving an image into regions of common texture properties. [4]

texture-defined object or contrast-defined object   An object that is defined by differences in contrast, or texture, but not by luminance. [8]

thermoreceptor A sensory receptor that signals information about changes in skin temperature. [13]

threshold tuning curve A graph plotting the thresholds of a neuron or fiber in response to sine waves with varying frequencies at the lowest intensity that will give rise to a response. [9]

tilt To attain a sloped position like that of the Leaning Tower of Pisa. [12]

tilt aftereffect The perceptual illusion of tilt, produced by adaptation to a pattern of a given orientation. [3, 6]

timbre The psychological sensation by which a listener can judge that two sounds with the same loudness and pitch are dissimilar. Timbre quality is conveyed by harmonics and other high frequencies. [9, 10]

time to collision (TTC) The time required for a moving object (such as a cricket ball) to hit a stationary object (such as a batsman's head). TTC = distance/rate. [8]

tip link A tiny filament that stretches from the tip of a stereocilium to the side of its neighbor. [9]

tip-of-the-nose phenomenon The inability to name an odor, even though it is very familiar. Contrary to the tip-of-the-tongue phenomenon, one has no lexical access to the name of the odor, such as first letter, rhyme, number of syllables, and so on, when in the tip-of-the-nose state. This is an example of how language and olfactory perception are deeply disconnected. [14]

tone chroma A sound quality shared by tones that have the same octave interval. [11]

tone height A sound quality corresponding to the level of pitch. Tone height is monotonically related to frequency. [11]

tonotopic organization An arrangement in which neurons that respond to different frequencies are organized anatomically in order of frequency. [9]

topographical mapping The orderly mapping of the world in the lateral geniculate nucleus and the visual cortex. [3]

touch The sensations caused by stimulation of the skin, muscles, tendons, and joints. [13]

transduce To convert from one form of energy to another (e.g., from light to neural electrical energy, or from mechanical movement to neural electrical energy). Neurons use electrical signals in their communications. [2, 12]

transmit To convey something (e.g., light) from one place or thing to another. [2]

transparent Referring to the characteristic of a material that allows light to pass through it with no interruption such that objects on the other side can be clearly seen. [2]

triangle test A test in which a participant is given three odorants to smell, of which two are the same and one is different. The participant is required to state which is the odd odor out. Typically, the order in which the three odorants are given (e.g., same, same, different; different, same, same; same, different, same) is manipulated and the test is repeated several times for greater accuracy. [14]

trichromacy or trichromatic theory of color vision The theory that the color of any light is defined in our visual system by the relationships of three numbers—the outputs of three receptor types now known to be the three cones. Also called the *Young-Helmholtz theory*. [5]

trigeminal (V) nerve The fifth cranial nerve, which transmits information about the "feel" of an odorant (e.g., mint feels cool, cinnamon feels warm), as well as pain and irritation sensations (e.g., ammonia feels burning). [14]

tritanope An individual who suffers from color blindness that is due to the absence of S-cones. [5]

trochlear (IV) nerves The fourth pair of cranial nerves, which innervate the superior oblique muscles of the eyeballs. [1]

tufted cells The next layer of cells after the juxtaglomerular neurons. They respond to fewer odorants than the juxtaglomerular cells, but more than neurons at the deepest layer of cells. [14]

two-point touch threshold The minimum distance at which two stimuli (e.g., two simultaneous touches) are just perceptible as separate. [1, 13]

two-tone suppression A decrease in the firing rate of one auditory nerve fiber due to one tone, when a second tone is presented at the same time. [9]

tympanic canal One of three fluid-filled passages in the cochlea. The tympanic canal extends from the round window at the base of the cochlea to the helicotrema at the apex. Also called *scala tympani*. [9]

tympanic membrane The eardrum; a thin sheet of skin at the end of the outer ear canal. The tympanic membrane vibrates in response to sound. [9]

U

umami The taste sensation produced by monosodium glutamate. [15]

uncrossed disparity The sign of disparity created by objects behind the plane of fixation (the horopter). The term *uncrossed* is used because images of objects located behind the horopter will appear to be displaced to the right in the right eye, and to the left in the left eye. [6]

unique hue Any of four colors that can be described with only a single color term: red, yellow, green, blue. Other colors (e.g., purple or orange) can also be described as compounds (reddish blue, reddish yellow). [5]

uniqueness constraint In stereopsis, the observation that a feature in the world is represented exactly once in each retinal image. This constraint simplifies the correspondence problem. [6]

unrelated color A color that can be experienced in isolation. [5]

utricle One of the two otolith organs. A saclike structure that contains the utricular macula. Also called *utriculus*. [12]

V

vanishing point The apparent point at which parallel lines receding in depth converge. [6]

vection An illusory sense of self-motion caused by moving visual cues when one is not, in fact, actually moving. [12]

velocity The speed and direction in which something moves. Mathematically, velocity is the integral of acceleration. In words, linear velocity is distance divided by time to traverse that distance; angular velocity is rotation angle divided by time to traverse that angle. [12]

velocity storage Prolongation of a rotational response by the brain beyond the duration of the rotational signal provided to the brain by the semicircular canals; typically yielding responses that are nearer the actual rotational motion than the signal provided by the canals. [12]

vergence A type of eye movement in which the two eyes move in opposite directions; for example, both eyes turn toward the nose (convergence) or away from the nose (divergence). [8]

vertigo A sensation of rotation or spinning. The term is often used more generally to mean any form of dizziness. [12]

vestibular canal One of three fluid-filled passages in the cochlea. The vestibular canal extends from the oval window at the base of the cochlea to the helicotrema at the apex. Also called *scala vestibuli*. [9]

vestibular organs The set of five sense organs—three semicircular canals and two otolith organs—located in each inner ear that sense head motion and head orientation with respect to gravity. See also *vestibular system*. [12]

vestibular system The vestibular organs as well as the vestibular neurons in cranial nerve VIII and the central neurons that contribute to the functional roles that the vestibular system participates in. [12]

vestibulo-ocular reflex (VOR) A short-latency reflex that helps stabilize vision by counterrotating the eyes when the vestibular system senses head movement. [12]

vestibulocochlear (VIII) nerves The eighth pair of cranial nerves, which connect the inner ear with the brain, transmitting impulses concerned with hearing and spatial orientation. The vestibulocochlear nerve is composed of the cochlear nerve branch and the vestibular nerve branch. [1]

vibration theory An alternative to *shape-pattern theory* for describing how olfaction works. Vibration theory proposes that every odorant has a different vibrational frequency and that molecules that produce the same vibrational frequencies will smell the same. [14]

Vieth-Müller circle The location of objects whose images fall on geometrically corresponding points in the two retinas. If life were simple, this circle would be the horopter, but life is not simple. [6]

visual acuity A measure of the finest detail that can be resolved by the eyes. [2]

visual angle The angle that an object subtends at the eye. [2, 3]

visual crowding The deleterious effect of clutter on peripheral object recognition. [3]

visual search Search for a target in a display containing distracting elements. [7]

visual-field defect A portion of the visual field with no vision or with abnormal vision, typically resulting from damage to the visual nervous system. [7]

vitalism The idea that there is a force in life that is distinct from physical entities. [1]

vitreous humor The transparent fluid that fills the vitreous chamber in the posterior part of the eye. [2]

vocal tract The airway above the larynx used for the production of speech. The vocal tract includes the oral tract and nasal tract. [11]

volley principle The idea that multiple neurons can provide a temporal code for frequency if each neuron fires at a distinct point in the period of a sound wave but does not fire on every period. [9]

vomeronasal organ (VNO) Found in nonhuman animals, it is a chemical-sensing organ at the base of the nasal cavity with a curved tubular shape. The VNO evolved to detect chemicals that cannot be processed by ORs, such as large and/or aqueous molecules, the types of molecules that constitute pheromones. Also called *Jacobson's organ*. [14]

W

warmth fiber A sensory nerve fiber that fires when skin temperature increases. [13]

wave An oscillation that travels through a medium by transferring energy from one particle or point to another without causing any permanent displacement of the medium. [2]

wavelength The distance required for one full cycle of oscillation for a sine wave. [1]

Weber fraction The constant of proportionality in Weber's law. [1]

Weber's law The principle describing the relationship between stimulus and resulting sensation that says the just noticeable difference (JND) is a constant fraction of the comparison stimulus. [1]

white noise Noise consisting of all audible frequencies in equal amounts. White noise in hearing is analogous to white light in vision, for which all wavelengths are present. [9]

References

A

Abraira, V. E. and Ginty, D. D. (2013). The sensory neurons of touch. *Neuron* 79: 618–639.

Abrams, J., Nizam, A. and Carrasco, M. (2012). Isoeccentric locations are not equivalent: The extent of the vertical meridian asymmetry. *Vision Res* 52: 70–78.

Ackerman, D. (1990). *A Natural History of the Senses*. New York: Random House.

Addams, R. (1834). An account of a peculiar optical phenomenon seen after having looked at a moving body, etc. *Lond Edinb Philos Mag J Sci* 5: 373–374.

Adelson, E. H. (1993). Perceptual organization and the judgment of brightness. *Science* 262: 2042–2044.

Adelson E. H. (2001). On seeing stuff: The perception of materials by humans and machines. In B. E. Rogowitz and T. N. Pappas (Eds.), *Proceedings SPIE Human Vision and Electronic Imaging VI* (Vol. 4299, pp. 1–12).

Adelson, E. H. and Bergen, J. R. (1985). Spatiotemporal energy models perception of motion. *J Opt Soc Am A* 2: 284–299.

Agrawal, Y., Carey, J. P., Della Santina, C. C., Schubert, M. C., and Minor, L. B. (2009). Disorders of balance and vestibular function in US adults: Data from the National Health and Nutrition Examination Survey, 2001–2004. *Arch Intern Med* 169(10): 938–944.

Ahissar, M. and Hochstein, S. (2004). The reverse hierarchy theory of visual perceptual learning. *Trends Cogn Sci* 8: 457–464.

Alais, D. and Blake, R. (2005). *Binocular Rivalry and Perceptual Ambiguity*. Cambridge, MA: MIT Press.

Alberti, L. B. (1970). *On Painting* (translated with Introduction and Notes by John R. Spencer). New Haven: Yale University Press.

Alexander, J. A. and Kluender, K. R. (2010). Temporal properties of perceptual calibration to local and broad spectral characteristics of a listening context. *J Acoust Soc Am* 128: 3597–3613.

Alexander, J. M. (2013). Individual variability in recognition of frequency-lowered speech. *Semin Hear* 34: 86–109.

Alexander, J. M. and Kluender, K. R. (2009). Spectral tilt change in stop consonant perception by listeners with hearing impairment. *J Speech Lang Hearing Res* 52: 653–670.

Alpern, M., Kitahara, K., and Krantz, D. H. (1983). Classical tritanopia. *J Physiol* 335: 655–681.

Alvarez, G. A. (2011). Representing multiple objects as an ensemble enhances visual cognition. *Trends Cogn Sci* 15: 122–131.

Amano, K., Wandell, B. A., and Dumoulin, S. O. (2009). Visual field maps, population receptive field sizes, and visual field coverage in the human MT+ complex. *J Neurophysiol* 102: 2704–2718.

American Standards Association. (1960). *Acoustical Terminology SI, 1-1960*. New York: American Standards Association.

Anderson, J. A., Silverstein, J. W., Ritz, S. A., and Jones, R. S. (1977). Distinctive features, categorical perception, and probability learning: Some applications of a neural model. *Psychol Rev* 84: 413–451.

Anderson, J. S., Lampl, I., Gillespie, D. C., and Ferster, D. (2000). Contribution of noise to contrast invariance of orientation tuning in cat visual cortex. *Science* 290: 1968–1972.

Anderson, P. W. and Zahorik, P. (2014). Auditory/visual distance estimation: Accuracy and variability. *Front Psychol* 5: 1097.

Andre, T., Lefèvre, P., and Thonnard, J. L. (2009). A continuous measure of fingertip friction during precision grip. *J Neurosci Meth* 179: 224–229.

Angelaki, D., McHenry, M., Dickman, J. D., Newlands, S., and Hess, B. (1999). Computation of inertial motion: Neural strategies to resolve ambiguous otolith information. *J Neurosci* 19: 316–327.

Anzai, A. and DeAngelis, G. C. (2010). Neural computations underlying depth perception. *Curr Opin Neurobiol* 20: 367–375.

Archie, P., Bruera, E., and Cohen, L. (2013). Music-based interventions in palliative cancer care: A review of quantitative studies and neurobiological literature. *Support Care Cancer* 21: 2609–2624.

Arend, L. and Reeves, A. (1986). Simultaneous color constancy. *J Opt Soc Am A* 3: 1743–1751.

Arshamian, A., Iannilli, E., Gerber, J. C., Willander, J., Persson, J., Seo, H.-S. Hummel, T., and Larsson, M. (2013). The functional neuroanatomy of odor-evoked autobiographical memories cued by odors and words. *Neuropsychologia* 51: 123–131.

Arzi, A., Holtzman, Y., Samnon, P., Eshel, N., Harel, E., and Sobel, N. (2014). Olfactory aversive conditioning during sleep reduces cigarette-smoking behavior. *J Neurosci* 34: 15382–15393.

Aschenbrenner, K., Hummel, C., Teszmer, K., Krone, F., Ishimaru, T., Seo, H. S., and Hummel, T. (2008). The influence of olfactory loss on dietary behaviors. *Laryngoscope* 118: 135–144.

Assad, J. A. (2014). Neuroscience: Updating views of visual updating. *Nature* 507: 434–435.

Athos, E. A., Levinson, B., Kistler, A., Zemansky, J., Bostrom, A., and Freimer, N. (2007). Dichotomy and perceptual distortions in absolute pitch ability. *Proc Nat Acad Sci USA* 104: 14795–14800.

Attneave, F. and Olson, R. K. (1971). Pitch as a medium: A new approach to psychophysical scaling. *Am J Psychol* 84: 147–166.

Au, R., Joung, P., Nicholas, M., Obler, L. K., Kass, R., and Albert, M. L. (1995). Naming ability across the adult life span. *Aging Neuropsychol Cogn* 2: 300–311.

Aubert, H. (1861). Eine scheinbare bedeutende Drehung von Objekten bei Neigung des Kopfes nach rechts oder links. *Virchows Arch* 20: 381–393.

Aubert, H. (1886). Die Bewegungsempfindung. *Arch Ges Physiol* 39: 347–370.

Ayabe-Kanamura, S., Schicker, I., Laska, M., Hudson, R., Distel, H., Kobayakawa, T., and Saito, S. (1998). Differences in perception of everyday odors: A Japanese-German cross-cultural study. *Chem Senses* 23: 31–38.

B

Babadi, B., Casti, A., Xiao, Y., Kaplan, E., and Paninski, L. (2010). A generalized linear model of the impact of direct and indirect inputs to the lateral geniculate nucleus. *J Vis* 10: 22.

Bahill, A. T. and Stark, L. (1979). The trajectories of saccadic eye movements. *Sci Am* 240: 108–117.

Baldauf, D. and Desimone, R. (2014). Neural mechanisms of object-based attention. *Science* 344: 424–427.

Baloh, R. and Halmagyi, G. M. (Eds.). (1996). *Disorders of the Vestibular System.* Oxford, UK: Oxford University Press.

Bandyopadhyay, S., Shamma, S. A., and Kanold, P. O. (2010). Dichotomy of functional organization in the mouse auditory cortex. *Nat Neurosci* 13: 361–368.

Banks, M. S., Aslin, R. N., and Letson, R. D. (1975). Sensitive period for the development of human binocular vision. *Science* 190: 675–677.

Barclay, C. D., Cutting, J. E., and Kozlowski, L. T. (1978). Temporal and spatial factors in gait perception that influence gender recognition. *Percept Psychophys* 23: 145–152.

Baringa, M. (2002). How the brain's clock gets daily enlightenment. *Science* 295: 955–957.

Barlow, H. B. (1972). Single units and sensation: A neuron doctrine for perceptual psychology. *Perception* 1: 371–394.

Barlow, H. B. (1995). The neuron doctrine in perception. In M. S. Gazzaniga (Ed.), *The Cognitive Neurosciences* (pp. 415–435). Cambridge, MA: MIT Press.

Barlow, H. B. and Levick, W. R. (1965). The mechanism of directionally selective units in rabbit's retina. *J Physiol* 178: 477–504.

Barlow, H. B., Blakemore, C., and Pettigrew, J. D. (1967). The neural mechanism of binocular depth discrimination. *J Physiol* 193: 327–342.

Barr, C. C., Schultheis, L. W., and Robinson, D. A. (1976). Voluntary, non-visual control of the human vestibulo-ocular reflex. *Acta Otolaryngol* 81: 365–375.

Barry, S. R. (2009). *Fixing My Gaze.* New York, NY: Basic Books.

Bartoshuk, L. M. (1975). Taste mixtures: Is mixture suppression related to compression? *Physiol Behav* 14: 643–649.

Bartoshuk, L. M. (1978). History of taste research. In E. C. Carterette and M. P. Friedman (Eds.), *Tasting and smelling* (Vol. VIA, pp. 3–18). New York: Academic Press.

Bartoshuk, L. M. (1979). Bitter taste of saccharin: Related to the genetic ability to taste the bitter substance 6-*n*-propylthiouracil (PROP). *Science* 205: 934–935.

Bartoshuk, L. M. (1991). Taste, smell and pleasure. In R. C. Bolles (Ed.), *The Hedonics of Taste* (pp. 15–28). Hillsdale, NJ: Erlbaum.

Bartoshuk, L. M., Cartalanotto, J. A., Hoffman, H. J., Logan, H. L., and Snyder, D. J. (2012). Taste damage (otitis media, tonsillectomy and head and neck cancer) can intenify oral sensations. *Physiol Behav* 107: 516–526.

Bartoshuk, L. M., Fast, K., and Snyder, D. (2005). Differences in our sensory worlds: Invalid comparisons with labeled scales. *Curr Dir Psychol Sci* 14: 122–125.

Bartoshuk, L. M. and Klee, H. J. (2013). Better fruits and vegetables through sensory analysis. *Curr Biol* 23: R374–R378.

Bartoshuk, L. M., Marino, S., Snyder, D. J., and Stamps, J. (2013). Head trauma, taste damage and weight gain. *Chem Senses* 38: 626.

Bartoshuk, L. M. and Wolfe, J. M. (1990). Conditioned taste aversions in humans: Are they olfactory aversions? *Chem Senses* 15: 551.

Bashford, J. A. and Warren, R. M. (1987). Multiple phonemic restorations follow the rules for auditory induction. *Percept Psychophys* 42: 114–121.

Basson, M. D., Bartoshuk, L. M., Dichello, S. Z., Weiffenbach, J., and Duffy, V. B. (2003). Colon cancer and genetic variation in taste. *Chem Senses* 28: 109.

Bates, L. A., Sayialel, K. N., Njiraini, N. W., Moss, C. J., Poole, J. H., and Byrne, R. W. 2007. Elephants classify human ethnic groups by odor and garment color. *Curr Biol* 17: 1938–1942.

Bautista, D. M., Siemens, J., Glazer, J. M., Tsuruda, P. R., Basbaum, A. I., Stucky, C. L., Jordt, S. E., and Julius, D. (2007). The menthol receptor TRPM8 is the principal detector of environmental cold. *Nature* 448: 204–208.

Beck, J. (1982). Textural segmentation. In J. Beck (Ed.), *Organization and Representation in Perception* (pp. 285–317). Hillsdale, NJ: Erlbaum.

Behrmann, M. and Avidan, G. (2005). Congenital prosopagnosia: Face-blind from birth. *Trends Cogn Sci* 9: 180–187.

Benson, P. J., Beedie, S. A., Shephard, E., Giegling, I., Rujescu, D., and St. Clair, D. (2012). Simple viewing tests can detect eye movement abnormalities that distinguish schizophrenia cases from controls with exceptional accuracy. *Biol Psychiatry* 72: 716–724.

Bergen, J. R. and Adelson, E. H. (1988). Early vision and texture perception. *Nature* 333: 363–364.

Berger, A., Henderson, M., Nadoolman, W., Duffy, V. B., Cooper, D., Saberski, L., and Bartoshuk, L. (1995). Oral capsaicin provides temporary relief for oral mucositis pain secondary to chemotherapy/radiation therapy. *J Pain Symptom Manage* 10: 243–248.

Berlin, B. and Kay, P. (1969). *Basic Color Terms: Their Universality and Evolution.* Berkeley: University of California Berkeley.

Bermúdez Rey, M. C., Clark, T. K., Wang, W., Leeder, T., Bian, Y., and Merfeld, D. M. (2016). Vestibular perceptual thresholds increase above the age of 40. *Front Neurol* 7: 162.

Bernstein, I. L. (1978). Learned taste aversions in children receiving chemotherapy. *Science* 200: 1302–1303.

Berthoz, A., Israel, I., Georges-Francois, P., Grasso, R., and Tsuzuku, T. (1995). Spatial memory of body linear displacement: What is being stored? *Science* 269: 95–98.

Bertino, M., Beauchamp, G. K., and Engelman, K. (1982). Long-term reduction in dietary sodium alters the taste of salt. *Am J Clin Nutr* 36: 1134–1144.

Bertolini, G., Ramat, S., Laurens, J., Bockisch, C. J., Marti, S., Straumann, D., and Palla, A. (2011). Velocity storage contribution to vestibular self-motion perception in healthy human subjects. *J Neurophysiol* 105: 209–223.

Best, C. T., McRoberts, G. W., and Sithole, N. T. (1988). Examination of perceptual reorganization for non-native speech contrasts: Zulu click discrimination by English-speaking adults and infants. *J Exp Psychol Hum Percept Perform* 14: 345–360.

Bhutani, S., Gottfried, J., and Kahnt, T. (2017). *Central olfactory mechanisms underlying sleep-dependent changes in food processing.* Paper presented at the Cognitive Neuroscience Society Annual Meeting, San Francisco, March 27, 2017.

Bialystok, E. and Hakuta, K. (1994). *In Other Words: The Science and Psychology of Second-Language Acquisition.* New York: Basic Books.

Biederman, I. (1987). Recognition-by-components: A theory of human image understanding. *Psychol Rev* 94: 115–147.

Birch, E. E. (1993). Stereopsis in infants and its developmental relation to visual acuity. In K. Simons (Ed.), *Early Visual Development Normal and Abnormal* (pp. 224–234). New York: Oxford University Press.

Birch, E. and Petrig, B. (1996). FPL and VEP measures of fusion, stereopsis and stereoacuity in normal infants. *Vision Res* 36: 1321–1326.

Bird, C. M., Berens, S. C., Horner, A. J., and Franklin, A. (2014). Categorical encoding of color in the brain. *Proc Nat Acad Sci USA* 111: 4590–4595.

Birznieks, I., Macefield, V. G., Westling, G., and Johansson, R. S. (2009). Slowly adapting mechanoreceptors in the borders of the human fingernail encode fingertip forces. *J Neurosci* 29: 9370–9379.

Björnsdotter, M., Löken, L., Olausson, H., Vallbo, A., and Wessberg, J. (2009). Somatotopic organization of gentle touch processing in the posterior insular cortex. *J Neurosci* 29: 9314–9320.

Blake, R. (1988). Cat spatial vision. *Trends Neurosci* 11: 78–83.

Blake, R. and Logothetis, N. K. (2002). Visual competition. *Nat Rev Neurosci* 3: 13–21.

Blake, R. and Wilson, H. (2011). Binocular vision. *Vision Res* 51: 754–770.

Blake, R., Sloane, M., and Fox, R. (1981). Further developments in binocular summation. *Percept Psychophys* 30: 266–276.

Blakemore, C. and Campbell, F. W. (1969). On the existence of neurons in the human visual system selectively sensitive to the orientation and size of images. *J Physiol* 203: 237–260.

Blakemore, S.-J., Wolpert, D. M., and Frith, C. D. (1998). Central cancellation of self-produced tickle sensation. *Nat Neurosci* 1: 635–640.

Blasdel, G. G. and Salama, G. (1986). Voltage-sensitive dyes reveal a modular organization in monkey striate cortex. *Nature* 321: 579–585.

Block, E., Jang, S., Matsunami, H., Sekharan, S., Dethier, B., Ertem, M. Z., Gundala, S., et al. (2015). Implausibility of the vibrational theory of olfaction. *Proc Natl Acad Sci USA* 112: E2766–E2774.

Blood, A. J. and Zatorre, R. J. (2001). Intensely pleasurable responses to music correlate with activity in brain regions implicated in reward and emotion. *Proc Natl Acad Sci USA* 98: 11818–11823.

Blumenfeld, H. (2002). *Neuroanatomy through Clinical Cases.* Sunderland, MA: Sinauer.

Blumenfeld, H. (2010). *Neuroanatomy through Clinical Cases* (2nd ed.). Sunderland, MA: Sinauer.

Blundell, J. and Hill, A. J. (1986). Paradoxical effects of an intense sweetener (aspartame) on appetite. *Lancet* 1: 1092–1093.

Boesveldt, S., Lindau, S. T., McClintock, M. K., Hummel, T., and Lundstrom, J. N. (2011). Gustatory and olfactory dysfunction in older adults: A national probability study. *Rhinology*, 49: 324–330.

Bolton, T. L. (1894). Rhythm. *Am J Psychol* 6: 145–238.

Bompas, A., Kendall, G., and Sumner, P. (2013). Spotting fruit versus picking fruit as the selective advantage of human colour vision. *i-Perception* 4: 84–94.

Boothe, R. G., Dobson, V., and Teller, D. Y. (1985). Postnatal development of vision in human and non-human primates. *Annu Rev Neurosci* 8: 495–545.

Boring, E. G. (1942). *Sensation and Perception in the History of Experimental Psychology by Edwin G. Boring.* Appleton-Century-Crofts.

Boring, E. G. (1950). *A History of Experimental Psychology* (2nd ed.). New York: Appleton-Century-Crofts.

Bortolami, S. B., Pierobon, A., DiZio, P., and Lackner, J. R. (2006). Localization of the subjective vertical during roll, pitch, and recumbent yaw body tilt. *Exp Brain Res* 173: 364–373.

Boycott, B. B. and Dowling, J. E. (1969). Organization of the primate retina: Light microscopy. *Philos Trans R Soc Lond B Biol Sci* 255: 109–176.

Brady, P. T. (1970). Fixed scale mechanism of absolute pitch. *J Acoust Soc Am* 48: 883–887.

Brady, T. F., Konkle, T., Alvarez, G. A., and Oliva, A. (2008). Visual long-term memory has a massive storage capacity for object details. *Proc Natl Acad Sci USA* 105: 14325–14329.

Brady, T. F., Shafer-Skelton, A., and Alvarez, G. A. (2017). Global ensemble texture representations are critical to rapid scene perception. *J Exp Psychol Hum Percept Perform* 43: 1160–1176. Published by APA; reprinted with permission.

Brainard, D. H. (2009). Bayesian approaches to color vision. In M. S. Gazzaniga (Ed.), *The Cognitive Neurosciences* (4th ed., pp. 395–408). Cambridge, MA: MIT Press.

Brainard, D. H. and Freeman, W. T. (1997). Bayesian color constancy. *J Opt Soc Am A* 14: 1393–1411.

Brainard, D. H. and Hurlbert, A. C. (2015). Colour vision: Understanding #TheDress. *Curr Biol* 25: R551–R554.

Bramble D. M. and Lieberman, D. E. (2004). Endurance running and the evolution of Homo. *Nature* 432: 345–352.

Brand, A., Behrend, O., Marquardt, T., McAlpine, D., and Grothe, B. (2002). Precise inhibition is essential for microsecond interaural time difference coding. *Nature* 417: 543–547.

Breedlove, S. M. and Watson, N. V. (2013). *Biological Psychology: An Introduction to Behavioral, Cognitive, and Clinical Neuroscience* (7th ed.). Sunderland, MA: Sinauer.

Breedlove, S. M., Rosenzweig, M. R., and Watson, N. V. (2007). *Biological Psychology: An Introduction to Behavioral, Cognitive, and Clinical Neuroscience* (5th ed.). Sunderland, MA: Sinauer.

Breedlove, S. M., Watson, N. V., and Rosenzweig, M. R. (2010). *Biological Psychology: An Introduction to Behavioral, Cognitive, and Clinical Neuroscience* (6th ed.). Sunderland, MA: Sinauer.

Brefczynski, J. A. and DeYoe, E. A. (1999). A physiological correlate of the "spotlight" of visual attention. *Nat Neurosci* 2: 370–374.

Bremner, E. A., Mainland, J. D., Khan, R. M., and Sobel, N. (2003). The prevalence of androstenone anosmia. *Chem Senses* 28: 423–432.

Bressler, S., Masud, S., Bharadwaj, H., and Shinn-Cunningham, B. (2014). Bottom-up influences of voice continuity in focusing selective auditory attention. *Psych Res* 78: 349–360.

Breuer, J. (1874). Ueber die Funktion der Bogengänge des Ohrlabyrinths [About the functions of the semicircular canals of the ear labyrinth]. *Med Jahrbücher* 2nd series 4: 72–124.

Bridgeman, B. (2014). Restoring adult stereopsis: A vision researcher's personal experience. *Optom Vis Sci* 91: e135–139.

Brown, A. C. (1874). The sense of rotation and the anatomy and physiology of the semicircular canals of the internal ear. *J Anat Physiol* 8: 327–331.

Bruce, V. and Young, A. (1986). Understanding face recognition. *Br J Psychol* 77(Pt.3): 305–327.

Brugge, J. F. and Howard, M. A. (2002). Hearing. In V. S. Ramachandran (Ed.), *Encyclopedia of the Human Brain* (pp. 429–448). New York: Academic Press.

Brughera, A., Dunai, L., and Hartman, W. M. (2013). Human interaural time difference thresholds for sine tones: The high-frequency limit. *J Acoust Soc Am* 133: 2839–2855.

Brungart, D. S., Durlach, N. I., and Rabinowitz, W. M. (1999). Auditory localization of nearby sources. II. Localization of a broadband source. *J Acoust Soc Am* 106: 1956–1968.

Buchsbaum, G. (1980). A spatial processor model for object colour perception. *J Franklin Inst* 310: 1–26.

Buchsbaum, G. and Gottschalk, A. (1983). Trichromacy, opponent colours coding and optimum colour information transmission in the retina. *Proc R Soc Lond B Biol Sci* 220: 89–113.

Buck, L. and Axel, R. (1991). A novel multigene family may encode odorant receptors: A molecular basis for odor recognition. *Cell* 65: 175–187.

Buck, S. (2015). Brown. *Curr Biol* 25: R536–R537.

Burgess, A. E. (2010). Signal detection in radiology. In E. Samei and E. A. Krupinski (Eds.), *The Handbook of Medical Image Perception and Techniques* (pp. 26–46). Cambridge, UK: Cambridge University Press.

Burton, A. M. (2013). Why has research in face recognition progressed so slowly? The importance of variability. *Q J Exp Psychol* 66: 1467–1485.

Bushdid, C. M., Magnasco, O., Vosshall, L. B. Keller, A. (2014). Humans can discriminate more than 1 trillion olfactory stimuli *Science* 343: 1370–1372.

Bushnell, B. N., Harding, P. J., Kosai, Y., and Pasupathy, A. (2011). Partial occlusion modulates contour-based shape encoding in primate area V4. *J Neurosci* 31: 4012–4024.

Busskamp, V., Duebel, J., Balya, D., Fradot, M., Viney, T. J., Siegert, S., Groner, A. C., et al. (2010). Genetic reactivation of cone photoreceptors restores visual responses in retinitis pigmentosa. *Science* 329: 413–417.

Bylinskii, Z., Isola, P., Bainbridge, C., Torralba, A., and Oliva, A. (2015). Intrinsic and extrinsic effects on image memorability. *Vision Res* 116(Pt.B): 165–178.

Byrne, A. (Summer 2014 Edition). Inverted qualia. In E. N. Zalta (Ed.), *The Stanford Encyclopedia of Philosophy*, plato.stanford.edu/archives/sum2014/entries/qualia-inverted/.

C

Cadiou, H., Aoudé, I., Tazir, B., Molinas, A., Fenech, C., Meunier, N., and Grosmaitre, X. (2014). Postnatal odorant exposure induces peripheral olfactory plasticity at the cellular level. *J Neurosci* 34: 4857–4870.

Cahill, L., Babinsky, R., Markowitsch, H. J., and McGaugh, J. L. (1995). The amygdala and emotional memory. *Nature* 377: 295–296.

Cain, W. S. and Engen, T. (1969). Olfactory adaptation and the scaling of odor intensity. In C. Pfaffmann (Ed.), *Olfaction and Taste III* (pp. 127–141). New York: Rockefeller University Press.

Cain, W. S. and Johnson, F., Jr. (1978). Lability of odor pleasantness: Influence of mere exposure. *Perception* 7: 459–465.

Cameron, E. L. (2007). Measures of human olfactory perception during pregnancy. *Chem Senses* 32: 775–782.

Campbell, F. W. and Green, D. G. (1965). Optical and retinal factors affecting visual resolution. *J Physiol* 181: 576–593.

Campbell, F. W. and Robson, J. G. (1968). Application of Fourier analysis to the visibility of gratings. *J Physiol* 197: 551–556.

Campbell, R., Pascalis, O., Coleman, M., Wallace, B., and Benson, P. J. (1997). Are faces of different species perceived categorically by human observers? *Proc R Soc Lond B Biol Sci* 264: 1429–1434.

Canzoneri, E., Ubaldi, S., Rastelli, V., Finisguerra, A., Bassolino, M., and Serino, A. (2013). Tool-use reshapes the boundaries of body and peripersonal space representations. *Exp Brain Res* 228: 25–42.

Capaldi, E. D., Hunter, M. J., and Privitera, G. J. (2004). Odor of taste stimuli in conditioned "taste" aversion learning. *Behav Neurosci* 118: 1400–1408.

Carskadon, M. A., Wyatt, J., Etgen, G., and Rosekind, M. R. (1989). Nonvisual sensory experiences in dreams of college students. *Sleep Res* 18: 159.

Carskadon, M. and Herz, R. S. (2004). Minimal olfactory perception during sleep: Why odor alarms will not work for humans. *Sleep* 27: 402–405.

Casagrande, V. A., Yazar, F., Jones, K. D., and Ding, Y. (2007). The morphology of the koniocellular axon pathway in the macaque monkey. *Cereb Cortex* 17: 2334–2345.

Castelhano, M. S. and Heaven, C. (2010). The relative contribution of scene context and target features to visual search in scenes. *Atten Percept Psychophys* 72: 1283–1297.

Castet, E., Jeanjean, S., and Masson, G. S. (2001). "Saccadic suppression"—no need for an active extra-retinal mechanism. *Trends Neurosci* 24: 316–318.

Castro, J. B., Ramanathan, A., and Chennubhotla, C. S. (2013). Categorical dimensions of human odor descriptor space revealed by non-negative matrix factorization. *PLoS One* 8: e73289.

Cavanagh, P. and Leclerc, Y. G. (1989). Shape from shadows. *J Exp Psychol Hum Percept Perform* 15: 3–27.

Cavanagh, P., Hunt, A. R., Afraz, A., and Rolfs, M. (2010). Visual stability based on remapping of attention pointers. *Trends Cogn Sci* 14: 147–153.

Cave, K. R. and Bichot, N. P. (1999). Visuo-spatial attention: Beyond a spotlight model. *Psychon Bull Rev* 6: 204–223.

Cazakoff, B. N., Lau, B. Y. B., Crump, K. L., Demmer, H. S., and Shea, S. D. (2014). Broadly tuned and respiration-independent inhibition in the olfactory bulb of awake mice *Nat Neurosci* 17: 569–576.

Chabris, C. F. and Simons, D. J. (2011). You do not talk about Fight Club if you do not notice Fight Club: Inattentional blindness for a simulated real-world assault. *i-Perception* 2, i-perception. perceptionweb.com.

Champagne, F. A. (2008). Epigenetic mechanisms and the transgenerational effects of maternal care. *Front Neuroendocrinol* 29: 386–397.

Chang, E. F., Rieger, J. W., Johnson, K., Berger, M. S., Barbaro, N. M., and Knight, R. T. (2010). Categorical speech representation in human superior temporal gyrus. *Nat Neurosci* 13: 1428–1432.

Changizi, M. A., Zhang, Q., and Shimojo, S. (2006). Bare skin, blood and the evolution of primate colour vision. *Biol Lett* 2: 217–221.

Chapman, C. E., Jiang, W., and Lamarre, Y. (1988). Modulation of lemniscal input during conditioned arm movements in the monkey. *Exp Brain Res* 72: 316–334.

Chapuis, J., Messaoudi, B., Ferreira, G., and Ravel, N. (2007). Importance of retronasal and orthonasal olfaction for odor aversion memory in rats. *Behav Neurosci* 121: 1383–1392.

Chaudhari, N. and Roper, S. D. (2010). The cell biology of taste. *J Cell Biol* 190: 285–296.

Chaudhari, N., Pereira, E., and Roper, S. D. (2009). Taste receptors for umami: the case for multiple receptors. *Am J Clin Nutr* 90: 738S–742S.

Cheeseman, J. R., Norman, J. F., and Kappers, A. M. L. (2016). Dynamic cutaneous information is sufficient for precise curvature discrimination. *Nat Sci Rep* 6: 25473.

Chen, X., Gabitto, M., Peng, Y., Ryba, N. J. P., and Zuker, C. S. (2011). A gustotopic map of taste qualities in the mammalian brain. *Science* 333: 1262–1266.

Cheung, C., Hamilton, L. S., Johnson, K., and Chang, E. H. (2016). The auditory representation of speech sounds in human motor cortex. *eLife* 5: e12577.

Chino, Y. M., Smith, E. L., III, Hatta, S., and Cheng, H. (1997). Postnatal development of binocular disparity sensitivity in neurons of the primate visual cortex. *J Neurosci* 17: 296–307.

Chong, S. C. and Treisman, A. (2003). Representation of statistical properties. *Vision Res* 43: 393–404.

Chu, S. and Downes, J. J. (2000). Long live Proust: The odour-cued autobiographical memory bump. *Cognition* 75: B41–B50.

Chubb, C. and Landy, M. S. (1994). Orthogonal distribution analysis: A new approach to the study of texture perception. In M. S. Landy and J. A. Movshon (Eds.), *Computational Models of Visual Processing* (pp. 291–301). Cambridge, MA: MIT Press.

Chun, M. M. and Potter, M. C. (1995). A two-stage model for multiple target detection in RSVP. *J Exp Psychol Hum Percept Perform* 21: 109–127.

Chun, M. M., Golomb, J. D., and Turk-Browne, N. B. (2011). A taxonomy of external and internal attention. *Annu Rev Psychol* 62: 73–101.

Cimmino, R. L., Spitoni, G., Serino, A., Antonucci, G., Catagni, M., Camagni, M., Haggard, P., et al. (2013). Plasticity of body representations after surgical arm elongation in an achondroplasic patient. *Restor Neurol Neurosci* 31: 287–298.

Clark, F. J. and Horch, K. W. (1986). Kinesthesia. In K. R. Boff, L. Kaufman, and J. P. Thomas (Eds.), *Handbook of Perception & Human Performance*, Vol. 1: *Sensory Processes and Perception* (pp. 13–1 to 13–62). New York: Wiley.

Classen, C., Howes, D., and Synnott, A. (1994). *Aroma: The Cultural History of Smell.* London: Routledge.

Cleary, A. M., Konkel, K. E., Nomi, J. S., and McCabe, D. P. (2010). Odor recognition without identification. *Mem Cognit* 38: 452–460.

Clifford, C. W. G. (2009). Binocular rivalry. *Curr Biol* 19: R1022–R1023.

Coady, J. A., Kluender, K. R., and Rhode, W. S. (2003). Effects of contrast between onsets of speech and other complex spectra. *J Acoust Soc Am* 114: 2225–2235.

Coan, J. A., Schaefer, H. S., and Davidson, R. J. (2006). Lending a hand: Social regulation of the natural response to threat. *Psychol Sci* 17: 1032–1039.

Cohen, M. A., Dennett, D. C., and Kanwisher, N. (2016). What is the bandwidth of perceptual experience? *Trends Cogn Sci* 20: 324–335.

Cohen, M. R. and Maunsell, J. H. (2009). Attention improves performance primarily by reducing interneuronal correlations. *Nat Neurosci* 12: 1594–1600.

Cole, J. (1991). *Pride and a Daily Marathon.* Boston: MIT Press.

Conard, N., Malina, M., and Münzel, S. (2009). New flutes document the earliest musical tradition in southwestern Germany. *Nature* 460: 737–740.

Cong, X., Ludington-Hoe, S. M., Hussain, N., Cusson, R. M., Walsh, S., Vazquez, V., Briere, C. E., et al. (2015). Parental oxytocin responses during skin-to-skin contact in pre-term infants. *Early Hum Dev* 91: 401–406.

Conway, B. R. (2014). Color signals through dorsal and ventral visual pathways. *Vis Neurosci* 31 (Special Issue 02): 197–209.

Conway, B. R., Kitaoka, A., Yazdanbakhsh, A., Pack, C. C., and Livingstone, M. S. (2005). Neural basis for a powerful static motion illusion. *J Neurosci* 25: 5651–5656.

Conway, B. R., Moeller, S., and Tsao, D. Y. (2007). Specialized color modules in macaque extrastriate cortex. *Neuron* 56: 560–573.

Cornsweet, T. N. (1970). *Visual Perception.* New York: Academic Press.

Coss, R. G., Gusé, K. L., Poran, N. S., and Smith, D. (1993). Development of antisnake defense in California ground squirrels (*Sperophilus beecheyi*). II. Microevolutionary effects of relaxed selection from rattlesnakes. *Behavior* 124: 137–165.

Craft, E., Schütze, H., Niebur, E., and von der Heydt, R. (2007). A neural model of figure-ground organization. *J Neurophysiol* 97: 4310–4326.

Craig, J. C. and Johnson, K. O. (2000). The two-point threshold: Not a measure of tactile spatial resolution. *Curr Dir Psychol Sci* 9: 29–32.

Crick, F. (1984). Function of the thalamic reticular complex: The searchlight hypothesis. *Proc. Natl. Acad. Sci. USA* 81: 4586–4590.

Cronin, T. W., Jarvilehto, M., Weckstrom, M., and Lall, A. B. (2000). Tuning of photoreceptor spectral sensitivity in fireflies (Coleoptera: Lampyridae). *J Comp Physiol A* 186: 1–12.

Croy, I., Luong, A., Triscoli, C., Hofmann, E., Olausson, H., and Sailer, U. (2016). Interpersonal stroking touch is targeted to C tactile afferent activation. *Behav Brain Res* 297: 37–40.

Croy, I., Symmank, A., Schellong, J., Hummel, C., Gerber, J., Joraschky, P., and Hummel, T. (2014). Olfaction as a marker for depression in humans. *J Affect Disorders* 160: 80–86.

Crystal, S. R. and Bernstein, I. L. (1995). Morning sickness: Impact on offspring salt preference. *Appetite* 25: 231–240.

Cullen, K. E. (2011). The neural encoding of self-motion. *Curr Opin Neurobiol* 21: 587–595.

Curcio, C. A., Sloan, K. R., Kalina, R. E., and Hendrickson, A. E. (1990). Human photoreceptor topography. *J Comp Neurol* 292: 497–523.

Curthoys, I., Blanks, R., and Markham, C. (1977). Semicircular canal functional anatomy in cat, guinea pig, and man. *Acta Otolaryngol* 83: 258–265.

Czeisler, C. A., Shanahan, T. L., Klerman, E. B., Martens, H., Brotman, D. J., Emens, J. S., Klein, T. and Rizzo, J. F., III (1995). Suppression of melatonin secretion in some blind patients by exposure to bright light. *N Engl J Med* 332: 6–11.

D

Dai, M., Cohen, B., Cho, C., Shin, S., and Yakushin, S. B, (2017). Treatment of the Mal de Debarquement Syndrome: A 1-year follow-up. *Front Neurol* 8: 175.

Dalton, P. (1996). Odor perception and beliefs about risk. *Chem Senses* 21: 447–458.

Dalton, P. (2002). Olfaction. In H. Pashler, S. Yantis, D. Medin, R. Gallistel, and J. Wixted (Eds.), *Stevens' Handbook of Experimental Psychology* (3rd ed.), Vol. 1: *Sensation and Perception* (pp. 691–746). New York: Wiley.

Dalton, P., Doolittle, N., and Breslin, P. A. S. (2002). Gender-specific induction of enhanced sensitivity to odors. *Nat Neurosci* 5: 199–200.

Dalton, P., Wysocki, C. J., Brody, M. J., and Lawley, H. J. (1997). Perceived odor, irritation and health symptoms following short-term exposure to acetone. *Am J Ind Med* 31: 558–569.

Damasio, A. R., Damasio, H., and Van Hoesen, G. W. (1982). Prosopagnosia. *Neurology* 32: 331.

Damper, R. I. and Harnad, S. R. (2000). Neural network models of categorical perception. *Percept Psychophys* 62: 843–867.

Darwin, C. (1859). *The Origin of Species, by Means of Natural Selection or the Preservation of Favoured Races in the Struggle for Life.* New York: New York American Library.

Darwin, C. (1871). *The Descent of Man, and Selection in Relation to Sex.* New York: Burt.

Darwin, C. J. (1984). Perceiving vowels in the presence of another sound: Constraints on formant perception. *J Acoust Soc Am* 76: 1636–1647.

Davidoff, J., Davies, I., and Roberson, D. (1999). Is colour categorisation universal? New evidence from a stone-age culture. *Nature* 398: 203–204.

Davidson, R. J. (1984). Affect, cognition, and hemispheric specialization. In S. E. Izard, J. Kagan, and R. Zajonc (Eds.), *Emotions, Cognition and Behavior* (pp. 320–365). Cambridge, UK: Cambridge University Press.

Davidson, R. J., Putnam, K. M., and Larson, C. L. (2000). Dysfunction in the neural circuitry of emotion regulation—A possible prelude to violence. *Science* 289: 591–594.

Davidson, S., Zhang, X., Khasabov, S. G., Simone D. A., and Giesler, G. J., Jr. (2009). Relief of itch by scratching: State-dependent inhibition of primate spinothalamic tract neurons. *Nat Neurosci* 12: 544–546.

Davidson, T. L. and Swithers, S. E. (2004). A Pavlovian approach to the problem of obesity. *Int J Obes Relat Metab Disord* 28: 933–935.

Davis, C. M. (1928). Self selection of diet by newly weaned infants: An experimental study. *Am J Dis Child* 36: 651–679.

Davis, M. (2006). Neural systems involved in fear and anxiety measured with fear-potentiated startle. *Am Psych* 61: 741–756.

Davis, M. and Whalen, P. J. (2001). The amygdala: Vigilance and emotion. *Mol Psychiatry* 6: 13–34.

De Gelder, B., Teunisse, J. P., and Benson, P. J. (1997). Categorical perception of facial expressions: Categories and their internal structure. *Cogn Emot* 11: 1–23.

De Valois, R. L., Abramov, I., and Jacobs, G. H. (1966). Analysis of response patterns of LGN cells. *J Opt Soc Am A* 56: 966–977.

De Valois, R. L., Albrecht, D. G., and Thorell, L. G. (1982). Spatial frequency selectivity of cells in macaque visual cortex. *Vision Res* 22: 545–559.

De Valois, R. L., Yund, E. W., and Hepler, N. (1982). The orientation and direction selectivity of cells in macaque visual cortex. *Vision Res* 22: 531–544.

DeCasper, A. J. and Fifer, W. P. (1980). Of human bonding: Newborns prefer their mother's voices. *Science* 208: 1174–1176.

DeCasper, A. J. and Spence, M. J. (1986). Prenatal maternal speech influences newborns' perception of speech sounds. *Infant Behav Dev* 9: 133–150.

Descartes, R. (1664). *Le Monde.* Paris: Jacques Le Gras.

DeSimone, J. A., Phan, T.-H. T., Heck, G. L., Ren, Z., Coleman, J., Mummalaneni, S., Melone, P., and Lyall, V. (2011). Involvement of NADPH-dependent and cAMP-PKA sensitive H^+ channels in the chorda tympani nerve responses to strong acids. *Chem Senses* 36: 389–403.

Deutsch, D. (2013). Absolute pitch. In D. Deutsch (Ed.) *The Psychology of Music* (2nd ed.), pp. 141–182. San Diego: Academic Press.

Deutsch, D., Le, J., Shen, J., and Li, X. (2011). Large-scale direct-test study reveals unexpected characteristics of absolute pitch. *J Acoust Soc Am* 130: 2398.

DeWitt, L. A. and Samuel, A. G. (1990). The role of knowledge-based expectations in music perception: Evidence from musical restoration. *J Exp Psychol Gen* 119: 123–144.

Di Lollo, V., Kawahara, J., Shahab Ghorashi, S. M., and Enns, J. T. (2005). The attentional blink: Resource depletion or temporary loss of control? *Psychol Res* 69: 191–200.

Diamond, J., Dalton, P., Doolittle, N., and Breslin, P. A. (2005). Gender-specific olfactory sensitization: Hormonal and cognitive influences. *Chem Senses* Supp.1: i224–i225.

DiCarlo, J. J., Johnson, K. O., and Hsiao, S. S. (1998). Structure of receptive fields in area 3b of primary somatosensory cortex in the alert monkey. *J Neurosci* 18: 2626–2645.

Dieterich, M. and Brandt, T. (2008). Functional brain imaging of peripheral and central vestibular disorders. *Brain* 131(Pt.10): 2538–2552.

Dilks, D. D., Dalton, P., and Beauchamp, G. K. (1999). Cross-cultural variation in responses to malodors. *Chem Senses* 24: 599.

Ding, J. and Levi, D. M. (2011). Recovery of stereopsis through perceptual learning in human adults with abnormal binocular vision. *Proc Natl Acad Sci USA* 108: e733–741.

Dittman, A. and Quinn, T. (1996). Homing in Pacific salmon: Mechanisms and ecological basis. *J Exp Biol* 199(Pt.1): 83–91.

Djordjevic, J., Zatorre, R. J., Petrides, M., Boyle, J. A., and Jones-Gotman, M. (2005). Functional neuroimaging of odor imagery. *Neuroimage* 24: 791–801.

Dong, W. and Olson, E. S. (2013). Detection of cochlear amplification and it activation. *Biophys J* 105: 1067–1078.

Doty, R. L. (2010). *The Great Pheromone Myth.* Baltimore: Johns Hopkins University Press.

Doty, R. L. and Bromely, S. M. (2004). Effects of drugs on olfaction and taste. *Otolaryngol Clin North Am* 37: 1229–1254.

Doty, R. L. and Cameron, E. L. (2009). Sex differences and reproductive hormone influences on human odor perception. *Physiol Behav* 97: 213–228.

Doty, R. L., Heidt, J. M., MacGillivray, M. R., Dsouza, M., Tracey, E. H., Mirza, N., and Bigelow, D. (2016). Influences of age, tongue region, and chorda tympani nerve sectioning on signal detection measures of lingual taste sensitivity. *Physiol Behav* 155: 202–207.

Doty, R. L., Shaman, P., Applebaum, S. L., Giberson, R, Siksorski, L., and Rosenberg, L. (1984). Smell identification ability: Changes with age. *Science* 226: 1441–1443.

Doty, R. L., Shaman, P., Dann, M. (1984). Development of the University of Pennsylvania Smell Identification Test: A standardized microencapsulated test of olfactory function. *Physiol Behav* 32: 489–502.

Doty, R. L., Snyder, P., Huggins, G., and Lowry, L. D. (1981). Endocrine, cardiovascular and psychological correlates of olfac-tory sensitivity changes during the human menstrual cycle. *J Comp Physiol Psychol* 95: 45–60.

Downing, P., Liu, J., and Kanwisher, N. (2001). Testing cognitive models of visual attention with fMRI and MEG. *Neuropsychologia* 39: 1329–1342.

Drew, T., Vo, M. L.-H., and Wolfe, J. M. (2013). The invisible gorilla strikes again: Sustained inattentional blindness in expert observers. *Psychol Sci* 24: 1848–1853.

Driver, J. (1998). The neuropsychology of spatial attention. In H. Pashler (Ed.), *Attention* (pp. 297–340). Hove, East Sussex, UK: Psychology Press.

Dubin, M. W. and Cleland, B. G. (1977). Organization of visual inputs to interneurons of lateral geniculate nucleus of the cat. *J Neurophysiol* 40: 410–427.

Duchaine, B. and Yovel, G. (2015). A revised neural framework for face processing. *Annu Rev Vis Sci* 1: 393–416.

Duffy, V. B., Bartoshuk, L. M., Striegel-Moore, R., and Rodin, J. (1998). Taste changes across pregnancy. In C.

Murphy (Ed.), *Olfaction and Taste XIX: An International Symposium* (Vol. 855, pp. 805–809). New York: Annals of the New York Academy of Sciences.

Duffy, V. B., Davidson, A. C., Kidd, J. R., Kidd, K. K., Speed, W. C., Pakstis, A. J., Reed, D. R., Snyder, D. J., and Bartoshuk, L. M. (2004). Bitter receptor gene (TAS2R38), 6-*n*-propylthiouracil (PROP) bitterness and alcohol intake. *Alcohol Clin Exp Res* 28: 1629–1637.

Duffy, V. B., Lanier, S. A., Hutchins, H. L., Pescatello, L. S., Johnson, M. K., and Bartoshuk, L. M. (2007). Food preference questionnaire as a screening tool for assessing dietary risk of cardiovascular disease within health risk appraisals. *J Am Diet Assoc* 107: 237–245.

Duffy, V. B., Lucchina, L. A., and Bartoshuk, L. M. (2004). Genetic variation in taste: Potential biomarker for cardiovascular disease risk? In J. Prescott and B. J. Tepper (Eds.), *Genetic Variations in Taste Sensitivity: Measurement, Significance and Implications* (pp. 195–228). New York: Dekker.

Duhamel, J. R., Colby, C. L., and Goldberg, M. E. (1992). The updating of the representation of visual space in parietal cortex by intended eye movements. *Science* 255: 90–92.

Durgin, F. H., Proffitt, D. R., Olson, T. J., and Reinke, K. S. (1995). Comparing depth from motion with depth from binocular disparity. *J Exp Psychol Hum Percept Perform* 21: 679–699.

E

Ehinger, K. A., Hidalgo-Sotelo, B., Torralba, A., and Oliva, A. (2009). Modelling search for people in 900 scenes: A combined source model of eye guidance. *Vis Cogn* 17: 945–978.

Ehrsson, H. H. (2007). The experimental induction of out-of-body experiences. *Science* 317: 1048.

Eich, E. (1995). Mood as a mediator of place dependent memory. *J Exp Psychol* 124: 293–308.

Eichenbaum, H. (2001). The hippocampus and declarative memory: Cognitive mechanisms and neural codes. *Behav Brain Res* 127: 199–207.

Eippert, F., Finsterbusch, J., Bingel, U., and Büchel, C. (2009). Direct evidence for spinal cord involvement in placebo analgesia. *Science* 326: 404.

Ellingsen, D-M., Wessberg, J., Eikemo, M., Liljencrantz, J., Endestad, T., Olausson, H., and Leknes, S. (2013). Placebo improves pleasure and pain

through opposite modulation of sensory processing. *Proc Nat Acad Sci USA* 110: 17993–17998.

Endevelt-Shapira, Y., Shushan, S., Roth, Y., Sobel, N. (2014). Disinhibition of olfaction: Human olfactory performance improves following low levels of alcohol, *Behav Brain Res* 272: 66–74.

Engen, T. (1972). The effect of expectation on judgments of odor. *Acta Psychol* 36: 450–458.

Engen, T. (1982). *The Perception of Odors.* Toronto: Academic Press.

Engen, T. (1991). *Odor Sensation and Memory.* New York: Praeger.

Engen, T. and Ross, B. M. (1973). Long-term memory odours with and without verbal descriptions. *J Exp Psychol* 100: 221–227.

Engen, T., Kuisma, J. E., and Eimas, P. D. (1973). Short-term memory of odors. *J Exp Psychol* 99: 222–225.

Enns, J. T. and Rensink, R. A. (1990). Scene based properties influence visual search. *Science* 247: 721–723.

Enroth-Cugell, C. and Robson, J. G. (1984). Functional characteristics and diversity of cat retinal ganglion cells: Basic characteristics and quantitative description. *Invest Ophthalmol Vis Sci* 25: 250–267.

Epstein, R. and Kanwisher, N. (1998). A cortical representation of the local visual environment. *Nature* 392: 598–601.

Epstein, R., Harris, A., Stanley, D., and Kanwisher, N. (1999). The parahippocampal place area: Recognition, navigation, or encoding? *Neuron* 23: 115–125.

Eriksen, C. W. and Yeh, Y. Y. (1985). Allocation of attention in the visual field. *J Exp Psychol Hum Percept Perform* 11: 583–597.

Ernst, M. O. and Banks, M. S. (2002). Humans integrate visual and haptic information in a statistically optimal fashion. *Nature* 415: 429–433.

Eskew, R. T., Jr. (2008). Chromatic detection and discrimination. In R. H. Masland and T. D. Albright (Eds.), *The Senses: A Comprehensive Reference*, Vol. 2: *Vision II* (pp. 101–117). New York: Academic Press.

Esteva, A., Kuprel, B., Novoa, R. A., Ko, J., Swetter, S. M., Blau, H. M., and Thrun, S. (2017). Dermatologist-level classification of skin cancer with deep neural networks. [Letter]. *Nature* 542: 115–118.

F

Fahle, M. (1982). Binocular rivalry: Suppression depends on orientation and spatial frequency. *Vision Res* 22: 787–800.

Fairhurst, M. T., Loken, L., and Grossmann, T. (2014). Physiological and behavioral responses reveal 9-month-old infants' sensitivity to pleasant touch. *Psychol Sci* 25: 1124–1131.

Fancher, R. E. (1990). *Pioneers of Psychology* (2nd ed.). New York: Norton.

Farris, H. (2017). Perception drives the evolution of observable traits. *Science* 355: 25–26.

Farroni, T., Menon, E., Rigato, S., and Johnson, M. H. (2007). The perception of facial expressions in newborns. *Eur J Dev Psychol* 4: 2–13.

Fast, K. (2004). *Developing a Scale to Measure Just About Anything: Comparisons across Groups and Individuals.* New Haven, CT: Yale University School of Medicine.

Fechner, G. (1903/1921). *Nanna: Oder Über das Seelenleben der Pflanzen* [Nanna, or Concerning the Mental Life of Plants]. Leipzig: Leopold Voss.

Fedderson, W. E., Sandel, T. T., Teas, D. C., and Jeffress, L. A. (1957). Localization of high frequency tones. *J Acoust Soc Am* 29: 988–991.

Federer, F., Ichida, J. M., Jeffs, J., Schiessl, I., McLoughlin, N., and Angelucci, A. (2009). Four projection streams from primate V1 to the cytochrome oxidase stripes of V2. *J Neurosci* 29: 15455–15471.

Feldman, H. M. and Reiff, M. I. (2014). Attention Deficit-Hyperactivity Disorder in Children and Adolescents. *N Engl J Med* 370: 838–846.

Felleman, D. J. and Van Essen, D. C. (1991). Distributed hierarchical processing in the primate cerebral cortex. *Cereb Cortex* 1: 1–47.

Fernandez, C. and Goldberg, J. (1971). Physiology of peripheral neurons innervating semicircular canals of the squirrel monkey. II. Response to sinusoidal stimulation and dynamics of peripheral vestibular system. *J Neurophysiol* 34: 661–675.

Ferrandiz-Huertas, C., Mathivanan, S., Wolf, C. J., Devesa, I., and Ferrer-Montiel, A. (2014). Trafficking of thermo TRP channels. *Membranes* 4: 525–564.

Fettiplace, R. and Hackney, C. M. (2006). The sensory and motor roles of auditory hair cells. *Nature* 7: 19–29.

Field, D. J., Hayes, A., and Hess, R. F. (1992). Contour integration by the human visual system: Evidence for a local "association field." *Vision Res* 33: 173–193.

Field, T. M., Schanberg, S. M., Scafidi, F., Bauer, C. R., Vega-Lahr, N., Garcia, R., Nystrom, J., and Kuhn, C. M. (1986). Tactile/kinesthetic stimulation effects on preterm neonates. *Pediatrics* 77: 654–658.

Fielder, A. R. and Moseley, M. J. (1996). Does stereopsis matter in humans? *Eye* 10: 233–238.

Firestein, S. (2001). How the olfactory system makes sense of scents. *Nature* 413: 211–218.

Fischer, R. and Griffin, F. (1964). Pharmacogenetic aspects of gustation. *Drug Res* 14: 673–686.

Fisher, S. K. and Ciuffreda, K. J. (1988). Accommodation and apparent distance. *Perception* 17: 609–621.

Flegal, K. M., Carroll, M. D., Ogden, C. L., and Johnson, C. L. (2002). Prevalence and trends in obesity among U.S. adults, 1999–2000. *JAMA* 14: 1723–1727.

Flege, J. E., Bohn, O. S., and Jang, S. (1997). Effects of experience on non-native speakers' production and perception of English vowels. *J Phon* 25: 437–470.

Fleming, R. W. (2014). Visual perception of materials and their properties. *Vis Res* 94: 62–75.

Fletcher, H. (1940). Auditory patterns. *Rev Mod Phys* 12: 47–65.

Fletcher, H. and Galt, R. H. (1950). The perception of speech and its relation to telephony. *J Acoust Soc Am* 22: 89–151.

Florida Atlantic University. (2017, July 20). "Sound" research shows slower boats may cause manatees more harm than good: Manatee alerting device research points to better solution. *ScienceDaily.* Retrieved from www.sciencedaily.com/releases/2017/07/170720095358.htm.

Foster, D. H. (2011). Color constancy. *Vision Res* 51: 674–700.

Fox, A. L. (1931). Six in ten "tasteblind" to bitter chemical. *Sci News Lett* 9: 249.

Fox, R. and Blake, R. R. (1971). Stereoscopic vision in the cat. *Nature* 233: 55–56.

Francis, D., Diorio, J., Liu, D., and Meaney, M. J. (1999). Nongenomic transmission across generations of maternal behavior and stress responses in the rat. *Science* 286: 1155–1158.

Francis, S. T., Rolls, E. T., Bowtell, R., McGlone, F., O'Doherty, J. O., Browning, A., Clare, S., et al. (1999). The representation of pleasant touch in the brain and its relationship with taste and olfactory areas. *Neuroreport* 10: 453–459.

Franco, M. I., Turin, L., Mershin, A., and Skoulakis, E. M. C. (2011). Molecular vibration sensing component in *Drosophila melanogaster* olfaction. *Proc Natl Acad Sci USA* 108: 3797–3802.

Freedman, D. J., Riesenhuber, M., Poggio, T., and Miller, E. K. (2001). Categorical perception of visual stimuli in the primate prefrontal cortex. *Science* 291: 312–316.

Freire, A., Lewis, T. L., Maurer, D., and Blake, R. (2006). The development of sensitivity to biological motion in noise. *Perception* 35: 647–657.

Frenzel, H., Bohlender, J., Pinsker, K., Wohlleben, B., Tank, J., Lechner, S. G., Schiska, D., et al. (2012). A genetic basis for mechanosensory traits in humans. *PLoS Biology* 10: e1001318.

Frisby, J. P. and Stone, J. V. (2010). *Seeing: The Computational Approach to Biological Vision.* MIT Press: Cambridge, MA.

Fuentes, C. T., Longo, M. R., and Haggard, P. (2013). Body image distortions in healthy adults. *Acta Psychol (Amst)* 144: 344–351.

G

Galanter, E. (1962). Direct measurement of utility and subjective probability. *Am J Psychol* 75: 208–220.

Galef, B. G. and Wigmore, S. W. (1983). Transfer of information concerning distant foods: A laboratory investigation of the "information-centre" hypothesis. *Anim Behav* 31: 748–758.

Gallace, A., Tan, H. Z., and Spence, C. (2007). Do "mudsplashes" induce tactile change blindness? *Percept Psychophys* 69: 477–486.

Gallant, J. L., Braun, B., and Van Essen, D. C. (1993). Selectivity for polar, hyperbolic, and cartesian gratings in macaque visual cortex. *Science* 259: 100–103.

Gandhi, S. P., Heeger, D. J., and Boynton, G. M. (1998). Spatial attention affects brain activity in human primary visual cortex. *Proc Natl Acad Sci USA* 96: 3314–3319.

Gangrade, A. (2011). The effect of music on the production of neurotransmitters, hormones, cytokines, and peptides: A review. *Music Med* 3(3) [Published online before print]. doi: 10.1177/1943862111415117.

Gauthier, I., Williams, P., Tarr, M. J., and Tanaka, J. (1998). Training "greeble" experts: A framework for studying expert object recognition processes. *Vision Res* 38: 2401–2428.

Gegenfurtner, K. R. (2003). Cortical mechanisms of colour vision. *Nat Rev Neurosci* 4: 563–572.

Gegenfurtner, K. R. (2016). The interaction between vision and eye movements. *Perception* 45: 1333–1357.

Gegenfurtner, K. R., Bloj, M., and Toscani, M. (2015). The many colours of 'the dress.' *Curr Biol* 25: R543–R544.

Geisler, C. D. (1998). *From Sound to Synapse: Physiology of the Mammalian Ear*. New York: Oxford University Press.

Geisler, W. S. and Perry, J. S. (2009). Contour statistics in natural images: Grouping across occlusions. *Vis Neurosci* 26: 109–121.

Geldard, F. A. (1972). *The Human Senses* (2nd ed.). New York: Wiley.

Gelstein, S., Yeshurun, Y., Rozenkrantz, L., Shushan, S., Frumin, I., Roth, Y., and Sobel, N. (2011). Human tears contain chemosignal. *Science* 331: 226–230.

Gerkin, R. C. and Castro, J. B. (2015). The number of olfactory stimuli that humans can discriminate is still unknown. *Elife* 4: e08127.

Gerstein, E. R. (2002). Manatees, bioacoustics, and boats: Hearing tests, environmental measurements, and acoustic phenomena may together explain why boats and animals collide. *Am Sci* 90: 154–156.

Gescheider, G. A. (1974). *Temporal Relations in Cutaneous Stimulation* (Conference on Cutaneous Communication Systems and Devices). Oxford, UK: Psychonomic Society.

Getty, D. J., D'Orsi, C., and Pickett, R. M. (2008). Stereoscopic digital mammography: Improved accuracy of lesion detection in breast cancer screening. In E. A. Krupinski (Ed.), *Digital Mammography: 9th International Workshop, IWDM 2008 Tucson, AZ, USA, July 20–23, 2008 Proceedings* (Lecture Notes in Computer Science, no. 5116) (pp. 74–79). Berlin: Springer.

Giaschi, D., Lo, R., Narasimhan, S., Lyons, C., and Wilcox, L. M. (2013). Sparing of coarse stereopsis in stereodeficient children with a history of amblyopia. *J Vis* 13: 17.

Gibson, J. J. (1957). Optical motions and transformations as stimuli for visual perception. *Psychol Rev* 64: 288–295.

Gibson, J. J. (1966). *The Senses Considered as Perceptual Systems*. Boston: Houghton Mifflin.

Gilad, Y., Wiebe, V., Przeworski, M., Lancet, D., and Paabo, S. (2004). Loss of olfactory receptors genes coincides with the acquisition of full trichromatic vision in primates. *PLoS Biol* 2: 120–125.

Gilad, Y., Wiebe, V., Przeworski, M., Lancet, D., and Pääbo, S. (2007). Correction. Loss of olfactory receptor genes coincides with the acquisition of full trichromatic vision in primates. *PLoS Biol* 5: e148.

Gilbertson, T. A. (1998). Gustatory mechanisms for the detection of fat. *Curr Opin Neurobiol* 8: 447–452.

Gillam, B. (1980). Geometrical illusions. *Sci Am* 242: 102–111.

Glasser, D. M., Tsui, J. M. G., Pack, C. C., and Tadin, D. (2011). Perceptual and neural consequences of rapid motion adaptation. *Proc Nat Acad Sci USA* 108: E1080–E1088.

Goddard, G. W. (1951). Our eyes aloft spy out the enemy. *Popular Mechanics* 96: 97–102. Reprinted with permission.

Goff, S. A. and Klee, H. J. (2006). Plant volatile compounds: Sensory cues for health and nutritional value? *Science* 311: 815–819.

Goldberg, J. M. and Fernandez, C. (1971). Physiology of peripheral neurons innervating semicircular canals of the squirrel monkey, Parts 1, 2, 3. *J Neurophysiol* 34: 635–684.

Goldberg, J. M. and Fernandez, C. (1976). Physiology of peripheral neurons innervating otolith organs of the squirrel monkey, Parts 1, 2, 3. *J Neurophysiol* 39: 970–1008.

Goncalves, N. R. and Welchman, A. E. (2017). "What not" detectors help the brain see in depth. *Curr Biol* 27: 1403–1412.

Govardovskii, V. I. (1983). On the role of oil drops in colour vision. *Vision Res* 23: 1739–1740.

Goycoolea, M. V., Goycoolea, H. G., Farfan, C. R., Rodriguez, L. G., Martinez, G. C., and Vidal, R. (1986). Effect of life in industrialized societies on hearing in natives of Easter Island. *Laryngoscope* 96: 1391–1396.

Grabherr, L., Nicoucar, K., Mast, F. W., and Merfeld, D. M. (2008). Direction detection thresholds for yaw rotation about an earth-vertical axis as a function of frequency. *Exp Brain Res* 186: 677–681.

Graham, N. and Nachmias, J. (1971). Detection of grating patterns containing two spatial frequencies: A comparison of single-channel and multiple-channel models. *Vision Res* 11: 251–259.

Grant S. and Moseley, M. J. (2011). Amblyopia and real-world visuomotor tasks. *Strabismus* 19: 119–128.

Green, B. G. (1993). Evidence that removal of capsaicin accelerates desensitization on the tongue. *Neurosci Lett* 150: 44–48.

Green, C. S. and Bavelier, D. (2003). Action video game modifies visual attention. *Nature* 423: 534–537.

Green, D. M. and Swets, J. (1966). *Signal Detection Theory and Psychophysics*. New York: Wiley.

Greene, M. R. and Oliva, A. (2009). The briefest of glances: The time course of natural scene understanding. *Psychol Sci* 20: 464–472.

Gregory, R. L. (1966). *Eye and Brain*. New York: World University Library.

Gregory, R. L. (1970). *The Intelligent Eye*. London: Weidenfeld and Nicolson.

Grill-Spector, K. and Malach, R. (2004). The human visual cortex. *Annu Rev Neurosci* 27: 649–677.

Gross, C. G., Rocha-Miranda, C. E., and Bender, D. B. (1972). Visual properties of neurons in inferotemporal cortex of the macaque. *J Neurophysiol* 35: 96–111.

Grushka, M. and Bartoshuk, L. M. (2000). Burning mouth syndrome and oral dysesthesias. *Can J Diagn* 17: 99–109.

Guedry, F. (1974). Psychophysics of vestibular sensation. In H. H. Kornhuber (Ed.), *Vestibular System* (Handbook of Sensory Physiology, vol. 6) (pp. 1–154). New York: Springer.

Gurnsey, R. and Browse, R. A. (1987). Micropattern properties and presentation conditions influencing visual texture discrimination. *Percept Psychophys* 41: 239–252.

Guyton, A. C. (1991). *Textbook of Medical Physiology* (8th ed). Philadelphia: Saunders.

H

Haenny, P. E. and Schiller, P. H. (1988). State dependent activity in monkey visual cortex. I. Single cell activity in

V1 and V4 on visual tasks. *Exp Brain Res* 69: 225–244.

Haggard, P., Newman, C., Blundell, J., and Andrew, H. (2000). The perceived position of the hand in space. *Percept Psychophys* 68: 363–377.

Haller, R., Rummel, C., Henneberg, S., Pollmer, U., and Koster, E. P. (1999). The influence of early experience with vanillin on food preference in later life. *Chem Senses* 24: 465–467.

Han, S. E., Sundarajan, J., Bowling, D. L., Lake, J., and Purves, D. (2011). Co-variation of tonality in the music and speech of different cultures. *PLoS One* 6: e20160–e20160.

Handel, S. (1989). *Listening: An Introduction to the Perception of Auditory Events*. Cambridge, MA: MIT Press.

Handel, S. and Oshinsky, J. S. (1981). The meter of syncopated auditory poly-rhythms. *Percept Psychophys* 30: 1–9.

Hänig, D. (1901). Zur Psychophysik des Geschmackssinnes. *Philosophische Studien* 17: 576–623.

Hare, R. M., Schlatter, S., Rhodes, G., and Simmons, L. W. (2017). Putative sex-specific human pheromones do not affect gender perception, attractiveness ratings or unfaithfulness judgements of opposite sex faces. *Roy Soc Open Sci* 4: 160831.

Harkness, L. (1977). Chameleons use accommodation cues to judge distance. *Nature* 267: 346–349.

Harmon, L. D. and Julesz, B. (1973). Masking in visual recognition: Effects of two-dimensional filtered noise. *Science* 180: 1194–1197.

Hartline, H. K. (1940). The nerve messages in the fibers of the visual pathway. *J Opt Soc Am* 30: 239–247.

Haxby, J. V., Hoffman, E. A., and Gobbini, M. I. (2000). The distributed human neural system for face perception. *Trends Cogn Sci* 4: 223–233.

Hayes, J. E., Bartoshuk, L. M., Kidd, J. R., and Duffy, V. B. (2008). Supertasting and PROP bitterness depends on more than the *Tas2r38* gene. *Chem Senses* 33: 255–265.

Hedger, S. C., Heald, S. L. M., and Nusbaum, H. C. (2013). Absolute pitch may not be so absolute. *J Acoust Soc Am* 24: 1496–1502.

Hedner, M., Larsson, M., Arnold, N., Zucco, G. M., and Hummel, T. (2010). Cognitive factors in odor detection, odor discrimination, and odor identi-

fication tasks. *J Clin Exp Neuropsych* 32: 1062–1067.

Heeger, D. (2006). Visual motion perception. Lecture notes. New York University, Department of Psychology. cns.nyu.edu/~david/courses/perception/lecturenotes/motion/motion.html

Heider, E. R. (1972). Universals in color naming and memory. *J Exp Psychol* 93: 10–20.

Heise, G. A. and Miller, G. A. (1951). An experimental study of auditory patterns. *Am J Psychol* 64: 68–77.

Heiser, C., Baja, J., Lenz, F. Sommer, J. U., Hormann, K., Herr, R. M., and Stuck, B. A. (2012). Effects of an artificial smoke on arousals during human sleep. *Chemosens Percept* 5: 274–279.

Held, R. T. and Hui, T. T. (2011). A guide to stereoscopic 3D displays in medicine. *Acad Radiol* 18: 1035–1048.

Held, R. T., Cooper, E. A., and Banks, M. S. (2012). Blur and disparity are complementary cues to depth. *Curr Biol* 22: 426–431.

Held, R., Ostrovsky, Y., deGelder, B., Gandhi, T., Ganesh, S., Mathur, M., and Sinha, P. (2011). Newly sighted cannot match seen with felt. *Nat Neurosci* 14: 551–553.

Helmholtz, H. von. (1924). *Helmholtz's Treatise on Physiological Optics* (translated from the 3rd German ed.; edited by J. P. C. Southall). Rochester, NY: Optical Society of America.

Hendry, S. H. and Reid, R. C. (2000). The koniocellular pathway in primate vision. *Annu Rev Neurosci* 23: 127–153.

Hering, E. (1878). *Zur Lehre vom Lichtsinn*. Vienna: Gerold.

Herness, S., Zhao, F.-L., Kaya, N., Shen, T., Lu, S.-G., and Cao, Y. (2005). Communication routes within the taste bud by neurotransmitters and neuropeptides. *Chem Senses* 30 (Suppl.1): i37–i38.

Herz, R. S. (1997). Emotion experienced during encoding enhances odor retrieval cue effectiveness. *Am J Psychol* 110: 489–505.

Herz, R. S. (1998). Are odors the best cues to memory? A cross-modal comparison of associative memory stimuli. *Ann NY Acad Sci* 855: 670–674.

Herz, R. S. (2000). Scents of time. *Sciences* 40: 34–39.

Herz, R. S. (2001). Ah, sweet skunk: Why we like or dislike what we smell. *Cerebrum* 3: 31–47.

Herz, R. S. (2004). A comparison of autobiographical memories triggered by

olfactory, visual, and auditory stimuli. *Chem Senses* 29: 217–224.

Herz, R. (2007). *The Scent of Desire: Discovering Our Enigmatic Sense of Smell*. New York: Morrow.

Herz, R. S. (2009). Aromatherapy facts and fictions: A scientific analysis of olfactory effects on mood, physiology and behavior. *Int J Neurosci* 119: 263–290.

Herz, R. S. (2016). The role of odor-evoked memory in psychological and physiological health. *Brain Sci* 6: 22.

Herz, R. S., Beland, S. L., and Hellerstein, M. (2004). Changing odor hedonic perception through emotional associations in humans. *Int J Comp Psychol* 17: 315–339.

Herz, R. S. and Cupchik, G. C. (1992). An experimental characterization of odor-evoked memories in humans. *Chem Senses* 17: 519–528.

Herz, R. S. and Cupchik, G. C. (1995). The emotional distinctiveness of odor-evoked memories. *Chem Senses* 20: 517–528.

Herz, R. S., Eliassen, J. C., Beland, S. L., and T. Souza. (2004). Neuroimaging evidence for the emotional potency of odor-evoked memory. *Neuropsychologia* 42: 371–378.

Herz, R. S. and Schooler, J. W. (2002). A naturalistic study of autobiographical memories evoked by olfactory and visual cues: Testing the Proustian hypothesis. *Am J Psychol* 115: 21–32.

Herz, R. S., Van Reen, E., Barker, D., Bartz, A., and Carskadon, M. A. (2017b). *Olfactory sensitivity declines with number of hours awake*. Paper presented at the Association for Chemoreception Sciences Annual Meeting, Bonita Springs, April 29, 2017.

Herz, R. S., Van Reen, E., Barker, D., and Carskadon, M. A. (2017a, under review). The influence of circadian timing on odor detection. *Chem Senses* doi:10.1093/chemse/bjx067

Herz, R. S. and von Clef, J. (2001). The influence of verbal labeling on the perception of odors: Evidence for olfactory illusions? *Perception* 30: 381–391.

Hickox, A. E. and Liberman, M. C. (2014). Is noise-induced cochlear neuropathy key to the generation of hyperacusis or tinnitus? *J Neurophysiol* 111: 552–564.

Hinton, P. B. and Henley, T. B. (1993). Cognitive and affective components of stimuli presented in three modes. *B Psychonomic Soc* 31: 595–598.

Hochstein, S. and Ahissar, M. (2002). View from the top: Hierarchies and reverse hierarchies in the visual system. *Neuron* 36: 791–804.

Hoffman, D. D. and Richards, W. A. (1984). Parts of recognition. *Cognition* 18: 65–96.

Hofman, P. M., Van Riswick, J. G. A., and Van Opsal, A. J. (1998). Relearning sound localization with new ears. *Nat Neurosci* 1: 417–421.

Hohmann A. and Creutzfeldt, O. D. (1975). Squint and the development of binocularity in humans. *Nature* 254: 613–614.

Holbrook, E. H., Wu, E., Curry, W. T., Lin, D. T., and Schwob, J. E. (2011). Immunohistochemical characterization of human olfactory tissue. *Laryngoscope* 121: 1687–701.

Hollins, M. (2002). Touch and haptics. In H. Pashler and S. Yantis (Eds.), *Stevens Handbook of Experimental Psychology* (3rd ed.), Vol. 1: *Sensation and Perception* (pp. 585–618). New York: Wiley.

Hoon, M. A., Adler, E., Lindemeier, J., Battey, J. F., Ryba, N. J., and Zuker, C. S. (1999). Putative mammalian taste receptors: A class of taste-specific GPCRs with distinct topographic selectivity. *Cell* 96: 541–551.

Horak, F., Nashner, L., and Diener, H. (1990). Postural strategies associated with somatosensory and vestibular loss. *Exp Brain Res* 82: 167–177.

Horii, A., Russell, N. A., Smith, P. F., Darlington, C. L., and Bilkey, D. K. (2004). Vestibular influences on CA1 neurons in the rat hippocampus: An electrophysiological study in vivo. *Exp Brain Res* 155: 245–250.

Horikawa, T., Tamaki, M., Miyawaki, Y., and Kamitani, Y. (2013). Neural decoding of visual imagery during sleep. *Science* 340: 639–642.

Horton, J. C. and Hocking, D. R. (1996). An adult-like pattern of ocular dominance columns in striate cortex of newborn monkeys prior to visual experience. *J Neurosci* 16: 1791–1807.

Horton, J. C. and Hoyt, W. F. (1991). The representation of the visual field in human striate cortex. A revision of the classic Holmes map. *Arch Ophthalmol* 109: 816–824.

Horton, J. C. and Trobe, J. D. (1999). Akinetopsia from nefazodone toxicity. *Am J Ophthalmol* 128: 530–531.

Horwitz, G. D. and Hass, C. A. (2012). Nonlinear analysis of macaque V1 color tuning reveals cardinal directions for cortical color processing. *Nat Neurosci* 15: 913–919.

Howard, I. P. and Rogers, B. J. (1995). *Binocular Vision and Stereopsis.* New York: Oxford University Press.

Howard, I. P. and Rogers, B. J. (2001). *Seeing in Depth.* Toronto: Porteous.

Howard, J. D., Plailly, J., Grueschow, M., Hayens, J.-D., and Gottfried, J. A. (2009). Odor quality coding and categorization in human posterior piriform cortex. *Nat Neurosci* 12: 932–938.

Hubel, D. H. (1982). Exploration of the primary visual cortex, 1955–78. *Nature* 299: 515–524.

Hubel, D. H. (1988). *Eye, Brain, and Vision.* New York: Scientific American Library.

Hubel, D. and Wiesel, T. N. (1961). Integrative action in the cat's lateral geniculate body. *J Physiol* 155: 385–398.

Hubel, D. H. and Wiesel, T. N. (1962). Receptive fields, binocular interaction and functional architecture in the cat's visual cortex. *J Physiol* 160: 106–154.

Hubel, D. H. and Wiesel, T. N. (1973). A re-examination of stereoscopic mechanisms in area 17 of the cat. *J Physiol* 232: 29P–30P.

Hubel, D. H., Wiesel, T. N., and Stryker, M. P. (1978). Anatomical demonstration of orientation columns in macaque monkey. *J Comp Neurol* 177: 361–380.

Hudspeth, A. J. (1997). How hearing happens. *Neuron* 19: 947–950.

Hudspeth, A. J. (2013). Snapshot: Auditory transduction. *Neuron* 80: 536.e1

Hughes, A. (1977). The topography of vision in mammals of contrasting life styles: Comparative optics and retinal organization. In F. Crescitelli (Ed.), *Handbook of Sensory Physiology*, Vol. VII/5: *The Visual System in Vertebrates* (pp. 613–756). New York: Springer.

Hughes, S., Jagannath, A., Rodgers, J., Hankins, M. W., Peirson, S. N., and Foster, R. G. (2016). Signalling by melanopsin (OPN4) expressing photosensitive retinal ganglion cells. *Eye (Lond)* 30: 247–254.

Huk, A. C., Ress, D., and Heeger, D. J. (2001). Neuronal basis of the motion aftereffect reconsidered. *Neuron* 32: 161–172.

Hummel, T., Futschik, T., Frasnelli, J., and Huttenbring, K. B. (2003). Effects of olfactory function, age and gender on trigeminally mediated sensations: A study based on the lateralization of chemosensory stimuli. *Toxicol Lett* 140: 273–280.

Hummel, T., Kobel, G., Gudziol, H., and Mackay-Sim, A. (2007). Normative data for the "Sniffin' Sticks" including tests of odor identification, odor discrimination, and olfactory thresholds: An upgrade based on a group of more than 3,000 subjects. *Eur Arch Otorhinolaryngol* 264: 237–243.

Hummel, T., von Mering, R., Huch, R., and Kolble, N. (2002). Olfactory modulation of nausea during early pregnancy? *BJOG* 109: 1394–1397.

Hurvich, L. and Jameson, D. (1957). An opponent process theory of color vision. *Psychol Rev* 64: 384–404.

Hutchison, R. M., Culham, J. C., Everling, S. Flanagan, J. R., and Gallivan, J. P. (2014). Distinct and distributed functional connectivity patterns across cortex reflect the domain-specific constraints of object, face, scene, body, and tool category-selective modules in the ventral visual pathway. *Neuroimage* 96: 216–236.

Huterer, M. and Cullen, K. E. (2002). Vestibuloocular reflex dynamics during high-frequency and high-acceleration rotations of the head on body in rhesus monkey. *J Neurophysiol* 88: 13–28.

I

Imai, S., Flege, J., and Wayland, R. (2002). Perception of cross-language vowel differences: A longitudinal study of native Spanish learners of English. *J Acoust Soc Am* 111: 2364–2364.

Inagaki, T., K. and Eisenberger, N. I. (2013). Shared neural mechanisms underlying social warmth and physical warmth. *Psychol Sci* 24: 2272–2280.

Iriki, A., Tanaka, M., and Iwamura, Y. (1996). Coding of modified body schema during tool use by macaque postcentral neurons. *Neuroreport* 7: 2325–2330.

Irwin, D. E., Zacks, J. L., and Brown, J. S. (1990). Visual memory and the perception of a stable visual environment. *Percept Psychophys* 47: 35–46.

Ishiyama, S. and Brecht, M. (2016). Neural correlates of ticklishness in the rat somatosensory cortex. *Science* 354: 757–760.

Itatani, N. and Klump, G. M. (2017). Animal models for auditory streaming. *Philos Trans R Soc Lond B Biol Sci* 372: 1–11.

J

Jacob, S., Hayreh, D. J. S, and McClintock, M. (2001). Context-dependent effects of steroid chemosignals on human physiology and mood. *Physiol Behav* 74: 15–27.

Jacobs, L. F., Arter, J., Cook, A., and Sulloway, F. J. (2015). Olfactory orientation and navigation in humans. *PLoS One* 10: e0129387.

Jacoby, N. and McDermott, J. H. (2017). Integer ratio priors on musical rhythm revealed cross-culturally by iterated reproduction. *Curr Biol* 27: 359–370.

Jakubiak, B. K. and Feeney, B. C. (2017). Affectionate touch to promote relational, psychological, and physical well-being in adulthood. *Pers Soc Psychol Rev* 21: 228–252.

James, W. (1890). *The Principles of Psychology* (2 vols.). New York: Holt.

Jeffress, L. A. (1948). A place theory of sound localization. *J Comp Physiol Psychol* 41: 35–39.

Jeon, T.-I., Zhu, B., Larson, J. L., and Osborne, T. F. (2008). SREBP-2 regulates gut peptide secretion through intestinal bitter taste receptor signaling in mice. *J Clin Invest* 118: 3693–3700.

Johansson, G. (1975). Visual motion perception. *Sci Am* 232: 76–88.

Johansson, R. S. and Vallbo, A. B. (1983). Tactile sensory coding in the glabrous skin of the human hand. *Trends Neurosci* 6: 27–32.

Johnson, E. N., Hawken, M. J., and Shapley, R. (2001). The spatial transformation of color in the primary visual cortex of the macaque monkey. *Nat Neurosci* 4: 409–416.

Johnson, K. O. (2002). Neural basis of haptic perception. In H. Pashler and S. Yantis (Eds.), *Stevens Handbook of Experimental Psychology* (3rd ed.), Vol. 1: *Sensation and Perception* (pp. 537–583). New York: Wiley.

Jolicoeur, P., Gluck, M. A., and Kosslyn, S. M. (1984). Pictures and names: Making the connection. *Cogn Psychol* 16: 243–275.

Jones, B. and Mishkin, M. (1972). Limbic lesions and the problem of stimulus–reinforcement associations. *Exp Neurol* 36: 362–377.

Jones, H. G., Koka, K., Thornton, J. L., and Tollin, D. J. (2011). Concurrent development of the head and pinnae and the acoustic cues to sound location in a precocious species, the chinchilla (*Chinchilla lanigera*). *J Assoc Res Otolaryngol* 12: 127–140.

Jones, L. A. (1999). Somatic senses 3: Proprioception. In H. Cohen (Ed.), *Neuroscience for Rehabilitation* (2nd ed.), pp. 111–130. Philadelphia: Lippincott.

Jones, M. and Love, B. C. (2011). Bayesian Fundamentalism or Enlightenment? On the explanatory status and theoretical contributions of Bayesian models of cognition. *Behav Brain Sci* 34: 169–188.

Jones, R. K. and Lee, D. N. (1981). Why two eyes are better than one: The two views of binocular vision. *J Exp Psychol Hum Percept Perform* 7: 30–40.

Jordan, G., Deeb, S. S., Bosten, J. M., and Mollon, J. D. (2010). The dimensionality of color vision in carriers of anomalous trichromacy. *J Vis* 10: 12–12.

Joris, P. X., Smith, P. H., and Yin, T. C. T. (1998). Coincidence detection in the auditory system: 50 years after Jeffress. *Neuron* 21: 1235–1238.

Julesz, B. (1964). Binocular depth perception without familiarity cues. *Science* 45: 356–362.

Julesz, B. (1971). *Foundations of Cyclopean Perception.* Chicago: University of Chicago Press.

Julius, D. (2013). TRP channels and pain. *Annu Rev Cell Dev Biol* 29: 355–384.

K

Kadohisa, M. and Wilson, D. A. (2006). Olfactory cortical adaptation facilitates detection of odors against background. *J Neurophysiol* 95: 1888–1896.

Kaim, L. and Drewing, K. (2009). *Finger force of exploratory movements is adapted to the compliance of deformable objects.* Paper presented at the IEEE World Haptics Conference 2009, 565–569.

Kanwisher, N. (2010). Functional specificity in the human brain: A window into the functional architecture of the mind. *Proc Natl Acad Sci USA* 107: 11163–11170.

Kanwisher, N. (2017). The quest for the FFA and where it led. *J Neurosci* 37: 1056–1061.

Kanwisher, N. and Dilks, D. D. (2013). The functional organization of the ventral visual pathway in humans. In L. M. Chalupa and J. S. Werner (Eds.), *The New Visual Neurosciences* (pp. 733–746). Cambridge: MIT Press.

Kanwisher, N., McDermott, J., and Chun, M. M. (1997). The fusiform face area: A module in human extrastriate cortex specialized for face perception. *J Neurosci* 17: 4302–4311.

Kapfer, C., Seidl, A. H., Schweizer, H., and Grothe, B. (2002). Experience-dependent refinement of inhibitory inputs to auditory coincidence-detector neurons. *Nat Neurosci* 5: 247–253.

Kappers, S. (2007). Haptic space perception. *Can J Exp Psychol* 61: 208–218.

Kay, K. N., Naselaris, T., Prenger, R. J., and Gallant, J. L. (2008). Identifying natural images from human brain activity. *Nature* 452: 352–355.

Kaya, E. M. and Elhilali, M. (2017). Modelling auditory attention. *Philos Trans R Soc Lond B Biol Sci* 372: 1–10.

Keats, J. (2014). 20 Things You Didn't Know About…Noise. *Discover Magazine* June.

Keller, A. and Vosshall, L. B. (2004). A psychophysical test of the vibration theory of olfaction. *Nat Neurosci* 7: 337–338.

Keller, A. and Vosshall, L. B. (2016). Olfactory perception of chemically diverse molecules. *BMC Neurosci* 17: 55.

Keller, A., Gerkin, R. C., Guan, Y., Dhurandhar, A., Turu, G., Szalai, B., Mainland, J. D., et al. (2017). Predicting human olfactory perception from chemical features of odor molecules. *Science* 355: 820–826.

Keller, A., Zhuang, H., Chi, Q., Vosshall, L. B., and Matsunami, H. (2007). Genetic variation in a human odorant receptor alters odour perception. *Nature* 449: 468–472.

Kellman, P. J. (1998). An update on gestalt psychology. In *Perception, Cognition, and Language: Essays in Honor of Henry and Lila Gleitman* (pp. 157–190). Cambridge, MA: MIT Press.

Kellman, P. J. and Shipley, T. F. (1991). A theory of visual interpolation in object perception. *Cogn Psychol* 23: 141–221.

Kepecs, A., Uchida, N., and Mainen, Z. F. (2007). Rapid and precise control of sniffing during olfactory discrimination in rats. *J Neurophysiol* 98: 205–213.

Kern, R. C., Conley, D. B., Haines, G. K., and Robinson, A. M. (2004). Pathology of the olfactory mucosa: Implications for the treatment of olfactory dysfunction. *Laryngoscope* 114: 279–285.

Kersten, D., Mamassian, P., and Yuille, A. (2004). Object perception as Bayesian inference. *Annu Rev Psychol* 55: 271–304.

Kessel, R. G. and Kardon, R. H. (1979). *Tissues and Organs: A Text-Atlas of Scanning Electron Microscopy.* San Francisco: Freeman.

Khan, R. M., Luk, C. H., Flinker, A., Aggarwal, A., Lapid, H., Haddad, R., and Sobel, N. (2007). Predicting odor pleasantness from odorant structure: Pleasantness as a reflection of the physical world. *J Neurosci* 27: 1–9.

Kiang, N. Y. S. (1965). *Discharge Patterns of Single Fibers in the Cat's Auditory Nerve.* Cambridge, MA: MIT Press.

Kiefte, M. and Kluender, K. R. (2005). The relative importance of spectral tilt in monopthongs and diphthongs. *J Acoust Soc Am* 117: 1395–1404.

Kiefte, M. and Kluender, K. R. (2008). Absorption of reliable spectral characteristics in auditory perception. *J Acoust Soc Am* 123: 366–376.

Kikuta, S., Fletcher, M. L. Homma, R. Yamasoba, T., and Nagayama, S. (2013). Odorant Response Properties of individual neurons in an olfactory glomerular module. *Neuron* 77: 1122–1135.

Kim, U. K., Jorgenson, E., Coon, H., Leppert, M., Risch, N., and Drayna, D. (2003). Positional cloning of the human quantitative trait locus underlying taste sensitivity to phenylthiocarbamide. *Science* 299: 1221–1225.

Kirchner, H. and Thorpe, S. J. (2006). Ultra-rapid object detection with saccadic eye movements: Visual processing speed revisited. *Vision Res* 46: 1762–1776.

Kistler, D. J. and Wightman, F. L. (1992). A model of head-related transfer functions based on principal components analysis and minimum-phase reconstruction. *J Acoust Soc Am* 91: 1637–1647.

Klatzky, R. L., Lederman, S. J., and Metzger, V. (1985). Identifying objects by touch: An "expert system." *Percept Psychophys* 37: 299–302.

Klein, R. M. (2000). Inhibition of return. *Trends Cogn Sci* 4: 138–147.

Klein, R. M. and MacInnes, W. J. (1999). Inhibition of return is a foraging facilitator in visual search. *Psychol Sci* 10: 346–352.

Klerman, E. B., Shanahan, T. L., Brotman, D. J., Rimmer, D. W., Emens, J. S., Rizzo, J. F., III, and Czeisler, C. A. (2002). Photic resetting of the human circadian pacemaker in the absence of conscious vision. *J Biol Rhythms* 17: 548–555.

Kluender, K. R. and Alexander, J. M. (2008). Perception of speech sounds. In A. I. Basbaum, A. Kaneko, G. M. Shepard, and G. Westheimer (Eds.), *The Senses: A Comprehensive Reference*, Vol. 3: *Audition* (P. Dallos and D. Oertel, Eds.) (pp. 829–860). San Diego: Academic Press.

Kluender, K. R., Diehl, R. L., and Killeen, P. R. (1987). Japanese quail can learn phonetic categories. *Science* 237: 1195–1197.

Kluender, K. R. and Jenison, R. L. (1992). Effects of glide slope, noise intensity, and noise duration on the extrapolation of FM glides through noise. *Percept Psychophys* 51: 231–238.

Kluender, K. R., Lotto, A. J., and Holt, L. L. (2005). Contributions of nonhuman animal models to understanding human speech perception. In S. Greenberg and W. Ainsworth (Eds.), *Listening to Speech: An Auditory Perspective* (pp. 203–220). Mahwah, NJ: Erlbaum.

Kluender, K. R., Lotto, A. J., Holt, L. L., and Bloedel, S. L. (1998). Role of experience for language-specific functional mapping of vowel sounds. *J Acoust Soc Am* 104: 3596–3582.

Kluender, K. R., Stilp, C. E., and Kiefte, M. (2013). Perception of vowel sounds within a biologically realistic model of efficient coding. In G. S. Morrison and P. F. Assmann (Eds.), *Vowel Inherent Spectral Change: Modern Acoustics and Signal Processing* (pp. 117–151). Berlin, Heidelberg: Springer-Verlag.

Klumpp, R. G. and Eady, H. R. (1956). Some measurements of interaural time-difference thresholds. *J Acoust Soc Am* 28: 859–860.

Klüver, H. and Bucy, P. C. (1938). An analysis of certain effects of bilateral temporal lobectomy in the rhesus monkey, with special reference to "psychic blindness." *J Psychol* 5: 33–54.

Klüver, H. and Bucy, P. C. (1939). Preliminary analysis of functions of the temporal lobes in monkeys. *Arch Neurol Psychiatry* 42: 979–1000.

Ko, H. K., Poletti, M., and Rucci, M. (2010). Microsaccades precisely relocate gaze in a high visual acuity task. *Nat Neurosci* 13: 1549–1553.

Koenigsberger, L. (1906/1965). *Hermann von Helmholtz* (translated by F. A. Welby). Repr. New York: Dover.

Kolarik, A. J., Moore, B. C. J., Zahorik, P., Cirstea, S., and Pardhan, S. (2016). Auditory distance perception in humans: A review of cues, development, neuronal bases, and effects of sensory loss. *Atten Percept Psychophys* 78: 373–395.

Kondo, H. M., van Loon, A. M., Kawahara, J.-I., and Moore, B. C. J. (2017). Auditory and visual scene analysis: An overview. *Philos Trans R Soc Lond B Biol Sci* 372: 1–6.

Konen, C. S. and Kastner, S. (2008). Two hierarchically organized neural systems for object information in human visual cortex. *Nat Neurosci* 11: 224–231.

Koreimann, S., Gula, B., and Vitouch, O. (2014). Inattentional deafness in music. *Psych Res* 78: 304–312.

Kosslyn, S. M., Thompson, W. L., Kim, I. J., and Alpert, A. M. (1995). Topographic representations of mental images in primary visual cortex. *Nature* 378: 496–498.

Koulakov, A. A. and Rinberg, D. (2011). Sparse incomplete representations: a potential role of olfactory granule cells. *Neuron* 72: 124–136.

Kourtzi, Z. and Connor, C. E. (2011). Neural representations for object perception: Structure, category, and adaptive coding. *Annu Rev Neurosci* 34: 45–67.

Kovacs, I. and Julesz, B. (1993). A closed curve is much more than an incomplete one: Effect of closure in figure-ground segmentation. *Proc Natl Acad Sci USA* 90: 7495–7497.

Kovacs, I., Papathomas, T., Yang, M., and Feher, A. (1996). When the brain changes its mind: Interocular grouping during binocular rivalry. *Proc Natl Acad Sci USA* 93: 15508–15511. © (1996) National Academy of Sciences U.S.A.

Kowler, E. and Collewijn, H. (2010). The eye on the needle. *Nat Neurosci* 13: 1443–1444.

Krauskopf, J., Williams, D. R., and Heeley, D. W. (1982). Cardinal directions of color space. *Vision Res* 22: 1123–1131.

Krestel, D., Passe, D., Smith, J. C., and Jonsson, L. (1984). Behavioral determinants of olfactory thresholds to amyl acetate in dogs. *Neurosci Biobehav Rev* 8: 169–174.

Krusemark, E. A., Novak, L. R., Gitelman, D. R., and Li, W. (2103). When the sense of smell meets emotion: anxiety state dependent olfactory processing and neural circuitry adaption. *J Neurosci* 33: 15324–15332.

Kubovy, M. and Cohen, D. J. (2001). What boundaries tell us about binding. *Trends Cogn Sci* 5: 93–95.

Kuffler, S. W. (1953). Discharge patterns and functional organization of mammalian retina. *J Neurophysiol* 16: 37–68.

Kuhl, P. K. (1981). Discrimination of speech by nonhuman animals: Basic sensitivities conducive to the perception of speech sound categories. *J Acoust Soc Am* 70: 340–349.

Kuhl, P. K. and Miller, J. D. (1978). Speech perception by the chinchilla: Identification functions for synthetic VOT stimuli. *J Acoust Soc Am* 63: 905–917.

Kuhl, P. K., Williams, K. A., Lacerda, F., Stevens, K. N., and Lindblom, B. (1992). Linguistic experience alters phonetic perception in infants six months of age. *Science* 255: 606–608.

Kuhn, G. and Kingstone, A. (2009). Look away! Eyes and arrows engage oculomotor responses automatically. *Atten Percept Psychophys* 71: 314–327.

Kumagami, T., Zhang, B., Smith, E. L., III, and Chino, Y. M. (2000). Effect of onset age of strabismus on the binocular responses of neurons in the monkey visual cortex. *Invest Ophthalmol Vis Sci* 41: 948–954.

Kurz, J. (2008, December 26). Getting to the root of the great cilantro divide. *National Public Radio*, www.npr.org.

Kwok, R. H. M. (1968). Chinese-restaurant syndrome. *N Engl J Med* 278: 796.

Kwok, V., Niu, Z., Kay, P., Zhou, K., Mo, L., Jin, Z., So, K.-W., et al. (2011). Learning new color names produces rapid increase in gray matter in the intact adult human cortex. *Proc Natl Acad Sci USA* 108: 6686–6688.

L

Lafer-Sousa, R., Hermann, K. L., and Conway, B. R. (2015). Striking individual differences in color perception uncovered by 'the dress' photograph. *Curr Biol* 25: R545–R546.

Laing, D. G. and Francis, G. W. (1989). The capacity of humans to identify odors in mixtures. *Physiol Behav* 46: 809–814.

Laing, D. G. and Glemarec, A. (1992). Selective attention and the perceptual analysis of odor mixtures. *Physiol Behav* 33: 309–319.

Lam, R. S. and Mombaerts, P. (2013). Odorant responsiveness of embryonic mouse olfactory sensory neurons expressing the odorant receptors S1 or MOR23. *Eur J Neurosci* 38: 2210–2217.

LaMotte, R. H. and Srinivasan, M. A. (1991). Surface microgeometry: Tactile perception and neural encoding. In O. Franzen and J. Westman (Eds.), *Information Processing in the Somatosensory System* (pp. 49–58). London: Macmillan.

Land, E. H. and McCann, J. J. (1971). Lightness and retinex theory. *J Opt Soc Am* 61: 1–11.

Larsson, M. and Willander, J. (2009). Autobiographical odor memory. *Ann NY Acad Sci* 1170: 318–323.

Laska, M., Koch, B., Heid, B., and Hudson, R. (1996). Failure to demonstrate systematic changes in olfactory perception in the course of pregnancy: A longitudinal study. *Chem Senses* 21: 567–571.

Latorre, R., Zaelzer, C., and Brauchi, S. (2009). Structure-functional intimacies of transient receptor potential channels. *Q Rev Biophys* 42: 201–246.

Lawless, H. and Engen, T. (1977). Associations to odors: Interference, mnemonics, and verbal labelling. *J Exp Psychol* 3: 52–59.

Lawo, V. and Koch, I. (2014). Dissociable effects of auditory attention switching and stimulus–response compatibility. *Psych Res* 78: 379–386.

Lecanuet, J. P., Granier-Deferre, C., Cohen, C., Le Houezec, R., and Busnel, M. C. (1986). Fetal responses to acoustic stimulation depend on heart rate variability pattern stimulus intensity and repetition. *Early Hum Dev* 13: 269–283.

Lederman, S. J. and Klatzky, R. L. (1987). Hand movements: A window into haptic object recognition. *Cogn Psychol* 19: 342–368.

Lederman, S. J. and Klatzky, R. L. (1997). Relative availability of surface and object properties during early haptic processing. *J Exp Psychol Hum Percept Perform* 23: 1680–1707.

Lederman, S. J., Klatzky, R., Chataway, C., and Summers, C. (1990). Visual mediation and the haptic recognition of two-dimensional pictures of common objects. *Percept Psychophys* 47: 54–64.

Lederman, S. J., Thorne, G., and Jones, B. (1986). The perception of texture by vision and touch: Multidimensionality and intersensory integration. *J Exp Psychol Hum Percept Perform* 12: 169–180.

Ledgeway, T. (1994). Adaptation to second-order motion results in a motion aftereffect for directionally-ambiguous test stimuli. *Vision Res* 34: 2879–2889.

Ledgeway, T. and Smith, A. T. (1994). The duration of the motion aftereffect following adaptation to first-order and second-order motion. *Perception* 23: 1211–1219.

Lee, C.-Y. and Lee, Y.-F. (2010). Perception of musical pitch and lexical tones by Mandarin speaking musicians. *J Acoust Soc Am* 127: 481–490.

Lee, D. N. (1976). A theory of visual control of braking based on information about time-to-collision. *Perception* 5: 437–459.

Lee, S.-H. and Blake, R. (1999). Visual form created solely from temporal structure. *Science* 284: 1165–1168.

LeGates, T. A., Fernandez, D. C., and Hattar, S. (2014). Light as a central modulator of circadian rhythms, sleep and affect. [Review]. *Nat Rev Neurosci* 15: 443–454.

Legge, G. E., Madison, C., Vaughn, B. N., Cheong, A. M. Y., and Miller, J. C. (2008). Retention of high tactile acuity throughout the life span in blindness. *Percept Psychophys* 70: 1471–1488.

Lehman, C. D., Bartoshuk, L. M., Catalanotto, F. C., Kveton, J. F., and Lowlicht, R. A. (1995). The effect of anesthesia of the chorda tympani nerve on taste perception in humans. *Physiol Behav* 57: 943–951.

LeVay, S., Hubel, D. H., and Wiesel, T. N. (1975). The pattern of ocular dominance columns in macaque visual cortex revealed by a reduced silver stain. *J Comp Neurol* 159: 559–576.

Levi, D. M. (2008). Crowding—an essential bottleneck for object recognition: A mini-review. *Vision Res* 48: 635–654.

Levi, D. M. and Li, R. W. (2009). Perceptual learning as a potential treatment for amblyopia: A mini review. *Vision Res* 49: 2535–2549.

Levi, D. M., Klein, S. A., and Aitsebaomo, A. P. (1985). Vernier acuity, crowding and cortical magnification. *Vision Res* 25: 963–977.

Levin, D. T. and Beale, J. M. (2000). Categorical perception occurs in newly learned faces, other-race faces, and inverted faces. *Atten Percept Psychophys* 62: 386–401.

Levine, M. W. (2000). *Levine & Shefner's Fundamentals of Sensation and Perception* (3rd ed.). Oxford, UK: Oxford University Press.

Levinson, S. C. (2000). Yeli Dnye and the theory of basic color terms. *J Linguist Anthropol* 10: 3–55.

Li, B., Peterson, M. R., and Freeman, R. D. (2003). Oblique effect: A neural basis in the visual cortex. *J Neurophysiol* 90: 204–217.

Li, F. F., VanRullen, R., Koch, C., and Perona, P. (2002). Rapid natural scene categorization in the near absence of attention. *Proc Natl Acad Sci USA* 99: 9596–9601.

Li, H.-H., Rankin, J., Rinzel, J., Carrasco, M., and Heeger, D. J. (2017). Attention model of binocular rivalry. *Proc Natl Acad Sci USA* 114: E6192–E6201.

Li, R. W., Ngo, C., Nguyen, J., and Levi, D. M. (2011). Videogame play induces plasticity in the visual system of adults with amblyopia. *PloS Biology* 9: e1001135.

Li, W., Lopez, L., Osher, J., Howard, J. D., Parrish, T. B., and Gottfried, J. A. (2010). Right orbitofrontal cortex mediates conscious olfactory perception. *Psychol Sci* 21: 1454–1463.

Liberman, A. M. and Mattingly, I. G. (1985). The motor theory of speech perception revised. *Cognition* 21: 1–36.

Liberman, A. M., Cooper, F. S., Shankweiler, D. P., and Studdert Kennedy, M. (1967). Perception of the speech code. *Psychol Rev* 74: 431–461.

Liberman, A. M., Harris, K. S., Hoffman, H. S., and Griffith, B. C. (1957). The discrimination of speech sounds within and across phoneme boundaries. *J Exp Biol* 54: 358–368.

Lieberman, P. (1984). *The Biology and Evolution of Language.* Cambridge, MA: Harvard University Press.

Liem, D. G. and Mennella, J. A. (2003). Heightened sour preferences during childhood. *Chem Senses* 28: 173–180.

Lima, C. F., Krishnan, S., and Scott, S. K. (2016). Roles of supplementary motor areas in auditory processing and auditory imagery. *Trends Neurosci* 39: 527–542.

Lin, J. Y., Murray, S. O., and Boynton, G. M. (2009). Capture of attention to threatening stimuli without perceptual awareness. *Curr Biol* 19: 1118–1122.

Lindeman, H. H. (1973). Anatomy of the otolith organs. *Adv Otorhinolaryngol* 20: 404–433.

Lindsey, D. T. and Brown, A. M. (2006). Universality of color names. *Proc Natl Acad Sci USA* 103: 16608–16613.

Lindsey, D. T. and Brown, A. M. (2014). The color lexicon of American English. *J Vis* 14: 17.

Lindsey, D. T., Brown, A. M., Reijnen, E., Rich, A. N., Kuzmova, Y., and Wolfe, J. M. (2010). Color channels, not color appearance or color categories, guide visual search for desaturated color targets. *Psychol Sci* 21: 1208–1214.

Linhares, J. M. M., Pinto, P. D., and Nascimento, S. M. C. (2008). The number of discernible colors in natural scenes.

J Opt Soc Am A Opt Image Sci Vis 25: 2918–2924.

Lisker, L. (1986). "Voicing" in English: A catalogue of acoustic features signaling /b/ versus /p/ in trochees. *Lang Speech* 29: 3–11.

Livingstone, M. and Hubel, D. (1988). Segregation of form, color, movement, and depth: Anatomy, physiology, and perception. *Science* 240: 740–749.

Llanos, F., Jiang, Y., and Kluender, K. R. (2014). Exploiting 2nd-order statistics improves statistical learning of vowels. Paper presented at the 168th Meeting of the Acoustical Society of America, October, 2014, Indianapolis, IN.

Locke, J. (1689/1975). *Essay Concerning Human Understanding,* Oxford: Oxford University Press.

Löfvenberg, J. and Johansson, R. S. (1984). Regional differences and interindividual variability in sensitivity to vibration in the glabrous skin of the human hand. *Brain Res* 301: 65–72.

Logothetis, N. K. and Schall, J. D. (1989). Neuronal correlates of subjective visual perception. *Science* 245: 761–763.

Logothetis, N. K., Pauls, J., and Poggio, T. (1995). Shape representation in the inferior temporal cortex of monkeys. *Curr Biol* 5: 552–563.

Loomis, J. M. (1981). On the tangibility of letters and braille. *Percept Psychophys* 29: 37–46.

Loomis, J. M. (1990). A model of character recognition and legibility. *J Exp Psychol Hum Percept Perform* 16: 106–120.

Lorig, T. (1999). On the similarity of odor and language perception. *Neurosci Biobehav Rev* 23: 391–398.

Lowe, D. G. (1985). *Perceptual Organization and Visual Recognition.* Boston: Kluwer.

Lu, Z.-L. and Dosher, B. A. (1998). External noise distinguishes attention mechanisms. *Vision Res* 38: 1183–1198.

Lundstrom, J. N. and Olsson, M. J. (2005). Subthreshold amounts of a social odorant affect mood, but not behavior, in heterosexual women when tested by a male, but not a female experimenter. *Biol Psychol* 60: 197–204.

Lynch, M. P. and Eilers, R. E. (1990). Innateness, experience, and music perception. *Psychol Sci* 1: 272–276.

M

Ma, Q. (2010). Labeled lines meet and talk: Population coding of somatic sensations. *J Clin Invest* 120: 3773–3778.

Mach, E. (1875/2001). *Fundamentals of the Theory of Movement Perception* (republished with translations in 2001). New York: Kluwer/Plenum.

Macknik, S. L., Martinez-Conde, S., and Conway, B. (2015). How "The Dress" became an illusion unlike any other. *Sci Am Mind* 26(4).

MacLeod, D. I. and Lennie, P. (1976). Red-green blindness confined to one eye. *Vision Res* 16: 691–702.

Macmillan, N. A. and Creelman, C. D. (2005). *Detection Theory.* Mahwah, NJ: Erlbaum.

Maddieson, I. (1984). *Patterns of Sound.* Cambridge, UK: Cambridge University Press.

Maffei, L. and Fiorentini, A. (1973). The visual cortex as a spatial frequency analyzer. *Vision Res* 13: 1255–1267.

Maison, S. F., Usubuchi, H., and Liberman, M. C. (2013). Efferent feedback minimizes cochlear neuropathy from moderate noise exposure. *J Neurosci* 13: 5542–5552.

Majid, A. and Burenhult, N. (2014). Odors are expressible in language, as long as you speak the right language. *Cognition* 130: 266–270.

Malik, J. and Perona, P. (1990). Preattentive texture discrimination with early vision mechanisms. *J Opt Soc Am A* 7: 923–932.

Maloney, L. T. (1986). Evaluation of linear models of surface spectral reflectance with small numbers of parameters. *J Opt Soc Am A* 3: 1673–1683.

Mancini, F., Bauleo, A., Cole, J., Lui, F., Porro, C. A., Haggard, P., and Iannetti, G. D. (2014). Whole-body mapping of spatial acuity for pain and touch. *Ann Neurol* 75: 917–924.

Mancini, F., Sambo, C. F., Ramirez, J. D., Bennett, D. L. H., Haggard, P., and Ianetti, G. D. (2013). A fovea for pain at the fingertips. *Curr Biol* 23: 496–500.

Maquet, P., Peters, J., Aerts, J., Delfiore, G., Degueldre, C., Luxen, A., and Franck, G. (1996). Functional neuroanatomy of human rapid-eye-movement sleep and dreaming. *Nature* 383: 163–166.

Maresh, A., Gil, D. R., Whitman, M. C., and Greer, C. A. (2008). Principles of glomerular organization in the human olfactory bulb—Implications for odor processing. *PLoS One* 3: 1–6.

Marks, L. E., Stevens, J. C., Bartoshuk, L. M., Gent, J. G., Rifkin, B., and Stone, V. K. (1988). Magnitude matching: The measurement of taste and smell. *Chem Senses* 13: 63–87.

Marotta, A., Ferre. E. R., and Haggard, P. (2015). Transforming the thermal grill effect by crossing the fingers. *Curr Biol* 25: 1069–1073.

Marr, D. and Poggio, T. (1979). A computational theory of human stereo vision. *Proc R Soc Lond B Biol Sci* 204: 301–328.

Marshall, J. and Arikawa, K. (2014). Unconventional colour vision. *Curr Biol* 24: R1150–R1154.

Martinez, A., Anllo-Vento, L., Sereno, M. I., Frank, L. R., Buxton, R. B., Dubowitz, D. J., Wong, E. C., Hinrichs, H., Heinze, H. J., and Hillyard, S. A. (1999). Involvement of striate and extrastriate visual cortical areas in spatial attention. *Nat Neurosci* 2: 364–369.

Maruniak, J. A., Silver, W. L., and Moulton, D. G. (1983). Olfactory receptors respond to blood-borne odorants. *Brain Res* 265: 312–316.

Masland, R. H. (2017). Vision: Two speeds in the retina. *Curr Biol* 27: R303–R305.

Mather, G. and Murdoch, L. (1994). Gender discrimination in biological motion displays based on dynamic cues. *Proc R Soc Lond B Biol Sci* 258: 273–279.

Matin, L., Picoult, E., Stevens, J. K., Edwards, M. W., Jr., Young, D., and MacArthur, R. (1982). Oculoparalytic illusion: Visual-field dependent spatial mislocalizations by humans partially paralyzed with curare. *Science* 216: 198–201.

Matsui, A., Go, Y., and Niimura, Y. (2010). Degeneration of olfactory receptor gene repertories in primates: No direct link to full trichromatic vision. *Mol Biol Evol* 27: 1192–1200.

Matsunami, H. (2011). *Recent advances in understanding olfactory molecular biological mechanisms.* Paper presented at the AChemS Annual Meeting, St. Petersburg, FL.

Maurer, D., Lewis, T. L., Brent, H. P., and Levin, A. V. (1999). Rapid improvement in the acuity of infants after visual input. *Science* 286: 108–110.

Mays, L. E. and Sparks, D. L. (1980). Dissociation of visual and saccade-related responses in superior colliculus neurons. *J Neurophysiol* 43: 207–232.

McConkie, G. W. and Currie, C. (1996). Visual stability across saccades while viewing complex pictures. *J Exp Psychol Hum Percept Perform* 22: 563–581.

McDermott, J. H., Schultz, A. F., Undurraga, E. A., and Godoy, R. A. (2016). Indifference to dissonance in native Amazonians reveals cultural variation in music perception. *Nature* 535: 547–550.

McDermott, J. H., Wroblewski, D., and Oxenham, A. J. (2011). Recovering sound sources from embedded repetition. *Proc Natl Acad Sci USA* 108: 1188–1193.

McGann, J. P. (2017). Poor human olfaction is a 19th-century myth. *Science* 356(6338): eaam7263.

McGlone, F., Vallbo, A. B., Olausson, H., Loken, L. S., and Wessberg, J. (2007). Discriminative touch and emotional touch. *Can J Exp Psychol* 61: 173–183.

McGowan, P. O., Sasaki, A., D'Alessio, A. C., Dymov, S., Labonté, B., Szy, M., Turecki, G., and Meaney, M. J. (2009). Epigenetic regulation of the glucocorticoid receptor in human brain associates with childhood abuse. *Nat Neurosci* 12: 342–348.

McGurk, H. and MacDonald, J. (1976). Hearing lips and seeing voices. *Nature* 264: 746–748.

McKee, S. P. (1983). The spatial requirements for fine stereoacuity. *Vision Res* 23: 191–198.

McKee, S. P. and D. G. Taylor (2010). The precision of binocular and monocular depth judgments in natural settings. *J Vis* 10: 5.

McMains, S. A. and Somers, D. C. (2004). Multiple spotlights of attentional selection in human visual cortex. *Neuron* 42: 677–686.

McRae, J. F., Jaeger, S. R., Bava, C. M., Beresford, M. K., Hunter, D., Jia, Y., Chheang, S. L., et al. (2013). Identification of regions associated with variation in sensitivity to food-related odors in the human genome. *Curr Biol* 23: 1596–600.

Mehler, J., Jusczyk, P., Lambertz, C., Halsted, N., Bertoncini, J., and Amiel-Tison, C. (1988). A precursor of language acquisition in young infants. *Cognition* 29: 143–178.

Melin, A. D., Kline, D. W., Hickey, C. M., and Fedigan, L. M. (2013). Food search through the eyes of a monkey: A functional substitution approach for assessing the ecology of primate color vision. *Vision Res* 86: 87–96.

Melzack, R. and Wall, P. D. (1988). *The Challenge of Pain* (2nd ed.). New York: Penguin.

Menashe, I., Man, O., Lancet, D., and Gilad, Y. (2003). Different noses for different people. *Nat Genet* 34: 143–144.

Mennella, J. A. and Beauchamp, G. K. (1991). The transfer of alcohol to human milk: Effects on flavor and the infant's behavior. *N Engl J Med* 325: 981–985.

Mennella, J. A. and Beauchamp, G. K. (1993). The effects of repeated exposure to garlic-flavored milk on the nursling's behavior. *Pediatr Res* 34: 805–808.

Mennella, J. A., Johnson, A., and Beauchamp, G. K. (1995). Garlic ingestion by pregnant women alters the odor of amniotic fluid. *Chem Senses* 20: 207–209.

Merfeld, D. M., Young, L., Oman, C., and Shelhamer, M. (1993). A multi-dimensional model of the effect of gravity on the spatial orientation of the monkey. *J Vestib Res* 3: 141–161.

Merfeld, D., Zupan, L., and Peterka, R. (1999). Humans use internal models to estimate gravity and linear acceleration. *Nature* 398: 615–618.

Mesgarani, N., Cheung, C., Johnson, K., and Chang, E. F. (2014). Phonetic feature encoding in human superior temporal gyrus. *Science* 343: 1006–1010.

Meyerhof, W., Batram, C., Kuhn, C., Brockhoff, A., Chudoba, E., Bufe, B., Appendino, G., et al. (2010). The molecular receptive ranges of human TAS2R bitter taste receptors. *Chem Senses* 35: 157–170.

Miller, G. A. and Heise, G. A. (1950). The trill threshold. *J Acoust Soc Am* 22: 637–638.

Miller, G., Tybur, J. M., and Jordan, B. D. (2007). Ovulatory cycle effects on tip earnings by lap dancers: Economic evidence for human estrus? *Evol Hum Behav* 28: 375–381.

Miller, S. L. and Maner J. K. (2010). Scent of a woman: Men's testosterone responses to olfactory ovulation cues. *Psychol Sci* 21: 276–283.

Ming, D., Ninomiya, Y., and Margolskee, R. F. (1999). Blocking taste receptor activation of gustducin inhibits gustatory responses to bitter compounds. *Proc Natl Acad Sci USA* 96: 9903–9908.

Miranda, M. I. (2012). Taste and odor recognition memory: The emotional flavor of life. *Rev Neuroscience* 23: 481–499

Miyawaki, Y., Uchida, H., Yamashita, O., Sato, M., Morito, Y., Tanabe, H., Sadato, N., et al. (2008). Visual image reconstruction from human brain activity using a combination of multiscale local image decoders. *Neuron* 60: 915–29.

Mollon, J. D. (1989). "Tho' she kneel'd in that place where they grew...": The uses and origins of primate colour vision. *J Exp Biol* 146: 21–38.

Mombaerts, P., Wang, F., Dulac, C., Chao, S. K., Nemes, A., Mendelsohn, M., Edmondson, J., and Axel, R. (1996). Visualizing an olfactory sensory map. *Cell* 87: 675–686.

Moncrieff, R. W. (1966). *Odour Preferences.* New York: Wiley.

Mondloch, C. J., Lewis, T. L., Budreau, D. R., Maurer, D., Dannemiller, J. L., Stephens, B. R., and Kleiner-Gathercoal, K. A. (1999). Face perception during early infancy. *Psychol Sci* 10: 419–422.

Moore, B. C. J. (2003). *An Introduction to the Psychology of Hearing* (5th ed.). London: Academic Press.

Moraga-Amaro, R., Cortes-Rojas, A., Simon, F., and Stehberg, J. (2013). Role of the insular cortex in taste familiarity. *Neurobio Learn Mem* 109: 37–45.

Moran, J. and Desimone, R. (1985). Selective attention gates visual processing in the extrastriate cortex. *Science* 229: 782–784.

Mori, E., Petters, W., Schriever, V. A., Valder, C., and Hummel, T. (2015). Exposure to odours improves olfactory function in healthy children. *Rhinology* 53: 221–226.

Moskowitz, H. R., Dravnieks, A., and Klarman, L. A. (1976). Odor intensity and pleasantness for a diverse set of odorants. *Percept Psychophys* 19: 122–128.

Motohashi, K. and Umino, M. (2001). Heterotopic painful stimulation decreases the late component of somatosensory evoked potentials induced by electrical tooth stimulation. *Brain Res Cogn Brain Res* 11: 39–46.

Mounts, J. R. (2000). Evidence for suppressive mechanisms in attentional selection: Feature singletons produce inhibitory surrounds. *Percept Psychophys* 62: 969–983.

Mozer, M. C. (1991). *The Perception of Multiple Objects: A Connectionist Approach.* Cambridge, MA: MIT Press.

Mullane, J. C. and Klein, R. M. (2008). Visual search by children with and without ADHD. *J Attention Disord* 12: 44–53.

Mullen, K. T. (1985). The contrast sensitivity of human colour vision to red-green and blue-yellow chromatic gratings. *J Physiol* 359: 381–400.

Müller, J. (1838/1912). *Handbook of Physiology* (translation from B. Rand [1912], *The Classical Psychologists*). Repr. Boston: Houghton-Mifflin.

Murphy, C., Cain, W. S., Gilmore, M. M., and Skinner, R. B. (1991). Sensory and semantic factors in recognition memory for odors and graphic stimuli: Elderly versus young persons. *Am J Psychol* 104: 161–192.

Murphy, S. and Dalton, P. (2016). Out of touch? Visual load induces inattentional numbness. *J Exp Psychol Hum Percept Perform* 42: 761–765.

Musiek, F. E. (2003). What can the acoustic startle reflex tell us? *Hear J* 56: 55.

N

Nachev, V., Stich, K. P., Winter, C., Bond, A., Kamil, A., and Winter, Y. (2017). Cognition-mediated evolution of low-quality floral nectars. *Science* 355: 75–78.

Nadler, J. W., Angelaki, D. E., and DeAngelis, G. C. (2008). A neural representation of depth from motion parallax in macaque visual cortex. *Nature* 452: 642–645.

Nassi, J. and Callaway, E. M. (2009). Parallel processing strategies of the primate visual system. *Nat Rev Neurosci* 10: 360–372.

Nathans, J. (1986). Molecular genetics of inherited variation in human color vision. *Science* 232: 203–210.

Nathans, J., Thomas, D., and Hogness, D. S. (1986). Molecular genetics of human color vision: The genes encoding blue, green, and red pigments. *Science* 232: 193–202.

National Eye Institute. *Facts about age-related macular degeneration.* August 2010, www.nei.nih.gov/health/maculardegen/armd_facts.asp.

Nauhaus, I., Benucci, A., Carandini, M., and Ringach, D. L. (2008). Neuronal selectivity and local map structure in visual cortex. *Neuron* 57: 673–679.

Navon, D. (1977). Forest before the trees: The precedence of global features in visual perception. *Cogn Psychol* 9: 353–383.

Negoias, S., Croy, I., Gerber, J., Puschmann, S., Petrowski, K., Joraschky, P., and Hummel, T. (2010). Reduced olfactory bulb volume and olfactory

sensitivity in patients with acute major depression. *Neuroscience* 169: 415–421.

Neitz, J., Geist, T., and Jacobs, G. H. (1989). Color vision in the dog. *Vis Neurosci* 3: 119–125.

Nerger, J. L., Volbrecht, V. J., and Ayde, C. J. (1995). Unique hue judgments as a function of test size in the fovea and at 20-deg temporal eccentricity. *J Opt Soc Am A Opt Image Sci Vis* 12: 1225–1232.

Neri, P., Luu, J. Y., and Levi, D. M. (2006). Meaningful interactions can enhance visual discrimination of human agents. *Nat Neurosci* 9: 1186–1192.

Neri, P., Morrone, M. C., and Burr, D. C. (1998). Seeing biological motion. *Nature* 395: 894–896.

Netter, F. (1983). *Nervous System: Anatomy and Physiology.* West Caldwell, NJ: CIBA Pharmaceutical Company.

Newcombe, F. and de Haan, E. H. F. (1994). Category specificity in visual recognition. In M. J. Farah and G. Ratcliff (Eds.), *The Neuropsychology of High-Level Vision: Collected Tutorial Essays* (Carnegie Mellon Symposia on Cognition) (pp. 103–132). Hillsdale, NJ: Erlbaum.

Newell, F. N. and Bülthoff, H. H. (2002). Categorical perception of familiar objects. *Cognition* 85: 113–143.

Newell, F. N., Ernst, M. O., Tjan, B. S., and Bulthoff, H. (2001). Viewpoint dependence in visual and haptic object recognition. *Psychol Sci* 12: 37–42.

Newsome, W. T. and Pare, E. B. (1988). A selective impairment of motion perception following lesions of the middle temporal visual area (MT). *J Neurosci* 8: 2201–2211.

Niimura, Y., Matsui, A., and Touhara, K. (2014). Extreme expansion of the olfactory receptor gene repertoire in African elephants and evolutionary dynamics of orthologous gene groups in 13 placental mammals. *Genome Res* 24: 1485–1496.

Nishimoto, S., Vu, A. T., Naselaris, T., Benjamini, Y., Yu, B., Gallant, J. L. (2011). Reconstructing visual experiences from brain activity evoked by natural movies. *Curr Biol* 21: 1641–1646.

Nityananda, V., Tarawneh, G., Jones, L., Busby, N., Herbert, W., Davies, R., and Read, J. C. A. (2015). The contrast sensitivity function of the praying mantis *Sphodromantis lineola. J Comp Physiol A* 201: 741–750.

Nityananda, V., Tarawneh, G., Rosner, R., Nicolas, J., Crichton, S., and Read, J.

(2016). Insect stereopsis demonstrated using a 3D insect cinema. *Sci Rep* 6: 18718.

Nobre, A. C. and Kastner, S. (2014). *Oxford Handbook of Attention*. New York: Oxford University Press.

Nodine, C. F., Mello-Thoms, C., Kundel, H. L., and Weinstein, S. P. (2002). Time course of perception and decision making during mammographic interpretation. *Am J Roentgenol* 179: 917–923.

Norcia, A. M., Tyler, C. W., and Hamer, R. D. (1990). Development of contrast sensitivity in the human infant. *Vision Res* 30: 1475–1486.

Norman-Haignere, S., Kanwisher, N. G., and McDermott, J. H. (2015). Distinct cortical pathways for music and speech revealed by hypothesis-free voxel decomposition. *Neuron* 88: 1281–1296.

O

O'Craven, K. M. and Kanwisher, N. (2000). Mental imagery of faces and places activates corresponding stimulus-specific brain regions. *J Cogn Neurosci* 12: 1013–1023.

O'Dell, C. and Boothe, R. G. (1997). The development of stereoacuity in infant rhesus monkeys. *Vision Res* 37: 2675–2684.

O'Regan, K. (1992). Solving the "real" mys-teries of visual perception: The world as an outside memory. *Can J Psychol* 46: 461–488.

Ogle, K. N. (1952b). On the limits of stereoscopic vision. *J Exp Psychol* 44: 253–259.

Ohzawa, I. and Freeman, R. D. (1986a). The binocular organization of simple cells in the cat's visual cortex. *J Neurophysiol* 56: 221–242.

Ohzawa, I. and Freeman, R. D. (1986b). The binocular organization of complex cells in the cat's visual cortex. *J Neurophysiol* 56: 243–259.

Okano, T., Fukada, Y., and Yoshizawa, T. (1995). Molecular basis for tetrachromatic color vision. *Comp Biochem Physiol B* 112: 405–414.

Olausson, H., Cole, J., Rylander, K., McGlone, F., Lamarre, Y., Wallin, B. G., Krämer H., et al. (2008). Functional role of unmyelinated tactile afferents in human hairy skin: Sympathetic response and perceptual localization. *Exp Brain Res* 184: 135–140.

Oliva, A. and Torralba, A. (2001). Modeling the shape of the scene: A holistic representation of the spatial envelope. *Int J Comput Vis* 42: 145–175.

Olivers, C. N. and Meeter, M. (2008). A boost and bounce theory of temporal attention. *Psychol Rev* 115: 836–863.

Olney, J. W. and Sharpe, L. G. (1969). Brain lesions in an infant rhesus monkey treated with monosodium glutamate. *Science* 166: 386–388.

Oman, C. (1990). Motion sickness: A synthesis and evaluation of the sensory conflict theory. *Can J Physiol Pharmacol* 68: 294–303.

Ooi, T. L., Wu, B., and He, Z. J. (2001). Distance determined by the angular declination below the horizon. *Nature* 414: 197–200.

Ooi, T. and He, Z. (1999). Binocular rivalry and visual awareness: The role of attention. *Perception* 28: 551–574.

Orefice, L. L., Zimmerman, A. L., Chirila1, A. M., Sleboda1, S. J., Head, J. P., and Ginty, D. D., (2016). Peripheral mechanosensory neuron dysfunction underlies tactile and behavioral deficits in mouse models of ASDs. *Cell* 166: 299–313.

Otte, R. J., Agterberg, M. J. H., Van Wanrooij, M. M., Snik, A. F. M., and Van Opstal, A. J. (2013). Age-related hearing loss and ear morphology affect vertical but not horizontal sound-localization performance. *J Assoc Res Otolaryngol* 14: 261–273.

Owens, D. A. (1987). Oculomotor information and perception of three-dimensional space. In H. Heuer and A. F. Sanders (Eds.), *Perspectives on Perception and Action* (pp. 215–248). Hillside, NJ: Erlbaum.

Oxbury, J. M., Oxbury, S. M., and Humphrey, N. K. (1969). Varieties of colour anomia. *Brain* 92: 847–860.

Oyster, C. W. (1999). *The Human Eye: Structure and Function*. Sunderland, MA: Sinauer.

P

Paik, S. B. and Ringach, D. L. (2011). Retinal origin of orientation maps in visual cortex. *Nat Neurosci* 14: 919–925.

Palmer, J. (1995). Attention in visual search: Distinguishing four causes of a set size effect. *Curr Dir Psychol Sci* 4: 118–123.

Palmer, S. E. (1992). Common region: A new principle of perceptual grouping. *Cogn Psychol* 24: 436–447.

Palmer, S. E. (1999). Color, consciousness, and the isomorphism constraint.

Behav Brain Sci 22: 923–943; discussion 944–989.

Palmer, S. E. and Ghose, T. (2008). Extremal edges: A powerful cue to depth perception and figure-ground organization. *Psychol Sci* 19: 77–84.

Palmisano, S., Gillam, B., Govan, D. G., Allison, R. S., and Harris, J. M. (2010). Stereoscopic perception of real depths at large distances. *J Vis* 10: 19.

Panum, P. L. (1940). *Physiological Investigations Concerning Vision with Two Eyes* (translated from German by C. Hubscher). Hanover, NH: Dartmouth Eye Institute. (Original work published 1858.)

Papoiu, A. D. P., Nattkemper, L. A., Sanders, K. M., Kraft, R. A., Chan, Y.-H., Coghill, R. C., and Yosipovitch, G. (2013). Brain's reward circuits mediate itch relief. A functional MRI study of active scratching. *PLoS One* 8: e82389.

Parker, A. J. (2007). Binocular depth perception and the cerebral cortex. *Nat Rev Neurosci* 8: 379–391.

Parr, W. V., Heatherbell, D. A., and White, K. G. (2002). Demystifying wine expertise: Olfactory threshold, perceptual skill, and semantic memory in expert and novice wine judges. *Chem Senses* 27: 747–755.

Parrish, E. E., Giaschi, D. E., Boden, C., and Dougherty, R. (2005). The maturation of form and motion perception in school age children. *Vision Res* 45: 827–837.

Pascual-Leone, A. and Hamilton, R. (2001). The metamodal organization of the brain. *Prog Brain Res* 134: 427–445.

Pastor, A., Fernández-Aranda, F., Fitó, M., Jiménez-Murcia, S., Botella, C., Fernández-Real, J. M., Frühbeck, G., et al. (2016). A lower olfactory capacity is related to higher circulating concentrations of endocannabinoid 2-arachidonoylglycerol and higher body mass index in women. *PLoS One* 11: e0148734.

Patterson, R. D. and Johnsrude, I. S. (2008). Functional imaging of the auditory processing applied to speech sounds. *Philos Trans R Soc B Biol Sci* 363: 1023–1035.

Pawling, R., Cannon, P. R., McGlone, F. P., and Walker, S. C. (2017). C-tactile afferent stimulating touch carries a positive affective value. *PLoS One* 12: e0173457.

Peirs, C. and Seal, R. P. (2016). Neural circuits for pain: Recent advances and current views. *Science* 354: 578–584.

Pelchat, M. L., Bykowski, C., Duke, F. F., and Reed, D. R. (2011). Excretion and perception of a characteristic odor in urine after asparagus ingestion: A psychophysical and genetic study. *Chem Senses* 36: 9–17.

Penfield, W. and Rasmussen, T. (1950). *The Cerebral Cortex of Man: A Clinical Study of Localization of Function*. New York: Macmillan.

Perini, I., Olausson, H., and Morrison, I. (2015). Seeking pleasant touch: Neural correlates of behavioral preferences for skin stroking. *Front Behav Neurosci* 9: 8.

Perlman, M. and Krumhansl, C. L. (1996). An experimental study of internal interval standards in Javanese and Western musicians. *Music Percept* 14: 95–116.

Peterhans, E., von der Heydt, R., Baumgartner, G., Pettigrew, J. D., Sanderson, K. J., and Levick, W. R. (1986). Neuronal responses to illusory contour stimuli reveal stages of visual cortical processing. In J. D. Pettigrew, K. J. Sanderson, and W. R. Levick (Eds.), *Visual Neuroscience* (pp. 343–351). Cambridge, UK: Cambridge University Press.

Peterka, R. J. (2002). Sensorimotor integration in human postural control. *J Neurophysiol* 88: 1097–1118.

Peterson, M. A. and Skow, E. (2008). Inhibitory competition between shape properties in figure-ground perception. *J Exp Psychol Hum Percept Perform* 34: 251–267.

Petkov, C. I., O'Connor, K. N., and Sutter, M. L. (2003). Illusory sound perception in macaque monkeys. *J Neurosci* 23: 9155–9161.

Petkov, C. I., O'Connor, K. N., and Sutter, M. L. (2007). Encoding of illusory continuity in primary auditory cortex. *Neuron* 54: 153–165.

Pettigrew, J. D., Nikara, T., and Bishop, P. O. (1968). Binocular interaction on single units in cat striate cortex: Simultaneous stimulation by single moving slit with receptive fields in correspondence. *Exp Brain Res* 6: 391–410.

Pfaffmann, C. (1974a). The sensory coding of taste quality. *Chem Senses Flavor* 1: 5–8.

Pfaffmann, C. (1974b). Specificity of the sweet receptors of the squirrel monkey. *Chem Senses Flavor* 1: 61–67.

Phelps, M. E. (2000). Positron emission tomography provides molecular imaging of biological processes. *Proc Natl Acad Sci USA* 97: 9226–9233.

Pierce, J. D., Jr., Wysocki, C. J., Aronov, E. V., Webb, J. B., and Boden, R. M. (1996). The role of perceptual and structural similarity in cross-adaptation. *Chem Senses* 21: 223–237.

Pignatiello, M. F., Camp, C. J., and Rasar, L. A. (1986). Musical mood induction: An alternative to the Velten technique. *J Abnorm Psychol* 95: 295–297.

Plailly, J., Delon-Martin, C., and Royet, J.-P. (2011). Experience induces functional reorganization in brain regions involved in odor imagery in perfumers. *Hum Brain Mapp* 33: 224–234.

Plailly, J., Howard, J. D., Gitelman, D. R., and Gottfried, J. A. (2008). Attention to odor modulates thalamocortical connectivity in the human brain. *J Neurosci* 28: 5257–5267.

Plaisier, M. A., Bergmann Tiest, W. M., and Kappers, A. M. L. (2009). Salient features in 3-D haptic shape perception. *Atten Percept Psychophys* 71: 421–430.

Plomp, R. (1976). *Aspects of Tone Sensation—A Psychophysical Study*. New York: Academic Press.

Plotkin, A., Sela, L., Weissbord, A., Kahana, R., Haviv, L., Yeshurun, Y., and Soroker, N. (2010). Sniffing enables communication and environmental control for the severely disabled. *Proc Natl Acad Sci USA* 107: 14413–14418.

Poggio, G. F. and Talbot, W. H. (1981). Mechanisms of static and dynamic stereopsis in foveal cortex of the rhesus monkey. *J Physiol* 315: 469–492.

Pointer, M. R. and Attridge, G. G. (1998). The number of discernible colours. *Color Res Appl* 23: 52–54.

Polat, U. and Sagi, D. (1993). Lateral interactions between spatial channels: Suppression and facilitation revealed by lateral masking experiments. *Vision Res* 33: 993–999.

Poletti, M., Listorti, C., and Rucci, M. (2010). Stability of the visual world during eye drift. *J Neurosci* 30: 11143–11150.

Poletti, M., Listorti, C., and Rucci, M. (2013). Microscopic eye movements compensate for nonhomogeneous vision within the fovea. *Curr Biol* 23: 1691–1695.

Pollan, M. (2006). *The Omnivore's Dilemma: A Natural History of Four Meals*. New York: Penguin.

Ponzo, M. (1913). Rapports entre quelque illusions visuelles de contraste angulaire et l'appréciation de grandeur astres à l'horizon. *Arch Ital Biol* 58: 327–329.

Poran N. S. and Coss, R. G. (1990). Development of antisnake defenses in California ground squirrels (*Spermaphilus beecheyi*): I. Behavioral and immunological relationships. *Behavior* 112: 222–245.

Porter, J., Carven, B., Khan, R. M., Chang, S. J., Kang, I., Judkewicz, B., Volpe, J., et al. (2007). Mechanisms of scent-tracking in humans. *Nat Neurosci* 10: 27–29.

Posner, M. I. (1980). Orienting of attention. *Q J Exp Psychol* 32: 3–25.

Pospichalova, K., Vodicka, J., and Kopal, A. (2016). New test of odor pleasantness in Parkinson's disease. *Funct Neurol* 31: 149–155.

Potter, M. C. (1975). Meaning in visual search. *Science* 187: 965–966.

Potter, M. C. (1976). Short-term conceptual memory for pictures. *J Exp Psychol Hum Learn Mem* 2: 509–522.

Potter, M. C., Wyble, B., Hagmann, C. E. H., and McCourt, E. (2013). Detecting meaning in RSVP at 13 ms per picture. *Atten Percept Psychophys* 76: 270–279.

Prescott, J. (2004). Effects of added glutamate on liking for novel flavors. *Appetite* 42: 143–150.

Preston, T. J., Li, S., Kourtzi, Z., and Welchman, A. E. (2008). Multivoxel pattern selectivity for perceptually relevant binocular disparities in the human brain. *J Neurosci* 28: 11315–1132.

Price, D. D. (2000). Psychological and neural mechanisms of the affective dimension of pain. *Science* 288: 1769–1772.

Price, D. D., Wu, J. W., Dubner, R., and Gracely, R. H. (1977). Peripheral suppression of first pain and central summation of second pain evoked by noxious heat pulses. *Pain* 3: 57–68.

Prinzmetal, W. and Beck, D. M. (2001). The tilt-constancy theory of visual illusions. *J Exp Psychol Hum Percept Perform* 27: 206–217.

Prinzmetal, W., Shimamura, A. P., and Mikolinski, M. (2001). The Ponzo illusion and the perception of orientation. *Percept Psychophys* 63: 99–114.

Pritchard, T. C. and Norgren, R. (2004). Gustatory system. In G. Paxinos and J. K. Mai (Eds.), *The Human Nervous System* (2nd ed., pp. 1171–1196). Amsterdam: Elsevier.

Proust, M. (1928). *Swann's Way*. New York: Modern Library.

Pugh, M. C., Ringach, D. L., Shapley, R., and Shelley, M. J. (2000). Computational modeling of orientation tuning dynamics in monkey primary visual cortex. *J Comput Neurosci* 8: 143–159.

Purves, D., Augustine, G. J., Fitzpatrick, D., Hall, W. C., LaMantia, A.–S., and White, L. E. (2017). *Neuroscience* (6th ed.). Sunderland, MA: Sinauer.

Q

Qiu, F. T. and von der Heydt, R. (2007). Neural representation of transparent overlay. *Nat Neurosci* 10: 283–284.

Quilliam, T. A. (1978), The structure of finger print skin. In G. Gordon (Ed.), *Active Touch: The Mechanisms of Recognition of Objects by Manipulation. A Multidisciplinary Approach* (pp. 1–15). Oxford, UK: Pergamon.

Quiroga, R. Q., Reddy, L., Kreiman, G., Koch, C., and Fried, I. (2005). Invariant visual representation by single neurons in the human brain. *Nature* 435: 1102–1107.

R

Rabin, M. D. and Cain, W. S. (1984). Odor recognition, familiarity, identifiability and encoding consistency. *J Exp Psychol Learn Mem Cogn* 10: 316–325.

Rader, A. A., Oman, C. M., and Merfeld, D. M. (2011). Perceived tilt and translation during variable-radius swing motion with congruent or conflicting visual and vestibular cues. *Exp Brain Res* 210: 173–184.

Raichlen, D. A. and Gordon, A. D. (2011). Relationship between exercise capacity and brain size in mammals. *PLoS One* 6: e20601.

Rainville, P., Duncan, G. H., Price, D. D., Carrier, B., and Bushnell, M. C. (1997). Pain affect encoded in human anterior cingulate but not somatosensory cortex. *Science* 277: 968–971.

Ramachandran, R. and Lisberger, S. G. (2005). Normal performance and expression of learning in the vestibulo-ocular reflex (VOR) at high frequencies. *J Neurophysiol* 93: 2028–2038.

Ramachandran, V. S. (1993). Behavioral and magnetoencephalographic correlates of plasticity in the adult human brain. *Proc Natl Acad Sci USA* 90: 10413–10420.

Raphan, T., Matsuo, V., and Cohen, B. (1977). A velocity storage mechanism responsible for optokinetic nystagmus (OKN), optokinetic after-nystagmus (OKAN) and vestibular nystagmus. In R. Baker and A. Berthoz (Eds.), *Control of Gaze by Brain Stem Neurons: Proceedings of the Symposium Held in the Abbaye de Royaumont, Paris, France on July 12–15, 1977* (Developments in Neuroscience, vol. 1) (pp. 37–47). Amsterdam: Elsevier/North Holland.

Rasch, B., Buchel, C., Gais, S., and Born, J. (2007). Odor cues during slow-wave sleep prompt declarative memory consolidations. *Science* 315: 1426–1429.

Rasch, R. A. (1978). The perception of simultaneous notes such as in polyphonic music. *Acustica* 40: 1–72.

Raudenbush, B., Corley, N., and Eppich, W. (2001). Enhancing athletic performance through the administration of peppermint odor. *J Sport Exerc Psychol* 23: 156–160.

Raudenbush, B., Grayhem, R., Sears, T., and Wilson, I. (2009). Effects of peppermint and cinnamon odor administration on simulated driving alertness, mood and workload. *N Am J Psychol* 11: 245–256.

Raymond, J. E. (1993). Complete interocular transfer of motion adaptation effects on motion coherence thresholds. *Vision Res* 33: 1865–1870.

Rayner, K. (1978). Eye movements in reading and information processing. *Psychol Bull* 85: 618–660.

Rayner, K., Liversedge, S. P., White, S. J., and Vergilino-Perez, D. (2003). Reading disappearing text: Cognitive control of eye movements. *Psychol Sci* 14: 385–388.

Reale, R. A., Calvert, G. A., Thesen, T., Jenison, R. L., Kawasaki, H., Oya, H., Howard, M. A., and Brugge, J. F. (2007). Auditory-visual processing represented in the human superior temporal gyrus. *Neuroscience* 145: 162–184.

Reason, J. and Brand, J. (1975). *Motion Sickness.* London: Academic Press.

Reed, C. L. and Caselli, R. J. (1994). The nature of tactile agnosia: A case study. *Neuropsychologia* 32: 527–539.

Reed, C. L., Caselli, R. J., and Farah, M. J. (1996). Tactile agnosia: Underlying impairment and implications for normal tactile object recognition. *Brain* 119: 875–888.

Reed, C. L., Klatzky, R. L., and Halgren, E. (2005). What versus where in touch: An fMRI study. *Neuroimage* 25: 718–726.

Reed, C. L., Shoham, S., and Halgren, E. (2004). Neural substrates of tactile object recognition: A fMRI study. *Hum Brain Mapp* 21: 236–246.

Reese, A., List, N. H., Kongsted, J., and Solov'yov, I. A. (2016). How far does a receptor influence vibrational properties of an odorant? *PLoS One* 11: e0152345.

Regan, B. C., Julliot, C., Simmen, B., Viénot, F., Charles-Dominique, P., and Mollon, J. D. (2001). Fruits, foliage, and the evolution of primate colour vision. *Phil Trans R Soc Lond B* 356: 229–283.

Regan, D. (1991). Depth from motion and motion in depth. In D. Regan (Ed.), *Binocular Vision* (pp. 137–169). London: Macmillan.

Reichardt, W. (1986). Processing of optical information by the visual system of the fly. *Vision Res* 26: 113–126.

Reichert J. L. and Schöpf, V. (2017). Olfactory loss and regain: Lessons for neuroplasticity. *Neuroscientist* [Epub ahead of print]. doi: 10.1177/1073858417703910.

Reid, V. M., Dunn, K., Young, R. J., Amu, J., Donovan, T., and Reissland, N. (2017). The human fetus preferentially engages with face-like visual stimuli. *Curr Biol* 27: 1825–1828.

Rensink, R. A. (2000). Seeing, sensing, and scrutinizing. *Vision Res* 40: 1469–1487.

Rensink, R. A., O'Regan, J. K., and Clark, J. J. (1997). To see or not to see: The need for attention to perceive changes in scenes. *Psychol Sci* 8: 368–373.

Reynolds, J. H. and Chelazzi, L. (2004). Attentional modulation of visual processing. *Annu Rev Neurosci* 27: 611–647.

Reynolds, J. H. and Heeger, D. J. (2009). The normalization model of attention. *Neuron* 61: 168–185.

Richard, M. C., Taylor, S. R., and Greer, C. A. (2010). Age-induced disruption of selective olfactory bulb synaptic circuits. *Proc Nat Acad Sci USA* 107: 15613–15618.

Riecke, L., Esposito, F., Bonte, M., and Formisano, E. (2009). Hearing illusory sounds in noise: The timing of sensory-perceptual transformations in auditory cortex. *Neuron* 64: 550–561.

Riecke, L., van Opstal, A. J., Goebel, R., and Formisano, E. (2007). Hearing illusory sounds in noise: Sensory-perceptual transformations in primary auditory cortex. *J Neurosci* 27: 12684–12689.

Rind, F. C. and Simmons, P. J. (1999). Seeing what is coming: Building collision-sensitive neurones. *Trends Neurosci* 22: 215–220.

Robinson, D. (1977). Vestibular and optokinetic symbiosis: An example of explaining by modelling. In R. Baker and A. Berthoz (Eds.), *Control of Gaze by Brain Stem Neurons: Proceedings of the Symposium Held in the Abbaye de Royaumont, Paris, France on July 12–15, 1977* (Developments in Neuroscience, vol. 1) (pp. 49–58). Amsterdam: Elsevier/North Holland.

Robson, J. and Campbell, F. (1997). A quick demonstration of your own contrast sensitivity function. In D. G. Pelli and A. M. Torres, *Thresholds: Limits of Perception.* New York: NY Arts Magazine.

Rock, I. and Victor, J. (1964). Vision and touch: An experimentally created conflict between the two senses. *Science* 143: 594–596.

Rodieck, R. W. (1998). *The First Steps in Seeing.* Sunderland, MA: Sinauer.

Roe, A. W., Chelazzi, L., Connor, C. E., Conway, B. R., Fujita, I., Gallant, J. L., Lu, H., et al. (2012). Toward a unified theory of visual area V4. *Neuron* 74: 12–29.

Rogers, B. J. and Collett, T. S. (1989). The appearance of surfaces specified by motion parallax and binocular disparity. *Q J Exp Psychol A* 41: 697–717.

Rolls, B. J. (1986). Sensory-specific satiety. *Nutr Rev* 44: 93–101.

Rolls, E. T. (2006). Brain mechanisms underlying flavor and appetite. *Philos Trans R Soc Lond B Biol Sci* 361: 1123–1136.

Roorda, A. and Williams, D. R. (1999). The arrangement of the three cone classes in the living human eye. *Nature* 397: 520–522.

Roper, S. D. (2006). Cell communication in taste buds. *Cell Mol Life Sci* 63: 1494–1500.

Roper, S. D. (2013). Taste buds as peripheral chemosensory processors. *Sem Cell Dev Biol* 24: 71–79.

Roper, S. D. and Chaudhari, N. (2009). Processing umami and other tastes in mammalian taste buds. *Ann NY Acad Sci* 1170: 60–65.

Roper, S. D. and Chaudhari, N. (2017). Taste buds: Cells, signals and synapses. *Nat Rev Neurosci* 18: 485–497.

Rosen, S., Wise, R. J. S., Chadha, S., Conway, E.-J., and Scott, S. K. (2011). Hemispheric asymmetries in speech perception: Sense, nonsense, and modulations. *PLoS One* 6: e24672.

Rosenzweig, M. R., Breedlove, S. M., and Leiman, A. L. (2002). *Biological Psychology* (3rd ed.). Sunderland, MA: Sinauer.

Rosenzweig, M. R., Breedlove, S. M., and Watson, N. V. (2005). *Biological Psychology: An Introduction to Behavioral and Cognitive Neuroscience* (4th ed.). Sunderland, MA: Sinauer.

Ross, J., Morrone, M. C., Goldberg, M. E., Burr, D. C. (2001). Changes in visual perception at the time of saccades. *Trends Neurosci* 24: 113–121.

Ross, S E. (2011). Pain and itch: Insights into the neural circuits of aversive somatosensation in health and disease. *Curr Opin Neurobiol* 21: 880–887.

Rossetti, Y., Rode, G., and Boisson, D. (1995). Implicit processing of somaesthetic information: A dissociation between where and how? *Neuroreport* 15: 506–510.

Rothschild, G., Nelken, I., Mizrahi, A. (2013). Functional organization and population dynamics in the mouse primary auditory cortex. *Nat Neurosci* 13: 353–360.

Rowe, T. B., Macrinin, T. E., and Luo, Z.-X. (2011). Fossil evidence on origin of the mammalian brain. *Science* 332: 955–957.

Roy, M., Peretz, I., and Rainville, P. (2007). Emotional valence contributes to music-induced analgesia. *Pain* 1–2: 140–147.

Royden, C. S., Banks, M. S., and Crowell, J. A. (1992). The perception of heading during eye movements. *Nature* 360: 583–585.

Royet, J.-P. and Plailly, J. (2004). Lateralization of olfactory processes. *Chem Senses* 29: 731–745.

Rozin, E. and Rozin, P. (1981). Culinary themes and variations. *Natural History* 90: 6–14.

Rozin, P. (Ed.). (1967). *Thiamin Specific Hunger* (Vol. 1). Washington, DC: American Physiological Society.

Rozin, P., Gruss, L., and Berk, G. (1979). The reversal of innate aversions: Attempts to induce a preference for chili peppers in rats. *J Comp Physiol Psychol* 93: 1001–1014.

Rozin, P. and Schiller, D. (1980). The nature and acquisition of a preference for chili pepper by humans. *Motiv Emot* 4: 77.

Rubin, D. C., Groth, E., and Goldsmith, D. J. (1984). Olfactory cuing of autobiographical memory. *Am J Psychol* 97: 493–507.

Ruijschop, R. M. A. J., Boelrijk, A. E. M., de Ru, J. A., de Graaf, C., and Westerterp-Plantenga, M. S. (2008). Effects of retro-nasal aroma release on satiation. *Br J Nutr* 99: 1140–1148.

Rupp, C. I., Kurz, M., Kemmler, G., Mair, D., Hausmann, A., Hinterhuber, H., and Fleischhacker, W. W. (2003). Reduced olfactory sensitivity, discrimination, and identification in patients with alcohol dependence. *Alcohol Clin Exp Res* 27: 432–439.

Rushton, W. (1972). Visual pigments in man. In H. Dartnall (Ed.), *Photochemistry of Vision* (Vol. VII/1, pp. 364–394). New York: Springer.

S

Saal, H. P., Wang, X., and Bensmaia, S. J. (2016). Importance of spike timing in touch: An analogy with hearing? *Curr Opin Neurobiol* 40: 142–149.

Sabesan, R., Schmidt, B. P., Tuten, W. S., and Roorda, A. (2016). The elementary representation of spatial and color vision in the human retina. *Sci Adv* 2: e1600797.

Sachse, S., Rueckert, E., Keller, A., Okada, R., Tanaka, N. K., Ito, K., and Vosshall, L. B. (2007). Activity dependent plasticity in an olfactory circuit. *Neuron* 56: 838–850.

Sacks, O. (2006, June 19). A neurologist's notebook: "Stereo Sue." *New Yorker* 64.

Saffran, J. R. (2001). Words in a sea of sounds: The output of statistical learning. *Cognition* 81: 149–169.

Saffran, J. R. (2002). Constraints on statistical language learning. *J Mem Lang* 47: 172–196.

Saffran, J. R., Aslin, R. N., and Newport, E. L. (1996). Statistical learning by 8-month-old infants. *Science* 274: 1926–1928.

Saffran, J. R., Johnson, E. K., Aslin, R. N., and Newport, E. L. (1999). Statistical learning of tone sequences by human infants and adults. *Cognition* 70: 27–52.

Saffran, J. R., Loman, M. M., and Robertson, R. R. W. (2000). Infant memory for musical experiences. *Cognition* 77: B15–B23.

Salzman, C. D., Britten, K. H., and Newsome, W. T. (1990). Cortical microstimulation influences perceptual judgements of motion direction. *Nature* 346: 174–177.

Sarrafchi, A., Odhammer, A. M., Salazar, L. T. H., and Laska, M. (2013). Olfactory sensitivity for six predator odorants in CD-1 mice, human subjects, and spider monkeys. *PLoS One* 8: e80621.

Sayles, M., Fontaine, B., Smith, P. H., and Joris, P. X. (2017). *Inter-aural time sensitivity of superior-olivary-complex neurons is shaped by systematic cochlear disparities.* Paper presented at the 40th Annual MidWinter Meeting of the Association for Research in Otolaryngology, Baltimore, Maryland.

Sceniak, M. P., Ringach, D. L., Hawken, M. J., and Shapley, R. (1999). Contrast's effect on spatial summation by macaque V1 neurons. *Nat Neurosci* 2: 733–739.

Schaal, B., Marlier, L., and Soussignan, R. (1995). Responsiveness to the odor of amniotic fluid in the human neonate. *Biol Neonate* 671: 397–406.

Schaal, B., Marlier, L., and Soussignan, R. (1998). Olfactory function in the human fetus: Evidence from selective neonatal responsiveness to the odor of amniotic fluid. *Behav Neurosci* 112: 1438–1449.

Scheibert, J., Leurent, S., Prevost, A., and Debrégeas, G. (2009). The role of fingerprints in the coding of tactile information probed with a biomimetic sensor. *Science* 323: 1503–1506.

Schier, L. A., Hashimoto, K., Bales, M. B., Blonde, G. D., and Spector, A. C. (2014). High-resolution lesion-mapping strategy links a hot spot in rat insular cortex with impaired expression of taste aversion learning. *Proc Nat Acad Sci USA* 111: 1162–1167.

Schild, D. and Restrepo, D. (1998). Transduction mechanism in vertebrate olfactory receptor cells. *Physiol Rev* 37: 369–375.

Schiller, P. H. and Sandell, J. H. (1983). Interactions between visually and electrically elicited saccades before and after superior colliculus and frontal eye field ablations in the rhesus monkey. *Exp Brain Res* 49: 381–392.

Schleidt, M., Hold, B., and Attila, G. (1981). A cross-cultural study on the attitude towards personal odors. *J Chem Ecol* 7: 19–31.

Schnapf, J. L., Kraft, T. W., and Baylor, D. A. (1987). Spectral sensitivity of human cone photoreceptors. *Nature* 325: 439–441.

Schoonevelt, G. P. and Moore, B. C. J. (1989). Comodulation masking release (CMR) as a function of masker bandwidth, modulator bandwidth, and signal duration. *J Acoust Soc Am* 85: 273–281. (With permission of the Acoustical Society of America.)

Schütz, A. C., Braun, D. I., and Gegenfurtner, K. R. (2011). Eye movements and perception: a selective review. *J Vis* 11(5).

Sclafani, A. (1997). Learned controls of ingestive behaviour. *Appetite* 29: 153–158.

Seay, C. F. (1975). *First Thoughts on a Theology of Music from the Psalter.* Dallas, TX: Dallas Theological Seminary.

Seeba, F. and Klump, G. M. (2009). Stimulus familiarity affects perceptual restoration in the European starling (*Sturnus vulgaris*). *PLoS One* 4: e5974.

Seidl, A. H. and Grothe, B. (2005). Development of sound localization mechanisms in the Mongolian gerbil is shaped by early acoustic experience. *J Neurophysiol* 94: 1028–1036.

Selfridge, O. G. (1959). Pandemonium: A paradigm for learning. In D. V. Blake and A. M. Uttley (Eds.), *Proceedings of the Symposium on the Mechanisation of Thought Processes* (pp. 511–529). London: Her Majesty's Stationery Office.

Seow, Y. X., Ong, P. K., and Huang, D. (2016). Odor-specific loss of smell sensitivity with age as revealed by the specific sensitivity test. *Chem Sens* 41: 487–495.

Serences, J. T. and Yantis, S. (2006). Selective visual attention and perceptual coherence. *Trends Cogn Sci* 10: 38–45.

Serre, T., Oliva, A., and Poggio, T. (2007). A feedforward architecture accounts for rapid categorization. *Proc Natl Acad Sci USA* 104: 6424–6429.

Shapiro, K. L. (1994). The attentional blink: The brain's eyeblink. *Curr Dir Psychol Sci* 3: 86–89.

Shapley, R. and Hawken, M. J. (2011). Color in the cortex: Single- and double-opponent cells. *Vision Res* 51: 701–717.

Sharan, L., Rosenholtz, R., and Adelson, E. H. (2009). Material perception: What can you see in a brief glance? *J Vis* 9: 784.

Shepard, R. N. (1967). Recognition memory for words, sentences, and pictures. *J Verbal Learn Verbal Behav* 6: 156–163.

Sherrick C. and Cholewiak, R. (1986). Cutaneous sensitivity. In K. R. Boff, L. Kaufman, and J. P. Thomas (Eds.), *Handbook of Perception and Human Performance* (Vol 1., pp. 12.1–12.58). New York: Wiley.

Shevell, S. K. (2003). Color appearance. In S. K. Shevell (Ed.), *The Science of Color* (2nd ed., pp. 149–190). Oxford, UK: Elsevier.

Simon, R., Holderied, M. W., Koch, C. U., and von Helversen, O. (2011). Floral acoustics: Conspicuous echoes of a dish-shaped leaf attract bat pollinators. *Science* 333: 631–633.

Simons, D. J. and Chabris, C. F. (1999). Gorillas in our midst: Sustained inattentional blindness for dynamic events. *Perception* 28: 1059–1074.

Simons, D. J. and Levin, D. T. (1997). Change blindness. *Trends Cogn Sci* 1: 261–267.

Singer, W. (1999). Neuronal synchrony: A versatile code for the definition of relations? *Neuron* 24: 49–65.

Sinha, R., Hoon, M., Baudin, J., Okawa, H., Wong, R. O., and Rieke, F. (2017). Cellular and circuit mechanisms shaping the perceptual properties of the primate fovea. *Cell* 168: 413–426.

Sipiora, M. L., Murtaugh, M. A., Gregoire, M. B., and Duffy, V. B. (2000). Bitter taste perception and severe vomiting during pregnancy. *Physiol Behav* 69: 259–267.

Sjöström, L. B. and Cairncross, S. E. (1955). Role of sweeteners in food flavor. In *Use of Sugars and other Carbohydrates in the Food Industry* (pp. 108–113). Washington, D.C.: American Chemical Society.

Skedung, L., Arvidsson, M., Chung, J. Y., Stafford, C. M., Berglund, B., and Rutland, M. W. (2013). Feeling small: Exploring the tactile perception limits. *Sci Rep* 3: 2617.

Sloboda, J. A. (1999). Music: Where cognition and emotion meet. *Psychologist* 12: 450–455.

Small, D. M., Gerber, J. C., Mak, Y. E., and Hummel, T. (2005). Differential neural responses evoked by orthonasal versus retronasal odorant perception in humans. *Neuron* 47: 593–605.

Smith, J. D., Kemler Nelson, D. G., Grohskopf, L. A., and Appleton, T. (1994). What child is this? What interval was that? Familiar tunes and music perception in novice listeners. *Cognition* 52: 23–54.

Smith, W. M., Davidson, T. M., and Murphy, C. (2009). Toxin–induced chemosensory dysfunction: A case series and review. *Am J Rhinol Allergy* 23: 578–581.

Smithson, H. E. (2005). Sensory, computational and cognitive components of human colour constancy. *Philos Trans R Soc Lond B Biol Sci* 360: 1329–1346.

Snyder, D. J., Davidson, A. C., Kidd, J. R., Kidd, K. K., Speed, W. C., Pakstis, A. J., Cubells, J. F., et al. (2005). *Oral sensation influences tobacco use: Genetic and psychophysical evidence*. Paper presented at the Society for Research on Nicotine and Tobacco, Prague, Czech Republic.

Snyder, D. J., Dwivedi, N., Mramor, A., Bartoshuk, L. M., and Duffy, V. B. (2001). *Taste and touch may contribute to the localization of retronasal olfaction: Unilateral and bilateral anesthesia of cranial nerves V/VII*. Paper presented at the Society of Neuroscience Abstract, San Diego, CA.

Snyder, J. S. and Alain, C. (2007). Toward a neurophysiological theory of auditory stream segregation. *Psychol Bull* 133: 780–799.

Sollberger, B., Reber, R., and Eckstein, D. (2003). Musical chords as affective priming context in a word-evaluation task. *Music Percept* 20: 263–283.

Sommers, M. S., Hale, S., Myerson, J., Rose, N., Tye-Murray, N., and Spehar, B. (2011). Listening comprehension across the adult lifespan. *Ear Hear* 32: 775–781.

Soria-Gómez, E., Bellocchio, L., Reguero, L., Lepousez, G., Martin, C., Bendahmane, M., Ruehle, S., et al. (2014). The endocannabinoid system controls food intake via olfactory processes. *Nat Neurosci* 17: 407–415.

Spence, C., Nicholls, M. E. R., and Driver, J. (2001). The cost of expecting events in the wrong sensory modality. *Percept Psychophys* 63: 330–336.

Spence, C., Pavani, F., and Driver, J. (2000). Crossmodal links between vision and touch in covert endogenous spatial attention. *J Exp Psychol Hum Percept Perform* 26: 1298–1319.

Spencer, N. A., McClintock, M. K., Sellergren, S. A., Bullivant, S., Jacob, S., and Mennella, J. A. (2004). Social chemosignals from breastfeeding women increase sexual motivation. *Hum Behav* 46: 362–370.

Sperling, G. and Weichselgartner, E. (1995). Episodic theory of the dynamics of spatial attention. *Psychol Rev* 102: 503–532.

Spoor, F., Wood, B., and Zonneveld, F. (1994). Implications of early hominid labyrinthine morphology for evolution of human bipedal locomotion. *Nature* 369: 645–648.

Sreenivasan, V., Babinsky, E. E., Wu, Y., and Candy, T. R. (2016). Objective measurement of fusional vergence ranges and heterophoria in infants and preschool children. *Invest Ophthalmol Vis Sci* 57: 2678–2688.

Stabell, B. and Stabell, U. (2002). Effects of rod activity on color perception with light adaptation. *J Opt Soc Am A Opt Image Sci Vis* 19: 1249–1258.

Stager, D. R. and Birch, E. (1986). Preferential-looking acuity and stereopsis in infantile esotropia. *J Pediatr Ophthalmol Strabismus* 23: 160–165.

Standing, L. (1973). Learning 10,000 pictures. *Q J Exp Psychol* 25: 207–222.

Standing, L., Conezio, J., and Haber, R. N. (1970). Perception and memory for pictures: Single trial learning of 2500 visual stimuli. *Psychon Sci* 19: 73–74.

Stein, L. J., Cowart, B. J., Epstein, A. N., Pilot, L. J., Laskin, C. R., and Beauchamp, G. K. (1996). Increased liking for salty foods in adolescents exposed during infancy to a chloride-deficient feeding formula. *Appetite* 27: 65–77.

Stein, M., Ottenberg, M. D., and Roulet, N. (1958). A study of the development of olfactory preferences. *Arch Neurol Psychiatry* 80: 264–266.

Steiner, J. E. (1973). The gustofacial response: Observation on normal and anencephalic newborn infants. In J. F. Bosma (Ed.), *Development in the Fetus and Infant* (pp. 254–278). Washington, DC: U.S. Government Printing Office.

Stellman, S. D. and Garkinfel, L. (1988). Patterns of artificial sweetener use and weight change in an American Cancer Society Prospective Study. *Appetite* 11: 85–91.

Stevens, J. C. (1959). Cross-modality validation of subjective scales for loudness, vibration, and electric shock. *J Exp Psychol* 57: 201–209.

Stevens, J. C. and Cain, W. S. (1987). Old-age deficits in the sense of smell as gauged by thresholds, magnitude matching and odor identification. *Psychol Aging* 2: 36–42.

Stevens, S. S. (1962). The surprising simplicity of sensory metrics. *Am Psychol* 17: 29–39.

Stevens, S. S. (1975). *Psychophysics*. New York: Academic Press.

Stevens, S. S. and Galanter, E. H. (1957). Ratio scales and category scales for a dozen perceptual continua. *J Exp Psychol* 54: 377–411.

Stevens, S. S., Carton, A. S., and Shickman, G. M. (1958). A scale of apparent intensity of electric shock. *J Exp Psychol* 56: 328–334.

Stilp, C. E., Alexander, J. M., Kiefte, M., and Kluender, K. R. (2010). Auditory color constancy: Calibration to reliable spectral characteristics across speech and nonspeech contexts and targets. *Atten Percept Psychophys* 72: 470–480.

Stilp, C. E. and Kluender, K. R. (2010). Cochlea-scaled entropy, not consonants, vowels, or time, best predicts speech intelligibility. *Proc Natl Acad Sci USA* 107: 12387–12392.

Stilp, C. E. and Kluender, K. R. (2012). Efficient coding and statistically optimal weighting of covariance among acoustic attributes in novel sounds. *PLoS One* 7: e30845.

Stilp, C. E. and Kluender, K. R. (2016). Stimulus statistics change sounds from near-indiscriminable to hyperdiscriminable. *PLoS One* 11: e0161001.

Stilp, C. E., Rogers, T. T., and Kluender, K. R. (2010). Rapid efficient coding of correlated complex acoustic properties. *Proc Natl Acad Sci USA* 107: 21914–21919.

Stockman, A. and Brainard, D. H. (2010). Color vision mechanisms. In M. Bass (Ed.), *OSA Handbook of Optics* (3rd ed., pp. 11.11–11.104). New York: McGraw-Hill.

Stryker, M. P. and Schiller, P. H. (1975). Eye and head movements evoked by electrical stimulation of monkey superior colliculus. *Exp Brain Res* 23: 103–112.

Sulmont, C., Issanchou, S., and Koster, E. P. (2002). Selection of odorants for memory tests on the basis of familiarity, perceived complexity, pleasantness, similarity and identification. *Chem Senses* 27: 307–317.

Sun, H.-C., Welchman, A. E., Chang, D. H. F., and Di Luca, M. (2016). Look but don't touch: Visual cues to surface structure drive somatosensory cortex. *NeuroImage* 128: 353–361.

Sun, P., Chubb, C., Wright, C. E., and Sperling, G. (2016). Human attention filters for single colors. *Proc Natl Acad Sci USA* 113: E6712–E6720.

Sun, Y.-G., Zhao, Z.-Q., Meng, X.-L., Yin, J., Liu, X.-Y., and Chen, Z.-F. (2009). Cellular basis of itch sensation. *Science* 325: 1531–1534.

Suzuki, Y. and Takeshima, H. (2004). Equal-loudness-level contours for pure tones. *J Acoust Soc Am* 116: 918–933.

Svaetichin, G. and Macnichol, E. F., Jr. (1959). Retinal mechanisms for chromatic and achromatic vision. *Ann NY Acad Sci* 74: 385–404.

Szmajda, B. A., Grünert, U., and Martin, P. R. (2008). Retinal ganglion cell inputs to the koniocellular pathway. *J Comp Neurol* 510: 251–268.

T

Takeuchi, A. H. and Hulse, S. H. (1993). Absolute pitch. *Psychol Bull* 113: 345–361.

Tanaka, Y., Bergmann Tiest, W. M., Kappers, A. M. L., and Sano, A. (2014). Contact force and scanning velocity during active roughness perception. *PLoS One* 9: e93363.

Tang, C., Hamilton, L. S., and Change, E. H. (2017). Intonational speech prosody encoding in the human auditory cortex. *Science* 357: 797–801.

Taube, J. S. (2007). The head direction signal: Origins and sensory-motor integration. *Annu Rev Neurosci* 30: 181–207.

Teller, D. Y. and Movshon, J. A. (1986). Visual development. *Vision Res* 26: 1483–1506.

Temussi, P. (2007). The sweet taste receptor: A single receptor with multiple sites and modes of interaction. In S. Taylor (Ed.), *Advances in Food and Nutrition Research* (Vol. 53, pp. 199–239). Elsevier, New York.

Thaler, L., Arnott, S. R., and Goodale, M. A. (2011). Neural correlates of natural human echolocation in early and late blind echolocation experts. *PLoS One* 6: e20162.

Thaler, L. and Goodale, M. A. (2016). Echolocation in humans: An overview. *WIREs Cogn Sci* 7: 382–393.

Thompson, P. (1980). Margaret Thatcher: A new illusion. *Perception* 9: 482–484.

Thorpe, S., Fize, D., and Marlot, C. (1996). Speed of processing in the human visual system. *Nature* 381: 520–552.

Tieman, D., Bliss, P., McIntyre, L. M., Blandon-Ubeda, A., Bies, D., Odabasi, A. Z., Rodriguez, G. R., et al. (2012). The chemical interactions underlying tomato flavor preferences. *Curr Biol* 22: 1–5.

Tinsley, J. N., Molodtsov, M. I., Prevedel, R., Wartmann, D., Espigulé-Pons, J., Lauwers, M., and Alipasha Vaziri, A. (2016). Direct detection of a single photon by humans. *Nat Comm* 7: Article 12172 (2016).

Tipper, S. P. and Behrmann, M. (1996). Object-centered not scene-based visual neglect. *J Exp Psychol Hum Percept Perform* 22: 1261–1278.

Tochitsky, I., Polosukhina, A., Degtyar, V. E., Gallerani, N., Smith, C. M., Friedman, A., Van Gelder, R. N., et al. (2014). Restoring visual function to blind mice with a photoswitch that exploits electrophysiological remodeling of retinal ganglion cells *Neuron* 81: 800–813.

Todd, A. J. (2010). Neuronal circuitry for pain processing in the dorsal horn. *Nat Rev Neurosci* 11: 823–836.

Tomchek, S. D. and Dunn, W. (2007). Sensory processing in children with and without autism: A comparative study using the short sensory profile. *Am. J. Occup Ther* 61: 190–200.

Tomko, D., Barbaro, N., and Ali, F. (1981). Effect of body tilt on receptive field orientation of simple visual cortical neurons in unanesthetized cats. *Exp Brain Res* 43: 309–314.

Tong, F., Meng, M., and Blake, R. (2006). Neural bases of binocular rivalry. *Trends Cogn Sci* 10: 502–511.

Tong, F., Nakayama, K., Vaughan, J. T., and Kanwisher, N. (1998). Binocular rivalry and visual awareness in human extrastriate cortex. *Neuron* 21: 753–759.

Treisman, A. (1986a). Features and objects in visual processing. *Sci Am* 255: 114–125.

Treisman, A. (1986b). Properties, parts, and objects. In K. R. Boff, L. Kaufmann, and J. P. Thomas (Eds.), *Handbook of Perception and Human Performance*, Vol. 2: *Cognitive Processes and Performance* (pp. 35.31–35.70). New York: Wiley.

Treisman, A. (1996). The binding problem. *Curr Opin Neurobiol* 6: 171–178.

Treisman, A. M. and Schmidt, H. (1982). Illusory conjunctions in the perception of objects. *Cogn Psychol* 14: 107–141.

Treisman, A. and Gelade, G. (1980). A feature-integration theory of attention. *Cogn Psychol* 12: 97–136.

Treisman, M. (1977). Motion sickness: An evolutionary hypothesis. *Science* 197: 493–495.

Tresilian, J. R. (1999). Visually timed action: Time-out for "tau"? *Trends Cogn Sci* 3: 301–310.

Treue, S. and Trujillo, J. C. M. (1999). Feature-based attention influences motion processing gain in macaque visual cortex. *Nature* 399: 575–579.

Troscianko, T., Baddeley, R., Parraga, C. A., Leonards, U., and Troscianko, J. (2003). Visual encoding of green leaves in primate vision. *J Vis* 3: 137–137.

Tse, P. U. (1999). Volume completion. *Cogn Psychol* 39: 37–68.

Tse, P. U. (2005). Voluntary attention modulates the brightness of overlapping transparent surfaces. *Vision Res* 45: 1095–1098.

Tsotsos, J. K. (1990). Analyzing vision at the complexity level. *Behav Brain Sci* 13: 423–469.

Tsuruhara, A., Corrow, S., Kanazawa, S., Yamaguchi, M. K., and Yonas, A. (2014). Measuring young infants' sensitivity to height-in-the-picture-plane by contrasting monocular and binocular preferential-looking. *Dev Psychobiol* 56: 109–116.

Turin, L. (1996). A spectroscopic mechanism for primary olfactory reception. *Chem Senses* 21: 773–791.

Turin, L., Gane, S., Georganakis, D., Maniati, K., and Skoulakis, E. M. (2015). Plausibility of the vibrational theory of olfaction. *Proc Natl Acad Sci USA* 112: E3154.

Tyler, C. W. (1991). Cyclopean vision. In D. Regan (Ed.), *Binocular Vision* (Vol. 9, pp. 38–74). Boca Raton, FL: CRC Press.

U

Ungerleider, L. G. and Bell, A. H. (2011). Uncovering the visual "alphabet": Advances in our understanding of object perception. *Vision Res* 51: 782–799.

Ungerleider, L. G. and Mishkin, M. (1982). Two cortical visual systems. In D. J. Ingle, M. A. Goodale, and R. J. W. Mansfield (Eds.), *Analysis of Visual Behavior* (pp. 549–586). Cambridge, MA: MIT Press.

Uppenkamp, S., Johnsrude, I. S., Norris, D., Marslen-Wilson, W., and Patterson, R. D. (2006). Locating the initial stages of speech-sound processing in human temporal cortex. *Neuroimage* 31: 1284–1296.

V

Vaina, L. M. and Cowey, A. (1996). Impairment of the perception of second order motion but not first order motion in a patient with unilateral focal brain damage. *Proc R Soc Lond B Biol Sci* 263: 1225–1232.

Vaina, L. M., Makris, N., Kennedy, D., and Cowey, A. (1998). The selective impairment of the perception of first-order motion by unilateral cortical brain damage. *Vis Neurosci* 15: 333–348.

Valko, Y., Priesol, A. J., Lewis, R., and Merfeld, D. (2012). Vestibular labyrinth contributions to human whole-body motion discrimination *J Neurosci* 32: 13537–13542.

van Noorden, L. P. A. S. (1975). *Temporal Coherence in the Perception of Tone Sequences.* PhD diss., Technical University, Eindhoven, Netherlands.

Vandewalle, G., Collignon, O., Hull, J. T., Daneault, V., Albouy, G., Lepore, F., Phillips, C., et al. (2013). Blue light stimulates cognitive brain activity in visually blind individuals. *J Cogn Neurosci* 25: 2072–2085.

Verhagen, J. V., Wesson, D. W., Netoff, T. I., White, J. A., and Wachowiak, M. (2007). Sniffing controls an adaptive filter of sensory input to the olfactory bulb. *Nat Neurosci* 10: 631–639.

Vermetten, E., Schmahl, C., Southwick, S. M., and Bremner, J. D. (2007). A positron tomographic emission study of olfactory induced emotional recall in veterans with and without combat-related posttraumatic stress disorder. *Psychopharmacol Bull* 40: 8–30.

Verrillo, R. T. (1963). Effect of contactor area on the vibrotactile threshold. *J Acoust Soc Am* 35: 1962–1966.

Vickers, A. J., Savage, C. J., Hruza, M., Tuerk, I., Koenig, P., Martinez-Pineiro, L., Janetschek, G., et al. (2009). The surgical learning curve for laparoscopic compared to open radical prostatectomy: A retrospective cohort study. *Lancet Oncol* 10: 475–480.

Vickery, T. J., King, L.-W., and Jiang, Y. (2005). Setting up the target template in visual search. *J Vis* 5: 81–92.

Vishwanath, D., Girshik, A. R., and Banks, M. (2005). Why pictures look right when viewed from the wrong place. *Nat Neurosci* 8: 1401–1410.

Vockely, J. and Ensenauer, R. (2006). Isovaleric acidemia: new aspects of genetic and phenotypic heterogeneity. *Am. J Med Genet C Semin Med Genet* 142: 95–103.

Volkow, N. D. and Swanson, J. M. (2013). Adult Attention Deficit-Hyperactivity Disorder. *N Engl J Med* 369: 1935–1944.

von der Heydt, R., Peterhans, E., and Baumgartner, G. (1984). Illusory contours and cortical neuron responses. *Science* 224: 1260–1262.

Von Holst, E. and Mittelstaedt, H. (1950). Das Reafferenzprinzip (Wechselwirkungen zwischen Zentralnerven-

system und Peripherie) [The principle of reafference]. *Naturwissenschaften* 37: 464–476.

Voss, P. and Zatorre, R. J. (2012). Organization and reorganization of sensory-deprived cortex. *Curr Biol* 22: 168–173.

W

Wade, N. J. (2000). William Charles Wells (1757–1817) and vestibular research before Purkinje and Flourens. *J Vestib Res* 10: 127–137.

Wagemans, J., Feldman, J., Gepshtein, S., Kimchi, R., Pomerantz, J. R., van der Helm, P. A., and van Leeuwen, C. (2012). A century of Gestalt psychology in visual perception: II. Conceptual and theoretical foundations. *Psychol Bull* 138: 1218–1252.

Walker, R. and Lupien, J. R. (2000). The safety evaluation of monosodium glutamate. *J Nutr* 130 (4S Suppl.): 1049S–1052S.

Walla, P. (2008). Olfaction and its dynamic influence on word and face processing: Cross-modal integration. *Prog Neurobiol* 84: 192–209.

Walla, P., Hufnagl, B., Lehern, J., Mayer, D., Lindinger, G., Imhof, H., Deeke, L., and Lang, W. (2003). Olfaction and depth of word processing: A magnetoencephalographic study. *Neuroimage* 18: 104–116.

Wallisch, P. (2017). Illumination assumptions account for individual differences in the perceptual interpretation of a profoundly ambiguous stimulus in the color domain: "The dress." *J Vis* 17: 5.

Wandell, B. A. and Chichilnisky, E. J. (2012). Squaring cortex with color. *Nat Neurosci* 15: 809–810.

Wandell, B. A. and Winawer, J. (2011). Imaging retinotopic maps in the human brain. *Vision Res* 51: 718–737.

Wang, Y. and Frost, B. J. (1992). Time to collision is signalled by neurons in the nucleus rotundus of pigeons. *Nature* 356: 236–238.

Ward, W. D. (1954). Subjective musical pitch. *J Acoust Soc Am* 26: 369–380.

Warman, P. H. and Ennos, A. R. (2009). Fingerprints are unlikely to increase the friction of primate fingerpads. *J Exp Biol* 212: 2016–2022.

Warren, R. M. (1984). Perceptual restoration of obliterated sounds. *Psychol Rev* 96: 371–385.

Warren, R. M. and Obusek, C. J. (1971). Speech perception and phonemic

restorations. *Percept Psychophys* 9: 358–362.

Warren, W. H., Jr. and Hannon, D. J. (1990). Eye movements and optical flow. *J Opt Soc Am A* 7: 160–169.

Warren, W. H., Jr. and Saunders, J. A. (1995). Perceiving heading in the presence of moving objects. *Perception* 24: 315–331.

Warren, W. H., Jr. and Verbrugge, R. R. (1984). Auditory perception of breaking and bouncing events: A case study in ecological acoustics. *J Exp Psychol Hum Percept Perform* 10: 704–712.

Warren, W. H., Jr., Morris, M. W., and Kalish, M. (1988). Perception of translational heading from optical flow. *J Exp Psychol Hum Percept Perform* 14: 646–660.

Webster, M. A. (2017). Color vision. In J. T. C. Wixted (Ed.), *The Stevens' Handbook of Experimental Psychology and Cognitive Neuroscience* (4th ed.). New York: Wiley and Sons.

Weiland J. D., Cho, A. K., and Humayun, M. S. (2011). Retinal prostheses: Current clinical results and future needs. *Ophthalmology* 118: 2227–2237.

Weinstein, S. (1968). Intensive and extensive aspects of tactile sensitivity as a function of body part, sex, and laterality. In D. R. Kenshalo (Ed.), *The Skin Senses* (pp. 195–222). Springfield, IL: Thomas.

Weiss, T., Snitz, K., Yablonka, A., Khan, R. M., Gafsou, D., Schneidman, E., and Sobel, N. (2012). Perceptual convergence of multi-component mixtures in olfaction implies an olfactory white. *Proc Nat Acad Sci USA* 109: 19959–19964.

Wells, G. L. and Olson, E. A. (2003). Eyewitness testimony. *Annu Rev Psychol* 54: 277–295.

Wells, W. (1792). *An Essay upon Single Vision with Two Eyes: Together with Experiments and Observations on Several Other Subjects in Optics.* London: Cadell.

Werker J. F. and Tees, R. C. (1984). Cross-language speech perception: Evidence for perceptual reorganization during the first year of life. *Infant Behav Dev* 7: 49–63.

Werner, J. S., Peterzell, D. H., and Scheetz, A. J. (1990). Light, vision, and aging. *Optom Vision Sci* 67: 214–229.

Wertheim, A. H., Mesland, B. S., and Bles, W. (2001). Cognitive suppression of tilt sensations during linear horizontal self-motion in the dark. *Perception* 30: 733–741.

Wessel, D. L. (1979). Timbre space as a musical control structure. *Comput Music J* 3: 45–52.

Westling, G. and Johansson, R. S. (1984). Factors influencing the force control during precision grip. *Exp Brain Res* 53: 277–284.

Wever, E. G. (1949). *Theory of Hearing.* New York: Wiley.

Wheatstone, C. (1838). Contributions to the physiology of vision. Part the first: On some remarkable, and hitherto unobserved, phenomena of binocular vision. *Philos Trans R Soc Lond* 1838: 371–394.

Wheatstone, C. (1852). Some remarkable and hitherto unobserved phenomena of binocular vision: Part two. *Philos Mag* 4: 504–523.

Whitney, D. and Levi, D. M. (2011). Visual crowding: A fundamental limit on conscious perception and object recognition. *Trends Cogn Sci* 15: 160–168.

Wiener, A., Shudler, M., Levit, A., Niv. M. Y. (2012). BitterDB: A database of bitter compounds. *Nucleic Acids Res* 40(Database issue): D413–419.

Wiesel, T. N. (1982). Postnatal development of the visual cortex and the influence of environment. *Nature* 299: 583–591.

Wightman, F. L. and Jenison, R. (1995). Auditory spatial layout. In W. Epstein and S. Rogers (Eds.), *Perception of Space and Motion* (pp. 365–400). San Diego, CA: Academic Press.

Wightman, F. L. and Kistler, D. J. (1993). Sound localization. In W. A. Yost, A. N. Popper, and R. R. Fay (Eds.), *Human Psychophysics*, Vol. 3: *Springer Handbook of Auditory Research*. New York: Springer.

Wightman, F. and Kistler, D. (1998). Of Vulcan ears, human ears and "earprints." *Nat Neurosci* 1: 337–339.

Wijntjes, M. W. A., Sato, A., Hayward, V., and Kappers, A. M. L. (2009). Local surface orientation dominates haptic curvature discrimination. *IEEE Trans Haptics* 2: 94–102.

Wilcox, L. M. and Allison, R. S. (2009). Coarse-fine dichotomies in human stereopsis. *Vision Res* 49: 2653–2665.

Wilkins, L. and Richter, C. P. (1940). A great craving for salt by a child with cortico-adrenal insufficiency. *J Am Med Assoc* 114: 866–868.

Willander, J. and Larsson, M. (2007). Olfaction and emotion: The case of au-to-biographical memory. *Mem Cognit* 35: 1659–1663.

Willems, C. and Martens, S. (2016). Time to see the bigger picture: Individual differences in the attentional blink. *Psychon Bull Rev* 23: 1289–1299.

Williams, D. W. and Sekuler, R. (1984). Coherent global motion percepts from stochastic local motions. *Vision Res* 24: 55–62.

Williford, J. R. and von der Heydt, R. (2016). Figure-ground organization in visual cortex for natural scenes. *eNeuro* 3(6). doi: 10.1523/ENEURO.0127-16.2016

Willis, C. M., Church, S. M., Guest, C. M., Cook, W. A., McCarthy, N., Bransbury, A. J., Church, M. R. T., et al. (2004). Olfactory detection of human bladder cancer by dogs: Proof of principle study. *Br Med J* 329: 712–714.

Wilson, D. A., Best, A. R., and Sullivan, R. M. (2004). Plasticity in the olfactory system: Lessons for the neurobiology of memory. *Neuroscientist* 10: 513–524.

Wilson, F. A. W. and Rolls, E. T. (2005). The primate amygdala and reinforcement: A dissociation between rule-based and associatively-mediated memory revealed in neuronal activity. *Neuroscience* 133: 1061–1072.

Wilson, H. C. (1992). A critical review of menstrual synchrony research. *Psychoneuroendocrinology* 17: 565–591.

Wilson, V. J. and Melvill Jones, G. (1979). *Mammalian Vestibular Physiology.* New York: Plenum.

Winawer, J., Witthoft, N., Frank, M. C., Wu, L., Wade, A. R., and Boroditsky, L. (2007). Russian blues reveal effects of language on color discrimination. *Proc Natl Acad Sci USA* 104: 7780–7785.

Winberg, J. and Porter, R. H. (1998). Olfaction and human neonatal behaviour: Clinical implications. *Acta Paediatr* 87: 6–10.

Witzel, C. and Gegenfurtner, K. R. (2016). Categorical perception for red and brown. *J Exp Psychol Hum Percept Perform* 42: 540–570.

Wolfe, J. M. (1994). Guided Search 2.0: A revised model of visual search. *Psychon Bull Rev* 1: 202–238.

Wolfe, J. M. and Bennett, S. C. (1997). Preattentive object files: Shapeless bundles of basic features. *Vision Res* 37: 25–43.

Wolfe, J. M. and DiMase, J. S. (2003). Do intersections serve as basic features in visual search? *Perception* 32: 645–656.

Wolfe, J. M. and Held, R. (1981). A purely binocular mechanism in human vision. *Vision Res* 21: 1755–1759.

Wolfe, J. M. and Horowitz, T. S. (2017). Five factors that guide attention in visual search. [Review Article]. *Nat Hum Behav* 1: Article 0058. doi: 10.1038/s41562-017-0058.

Wolfe, J. M., Cave, K. R., and Franzel, S. L. (1989). Guided search: An alternative to the feature integration model for visual search. *J Exp Psychol Hum Percept Perform* 15: 419–433.

Wolfe, J. M., Reinecke, A., and Brawn, P. (2006). Why don't we see changes? The role of attentional bottlenecks and limited visual memory. *Vis Cogn* 14: 749–780.

Wolfe, J. M., Vo, M. L.-H., Evans, K. K., and Greene, M. R. (2011). Visual search in scenes involves selective and non-selective pathways. *Trends Cogn Sci* 15: 77–84.

Womelsdorf, T., Anton-Erxleben, K., Pieper, F., and Treue, S. (2006). Dynamic shifts of visual receptive fields in cortical area MT by spatial attention. *Nat Neurosci* 9: 1156–1160.

Woodrow, H. (1909). A quantitative study of rhythm. *Arch Psychol* 14: 1–66.

Wrzesniewski, A., McCauley, C., and Rozin, P. (1999). Odor and affect: Individual differences in the impact of odor on liking for places, things and people. *Chem Senses* 24: 713–721.

Wurtz, R. H. (2008). Neuronal mechanisms of visual stability. *Vision Res* 48: 2070–2089.

Wyert, C., Webster, W. W., Chen, J. H., Wilson, S. R., McClary, A., Khan, R. M., and Sobel, N. (2007). Smelling a single component of male sweat alters levels of cortisol in women. *J Neurosci* 27: 1261–1265.

Wysocki, C. J., Dalton, P., Brody, M. J., and Lawley, H. J. (1997). Acetone odor and irritation thresholds obtained from acetone-exposed factory workers and from control (occupationally non-exposed) subjects. *Am Ind Hyg Assoc J* 58: 704–712.

Wysocki, C. J., Dorries, K. M., and Beauchamp, G. K. (1989). Ability to perceive androstenone can be acquired by ostensibly anosmic people. *Proc Natl Acad Sci USA* 86: 7976–7978.

X

Xiao, Y. (2014). Processing of the S-cone signals in the early visual cortex of primates. *Vis Neurosci* 31 (Special Issue 02): 189–195.

Y

Yabuta, N. H. and Callaway, E. M. (1998). Functional streams and local connections of layer 4C neurons in primary visual cortex of the macaque monkey. *J Neurosci* 18: 9489–9499.

Yang, Z. and Schank, J. C. (2006). Women do not synchronize their menstrual cycles. *Hum Nat* 17: 433–447.

Yantis, S. (1993). Stimulus-driven attentional capture. *Curr Dir Psychol Sci* 2: 156–161.

Yarbus, A. L. (1967). *Eye Movements and Vision.* New York: Plenum.

Yates, B. J., Bolton, P. S., and Macefield, V. G. (2014). Vestibulo-sympathetic responses. *Compr Physiol* 4: 851–887.

Yates, B. and Miller, A. (1998). Physiological evidence that the vestibular system participates in autonomic and respiratory control. *J Vestib Res* 8: 17–26.

Yee, K. K., Sukumaran, S. K., Kotha, R., Gilbertson, T. A., and Margolskee, R. F. (2011). Glucose transporters and ATP-gated K+ (K$_{ATP}$) metabolic sensors are present in type 1 taste receptor 3 (T1r3)-expressing taste cells. *Proc Natl Acad Sci USA* 108: 5431–5436.

Yeshurun, Y., Lapid, H., Dudai, Y., and Sobel, N. (2009). The privileged brain representation of first olfactory associations. *Curr Biol* 19: 1869–1874.

Yesilyurt, B., Whittingstall, K., Ugurbil, K., Logothetis, N. K., and Uludag, K. (2009). Relationship of the BOLD signal with VEP for ultrashort duration visual stimuli (0.1 to 5 ms) in humans. *J Cereb Blood Flow Metab* 30: 449–458.

Yin, C., Kellman, P. J., and Shipley, T. F. (1997). Surface completion complements boundary interpolation in the visual integration of partly occluded objects. *Perception* 26: 1459–1479.

Yin, T. C. and Chan, J. C. (1990). Interaural time sensitivity in medial superior olive of cat. *J Neurophysiol* 65: 465–488.

Yonas, A., Craton, L. G., and Thompson, W. B. (1987). Relative motion: Kinetic information for the order of depth at an edge. *Percept Psychophys* 41: 53–59.

Young, L. R. (1984). Perception of the body in space: Mechanisms. In I. Darian-Smith (Ed.), *Handbook of Physiology—The Nervous System* (Vol. 3[2], pp. 1023–1066). Bethesda, MD: American Physiological Society.

Young, L. R., Shelhamer, M., and Modestino, S. (1986). M.I.T./Canadian vestibular experiments on the Spacelab-1 mission. 2. Visual vestibular tilt interaction in weightlessness. *Exp Brain Res* 64: 299–307.

Yu, K. and Blake, R. (1992). Do recognizable figures enjoy an advantage in binocular rivalry? *J Exp Psychol Hum Percept Perform* 18: 1158–1173.

Yuille, A. and Kersten, D. (2006). Vision as Bayesian inference: Analysis by synthesis? *Trends Cogn Sci* 10: 301–308.

Yuodelis, C. and Hendrickson, A. (1986). A qualitative and quantitative analysis of the human fovea during development. *Vision Res* 26: 847–855.

Z

Zadra, A., Nielsen, T. A., and Donderi, D. C. (1998). Prevalence of auditory, olfactory, and gustatory experiences in home dreams. *Percept Mot Skills* 87: 819–826.

Zahorick, P. and Wightman, F. L. (2001). Loudness constancy with varying sound source distance. *Nat Neuro* 4: 78–83.

Zahorik, P. (2002). Assessing auditory distance perception using virtual acoustics. *J Acoust Soc Am* 111: 1832–1846.

Zaidi, Q. (1997). Decorrelation of L- and M-cone signals. *J Opt Soc Am A Opt Image Sci Vis* 14: 3430–3431.

Zaidi, Q., Ennis, R., Cao, D., and Lee, B. (2012). Neural locus of color afterimages. *Curr Biol* 22: 220–224.

Zatorre, R. J. (2001). Do you see what I'm saying? Interactions between auditory and visual cortices in cochlear implant users. *Neuron* 1: 13–14.

Zeki, S. (1983a). Colour coding in the cerebral cortex: The reaction of cells in monkey visual-cortex to wavelengths and colours. *Neuroscience* 9: 741–765.

Zeki, S. (1983b). Colour coding in the cerebral cortex: The responses of wavelength-selective and colour-coded cells in monkey visual cortex to changes in wavelength composition. *Neuroscience* 9: 767–781.

Zeki, S. (1990). A century of cerebral achromatopsia. *Brain* 113 (Pt. 6): 1721–1777.

Zelano, C., Bensafi, M., Porter, J., Mainland, J., Johnson, B., Bremner, E., Telles, C., Khan, R., and Sobel, N. (2005). Attentional modulation in human primary olfactory cortex. *Nat Neurosci* 8: 114–120.

Zellner, D. A., Rozin, P., Aron, M., and Kulish, C. (1983). Conditioned enhancement of human's liking for flavor by pairing with sweetness. *Learn Motiv* 14: 338–350.

Zhang, B., Zheng, J., Watanabe, I., Maruko, I., Bi, H., Smith, E. L., III, and Chino, Y. (2005). Delayed maturation of receptive field center/surround mechanisms in V2. *Proc Natl Acad Sci USA* 102: 5862–5867.

Zhao, G. Q., Zhang, Y., Hoon, M. A., Chandrashekar, J., Erlenbach, I., Ryba, N. J., and Zuker, C. S. (2003). The receptors for mammalian sweet and umami taste. *Cell* 115: 255–266.

Zheng, J., Zhang, B., Bi, H., Maruko, I., Watanabe, I., Nakatsuka, C., Smith, E. L., III, et al. (2007). Development of temporal response properties and contrast sensitivity of V1 and V2 neurons in macaque monkeys. *J Neurophysiol* 97: 3905–3916.

Zhou, B., Feng, G., Chen, W., and Zhou, W. (2017). Olfaction warps visual time perception. *Cereb Cortex* [Epub ahead of print]. doi: 10.1093/cercor/bhx068

Zhou, H., Friedman, H. S., and von der Heydt, R. (2000). Coding of border ownership in monkey visual cortex. *J Neurosci* 20: 6594–6611.

Zhou, W. and Chen, D. (2009). Binaral rivalry between the nostrils and the cortex. *Curr Biol* 19: 1561–1565.

Zhou, W., Jiang, Y., He, S., and Chen, D. (2010). Olfaction modulates visual perception in binocular rivalry. *Curr Biol* 20: 1356–1358.

Zipser, K., Lamme, V. A., and Schiller, P. H. (1996). Contextual modulation in primary visual cortex. *J Neurosci* 16: 7376–7389.

Zirnsak, M., Steinmetz, N. A., Noudoost, B., Xu, K. Z., and Moore, T. (2014). Visual space is compressed in prefrontal cortex before eye movements. *Nature* 507: 504–507.

Zotterman, Y. (1939). Touch, pain and tickling: An electrophysiological investigation on cutaneous sensory nerves. *J Physiol* 95: 1–28.

Zou, Z., Li, F., and Buck, L. B. (2005). Odor maps in the olfactory cortex. *Proc Natl Acad Sci USA* 102: 7724–7729.

Zucco, G. M., Aiello, L., Turuani, L., and Köster, E. (2012). Odor-evoked autobiographical memories: Age and gender differences along the life span. *Chem Senses* 37: 179–189.

Photo Credits

Index

Entries with an italic *f* next to the page number indicate that the information will be found in a figure. Entries with an italic *t* next to the page number indicate that the information will be found in a table.

ABOUT THE BOOK

Editor: Sydney Carroll

Production Editor: Danna Lockwood

Copyeditor: Louise Doucette

Indexer: Hughes Analytics

Production Manager: Christopher Small

Book Design and Production: Ann Chiara

Cover Design: Ann Chiara

Illustration Program: Dragonfly Media Group